Ezekiel 21–48

CONCORDIA COMMENTARY

A Theological Exposition of Sacred Scripture

EZEKIEL
21–48

Horace D. Hummel

Concordia Publishing House
Saint Louis

Library of Congress Cataloging-in-Publication Data

Hummel, Horace D.
    Ezekiel 21–48 / Horace D. Hummel.
        p.   cm. — (Concordia commentary)
    Includes bibliographical references and indexes.
    ISBN 978-0-7586-1001-0
    1. Bible. O.T. Ezekiel XXI–XLVIII—Commentaries. I. Title. II. Series.

    BS1545.53.H792   2007
    224'.4077—dc22

                                                                    2007005400

1   2   3   4   5   6   7   8   9   10   16   15   14   13   12   11   10   09   08   07

To Ruth
The desire of my eyes
(See מַחְמַד עֵינֶיךָ, *Ezek 24:16)*

Contents

Pages 1–615 are in *Ezekiel 1–20*.

Editors' Preface

What may a reader expect from the Concordia Commentary: A Theological Exposition of Sacred Scripture?

The purpose of this series, simply put, is to assist pastors, missionaries, and teachers of the Scriptures to convey God's Word with greater clarity, understanding, and faithfulness to the divine intent of the text.

Since every interpreter approaches the exegetical task from a certain perspective, honesty calls for an outline of the presuppositions held by those who have shaped this commentary series. This also serves, then, as a description of the characteristics of the commentaries.

First in importance is the conviction that the content of the scriptural testimony is Jesus Christ. The Lord himself enunciated this when he said, "The Scriptures ... testify to me" (Jn 5:39), words that have been incorporated into the logo of this series. The message of the Scriptures is the Good News of God's work to reconcile the world to himself through the life, death, resurrection, ascension, and everlasting session of Jesus Christ at the right hand of God the Father. Under the guidance of the same Spirit who inspired the writing of the Scriptures, these commentaries seek to find in every passage of every canonical book "that which promotes Christ" (as Luther's hermeneutic is often described). They are Christ-centered, *Christological* commentaries.

As they unfold the scriptural testimony to Jesus Christ, these commentaries expound Law and Gospel. This approach arises from a second conviction—that Law and Gospel are the overarching doctrines of the Bible itself and that to understand them in their proper distinction and relationship to one another is a key for understanding the self-revelation of God and his plan of salvation in Jesus Christ.

Now, Law and Gospel do not always appear in Scripture labeled as such. The palette of language in Scripture is multicolored, with many and rich hues. The dialectic of a pericope may be fallen creation and new creation, darkness and light, death and life, wandering and promised land, exile and return, ignorance and wisdom, demon possession and the kingdom of God, sickness and healing, being lost and found, guilt and righteousness, flesh and Spirit, fear and joy, hunger and feast, or Babylon and the new Jerusalem. But the common element is God's gracious work of restoring fallen humanity through the Gospel of his Son. Since the predominant characteristic of these commentaries is the proclamation of that Gospel, they are, in the proper sense of the term, *evangelical.*

A third, related conviction is that the Scriptures are God's vehicle for communicating the Gospel. The editors and authors accept without reservation that the canonical books of the Old and New Testaments are, in their entirety, the inspired, infallible, and inerrant Word of God. The triune God is the ultimate author of the Bible, and every word in the original Hebrew, Aramaic, and Greek is inspired by the Holy Spirit. Yet rather than mechanical dictation, in the mysterious process by which the Scriptures were divinely inspired (e.g., 2 Tim 3:16; 2 Pet 1:21), God made use of the human faculties, knowledge, interests, and styles of the biblical writers, whose individual books surely are marked by distinctive features. At the same time, the canon of Scripture has its own inner unity, and each passage must be understood in harmony with the larger context of the whole. This commentary series pays heed to the smallest of textual details because of its acceptance of *plenary and verbal inspiration* and interprets the text in light of the whole of Scripture, in accord with the analogy of faith, following the principle that *Scripture interprets Scripture*. The entirety of the Bible is God's Word, *sacred* Scripture, calling for *theological* exposition.

A fourth conviction is that, even as the God of the Gospel came into this world in Jesus Christ (the Word incarnate), the scriptural Gospel has been given to and through the people of God, for the benefit of all humanity. God did not intend his Scriptures to have a life separated from the church. He gave them through servants of his choosing: prophets, sages, evangelists, and apostles. He gave them to the church and through the church, to be cherished in the church for admonition and comfort and to be used by the church for proclamation and catechesis. The living context of Scripture is ever the church, where the Lord's ministry of preaching, baptizing, forgiving sins, teaching, and celebrating the Lord's Supper continues. Aware of the way in which the incarnation of the Son of God has as a consequence the close union of Scripture and church, of Word and Sacraments, this commentary series features expositions that are *incarnational* and *sacramental*.

This Gospel Word of God, moreover, creates a unity among all those in whom it works the obedience of faith and who confess the truth of God revealed in it. This is the unity of the one holy Christian and apostolic church, which extends through world history. The church is to be found wherever the marks of the church are present: the Gospel in the Word and the Sacraments. These have been proclaimed, confessed, and celebrated in many different cultures and are in no way limited nor especially attached to any single culture or people. As this commentary series seeks to articulate the universal truth of the Gospel, it acknowledges and affirms the confession of the scriptural truth in all the many times and places where the one true church has been found. Aiming to promote *concord* in the confession of the one scriptural Gospel, these commentaries seek to be, in the best sense of the terms, *confessional, ecumenical,* and *catholic*.

All of those convictions and characteristics describe the theological heritage of Martin Luther and of the confessors who subscribe to the *Book of Concord* (1580)—those who have come to be known as Lutherans. The editors and authors forthrightly confess their subscription to the doctrinal exposition of Scripture in the *Book of Concord*. As the publishing arm of The Lutheran

Church—Missouri Synod, Concordia Publishing House is bound to doctrinal agreement with the Scriptures and the Lutheran Confessions and seeks to herald the true Christian doctrine to the ends of the earth. To that end, the series has enlisted confessional Lutheran authors from other church bodies around the world who share the evangelical mission of promoting theological concord.

The authors and editors stand in the exegetical tradition of Martin Luther and the other Lutheran reformers, who in turn (as their writings took pains to demonstrate) stood in continuity with faithful exegesis by theologians of the early and medieval church, rooted in the hermeneutics of the Scriptures themselves (evident, for example, by how the New Testament interprets the Old). This hermeneutical method, practiced also by many non-Lutherans, includes (1) interpreting Scripture with Scripture according to the analogy of faith, that is, in harmony with the whole of Christian doctrine revealed in the Word; (2) giving utmost attention to the grammar (lexicography, phonetics, morphology, syntax, pragmatics) of the original language of the text; (3) seeking to discern the intended meaning of the text, the "plain" or "literal" sense, aware that the language of Scripture ranges from narrative to discourse, from formal prose to evocative poetry, from archaic to acrostic to apocalyptic, and it uses metaphor, type, parable, and other figures; (4) drawing on philology, linguistics, archaeology, literature, philosophy, history, and other fields in the quest for a better understanding of the text; (5) considering the history of the church's interpretation; (6) applying the text as authoritative also in the present milieu of the interpreter; and (7) above all, seeing the present application and fulfillment of the text in terms of Jesus Christ and his corporate church; upholding the Word, Baptism, and the Supper as the means through which Christ imparts salvation today; and affirming the inauguration, already now, of the eternal benefits of that salvation that is yet to come.

To be sure, the authors and editors do not feel bound to agree with every detail of the exegesis of our Lutheran forefathers. Nor do we imagine that the interpretations presented here are the final word about every crux and enigmatic passage. But the work has been done in harmony with the exegetical tradition that reaches back through the Lutheran confessors all the way to the biblical writers themselves, and in harmony with the confession of the church: grace alone, faith alone, Scripture alone, Christ alone.

The editors wish to acknowledge their debt of gratitude for all who have helped make possible this series. It was conceived at CPH in 1990, and a couple of years of planning and prayer to the Lord of the church preceded its formal launch on July 2, 1992. During that time, Dr. J. A. O. Preus II volunteered his enthusiasm for the project because, in his view, it would nurture and advance the faithful proclamation of the Christian faith as understood by the Lutheran church. The financial support that has underwritten the series was provided by a gracious donor who wished to remain anonymous. Those two faithful servants of God were called to heavenly rest a few short years later.

During the early years, former CPH presidents Dr. John W. Gerber and Dr. Stephen J. Carter had the foresight to recognize the potential benefit of such a landmark work for the church at large. CPH allowed Dr. Christopher W. Mitchell to devote his time and energy to the conception and initial development of the project. Dr. Mitchell has remained the CPH editor and is also the Old Testament editor. Dr. Dean O. Wenthe has served on the project since its official start in 1992 and is the general editor, as well as a commentary author. Mrs. Julene Gernant Dumit (M.A.R.) has been the CPH production editor for the entire series. In 1999 Dr. Jeffrey A. Gibbs, already a commentary author, joined the editorial board as the New Testament editor.

CPH thanks Concordia Theological Seminary, Fort Wayne, Indiana, for kindly allowing its president, Dr. Dean O. Wenthe, to serve as the general editor of the series and to dedicate a substantial portion of his time to it for many years. CPH also thanks Concordia Seminary, St. Louis, Missouri, for permitting Dr. Jeffrey A. Gibbs to devote a significant share of his time to his capacity as the New Testament editor. Those two seminaries have thereby extended their ministries in selfless service for the benefit of the church.

The editors pray that the beneficence of their institutions may be reflected in this series by an evangelical orientation, a steadfast Christological perspective, an eschatological view toward the ultimate good of Christ's bride, and a concern that the wedding feast of the King's Son may be filled with all manner of guests (Mt 22:1–14).

> Now to him who is able to establish you by my Gospel and the preaching of Jesus Christ, by the revelation of the mystery kept secret for ages past but now revealed also through the prophetic Scriptures, made known to all the nations by order of the eternal God unto the obedience of faith—to the only wise God, through Jesus Christ, be the glory forever. Amen! (Rom 16:25–27)

Author's Preface

There is a German saying that can be freely translated, "When I am finished, I also begin." That is hyperbolic, at least in my case, at the conclusion of essaying a commentary on a book, especially one as sometimes seemingly opaque as Ezekiel.

Inevitably, there are afterthoughts. When there were choices between viable options, did I make the right choice? Certain sections of the book remain question marks in my mind, for example, the precise background of the oracle against the king of Tyre in chapter 28, the identification of the guide (e.g., 40:3–4) and of the "Prince" (נָשִׂיא) in chapters 40–48, and so on.

Writing a somewhat technical commentary, based on the original language, inevitably reinforces in one's mind the truism that "every translation is an interpretation." Hence, a comparison of the renditions in the major English translations was often at least as enlightening as other commentaries. (I limited myself to commonly used versions.)

Perhaps the major overriding issue for me throughout was the simultaneous tension and unity of the historical and the Christological. It is axiomatic among us that a confessional commentary must do justice to both aspects. But the task is far easier said than done! The commentary is basically structured in a division between the text's philological and Christological perspectives. But their distinction is often artificial. For the grammatical aspects, there are relatively clear and commonly agreed upon rules to follow. But what rules shall one follow in expounding the Christological sense of an Old Testament text? There are, of course, certain general hermeneutical principles to follow, but, except where there is a clear New Testament reference (rare in Ezekiel), one can only pray that the Holy Spirit has informed him sufficiently. The user of this commentary must be the final judge of especially that aspect of my efforts.

Or to put the matter differently, it is a reminder of the extent to which the church must always steer between the Scylla of historicism on the one hand and the Charybdis of allegory on the other. Modern commentaries have, to one degree or the other, succumbed to the former, leaving the Old Testament especially as an ancient, largely irrelevant record of "spirituality." In even conservative churches, at least since the Enlightenment (and certainly no less so in a so-called "postmodern era"), those cultural changes always seek to infiltrate. We may have exorcized the grosser manifestations of historicism (JEDP, an imagined Second Isaiah, etc.), but in subtler ways those pressures never cease to threaten. No further evidence is needed than to note the distinctly subcanonical status the Old Testament holds in the actual piety and practice of the church.

No less a perennial threat are the countless sermons and meditations one hears that, at best, can only be labeled "allegorical."[1] Even though we can

---

[1] A very instructive illustration of patristic exegesis, which, in its own way, was also text-based, is this study of ancient Christian commentary on Ezekiel 1: Christman, "What Did Ezekiel See?"

hardly own that precise method, at least its overriding concern was with the text's possible message about the triune God who has revealed himself in the life, death, and resurrection of our Savior. In a good sense, concern with historical matters has entered our consciousness in a way that it did not confront antiquity, and, if properly deployed, lends reinforcement to basic doctrines such as the incarnation, resurrection of the body, and the Sacraments.

When it comes to those to whom I owe special thanks, I hardly know where to start. Perhaps I must begin with the sainted Dr. Walter Roehrs at Concordia Seminary, St. Louis, who first introduced me to the hidden treasures of the Hebrew language and its ancient Near Eastern environment. I had taught electives in Ezekiel several times before embarking on this commentary, and inevitably, one learns from interaction with the students. Here I must single out Carl Hanson, now a missionary in Taiwan, who compiled an exhaustive bibliography on Ezekiel for me. (The vast majority of the titles, if accessible, I found to be either too popular for my purposes or too "far out" even to merit refutation.) The editors of this commentary, Dr. Chris Mitchell and Mrs. Julene Dumit, have labored over and improved on my manuscript to a greater extent than I will ever know. And last, but by no means least, I must remember my wife, Ruth, who tolerated no little neglect of other matters while I wrestled with Ezekiel.

July 21, 2005
Feast of St. Ezekiel[2]

---

[2] *LSB* follows the Maronite calendar in commemorating St. Ezekiel on July 21. In the Greek Orthodox calendar, the day for Ezekiel is July 23.

Principal Abbreviations

Books of the Bible

Gen	2 Ki	Is	Nah	Rom	Titus
Ex	1 Chr	Jer	Hab	1 Cor	Philemon
Lev	2 Chr	Lam	Zeph	2 Cor	Heb
Num	Ezra	Ezek	Hag	Gal	James
Deut	Neh	Dan	Zech	Eph	1 Pet
Josh	Esth	Hos	Mal	Phil	2 Pet
Judg	Job	Joel	Mt	Col	1 Jn
Ruth	Ps (pl. Pss)	Amos	Mk	1 Thess	2 Jn
1 Sam	Prov	Obad	Lk	2 Thess	3 Jn
2 Sam	Eccl	Jonah	Jn	1 Tim	Jude
1 Ki	Song	Micah	Acts	2 Tim	Rev

Books of the Apocrypha and Other Noncanonical Books of the Septuagint

1–2 Esdras	1–2 Esdras
Tobit	Tobit
Judith	Judith
Add Esth	Additions to Esther
Wis Sol	Wisdom of Solomon
Sirach	Sirach/Ecclesiasticus
Baruch	Baruch
Ep Jer	Epistle of Jeremiah
Azariah	Prayer of Azariah
Song of the Three	Song of the Three Young Men
Susanna	Susanna
Bel	Bel and the Dragon
Manasseh	Prayer of Manasseh
1–2 Macc	1–2 Maccabees
3–4 Macc	3–4 Maccabees
Ps 151	Psalm 151
Odes	Odes
Ps(s) Sol	Psalm(s) of Solomon

Reference Works and Scripture Versions

AASOR	Annual of the American Schools of Oriental Research
ABD	*Anchor Bible Dictionary.* Edited by D. N. Freedman. 6 vols. New York: Doubleday, 1992
AC	Augsburg Confession
AE	American ed. of *Luther's Works.* 55 vols. St. Louis: Concordia; Philadelphia: Fortress, 1955–1986
AJA	*American Journal of Archaeology*
ANEP	*The Ancient Near East in Pictures Relating to the Old Testament.* Edited by J. B. Pritchard. 2d ed. Princeton: Princeton University Press, 1969
ANET	*Ancient Near Eastern Texts Relating to the Old Testament.* Edited by J. B. Pritchard. 3d ed. Princeton: Princeton University Press, 1969
ANF	*The Ante-Nicene Fathers.* Edited by A. Roberts and J. Donaldson. 10 vols. Repr. Peabody, Mass.: Hendrickson, 1994
Ap	Apology of the Augsburg Confession
BASOR	*Bulletin of the American Schools of Oriental Research*
BDB	Brown, F., S. R. Driver, and C. A. Briggs. *A Hebrew and English Lexicon of the Old Testament.* Oxford: Clarendon, 1979
BHS	*Biblia Hebraica Stuttgartensia*
BZAW	Beihefte zur Zeitschrift für die alttestamentliche Wissenschaft
CBQ	*Catholic Biblical Quarterly*
CCSL	Corpus Christianorum: Series latina. Turnhout: Brepols, 1953–
CTA	*Corpus des tablettes en cunéiformes alphabétiques découvertes à Ras Shamra-Ugarit de 1929 à 1939.* Edited by Andrée Herdner. Paris: P. Geuthner, 1963.
DCH	*The Dictionary of Classical Hebrew.* Edited by D. J. A. Clines. Sheffield: Sheffield Academic Press, 1993–
Ep	Epitome of the Formula of Concord
ESV	English Standard Version of the Bible
ET	English translation
FC	Formula of Concord
GKC	*Gesenius' Hebrew Grammar.* Edited by E. Kautzsch. Translated by A. E. Cowley. 2d ed. Oxford: Clarendon, 1910

GTJ	*Grace Theological Journal*
HALOT	Koehler, L., W. Baumgartner, and J. J. Stamm. *The Hebrew and Aramaic Lexicon of the Old Testament.* Translated and edited under the supervision of M. E. J. Richardson. 5 vols. Leiden: Brill, 1994–2000
IDB	*The Interpreter's Dictionary of the Bible.* Edited by G. A. Buttrick. 5 vols. Nashville: Abingdon, 1962, 1976
Jastrow	Jastrow, M., comp. *A Dictionary of the Targumim, the Talmud Babli and Yerushalmi, and the Midrashic Literature.* 2 vols. Brooklyn: P. Shalom, 1967
JBL	*Journal of Biblical Literature*
Joüon	Joüon, P. *A Grammar of Biblical Hebrew.* Translated and revised by T. Muraoka. 2 vols. Subsidia biblica 14/1–2. Rome: Editrice Pontificio Istituto Biblico, 1991
KJV	King James Version of the Bible
LEH	Lust, J., E. Eynikel, and K. Hauspie. *A Greek-English Lexicon of the Septuagint.* 2 vols. Stuttgart: Deutsche Bibelgesellschaft, 1992–1996
LSB	*Lutheran Service Book.* St. Louis: Concordia, 2006
LW	*Lutheran Worship.* St. Louis: Concordia, 1982
LXX	Septuagint
MT	Masoretic Text of the Hebrew Old Testament
NASB	New American Standard Bible
NIV	New International Version of the Bible
NKJV	New King James Version of the Bible
NRSV	New Revised Standard Version of the Bible
NT	New Testament
OT	Old Testament
PL	Patrologia latina. Edited by J.-P. Migne. 217 vols. Paris, 1844–1864
RSV	Revised Standard Version of the Bible
SA	Smalcald Articles
SC	Small Catechism by M. Luther
SD	Solid Declaration of the Formula of Concord
Soncino ed.	Hebrew-English Edition of the Babylonian Talmud. Edited by I. Epstein. 30 vols. London: Soncino, 1984–1990
TLH	*The Lutheran Hymnal.* St. Louis: Concordia, 1941
VT	*Vetus Testamentum*
VTSup	Supplements to Vetus Testamentum

WA DB	Weimar Ausgabe Deutsche Bibel ("German Bible"). *Luthers Werke: Kritische Gesamtausgabe. Deutsche Bibel.* 12 vols. Weimar: Böhlau, 1906–1961
Waltke-O'Connor	Waltke, B. K., and M. O'Connor. *An Introduction to Biblical Hebrew Syntax.* Winona Lake, Ind.: Eisenbrauns, 1990
Williams	Williams, R. J. *Hebrew Syntax: An Outline.* 2d ed. Toronto: University of Toronto Press, 1976
ZAW	*Zeitschrift für die alttestamentliche Wissenschaft*

Icons

These icons are used in the margins of this commentary to highlight the following themes:

Trinity

Temple, Tabernacle

Incarnation

Passion, Atonement

Death and Resurrection,
Theology of the Cross,
the Great Reversal

Christus Victor,
Christology

Baptism

Catechesis,
Instruction, Revelation

Lord's Supper

Ministry of Word and Sacrament,
Office of the Keys

The Church,
Christian Marriage

Worship

Sin, Law Breaking,
Death

Hope of Heaven,
Eschatology

Justification

Bibliography

Albright, William Foxwell. *Archaeology and the Religion of Israel.* 4th ed. Baltimore: Johns Hopkins University Press, 1956.

———. "The Babylonian Temple-Tower and the Altar of Burnt-Offering." *Journal of Biblical Literature* 39 (1920): 137–42.

Alexander, Ralph. *Ezekiel.* Chicago: Moody, 1976.

Allen, Leslie C. *Ezekiel.* 2 vols. Word Biblical Commentary 28–29. Dallas: Word, 1990 (vol. 2), 1994 (vol. 1).

Block, Daniel I. "*Bny ʿmwn*: The Sons of Ammon." *Andrews University Seminary Studies* 22 (1984): 197–212.

———. *The Book of Ezekiel.* 2 vols. New International Commentary on the Old Testament. Grand Rapids: Eerdmans, 1997–1998.

Boadt, Lawrence E. *Ezekiel's Oracles against Egypt: A Literary and Philological Study of Ezekiel 29–32.* Biblica et Orientalia 37. Rome: Biblical Institute Press, 1980.

———. "Mythological Themes and the Unity of Ezekiel." Pages 211–31 in *Literary Structure and Rhetorical Strategies in the Hebrew Bible.* Edited by L. J. de Regt, J. de Waard, and J. P. Fokkelman. Assen, The Netherlands: Van Gorcum, 1996.

Bøe, Sverre. *Gog and Magog: Ezekiel 38–39 as Pre-Text for Revelation 19, 17–21 and 20, 7–10,* Wissenschaftliche Untersuchungen zum Neuen Testament 2/135. Tübingen: Mohr Siebeck, 2001.

Brighton, Louis A. *Revelation.* Concordia Commentary. St. Louis: Concordia, 1999.

Chemnitz, Martin. *The Two Natures in Christ.* Translated by J. A. O. Preus. St. Louis: Concordia, 1971.

Christensen, Duane L. *Transformations of the War Oracle in Old Testament Prophecy: Studies in the Oracles against the Nations.* Harvard Dissertations in Religion 3. Missoula, Mont.: Scholars Press, 1975.

Christman, Angela Russell. "What Did Ezekiel See? Patristic Exegesis of Ezekiel 1 and Debates about God's Incomprehensibility." *Pro Ecclesia* 8/3 (Summer 1999): 338–63.

Cook, Stephen L., and Corrine L. Patton, ed. *Ezekiel's Hierarchical World: Wrestling with a Tiered Reality.* Leiden: Brill, 2004.

Cooke, G. A. *A Critical and Exegetical Commentary on the Book of Ezekiel.* International Critical Commentary 21. Edinburgh: T&T Clark, 1936.

Dahood, Mitchell. *Psalms.* 3 vols. Anchor Bible 16–17A. Garden City, N.Y.: Doubleday, 1966–1970.

Davies, W. Vivian, and Louise Schofield, eds. *Egypt, the Aegean and the Levant: Interconnections in the Second Millennium BC.* London: British Museum Press, 1995.

Deterding, Paul E. *Colossians.* Concordia Commentary. St. Louis: Concordia, 2003.

Dijk, H. J. van. *Ezekiel's Prophecy on Tyre (Ez. 26,1–28,19): A New Approach.* Biblica et orientalia 20. Rome: Pontifical Biblical Institute, 1968.

Eichrodt, Walther. *Ezekiel: A Commentary.* Translated by Cosslett Quin. Old Testament Library. Philadelphia: Westminster, 1970.

Finegan, Jack. *Handbook of Biblical Chronology.* Rev. ed. Peabody, Mass.: Hendrickson, 1998.

Fohrer, Georg. *Ezechiel.* Handbuch zum Alten Testament (First Series) 13. Tübingen: Mohr (Siebeck), 1955.

———. *Die symbolischen Handlungen der Propheten.* 2d ed. Zurich: Zwingli Verlag, 1968.

Freedy, K. S., and D. B. Redford. "The Dates in Ezekiel in Relation to Biblical, Babylonian and Egyptian Sources." *Journal of the American Oriental Society* 90 (1970): 462–85.

Friebel, Kelvin. *Jeremiah's and Ezekiel's Sign-Acts: Rhetorical Nonverbal Communication.* Journal for the Study of the Old Testament: Supplement Series 283. Sheffield: Sheffield Academic Press, 1999.

Garfinkel, S. P. *Studies in Akkadian Influences in the Book of Ezekiel.* Ann Arbor: University Microfilms, 1983.

Gerhard, Johann. *On the Nature of Theology and Scripture.* Theological Commonplaces. Translated by Richard J. Dinda. Saint Louis: Concordia, 2006.

Gese, Hartmut. *Der Verfassungsentwurf des Ezechiel (Kap. 40–48): Traditionsgeschichtlich Untersucht.* Beiträge zur historischen Theologie 25. Tübingen: Mohr (Siebeck), 1957.

Gibbs, Jeffrey A. *Matthew 1:1–11:1.* Concordia Commentary. St. Louis: Concordia, 2006.

Gibson, John C. L. *Canaanite Myths and Legends.* Edinburgh: T&T Clark, 1977.

Gray, Theodosia, trans. *The Homilies of St. Gregory the Great on the Book of the Prophet Ezekiel.* Etna, Calif.: Center for Traditionalist Orthodox Studies, 1990.

Greenberg, Moshe. "The Design and Themes of Ezekiel's Program of Restoration." *Interpretation* 38 (1984): 181–208.

———. *Ezekiel.* 2 vols. Anchor Bible 22–22A. Garden City, N.Y.: Doubleday, 1983–1997.

Hals, Ronald M. *Ezekiel.* The Forms of the Old Testament Literature 19. Grand Rapids: Eerdmans, 1989.

Harstad, Adolph L. *Joshua.* Concordia Commentary. St. Louis: Concordia, 2004.

Hengstenberg, E. W. *Christology of the Old Testament and a Commentary on the Messianic Predictions.* Translated by James Martin. 2d ed. Vol. 3. Edinburgh: T&T Clark, 1864.

Herrmann, Johannes. *Ezechiel.* Kommentar zum alten Testament 11. Leipzig: Deichert, 1924.

Hoekema, Anthony A. *The Bible and the Future*. Grand Rapids: Eerdmans, 1979.

Howie, Carl G. *The Date and Composition of Ezekiel*. Journal of Biblical Literature Monograph Series 4. Philadelphia: Society of Biblical Literature, 1950.

Hummel, Horace D. "Enclitic *Mem* in Early Northwest Semitic, Especially Hebrew." *Journal of Biblical Literature* 76 (1957): 85–107.

———. *Ezekiel 1–20*. Concordia Commentary. St. Louis: Concordia, 2005.

Just, Arthur A., Jr. *Luke 1:1–9:50*. Concordia Commentary. St. Louis: Concordia, 1996.

———. *Luke 9:51–24:53*. Concordia Commentary. St. Louis: Concordia, 1997.

Keil, Carl Friedrich. *Biblical Commentary on the Prophecies of Ezekiel*. Translated by James Martin. 2 vols. Edinburgh: T&T Clark, 1876. Repr., Grand Rapids: Eerdmans, 1978. Translation of *Biblischer Commentar über den Propheten Ezechiel*. Biblischer Commentar über das Alte Testament, vol. 3 of part 3, by C. F. Keil and Franz Delitzsch. Leipzig: Dörffling & Franke, 1868.

Kesler, Andreas. "Hesekiel." Pages 953–1016 in the Old Testament portion of *Biblia, das ist die ganze heilige Schrift Alten und Neuen Testaments verdeutscht von Doctor Martin Luther, und auf Herzog Ernst's Verordnung von etlichen reinen Theologen dem eigentlichen Wortoerstand nach erklärt*. Das Weimarische Bibelwerk. 2d ed. 1768. Repr., St. Louis: Fr. Dette, 1880. The first edition was published in 1640.

Kleinig, John W. *Leviticus*. Concordia Commentary. St. Louis: Concordia, 2003.

Kliefoth, Theodor. *Das Buch Ezechiels*. 2 vols. in 1. Rostock: Hinstorff'sche Verlagsbuchhandlung, 1864–1865.

Kutsko, John F. *Between Heaven and Earth: Divine Presence and Absence in the Book of Ezekiel*. Winona Lake, Ind.: Eisenbrauns, 2000.

Lessing, R. Reed. *Jonah*. Concordia Commentary. St. Louis: Concordia, 2007.

Levenson, Jon Douglas. *Theology of the Program of Restoration of Ezekiel 40–48*. Harvard Semitic Monograph 10. Cambridge, Mass.: Scholars Press, 1976.

Levy, Abraham J. *Rashi's Commentary on Ezekiel 40–48*. Philadelphia: Dropsie College, 1931.

Lockwood, Gregory J. *1 Corinthians*. Concordia Commentary. St. Louis: Concordia, 2000.

Luther's Small Catechism with Explanation. St. Louis: Concordia, 1986, 1991.

Malamat, Abraham. "The Last Kings of Judah and the Fall of Jerusalem: An Historical-Chronological Study." *Israel Exploration Journal* 18 (1968): 137–56.

Manning, Gary T. *Echoes of a Prophet: The Use of Ezekiel in the Gospel of John and in Literature of the Second Temple Period*. London: T&T Clark, 2004.

Mitchell, Christopher W. *Our Suffering Savior: Exegetical Studies and Sermons for Ash Wednesday through Easter Based on Isaiah 52:13–53:12*. St. Louis: Concordia, 2003.

———. *The Song of Songs*. Concordia Commentary. St. Louis: Concordia, 2003.

Neumann, Wilhelm. *Die Wasser des Lebens: Ein exegetischer versuch uber Ezechiel 47, 1–12*. Berlin: Enslinsche, 1848.

Neuss, Wilhelm. *Das Buch Ezechiel in Theologie und Kunst bis zum Ende des XII. Jahrhunderts*. Münster: Aschendorff, 1912.

Pieper, Francis. *Christian Dogmatics*. 3 vols. St. Louis: Concordia, 1950–1953.

Pope, Marvin H. *El in the Ugaritic Texts*. Supplements to Vetus Testamentum 2. Leiden: Brill, 1955.

Raabe, Paul R. *Obadiah*. Anchor Bible 24D. New York: Doubleday, 1996.

———. "Why Prophetic Oracles against the Nations?" Pages 236–57 in *Fortunate the Eyes That See: Essays in Honor of David Noel Freedman in Celebration of His Seventieth Birthday*. Edited by Astrid B. Beck, Andrew H. Bartelt, Paul R. Raabe, and Chris A. Franke. Grand Rapids: Eerdmans, 1995.

Taylor, John B. *Ezekiel: An Introduction and Commentary*. Tyndale Old Testament Commentaries. Downers Grove, Ill.: Inter-Varsity, 1969.

Tov, Emanuel. *Textual Criticism of the Hebrew Bible*. 2d rev. ed. Minneapolis: Fortress, 1992, 2001.

Tuell, Steven Shawn. *The Law of the Temple in Ezekiel 40–48*. Harvard Semitic Monographs 49. Atlanta: Scholars Press, 1992.

Ulrich, Dean. "Dissonant Prophecy in Ezekiel 26 and 29." *Bulletin for Biblical Research* 10/1 (2000): 121–41.

Whiston, William, trans. *The Works of Josephus*. Complete and unabridged in 1 vol. New updated ed. Peabody, Mass.: Hendrickson Publishers, 1987.

Yeivin, Israel. *Introduction to the Tiberian Masorah*. Translated and edited by E. J. Revell. Masoretic Studies 5. Missoula, Mont.: Scholars Press, 1980.

Zimmerli, Walther. *Ezekiel*. Translated by Ronald E. Clements. 2 vols. Hermeneia. Philadelphia: Fortress, 1979–1983.

Ezekiel 4–24

Prophecies of Judgment against Israel

Ezekiel 21:1–37 (ET 20:45–21:32)
Yahweh's Punishing Sword Is Drawn

Translation

21 ¹The Word of Yahweh came to me: ²"Son of man, set your face toward Teman, preach against Darom, and prophesy against the scrub forest of the Negev. ³Say to the Negev scrub, 'Hear the Word of Yahweh! Thus says the Lord Yahweh: I am about to kindle in you a fire, and it will devour in you every green tree and every dry tree. The blazing flame will not be extinguished, and every face will be scorched by it, from south to north. ⁴Everyone will see that I, Yahweh, have kindled it; it will not be extinguished.'"

⁵Then I said, "Oh, Lord Yahweh, they are saying about me, 'Doesn't he love to talk in riddles?'"

⁶Then the Word of Yahweh came to me: ⁷"Son of man, set your face toward Jerusalem, preach against the sanctuaries, and prophesy against the land of Israel. ⁸Say to the land of Israel, 'Thus says Yahweh: I am against you, and I will draw out my sword from its scabbard and cut off from you both righteous and wicked. ⁹Because I have resolved to cut off from you both righteous and wicked, therefore my sword will come out of its scabbard against everyone from south to north. ¹⁰Then everyone will know that I, Yahweh, have drawn my sword from its scabbard; it will not return [to its sheath] again.' ¹¹Now you, son of man, groan as though doubled up in pain; groan in front of them as though in bitter anguish. ¹²When they ask you, 'Why are you groaning?' say, 'Because of the news that is coming. Then every heart will melt, all hands will hang limp, every spirit will faint, and all knees will run with water. It is coming, and it will happen, says the Lord Yahweh.'"

¹³The Word of Yahweh came to me: ¹⁴"Son of man, prophesy and say, 'Thus the Lord says:

" 'A sword, a sword has been sharpened,
>   and it is polished too.
¹⁵It has been sharpened for slaughter,
>   polished to flash like lightning.
Or shall we rejoice, staff of my son?
>   [The sword] despises every tree.
¹⁶But the sword has been given to be polished,
>   to be grasped by the hand.
It has been sharpened, and it has been polished
>   to be put into the hand of a killer.
¹⁷Cry out and wail, son of man,
>   because it is against my people;
>   it is against all the princes of Israel.

They have been thrown to the sword together with my people.

 Therefore, slap [your] thigh.

¹⁸For it has been tested. Now what?

If even a staff, which [the sword] despises, will not be … ?

 says the Lord Yahweh.'

¹⁹"Now you, son of man, prophesy.

 Clap your hands.

Let the sword strike twice, even thrice.

 It is a sword of the slain,

a sword that slays also great men,

 [a sword] that pursues even into their private homes,

²⁰so that hearts may melt

 and those who stumble may multiply.

At all their gates

 I have set the point of the sword.

Ah, it is made to flash like lightning,

 unsheathed for slaughter.

²¹Focus on the right, turn to the left,

 whenever your blade is turned.

²²I myself will also clap my hands

 and satisfy my wrath.

I, Yahweh, have spoken."

²³The Word of Yahweh came to me: ²⁴"Now you, son of man, mark out two roads for the sword of the king of Babylon to come. Both of them should originate in the same country. Make a signpost; make it at the fork of the road to the city. ²⁵Mark out a road for the sword to come to Rabbah of the sons of Ammon or to Judah in fortified Jerusalem. ²⁶For the king of Babylon will stand at the fork of the road, at the beginning of the two roads, in order to practice divination. He will shake the arrows, consult the teraphim, and examine the liver. ²⁷In his right hand will be the omen for Jerusalem, to erect battering rams, to open mouths for shouting, to sound the battle cry, to set battering rams against the gates, to throw up a ramp, to build a siege wall. ²⁸But to them it will seem like false divination. They have sworn solemn oaths, but he [Yahweh] will bring their iniquity to mind, resulting in their being captured. ²⁹Therefore, thus says the Lord Yahweh: Because you have brought to mind your iniquity by your rebellious acts being disclosed, so that your sins are revealed in all your misdeeds—because you have been brought to mind, you will be taken in hand. ³⁰And you, you wicked corpse, prince of Israel, whose day has come at the time of final punishment, ³¹thus says the Lord Yahweh: Remove the turban; take off the crown. Everything will be changed. Raise the low; bring down the high. ³²Ruin, ruin, ruin I will make it. But this will not be until the one to whom judgment belongs comes and to whom I will give it."

³³"Now you, son of man, prophesy and say, 'Thus says the Lord Yahweh concerning the sons of Ammon and their taunts.' Say, 'Sword, sword, unsheathed for

slaughter, polished to consume, to flash like lightning, ³⁴when false visions were seen about you, when deceitful divinations were made about you, to put you on the necks of corpses of wicked men, whose day had come at the time of final punishment. ³⁵Put [your sword] back in its scabbard. In the place where you were created, in the land of your origin, I will judge you. ³⁶I will pour out my wrath on you; I will blow the fire of my fury upon you; I will deliver you into the hands of brutal men, expert destroyers. ³⁷You will be fuel for the fire; your blood will flow all over the land; and you will no longer be remembered, for I, Yahweh, have spoken.' "

Textual Notes

21:2 בֶּן־אָדָם—For Ezekiel as a "son of man," see the second textual note and the commentary on 2:1.[1]

שִׂים פָּנֶיךָ—The Qal of שִׂים is the first of three imperatives in 21:2 (ET 20:46), all of which will be repeated in 21:7 (ET 21:2). "Set *your* face" is a recurring expression in Ezekiel[2] that is related to the so-called hostile orientation formula, "behold, I am against you."[3] Similar expressions use essentially synonymous vocabulary (e.g., 4:3; 15:7). The expression is an obvious derivative of the universal practice of facing the person to whom one is speaking, although here and in 6:2, where we first met it, the addressees are inanimate. An actual gesture or facial expression may be implied as a sort of action prophecy,[4] but in Ezekiel's usage the expression is mostly figurative, merely indicating hostile disposition toward the object.

תֵּימָנָה ... דָּרוֹם ... נֶגֶב—A virtual crux is involved in trying to decide whether the three nouns are proper place names or essentially synonymous terms for the direction south. Most English translations from KJV on opt for the latter alternative. After some debate, I have decided with the LXX and others that taking them as place names is more likely. The original audience would have associated them with the south, but that is exegesis, not translation. First of all, it seems strange to me that three essentially synonymous words for "south" would be used in a row. Second, all three words are used as place names elsewhere in the Bible. "Teman" is somewhere in Edom, south-southeast of Jerusalem. "Darom" is known from the Mishnah as a region north of Beersheba. It is a favorite term of Ezekiel, whose book includes thirteen of the seventeen OT occurrences. Elsewhere Ezekiel always uses it with the definite article as a directional term, "the south." Only here in Ezekiel is it anarthrous, and only here in the OT is it a proper place name. Perhaps its directional use is derivative from the place name. "Negev," usually reckoned as beginning south of Beersheba, is the best known name of the three names. Sometimes נֶגֶב is transliterated as

---

[1] The introduction and the textual notes and commentary on the first twenty chapters of Ezekiel are in Hummel, *Ezekiel 1–20*.

[2] See the textual note on 6:2. The expression occurs in 6:2; 13:17; 21:2, 7 (ET 20:46; 21:2); 25:2; 28:21; 29:2; 35:2; 38:2.

[3] For this formula, see page 9 in the introduction and the commentary on 5:8.

[4] See "Ezekiel's Action Prophecies" in Hummel, *Ezekiel 1–20*, 148–50.

"Negeb," but phonetically a *bet* without *daghesh* is pronounced like "v." Above all, since this first part of the oracle is a parable and its interpretation in 21:6–12 (ET 21:1–7) applies it to Jerusalem, it seems more natural for actual places (in the south) to stand for another place (Jerusalem).

The final phrase, יַעַר הַשָּׂדֶה נֶגֶב, is accented so that (literally) "forest of the field" is followed by "Negev" in apposition. Since the next verse has simply יַעַר הַנֶּגֶב ("the Negev scrub"), שָׂדֶה here is widely taken as a gloss.[5] The LXX read (or interpreted) שָׂדֶה as שַׂר ("chief"), while the Syriac does not reflect שָׂדֶה at all. If the MT is to be defended, there seem to be two alternatives. First, Eastern and some other Hebrew manuscripts have נֶגְבָּה (with directive *he*), placing the word in apposition to the preceding prepositional phrase with אֶל. The MT's נֶגֶב may simply be assuming that. A bit more radically, one may with the Vulgate and Targum attach the article to נֶגֶב rather than שָׂדֶה to form a three-word construct chain. I have translated "the scrub forest of the Negev" without necessarily endorsing an emendation.

וְהַטֵּף is the Hiphil imperative of נָטַף. In the Qal, it usually means "to drip." In the Hiphil too, Hebrew can use it in its native application to liquids (Amos 9:13), but somehow its Hiphil came to be used most commonly of speech. Here it is essentially synonymous with the following Niphal imperative הִנָּבֵא, "prophesy," but perhaps is more picturesque.

21:3 וְאָמַרְתָּ—Following the three imperatives in 21:2 (ET 20:46), this perfect with *waw* consecutive ("say") has imperatival force (Joüon, §119 l).

הִנְנִי מַצִּית—The interjection הִנֵּה (with first common singular suffix) followed by the Hiphil participle of יָצַת probably signals imminence (*futurum instans*, GKC, § 116 p): "I am about to kindle."

Four rhetorical devices are used to emphasize the extent and severity of the conflagration. First, כָּל, "every," is used three times. Second, there are two uses of merism, wherein the whole is represented by the two boundaries: "green" and "dry," and "from south to north," which is the opposite of the common "Dan to Beersheba" direction (e.g., Judg 20:1), probably because of the previous concentration on the south in Ezek 21:2–3a (ET 20:46–47a). Third, there are two assertions that the blaze will not be extinguished (21:3–4 [ET 20:47–48]). Fourth, the rhyming and rhythmic construct phrase לֶהֶבֶת שַׁלְהֶבֶת, literally, "flame of flame," is redundant but also emphatic. לֶהֶבֶת can be used as an absolute form or as the construct of לֶהָבָה, a common Hebrew word for "flame." The masculine form לַהַב also appears in the OT. The absence of an article on the *nomen rectum*, שַׁלְהֶבֶת, is a devise of high, poetic style. שַׁלְהֶבֶת is an augmented form of לֶהֶבֶת with the preformative שׁ. The use of שׁ as a noun preformative probably derives from the use of שׁ as a verb preformative in Akkadian, Ugaritic, and Aramaic, which use the Shaphel conjugation instead of the Hebrew Hiphil. In the Bible שַׁלְהֶבֶת occurs elsewhere only in Job 15:30 and Song 8:6. שַׁלְהֶבֶת also appears in Rabbinic Hebrew.

וְנִצְרְבוּ—The verb צָרַב is a hapax, but there are cognate nominal and adjectival forms in Hebrew, as well as an Akkadian cognate. For this Niphal (third common

---

[5] So Zimmerli, *Ezekiel*, 1:420; Allen, *Ezekiel*, 2:19.

plural perfect with *waw* consecutive) "burn" (KJV) is a possible translation, but "scorch" is more commonly employed for variation.

21.4 כָּל־בָּשָׂר—Literally, "all flesh," this common OT expression, which recurs in 21:9–10 (ET 21:4–5), is translated idiomatically as "everyone." בָּשָׂר can mean the "body" of a creature (10:12) or the "flesh" on bones (37:6, 8), but with כָּל, it generally implies "all humanity."

בְּעַרְתִּיהָ—This Piel (first common singular perfect with third feminine singular suffix) of בָּעַר, "kindle," is a synonym of the Hiphil participle מַצִּית in 21:3 (ET 20:47).

21:5 הֲלֹא מְמַשֵּׁל מְשָׁלִים הוּא—The negative לֹא with interrogative הֲ implies that the answer to the question is obvious and that everybody will answer it affirmatively. My free translation of the Hebrew cognate construction מְמַשֵּׁל מְשָׁלִים, literally, "prattler of parables," is an attempt to reproduce the frequentative force of the Piel participle מְמַשֵּׁל (in contrast to the Qal of מָשַׁל in 17:2). The noun מָשָׁל may be rendered in various ways, including "riddle, parable, allegory," but in general it refers to words that are obscure or difficult to understand. Compare the use of παραβολή in Mt 13:10.

21:7 The structure and vocabulary of this verse correspond almost exactly to those of 21:2 (ET 20:46). Less precise is the correspondence between 21:8–10 (ET 21:3–5) and 21:3–5 (ET 20:47–49).

בֶּן־אָדָם שִׂים פָּנֶיךָ אֶל־—The only structural variation between this clause and the corresponding one in 21:2 (ET 20:46) is that after "set your face," 21:7 (ET 21:2) uses the preposition אֶל, whereas 21:2 (ET 20:46) used דֶּרֶךְ, which clearly meant "toward." Then 21:2 (ET 20:46) went on to use אֶל twice in the sense of "against." The question arises whether here too אֶל should be translated "against" instead of "toward." The preposition אֶל is supple enough that both translations are equally possible—and equally plausible. The ultimate difference in meaning, however, is minor.

מִקְדָּשִׁים—This plural noun raises questions. If taken as a true plural, it must refer to all the pagan shrines in addition to the temple of Yahweh. Greenberg's explanation that the form is "a plural of extension, indicating that the referent of the noun is inherently large or complex"[6] strikes me as forced. A few manuscripts have מִקְדָּשָׁם ("their sanctuary"), with the plural suffix referring to the people of Jerusalem. This reading is followed by the Syriac and perhaps the LXX. It is easier but requires a difficult emendation. Other pronominal suffixes are found in a few other manuscripts or have been proposed by modern scholars, but all lack any real support.

21:8 כֹּה אָמַר יְהֹוָה—On this shorter form of the citation formula, see the third textual note on 11:5.

הִנְנִי אֵלֶיךָ—This clause, literally, "behold, I am against you," corresponds to הִנְנִי מַצִּית in 21:3 (ET 20:47). Clearly אֶל has the hostile sense of "against." NRSV has "I am coming against you," but without support, ancient or modern (other translations). The MT verbless expression is much stronger.

וְהוֹצֵאתִי חַרְבִּי מִתַּעְרָהּ—For unsheathing the sword (חֶרֶב) from its "scabbard" (תַּעַר), this clause uses the Hiphil of יָצָא (first common singular perfect with *waw* consecutive) instead of the usual שָׁלַף (1 Sam 17:51) or הֵרִיק (Ezek 5:2), possibly

---

[6] Greenberg, *Ezekiel*, 2:419; similarly, Cooke, *Ezekiel*, 227–28.

because of assonance between וְהוֹצֵאתִי and מֵצִית in 21:3 (ET 20:47). The next verse uses the Qal of יָצָא to say the sword "will come out."

21:9 יַעַן אֲשֶׁר־הִכְרַתִּי מִמֵּךְ צַדִּיק וְרָשָׁע—Elsewhere יַעַן אֲשֶׁר usually functions as a conjunction meaning "because." Here Block takes it as telic ("so") as in 12:12.[7] The general consensus for it here seems to favor a circumstantial or result meaning ("because"; KJV: "seeing then that …"). הִכְרַתִּי, the Hiphil (first common singular) perfect of כָּרַת, is a sort of prophetic perfect, but apparently with the nuance of "a fixed resolve,"[8] as I have translated it: "because *I have resolved to cut off* from you both righteous and wicked."

מִנֶּגֶב צָפוֹנָה:—One would expect צָפוֹן to have the directive ending (צָפוֹנָה) for "to the north," as at the end of 21:3 (ET 20:47). Some Eastern and other manuscripts do add it, but there are enough examples of its omission that it should be construed as simply a stylistic variant. Hebrew commonly uses a noun as an adverbial accusative (Joüon, § 125 n). In the absence of case endings, that the noun is an accusative is evident only from context.

21:11 My translation tries to reproduce the natural parallelism of the verse. The Masoretic *athnach* would put the major break after the first "groan": "son of man, groan; in breakage of torso and bitterness, groan before them." That accentuation does provide a balance with the beginning of 21:19 (ET 21:14), but that verse is far off in a different division of the chapter, and the result makes for a lopsided expression.

My translation is otherwise free, both because of the vocabulary and because Yahweh here commands an action prophecy. There is no simile ("as though") in the original, but plainly the description is not of Ezekiel's actual physical condition. He should first mime pain caused by a "breakdown/collapse of the lumbar region." The noun שִׁבָּרוֹן is obviously a derivative of the common verb שָׁבַר, "break." The traditional translation of מָתְנַיִם as "loins" (KJV) is not only archaic, but misleading. The word refers to the strong musculature that unites the upper and lower parts of the body, that is, the hips and small of the back and/or lower abdomen. The total picture is that of such crippling pain in that region that a person can barely stand up. The parallel word מְרִירוּת is a hapax, but obviously derivative from מָרַר, "be bitter, afflicted."

21:12 This is the only occurrence in Ezekiel of the interrogative phrase עַל־מָה, "for what reason, why?" Ezekiel uses the more common interrogatives מַדּוּעַ in 18:19 and לָמָּה (disparagingly) in 18:31 and 33:11.

My translation follows the Masoretic accents. If that is done, a period or other major disjunction must come after בָּאָה ("…is coming"), not after שְׁמוּעָה as in RSV. The accent on the ultima of בָּאָה also shows that it is the (feminine singular) participle of בּוֹא, not a prophetic perfect (Qal third feminine singular), as in NRSV. Likewise, בָאָה later in the verse is the participle.

The dual forms יָדַיִם, "hands," and בִּרְכַּיִם, "knees," are used when plurals might be expected. The duals apparently individualize what will happen to each person

---

[7]   Block, *Ezekiel*, 1:665, including n. 42.

[8]   Cooke, *Ezekiel*, 228.

(since each has a pair of these limbs). That knees "will run with water" apparently expresses a loss of bladder control from sheer terror. The same idiom occurred earlier in 7:17; see the textual note there. This verse may be an amplification of 7:17, where only external organs were mentioned (hands, knees), since here those external organs are supplemented here (in alternating order) by the internal factors of "heart" (which "melts," וְנָמֵס, Niphal perfect of מָסַס) and "spirit" (which "faints," וְכִהֲתָה, Piel perfect of כָּהָה). To one extent or the other, all the images used here are relative commonplaces in comparable circumstances.

הִנֵּה בָאָה וְנִהְיָתָה—The referent of the feminine participle בָאָה and the subject of the feminine verb נִהְיָתָה (Niphal third singular perfect of הָיָה with *waw* consecutive) is still the feminine noun שְׁמוּעָה ("the news") midway through the verse. The meaning of the Niphal of הָיָה is scarcely distinguishable from the meaning of the Qal, although possibly somewhat more emphatic: "be done, be brought about" (BDB, Niphal, 1).

21:14 כֹּה אָמַר אֲדֹנָי אֱמֹר—Elsewhere the citation formula is "thus says the *Lord Yahweh*" (see the fourth textual note and the commentary on 2:4). The use in this formula of אֲדֹנָי alone is without parallel in Ezekiel. The text-critical case for it is sort of a draw: the Vulgate (*Dominus Deus*) and Syriac Peshitta (ܡܪܝܐ ܐܠܗܐ) have their usual translations for אֲדֹנָי יהוה, while the LXX's κύριος is ambiguous, and the Targum has יוי without a second divine name or title (in other places, e.g., 21:18, 29 [ET 21:13, 24], it translates אֲדֹנָי יהוה as יוי אֱלֹהִים). Possibly the MT has the edge as the *lectio difficilior*. The anomaly may be connected with the seemingly redundant imperative אֱמֹר, which many delete as a gloss or construe as a garbled remnant of the original יהוה. But in 21:33 (ET 21:28), which echoes this verse, the common form וְאָמַרְתָּ seems dependent on אֱמֹר being present here. Nothing substantial seems to be at stake in these two related questions, but, in a way, they help steel us at the outset for the host of irregularities throughout the subsequent Song of the Sword.

A common dilemma when translating the prophets is whether the text should be set as poetry or prose. Much of prophecy is at least quasi-poetic, or a poetry of its own type—if one can even find agreement on what constitutes Hebrew "poetry" (a topic about which there is much debate). I am disposed to agree with *BHS* that 21:14b–22 should be set as poetry. Although the sword theme continues throughout the chapter, these verses are set off by the word-event formula ("the Word of Yahweh came to me") and the address "son of man" both before (21:13 [ET 21:8]) and after (21:23–24 [ET 21:18–19]).

חֶרֶב חֶרֶב הוּחַדָּה וְגַם־מְרוּטָה:—The repetition of חֶרֶב obviously indicates excitement and/or emphasis. There are many parallels; probably all languages use repetition for emphasis. In 21:32 (ET 21:27), "ruin" will be used three times.

הוּחַדָּה is the third feminine singular Hophal perfect of the geminate verb חָדַד, "sharpen." The *daghesh forte* of the inflected form (-דָּ-) marks the second, assimilated ד. The pairing of this perfect with a participle (מְרוּטָה, Qal passive participle of מָרַט, "polish") is unexpected. I have tried to reflect the different forms in translation, but usually this is not done. In 21:15–16 (ET 21:10–11), the Hophal perfect הוּחַדָּה was followed by מֹרָטָה, the third feminine singular Pual (or Qal passive) perfect of

מָרַט, suggesting that here a perfect (instead of a participle) could have been used. The participle here, מְרוּטָה, appears again in 21:33 (ET 21:28), but there it is paired with another passive participle.

21:15 The first two lines of the verse are basically clear, the last two lines anything but. The first two lines are both introduced by לְמַעַן, "for, in order that."

לְמַעַן טְבֹחַ טֶבַח הוּחַדָּה—This first line repeats הוּחַדָּה, "sharpened," from 21:14 (ET 21:9). The cognate accusative construction, "to slaughter a slaughter," uses the Qal infinitive construct of טָבַח as a gerund plus the noun טֶבַח from the same root. This construction does not necessarily imply a superlative, as many translations render it.

לְמַעַן־הֱיֵה־לָהּ בָּרָק מֹרָטָּה—This is, literally, "so that it might have lightning, it is polished" (cf. 21:33 [ET 21:28]). The idiom הָיָה לְ often means "be(long) to," hence "have." Unlike the preceding line, it does not have an infinitive construct (which would be הֱיוֹת); instead it uses the imperative הֱיֵה. Greenberg suggests a "colloquialism" where, on the analogy of the strong verb, the imperative and infinitive construct are identical in form.[9] The antecedent of the third feminine singular pronominal suffix on לָהּ is obviously the sword. The comparison of a flashing sword with lightning is readily comprehensible. And a polished, flashing sword is obviously ready to use—if not already in use. The verb מָרַט is repeated from 21:14 (ET 21:9), but in a different form: מֹרָטָּה is a Pual (or Qal passive) third feminine singular perfect. The anomalous doubling of the third radical in מֹרָטָּה in 21:15–16 (ET 21:10–11) appears to have been used for euphonic reasons to match the *daghesh forte* in הוּחַדָּה in 21:14–16 (ET 21:9–11).

אוֹ נָשִׂישׂ שֵׁבֶט בְּנִי מֹאֶסֶת כָּל־עֵץ׃—In complete contrast to the preceding two lines, 21:15c–d (ET 21:10c–d) is utterly opaque. Greenberg quotes a certain Rothstein: "This verse is both unintelligible and unimprovable."[10] The ancient versions all reflect the existence of the half verse but are clearly no more able to make sense of the words than modern commentators and translators are (as any quick comparison of their attempts will demonstrate). There is no point in even trying to list all the variations, ancient and modern.

My translation attempts to simply reproduce the surface translation of the Hebrew words, as far as that is possible. What the question (if it is that) ultimately means is another matter. In fact, one might offer it as a parade example of the translation theory known as "formal equivalence," which tries to adhere as closely as possible to the original text, leaving it to the readers in the receptor language to make sense out of it as best they can.

Not that even my literalism is beyond dispute. The initial אוֹ is ordinarily translated "or." Most English translations, beginning with KJV, treat it as an interrogative particle, which today is known to have an Akkadian cognate. However, another sim-

---

[9] Greenberg, *Ezekiel*, 2:422.
[10] Greenberg, *Ezekiel*, 2:422.

ilar Akkadian word has prohibitive force, so Block translates: "Let us not …"[11] Second, the most recent possible antecedent for the feminine participle מֹאֶסֶת is שֵׁבֶט, but in every other OT passage שֵׁבֶט is masculine.[12] My translation ("[The sword] despises every tree") assumes the feminine participle is still governed by the feminine noun חֶרֶב, which the NIV supplies in its "dynamic equivalent" translation.

The phrase שֵׁבֶט מֹאֶסֶת will occur in 21:18 (ET 21:13; see the discussion there), which suggests that it and 21:15c–d (ET 21:10c–d) should be considered together. Indeed, in neither verse do these words fit easily into the context. Ezek 21:16 (ET 21:11) follows naturally after 21:15b (ET 21:10b), and the same apparent intrusiveness appears with 21:18 (ET 21:13), which is unique in other ways. This disconnect inevitably leads critical scholars to the widespread conclusion that 21:15c–d (ET 21:10c–d) and 21:18 (ET 21:13) are later additions,[13] with 21:15c–d (ET 21:10c–d) perhaps being a marginal comment on "every tree" in 21:3 (ET 20:47).[14] I have a rather congenital aversion to such expedients, but as good a case as anywhere can be made for such explanations here. There is no doubt that such things did happen in textual history, and sometimes (though not here) demonstrably so. If something of that sort is the explanation here, the attestation of these verses in all the ancient versions (though translated variously) indicates that the glossation occurred at an extremely early date in the history of the text (pre-LXX). Theologically, how we regard the disputed lines might depend upon whether the glossarist was Ezekiel himself or some later copyist. In the former case, we are bound to regard them as part of the inspired text and interpret them as best we can. In the latter case, they belong to the history of exegesis and are not strictly pertinent to a *biblical* commentary.

On the principle of *in dubito, pro traditione*, in my commentary I shall offer one ancient interpretation, still defended by more conservative commentators (e.g., Keil and Block[15]) and clearly reflected in the NIV's translation. It is a plausible and congenial understanding of the words, but not one that I can put forward as certain.

21:16 וַיִּתֵּן אֹתָהּ לְמָרְטָה—"But the sword has been given to be polished" takes the *waw* as adversative. The *waw*, of course, can be rendered in many ways. Construing it as adversative makes 21:16 (ET 21:11) a continued (?) corrective of the point of view expressed by Ezekiel's hearers in the last half of the previous verse (see the commentary on 21:15 [ET 21:10]). This interpretation stands or falls with the exegesis offered for that half verse.

The impersonal Qal וַיִּתֵּן, literally, "he/someone gave," is often rendered as a passive ("it has been given"), although in the context, there can be no doubt who the

---

[11]   Block, *Ezekiel*, 1:672, including n. 79.

[12]   The best way to understand שֵׁבֶט מֹאֶסֶת in 21:18 (ET 21:13) is that שֵׁבֶט is not the subject, but the object, of the feminine participle מֹאֶסֶת, so that verse is not an exception to the regular construal of שֵׁבֶט as masculine.

[13]   See, for example, Zimmerli, *Ezekiel*, 1:426–28.

[14]   Allen, *Ezekiel*, 2:19.

[15]   Keil, *Ezekiel*, 1:292–94; Block, *Ezekiel*, 1:677–78.

Giver was. My translation clarifies the third feminine singular pronominal object אֹתָהּ, "she/it," with the specific "sword" (חֶרֶב) as its feminine singular referent. In a passive construction, the object becomes the subject: "the sword has been given." In the translation, "sword" is included here rather than at the location of the otiose חֶרֶב in the second half of the verse, which occurs between two more feminine pronouns (הִיא ... חֶרֶב וְהִיא). לְמָרְטָה is a Qal infinitive construct of מָרַט of the feminine form, used gerundivally: literally, "for polishing."

The text reveals no more about to whom the sword shall be given or who shall grasp it and proceeds to the "killing fields."

הִיא־הוּחַדָּה חֶרֶב וְהִיא מֹרָטָה—Ezek 21:16c (ET 21:11c) is essentially a repetition of elements of 21:14b–15b (ET 21:9b–10b). It excitedly repeats the feminine pronoun הִיא ... וְהִיא ("it ... and it") referring to the sword, whereas 21:14b (ET 21:9b) began with the repeated חֶרֶב ("sword"). Even the euphonic doubling of the third radical of the verb מֹרָטָה in 21:15 is duplicated here.

לָתֵת אוֹתָהּ בְּיַד־הוֹרֵג:—The verb is the Qal infinitive construct (with ל) of נָתַן. The idiom נָתַן בְּיַד, "deliver into the hand of, hand over," was also used in 7:21; 11:9; 16:39. It will be used again in 21:36 (ET 21:31); 23:9, 28, 31; 31:11; 39:23.

21:17 זְעַק וְהֵילֵל—The imperatives "cry out" and "wail" (Hiphil of יָלַל) are a standard pair of onomatopoetic verbs, found only in the prophets (especially frequently in Jeremiah). Vocal activity of that sort was sometimes accompanied by gestures of distress, for example, wearing sackcloth, placing dust on one's head, and so forth (as in 27:30–31). Such a gesture is mentioned at the end of the verse.

כִּי־הִיא הָיְתָה בְעַמִּי—The antecedent of הִיא (twice in this verse) continues to be the feminine noun חֶרֶב, "sword," which dominates the entire song. The idiom הָיָה בְּ ("be against/upon") frequently has hostile implications. הָיְתָה is a perfect, normally past tense, but here undoubtedly a prophetic perfect.

מְגוּרֵי אֶל־חֶרֶב הָיוּ אֶת־עַמִּי—This is the most difficult expression in the verse. מְגוּרֵי must modify the preceding "princes of Israel." It is the masculine plural Qal passive participle in construct, from מָגַר, a rare verb meaning "throw (down)," that appears elsewhere in the OT only in the Piel in Ps 89:45 (ET 89:44) and the Aramaic Pael in Ezra 6:12. In Hebrew prophecy and poetry, a participle can be used in construct with a prepositional phrase, as here, where מְגוּרֵי is in construct with אֶל־חֶרֶב. See GKC, § 130 a; Joüon, § 129 m. Literally, "thrown to the sword they shall be with my people," this is translated, "they have been thrown to the sword together with my people."

Many prefer to repoint the word as מֻגָּרֵי, a Hophal participle (masculine plural in construct) of נָגַר, "pour out," here meaning "delivered, abandoned." Ezekiel uses the Hiphil of נָגַר with the corresponding active meaning sense in 35:5. Neither text critically nor in meaning is the difference great; both involve the syntax of a participle in construct with a prepositional phrase. The change appears, at best, to be unnecessary.

A third possible alternative appears in the translations "terrors by reason of the sword" in KJV and "terrors including the sword" in NKJV. Those translations understand מְגוּרֵי to be the plural in construct of the noun מָגוֹר, "fear, terror," which occurs nine other places in the OT. The underlying verb, גּוּר III (there are two other homonyms), means, "be afraid, dread," and occurs a dozen times in the OT.

סְפֹק אֶל־יְרֵכֶךְ—To "slap the thigh" was clearly in the culture of the times a gesture of alarm or horror (also used in Jer 31:19).[16] NIV offers the dynamic equivalent in our culture (?) of "beat your breast."

21:18 This verse is every bit as intractable in releasing its meaning as 21:15c–d (ET 21:10c–d), to which it is obviously related. Its problems and proposed solutions (some commentators attempt none!) run quite parallel to the earlier verse. Again, I have offered a possible literal(istic?) translation, with no pretense that I understand what the verse is about.

כִּי בֹחַן וּמָה—In form בֹחַן could be a Pual third masculine singular perfect. It is separated from the rest of the verse by a *zaqeph qaton* accent (-בֹ). The verb בָּחַן is fairly common, meaning to "test." With the same pointing, the word can also be construed as a noun, as in Isaiah's famous phrase אֶבֶן בֹּחַן, traditionally translated "tested stone/touchstone" (Is 28:16). But here, whether it is the verb or noun, to what does it refer? NIV freely ventures "testing will surely come." Any number of possibilities arise, depending on the syntax of the rest of the verse. Besides sundry guesses, various additions (italicized in traditional translations) are usually made in order to wrest some sort of coherent meaning out of the words. The MT indicates that it understands וּמָה independently, perhaps aposiopesis. Since, as in 21:15c–d (ET 21:10c–d), the masculine noun שֵׁבֶט cannot govern the feminine participle מֹאֶסֶת, it seems one must again supply חֶרֶב as the participle's subject. Then one must connect שֵׁבֶט with לֹא יִהְיֶה, but what is the sense of "the staff ... will not be"? Will not prevail? Will not survive?

A final challenge is that one does not expect to meet the signatory formula ("says the Lord Yahweh") in the middle of an oracle.[17] For it, see the second textual note on 5:11.

21:19 What should probably be taken as the second strophe of the song (21:19–22 [ET 21:14–17]) now emphasizes the sword's deadly work. Most divine commands to "prophesy" (הִנָּבֵא) are followed by "say" or the like and the words of Yahweh that the prophet should speak. Instead of words, we have here an action prophecy, followed by the meaning of the action.

וְהַךְ כַּף אֶל־כָּף—"Clap your hands" is, literally, "strike palm upon palm," using the apocopated Hiphil imperative of נָכָה. The same idiom appears in 21:22 (ET 21:17). For the significance of the action, see the second textual note on 6:11, which uses the similar idiom הַכֵּה בְכַפְּךָ.

וְתִכָּפֵל חֶרֶב שְׁלִישְׁתָה—The verb כָּפַל is used five times in the OT, only here in the Niphal, a third feminine singular imperfect with jussive meaning ("may/let ..."). The OT also has two occurrences of a derivative noun. A literal translation is "let the sword be doubled," or more freely, "let the sword strike twice." שְׁלִישְׁתָה, a "third" (?),

---

[16] This idiom is evident also in the *Odyssey* of Homer (13.198–99).

[17] For this formula, see the pages 8–9 in the introduction and the second textual note on 5:11.

is more problematic. The unusual final *he* may be paragogic, that is, a meaningless poetic enclitic. Perhaps Hebrew idiom did not require the addition of a word such as פַּעַם to make "a third *time*." The LXX and other ancient versions clearly attest to the MT. KJV has "let the sword be doubled the third time," and NKJV, "the third time let the sword do double damage." Following the Syriac, many today prefer to emend שְׁלִישָׁ֫תָה to a Pual participle, שֻׁלָּשָׁה, "let it be tripled," but that form should begin with a *mem* and is obviously the *lectio facilior*. Possibly the Peshitta was only being free, and so can we. See further the commentary.

חֲלָלִים—"Slain (ones)" is, literally, "those pierced."

חֶרֶב חָלָל הַגָּדוֹל—It is unclear what sense is conveyed here by the singular חָלָל in contrast to the preceding plural חֲלָלִים. Furthermore, the adjective with the article, הַגָּדוֹל, "the great," follows two anarthrous nouns. Poetry often omits articles. Since "sword" is feminine, the adjective גָּדוֹל must modify חָלָל. Keil thinks of the king; the sword will slay not only the masses.[18] That strikes me as forced, however, so I have taken it as a collective, not in the sense of "the great mass of slain," but of a sword that indiscriminately slays "great" as well as small.

הַחֹדֶרֶת לָהֶם:—The verb חֹדֶרֶת apparently is the Qal feminine singular participle of חָדַר, which is a hapax. The feminine form shows that "sword" is its subject. The LXX and other ancient versions apparently transposed the *resh* and *dalet* since they translated "frighten," but the Hebrew verb in the Qal probably is intransitive. The Syriac cognate verb means "surround, beset," which is the most common modern translation (RSV, ESV, NIV). But I am attracted to the tradition, at least as old as the medieval Jewish interpreter Rashi, that associates the verb with the common noun חֶדֶר, an "inner room," as in Ezekiel's vision in 8:12. Thus KJV has "which entereth into their privy chambers," and NKJV updated to "that enters their private chambers." The preposition with suffix לָהֶם functions as a possessive in the translation: "pursues even into *their* private homes." Being a hapax, the verb cannot be pushed further, and this translation fits the context at least as well as the alternatives.

21:20 This verse teems with uncertainties and difficulties. After לְמַעַן, the use of לְ with the infinitive (לָמוּג) appears to be pleonastic, unless, as Zimmerli suggests,[19] a deliberate attempt was made to achieve alliteration by combining the first three words, all beginning with לְ. The verb מוּג may mean either "waver/quake" or "melt." The scales probably tip toward the latter because of the use of the synonym נָמֵס, "melt," in 21:12 (ET 21:7), which uses additional metaphors to express a similar thought.

With Greenberg, I take הַרְבֵּה as an infinitive in a colloquial form.[20] (See the textual note on הֱיֵה, a colloquial imperative, in 21:15 [ET 21:10]). Literally, then, the translation of the phrase would be "to multiply occasions to fall (by the sword)," perhaps also including a picture of blind panic as people stumble over anything and everything in their desperate attempt to escape pursuers.

---

[18] Keil, *Ezekiel*, 1:294.

[19] Zimmerli, *Ezekiel*, 1:429–30.

[20] Greenberg, *Ezekiel*, 2:425.

See the textual note on מִכְשׁוֹל in 3:20 and on the phrase מִכְשׁוֹל עָוֺן ("stumbling block of iniquity") in 7:19 (also 14:3, 4, 7; 18:30; 44:12). Many wish to emend מִכְשֹׁלִים to מֻכְשָׁלִים, a Hophal participle, "those who are made to stumble." The LXX and Syriac so translate here, perhaps freely substituting a personal or concrete word for an abstraction. But neither version translates the Hophal participle in the same way in its only OT occurrence, in Jer 18:23. Hence, while I too have given a personal translation ("those who stumble"), I regard it as a matter of translator's license, not necessitating any emendation of the Hebrew text.

אִבְחַת־חָרֶב—The word in construct is a hapax. Since there is neither known cognates nor etymology to help us out, translation is a free-for-all, and naturally the guesses are many. Following the LXX, many wish to emend to טִבְחַת, "slaughter of," but other words from that root are already overworked in the context (21:15, 33 [ET 21:10, 28], as well as the end of 21:20 [ET 21:15]). In a total vacuum of controls, the ancient (at least medieval) understanding, "*point* of the sword," seems as appropriate as anything.[21] That is, guards with drawn swords are stationed at all exits, so if the mob rushes madly forward, it will only impale itself.

Even the little exclamation אָח occasions debate and emendations. It may be a short form of הֶאָח, used in 25:3; 26:2; and 36:2, which the LXX translates as εὖγε in the latter two verses, but these others all tend to express joy or congratulations rather than pain or grief, which one would expect here. Possibly we have an anticipation of Yahweh's expression of satisfaction in 21:22 (ET 21:17), and this verse too has Yahweh speaking in the first person. But there is a limit to which little emotivities like this are subject to rational analysis—in any language.

The verse's final conundrum is מְעֻטָה. It is another hapax. The MT points it as a Pual participle of עָטָה, "wrap, cover." The verb is not rare, but its Pual is attested nowhere else, and the meaning appears to be precisely the opposite of what the context seems to demand. There is a homonym, עָטָה II, meaning to "grasp," which has possibilities (so NKJV, NIV), but it too is attested only in the Qal. Probably the most popular solution is to emend to a Pual participle of מָרַט, "polish," a root already used prominently in 21:14–16 (ET 21:9–11). An ideal solution, suggested already by Keil,[22] appeals to an Arabic cognate (מעט in Hebrew script) meaning to "unsheathe/draw from the scabbard."

21:21   There is little unanimity on this verse. הִתְאָחֲדִי appears to be the feminine singular Hithpael imperative of a verb related to אֶחָד, the numeral "one." I understand the word in the sense of "focus/act single-mindedly" or the like. Cf. KJV: "Go thee one way or other." Although such a verb is unattested elsewhere, it appears to be preferable to the frequent emendation (following the LXX) to הִתְחַדִּי, "sharpen yourself," the Hithpael imperative of חָדַד, already used in the MT in 21:14–16 (ET 21:9–11). Cooke's free translation of "cut sharply to right"[23] is copied in RSV and

---

[21]   That is the translation of KJV, NKJV, and NRSV, but not RSV!

[22]   Keil, *Ezekiel*, 1:295.

[23]   Cooke, *Ezekiel*, 231.

may underlie NRSV's "attack to the right!" and perhaps NIV's "slash to the right." NKJV is free: "swords at the ready!"

הֵימָנִי is the Hiphil feminine singular imperative of יָמַן, "go to the right" (BDB), clearly related to יָמִין, "right hand/side."

With הָשִׂימִי, the Hiphil feminine singular imperative of שִׂים, we probably should supply פָּנַיִךְ, "your face," meaning "your edge" or "your blade" as in the next clause. Since הָשִׂימִי is not represented in the LXX and other ancient witnesses, many delete it as a mutilated dittograph of the following word, הַשְׂמִילִי. But that leaves us with a very compact "focus (head) right, left," which appears less likely to me.

הַשְׂמִילִי, the Hiphil feminine singular imperative of שָׂמַל or שָׂמְאַל, which only occurs in the Hiphil, means "go to the left" (BDB, s.v. שָׂמְאַל, Hiphil, 1). In many manuscripts, it is spelled הַשְׂמָאִי׳לִי, which is a more regular spelling because שְׂמֹאל, "left," is usually written with an *aleph*. The quiescence of א in pronunciation would easily lead to its omission in writing.

אָנָה פָּנַיִךְ מֻעָדוֹת:—The final Hophal participle of יָעַד, "to order, direct," is feminine plural, apparently reflecting late Hebrew construal of פָּנִים as feminine. Otherwise in the OT, פָּנִים is always masculine. But Ezekiel's text evinces enough late Hebrew influences that emendation is not necessary. Here פָּנִים (with second feminine singular suffix, פָּנַיִךְ, "your face") must refer to the sword's "edge" or "blade."

21:22 וַהֲנִחֹתִי חֲמָתִי—See the textual note and commentary on this same clause in 5:13 (also 16:42; cf. 24:13).

21:24 שִׂים־לְךָ—This idiom, used only here in Ezekiel, would most naturally be translated "appoint/establish/make for yourself." However, the dative of advantage (לְ?) usually is not translated, and here the imperative of שִׂים must mean something like "sketch, mark out, incise." The double use of בָּרֵא in the second half of the verse (see the last textual note on this verse) points in that direction too but does not enable us to determine more precisely the type of action Ezekiel is commanded to take. Cooke's idea that Ezekiel is to "trace on the sand"[24] is very plausible, but there are other possibilities. In 4:1 a city plan had been scratched on a brick, although the more precise verb חָקַק is used there. But the exact method Ezekiel is to use is of no significance.

מֵאֶרֶץ אֶחָד—The use of the masculine אֶחָד with the feminine noun אֶרֶץ ("from one land") is unusual. Greenberg suggests that it is for the sake of assonance with הָתְאַחֲדִי in 21:21 (ET 21:16).[25] However, אֶרֶץ is construed as masculine also in Gen 13:6. It may be no more than a colloquialism or another example of Ezekiel's relaxedness about grammatical precision (especially gender in chapter 1).

וְיָד בָּרֵא בְּרֹאשׁ דֶּרֶךְ־עִיר בָּרֵא:—"Sign(post)" is a favored translation of יָד that is supported by many parallel passages, in which it is sometimes translated "monument," although an incision on some hard surface might be implied. Since נֵס is often used of a sign or signal, יָד, on the other hand, may signify a mere post or other marker.

The exact meaning of the Piel verb (here the masculine imperative, בָּרֵא) is uncertain. BDB lists it as the Piel of בָּרָא, whose Qal means "create," but more likely

---

24 Cooke, *Ezekiel*, 231.

25 Greenberg, *Ezekiel*, 2:426.

the Piel verb is a separate homograph. It is used only three times elsewhere: in Josh 17:15, 18, it describes the clearing of a forest, and in Ezek 23:47, it refers to the execution (cutting down) of the two whores. Greenberg champions "clear" here also.[26] That, in turn, forces him to render יָד as "place," a possibility (cf. Num 2:17; Deut 23:13 [ET 23:12]; Jer 6:3), but יָד is too polysemous in its metaphorical applications to build much of a case on. "Clear a place" seems singularly inappropriate here: Nebuchadnezzar is not blazing a trail through unknown territory but is traveling on one of the major thoroughfares of the region (see below). KJV translates יָד as "place" too, but translates the verb as "choose." For בָּרָא, we have settled for the general verb "make."

That רֹאשׁ דֶּרֶךְ ("head/beginning of the road") means the "fork of the road" (cf. 16:25) will be clarified by another idiom in 21:26 (ET 21:21).

The LXX has a shorter text since it omits a translation of the first בָּרָא. It translates the end of 21:24 (ET 21:19) as ἐπ' ἀρχῆς, as if reading בְּרֹאשׁ in place of the second בָּרָא, and these two Greek words begin a clause continued in 21:25 (ET 21:20): "at the head [25]of the way, you shall arrange …"

The syntax of 21:24–25 (ET 21:19–20) apparently implies a main thought of "mark out two roads … to Rabbah … or to … Jerusalem." But in 21:24b (ET 21:19b), Ezekiel digresses and fills in details about the "one/same country" and the "signpost." As Greenberg dryly observes: "In Ezekiel the presumption of original simplicity [almost axiomatic for many cities] is not strong."[27] Allen develops the kind of ingenious hypothetical reconstruction of the history of the text in which he often seems to delight,[28] and others too rewrite the received text.

21:25 אֵת רַבַּת … וְאֶת־יְהוּדָה—Most likely the direct object marker, אֵת, is used idiomatically here twice, where אֶל might be expected, to indicate the destination "to" which one comes. אֵת is so used with הָלַךְ in Judg 19:18 and with נָגַשׁ in 1 Sam 30:21. Somewhat parallel is the use of אֵת with יָצָא (the antonym of בּוֹא) for "come out *from* a city" in Gen 44:4 and Ex 9:29.

"Rabbah of the sons of Ammon" is the full name of the capital of ancient Ammon (modern Amman, the capital of the modern kingdom of Jordan). In his Gentile oracle against Ammon, Ezekiel will use the shorter form Rabbah ("the great/large one") in 25:5, but the fuller designation distinguishes it from other cities by that name, for example, the "Rabbah" in Judah (Josh 15:60).

I have followed the technically correct full translation "the sons of Ammon." For whatever reason, the name "Ammon" appears alone in the Bible only twice (1 Sam 11:11; Ps 83:8 [ET 83:7]), but over a hundred times in combination with "the sons of." (This practice also accords with ancient Assyrian usage.) In most cases, the phrase seems to refer more to the country itself than it citizens. For example, the oracle against "the sons of Ammon" (25:1–7) is followed by oracles against "Moab" (25:8–11) and "Edom" (25:12–14). In such places, the phrase could be rendered as the name of the

---

[26] Greenberg, *Ezekiel*, 2:426–27.

[27] Greenberg, *Ezekiel*, 2:427.

[28] Allen, *Ezekiel*, 2:20–21.

nation ("The Sons of Ammon").[29] Thus unlike "the sons of Israel" and similar phrases, "the sons of Ammon" should not automatically be dissolved into a gentilic, "the Ammonites." A gentilic form exists and is readily used. However, in some contexts, it is ambiguous whether the country or its people is more in view (and once, in 2 Chr 20:1, "the sons of Ammon" occurs with "the sons of Moab"). I have tried to retain that ambiguity with the translation "the sons of Ammon."

After "Rabbah of the sons of Ammon," we might expect as a parallel "Jerusalem of Judah." Instead, the word order is inverted ("to Judah in fortified Jerusalem"), probably for the sake of climax. As was common in times of siege, the populace was crowded into the walled cities, and here Judah's population is concentrated in the fortified capital. בְּצוּרָה, the Qal passive participle (only occurring in the feminine) of בָּצַר, "to make inaccessible, fortify," is somewhat superlative in force, implying especially reinforced bastions. Maybe the word is intended as a foil to the devastating power of the coming sword. בְּצוּרָה lacks the expected definite article (since "Jerusalem" and all city names are intrinsically definite), but the article is omitted sometimes elsewhere when a proper noun is being qualified. The LXX has ἐν μέσῳ αὐτῆς, "in the midst of her," apparently reading בְּתוֹכָה instead of בְּצוּרָה. That reading perhaps is smoother (and many critics prefer it), but it is also a more bland, less powerful rendering.

21:26 The initial כִּי is not causal, but simply indicates that the interpretation of Ezekiel's nonverbal actions in 21:24–25 (ET 21:19–20) now begins.

Throughout 21:26–27 (ET 21:21–22), the Hebrew consistently uses perfect verb forms, but since the perfect is not really a "tense" in the Western sense, the translator must decide which tense to use. Any quick survey of English translations will find past, present, and future renderings, and all three are grammatically permissible. The decision depends largely upon how one envisions the scene. It seems unlikely that Ezekiel is reporting events that have already taken place, or even ones that are occurring as he speaks. Since we are dealing with prophecy (prediction), the future tense seems most appropriate. We need not press the idea so far that everything necessarily occurred precisely as presented, but there is no reason to rule that out either. In a sense, the total montage presented vividly is more important than any individual element.

What Nebuchadnezzar is depicted as about to do certainly accords in general with all that we know about the preparation for warfare in the ancient Near East. There are many parallels from Mesopotamia and elsewhere in antiquity showing that battles were not undertaken without resort to various divinatory techniques. More than one method was often used in the hope that all methods would concur. Sometimes the practices were continued over a period of time, perhaps until the desired result was achieved. Certain external similarities can be discerned in Israel, although to what degree is hard to determine. God himself provided the Urim and Thummim kept in the high priest's ephod (Ex 28:30; Num 27:21), and consulting them was not regarded as practicing divination (קָסַם, e.g., Deut 18:10, 14). However, God strictly forbade necromancy, mediums, and other occult methods of divination (Deut 18:9–14).

---

[29] See Block, "*Bny ʿmwn*: The Sons of Ammon."

Toward the end of his life, Saul sought advice from Urim (1 Sam 28:6), and when no answer was forthcoming, he resorted to the witch (medium) at Endor (1 Sam 28:7–25). On the Urim and Thummim, see the commentary below. The casting of lots, frequent in the OT and also practiced in the NT (Acts 1:23–26), probably falls into the same category as a divinely approved method.

Two essentially synonymous expressions are used of the junction where Nebuchadnezzar must make a decision. The first, אֵם הַדֶּרֶךְ, is, literally, "the mother of the way/route/road." It may be a more comprehensive expression. In his bluster in connection with the First Gulf War, Saddam Hussein's threats of a "mother of all wars" alerted the West to the myriad of idioms involving "mother" in all Semitic languages, usually connoting something great, impressive, or initiatory. The second expression, בְּרֹאשׁ שְׁנֵי הַדְּרָכִים, literally, "at the head of the two ways," uses the same idiom we met in 21:24 (ET 21:19), בְּרֹאשׁ דֶּרֶךְ.

לִקְסָם־קָסֶם—The cognate accusative construction, literally, "to divine divination" (Qal infinitive of קָסַם followed by the noun קֶסֶם in pause) is here used generically to introduce the specific procedures that follow. By itself, it implies trying to divine the gods' will by casting lots. With the apparent exception of Prov 16:10, these words are always used negatively in the OT, often tantamount simply to "false prophecy." Ezekiel uses קָסַם and/or קֶסֶם in that sense in 13:6, 9, 23 and 22:28 (also 21:26–28, 34 [ET 21:21–23, 29]). The Qal participle of קָסַם occurs in a semi-fixed phrase together with the Poel participle of עָנַן in Deut 18:10, 14 and Jer 27:9, where the pair are translated "diviners and soothsayers," "mediums and spiritists," or the like.

Next, three different divinatory techniques are used, presumably to try to be certain of the divine will.

קִלְקַל בַּחִצִּים—First, the king or his servant will "shake the arrows." The verb is the Pilpal third masculine singular perfect of קָלַל, possibly a homonym of the verb's common meaning of "be small, light." Here, as with the next two verbs in the series, the object is introduced by בְּ. The practice is known technically as belomancy. It is mentioned nowhere else in the OT. St. Jerome has favored us with a description of the practice: arrows are inscribed with the names of individuals or nations, then put in a quiver, mixed, and one is finally withdrawn.[30] The practice was also known among the ancient Greeks and pre-Islamic Arabs (Muhammad in Sura 5:3 expressly forbids using this practice to divide portions of meat). There is no mention of this practice, however, in extant Mesopotamian sources, which leads some critics to think its appearance here is the result of the prophet's imagination, drawing on practices familiar to him. But there is no reason to doubt that Nebuchadnezzar, to be on the safe side, would also make use of the specific practices presumably favored by the gods of the region.

שָׁאַל בַּתְּרָפִים—Second, Nebuchadnezzar consults the teraphim. They are often thought to relate to a uniquely Israelite practice. Since there is not clear evidence of their use in Babylonia (unless they appear under some other name), some of the same

---

[30] Jerome, *Commentariorum in Hiezechielem* (CCSL 75:289).

questions are raised as with the arrow divination just mentioned. Their prominence in the narrative of Jacob leaving Laban (Gen 31:19–35) indicates that they were at least known in Aram Naharaim (upper Mesopotamia between the Tigris and the Euphrates).

Some translations offer "gods" or "idols," and while this may not be entirely incorrect, it is entirely too vague and general for this context. Teraphim are mentioned in every OT period. In Israelite contexts, they are virtually always condemned and mostly associated with divination, as here. Unfortunately, however, we are never told how they were consulted, or even what they looked like. The singular of תְּרָפִים never occurs, and all proposed etymologies are speculative. Currently most favored is the Hittite *tarpish*, referring to some kind of spirit, sometimes protective, sometimes evil.

That Rachel can put teraphim in her camel's saddle and sit on them and decline to get up, claiming it is the time of her period (Gen 31:34–35), suggests relatively small objects. When Michal, on the other hand, can place them in (or beside?) David's bed to help him escape Saul (1 Sam 19:13–16), more or less life-size figures are suggested.

The most common assumption is that they were private household gods (like the Roman Penates) used for daily needs and protection, in contrast to the remote official pantheon. The presence of teraphim alongside an ephod in Micah's private shrine (Judg 17:5) tends to confirm this supposition. For a time, on the basis of archaeological evidence (Hurrian Nuzi), it was thought that Laban and Rachel were so concerned about the teraphim because they signified an inheritance claim, but this view is now largely abandoned. Rachel's interest may have been primarily apotropaic, to ward off demons on the long journey and so on. But of their specifically divinatory role, we remain completely uninformed.

רָאָה בַּכָּבֵד:—Finally, Nebuchadnezzar examines the liver. Possibly it is mentioned last as climactic, as the procedure in which the king has the most confidence. No doubt, we have here a genuine and major Mesopotamian practice. Extispicy, divination from the internal organs of sacrificed animals, and especially of the liver (hepatoscopy), was extremely common. Clay models of livers, probably for training, are found in great numbers.[31] An especially famous one from early Babylon is divided into more than fifty segments, on which are drawn important marks for interpretation. At the Amorite site of Mari on the middle Euphrates, over thirty liver models were found. Others come from all over the ancient Near East, including Megiddo and Hazor in Canaan. We have entire textbooks on liver interpretation. The later Romans considered the practice of great importance, and we even meet it as late as the eighth century A.D. among a small pagan community that still existed at Haran. For all of that, the Bible mentions the practice nowhere else, and the details of its use are still very poorly understood.

21:27 בִּימִינוֹ—The antecedent to the third masculine singular suffix is unclear. My translation, "in his right hand," implies that the reference is to Nebuchadnezzar or to

---

[31] See *ANEP*, §§ 594, 595, 844 for photographs.

whomever performed the divinatory act. It is very possible, however, that the antecedent is the liver, the immediately preceding word (כָּבֵב at the end of 21:26 [ET 21:21]). Then the correct translation would be "on its [the liver's] right side." We do know that the right side of the liver was considered lucky for those consulting the liver (not for the enemy). Precisely how or if that would apply here is uncertain.

For reasons that escape me, many modern interpreters take the arrow divination as the definitive one of the three methods, but both textually and culturally, based on the Mesopotamian evidence, the liver probably would be the most important one.

הַקֶּסֶם יְרוּשָׁלִַם—Here קֶסֶם apparently refers to the results of the divination (cf. Prov 16:10). The result implied a decision to attack Jerusalem first and Rabbah later. I have added "*for* Jerusalem" for the sake of a fluent translation. Nebuchadnezzar's decision makes historical sense too. We know that Pharaoh Hophra (Apries) had dispatched an army to aid Jerusalem (Jer 37:5–10). If Nebuchadnezzar first defeated both that Egyptian army and Jerusalem, then Rabbah would be a much easier target.

After "Jerusalem" come six infinitive phrases, describing the Babylonian preparations for a siege of the city. They are structured into two tricola, each beginning with לָשׂוּם כָּרִים ("to set up/erect battering rams"). Because of the repetition, the first is often deleted as an addition, but it is attested already by the LXX. If it is deleted, various reconstructions of the verse are often proposed, but none seem necessary or convincing.

לִפְתֹּחַ פֶּה בְּרֶצַח—"To open mouth(s)" is clear. The noun רֶצַח is from the verb רָצַח, "murder," but that verb is not elsewhere used of killing in war (contra the pacifists who love to cite its use in the Fifth Commandment to support their cause). "To open the mouth in killing" is a strange expression, and the next expression uses תְּרוּעָה, often used of shouts of various sorts, including a war cry. Since the LXX translates בְּרֶצַח by ἐν βοῇ, I have reluctantly acceded to the common judgment that we have in the MT a classical case of metathesis of two consonants, a common and easy copyist's error. That leaves us with an original בְּצֶרַח, an otherwise unattested noun (although a similar problem appears in Jer 4:31), but the verb צָרַח, "yell, shriek," is used in Is 42:13 and Zeph 1:14. Hence my translation is "to open mouths for shouting." The expression is similar to the next one, לְהָרִים קוֹל בִּתְרוּעָה, literally, "to raise [Hiphil infinitive of רוּם] a voice in a shout," that is, "to sound the battle cry."

The nouns at the end of the verse, סֹלְלָה, "ramp," and דָּיֵק, "siege wall," also appear (in reverse order) in Ezekiel's action prophecy in 4:2 (see the textual note there); in 17:17; and in 26:8.

21:28 The sense of the verse is difficult to discern, mostly because the antecedents of all three of the third masculine plural pronouns (הֶם-) are not self-evident. As I understand it, only the following verse makes this verse relatively clear.

The Kethib כִּקְסָום looks like a Qal infinitive construct of קָסַם written *plene*. The Qere directs us to read a defective spelling of the same infinitive, כִּקְסָם, in which the last vowel is shortened from *holem* to *qamets chatuph* because the infinitive is connected to שָׁוְא with a *maqqeph* and so has lost its accent. Many critical scholars vocalize the consonants as the noun קֶסֶם, but the difference in meaning between the noun, "divination," and the infinitive, "the act of divination," is of no consequence.

In both this and the following clause לָהֶם ("belonging to them") refers to the same group, namely, the Israelites. Most scholars agree with that application in its first appearance, but think the referent in the second case is the Babylonians.

On that decision turns how we understand the following שְׁבֻעֵי שְׁבֻעוֹת. The expression itself is unclear. Both the LXX and the Syriac omit it, perhaps because they did not understand it, or, more likely, the Hebrew text they were translating from did not have it. If so, it is easy to "solve" the present problem by labeling it a later addition.[32] Traditionally, שְׁבֻעֵי has been construed as the construct form of the masculine plural Qal passive participle of שָׁבַע, whose common Niphal means "to swear," but the Qal of this verb is found nowhere else. If one attempts a translation of MT nonetheless, it will apparently be something like "those who have persons under oath to them." One might attempt to read שְׁבֻעֵי as a plural noun in construct, so that the phrase is "oaths of oaths," that is, a superlative, "the most solemn oaths." However, the normal form of the noun for "oath" is feminine, שְׁבֻעָה, as shown by the following plural absolute form, שְׁבֻעוֹת. One may, of course, appeal to Ezekiel's occasional disregard of gender. Or one may regard it as an attempt to make clear that the first word is intended to be a construct form; if it were feminine plural, its absolute and construct forms would be indistinguishable.[33] One gets the same translation if one appeals to elative formations found in postbiblical Hebrew.[34]

וְהוּא־מַזְכִּיר עָוֹן לְהִתָּפֵשׂ:—To whom or what the pronoun הוּא refers will be determined by one's understanding of the whole verse. See the commentary. The Hiphil participle מַזְכִּיר is easy to translate ("remember, bring to mind"). Attention should be called to the hypothesis, especially popular among German commentators, that the reference is to a *person*, a public prosecutor whose office would bring indictments. But Greenberg points out that no such functionary is known in Israel or elsewhere in ancient Near Eastern culture.[35]

As often in Hebrew (and essentially as in English with "to"), לְ on the Niphal infinitive לְהִתָּפֵשׂ ("to be captured") functions to indicate purpose (as does the longer לְמַעַן, "in order that/so that," 21:15, 20, 33 [ET 21:10, 16, 28]). My translation is free but captures (no pun intended) the sense.

21:29 As frequently in Hebrew, לָכֵן does not here introduce a result or apodosis of what precedes. Rather, it simply underscores what has already been said, here by restating the contents of the previous verse in God's own words, as it were.

יַעַן הַזְכַּרְכֶם עֲוֹנְכֶם ... יַעַן הִזָּכֶרְכֶם—By repeating the protasis twice, first with the Hiphil infinitive הַזְכַּרְכֶם (like the Hiphil participle at the end of 21:28) and then

---

[32] So Allen, *Ezekiel*, 2:21, and Zimmerli, *Ezekiel*, 1:437–38, although with considerable discussion.

[33] Cf. Keil, *Ezekiel*, 1:300–301.

[34] Cf. Greenberg, *Ezekiel*, 2:431, citing Matitiahu Tsevat, "The Neo-Assyrian and Neo-Babylonian Vassal Oaths and the Prophet Ezekiel," *JBL* 78 (1959): 202.

[35] Greenberg, *Ezekiel*, 2:432, citing I. L. Seeligmann, "Zur Terminologie für das Gerichtsverfahren im Wortschatz des biblischen Hebräisch," in *Hebräische Wortforschung: Festschrift zum 80. Geburtstag von Walter Baumgartner* (VTSup 16; Leiden: Brill, 1967), 260–61.

with the Niphal infinitive הִזָּכֶרְכֶם, both with second masculine plural suffix, the gravity of the offense ("brought to mind") is underscored.

בַּכַּף תִּתָּפֵשׂוּ:—The apodosis uses the Niphal (second masculine plural imperfect) of תָּפַשׂ ("you will be captured/taken"), as in 21:28 (ET 21:23), but adds בַּכַּף, "in the hand." The precise figure intended by the addition is uncertain. I have followed NKJV in translating "taken in hand," which, unfortunately, loses the connection with the previous verse (where the verb was translated "captured") but enables the literal rendition בַּכַּף. Zimmerli adds "strong," "with a (strong) hand,"[36] recalling the frequent use of יָד חֲזָקָה for Yahweh's "strong hand," that is, miraculous interventions (e.g., Ex 13:9). Keil thinks it points back to בְּיַד־הֹרֵג in Ezek 21:16 (ET 21:11).[37] If so, the fugitive Israelites here are grasped by the hand of the same "killer" into whose hand the sword was placed.

21:30 וְאַתָּה חָלָל רָשָׁע—This is translated literally as a vocative, "and you, you wicked corpse." However, there is sharp disagreement about the meaning of the חָלָל here. Hebrew has two homonymous חלל roots (and possibly more, which are not relevant here). One means "pierce (by the sword), strike dead," which is the root of the noun חָלָל, "slain," in 21:19 (ET 21:14). Piel verbal forms of the other mean "profane, desecrate," as in, for example, 20:13, 16. Already the LXX and Syriac opted for the latter and translated "defiled." Most English translations translate similarly: "profane" (KJV, NKJV, NIV), "unhallowed" (RSV), "vile" (NRSV). Many commentators agree: Cooke, who calls the first choice "possible, but not so suitable"; Allen, who explicitly rejects the first alternative; and Block, who terms it ill-advised.[38]

However, the linguistic evidence is entirely in the opposite direction. There is no other instance where the noun חָלָל means "profaned," with the possible exception of Lev 21:7, 14 (of a violated, deflowered woman). The words used here are essentially repeated in Ezek 21:34 (ET 21:29); see the textual note on that verse. All agree that חָלָל should be translated "slain" or the like in 21:19 (ET 21:14), similarly in 21:34 (ET 21:29). Following Greenberg,[39] I have translated "corpse." The possible translation "pierced" does not communicate well. The sense, as the rest of the verse seems to make clear, is that the wicked prince of Israel is "as good as dead."

Because in the analogous plural parallel in 21:34 (ET 21:29) the first word is in the construct ("corpses of wicked men"), many wish to repoint חָלָל as the construct form חֲלַל, but the change is unnecessary.

נְשִׂיא יִשְׂרָאֵל—Syntactically, this construct phrase, "prince of Israel," stands in apposition to the preceding vocative address to him as "you wicked corpse." This phrase too probably is a vocative. The use of נָשִׂיא, "prince," may reflect Ezekiel's refusal to dignify Israel's apostate royalty as מֶלֶךְ, "king," especially for Zedekiah, who was not in the valid line of succession. See the second textual note on 7:27 and the commentary on 12:10.

---

[36] Zimmerli, *Ezekiel*, 1:438.

[37] Keil, *Ezekiel*, 1:301.

[38] Cooke, *Ezekiel*, 234; Allen, *Ezekiel*, 2:21; Block, *Ezekiel*, 1:682–83, n. 153.

[39] Greenberg, *Ezekiel*, 2:432–33. Cf. also Keil, *Ezekiel*, 1:301–2.

יוֹמוֹ—"His day" here is obviously a final, definitive day of doom or death. This usage of "day" has many parallels (cf. 7:7, 10, 12 and also 1 Sam 26:10). It is also frequently used of a portentous event in the history of a city or nation (e.g., Midian in Is 9:3 [ET 9:4]; Egypt in Ezek 30:9).

בְּעֵת עֲוֹן קֵץ:—In contrast to "day," this phrase, "the time of final punishment," appears to be Ezekiel's own coinage. It will recur in 21:34 (ET 21:29) and 35:5.

21:31 הַשְׁפִּיל ... הַגְבֵּהַ ... וְהָרִים ... הָסִיר'—Context requires that all four of these verbs be imperatives ("remove ... take off ... raise ... bring low"). Yet only הַגְבֵּהַ is imperative in form. One would expect a *mappiq* in its final *he*, which is consonantal, not a vowel letter, but Leningradensis mistakenly omits the *mappiq* (as also in the *he* in the following cognate noun, וְהַגְבֵּהַ), so it does not appear in most contemporary printings of the Hebrew Bible. The other three verbs are vocalized as infinitive constructs. Most modern commentators almost reflexively "correct" the vocalizations to make them imperatives. Yet there are other instances (Jer 17:18; Ps 94:1) where infinitive constructs serve as imperatives. (Infinitive absolutes sometimes serve as surrogates for virtually any finite verb form, including imperatives, and הַגְבֵּהַ could also be an infinitive absolute.) Greenberg harshly, but correctly, calls the emendations of the three verbs "sheer pedantry. ... Evidently these forms, so close in vocalization and meaning, were not always distinguished."[40] One may note a possible parallel in the geminate verbs, where all three forms (imperative and both infinitives) are usually identical.

הָעֲטָרָה ... הַמִּצְנֶפֶת—Does the text speak of the downfall of not only the monarchy, but also of the priesthood? Commentators disagree (see the commentary below). The first term for headgear, מִצְנֶפֶת, everywhere else in the OT refers to the high priest's "turban, miter, tiara" (the first translation is the least encumbered by later ecclesiastical associations). A related word, צָנִיף, is used in Zech 3:5, that postexilic prophet's vision of the "turban" of Joshua, the high priest. But in Is 62:3, צָנִיף is used as a synonym in parallel to עֲטָרָה, "crown," which is also the second word used in Ezek 21:31 (ET 21:26) and which describes royal headgear. Historical-critical presuppositions may enter the discussion. At least early higher criticism was quite sure that the high priesthood was a later institution, probably postexilic and that its vestments were modeled after those of the then-defunct monarchy. Although the Bible never addresses the question of the relationship between priestly and royal vestments, the relationship, if anything, should be the other way around. The priesthood and its vestments were established in the Torah of Moses (fifteenth century B.C.). Kingship was a later institution in Israel (Saul, ca. 1050 B.C.). When later apostate kings arrogated priestly prerogatives to themselves, it would have been natural for them to appropriate or adopt priestly regalia too. But then again, there may be no connection whatsoever between the two kinds of vestments.

זֹאת לֹא־זֹאת—"This [is/will be] not this" demands some periphrastic translation. Cooke, speaking of both this and the following expression, is widely followed: these

---

[40] Greenberg, *Ezekiel*, 2:433.

are "proverbial expressions for a complete upset of the familiar order: this is no more this; everything is turned topsy-turvy,"[41]

הַשָּׁפָלָה הַגְּבֵהַ—The meaning is clear: "raise the low." The verb is the Hiphil infinitive absolute of גָּבַהּ with imperatival meaning. The final *he* on הַשָּׁפָלָה is unaccented, indicating that the Masoretes did not want it to be taken for the feminine ending, evidently so that the word ("the low") could accord with the masculine parallel הַגְּבֹהַ ("the high"). (A similar problem occurred with הַשְּׁמַלָה in 8:2, used for a word that is otherwise masculine.) According to the MT, the word here is a form of the masculine adjective with article, הַשָּׁפֵל, used as a substantive. The OT also has a masculine noun שֵׁפֶל, "lowliness," and a feminine noun שִׁפְלָה, "humiliation." The *he* on הַשָּׁפֵלָה may be paragogic, an inert enclitic, possibly serving a rhythmic, ornamental, or emphatic function (cf. GKC, § 90 f). If one wants to think of scribal error, the final *he* could be dittographic, if both the two antonymous nouns were originally masculine. On the other hand, if we disregard the accent and take הַשָּׁפֵלָה as feminine, perhaps its parallel might originally have been the feminine הַגֻּבְהָה, whose final *he* might have been lost by parablepsis. Fortunately, translation is unaffected.

21:32 עַוָּה עַוָּה עַוָּה אֲשִׂימֶנָּה—The noun עַוָּה is repeated thrice, probably as a superlative; compare the Trisagion, Is 6:3. Unfortunately, it is a hapax, and its meaning must basically be derived from the context. If one can argue from etymology (always risky), it may be derived from the verb עָוָה, "twist, distort," and possibly be related to the noun עִי, "ruin, rubble," and thus possibly the place name "Ai." There may be a play on עָוֹן ("punishment for iniquity") in 21:30 (ET 21:25), which may or may not be derived from the same root.

The favorite English translation seems to be "ruin," and it is hard to improve upon. KJV translates it as a verb ("I will overturn ... it"), essentially merging it with the following verb אֲשִׂימֶנָּה. NKJV corrects slightly to "overthrown, overthrown, I will make it overthrown!" Although more free, the sense is essentially the same as "ruin ... I will make it."

גַּם־זֹאת לֹא הָיָה—Quite varying translations are offered for this clause, partly depending on the understanding of the rest of the verse. A basic question is whether הָיָה is to be understood in the past tense or as a prophetic perfect (i.e., future tense). If one follows the first option, NRSV's parenthetical "such has never occurred" seems basically on target. Most interpreters, however, understand it as a prophetic perfect.

In any case, the disagreement in gender between the masculine verb הָיָה and its feminine subject, the pronoun זֹאת, is disquieting. The best explanation may be in the לֹא that intervenes. Zimmerli follows Moran in taking הָיָה as an abbreviation of an original תִּהְיֶה, but that is speculative emendation.[42]

To what does זֹאת refer? It seems to reiterate זֹאת לֹא־זֹאת (translated as "everything will be changed") in 21:31 (ET 21:26). That is, the calamitous reversals just spo-

---

[41] Cooke, *Ezekiel*, 235.

[42] Zimmerli, *Ezekiel*, 1:438, citing William L. Moran, "Gen 49,10 and Its Use in Ez 21,32," *Biblica* 39 (1958): 421–22.

ken of will not take place "until" (… עַד) whatever is referred to by that clause. See further the commentary.

עַד־בֹּא אֲשֶׁר־לוֹ הַמִּשְׁפָּט וּנְתַתִּיו׃—A final question is raised by the antecedent of the third masculine singular object suffix on the last verb, וּנְתַתִּיו, "and I will give it." If "it" refers to הַמִּשְׁפָּט, "judgment," which is the closest noun, we would expect וּנְתַתִּיו to be followed by לוֹ, "I will give it [judgment] *to him*." Cooke emends by adding לוֹ on the basis of the Greek παραδώσω αὐτῷ.[43] But in Hebrew a pronominal suffix on a verb can serve as an indirect object, so וּנְתַתִּיו can mean "And I will give to him," with "judgment" as the implied direct object. Thus no emendation is required. As often in Hebrew, the direct object can and must be supplied.

21:33–37 No word-event formula ("the Word of Yahweh came …") or other device sets the remainder of the chapter off from what precedes. Yet, both style and content require regarding it as a separate oracle. At the same time, all kinds of links with earlier parts of the chapter require that we keep them in mind.

This entire section divides fairly easily into two parts on the basis of literary style: 21:33–34 (ET 21:28–29) and 21:35–37 (ET 21:30–32). On the subjects of the two parts, there is, however, considerable diversity of views. It may be noted initially that feminine singular forms predominate throughout. That is, the grammatical subject is חֶרֶב, "sword," although that by itself does not tell us who wields the sword or against whom. After 21:33a (ET 21:28a), the prophecy itself is not directed to anyone in particular. Following Greenberg, I have adopted the view that, since the language, at least through 21:34 (ET 21:29), is so similar to that of the preceding sections predicting Nebuchadnezzar's attack on Judah, "a continuation of that theme seems to be the most plausible line of interpretation."[44] Further details will be discussed as met, either in the textual analysis or in the commentary.

21:33 כֹּה אָמַר אֲדֹנָי יְהוִֹה אֶל־בְּנֵי עַמּוֹן וְאֶל־חֶרְפָּתָם—After אָמַר, both instances of אֶל must be translated as what Yahweh "says *concerning*," not "says to." This is unusual in Ezekiel, but not unparalleled (e.g., 2 Ki 19:32; Jer 22:18). Ezekiel used אָמַר לְ in 12:19 for what Yahweh "says concerning/about."

On the rendition of בְּנֵי עַמּוֹן as "the sons of Ammon," see the discussion in the textual note on 21:25 (ET 21:20). Here the plural suffix on חֶרְפָּתָם, "*their* taunts," could indicate that the people are more in view here than the country itself. חֶרְפָּתָם could refer either to "their disgrace," which they endured, or more actively to "their scorn/taunts" toward Israel. The latter is obviously meant here.

וְאָמַרְתָּ חֶרֶב חֶרֶב—This oracle begins in almost the same way as the oracle that begins in 21:14 (ET 21:9), אֱמֹר חֶרֶב חֶרֶב. Here "sword, sword" is vocative. In 21:34 (ET 21:29), Yahweh continues to speak to the sword as "you" (feminine singular in Hebrew, since חֶרֶב is a feminine noun).

פְּתוּחָה לְטֶבַח—The feminine singular Qal passive participle פְּתוּחָה, literally, "opened, exposed," means the sword is "drawn, unsheathed." Here it replaces הוּחַדָּה,

---

[43] Cooke, *Ezekiel*, 239.

[44] Greenberg, *Ezekiel*, 2:435.

"sharpened," in 21:14 (ET 21:9). מֶבַח ("slaughter") is the same noun used in 21:15, 20 (ET 21:10, 15),

מְרוּטָה לְהָכִיל לְמַעַן בָּרֶק:—The same Qal passive participle (מְרוּטָה, "polished") was in 21:14 (ET 21:9). לְהָכִיל is most easily parsed as a Hiphil infinitive construct of כּוּל, "to contain," but that makes no sense in this context. Two explanations, neither requiring emendation, are possible. One takes it as a syncopated form of לְהַאֲכִיל, "to cause to eat/devour," the Hiphil infinitive construct of אָכַל with the weak *aleph* disappearing as occurs in other verbs beginning with *aleph*.[45] Second, especially since the LXX has εἰς συντέλειαν ("for completion/destruction"), the form here may be from a verb כּוּל that is a synonym and biform of כָּלָה, "to end, consume." Its Hiphil infinitive construct would have a causative meaning: "to bring to an end, cause to be consumed." Usually after לְמַעַן, which begins a purpose clause, Hebrew uses a verb, but here we find the noun בָּרֶק, "lightning." For smooth English, the translation adds a verb, "to flash like lightning." Some advocate revocalizing the noun as a Qal infinitive construct, בְּרֹק, but the meaning remains the same (cf. 21:20 [ET 21:15]).

21:34 Any translation of this verse must be tentative because it is unclear in the context who or what is being talked about. The first part of the verse has no finite verbs, but three Qal infinitive constructs with prepositions (בַּחֲזוֹת ... בִּקְסָם ... לָתֵת). Initially, the language of 21:28a (ET 21:23a) and 21:30 (ET 21:25) is reworked. The near synonyms שָׁוְא and כָּזָב are combined again in connection with false prophecy and divination in 13:6–9 and 22:28 (see also 13:23). The figure of speech that the sword will be put upon people's necks occurs only here in the OT. The phrase חַלְלֵי רְשָׁעִים is a plural variation of חֲלַל רָשָׁע in 21:30 (ET 21:25). As there, חָלָל again means a virtual "corpse," a condemned person who is as good as dead. The final clause is a variation of the clause at the end of 21:30 (ET 21:25) with a third masculine plural suffix on יוֹם rather than a third masculine singular one.

21:35 הָשֵׁב אֶל־תַּעְרָהּ—The Hiphil of שׁוּב ("return") has an unusual form if this is the masculine singular imperative. Ordinarily the imperative is pointed הָשֵׁב and has a *patach* (-ַשׁ-) in the ultima only when in pause (Is 42:22). However, we should have long since ceased to be surprised by such minor irregularities in Ezekiel. The form could also be the Hiphil infinitive absolute, which can serve as a sort of all-purpose shorthand for any person, number, gender, or mood, including an imperative, so the meaning would be the same.

Here the verb has no stated object, although that is not unusual in Hebrew usage, and obviously it is the "sword," as confirmed by the third feminine singular suffix on תַּעְרָהּ ("*its* scabbard"). The shift to the third person (speaking *about* the sword, rather than *to* it as in 21:33b–34 [ET 21:18b–19]) would imply that some other unidentified actor is being addressed by the masculine imperative. Probably it is addressed to the Babylonians, who wield the sword in this pericope.

Some take an easy way out by making a radical emendation of הָשֵׁב to the Qal feminine singular imperative שֻׁבִי, which would command the sword to "return."

---

45 Keil, *Ezekiel*, 1:306, and others.

מְכֻרֹתַיִךְ—This is the plural of the feminine noun מְכוּרָה with second feminine singular suffix, which must refer to the sword. See the discussion of מְכוּרָה in the first textual note on 16:3. The word will be used again in 29:14.

21:36 וְשָׁפַכְתִּי עָלַיִךְ זַעְמִי—Ordinarily in contexts of God's wrath, the verb שָׁפַךְ ("pour out") is used with the object חֵמָה, "heat, anger." In Ezekiel, the combination used here recurs only in 22:31, and the noun זַעַם occurs only once more, in 22:31. This noun is sometimes translated "indignation" or "curse," but it is parallel to various OT words for "wrath," and so, for all practical purposes, it may be considered synonymous.

אָפִיחַ—The verb פוּחַ (here Hiphil first common singular imperfect), "blow," occurs only here in Ezekiel, but is related to נָפַח in 22:20–21. The literal use of "blow fire" is at home in the realm of metallurgy (smelting).

וּנְתַתִּיךְ בְּיַד אֲנָשִׁים בֹּעֲרִים—The idiom נָתַן בְּיַד, "deliver into the hand of," was used in 21:16 (ET 21:11). The verb בָּעַר can mean to "burn," and some have thought the expression here might refer to "men burning with wrath." Although that sort of language appears in the OT, בָּעַר is never used to express it. There might be some intent to evoke the בְּעַרְתִּיהָ ("I have kindled it") at the beginning of the (Hebrew) chapter, 21:4 (ET 20:48). See the commentary on the possibility of an "inclusion" around the chapter involving the fire. But as far as translation is concerned, בֹּעֲרִים probably is a homonym, the Qal masculine plural participle of בָּעַר II, which has nothing to do with "burning," but rather means "to be like an animal, stupid, foolish, brutish." In Pss 92:7 (ET 92:6) and 94:8, some form of the root is paralleled with כְּסִיל, "foolish (one)." Interestingly, the LXX translates the phrase here ἀνδρῶν βαρβάρων, "barbarians," chosen possibly because of its phonic similarity with בֹּעֲרִים, but also nicely capturing the double emphasis of wildness and disorder that is probably implicit in the Hebrew.[46] Keil probably correctly notes that OT thought "associated the idea of godlessness with folly, and that cruelty naturally follows in its train."[47]

חָרָשֵׁי מַשְׁחִית:—This final phrase is in apposition to the preceding ("brutal men"). A חָרָשׁ is a "craftsman," an expert or specialist in almost anything. Here the expertise is specified by the noun מַשְׁחִית, "destruction."

21:37 לָאֵשׁ תִּהְיֶה לְאָכְלָה—The Hebrew is, literally, "for the fire you will be for consuming." Since in 21:35b–36 Yahweh was speaking to the sword ("you") in the second person feminine (see the commentary on those verses), here one would expect another second person feminine verb, תִּהְיִי instead of תִּהְיֶה, which could be either second masculine or third feminine. On the basis of the irregularity, Zimmerli deletes the entire phrase as a careless subsequent insertion,[48] but lacking any textual evidence for that, one looks for a better explanation. It could be a copyist's slip; it could be merely another example of Ezekiel's occasional laxity about grammatical correctness; or it may reflect the increasing reluctance in late Hebrew to use feminine forms.

---

[46] Zimmerli, *Ezekiel*, 1:440.

[47] Keil, *Ezekiel*, 1:309.

[48] Zimmerli, *Ezekiel*, 1:440.

דָּמֵךְ יִהְיֶה בְּתוֹךְ הָאָרֶץ—This clause, literally, "your blood will be in the midst of the land," is not exactly pellucid. Translations vary. Some simply reproduce the Hebrew and leave it up to the readers to make sense of it as best they can. This is the common approach of "formal equivalent" translations (so KJV, NKJV, RSV, and ESV here). "Dynamic equivalent" versions usually risk some interpretation. They vary slightly in detail, but most offer something comparable to my venture: "your blood will flow all over the land." For example, NRSV has "your blood shall enter the earth," and NIV gives "your blood will be shed in your land."

Commentary
Outline of Ezekiel 21

This entire Hebrew chapter is structurally a series of four oracles united by a common subject: the sword.[a] Mostly it is the sword of Yahweh, although at times the sword is poetically personified and appears to act of its own volition.[49] That uniting feature alone (prescinding momentarily from the vast differences in the style and vocabulary of the four oracles compared to the surrounding material) suffices to demonstrate the superiority of the Hebrew chapter division. The LXX agrees with the Hebrew division and thus is a happy construction. The Vulgate put the break between chapters 20 and 21 after MT 21:5. Why the Vulgate made the break at so obviously inappropriate a place is past finding out. English Bibles follow the Vulgate by including MT 21:1–5 in the previous chapter (ET 20:45–49).

(a) Ezek 21:1–12 (ET 20:45–21:7); 21:13–22 (ET 21:8–17); 21:23–32 (ET 21:18–27); 21:33–37 (ET 21:28–32)

The "sword" (חֶרֶב) is one of Ezekiel's favorite terms for the forces of war, death, and destruction. Of the various synonyms for those forces, this is the only one that dominates entire oracles. חֶרֶב occurs some ninety times in the book and fifteen times in this chapter alone. The word will be featured again in 32:11–15, which refers to other activities of Nebuchadnezzar.

None of the oracles in this chapter is dated, but all of them seem to refer to events closely related to Jerusalem's capitulation in the summer of 586. Other parts of the chapter may well have been composed separately and later joined editorially, but if so, the prime candidate for "editor" is Ezekiel himself.

The chapter is easily divisible into four discrete oracles:

1. The riddle of the sword and its interpretation (21:1–12 [ET 20:45–21:7])
2. The Song of the Sword (21:13–22 [ET 21:8–17])
3. The historical activity of the sword and its consequences (21:23–32 [ET 21:18–27])
4. The return of the sword to its scabbard (21:33–37 [ET 21:28–32])

These divisions are not arbitrary, since they are clearly marked by common prophetic formulae. The first three open with the word-event formula, "the Word of Yahweh came (to me)" (21:1, 13, 23 [ET 20:45; 21:8, 18]; also 21:6

---

[49] Allen, *Ezekiel*, 2:17, entitles his treatment of the chapter "The Sword of Damocles."

[ET 21:1]),[50] followed by commands to do something. The fourth begins with a command to prophesy plus the citation formula ("thus says the Lord Yahweh," 21:33 [ET 21:28]).[51] A clear progression in the sword's involvement is also evident: (1) in the first oracle, Yahweh himself wields the sword; (2) in the second, the sword seems to act independently; (3) in the third, Yahweh gives the sword to his agent to act for him; and (4) in the final oracle, the sword is returned to its sheath after doing its job.

All four oracles are closely tied to historical circumstances, so their theological yield for the church requires an understanding of that history. The chapter contains little overt theological expatiation, but has important Christological implications (see especially the commentary on 21:10, 23–27, 28, 32, 37 [ET 21:5, 18–22, 23, 27, 32]).

It also abounds in textual difficulties. In that respect, it is often compared with 7:1–27 (the Day of Yahweh) or 1:4–28 (the inaugural vision). Some verses defy certain translation—or perhaps translation at all. The fact that much of the chapter is at least semi-poetic, or that an actual poem or song may underlie it, may account for many of the textual problems. English translations, like modern editions of the Hebrew Bible, often use poetic typography where the text is so judged, but a cursory comparison shows that those judgments about Ezekiel 21 vary widely.[52] The many linguistic problems, "repetitions, exclamations, choppy staccato constructions, incomplete and garbled sentences, unusual forms, absence of rhythm, and puzzling motifs," as Block summarizes them, are often considered corruptions, and some may be. But Block's working hypothesis, that they more likely reflect Ezekiel's "heightened emotional condition," seems to be more circumspect.[53]

The Riddle of the Sword and Its Interpretation (21:1–12 [ET 20:45–21:7])

21:1–2 (ET 20:45–46)   The first sword oracle (21:1–12 [ET 20:45–21:7]) consists of two parts. Its first half (21:1–5 [ET 20:45–49]) is a parable or riddle (see the plural of מָשָׁל, "parable, riddle," in 21:5 [ET 20:49]), and its second half is the interpretation (21:6–12 [ET 21:1–7]).

Ezekiel is preaching to an audience of Israelites in exile in Babylon. Whether Ezekiel intended to use three essentially synonymous terms for "south," or whether they are all place names (as I have translated; see the third textual note on 21:2 [ET 20:46]), his audience surely would have thought "south" because of the application to Jerusalem in 21:7 (ET 21:2). For a

---

[50] For this formula, see page 8 in the introduction and the textual note on 3:16.

[51] For this formula, see pages 8–9 in the introduction and the fourth textual note and the commentary on 2:4.

[52] For example, *BHS* has 21:14b–17, 19–22a (ET 21:9b–12, 14–17a) in poetic layout, whereas ESV has only 21:14b–15 (ET 21:9b–10) as poetry.

[53] Block, *Ezekiel*, 1:660, citing Daniel I. Block, "Text and Emotion: A Study in the 'Corruptions' in Ezekiel's Inaugural Vision (Ezekiel 1:4–28)," *CBQ* 50/3 (July 1988): 418–42.

southerly direction to make geographical sense, Ezekiel must have the homeland in mind. Those in Babylon would have easily grasped that because their hearts and thoughts were still very much back in Judah.

It is an attractive possibility, however, that we have the counterpart to the frequent description of the foe from the north (either exmythological,[54] or, geographically determined, the western leg of the fertile crescent). That reference to the north occurs quite frequently, especially in Jeremiah, and is discernible in Ezek 38:6, 15; 39:2.

Some commentators wonder whether the scrub of the Negev would provide enough fuel for a conflagration of the magnitude described in the next two verses. Those who live today in southern California would have no doubts about it!

21:3 (ET 20:47)   Even though the literary form is still parabolic, several of its elements clearly point toward the interpretation in 21:6–12 (ET 21:1–7). While לַהֶבֶת in "blazing flame" is most easily used of fire, the related masculine form לַהַב appears elsewhere of the flashing blade of a sword (Judg 3:22; Nah 3:3), and "sword" will become explicit in Ezek 21:8 (ET 21:3). The word probably even anticipates the "lightning" of 21:15, 20, 33 (ET 21:10, 15, 28). Thus the "fire" and "blazing flame" (21:3 [ET 20:47]) are those of war.

Ezekiel's primary concern is not with trees, but with people. Hence, the trees surely represent people, and the forest of 21:2 (ET 20:46) the entire population. The "green" and "dry" trees correspond to the "righteous" and the "wicked" (another merism) in 21:8 (ET 21:3; cf. Lk 23:31). "Every face will be scorched" because faces would be the first to feel the heat, but this is soon expanded by כָל־בָּשָׂר, "all flesh/everyone," in the next verse.

21:4 (ET 20:48)   The verse is an expansion and intensification of the previous ones. "Every face" becomes "all people, everyone." The verb "see, realize, recognize" (רָאָה) is used instead of יָדַע, "know," in "everyone will see that I, Yahweh, have kindled it," which (like clauses in 21:10 [ET 21:5] and 39:21) is a variant formulation of the recognition formula: "then you/they will know that I am Yahweh."[55] What will be seen or recognized is that the "fire" (21:3 [ET 20:47]) is caused by divine action and not something that can be explained by natural or inner-historical causes. The repetition of "(It) will not be extinguished" underscores the irrevocability of Yahweh's decision (cf. 6:10 and 14:23).

21:5 (ET 20:49)   Once again we have one of those rare occasions where Ezekiel's own voice is heard. Oracles like the one just uttered, plus his sometimes bizarre action prophecies, make it easy to understand that the people

---

[54] By "exmythological," this commentary refers to ideas or motifs that were utilized in the religious mythology of Israel's pagan neighbors and that sometimes are used also in the OT, where, of course, their theological meaning is quite different in the context of faith in Yahweh, the one true God.

[55] For this formula, see page 9 in the introduction and the commentary on 6:7.

would think of him as a master entertainer. When the "elders" are reported to be with him in chapters 8, 14, and 20, the motivation may have been mostly mere curiosity to see what he would do next. And such a view of his actions and words would surely call into question his authority as a genuine prophet and discredit, or at least neutralize, the impact of his ministry. Rough parallels among some clergymen today would surely not be hard to find!

Implicit in Ezekiel's complaint is a request that the riddle just uttered be explained. The request is readily granted by Yahweh, first by an interpretation of the simile in 21:6–12 (ET 21:1–7) and expanded still more in 21:13–22 (ET 21:8–17).

21:7 (ET 21:2) Almost in the form of a strict allegory, the three figurative representations of the south in 21:2 (ET 20:46) are here specifically identified. Teman is Jerusalem, Darom is her sanctuaries, and the Negev is the entire land of Israel. The repetition of the same three verbs, "set ... preach ... prophesy," from 21:2 (ET 20:46) confirms the matches.

21:8 (ET 21:3) The figures of fire (from the riddle in 21:2–4 [ET 20:46–48]) and sword interpenetrate in this and the next two verses. Ezekiel employs both as Yahweh's agents of death, but nowhere else in the OT are they so closely equated as here. There is a Babylonian parallel, however, in the Erra Epic,[56] and it is just possible that Ezekiel is adapting a literary motif from his exilic cultural environment. The verb אָכַל, "eat/devour," used of the fire in 21:3 (ET 20:47), could provide an easy link, since it is frequently used of the sword (e.g., Deut 32:42), but here the verb הִכְרִית, "cut off," has been substituted.

Superficially, the statement that the righteous as well as the wicked will be punished appears in frontal contradiction to earlier statements to the contrary, especially in chapter 18 (cf. also 9:4–6 and 14:12–20). (The LXX "corrected" the problem by apparently deliberately translating צַדִּיק, "righteous," as ἄδικον, "lawless," instead of the correct δίκαιον, "righteous.") The structure of the oracle, however, indicates that this statement of polar opposites is the interpretation of the "green" and "dry" trees in 21:3 (ET 20:47). That is, we have another merism, indicating an undifferentiated totality. Ezekiel is no systematic theologian. Here he is not addressing the issue of individual accountability before God, but of simply the external, empirical side of things. Just as a raging forest fire consumes everything in its path, so in the horrors of war, innocent civilians often suffer just as much as the combatants, and righteous believers may be killed together with wicked unbelievers. Block may be correct in adding that the expression is not merely a literary merism, but also "a deliberately offensive rhetorical device intended to shock, designed to awaken his [Ezekiel's] audience out of their spiritual lethargy."[57]

---

[56] See Stephanie Dalley, *Myths from Mesopotamia: Creation, the Flood, Gilgamesh, and Others* (Oxford: Oxford University Press, 1989), cited in Block, *Ezekiel*, 1:670, n. 65.

[57] Block, *Ezekiel*, 1:670.

21:9 (ET 21:4)   Although the correspondence to 21:3 (ET 20:47) is not quite so close as it was in 21:8, this verse apparently interprets the scorching of every face at the end of 21:3 (ET 20:47). "Everyone" again translates כָּל־בָּשָׂר. Previously in 21:4 (ET 20:48), the phrase had applied to witnesses of the judgment. Here it applies to all the refugees of Judah, where the horrors of war continue to afflict "everyone" indiscriminately.

21:10 (ET 21:5)   The recognition formula[58] here obviously corresponds to that of 21:4 (ET 20:48), only now using the common verb יָדַע, "know," for the formula, instead of the infrequent רָאָה, "see," which was in 21:4 (ET 20:48). "Everyone" again translates כָּל־בָּשָׂר, but here apparently in a wider sense than in 21:9 (ET 21:4), namely, the world at large will recognize that Yahweh is punishing his own people for their infidelity.

Greenberg points to a "logical difficulty" that occurs frequently. He observes that in the Gentile oracles of the book, Yahweh repeatedly states that the foreign nations will be annihilated; "then they/you [the foreign nation] will know that I am Yahweh" (25:7, 11, 17; 26:6; 39:6). Even in Ex 14:4, Yahweh paradoxically asserts that he must destroy Pharaoh and his army for the same reason.[59] If these unbelievers are destroyed, how will they know that he is Yahweh? Some of the answer has to do with the epic or poetic use of language, including hyperbole, but part of it is profoundly theological: if even believers must die with Christ on the cross, no wonder that those still outside the pale must be annihilated, at least in their old identity, before God can effect his new creation also upon as many of them as will repent and believe (cf. Rom 6:1–4; 2 Cor 5:17; Col 2:11–13; Titus 3:5–7).

The very end of the verse raises a similar problem. As it stands, it asserts that God's wrath, now aroused, will never subside. However, such a picture of God as eternally, essentially wrathful would contradict much of the rest of Scripture, including 21:35 (ET 21:30). Again we have a hyperbolic statement of what needs to be emphasized at the moment. One might restate its intent that the sword will not be sheathed until it has accomplished the result predicted in 21:8 (ET 21:3; cf. Is 55:11). In fact, that becomes explicit in 21:35 (ET 21:30).

21:11 (ET 21:6)   Even after the initial riddle has been explained, the people are apparently still too dismissive of Ezekiel as a mere actor or jester to understand or take seriously what he has just tried to communicate. Accordingly, Yahweh commands Ezekiel to perform another action prophecy, predicting nonverbally what the future conduct of the people will be. The immediate intent is to provoke them to ask seriously what the action meant, and the next verse shows that that objective was readily accomplished.

21:12 (ET 21:7)   The reply Ezekiel is to give his questioners remains rather cryptic. He is to speak only of "news" that will be paralyzing and de-

---

[58] For this formula, see page 9 in the introduction and the commentary on 6:7.

[59] Greenberg, *Ezekiel*, 2:420.

moralizing. The "news" is practically expanded in the Song of the Sword in 21:13–22 (ET 21:8–17), but even then no explicit clarification is forthcoming. One surely must assume that the reference is to the approach of Nebuchadnezzar for the fateful siege that will lead to the fall of Jerusalem itself. Yahweh may still hope to evoke some genuine repentance before the sword falls. However, the chapter does not indicate that any believed the prophecy or repented. Rather, it seems that the people persisted in their self-denial and false sense of security. Yet the time would soon come when they would imitate Ezekiel's behavior.

The Song of the Sword (21:13–22 [ET 21:8–17])

21:13–14 (ET 21:8–9) A new section of the chapter begins here. Ezek 21:13–14a (ET 21:8–9a) introduces what is almost universally known as the Song of the Sword, 21:14b–21:22 (ET 21:9b–17). As "song" indicates, it is mostly written in a highly turgid and poetic style. Probably for that very reason, its Hebrew teems with an unusual number of textual and syntactical difficulties. Poetry, almost by definition, is written in an unusual style and with unique vocabulary (which, in turn, greatly increased the chances that later scribes would not understand or would otherwise miscopy). There is no way of determining whether the song is an original composition Yahweh inspired Ezekiel to write or if it was a preexistent piece that Yahweh directed the prophet to adapt for use here. A poetic proclivity of the prophet is generally not in great evidence in his book. In any case, the present form of the song has been thoroughly mortised into its larger context.

What is striking about the song is that the "sword" is apostrophized and thus appears to take on an independent existence. That it remains Yahweh's sword is, of course, in no doubt, but the literary (and thence the theological) impact of its personification is great. (There may be an exmythological remote origin of the figure, in which kind of thought, the sword would have been objectified and deified, but except perhaps as a foil for an Israelite audience, such a possible background is irrelevant to biblical meaning.)

The figure is not unique to Ezekiel. As "a man of war" (Ex 15:3), Yahweh is often depicted as not only wielding the sword himself, but as commanding it to execute judgment. Various Hebrew verbs are employed: Yahweh may "command" (צִוָּה, Amos 9:4; cf. Josh 11:12) or "send" (שָׁלַח, e.g., Jer 9:15 [ET 9:16]; 24:10) the sword. The sword can even be described as getting drunk on the blood of its victims (רָוְה, Is 34:5; Jer 46:10). Other passages where the sword is addressed personally or is described as raging independently include Jer 47:6–7; 50:35–37; and Zech 13:7, which is cited in Mt 26:31 and Mk 14:27 as fulfilled in our Lord's passion.

The verbal forms describing the sword in Ezek 21:14b–c (ET 21:9b–c) are both repeated and applied in the following verses.

21:15 (ET 21:10) The first two lines simply expand on 21:14 (ET 21:9) and require no further comment. The third and fourth lines are a genuine crux, however. As indicated in my textual comments (which see), I present as an attractive (though far from certain) translation: "Or shall we rejoice, staff of my son? [The sword] despises every tree." This interpretation takes its under-standing from the blessing of Jacob in Gen 49:10, clearly alluded to in Ezek 21:32 (ET 21:27) below. These lines probably also allude to Nathan's oracle to David in 2 Samuel 7. They can then be interpreted as a sort of protest by the people, appealing to the ancient messianic promises.[60]

The people have misunderstood the announcement of a sword prepared for slaughter as good news that Yahweh will soon deliver them from Babylon. The basis of their false hope is summarized in the slogan "staff of my son" (or, if vocative instead of construct, "staff, my son"), which they claim will defend them from the menacing sword. שֵׁבֶט could be understood as Yahweh's "rod" of discipline (so RSV and NRSV; also KJV, but probably in a different sense). שֵׁבֶט is so used in 2 Sam 7:14: "when he does iniquity, I will discipline him with the *rod* of men." But the interpretation here is that the word denotes "scepter," symbolizing political power (so NKJV, NIV). If so translated, the appeal to Genesis 49 and the royal promise in 2 Samuel 7 becomes likely. The phrase בְּנִי, "my son," derives from Gen 49:9, where the patriarch addresses Judah, comparing him to a young lion (NIV adds "Judah" as an appositive to "my son" in Ezek 21:15 [ET 21:10]), as well as to 2 Sam 7:14, where Yahweh says about David's S/son, "I will be his Father, and he will be my S/son" (cf. Ps 2:7, 12). שֵׁבֶט is used of the royal scepter of David's S/son in Ps 2:9: "you will rule them with an iron *rod*." If כָּל־עֵץ in Ezek 21:15 (ET 21:10) is then translated as "all wood," which is despised, the idea is that Judah's scepter rejects every other ruler's staff as bad wood—which, as such, would be correct, except for the application Ezekiel's contemporaries were making of it.

Block retains the "every tree" translation and, referring back to 21:3 (ET 20:47), applies it to every resident, including the royal family.[61] That is, Yahweh's "sword" (as the most likely grammatical subject of the verb) "rejects" (מֹאֶסֶת) the people's futile claim that the ancient promise grants them automatic immunity from the looming catastrophe, regardless of their unfaithfulness.

Such a line of interpretation accords well with many of Ezekiel's other preachments to his contemporaries. Because of the difficulty of the Hebrew, achieving that result almost seems more like cryptography than exegesis, but no alternative commends itself either!

21:16–17 (ET 21:11–12)   These verses add little that was not already contained in 21:14b–15b (ET 21:9b–10b). Typical of poetry, they remain allusive, never stating who is handing the sword to whom—although in the context that is easy to surmise: Yahweh hands it to the king of Babylon to use to defeat Judah. The repeated "my people" should not be understood as an anthropopathism expressing Yahweh's regret over the painful action he must take in

---

[60] Keil, *Ezekiel*, 1:291, suggests adding "saying": "shall we rejoice (saying), ..." This clarifies the sense, but the interpretation above does not depend on this addition.

[61] Block, *Ezekiel*, 1:678.

punishing his people, as it often does in the prophets (e.g., Is 1:3; Micah 6:3; also in Ezek 13:10). Rather, it underscores the depths of the estrangement of covenant partners. Dare we compare it to the vindictiveness often seen in human divorces?

The only substantive question is whether the crying out, wailing, and slapping the thigh that frame 21:17 (ET 21:12) are mere literary figures or action prophecies by the prophet. In either case, the import is predictive. My judgment would be that they were acted out, as was already the case in 21:11–12 (ET 21:6–7) and as will appear to be the case again in 21:19 (ET 21:14). Everything has to do with the impending judgment upon Jerusalem and the people's inevitable reactions to the event.

21:18 (ET 21:13)   This difficult Hebrew verse is virtually unintelligible, like the related 21:15c–d (ET 21:10c–d). It can be, has been, and is understood and translated in many disparate ways, and almost no one claims any certainty. If the line of interpretation tentatively offered in 21:15c–d (ET 21:10c–d) is continued, the שֵׁבֶט, "rod," is again the scepter of Judah (Gen 49:10). But the present heirs of Judah have failed the test, so the sword of God's judgment will … ; the text seems to leave it to the audience to supply the answer or fill in the blank! Ezekiel has already provided the answer many times and will continue to do so.

21:19 (ET 21:14)   That Ezekiel's "prophecy" (usually understood as verbalization) is to consist of an action prophecy is also as good an illustration as any of the virtual synonymity of prophecy and typology (nonverbal). Also parallel is the complementarity of Word and Sacrament. God's Word is a spoken "Sacrament," and a Sacrament is a visible form of the Word.[62]

The precise meaning of the jussive, literally, "let the sword be doubled a third," is unclear (see the textual note). I have acceded to the common view that "a third" is akin to another jussive, "let it be tripled." Since the reference is scarcely to a multiplication of the number of swords, the picture would then be that of the rapid back-and-forth vacillation of a sword in action, which to the eye, however, would create such an illusion. Hence the paraphrase "let the sword strike twice, even thrice."

The Hebrew text, however, raises suspicions that more is implied. The MT's simple "third" may recall the "third" of the hair—representing the people—to be struck down by the sword in 5:2, 12. Zimmerli, citing Zech 13:8, asks whether the MT means to say that the sword will redouble its portion, that is, devour two-thirds.[63] Zech 13:8 speaks of two-thirds being cut off by the sword. If this is not mere coincidence, it could be that Zechariah (who frequently "recycles" earlier prophecy) is dependent on Ezekiel. Greenberg suggests literary artistry: after the double "a sword, a sword" at the beginning of

---

[62]   See further pages 2–4, 6, 10, 16 in the introduction.

[63]   Zimmerli, *Ezekiel*, 1:429.

the song in 21:14b (ET 21:9b) and its double use again in 21:16–17 (ET 21:11–12), we have here a sort of accusative of extent to which, that is, the sword's deprivations "up to a third time."[64]

The text emphasizes that the sword will result in those "slain." The word חָלָל also has overtones of judicial execution. As the divine Judge, Yahweh is also commissioning the sword to execute his forensic sentence—the opposite of justification (cf. Rom 5:12–21).

No matter what the translation of the hapax (הַחֹדֶרֶת, translated "that pursues even into private homes"; see the textual note), the last line of the verse describes the horror of the sword's inescapable action.

21:20 (ET 21:15)   It must not escape our attention that in this verse for the first time in the song Yahweh speaks of himself in the first person: "I have set the point of the sword." This is continued even more sharply in 21:22 (ET 21:17). Thus all three actors in the song come into view: (1) the people (Babylonians) who wield the sword (sometimes the apostrophized sword itself); (2) the prophetic messenger; and (3) Yahweh himself, who really directs everything, even if mediately.

The confused panic, as all avenues of escape are cut off, may reflect the common theme of Israel's "holy war" (which today probably should be called "Yahweh's war," lest it be confused with the *jihad* of Islam), in which Yahweh brings victory by inducing panic in the hearts of the enemy or takes away their will to fight. Here, however, Yahweh will be employing that tactic on his own apostate people.

21:21 (ET 21:16)   Yahweh here addresses the sword directly, commanding it to perform its gruesome task insatiably and fully.

21:22 (ET 21:17)   The final verse of the song uses about the most emphatic language possible (וְגַם־אֲנִי, "I myself ... also") and one of the strongest anthropomorphisms in the book: "I myself will also clap my hands." Yahweh himself will do what he had commanded the prophet to do in 21:19 (ET 21:14), so both he and his prophet anticipate the victory over the sword's enemies. By clapping his own hands, he will arouse the sword to full fury. And in so doing he will "satisfy" his own "fury/wrath." We met the idiom of Yahweh (literally) "causing his wrath to rest" in 5:13 (which see) and 16:42, and we will encounter it again in 24:13. Probably not accidentally, a prophecy on the use of Yahweh's sword against his own people concludes in 5:17 with these words: "I, Yahweh, have spoken." The Song of the Sword concludes the same way.

That Yahweh himself will satisfy his own wrath by executing judgment is a prototype of God's climactic, vicarious satisfaction of his wrath on Calvary. The same thought underlies the propitiatory efficacy of all OT sacrifice, and the NT explicitly applies it to the work of Christ (Rom 3:25; 1 Jn 2:2). The sinless Son of God became incarnate to "save his people from their sins" (Mt 1:21)

---

[64] Greenberg, *Ezekiel*, 2:424.

through his perfect life of obedience; his atoning death on the cross, where he endured the punishment for the sins of all humanity; and his glorious resurrection, portending the resurrection of all believers in Christ to life everlasting.

The Historical Activity of the Sword and Its Consequences (21:23–32 [ET 21:18–27])

21:23–27 (ET 21:18–22) The word-event formula,[65] "the Word of Yahweh came to me" (21:23 [ET 21:18]), begins an entirely new section of the chapter, connected to what precedes only by the prominence of חֶרֶב, "sword." This section continues through 21:32 (ET 21:27). Then the citation formula in 21:33 (ET 21:28) signals a separate, but closely related final sword account (21:33–37 [ET 21:28–32]).

Now the subject is the final campaign of Nebuchadnezzar, king of Babylon, against Jerusalem, and at the same time, against Ammon. It seems all but certain that this oracle (21:23–32 [ET 21:18–27]) can be dated to late 588 or very early 587 B.C. (cf. 2 Ki 25:1; Jer 39:1), after Zedekiah, king of Judah, rebelled against Babylon as his overlord, as also did the nation of Ammon. At a certain point in the itinerary of Nebuchadnezzar, king of Babylon, he must decide which of the two countries to target first. At the time of this oracle, his decision apparently had not yet been made, and Ezekiel's hearers (the exiles in Babylon, mindful of their kinsmen in Judah) were probably awaiting it anxiously.

Ezekiel's action of sketching out the fork in the road may be described as another action prophecy. It required no particular prescience, let alone supernatural revelation, to know that a decision would have to be made at the place where the roads divided. At the junction, Nebuchadnezzar could either continue south on the King's Highway (cf. Num 20:17; 21:22) to Rabbah, the capital of Ammon, or turn right toward Jerusalem. Damascus is often pinpointed as the site where the crucial decision had to be made. No doubt, Damascus was (and is) a major crossroads of the Near East, but there are any number of other places farther south where the army could have veered off to the right and west. But that sort of detail is of no importance here.

Ezek 21:23–27 (ET 21:18–22) dramatically predicts Nebuchadnezzar's fateful decision to attack Jerusalem before Ammon. These verses give us considerable information about some of the divinatory and military practices of antiquity. However, even these pagan divination practices, which may appear to us to have been games of chance, were made subservient to Yahweh's redemptive purposes, and Nebuchadnezzar's decision ultimately was determined by God. The judgment of Jerusalem must take place as part of Yahweh's plan to bring redemption to the entire world. The same dynamic pertains to the atonement of Christ, who suffered divine judgment, executed in part through

---

[65] For this formula, see page 8 in the introduction and the textual note on 3:16.

a game of chance, but in fulfillment of Scripture, according to God's plan (Ps 22:19 [ET 22:18]; Mt 27:35).

21:28 (ET 21:23) The first clause clearly describes the Israelites as dismissing Nebuchadnezzar's divinations and his decision based on them as meaningless or fraudulent (שָׁוְא). Does Ezekiel mean to say that the Israelites doubted that the king would actually attack them? That question is not addressed, but the issue of oaths is immediately broached: the Israelites "have sworn solemn oaths." To whom have their oaths been made? Commentaries give a great variety of answers to that question. Nebuchadnezzar has been suggested. The NIV's periphrastic translation seems to assume that. But if those oaths are still in force, that would seem to imply that Zedekiah had not yet revolted from Babylon's dominion over Judah, and thus that Nebuchadnezzar's third campaign to the area had not yet begun. His first campaign was after his victory over Egypt at Carchemish in 605 B.C., at which time Daniel and a few other token candidates were carried back from Judah to Babylon (Dan 1:1–4). Nebuchadnezzar's second campaign ended in 597 with the surrender of Jehoiachin and a second deportation, during which Ezekiel was taken to Babylon. Here, however, Ezekiel must have in view the third campaign that ended with the destruction of Jerusalem in summer 586.

Greenberg floats the possibility that the Israelites' oaths were to the Egyptians, with whom Jerusalem had made an alliance. Greenberg calls attention to 29:16, where Ezekiel describes that alliance as being to the Judahites (literally) "an object of trust, bringing iniquity to mind" (מִבְטָח מַזְכִּיר עָוֹן), but Yahweh emphasizes its futility.[66] (That alliance also was alluded to and denounced in 16:26.) I will grant this possibility as a valid option, but in my judgment, there is a better one, especially in the light of the next verse, which again uses the verb זָכַר, "bring to mind, remember."

The most solemn oath of all sworn by the Israelites was that to God. The covenant is frequently described in terms of an oath, and the fact that its essence was God's oath (promise) to them, not their promise to be faithful to it, only made it more "solemn."[b] But in line with the major theme of Ezekiel and other prophets, the people had forgotten that while God's promise was indeed unconditional, it was not magic, and they had the power to forfeit it by unfaithfulness—as, indeed, they had done. Ezekiel is not more specific, but there may be specific reference to the promise of the inviolability of Zion (that is, of "the city of God," of the true church, in its narrow sense), not the inviolability of Jerusalem, the earthly city, as they were disposed to misunderstand it.[67] And since "Zion" and "David" go together, Zedekiah, the present regent, may also

(b) See, e.g., Gen 22:16–18; 24:7; 26:3–4; Deut 1:35; 4:31; 7:8, 12, 13

---

[66] Greenberg, *Ezekiel*, 2:431.

[67] The inviolability of Zion is God's promise, reiterated throughout both the OT and the NT, that God will preserve his church to everlasting salvation (e.g., Mt 16:18). However, this promise does not mean that individuals can sin with impunity; those who apostatize from the true faith thereby forfeit their own salvation. See also the discussion in Hummel, *Ezekiel 1–20*, 256–57, 274–75, 371, 471. The true church in its narrow sense consists of all believ-

be on the horizon; he may have thought that he could break his oath of fealty to Nebuchadnezzar with impunity.

The antecedent of הוּא, "but *he* will bring their iniquity to mind" (21:28 [ET 21:23]), is uncertain, like so many other details in this verse. "Yahweh" seems to me to be the obvious choice. By translating the preceding conjunction adversatively ("but"), the gravamen of the verse is emphasized: they "trusted" in Yahweh, or so they thought, but the "Yahweh" in whom they trusted was a figment of their own "theology of glory" rather than the God who calls his people to be "crucified" with him. Such dying to sin and rising to new life is the only way people will ever learn that he is Yahweh.[68] To make Yahweh the subject does not eliminate secondary means that he used to accomplish his purpose. Obviously, Nebuchadnezzar was the historical agent through whom Yahweh reminded his people of their iniquity. He could just as well be called "the rod of my anger," as the Assyrians are labeled in Is 10:5, although neither Nebuchadnezzar nor the Assyrians had a clue to the fact that Yahweh was using them for his own purposes.

Block takes קֶסֶם, "divination" (Ezek 21:26–27 [ET 21:21–22]), as the antecedent,[69] and while that strikes me as less likely, we need not exclude it from the total picture. Obviously, God uses the pagan oracle as a means of determining Nebuchadnezzar's decision.

"Bring … to mind" (מַזְכִּיר) may be taken with a double reference. Obviously, the punishment will remind the people of their real status as sinners before God. As with all people, they will have to learn the hard way—in a sense, by dying with Christ, which is the only way true repentance is ever kindled. Also involved may be the common biblical anthropomorphism of God remembering (and so not forgetting) sins. In the same vein, it will be the cumulative effect of all of Israel's infidelities that is finally reminding Yahweh that since the people have spurned the covenant's blessings, now is the time to bring its curses to bear on them (see especially Deuteronomy 27–28). The verb (Niphal of תָּפַשׂ) that ends both 21:28 (ET 21:23; "being captured") and also 21:29 (where it is translated "taken") summarizes the form of the curse. This verb implies not only "capture" in some general sense, but to be caught *in flagrante*. It is so used in Num 5:13 of the adulterous wife (cf. Ezekiel 16 and 23, which picture Israel as Yahweh's adulterous wife).

21:29 (ET 21:24)   The verse is a commentary on the preceding one. That this is the end game of Yahweh's dealings with preexilic Israel, or (to change the metaphor) the straw that breaks the camel's back of God's patience with

---

ers. It is to be distinguished from the visible, outward church, which includes some hypocrites and unbelievers.

[68] For the recognition formula, "(Then) you/they will know that I am Yahweh," a favorite expression of Ezekiel, see page 9 in the introduction and the commentary on 6:7. Variations of this formula occur in 21:4 (ET 20:48) and 21:10 (ET 21:5).

[69] Block, *Ezekiel*, 1:688, including n. 180.

Israel, is indicated by the accumulation of four different, but essentially synonymous, expressions for sin: עָוֹן, "iniquity"; פְּשָׁעִים, "rebellions/rebellious acts"; חַטָּאוֹת, "sins/missing the mark"; and עֲלִילוֹת, "misdeeds." Corresponding to the four nouns are four verbs: the Hiphil of זָכַר, "bring to mind, remind"; the Niphal of גָּלָה, "be disclosed"; the Niphal of רָאָה, "be revealed, seen"; and the Niphal of זָכַר, "be brought to mind."

Finally, it should not be overlooked that in this and the next verse, Yahweh no longer uses the third person for his people, but the second person of direct address ("you … your"). The people's lostness is no longer being spoken *about*. They are being confronted personally by the righteous Judge they had tried to evade.

21:30 (ET 21:25)   Ezekiel now suddenly focuses all his fury on Zedekiah, the "prince of Israel" who has frequently been targeted in this book and will be again. Block calls this verse "a tirade … unequalled in this book or any other prophet for its forthrightness and harshness."[70] The עָוֹן, "iniquity," spoken of in the previous verses (21:28–29 [ET 21:23–24]) is corporate, committed by all of Israel, but Zedekiah is the "head of the body," and ultimately the responsibility for the iniquity that brought the "final punishment" on Jerusalem was Zedekiah's. We know that Jerusalem just before the fall was torn by pro- and anti-Egyptian factions, but Zedekiah ultimately cast his lot with the former, and with that revolt against Babylon's rule, and against Yahweh's, the whole "house of Israel" (e.g., 3:1) would soon collapse.

After having called him a "corpse" or "walking dead man," no further explanation is required of what would happen on his "day" when Yahweh would intervene. The parallel "time of [your] final *punishment*" uses עָוֹן now in the sense of "the consequence of iniquity" (עָוֹן meant "iniquity" itself in 21:28–29 [ET 21:23–24]). This punishment will be meted out at a set time (קֵץ, "*final punishment*") in the counsel of God when the cup of his wrath will finally spill over.

21:31 (ET 21:26)   There is some question whether Ezekiel envisions the unfrocking of both high priest and king or only the latter. Lexically, both understandings are possible (see the textual note). Since Ezekiel plainly envisions a total revolution involving all strata of society, inclusion of the priesthood would help paint a more comprehensive picture. On the other hand, a reference to the priesthood seems rather intrusive in this royal context.

The inversion of the low and the high in the verse inevitably reminds one of Jesus' logion in Mt 23:12 and Lk 14:11 and many similar statements (e.g., Lk 3:5; 18:13; 1 Pet 5:6). The NT contexts are generally focused more on individuals, although Zedekiah is in the fore here in Ezekiel too. Ultimately, however, the theme is almost a *cantus firmus* throughout Scripture: God ultimately overcomes all human pride and lofty striving that will not let him be

---

[70] Block, *Ezekiel*, 1:689.

God. Conversely, he lifts up the lowly and exalts them to the highest place with his Son (see, e.g., Lk 1:52; 1 Cor 1:26–29; Phil 2:5–11).

21:32 (ET 21:27) The previous verse's picture of everything turned upside down is repeated and intensified. The first person subject of the first verb "I will make it" should be noted: this is no anarchy for which political and social explanations might suffice. Rather it is Yahweh himself who will bring events that can almost be described as apocalyptic in nature.

The major exegetical issue in the verse is the meaning of the עַד ("until …") clause. Very early on, interpreters noticed a certain similarity between this clause: עַד־בֹּא אֲשֶׁר־לוֹ הַמִּשְׁפָּט, literally, "until the one comes to whom belongs judgment/justice/the right," and a clause in the Shiloh prophecy of Gen 49:10, which foretells that rulers shall continue from the tribe and line of Judah until the advent of the Ruler:

> The scepter shall not depart from Judah,
> nor the ruler's staff from between his feet,
> until Shiloh comes [עַד כִּי־יָבֹא שִׁילֹה],
> and to him [וְלוֹ] shall be the obedience of peoples.

"Shiloh" (שִׁילֹה) is a crux that can be interpreted in various ways, including "the one to whom it belongs" (if שׁ is the relative pronoun and לֹה is an archaic spelling of לוֹ). In light of Gen 49:10, Ezek 21:32 (ET 21:27) would mean that Israel shall be in ruins and desolated until the One comes to whom justice belongs, and God shall give to him the administration of justice—both judgment of unbelievers and justification of believers.

The comparison of these two verses seems to have been made even among many early Jewish interpreters, although not necessarily in a messianic way.[71] It is the apparent import of the LXX, which translates Ezek 21:32 with καθήκει, "for whom it is fitting" (although the LXX translates Gen 49:10 differently). After the coming of the promised Messiah, Jesus Christ, "messianic" naturally came to mean "Christological," and inevitably Judaism shied away from that understanding. Early Christian scholars, such as St. Jerome, clearly interpreted Ezek 21:32 as referring to Jesus Christ,[72] and until rather recent times, so did the vast majority of Christian exegetes. This view still has its defenders.[73]

Today, I think it safe to say that majority commentary opinion inclines against that long tradition. Most commentators now claim that this is not a result of non-Christian views or of a historicistic hermeneutic of the OT, but of

---

[71] Targum Jonathan applies the text to Zedekiah and Gedaliah (both of whom it mentions by name in Ezek 21:31 [ET 21:26]) and renders 21:32 (ET 21:27): "… according to their sins I will exact payment from them. Also, it will not be established for him until I bring upon him judgment—Ishmael son of Nathaniah [who murdered Gedaliah; see 2 Ki 25:25]—and I will deliver him into his hand."

[72] Jerome, *Commentariorum in Hiezechielem* (CCSL 75:290–91).

[73] E.g., Keil, *Ezekiel*, 1:305; Taylor, *Ezekiel*, 165.

philology. The issue really turns on how מִשְׁפָּט is to be translated and understood in Ezek 21:32 (ET 21:27). Already KJV translated it "right" ("whose right it is"), and with only minimal variation this rendering continues in most modern translations. For example, NRSV uses exactly the same words, and NIV has "to whom it rightfully belongs." However, ESV has "the one to whom judgment belongs."

In Ezekiel, מִשְׁפָּט often refers to God's "judgment" against his apostate people. It can also refer to God's revealed "ordinances"[74] or his "justice," given to his people to practice,[75] or even to what is "due" or "owed" to a member of the covenant people.[76] The closest verbal parallel to the wording in 21:32 (ET 21:27) might be 23:24b, where we again meet נָתַתִּי ... מִשְׁפָּט, but this clause is immediately clarified by adding (literally) "they will judge you with their judgments." (The context is the former lovers' judgment on whoring Oholibah, that is, Jerusalem.) The translation "judgment" fits our context perfectly also. And the person to whom Yahweh has given or assigned the task of carrying out his judgment on the "wicked corpse" 21:30 (ET 21:25) is none other than Nebuchadnezzar himself.

This nontraditional understanding need not, and probably does not, mean that Gen 49:10 is out of the picture. In fact, it is thoroughly in character for Ezekiel to take the ancient promise and make it into the vehicle of a message of total punishment. Ezekiel is not negating the messianic import of Gen 49:10, but he is saying that the apostate Jerusalemites have long since forfeited its applicability to them. When Nebuchadnezzar invests their city, no Messiah will intervene. "The prophet has turned a sacred text upside down in order to expose a twisted world and to annul false bases of hope."[77]

The almost redundant נְתַתִּיו, "I will give it," at the end of the verse (the same verb used in the already cited 23:24b) is a final divine reminder that Nebuchadnezzar will serve as Yahweh's agent.

The Return of the Sword to Its Scabbard (21:33–37 [ET 21:28–32])

21:33 (ET 21:28) I take this and the remainder of the final section of the chapter as basically concerned with the Babylonians, although addressed to the sword. A curve has been thrown to interpreters by the initial mention of the Ammonites, which has led many to understand at least this verse as addressed to them. Thus Block understands 21:33 (ET 21:28) to be the Ammonite version of the Song of the Sword (see 21:14–15 [ET 21:9–10]).[78] This view has a

---

[74] See the first textual note and the commentary on 5:6.

[75] See the textual note and commentary on 18:5.

[76] See the second textual note and the commentary on 22:29.

[77] Block, *Ezekiel*, 1:693.

[78] Block, *Ezekiel*, 1:696–97.

certain plausibility, because one can easily hypothesize that after the decision to attack Jerusalem first, the Ammonites, who were previously allied with Israel in revolt, would now betray their former friends and in *Schadenfreude* ("malicious joy at another's defeat") taunt the Israelites as they approached their fate. This view also resolves the perceived problem of the relation between this oracle and the Gentile oracle against Ammon in 25:1–7. While the latter is concerned with Ammonite glee *after* the fall of Jerusalem, here the catastrophe is still in the future. But a difficulty with this view is that 21:33 (ET 21:28) seems to promise punishment upon the Ammonites for their gloating (חֶרְפָּתָם, "their taunts"). Furthermore, the words here seem to imply some otherwise unattested Ammonite attack on Jerusalem.

Others understand the passage as referring to Nebuchadnezzar's attack on Ammon after he was finished with Judah. That too is plausible, although we lack historical confirmation of such an event. Still a third, rather mediating position understands the Ammonites as only an audience. They are allegedly singled out because of their previous mention (21:25 [ET 21:20]), but the intent is to reprove the premature rejoicing of all of Israel's neighbors. But the text itself says only that the Ammonites and their taunts are to be the occasion for an address to an anonymous sword.

Although it too is daring, I am attracted to the view of Greenberg that "Ammonites" (as he translates בְּנֵי עַמּוֹן) is code for the Babylonians. He compares it with Jeremiah's use of the code name "Sheshach" for Babylon (Jer 25:26). He notes that it was dangerous for Ezekiel in Babylon to make an explicit prophecy of Babylonia's ultimate destruction when it was at the height of its power. By describing the prophecy as "concerning the Ammonites/sons of Ammon and their taunts," and by inserting it at this point, Ezekiel could deflect any possible Babylonian suspicion by relating it here both to the present situation (Ezek 21:24–27 [ET 21:19–22]) and to the post-fall setting of 25:3–7.[79] This view, strained as it might seem at first blush, seems to me to be confirmed by the rest of the chapter.

21:34 (ET 21:29) To exegete this verse, one must know what the referents are, and, as in the previous verse, any certainty eludes us. If one thinks of the Ammonites as the subject, it would be a reference to their own soothsayers who either influenced Ammonite policy or assured them that they had nothing to fear from Nebuchadnezzar. But I have already given my reasons why I dismiss this view.

It is just possible that the reference is to the deceits of prophetic attempts by the Judeans and/or the exiles themselves, which would have encouraged their tendency to dismiss the Babylonian divinations as שָׁוְא, "false," as reported in 21:28 (ET 21:23). Jer 27:9 indicates that such activity was not unknown among those groups.

---

[79] Greenberg, *Ezekiel*, 2:436.

If my understanding of the entire section of 21:33–37 (ET 21:28–32) is correct, this verse should be taken as a reference to Nebuchadnezzar's divinations at the crossroads (21:24–27 [ET 21:19–22]). Unbeknownst to him, these divinations had led him to do Yahweh's bidding and turn toward Jerusalem. But still hidden from him was what would happen to Babylon later: its demise and destruction, as 21:35–37 (ET 21:30–32) will proceed to proclaim.

21:35 (ET 21:30)   The point of the entire section now comes into clear focus. Now that the bloody work of the sword is finished (as far as Ezekiel is concerned in this pericope), it, that is, Nebuchadnezzar's force, is to be sheathed, that is, withdrawn from Judah and returned to its homeland (Babylon), there to face God's judgment itself.

Of special significance is the description of Babylonia as "the place where you were created." The verb is the Niphal of בָּרָא. Throughout the OT, Qal forms always have God as subject and refer to him "creating" something out of nothing (*ex nihilo*), as in Gen 1:1. The Niphal forms too refer exclusively to divine activity, though here the Babylonians (represented by the sword) had been generated through the normal human process. Even with all our scientific knowledge and techniques, we must still admit that it is finally only God who opens the womb to give life (e.g., Gen 29:31) or who closes the womb (1 Sam 1:5–6), to use the common biblical expressions. For this reason all human life is sacred to God, from the moment of conception to life's natural end, and any violation of it (e.g., abortion, infanticide, euthanasia) incurs God's judgment.

The Niphal (passive) of בָּרָא, "created," will be used again of the king of Tyre in 28:13, 15. Yahweh had created him, and had overseen the king's life since the moment of his conception. One thinks of Yahweh's similar role in the rise of Cyrus, who would terminate the exile by permitting the Israelites to return to Judah (Is 44:28). The arrogant superpower and its monarch are only creatures, as vulnerable to God's judgment as any other mortal. That Nebuchadnezzar had unwittingly served as God's agent of judgment upon Jerusalem did not absolve him of accountability before his Creator. We need not search for any particular misconduct on Nebuchadnezzar's part to make that point. Despite his momentary conversions recorded in the book of Daniel (2:47; 3:28–29; 4:31–34 [ET 4:34–37]), the mere fact that he lacked faith in the one true and triune God sufficed to make him subject to condemnation.

It is often suggested that Ezekiel models this recall of Nebuchadnezzar on the account in 2 Kings 19 (∥ Isaiah 37) of Sennacherib's withdrawal from the siege of Jerusalem, only to be assassinated by his own sons upon his return to Nineveh. Any such connection is speculative, at best. At any rate, Nebuchadnezzar met no such fate upon his return, no does Ezekiel say he did. As a matter of fact, we know little of the last thirty years of his reign. He died in 562 and was succeeded (apparently peacefully) by his son Amel-Marduk, whose name is deliberately defaced in the OT by its Hebrew rendition as אֱוִיל מְרֹדַךְ, "Evil-Merodach" (2 Ki 25:27; Jer 52:31). He, in turn, reigned scarcely two years before being killed in a plot led by his brother-in-law. Nebuchadnezzar's "dynasty" was thus short-lived, but as is apparent already in this verse, the text merges the person of Nebuchadnezzar with that of the country, Babylonia. After this verse, the country appears to be the total topic.

21:36 (ET 21:31) Different figures are now used to describe God's judgment. The figure of fire becomes prominent, perhaps forming a framework or inclusion with the beginning of the (Hebrew) chapter, 21:1–4 (ET 20:45–48). But while that first one was a forest fire, here it is the fire of a forge or foundry. Like a smelter, Yahweh will pour his wrath upon his erstwhile agents. Or in a slight shift of the metaphor, he will blow the fire of his fury upon them—perhaps an allusion to bellows. The noun מַפֻּחַ, "bellows" (Jer 6:29), is derived from the verb here, פּוּחַ, or from the related verb נָפַח, both of which mean "blow."

Perhaps now Ezekiel is abandoning figurative language and replacing it with the nonmetaphorical language of new wielders of God's sword, who will do to the Babylonians as they have done to others. God will allow brutal, barbarous invaders to wreak their carnage and devastation on the land. None are named, but the Caucasus region to the north teemed with people who could be described as "expert destroyers." If we look for people relatively close to the Babylon at Ezekiel's time who would fit that description, we might think first of the Medes, who had a reputation of being ruthless murderers, and whose values were not those of civilized peoples (Is 13:17–18). Later it was the Medes, by that time incorporated into the Persian Empire, who captured Babylon and ended its empire in 539 under Cyrus the Mede. In any case, people of this sort all but form the stuff of history: Mongols, Huns, Vandals, Goths, Vikings, and countless more. God allows them to destroy nations, yet he constantly preserves and rebuilds his church.

21:37 (ET 21:32) Apparently using the figures of fire and blood, we have here the picture of a violent bloodbath. The picture of fire is now familiar, but mention of blood is new. It appears to me simply to underscore the shedding of blood, sometimes in vast amounts, that unfortunately nearly always accompanies warfare, ancient or modern. Greenberg, after analyzing other Ezekelian uses of "blood in the midst of," argues that the phrase, rather than simply predicting widespread bloodshed, accents rather the iniquity of this bloodshed (presumably that which the Babylonians themselves have been responsible for with their many victims), which will entail punishment upon Babylon.[80] While such a thought is compatible with the context and with biblical thought otherwise, it seems to me to introduce an alien emphasis at this point. From 21:33 (ET 21:28) on, there has been little detailing of the Babylonians' specific atrocities, which will now bring judgment upon them too. Rather, there has simply been a poetic description of God's turning of the tables. No earthly power ever becomes so mighty that it escapes the scrutiny and verdict of the Lord of history.

---

[80] Greenberg, *Ezekiel*, 2:438.

Although it will ultimately be true, we make difficulties for ourselves if we press too far the final prediction that Babylon "will no longer be remembered." The expression is a rather stereotyped commonplace. Indeed, in about half a century (539 B.C.), Babylonian (really Chaldean or Aramean!) hegemony will be over. All ancient reports indicate that by that time, the local populace was so exasperated by the dereliction of Nabonidus, king of Babylon, that they welcomed Cyrus the Great as a liberator; their city could thus be taken with minimal bloodshed. Although deprived of independent political power, the city of Babylon, with only brief interruptions, continued to be a great city during subsequent Persian, Seleucid, Parthian, and Sassanid rule. Only with the city's conquest by the Arabs in A.D. 641 does power and significance finally begin to leave the city for points north, especially Baghdad. This means that it was a good millennium after Ezekiel that dust began to cover the abandoned city. The tourist today can visit the only partially excavated site. As someone has said, "God's mills grind slowly, but they grind very fine."

(c) Also Ezek 17:21; 26:14; 37:14; cf. Ezek 23:34; 26:5; 28:10; 39:5

The final כִּי clause, "for I, Yahweh, have spoken," occurred first in 5:13.[c] Thus the biblical connection between the spoken Word and "word" in the sense of history ("his-story") is drawn very clearly.

Allen makes the point that the chapter's conclusion is that God's final word is not the sword; it must be sheathed. This "implicitly lets a chink of light into the dark early messages of Ezekiel. Beyond hopelessness there might yet be hope."[81] Babylon, like all the kingdoms of this world, must ultimately fall (the message of the Gentile oracles, Ezekiel 25–32), but God's eternal kingdom will not. Jerusalem too will fall, but exiles will return from the grave of the exile (37:1–14).

Christ, as antitype and Israel/humanity reduced to one, will also enter the grave, but will rise victoriously on the third day. And this is the heart of the Christian credo, that all who are baptized into him and believe will rise with him (Acts 2:38–39; 22:16; Rom 6:1–4; 1 Pet 3:21). They will not be forgotten, their only memorial a neglected tombstone in some forgotten cemetery, but they will reign as kings and priests with him through all eternity (1 Pet 2:5–9; Rev 1:6; 5:10; 20:6).

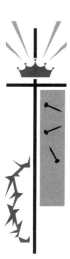

---

[81] Allen, *Ezekiel*, 2:29.

Judgment on the Bloody City
for Her Abominations

Translation

22 ¹The Word of Yahweh came to me: ²"You, son of man, will you arraign, will you arraign the bloody city? Then tell her all her abominations. ³Say, 'This is what the Lord Yahweh says: O city that sheds blood in her midst, bringing on her time, and manufactures idols all over herself, defiling [herself]. ⁴Because of the blood you have shed, you have become guilty, and because of the idols you have made, you have become defiled. You have brought near your [final] days; you have arrived at [the end of] your years. Therefore, I have made you a disgrace to the nations and ridicule to all the countries. ⁵Those nearby and those far away from you will ridicule you, impure in name and great in confusion. ⁶Look at the rulers of Israel: each one present in you uses his power to shed blood. ⁷Father and mother they have dishonored in you; the alien in your midst they have exploited; and the orphan and the widow they have mistreated in you. ⁸You have despised my holy things and profaned my Sabbaths. ⁹In you slanderers are present to shed blood. In you are those who eat on the mountains and act depravedly in your midst. ¹⁰In you a man uncovers the nakedness of [his mother, reserved for his] father, and they force themselves on women unclean during their periods. ¹¹In you some commit an abomination with a neighbor's wife; some depravedly defile a daughter-in-law; and some force themselves on a sister, their father's daughter. ¹²In you they take bribes to shed blood; you demand interest in advance and then refuse to repay it, thus defrauding your neighbor by extortion; and you have forgotten me, says the Lord Yahweh. ¹³Therefore, I clap my hands at the fraudulent profit you have made and over the bloodshed in your midst. ¹⁴Will your courage endure or your hands remain strong in the days when I deal with you? I, Yahweh, have spoken, and I will accomplish [it]. ¹⁵I will scatter you among the nations, disperse you throughout the countries, and eliminate your uncleanness from you. ¹⁶After you have been defiled in you in the eyes of the nations, you will know that I am Yahweh.'"

¹⁷The Word of Yahweh came to me: ¹⁸"Son of man, the house of Israel has become dross to me. All of them are copper, tin, iron, and lead inside a furnace. They have become the dross of silver. ¹⁹Therefore, this is what the Lord Yahweh says: Because you have all become dross, I am about to gather you inside Jerusalem. ²⁰As silver, copper, iron, lead, and tin are gathered inside a furnace to blast it with fire and melt it, so I will gather [you] in my anger and my wrath, throw [you] in, and melt you. ²¹I will gather you and blast you with the fire of my fury, and you will be melted inside her [the city]. ²²As silver is melted inside a

furnace, so you will be melted inside her [the city]. Then you will know that I, Yahweh, have poured out my wrath upon you."

²³The Word of Yahweh came to me: ²⁴"Son of man, say to her, 'You are a land not cleansed, not rained upon in the day of rage.' ²⁵Her princes within her are like a roaring lion, tearing its prey. They devour people, expropriate treasures and precious things, and make many her widows within her. ²⁶Her priests do violence to my Torah by profaning what is holy to me, by not distinguishing between the holy and the common or teaching the difference between the unclean and the clean. They disregard my Sabbaths, with the result that I am profaned among them. ²⁷Her officials inside her are like wolves, tearing their prey, shedding blood, and destroying lives in order to make dishonest profits. ²⁸Her prophets daub whitewash for them, seeing false visions and divining lies for them, saying, 'Thus says the Lord Yahweh,' when Yahweh has not spoken at all. ²⁹Ordinary citizens too practice extortion and commit robbery. They oppress the poor and the needy and unjustly deprive the alien of his due. ³⁰I looked for someone among them who would repair the wall and stand in the breach before me on behalf of the land so that I would not destroy her, but I found no one. ³¹Therefore, I will pour out my rage upon them. In the fire of my fury, I will make an end of them. I will place their conduct on their own head, says the Lord Yahweh."

Textual Notes

22:3   עִיר שֹׁפֶכֶת דָּם בְּתוֹכָהּ—After the citation formula ("this is what the Lord Yahweh says"), the feminine noun עִיר, "city," is apparently a vocative, even though vocatives often have the article and עִיר here lacks it. The article is unnecessary especially when mental constructs are being addressed. The rest of the verse is dependent on that vocative and qualifies or defines it, first by a participle (שֹׁפֶכֶת, "sheds"), then by a perfect in the next clause (וְעָשְׂתָה, "manufactures"), so that both indicate habitual, continuous actions. After a vocative, the change from second to third person (starting with בְּתוֹכָהּ, "in *her* midst") has parallels; see 2 Ki 9:31 and Is 22:16. For better English idiom, I have freely changed the participle into a finite verb ("sheds").

The noun תָּוֶךְ is used as a preposition with בְּ and a third feminine singular suffix (בְּתוֹכָהּ, literally, "in her midst") in 22:3, 21, 22, 25. תָּוֶךְ with בְּ recurs with a second feminine singular suffix (בְּתוֹכֵךְ, "in your midst") in 22:7, 9, 13. Just the preposition בְּ with second feminine singular suffix, בָּךְ, "in you," occurs eleven times in 22:5–16. The cumulative effect of all these prepositions is to imply that the sins are occurring at the heart of the city, in its very bones and marrow, as it were. It is corrupt to the core.

לָבוֹא עִתָּהּ—The use of לְ with the infinitive construct of בּוֹא is an abbreviated expression for a result clause (elsewhere often expressed with לְמַעַן, "so that"). I have freely used an English participle, *bringing on* her time." This agrees with the participial translation of the infinitive construct לְטָמְאָה, "defiling [herself]," at the end of the verse (see the next textual note).

"Her time" (עֵת with third feminine singular suffix) is obviously of doom, synonymous with the use of יוֹם, "day," in that same ominous sense. In 21:30 (ET 21:25), these two words together virtually formed a hendiadys. See both also in 7:7, 12; 12:27;

21:34 (ET 21:29); 30:3. The OT contains many uses of both nouns in this sense, and the NT uses comparable Greek words in the same way.

וְעָשְׂתָה גִלּוּלִים עָלֶיהָ לְטָמְאָה—I have usually rendered גִּלּוּלִים as "fecal deities" to bring out Ezekiel's contempt. See the textual note on it in 6:4. Here, however, I have used the more generic "idols," because "fraudulent profit" and "bloodshed" in 22:13 (the summary of the first section of the chapter) may be an inverted equivalent of the two "abominations" (22:2) listed in 22:3, "sheds blood" and now "manufactures idols," as Greenberg suggests.[1] The commentary on 22:3 explains the close, internal connection between 22:3 and 22:13.

The prepositional phrase עָלֶיהָ ("all over herself") is a strange expression in this context. I take it as a near parallel to בְּתוֹכָהּ. The behavior envelopes the entire city, almost like a fog or a thick cloud cover.

The Qal infinitive construct of טָמֵא always has the so-called feminine form (see Joüon, § 49 d), טָמְאָה (so also in 44:25, as well as Lev 15:32; 18:20, 23; 19:31; 22:8). The translation of לְטָמְאָה adds the implied object, "defiling *herself*."

22:4 The shift to the second person indicates the formal announcement of charges. Two parallel charges, "because of the blood you have shed, you have become guilty" and "because of the idols you have made, you have become defiled," essentially repeat the third person statements of the previous verse ("O city that sheds blood ... and manufactures idols," 22:3). Then "bringing on her time" from 22:3 is expanded into two parallel statements: "you have brought near your final days; you have arrived at the end of your years" (22:4). A verdict of the result ("therefore ...") concludes the verse.

בְּדָמֵךְ—The first charge, literally, begins with "by [בְּ] your blood," that is, the blood of "your" (the city's) victims.

אָשַׁמְתְּ—Ezekiel uses אָשַׁם, "be guilty," elsewhere only in 6:6 and 25:12 (possibly also in 35:6). He uses the cognate noun אָשָׁם, referring to a type of sacrifice traditionally called "guilt offering" (the subject of Leviticus 5) in Ezek 40:39; 42:13; 44:29; 46:20. The verb אָשַׁם focuses on trespasses on the domain of the holy, especially by idolatrous worship practices. טָמֵא, "be defiled," which follows in 22:4, refers to ceremonial uncleanness and is a natural parallel.

וַתַּקְרִיבִי יָמַיִךְ וַתָּבוֹא עַד־שְׁנוֹתָיִךְ—Forms of the verb קָרֵב frequently denote the imminence of judgment (e.g., Is 41:1; Ezek 9:1; Mal 3:5). Here the Hiphil of קָרֵב (second feminine singular imperfect with *waw* consecutive), "to bring near," is paralleled by the idiom בּוֹא עַד, that is, "arrive at" the goal or conclusion. וַתָּבוֹא is a third feminine singular (or second masculine singular) Qal imperfect of בּוֹא with *waw* consecutive, instead of the expected second feminine singular תָּבוֹאִי. Since the LXX and the Vulgate apparently read a Hiphil, many would emend the word further to תָּבִיאִי, sometimes in conjunction with a change of עַד to עֵת, as in 22:3.[2] However, we met this same phenomenon before in 21:37 (ET 21:32); see the first textual note there. It occurs again in 23:32 and 26:14.

---

[1] Greenberg, *Ezekiel*, 2:452.

[2] Cf. Zimmerli, *Ezekiel*, 1:452.

"Your days" and "your years" might have been clear enough by themselves in the context, but I have supplemented both of them for clarity: "your [final] days … [the end of] your years." Many are tempted to emend "days" to the singular, but the plural has already been used in a similar context in 12:23. The expression בָּא בַיָּמִים is used in Gen 18:11; 24:1; and Josh 13:1 for old age and the approach of death. The plural of "years" here, then, may be a case of attraction.

נְתַתִּיךְ חֶרְפָּה ֹ … וְקַלָסָה—The last sentence shifts easily into the prophetic perfect (Qal of נָתַן). חֶרְפָּה, "disgrace," is a common noun. קַלָסָה, "ridicule, scorn," is technically a hapax, but a masculine equivalent, קֶלֶס, occurs in Jer 20:8; Pss 44:14 (ET 44:13); 79:4, and the verb appears in both the Piel (Ezek 16:31) and the Hithpael (e.g., יִתְקַלְּסוּ, Ezek 22:5, the next verse).

22:5 טֻמְאַת הַשֵּׁם—"Impure" is the feminine adjective טְמֵאָה (in construct), which is cognate to the verb טָמֵא, "defiled," in 22:3–4. The construct phrase is epexegetical (Waltke-O'Connor, § 9.5.3c; cf. Joüon, § 129 i), since "the name" (הַשֵּׁם) is characterized as "impure."

22:6–12 Here commences a list enumerating the various, typical sins being committed in Jerusalem, adding up to a picture of total lawlessness and disobedience. There is no quasi-historical review here, as, for example, in chapter 20, but simply reference to laws that the follower of the Torah would heed as a matter of course. The list divides itself into three groups of sins, signaled formally by the threefold repetition of the phrase לְמַעַן שְׁפָּךְ־דָּם, "(in order) to shed blood," in 22:6, 9, and 12. Ezek 22:6–7 and 22:9–12 use בָּךְ, "in you" (feminine singular, referring to Jerusalem), and 22:7 and 22:9 use its stylistic variant, בְּתוֹכֵךְ, "in your midst." The first group of sins (22:6–8) scores various infractions, both liturgical and moral. The second (22:9–11) berates sexual depravity, especially incest. The third (22:12) upbraids economic crimes.

Zimmerli toys with the possibility of "whether a conscious decalogue series was intended" since there are a total of nine uses of בָּךְ in the list (22:6, 7 [twice], 9 [twice], 10 [twice], 11, 12) plus two of בְּתוֹכֵךְ (22:7, 9), approximating the number ten. (In the chapter, בָּךְ also occurs twice outside the list: in 22:5, 16.) He finally dismisses the idea but suggests that "a 'decalogue' could at most stand in the background."[3]

22:6 הִנֵּה ֹ נְשִׂיאֵי יִשְׂרָאֵל—It is debated whether נְשִׂיאִים are specifically the "*kings* of Israel" (whom Ezekiel will never label as such by מְלָכִים) or whether the word has a more general connotation of "rulers." The former option seems more likely to me.

אִישׁ לִזְרֹעוֹ הָיוּ בָךְ—The clause literalistically translates as "each (according) to his arm were in you." The similar construct phrase אִישׁ־זְרוֹעַ ("man of arm") occurs in Job 22:8 and means a strong-armed, violent man who does not hesitate to resort to force to get his way.

22:8 Note the abrupt transition from the third person plurals in 22:7 ("they have …") to the second person singular in 22:8 ("you have …"), which dominates the rest of the first oracle (through 22:16). That is, Jerusalem is addressed directly, almost apostrophized. Together with the continuing בָּךְ in subsequent verses, it stresses the

---

3 Zimmerli, *Ezekiel*, 1:457.

lethal damage the city is doing to itself. In 22:26 the offenses attributed to the city are ascribed to the priests, a natural parallel because the verse speaks of violations of specifically sacral Law.

22:9 The second group of indictments begins here and continues through 22:11. They all specify sexual misbehavior except for the first clause, which condemns אַנְשֵׁי רָכִיל, "men of slander," that is, "malicious gossips, talebearers." (The LXX overtranslates it by including λῃσταί, "robbers, bandits.") Since a prohibition of such behavior occurs in the OT only in Lev 19:16, and since there too it is associated with bloodshed, that probably is the basis of Ezekiel's condemnation here. Frequently the noun רָכִיל is used with the verb הָלַךְ, meaning "to walk around slandering" (Jer 6:28; 9:3 [ET 9:4]; Prov 11:13; 20:19). Etymologically, the noun probably derives from the root רָכַל, meaning to "trade, act as a merchant," and the phrase with הָלַךְ then means something like "to go about as a traveling salesman." The connection apparently is that such a person would be in a unique position to hear and spread all the latest gossip, probably hoping to ingratiate himself with potential customers by such behavior. If this clause relates to the sexual focus of the following verses, it would be that gossip of that sort would probably be the most delicious of all, while its purveyor could pose as himself a paragon of moral probity.

22:11 Each of the three accusations in the Hebrew begins with אִישׁ, "man," used in a collective sense, followed by an object with a third person singular suffix and the third person singular verb. My translation of אִישׁ as "some" retains the plural of the previous verses but necessitates changes in number and omission of some suffixes.

וְאִישׁ ׀ אֶת־אֵשֶׁת רֵעֵהוּ עָשָׂה תּוֹעֵבָה—Here אֶת must be the preposition "*with* his neighbor's wife." (In the next two accusations, אֵת is the sign of the direct object.) The direct object of עָשָׂה, "do, commit," is תּוֹעֵבָה, "abomination." There is no other OT verse with the idiom "commit abomination with." It apparently is Ezekiel's variation on Lev 18:20, which uses the euphemistic idiom נָתַן שְׁכָבְתּ לְזֶרַע, "give copulation for seed," and Lev 20:10, which uses the specific verb for committing adultery, נָאַף, as in Ex 20:14; Deut 5:18.

אֲחֹתוֹ בַת־אָבִיו—"His (half-)sister" is strengthened by adding "daughter of his father." The prohibition of sexual union with paternal sisters in Lev 18:9 and with maternal sisters in Lev 18:11 suggests that sibling incest was a common infraction of biblical morality.

22:12 נֶשֶׁךְ וְתַרְבִּית לָקָחַתְּ—The MT had begun in the third masculine plural ("they take bribes …"), but here in the middle of the verse, it reverts to the second feminine singular: "you demand …" In contrast, the LXX and the Syriac continue here with verbs in the third person. The MT's sudden shift is jarring, although somewhat mitigated by the repeated בָּךְ. The MT seems to be the more likely reading, even more certainly by the way it forms the transition to the final accusation in the entire list of sins from 22:6 on.

We met the obscure pair נֶשֶׁךְ וְתַרְבִּית previously; see the textual note on it in 18:8. As already in Lev 25:36–37, the context makes plain that activity involving these nouns consists of some type of illicit and/or fraudulent profit-taking. However, we do not know enough about Israelite mercantile practices to determine precisely what was involved. My translation ("demand interest in advance and then refuse to repay it") seeks to be consistent with my interpretation of 18:8, namely, that a lender withholds part of the amount lent at the time of the loan and then demands the full amount in repayment. Others take the two words as hendiadys for usurious interest on loans. The other major interpretation thinks that Leviticus 25 is distinguishing between loans of money and loans of edibles, but the evidence adduced is not decisive.

22:13 הִכֵּיתִי כַפִּי—The idiom for hand-clapping is the same as in 6:11; 21:19, 22 (ET 21:14, 17). See the textual note on it in 6:11. This gesture conveys anger and vexation, indicating that the subject has had enough and is about to take action. Here the singular כַפִּי ("my hand") is used. However, "to clap," as the Hiphil of נָכָה, "strike," is virtually always translated in this idiom, is rather difficult to do with only one hand! But as 21:19 (ET 21:14) shows, this idiom probably is a contracted form of הִכָּה כַף אֶל־כַּף, "strike a hand against a hand," or at least there were several acceptable forms of the idiom in Biblical Hebrew. The (Hiphil first common singular) perfect form of הִכֵּיתִי is performative or instantaneous in nature, indicating an act performed as the verb is spoken ("I clap"). Here, as also in 21:22 (ET 21:17), Yahweh himself does the clapping, whereas in 6:11 and 21:19 (ET 21:14), Yahweh commanded Ezekiel to clap on his behalf.

וְעַל־דָּמֵךְ אֲשֶׁר הָיוּ בְתוֹכֵךְ:—The singular subject דָּמֵךְ ("your bloodshed") does not agree in number with the plural verb הָיוּ. It is debatable whether or not that is a problem. The LXX makes both plural, while the Aramaic Targum and the Syriac Peshitta make both singular. The singular form of דָּם in 22:12 might have influenced the word here. In any case, meaning is at stake only to the extent of whether an apostrophized city or its inhabitants is the subject; context would seem to prefer the latter.

22:14 הֲיַעֲמֹד לִבֵּךְ—The first rhetorical question is, literalistically, "will your heart stand?" "Heart" in the sense of courage is still used in English, and עָמַד implies "stand firm, endure." We met the opposite idiom in 21:12 (ET 21:7), where "[the] heart will melt."

אִם־תֶּחֱזַקְנָה יָדַיִךְ:—The second question can be translated literally without explanation: "will … your hands remain strong?" Again, we met the opposite idiom in 21:12 (ET 21:7), where "hands will hang limp."

אֲנִי יְהוָה דִּבַּרְתִּי וְעָשִׂיתִי:—This self-introduction, "I, Yahweh, have spoken, and I will accomplish [it]," already appeared in 17:24 and will be repeated in 36:36 and 37:14 in contexts similar to the one here. It might arguably be better placed at the beginning of 22:15, where the actual sentence is announced. This self-introduction is an expanded form of the simple אֲנִי יְהוָה so frequent in Ezekiel. Yahweh's Word (the noun דְּבָר) does not return to him empty (Is 55:11). His very speech (the Piel verb here, דִּבַּרְתִּי) entails action. The Hebrew noun and verb each comprise both speech and action, a duality impossible to reproduce in English.

22:16 וְנִחַלְתְּ בָּךְ—There is considerable debate about these first two words, and as usual, exegesis very much involves their meaning. The LXX (καὶ κατακληρονομήσω ἐν σοί, "and I will apportion in you"), the Vulgate (*et possidebo te*), and the KJV ("and thou shalt take thine inheritance") evidently parsed וְנִחַלְתְּ as the Piel of נָחַל, "to inherit, possess," which in the Piel means "give, apportion as a possession." Whereas וְנָחַלְתְּ is a second feminine singular perfect, all the ancient versions read a first person singular verb. Although the concept of the promised land as the inheritance given Israel by Yahweh is common in Deuteronomy and Joshua, which often use נָחַל and the noun נַחֲלָה, this usage is not found in Ezekiel until the later prophecies of restoration (נָחַל in 46:18; 47:13–14; נַחֲלָה in, e.g., 35:15; 36:12; 44:28; 45:1). It would seem to inject a positive, promissory note that does not seem appropriate here.

The alternative is that וְנָחַלְתְּ can be the Niphal second feminine singular perfect of חָלַל, "defile, profane," whose Niphal usually has a passive meaning, "be defiled." Modern commentaries widely advocate that meaning and follow the ancient versions in reading a first singular form, resulting in something like this: "I (Yahweh) was defiled in you (Israel)."[4] Arguments in favor of that understanding include the use of בָּךְ ("in you") and the fact that the following phrase, לְעֵינֵי גוֹיִם, commonly accompanies mention of Yahweh being profaned (20:9, 14, 22; cf. 36:20, 23). The Piel of חָלַל was used in 22:8 to refer to "profaning" Yahweh's Sabbaths, and it will be used in 22:26 to speak of "profaning" Yahweh's holy things.

However, the context of 22:16 does not support the idea that it is Yahweh who is profaned here, so there is no need to emend the second feminine singular verb וְנָחַלְתְּ, "you [Israel] have been defiled." The awkward בָּךְ, "in you," then indicates a climax to the series of scandals found "in you" (22:6–7, 9–11) and "in the midst of you" (22:7, 9). בָּךְ may strengthen the force of the Niphal, approaching a reflexive translation, "you defiled yourself through/because of you," although here the Niphal functions primarily as a passive ("have been defiled"). Thus an almost perfect match with 22:26 is achieved: as the people defiled (dishonored) Yahweh (22:26), they too will be defiled (22:16). Finally, the concluding recognition formula follows better from some calamity that has befallen people (they, not God, are "defiled"), which causes them to acknowledge Yahweh. That the versions read the verb as first person may represent either a harmonization with related texts or their difficulty in comprehending an unusual expression.

22:18 לְסוּג—The Kethib could be vocalized לָסוּג, the Qal infinitive construct (with לְ) of סוּג, to "backslide, prove recreant to [Yahweh]" (BDB). However, its place in this sentence indicates that it is more likely a noun, as indicated by the Qere, לְסִיג, "become [לְ] dross [סִיג]." When the noun is repeated at the end of 22:18 and in 22:19a, as well as everywhere else in the OT, it is always in the plural, סִיגִים. (The singular noun שִׂיג in 1 Ki 18:27 could mean "a journey.") The singular Qere (סִיג) may be only a partial correction if proper usage calls for a plural, but we know too little of ancient Hebrew usage to be sure. An original final *mem* may have been dropped by scribal accident, or the now-otiose enclitic *mem* of archaic Hebrew may have been considered dispensable, although Ezekiel writes late enough that one would hardly expect that aspect of the evolution of the language to still be occurring.

In any case, the word appears to derive from the root סוּג, "to deviate, separate off," and thus denotes the separating off of the worthless material in the process of

---

4   Allen, *Ezekiel*, 2:32; Zimmerli, *Ezekiel*, 1:454; RSV and NRSV.

smelting, especially the refining of silver. This was a two-phase process. In the first phase, sulfur elements in the ore were removed, leaving a mixture of silver and lead. Sometimes סִיגִים refers to this intermediate ore, a very impure form of silver. In the second phase, the lead is removed also. However, this second phase was more difficult and easily could go wrong, leaving a silver-like substance, also called "dross" or סִיגִים. Since ores containing silver are not found in Israel, it seems likely that Ezekiel is referring to the second stage, a processing of partially processed ingots that had been imported.[5]

Be that as it may, the context makes plain that "the house of Israel" has become useless material, most likely a "rejected silver" (Jer 6:30), still full of impurities. Is 1:25 speaks of a successful second part of the process or refining, but the picture here is completely the opposite. Then we can easily understand the סִגִים כֶּסֶף at the end of Ezek 22:18 as "dross of silver," the impure substance remaining after a failed second process. But questions remain; see the last textual note on 22:18.

נְחֹשֶׁת—This noun may mean either "copper" or "bronze," which is an alloy of copper and tin. "Copper" in its natural state had been known from high antiquity, though rare, and bronze does not appear until about 2000 B.C., long before Ezekiel's day. Thus both translations are theoretically possible, but "copper" seems more likely because the text is speaking of unprocessed, natural ores. "Brass" (KJV), an alloy of copper and zinc, was unknown in biblical times.

בְּתוֹךְ כּוּר—The use of בְּתוֹךְ, "in the midst of," with כּוּר, "furnace," meaning Jerusalem, links this oracle with the preceding one. See (with suffixes) -בְּתוֹכֵ in 22:3, 7, 9, 13.

סִגִים כֶּסֶף הָיוּ:—The LXX's reading, ἐν μέσῳ ἀργυρίου ἀναμεμειγμένος ἐστίν, seems to reflect בְּתוֹךְ כֶּסֶף סִגִים הָיוּ ("in the midst of silver, dross they have become") instead of the MT's בְּתוֹךְ כּוּר סִגִים כֶּסֶף הָיוּ ("... inside a furnace. The dross of silver they have become"). Ezek 22:20 describes the actual process on which the metaphor is based, and silver is included among the elements of the ore put in the furnace. This leads to speculation that כֶּסֶף at the end of 22:18 is a gloss: it was mistakenly inserted in the earlier part of 22:18 to supply the missing metal put into the furnace,[6] then somehow this gloss migrated to the end of the verse in the MT. But this speculation is entirely arbitrary, "a quite unnecessary intrusion into the text where the writer is being significantly silent."[7] Ezekiel avoids any mention of "silver" in connection with Israel until the end of the verse, where כֶּסֶף simply specifies what type of סִגִים Israel is: "dross of silver." The gist of 22:18 seems to be that the whole operation is a waste of effort; what silver still remains in Israel is all dross, completely worthless.

22:19 לָכֵן ... לָכֵן—The Hebrew repeats the opening word, לָכֵן, before the apodosis, but the repetition seems superfluous in translation. The LXX adds an imperative af-

---

[5] Allen, *Ezekiel*, 2:37, thinks that Ezekiel is referring "only to the preliminary stage of smelting," unlike Isaiah (1:21–26), who refers to the whole refining process and the resulting valuable end product.

[6] Allen, *Ezekiel*, 2:32; also RSV and NRSV.

[7] Taylor, *Ezekiel*, 168.

ter its translation of the opening לָכֵן, producing διὰ τοῦτο εἰπόν, "therefore *say*," as if אֱמֹר were there. If one wished to accept the LXX text, the addition would be manageable.

הִנְנִי קֹבֵץ—I have translated הִנְנִי followed by the Qal participle as a *futurum instans*, "I am *about* to gather," implying imminence of action. One may quibble whether or not it has that precise force here, although it fits the historical situation. In a sense, prophecy always implies imminence of action in the "eternal now" of the vertical relationship with God. The clause here may, however, simply have futuristic force or imply action that God is already engaged in.

22:20 קְבֻצַת כֶּסֶף—The first noun, קְבֻצָה in construct, means "gathering." It is technically a hapax, although the verb קָבַץ, "gather," is not rare. Literally, the Hebrew has the protasis, "the gathering of …" followed by the verb in the apodosis, כֵּן אֶקְבֹּץ, "so I will gather …" I have rendered the noun with a passive ("are gathered"). I have also begun the protasis with the comparative adverb "as," as do all the versions, but probably for idiomatic reasons. The comparative function of the noun phrase was evidently considered implicit, requiring no explicit preposition (כְּ, "as, like") to match the כֵּן ("so") beginning the apodosis. An initial כְּ does precede another hapax at the beginning of 22:22. This leads to much speculation that one originally appeared here and was lost in transmission, but that appears to be unnecessary.

לָפַחַת־עָלָיו אֵשׁ—"To blast it with fire" is, literally, "blow upon it fire." לָפַחַת is the Qal infinitive construct (with לְ) of נָפַח, "to blow, breathe," which recurs in a finite form in 22:21. The expression probably assumes the use of bellows.

לְהַנְתִּיךְ—The verb is the Hiphil infinitive construct (with לְ) of נָתַךְ, whose Hiphil means "pour out, melt." The failure of the *nun* to assimilate (-נְ-) is frequently evidenced in pausal forms of first *nun* verbs. The momentary slowing in the pronunciation of a word in pause allows sounds that are usually elided to be preserved. Note that the *nun* is assimilated when the Hiphil of נָתַךְ recurs at the end of the verse: וְהִתַּכְתִּי is the Hiphil first common singular perfect with *waw* consecutive. Its Niphal (וְנִתַּכְתֶּם) in 22:21 and Hophal (תֻּתְּכוּ) in 22:22 both have the passive meaning, "you will be melted."

וְהִנַּחְתִּי—This is the Hiphil first common singular perfect of נוּחַ. It has *waw* consecutive, so the accent has shifted to the final syllable (-תִּי). This verb has two Hiphil conjugations. Forms of this second conjugation include a *daghesh* in the *nun* (as if from a root ננח) and ordinarily mean "put, set, leave." "Throw" would be an unusual meaning. (The Hiphil of שָׁלַךְ is the common OT verb for "throw.") Or should we translate it in its ordinary sense, that God will "leave" (KJV, NKJV) or "put" (RSV, NRSV, NIV) Israel in the furnace? The LXX has συνάξω, "I will gather," which could be a translation of וְכִנַסְתִּי at the start of 22:21 (where the LXX omits any translation of it). This leads many critics to construct elaborate histories of the MT,[8] but unconvincingly so.

22:21 וְכִנַסְתִּי אֶתְכֶם—The verb כָּנַס is relatively rare in Biblical Hebrew. Both its Qal and Piel (here first common singular perfect with *waw* consecutive) mean "to

---

8   Zimmerli, *Ezekiel*, 1:462; Allen, *Ezekiel*, 2:32; cf. Block, *Ezekiel*, 1:715, n. 13.

gather." It probably recurs in 39:28. It occurs mainly in later OT books.[a] However, it is very common in Mishnaic and modern Hebrew. It is the root of "Knesset," modern Israel's parliament.

בְּתוֹכָהּ—"In the midst of/inside her" refers to the city. I have made the antecedent of the pronoun explicit here and again in the next verse (בְּתוֹכָהּ).

22:22 כְּהִתּוּךְ—The noun הִתּוּךְ, "melting," is derived from the verb נָתַךְ, "melt," used in 22:20–22. Technically it is another hapax, like קֻבְצָה (see the first textual note on 22:20). As noted there, the expected כְּ is used here.

22:24 אֱמָר־לָהּ אַתְּ אֶרֶץ—The referent of לָהּ must be אֶרֶץ, the "land" (no longer the city), as the following identification of the addressee makes plain. In this case, the pronoun on לָהּ has been placed before the noun (אֶרֶץ) to which it refers. "The prophet's thoughts appear to be running ahead of his mouth/pen."[9]

אַתְּ אֶרֶץ לֹא מְטֹהָרָה הִיא לֹא גֻשְׁמָה—The feminine singular Pual participle מְטֹהָרָה, "cleansed," is from the common verb טָהֵר, "be clean," although the Pual is used nowhere else. Because the LXX has βρεχομένη, implying some original form from מָטַר, "to rain," and especially because this makes a better parallel with the following גֻשְׁמָה, "rained upon" (third feminine singular Pual perfect from גָּשַׁם, related to the common noun גֶּשֶׁם, "rain"), a large number of commentators emend in that direction.[10] But of the translations tracked in this commentary, only NIV ("has had no rain") follows the LXX. As such, this translation is compatible with biblical usage, where rain is often referred to as a sign of divine favor and blessing, or its lack a sign of Yahweh's disfavor or wrath.[b] But it is not evident that this fits the context, which seems, especially by the use of זַעַם at the end of the verse (see below), to imply something more sudden and cataclysmic. The same stricture would apply to Keil's apparently unique attempt. Noting the lack of parallelism, he relates the form to the *noun* טֹהַר used in Ex 24:10 of "splendor, brightness,"[11] but a related verb is unknown (cf. the noun זֹהַר in Ezek 8:2). Ezekiel would be saying that the land had neither sunlight nor rain—but that is forced.

Hebrew poetry (and also heightened prose) can exhibit many different kinds of parallelism (e.g., synthetic and even antithetical), not just synonymous parallelism, so the argument that מְטֹהָרָה should be emended to produce a synonym to גֻשְׁמָה is not compelling. But if the following גֻשְׁמָה is understood as a more torrential downpour with a certain cleansing ensuing, we obtain a meaning akin to at least partially synonymous parallelism after all. With that understanding, a link is also maintained with the preceding oracle, where the thought of the cleansing of ore was central. Furthermore, we hear an echo of the "impure in name" in 22:5. That a passive verbal form (מְטֹהָרָה, "cleansed") is used instead of a simple adjective (טְהוֹרָה, "clean") may imply that attempts had been made to cleanse the land, but had failed.

The semi-parallel גֻשְׁמָה is also problematic, although the root is not in doubt. The form is a hapax because the Pual occurs only here. The lack of doubling of the mid-

(a) Pss 33:7; 147:2; Eccl 2:8, 26; 3:5; Esth 4:16; Neh 12:44; 1 Chr 22:2

(b) E.g., Lev 26:3–5; Deut 11:16–17; 28:1, 12, 15, 23–24

---

[9] Block, *Ezekiel*, 1:722, n. 18.

[10] E.g., Zimmerli, *Ezekiel*, 1:465; Allen, *Ezekiel*, 2:32.

[11] Keil, *Ezekiel*, 1:317.

dle radical is not unusual with a vowelless sibilant (-שְׁ-), but the *mappiq* in the final *he* is difficult and might be explained as "euphonic."[12] The form might possibly be the noun גֶּשֶׁם with third feminine singular suffix, which normally has the *mappiq* (הּ-), meaning "its rain," but the expected form of a so-called *qitl* type of segholate noun with suffix would be -גִּשְׁמוֹ, and the syntax of the clause would be unusual (to say the least) if the form were a noun. The use of a third person verb probably facilitates the shift from second person ("you are …") to third person in the following verses.

Translation of the verse is complicated further by the lack of the relative אֲשֶׁר or other conjunction before לֹא מְטֹהָרָה. The pronoun הִיא is readily comprehensible as a resumptive pronoun (referring back to אֶרֶץ), which often functions as a virtual copula in a language that technically has none.

בְּיוֹם זָעַם:—It is not easy to capture the best nuance for the noun זַעַם, which recurs in 22:31 and otherwise in Ezekiel only in 21:36 (ET 21:31), although it is common in other prophets. "Indignation" is a common translation, but it is used so often of Yahweh's intervention in judgment and paralleled with other words for "wrath, fury" that a stronger term is called for. I have settled on "rage." In Dan 8:19 and 11:36, the word begins to be used more technically in connection with the periodicity of apocalyptic idiom.

22:25 קֶשֶׁר נְבִיאֶיהָ בְּתוֹכָהּ—The MT has "the conspiracy [קֶשֶׁר] of her prophets," but there is virtual unanimity among commentators,[13] reflected in most translations except KJV and NKJV, that in this instance the LXX (ἧς οἱ ἀφηγούμενοι) has preserved a superior text, אֲשֶׁר נְשִׂיאֶיהָ, "whose princes." NIV has preserved קֶשֶׁר but reads "princes" ("there is a conspiracy of her princes"), which involves the change of only one consonant, although it is a type of change that is not easy to explain because the letters בּ and שׁ are not similar in any stage of their development. The main reason for accepting the change is that mention of prophets is premature; their turn comes in 22:28. What is said of the "princes" here is very similar to what the "officials" are faulted for in 22:27. And if that is not considered persuasive evidence, there is the parallel in Zeph 3:3, which is very similar.[14] (Ezekiel substitutes Zephaniah's שֹׁפְטִים with the more general שָׂרִים in 22:27 in accordance with his apparent avoidance of the former, but that also necessitates the change here of Zephaniah's שָׂרִים to נְשִׂיאִים, one of Ezekiel's favorite words.) The interchangeability of the various labels indicates that we should not try too hard to distinguish these leaders, but probably the נְשִׂיאִים are members of the Davidic dynasty, while the שָׂרִים in 22:27 are lay nobility of lower status in the ruling hierarchy and hence compared with wolves rather than with lions; compare the use of lion imagery for the נְשִׂיאִים already in 19:1–7.

The MT's reading, "prophets," is not defenseless, however. St. Jerome clearly so translates, and perhaps the Targum's "scribes" reflects it. That is, the error crept into

---

[12] Greenberg, *Ezekiel*, 2:460.

[13] Even Keil, *Ezekiel*, 1:318!

[14] Zephaniah prophesied during the reign of Josiah (Zeph 1:1), who reigned from 640 to 609 B.C.

the text at an early stage of its long history. If "prophets" is to be defended at all, it implies that, implicitly or explicitly (especially if קֶשֶׁר is retained also), they legitimized or at least failed to denounce the behavior of the ruling classes.

טֹרֵף טָרֶף—This phrase, the Qal participle of טָרַף and the cognate accusative noun טֶרֶף, "preying upon prey," will recur but with the plural participle in 22:27. As noted, the simile of a lion appeared already in 19:1–7, and even the following metaphor of cannibalism may echo that passage.

נֶפֶשׁ אָכָלוּ—As the life principle or human soul, נֶפֶשׁ is what distinguishes a living person from a corpse. It is used collectively here, hence, "they devour people." The rulers' behavior violated the Fifth Commandment just as surely as if they had literally murdered.

חֹסֶן וִיקָר יִקָּחוּ—As evidence of such a serious charge, Ezekiel adduces legal theft, apparently through an endemic miscarriage of justice. The two object nouns, חֹסֶן and יְקָר, are near synonyms. Both are rare, and both may reflect Aramaic influence. חֹסֶן is rendered "treasures." יְקָר is, literally, "preciousness," an abstract used collectively for concrete "precious things." The two words are used together elsewhere only in Jer 20:5, a prediction of the Babylonian looting of Jerusalem. If Ezekiel was familiar with that prophecy, as he well may have been, he implies that Israel's rulers are anticipating the behavior of the enemy.

The imperfect verb יִקָּחוּ (from לָקַח), "take, expropriate," is unexpected between the two surrounding prophetic perfects (אָכָלוּ ... הִרְבּוּ). Like my translation, the versions smooth out the difference, which leads to suggestions that here we should read another perfect, לָקְחוּ. But Zimmerli points to the same phenomenon in 18:5–9, 10–13,[15] and Greenberg notes that the interchangeability of "tenses" is especially common in statements of general truths.[16]

אַלְמְנוֹתֶיהָ הִרְבּוּ—The verb is the Hiphil third common plural perfect of רָבָה in a causative sense, "make many, multiply." With the multiplication of "her [Jerusalem's] widows," Ezekiel returns to the theme of actual or de facto murder.

22:26 Using a different word order, the first two clauses are an almost verbatim repetition of Zeph 3:4b.

כֹּהֲנֶיהָ חָמְסוּ תוֹרָתִי—The verb חָמַס, "do violence," is used only seven times in the whole OT. It takes תּוֹרָה as its object elsewhere only in the Zephaniah parallel (Zeph 3:4). The verb and corresponding noun, חָמָס, usually "violence," apparently may refer both to physical violence as well as to other types of perversion of the nature or intent of something. The first uses of the noun חָמָס occur in God's explanation of why the flood was necessary (Gen 6:11, 13). The word occurs six times in Ezekiel; see the textual note on it in 7:23.

"Law" or even "instruction, teaching" is not an adequate equivalent to תּוֹרָה, Torah, although with sufficient understanding they might be as appropriate in this context as anywhere. The OT תּוֹרָה was, first of all, history, a narrative of what Yahweh

---

[15] Zimmerli, *Ezekiel*, 1:465–66.

[16] Greenberg, *Ezekiel*, 2:462.

had done to redeem his people, and only secondarily instructions of the appropriate response of the people. Likewise, the *nova lex* of Christianity, "love" (Rom 13:10), or the third use of the Law, divorced from the history of salvation now climaxed in Christ, is sheer legalism or subjective sentimentality. In principle, it was no different in the OT. Hence, I have left תּוֹרָה untranslated. It is one of those theological words the true meaning of which the faithful simply need to be taught.

The rest of the verse simply gives major genres of "doing violence" to the Torah. Instead of the Hebrew's idiomatic parataxis ("and … and …"), I have tried to indicate the connection by subordinating the various clauses. Only with regard to the Sabbath is a separate idiom used, and so I have treated it independently.

וַיְחַלְּלוּ קָדָשַׁי—The noun קֹדֶשׁ ("what is holy") is singular in Zephaniah but plural here with first common singular suffix, קָדָשַׁי, "my holy things," rendered "what is holy to me." It was Yahweh, "the holy one of Israel" (Isaiah),[17] who determined what was holy to begin with. קָדָשִׁים is a very comprehensive term, including the whole sphere of objects and actions, "wholly other," set apart for Yahweh's service. The charge here is similar to 22:8, except that it used the general verb בָּזָה, "despise," instead of the specifically cultic חִלֵּל, "desecrate, profane," employed here.

בֵּין־קֹדֶשׁ לְחֹל לֹא הִבְדִּילוּ—The natural alternative to the noun קֹדֶשׁ (or the adjective קָדוֹשׁ) would be חֹל, the "common," everyday, quotidian action or object that is not "set apart" for Yahweh's liturgical service. "Distinguish" seemed to be the best rendition of the Hiphil of בָּדַל in this context, but often its idea is better conveyed by "separate" or "divide." Beginning with the first day of creation, God "separated" (הִבְדִּיל) light from darkness (Gen 1:4). The concept is an important one in the Bible, ritually, morally, and doctrinally. Rabbinic Judaism makes a great deal of הַבְדָּלָה (an apparently later noun formation from the biblical root), although increasingly in a casuistic and legalistic direction. But the basic concern with distinguishing truth from falsehood, moral from immoral, and so on remains constitutive of orthodox Christianity.

וּבֵין־הַטָּמֵא לְטָהוֹר לֹא הוֹדִיעוּ—Many suggest dropping the article on טָמֵא since קֹדֶשׁ, חֹל, and טָהוֹר are all anarthrous, as is טָמֵא in the positive parallel in 44:23. A few Hebrew manuscripts have anarthrous טָמֵא here. On the other hand, in 42:20, a sequence of a determinate form (הַקֹּדֶשׁ) and an indeterminate one (חֹל) suggests that such a usage was acceptable Hebrew, at least to Ezekiel. Fortunately, meaning is not affected.

The preceding "holy" versus "common" is not entirely correlative with "clean" (טָהוֹר) versus "unclean" (טָמֵא) here. The first antithesis is much more liturgically oriented than the second, while the second concerns itself more with diet, hygiene, and matters of health. But a handy rule of thumb describes the "holy" as the *presence* of some divine force (sometimes facetiously compared with an electric charge), while "*un*clean" implies the *absence* of divine sanction.

וּמִשַּׁבְּתוֹתַי הֶעְלִימוּ עֵינֵיהֶם—"They disregard my Sabbaths" is a free translation of "from [מִן] my Sabbaths they hide [Hiphil of עָלַם] their eyes [עֵינֵיהֶם]." Greenberg

---

[17] This phrase is used by Isaiah twenty-five times, including Is 1:4; 54:5; and 60:9.

suggests the idiom "turned a blind eye to."[18] On exactly how the priests did that, see the commentary.

22:27 שָׂרֶיהָ בְקִרְבָּהּ כִּזְאֵבִים — "Her officials" renders the plural (with third feminine singular suffix) of שַׂר, apparently a quite general term referring to the entire lay nobility who were to see to the everyday rule or administration of the city. Since they are a notch lower in rank than the "princes" who were like "a lion" (22:25), they are compared to "wolves" (זְאֵבִים), predators next in menace after lions, as also in Gen 49:9, 27 and in Zeph 3:3. Ezekiel's dependence on Zephaniah is indicated by his use of בְקִרְבָּהּ (as in Zeph 3:3) instead of the usual Ezekelian בְּתוֹכָה (e.g., 22:21, 22, 25) for "inside her/in her midst." Besides 22:27, קֶרֶב is found in Ezekiel only in 11:19 and 36:26–27.

The "officials" are found guilty of essentially the same avaricious behavior as the "princes" in 22:25. There are only a few minor changes in vocabulary. While the princes "eat/devour people" (נֶפֶשׁ אָכָלוּ) people, the officials are "destroying lives" (לְאַבֵּד נְפָשׁוֹת). The Piel (infinitive construct with לְ) of אָבַד, has a causative meaning, "cause to perish, destroy." Both phrases have the same object, נֶפֶשׁ, but for the plural here "lives" seemed preferable to "people" to convey the full force of the Hebrew. לְאַבֵּד נְפָשׁוֹת is not represented in the LXX, so many[19] would delete it, but that sort of argumentation seems singularly weak.

לְמַעַן בְּצֹעַ בָּצַע — Instead of the princes' expropriation (חֹסֶן וִיקָר יִקָּחוּ, 22:25), we here have a purpose clause (לְמַעַן, "in order to") with the Qal infinitive בְּצֹעַ and the cognate accusative noun בָּצַע in pause, literally, "in order to profit a profit," but obviously with implications of dishonesty (cf. 22:12; 33:31). The root בָּצַע is technically a weaver's term for cutting off the woof,[20] so the English colloquialism of "get one's cut" would carry about the same metaphor as the Hebrew does.

22:28 טָחוּ לָהֶם ... וְקֹסְמִים לָהֶם — The repeated לָהֶם is of uncertain force. It might be the idiomatic Hebrew ethical dative (or dative of [dis]advantage), "for themselves," which would imply that the prophets' behavior was self-serving, intended to enhance their prestige, increase their wealth, or both. Or it might mean "for them" and refer back to the "officials" of 22:27, implying that the prophets in 22:28 were working "for" the officials, justifying and encouraging the rulers' outrageous behavior. My translation takes the second tack, but either understanding is equally plausible.

22:29 עַם הָאָרֶץ — The subject is this construct phrase, literally, "the people of the land," a fairly frequent expression in the OT. The phrase already appeared in 7:27, with "the king" and "the prince." Most translations reproduce it literally, but in my judgment, that communicates too little. The idiom, which I have rendered as "ordinary citizens," refers to free citizens, those with full civil rights, who are probably landowners.

Most of the vocabulary in 22:29 we have already met in 18:12, 18, where it was used to describe the wicked in general.

---

[18] Greenberg, *Ezekiel*, 2:462.

[19] E.g., Zimmerli, *Ezekiel*, 1:466.

[20] See D. Kellermann, "בצע," *TDOT* 2:206–7.

וְאֶת־הַגֵּר עָשְׁקוּ בְּלֹא מִשְׁפָּט׃—Only this last charge ("they … unjustly deprive the alien of his due") appears to root in Jeremiah (7:6 and 22:13). The verb עָשְׁקוּ rouses many commentators' suspicions since it also occurred near the beginning of the verse; some who allow it to stand judge בְּלֹא מִשְׁפָּט to be redundant. Many read עָשׂוּ as in 22:7 (cf. LXX 22:29: ἀναστρεφόμενοι), instead of עָשְׁקוּ, leading to a translation "deal unjustly" or the like. The change in meaning is not great, but the repetition of עָשְׁקוּ in the MT has an Ezekelian ring to it. Perhaps inconsistently, then, I have used the paraphrase of Greenberg,[21] who offers a spirited defense of the MT.[22]

22:30 וָאֲבַקֵּשׁ מֵהֶם אִישׁ גֹּדֵר־גָּדֵר וְעֹמֵד בַּפֶּרֶץ—The verb (Piel first common singular imperfect of בָּקַשׁ with *waw* consecutive) has a past-tense meaning: "I looked for." The preposition with suffix מֵהֶם is clearly partitive, "from/among them," and אִישׁ is used in the sense of "anyone."

The two (Qal masculine singular) participle clauses, with גֹּדֵר and עֹמֵד, serve, in effect, as relative clauses. Hebrew has no real way to express modalities, but "would" or even "could" is implied: "who *would* repair … and stand." The cognate accusative construction with the participle גֹּדֵר, "walling up," and noun גָּדֵר, "a wall," might mean simply "building a wall," but the parallel "and standing [וְעֹמֵד] in the breach [בַּפֶּרֶץ]" suggests that "*repairing* the wall" is more likely. פֶּרֶץ ("breach") indicates that the enemy has already breached the wall and will soon come pouring in unless the gap is quickly closed. The language recalls 13:5.

לְפָנַי בְּעַד הָאָרֶץ—This idiomatic phrase, "before me on behalf of the land," almost certainly has intercessory overtones; see the commentary. It implies, as Ezekiel has many times before, that at this point Yahweh is the enemy, who is merely using the Babylonians as his agents of judgment. This is reinforced by the following לְבִלְתִּי שַׁחֲתָהּ, literally, "so as not to destroy her [the land]." The Piel infinitive construct of שָׁחַת with third feminine singular suffix (referring to הָאָרֶץ) requires the subject "I," that is, Yahweh, to be supplied from the context. English translation requires that this be made explicit.

22:31 וָאֶשְׁפֹּךְ … כִּלִּיתִים … נָתַתִּי—These verbs, all first common singular, are an imperfect (Qal of שָׁפַךְ) with *waw* consecutive and two perfects: Piel of כָּלָה with third masculine plural suffix and Qal of נָתַן. Ordinarily they would be translated as past tense, so they sound as though the viewpoint is after the fall of Jerusalem. Hence, most critics take at least the last two verses of the oracle (if not the entire third oracle, 22:23–31) as a later addendum. But presuppositions have determined conclusions. There is no compelling reason why all the verbs in these two verses should not be treated as prophetic perfects. The inspired prophets often speak of the future using perfect verbs to convey the certainty of the prophesied events.

וָאֶשְׁפֹּךְ עֲלֵיהֶם זַעְמִי—"I will pour out on them my rage" seems to be taken directly from Zeph 3:8, which is identical except that there the verb (Qal of שָׁפַךְ) is in the form of an infinitive: לִשְׁפֹּךְ עֲלֵיהֶם זַעְמִי (cf. also Ezek 21:36 [ET 21:31]; 22:22).

---

[21] Greenberg, *Ezekiel*, 2:451.

[22] Greenberg, *Ezekiel*, 2:463.

בְּאֵשׁ עֶבְרָתִי כִּלִּיתִים—The construct phrase ("the fire of my fury") is identical to that in 21:36 (ET 21:31); 22:21; and 38:19.

דַּרְכָּם בְּרֹאשָׁם נָתַתִּי—The expression "place their conduct [דֶּרֶךְ] on their own head" regularly climaxes predictions of punishment (9:10; 11:21; 16:43). See the textual note on the identical clause in 9:10; there and in 11:21, which also has the same clause, it was treated as a prophetic perfect.

Commentary
Three Oracles Comprise Ezekiel 22

This chapter consists of three separate oracles: (1) 22:1–16; (2) 22:17–22; and (3) 22:23–31. The same word-event formula, "the Word of Yahweh came to me,"[23] introduces each of the three oracles, since it is repeated in 22:1, 17, 23. Comparably, the recognition formula, "you will know that I am Yahweh,"[24] concludes the first oracle (22:16) and a variation of it concludes the second oracle (22:22). The signatory formula, "says the Lord Yahweh,"[25] ends 22:31 and closes the chapter.

Formally, the three oracles are addressed to different audiences, although in reality they are identical: (1) the bloody city; (2) the house of Israel; and (3) the unclean land. The themes of the three are similar, but with different approaches or metaphors: (1) a general indictment of Jerusalem for a great variety of moral and ceremonial violations; (2) the use of metallurgical imagery to describe "the house of Israel" (22:18) as all dross that must be purged in the fire of judgment; and (3) the offenses of all classes of Israelite society.

There is widespread agreement that the three oracles were uttered and composed at different times and only later joined "editorially." That may well be, but there is no way to test the supposition—and it is scarcely worth testing. The only tangible issue in terms of date arises with the third oracle. The first two oracles explicitly place the punishment in the future. In contrast, the third oracle seems to look back on an already devastated land. For that reason, many critics judge it to be a post-destruction composition.[26] However, it is just as plausible that greater use is made in this third oracle of the prophetic perfect,[27] an idiom we have already met frequently in Ezekiel. There is no compelling reason why all three oracles should not be dated sometime just before the Babylonian conquest of Jerusalem in summer 586 B.C., although it is not possible to be more precise.

---

[23] For this formula, see page 8 in the introduction and the textual note on 3:16.

[24] For this formula, see page 9 in the introduction and the commentary on 6:7.

[25] For this formula, see pages 8–9 in the introduction and the second textual note on 5:11.

[26] E.g., Zimmerli, *Ezekiel*, 1:467.

[27] See the textual note on 22:31.

The Bloody City (22:1–16)

The first oracle (22:1–16) may be subdivided into three parts: (1) a general indictment and a prediction of public disgrace after the judgment (22:1–5); (2) a detailed indictment (22:6–12), grouped in three clusters, each involving the leitmotif of "shed blood" (שָׁפְךּ־דָּם in 22:6, 9, 12); and (3) Yahweh's vigorous reaction (22:13–16). Throughout the Hebrew, we meet repeated shifts in person, number, and gender.

22:2   The general indictment of Jerusalem opens with the same rhetorical questions that we met in 20:4. The repetition ("will you arraign, will you arraign?") indicates that, despite all the intervening variation, the overarching theme has been reproof of the city. The use of the question twice here indicates excitement. As in 20:4, the use of the interrogative particle implies indignation and virtually turns the question into an imperative ("arraign!"). Since the prophet himself is not the one who will effect the judgment, "arraign" is a more suitable translation of שָׁפַט than a literalistic "judge"; it is Yahweh who will execute the judgment.

The epithet "bloody city" is, literally, "city of bloodshed" (עִיר הַדָּמִים, 22:2), which will be repeated in 24:6, 9. The plural דָּמִים ("bloods") is regularly used idiomatically for "murder, bloodshed," conceivably because of the drops or pools of blood involved. As the context will make plain, the primary reference is to judicial murder, an actionable abuse of administrative power. We have heard Jerusalem or Israel described in similar terms in 7:23; 9:9; 11:6; 16:38, and we will meet such descriptions again in 23:45 and 24:6–9. But we must struggle to hear the phrase in Ezekiel's priestly frame of reference. "Bloodguilt" is a quite comprehensive category of guilt. It involves not only the taking of a person's physical life, but also social oppression and ritual misbehavior, which we would probably classify separately. For example, its applicability to ritual is illustrated in Lev 17:3–4, where improper slaughter of animals is considered "bloodguilt."

Much of the cogency of the epithet "bloody city" (Ezek 22:2) at least to the original audience, lay in the fact that Ezekiel appears to have taken it from the prophet Nahum (3:1), who was active sometime in the half century preceding (the second half of the seventh century B.C.). Nahum had applied it to the Assyrians, who were infamous because of their brutal treatment of captives, a reputation of which they seem to have been proud. One can easily imagine the shock value that the epithet's application to Jerusalem would have to the city's inhabitants.

Somewhat coincidentally at this point, but noteworthy nonetheless, is the light that this citation from an earlier prophet may shed on the history of the OT canon, a topic about which we know very little. Toward the end of this chapter, we will see extensive dependence on the prophet Zephaniah, who probably was active a bit later than Nahum, closer still in time to Ezekiel. Add to these two examples of Ezekiel's citations from earlier prophets his great dependence on the Pentateuch (see the commentary on 22:7, 8, 26, 29) and apparent adaptations especially of Isaiah and Jeremiah, and we get a sense that, humanly speaking, the OT canon was, slowly but surely, being fixed already, and that the process began very shortly after the books were first composed.[28]

The second half of the verse (22:2) is a sort of an apodosis of the first half, and it continues in 22:3. "Tell her [וְהוֹדַעְתָּהּ, Hiphil of יָדַע] all her abominations" implies far more than merely to "make them known" in a cognitive sense. Intellectually, Jerusalem was well aware of the inadvisability of its actions, but acknowledging them as תוֹעֵבוֹת (conventionally, "abominations") was something else. Ezekiel had earlier used that favorite word of his for Israel's idolatrous (e.g., 5:11; 7:20) and sexual offenses (e.g., 16:22, 36), but in the following verses the two accents converge.

22:3   "Shedding blood" and "manufacturing idols" are mentioned in the same breath. These twin "abominations" (22:2) equally bring defilement and judgment. As Zimmerli well summarizes: "where a proper fear before the One, who alone is holy, is lost and men impiously prepare their unclean idolatry, there reverence for life and the life of one's neighbor disappears."[29]

22:4–5   The two interlocked atrocities of murder and impurity or defilement because of idolatrous practices will, in the short term, precipitate the mockery and taunts of all who hear of Jerusalem and, in the long term, hasten the day of reckoning. The ridicule is intensified because of the disconnection between what the people claimed to be and their behavior in the eyes of outsiders—as is still the case with the church and supposedly devout believers. Far from being the holy city, even uniformed unbelievers would laugh at her sexual and social offenses specified in the following verses (22:6–12).

The "name" (22:5) of the city is probably more than mere reputation. In OT thought, a "name" was not only an identification, but a window to a person's or entity's interior being. This is evident in many biblical birth narratives, at least in the hopes and prayers of parents, and especially when a name is divinely ordained.[c] *Nomen est omen.* The same idea inheres in the "Christian" names we are given at Baptism or "*christ*ening," although consciousness of that usage has fallen into desuetude in our secular culture, even within the church. For Yahweh, Jerusalem had become so irreparably polluted that in the vision given Ezekiel of the new Jerusalem, it is given a new name, יְהוָה ׀ שָׁמָּה, "Yahweh is there," the very last words of the book (48:35). Compare similarly Is 62:2, 4; Rev 2:17; 3:12—not to speak of the host of other "new" things God creates (Ps 51:12 [ET 51:10]; 2 Cor 5:17; Rev 21:1–5).

The final phrase, "great in confusion/turmoil/tumult" (מְהוּמָה, Ezek 22:5), aptly summarizes a society that has lost both chart and compass (cf. Amos 3:9). One is tempted to apply it to contemporary Western culture.

(c) Cf. 2 Sam 12:25; Is 7:14; 9:5 (ET 9:6); Mt 1:20–21; Lk 1:13, 31–33, 59–63

---

[28]   The Pentateuch dates from the time of Moses, its primary author (fifteenth century B.C.). Isaiah prophesied and wrote around 740–681 B.C., while Jeremiah did so about 625–575 B.C., thus overlapping his later contemporary Ezekiel, who ministered from 593 to 571 B.C.

[29]   Zimmerli, *Ezekiel*, 1:456.

22:6   The first group of condemnations involving bloodshed (שָׁפְכוּ־דָם, 22:6) consists of 22:6–8. Whether "rulers" refers specifically to kings or to anyone in authority, this verse speaks of leaders whose motto is "might makes right." Even the nonbiblical literature of antiquity describes rulers whose duty it is to take care of the widow and the orphan, who usually were the most powerless members of ancient society. But the rulers of Jerusalem, instead of maintaining justice, had set an example that undermined divine norms. They had forgotten that the strong arm of dominion and deliverance belongs to God alone (see, e.g., Deut 4:34; Jer 21:5; Ezek 20:33–34), who also breaks the arm of the wicked (Ps 10:15).

22:7   Ezekiel's dependence on the Torah of Moses is obvious in this verse. Often, especially in Deuteronomy, "the alien/sojourner … the orphan and widow," who are easily victimized, even appear in this same order (e.g., Deut 24:17, 19–21). Also reflected here are other parts of the Torah: the so-called Covenant Code (Ex 22:20–21 [ET 22:21–22]) and the Holiness Code (Lev 19:33–34). (I use the traditional scholarly terminology, minus the critical baggage often accompanying it, and affirming Mosaic authorship of the Pentateuch. "Code" is misleading because these passages offered examples more than legal precedents.)

Singular collectives ("father and mother …") are used throughout this verse to speak of the individuals who are being mistreated. The abusive subjects of the verb, "*they* have dishonored," apparently are not to be limited to the rulers denounced in the previous verse, but refer to undefined persons, probably to virtually anyone in a position to behave that way. Compare similarly 22:9b. The first outrage clearly refers to disobedience to the Fourth Commandment. The Hebrew verb (הֵקֵלּוּ) rendered "dishonored" is an absolute antithesis to the one used in that commandment: כַּבֵּד (Ex 20:12; Deut 5:16), a Piel imperative of a root that in the Qal means "to be heavy" and so in the Piel means to treat or regard as a "heavy," someone important, influential, or authoritative—traditionally translated "honor." Here Ezekiel uses the Hiphil of קָלַל, "to be light," and thus to treat someone as a "lightweight," of no real importance, triflingly, contemptuously, and so on. The English "*dis*honor" linguistically expresses the Hebrew antonym.

The remaining two verbs are virtually interchangeable. Ezekiel could have used the simple verb עָשַׁק, "to cheat someone of his due, take advantage of, exploit." Instead, he uses the cognate noun, עֹשֶׁק, preceded with עָשָׂה, so עָשׂוּ בַעֹשֶׁק is, literally, "treat with exploitation." This construction possibly indicates ongoing behavior, not merely a solitary offense (cf. עָשַׁק עֹשֶׁק, "practices extortion," in 18:18).

The Torah too is much concerned with the גֵּר, "alien" (22:7), a refugee or temporary resident, who is partially protected by law, but whose rights are also curtailed, and hence who is easily taken advantage of, whether out of xenophobia or unscrupulousness. Today one can hardly help but think of the masses of immigrants, legal or otherwise, who flood the United States. Government programs and the law can do only so much; the responsibility to a large extent depends upon individual concern, which, however, is easily forgotten. An orthodox church's concern with doctrinal integrity or justifiable fear of a "social gospel" is neutralized (at best) if it and its members disregard the needs of the disadvantaged "in [their] midst" (22:7).

22:8   The verse seems to be formulated as a direct contrast to the commands of Lev 19:30. Ezekiel gives it his own touch by reversing the order of the two clauses. Yahweh uses almost exactly antonymous verbs from those in Lev 19:30 to make the accusation. Instead of "you shall fear/revere/reverence [יָרֵא] my sanctuary" (Lev 19:30), here Yahweh says, "You have despised [בָּזָה] my holy things," using a verb Ezekiel employs elsewhere to describe contempt of the covenant oath (16:59; 17:19; cf. 17:16, 18). And instead of "you shall keep/guard [שָׁמַר] my Sabbaths" (Lev 19:30), Yahweh accuses, "You have … profaned [חִלֵּל] my Sabbaths."

Ezekiel also broadens the scope of the transgression by expanding מִקְדָּשִׁי, "my sanctuary," in Lev 19:30 to קָדָשַׁי, "my holy things," a very comprehensive term involving not only the sanctuary, but all other *sacra*: the sacrifices, the temple accoutrements, the rituals, and so forth. In modern times, to "despise" these might signify secularism, but in antiquity it would undoubtedly mean the transfer of religious devotion to other cults.

As in Lev 19:30, one plural noun, here "my holy things," is paralleled by a second: "my Sabbaths." The plural may refer only to Sabbath *days*, but may also mean to include the expansion of "rest" in the sphere of time to the realm of space, the Sabbatical Years and the Jubilee (Leviticus 25). The centrality of these observances to Israelite identity and theology can hardly be overstated. Christians celebrate the fulfillment of this "rest" in Christ's Easter victory, although on earth only proleptically.[30]

22:9   The second group of condemnations (22:9–11) involving bloodshed (שֹׁפְכֵי־דָם, 22:9) seems to inch gradually into its main concern with sexual transgressions. How slander or gossip connects is not self-evident, except possibly by the association of the Hebrew word translated "slanderers" with itinerant merchants (see the textual note on 22:9). The text's own immediate association is that "slanderers are present to shed blood" (22:9). It is not immediately apparent what the connection is between slander and bloodshed. Lev 19:16, to which Ezekiel is probably referring, makes the same connection. Cooke is probably correct in understanding the connection as efforts "to get rid of persons obnoxious to those in power by means of false accusations."[31]

That practice is scarcely unknown today. Nor has the Christian church been particularly successful in eliminating such behavior, not even in its own internal politics. If one looks for evidence of original sin, few examples will serve

---

[30] For the theological significance of the Sabbatical Years and the Jubilee, one may see Kleinig, *Leviticus*, 551–55.

[31] Cooke, *Ezekiel*, 241.

better. It is noteworthy also that the OT mentions slander as such a common, everyday sin (so much so that we almost fail to acknowledge it as sinful) virtually in the same breath with the gross immoralities to be targeted shortly. How readily the malice or hate involved in malicious gossip involves or turns into bloodshed is developed in the Sermon on the Mount (Mt 5:21–26). Many other biblical passages could also be cited of course.

"Eat on the mountains" (Ezek 22:9) undoubtedly refers to participation in pagan ritual meals on the high places. This was already condemned in 18:6. The connection with sexual debauchery is now quite clear: the apparently orgiastic character of the pagan rituals.

The last clause in the verse, "act depravedly in your midst" (22:9), serves as an explicit transition to the next two verses. זִמָּה, "depravity, lewdness," is one of the strongest and most comprehensive biblical terms for unchastity and forbidden sexual unions. Five specific examples appear in 22:10–11.

22:10   The translation is deliberately free to accord with English usages. The Hebrew here does not use the common שָׁכַב, "lie with," that is, "sleep with" in a sexual sense. Instead, for cohabitation with one's mother, it uses גִּלָּה (Piel perfect of גָּלָה), literally, "[He] uncovers the nakedness of a father," meaning that he uncovers his mother's nakedness, which is lawfully uncoverable only to the father (Lev 18:8; 20:11).[32] According to Lev 20:11, violation of this was a capital crime. The MT of Ezek 22:10 has the singular verb גִּלָּה, "[He] uncovers" (as in Lev 20:11), while all the versions have a plural verb, matching the parallel plural verb עִנּוּ (Piel perfect of עָנָה), men "force themselves" upon women. The singular may be a sort of deliberate euphemism for the shocking expression.

The clause describing the violated women is harder to translate literally. The Hebrew places the object (a construct phrase) before the verb, literally, "the unclean of menstruation they violate in you" (טְמֵאַת הַנִּדָּה עִנּוּ־בָךְ). The uncleanness of women for seven days during menstruation is part of the ceremonial law (Lev 15:19), mentioned earlier in Ezek 18:6. In Lev 18:19, the euphemistic קָרֵב, "approach," was used in the prohibition of intimacy during menstruation, but Ezekiel uses the stronger verb עִנּוּ, "they violate, humiliate, subdue, overpower, force themselves upon," implying the woman's unwillingness to acquiesce. The singular of the same verb (עִנָּה) recurs in the last clause of 22:11. "Rape," of course, is a possible translation but may be a bit too strong, depending upon precisely how the word is defined.

The parallelism between 22:8 and 22:10 is a good example of how the OT places moral and ceremonial laws beside each other without the sharp distinction between them later made by Christians. Christ fulfilled the entirety of the OT for our sakes. The ceremonial law has been rendered obsolete, and indeed since the destruction of the temple in A.D. 70 much of it is impossible to perform, but God's moral law remains normative for Christians and for all peoples. To the

---

[32] For this terminology, see Kleinig, *Leviticus*, 376–77.

best of my knowledge, no Christians prohibit intimacy during menstruation. However, even most secular societies regard mother son incest as heinous, and this is also an excellent example of "natural law" (cf. Oedipus).

22:11 The mores of our society still tend to disapprove of the three sexual aberrations listed in this verse, but it is no longer a matter of law, except for the suggestion of rape in the third instance: "some force themselves [עִנָּה] on a sister" (for the verb, see the commentary on 22:10). Believers who view these three as more than "mores," however, will be aware that there are self-styled "progressive" or "liberated" groups who believe that they are little more than ancient taboos that may be discarded and who lobby to that effect.

22:12 The sins in the third group involving bloodshed (שְׁפָךְ־דָּם, 22:12) are all covered by this single verse. Although the specifics are debated (see the textual note), the gist is perfectly clear. It turns from sexual to economic transgressions. Fallen man's unruly sexual impulses and greed are mentioned in the same breath, as it were. Of course, Ezekiel's perspective is that of the Torah, but the problems are universal. Both problems are, at best, barely held in check by law but will yield only to a change of heart, which will never be fully realized in this world. The secular temptation is always to try to solve the problem by a new "system," or at least by multiplying rules and regulations. The twentieth century was convulsed by the battle between capitalism and socialism/Communism, or some amalgam of each. The West is largely convinced that some version of "free enterprise" is, at least, the lesser of two evils, but even here, without playing politics, Christians may serve as salt to remind capitalists that the profit motive built into the system easily falls prey to unvarnished greed—an amoral concern with only "the bottom line," the mantra that "our first obligation is to our stockholders," and so forth.

But the theological pièce de résistance of the entire section comes in the final two Hebrew words of the bill of indictment: וְאֹתִי שָׁכַחַתְּ, literally, "me you have forgotten." If one is not careful, it is easy to overlook the tremendous significance of this clause as merely the last in a list of discrete offenses of various sorts. Instead, it clearly is a climactic and comprehensive charge, encompassing all of the individual ones preceding. Underlying the objective reality of broken laws is the personal offense of having forgotten Yahweh and all his redemptive acts and promises. The "I" of a personal Creator-Redeemer-Sanctifier confronts the "you" of an apostate city. The people might have fostered some hidden "spirituality" of their own syncretistic manufacture, but those who remember Yahweh know that confession of his name manifests itself in loyalty in all the multiplicity of concrete situations of everyday life.

It is true that Ezekiel does not often speak so plainly of faith, and thus it becomes easy to dismiss him as only another legalist. He speaks of forgetting Yahweh only once more, in 23:35.[33] It joins the list of other important, main-

---

[33] Ezek 22:12 and 23:35 are the only two verses in the book with שָׁכַח, "to forget," and in both the direct object is אֹתִי, "me."

line theological expressions that occur only once in the book: the use of בָּחַר, "to choose," only in 20:5; מָלַךְ, "to rule (as king)," applied to Yahweh only in 20:33; and זָכַר, "to remember," has Yahweh as its object only in 6:9, where "will remember me" is the counterpart of "forgetting me" in 22:12 and 23:35. "To remember" is shorthand for saving faith, while "to forget" implies apostasy and complete loss of faith.

Like all biblical writers, Ezekiel has his own favorite way of expressing things; compare the writings of St. John with those of St. Paul in the NT. Ezekiel's own characteristic way of expressing that everything depends on faithful remembering is by use of antonyms such as the verb מָרָה, "to rebel" (5:6; 20:8, 13, 21), and his description of the city and its people not as "the house of (true) Israel," but (literally) "a house of rebellion" (מְרִי).[d]

(d) Ezek 2:5, 6, 8; 3:9, 26, 27; 12:2, 3, 9, 25; 17:12; 24:3; 44:6

If all this is overlooked by the reader, Ezekiel will easily be read as a major exemplar of a legalistic OT religion—especially if one is disposed to view the OT as an antithesis to the NT to begin with. Nor should the church—which is "the Israel of God" (Gal 6:16), the spiritual heir of the OT "house of Israel"— think that it is immune from committing the same sins Ezekiel condemns in Israel (cf. 1 Cor 10:1–13). We forget that, in principle, we confess "sin," that we *are* sinners, before we confess specific sins. Or put positively, although "love is the fulfilling of the Law" (Rom 13:10), yet because "we daily sin much,"[34] we are still bound to what dogmaticians call "the third use of the Law."[35]

We forever teeter on the ledge between legalism and antinomianism. And here one of the great fault lines of Protestantism emerges. The Reformed tradition with its "Gospel as preparation for the Law" orientation easily slides into (quasi-)legalistic preoccupation with rules and empirical experience. Lutheranism, however, proclaims that the Law has condemned the old Adam, who has been crucified and buried with Christ, and the baptized believer is now raised with Christ and thus has been set free from the Law (e.g., Rom 6:1–14). Yet Lutheranism is always tempted to soft-pedal the third use of the Law and at times even to deny its very existence or applicability for a particular behavior. The church, whose doctrine and life are drawn from and normed by the Scriptures alone (*sola Scriptura*), needs constantly to ponder the whole counsel of God in the Scriptures to maintain the proper distinction and application of Law and Gospel to the Christian faith and life.[36]

22:13 After the long list of tergiversations (22:6–12) follows the announcement of the sentence in 22:13–16. Only the people's fraudulent business practices and their bloodguiltiness are mentioned again, but they obviously are

---

[34] SC III 16 (*Luther's Small Catechism with Explanation*, 19).

[35] On the basis of Scripture, the Lutheran Confessions affirm that God's Word is the rule and norm that instructs Christians about godly life and behavior in accord with God's immutable will. See FC Ep and SD VI.

[36] See FC, Ep, Rule and Norm, 1–2, and SD, Rule and Norm, 1–3.

a sort of shorthand for the whole catalog of sins mentioned earlier. Here Yahweh himself is anthropomorphically described as clapping his hands, a gesture of exasperation indicating that his patience is exhausted. Israel may have forgotten him (22:12), but he has not forgotten the Israelites, and "it will be sheer terror to understand the message" (Is 28:19).

22:14 In two rhetorical questions that assume negative replies, Yahweh virtually mocks Jerusalem's bravado and machismo. In contrast, by adducing his own efficacious Word (דִּבַּרְתִּי, "I … have spoken"), Yahweh virtually takes an oath that the promised judgment will not fail to come. The following verses describe the nature of the judgment.

22:15 Singular forms continue to be used, but the reference is now clearly to the inhabitants of the city, not the city as such—although it is a distinction Ezekiel barely makes. The judgment will consist in the scattering of the people in all directions at the same time that their uncleanness will be purged. The verb תֻּמֹּם ("I will … *eliminate* your uncleanness") will be used again in 24:10–11 and 47:12. Here the removal of uncleanness is not a reassuring statement (as it will be in 36:25), but a remorseless annihilation of every stain. At this point we have pure Law.

22:16 The verb used here, "defiled, desecrated, dishonored" (וְנִחַלְתְּ, Niphal of חָלַל), is essentially synonymous with טֻמְאָה, "uncleanness," of the previous verse. If we followed the ancient versions (also RSV and NRSV) in emending to a first person, so that Yahweh is the one who will be "profaned," the idea would be that the nations fail to recognize Yahweh's judicial role in the destruction of Jerusalem and take it as evidence of his inability to save his people. But the MT seems to be describing the last and climactic punishment: the people will be "defiled … in the eyes of the nations." Ezekiel seems to pick up on the Deuteronomic picture that in exile the people initially will be able to defile themselves to their hearts' content (Deut 4:27–28; 28:36–37, 64), but when they finally realize the depths to which they have fallen, only *de profundis*, "out of the depths" (Ps 130:1 [Vulgate 129:1]), will they again cry out to Yahweh and know him.

The House of Israel (22:17–22)

22:17 With this verse begins one of the shortest oracles in the book; it continues only through 22:22, whose ending is similar to the recognition formula concluding 22:16 ("you will know …"). The legal atmosphere of the previous verses is replaced by a metaphor in the third person drawn from the realm of metallurgy. With a variety of verbs, Yahweh is described as a smelter, extracting valuable metals from ore. The picture is not unique to Ezekiel. Lexical links with Is 1:21–23, 25 and Jer 6:28–30 indicate a likelihood that Ezekiel was drawing on common prophetic imagery.

22:18 The harsh message of this oracle is summarized in this verse. That Israel in Yahweh's eyes had become only worthless slag is a metaphor that requires little explanation. But we must hear the picture against the backdrop of other biblical passages where Israel is described as God's סְגֻלָּה, his special,

687

personal, prized "treasure," especially Ex 19:5, but also Deut 7:6; 14:2; 26:18; Mal 3:17; Ps 135:4. Naturally, such a self-understanding would be cherished infinitely more than the one presented here. Of course, Yahweh had not changed, had not revoked his election promises, but the people most certainly had. That the Exodus 19 passage could be quoted almost verbatim in 1 Pet 2:9 and applied to Christians suggests the ease with which the oracle can be applied to us as much as to ancient Israel—and perhaps more so because "to whom much is given, much will be required from him" (Lk 12:48). The message here parallels that contained in the metaphor or allegory of the vine in Ezekiel 15. Compare also our Lord's similar use of the vine metaphor in Jn 15:1–11.

Because Ezekiel himself does not elaborate, we must use our imagination a bit in attempting to understand the role that silver plays in the oracle. If our exegesis is correct, it must be noted that the concluding words of the verse indicated that the one precious metal, silver, is indeed present but has not yet been successfully extracted. If "the house of Israel" can be distinguished from the "silver" (22:18), the latter may be a reference to Ezekiel's present audience in exile with him. God's future plans lie with the exiles, while those momentarily spared back in Judah soon will be skimmed off as dross. The remaining verses in the oracle will have more to say about the "silver."

22:19 As the metaphor of the disposition of the slag continues, the introductory thesis, "because you have all become dross, I am about to gather you inside Jerusalem," introduces the pair of similes in 22:20–22a. If it were not already evident, the verse clearly identifies Yahweh as the smelter who gathers the ore for the furnace. It also identifies the furnace as Jerusalem. In the face of Nebuchadnezzar's imminent siege, the people may have gathered behind Jerusalem's walls for safety (common behavior in antiquity), perhaps still deluding themselves into expecting miraculous divine intervention. But Ezekiel declares that their action was a deliberate act of Yahweh, setting them up for his intended judgment.

To follow the line of Ezekiel's thought in 22:19–22, it is necessary that the reader note that the metallurgical metaphor from here on is somewhat different from 22:18. In 22:18, the metals listed were elements in the dross to be removed from the furnace after the ore had been heated. In 22:19–22, the picture is that of the earlier refining process; the metals are raw material thrown into the furnace to be melted down. That is, the order of the verses (22:18, followed by 22:19–22) is the reverse of what would actually happen in the smelting process. First, a smith would do the refining (22:19–22), and only after that would he discover that the ores are all worthless dross (22:18). But in the prophecy, the result was placed first (22:18), before the process that led to the result (22:19–22), to emphasize the coming punishment—the near obliteration of the people, which is the prophet's main point.

22:20–22 It is doubtful if anything can be made of the mention of "silver" in 22:20, 22. If my interpretation of 22:18 correctly identified the "silver" as Ezekiel's present audience in exile with him (versus the "dross" in

Jerusalem), the repetition of "silver" in 22:20, 22 may be intended to caution that the exiles too must continue to experience Yahweh's fiery wrath before any pure and useful silver will be available. Ezekiel himself is here silent about the ultimately salutary effects of the remnant from which Yahweh will restore his people. But once they have acknowledged and digested the fact that their exile was all because of Yahweh's anger at their relentless sinfulness, the possibility presents itself that Yahweh may once again do something positive with them. This is the Law-Gospel dynamic that is at work throughout the Scriptures: the Law must do its preparatory work of driving us sinners to repentance (e.g., Romans 2–3) before we can receive the Gospel as the Good News of forgiveness through the atoning death and resurrection of Jesus Christ, whose grace empowers our new life in the service of God (e.g., Romans 4–6).

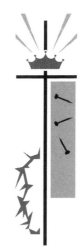

The Unclean Land (22:23–31)

22:23 Now begins the final oracle of the chapter, a sort of miscellany detailing aspects of the all-pervasive ungodliness of all strata of society, necessitating in God's justice, a final judgment upon Jerusalem. Rulers, priests, prophets, and even the ordinary citizenry openly flout God's will. The oracle divides itself into two uneven parts: after the survey of the pervasive corruption in 22:23–29, the final two verses (22:30–31) describe how, after Yahweh has vainly sought for someone to stand in the breach before him, he is left with no alternative but to carry out the judgment.

Commentators have long noted a striking similarity between this oracle and Zeph 3:3–4, written probably about a half-century earlier (early in the reign of Josiah, whose reign began in 640 B.C.). It is very plausible that Ezekiel has deliberately expanded Zephaniah's rebukes and applied them to his own day.

The oracle is full of Hebrew perfect verbs, which tempts many critics to read it as a late retrospective addition written by Ezekiel or some other redactor after the fall of Jerusalem in summer 586 B.C. While this possibility cannot be ruled out of court, it is more likely that they are prophetic perfects, which describe the future as already past ("as good as done"), since Ezekiel uses them often.

22:24 This verse is thetical and rather general. It is addressed to the "land," although Ezekiel's main concern is with those whom Yahweh is presently allowing to occupy it. Nevertheless, the mention of the land should not be dismissed as simply metonymic. Although the Bible does not dwell on the point, it is almost a commonplace of its thought that the land shared in the primeval curse upon Adam (Gen 3:17–18) and continues to be inseparable from blessings and curses upon Adam's descendants, ultimately even awaiting its own deliverance from its "bondage to decay" (Rom 8:19–22). And beginning with Lev 26:43, the assertion is frequently made that in the B.C. order of creation, the land itself will finally enjoy its Sabbaths. Yahweh had commanded the Israelites to let the land lie fallow every seventh (sabbatical) year, but Israel's antinomian farmers had ignored that command. One of the ways by which the Bible calculates the beginning and end of the seventy years' exile, which Jeremiah (25:12) had predicted, was "until the land had enjoyed its Sabbaths" (2 Chr 36:21).

The Hebrew verb מְטֹהָרָה in Ezek 22:24 clearly speaks of the land not being "cleansed" or "purged" by torrential rain. The text is disputed (see the textual note), but the difference is more a matter of degree than of kind. If we followed the LXX, the picture would be that of a severe drought that had not yet sparked repentance—a common enough biblical picture. But the MT yields an even stronger picture, the metaphor of a torrential deluge—that is, exile—that will be needed to cleanse the land. That will occur "on the day of rage" (בְּיוֹם זָעַם). "Rage" (זַעַם), used both here and in 22:31, forms an inclusion or framework for the entire oracle.

Ezekiel had used the same kind of language and metaphor in 13:11, 13 for torrential "rain" (גֶּשֶׁם; cf. גִּשְׁמָה in 22:24) that would dissolve the flimsy plaster the false prophets had used to deny the problem. Here it is given a more eschatological application, which will appear again in 38:22. Behind the metaphor may well stand the narrative of the worldwide deluge in Genesis 6, implying it as a type of the final judgment. 1 Pet 3:20–21 reminds us that *coram Deo*, not only eschatologically, but also in the existential sense, every day is Judgment Day, and that the Sacrament of Baptism saves us through the resurrection of Jesus Christ. As reprobate humanity perished in the flood, so the sinful nature must perish in Baptism—daily—and be buried with Christ (cf. Rom 6:1–4; Col 2:11–13). As the "eight" (1 Pet 3:20) saved through the ark began humanity anew (eight representing the start of a new week and a new creation), so also Christ's resurrection on the first day of the new week has begun the new creation for all in Christ, the firstfruits (cf. 1 Cor 15:20; 2 Cor 5:17; James 1:18).

22:25 Presuming that we should read "princes" with the LXX, not "prophets" as in the MT (see the textual note), we have a picture of a thoroughly corrupt and avaricious royal house, which, with the collusion of an equally corrupt judiciary, will stop at nothing, not even "legalized" murder, to aggrandize its power and wealth. Prophets apparently receive their "cut" too, or at least "bless" such behavior—but that will be the subject of 22:28. The episode of 1 Kings 21, describing Ahab and Jezebel's murder of Naboth and the confiscation of his property, is a classical illustration of this verse's lament, and we are given to understand that such deportment was not particularly rare, especially when "Elijahs" were not to be found. Of course, the other writing prophets are replete with denunciations similar to that of Ezekiel's here. Jeremiah was the only other one active at Ezekiel's time, and he himself records the hostile reception he received. False prophets, who prophesy "smooth things" (Is 30:10), on the other hand, are always welcomed.

22:26 This is virtually the only verse in the book where Ezekiel, himself a priest (1:3), reprimands his fellow priests, although in the vision of the eschatological temple, certain Levites will be severely criticized and restricted in their functions (see the comments on 44:10–14). The punishment in 7:26 was that "instruction [תּוֹרָה, Torah] will perish from the priest" because of the bloodshed and violence in the land, but that passage had no strictures of the priesthood itself.

Ezek 22:26 apparently gives us only a generalized description of how the "priests do violence to my Torah." The language suggests a blatant disregard for the spirit, if not also the letter of the Torah. The suggestion is that they twisted it and interpreted it arbitrarily for their own ends, forgetting that it can only be received as a gift and communicated scrupulously. Whenever "Torah" degenerates into mere "law," all kinds of sophistries, new "understandings," and the like will be found to evade the clear intent of the original. As a priest (1:3) denouncing fellow priests, Ezekiel concentrates on ceremonial violations of the Torah, but its moral implications are surely included (the OT itself barely makes a distinction between the ceremonial and moral stipulations). A somewhat parallel passage, Mal 2:7–8, illustrates a wider scope of priestly dereliction than is specified here.

Yahweh's "holy" things might be profaned in many ways. We find an example in the behavior of Eli's sons (1 Sam 2:12–25). Or it would have been easy to eat the sacred offerings when in a state of impurity (Lev 22:1–9). Any number of other regulations governing sacrifice could have been ignored, and hypocritical priests might easily have failed to set an example of holy living.

The distinction between the sacred and the profane is first enjoined in Lev 10:10, and in Ezek 44:23, Ezekiel is careful to require its inculcation in the eschatological priesthood. Like the difference between clean and unclean, much of this will be a matter of literal obligation only in the B.C. era, but the general idea of proper reverence for God's Word, for preaching and administering the Sacraments faithfully, is no less mandatory in the years of our Lord (A.D.).

All the evidence we have indicates that in addition to their liturgical responsibilities, it was the priests' obligation to "teach," or, literally, "cause [people] to know" (Hiphil of יָדַע in 22:26) Yahweh's Torah.[37] In a way, it is surprising that the OT places as little explicit emphasis on this as it does. But the pedagogical duties of the priests come through clearly at points: Lev 10:11; Deut 33:10; Hos 4:6; Hag 2:11; Mal 2:6–8. It matters little whether Ezekiel and these other prophets have in mind sins of omission (neglect) or commission (false teaching); both are equally injurious. Certainly in this respect, the concern is no less urgent for the Christian church. The traditional period of catechesis leading up to the Easter Vigil illustrates the prominence of pastoral teaching in the early church, and not a few of the problems perennially besetting the church can be attributed to incompetent and/or insufficient catechesis. Parents, pastors, and teachers in academic settings on whatever level, all must rank Christian education as among their highest priorities.

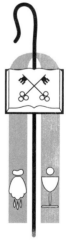

---

[37] See, for example, the Hiphil of יָדַע of Moses in Ex 18:16, 20 and of parents in Deut 4:9; Josh 4:22. The Hiphil of יָרָה is the synonym translated "teach" in God's mandate that the priests "teach" in Lev 10:11; Deut 17:10–11; 24:8; 33:10.

Finally, by different diction, Ezekiel, as we have noted many times before, places special emphasis on the Sabbath (literally, "from my Sabbaths they hide their eyes," 22:26). We are left to speculate what all "hiding the eyes" from the Sabbath entailed, but it may well have included both the priests' own disregard for the Sabbath rest as well as the failure to reprove those who did likewise. We regularly restate the Third Commandment (Ex 20:8; Deut 5:12) to help apply it to "the Lord's day" (Rev 1:10) of the new covenant.

And that all this was far more serious than superficial infractions of "law" is shown by the final clause, "with the result that I am profaned among them." To treat God's will as mere custom or a matter of personal choice is finally to treat God himself as though, at best, he were only another take-it-or-leave-it moralizer; no matter what sort of "spirituality" remains, this is to deify oneself.

22:27 With only slightly different expressions, the "officials" (people of lesser power) are accused of essentially the same thing as the "princes" were in 22:25.

22:28 A harsher assessment of the prophets is scarcely imaginable. The tone is very similar to Jeremiah's in Jer 23:23–40. And we have heard almost exactly the same language earlier in Ezekiel 13: whitewashing the truth (13:10–16), giving lying visions and oracles (13:6–9), and perhaps most heinous of all, claiming to be speaking God's Word when Yahweh has never been in communication with them (13:6–7).

However, when false prophets use exactly the same formula ("hear the Word of Yahweh," 13:2) as Ezekiel and other true prophets do,[e] we sense how hard it must have been for the masses, who probably were only minimally instructed in the Torah, to decide who was a true prophet and who was false. It is, in principle, not at all different today. "Religious" spokesmen talk glibly about "God," "the Lord," "Jesus"—whatever—and perhaps even profess a belief in a "verbally inspired, inerrant Scripture," but their message may not be scriptural in substance or evangelical (in the historic sense) at all.

22:29 So pervasive is the amoral atmosphere that even the ordinary citizenry behaves as consciencelessly as the upper classes, especially to the detriment of those without full rights (aliens) or those in need of special assistance such as the "the poor and the needy" (two common virtual synonyms are used). The Torah already contained admonitions against such abuses (e.g., Deut 24:14), and the true prophets since the days of Amos (eighth century B.C.) had condemned them (e.g., Amos 8:4–14). But obviously all of that meant nothing in such a society.

22:30 The last two verses quickly bring the third and last oracle (22:23–31) to a close. They describe Yahweh's response to the wholesale defection of his people. This verse portrays his futile attempt to find someone who could intervene and avert the impending invasion of the land and the destruction of the city.

(e) E.g., 1 Ki 22:19; Is 1:10; Jer 2:4; Ezek 16:35; 21:3 (ET 20:47); 34:7, 9

"Someone among them" (מֵהֶם אִישׁ) casts a wide net, referring to all the classes of society previously mentioned. Here pedigree does not count, but only someone with sufficient "standing" before God to satisfy his wrath. In the broader biblical context, this can only refer to some "righteous person"—and not in a moralistic sense, but who by justification has received an alien righteousness. Christians cannot think such thoughts without reference to Jesus Christ, our μεσίτης, "mediator, intermediary, arbiter," before the Father (1 Tim 2:5).

The metaphor of our text, where someone closes a breach in a wall is, as such, not specifically developed in the NT. However, virtually the same thing is developed in sundry ways throughout the NT and by preachers in expository and homiletical contexts. A breach in the wall surrounding a city represents an attacking enemy who soon would rush through the breach and annihilate the city's inhabitants. To take one's stand in the breach makes one vulnerable to the full force of the enemy, risking death for the sake of saving the inhabitants. It is not hard to apply this picture to Christ's entire vicarious redemptive work on our behalf, using the metaphor that he closed the breach between God and man caused by our sin. Jesus willingly sacrificed himself on the cross to absorb God's righteous judgment against humanity's sin, thus averting judgment from all believers in him, and, rising on the third day, he defeated Satan and death on our behalf.

The picture of a breach plays a somewhat more explicit role in the OT, even when the root פֶּרֶץ ("breach") is not used. It is very possible, as many commentators think, that Ezekiel is here echoing Jer 5:1–6, where God commands that prophet to search throughout Jerusalem for someone who was faithful. Zeph 1:12 describes Yahweh himself as searching Jerusalem with lamps (bringing superficial comparisons with Diogene's lantern), but there the idea seems to be to search out and punish the evil—almost the opposite of the thrust of Ezekiel here. The enigmatic פֹּרֵץ, "one who breaches," of Micah 2:13 seems to be a messianic figure who breaks out and leads God's people through the gate (almost an answer to Ezek 22:30, if the contexts were at all related). In different vocabulary, Is 63:1–6 describes Yahweh coming from Edom to save his people after he found no one to do it for him.[38] In a specifically historical context, David names the site near Jerusalem where he won his epochal victory over the Philistines, "Baal-perazim," that is, "the Lord of breaches/breaking through," in effect crediting Yahweh with the victory (2 Sam 5:20). Perhaps Isaiah (28:21) refers to the same event—in the verse that in the Vulgate uses the phrase *alienum opus* ("alien/foreign work"), so prominent in Luther's thought.[39]

---

[38] Cf. the hymn "Who Is This That Comes from Edom" (*TLH* 209).

[39] E.g., AE 2:134; 14:335.

Ps 106:23, using virtually identical language as this verse, speaks of Moses as the one who "stood in the breach before him [God]" (עָמַד בַּפֶּרֶץ לְפָנָיו) and averted God's destructive wrath. The reference is obviously to Ex 32:11–14, where, by his intercessory prayer, Moses dissuades God from destroying the Israelites after the golden calf apostasy. The use of the nearly identical phrase here in Ezekiel (וְעֹמֵד בַּפֶּרֶץ לְפָנַי, 22:30) plainly makes the intercessory idea at least as prominent as the martial one. And that concept can hardly be considered without mentioning the famous episode of Gen 18:22–33, where Abraham bargains God down to only ten righteous people, who, if found within Sodom, would be sufficient to spare the city.

But all of this seems to leave the impression that the mere presence of one "righteous" person (a sinner justified by grace) would have been enough to save Jerusalem. Obviously that would contradict 14:12–20, not to speak of virtually the whole of chapter 20 as well as 3:16–21 and 33:7–20 (cf. similarly Jer 5:1–9; 6:13; 8:6, 10). Ezekiel surely does not contradict Ezekiel any more than Scripture contradicts Scripture! The presence of God the Son would be another matter. But Ezekiel is a book of biblical, exegetical theology, not of systematics or dogmatics. Greenberg summarizes it well: "But each proposition is a rhetorical necessity in its context. … Rhetoric that serves a given context may contradict that of another context. … For all his love of rules Ezekiel was not a systematic theologian."[40]

22:31 In relatively formulaic language, the point of the entire oracle is summarized here. Since everyone was too busy with his own nefarious activities to dissuade Yahweh (portrayed here as the enemy) from sending the Babylonian hordes through the breach that the people's attitude has opened up in the city's wall, the catastrophe becomes inevitable.

The oracle ends abruptly and almost ominously with the divine signatory formula, "says the Lord Yahweh."[41] Yahweh, the commander in chief, has signed his own order to destroy Jerusalem, and there will be no reprieve.

---

[40] Greenberg, *Ezekiel*, 2:469.

[41] For this formula, see pages 8–9 in the introduction and the second textual note on 5:11.

Two Lewd Sisters Whore against Yahweh

Translation

23 ¹The Word of Yahweh came to me: ²"Son of man, there were two women, daughters of the same mother. ³They acted as whores in Egypt; they whored in their youth. There they let their breasts be fondled, and there they let men caress their virgin nipples. ⁴Their names were Oholah, the older sister, and Oholibah, her sister. They became mine and bore sons and daughters. (As for their names, Samaria is Oholah and Jerusalem is Oholibah.)

⁵"Oholah played the whore instead of being faithful to me. She lusted after her lovers, the Assyrians—bodyguards ⁶clothed in purple, governors and commanders, all of them desirable young men, charioteers driving horses. ⁷She bestowed her favors upon them, all the elite of the Assyrians, and with all for whom she lusted she defiled herself with all their fecal deities. ⁸She did not give up the whorings she had practiced since Egypt, when men laid her in her youth, caressed her virgin nipples, and poured out their lust upon her. ⁹Therefore, I delivered her into the hands of her lovers, into the hands of the Assyrians, after whom she had lusted. ¹⁰They exposed her nakedness, took away her sons and her daughters, and killed her by the sword. She became a byword among women because of the punishments they inflicted upon her.

¹¹"Although her sister, Oholibah, saw this, she behaved even more depravedly in her lustfulness than her [sister], and her whorings were even worse than her sister's nymphomania. ¹²She lusted after the Assyrians—governors, commanders, bodyguards clothed in gorgeous uniforms, and charioteers driving horses, all of them desirable young men. ¹³Then I saw that she too had defiled herself. (Both of them had gone the same way.) ¹⁴In fact, she intensified her whorings by looking at figures of men engraved on the wall, images of Chaldeans incised in vermilion, ¹⁵with belts around their waists and flowing turbans on their heads. All of them looked like noblemen, resembling Babylonians whose native land was Chaldea. ¹⁶She lusted after them at the mere sight and sent messengers to them in Chaldea. ¹⁷The Babylonians came to her to make love and defiled her by their whoredom. But after she had been defiled by them, she turned from them in disgust. ¹⁸Because she whored so openly and exposed her nakedness, I turned away from her in disgust just as I had turned away in disgust from her sister. ¹⁹Yet she increased her whorings, remembering the days of her youth when she played the whore in the land of Egypt. ²⁰She lusted after her deviant lovers whose penises were like those of asses and whose ejaculate was like that of horses. ²¹So you reverted to the lewdness of your youth when your nipples were caressed in Egypt and your young breasts fondled.

²²"Therefore, Oholibah, thus says the Lord Yahweh: I am about to rouse your lovers against you, those from whom you had turned away in disgust, and bring

695

them against you from all sides: ²³the Babylonians and all the Chaldeans, Pekod, Shoa, and Koa, and all the Assyrians with them, desirable young men, governors and commanders all of them, noblemen and men of high rank, all of them riding on horses. ²⁴They will come against you with weapons, wheeled chariots, and a horde of people. With shield, buckler, and helmet, they will take up positions against you on all sides. I will give you up to them for judgment, and they will punish you according to their own standards. ²⁵I will turn my zeal against you, and they will deal with you in wrath. They will cut off your nose and your ears, and the rest of you will fall by the sword. They will take away your sons and your daughters, and the rest of you will be devoured by fire. ²⁶They will strip you of your clothes and take away your beautiful jewelry. ²⁷I will put an end to your depravity and the whoring you began in the land of Egypt. You will not lift up your eyes to them or remember Egypt anymore. ²⁸For thus says the Lord Yahweh: I am about to deliver you into the hands of those you hate, into the hands of those from whom you turned away in disgust. ²⁹They will treat you hatefully, take away everything you have worked for, and leave you stark naked, your whorish nakedness being exposed. Your depravity and your whoredom ³⁰have brought those things upon you because of your whoring after the nations, because you defiled yourself with their fecal deities. ³¹Because you walked in the way of your sister, I will put her cup into your hand.

³²"Thus says the Lord Yahweh:

You will drink your sister's cup,
　　a cup deep and wide.
It will cause derision and scorn
　　because it contains so much.
³³You will be filled with drunkenness and grief,
　　the cup of horror and devastation,
　　the cup of your sister, Samaria.
³⁴You will drink it and drain it.
　　You will gnaw its shards
　　and tear out your breasts.

For I have spoken, says the Lord Yahweh.

³⁵"Therefore, thus says the Lord Yahweh: Because you have forgotten me and cast me behind your back, you yourself must also bear [the penalty of] your depravity and your whoredom."

³⁶Yahweh said to me: "Son of man, will you arraign Oholah and Oholibah? Make their abominations known to them. ³⁷For they have committed adultery, and blood is on their hands. They have committed adultery with their fecal deities, and even their children, whom they bore to me, they have offered up to them as food. ³⁸Furthermore, they have done this to me: they defiled my sanctuary on the same day they desecrated my Sabbaths. ³⁹When they slaughtered their children to their fecal deities, they entered my sanctuary on that same day to defile it. This is what they did in my own house. ⁴⁰Furthermore, they sent for men to come from afar, to whom a messenger had been sent, and they came. For them

you bathed, applied eye shadow, and put on your jewelry. ⁴¹You sat on a glorious couch with a set table before it, on which you placed my incense and my oil. ⁴²The noise of a carefree crowd was around her. In addition to the large throng of ordinary people were brought drunkards from the desert, and they put bracelets on their arms and beautiful crowns on their heads. ⁴³Then I said about the woman worn out with adulteries, 'Now her whoredom itself will go whoring.' ⁴⁴They used her as one uses a whore. So they used Oholah and Oholibah, those depraved women. ⁴⁵But righteous men will punish them with the punishment due adulteresses and the punishment due murderesses, for they are adulteresses and blood is on their hands.

⁴⁶"For thus says the Lord Yahweh: I will bring an army against them and hand them over to terror and plunder. ⁴⁷The army will stone them and cut them down with their swords. They will slaughter their sons and daughters and burn down their houses. ⁴⁸Thus I will remove depravity from the land so that all women may take warning not to act as depravedly as you. ⁴⁹They will impose upon you [the penalty for] your depravity, and you will bear [the punishment for] your sinful worship of your fecal deities. Then you will know that I am the Lord Yahweh."

Textual Notes

23:3 וַתִּזְנֶינָה בְמִצְרַיִם בִּנְעוּרֵיהֶן זָנוּ—The Qal of זָנָה occurs seven times in this chapter (23:3 [twice], 5, 19, 30, 43, 44). Its finite forms are translated "act as a/play the whore" or "to whore," while the participle (זוֹנָה in 23:44) is rendered "a whore." The Qal of זָנָה occurred eleven times in chapter 16 (and the Pual once) in the same sense. Other OT books use זָנָה literally for a prostitute (e.g., Lev 21:7; Josh 2:1; 1 Ki 3:16) or theologically for Israel's unfaithfulness to Yahweh.[a] The idea here that the women began to whore "in Egypt" (בְמִצְרַיִם) when still "in their youth" (בִּנְעוּרֵיהֶן) will be repeated with slightly different Hebrew in later places in the chapter (e.g., see the first textual note on 23:8).

שָׁמָּה מֹעֲכוּ שְׁדֵיהֶן—As often, the final *he* on שָׁמָּה is not a *he* directive ("thither") but is used in a purely local sense ("there"), entirely synonymous with the following וְשָׁם. Probably the *he* is added for purely euphonic reasons, to avoid a fusion of the two *mems* (-מ מָּה-) if it had not been added.

The Pual (third common plural perfect) מֹעֲכוּ is a hapax since מָעַךְ occurs elsewhere only in the Qal (Qal passive participles in Lev 22:24; 1 Sam 26:7), meaning "press, squeeze." Block is probably correct in understanding this Pual as having a tolerative sense ("let …") and as a passive of the Qal:[1] "they let their breasts be fondled." (The Niphal more commonly has a tolerative sense.) The subject, שְׁדֵיהֶן, is the dual (שָׁדַיִם) with third feminine plural suffix of שַׁד, the female "breast." It is always used in the dual (except in Lam 4:3), as is customary for Hebrew words for body parts that occur in pairs. Its dual occurred in Ezek 16:7 and recurs in 23:21, 34.

(a) E.g., Ex 34:15; Lev 20:6; Deut 31:16; Is 1:21; Hos 1:2

---

[1]   Block, *Ezekiel*, 1:732, including n. 14.

וְשָׁם עִשּׂוּ דַּדֵּי בְּתוּלֵיהֶן׃—"There they let men caress their virgin nipples" uses the Piel (third common plural perfect) of עָשָׂה. This may be a specialized meaning of the common verb עָשָׂה, whose Qal means "to do," or it could be a homograph, עָשָׂה II, "press, squeeze" (BDB; similar is *HALOT*). It recurs in the OT only in 23:8, where the identical Piel (עִשּׂוּ) has the active meaning, "they caressed," and in Qal in 23:21. The translation uses two varied and appropriate synonyms for the preceding verb and this one: "fondled [מֹעֲכוּ] … let … caress [עִשּׂוּ]." Since this whole clause is parallel to the preceding clause, the Piel verb here can be translated in a tolerative sense: "they let men …" like the preceding tolerative Pual. The form is impersonal with no explicit subject; I have added "men" for clarity. Some wish to revocalize עִשּׂוּ as a Pual (עֻשּׂוּ) to correspond to the previous Pual (מֹעֲכוּ), but this is unnecessary, especially in the light of Ezekiel's love of variety.

In slight contrast to שְׁדֵיהֶן in the preceding clause ("their breasts"), the plural of דַּד (in construct, דַּדֵּי), which can also refer to the entire breast, should be translated "nipples" in 23:3, 8, 21. Hebrew parallelism characteristically uses near, but not total synonyms. The abstract plural noun בְּתוּלִים means "virginity" (BDB), and in the construct phrase, דַּדֵּי בְּתוּלֵיהֶן, the second word serves as an attributive or adjectival genitive modifying the first noun: "the nipples of their virginity" means "their virgin nipples" (similarly in 23:8).

23:4 וּשְׁמוֹתָן … וּשְׁמוֹתָן—The first and fourth clauses begin with an independent "[as for] their names." This is the only place in the OT where this contracted form of the third plural feminine suffix (ָן-) occurs on the feminine plural noun ending, וֹת-. (The noun שֵׁם is masculine, but the form of its plural is שֵׁמוֹת.) Normally one would expect שְׁמוֹתֵיהֶן. But the form here may be compared with אַתֵּן in 16:54 among other examples. It seems to be a rare, but permissible (dialectical?) variation.

הַגְּדוֹלָה—Ordinarily, this would be translated as "the larger," and some commentators insist it should be so rendered here. Geographically, (northern) Israel was far larger than Judah, but in the context of the metaphor here, "older" seems required. The adjective clearly can have that sense (e.g., Gen 27:1; 29:16). Perhaps a clever double entendre is intended.

וַתִּהְיֶינָה לִי—"They became mine" is idiomatic for marriage, with the לְ of possession (BDB, s.v. לְ, 5 b (*a*)). All the ritual acts of the marriage ceremony described in 16:8–13 are passed over completely in chapter 23.

Critical opinion quite unanimously assumes that the last sentence in the verse, which explicitly identifies "Samaria" and "Jerusalem" as the referents of the symbolic names, is a later interpretive gloss, possibly precipitated by 23:33. Indeed, one might have expected this identification earlier, after the first שְׁמוֹתָן clause in 23:4. But the intent of the odd positioning may be to emphasize at the outset that the allegorical narrative following is entirely transparent in meaning. I have used parentheses around its translation, but without intending to address the text-critical issue.

23:5 וַתִּזֶן אָהֳלָה תַּחְתָּי—For clarity, I have expanded תַּחְתָּי (תַּחַת with first common singular suffix) into "instead of *being faithful to* me." After the marriages in 23:4, the context now is of married women expected to be faithful to their husband, not merely of wild, unattached young women. The specific verb נָאַף, "commit adultery," will occur in 23:37, 45 (as in Ex 20:14; Deut 5:18; Ezek 16:32, 38).

וַתַּעְגַּב עַל־מְאַהֲבֶיהָ—The Qal verb עָגַב, to "have inordinate affection" or "*lust* after (עַל־)" (BDB), recurs in 23:7, 9, 12, 16, 20. Elsewhere in the OT, it occurs only in the thematically related Jer 4:30. It is an extremely strong word, denoting an almost pathological eroticism. It may be related to עוּגָב, a type of pipe or flute, associated in rabbinical writings with erotic music; compare Pan, the satyr of Greek mythology, who uses some such instrument for seductions. The form here (third feminine singular imperfect with *waw* consecutive) is slightly irregular. Instead of the *patach* under the preformative (-וַתַּ), we would expect a *seghol* (-וַתֶּ), which is found in some Eastern codices. The form here may be influenced by the Qere in 23:16 and the same form in 23:20, which is the lengthened form with paragogic *he*, וַתַּעְגְּבָה. The shift in accent in the lengthened form explains its *patach*.

The subject, מְאַהֲבִים with third feminine singular suffix, is the masculine plural Piel participle of אָהַב, "to love." In Jeremiah, Hosea, Ezekiel,[b] and Lamentations, the Piel participle always refers to adulterous lovers. In Zech 13:6 it means "friends."

אֶל־אַשּׁוּר קְרוֹבִים:—The MT has "Assyria," the name of the city or country, rather than "Assyrians," as do the LXX and Syriac. In 23:7, 9, 12, 23, we meet the easier בְּנֵי־אַשּׁוּר, "sons of Assyria," that is, "Assyrians." Critics commonly delete the name here as a premature anticipatory gloss.

The final word, קְרוֹבִים, is very difficult. A first instinct would be to take it as the masculine plural of the adjective קָרוֹב, "near," and translate it as "those who are her neighbors," as in the LXX (τοὺς Ἀσσυρίους τοὺς ἐγγίζοντας αὐτῇ) and, predictably, KJV and NKJV. However, this contradicts geographic reality. Assyria was not "near" Samaria, especially in the light of the lengthier travel times required in antiquity than today. Keil senses this and other problems, but his suggestion that the term is not meant in a local, but an "inward or spiritual nearness"[2] is an intrusive idea in the context.

There are also syntactical difficulties. If the word were in apposition to אַשּׁוּר, it would require the article and probably also be singular and followed by a preposition (הַקָּרוֹב עָלֶיהָ, "which is near to her"). All this, plus the fact that the anarthrous plural word recurs in 23:12 (and perhaps also in 23:23, if the text is emended), suggests that the word should be approached from an entirely different angle.

Virtually everyone (myself included) agrees that the verse division is faulty and that קְרוֹבִים should begin 23:6 as the first of a series of titles of Assyrian officials. Since the LXX and the other ancient versions agree with the MT in taking the word as the end of 23:5, this verse division was part of the tradition very early in the history of the text. It seems that the verse division was established after the Akkadian language and Assyrian culture had been forgotten or replaced by Persian and/or Aramaic ones, but before the era of the LXX (ca. 200 B.C.), so perhaps in the fifth or fourth centuries B.C.

(b) Ezek 16:33, 36, 37; 23:5, 9, 22

---

[2] Keil, *Ezekiel*, 1:323.

Most commonly now, קְרוֹבִים is considered a derivative of the Aramaic קְרָב, "battle," and so means those "able to fight" (*HALOT*, s.v. קְרוֹב II) or "warriors" (RSV, NRSV, NIV). However, since the native language of Assyria was Akkadian, not Aramaic, the word is better understood as a hebraization of Akkadian *qurubu*, "bodyguard," or other staff officer close to the king. Thus Hebrew קְרוֹב in its ordinary sense of "near" may be a distant cognate of the Akkadian word, but in a vastly different sense.

23:5c–6 קְרוֹבִים: לְבֻשֵׁי תְכֵלֶת —"Bodyguards," which should be at the head of 23:6, is now modified by "clothed" (masculine plural construct of the Qal passive participle of לָבֵשׁ) in "purple." Was תְכֵלֶת the color purple or blue? Translations alternate unpredictably between the two, and commentators are also divided. It is impossible to determine exactly where on the spectrum this color fell. Various shades and hues could be achieved through blending and other processes.

The OT uses two main Hebrew words, תְכֵלֶת and אַרְגָּמָן. The latter, via Greek and Latin translations, corresponds to our word "purple," but a connection to our modern *word* does not necessarily imply that the ancient term referred to the same color in antiquity. It seems that אַרְגָּמָן implied various blends of an acid derived from the dried bodies of the females of a scale insect (kermes) with an extract from various shellfish, often translated "red violet, purple." In contrast, תְכֵלֶת implied a dye based more exclusively on various marine snails, especially common around Tyre, producing a deep blue violet. If this summary is at all accurate, "blue" might be preferred to "purple," if one has to choose. But "purple" has come to be associated with wealth and regal authority ("born to the purple," etc.) in a way that "blue" has not, and hence "purple" has better symbolic associations and thus is my translation.

The colorful attire of Assyrian soldiery is often depicted on wall paintings. The practice of beautifully dyed garments extends at least from Middle Bronze II (ca. 1500 B.C.) until well into the Roman era. (Compare the soldiers who mock Jesus' status by dressing him in purple [Mk 15:17; Jn 19:2].) Perhaps the best modern equivalent is the colorful garb of the Swiss guard of the Vatican.

פַּחוֹת וּסְגָנִים —"Governors" and "commanders" translate these loanwords from Assyrian administrative vocabulary. Both words appear at other times under different regimes, and the precise status and responsibilities involved varied accordingly.

פָּרָשִׁים רֹכְבֵי סוּסִים: —The same phrase recurs in 23:12. Just רֹכְבֵי סוּסִים recurs in 23:23. There is no agreement whether פָּרָשׁ means "charioteer" or "horseman, cavalryman." The latter is usually preferred, but then "riding [Qal masculine plural participle in construct of רָכַב] on horses [סוּסִים]" seems redundant. NIV offers "mounted horsemen" (NKJV is similar). There is no doubt that organized cavalry played a major role in Assyrian military strategy.[3] On the other hand, there is again an Akkadian cognate that means "horse chariot." And there is no doubt that the chariot units from which soldiers fought with bows also played a major role in offensive tactics.

---

[3] Cf. *ANEP*, § 375.

Some of the confusion may arise in that in earlier Semitic, a different word for "horse" (not the common סוּס) merged with "horsemen/rider." If פָּרָשִׁים here means a team of horses hitched to a chariot, and we accept the proposal that רָכַב be translated "drive" rather than "ride," the difficulty disappears. (The ordinary Hebrew word for "charioteer" is רַכָּב.) Largely following Block[4] here, I have translated, "charioteers driving horses," but one cannot be dogmatic.

23:7 וַתִּתֵּן תַּזְנוּתֶיהָ—"She bestowed her favors" is English idiom for what is, literally, "she gave her whoredom, engaged in obscene behavior." On the form תַּזְנוּתֶיהָ, see the third textual note on 16:15.

וּבְכָל ... בְּכָל־—The phrases beginning "with all …" define the first clause more precisely. Zimmerli[5] and others delete them as a clumsy gloss, introducing the subject of idolatry into a context that is largely political. Zimmerli literalistically intimates that the phrase implies intercourse with Assyrian idols. But the antecedent of the pronoun in גִּלּוּלֵיהֶם, *their* fecal deities," is מִבְחַר בְּנֵי־אַשּׁוּר, the "elite of the Assyrians." For גִּלּוּלִים as "fecal deities," see the fourth textual note on 6:4.

23:8 The verse is brutally frank, to the point of vulgarity, but of the sort one soon becomes accustomed to in Ezekiel, no matter what the topic.

וְאֶת־תַּזְנוּתֶיהָ מִמִּצְרַיִם לֹא עָזָבָה—The first clause is, literally, "but her whorings from Egypt she did not abandon." In idiomatic Hebrew, a temporal מִן before a place name implies time beginning at that place and continuing since. Whoring had become a way of life.

כִּי אוֹתָהּ שָׁכְבוּ בִנְעוּרֶיהָ—This כִּי clause probably also has a temporal sense. Commentators routinely emend אוֹתָהּ, the sign of the direct object with the third feminine singular suffix, to the preposition with suffix, אִתָּהּ, "with her," or at least translate it as such, possibly for euphemistic reasons. However, while the Hebrew euphemism שָׁכַב עִם ("lie with") is common, שָׁכַב אֶת־ in a sexual sense is unattested in the MT. Here and elsewhere when שָׁכַב takes אֶת, the form of אֶת shows that it is not the preposition אֶת־, "with" (synonymous with עִם), since wherever a suffix is added, its form, אֹת־, is that for a definite direct object, as in, for example, וַיִּשְׁכַּב אֹתָהּ, "he laid/raped her" (Gen 34:2). Furthermore, שָׁכַב is used with object suffixes. The Niphal and Pual of שָׁכַב are used with passive meanings as the Qere in Is 13:16; Jer 3:2; Zech 14:2, verses where the Kethib is a form of שָׁגַל, which the Masoretes considered to be obscene.

What all this means is that Hebrew could use שָׁכַב transitively when it refers to vulgar intimacy. I have dared to reproduce this usage literally as "men laid her," which is possible in colloquial English, even though that use of transitive "lay" in a sexual sense is usually considered vulgar. Greenberg, who discusses the issue at length, suggests using the verb "bed" in a transitive and sexual sense,[6] which is more decorous but fails to reproduce the Hebrew directly when it is easy to do so.

---

[4] Block, *Ezekiel*, 1:737, translates the phrase this way: "charioteers, men driving horses" (see also 1:739).

[5] Zimmerli, *Ezekiel*, 1:485.

[6] Greenberg, *Ezekiel*, 2:476–77.

וַיִּשְׁפְּכוּ תַזְנוּתָם עָלֶיהָ—"They … poured out their *lust* upon her" translates תַזְנוּת, the common noun usually translated "whorings" or "whoredom" (23:8a, 11, 14, 17, 18, 19, 29, 35, 43; "favors" in 23:7). As the object of the verb שָׁפַךְ, the reference is obviously to ejaculation.

23:10 הֵמָּה גִּלּוּ עֶרְוָתָהּ—The idiom גִּלָּה עֶרְוָה is, literally, "expose, reveal, uncover [Piel of גָּלָה] nakedness." The motif of exposing an adulteress in the sight of her lovers is a common one in the ancient Near East. See the commentary on 16:37.

בָּנֶיהָ וּבְנוֹתֶיהָ לָקָחוּ—Literally, "her sons and her daughters they took" is a brief summary of the deportation of large segments of Samaria's population to Mesopotamia (2 Ki 17:6).

וַתְּהִי־שֵׁם לַנָּשִׁים—This is, literally, "and she will be a name to the women." Here שֵׁם means "byword," that is, a proverbial, well-known example of someone shamefully punished. A personal or place name can become a common noun or adjective for a type of action, for example, sodomy, quisling, Machiavellian, and so on.

וּשְׁפוּטִים עָשׂוּ בָהּ—The plural noun שְׁפוּטִים, "punishments," appears only here in the OT. It may be an intensive plural. Its singular שְׁפוֹט occurs in 2 Chr 20:9. Much more common is שְׁפָטִים (e.g., Ezek 5:10; 16:41), probably the plural of the singular שֶׁפֶט. The verbal root שָׁפַט, "judge," and the noun מִשְׁפָּט are, of course, extremely common.

23:11 The verse is not easy to translate, not because of unclarity, but because Ezekiel piles up words to summarize at the outset how much worse Jerusalem's carnality is than Samaria's.

וַתַּשְׁחֵת עַגְבָתָהּ מִמֶּנָּה—This is, literally, "she made her [own] lustfulness more corrupt than her [sister]." The noun עֶגְבָה (with third feminine singular suffix), "lustfulness," is cognate to the verb עָגַב (see the second textual note on 23:5). It is intensified by being the object of וַתַּשְׁחֵת, the Hiphil (third feminine singular imperfect with *waw* consecutive) of שָׁחַת, which commonly refers to destructive or ruinous behavior. Ezekiel uses it also in 33:31–32, and here the reference is obviously to moral corruption.

וְאֶת־תַּזְנוּתֶיהָ מִזְּנוּנֵי אֲחוֹתָהּ—This phrase is a second direct object of the verb וַתַּשְׁחֵת in the preceding clause. It too uses the preposition מִן (on מִזְּנוּנֵי) in a comparative sense ("more than"). With that preposition Ezekiel uses the construct of זְנוּנִים, apparently as a variation from the immediately preceding noun תַּזְנוּת. To reflect the variation, זְנוּנִים is translated "nymphomania." Although used in Ezekiel again only in 23:29, זְנוּנִים occurs six times in Hosea with similar meaning.

23:12 The verse obviously echoes 23:5b–6; see the textual notes on those verses. Besides differences in word order, the major change is in the description of the bodyguards' uniforms; they are described as clothed in מִכְלוֹל (23:12; for the syntax, see Joüon, § 121 o) rather than in תְּכֵלֶת (23:6). Partly the different word is merely an assonant variation, but beyond the wordplay, its precise meaning is not entirely clear. Usually מִכְלוֹל is taken as a derivative of כָּלַל, thus "perfectly/splendidly attired" or the like. The standard of perfection apparently involves color, but exactly how is unknown. An Akkadian cognate implies some specially dyed garment. מִכְלוֹל recurs in 38:4, also in a military context. If it is essentially the same word as מַכְלוּל in 27:24, which refers to gorgeous attire of some sort, the interpretation is strengthened, but still not totally clarified.

23:14 אַנְשֵׁי מְחֻקֶּה עַל הַקִּיר—Literally "men of engraving on the wall," this is translated "figures of men engraved on the wall." The phrase מְחֻקֶּה עַל־הַקִּיר was used already in 8:10. מְחֻקֶּה is the Pual masculine singular participle ("engraved") of חָקָה used as a noun ("engraving, carved art"). חָקָה is a variant of חָקַק, whose Qal passive participle (חֲקֻקִים) is used at the end of the verse.

כַּשְׂדִּיִּים—The Qere, כַּשְׂדִּים, is simply the common spelling for "Chaldeans." The Kethib, כַּשְׂדַּיִּים, occurs elsewhere only in 2 Chr 36:17.

בַּשָּׁשַׁר—The noun שָׁשַׁר may also be an Akkadian derivative, referring to some type of bright red pigment for painting, probably red ocher, an iron oxide.

23:15 This verse is really a single unit with 23:14. The verse division is artificial.

חֲגוֹרֵי אֵזוֹר בְּמָתְנֵיהֶם—The adjective חָגוֹר, "girded," is a hapax, though the cognate noun חֲגוֹר, "belt, sash," occurs thrice in the OT (1 Sam 18:4; 2 Sam 20:8; Prov 31:24), and the verb חָגַר is common. The plural adjective is in construct with אֵזוֹר, "waistcloth," so the phrase is, literally, "girded of [with] waistcloth on their loins." One might expect the Qal passive participle of the common verb חָגַר to form חֲגוּרֵי אֵזוֹר, "girded with waistcloth," but Greenberg plausibly suggests that חֲגוֹרֵי is a deliberate attempt to achieve assonance with the following סְרוּחֵי.[7]

סְרוּחֵי טְבוּלִים—The word in construct, סְרוּחֵי, another genitival construction, is apparently the masculine plural Qal passive participle of סָרַח, although it could be a related adjective. It apparently means that the Chaldeans are *"overhung of turbans"* (BDB, s.v. סָרַח, Qal, 2), referring to lofty turbans known from Assyrian art. Hence it is usually translated "flowing, trailing, pendulous," or the like. The noun טְבוּלִים is a hapax, unrelated to the common טָבַל, "dip," which later in Aramaic was used of Baptism. An Akkadian cognate of טְבוּלִים leads to the nearly universal translation today of "turban." There is an Arabic root, טבל in Hebrew characters, which refers to dyeing, and thus KJV's "dyed attire." Some color connotation thus may be implied, but it does not seem to be the major import of the word.

שָׁלִשִׁים—The noun שָׁלִישׁ is almost certainly related to the numeral three. Until recently, modern commentators, following certain Assyrian usages, understood the word as referring to the third man in a chariot. This third man was a shield bearer for the driver and the archer, and he could hand arrows to the archer. This translation is still followed by Zimmerli,[8] but this interpretation has now been largely abandoned. Especially if related to the numeral, the word may refer to a nobleman of the third rank, although his specific duties, if any, are uncertain. Some think it refers to the "secret service" protecting the king. 2 Ki 15:25 refers to Pekah, who led a coup against Pekahiah, as a שָׁלִישׁ, and a seal showing him with a javelin in his hand is extant. The following phrase indicates a connection with the court, so modern translations have "officers," "captains," and so on. Ironically, such translations approximate KJV's

---

[7] Greenberg, *Ezekiel*, 2:479.

[8] Zimmerli, *Ezekiel*, 1:472.

"princes" (or St. Jerome's "rulers, commanders") from long before modern discoveries.

דְּמוּת בְּנֵי־בָבֶל אֶרֶץ מוֹלַדְתָּם:—In 23:14, the pictures had been described as צַלְמֵי כַשְׂדִּים (masculine plural construct of צֶלֶם), "images of Chaldeans." Here דְּמוּת, "likeness," is used for the comparison and is translated "resembling." צֶלֶם and דְּמוּת are a standard word pair in the OT (Gen 1:26–27; 5:1, 3) and in related Semitic languages. Here the phrase בְּנֵי־בָבֶל, "Babylonians," intervenes here before כַשְׂדִּים, making clear that the reference is to the ruling classes. The final phrase is, literally, "Babylonians, [i.e.,] Chaldea [being] the land of their birth." כַשְׂדִּים may refer either to the territory, "Chaldea," or to its inhabitants, "Chaldeans." Ezekiel thus shows an awareness that the current ruling class was not autochthonous, but originated in Aramean territory to the west.

23:16 וַתַּעְגַּב—The Qere, וַתַּעְגְּבָה, is a lengthened form of the Qal third feminine singular imperfect with *waw* consecutive (GKC, § 48 d; Joüon, § 45 a, footnote 1). Its form resembles that of a cohortative, which normally occurs only in the first person. The Kethib is וַתַּעְגַּב, the same form that occurred in 23:5; see the second textual note on 23:5. In 23:20 the sole reading is וַתַּעְגְּבָה.

23:17 לְמִשְׁכַּב דֹּדִים—Literally, "for a bed of lovemaking" or "for a lying of lovemaking," this is translated, "to make love." The noun מִשְׁכָּב is from the verb שָׁכַב, commonly used in the Hebrew idiom "to lie with." The Hebrew abstract plural noun דֹּדִים requires a euphemistic "love" in translation (cf. its use in 16:8). While our currently cruder and franker speech might retain the euphemism of "love," it more likely would say "have sex." The abstract plural is also used in the Song of Songs (1:2, 4; 4:10; 5:1; 7:13 [ET 7:12]), where its singular, דּוֹד, is used by the beloved woman to refer to Solomon as her "lover" (e.g., 1:13–14).[9]

וַתֵּקַע נַפְשָׁהּ מֵהֶם:—This final clause is difficult to translate, both because of the rarity of the verb יָקַע and especially because of the lack of a single adequate English equivalent of נֶפֶשׁ. The verb יָקַע and נֶפֶשׁ are used together only in Jer 6:8 and Ezek 23:17–18, while נָקַע and נֶפֶשׁ occur together in 23:18, 22, 28. In all these Ezekiel verses, I have translated the idiom as "turn away in disgust."

The verb יָקַע (without נֶפֶשׁ) is used in Gen 32:26, where it refers to the dislocation of Jacob's hip socket at Penuel. וַתֵּקַע, which occurs in Ezek 23:17–18, is the Qal third feminine singular imperfect with *waw* consecutive of יָקַע. The form נָקְעָה in 23:18, 22, 28 is the third feminine singular Qal perfect of נָקַע, which obviously is related and synonymous. The basic meaning of both verbs appears to be something like "separate, fall apart (suddenly)." In this context, there are clearly overtones of emotional alienation or disgust, and the verb is followed by מִן, "from," or מֵעַל, "from upon," attached to a noun or pronoun, telling from whom the subject turned in disgust. The subject, נֶפֶשׁ, here could refer to the woman's "person" or her "desire, appetite," rooting in the word's ultimate physical foundation in the esophagus, but only in the abstract is it possible to talk about one without the other. Various expedients

---

[9] For this terminology, one may see Mitchell, *The Song of Songs*, 386–93, 562–65.

are used in translation. Least satisfactory is probably KJV's "mind," for while one's mind is undoubtedly engaged in such situations, the action is probably more a rationalization than a rational decision. Different terminology is used for the corresponding sudden sexual revulsion on the male side in 2 Sam 13:15 after Amnon's rape of his half sister.

23:18 The translation is somewhat free. The verb וַתְּגַל (Piel third feminine singular imperfect with *waw* consecutive of גָּלָה), "she exposed, uncovered, revealed," is used twice, the first time without the accusative sign אֶת־ before the definite direct object, the second time with it. The variation is apparently only stylistic. Twice more in this chapter, in the first clause of 23:27 and the last clause of 23:35, the first definite direct object lacks אֶת־ but the second has it.

23:19–20 In these two verses, the verbs are third person (feminine singular), but they will shift in 23:21 to second person (feminine singular) for direct address ("you").

23:20 The language is crude and suggests unrestrained prurience. The Egyptians are pictured as dissolute degenerates. Some of the details, possibly reflecting bawdy street speech, are unclear. There is obviously a fair degree of parody in the language, although to what degree is hard to say. There is no reason to believe that Egyptian culture of the time was particularly sybaritic. The purpose of such hyperbole, then, is primarily rhetorical, that is, to register disapproval of Zedekiah's appeal to Egypt for help.

וַתַּעְגְּבָה עַל פִּלַגְשֵׁיהֶם—For the verb, see the textual note on 23:16. An immediate conundrum arises with פִּלַגְשֵׁיהֶם, the plural of פִּלֶגֶשׁ with third masculine plural suffix, which normally would mean "their [the Egyptians'] concubines." The quadriliteral form of פִּלֶגֶשׁ indicates that it is probably of non-Semitic origin, but that does not clarify its meaning. Everywhere else in the OT פִּלֶגֶשׁ simply means "concubine," apparently almost synonymous with the native Hebrew אָמָה. Elsewhere פִּלֶגֶשׁ (sometimes spelled פִּילֶגֶשׁ) always refers to a female "concubine," even though grammatically it is always declined as a masculine noun. A jaded modern audience might think that its use here might refer to lesbianism, but the rest of the verse eliminates that possibility. No other use of the word to refer to a man is known. One traditional interpretation has been that the word refers to the סָרִיסִים, the male "eunuchs" or "courtiers" of ancient oriental palaces.[10] The implication would be that her sexual appetite was so boundless that she even used Egyptian servants. That fits the context, but it is a guess, and no certain explanation can be given. I have translated it "her deviant lovers."

בְּשַׂר־חֲמוֹרִים בְּשָׂרָם—Twice here בָּשָׂר ("flesh, meat") refers to the *membrum virile*. See the first textual note on 16:26. There too the allegedly oversize genitals of the Egyptians had been referred to, and the picture of equine lasciviousness was apparently commonplace in the ancient world (attested also in classical literature). Bestial imagery for libertine sexual behavior is frequent also in Jeremiah (2:23–24; 5:8; 13:27; 50:11).

---

[10] Keil, *Ezekiel*, 1:327. Cf. Greenberg, *Ezekiel*, 2:480, who says: "No solution is satisfactory."

וְזִרְמַת סוּסִים זִרְמָתָם—The noun זִרְמָה occurs in the OT only here (twice). Apparently it is related to the verb זָרַם, "to rain, pour forth in floods," and masculine noun זֶרֶם, which refers to a "cloudburst" or "downpour." Some, following the LXX (αἰδοῖα) and Syriac (ﺳﻨ), both of which mean "privy parts," think that there has been a metathesis of the ר and the מ, and so the original term here was זְמוֹרָה, "shoot, twig," a euphemism for "phallus" (cf. זְמוֹרָה in 8:17). That results in parallelism between the organs of the asses (see the preceding textual note) and those of the horses here. However, a certain development of meaning seems more likely and requires no emendation of the MT.

23:21 This verse at the end of the indictment (23:3–21) appears to form an inclusion or closure to its beginning in 23:3. But, for whatever reason, it has an unusual number of difficult words, prompting proposals for repointings and emendations. The shift from third to second person in 23:21 appears premature before an entire section of the chapter of direct address, beginning in the next verse (23:22–35), but there are many parallels, and it may deliberately intend to make the transition less abrupt.

וַתִּפְקְדִי—The general meaning of the common, but rather multivalent, Qal of פָּקַד (here second feminine singular imperfect with *waw* consecutive) is something like "administer, take care of." Its precise nuance here is debatable. "To long for," as a sort of parallel to זָכַר in 23:19, which this entire verse recapitulates and intensifies, is often suggested, but פָּקַד is usually less laden with emotion. Hence, "search for, revert to" seems more accurate. There are other instances where the verb implies a return to a situation that had not been attended to for a time (Ex 4:31; Judg 15:1).

זִמַּת נְעוּרָיִךְ—The noun זִמָּה, "lewdness," is a very strong term that will be used

(c) Ezek 23:21, 27, 29, 35, 44, 48 (twice), 49

eight times in the chapter.[c] See the third textual note on 16:27.

בַּעְשׂוֹת מִמִּצְרַיִם דַּדַּיִךְ—The verb is the Qal infinitive construct (gerund) with בְּ of the עָשָׂה meaning "squeeze, caress," whose Piel was in 23:3, 8 (see the third textual note on 23:3). An infinitive can have either an active or a passive meaning (Joüon, § 124 s), and the context here requires a passive translation: "your nipples were caressed." One would expect a *chateph* vowel (-ֲ-) under the guttural ע. Some propose repointing the infinitive to be Piel (בְּעַשּׂוֹת) to match the Piel in 23:3, 8, or to Pual (בְּעֻשּׂוֹת) for the passive meaning, but neither emendation is needed.

As for מִמִּצְרַיִם, it literally meant "from Egypt" in 23:8, where the translation "since Egypt," implying duration, was appropriate, but that makes no sense in this context. Two Hebrew manuscripts read simply מִצְרַיִם, that is, "the Egyptians" as subject, as in 23:19 and 23:27. A superfluous מ could have been added under the influence of 23:8 or for other reasons. The easiest reading would appear to be that of the LXX, Syriac, and Vulgate, which translate as if the text were בְּמִצְרַיִם, "in Egypt." The text-critical dislike of easier readings is subject to exception, and I have taken this as one example.

לְמַעַן שְׁדֵי נְעוּרָיִךְ׃—The use of לְמַעַן, "for the sake of, because of," is strange here, at best. The NKJV adopts that translation, but otherwise there is near unanimity, which I join, in emending to a form of מָעַךְ, "fondle," with the preposition לְ: either לִמְעֹךְ, the Qal infinitive, or לְמַעֵךְ, the Piel infinitive. In 23:3 the Pual of מָעַךְ was used with שָׁדַיִם, which also is here. Whether the emendation is to the Qal or Piel here,

706

the (gerundival) active infinitive would have a passive meaning: "your young breasts were fondled." The meaning of the construct phrase שְׁדֵי נְעוּרָיִךְ is similar to that of בְּתוּלֵיהֶן ‏ ‏ ‏ (see the third textual note on 23:3).

23:22 הִנְנִי מֵעִיר אֶת־מְאַהֲבַיִךְ עָלַיִךְ—I have taken הִנֵּה (with first common singular suffix) before the participle (Hiphil of עוּר) as a *futurum instans*: "I am about to rouse ..." This construction will be repeated in 23:28 (הִנְנִי נֹתְנָךְ) at the beginning of a sort of subdivision within the entire sentence of judgment, which begins in 23:22 and continues through 23:34 or 23:35, which has a brief concluding summary of all the charges and their consequences.

This verse introduces the great reversal, which the following verses will detail. All the roles described in 23:10–21 are now reversed by the rejected husband, Yahweh. Clearly he is the one who is going to "rouse, stir up, incite" (מֵעִיר) Babylon, the scorned political lover (23:17), together with its allies, to punish Judah. Babylon's military machismo, once so attractive to Israel, will now boomerang. Ezekiel says nothing about Babylon's motivation, whether it was retaliation or simple opportunism. But Babylon's action is God's work *sub contrario* to filter out a faithful remnant in Israel. God works "under opposites": his execution of judgment also brings about salvation for all who believe. This is supremely true of the vicarious death of Christ under judgment for humanity's sin, which accomplished the redemption of the world.

23:23 Apparently rather randomly Ezekiel specifies first by nationality, then by status, those allied in the attack. Clearly leading the assault are the Babylonians, the oldest settled inhabitants of the city of Babylon, distinguished from the Aramean Chaldeans, the current ruling class.

The following three names are somewhat elusive. The presumption would be that they are political or ethnic entities, probably incorporated into the Babylonian Empire, but probably due to our scanty knowledge, they are not easy to identify clearly. The first, Pekod, is the most distinct of the three. It is mentioned in Jer 50:21, also in connection with Babylon, and is the only one of the three to be mentioned on a famous prism of Nebuchadnezzar, listing the various political and ethnic entities of the empire.[11] Earlier references to Pekod also occur in Assyrian records. It was a strong east Aramean group, occupying territory east of the lower Tigris River. Often refractory, at Ezekiel's time, Pekod was apparently subservient.

The other two names are more elusive. Shoa is mentioned nowhere else, except possibly in Is 22:5, where, however, שׁוֹעַ may be a common noun meaning "cry for help." Shoa might be identified as the Sutu or Sutaeans, although the phonetic correspondence between the names is distant. The Sutu were a seminomadic group, apparently also centered east of the Tigris, which raided Assyrian and Babylonian territory for centuries in the second and first millennia.

Koa (also transliterated Qoa) is the most difficult. It is often tentatively identified with the Quti (more often transliterated as Guti). Again, however, there is a lack

---

[11] *ANET*, 307–8, where the name is spelled Puqudu.

of phonetic correspondence. The Guti first appear as formidable barbarians of the lower eastern Tigris who destroyed the Semitic kingdom of Akkad around 2200 B.C. By the first millennium, the term had apparently lost its gentilic sense and become a geographical one referring to the entire Transtigridian region.

If all three names are of peoples or countries, they must have been incorporated into the Babylonian Empire by Ezekiel's time, or at least, groups of them had been employed as mercenaries. Eichrodt long ago noted a possible wordplay in the names, especially in the three "o" sounds.[12] He pointed out that Pekod sounds like the Hebrew verb for "punish" (פָּקַד), Shoa sounds like "cry for help" (שׁוֹעַ, as in Is 22:5), and Koa might resemble "shriek" (although no plausible root קוע with that meaning is known until much later Hebrew). Such paronomasia is, as such, neutral with respect to the historicity of the three names, but it may suggest that Yahweh chose just these three for rhetorical effect. Some suggest that Yahweh even deliberately distorted the names (compare the proposed identifications above) in order to achieve that effect, thus describing the fate in store for Judah in a forceful way.

Keil argues from the omission of the copula before פְּקוֹד that all three were common nouns in apposition with כָּל־כַּשְׂדִּים. He notes that שׁוֹעַ in Is 32:5 and Job 34:19 refers to wealthy men of high rank, and then explains פְּקוֹד in the sense of "overseer, or ruler" (a meaning well attested for פָּקִיד). Keil offers no explanation for Koa. He translates the three words as "rulers, lords, and nobles."[13] Keil's argument seems weak, since it does not explain why Yahweh did not use well-known words of similar meaning, like those that follow in 23:23. I know of none who has followed him.

"All the Assyrians" is a bit problematic because, as a political and military entity, Assyria had ceased to exist a good two decades earlier.[14] But it is easy to assume that the reference is either to mercenaries of Assyrian extraction or even of intact military units of the defeated enemy that the Babylonians pressed into service.

The remaining vocabulary in the verse simply echoes the lists of previous types of lovers in 23:5–6, 12, although in different order. That is, the entire political and military nobility of the Babylonian world is again represented. The only significant change is the substitution of קְרֻאִים, instead of the קְרֹבִים ("bodyguards") of 23:5, 12. Naturally, a few wish to harmonize all three by emendation here (so RSV, NRSV), but most follow the MT, which is confirmed by the LXX and the Vulgate, and retain קְרֻאִים, the masculine plural Qal passive participle of קָרָא, "to call." It must mean "called ones" in some sense like "select officers, men of high rank." The word is used elsewhere in the censuses of Num 1:16 (Qere) and Num 26:9 (Kethib).

Here I have rendered רֹכְבֵי סוּסִים as *riding* on horses" (its more natural meaning), instead of "driving horses," as its connection with פָּרָשִׁים seemed to mandate in 23:6, 12.

23:24 The syntax of the first part of the verse is unusual in its paucity of prepositions. After the opening verbal clause (וּבָאוּ עָלַיִךְ), we meet three prepositionless nouns in a

---

[12] Eichrodt, *Ezekiel*, 328.

[13] Keil, *Ezekiel*, 1:328–29.

[14] Zimmerli, *Ezekiel*, 1:488, and others delete the phrase as a gloss.

row (הֹצֶן רֶכֶב וְגַלְגַּל), followed by a phrase with the expected preposition (וּבִקְהַל עַמִּים). This is followed again by three more nouns without prepositions (צִנָּה וּמָגֵן וְקוֹבָע). All six can—and must—be construed as adverbial accusatives ("with …"). Perhaps a certain symmetry was intended by this relatively unique diction.

הֹצֶן—This noun is a hapax, and there is not even a good clue to its meaning. All sorts of guesses, ancient and modern, inevitably ensue. Both the Targum and the Syriac understand it as something like "weapons, armor," or the like. If we understand this as a heading for the following list, it is as suitable an expedient as any. The major alternative follows the LXX, which apparently read מִצָּפוֹן, "from the north" (so RSV). Presuming the LXX did not have a different Hebrew text, that translation seems to have been suggested by 26:7, where in a somewhat similar context, Nebuchadnezzar is described as descending upon Tyre from the north. Ezekiel also alludes to the thought in 39:2. Jeremiah also makes frequent reference to an enemy from the north, already in his call vision (Jer 1:13–15) and numerous times later. A modern twist (evidently followed in NKJV) builds on the use of פָּרָשׁ ("horseman") before גַּלְגַּל וָרֶכֶב in Ezek 26:10 and similar language in Jer 47:3, and emends הֹצֶן to חָצָן, equivalent to an Arabic word for "stallion."

רֶכֶב וְגַלְגַּל—I understand "chariotry and wheel" as a hendiadys: "wheeled chariots."

צִנָּה וּמָגֵן—These refer to two different types of shields. The צִנָּה was a large body shield, often carried by an assistant, as for Goliath in 1 Sam 17:7, who must have required an unusually large one! The מָגֵן, traditionally translated "buckler," was smaller, often round, and held or worn on the combatant's arm. For reasons that elude me, KJV and most modern translations confuse the two and mention the buckler first. Of those translations surveyed in this commentary, only NIV is basically correct with its "large and small shields."[15]

וְקוֹבָע—This spelling for "helmet" is found only here and in 1 Sam 17:38. The usual spelling is כּוֹבַע, as in Ezek 27:10; 38:5.

יָשִׂימוּ עָלַיִךְ סָבִיב—Literally, "they will set upon you around," this is rendered as "they will take up positions against you on all sides." The expression could also be rendered "they will attack you." It apparently is a military expression for any device or tactic used in besieging a city; it was used specifically with "battering rams" in Ezek 4:2. A similar idiom using the synonymous שִׁית instead of שִׂים is used in Ps 3:7 (ET 3:6).

וְנָתַתִּי לִפְנֵיהֶם מִשְׁפָּט—Israel is the implied object of the verb, and נָתַן לִפְנֵי ("place before") has the sense of "give up to, hand over to," hence, "I will give [you] up to them [for] judgment." לִפְנֵי is used in the same sense in, for example, Gen 13:9; 24:51.

וּשְׁפָטוּךְ בְּמִשְׁפְּטֵיהֶם:—The root שׁפט is present in all three of the final words of this verse: the verb שָׁפַט (Qal third common plural perfect with second feminine singular suffix and waw consecutive) and the noun מִשְׁפָּט (plural with third common plural suffix and בְּ) here, as well as the noun מִשְׁפָּט at the end of the preceding clause,

---

[15] For illustrations, see *ANEP*, §§ 368, 372, 373.

where it meant "judgment." Elsewhere the verb can be rendered "to judge," since it can refer to acquittal (justification) as well as condemnation, but in this context, the verb must mean "impose a sentence of judgment, carry out punishment." The final מִשְׁפָּט is used in the sense of "standard, custom, procedure," hence בְּמִשְׁפְּטֵיהֶם is "according to their own standards."

23:25 וְנָתַתִּי קִנְאָתִי בָּךְ—Compare the use of נָתַן here ("I will *turn* my zeal against you") with that in the previous verse (see the seventh textual note on 23:24). These are merely two examples of how widely varied the English translations of this verb must be.

אַפֵּךְ וְאָזְנַיִךְ יָסִירוּ—Literally, "your nose and your ears they will remove," the Hiphil of סוּר is translated "cut off."

וְאַחֲרִיתֵךְ בַּחֶרֶב תִּפּוֹל ... וְאַחֲרִיתֵךְ תֵּאָכֵל בָּאֵשׁ:—In each of these clauses, אַחֲרִית is used as a substantive noun. Its meaning is unclear and may or may not be the same in both instances. אַחֲרִית ("what is behind, after") may have either spatial or temporal applications. Here the second alternative seems appropriate. The word sometimes implies "posterity, remnant," but so distant a vision does not seem to be involved here. I have taken the word as used in essentially the same way both times. Some Israelites will be mutilated, "and *the rest* of you will fall by the sword. They will take away your sons and your daughters, and *the rest* of you will be devoured by fire" in the torching of the city.

The catastrophes described in this verse echo those predicted in lesser detail about Oholah and her children in 23:10.

23:27 וְהִשְׁבַּתִּי זִמָּתֵךְ מִמֵּךְ וְאֶת־זְנוּתֵךְ מֵאֶרֶץ מִצְרָיִם—The first part of this sentence is, literally, "I will put an end to your depravity from you," but "from you" is omitted in translation for the sake of English idiom. "Your whoring from the land of Egypt" means "the whoring you began in the land of Egypt," similar to the use of מִמִּצְרַיִם in 23:8 in a temporal sense. זְנוּת is found in Ezekiel only here and in 43:7, 9. Elsewhere Ezekiel usually uses the synonym תַּזְנוּת. Zimmerli[16] and others entertain the idea that a ת has somehow dropped out here, and זְנוּת should be emended to תַּזְנוּת, but that is entirely unnecessary. זְנוּת is used elsewhere in the OT (e.g., Num 14:33; Jer 3:2), and it seems to be merely a stylistic variant.

23:28 The first half of the verse is comparable to 16:37 and the second half to 23:17 above.

כִּי כֹה אָמַר אֲדֹנָי יְהוִה—The use of כִּי with the citation formula links the following material closely with what had preceded.

הִנְנִי נֹתְנָךְ—This identical phrase recurs in 25:4 (cf. 29:19). Here again we have the instant-future idiom, הִנְנִי plus a participle (here the Qal of נָתַן), "I am about to deliver you ..." For this idiom, see the first textual note on 23:22. The object is expressed by attaching the second feminine singular object suffix directly to the participle (נֹתְנָךְ).

בְּיַד אֲשֶׁר ... בְּיַד אֲשֶׁר—Twice אֲשֶׁר is used as a compound relative in a genitive relationship, "into the hand of those ...."

---

[16] Zimmerli, *Ezekiel*, 1:476.

23:29 וְלָקְחוּ כָּל־יְגִיעֵךְ—The noun יְגִיעַ may mean "labor, exertion," but in context here, as often, it means "the result of your labors, produce, property, gain": "they will … take away everything you have worked for."

וַעֲזָבוּךְ עֵירֹם וְעֶרְיָה—The hendiadys עֵירֹם וְעֶרְיָה, consisting of two virtual synonyms, is rendered "stark naked." The same expression occurs in 16:7, 22, 39, where it is rendered "naked and nude."

וְנִגְלָה עֶרְוַת זְנוּנָיִךְ—This clause preserves the connection to the whole context of Oholibah's adultery: her judgment is not merely typical politico-military vengeance. The construct chain עֶרְוַת זְנוּנָיִךְ is, literally, "the nakedness of your whorings," but the genitive is rendered adjectivally: "your whorish nakedness." Hebrew typically prefers a construct chain to a noun and adjectival modifier.

Since the subject, עֶרְוָה (the word in construct), is feminine, some commentators are tempted to emend וְנִגְלָה (Niphal of גָּלָה, "be revealed"), which at first glance might be taken as the third masculine singular perfect with *waw* consecutive, into the third feminine singular perfect, וְנִגְלְתָה.[17] However, וְנִגְלָה can also be the Niphal feminine singular participle, introducing a circumstantial clause (as I have tried to indicate in translation), so the difficulty evaporates.[18]

וְזִמָּתֵךְ וְתַזְנוּתָיִךְ—As the MT stands, these two nouns, together with the preceding עֶרְוַת זְנוּנָיִךְ, form a triple compound subject for the preceding singular verb, וְנִגְלָה. Such a subject might have required a plural verb (whether it is a perfect or a participle). However, with most modern commentators and translations, I am assuming that the MT's verse division is incorrect, or at least infelicitous, and that 23:30 should begin with these two words. This assumption is supported by the beginning of Jer 4:18 (דַּרְכֵּךְ וּמַעֲלָלַיִךְ עָשׂוֹ אֵלֶּה לָךְ), since it has two nouns similar to these two at the end of Ezek 23:29, followed by an infinitive absolute phrase almost identical to the phrase that begins Ezek 23:30 (see the next textual note). No significant change in the meaning of either verse is involved. If the MT's versification is retained, the Hebrew text will display the clustering of three key words in the chapter (זְנוּנָיִךְ וְזִמָּתֵךְ וְתַזְנוּתָיִךְ), namely, זְנוּנִים וְזִמָּה וְתַזְנוּת (each with second feminine singular suffix). These three words follow in succession even if the last two are connected to the start of 23:30.

23:30 עָשֹׂה אֵלֶּה לָךְ—On the versification, see the previous textual note. עָשֹׂה is an infinitive absolute (Qal of עָשָׂה, "do"), which can function as a surrogate for any verb form. If we reversify as most do, the compound (dual) subject poses no problem whatsoever for this verb ("your depravity and your whoredom *have brought* …"). A few manuscripts read עָשׂוּ, which could be vocalized as the easier third common plural perfect עָשׂוּ or as the alternative spelling for the infinitive absolute, עָשׂוֹ, found in the parallel Jer 4:18. However, already Cooke noted that no change is necessary,[19] and Zimmerli's sarcasm is unwarranted.[20]

---

[17] Zimmerli, *Ezekiel*, 1:476, for example, mentions this as a possibility.

[18] See Allen, *Ezekiel*, 2:44; Block, *Ezekiel*, 1:752.

[19] Cooke, *Ezekiel*, 261–62.

[20] Zimmerli, *Ezekiel*, 1:476, wrongly claims that עָשֹׂה is "a vocalization of embarrassment made necessary in consequence of the false verse division."

If the MT's versification is retained, the infinitive absolute must be construed differently. KJV, NKJV, and Block[21] translate, "I [Yahweh] will do ... ," syntactically construing it as a continuation of the distant construction הִנְנִי נֹתְנָךְ toward the beginning of 23:28. This construal makes explicit Yahweh as the ultimate actor, but even without it, Yahweh's agency is implicit here and will become explicit in 23:31. Greenberg construes the infinitive absolute as a future passive ("shall be done"),[22] which is possible.

בִּזְנוֹתֵךְ אַחֲרֵי גוֹיִם—The preposition בְּ with the Qal infinitive construct of זָנָה is understood causally, "because of your whoring" (as עַל אֲשֶׁר in the next clause also is causal). גוֹיִם is anarthrous, as already in 7:24; 19:4, 8; 22:16.

23:31 בְּדֶרֶךְ אֲחוֹתֵךְ הָלָכְתְּ—"Walk in the way of" is standard biblical usage, continuing into the NT and even into Christian usage. It is usually figurative for faith and life.

וְנָתַתִּי כוֹסָהּ בְּיָדֵךְ:—This clause introduces the metaphor of the "cup" (the feminine noun כּוֹס), a familiar figure in Hebrew poetry, to which the next three verses will be devoted. To the extent that one can locate a specific origin, it is usually assumed that the picture is of a banquet where the host would pour wine into the cup of each of his guests (a custom which, interestingly, has survived the millennia). Since God is the host in the Bible, however, guests are usually described as powerless to refuse it. Thus sometimes the cup implies one's lot in life, whether for good or ill. A well-known example of the former is a verse that Christians can hardly read without thinking of the Eucharist, namely, Ps 116:13: "I will take the cup of salvation, and call upon the name of the LORD" (KJV). The fact that wine is one of God's good gifts if used properly (e.g., to gladden the human heart [Ps 104:14–15]) may explain why "eucharistic" libations of wine play a role in Israel's sacrificial ritual, although we are given few details about their precise role. More often, as here, however, the cup is a figure of God's wrath and the resulting woe. Ezekiel's use of it here may have been influenced by Jeremiah's warning in 25:15–29.[23] Jesus in Gethsemane refers to this "cup" of God's wrath (Mt 26:39), which he would (metaphorically) drink on the cross. Since he suffered the entirety of divine wrath at humanity's sin, he is able to furnish the cup of salvation with his blood, shed for the forgiveness of sins (Mt 26:27–28).

23:32 In developing the theme of the cup, Yahweh composes a poem, as indicated by the poetic typography of most modern translations. Whatever its earthly origins, Ezekiel underscores that it is God's Word by using the citation formula at its beginning (32:32) and the signatory formula at the end (32:34).[24] Each of the three verses or divisions of the song begins with some reference to Oholibah's drinking. Partly because it is poetry and for other reasons, it is not the easiest material to translate. As

---

[21] Block, *Ezekiel*, 1:752–53.

[22] Greenberg, *Ezekiel*, 2:483, citing GKC, § 113 ff; Joüon, § 123 w.

[23] For an excellent overview of the entire ambience of the picture, see the excursus "Drinking the Cup of Yahweh's Wrath" in Raabe, *Obadiah*, 206–42, especially pages 213–36, where the fourteen texts employing the metaphor of drinking the cup of divine wrath, including Ezek 23:31–34, are considered in some detail.

[24] For the citation formula, see pages 8–9 in the introduction and the fourth textual note and the commentary on 2:4. For the signatory formula, see pages 8–9 in the introduction and the second textual note on 5:11.

Block summarizes: "The internal disjointedness, redundancy, and inconsistency of rhythm may be attributed to the prophet's heightened emotional state. But the incoherence also reflects the speech of one literally intoxicated with alcohol."[25]

תִּהְיֶה לִצְחֹק וּלְלַעַג—The first clause of the poem was addressed to Oholibah in the second person, but this line apparently shifts to the third person and describes the "cup." תִּהְיֶה in this context must be the third feminine singular (Qal imperfect), and its subject is the feminine noun כּוֹס in the preceding clause: "it [the cup] will be for [cause] derision and scorn." Nevertheless, since Oholibah is drinking the cup's contents, there is still ultimate reference to her. תִּהְיֶה could also be second masculine singular, but that would not fit here since its subject must be either the feminine "cup" or the sister Oholibah. Because of the shift, and since the entire line is missing the LXX, many critics want to delete it as a marginal gloss.[26]

The nouns צְחֹק, "laughing, derision," and לַעַג, "mocking, scorn," are near synonyms, as can be the verbs (צָחַק and לָעַג) from which they are derived. The first refers more neutrally to laughing, but with לַעַג and its more specific implications of ridicule, its poetic mate takes on the same overtones.

מִרְבָּה לְהָכִיל:—The feminine noun מִרְבָּה is a hapax meaning "much" (BDB, under the root רבה). Many advocate repointing it to מַרְבָּה, the Hiphil feminine singular participle.[27] However, in my judgment, there is insufficient reason to make even that minor change. If one takes the hapax as simply that, a word otherwise unattested in the Bible but not necessarily suspect for that reason, we get a literal translation of "the magnitude to hold (much)" or the like, that is, simply a further description of the cup.

23:33 The LXX attests only one of the two synonymous terms שַׁמָּה וּשְׁמָמָה. This is the only place שַׁמָּה appears in Ezekiel, while it is common in Jeremiah. Ezekiel usually prefers the phrase שְׁמָמָה וּמְשַׁמָּה (6:14; 33:28, 29; 35:3) and uses שְׁמָמָה a total of twenty-one times. For those reasons many consider שַׁמָּה here to be an addition.[28] But it is almost a dispute about nothing: all three words are derivatives of שׁמם and virtually synonymous, and this is far from the only instance of stylistic variation in Ezekiel.

שֹׁמְרוֹן is missing in the original text of LXX codex Vaticanus,[29] but Block observes that it makes an assonantal inclusio for the strophe: שֹׁמְרוֹן ... שִׁכָּרוֹן.[30]

23:34 וְאֶת־חֲרָשֶׂיהָ תְּגָרֵמִי—I have translated this as "you will gnaw its shards." The verb גָּרַם is rare, and its other uses are of debatable meaning. It is probably a denominative from גֶּרֶם, "bone," hence perhaps basically "break bones." In Num 24:8, it is paralleled by אָכַל, "eat." Of the ancient versions, only the Vulgate translates in such a sense here; the others seem not to understand it at all. The picture seems to be that

---

[25] Block, *Ezekiel*, 1:755.

[26] See, for example, Zimmerli, *Ezekiel*, 1:477; Allen, *Ezekiel*, 2:44.

[27] Greenberg, *Ezekiel*, 2:483, takes it as merely "an unusual variant" of that form and points to a possible analogy in 2 Chr 24:7 (מַרְשַׁעַת for מְרֻשַּׁעַת).

[28] E.g., Zimmerli, *Ezekiel*, 1:477.

[29] Zimmerli, *Ezekiel*, 1:477, takes it as possibly "an old interpretative addition."

[30] Block, *Ezekiel*, 1:755.

of breaking the ceramic cup and attempting to suck out any wine that had soaked into the vessel. Various emendations are proposed, but all are arbitrary.

וְשָׁדַיִךְ תְּנַתֵּקִי—This clause is grotesque. Some translations soften the meaning of נָתַק to merely "tear at, lacerate," but the other passages with the verb overwhelmingly indicate a stronger meaning, "tear out, pull out," although it may be hyperbolic here.

23:36 וַיֹּאמֶר יְהוָה אֵלַי—This introductory clause, "Yahweh said to me," is unique in Ezekiel, although it is common in Deuteronomy (spoken by Moses) and Jeremiah. It is only the first of a series of stylistic (and text-critical) difficulties in this final section of the chapter (23:36–49), where the influence of chapter 16 is more evident than before. One challenge is the alternation between third person (generally plural) narrative (23:36b–40a, 42–48) and the second singular of direct address (23:40b–41, 49). To critics that can only mean that the passage is a pastiche of contributions from many hands. But Block is more on target when he understands them "to reflect the tension between the prophet's roles as recipient and as transmitter of the divine message."[31]

This section divides itself into the same two parts as the preceding section: (1) a statement of the charges (23:36–45) and (2) the announcement of the punishment (23:46–49).

הֲתִשְׁפּוֹט ... וְהַגֵּד—As in 20:4 and 22:2, the interrogative particle (הֲ-) with the verb תִשְׁפּוֹט ("will you arraign?") is, in effect, an indignant affirmative imperative for the prophet: "arraign!" This is confirmed by the following imperative (Hiphil of נָגַד), "make known." As in the parallel verses, only Yahweh can finally execute judgment, so "arraign" is a more appropriate translation for שָׁפַט in this context than "judge."

תוֹעֲבוֹתֵיהֶן:—The abstract "their abominations" is concrete in import: "abominable acts."

23:39 וּבְשַׁחֲטָם אֶת־בְּנֵיהֶם לְגִלּוּלֵיהֶם—The masculine pronouns on the verb (infinitive of שָׁחַט) and the nouns are unexpected. Until now feminine forms have been used to refer to the two sisters, but now in this verse masculine forms are used. The metaphor of the sisters recedes while Yahweh speaks literally of the Israelites they represented.

23:40 וְאַף כִּי תִשְׁלַחְנָה—"Furthermore" translates אַף כִּי, not the same as the phrase so translated in 23:38. Another episode in wild living is thus introduced. Gender and number are especially inconsistent through 23:44. In 23:36b–40a we had third plural, 23:40b–41 has second singular, 23:42a third singular, 23:42b third plural, 23:43–44a third singular, with 23:44b third plural again. It is as though the prophet's mind flits from the metaphor of the woman to what she represents.

The verb תִשְׁלַחְנָה could be either third or second feminine plural. The first option seems more likely. The imperfect form represents an old preterit of a type that is especially common in poetry.

בָּאִים—The use of this participle instead of an infinitive construct to express purpose ("to come") may reflect Aramaic influence.

לַאֲשֶׁר רָחָצְתְּ—This use of a preposition with אֲשֶׁר in this sense (literally, *"for whom* you bathed") is very rare. We might have expected לָהֶם, "for them," but the

---

[31] Block, *Ezekiel*, 1:756.

sense is the same. Beginning with רָחַצְתְּ (Qal perfect of רָחַץ), the verbs suddenly are singular (second feminine) again.

כָּחַלְתְּ עֵינָיִךְ—The verb כָּחַל is technically a hapax, although we know the verb from outside the Bible. It is obviously related to "kohl" (כֹּחַל in extrabiblical Hebrew), a preparation still used in the Near East to darken the edges of the eyelids. Since the preceding clause had a perfect referring to the past (רָחַצְתְּ), we might have expected imperfect verbs with *waw* consecutive to continue to refer to the past, instead of the perfect כָּחַלְתְּ (and the following perfect וְעָדִית). The non-use of the *waw* consecutive, whose use is a characteristic feature of classical Hebrew, may be a sign of the gradual loss of that idiom in later OT books. It disappears entirely in postbiblical Hebrew.

23:41 וְיָשַׁבְתְּ עַל־מִטָּה כְבוּדָּה—It is not easy to find a good English equivalent for מִטָּה because of cultural differences. One must have a mental picture of ancient oriental (and Greco-Roman) dining customs to understand the passage. The word here can mean "bed," but that would probably be misleading. "Couch" is usually the preferred alternative. What Yahweh is referring to here is probably something like the Greco-Roman triclinium, a couch specifically for reclining at meals and extending around three sides of a table. We see similar scenes in Assyrian art.[32]

Its modifying feminine adjective, כְבוּדָּה, "glorious" (BDB, s.v. כָּבוֹד I), occurs only here and in Ps 45:14 (ET 45:13), where the identical feminine form refers to a princess in bridal array. Presumably, the masculine form would be the same as the common noun כָּבוֹד, "glory." Greenberg compares the form of the feminine adjective to עֲרֻמָּה, from עָרוֹם.[33] In this context, "glorious" would mean something like "covered with glorious cushions," as the Targum paraphrases the word. Many commentators,[34] citing the LXX, emend to רְבוּדָה, "decked, spread," the root used of the seductive action of the strange woman in Prov 7:16. But both Greenberg[35] and Allen[36] contest that explanation of the LXX's translation. Letting the MT stand seems preferable.

עָלֶיהָ:—The feminine suffix would suggest the feminine noun מִטָּה ("couch") as its antecedent, but "incense" and "oil" more likely would have been placed on the "table," so שֻׁלְחָן must be the referent. While שֻׁלְחָן is usually masculine, its plural is usually ־וֹת, and as a neuter object, it could easily be expressed by a feminine in Hebrew. Hence, there is no reason to assume that the MT is erroneous.

23:42 The verse is anything but clear. The ancient versions are all over the place in their renditions. The phrase וְקוֹל הָמוֹן שָׁלֵו בָהּ is translated as "the noise of a carefree crowd was around her." קוֹל can mean "voice" but here probably has a broader meaning, "noise," since הָמוֹן always denotes a noisy, boisterous crowd or mob. שָׁלֵו, "carefree, heedless," must modify הָמוֹן. The Targum's paraphrase seems to wrest meaning from the phrase: "The sound of their noisy crowds was that of thoughtless unconcern

---

[32] See *ANEP*, § 451.

[33] Greenberg, *Ezekiel*, 2:486.

[34] E.g., Zimmerli, *Ezekiel*, 1:478.

[35] Greenberg, *Ezekiel*, 2:486.

[36] Allen, *Ezekiel*, 2:44.

in her midst." The import of the context seems to be that the banquet was open to the public. Keil tries to press the phrase to mean "the loud noise became still threat,"[37] but such a thought accords with neither what precedes nor what follows.

וְאֶל־אֲנָשִׁים מֵרֹב אָדָם—This phrase is also difficult. It seems to mean, literally, "to men from [out of?] a multitude of humanity." This phrase seems to repeat, in effect, the previous statement: large numbers of people from the general population. KJV, NKJV, and RSV have "(the) men of the common sort." NRSV introduces the idea of "the rabble," but this goes beyond the text. I have translated it as "in addition to the large throng of ordinary people," and the additional people who are brought "to" (וְאֶל) them are in the next phrase.

מוּבָאִים סׇבָאִים מִמִּדְבָּר—To the crowd in the preceding phrase additional men "were brought" (מוּבָאִים), the Hophal masculine plural participle of בּוֹא. Apparently they were invited (23:40). They were "from the desert" (מִמִּדְבָּר).

Who came? The Qere is סָבָאִים, "Sabeans," a people, perhaps nomadic, mentioned elsewhere only in Is 45:14. The OT also twice refers to a place called "Seba" (Is 43:3; Ps 72:10), which should not be confused with "Sheba"; the Hebrew sibilants are unrelated, and Ps 72:10 distinguishes the two places. Many English translations assume that both שְׁבָאִים in Joel 4:8 (ET 3:8) and שְׁבָא in Job 1:15 also refer to the "Sabeans." They are associated with the Arabian desert, which accords with מִמִּדְבָּר, "from the desert."

However, the Kethib is סוֹבָאִים. That seems to be the plural of a hapax noun meaning "drunkard" (so BDB, s.v. סָבָא [II]). The consonantal text could also be vocalized as סֹבְאִים, the Qal masculine plural participle of the verb סָבָא, "drink, be drunk," whose participle elsewhere means "drunkard" (Deut 21:20; Prov 23:20–21). That meaning could hardly fit the context better.

וַיִּתְּנוּ—This third masculine plural (Qal imperfect of נָתַן with *waw* consecutive) normally would imply that it is the men who "put" ornaments on the women. In an atmosphere of carousal, that would hardly be out of the question. However, in the light of the general preference for masculine forms instead of feminine ones, especially in later Hebrew, the subject might be the women, who here would continue their self-adornment as described already in 23:40. In either case, the bracelets and crowns are probably to be understood as payment or reward for sexual services. My translation ("they put") reproduces the ambiguity of the original.

23:43 This verse is even more difficult than the preceding one, and its end is almost unintelligible. Zimmerli does not even attempt a translation,[38] and Greenberg says: "Any rendering is guesswork."[39] The ancient versions seem to have had the MT in front of them, but their translations make little sense. When one surveys the wide variety of modern commentaries and translations, one must sometimes at least regard some of them as monuments to exegetical despair and ingenuity.

---

[37] Keil, *Ezekiel*, 1:332, 335–36.

[38] Zimmerli, *Ezekiel*, 1:479.

[39] Greenberg, *Ezekiel*, 2:486.

וָאֹמַר לַבָּלָה נְאוּפִים—"Then I said" may introduce this verse as spoken by Ezekiel since וָאֹמַר sometimes introduces speech by the prophet (e.g., 4:14; 9:8, 11:13; 21:5 [ET 20:49]), but it can also be spoken by Yahweh (e.g., 16:6; 20:7, 8, 13, 18). This verse comments on only one woman, whereas 23:42 had ended with a plurality of women. A shift from plural to singular (or vice versa) is not unusual in this section, as noted earlier. לַבָּלָה is the preposition לְ and the definite article attached to בָּלָה, the feminine of the adjective בָּלֶה, "worn out," used elsewhere for worn-out clothing (Josh 9:4–5). It derives from the verb בָּלָה, which can be used of an old, worn-out woman; Sarah uses it for herself in Gen 18:12. The plural noun נְאוּפִים, "adulteries," is used elsewhere only in Jer 13:27. Greenberg cites a rabbinical record of Aquila's otherwise lost Greek translation of the phrase here as παλαιὰ πόρνη, "old [= worn-out] whore."[40]

עַתָּ יִזְנֶה תַזְנוּתֶהָ וָהִיא:—The Qere for the first two words is עַתָּה יִזְנוּ, "now [her whorings/whoredom, תַזְנוּתֶהָ] will go whoring." The Kethib of the first word, עַתָּ, lacks the usual final vowel letter *he*. עַתָּ (with the same Qere) appears in the OT elsewhere only in Ps 74:6 but is common in ancient extrabiblical writing. Meaning is not involved.

The second Qere is more substantive. The Kethib is apparently the masculine singular (Qal imperfect) יִזְנֶה, "he will whore." The Qere is the masculine plural (also Qal imperfect), "they will whore," which fits better if the subject is the abstract plural noun, "her whorings/whoredom" (תַזְנוּתֶהָ), although that noun is feminine. Alternatively, the plural noun could be the object of the verb, "they whore her whorings," but that makes less sense.

With either the Kethib or Qere, the final וָהִיא, "and she," remains obscure. Without adding something, the final וָהִיא stands alone, either at the beginning of a statement lost in transmission or in the prophet's sudden change of mind. For better or for worse, I am indebted in my translation to Keil, who seems to me to make the best of the situation. He follows the Kethib and takes תַזְנוּתֶהָ ("her whorings/whoredom") as the subject of the verb, not its object. He argues that in Hebrew idiom the abstract feminine plural noun could be the subject of a preceding masculine verb. And the pendant וָהִיא he construes as emphasizing both the noun and its suffix.[41] It is reflected in my translation: "now her whoredom *itself* will go whoring." This exegesis is certainly not beyond challenge, but the burden of proof is on other interpretations (too many even to list here) to demonstrate their superiority. It is certainly better than regarding it all as gibberish and simply leaving a blank.

23:44 וַיָּבוֹא אֵלֶיהָ כְּבוֹא אֶל־אִשָּׁה זוֹנָה—The subject of the singular verb (Qal of בּוֹא) must be the (plural) men in 23:42 and the preceding verses. וַיָּבוֹא was followed by a plural subject (אֲנָשִׁים) in 14:1; see the textual note there. In both places, the marginal Masoretic note (a *sebir*) warns against emending the verb to the plural. The versions and the Dead Sea fragment of Ezekiel (4QEz^a) have a plural verb, which translators

---

[40] Greenberg, *Ezekiel*, 2:486, citing *Midrash Rabbah Leviticus*, 33.6 (on Lev 25:14).

[41] Keil, *Ezekiel*, 1:337.

and scribes would naturally prefer to smooth out the grammar. The idiom בּוֹא אֶל, twice in this clause (כְּבוֹא is the infinitive with כְּ), is the common biblical idiom for sexual congress. Both times I have freely rendered it "used" because that appears to be the import of this language in the present context. See the commentary.

Note the switch in number from the singular ("her") in the first half of the verse to the plural ("women") in the second half.

אִשֹּׁת הַזִּמָּה:—Only here in the OT is אִשֹּׁת, "women," used as the plural of אִשָּׁה. The normal plural is נָשִׁים. However, this form is known from Phoenician, as well as from an Akkadian cognate.

23:45 וַאֲנָשִׁים צַדִּיקִם הֵמָּה יִשְׁפְּטוּ אוֹתְהֶם—Hebrew often uses a resumptive pronoun (here הֵמָּה) for emphasis and/or contrast: "righteous men, *they* will punish them." The verb שָׁפַט is translated "punish," not "judge," for in Ezekiel, the latter prerogative is reserved for God, and human agents merely execute the verdict. The form of the direct object, אוֹתְהֶם (אֵת with third masculine plural suffix), is thoroughly irregular according to the canons of classical Hebrew. First, we would expect a feminine (third plural) suffix (הֶן-). Second, the retention of the *holem* (אוֹ-) with a biconsonantal suffix (הֶם-) is unique. In the next verse, the expected אֶתְהֶן occurs, but in 23:47 we have אוֹתְהֶן, with a feminine suffix but also with a *holem*, again unique. The use of masculine suffixes where feminine ones would be expected peaks in 23:45–49, and they regularly alternate in 23:46–47. Greenberg comments: "It is as though the copyist preserved maximal variants in a text tradition that vacillated on such fine points."[42] In chapter 1 too, there was much vacillation and inconsistency in grammatical gender.

23:46 הַעֲלֵה עֲלֵיהֶם קָהָל—The verb הַעֲלֵה may be the Hiphil imperative of עָלָה, but since the Qal infinitive absolute נָתֹן follows, it is probably best to construe הַעֲלֵה too as an infinitive absolute. In either case, it means "bring (up)." Since infinitive absolutes often function as lapidary shorthand for any form of the finite verb, it falls to the translator to decide which inflected form is implied here. KJV opted for first singular imperfect, implying Yahweh as the speaker ("I will bring up"). Beginning with RSV, however, modern translations (including NIV) prefer to understand the words as imperatives, apparently with Yahweh speaking to some unidentified executioners (like those in chapter 9). However, the actual executioners are the "army" (קָהָל), the stated object in the text, and thus an imperative requires awkward redundancy (executioners would bring up the army). There ultimately will not be much difference in meaning in either case, but in my judgment, a smoother reading is achieved by choosing a first person reading: "I will bring an army against them." This connects naturally with the first person verb of 23:48.

The general noun קָהָל, "company, assembly," is translated "army." The same noun was used in a similar context in 23:24, as already in 16:40. The picture in the context is as much of a mob as of a disciplined army, but on the other hand, קָהָל does imply an orderly group, so "army" remains the best rendition.

---

[42] Greenberg, *Ezekiel*, 2:487.

לְזַעֲוָה—The noun זַעֲוָה, "terror," occurs here and in Deut 28:25, to which Ezekiel may be alluding. It also is the Qere in four verses in Jeremiah and one in 1 Chronicles, in those verses the Kethib is זְוָעָה, which also occurs in Is 28:19. Both nouns are related to the verb זוּעַ, "to tremble with fear."

23:47 This verse repeats much of 23:25 but with more intensity.

וְרָגְמוּ עֲלֵיהֶן אֶבֶן קָהָל—The collective and anarthrous noun קָהָל, "army," must be the subject of both רָגְמוּ and the Piel infinitive absolute in the next clause, וּבָרֵא. The anarthrous form and position of קָהָל led to theories that רָגְמוּ was originally an infinitive absolute, רָגֹם.[43] But in the light of all the other idiosyncrasies of the context, so convoluted a text history need not be theorized. רָגַם, "to stone," is normally used with אֶבֶן ("stone") as an adverbial accusative: "to stone with stones." The redundancy need not be reproduced in English. The same will be true of שָׂרַף with אֵשׁ ("burn with fire") at the end of the verse.

וּבָרֵא אוֹתְהֶן בְּחַרְבוֹתָם—The Piel of בָּרָא (here the infinitive absolute) is ordinarily used of chopping down trees in clearing forests. See the last textual note on 21:24 (ET 21:19), where its Piel imperative is used twice. Its use here is vivid and more forceful than כָּרַת or another verb for "cut." The corresponding verse in chapter 16 used בָּתֵק, "slaughter" (16:40).

23:48 וְהִשְׁבַּתִּי—"Remove" is used to translate the Hiphil (first common singular perfect with *waw* consecutive) of שָׁבַת because of the following מִן. The Hiphil of this verb usually means "to make cease, put an end to."

וְנִוַּסְּרוּ—This is a Nithpael (third common plural perfect with *waw* consecutive) of יָסַר, meaning "be disciplined, corrected" (BDB) or "take warning." This conjugation resembles both a Niphal and a Hithpael: it combines the *nun* preformative of the Niphal with Hithpael vocalization. In place of וְנִתְוַסְּרוּ, the ת of the prefix has been assimilated and is marked by the *daghesh* in the consonantal *waw* (-וַּ-). See GKC, § 55 k; Joüon, § 59 f. The only other Nithpaels in the OT are נְכַּפֵּר, "be atoned for," in Deut 21:8, and נִשְׁתַּוָּה in Prov 27:15. In Mishnaic Hebrew, it became a regular conjugation. Like the Hithpael, it can have a reflexive, middle, or passive sense.

כְּזִמַּתְכֶנָה:—This is the noun זִמָּה, "lewdness," with the preposition כְּ and the longer, infrequently used second feminine plural suffix כֶנָה- that recurs on the same word in 23:49 (זִמַּתְכֶנָה).

23:49 Literal translations of the first two clauses do not communicate well in English, so I have been relatively free.

וְנָתְנוּ זִמַּתְכֶנָה עֲלֵיכֶן—This is, literally, "they will lay your lewdness upon you." The idiom נָתַן עַל, meaning "impose [a penalty] upon," was used already in 7:3. It does not merely mean "charge you with." If we remember that the implied subjects here ("they") are the executioners in 23:47, the topic is not the activity of a plaintiff or a judge, but of those who carry out the penalty.

---

[43] Zimmerli, *Ezekiel*, 1:480, and Allen, *Ezekiel*, 2:45. The theory is that the finite verb in the MT arose by parallel assimilation to 16:40 and קָהָל was a later gloss added to clarify the subject of the verb in the MT.

וַחֲטָאֵי גִלּוּלֵיכֶן תִּשֶּׂאינָה—This clause too requires supplying words in English: "you will bear [the punishment for] the sins of your fecal deities." Elsewhere Ezekiel uses נָשָׂא with the object עָוֹן, "bear punishment/iniquity" (4:4–6; 14:10; 44:10; see also 18:19–20). Here the object is the plural (in construct) of חֵטְא, "sin," the only occurrence in Ezekiel of this masculine noun, which is virtually synonymous with עָוֹן. The problem lies in capturing the sense of the construct chain וַחֲטָאֵי גִלּוּלֵיכֶן. Obviously, it is not the "fecal deities" who have "sin," so it is not a subjective genitive, but a sort of objective genitive. Since חֵטְא here is no mere abstraction, but the rites and deeds associated with reverence for the גִלּוּלִים, I have translated, "your sinful worship of your fecal deities."

וִידַעְתֶּם כִּי אֲנִי אֲדֹנָי יְהוִה:—Of the around eighty uses in the OT of the recognition formula, "(Then) you/they will know that I am (the Lord) Yahweh," this is one of only five times where אֲדֹנָי precedes the Tetragrammaton. The other four are in 13:9; 24:24; 28:24; 29:16. If the addition makes any difference at all, it makes for a stronger, more emphatic statement.

Commentary

That chapter 23 is a sort of sequel to chapter 16 is obvious. In both, sexual imagery is pressed almost to the limit—in about the same hyperbolic way Ezekiel treats other topics. Chapter 23 is commonly judged to go beyond chapter 16 in this respect ("the locus classicus for bawdy vocabulary"[44]), but the question is debatable. It is probably coincidental that chapter 16 is the longest chapter in the book and chapter 23 is the second longest. But, it must be stressed, in both chapters the aim is not to titillate the audience with pornography, but to shock it, to dramatize how such behavior departed from Yahweh's will as sharply as the people's attitude toward him did in other respects.

If this historical and theological context is borne in mind, feminist critiques of this chapter prove to be as beside the point as they were of chapter 16. It is anything but a case of blaming the victim for something domineering males forced upon them. It is clear in the text that the two "sisters" were not only willing "victims," but took the initiative in what is usually and more accurately described as nymphomania—a metaphor here of a theological pathology. Ezekiel's audience, male and female alike, surely agreed with his pillorying of such behavior. As Greenberg summarizes:

> The feminist project, promoting a new female reality, necessarily clashes with Scripture—one of the fashioners of the reality to be superseded. At bottom, what feminists criticize is not what the texts meant to those who composed and received them in their historical context. ... Ezekiel is but a negative countertext, whose male-centered agenda must be exposed and disarmed in terms of today's values, psychology, and anthropology.[45]

---

[44] Block, *Ezekiel*, 1:729.

[45] Greenberg, *Ezekiel*, 2:494.

For all the surface similarities between chapters 16 and 23, the basic imagery of sexual promiscuity is developed in different ways, some of which we can best note as we go along. The most obvious one is that whereas Jerusalem's "sister," Samaria, is mentioned in chapter 16 only in passing, here an entire section (23:5–10) is devoted to her, although the overwhelming concentration of chapter 23 remains on Jerusalem. It is generally agreed that the focus of chapter 23 is much more on political entanglements, in contrast to the greater concern in chapter 16 with cultic "whoredom"—although the two often went hand in hand in the ancient world. And, perhaps, most notably of all, while chapter 16 had closed with the eschatological note of the great reversal and a new covenant, here there is no hint of that in chapter 23—only judgment (Law). At most, other women are to learn a lesson (23:48), even if Oholibah did not, but that is hardly Gospel kerygma.

Redaction-critical gamesmanship has exercised itself sufficiently on the chapter, and a few problems occasioning such critiques will be considered passim. Generally speaking, 23:36–49 is commonly considered a secondary addition. Zimmerli allows only parts of twenty-one verses (all in 23:1–27) to be authentic,[46] and there are even more radical voices.

As the book stands, it may be divided simply into a main oracle (23:1–35) and a subordinate one dependent on it (23:36–49). In slightly more detail, we may distinguish (1) an introduction in 23:1–4; (2) the fate of Oholah in 23:5–10; (3) the fate of Oholibah in 23:11–35; and (4) a review of the profligacy of both sisters and the judgment on both (23:36–49). Various further subdivisions are possible, of course.

Finally by way of introduction, we should note the common opinion that this chapter in Ezekiel was inspired by Jer 3:6–11. Although Ezekiel greatly expands on his compatriot's oracle and develops it in somewhat different ways, there is enough commonality in vocabulary and diction that the connection seems undeniable. We shall later note a similar relationship between Jer 23:1–4 and Ezekiel 34.

Oracle about the Lewd Sisters (23:1–35)

Introduction (23:1–4)

23:1–2 Other than the usual word-event formula[47] and God's continuing address of Ezekiel as "son of man,"[48] the chapter opens abruptly without any charge to the prophet to speak or to set his face against someone (as in, e.g., 4:3; 13:17). In fact, the use of the third person until 23:21 indicates that Yahweh is depicted as simply narrating to the prophet a rhetorical account of the lives of the two sisters. The kingdoms of Israel and Judah are called "sisters"

---

[46] Zimmerli, *Ezekiel*, 1:480–81.

[47] For this formula, "The Word of Yahweh came to me," see page 8 in the introduction and the textual note on 3:16.

[48] See the second textual note and the commentary on 2:1.

because of their common origin in the patriarchal era and exodus redemption through the united kingdom of David and Solomon. No attempt is made to arouse sympathy for the sisters, as was the case with the "foundling" in the opening verses of chapter 16 (16:2–5). Neither is the character of the "mother" adduced to explain the debased character of the daughters, as was done in 16:44.

23:3 In chapter 16, Jerusalem's immorality had been traced back only to its roots in Canaan, but here the beginnings of the sisters' uncontrolled sexual appetites are located in their premarital (cf. the next verse) youth in Egypt. However, 20:7–12 had already referred to disobedience as early as the Egyptian period. There the accent was on idolatry, but 23:1–25 as a whole shows a greater interest in the political aspect of the relationship. In the metaphor here, the sisters are pictured as readily assenting to the Egyptian sexual advances and, once awakened, kept coming back for more the rest of their lives (23:8, 19–21). As noted earlier, it is fruitless to look for any specific historical referent, although there is no reason to doubt the main theological point: Yahweh elected the Israelites too while they were still sinners (Rom 5:8). Block plausibly suggests that Yahweh is putting "a political spin" on the Israelites' frequent longing backward glances at the fleshpots of Egypt while in the wilderness (e.g., Num 11:18).[49] In any case, Ezekiel's overriding concern is rhetorical and theological, not historical.

23:4 The simple assertion of marriage against the background given in 23:3 makes plain that the women were already given in venery (unlike the foundling of 16:8). The metaphor thus parallels Yahweh's command to Hosea to marry Gomer, "a woman of whoredom" (Hos 1:2), who may or may not be identical with the "adulteress" of Hosea 3, whom he is to "love" (Hos 3:1). This context heightens and gives poignancy to the expressions of Yahweh's wrath: he is a husband jealous for his marriage (explicit in the קִנְאָה, "zeal," of 23:25; see also Yahweh as "jealous" in Ex 20:5; 34:14; Deut 4:24; 5:9; 6:15). In general, though, the following verses stress not so much the sisters' unfaithfulness to their true husband as their promiscuous moving from one lover to another.

Like the woman of 16:20, the sisters here bear "sons and daughters" (23:4). These are not labeled as "children of whoredom" as Hosea's were (Hos 1:2), but apparently merely provide concrete proof that the marriage had been consummated.

It must surely strike the reader that the allegory depicts Yahweh as bigamous. There is archaeological evidence (Kuntillet ʿAjrud and Khirbet el-Kom) that demonstrates that there were syncretistic cults that depicted Yahweh as having an "Asherah" wife and perhaps other consorts.[50] But it must have been

---

[49] Block, *Ezekiel*, 1:734.

[50] See John S. Holladay, "Kom, Khirbet El-," *ABD* 4:98; William G. Dever, "Asherah, Consort of Yahweh? New Evidence from Kuntillet ʿAjrud," *BASOR* 255 (Summer 1984): 21–37.

common knowledge to the orthodox that Yahweh was beyond the realm of sexual activity. He alone is God, and there is no goddess. The only "wife" he takes is his people Israel in a metaphorical and theological sense, just as in the NT the church is the bride of Christ.

The Mosaic Torah permitted polygamy (Deut 21:15), although probably only a small minority could afford more than one wife. Yet this provision did not in any way reflect the character or behavior of their Deity. The best proof of this is that Ezekiel does not even bother to comment on that aspect of the picture. Like divorce, which the Torah also permitted, polygamy was not Yahweh's will, but the result of human sinfulness (cf. Mt 19:8; Mk 10:5).[51] So too, God called Israel to be one people (his one wife), and it was the northern tribes' rebellion against Judah and the Davidic monarchy (hence against Yahweh) that rent the people, leaving Yahweh with two "wives."

Obviously—and the prophet's audience would have had no trouble understanding this—the image is constructed artificially as the allegory required. In the background probably stands the assumption, which all the prophets seem to share, that "Israel" was really one undivided people of God, even though politically the people had been divided into two kingdoms for centuries, as well as the assumption that at least eschatologically their primal unity would be restored (Ezek 37:15–28). Likewise, the far greater division between Jew and Gentile is overcome in Christ, and eschatologically all believers without distinction shall be part of the one new Jerusalem (Gal 3:26–29; 4:26; Heb 12:22; Revelation 21).

The assumption of Israel's unity may even give us a clue to the much debated question of what the names "Oholah" and "Oholibah" meant. Since "Israel" for Ezekiel meant the whole people of God, some device was needed to suggest that as siblings they were distinct, yet one. Some have noted that in Hebrew both Oholah (אָהֳלָה) and Samaria (שֹׁמְרוֹן) have two syllables, while Oholibah (אָהֳלִיבָה) and Jerusalem (the older יְרוּשָׁלֵם without the final diphthong) both have three syllables. Allen compares the matching quality of the names to "Tweedledum" and "Tweedledee," that is, entities that are practically indistinguishable.[52] All of these observations regard the names as purely artificial constructs without intrinsic meaning.

If the possible parallel in Jer 3:11 is pertinent, there the two sisters are labeled מְשֻׁבָה יִשְׂרָאֵל, "backsliding Israel," and בֹּגֵדָה יְהוּדָה, "treacherous Judah." That may suggest that we are to look for some meaning in Ezekiel's names also.

By far the most common and traditional interpretation for Oholah (אָהֳלָה) and Oholibah (אָהֳלִיבָה) is to take אֹהֶל ("tent"), which is an element in both

---

[51] For a Christian perspective on polygamy in the OT compared to monogamy in the NT, one may see Mitchell, *The Song of Songs*, 120–27.

[52] Allen, *Ezekiel*, 2:48. Many scholars have adduced the similarity in the names of the sons of the caliph Ali (son-in-law of Muhammad): Hasan and Hussein.

names,[53] as a reference to the אֹהֶל מוֹעֵד, "tent of meeting," a common designation of the wilderness tabernacle (e.g., Exodus 29–30; 38–40). Oholah then means "her [own] tent," indicative of the unsanctioned worship of the northern kingdom at the idolatrous shrines in Dan and Bethel. Similarly, but with the opposite theological implication, Oholibah means "my tent [is] in her," which refers to the temple in Jerusalem (successor to the tabernacle) as the legitimate place where Yahweh caused his name to dwell, even though it was currently contaminated by the people's uncleanness.

Initially, this understanding makes good sense, even though it has minor difficulties. First of all, the thrust of the chapter is not the disparagement of the northern kingdom—in fact, at times, the southern kingdom is depicted as worse (23:11). Second, Ezekiel refers to the Jerusalem sanctuary as an אֹהֶל only once elsewhere, in 41:1, in his eschatological vision. Third, if the ה at the end of both names is the third feminine singular pronominal suffix ("her"), it should have a *mappiq* in it, but it does not. An example of the expected usage with *mappiq* is illustrated by the name חֶפְצִי־בָהּ, "Hephzibah," meaning "my delight is in her," in 2 Ki 21:1 and Is 62:4. As Oholah and Oholibah are written, they could simply be two undeclined feminine nouns (feminine apparently because they refer to cities or countries).

Hence, other proposals have been made, although none has a wide following. With a slight revocalization, Oholah may be translated "a tenter, one who has a tent." For Oholibah, instead of the pronoun "my," the *yod* in אָהֳלִיבָה may be taken as a paragogic or companionate letter (*yod compaginis*), added perhaps for rhythmic reasons (although grammarians attach those labels when they have no other explanation). If so, Oholibah may simply mean "a tent in her." Both names can be heard as rebukes for pagan tents or high places. But this is clearly strained.

Another counsel of desperation is to connect the names somehow with the אֹהֶל of 2 Sam 16:22, where the reference is to a marriage tent (wherein Absalom slept with David's concubines). Such an association accords with the flavor of chapter 23, but otherwise is a long shot.

Finally, we may mention Zimmerli, who argues that the names are evocative of tent-dwelling shepherds (in contrast to the Egyptians) and points to other early Israelite names formed from אֹהֶל: Oholibamah, the name of one of Esau's wives (Gen 36:2) as well as the chief of an Edomite tribe (Gen 36:40–41), and Oholiab, a Danite (Ex 31:6).[54] However, "Ohel" formations appear also in other periods (e.g., Ohel, a descendant of Zerubbabel, 1 Chr 3:19–20), and they are known in the onomastica of Israel's Phoenician neighbors. Hence, even if true, this interpretation does not carry us very far.

---

[53] With the addition of the suffixes (-אָהֳל), the *holem* in אֹהֶל is reduced to the short "o" vowel, *qamets chatuph* (-אָ), and the composite *shewa* under the *he* likewise has *chateph qamets* (-הֳ-).

[54] Zimmerli, *Ezekiel*, 1:483–84.

I must confess that I retain an emotional preference for the common traditional understanding, in spite of its problems, although it cannot be demonstrated or insisted upon. To my ears, the fact that Yahweh's "tent" (tabernacle) was in Jerusalem contributes to the chapter's later judgment that Jerusalem's behavior was even worse than Samaria's (23:11–21).

The Whorings and Judgment of Oholah (23:5–10)

Accusation of Oholah's Whorings (23:5–8)

23:5–7 Oholah "has taste; she is infatuated particularly by Assyria's upper crust."[55] Not exactly run-of-the-mill camp followers, the northern Israelites might more easily be compared with the groupies surrounding the modern entertainment demimonde. Several examples of men of higher rank whom Oholibah might find "desirable" are listed. Some translations render בַּחוּרֵי חֶמֶד as "handsome young men," but in this context that is probably too weak. The noun חֶמֶד ("desire") is from the verb חָמַד, which is used in the Ninth and Tenth Commandments (Ex 20:17; Deut 5:21a; Deut 5:21b uses the synonym הִתְאַוָּה) and which implies an inordinate "coveting" of someone or something. Here the accent is on the young men's potential for satisfying the woman's insatiable lust. In chapter 16, the accent had been that the woman capitalized on her beauty, and there Yahweh's rivals are idols. Here the paramours are human, and the accent is on the physical attractiveness of young men, and all the more if they possessed power and wealth.

But with that understanding, the fourfold כֹּל, "all," in 23:6–7 emphasizes Oholah's total lack of discrimination or restraint. Ezek 23:7b combines religious with political promiscuity (as 16:26–29 had added the political to the religious). In the ancient world, the two went hand in glove to such an extent that there is not the slightest reason to doubt their virtual synonymity.

23:8 In his very brief summary (23:5–10), Ezekiel has completely passed over most of Israel's history from the sojourn in Egypt (nineteenth–fifteenth centuries B.C.) to the Assyrian period (ninth–seventh centuries B.C.) shortly before his own day. But here he reminds his audience that his historical omission does not imply any hiatus in Oholah's unrestrained adulteries.

It is not easy to specify what historical occasions Ezekiel had in mind in this broadside against Oholah in 23:5–8. Generally, the northern kingdom was anti-Assyrian in political posture, like most of the neighboring Levantine countries threatened by the Assyrian juggernaut. A classic illustration is Ahab's leadership in the coalition opposing Shalmaneser III at the great battle at Qarqar on the Orontes in 853. There were occasional exceptions, however. About twelve years later, when the coalition dissolved, Jehu voluntarily submitted to and paid tribute to Shalmaneser for protection from Hazael of Damascus, as recorded on the famous Black Obelisk.[56] Similarly, a little over a century later,

---

[55] Block, *Ezekiel*, 1:738.

[56] *ANEP*, §§ 351, 355.

Menahem bought off Tiglath-Pileser III in 738 (2 Ki 15:19–20). But in 722, after a final rebellion *against* Assyria, Samaria is wiped off the map by Shalmaneser V, and the population deported by his successor, Sargon II. Similar to his broad strokes in previous chapters, it appears that Ezekiel has generalized Israel's occasional flirtations with Assyria into characteristic behavior.

The Judgment upon Oholah (23:9–10)

23:9–10 These two verses summarize briefly the result of Oholah's behavior. It is a short version of 16:35–43, which announced the judgment of Jerusalem the whore. More immediately, it is also a briefer version of the much longer judgment oracle on the sister Oholibah in 23:22–35. Ezek 23:9 puts the punishment in theological perspective, and 23:10 summarizes it historically. Since Oholah's desire for Assyrian "love" cannot be slaked, Yahweh gives her what she thinks she wants, but what she gets turns out to be a total travesty. It is Yahweh who causes those she pursued so avidly to become the agents of his judgment. 2 Kings 17 is a long theological meditation on the same events, as Samaria is obliterated, her citizens deported, and non-Israelites brought in as replacements. The turn of events here reminds one of the primordial sin in paradise: the temptation to "be like God, knowing good and evil" (Gen 3:5) is satisfied in a sense, but in a vastly different way than anticipated (Gen 3:22–23).

The Fate of Oholibah (23:11–35)

From 23:11 through 23:35, we have Ezekiel's indictment of Oholibah, the sister, Jerusalem. That the prophet's major concern lies here rather than with the long-gone northern kingdom is evident in the far greater number of verses used: twenty-five for Oholibah (23:11–35) versus only six for Oholah (23:5–10). In spite of the larger number of verses, the overall structure of the two units is parallel: (1) a presentation of the charges, 23:11–21, corresponding to 23:5–8, and (2) the sentence pronounced, 23:22–35, corresponding to 23:9–10.

Accusation of Oholibah's Whorings (23:11–21)

23:11 In very strong language, 23:11 states the thesis that Oholibah had not learned anything from her sister's fate and far exceeded her in flagrancy. The succeeding verses expand upon that thesis.

23:12–13 At first, the point is established that Oholibah veered off the straight and narrow path in essentially the same way that her sister had. Her inordinate affection for Assyria is described in 23:12 in virtually the same language as that describing Oholah (23:5). The historical referent is again uncertain, and, as usual in Ezekiel's "surveys," we cannot always find clear correspondences. In this case, the clearest reference appears to be Ahaz's appeal to Tiglath-Pileser III for help against Pekah of Israel and Rezin of Damascus (2 Ki 16:5–20). This fateful move was forcefully denounced by Isaiah (chapter 7), the backdrop of the prophecy of Immanuel (Is 7:14). There the accent is not so much on Israel's errant "love" as on her placing her trust in human machinations instead of in Yahweh's sure promise (although ultimately the two sins amount to the same thing). Nevertheless, Israel's misplaced faith would not prevent the fulfillment of the promise of Immanuel to be born of a virgin—Jesus Christ (Is 7:14; Mt 1:23; cf. Is 8:8; 9:5 [ET 9:6]).

23:14–16   With 23:14, the theme enunciated in 23:11 is taken up again, namely, that Oholibah's behavior is even more outré than Oholah's.[57]

Ezek 23:14 illustrates how flighty and fickle Oholibah is. To judge from Ezekiel's portrayal, she shifts her affections from the Assyrians to the Babylonians without a thought. The historical occasion remains opaque. 2 Ki 20:12–21 records the cordial reception Hezekiah gave to the Babylonian rebel Merodach-Baladan, apparently making common cause against Assyria, but drawing a dire rebuke from Isaiah (39:5–8). The initiative here, however, appears to be from Jerusalem, and, if that can be pressed, could imply prior unrecorded overtures from Judah. Because of the greater detail given here, others think of something more recent. Zimmerli[58] and others think of Josiah's fatal attempt at Megiddo in 609 to intercept Pharaoh Neco's march north to Carchemish, and interpret it as implying that Josiah had cast his lot with Babylon as the certain successor to fallen Assyria. This is speculative in the extreme, however; Josiah's action is more commonly understood as an attempt to establish Judah's independence from any foreign hegemony.

We are not told where Oholibah saw the painted engravings of Babylonian officers, but as any handbook on Assyrian culture will amply illustrate, the verbal portraits here accord readily with sculptures and paintings on the inner walls of various Assyrian palaces at Kuyunjik (Nineveh), Khorsabad, Nimrud, and elsewhere. Presumably such art was common enough that Ezekiel and his fellow exiles might well have seen examples with their own eyes.

The escalation of Oholibah's degeneracy consists in the fact that she not only lusts for men in the flesh but is inflamed with passion by gazing at mere pictures of them. One gets the impression that almost any man might have served, but the magnificent and colorful garb of Babylonian officialdom, with its implications of power and wealth, intensified her craze.

Possibly, Oholibah's behavior would have seemed more bizarre to Ezekiel's audience than it does to modern readers. At the gutter level, such behavior probably has been a constant of fallen humanity. However, we cannot forget the extent to which pornography of all sorts has flooded our culture in especially the last generation, usually excused with an appeal to the First Amendment of the United States Constitution. Such abuse supports the dictum "patriotism is the last refuge of a scoundrel."[59] Traditionally, this means of sexual excitation has been associated with men more than women, but many strains

---

[57] This does not support the suspicion of Zimmerli, *Ezekiel*, 1:486, that 23:12–14a is only an "elaborative addition."

[58] Zimmerli, *Ezekiel*, 1:486.

[59] Samuel Johnson, April 7, 1775 (Boswell, *Life of Johnson*).

of feminism have made it at least as socially acceptable among women. Statistics confirm the tremendous profitability of the pornography industry, and the anonymity afforded by cable, the Internet, and so on has obviously emboldened many who previously abstained for fear of exposure. Only God knows how many "good" Christians and Lutherans are among them. Confession and absolution are an essential part of the needed treatment for this addictive behavior.

Ezek 23:16 confirms that pictures alone had aroused Oholibah so much that she invites the Babylonians to an orgy from afar.

23:17 The Babylonians are not at all reluctant to accept her invitation. But the relationship sours even more quickly than it began, implying not only fickleness on Judah's part, but emotional—and spiritual—instability as well. Again the most likely historical setting might be a shift from generally pro-Babylonian sentiments throughout the seventh century to rebellion against Babylon under Jehoiakim and Zedekiah, here metaphorized into a sudden shift in extramarital affections. Minus the sexual metaphor, some of the same situation is reflected in Habakkuk, which laments the substitution of Assyrian tyranny with Babylonian.

23:18 Because she flaunted her body so openly to multiple lovers, Yahweh reacts in a disgust comparable to her own recoil from Babylonian embrace (23:17). Ezekiel obviously pushes the metaphor of Israel as Yahweh's wife about as far as he dares. Biblical usage forbids attribution of sexual desire to Yahweh, but otherwise the metaphor of the covenant as a marriage is almost foundational in Scripture. If possible, the applicability of the metaphor to the church as the virgin bride of Christ is even stronger (e.g., 2 Cor 11:2–3).

23:19–21 These verses use nearly obscene imagery to bring the indictment to a climatic close. Jerusalem is depicted as caring not a wit about her progressive alienation from Yahweh, to the point of a complete rupture of the relationship on her side. She nostalgically reveals the frissons of her initiation into sex as a young girl in Egypt, and now, as an old, worn-out whore, she returns to the "house of bondage," as Egypt is frequently called (e.g., Ex 13:3, 14; 20:2), where her steady slide into incorrigible depravity had begun. The sudden use of direct address (second person, "you," 23:21) signals that the time of reckoning has come. The judgment in 23:22–35 parallels the sentence on the זוֹנָה, "whore," in 16:35–52.

The Judgment upon Oholibah (23:22–35)

23:22–23 The turning of the tables (often expressed in the phrase שׁוּב אֶת־שְׁבוּת, "bring about the restoration of" [16:53; 29:14; 39:25; see also, e.g., Deut 30:3; Jer 33:7, 11, 26]) is a common concept in the OT for God's redemptive (often eschatological) intervention on behalf of Israel; as Christians recognize, this climaxed on Good Friday and Easter. But God can also turn the tables in the other direction too. All those lovers whom Oholibah had so wantonly pursued are now roused by God to pursue her—in the judgment of invasion and war. The repetition in 23:23 of much of the earlier description of the "lovers" illustrates what a total turnabout it will be.

23:24 Previously, Oholibah was attracted by the luxurious garb of the nobility (23:12, 14–15; cf. 23:6), but now such men approach her hostilely in the full panoply of armaments. The emphasis that Yahweh allows the enemy, as his agents, to follow their own traditions, "according to their own standards" of justice, is intended to introduce the non-Israelite type of treatment of prisoners of war, which is described in the following verses.

23:25 The atrocities mentioned here are expanded somewhat in the next few verses. All of them are amply illustrated in Assyrian records, both in connection with war and with individual offenders, as the Israelites would have been well aware. What is more, the Assyrians typically boasted and gloated about their behavior. In general, the Babylonians were more humane conquerors than the Assyrians, but it was probably more of a difference in degree than in kind. The modern world is certainly no stranger to comparable "war crimes." Even if it is not official state policy, all kinds of horrors are typically perpetrated without official sanction by individuals or localized groups. It remains to be seen whether the Hague, the United Nations, and other international tribunals will succeed in achieving much long-term and global improvement.

It is hardly surprising that similar barbarism did occur in Israel's wars (e.g., 2 Ki 15:16), but the biblical sense of the sanctity of all human life and of ultimate accountability to the Creator seems to have tempered the impulse. The laws of חֵרֶם, the sacral ban to "destruction," as illustrated vividly in the case of Achan (Joshua 7) and applicable to entire groups (e.g., the verb הַחֲרֵם in Deut 7:2), should not be understood as on the same plane as Gentile savagery. It was of a piece with the laws governing "Yahweh's war": the intent was to keep Israel (both God's "church" and his state) free from syncretistic contamination, and there certainly was to be no gloating about it. Although Yahweh does not develop it in these terms in Ezekiel, it was precisely Israel's failure to keep such laws (as shown already in the book of Judges) that led to the extremities with which Yahweh had to deal. Freed from political considerations, the Christian church is charged with comparable injunctions not be "conformed to this world" (Rom 12:2), to keep oneself "unspotted from the world" (James 1:27), and so on, that is, the unending "Christ versus culture" challenge.

23:26 The same judgment as here was also described in 16:39 following a detailed account of the beautiful wardrobe Yahweh had given the foundling (see the commentary there). There are other biblical references to this common humiliation (Jer 13:22, 26; Hos 2:12 [ET 2:10]; Nah 3:5). It is especially associated with punishment for adultery, as here. The punishment matches the offense: as she had voluntarily bared herself to all her lovers, now they will forcefully and publicly strip her bare.

23:27 This last verse of the first phase of the indictment (23:22–27) envisions a total change in Oholibah's outlook. "Lift up … eyes" in this context probably has primary reference to amorous intent (as with Potiphar's wife in Gen 39:7). But the phrase can also imply "look for help" (Ps 121:1), and so Ezekiel with one phrase can also make reference to Jerusalem abandoning her current expectation of help from Egypt in the face of the Babylonian threat.

"Remember," as so often in biblical usage, refers not so much to mere memory of a bare fact as to an orientation or way of life in relation to something. In the context of this chapter, we think primarily of Jerusalem not remembering Egypt because of the obliteration of the northern kingdom in judgment. But if we peer between the lines, we may see a hint of the "new heart" and "new spirit," of which Ezekiel spoke in 11:19 and 18:31 and will speak about further in due time (36:25–27; see also the gift of the "Spirit" in 37:14; 39:29).

23:28 The second phase of the indictment (23:28–35) is supplemental to what has already been predicted. Ezek 23:28–30 largely reiterates previous material, but 23:31–34 returns to consider the sister, Oholah, and compare the fate of the two sisters.

In 23:28–29, the verb שָׂנֵא, "to hate," and the noun שִׂנְאָה, "hate," become prominent. They are an obvious foil to the repeated previous use of a participle of אָהַב, "love," for the women's "lovers" (23:5, 9, 22). "Your lovers" (מְאַהֲבַיִךְ, 23:22) could be ambiguous without its context: the suffix, "your," could be either an objective or subjective genitive, though the context showed that it was subjective; she sought out her paramours. However, even without context, there is no such ambiguity about "those you hate" (אֲשֶׁר שָׂנֵאת) in 23:28. Yet Yahweh will turn the tables again—with the devastating consequences described in the next two verses.

23:29–30 In these climactic verses reiterating Oholibah's sentence, note how Ezekiel is gradually easing into a linkage of the judgment on *both* sisters, which will continue throughout the rest of the chapter. In 23:29 Oholibah is stripped, robbed, and abandoned as Oholah had been (23:10). Her defilement with the idols of the nations—perhaps the images on the walls that had once infatuated her (23:13–16), which in principle had been Oholah's offense (23:7b)—is here for the first time asserted as Oholibah's offense as well.

23:31–32 Oholibah will be given the same "cup" of God's wrathful judgment (see the second textual note on 23:31) as Oholah because she had refused to learn her lesson from her sister's fate and instead had behaved in essentially the same way. As such, 23:32 is about the cup and its capaciousness. It takes little thought to realize that anyone who drinks that much will become thoroughly intoxicated and will be an object of laughter and ridicule, as had already been asserted of Oholah (23:10). The obvious application of such a picture is to the intensity of the coming judgment. Jerusalem could no more escape that due reward of her behavior, enjoyable as it might have momentarily been, than one who has overindulged in alcoholic beverages can escape the inevitable result.

23:33 The verse edges gradually toward the grotesque scene of the next verse. Two literary devices are used to develop the picture. First, שִׁכָּרוֹן וְיָגוֹן,

"drunkenness and grief," is zeugmatic, meaning "the drunkenness that leads to grief/sorrow." יָגוֹן indicates intense inner grief and emotional anguish, the hangover and depression after imbibing far too much. It is followed by a virtual hendiadys: "the cup of horror and devastation" (שַׁמָּה וּשְׁמָמָה), the horror or appallment after devastation or desolation. As in English, these terms can be used for both psychological and physical destruction. Thus the symbol and the reality converge, and as the last phrase of the verse shows, the real subject is the city, Jerusalem.

23:34 The final picture is that of a woman's alcohol-intensified remorse so extreme that her actions approach dementia. As she earlier shamelessly pursued her lovers, now she will smash the cup and try to retrieve any wine that had been absorbed by it. And in ultimate frenzy, she will use the sharp sherds (cf. Job scraping his sores with them in Job 2:7–8) to "destroy 'the peccant members' ... , around which erotic memories lingered."[60] She who had once craved the fondling of her breasts will now mutilate herself so much that her erstwhile paramours will be revolted and abhor her. As is his custom, Ezekiel pushes the metaphor of the drunken woman to the extreme.

The double formulaic conclusion, "for I have spoken, says the Lord Yahweh," underscores the horror and certainty of the reality expressed by the metaphor.

23:35 Ezek 23:34 has brought the metaphor to a dramatic climax. It might appear as if nothing more need be said. But Yahweh makes a non-metaphorical assertion to drive the theological point home.

As elsewhere (e.g., 16:43; 22:12), Yahweh underscores the core of Israel's sin, and of all sin: the people had forgotten Yahweh, which was tantamount to worshiping other gods. The point is made vivid by use of the picture that the people "cast" God "behind [their] back," an idiom used elsewhere only in 1 Ki 14:9 and Neh 9:26. Instead of facing him in adoration and thanksgiving, they have turned their backs on him while facing (worshiping) other deities, as in Ezek 8:16: "their backsides to the temple of Yahweh, and their faces eastward— and they were prostrating themselves eastward to the sun."

After the motive clause beginning with יַעַן, "because," one would expect the apodosis to begin with לָכֵן, "therefore." Instead, it is shortened to גַּם, "you yourself must *also* bear ..." The implication is that, like many who stray, Israel deluded herself into thinking that she was somehow exempt from Yahweh's universal law. Exemption was available only through repentance and faith, and that she had scorned.

The verb "bear" (שָׂאִי) needs and has no object in Hebrew, but in English "penalty, consequences" must be supplied. The picture is that of sin as a burden that will crush the one who carries it unless another party relieves him of

---

[60] Greenberg, *Ezekiel*, 2:484, quoting G. R. Driver, "Ezekiel: Linguistic and Textual Problems," *Biblica* 35/2 (1954): 155.

it. The traditional wording of the Agnus Dei speaks of Christ *bearing (tollis, trägst)* the burden of the world's sin for us. The more recent translation "take away" loses that picture.

Review of the Profligacy and Judgment of Both Sisters (23:36–49)

Summary of the Charges against the Sisters (23:36–45)

23:36   The section that begins with this verse and extends through 23:49 is the climax of the entire chapter: Ezekiel's authorization to play the role of prosecutor in the heavenly court. The charges are repeated in 23:36–45, although a few appear that have not surfaced in this chapter before, then the verdict of guilty and the sentencing come in 23:46–49.

It is noteworthy that the charges are against *both* Oholah and Oholibah, that is, against both Israel and Judah. Historically, this is artificial, because the northern kingdom (Oholah) had disappeared from the map in 722 B.C., over a century before the time of Ezekiel. But earthly history does not always reflect God's ultimate will. Yahweh had established an *Una Sancta* ("one holy catholic and apostolic church" in the words of the Nicene Creed) that in God's good time (perhaps eschatological "time") would be reestablished, as Ezekiel will emphasize later, especially in chapters 34–37, and political divisions can never thwart the divine will. God, not people, makes his kingdom come *ubi et quando visum est* ("where and when it pleases") him,[61] and the new Jerusalem will exceed the bounds of human language to articulate (Ezekiel 40–48; Revelation 21–22).

Having made that important point, however, beginning with 23:38 it will be clear that Ezekiel's chief target is Jerusalem (Oholibah).

23:37   A causal כִּי, "for," leads to a description of the sisters' sins. After the repeated use of זָנָה, "be a whore," and cognate nouns in the preceding material, one is surprised to meet נָאַף, "commit adultery," twice in this verse. Nouns derived from that verb will be used in following verses: נִאוּפִים, "adulteries," in 23:43, and נֹאֲפוֹת, "adulteresses," in 23:45. These terms are stronger in that they emphasize a woman's violation of her marriage covenant; these are offenses against her husband. A stronger verb means far more serious infractions. The basic biblical picture of Israel as Yahweh's wife, wed to him at the exodus, has always hovered in the background and now comes to the fore. Its NT counterpart is the depiction of the church as the bride of Christ (e.g., 2 Cor 11:2–3; Eph 5:21–33; Revelation 21–22; cf. Mt 22:1–14; 25:1–13).

Nor have we heard of bloodshed for a time. Other charges, new to this context, are "recycled" from chapter 16 (various verses, perhaps especially 16:17, 20–21, 32, 36, and 38).

After the general charges, clarification of each follows. Consorting with foreign nations inevitably involved the adultery of idolatry, that is, taking other husbands instead of Yahweh—or alongside of him, if that were possible (as the

---

[61] AC V on the holy ministry.

people might well have supposed). This is not merely Israelite propaganda; Near Eastern kings, while not actually deified as in Egypt, were closely identified with gods, and sometimes both kings and gods appear on paintings side by side in identical pose and attire.

Again the outrage of Molech worship is added to the indictment. See the commentary on 16:20–21 and 20:31.

23:38–39 These verses combine violations of the sanctity of both sanctuary and Sabbath (cf. 5:11; and 20:13, 16, 21; 22:8, respectively). The two are linked already in Lev 19:30. The first has to do with sacred space, the second with sacred time. Both were set apart from ordinary space and time. Paradoxically, the sacred space and time of paradise were "sacramentally" present in them (the eternal now/today), and they also were God's bridgeheads for reclaiming the whole of creation, which had been befouled in the fall. In Christ, the reclamation has come near (cf. Mt 4:17), but the consummate stage is still awaited and longed for (Revelation 21–22).

The phrase "on the/that same day" in both 23:38 and 23:39 stresses that all the offenses were contiguous.[62] In 22:26 defilement of holy things was attributed to priestly neglect, but here it is associated specifically with child sacrifice. Having already defiled themselves by bloodshed and idolatry, the people defile the temple by entering it in an adulterous rupture of proper relation to Yahweh. And the mention of the Sabbath in the same breath suggests that they had compounded the offense by doing it on the Sabbath, thus denying Yahweh's lordship of time as well. The concern with temple trespasses reminds one of the temple abominations described in chapter 8.

The pronouns in "*my* sanctuary" and "*my* own house" underscore all the other personal pronouns referring to Yahweh in these chapters. As with Christianity, the sins were no mere violations of rules and abstract principles, but a personal affront to a personal God—in fact, a "husband." Getting and keeping this straight is part and parcel of the proclamation that biblical faith is Gospel, not Law.

23:40–41 The scene shifts to the past elaborate efforts of the adulteress to lure her lovers—as though that really had been necessary. It is futile even to ask which nation(s) are in mind as her lovers. Such behavior had become virtually instinctual and a way of life for the women. The scene is similar to that described in 16:16–19.

God refers to "my incense" and "my oil," not only because they came from him as the Creator, but also because he, as the people's Redeemer, had specified that the highest use of these gifts was in the portion to be returned to him as a eucharistic offering. For their proper use in worship, see, for example, Ex 25:6, 29; 27:20; Exodus 29–31; Leviticus 2; 8; 14; 16:12–13; Numbers 7.

---

[62] For some reason, this phrase is missing in the LXX of both verses, resulting in a weaker charge.

Instead, the woman meretriciously squanders them.

23:42   The import of this difficult verse (see the textual notes) seems to be that the women have fallen so low that they welcome to their beds not only the ordinary populace (i.e., not merely the nobility with whom earlier verses seemed to limit their liaisons) but also drunken, nomadic men from the desert to satisfy their yen for kinky experiences.

23:43   This most opaque verse (see the textual notes) could be spoken by Yahweh, or it could be an expression of the prophet's personal outrage at Oholibah and what she represents—a vantage point that may continue through 23:45. Although Ezekiel rarely interposes personal observations, this may be an instance. The entirety of Scripture consists of the *ipsissima verba* ("very words") of God, the divine author, yet part of the mystery of inspiration is that the human author can express himself personally while conveying God's words.

If my (and Keil's)[63] take on the rest of the verse is correct, it expresses the idea that the old whore, though now worn out, will continue her nauseating behavior, although almost more as an impersonal, diabolical force than as an active, personal agent. Whoredom has virtually become personified and/or abstracted as a propensity that continues in full force even after the capacity of the woman herself is exhausted. That "whoredom itself will go whoring" almost sounds like a summary of humanity's condition that led Christ to lead captivity captive (Ps 68:19 [ET 68:18]; Eph 4:8) in his death and resurrection.

23:44   The depth of degradation is indicated here by the use of two pejorative phrases, first of the one "woman" as a "whore" (אִשָּׁה זוֹנָה) and then of both Oholah and Oholibah as "depraved women" (אִשֹּׁת הַזִּמָּה). In their sex lives, there is only lust, no love; their partners need not be concerned about whether they are married or not; their beds are in the common domain (contrast Heb 13:4).

23:45   Whether we think of this verse as concluding the prophet's reaction (23:43–45) or of expressing the plans of Yahweh (if he is the speaker of 23:43–45) is of no moment, but the verse does anticipate or introduce the formal sentencing of Oholah and Oholibah in the remaining verses of the chapter.

The previous verse had described the women as behaving and being treated as unattached free agents, but the double use of נֹאֲפוֹת, "adulteresses," in this verse signals that Yahweh takes his marriage covenant seriously and will hold them accountable for their failure to do likewise. The references to murder are probably reminiscences of the atrocities, including child sacrifice, connected with the worship of Molech (see the commentary on 16:20–21 and 20:31). Both adultery and murder were, of course, capital crimes.

The phrase וַאֲנָשִׁים צַדִּיקִם at the beginning of the verse must be translated "righteous men," but that can be misleading. As stressed many times, in the

---

[63]   Keil, *Ezekiel*, 1:337. See the last textual note on 23:43.

biblical usage of both Testaments, the word's primary accent is not on deeds (sanctification), but on the alien righteousness of Jesus Christ that is imputed to the believer, who then is reckoned as righteous (Gen 15:6; Romans 4)—a condition or relationship of which God in Christ is the source and author: justification. Thus the righteous person is first of all one who is right before God, whose sins have been atoned for by Christ, and who receives Christ's righteousness through faith (2 Cor 5:21). Since "Scripture is to be interpreted by Scripture," the OT must be read Christologically in this way.

The punishment of the women by "righteous men" indicates that their judgment will be righteous because it is in accord with Yahweh's own holiness and is ordained by him. Yahweh does not specify what people or historical agents he will use. If this is taken to refer to pagan conquerors such as the Babylonians (or later, the Greeks and Romans), then he is not using the word "righteous" in any strict theological sense at all here, but only in the same relative sense as the related verb צָדֵק was used in 16:51–52, where Yahweh said that Jerusalem had made Sodom and Samaria appear more "righteous" because she had fallen even farther than they.

The Guilty Verdict and Sentencing of the Sisters (23:46–49)

23:46   The chapter ends with the sentencing of Oholah and Oholibah. In principle, the material is similar to previous oracles of doom, but it is the almost inevitable conclusion to a narrative of a pair of hardened and habitual reprobates. The oscillation between the metaphor of the sisters and the countries or cities they represent continues in these verses. The reference to "terror and plunder" indicates that in this verse (as in 23:47), the primary concern is with the cities, but in 23:48–49, the two sisters are once more front and center.

23:47   The ruthlessness of those who carry out the sentence recalls 16:41 and 23:25–26.

23:48–49   The ridding of the land of depravity is similar to 16:41b. Women in general were mentioned in 23:10 (Oholah will be "a byword among women"). Here the punishment of the sisters is described in stronger terms as well deserved. With the goal that "all women may take warning," the verse also takes a didactic direction and considers not only the nation corporately, but also individuals. This is a reminder that Ezekiel took his pastoral role as a "watchman" (3:17; 33:7) seriously. It is also a correction of the common canard that the OT has minimal concern with the sin of individuals. That canard is also disproven by Ezek 3:16–21; chapter 18; and 33:1–20. And, if needed, we may note with Block that "this appeal to women balances earlier appeals that had primarily men in view."[64]

---

[64]   Block, *Ezekiel*, 1:764, n. 208.

The Cooking Pot, and the Death of Ezekiel's Wife

Translation

24 ¹The Word of Yahweh came to me in the ninth year, in the tenth month, on the tenth [day] of the month: ²"Son of man, record this date, this very day: the king of Babylon laid siege to Jerusalem on this very day. ³Tell a parable to the rebellious house, and say to them, 'Thus says the Lord Yahweh:

" 'Put the pot on; put it on;
 and pour water in it too.
⁴Gather its pieces of meat into it,
 every good piece,
thigh and shoulder;
 fill it with the choicest limbs.
⁵Take the best of the flock.
 Pile up the logs under it,
and boil thoroughly,
 so that the limbs in it are well cooked.

⁶" 'Therefore, thus says the Lord Yahweh: Woe to the bloody city, a pot whose filth is inside it, whose filth has not gone out of it! Take out its cuts piece by piece. No lot has fallen on it. ⁷For the blood she shed remains within her. She placed it on a bare rock; she did not pour it on the ground, where the soil would cover it. ⁸To rouse wrath and exact requital, I have placed her blood on a bare rock so that it would not be covered.

⁹" 'Therefore, thus says the Lord Yahweh: Woe to the bloody city! I myself will enlarge the pyre. ¹⁰Add more logs; light the fire; do away with the meat; pour out the broth; let the bones be charred. ¹¹Stand the empty pot on the coals so it becomes hot and its copper glows, the uncleanness inside it is melted, and its filth is done away with. ¹²It has wearied me with its wickedness; its great filth has not gone out of it. Into the fire with its filth! ¹³On account of your depraved impurity, because I tried to cleanse you, but you did not become clean, you will not be clean again from your impurity until I have satisfied my wrath upon you. ¹⁴I, Yahweh, have spoken. It is coming, and I will do it. I will not neglect it; I will not spare; and I will not relent. According to your behavior and your misdeeds, they will punish you, says the Lord Yahweh.' "

¹⁵The Word of Yahweh came to me: ¹⁶"Son of man, I am taking away from you the desire of your eyes by a stroke. You must neither mourn nor cry; your tears must not come. ¹⁷Groan silently; perform no mourning rites for the dead. Bind your turban on yourself; put your sandals on your feet; do not cover your upper lip; and do not eat the food men bring to mourners."

[18]So I spoke to the people that morning, and in the evening my wife died. The next morning I did as I had been commanded. [19]Then the people asked me, "Won't you tell us what these things [you are doing mean] for us?"

[20]I answered them, "The Word of Yahweh came to me: [21]Say to the house of Israel, "Thus says the Lord Yahweh: I am about to desecrate my sanctuary, the stronghold of which you are so proud, the desire of your eyes, the yearning of your hearts; and your sons and your daughters whom you have left behind will fall by the sword. [22]You will do as I have done: you will not cover your upper lip and will not eat the food men bring to mourners. [23]Your turbans will be on your heads and your sandals on your feet. You will neither mourn nor cry but pine away because of your iniquities and groan to one another. [24]Thus Ezekiel will be a sign to you: you will do according to all that he has done. When it comes, you will know that I am the Lord Yahweh."

[25]" 'And you, son of man, will it not be that on the day when I take away from them their stronghold, their joy and glory, the desire of their eyes, and that on which they set their minds—their sons and their daughters as well— [26]on that day a survivor will come to you to let you hear it with your own ears? [27]On that day, your mouth will be opened with the coming of the survivor, and you will speak and be speechless no longer. You will be a sign to them, and they will know that I am Yahweh.' "

Textual Notes

24:1 The alert reader of the Hebrew will note at once the strange formulation of the date notice, although the difference might get lost in translation. If we turn back to 20:1, we see the usual pattern Ezekiel follows: after the opening וַיְהִי, the date follows immediately. Shortly thereafter follows the word-event formula, literally, "and the Word of Yahweh was/came [וַיְהִי or הָיָה] (to me, saying) [לֵאמֹר]" (e.g., 20:2). Here the word-event formula is broken up: the verse begins with most of the formula (וַיְהִי דְבַר־יְהוָה אֵלַי); then comes the date notice; and לֵאמֹר, the word that concludes the formula in most of its occurrences, ends 24:1. Here and elsewhere לֵאמֹר is not translated as "saying," but is reflected in my translation and others only by a colon and quotation marks beginning the following quote. (The pattern in 29:1 is the same as in 20:1 except that the verse does not begin with וַיְהִי.) This verse also exhibits a deviation regarding the month. In date notices that include the month, usually it is indicated simply by the ordinal number with בְּ, for example, בַּחֲמִשִׁי, "in the fifth [month]" (20:1). In contrast here (בַּחֹדֶשׁ הָעֲשִׂירִי), the ordinal הָעֲשִׂירִי modifies the preceding בַּחֹדֶשׁ, hence, "in the tenth month."

Why the variations from Ezekiel's usual (idiosyncratic) pattern? It seems that for this pivotally significant date, Ezekiel chose a distinctive formulation used also by Jeremiah and the author of Kings. We find almost the identical formulation if we turn to 2 Ki 25:1 and Jer 52:4. Jeremiah has the identical Hebrew wording (plus לְמָלְכוֹ) as Ezekiel, and the wording of 2 Ki 25:1 is almost identical. The expression of this date in the same form by these three biblical authors reinforces its critical significance and historicity, and testifies to the impact it had on ancient Israel, much as when the three synoptic evangelists record words or deeds of Jesus using nearly identical language.

The wording of the date notice in Ezek 24:1 is almost identical to the date notices in 2 Ki 25:1 and Jer 52:4, but has Ezekiel deviated not only from his usual wording but also from his customary system of reckoning, which is based on the exile of Jehoiachin (see the textual note on Ezek 1:2 and the commentary on 1:1)?

Block argues that Ezekiel has deviated from his usual system of reckoning. The time span between the beginning of the siege (24:1) and Ezekiel's awareness of its end (33:21–22) is just short of three years if we assume that both of these Ezekiel passages give dates based on the same calendar. If, as Block advocates, the siege of Jerusalem lasted eighteen months, that leaves about a year and a half for the news of the fall to travel from Jerusalem to Ezekiel in exile. However, a פָּלִיט ("survivor," 24:26–27) bringing the dreaded news might reasonably have taken up to six months (cf. Ezra 7:6–9, where returnees after the exile take four months to make the trip). To resolve this apparent conflict, Block argues that in 24:1 Ezekiel has abandoned his customary system of reckoning in favor the one used by 2 Ki 25:1, based on the regnal years of Zedekiah.[1]

However, if the siege of Jerusalem lasted two and a half years (see the discussion in figure 1), the apparent discrepancy between 24:1 and 33:21–22 disappears: the siege of Jerusalem begins in January 588 (24:1); the city falls two and a half years later in July 586; and a survivor arrives to tell Ezekiel the news in January 585 (33:21–22), about six months after the city fell and five months after it was burned in August 586.

Even though the wording of Ezekiel's date notice in 24:1 agrees with that in Jeremiah and 2 Kings, this does not require that Ezekiel changed his system of reckoning (for this date only) and instead used the system that prevails in those other books. As Greenberg notes: "By a fortunate coincidence the date [in our modern calendrical system: January 588] is the same whether one follows the Tishri-Elul regnal year of Kings or the Nisan-Adar year of 'our exile' [e.g., 1:2] in Ezekiel."[2]

Ezekiel's precision certainly must have had the effect of authenticating his message. When word came to the exiles of the city's collapse (33:21–22), the date Ezekiel had predicted in 24:1 easily could have been compared with the date reported by the surviving eyewitnesses and confirmed as true.

Critical commentators usually posit that the date in 24:1 is the result of some type of later editorial revision, added to authenticate Ezekiel's prophecy. However, the date appears in 24:1 in all the ancient versions, and so it must have been part of the traditional text from very early on. Many critics suppose that originally no date appeared in the word-event formula, partly because the oracle (מָשָׁל, 24:3) in 24:3–14 does not seem to be concerned with the question of date at all. Some unknown glossator allegedly noted the concern with "this very day" in 24:2 and copied the text of 2 Kings into the margin of Ezekiel, whence it eventually found its way into the prophetic text. For some earlier, more radical scholars, the precision of the date counted as major evidence that Ezekiel's ministry was really in Jerusalem rather than in the exile, but I doubt if anyone takes such a position today.

---

[1]   Block, *Ezekiel*, 1:772–74.

[2]   Greenberg, *Ezekiel*, 1:8, 10.

Rejecting that speculation, then, we must conclude that the date was part of the original text of 24:1 and was given to Ezekiel by "direct supernatural revelation."[3] Taylor observes that this "appears to be so much more in keeping with Ezekiel's characteristic God-consciousness and would be yet another authentication of his prophetic gifts."[4] This verse certainly highlights the biblical doctrine of the divine inspiration of the Scriptures (2 Tim 3:16 and 2 Pet 1:19–21; see also the commentary on Ezek 1:1).

24:2 כְּתָוב־לְךָ—The Kethib is the Qal imperative כְּתוֹב, written fully (*plene*). Rarely elsewhere are masculine singular Qal imperatives written *plene*. The Qere, כְּתָב־, regularizes the orthography to its usual defective form (כְּתֹב but in construct), like the Qal masculine singular imperatives שְׁפֹת in 24:3 (twice) and אֱסֹף in 24:4. The *holem* (-ֹ-) is shortened to *qamets chatuph* (-ָ-) because of the *maqqeph*, drawing the accent to the following לְךָ, which serves as an ethical dative or dative of advantage, literally, "write for yourself."

אֶת־שֵׁם הַיּוֹם—Literally, "the name of the day," this is the direct object of the imperative "write." Some commentators want to delete יוֹם here because of its redundancy with the following parallel phrase (see the next textual note) and because of its absence in the Vulgate. However, the full phrase is attested in the LXX, Peshitta, and Targum. The use of שֵׁם הַיּוֹם in the sense of "the/this date" is now confirmed by its appearance in an Arad ostracon.[5]

אֶת־עֶצֶם הַיּוֹם הַזֶּה—This phrase is a second direct object of "write" in apposition to the preceding direct object phrase. The noun עֶצֶם in the singular can mean "self," so the phrase means "this selfsame day" (BDB, s.v. עֶצֶם, 3), but it is commonly rendered "this very day" (cf. LXX: τῆς ἡμέρας ταύτης). Commonly this phrase (without the direct object marker) is introduced by בְּ and functions as a temporal adverbial phrase, as at the end of 24:2. The plural of עֶצֶם will mean "limbs" or "bones" in 24:4, 5, 10 ("bones" also in, e.g., 37:1, 3).

סָמַךְ מֶלֶךְ־בָּבֶל אֶל־יְרוּשָׁלַ͏ִם בְּעֶצֶם הַיּוֹם הַזֶּה:—This is, literally, "the King of Babylon leaned/pressed heavily on Jerusalem." The verbal idiom is translated "laid siege to." סָמַךְ is often used with an object and a preposition, such as "lay hands upon" (e.g., Ex 29:10). In the OT, only here and in Ps 88:8 (ET 88:7) is it intransitive, a use common in later Hebrew and Aramaic. It is unusual for the perfect verb סָמַךְ to precede the adverbial temporal phrase בְּעֶצֶם הַיּוֹם הַזֶּה. Everywhere else in the OT, that temporal phrase precedes a verb in the perfect (e.g., Gen 7:13; Ex 12:17; Ezek 40:1).

This clause is not causal (as would be expressed if it began כִּי סָמַךְ, "record this date … *because* the king …"). Rather, this entire clause is appositional to שֵׁם הַיּוֹם. Thus the "name" or title of the day, which Ezekiel is commanded to record, is this: "the king of Babylon laid siege to Jerusalem on this very day." The syntax thus stresses that the investment of the city had actually commenced. "It was the beginning of the end that the prophet had been predicting for years to an unbelieving community."[6]

---

[3] Taylor, *Ezekiel*, 177.

[4] Taylor, *Ezekiel*, 177.

[5] *ANET*, 569, including n. 28.

[6] Greenberg, *Ezekiel*, 2:497.

Figure 1

The Dates in Ezekiel

Fourteen dates appear in Ezekiel. All of them except the one in 1:1 are figured from 597 B.C., the first "year of the captivity of the king Jehoiachin" (1:2). According to the Babylonian Chronicle, Jerusalem surrenders to Nebuchadnezzar on Adar 2 (March 16), 597. In that year, Ezekiel is taken into captivity to Babylon along with Jehoiachin. Ezekiel seems to be following a calendar whose year begins in the month of Nisan, that is, March/April in our calendar (see the commentary on 40:1).†

Spring 597–spring 596: first year of captivity …

Spring 593–spring 592: fifth year of captivity

- The first date in Ezekiel, "in the thirtieth year, in the fourth [month], on the fifth [day] of the month" (**1:1**), most likely places Ezekiel's age at thirty ("in the thirtieth year") at the time of his inaugural vision, which occurs "on the fifth [day] of the [fourth] month … in the fifth year of the captivity of the king Jehoiachin" (**1:2**), that is, about July 31, 593.

Spring 592–spring 591: sixth year of captivity

- "In the sixth year, in the sixth [month], on the fifth day of the month" (**8:1**), that is, about September 18, 592, Yahweh gives Ezekiel the vision recorded in Ezekiel 8–11.

Spring 591–spring 590: seventh year of captivity

- "In the seventh year, in the fifth [month], on the tenth [day] of the month" (**20:1**), that is, around August 14, 591, Yahweh gives Ezekiel the oracle recorded in chapter 20.

Spring 590–spring 589: eighth year of captivity

Spring 589–spring 588: ninth year of captivity

- "In the ninth year, in the tenth month, on the tenth [day] of the month" (**24:1**), Yahweh instructs Ezekiel to record the date as the very day on which the siege of Jerusalem commences. The siege of Jerusalem, which lasts two and a half years, begins around January 15, 588.††

Spring 588–spring 587: tenth year of captivity

- "In the tenth year, in the tenth [month], on the twelfth [day] of the month" (**29:1**), that is, around January 7, 587, Yahweh gives Ezekiel an oracle against Egypt.

Spring 587–spring 586: eleventh year of captivity

- "In the eleventh year, in the first [month], on the seventh [day] of the month" (**30:20**), that is, around April 29, 587, Yahweh gives Ezekiel an oracle against Pharaoh.
- "In the eleventh year, in the third [month], on the first [day] of the month" (**31:1**), that is, about June 21, 587, Yahweh gives Ezekiel another oracle against Pharaoh.
- "In the eleventh year, on the first day of the month" (**26:1**), that is, sometime between spring 587 and spring 586, probably in spring 586, anticipating Jerusalem's fall in summer 586,†† Yahweh gives Ezekiel an oracle against Tyre.

Spring 586–spring 585: twelfth year of captivity

- "In the twelfth year of our captivity, in the tenth [month], on the fifth day of the month" (**33:21**), that is, around January 8, 585, Ezekiel receives word, via a survivor, that Jerusalem has fallen. The fall of Jerusalem had occurred the previous summer, around July 18, 586, and Jerusalem had been burned about a month later around August 14, 586.††

- "In the twelfth year, in the twelfth month, on the first [day] of the month" (**32:1**), that is, about March 3, 585, Yahweh instructs Ezekiel to give a lament for Pharaoh.

- "In the twelfth year on the fifteenth [day] of the month" (**32:17**), that is, also in March 585, Yahweh tells Ezekiel to give an elegy on Pharaoh's descent into Sheol.

Spring 585–spring 584: thirteenth year of captivity ...

Spring 573–spring 572: twenty-fifth year of captivity

- "In the twenty-fifth year of our captivity, at the beginning of the year, on the tenth of the month, in the fourteenth year after the fall of the city" (**40:1**), that is, around April 28, 573, Yahweh gives Ezekiel eschatological visions.

Spring 572–spring 571: twenty-sixth year of captivity

Spring 571–spring 570: twenty-seventh year of captivity

- "In the twenty-seventh year, in the first [month], on the first day of the month" (**29:17**), that is, around April 26, 571, Yahweh tells Ezekiel that he will give Egypt to Nebuchadnezzar in place of Tyre. Ezek 29:17–21 is Ezekiel's latest dated oracle.

† To a large extent, this figure follows the chronology advocated in Freedy and Redford, "The Dates in Ezekiel," 462–74; Malamat, "The Last Kings of Judah and the Fall of Jerusalem," 144–55; and Finegan, *Handbook of Biblical Chronology*, §§ 442, 450–53.

†† 2 Ki 25:1–4 and Jer 52:4–7 record that the siege of Jerusalem began in the ninth year of Zedekiah's reign, in the tenth month, on the tenth day of the month, and that the city fell in Zedekiah's eleventh year, in the fourth month, on the ninth day of the month. What are those dates according to our modern calendar? The issues involved in trying to answer that question include trying to synchronize all of the dates given in 2 Kings, Jeremiah, and Ezekiel for events in the final years of the Kingdom of Judah with each other and with dates available from extrabiblical sources. Unfortunately, the Babylonian Chronicle, which allows scholars to fix the date of Jehoiachin's surrender to the Babylonians as Adar 2 (March 16), 597, is not extant for the period covering the siege and fall of Jerusalem.

While there is some divergence of opinion about when the siege of Jerusalem began, many scholars are agreed on a date around January 15, 588. However, scholars are much more divided over when the city fell, with most scholars falling into one of two camps: those advocating July 587 and those advocating July 586.

The differences of opinion center around whether the regnal years of Zedekiah were reckoned by the author of Kings and by Jeremiah as having begun in the month of Tishri, in the fall, or as having begun in the month of Nisan, in the (previous) spring. If Zedekiah's regnal years were calculated as beginning in Tishri, with his first full year, beginning in Tishri 597, counted as year 1, the siege of Jerusalem began around January 15, 588, and the city fell after two and a half years around July 18, 586. If, on the other hand, Zedekiah's years were reckoned as beginning in Nisan 597, the siege of Jerusalem, which began around January 15, 588, lasted eighteen months, and the city fell in July 587.

The first view, with the fall of Jerusalem in 586, seems most consistent with the dates in Ezekiel. See, for instance, the textual note on 24:1, which discusses the relationship between the date notices in 24:1 and 33:21.

24:3 וּמְשֹׁל אֶל־בֵּית־הַמֶּ֫רִי מָשָׁל—The multivalence of the verb מָשַׁל (here Qal infinitive: וּמְשֹׁל) and the cognate noun מָשָׁל, meaning "compose a parable, proverb, allegory," was discussed in the textual note and commentary on 17:2. "Parable" seems most appropriate here. The construction with the cognate verb and noun is impossible to reproduce in English. For the verb, "tell, compose, utter, frame" all would work, and perhaps others as well. The variety reflects the question whether Ezekiel is to compose his own piece or merely to recite or adapt some already well-known ditty, but it does not much matter. That 24:3b–5 is poetic in form is indicated typographically in most translations. Taylor is often quoted in his comparison to a household cooking song, something like the British "Polly, put the kettle on."[7] The Bible contains several analogues or allusions to such songs, for example, the well-digging song in Num 21:17–18 and various vintage songs (cf. Is 9:2 [ET 9:3]).

The preposition אֶל might signify either "to" or "about." For בֵּית־הַמֶּ֫רִי, see the second textual note on 2:5.

שְׁפֹת הַסִּיר שְׁפֹת—The second Qal imperative שְׁפֹת is deleted by some commentators, following the LXX and the Syriac, but the Hebrew repetition emphasizes the exhortation and is characteristic of Ezekiel (cf., e.g., 20:4; 22:2; 37:9). It probably also contributes to the lilt of the poetry.

וְגַם־יְצֹק בּוֹ מָֽיִם:—The form of the Qal masculine singular imperative יְצֹק, "pour," does not follow the pattern of the root's behavior elsewhere. Many first *yod* verbs, like some first *nun* verbs, drop the first radical of the root for the imperative and have a segholate-type infinitive. Thus in 2 Ki 4:41, the Qal masculine singular imperative of this verb is צַק, and its infinitive is always צֶקֶת.

The noun סִיר, "pot," is usually feminine, and in 24:4, the feminine (third singular) pronouns on נְתָחֶ֫יהָ אֵלֶ֫יהָ refer to it. Therefore some argue that בּוֹ with the masculine suffix is an error for בָּהּ. But Jer 1:13 uses the masculine, and that may underlie the oracle here. (What is the gender of a cooking pot anyway?)

24:4 אֱסֹף נְתָחֶ֫יהָ אֵלֶ֫יהָ—The plural of נֶתַח, "piece of meat," with third feminine singular suffix (נְתָחֶ֫יהָ) is often thought to be an error for the simple plural (which the LXX and the Syriac have), perhaps by attraction to the following אֵלֶ֫יהָ. But emendation is not necessary. The implication of "*its* [the pot's] pieces" is that the meat has already been prepared for cooking. In contrast to 24:3, the feminine suffixes (נְתָחֶ֫יהָ אֵלֶ֫יהָ) refer to the pot as feminine, as is more common. Possibly the feminine appears here in anticipation of what the pot typifies: the city, Jerusalem (24:6 and 24:9), since cities and their names are feminine in Hebrew. Four words in 24:5 have feminine suffixes referring to the pot, as do additional words in 24:11.

"Every good piece" (כָּל־נֵתַח טוֹב) is then defined more minutely as "thigh and shoulder" (יָרֵךְ וְכָתֵף). And the pot is to be filled with מִבְחַר עֲצָמִים, literally, the "choice" (see the commentary) of the "limbs," as the masculine plural of עֶ֫צֶם can mean, not the inedible "bones" (as the feminine plural of עֶ֫צֶם will mean in 24:10).

24:5 מִבְחַר הַצֹּאן לָק֫וֹחַ—This verse is climactic: not only the "choicest" cuts (24:4) but also "the best of the flock" are to be used. מִבְחַר is repeated from 24:4 but here

---

[7] Taylor, *Ezekiel*, 178.

must be translated "best." A Qal infinitive absolute (לְקוֹחַ) is used for variety in lieu of another imperative.

וְגַם דּוּר הָעֲצָמִים תַּחְתֶּיהָ—The Qal imperative דּוּר, "pile up," is related to the derivative noun מְדוּרָה, "pyre," in 24:9. Semitic cognates indicate that the idea of a circle is involved, probably because of the common circular arrangement of the logs in a pyre. Compare the noun דּוּר in Is 22:18 and 29:3, perhaps meaning "circle, ball."

But it hardly makes sense for הָעֲצָמִים, "the limbs" or "the bones" (LXX: τὰ ὀστᾶ), to be the verb's object, constituting the fuel for the fire, both because they do not easily burn and because they have just been mentioned as being inside the pot (עֲצָמִים, "limbs," in 24:4). KJV has "burn also the bones under it." However, many commentators suggest that the MT's reading arose from a faulty word division; they emend הָעֲצָמִים to הָעֵצִים, the plural of עֵץ, meaning "pieces of wood, sticks, logs," and then append the second מ to the next word to produce מִתַּחְתֶּיהָ, "(from) underneath it." That emendation is followed by many translations (e.g., RSV, ESV). NIV tries to salvage the MT by translating, "pile wood beneath it for the bones," but one can hardly have it both ways.

רַתַּח רְתָחֶיהָ—Literally, "boil its boilings," this cognate accusative is the Piel imperative of רָתַח with the plural of רֶתַח (with third feminine singular suffix) as its object. Its onomatopoeia is poetic and may simply be emphatic. The LXX here confirms the MT. The verb רָתַח is used only two other times in the OT, both in Job (30:27 and 41:23). The cognate noun occurs nowhere else. In its place, two medieval manuscripts read נְתָחֶיהָ ("pieces of meat"), as in 24:4. Some are tempted to emend accordingly, but we lack sufficient evidence to make the change.

גַּם־בָּשְׁלוּ עֲצָמֶיהָ בְּתוֹכָהּ׃—Literally, "also its limbs cook in its midst," this is translated, "so that the limbs in it are well cooked." It uses the common verb בָּשַׁל, "to boil, cook," in an intransitive sense with עֲצָמֶיהָ as subject. I have taken גַּם with the perfect as the equivalent of וּבָשְׁלוּ, a perfect with *waw* consecutive, looking to the future. The Qal of בָּשַׁל occurs elsewhere only in Joel 4:13 (ET 3:13), where it has the intransitive meaning, "ripen." Many propose revocalizing the MT as a Piel singular imperative (בַּשֵּׁל) to continue the sequence of imperatives. The LXX has the singular imperative ἥψηται. However, it is not easy to see how the MT would have arisen from a singular imperative. Greenberg may correctly divine that the MT is here signaling a closure to the song by reversing the syntax from its previous sequence of transitive verb-object to the order here of intransitive verb-subject.[8]

24:6 סִיר אֲשֶׁר חֶלְאָתָה בָהּ—There is no agreement on the meaning of חֶלְאָה, a word found only in this verse (twice) and in 24:11. Its interpretation must relate somehow to 24:7 (literally, "its blood is in its midst") and to 24:11 ("its חֶלְאָה will be finished, consumed, burned away"). Thus the חֶלְאָה must be something unwanted inside the pot that can be removed only by overheating. Most modern versions (e.g., RSV, NRSV) and commentators follow the meaning proposed by BDB and *HALOT*: "rust." However, according to 24:11, the pot is made of copper or bronze (נְחֹשֶׁת). Copper does not rust, but after weathering, it develops a greenish patina or verdigris. The LXX's ἰός may refer to either rust or verdigris (or poison), and in the NT, it is used

---

[8] Greenberg, *Ezekiel*, 2:499.

more generally still of "corrosion" of gold and silver in James 5:3 (cf. βρῶσις in Mt 6:19–20 of the "corruption" of earthly treasures in general). However, it is doubtful if חֶלְאָה necessarily refers to metal at all. (The only known exception is Sirach 12:10, where it refers to bronze, but that is a far later text, probably written around 180 B.C.) חֶלְאָה is apparently an Aramaicized (with א replacing ה) noun formed from the common Hebrew verb חָלָה, "be sick, weak." At most, in this context that might imply a "copper sickness" or verdigris. But high heat does not eliminate verdigris, and heat would also not be needed to get rid of "scum" (KJV, NKJV; NIV speaks of an "encrusted" pot with a "deposit" on it). The best solution seems to be to understand the word as a rather general term for any unpleasant foulness. Hence my translation is "filth."[9]

The absence of a *mappiq* in the third feminine singular suffix on חֶלְאָתָה is usually explained as euphonic, an intentional quiescence before the stop in בָּה (GKC, § 91 e). Because the suffix is superfluous before the following בָּה ("its filth is in it"), some think of a simple scribal error for the absolute form, חֶלְאָה. The difference is slight, but an emendation is entirely conjectural and unnecessary.

לִנְתָחֶיהָ לִנְתָחֶיהָ הוֹצִיאָהּ—A literal translation of this clause could be "by its cuts, by its cuts, take it out." The repetition with *lamed* is clearly distributive in meaning, so it is translated, "take out its cuts piece by piece." However, the referent of the third feminine singular suffix on the Hiphil imperative (of יָצָא), הוֹצִיאָהּ, is unclear. Its most obvious antecedent would be the feminine noun וְחֶלְאָתָה, "its/whose filth," in the preceding clause, in which case the clause would mean "piece by piece take it [its filth] out," implying that the pieces constitute "its filth." Cooke and Allen[10] remove the *mappiq* (ה-) to form an emphatic imperative (הוֹצִיאָה) and eliminate the problem of the suffix's antecedent, but the MT clearly is the harder text. Nearly all English translations (already KJV) translate the verb as an imperative, as have I. Syntactically the clause seems to follow from the preceding "whose filth has not gone out," implying that removal of the cuts of meat is a figurative way of expressing the prosaic (factual) disposal of the pot's filth or impurity.

24:7 כִּי דָמָהּ בְּתוֹכָהּ הָיָה—"For" (כִּי) apparently connects this clause with the statement at the end of 24:6, "no lot has fallen on it," so a different verse division might be envisioned with that statement continuing through the end of this clause.

עַל־צְחִיחַ סֶלַע—The noun צְחִיחַ, a "shining, glaring surface," is a derivative of צָחַח, "to be dazzling, glaring, shining." But any glare is coincidental to the thrust of the sentence. The construct phrase צְחִיחַ סֶלַע means "bare rock" in the context here and when this phrase is repeated in 24:8.

לְכַסּוֹת עָלָיו עָפָר:—This clause with the Piel infinitive construct of כָּסָה is, literally, "to cover over it dust." The Piel of כָּסָה usually is transitive with a direct object, like the English "cover." But all languages deploy prepositions in their own way, and as with other verbs, Hebrew often uses a preposition (here עַל) instead of or as an

---

[9] With Greenberg, *Ezekiel*, 2:495, 499.

[10] Cooke, *Ezekiel*, 274; Allen, *Ezekiel*, 2:55.

alternative to the accusative. Often, as here, the preposition cannot be duplicated in English. The infinitive may denote either purpose ("in order that") or result ("so that"). I have freely translated, "where the soil would cover it."

24:8 לְהַעֲלוֹת חֵמָה לִנְקֹם נָקָם—Two purpose clauses with infinitive constructs are placed first for emphasis. The natural etymological meaning of the Hiphil of עָלָה is "raise up" or "rouse," as I have translated, but the word in some contexts has overtones of kindling (rousing) a fire. "Wrath, fury" (חֵמָה) is used elsewhere with this or similar verbs. The fire imagery present already here will be developed even more in 24:9–12.

The following cognate expression with the verb נָקַם and noun נָקָם is harder to do justice to (no pun intended) in translation. A common translation of the root is "avenge, take vengeance," but that is at least as susceptible to misunderstanding as God's "jealousy" (קִנְאָה). When people are the subject, "revenge, avenge" is appropriate, but with God as subject, the concern is his righting of wrongs ("*right*eousness"), establishing his justice, "justifying" (although some modern theology uses that word with other nuances). Here, of course, it is a matter of God righting the wrongs committed by his own people. But often נָקָם refers to God's righting of wrongs committed by enemies of his people, and then the noun is tantamount to "vindication, deliverance, rescue." An excellent example appears in Is 61:1–2, Jesus' text for his inaugural sermon in Lk 4:18–19, where God's "day of vengeance," as it is usually translated, is parallel to a series of other expressions of salvation.

24:10 הַרְבֵּה ... הַדְלֵק ... הָתֵם ... וְהַרְקַח—These four alliterative verb forms may be either Hiphil imperatives or Hiphil infinitive absolutes. Since the meaning will be the same in either case, one need not choose. However, the use of the jussive form of יֵחָרוּ at the end of 24:10 and of the imperative וְהַעֲמִידֶהָ at the beginning of 24:11 probably tips the scales toward parsing these four verbs as imperatives. The fact that they follow the first person indicative אַגְדִּיל ("I will enlarge") in 24:9 is probably stylistic as much as anything: Yahweh is pictured as talking or thinking to himself, or possibly commanding unnamed attendants or helpers.

The Hiphil imperatives of רָבָה ("increase, add more") and of דָּלַק ("light") are clear enough in meaning. Questions arise about the meanings of the other two, although the logical progression of thought is leading up to the near meltdown of the pot itself described in 24:11.

The third clause, הָתֵם הַבָּשָׂר, literally, "finish the meat," is ambiguous. It could mean "cook it well" or the like, as virtually all English translations render it, although the KJV's "consume the flesh" is about as ambiguous as the Hebrew. However, its translation should be compatible with 22:15 and 24:11, both of which have forms of תָּמַם, as well as with the call in 24:6 to *remove* the cuts of meat from the pot. Hence the translation of this phrase must convey the idea of overcooking until the pieces of meat are no longer edible or possibly are burned up. I have attempted that with my "do away with," which like הָתֵם (Hiphil second masculine singular imperative of תָּמַם) does not specify exactly how the elimination of the meat should be accomplished.

The following clause, וְהַרְקַח הַמֶּרְקָחָה, uses a verb (Hiphil imperative of רָקַח) whose Qal refers to mixing spices and fragrances in oil and a cognate noun (מֶרְקָחָה)

that occurs elsewhere only in Job 41:23 (ET 41:31) meaning "ointment pot." The clause may literally mean "anoint the ointment jar" or perhaps "season the seasoning." KJV has "spice it well," while others have "mix in the spices" (NKJV and NRSV; NIV is similar). It is less than pellucid what role spices or seasoning would have near the end of a process of overcooking. The best one might make of such a statement in the context is a comparison of the smell of a half-burned stew or the like to other aromas.

In my judgment, it is a clear case where emendation is called for, most likely one of simple metathesis of the last two radicals of the verb הַרְקַח to הַרְחֵק, "make distant/remove," and subsequent alteration of הַמֶּרְקָחָה into מָרָק, "broth." (Many propose changing the first verb into הָרֵק [Hiphil of רִיק], "empty out," but that is more distant from the MT.) Then a translation of "empty out the broth" (RSV) or the like is the result. The LXX (καὶ ἐλαττωθῇ ὁ ζωμός) appears to support such a change. The picture is that of the meat, which has fallen off the bones and nearly dissolved, being poured out, leaving only the bones in the pot (see the next clause).

וְהָעֲצָמוֹת יֵחָרוּ:—Since this final clause is missing in the LXX, it is often dismissed out of hand as a later addition. There are other anomalies in the clause, although explanations are possible. The change in word order, with the subject here before an intransitive verb, contrasts with the transitive verb–object sequence in the preceding clauses and probably effects a closure parallel to the one noted at the end of 24:5.

Already in 24:4 we noted the masculine plural עֲצָמִים in the sense of "limbs," which contrasts with the use of the feminine plural here of the now meatless "bones." יֵחָרוּ is the Niphal jussive (third plural masculine, where feminine would be expected) of חָרַר, "be scorched, charred," whose Niphal was also in 15:4–5. The change in verb form to jussive (a third person imperative) is understandable as simple variation and not out of place with imperatives both before and after. In 24:11 the Qal of חָרַר will be used of the fire's effect on the empty pot itself.

If I have interpreted the previous clause correctly and the pot has been emptied of everything but the bones, their charring will be the inevitable result with a hot fire still burning underneath. Greenberg summarizes: "Innocent cooking (vs. 5bᵞ) ends in ruthless cremation (vs. 10bᵝ)."[11]

24:11 וְהַעֲמִידֶהָ עַל־גֶּחָלֶיהָ רֵקָה—The Hiphil imperative of עָמַד (with third feminine singular suffix) fortunately can be translated quite literally in English: "stand it upon its coals empty." The translation makes explicit that the suffix refers to the pot: "stand [the empty pot] on the coals." The third feminine singular suffix is repeated on גֶּחָלֶיהָ but has been omitted in translation. The adjective רֵקָה (feminine of רִיק) is not reflected in the LXX and hence many omit it.[12] However, its presence in the MT strengthens the picture by making explicit that the pot is now "empty."

וְנִתְּכָה בְתוֹכָהּ טֻמְאָתָהּ—The Niphal of נָתַךְ (third feminine singular perfect with *waw* consecutive) is slightly ambiguous in context. It can mean simply "poured out,"

---

[11] Greenberg, *Ezekiel*, 2:502.

[12] E.g., Zimmerli, *Ezekiel*, 1:495.

but the repeated use of the verb in 22:20–22 for the smelting process suggests as more appropriate here "the uncleanness inside it is *melted*," If the parallel is pressed, it could imply that the pot itself with its verdigris liquefies. That is possible, but it seems more likely that the reference is to the contents (inhabitants of the city), which have at least become gelatinous enough that they pour.

תֵּתַּם חֶלְאָתָהּ—The verb is an Aramaicized Qal third feminine singular imperfect of the familiar root תָּמַם, "its filth is done away with, ceases" (see GKC § 67 g, q). Apparently this form is used merely for variety instead of the standard Hebrew תִּתֹּם (Gen 47:18; 1 Ki 7:22).

24:12 Not much about this verse is certain. The ancient versions evince the same perplexity. I have tried to give a reasonably literal translation. I perceive the verse to be a sort of meditation by God to himself as he watches the contents of the pot being poured into the fire.

תְּאֻנִים הֶלְאָת—These two words are not reflected in the LXX, with the result that they are commonly deleted as a blurred dittography of the last two words of the previous verse. As it stands, הֶלְאָת is an archaic form of the third feminine singular Hiphil perfect of לָאָה, "to make weary, exhaust," with the original final *taw*, before it was attenuated into a *he*. The implied subject must the pot, which has "wearied" Yahweh.

Its object, the preceding plural noun תְּאֻנִים, is a hapax. It must be an adverbial accusative, as translated: "… wearied me *with its wickedness*." The best guess (really a counsel of desperation) is to take it as a derivative of אָוֶן, "trouble, sorrow, wickedness, idolatry," although it is just as possibly from אוֹן, "strength, vigor." One finds paraphrases ranging all the way from "it has frustrated all efforts" (NIV) to "she hath wearied herself with lies" (KJV).

רַבַּת חֶלְאָתָהּ—The MT continues with (literally) "the abundance of its filth" not having left the pot, a thought rather parallel to 24:6.

בְּאֵשׁ חֶלְאָתָהּ—With some other interpreters, I take these final two abrupt and verbless words as an exclamation.

24:13 בְּטֻמְאָתֵךְ זִמָּה—These two words, טֻמְאָה ("uncleanness") and זִמָּה ("lewdness"), are synonyms. Conceivably, this is a short nominal sentence, as rendered by KJV: "In thy filthiness is lewdness" (similarly NKJV and NIV). Keil argues that it alludes to Lev 18:17 and 20:14, where זִמָּה refers to fleshly sins that are punishable by death.[13] RSV is more germane to the immediate context: it explicitly identifies the "rust" (or "filth") of the previous two verses as "your filthy lewdness." That point has, in effect, been made before, though not with the use of זִמָּה. My translation, "on account of your depraved impurity," takes זִמָּה as an epexegetical noun after בְּטֻמְאָתֵךְ, a noun with a suffix (second feminine singular). This construction is unusual, but Ezekiel has used it previously in 16:27 (מְדַרְכֵּךְ זִמָּה; see the third textual note on 16:27). The meaning is the same as if this were a construct chain: בְּטֻמְאַת־זִמָּתֵךְ.

יַעַן טִהַרְתִּיךְ—The causal conjunction יַעַן, "because," begins a new clause, but these two initial words still function somewhat as an appositive to the preceding two, as reflected in the translation. The Piel perfect (first common singular) with second

---

[13] Keil, *Ezekiel*, 1:347.

feminine singular suffix, טִהַרְתִּיךְ, literally is "I cleansed you." My translation, "I *tried to cleanse you*," is interpretive, partly in line with the gist of most of the book so far. **24:14** אֲנִי יְהוָה דִּבַּרְתִּי בָּאָה וְעָשִׂיתִי—Yahweh uses similar clauses elsewhere (17:24; 22:14; 36:36; 37:14) but without בָּאָה (Qal feminine singular participle of בּוֹא). Hence many critics omit בָּאָה even though it is attested already in the LXX. But since the entire point of chapter 24 (also what follows) is to stress the imminence of the disaster that is "coming" (in contrast to more distant events), it is entirely appropriate here.

לֹא־אֶפְרַע—The verb פָּרַע, although fairly frequent in the rest of the OT, appears only here in Ezekiel. Various nuances are possible: "I will not neglect, relent, hold back, annul."

וְלֹא־אָחוּס—Elsewhere in Ezekiel, חוּס, "to spare, have compassion," is always used with עַיִן, "eye," meaning "to look compassionately," though usually negated (5:11; 7:4, 9; 8:18; 9:5, 10; 16:5; 20:17; see the eighth textual note on 5:11). Here the anthropomorphism with "eye" is dropped.

וְלֹא אֶנָּחֵם—Older translations rendered the Niphal of נָחַם by saying that Yahweh does or (as here) does not "repent" (KJV, RSV), but more accurate is "relent, change his decision."[14] Because this negated verb is missing in the LXX and the clause "adds a third statement to the two preceding parallel expressions,"[15] Zimmerli and others delete it, but on tenuous grounds.

כִּדְרָכַיִךְ וְכַעֲלִילוֹתַיִךְ שְׁפָטוּךְ—"Behavior, conduct" is an inadequate rendering of דְּרָכִים, literally, "ways," because it easily gives a one-sidedly moralistic or legalistic flavor to the cause for judgment. עֲלִילוֹת often refers specifically to "evil deeds" (BDB, s.v. עֲלִילָה, 2 c). But both words (especially דְּרָכִים) ultimately involve also faith or its absence—the spiritual demeanor, orientation, and religious motivation (and there will always be one!) behind the deeds.

Probably the most debated form in the verse is the third common plural verb שְׁפָטוּךְ, "*they* will judge/punish you." The form is a prophetic perfect; the deed is as good as done. Although the word is commonly translated "judge," here there is not the slightest doubt what the verdict will be, so "punish" seems more appropriate. The versions and some later Hebrew manuscripts uniformly have the first person singular, "I will judge/punish you," which we might well expect after the emphatic introduction to the verse (אֲנִי יְהוָה) and the first person forms of the preceding verbs in the verse. Often in Ezekiel, Yahweh uses a first person singular Qal perfect of שָׁפַט with suffix (e.g., 7:3, 8; 16:38; 36:19). But Yahweh has also spoken explicitly of the foreigners he will incite against Judah to "punish" her (שָׁפַט in 23:24, 45). The MT is certainly the lectio difficilior. Theologically, it is a distinction without a difference. Whether mediately (through some historical agency) or through some immediate action, Israel's judgment will be God's doing.

The LXX has a verse-length addition to 24:14, in effect a summary of Israel's misdeeds. This is unusual, because generally in Ezekiel the LXX has a shorter text

---

[14] For the translation and theology, see the excursus "When Yahweh Changes a Prior Verdict" in Lessing, *Jonah*, 324–41.

[15] Zimmerli, *Ezekiel*, 1:496.

than the MT. There is no way to test it, but it seems unlikely that the Greek translator would have composed it himself, so it may well have been present in the Hebrew version from which he was translating. Nothing of substance that has not already been stated numerous times is gained or lost by its presence or absence.

24:16 הִנְנִי לֹקֵחַ—The interjection הִנֵּה (with first common singular suffix) followed by a participle (Qal of לָקַח) may, as often elsewhere, mean "I am about to." Yet the participle may also be taken in its basically tenseless sense, something in the process of happening but probably also to conclude very shortly. To convey this thought, the idiomatic English periphrasis "I am taking away" works very well.

מַחְמַד עֵינֶיךָ—The construct phrase, "the desire of your eyes," will be repeated in 24:21, 25. The noun מַחְמָד is a derivative of חָמַד, "to desire," traditionally rendered "covet" in the last two commandments (Ex 20:17; Deut 5:21a; Deut 5:21b uses the synonym הִתְאַוָּה). In the Decalogue, "you shall not desire the wife of your neighbor" (Ex 20:17b; Deut 5:21a) prohibits coveting someone other than one's own spouse (cf. Mt 5:27–32). Like greed, lust in effect establishes another "god" in violation of the First Commandment. Ezekiel has used the noun חֶמֶד, "desire," negatively: in 23:6, 12, 23, Yahweh refers to Israel's sexual lust for handsome men (rather than for her God and husband). But מַחְמָד may also refer to legitimate enjoyment and appreciation of people—a desire instilled by God the Creator and sanctioned by God the Redeemer, as is clearly required here in reference to Ezekiel's desire for his wife. This is the noun's meaning in Song 5:16, where Solomon's wife uses its intensive plural to describe her husband at the conclusion of her description of his bodily features (Song 5:10–16): וְכֻלּוֹ מַחֲמַדִּים, "all of him is exquisitely delightful."[16]

Most modern translations, apparently beginning with RSV, replace the literal "desire" with "delight": "the delight of your eyes." Perhaps there was a fear that in our sex-drenched culture, "desire" would carry too much erotic freight, but that need not be so—and in the context of marriage, it would scarcely be objectionable, even if it were to the point. However, "delight" is a perfectly acceptable translation too.

בְּמַגֵּפָה—"Stroke" is the traditional rendering of מַגֵּפָה, with בְּ, probably in an instrumental sense ("by means of"). This noun is used both of the result of a protracted sickness (Zech 14:12–18; 2 Chr 21:14) as well as a sudden, unexpected death by almost any means: battle, injury, or catastrophic malady, such as (what we would call) a heart attack or stroke. Here something of the latter sort seems likely, although we are given no specifics. The accent is entirely on Yahweh as the agent of death. The clause in 24:18, וַתָּמָת אִשְׁתִּי בָּעֶרֶב ("my wife died in the evening"), inevitably shapes our understanding of what Yahweh is predicting in 24:16.

וְלֹא תָבוֹא דִּמְעָתֶךָ:—This last clause, literally, "and your tear shall not come," is missing in the LXX and has no counterpart in 24:22–23. Commentators frequently delete it as superfluous after the two preceding prohibitions. Zimmerli makes much out of the fact that in this clause the negative particle is written fully (וְלֹא), because the plene writing of לֹא alone occurs nowhere in the book and וְלֹא occurs only here

---

[16] For this translation and its theological implications, one may see Mitchell, *The Song of Songs*, 939–41, 944–65.

and in 16:56.[17] However, its full spelling is common with an interrogative, הֲלֹא (e.g., 13:7; 24:25), and such minor orthographic variation seems too tiny a thread upon which to hang much of an argument. This clause contains three stresses (accented words) in contrast to the preceding two clauses, each of which had two stressed words, so it provides poetic variation.

24:17 Many details of the traditional mourning rites mentioned here are unclear.

הֵאָנֵק ׀ דֹּם—According to the MT's punctuation, the first prohibition comprises only these two words. הֵאָנֵק is the Niphal imperative of אָנַק, "groan" (as the Niphal meant in 9:4). Since the Qal is virtually synonymous (as in 26:15), the Niphal may have its usual reflexive force to make the point that this is something Ezekiel is to do to, or by, himself.

Most likely דֹּם too is to be parsed as an imperative (Qal of דָּמַם). Literally, then, "groan, be silent" is an oxymoron, but it expresses both Ezekiel's natural inner grief as well as his unnatural failure to give any audible or visible expression of it. Clearly the expression means "groan silently." Conceivably דֹּם is an infinitive, though the infinitive of דָּמַם is not otherwise attested in the OT. Complicating matters is the fact that Hebrew has two (BDB) or three (*HALOT*) homonymous geminate verbs דָּמַם. The one reflected in my translation is lexically classified as דָּמַם I (BDB; *HALOT*).

Zimmerli quibbles that דָּמַם more basically means "ceasing to move." He connects it with the following מֵתִים (raising other problems; see below) and translates, "deathly stiffness," then explains that "as the motionlessness of the dead or a fixed immobility in the face of coming death."[18] But, prescinding from the repunctuation involved, "silent(ly)" is still an acceptable translation for דֹּם, even if a picture of motionlessness lurks in the background.

If the punctuation of the Masoretic Text is ignored and the first three words of the verse, הֵאָנֵק ׀ דֹּם מֵתִים, are taken together, דֹּם could be the Qal imperative of דָּמַם II, "to wail, lament" (*HALOT*). The resultant translation would be "groan a moaning for the dead," which seems to me to be a highly unlikely redundancy. (However, the following words, "perform no mourning rites [אֵבֶל]," could stand by themselves.)

מֵתִים אֵבֶל לֹא־תַעֲשֶׂה—The MT's punctuation connects these words. The participle of מוּת and the noun אֵבֶל have often been translated "mourning for the dead," in effect reversing their order, as though the text were the construct chain אֵבֶל־מֵתִים. However, that is contrary to one of the most elementary rules of Hebrew grammar. It is better to construe both מֵתִים and אֵבֶל as accusative objects of the verb. A literal rendering is then "you shall not make the dead (the reason for) mourning (rites)," as, in effect, I have translated.

פְּאֵרְךָ חֲבוֹשׁ עָלֶיךָ—The first breach of mourning custom is that Ezekiel is to "bind, tie up, fasten" (חֲבוֹשׁ, imperative of חָבַשׁ) his פְּאֵר upon himself. That noun is rather generic for "headdress," whether of men, women, or priests. We may suspect that this word was chosen because the meaning of its root, the verb פָּאַר, is "to beau-

---

[17] Zimmerli, *Ezekiel*, 1:502.
[18] Zimmerli, *Ezekiel*, 1:502.

tify, glorify." If so, no ordinary headgear is meant, but a "festive turban" or the like, making all the greater contrast to the usual baring of the head and the sprinkling of dust or ashes on it —the same contrast as in Is 61:3.

וּנְעָלֶיךָ תָּשִׂים בְּרַגְלֶיךָ—Likewise, this command contrasts with the mourning custom of people denying themselves the comfort of sandals and walking about discalced (2 Sam 15:30; Is 20:2).

וְלֹא תַעְטֶה עַל־שָׂפָם—This clause prohibits Ezekiel from wrapping (Qal of עָטָה) his שָׂפָם, "moustache" (BDB; *HALOT*, 1) or "upper lip." The custom is utterly alien to us and must be explained. The turban was removed and it or another cloth was used to wrap the lower part of the face to the upper lip, thus covering the mustache and beard (a man's "ornaments"). Sometimes even the hair was shaved off together with the mustache (Micah 1:16).

וְלֶחֶם אֲנָשִׁים לֹא תֹאכֵל:—The final prohibition is against eating (literally) "bread [food] of men." Exactly what is meant is not clear. Theoretically it could imply a command to fast, but performing that mourning custom would send entirely the opposite signal from the other actions Ezekiel is to perform. Naturally, the temptation to emend is irresistible to many. A favorite is to change אֲנָשִׁים to אוֹנִים, "mourners,"[19] after a phrase found once in Hos 9:4 and perhaps supported by the Targum and Vulgate (so RSV, NRSV). The reference may ultimately be to the same thing, but the emendation, eliminating the *shin*, is a relatively radical emendation. Wellhausen's suggestion simply to repoint the consonants to אֲנֻשִׁים, "despairing, calamitous," is textually minor, but not clearly required.[20]

Most likely, לֶחֶם אֲנָשִׁים is simply a traditional expression for a custom (with certain distant parallels in our own customs) whereby friends would bring mourners their first meal after burial. There are various other OT references to the custom. Hos 9:4 probably does refer to the same custom, using different language. In 2 Sam 3:35, "all the people" bring food to David after Abner's funeral. Jer 16:5 may be relevant also, although the language gives one pause. Jeremiah is forbidden to enter a בֵּית מַרְזֵחַ, apparently referring to a place where sodalities celebrated feasts for the dead; these feasts apparently often degenerated into rather riotous and dissolute occasions (cf. Amos 6:7).

24:18 "I spoke to the people that morning" most naturally describes Ezekiel as addressing the people on the morning before his wife died; presumably the content of his preaching that morning was the message of 24:1–14 and also the substance of 24:16–17. Many commentators profess to find difficulties about the sequence of events. I have translated the three events in 24:18 in the order in which they appear in the text. My translation clarifies that the first בַּבֹּקֶר was *that* morning and that the second בַּבֹּקֶר is "the *next* morning."

Not all commentators are convinced the three events should be in this order, but the perceived inconcinnity seems almost inevitable in the transitions between pure narrative and the oracular material on either side. Although there is no support from

---

[19] Cf. Zimmerli, *Ezekiel*, 1:503.

[20] See Allen, *Ezekiel*, 2:56.

the ancient versions for shortening or rearranging the text, Zimmerli deletes the first clause,[21] while Allen places it between 24:19 and 24:20,[22] and there are other proposals.

24:19 הֲלֹא־תַגִּיד לָנוּ מָה־אֵלֶּה לָּנוּ—The second לָנוּ ("won't you tell us what these things [mean] *for us*?") is not reflected in the LXX and other versions, and hence is often deleted as an erroneous repetition of the first לָנוּ. But it is more likely that the versions erroneously omitted the second לָּנוּ, which is exegetically significant. See the commentary.

24:21 הִנְנִי מְחַלֵּל אֶת־מִקְדָּשִׁי—Again, הִנֵּה with first common singular suffix and a participle denotes imminent action: "I am about to …" מְחַלֵּל is the Piel participle of חָלַל, "to profane" what was holy, as in, for example, 13:19; 20:13, 16. מִקְדָּשׁ is the same term for "sanctuary" used in previous accusations that the people had defiled it (e.g., 5:11; 23:38–39).

וּמַחְמַל נַפְשְׁכֶם—This is translated as "the yearning of your hearts" and refers most directly to the sanctuary, as does the preceding phrase, "the desire of your eyes." Yet it may also allude to the exiles' children, mentioned at the end of the verse. The noun מַחְמָל is a hapax, but an obvious derivative of the common verb חָמַל, "to pity, care about, have compassion." Since that verb is used elsewhere of loving concern for children (Ex 2:6; Mal 3:17), it is probably transitional to the last thought in the verse. It suggests that many of Ezekiel's fellow exiles were older people whose children had been left behind in the doomed city. נֶפֶשׁ lacks any precise English equivalent; it implies a person's inner being, almost what he lives for. With many others, I have deemed the metaphor of "heart" to be a better carrier of that implication than "soul."

The parallel phrase in 24:25, מַשָּׂא נַפְשָׁם, uses the noun מַשָּׂא (from נָשָׂא, "carry, lift"). Therefore, many[23] derive מַחְמַל not from the common Hebrew verb, but from a cognate in Arabic, where *ḥml* is an almost exact synonym of the Hebrew נָשָׂא. The result would be that מַחְמָל would mean "that to which one lifts (his desire)," an almost precise parallel to the previous phrase in both 24:21 and 24:25: "the desire of your/their eyes." Such repetitiousness seems intrinsically unlikely, although Ezekiel does use different wording in 24:25 (מַשָּׂא נַפְשָׁם) to avoid repetition of the phrase here (וּמַחְמַל נַפְשְׁכֶם). As Greenberg observes, the appeal to Arabic "is ingenious but unnecessary."[24]

24:23 וּפְאֵרְכֶם—This is the plural of פְּאֵר (see the fourth textual note on 24:17) with second masculine plural suffix, written defectively for וּפְאֵרֵיכֶם. Many Hebrew manuscripts have the full spelling.

24:25 בֶּן־אָדָם—A new divine address to the prophet as "son of man" sets apart 24:25–27 somewhat from the preceding. At the same time, much of the vocabulary and the motif of 24:25 echo 24:21, although various stylistic changes appear. This

[21] Zimmerli, *Ezekiel*, 1:503.

[22] Allen, *Ezekiel*, 2:56.

[23] Zimmerli, *Ezekiel*, 1:503; Allen, *Ezekiel*, 2:56; even already Keil, *Ezekiel*, 1:349–50.

[24] Greenberg, *Ezekiel*, 2:511.

verse plays a transitional role. The forward-looking aspect of 24:25–27 will be evident by the appearance of פָּלִיט, "survivor," in 24:26–27, anticipating the fulfillment of the prediction when the פָּלִיט does arrive in 33:21–22.

הֲלֹוא—Literally, "is it not … ?" indicates that the sentence, which continues through the end of 24:26, is a rhetorical question, phrased as such to stress its importance. Many translations render 24:25–26 as a declarative sentence, but I have opted to retain the interrogative form.

מָעוּזָּם—The construct phrase in 24:21, גְּאֹון עֻזְּכֶם, "the stronghold of which you are so proud," is replaced by this an assonantal counterpart, the noun מָעֹוז with third masculine plural suffix, "their stronghold." Morphologically, the word is a hybrid. The doubling of its *zayin* before suffixes (-ֻזּ-) indicates a derivation from עָזַז, "to be strong." Without that doubling, we would assume that מָעֹוז is derived from עוּז, "to seek refuge" (the root under which BDB lists מָעֹוז). The meanings are complementary because strongholds or fortresses were inevitably also places of refuge. Perhaps a deliberate fusion of the two ideas was intended. Ezekiel uses מָעֹוז only once elsewhere, in 30:15 of Syene, an Egyptian stronghold. Of other OT passages with מָעֹוז, probably most relevant is Dan 11:31, where it is explicitly applied to the temple.

מְשֹׂושׂ תִּפְאַרְתָּם—This is, literally, "the joy of their glory" (KJV). However, both מָשֹׂושׂ and תִּפְאֶרֶת are used by themselves in other passages for the temple or for Jerusalem, where it was located. Thus many translations consider these two nouns to be separate objects (e.g., ESV: "when I take … their joy and glory"). מָשֹׂושׂ derives from שׂושׂ, whose cognates usually refer to extreme joy as at weddings and other celebrations (see, e.g., the noun שָׂשֹׂון in Is 61:3; Ps 45:8 [ET 45:7]). Jer 49:25 calls Jerusalem קִרְיַת מְשֹׂושִׂי, "the city of my rejoicing." The noun תִּפְאֶרֶת is from the same root (פאר) as פְּאֵר, "headdress, turban" (24:17, 23). The construct phrase בֵּית תִּפְאַרְתִּי, "the house of my glory," is used of the temple in Is 60:7, and תִּפְאֶרֶת pertains to the temple in Ps 96:6 and Lam 2:1.

One should not overlook the *athnach* under תִּפְאַרְתָּם in the MT. It is followed asyndetically by more temple epithets, two phrases, each introduced by the direct object marker אֵת. The first אֵת lacks a copula, which seems to indicate that the next two epithets ("the desire of their eyes" and "that on which they set their minds") are appositional to the previous two. At the same time, the next two are connected with "their sons and their daughters," who were also mentioned in 24:21. In that way, "the desire of (their) eyes," which in 24:15 had referred to a person (Ezekiel's wife) and in 24:21 to the temple, here does double duty, expressing that both the children and the temple were precious and desirable.

Thus the parallel between Ezekiel's action prophecy and the people's future actions is cemented. The people's loss of both the temple and the city with their children is further underscored by having מַשָּׂא נַפְשָׁם follow "the desire of their eyes." A similar, but not identical, expression had been used in 24:21 (with מַחְמָל instead of מַשָּׂא; see the second textual note on 24:21). That to which one lifts up his נֶפֶשׁ ("self/being") is that to which his heart is inclined, that on which his devotion is focused, and that for which he cherishes a desire or longing. Typologically, one thinks of Bach's famous "Jesu, Joy of Man's Desiring."

24:26 בַּיּוֹם הַהוּא יָבוֹא הַפָּלִיט אֵלֶיךָ—Syntactically בַּיּוֹם הַהוּא connects this verse both with הַיּוֹם in the previous verse and with the identical phrase at the beginning of 24:27. Content-wise, it introduces a new and climactic topic, the "survivor," whose significance is developed further in 24:27.

It is debatable whether or not the definite article on הַפָּלִיט is generic, that is, "*a* survivor/refugee," a person of that genus or status (so Joüon, § 137 n (2)), or whether it implies one specific person appointed by God for this purpose—whether he was aware of it or not. If theologically attuned, especially at this pivotal point in the history of salvation, the second option is very attractive. Grammatically, however, one cannot be dogmatic.

לְהַשְׁמָעוּת אָזְנָיִם:—This is, literally, "to cause ears to hear." הַשְׁמָעוּת (with לְ) is an Aramaic form of Hiphil infinitive of שָׁמַע (GKC, §§ 53 l; 54 k; Joüon, §§ 54 c, 88M j) or possibly a verbal noun substituting for the infinitive. The prophet is obviously the primary recipient and beneficiary of the news the פָּלִיט brings. Conceivably, the accent is on the physical aural faculties of the prophet because, in principle, he had long known it by divine revelation (24:1–2). My translation, "to let you hear it with your own ears," concentrates on the prophet, as do most ancient and modern translations. However, the lack of indication in the text of whose "ears" will hear may intend to imply that the message is also for the "ears" of the entire community. The next verse will speak further of the connection between the prophet and the exiles.

24:27 יִפָּתַח פִּיךָ אֶת־הַפָּלִיט—The subject of the passive verb (Niphal third masculine singular imperfect of פָּתַח), "will be opened," is פִּיךָ, "your mouth" (פֶּה with second masculine singular suffix). אֶת־הַפָּלִיט then must be "with the survivor," using the preposition אֵת, "with" (not the sign of the direct object). The wording is attested by the versions, although they interpret it in various ways. I have taken it temporally and freely translated, "with the coming of the survivor." Naturally, many critics take אֶת־הַפָּלִיט as a gloss intended to harmonize the discrepancy they perceive between 24:25, 27 and 33:21–22.[25] But this is of a piece with their theories about the redaction of this entire part of the book. See the introduction, the textual note on 24:1, and the commentary on 24:25–27.

וְלֹא תֵאָלֵם עוֹד—For the Niphal of אָלַם, "be speechless," which recurs in 33:22, see the second textual note on 3:26.

Commentary

By almost any reckoning, this is a central and pivotal chapter in the book of Ezekiel. By what is probably only a happy coincidence, by chapter count it is also the midpoint of the book (although if we count verses, we have to wait until the end of chapter 25, as the *Masorah finales*, the ancient compilation at the end of each book of the Hebrew Bible, informs us).

The chapter climaxes and in many ways summarizes everything Ezekiel has been preaching in especially the previous twelve chapters: the fatuity of

---

[25] See, for example, Zimmerli, *Ezekiel*, 1:504, 508; cf. Allen, *Ezekiel*, 2:56.

the people's illusions that Jerusalem is secure. But the time of reckoning has come. The chapter turns on two fateful days: the beginning of the siege of the city, announced in 24:1, and an anticipation of its fall, which would take place two and a half years later, although its fall is not recorded until 33:21.

Structurally, the chapter divides into two discrete sections: (1) a מָשָׁל, "parable" (24:3), of a cooking pot and its application (24:1–14) and (2) the action prophecy of Ezekiel's strange behavior when his wife dies and what it portends.

The Parable of the Cooking Pot and Its Application (24:1–14)

Prophecy of the Date of Jerusalem's Siege (24:1–2)

24:1 The date when the siege of Jerusalem commenced is not formulated in Ezekiel's usual way. Remarkably, the two other records of this date in the OT (2 Ki 25:1; Jer 52:4) are formulated in almost the identical wording used by Ezekiel. On our modern, Western calendar, this date probably was around January 15, 588. Ezekiel records this date at a time when neither he nor his fellow exiles could possibly know about the events in Judah apart from divine revelation. See further the textual note on 24:1 and figure 1, "The Dates in Ezekiel."

24:2 In very careful language, Ezekiel is literally commanded to record the "name" of the day: "the king of Babylon laid siege to Jerusalem on this very day." The beginning of the siege of Jerusalem was the beginning of the end for the politico-theological system begun by David and Solomon. When word would come nearly two years later of the city's fall, the reports of the few survivors would be found to match the prophet's prediction. Not only would that authenticate him as a true prophet to an unbelieving audience (cf. Deut 18:21–22), but in the meantime, it would give a sense of urgency to the prophet's preaching. Time was running out, not only in the general sense that one never knows the day or the hour (cf. Mt 24:36; 25:13) of future events, but in this pivotal moment in the history of God's people. The repeated "this very day" indicates that what follows is the culmination and fulfillment of all the prophecies of judgment in chapters 4–23.

The Parable of the Cooking Pot (24:3–5)

24:3–5 After the imperative command to note carefully the beginning of the siege ("record," 24:2), another imperative comes in 24:3 to "tell a parable" (the parable in 24:3–5), and yet another imperative ("take out," 24:6) occurs at the beginning of the application of the parable (24:6–14).

The parable is to be addressed to the בֵּית־הַמֶּרִי, "rebellious house" (literally, "house of rebellion" instead of the "house of Israel"), an epithet not voiced for some time (since 17:12). But the motif had been used already in 2:3, 5–8 in Ezekiel's prophetic commissioning. That is, after all of Ezekiel's labors, the people's orientation remained as refractory as ever, and even with the enemy at the gates, they were not about to relent.

The parable is to center on a סִיר, a cooking "pot." The process of boiling meat in it is described with eight imperatives in 24:3b–5, with three already in 24:3b. Yahweh had taken up the figure of a cooking pot once before, when he corrected the use of the metaphor by the deluded men of Jerusalem (11:3–11), who thought they were safe within the pot. That passage has affinities to this chapter. Especially significant is the use of מִבְחָר, "choice [cuts of meat]," in 24:4–5, which refers to the people's illusion of safety and superiority: the residents of Jerusalem considered themselves to be God's elect, safe within the vessel, despite the earlier deportation of supposedly inferior components of the population.

We are not told in this parable what sort of meal is being prepared. The impression is clearly given, however, that it will be no ordinary meal. Large quantities of the choicest portions of the choicest animals are to be cooked. And the סִיר is not the day pot of everyday life, but a copper cauldron (24:11). One plausible hypothesis, especially in the light of Ezekiel's concern with issues of purity and defilement, is that a cultic meal is in mind. If so, the meal would probably be the זֶבַח שְׁלָמִים, the "peace offering," or better, "communion sacrifice" (e.g., Lev 3:1, 3), celebrating both horizontal unity with other believers and vertical fellowship with Yahweh.[26] Thus Block may well be correct in supposing that "a Jerusalem audience would have undoubtedly received this song with great enthusiasm and interpreted it positively."[27]

The First Interpretation of the Parable (24:6–8)

24:6 As in 12:22–23, the interpretation of the parable (מָשָׁל) is introduced by לָכֵן, "therefore," which here, as often, is followed by the citation formula: "thus says the Lord Yahweh."[28] In fact, the guilt of the city is so great that Yahweh presents two complementary interpretations of the parable, each introduced by "therefore" and the citation formula (in 24:6 and 24:9). The first explanation of the parable (24:6–8) speaks of the imminent judgment on the inhabitants of Jerusalem, and the second (24:9–12) of the judgment on the city itself. In both, the figures in the parable and the facts to which they refer repeatedly intertwine, a situation that sometimes complicates both translation and understanding. Then 24:13 all but abandons the figures and shifts to the second person of direct address ("you"), and the conclusion of the section in 24:14 is anything but figurative.

The parable had been addressed to the "rebellious house" (24:3). Both interpretations of it are addressed to "the city of bloodshed" or "the bloody city" (עִיר הַדָּמִים, 24:6, 9), a theme that 24:7–8 will develop at length. Ezekiel had already used that epithet for the city in 22:2 (see the commentary there).

---

[26] See Kleinig, *Leviticus*, 84, 92–96.

[27] Block, *Ezekiel*, 1:776.

[28] For this formula, see pages 8–9 in the introduction and the fourth textual note and the commentary on 2:4.

Since the city is still full of "filth" (if that is the meaning of חֶלְאָה; see the first textual note on 24:6), that is, impurity and godlessness, the cuts of meat (the inhabitants of the city) will have to be removed one by one, or the city will never be purged. The implication is a frontal challenge to the people's perception of their status before God. Far from being choice cuts that would surely be saved, the residents of the city are stinking, rotten meat that must be charred and discarded.

The last clause of 24:6, "no lot has fallen on it," is somewhat obscure. The pronoun "it" must refer to the city or to its "cuts" (24:6), that is, residents considered collectively. Many interpretations have been proposed. My understanding is that no one in the city will be given any choice. No "lot" will consign only some to death and/or exile, while sparing others; all will, in effect, experience the same judgment. Since all are complicit in the same apostasy, all will suffer the same fate. There will be no need to cast lots to determine guilt (as in Joshua 7), because all have flaunted their blood guilt for all to see. All the meat in the pot is so rotten that no one will be interested in salvaging even a piece. (There are other interpretations or variations on the interpretation offered here, but there is no point in listing them all.)

24:7 "The blood she shed" is a semi-interpretative translation, since the Hebrew simply has "her blood is in her midst." Israel had many laws pertaining to blood, all centering on the understanding that "the life of the flesh is in the blood" (Lev 17:11) and explaining why blood played such a central role in sacrificial contexts of atonement and communion, as it still does in its Christian antitype, the Lord's Supper.

"For, because, seeing that" (כִּי) at the beginning of 24:7 suggests that 24:7a may continue the thought of 24:6 and have a different abuse in mind than the rest of the verse. If there is a connection, the hint of cooking a meal (which turned out to be inedible) in 24:6 may mean that in 24:7a Ezekiel has in mind violators of what today are usually referred to as the kosher laws. Especially Lev 17:10–16 lays down strict rules for eating only meat from which all the blood had been thoroughly drained. If Jerusalem, pictured as a cut of meat, still had its blood in its midst, it was unfit for human consumption. Far from being a choice cut, it was, from the sacral standpoint, in the same category as rotten meat, and no one would cast a lot for it (if that clause at the end of 24:6 is relevant here).

On the other hand, the entirety of 24:7 may refer to the same thing, that is, murder, the shedding of innocent blood, particularly if it was judicial murder as a result of the corruption of the legal system. That understanding would align the entire verse with 22:1–31, where the city had been termed "bloody" (22:2). The sacrificial slaughter of children to Molech, apparently especially on the בָּמוֹת ("high places," Jer 32:35) may again come into view here (see the commentary on Ezek 16:20–21; 20:31; 23:37). Even when animals or birds were slain for food, the blood was to be poured out and covered with earth (Lev 17:13; Deut 12:16, 23–24; 15:23). Blood that was not covered with earth and

buried is pictured as retaining some of its life force. In cases of murder, the blood cries out to heaven for vengeance—so, for the first time, said Yahweh to Cain after his murder of Abel (Gen 4:10). Job (16:18) requests that the earth not cover his blood, so that the outcry over his misfortunes would not cease to seek redress. In Jerusalem, no one had taken the trouble to atone for the people's murderous activity according to the Mosaic Law. It was not merely a matter of neglect; the people had deliberately poured the blood of their victims on the bare rock, where there was no soil, almost as if in boast of their "lifestyle."

24:8 There is a surprising shift to the first person as Yahweh himself speaks. Jerusalem's flaunting of its guilt is really God's doing. He himself is seeing to it that the blood on the bare rock remains exposed so that the city's crimes remain manifest, a reminder (a common biblical anthropomorphism) to him to execute his just judgment upon it. Zimmerli laudably terms it "a striking counterpart to the divine remembrance of his [God's] own mercy in the rainbow in Gen 9:12–17."[29] He will accomplish this judgment by his wrath at brazen, unrepented sin, thus requiting the wrongs the people have committed (see the textual note on 24:8 regarding נָקָם).

This is the first time that this oracle explicitly speaks of Yahweh's response to Jerusalem's sins. The verse forms a transition to the following verses, which will accent the wrath of Yahweh's judgment.

The Second Interpretation of the Parable (24:9–12)

24:9 The opening words, deliberately repeating 24:6a, lead into the theme of 24:9b–12, namely, that Yahweh himself will intervene directly and see to it that Jerusalem's deserved punishment is carried out thoroughly. Ezek 24:9b harks back to the parable itself and in a sense repeats part of 24:5, only now not in the imperative mood, addressing some unstated actor, but in the indicative of Yahweh himself assuming the role of cook. First of all, he sees to it that there is sufficient firewood to make an extremely hot fire. The word "pyre" here (מְדוּרָה) is a noun derivative of the verb דּוּר in 24:5, "pile up [the logs]."

24:10–11 For all their obscurities (see the textual notes), the gist of these verses seems reasonably clear. God directs the process, step by step, until all the filthy contents of the pot (and perhaps the pot itself) have been consumed in the fire. The language basically continues the metaphor, but words like טֻמְאָה, "uncleanness," and חֶלְאָה, "filth" (24:11), readily assume moral and theological overtones, which, of course, is the point of it all.

24:12 The verse is difficult but seems to say that since milder, less drastic means of cleansing the pot have proven ineffective, no alternative remained but to use the extreme measures pictured. Ezek 24:13 will repeat the thought but will abandon the picture to speak to the actual historical situation.

---

[29] Zimmerli, *Ezekiel*, 1:500.

Conclusion of the Prophecy of Jerusalem's Destruction (24:13–14)

The abandonment of the third person in favor of second person feminine forms ("you") in these two verses makes clear that this section is Yahweh's direct address to the "bloody city" (24:6, 9) itself.

24:13 Most of this verse is dominated by the verb טָהֵר, whose Piel (once here) means "cleanse," and whose Qal (twice here) means "become/be clean." This verse has the first appearance of the Piel of this verb in Ezekiel, and Yahweh's use of it for Israel virtually has to be translated as "I *tried to* cleanse you." By his own repeated testimony, Israel had been unclean and depraved from birth (16:3–5; cf. Ps 51:7 [ET 51:5]) and had never come clean in admitting its guilt, repenting, and changing its ways.

Exactly what does Yahweh mean when he speaks of his earlier attempts at cleansing his people? There are quite a number of possibilities, and perhaps it is a matter of the accumulation of all of them. The covenant of Moses included the sacrificial and liturgical cultus in Leviticus with its distinction between holy and profane, clean and unclean, which was provided by Yahweh to justify, sanctify, and cleanse his people.[30] Here Israel's failure to be cleansed may be considered a fulfillment of the picture in Lev 26:14–35, which depicts Yahweh's graduated futile chastisements on the people in an attempt to forestall their final judgment. The Bible records judgment after preliminary judgment in attempts to remind Israel of the exodus and Sinai events and all that followed from them, including Yahweh's provision of sanctifying worship at the tabernacle and temple.

Yahweh probably also intends to refer to his repeated threats and promises communicated through the prophets. Contemporary to this period of Ezekiel's ministry are the prophecies of Jeremiah in Jer 25:3–4 and 26:5, which speak in this vein. Especially 2 Chr 36:15–17, a little meditation on the fall of Jerusalem, may echo Ezekiel's oracle here. Jesus will speak similarly in Mt 23:37 (‖ Lk 13:34) and elsewhere, as will St. Stephen before his martyrdom (Acts 7, especially 7:51–53). "The hound of heaven"[31] never ceases to pursue the lost and straying, but (mixing metaphors) the time comes when the door is shut (Mt 25:10). It is not in principle different for groups of believers as for individuals: "it is appointed unto men once to die, but after this the judgment" (Heb 9:27 KJV).

That is precisely the point we hear in the final clause of the verse: "you will not be clean again from your impurity until I have satisfied my wrath upon you." For "satisfy wrath," see the third textual note and the commentary on 5:13, where Yahweh used the same vocabulary.

But if we read 24:13 (and 5:13) closely, we note a hint of Gospel rebirth in the words. The clear implication is that once God's righteous wrath is satis-

---

[30] See Kleinig, *Leviticus*, 1–13.

[31] "The Hound of Heaven" is a poem by Francis Thompson (1859–1907).

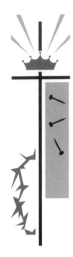

fied, he *will* make another attempt to cleanse his people—and succeed. The message is not one of total annihilation. This is not yet the time for Ezekiel to elaborate on the Gospel promise to a remnant (expounded in chapters 33–48), but it must be borne in mind as we read the next verse's final threat, the fire of judgment which the people must first experience. This judgment will come two and a half years hence, in the burning of Jerusalem in summer 586 B.C., a portent of the fiery baptism that Jesus Christ will undergo on the cross (Lk 12:49–50). There God's righteous wrath at humanity's sin will be fully satisfied, and God will reconstitute his new, cleansed Israel consisting of all in Christ (e.g., Gal 6:16).

24:14 Chapters 1–24 of Ezekiel consist almost exclusively of judgment oracles against Israel.[32] Since 24:1–14 is, in effect, the last of these oracles, it closes appropriately with about as strong an assertion of the certainty of imminent judgment as is imaginable. With seven verbs signifying completeness—three of them assertions, then three negated verbs, and a final one another assertion—the bell tolls, as it were, announcing the death of the city, the close of an era. This verse begins with the self-identification of the speaker, "I, Yahweh, have spoken,"[33] and closes with the signatory formula, "says the Lord Yahweh."[34] These phrases underscore all that the sacred name "Yahweh" carries with it, the God who had revealed himself to the chosen people as a God of covenant grace and promise, but also a God of zeal and justice. With him they had trifled, and him they finally mocked by their contumacy, so "the Day of Yahweh" (13:5; see also chapter 7) must be a "day of wrath" (Zeph 1:15), and it is just around the corner.

The Death of Ezekiel's Wife and the Destruction of the Temple (24:15–27)

The appearance in 24:15–16 of the word-event formula, "the Word of Yahweh came to me,"[35] and the use of "son of man"[36] (24:16) indicate that, for all practical purposes, a new chapter begins here. The message is still doom but is communicated now primarily by an action prophecy rather than through an ordinary oracle or sermon. The passage is undated, but according to the apparent sense of 24:18, the initial revelation of the impending death of Ezekiel's wife came on the evening of the same day—the day of the beginning of Jerusalem's blockade (24:1–2). That morning Ezekiel had preached to the people (24:18), and presumably his sermon consisted of the prophecy of 24:3–14 and the substance of 24:16–17. Later that day came the word concerning his wife's death, then the following morning the discussion with the people about

---

[32] See pages 10–12 in the introduction.

[33] See page 9 in the introduction.

[34] For this formula, see pages 8–9 in the introduction and the second textual note on 5:11.

[35] For this formula, see page 8 in the introduction and the textual note on 3:16.

[36] See the second textual note and the commentary on 2:1.

his strange behavior (24:18b–24). Ezek 24:25–27 is a distinct message, also undated. It may have come the same day as 24:1–17, or perhaps at some later date in the middle of the siege, though it is a fitting conclusion for this chapter.

Even if the date of reception of 24:15–24 and 24:25–27 was the same as the first part of the chapter, their shared subject is different. The first part of the chapter describes the inexorable process of Jerusalem's destruction, while in these verses we have a preview of the immediate aftermath of the fulfillment of that prophecy.

The half chapter, as already intimated, easily divides into two uneven parts: (1) 24:15–24, the prophet's action prophecy and what it portends, and (2) 24:25–27, a prediction of the prophet's release from dumbness. The first section, in turn, is easily divisible into (1) 24:15–17, Yahweh's foretelling of the death of Ezekiel's wife and the prohibition of showing any sign of mourning, and (2) 24:18–24, the prophet's explanation of his actions as a prefigurement of the people's behavior at the catastrophe.

The Death of Ezekiel's Wife and What It Portends (24:15–24)

24:16 It is customary, but appropriate, to digress here and note that this is one of the very few times where we get even a glimpse of Ezekiel's personal life. Generally, his apparently harsh and unyielding exterior, his zeal for the truth and the honor of God's holy name all but conceal the person behind them. Even here, Yahweh makes plain that the prophet's personal feelings are beside the point. But we do at least learn that he had a wife, who probably accompanied him into exile almost nine years earlier in 597 B.C. and whom he regarded as the "desire/delight of [his] eyes" (24:16). Indirectly, of course, one can infer a little more of Ezekiel's wide learning and interests from other parts of the book, but it is all indirect.

It is hard to guess how much of this persona accurately reflected the person and how much of it was imposed upon him (cf. 3:9 at his call, where Yahweh gave him a forehead "like the hardest stone, harder than flint"). In any case, Ezekiel never complains or laments his lot. In this respect, he forms a complete contrast to his contemporary Jeremiah, who carries his heart on his sleeve and often bitterly laments his circumstances (e.g., Jer 20:7–18), which are comparable, but not identical, to Ezekiel's. Jeremiah was not exiled, but if possible, was even more non grata among his contemporaries, and he apparently suffered physically for it far more than Ezekiel. Jeremiah was forbidden by Yahweh to marry (Jer 16:2) and to participate in ordinary social activities (Jer 16:5–8). As Jeremiah explains when questioned, his life, like that of Ezekiel, was a sort of living action prophecy of what the people's lot would be shortly.

Jeremiah is the exception among the prophets for revealing as much as he does about himself in his book; in that respect Isaiah probably is a distant second. The superscriptions of prophetic books often give us only the father's

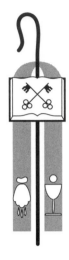

name and/or the place of birth. All that counts is God's Word, not the human "voice" (Is 40:6) chosen to deliver it. A cult of the pastor's personality easily competes with the cultus (worship) of the Savior.

Despite the differences, comparisons between OT prophetic ministry and the holy ministry are almost inevitable, not least in the heavy price ministers often must pay for their concern for scriptural truth—often in the face of indifference or outright hostility. And the great variety evident among the prophets is a reminder that God still uses "all sorts and conditions of men"[37] to make his Law and Gospel known. Pastors may be celibate (like Jeremiah) or married men (like Isaiah) or widowers (as Ezekiel now becomes), even as some of the apostles were married, while others were celibate or perhaps widowers (1 Cor 7:7–8; 9:5).[38] Both single and married men may serve in the holy ministry.[39]

Implicit in Ezek 24:16–24 is the biblical motif of Yahweh as the Husband of his people, his wife. Just as the prophet Ezekiel embodies Yahweh, so Ezekiel's wife represents Jerusalem, and her demise is correlated with that of the city. Ezekiel had developed the marriage motif of Yahweh and his wives in chapters 16 and 23, there tragically needing to stress the people's whoring. However, unlike whoring Israel and Hosea's adulterous wife (Hosea 1–3), nowhere does Yahweh indicate that Ezekiel's wife was guilty of any moral infraction that precipitated her death. The marriage motif that plays out tragically here will be developed positively at length in the NT in terms of Jesus Christ as the Bridegroom and his church as his virgin bride—a betrothal that has abundant implications for Christian family relationships and marriages (e.g., Eph 5:21–33).[40]

24:17 In general, Ezekiel's action prophecies are relatively typical of the genre by being dramatized or acted out.[41] That remains true of his avoidance of the customary behaviors and rituals of mourning, as prescribed in this verse. These actions generally were socially much more rigid and prescribed in traditional societies such as Israel and other societies in antiquity. Even so thoroughly non-traditional a culture as ours has not completely dropped a variety of mourning customs.

But it should not be overlooked that these formally typical action prophecies are set in the context of one that was far less common, namely, one that

---

[37] *All Sorts and Conditions of Men* is the title of a book by Walter Besant (1882).

[38] For the possibility that St. Paul was a widower, as Luther believed, see Lockwood, *1 Corinthians*, 234–36.

[39] See AC and Ap XXIII, "The Marriage of Priests."

[40] For a survey of OT passages depicting the "marriage" of God and Israel, and NT passages portraying the betrothal of the church to Jesus Christ, the Bridegroom, one may see Mitchell, *The Song of Songs*, 40–66.

[41] See "Ezekiel's Action Prophecies" in Hummel, *Ezekiel 1–20*, 148–50.

was experienced in the prophet's personal life and family. This is a type that was not entirely unique to Ezekiel. We have already noted the parallel to Yahweh's command that Jeremiah neither marry nor socialize (Jeremiah 16). And the roles played by the wives and children both of Hosea (chapters 1–3) and of Isaiah (7:3; 8:1–4, 18) are similar in that they too had prophetic significance. Hosea's unfaithful wife embodied unfaithful Israel, but Hosea bought her back just as Yahweh would redeem Israel. The names of Isaiah's children (7:3; 8:1, 3) were prophecies for Israel (8:18).

Christians will add that something similar in a climactic way is true of Christ, of whom all the prophets were forerunners and types and whom all the prophets foresaw. The Gospel rests on what Christ did and who he was and is as well as on what he said. Thus the Second Articles of the Apostles' and Nicene Creeds summarize the person and work of Christ.

What is then true of Christ's predecessors, the prophets, also works in the other A.D. direction as well. To be baptized into Christ means to be baptized into his death and resurrection that "we too might walk in newness of life" (Rom 6:3–4). In Christ we become "a new creation" (2 Cor 5:17). When we celebrate the blessed Sacrament, we say Christ's Words of Institution, and Christ himself is present in his body and blood, with all of our Savior's gifts: "for where there is forgiveness of sins, there is also life and salvation."[42] In an official way, Christ bestows his gifts upon his church particularly through the holy ministry as the pastor speaks and acts in Christ's stead. In a more general but no less real way, Christ is also present and active through the priesthood of all believers (e.g., 1 Pet 2:9). As baptized believers, we are witnesses to (perhaps "types" of) Christ, embodiments (*Christus in nobis*) of his life, death, resurrection, and coming again. "Whoever practices righteousness is righteous, just as that one [Christ] is righteous. ... By this is it manifest who are the children of God and who are the children of the devil: whoever does not practice righteousness is not of God, nor is he who does not love his brother" (1 Jn 3:7, 10). Whoever does not gather with Christ scatters (Mt 12:30 ‖ Lk 11:23).

24:18   We are not told what the prophet spoke to the people about on the first morning, but presumably he preached to them 24:1–14 and also reported 24:16–17. Since those verses do not specify who or what "the desire of [his] eyes" (24:16) was, it is easy to picture the people paying scant attention to what seemed to be merely some more strange talk by the prophet. What the phrase meant will become clear very shortly in 24:18, conceivably for the first time to the prophet himself. If one misreads the first clause of 24:18 ("so I spoke to the people that morning") as referring to the explanation in 24:21–24, given the morning after Ezekiel's wife died, all kinds of questions about the text and the actual sequence of events ensue (see the textual note on 24:18). As the text

---

[42] SC VI 6 (*Luther's Small Catechism with Explanation* 29).

stands, the people take note only when the prophet's wife dies and then, the next morning, Ezekiel fails to observe the usual conventions of mourning.

24:19 Not surprisingly, the people surmise that such weird behavior must have some significance. It is surely no accident that they do not merely ask about the sign's meaning in general, but what it means *"for us."* God has providentially caused them to accord the prophet more respect than ever before. God has disposed them to actually listen to his message more intently than on any earlier occasion, at least so far as we can tell (contrast 12:27; 21:5 [ET 20:49]).

24:20–21 The gravity of the message contained in the answer is underscored by introducing it with a triad of prophetic formulae, two of which ("the Word of Yahweh came to me" and "thus says the Lord Yahweh") emphasize the divine origin of the reply. The answer is as blunt as it is devastating.

The substance of the reply is contained in the verb and the first part of its compound object: "I am about to desecrate my sanctuary." ("Sanctuary" is followed by three appositives to it, then the final clause about the people's children.) Yahweh himself will desecrate or profane, that is, render unholy what had been his earthly holy place par excellence, his "sanctuary." To "desecrate" something is a far stronger expression than "take away" in 24:16, which 24:21 explains. For all practical purposes, the people themselves had already accomplished this desecration by their various syncretistic or outright pagan rites and subsequent behavior (see especially chapter 8), as Yahweh already said (5:11; 23:38–39). But as long as God's "Glory" (כָּבוֹד) remained "incarnate" there (Christologically),[43] the sanctuary was sanctified by the divine presence and could potentially mediate Yahweh's own holiness through the forgiveness of sins provided through the OT "sacraments" (sacrifices). But when Yahweh removed his Glory (11:22–23), the temple became only another meaningless structure of wood and stone. The historical reference of 24:21 is, of course, the temple's destruction by Nebuchadnezzar in summer 586 B.C., but the prophet's concern is with suprahistory, *"Hist*ory," the event's significance amid the history of salvation.

The first appositive, summarizing why the temple had become the opposite of Yahweh's intent, is, literally, "the pride of your strength." The phrase undoubtedly derives from Lev 26:19, where the reference is to pride and glorying in human power in general. But here עֹז, "strength," is not abstract as much as it is concrete: the people's false objectification of the temple as a stronghold. In Ps 78:61 "strength" and "glory" focus even more closely on the ark, above which Yahweh sat enthroned between the wings of the cherubim; his presence there was the focal point of the entire temple structure and all its rites. Similarly, in Ps 132:8 the entire building is termed "your mighty ark."

---

[43] See the textual notes and commentary on 1:26–28.

The problem, to which Ezekiel has alluded many times before, was that the people had come to regard the temple as a bit of magic, a talisman that should retain its power to protect them apart from faith and a life of faith.[44] Isaiah taught the inviolability of Zion, that the city would play a central role in God's economy of salvation because of God's election and promise,[a] as indeed it did as this promise was fulfilled in Christ's first advent. However, that teaching had become confused with the idea of the inviolability of the earthly city of Jerusalem, whether or not its people remained faithful (and they did not). God's promise that he would graciously "dwell" (שָׁכַן) there in the midst of his people (e.g., Ex 25:8; 29:45; Is 8:18) was an essential and oft-repeated component of the theology of Zion, but it was not irrevocable. In the fullness of time, God's Glory came to tabernacle (dwell permanently and irrevocably) in Jesus, the Word made flesh (Jn 1:14). The earthly temple, again desecrated by the people's infidelity and henceforth irrelevant to God's plan of salvation, was razed in A.D. 70, never to be rebuilt. The eschatological restoration of the new Jerusalem is the subject of Ezekiel 40–48 (with a temple) and Revelation 21–22 (without one).

More than a century before Ezekiel, Micah (3:11) had pinpointed the problem: in spite of all their malfeasance, "on Yahweh they lean, saying, 'Is not Yahweh in our midst? No harm can come upon us.' " And more or less contemporaneously with Ezekiel, Jeremiah had nearly been lynched after preaching his "temple sermon" (Jeremiah 7). See especially Jer 7:4, where he condemns the people's repetition of the mantra of "lying words: 'This is the temple of Yahweh, the temple of Yahweh, the temple of Yahweh.' " Jeremiah 26 is a parallel chapter detailing the circumstances accompanying the sermon.

"The desire of your eyes" (Ezek 24:21) obviously parallels Yahweh's description of Ezekiel's fondness for his wife (24:16). A parallel expression in Is 64:10 (ET 64:11) uses the same noun (מַחְמָד) as in Ezek 24:16, 21: the people call the temple "all our desirable things." Their affection for the temple was not objectionable per se, but they had made a building and an institution into ends in themselves rather than revering them as Yahweh's chosen means to an end.

The final appositional phrase, "the yearning of your hearts" (24:21), is perhaps a slight intensification of the preceding phrase, possibly expressing the people's anxiety because of their banishment from the temple, which will shortly be taken away from them.

The typology of Zion should be obvious, but it should not be taken for granted. Fulfilled in Christ, the incarnate temple, God continues through the Holy Spirit to employ temples, not only in the bodies of the baptized (1 Cor 6:19), where much of Protestantism would confine him, but also in congregations, many of them named "Zion" (cf. Heb 12:22), where his Word is preached faithfully and the Sacraments administered rightly, until the day of the new Jerusalem, where there will be no need of temples of any sort (Rev 21:22). In

(a) Is 1:27; 2:3; 4:3–5; 10:24; 12:6; 14:32; 18:7; 28:16; 52:1–2

---

[44] See also Hummel, *Ezekiel 1–20*, 256–57, 274–75, 371, 471, and the commentary on 21:28 (ET 21:23).

the meantime, the temptation is perennially present to confuse means and end, as ancient Israel had done.

24:22–23 For a moment, Ezekiel uses the first person ("you will do as *I* have done"), making unmistakable that his behavior, which the people have just witnessed at the death of his wife, will be duplicated by them when they will shortly be stunned by the news of Jerusalem's fall.

The clause "you will … *pine away because of/in* your *iniquities*" (24:23) has been used before, once in Lev 26:39 in a covenant curse for when the people would prove unfaithful, and by Ezekiel earlier in 4:17, there of the Israelites' physical starvation while Jerusalem is under siege. Here it is more of a spiritual and psychological destitution as each person sorrows silently. The picture is of overwhelming grief that no tears or lamentation can express adequately, with only an inner pain on account of the sins that had brought things to such a pass. The prophet's own silent groaning (24:17) will be paralleled by the people's inarticulate, unritualized expression of bereavement beyond words.

The verb "*groan* to one another" (נְהַם, 24:23, different from the verb for "groan" in 24:17) occurs only here in Ezekiel, but is used elsewhere in Is 5:29–30 for the roar of an attacking army compared to the roar of lions and the roar of ocean breakers (see also Prov 19:12; 20:2; 28:15). Here "groan" expresses that the people will try to reach out to console one another but lack the words to do so.

24:24 Now Yahweh speaks again and affirms what Ezekiel has just said. He even identifies the prophet by name, the only time Ezekiel's name appears in the book besides 1:3. The loaded word מוֹפֵת, "sign, portent, type," had been used in 12:6, 11 and will be repeated in 24:27, the only four times the word appears in the book. The word has various connotations. It is often paralleled with אוֹת, "sign" (e.g., Ex 7:3; Is 8:18). It can also be a synonym of פֶּלֶא, "wonder, miracle" (e.g., Is 9:5 [ET 9:6]; Ps 77:12, 15 [ET 77:11, 14]), implying something supernatural. That force is probably in the background here, in the sense that Ezekiel's behavior predicts the people's future. "Type" might work, not primarily in the theological sense, but in the sense of model, exemplar, prefigurement. In its context here, perhaps "action prophecy" could be used. The people would recognize that his had not been idle, meaningless gestures, but divine revelation intended to move them to repentance and faith.

"When *it* comes …" (24:24) refers to the predicted catastrophe for Jerusalem's residents and the destruction of the temple. The certainty of its coming Yahweh had averred in 24:14.

Some commentators take the recognition formula at the end of the verse, "you will know that I am the Lord Yahweh," as indicating true repentance.[45] Block, seeking an explanation for the silence of both Ezekiel and the people, looks ahead to 24:25–27, which promises that the prophet's mouth will be opened:

---

[45] E.g., Keil, *Ezekiel*, 1:350; Block, *Ezekiel*, 1:794.

The opening of the prophet's mouth signified a turning point in Israel's history: the old era of sin and judgment had come to an end; the new era of hope and salvation could begin. The exiles would refrain from mourning, not because they would be paralyzed by grief or calloused by sin, but because they would recognize the dawn of a new age.[46]

That is an enormously attractive construal, coming where it does in the structure of the entire book[47] and because such repentance and regeneration is the point of God's judgmental activity. Clearly, the Law has done its work, but it is not yet clear from the text itself that the Gospel (to be set forth in earnest in chapters 33–48) has yet penetrated the people's hearts. The refrain of recognizing Yahweh's lordship has sounded repeatedly where there was no implication that anything more than the second use of the Law (its righteous condemnation of sin) was in mind, and there is no clear indication in the text at this point that anything more is implied than an acknowledgment of the truth and mystery of Yahweh's holiness and actions in history. In my judgment, a better case for such an interpretation can be made when the formula is repeated in 24:27, at the very end of the chapter.

The Destruction of the Temple Brings Ezekiel's Release from Speechlessness (24:25–27)

24:25–27 These three verses, really a climactic and separate section of the chapter, are set apart by a new address to the prophet from Yahweh. At the same time there are many links with the preceding verses. One spots the repetition of the pregnant מוֹפֵת, "sign," for Ezekiel himself in 24:27 as in 24:24.

Ezek 24:25 is linked with the preceding in various ways. The use of לָקַח in 24:25 (בְּיוֹם קַחְתִּי), "on the day when *I take away* from them their stronghold," harks back to Yahweh's use of the same verb (הִנְנִי לֹקֵחַ) for the removal of Ezekiel's wife in 24:16: "*I am taking away* from you the desire of your eyes." And 24:25 is in many ways simply a restatement of 24:21, where Yahweh used the same construction as in 24:16 but with the devastating חִלֵּל instead of לָקַח, "*I am about to desecrate* [הִנְנִי מְחַלֵּל] my sanctuary."

Looking forward, "*on the day when* [בְּיוֹם] I take away" in 24:25 anticipates "*on that day* [בַּיּוֹם הַהוּא]" in both 24:26 and 24:27. On its surface that seems to imply that the "survivor" (24:26–27) would arrive in Babylon on the very day that Jerusalem fell—something not humanly possible, and conflicting with 33:21, which dates the survivor's arrival about six months later than the city's fall in summer 586 B.C. There are various ways out of the dilemma, however. The phrase בְּיוֹם frequently means simply "when(ever)," that is, with no concentration on a *day*, as such, but "at that time" (as NIV boldly renders it in 24:27), sometime in the future, undefined as to onset or length.

Furthermore, the accent is not so much on the calendar date of Jerusalem's fall, as such, as on the day when the news reached the exiles; at that time the

---

[46] Block, *Ezekiel*, 1:794.

[47] See the discussion of the "classical prophetic outline" on pages 10–12 in the introduction.

past event would become history for them (cf. "what these things [mean] for us" in 24:19). The six-month interval of time that it took the survivor to travel from conquered Jerusalem to the exiles in Babylon is passed over, or the conquest of Jerusalem and the survivor's arrival in Babylon are telescoped together,[48] in order to stress the inner connection between those two occasions and the end of Ezekiel's speechlessness.

May we compare this with the Gospel? The facts about the triune God and his works confessed in the Apostles' and Nicene Creeds are historically true regardless of whether or not anyone knows or believes them. At the same time, the Gospel truth of Christ's redemption benefits a person only when the objective fact is subjectively received through faith. Both the objective fact of Christ's Gospel and our faithful trust in it are confessed by the *pro nobis* ("for us") emphasis of Christian theology: "I believe … in one Lord Jesus Christ … who *for us men* and *for our salvation* came down from heaven" (Nicene Creed).

Yahweh has referred to פְּלִיטִים, "survivors," before in Ezekiel. In 6:8–9 and 7:16, the word was used of "survivors" of the various punishments sent by Yahweh—of those who, either voluntarily or involuntarily, were scattered to the four winds, like birds in the mountains (7:16). The cognate collective noun פְּלֵיטָה, "group of survivors/escapees," was used in 14:22, in partial anticipation of chapter 24, referring to those who would reach the exiles and console them by confirming that Yahweh's righteous judgments on the city were indeed justified.

And by no accident is מוֹפֵת, "sign," from 24:24 (also 12:6, 11) repeated in 24:27. As mentioned in the commentary on 24:24, it refers to the portentousness of Ezekiel's behavior at his wife's death for the people's own when they would hear that the city had actually fallen. But here the accent is on the veracity of the Word of Yahweh that Ezekiel had proclaimed, not only of the almost monotonously judgmental tone of all that he had preached until this time (beginning with 4:1), but also, at least potentially, of the future words of restoration (chapters 33–48). The opening of his mouth indicated the possibility of a new type of (Gospel) message and of an entirely new relationship between Yahweh and his audience; "they will know that a [true] prophet has been among them" (2:5; 33:33).

Inevitably, a new light is also shed on the recognition formula ("they will know that I am Yahweh")[49] when it is repeated in 24:27 compared to its use in 24:24. The text still does not dwell on the subjective reaction of either the prophet or the exiles (both those who had been with him all along and the new

---

[48] The prophets, looking at the future from afar, often "telescope" or perceive events as nearby, even though, when history unfolds, those events may be separated by quite some time. A classic example is the way Joel 3 (ET 2:28–32) foresees the events of Pentecost (the outpouring of the Spirit) followed immediately by the heavenly signs of the end of the world at Christ's second coming (Mt 24:27–31; Mk 13:24–27). We now know that those two events are separated by at least two millennia.

[49] For this formula, see page 9 in the introduction and the commentary on 6:7.

component that will arrive from the fallen city); it is not Ezekiel's habit to dwell on subjectivities of any sort. But the door is at least opened now for the populace to "know" Yahweh as more than the *Deus absconditus*, the hidden God of holy demand and righteous wrath (who for the Israelites had become part of some syncretistic mixture with the gods of the nations; see Ezekiel 8). Greenberg summarizes it eloquently:

> The moment of Ezekiel's deepest alienation from his community (due to their contrasting estimations of the disaster) would mark the turn toward his identification with them. Inhibitions upon his intercourse with them entailed by their hostility would be removed at a stroke. Their calamity would be the start of his fortune—his and God's—as the people would eventually realize the redemptive significance of Jerusalem's fall.[50]

Now they may come to "know" him as all that he had revealed himself to be to Moses, when his sacred name was given to Israel: as the *Deus revelatus* (at least in its OT fullness), the gracious God of the enduring covenant, with the promise of his still greater, definitive revelation in the Messiah, even if much of the NT Christological vocabulary was not yet used. The change wrought by Jerusalem's fall upon the Israelites' knowledge of Yahweh may be compared to the change wrought by the death of Jesus upon his disciples' understanding of who he was. Christ's crucifixion was a disastrous blow to the disciples' perception of Jesus (Lk 24:21), yet the dashing of their earthly hopes was necessary before they could gain the true knowledge of him and his mission (Lk 24:25–53).

Ezekiel 24:25–27 and the Composition of Ezekiel 25–32

A literary note may be anticlimactic here, but at this point of major change in the book's outline and contents, it is appropriate that we say a word about the composition of the book, or at least about the end result of that process: the text that the Holy Spirit inspired and preserved to be handed down to us. As I have indicated many times, speculation about the editorial process that (humanly speaking) produced the biblical book is a topic where the point of diminishing returns comes very early. If we must think of an editor or redactor, Ezekiel himself is far and away the most likely candidate. One can easily imagine a close group of disciples, amanuenses, and the like who assisted him in assembling his oracles, but we really have not a scintilla of evidence for such an association.

And cui bono? If some hermeneutical or theological insight is demonstrable or can even be made to seem likely, the enterprise may well be worthwhile, even when we must state our conclusions provisionally. But when the proposed results are purely literary (and when there is some modicum of agreement among the investigators), we learn nothing more than the putative skill of the author as a writer (or editor). If the primary concern is the Bible as literature, well and good. But I doubt if it is a major concern of most of those who will use this commentary, nor is it mine.

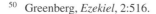

[50] Greenberg, *Ezekiel*, 2:516.

As the reader will note, other than an occasional inclusio or framing technique for a pericope, I have paid little attention to literary questions. It is widely supposed that the following section of Gentile oracles (chapters 25–32) was inserted at some later stage and that originally chapter 33 followed immediately after chapter 24. It is a matter of indifference to me whether that is true or not. But if one pursues that question, we must immediately explain why chapter 33 begins with a slightly expanded version of the watchman oracle of 3:16–21, and we must answer many other questions too.

I am much more excited by viewing the structure of the book in terms of the "classical prophetic outline" and the theological message it carries. As explained in the introduction,[51] I read chapters 1–24 as a manifestation of the principle summarized in 1 Pet 4:17: "the time has come for judgment to begin with the household of God" (RSV). That theme is followed by chapters 25–32, which consist of oracles against typical (representing all) nations and/or their gods, that is, all competitors to God's kingdom, and finally by chapters 33–48, mostly oracles of salvation for all who will believe. The result is a parallel to St. Paul's basic theme in Romans, especially 3:22–24: "The righteousness of God [is] through faith in Jesus Christ for all who believe. For there is no distinction [between Jew and Gentile], for all have sinned and fall short of the glory of God, being justified freely by his grace through the redemption that is in Christ Jesus."

My coolness toward redaction criticism focuses (of the commentators primarily consulted here) on especially Zimmerli and, to a slightly lesser extent, on Allen. With Block and Greenberg I generally find myself in agreement on such issues.

A good case study is the final three verses of chapter 24. After a short discussion, Zimmerli bluntly declares that these verses "are to be regarded as a redactional appendix, which is intended to form a bridge over the collection of oracles against foreign nations in Ezek 25–32 and to link up with Ezek 33."[52] Nor is that all. Ezek 24:26 must have been inserted between 24:25 and 24:27 because "a later hand noted the disagreement in 24:25, 27 as against 33:21f and has attempted to render the statement more precisely. ... Also the introduction of אֵת הַפָּלִיט ["with the survivor"] in v 27 ... must go back to the same hand. However, the text is not really clarified by this insertion."[53]

I have already proffered my exegesis of the material in 24:15–27, and I need not repeat. The topic will have to be revisited at 33:21–22 (see the commentary there). Obviously, a seam is evident in the book at that later point (surrounded by others in close proximity). But having noted the fact, I doubt if little (or anything) of merit is worth pursuing further concerning the sequence, complication, and so on.

---

[51] See the discussion of the "classical prophetic outline" on pages 10–12 in the introduction.

[52] Zimmerli, *Ezekiel*, 1:509.

[53] Zimmerli, *Ezekiel*, 1:508.

Ezekiel 25–32

Oracles against Other Nations

Introduction to Ezekiel 25–32:
Oracles against Other Nations

Oracles such as those in Ezekiel 25–32, which comprises the third major section of the book, are usually referred to by a title such as "oracles against other nations" or "Gentile oracles."[1]

This type of revelation from Yahweh was by no means unique or original to Ezekiel in the early sixth century B.C. In the eighth century, Isaiah (chapters 13–23) and Amos (chapters 1–2) devoted substantial parts of their books to such material, and the entire first half of Obadiah concerns Gentiles. Nahum, only slightly earlier than Ezekiel, is little but a Gentile oracle. Ezekiel's contemporary Jeremiah, in his retort to the challenge of Hananiah, asserts that earlier prophets "from ancient times prophesied against many countries and great kingdoms about war, about evil, and about pestilence" (Jer 28:8). In fact, depending on how one counts, something like thirteen to twenty percent of all the prophetic writing in the OT is of this sort.

The major question is that of the theological or exegetical significance of these oracles. To a certain extent, we may distinguish between the oracles as such and their position, usually in blocks, within the prophetic books. When the critical dogma reigned that a criterion of true prophecy was to preach judgment on Israel and Judah, the Gentile oracles could hardly be read otherwise than as the nationalism or chauvinism of false prophets. In more recent decades, however, the scholarly opinion has generally prevailed that they were basically proclamations of salvation for God's people through the elimination of their political and religious enemies. With this general outlook we can agree. Likewise, the NT describes the advent of God's salvation in Jesus Christ as the defeat of our enemies: Satan, our own sin, and death.[a]

(a) E.g., Lk 10:18; Jn 12:31; 1 Cor 15:24–26; Col 2:13–15; Rev 20:10, 14

As a general hermeneutical key to their theological interpretation and application, I would propose again the category of typology. The Gentile nations denounced in these oracles are types of all the kingdoms of this world; after the return of Christ, they all will finally be overcome by the kingdom of God. Many readers will be reminded of the memorable "Hallelujah Chorus" in Handel's *Messiah*: "The kingdoms of this world are become the kingdoms of our Lord and of his Christ; and he shall reign for ever and ever" (quoting Rev 11:15 KJV).

It is often difficult for us to know precisely why God moved his prophets to single out particular nations for censure and omitted other nations that might

---

[1] On this topic, see also "Ezekiel 24:25–27 and the Composition of Ezekiel 25–32" at the end of the commentary on 24:25–27. A major relevant essay is that of Raabe, "Why Prophetic Oracles against the Nations?" An earlier major study, that of Christensen, *Transformations of the War Oracle in Old Testament Prophecy: Studies in the Oracles against the Nations*, often reaches helpful conclusions but is often speculative in its developmental reconstructions.

have served equally well. Sometimes the reason for the choice is obvious (perhaps especially with Nahum). Ezekiel's choices (at least his major ones) are as related to his contemporary political situation as any, but in the case of many other prophets, the connection is remote.

Just as significant as the individual national names used typologically is the positioning of the oracles in the outline of the book. Ezekiel is a prime example of what I like to call the "classical prophetic outline": (1) judgment against Israel; (2) judgment against the heathen nations; and (3) salvation for Israel and for all.[2] The significance of this classical outline is essentially the Pauline thesis that there is "no distinction [between Jew and Gentile], for all have sinned and fall short of the glory of God" (Rom 3:22–23). Judgment begins with the household of God (1 Pet 4:17)—the Israelites in the OT (the first part of the outline). But judgment naturally rests also on the nations that have never received or accepted Yahweh's covenant (the second part of the outline: oracles against the nations). God's judgment against both Israel and the other nations is his response to their rebellion against him, their Creator. Yet despite this, he still wills to manifest "the righteousness of God through faith in Jesus Christ for all who believe" (Rom 3:21–22). Salvation is available for all alike as God's free gift of grace in Christ (Rom 6:23), which is the overarching theme of Ezekiel 33–48.

It is obvious that Ezekiel's Gentile oracles have been deliberately (editorially) gathered together into their present position, and the most likely "editor" is Ezekiel himself, under divine inspiration. The editorial arrangement is evident by the fact that these oracles about other nations separate two pericopes about Jerusalem that plausibly belong together: the prophecy of the impending fall of Jerusalem in 24:15–27 and the report of its actual fall in 33:21–22. Some deliberate arrangement of the collection is also evidenced by fact that the oracles that are dated are not in strictly chronological order. The dates, arranged from earliest to latest, are in 29:1; 30:20; 31:1; 26:1; 32:1; 32:17; and 29:17, the latest date in the entire book. See further figure 1, "The Dates in Ezekiel."

The fact cannot be overlooked that besides 25:12–14, another oracle against Edom appears separately in chapter 35, although this may partly reflect the course of events after the fall of Jerusalem; Edom's attempt to take advantage of Jerusalem's plight is also condemned by Obadiah. Sometimes the oracles against Gog and Magog in Ezekiel 38–39 are considered separate Gentile oracles too, but their quasi-apocalyptic character probably explains their later position before the eschatological vision of Israel in chapters 40–48.

Possibly an editorial device can be seen in the total number of seven nations addressed by the oracles: the Ammonites (25:1–7); Moab (25:8–11); Edom (25:12–14); the Philistines (25:15–17); Tyre (26:1–28:19); Sidon

---

[2] For a more detailed discussion, see pages 10–12 in the introduction.

(28:20–23); and Egypt (29:1–32:32). These sections vary greatly in length; the section against Egypt alone (chapters 29–32) equals the total length of the or-acles against the other six addressees in 25:1–28:23. And seven date notices also appear in the oracles (26:1; 29:1, 17; 30:20; 31:1; 32:1, 17). Moreover, there are seven discrete oracles against Egypt (chapters 29–32), each of which begins with the word-event formula, "the Word of Yahweh came to me,"[3] which consequently occurs seven times in those chapters.

Undoubtedly, the number seven was used because of its general symbol-ism of completeness: God's judgment will be universal. The ultimate source of this symbolism may root in the seven days of creation. An even closer im-plication may be to view them as a counterpart of the "seven nations" (Deut 7:1) of Canaan that Israel had to defeat before it could enter the promised land. At any rate, the association of the number seven appears already in the oracles of Amos 1–2 if one assumes the one against Judah to be Amos' unique addi-tion. (Since the oracle against Judah is the next to last oracle, the order of the oracles would represent a reversal of the order of judgment that would later crystallize in the classical outline.) Seven addresses are clearly to be seen in the Gentile oracles of Jeremiah 46–49, followed by a longer one in Jeremiah 50–51.[4]

Further evidence of deliberate structuring is obvious in the promissory or-acle in Ezek 28:24–26, at the transition between the oracles against Tyre and Sidon and those against Egypt. This is almost exactly the midway point of the Gentile oracles and thus, pointing both backwards and forwards, confirms the theological purpose of the surrounding oracles as backhanded messages of hope to Israel.

Nearly all commentators remark on the absence in Ezekiel of an oracle against Babylon. Already in the eighth century in Isaiah 13–14, and continu-ing even in the NT Apocalypse, "Babylon" served as a major symbol of the kingdoms of this world (Revelation 17–19). The absence of such a message in Ezekiel should not be attributed to a pro-Babylonian political stance (which some of Jeremiah's opponents wrongly seem to have attributed to him). Rather, during the historical period that included the ministries of Jeremiah and Ezekiel, Babylon was God's instrument of judgment upon unfaithful Judah. Thus one can understand the seemingly inordinate amount of attention given in Ezekiel to Tyre and Egypt, because those two countries represented the ma-jor obstacles at the time to the fulfillment of Babylon's mission to conquer Ju-

---

[3] For this formula, see page 8 in the introduction and the textual note on 3:16.

[4] Amos includes an oracle against both Israel and Judah in addition to six neighboring coun-tries, but Judah was not Gentile, whereas the apostate Northern Kingdom could easily be considered as bad as the Gentiles. In Jeremiah 46–49, we can count more or less than seven oracles depending on how the text is divided. Another Gentile oracle follows in Jeremiah 50–51, but it has a different introduction, a greater length, and a different character, and it ends with an action prophecy.

dah. Oracles proclaiming Babylon's own comeuppance would have to await another time and other prophetic mouthpieces.

Finally, although the subject matter in the Gentile oracles is obviously different from that in the prophetic oracles against Israel and Judah, their forms are alike. The reasons for judgment given in both are similar (e.g., hubris); the divine punishment will be the same; and in general, the vocabulary and tone are the same. Generally, the pattern is one familiar to us from other judgment oracles: (1) some introductory citation that declares that the oracle is a revelatory Word from Israel's God; (2) the indictment of the people's sins, introduced by יַעַן ("because"); (3) their punishment, introduced by לָכֵן ("therefore"); and (4) the result, often expressed by means of the recognition formula: "(then) you/they will know that I am Yahweh."[5] Unlike Amos (e.g., 1:3, 6), Ezekiel does not accent the irreversibility of the heavenly decision, but suggests the possibility of restoration after repentance. Thus in 29:13–14 Yahweh promises to "bring about the restoration of Egypt" after "forty years" (see further "Introduction to Ezekiel 29–32: Oracles against Egypt").[6]

If Ezekiel or other prophets were writing today, we can only speculate as to the examples God might choose to denounce through such oracles. On principle, we dare exclude no nation or people, not even our own. Certainly such oracles would apply to nations that have an official religion other than Christianity and use their civil power to persecute believers in Jesus. This would include Islamic states, whose god is opposed to the biblical God, and who by law condemn Christians to capital punishment. (Islam does not even recognize the distinction between the political and religious realms.) Such oracles would also apply to nations whose official religion is a form of atheism (e.g., Communism) and that oppose the one true faith.

Yet we must concede that these oracles can also pertain to nations where the church is accepted, and a Christian denomination may even be sanctioned as the state religion, but the church is subject to political control or even has virtually become an institutionalized "culture religion," so that the proclamation of the Gospel is suppressed or silenced for the sake of other agendas. Generally in the West there is, theoretically or practically, a separation between church and state, but sometimes the church seems to forget that its mission is thoroughly distinct from national interests.[7]

---

[5] For this formula, see page 9 in the introduction and the commentary on 6:7.

[6] Compare Jonah, where two groups of Gentiles are converted to saving faith in the one true God: the mariners in chapter 1 are converted through Jonah's confession (1:9), and the Ninevites are converted through Jonah's sermonette (3:4). See Lessing, *Jonah*, 127–42, 300–23.

[7] We must affirm the biblical teaching (e.g., Rom 13:1–7) that government authority is established by God and is to punish wrongdoing, protect its citizens, and maintain order and peace, so that the church can carry out its mission to proclaim the Gospel. The church may well wish to advertise its patriotism toward a benign government, but one may question whether it should go so far as to hold a special service specifically to celebrate a national holiday or display the nation's flag in the chancel. At the same time, we must protest the view

Moreover, society exerts a constant pressure on the church to circumscribe or contradict theological truth drawn from the Scriptures.[8] To the extent that the church compromises with and conforms to heathen society, it becomes liable to the denouncements in the prophetic oracles against the Gentiles. We Christians may also grow weary of waiting for the final deliverance promised in these oracles (cf. 2 Pet 3:4). In all these ways, these prophecies serve as a clarion call for self-examination and repentance, as well as a reminder that from "the sin that so easily entangles us" (Heb 12:1) and from all persecution by the enemies of Christ, we will, upon his return, finally be free.

---

of the state evident in the radical left wing of visible Christendom, where America and the capitalist West are instinctively condemned as purely evil agents of greed and exploitation. Of course, if civil authorities require people to do or say something that is sinful and contrary to Scripture, the Christian must refuse to comply.

[8] For example, biblical teachings that are currently under attack in the West include the inspiration and authority of Scripture; that salvation is through faith in Christ alone, since Jesus is the only way to God the Father; that only qualified men are to be ordained to the pastoral office; that abortion, infanticide, and euthanasia constitute murder; the sanctity of marriage as a lifelong and exclusive union; and that homosexuality is intrinsically sinful. No doubt in the future different biblical teachings will be the focus of society's assaults, just as other ones have been in the past.

Oracles against the Ammonites, Moab, Edom, and the Philistines

Translation

25 ¹The Word of Yahweh came to me: ²"Son of man, set your face toward the Ammonites and prophesy against them. ³Say to the Ammonites, 'Hear the Word of the Lord Yahweh. Thus says the Lord Yahweh: Because you said, "Aha!" against my sanctuary when it was desecrated and against the land of Israel when it was devastated and against the house of Judah when they went into exile, ⁴therefore, I am about to give you to the people of the East as available land. They will set up their encampments in you and place in you their dwellings. They will eat your produce, and they will drink your milk. ⁵I will make Rabbah into a camel pasture and Ammon into a sheepfold. Then you will know that I am Yahweh.

⁶" 'For thus says the Lord Yahweh: Because you clapped your hands, stamped your feet, and rejoiced with all your derision from the bottom of your heart against the land of Israel, ⁷therefore, I have stretched out my hand against you, and I have given you as booty to the nations. I have cut you off from the peoples, and I have made you perish out of the countries. I have exterminated you, and you will know that I am Yahweh.' "

⁸"Thus says the Lord Yahweh: Because Moab and Seir said, 'Look, the house of Judah is just like all the nations,' ⁹therefore, I am about to lay open the slope of Moab from the cities, from its cities, from its whole territory, the glory of the land, Beth-jeshimoth, Baal-meon, and Kiriathaim, ¹⁰to the people of the East in addition to the Ammonites. I will hand it over as available land so that the Ammonites will no longer be remembered among the nations. ¹¹I will execute judgments upon Moab, and they will know that I am Yahweh."

¹²"Thus says the Lord Yahweh: Because Edom has acted with vindictive vengeance toward the house of Judah and incurred grievous guilt by persisting in avenging themselves against them, ¹³therefore, thus says the Lord Yahweh: I will stretch out my hand against Edom, cut off man and beast from it, and turn it into a wasteland. From Teman to Dedan, they will fall by the sword. ¹⁴I will take my vengeance upon Edom by means of my people Israel, and they will act toward Edom with my anger and with my wrath. Thus they will know my vengeance, says the Lord Yahweh."

¹⁵"Thus says the Lord Yahweh: Because the Philistines acted vengefully and avenged themselves vindictively with utter contempt in order to destroy with everlasting enmity, ¹⁶therefore, thus says the Lord Yahweh: I am about to stretch out my hand against the Philistines, cut off the Cherethites, and destroy the remnant by the seacoast. ¹⁷I will act among them with great acts of vengeance and

with furious chastisements, and they will know that I am Yahweh when I lay my vengeance upon them.''

Textual Notes

25:1–17   See the map "The Ancient Near East."

25:2   שִׂ֥ים פָּנֶ֖יךָ אֶל־—This idiom also occurs, sometimes with עַל (twice) or דֶּ֣רֶךְ (used like a preposition once) in place of אֶל, in 6:2; 13:17; 21:2, 7 (ET 20:46; 21:2); 28:21; 29:2; 35:2; 38:2. See the second textual note on 6:2.

בְּנֵ֣י עַמּוֹן—As in 21:23–37 (ET 21:18–32; which see), this nation is literally called "the sons of Ammon." Overwhelming biblical usage and extrabiblical evidence, both textual and archaeological, make plain that this was the regular form of this nation's name. I have continued the long practice (KJV already) of using the gentilic form "the Ammonites," since "the sons of Ammon" sounds strange in English. However, a technically more correct rendition would simply be "Ammon."

In the following oracles, only the Philistines are referred to by a gentilic: the plural of פְּלִשְׁתִּי in 25:15.

25:3   יַ֧עַן אָמְרֵ֣ךְ הֶאָ֗ח—The accusations in 25:3, 6, 8, 12, 15 all use the same construction: the conjunction יַעַן, "because," followed by an infinitive construct, here the Qal of אָמַר with second feminine singular suffix.

Apparently that suffix deems the masculine plural phrase "the sons of Ammon" (בְּנֵ֣י עַמּוֹן, 25:2–3; see also the suffix on עֲלֵיהֶם in 25:2) to be a feminine singular entity, like a land or a city—perhaps the capital, רַבָּה, "Rabbah" (25:5). Such inconsistency in gender and number pervades the entire oracle. In the first part of the oracle (25:2–5), masculine plurals appear at the beginning and the end: the imperative שִׁמְעוּ, "hear" (25:3), and וִידַעְתֶּם, "then you will know" (25:5), both of which agree with "the sons of Ammon." In between (25:3b–4), the feminine singular is used, apparently because the reference is to the nation and/or its capital city. More enigmatically, the masculine singular rules the second address (25:6–7), possibly referring to the king as the embodiment of the nation. For example, in 25:6, the second masculine singular suffix is used on מַחְאֲךָ (Qal infinitive of מָחָא), "you clapped."

The little interjection הֶאָח (25:3) scarcely needs more than virtual transliteration into "aha!" It is used a number of times in the Bible (in Ezekiel again in 26:2 and 36:2) to express malicious glee, which German expresses so vividly by *Schadenfreude*.

אֶל־מִקְדָּשִׁ֣י כִֽי־נִחָ֔ל—Both אֶל and כִּי occur in all three parts of the indictment in 25:3. Each time, two alternative translations are possible for each. Often אֶל is used interchangeably for עַל and can be translated either "over" or "against." Similarly, כִּי can be taken either temporally ("when") or causally ("because/for"). In the context, the ultimate import will be essentially the same. I have preferred "against" for אֶל because it appears to anticipate that sense of עַל in 25:7 ("my hand *against* you"). I have chosen "when" for כִּי.

At first glance, we might be tempted to parse נִחָל (pausal for נִחַל) as the Piel third masculine singular perfect of נָחַל, "inherit," but sense eliminates that possibility. It is the Niphal third masculine singular perfect of the geminate verb חָלַל, "desecrate," whose Piel Ezekiel uses elsewhere for desecrating the sanctuary (23:39; 24:21; 44:7;

the Niphal is used with "sanctuaries" in 7:24). According to normal Hebrew orthography, the final consonant of the word cannot be doubled (נִחַל) to mark the second, assimilated ל of the root.

25:4 הִנְנִי נֹתְנָךְ—I have taken הִנְנִי plus a participle as *futurum instans*, as often elsewhere in Ezekiel. For the use of the feminine (second singular) suffix on the participle נֹתְנָךְ, see the first textual note on 25:3. This rare form of the suffix (instead of the expected ךְ ֵ) also occurred in 23:28. The feminine singular form of the suffix is understandable because of the parallel clause in 25:5 that uses the same verb (נָתַן) with the feminine capital, "Rabbah," as its object (וְנָתַתִּי אֶת־רַבָּה).

לִבְנֵי־קֶדֶם—Literally, "to the sons of the East," this translates idiomatically as "the people of the East." "Qedemites" might be permissible but would not communicate. The term does not refer to any single national or ethnic entity, but to the various nomadic groups migrating around the Arabian desert to the east and often opportunistically exploiting weaknesses in the settled communities to the west.

לְמֹורָשָׁה—The noun מֹורָשָׁה is rendered "available land" because it pertains to the transfer of property. Thus in conquest narratives, the verb יָרַשׁ can mean either "take possession of (land)" or "dispossess, drive out the inhabitants." The word is used exclusively of land, but, as here, taking possession of land involves expelling those who currently inhabit it.

וְיָשְׁבוּ טִירֹותֵיהֶם בָּךְ—The verb יָשְׁבוּ is the only OT occurrence of יָשַׁב in the Piel (third common plural perfect), although its Piel does occur in Rabbinic Hebrew. The common Qal is intransitive, while the Piel means "set up" (encampments, houses, etc.). An analogous Yiphil form of יָשַׁב with a causative meaning is also known in Phoenician.

The direct object is the plural (with third masculine plural suffix) of טִירָה, which generally refers to a nomadic settlement or "**encampment** protected by a stone wall" (*HALOT*, 1). Thus the plural of טִירָה will refer to "rows (of stones)" along the walls of the eschatological temple in Ezek 46:23 (where it is parallel to the synonym טוּר). In Gen 25:16, the plural of טִירָה stands in a series with חֲצֵרִים, "unwalled villages," and in Ps 69:26 (ET 69:25), the singular is parallel to אֹהָלִים, "tents."

מִשְׁכְּנֵיהֶם—The plural of מִשְׁכָּן (with third masculine plural suffix) then must refer to the individual "tents" or "dwellings" of the new inhabitants.

הֵמָּה יֹאכְלוּ פִרְיֵךְ—This and the next clause conspicuously repeat the grammatically unnecessary pronoun הֵמָּה, "they," to underscore the transfer of ownership and usufruct. "Fruit" is an archaic or poetic rendition of פְּרִי. Its application is broadly to "produce" of whatever sort.

וְהֵמָּה יִשְׁתּוּ חֲלָבֵךְ׃—"Milk" (חָלָב) is singled out and emphasized because of its prominence in the diets of nomadic herdsmen.

25:5 רַבָּה לִנְוֵה גְמַלִּים וְאֶת־בְּנֵי עַמֹּון לְמִרְבַּץ־צֹאן—The complete city name, רַבַּת בְּנֵי־עַמֹּון (as in 21:25 [ET 21:20]), is broken up into רַבָּה and then בְּנֵי עַמֹּון for the sake of parallelism. The noun נָוֶה is widely used for the open-range "pasture" of various creatures. Similarly, מַרְבֵּץ is, literally, "a place to stretch out" (from the verb רָבַץ), hence, "corral, animal enclosure, sheepfold."

וְיִדְעָתֶּם—Beginning with this verb and continuing in 25:6–7, the masculine is used for second person forms, probably signaling a shift in attention from the land to its inhabitants. After this masculine plural, the masculine singular is used in 25:6–7, probably referring to the king as the people's representative. Since the change to the masculine straddles 25:5–7 and the כִּי that begins 25:6 connects 25:6 to the preceding, 25:6–7 should not be considered a totally new and separate oracle against the Ammonites.

25:6 The entire verse has a certain Aramaicizing coloration, perhaps, as Greenberg opines, "to lend a foreign color to the address to the Ammonites."[1]

מַחְאֲךָ יָד—In 6:11; 21:19, 22 (ET 21:14, 17); and 22:13, the common Hiphil of נָכָה had been used with כַּף, the "palm," for "strike/clap the hand(s)" (see the second textual note on 6:11). Here we have the Aramaicizing Qal infinitive of מָחָא (with second masculine singular suffix), a verb used elsewhere in the OT only in expressions of joy in Is 55:12 and Ps 98:8. Its object here, יָד, probably was chosen to correspond with God's punishing יָדִי, "my hand," in 25:7.

וְרַקְעֲךָ בְּרֶגֶל—For this idiom, here, literally, "your stamping with foot," the see the third textual note on 6:11. וְרַקְעֲךָ is the Qal infinitive construct (with second masculine singular suffix), just like מַחְאֲךָ in the preceding clause. Usually the Qal infinitive has a *qotl* vocalization before a suffix, as with אָמְרֵךְ (with second feminine singular suffix) in 25:3. The use of *patach* (-רַ) in וְרַקְעֲךָ must be by assimilation to the preceding מַחְאֲךָ, where the *patach* appears because of the following guttural (-מָחָ). The gesture of stamping the feet is more common in Europe today than in America.

וַתִּשְׂמַח בְּכָל־שָׁאטְךָ בְּנֶפֶשׁ—This clause is difficult to capture in idiomatic English. The Qal of שָׂמַח, "rejoice," is usually used in benevolent contexts, but here it is obviously malevolent. The noun שָׁאט, "scorn, contempt," follows the Aramaic pattern of vocalization with a long "a." With a pronominal suffix, as here, the א quiesces into a monosyllabic base. In the OT, the root שׁאט is unique to Ezekiel. This noun recurs only in 25:6, 15; 36:5, while verbal forms occur only as plural Qal participles, שָׁאטִים (28:24, 26) and שָׁאטוֹת (16:57). The triconsonantal root שׁאט is itself a by-form of the hollow root שׁוּט, "treat with contempt." That kind of development from a hollow root is more common in later Hebrew. נֶפֶשׁ (with בְּ) only intensifies the phrase, referring to the inner, real "self" or "being." I have attempted to capture בְּנֶפֶשׁ with "from the bottom of your heart."

אֶל־אַדְמַת יִשְׂרָאֵל:—As in 25:3, אֶל, as an equivalent to עַל, could be translated either "over" or "against," and again I have opted for the latter to correspond to the use of עָלֶיךָ in 25:7 for Yahweh's "hand against you."

25:7 ... וְהַאֲבַדְתִּיךָ ... וְהִכְרַתִּיךָ ... וּנְתַתִּיךָ ... נָטִיתִי הִנְנִי—At least the first and perhaps all of these first person perfect verbs are governed by the initial הִנְנִי, a circumstance that occurs elsewhere in the OT only in Jer 44:26. The series of four prophetic perfects gives unusual emphasis to Yahweh's determination in this verse. In the eyes of God, the deeds are already past tense, as good as done.

---

[1] Greenberg, *Ezekiel*, 2:519.

לְבַנ—Virtually all ancient versions and modern commentators follow the Qere with the noun בַּ (with לְ) instead of the Kethib's unintelligible לְבַנ.

אַשְׁמִידְךָ—This imperfect (Hiphil first common singular of שָׁמַד) stands alone asyndetically after the four preceding perfect verbs, leading Zimmerli[2] and others to delete it as a gloss. Greenberg thinks it reflects a conflation of variant texts.[3] At any rate, it is clearly reflected in the versions. Its isolated abruptness may be read as the final bang of the gavel on God's irrevocable verdict.

25:8 מוֹאָב וְשֵׂעִיר—The MT has this compound subject, "Moab and Seir." The LXX and old Latin omit "Seir," as does the RSV. However, the Vulgate, Peshitta, and Targum have it, as do most English translations (e.g., KJV, NIV, ESV, NASB). The infinitive verb אֱמֹר could have either a single or compound subject. Usually שֵׂעִיר refers to the land or people of Edom. A separate oracle against Edom follows in 25:12–14. None of the other oracles address two nations, although 25:16 refers to both the "Philistines" and "Cherethites" (see the first textual note on 25:16). Allen suggests that וְשֵׂעִיר was added in the margin to draw attention to parallels between the oracle against Edom in 25:12–14 and the one against Mount Seir in 35:2–9, then was mistakenly written near 25:8 because of the similar beginnings of 25:8 and 25:12, and finally was inserted into the text here.[4]

25:9 הִנְנִי פֹתֵחַ אֶת־כֶּתֶף מוֹאָב—"Lay open" (Qal participle, פֹתֵחַ) apparently refers to the destruction of Moab's defenses, leaving it helpless against its enemies. כָּתֵף (here in construct) is most often used anatomically of a person's "shoulder(blade)" or upper arm, but it also has a number of derived, metaphorical meanings, including a "slope" or side of a hill. The reference here would appear to be the western edge of Moab with its steep escarpment down to the Jordan Valley and Dead Sea. Some, using more military language, translate "flank."

מֵהֶעָרִים מֵעָרָיו מִקָּצֵהוּ—These phrases, literally, "from the cities, from its cities, from its end/extremity," form a difficult expression of disputed meaning. The LXX lacks the repetitious "its cities," suggesting the possibility of conflation, but to follow it may be too easy a way out (not the *lectio difficilior*). If the MT stands, the question is what to do with the preposition מִן on all three words. Many take it privatively: "without/deprived of" cities, which are central to military and political control of a country. Grammatically, it seems more likely to me, however, that מִן here indicates source: "from the/its cities onward." One's decision about the first two words will inevitably determine how one views מִקָּצֵהוּ (קָצֶה with מִן and third masculine singular suffix). If the first option is followed, the reference to the land's "extremity" would be its western frontier. I have preferred, however, to understand the word as referring to its entire extent or "whole territory," all of which would be vulnerable if its western "slope" were lost.

---

2   Zimmerli, *Ezekiel*, 2:8.

3   Greenberg, *Ezekiel*, 2:520.

4   Allen, *Ezekiel*, 2:65.

צְבִי—"Glory" is not entirely a satisfactory translation. "Ornament," "desirability," or the like would be closer. This epithet may be given the land because of the Israelite (Reubenite) claim on it and/or because of the fertility of the Mishor (the Moabite plateau north of the Arnon River). The latter emphasis seems more likely in this context and would apply better to the relatively level interior of the land than to the precipitous western border.

The three cities mentioned can be identified with considerable certainty. Following Glueck,[5] Beth-jeshimoth (בֵּית הַיְשִׁמֹת) is usually equated with the modern Tell ʿAzeimeh, about a mile and a half northeast of the entrance of the Jordan into the Dead Sea, although a nearby Khirbet Suweimeh may preserve the ancient name. Baal-meon (בַּעַל מְעוֹן) is mentioned also in Num 32:38 and 1 Chr 5:8 and is called Beth-baal-meon in Josh 13:17 and Beth-meon in Jer 48:23. "Meon" is preserved in the modern Khirbet Maʿin, some thirteen miles southeast of Beth-jeshimoth, that is, five miles southwest of Medeba (today called Madaba, with a vocalic change), some eight miles east of the Dead Sea. Slightly more debated is the site of Kiriathaim, but probably it is to be identified with modern Khirbet Qureiyeh, some six miles west of Medeba. The Kethib, וְקִרְיָתְמָה, represents a defective or secondary spelling of the diphthong in a dual-appearing form. The Qere, וְקִרְיָתָיְמָה, with the additional *yod* normally found in such forms is to be preferred. Baal-meon and Kiriathaim (with the consonants *qrytn*) are also mentioned in the Mesha Inscription (Moabite Stone) as having been rebuilt by the Moabite king in the ninth century.[6]

These three sites form a line from the northwest to southeast. These places could trace a route of ascent for an attacking army: from Beth-jeshimoth near the Jordan, to Kiriathaim on the slope, to Baal-meon near the top of the plateau.[7] Questions arise, however, from the fact that none of them are in the undisputed Moabite heartland between the Zered and Arnon canyons. Rather, all of them are in the Mishor, north of the Arnon, which Joshua had allotted to the tribe of Reuben, although actual control see-sawed between Moab and Israel for quite a time. By Ezekiel's time, the territory had long been in Moabite hands, as both Is 15:1–9 and Jer 48:1–47 make clear. If Ezekiel intends to reassert the Reubenite claim to this territory, it is not clear how the capture of these cities by Israel would mean the demise of Moab proper. However, that seems unlikely, because in the next verse Ezekiel mentions their capture by the people of the East and the Ammonites. Is Ezekiel simply recognizing the historical fact that in his day these cities belonged to Moab? Has he already abandoned Israelite claims to the Transjordan on theological grounds? In his eschatological vision of Israel's boundaries (see 47:13–48:29), the Transjordan is not included as part of Israel. Compare earlier OT notices of suspicion or lack of cooperation between the tribes on either side of the Jordan: Numbers 32; Joshua 22.

---

[5] Nelson Glueck, *Explorations in Eastern Palestine, IV*, part 1: *Text*, vols. 25–28 of AASOR (New Haven: ASOR, 1951), 398–404.

[6] Mesha inscription, lines 9–10 (*ANET*, 320).

[7] Zimmerli, *Ezekiel*, 2:16, posits these geographical positions.

25:10 וּנְתַתִּיהָ—This verb (Qal of נָתַן, literally, "and I will give it") in the middle of the verse is the major curve thrown the translator. Its *waw* is redundant. A radical solution, proposed by some, would change the word order. A better solution, it seems to me, is to understand the preceding words in the verse as still governed by פֹּתֵחַ ("lay open") at the beginning of 25:9. Then we have a possibly faulty verse division if this verb should start a verse. At the very least, this verb begins an entirely new sentence (as in my translation). The opening words of the verse ("to the people of the East in addition to the Ammonites") fit better with the assumption that if Moab's western defenses fall before Yahweh's onslaught and its eastern frontier is overrun by desert nomads, all of Moab would soon become history (cf. on מִקָּצֵהוּ in 25:9 above). Regardless of how we understand the grammar, Moab must be the implied object of this verb and of the divine judgment, as the context requires. However, Moab is somewhat in the shadow of Ammon, the dominant power in Transjordan at the time, and Ammon almost dominates this verse.

לְמַעַן לֹא־תִזָּכֵר בְּנֵי־עַמּוֹן—The use of לְמַעַן לֹא instead of the classical Hebrew פֶּן to express negative purpose reflects late Hebrew usage. The use of the feminine singular verb (Niphal imperfect of זָכַר) is difficult because its subject is the masculine plural בְּנֵי־עַמּוֹן. Various solutions are proposed. Most commonly Rabbah, the feminine name of the capital city, is taken to be the implied subject, and the Syriac explicitly adds it. Others suggest that אֶרֶץ is implied. Zimmerli suggests that the verb is feminine singular by attraction to the preceding feminine singular suffix on וּנְתַתִּיהָ, referring to Moab.[8] If one of these solutions is not accepted, emendation may be required. Very radical proposals would delete both references to Ammon as later accretions.

25:12 יַעַן עֲשׂוֹת אֱדוֹם בִּנְקֹם נָקָם—The syntax is easier in the similar clause in 25:15 that begins the Philistine oracle (see the second textual note on that verse). Here, the infinitive construct עֲשׂוֹת (Qal of עָשָׂה), "to do," is followed by another infinitive construct phrase, בִּנְקֹם נָקָם the Qal of נָקַם and the cognate accusative noun נָקָם. (The same cognate accusative construction, לִנְקֹם נָקָם, occurred in 24:8.) In translation, perhaps "Edom's acting in avenging (with) vengeance" is as close as one can come. The syntax intends to convey the idea of malice aforethought, of excess far beyond any mere evening of the score or the like.

וַיֶּאְשְׁמוּ אָשׁוֹם—The Qal imperfect (third masculine plural) of אָשַׁם, "be guilty," is followed by the Qal infinitive absolute of the same verb to intensify the magnitude of Edom's vendetta even more. There is no hint of remorse by Edom here, so "incur grievous guilt" or inflict "an irreparable injury"[9] is implied. The expression appears to be derived from אָשֹׁם אָשַׁם in Lev 5:19, where the infinitive precedes the finite form. The verb אָשַׁם also occurs in Ezek 6:6 and 22:4. The root is not easy to translate. Traditionally, it has been rendered with "guilt," but with unclear distinction from various words for "sin." The cognate noun אָשָׁם refers to a type of sacrifice, traditionally

---

8   Zimmerli, *Ezekiel*, 2:9.

9   Cooke, *Ezekiel*, 284.

called the "guilt offering," but better is "reparation offering," because alone among the sacrifices, in this case the sinner, upon confession, must, in addition to the animal sacrifice, pay a penalty or "surcharge" of twenty percent. The noun occurs in 40:39; 42:13; 44:29; 46:20. It refers to the atonement made by the death of the Suffering Servant in Is 53:10.

וְנִקְמוּ בָהֶם׃—The Niphal perfect of נָקַם (instead of an imperfect with *waw* consecutive) makes clear that the guilt consisted in the very act of "avenging themselves," not that the vengeance was a consequence of the incurring of guilt.[10] Sometimes after an imperfect with *waw* consecutive (here וַיֶּאְשְׁמוּ), a perfect (וְנִקְמוּ here) has a frequentative sense, which certainly fits this context, and so I have rendered it.

25:13 וְהִכְרַתִּי ... וְנָטִתִי—Both of these verbs are first common singular perfects (Qal of נָטָה and Hiphil of כָּרַת, respectively) with *waw* consecutive, as indicated by the shift of the accent to the final syllable. Since *yethib* (-ֽטַ-) is prepositive, the last syllable of וְנָטִתִי is accented.

וּנְתַתִּיהָ חָרְבָּה מִתֵּימָן וּדְדָנֶה בַּחֶרֶב—As indicated in my translation, I concur with most commentators in punctuating the verse differently than the MT and connecting מִתֵּימָן with what follows (as if the *zaqeph qaton* were not on מִתֵּימָן, but on the preceding word, חָרְבָּה). Greenberg suggests that the MT represents a telescoping of "... a ruin from Teman [to Dedan], and [from Teman] to Dedan they shall fall."[11] My translation takes וְ ... מִן (on מִתֵּימָן וּדְדָנֶה) as equivalent to the common idiom מִן ... עַד. The directive *he* on וּדְדָנֶה is superfluous; the usage is attested also in Josh 15:4b. The directive *he* is normally preceded by a *patach*, but here by a *seghol*, probably by dissimilation. Its use with *seghol* is attested also in 1 Sam 21:2 (ET 21:1); 22:9; and 1 Ki 2:36, 42.

The locations of Teman and Dedan (mentioned together also in Jer 49:7–8) are not certain. תֵּימָן can mean "south" or "southern region" in general. Since Edom is south(east) of Israel, תֵּימָן may refer to Edom as a whole (so in Jer 49:7, 20 and Obad 9) or especially its "capital" around Bozrah. (It once was commonly identified with modern Tawilan near Petra, but this has been proven untenable.[12]) While Dedan may also refer to a territory rather than a specific site, it is usually identified as modern al-ʿUla (or nearby ruins), a major oasis on an ancient frankincense road from Yemen to Canaan. (Genealogically, Dedan appears as a grandson of Abraham by his second wife, Keturah, in Gen 25:3 along with other Arab tribes. Earlier Dedan is listed in Gen 10:7 as a descendant of Ham.) Since the region of Dedan was not usually considered a part of Edom, questions arise about the reason for its choice here. Perhaps they were literary more than geographical or political. The phrase is often compared to "from Dan to Beersheba" (e.g., Judg 20:1), with which Israel's borders did not always coincide exactly either.

25:15–16 The content and structure of these two verses aimed at the Philistines are very similar to the three preceding verses against Edom—and equally general in nature.

---

[10] Zimmerli, *Ezekiel*, 2:9, says it is "to be regarded hypotactically."

[11] Greenberg, *Ezekiel*, 2:522.

[12] See E. A. Knauf, "Teman," *ABD* 6:347–48.

25:15 פְּלִשְׁתִּים—In the four oracles of the chapter, the only gentilic nouns are the plurals of פְּלִשְׁתִּי, "Philistine" (25:15–16), and כְּרֵתִי, "Cherethite" (25:16). The use of these, rather than a name for a territory, theoretically condemns certain inhabitants rather than a nation as a whole. Possibly "Philistines" is used because there was no unified nation of Philistia, but only a confederation of five city-states.

בִּנְקָמָה וַיִּנָּקְמוּ נָקָם—Just as 25:12 used the verb נָקַם twice, along with the cognate noun נָקָם, so here the Niphal of the verb (third masculine plural with *waw* consecutive) is surrounded by the cognate nouns נְקָמָה (which also occurred twice in 25:14 and will occur twice in 25:17) and נָקָם.

בִּשְׁאָט בְּנֶפֶשׁ—This phrase echoes שָׁאט בְּנֶפֶשׁ in 25:6. In the absence of a suffix, the *aleph* in בִּשְׁאָט is not quiescent, but consonantal, and so takes a vowel. The phrase here is translated differently, "with utter contempt," because of the different context.

אֵיבַת עוֹלָם:—This construct phrase is adverbial ("with everlasting enmity") despite the lack of a preceding בְּ. It recurs in 35:5 and recalls אֵיבָה in Gen 3:15.

25:16 וְהִכְרַתִּי אֶת־כְּרֵתִים—Possibly to enable the alliterative wordplay of the verb and the noun with כרת, Ezekiel introduces the "Cherethites," parallel to the "Philistines" or a subgroup among them. כְּרֵתִי may be related to Crete, or Caphtor (Amos 9:7), from where the Philistines are said to have arrived.[13] If there was a difference between the Philistines and the Cherethites, it probably had largely disappeared by Ezekiel's day. If the reference to the "Cherethite Negev" in 1 Sam 30:14 is not simply synonymous with "Philistine land," it might indicate that the Cherethites were concentrated on the frontier with the Sinai Desert.

שְׁאֵרִית חוֹף הַיָּם:—"The remnant of [by] the shore of the sea" connects the Philistines, Cherethites, and seacoast dwellers, as also in Zeph 2:5. If the third component is not a sort of "etc." to the list, it alludes to other Sea Peoples north of the Philistines, whose territory seems to have extended roughly up to the Yarkon River on the north side of modern Tel Aviv.

25:17 נְקָמֹת ... נִקְמָתִי—The noun נְקָמָה appears twice more in Yahweh's mouth. In Ezekiel, it occurs only in 25:14, 15, 17, and the cognate verb נָקַם and noun נָקָם were in 25:12, 15. This repeated vocabulary links the oracle against the Philistines with the preceding one against Edom. In both oracles, some of this vocabulary occurs in the pronouncement of Yahweh's judgment (although his people's agency is not included here) and is incorporated in the recognition formula: "thus they will know my vengeance, says the Lord Yahweh" (25:14); "they will know that I am Yahweh when I lay my vengeance upon them" (25:17). The concern is Yahweh's deserts, to be expressed in his retributive justice. The pleonastic addition בְּתוֹכְחוֹת חֵמָה, "with furious chastisements," in 25:17 is derived from the same realm of thought (the noun תּוֹכַחַת is related to the verb יָכַח, which occurs mostly in the Hiphil, meaning "to settle quarrels" and the like).

This time Zimmerli is on the mark:

> The arrogant demand for justice on the part of Judah's two neighbors is countered by Yahweh with his own holy demand for justice. In נקם ("vengeance")

---

[13] See C. S. Ehrlich, "Cherethites," *ABD* 1:898–99.

there is not only the psychologically subjective "relishing of a thirst for revenge," but a strong forensic emphasis. In his vengeance Yahweh makes himself known as the one who does not suffer men to take from him what is his kingly right. Paul too, according to Rom 12:19, knows that "vengeance" is one of God's rights.[14]

Commentary

None of the oracles in chapter 25 include a date, and they cannot be dated precisely by any means. But since the destruction of Jerusalem seems to be presupposed, it is likely that these words from Yahweh arrived sometime shortly after Jerusalem's fall in summer 586 B.C. As a terminus ad quem, 582 seems likely, because by that time further insubordination in Canaan (Jer 40:1–43:7) and probably Ammon as well (Jer 40:13–16) had forced Nebuchadnezzar into still a fourth campaign in the area, after Moab and Ammon disappear from historical sight.[15]

An Oracle against the Ammonites (25:1–7)

25:2–3 Special attention is directed toward the Ammonites, as evidenced not only by their initial position in the series, but also by an order to address them directly ("say *to* the Ammonites," 25:3), in contrast to the other nations and peoples, which are only spoken of. The elaborate introduction includes a command for the prophet to (literally) set his face toward (or perhaps "against") his audience.[16] The phrase may be metaphorical, or it may represent the prophet's actual posture in a sort of action prophecy.

The special attention paid to Ammon is undoubtedly related to the long history of conflict between it and Israel, even though historically the Ammonites, like the Moabites, were related to the Israelites via descent from Lot (Gen 19:36–38). The conflict was exacerbated by the fact that the Ammonites' territory was poorly defined, although it apparently centered somewhat around the modern capital of Jordan—the city of Amman, which still bears the ancient name. The tribal list of Josh 13:15–20 assigns to the Israelites most of the territory north of the Arnon River (Gilead and Bashan to Mount Hermon) that the Israelites had conquered from the Amorite kingdoms of Sihon and Og (Num 21:10–35; 32:33–42). Moab had once possessed part of Sihon's territory north of the Arnon, which probably explains later conflicts between Moab and Gad, which received part of Gilead north of Reuben's allotment.

Just when the Ammonites appeared on the scene is uncertain. In the late fifteenth century B.C., Deut 2:19 asserts that Israel did not encroach on Ammonite land. In the early fourteenth century B.C., Josh 13:24–25 states that "half

---

[14] Zimmerli, *Ezekiel*, 2:19.

[15] "Josephus notes (*Ant* 10.9.7 §181) that Nebuchadnezzar subjected Ammon and Moab five years after the fall of Jerusalem, but neither Josephus nor the OT suggests that Edom was attacked on this occasion" (J. R. Bartlett, "Edom," *ABD* 2:293).

[16] See the second textual note on 6:2.

the land of the Ammonites" was allotted to the tribe of Gad—probably reflecting the conflicting claims. Jephthah fights the Ammonite king over disputed land in Judges 11. The Ammonite king Hanun's rebuff of David's irenic overtures led to David attacking and annexing the country (2 Samuel 10–12). At some later time, the Ammonites regained their independence, but under Uzziah and Jotham, they are again paying tribute to Judah (2 Chr 26:8; 27:5).

A century earlier, in the ninth century, King Mesha on the famous Moabite Stone boasts of recapturing cities north of the Arnon and evicting the Gadites.[17] Under Ahab's leadership, Ammon and other Levantine states join in confronting and checking the Assyrian advance, at least temporarily, at the famous Battle of Qarqar on the Orontes in 853. But such alliances were fleeting. In the eighth century B.C., Amos 1:13 denounces Ammonite atrocities in Gilead during Israel's century-long conflict with the Arameans to the north. Zephaniah condemns Ammon (and Moab) for reviling God's people and gloating over their territory (Zeph 2:8–9), and Jer 49:1 mentions an Ammonite occupation of Gad, but neither give specifics. Whatever all the details, the picture could hardly be clearer of ceaseless bad political blood, often erupting into open conflict.

In Ezekiel's own lifetime, Ammon, like the other Transjordanian nations, apparently submitted to Nebuchadnezzar after the Battle of Carchemish in 605. But its loyalty was superficial. On the one hand, Ammon aided the Babylonians in quelling Jehoiakim's rebellion against Babylon in 598 (in the aftermath of which Ezekiel was exiled [2 Ki 24:1–2]), but on the other hand, they joined Zedekiah a decade later in an anti-Babylonian cabal (Jer 27:3). Naturally, they welcomed Nebuchadnezzar's decision to attack Jerusalem first (Ezek 21:18–27), and Ezekiel's subsequent words indicate that Ammon did not escape unscathed either (21:28–32), but we lack specifics. After Judah's fall, Ammon, like Moab and Edom, accepted Judah's refugees, and King Baalis of Ammon was involved in the assassination of Gedaliah, whom the Babylonians had made governor of Judah (Jeremiah 40–41). We lack more detail, but Ammon, like Moab, continued to maneuver for independence, precipitating Nebuchadnezzar's 582 campaign against the area, which spelled the end of the ancient Ammonite and Moabite kingdoms.

What is exegetically significant, however, is that Ezekiel makes no mention of all this political and military intrigue swirling about him. Rather, the concern is theological. Ammon takes malicious delight, not only in Jerusalem's fall and the deportation of its inhabitants, but specifically in the profanation of Yahweh's מִקְדָּשׁ, "sanctuary" (25:3). In Ammon, the virtual identification of god(s), temple, and nation would hardly have differed enough from Judah's that the Ammonites would have failed to grasp the centrality of the Jerusalem temple in the official theology of the nation. Thus Ammon's glee was virtually

---

[17] *ANET*, 320.

explicit applause that Yahweh's own salvific purposes seemed to have been thwarted. Yahweh himself was being mocked.

25:4–5 The punishment will consist of Ammonite loss of title to the land they had received from Yahweh. The Ammonites will be weakened to the extent that the nomadic tribes to the east will find it easy to move in and help themselves to Ammon's land and property. This prophecy was fulfilled shortly after Nebuchadnezzar's 582 invasion and depopulation of the territory, which effectively terminated Ammonite identity. Jer 49:6 holds out hope of ultimate restoration for the Ammonites, but Ezekiel does not mention it. All evidence indicates that it was several centuries before "civilization" in its sense of central authority returned to the area. Judas Maccabaeus is reported to have waged war against the Ammonites in the second century B.C. (1 Macc 5:6), and even Justin Martyr in the second century A.D. mentions them,[18] but it is unclear whether these references are to a resurgence of the ancient nation or are more generally to whatever inhabitants lived in the territory still known by the ancient name.

As I can personally attest, as late as 1950, Amman was little more than a large village centered around the headwaters of the Jabbok at what is today known as the First Circle of a vast metropolis. For many centuries preceding, the Ottoman Turks had concerned themselves with little more than keeping open the pilgrimage route to Mecca. The proverbial conflict between "the desert and the sown" overstates the case. More often, as today with a strong central government, the nomadic and sedentary components of the society coexist in a generally peaceful, symbiotic relationship. But the climate and territory are such that in times of political weakness, the inhabitants find it relatively easy to revert to a nomadic way of life, and/or desert elements that had been held at bay sweep in and take control.

While Ezek 25:4 simply states the humiliation of the new situation, 25:5 does not let us forget that the subject is not sociology, but one part of Yahweh's process of establishing his status as Lord over all (cf. Psalm 110; Phil 2:6–11).

25:6–7 These verses could be considered a second oracle against Ammon, but it has extremely close links with the preceding verses: the continuation of masculine constructions (see the last textual note on 25:5), the connecting כִּי ("for") beginning 25:6, and essential similarity in content. Both the initial citation formula ("thus says the Lord Yahweh") and the concluding recognition formula ("you will know that I am Yahweh") are repeated (from 25:3 and 25:5, respectively), but are also emphatic. The language is less concrete than in the previous verses, but also more intense in its prophecy of judgment: Ammon will even be "exterminated" (25:7). As noted above, this prophecy was fulfilled in Nebuchadnezzar's 582 campaign in the region, after which Ammon as a distinct nation or people is heard from no more.

---

[18] Justin Martyr, *Dialogue with Trypho*, 119 (*ANF* 1:259).

An Oracle against Moab (25:8–11)

25:8 With this verse, an oracle against Moab commences. Genealogically a "brother" of Ammon (Gen 19:36–38), Moab is treated in this oracle almost as an adjunct of Ammon, which is specifically mentioned twice again in Ezek 25:10. Moab's relations with Israel and Judah closely paralleled Ammon's, and the specific judgments pronounced upon the Moabites are very similar to those upon the Ammonites.

Like Ammon, Moab's relations with the Israelites had been unfriendly from first contacts. Moab did everything in its power to foil Israelite attempts to invade Canaan—the subject of the Balak-Balaam narratives in Numbers 22–25. During the period of the judges, Eglon, king of Moab, gained some political control over Israel, with deliverance coming only through the daring feat of Ehud (Judg 3:12–30). The book of Ruth indicates that at least a truce obtained for a time then, but not long afterwards David conquered the land, dealing very harshly with it (2 Sam 8:2). In the ninth century, Mesha regained control of the Mishor, the Moabite plateau north of the Arnon that was also claimed by the tribe of Reuben (2 Kings 1–3; see also the famous Mesha Inscription, also known as the Moabite Stone).[19] 2 Chr 20:1–30 reports how Moab joined Ammon and Edom in an unsuccessful attack against Judah. The prophet Elisha is involved in various skirmishes with Moab, one concluding mysteriously with Israelite withdrawal after the Moabite king sacrifices his oldest son on the city wall, "and there came great wrath upon Israel" (2 Ki 3:27). 2 Ki 13:20 reports Moabite raids into Israel the year that prophet died.

In Ezekiel's day, Moab had joined Ammon in aiding Nebuchadnezzar's attack on Jehoiakim, then both had reversed fields and joined Zedekiah's coalition against Babylon. When Jerusalem fell, both taunted the stricken city, as intimated here in Ezekiel and referred to elsewhere (Jer 48:26–35; cf. Zeph 2:8). Finally, when both rebelled against Babylon in 582, both were all but erased from history by Nebuchadnezzar, Moab apparently sooner and more thoroughly than Ammon.

Ezekiel's oracle against Moab uses the third person rather than the second person of direct address employed for Ammon. Moab is not described as indulging in open celebration of Jerusalem's fall, but of using it as proof that Judah enjoyed no special status with heavenly powers, as it claimed, but was as vulnerable as all other nations. Some Hebrew manuscripts and the LXX have "the house of *Israel and* Judah" in 25:8, adding "Israel" in its theological sense as the covenanted people. This addition neutralizes the danger that "the house of Judah," used by the Moabites, might be misunderstood in purely political terms. It is accurate theologically: despite Moab's claim, the northern tribes too were not like other nations. The fact that Yahweh had indeed given his people a special status is linked to the incomparability of Yahweh himself. Thus Moab's language is simple blasphemy.

---

[19] *ANET*, 320.

One is reminded that Israel's desire for a king in 1 Sam 8:5 had been motivated by a desire to be like other nations. This desire was indeed a constant temptation for those elected to be a "special possession" and a "holy nation" (Ex 19:5–6), as it remains for the church (cf. 1 Pet 2:9). Moab had correctly discerned Israel's failure to live up to its high calling. Yet Moab, like unbelievers who fault the church for its failings, failed to realize that it was even more subject to judgment and had no license to give reign to its own conceits and hatreds.

25:9–11   Yahweh does not tolerate such blasphemous denials of his intrinsic uniqueness and incomparability and turns the tables. Like all the other kingdoms of this world, Moab must ultimately sink into oblivion.

An Oracle against Edom (25:12–14)

25:12   Edom runs a close second to Babylon, especially in the OT, as *the* symbol and type of the kingdoms of this world—of Satan's realm, which will be in unending conflict with the kingdom of God until the end of time.

The mutual enmity seems especially bitter because of the familial relationship between Edom and Israel. As is often the case, few feuds and grudges are as sharp and implacable as those between siblings. Jacob and Esau (the father of the Edomites) were twin sons of Isaac and Rebekah, and their rivalry, which will become one of the better-known narratives of the Bible, is foretold already at their birth (Gen 25:23). Genesis 32–33 indicates that Esau had settled in Edom already at the time of Jacob's return from Haran. Gen 36:31–39 reports that eight kings had already ruled in Edom before Saul became Israel's first. En route from Egypt to Canaan, Moses appeals in vain to the Edomites' relation as brothers for permission to traverse their territory (Num 20:14–21). Because of the relationship, Deut 23:8–9 (ET 23:7–8) even permits Israelites to intermarry with Edomites in the third generation. Closer to Ezekiel's time, both Amos and Obadiah highlight Edom's malicious behavior toward its brother. And the reader will not overlook that after the short oracle against Edom here, an entire chapter (Ezekiel 35) will be devoted to the coming judgment on Edom.

No written Edomite records have survived or been found (presuming there were some). For their history we are largely dependent on Israel's records in the inspired Scriptures. They indicate that relations between the two neighbors first became bitter when David conquered Edom and massacred many (2 Sam 8:13–14), although Edom was able to regain some independence under Solomon (1 Ki 11:14–22). The prize was the Gulf of Aqaba seaport of Eziongeber and/or Elath, and its control of trade routes, especially those between the Hejaz (western Saudi Arabia) and southern Sinai. A seesaw struggle continued until the time of Ahaz in the eighth century, after which Edom prevailed, although by this time as a vassal of Assyria. Initially, Edom joined Zedekiah's conspiracy against Nebuchadnezzar (Jer 27:3), but after Jerusalem fell Edom aided in the spoliation of the fallen city. It is especially this treachery which triggered the outrage expressed in Obad 11–14; Ps 137:7; and Lam 4:21.

The Edomite heartland was originally the mountainous territory east of the Arabah, from the Zered canyon on the border with Moab on the north, and extending as far south as the Gulf of Aqaba. Not long after Ezekiel, however, Edom's power began to wane, mostly because of pressure from the east. (Yahweh had mentioned enemies coming from the east against Ammon and Moab [25:4, 10], but does not for Edom.) Not long after the fall of Jerusalem, Nabonidus (father of the derelict king Belshazzar of Belshazzar's feast fame [Daniel 5]) campaigned to control desert trade routes, and Edom may have been adversely affected. Mal 1:3–4 indicates that eastern pressure had forced Edom out of its homeland then already. Shortly later, the opposition to Ezra and Nehemiah from the southeast came not from Edomites, but from one "Geshem the Arab" (Neh 2:19; 6:1–2). And by the fourth century B.C., Arabic Nabateans had begun to build their fabulous civilization in Petra. What was left of the ancient Edomites apparently gradually infiltrated southern Judah, where the memory of their origin was preserved in the name Idumea, given to the area. That name is best represented by Herod the Great, whose Idumean background[20] did not help endear him to his subjects.

Comparable to the close connection between the previous two oracles against Ammon (25:1–7) and Moab (25:8–11), the last two, against Edom (25:12–14) and Philistia (25:15–17), are very similar. The similarity is apparent both in their similarities of structure and in their shared vocabulary, including the verb נָקַם, "avenge, take vengeance" (25:12 [twice], 15), and the nouns derived from it, נָקָם (25:12, 15) and נְקָמָה (25:14 [twice], 15, 17 [twice]), both meaning "revenge, vengeance." In 25:12 the verb is used twice and the noun נָקָם once, while 25:14 uses the noun נְקָמָה twice. But in 25:12 Edom is the subject, while in 25:14 Yahweh is.

Throughout the OT, this difference in subject must be carefully noted, or serious misunderstandings result. When people or countries are the subjects who take vengeance, the root implies vindictive excess. However, when Yahweh is the actor, the word group often connotes his punitive defeat of the enemies of his people, which ensures his people's protection, vindication, and salvation. A major example is Is 61:2 (the text for our Lord's first sermon at Nazareth [Lk 4:16–27]), where "the year of Yahweh's favor" is parallel to "the day of vengeance for our God." See also Is 63:4, where "the day of vengeance" is parallel to "my year of redemption." It is translated "vengeance" in 25:14, where it refers to God judging Moab. Misunderstanding of God taking "vengeance" easily contributes to the canard that in the OT era God was characterized especially by wrath, and his love did not triumph until the NT.

Ezekiel does not specify what terrible malevolence Edom exercises toward Jerusalem, but the reference is almost certainly to its perfidy after Jerusalem's fall—not only betraying its previous alliance with its "brother" city, but gleefully joining in sharing the spoils. No wonder, even humanly speaking, that it

---

[20] See Josephus, *Antiquities*, 14.121 (14.7.3).

elicits such wounded outrage by Judah and prayers that Yahweh will exercise his vengeance and vindicate his people, as this oracle proceeds to promise (cf. Obadiah; Ps 137:7).

25:13 Yahweh's judgment is syntactically divisible into four declarations but may be summarized as consisting in depopulation and desolation, corresponding to the assonance of the two key words, חֶרֶב, "sword," and חָרְבָּה, "wasteland."

25:14 The punishment corresponds to the crime in the sense that Edom's vengeance triggers Yahweh's vengeance. See the commentary on 25:12 for the different connotations with human and divine subjects. (See also the reversal described in Obad 15 and 18.) More remarkable is the assertion that Yahweh will accomplish this through the agency of Israel. The pronominal suffix on עַמִּי, "*my* people," repeated with כְּאַפִּי וְכַחֲמָתִי, "with *my* anger and with *my* wrath," indicates that the prophet has more in mind than merely another round in an unending tit-for-tat human conflict. The suffix also suggests a time when God's covenant with Israel will be restored as before, even greater (see 16:60–62; 34:25; 37:26). The thrust of Ezekiel's thought is furthered by the transformation of the concluding recognition formula (25:7, 11) from a mere recognition of the person of Yahweh in general into a prediction that the Edomites will recognize Yahweh's avenging judgment in the actions of the Israelites (25:14). And the standard signatory formula, "says the Lord Yahweh,"[21] seals further the certainty of the fulfillment of the divine purpose.

It is not easy to locate times and places in the historical sphere when this prophecy was fulfilled because of Edom's imminent fading from that sphere (and this specific prophecy is not reiterated in chapter 35). The mutation of "Edom" into "Idumea" hardly ameliorates the problem. Instead, we must see the solution in transhistorical (eschatological) times, as, in a way, we must with all the Gentile oracles. Keil is profoundly correct when he asserts:

> On the ground, therefore, of the prophecies in Amos ix. 12 and Obad. vers. 17 sqq., that the people of God are to take possession of Edom, when the fallen tabernacle of David is raised up again, *i.e.* in the Messianic times ... we must seek for the complete fulfilment in the victories of the people of God over all their foes, among whom Edom from time immemorial had taken the leading place, at the time when the kingdom of God is perfected. For even here Edom is not introduced merely as a single nation that was peculiarly hostile to Judah, but also as a type of the implacable enmity of the heathen world towards the people and kingdom of God. ... The vengeance ... consists not merely in the annihilation of the national existence of Edom, which John Hyrcanus carried into effect by compelling the subjugated Edomites to adopt circumcision ... but chiefly in the wrathful judgment which Israel will execute in the person of Christ upon the arch-enemy of the kingdom of God by its complete extinction.[22]

---

[21] For this formula, see pages 8–9 in the introduction and the second textual note on 5:11.

[22] Keil, *Ezekiel*, 1:368.

An Oracle against the Philistines (25:15–17)

25:15 The inclusion of the Philistines is a bit puzzling in the absence of any overt conflicts between them and Jerusalem at Ezekiel's time. Perhaps it made for a traditional foursome: already Is 11:14 had included the Philistines with Edom, Moab, and Ammon as enemies whom Israel would attack and overcome after its dispersion was over. The ultimate origin of the Philistines is probably irrelevant here, but they are usually associated with the Sea Peoples, as the Egyptians called them, who wreaked havoc in the Levant and beyond in the thirteenth century B.C. The Bible (Amos 9:7) specifies Caphtor (usually identified with Crete) as the place of their origin. But the Table of Nations (Gen 10:14; 1 Chr 1:12) classifies them as Hamitic, leading many to hypothesize an earlier migration from Egypt to Crete. Excavations, both at Knossos in Minoan Crete and at Tell el-Dabʿa (probably ancient Avaris) in the eastern delta region of Egypt, attest to extensive cultural contacts.[23] But Minoan influence is also evident at Tel Kabri in northern Israel (Galilee).

The early conflicts between the Israelites and the Philistines are recounted in considerable detail in Judges and 1 Samuel and need not be repeated here. At Saul's death on Mount Gilboa (1 Samuel 31), the Philistines are poised to completely surround the Israelite hill country and subjugate Israel. David buys time by cunningly pretending allegiance with Achish, king of Gath (1 Samuel 27). But after becoming king in Jerusalem, he is able to deal the Philistines a decisive defeat in the outskirts of Jerusalem (narrated with surprising brevity in 2 Sam 5:17–25) so that never again are they any military menace.

Nevertheless, the Philistines were able to maintain their separate identity for centuries, although archaeology indicates that they acculturated rapidly. Subsequent relations with Israel were varied. We read of a couple of clashes at the city of Gibbethon, "which belonged to the Philistines" (1 Ki 15:27; 16:15), but any particular Philistine involvement is not mentioned. On the peaceful side, David employs, presumably as mercenaries, Cherethite (see the textual note above on 25:16) and Pelethite (that is, Philistine) bodyguards (2 Sam 8:18; 20:23; cf. 23:22–23) and maintains a core of Gittite troops (2 Sam 15:18).

Relations between the Philistines and the Assyrian Empire are equally unclear and seem to have varied from Philistine city to Philistine city. Assyrian records tell us that during Sennacherib's campaign against Hezekiah (which ended disastrously; see 2 Ki 19:35–37; Is 37:36–38; 2 Chr 32:21), Sennacherib deposed and deported Sidqia, king of Ashkelon, who had not submitted to him. But Padi, king of Ekron, whom Hezekiah had imprisoned, was released and profited from whatever temporary success Sennacherib had, along with Mitinti, king of Ashdod, and Sillibel, king of Gaza.[24] Something similar could have happened after Carchemish and Jehoiakim's revolt. But we know that when

---

[23] See Davies and Schofield, *Egypt, the Aegean and the Levant: Interconnections in the Second Millennium BC*.

[24] *ANET*, 287–88.

Ashkelon refused to pay tribute, Nebuchadnezzar leveled the city, and recent excavations at Ekron indicate a catastrophic destruction there at about the same time. One may compare Jeremiah 47, which suggests neo-Babylonian destruction of all Philistia. (A few Philistines from Ashdod become a problem for the postexilic community according to Neh 13:23–24, but that is much later.)

We have no extrabiblical evidence that Philistines joined Edomites and others in gloating at and profiting from Jerusalem's fall. That may imply that Yahweh builds this judgment oracle more on the "everlasting enmity" or "hatred immemorial"[25] mentioned in Ezek 25:15 than on specific, recent acts of spite in Ezekiel's lifetime.

It is only by a curiously coincidental act of spite over half a millennium later that a derivative of the name "Philistia" is still heard today in a national sense outside of biblical contexts. In exasperation after the second Jewish revolt in A.D. 135, the Romans renamed the province "Palestine" after Judah's archetypal enemy. Since the establishment of the modern Israeli state, speakers should be aware of the political connotations that "Palestine" has in connection with the ongoing conflict there.

25:16 By a triad of verbs we have seen associated previously (25:7), "stretch out my hand against," "cut off," and "destroy," God's justice on the Philistines is described. The use of שְׁאֵרִית ("remnant") may imply his will toward total elimination.

25:17 Since a translation of בְּתוֹכְחוֹת חֵמָה, "with furious chastisements," is missing in the LXX, the phrase is often considered a gloss, but it is typical of Ezekiel's expansiveness and seems especially appropriate in the conclusion.

---

[25] Greenberg, *Ezekiel*, 2:518, 522.

An Oracle against Tyre

Translation

26 ¹In the eleventh year, on the first day of the month, the Word of Yahweh came to me: ²"Son of man, because Tyre said about Jerusalem, 'Aha! The gateway to the peoples has been broken; it has been turned over to me. Because of her devastation, I will be satisfied,' ³therefore, thus says the Lord Yahweh: I am against you, Tyre, and I will raise up many nations against you as the sea raises up its waves. ⁴They will destroy the walls of Tyre and demolish her towers. I will scrape the debris off from her and make her a bare rock. ⁵In the middle of the sea, she will be only a place where fishing nets are spread out to dry, for I have spoken it, says the Lord Yahweh. She will become plunder for the nations, ⁶and her 'daughters' on the mainland will be slain by the sword. Then they will know that I am Yahweh.

⁷"For thus says the Lord Yahweh: I am bringing against Tyre Nebuchadnezzar, king of Babylon—from the north—king of kings, together with horses, chariots, horsemen, and a vast assembly of troops. ⁸Your 'daughters' on the mainland he will slay with the sword. He will set up a siege wall against you, heap up a ramp against you, and erect shields against you. ⁹He will direct the force of his battle against your walls, and your towers he will demolish with his swords. ¹⁰His horses will be so numerous that their dust will cover you. Your walls will shake from the noise of the horsemen, wheels, and chariots when he enters your gates as people enter a breached city. ¹¹With the hooves of his horses, he will trample all your streets; he will slay all your people with the sword; and your mighty pillars will topple to the ground. ¹²They will plunder your valuable property and take your merchandise as spoil. They will tear down your walls and demolish your magnificent houses. Your stones, your timbers, and your rubble they will throw into the water. ¹³I will put an end to the din of your songs, and the sound of your lyres will be heard no more. ¹⁴I will turn you into a bare rock. She will become a place where fishing nets are spread out to dry. She will never be rebuilt, for I, Yahweh, have spoken, says the Lord Yahweh.

¹⁵"Thus says the Lord Yahweh to Tyre: Will not the coastlands shudder at the sound of your downfall, when the victims groan, when the slain are slaughtered in your midst? ¹⁶All the princes of the sea will descend from their thrones, remove their robes, and take off their finely embroidered garments. Rather, in trembling they will clothe themselves; they will sit on the ground and tremble every moment, appalled at you. ¹⁷They will utter a lament over you and say to you:

" 'How you have perished,
    you who were inhabited from the seas,

a city that was celebrated,

> that was the strongest in the sea, she and her inhabitants,

who even inspired their terror

> —all of her inhabitants.

[18]Now the coastlands tremble

> on the day of your downfall.

The coastlands that are on the sea are terrified by your departure.'

[19]"For thus says the Lord Yahweh: When I make you a ruined city like the cities that are not inhabited, when I bring the deep up over you and the many waters cover you, [20]then I will bring you down to be with those who have descended to the pit, to the people of old. I will make you inhabit the underworld, like ancient ruins, to be with those who have descended to the pit, so that you will not be dwelt in or manifest glory in the land of the living. [21]I will make you an object of horror, and you will be no more. You will be sought but never found again, says the Lord Yahweh."

Textual Notes

26:1–21   See the map "The Ancient Near East."

26:1 וַיְהִי בְּעַשְׁתֵּי־עֶשְׂרֵה שָׁנָה בְּאֶחָד לַחֹדֶשׁ—The chapter opens with a date notice, which presents several difficulties. Many solutions have been proposed, but none have found common assent. The oracles in chapter 25 were all undated, but all assume a time shortly after Jerusalem's fall.

"On the first of the month" does not specify which month. The more immediate issue is that "the eleventh year" probably dates this oracle to before Jerusalem's fall (in summer 586 B.C.), since 33:21 reports that Ezekiel received news of Jerusalem's fall in the tenth month of the *twelfth* year. However, in the oracle itself, Tyre seems already to be rejoicing that Jerusalem has fallen. The suggestion that "eleventh" refers to the month, based in part on Albright,[1] has been widely followed. Many others note that Ezekiel in 30:20 and 31:1 expresses "in the eleventh year" by בְּאַחַת עֶשְׂרֵה שָׁנָה rather than the expression here. Some want to emend the text to בִּשְׁתֵּי עֶשְׂרֵה שָׁנָה, "in the *twelfth* year." This argument is seriously weakened, however, by the fact that the form of "eleven" used here (עַשְׁתֵּי־עֶשְׂרֵה) is well-attested elsewhere in the OT, and both terms occur in close sequence in 2 Ki 24:18 and 25:2 (∥ Jer 52:1, 5). Van Dijk considers the form used here an archaism.[2]

I am not convinced by any of the above arguments for emendation and am inclined to leave well enough alone, that is, let the MT stand in spite of the problems. Greenberg seems to me to argue convincingly: "By early spring of 586, after more than two years of siege, Jerusalem's fall and ruin might well have seemed a foregone

---

[1]   W. F. Albright, "The Seal of Eliakim and the Latest Preexilic History of Judah, with Some Observations on Ezekiel," *JBL* 51/2 (June 1932): 93.

[2]   Van Dijk, *Ezekiel's Prophecy on Tyre*, 3. This major study on the Tyre oracles should be noted and is frequently cited in chapters 26–28.

conclusion to any but its most fanatical defenders."[3] Regarding the siege of Jerusalem, which lasted two and a half years (according to the chronology advocated in this commentary), and the date of the city's fall in 586, see figure 1, "The Dates in Ezekiel," in the textual notes on chapter 24. Since this date notice does not specify a month, this oracle could have been delivered anytime between spring 587 and spring 586. However, it was probably delivered in spring 586, anticipating the city's fall in summer 586.

26:2 נִשְׁבְּרָה דַּלְתוֹת הָעַמִּים—It seems strange that the singular verb (Niphal third feminine perfect of שָׁבַר) has as its subject the feminine plural of דֶּלֶת (in construct), "doors," although there are many other instances of a feminine singular verb used with a plural subject. Often the incongruity in number here is explained by noting that דְּלָתוֹת refers to the two halves of a large door or gate, which could easily be thought of as a single object. Others explain the expression "doors of the peoples" as an epithet for Jerusalem, meaning that it is "the gateway to the peoples," as I have translated. Since the phrase refers to Jerusalem, the (feminine singular) city could be the implied subject of the feminine singular verb. Alternatively, according to van Dijk,[4] the verb form could be third feminine plural, as the identical form, נִשְׁבְּרָה, apparently is in 1 Ki 22:49, where it is the Kethib.

נָסֵבָּה אֵלָי—The verb is another third feminine singular Niphal perfect, of סָבַב (see GKC, § 67 t). It implies a change of hands or ownership. In Jer 6:12 the expression is used of houses. Here the subject is indeterminate ("*it* has been turned over to me"), apparently anything by which Jerusalem's fall will benefit Tyre.

אִמָּלְאָה הָחֳרָבָה:—I have freely connected the final two verbs in a causal clause ("because of her devastation, I will be satisfied") even though they stand independently without a connective. The verb מָלֵא means "be full," and this Niphal (first common singular cohortative) would mean "I shall be filled," but that literal translation sounds coarse, hence, I have freely used "I will be satisfied." הָחֳרָבָה is the Hophal third feminine singular perfect of חָרַב (which recurs in 26:19), referring to Jerusalem, meaning "she is devastated." The Hophal of חָרַב recurs in 29:12 of devastated cities. Van Dijk wants to repoint אִמָּלְאָה as a (transitive) Piel. He also wants to repoint הָחֳרָבָה as הַחַרְבָּה, which he claims would be the noun חֶרֶב, "sword," with the article serving as a personal suffix ("my") and a final *he* that is a fossilized remnant of the archaic accusative case ending.[5] Both the idiom of the devouring "sword" and various archaisms do appear in Ezekiel, but in this case, the emendations are unnecessary and unconvincing. The sense of the verse remains essentially the same.

26:3 כְּהַעֲלוֹת הַיָּם לְגַלָּיו:—After the transitive Hiphil (infinitive construct) of עָלָה, "to raise up," the *lamed* on לְגַלָּיו, "(to) its waves," is probably the Aramaic-type sign of the accusative: "the sea raises up its waves." The versions translate the verb as intransitive ("the sea rises with its waves"), but the sense and the parallelism favor retaining the MT's Hiphil.

---

[3] Greenberg, *Ezekiel*, 2:530.

[4] Van Dijk, *Ezekiel's Prophecy on Tyre*, 3–4.

[5] Van Dijk, *Ezekiel's Prophecy on Tyre*, 10–11.

26:4 The first half of this verse apparently still has גּוֹיִם רַבִּים, "many nations" (26:3), as its subject (those who will destroy Tyre), although the simile of the pounding breakers (26:3) may still be included. In the second half, Yahweh himself is the subject who scrapes the rock (Tyre) bare.

As we know from many illustrations from this period, the city wall had towers at set intervals. עָפָר normally is generic for "dust" or fine dirt, but as 26:12 will make plain, here the specific reference is to the rubble of the demolished city (doubtless, dusty enough!). For the construct phrase צְחִיחַ סֶלַע, see the second textual note on 24:7. It will be repeated in 26:14. The noun צְחִיחַ (in construct) has overtones of "brilliant, glaring surface," a translation that would heighten the transformation of the "rock," but perhaps be overkill; "bare" seems sufficient.

26:5 My translation is a bit expansive in order to bring out the full picture in idiomatic English.

מִשְׁטַח חֲרָמִים—The noun מִשְׁטָה (here in construct) means "spreading-place" (BDB), where things are spread out to dry, and is derived from the verb שָׁטַח, "spread out." The noun occurs in the OT only in 26:5, 14 in this identical phrase. (A similar phrase occurs in 47:10 but with the synonym מִשְׁטוֹחַ instead.) חֵרֶם II refers to a "net" for hunting or (as here and in 26:14; 47:10) fishing.

וְהָיְתָה לְבַז לַגּוֹיִם—The verse division seems to be an unhappy one. This final clause with a prophetic perfect ("she [Tyre] will become plunder for the nations") sounds like an unrelated addendum to the preceding part of 26:5, especially after the appeal to God's almighty Word and the signatory formula ("says the Lord Yahweh"). It forms a natural parallel to 26:6a, so my translation begins a new sentence with this clause.

26:6 וּבְנוֹתֶיהָ אֲשֶׁר בַּשָּׂדֶה—According to common Hebrew idiom, what we might call "suburbs" or at least satellite villages, often clustered just outside the city walls, are referred to as the city's "daughters." I have translated literally to retain the idiom but put the word in quotes because of its unfamiliarity in our culture. An island such as Tyre obviously could not have "suburbs" in the same sense as most cities. But it did have many satellite and partially dependent cities on the "mainland," here referred to by שָׂדֶה (often "field," that is, open country). Assyrian records bear eloquent testimony to how these villages (especially Ushu, on the mainland opposite Tyre) often bore the brunt of Assyrian frustration at its inability to eliminate Tyre itself,[6] and it surely was no different when it was Babylon's turn to attack.[7]

26:7 הִנְנִי מֵבִיא—As often elsewhere in Ezekiel, הִנֵּה (with first common singular suffix) followed by a participle (here the Hiphil of בּוֹא) denotes imminent action: "I am *about* to bring" or "I am bringing."

נְבוּכַדְרֶאאצַּר—One should not overlook the technically correct spelling of the king's name, Nebuchadrezzar, found in the Bible only here; 29:18–19; 30:10; and

---

[6] *ANET*, 287, 300.

[7] Van Dijk, *Ezekiel's Prophecy on Tyre*, 12–14, on the basis of the Ugaritic Keret Epic, tries to interpret "daughters" literally of women running to the cities for protection before an enemy onslaught, but the reference is forced, and biblical idiom weighs heavily against it.

throughout much of Jeremiah. (The LXX consistently renders the name with "n" in place of the first "r.") In the rest of the Bible, its spelling is נְבוּכַדְנֶאצַּר, probably to be explained linguistically as an example of regressive dissimilation.[8] The original Akkadian form of the name was *Nabu-kudurri-utsur*, meaning "may [the god] Nabu [biblical Nebo in Is 46:1] protect the son/offspring."

מִצָּפוֹן—The king will come "from the north" (cf. Jer 25:9, 26) even though Babylon is directly east of Jerusalem. Since the direct route was mostly some five hundred miles of trackless desert, both commercial and military traffic followed the line of the Fertile Crescent and came down the Levantine coast from the north. At times, "north" has exmythological connotations, apparently associated with Mount Zaphon, also known as Mount Casius (today on the Syrian-Turkish border), as the alleged home of Baal and the gathering place of the gods (cf. Olympus in Greece). Thus in biblical thought, it was the source of evil, of Satan and his cohorts, and so on (a classical example is in Jer 1:14), but it is doubtful if any such overtones are operative in this text.

"From the north" separates two titles, the preceding מֶלֶךְ־בָּבֶל and the following מֶלֶךְ מְלָכִים. Probably the separation is intended to underscore both, with the most comprehensive one coming second. The first, "king of Babylon," is common in Ezekiel and attested on a clay tablet by Nebuchadnezzar himself.[9] The more grandiose "king of kings" is attested widely all over the ancient Near East, but in Babylon itself so far only of its chief god, Marduk, not of the king himself.[10]

בְּסוּס וּבְרֶכֶב וּבְפָרָשִׁים—The Hebrew singulars "with horse [cavalry] and with chariotry" are both collectives. פָּרָשִׁים, however, is plural. There is some debate about the meaning of פָּרָשׁ because in earlier Semitic, a slightly different word, now a homonym, meant "horse" and, according to this understanding, is still so used in some seven Hebrew passages. That the meaning here must be "horse*man*" or "rider" is clear from 23:6, 12, where the word is explained as, literally, "riders of horses."

וְקָהָל וְעַם־רָב:—This last part of the verse is, literally, "and an assembly and many people." Syntactically, it could be an additional object of "I am bringing," but it seems to fit more naturally as the last in the series of things "with" which the king comes. The preposition בְּ ("with") on each of the three preceding nouns can carry over to this noun and phrase, a not uncommon Hebrew practice.[11] The LXX translation implies a hendiadys, and something of that sort must be the intent, so I have translated, "and a vast assembly of troops." Similar phrases with קָהָל and רָב appear in 38:15, where קָהָל גָּדוֹל in a military sense is parallel to חַיִל רָב.

26:8 וְנָתַן עָלַיִךְ דָּיֵק—Everywhere else in Ezekiel (4:2; 17:17; 21:27 [ET 21:22]), דָּיֵק, "siege wall," is the object of the verb בָּנָה, "build," whereas the verb here is נָתַן, but the difference is inconsequential.

---

[8] Other examples of the same phenomenon in the Bible appear in 1 Chr 3:18 (Shenazzar for Sharra-utsur) and Ezra 4:10 (Asnappar for Ashurbanipal).

[9] J. Starcky, "Une tablette araméenne de l'an 34 de Nabuchodonosor [AO.21.063]," *Syria* 37 (1960): 100, cited in Block, *Ezekiel*, 2:40, n. 74.

[10] See Marie-Joseph Seux, *Épithètes royales akkadiennes et sumériennes* (Paris: Letouzey & Ané, 1967), 318–19, cited in Block, *Ezekiel*, 2:40, n. 75.

[11] Cf. van Dijk, *Ezekiel's Prophecy on Tyre*, 15.

וְהֵקִים עָלַיִךְ צִנָּה:—Commentators disagree on the meaning of צִנָּה here. Elsewhere it denotes a large body shield (see the fourth textual note on 23:24). An ancient and still common rendition envisions a sort of roof of shields constructed over the battering ram to protect the attackers when the ram is brought up to the city walls. Something similar is well-known in Greco-Roman warfare. So far, however, there is no evidence that the practice had begun yet among the Assyrians and Babylonians. Body-length shields with backward-curved tops are common in Assyrian siege scenes,[12] and the Babylonians probably followed suit. Hence, I have taken the word in that sense and considered it a collective ("and erect shields against you").

26:9 וּמְחִי קָבְלּוֹ—Each of these two words is a hapax. All translations are guesses, and both ancient and modern ones vary widely. מְחִי is probably related to the verb מָחָה, "wipe out, destroy," or perhaps more closely to the Aramaicized verb מְחָא, "strike/clap [hands]" (25:6). Both may be related to Akkadian *maḫu*, "storm."

The presumed absolute singular of קָבְלּוֹ (with third masculine singular suffix) is קְבֹל, widely understood as "battering ram," but כַּר (used by Ezekiel in 4:2; 21:27 [ET 21:22]) is the usual Hebrew word for that major part of ancient "artillery." Since קְבֹל is cognate to the Akkadian *qablu*, "battle, warfare," a similar meaning is plausible. That background might help explain the unusual Masoretic vocalization of the suffixed form here, although vocalic assimilation may also be a factor. Possibly militating against an abstract translation ("battle") is the number of concrete weapons mentioned in the context.

וּמִגְדְּלֹתַיִךְ יִתֹּץ בְּחַרְבוֹתָיו:—The form of the plural of מִגְדָּל ("towers") is feminine here, while 26:4 had the masculine plural (מִגְדָּלֶיהָ), but there seems to be no discernible difference. Both refer to defensive towers on the city wall.

Ordinarily חֶרֶב means "sword, dagger" of some sort, but here the plural (בְּחַרְבוֹתָיו, with בְּ and third masculine singular suffix) are used to "tear down" (יִתֹּץ, Qal imperfect of נָתַץ) towers. "Axes" is offered by many translations (KJV already), but that meaning is entirely unattested. Daggers and swords are known to have been used to help pry apart walls. In 5:1 Ezekiel was instructed to use a חֶרֶב like a "razor," and if one wants a broader term than "swords" here, perhaps something like "iron tools" will satisfy.

26:10 מִשִּׁפְעַת סוּסָיו יְכַסֵּךְ אֲבָקָם—This clause reads, literally, "from the multitude of his horses he will cover you [with] their dust." אָבָק is a synonym of עָפָר and appears only here in Ezekiel. Van Dijk construes the final *mem* of אֲבָקָם not as the third masculine plural suffix, but as enclitic.[13] That would not materially change the meaning, but one expects minimal use of such an archaism in a late book like Ezekiel.

מִקּוֹל פָּרָשׁ—Here פָּרָשׁ, the collective "horsemen," is pointed as if in construct (so GKC, § 84ᵇ b). A once doubled *resh* in a *nomen opificum* (occupation) and compensatory doubling might be the explanation for retention of *qamets* in the first syllable (-פָּ).

---

[12] Greenberg, *Ezekiel*, 2:533.

[13] Van Dijk, *Ezekiel's Prophecy on Tyre*, 18.

וְגַלְגַּל וָרֶכֶב—"Wheel" and "chariot" are in a sense a unit (רֶכֶב וְגַלְגַּל, "wheeled chariots," 23:24), but here רֶכֶב is separated by the conjunction וְ.

כִּמְבוֹאֵי עִיר מְבֻקָּעָה:—The כְּ before the plural (construct) of מָבוֹא, "act of entrance, by violence" (BDB, 2), is the *kaph veritatis* (GKC, § 118 x), "just as people enter a breached city." The Pual feminine singular participle מְבֻקָּעָה (in pause: -קָ- in instead of -קְ-) is, literally, "split."

26:11 בְּפַרְסוֹת סוּסָיו יִרְמֹס—The assonance of sibilants in these first three words is worth noting from a literary standpoint. פַּרְסָה is technically a "cloven (split) hoof," characteristic of sheep and cattle, and hence among the prerequisites for an animal to be "clean" and edible according to the ceremonial law (especially Leviticus 11). Sometimes, as here, it is extended in meaning to apply to any "hoof," such as the hooves of horses.

וּמַצְּבוֹת עֻזֵּךְ—I have translated this as "your mighty pillars" rather than "pillars of your strength," following the idiomatic Hebrew propensity for construct chains over adjectival phrases. The more literalistic translation might better convey the significance of the pillars, although that could not erase the sense of literal, physical pillars. Exactly what the pillars were and what they signified is not fully understood. However, an Assyrian relief shows two external pillars on a Tyrian temple.[14] Herodotus speaks of two pillars, one of pure gold, the other of emerald, adorning the Tyrian temple of Heracles (i.e., Melkart, the native name of the city's chief deity).[15] Speculation has often sought to associate these and similar external pillars on ancient temples with the freestanding pillars named Jachin and Boaz in front of Solomon's temple, mentioned and described in 1 Ki 7:15–22 (‖ 2 Chr 3:15–17) but never explained. Very possibly the Tyrian pillars were symbols of the divine presence in which the Tyrians trusted for protection. One can compare similar language about the temple (גְּאוֹן עֻזְּכֶם, Ezek 24:21) and the ark (אֲרוֹן עֻזֶּךָ, Ps 132:8), although Yahweh is the referent of the suffix in the latter example.

תֵּרֵד:—As in 26:2, we meet a singular verb (Qal third feminine singular imperfect of יָרַד) with a plural subject (the plural of מַצֵּבָה in the construct phrase וּמַצְּבוֹת עֻזֵּךְ). Possibly the verb is influenced by the preceding feminine singular suffix on עֻזֵּךְ. But Greenberg notes that in 2 Ki 10:26 the plural of מַצֵּבָה is referred to by a singular (third feminine) suffix (on וַיִּשְׂרְפוּהָ) when the stelea in front of the Baal temple built in Samaria for Jezebel are destroyed. Given the Tyrian context both here and there (Jezebel was a fanatical devotee of the Tyrian Melkart), Greenberg inclines to the view that מַצֵּבוֹת here is really a singular and the Phoenician feminine singular afformative *-ath* has become *-oth*, but the native pronunciation has clung to this familiar object.[16]

26:12 The shift to plural verbs in this verse is easily explainable as an effort to portray the actions of Nebuchadnezzar's soldiers, or perhaps the "many nations" of 26:3.

---

[14] See Donald B. Harden, *The Phoenicians* (Harmondsworth: Penguin, 1971), plate 50, cited by Greenberg, *Ezekiel*, 2:534.

[15] Herodotus, *Histories*, 2.44.

[16] Greenberg, *Ezekiel*, 2:534. Van Dijk, *Ezekiel's Prophecy on Tyre*, 21–22, essentially seconds Greenberg.

In 26:5 "plunder" (the noun בַּז) was mentioned briefly. As the earlier verses are expanded here, the plundering (the verb וּבָזְזוּ) occurs immediately after the taking of the city (26:11).

וַעֲפָרֵךְ—As in 26:4, עָפָר here must mean the "rubble, debris" of the demolished city.

בְּתוֹךְ מַיִם יָשִׂימוּ:—The Qal of שִׂים, a common verb in Ezekiel, here must here have the sense of "throw," as in Gen 40:15, where it is equivalent to the Hiphil of שָׁלַךְ in Gen 37:24. One might have expected the Hiphil of שָׁלַךְ here.

The LXX and some other versions read הַיָּם, "the sea," instead of the MT's מַיִם, "water." Van Dijk thinks he finds evidence here of an enclitic *mem*, and redivides the words as בְּתוֹךְ־מ יָם, which he translates, "into the sea."[17] However, as in 26:10, it is doubtful if so ancient a feature of preclassical Hebrew should be expected in a text composed as late as Ezekiel. I stand by my earlier published judgment,[18] with which van Dijk takes explicit issue.[19] There is no substantial difference in meaning in any case.

26:13 Already Cooke noted the similarity between this verse and Amos 5:23.[20] Is 23:7 also describes Tyre as "exultant" (עַלִּיזָה). In general, ancient treaty curses are full of threats of the silencing of music as punishment for covenant infidelity.

26:14 With Tyre as the one being addressed, the context calls for second person feminine verbs. However, תִּהְיֶה and תִבָּנֶה (Niphal of בָּנָה) are both third feminine singular imperfects, evidently harking back to 26:4 and part of the verse's role as the conclusion of a section.

26:15 לְצוֹר ... אָמַר—Instead of "says ... to Tyre," van Dijk takes the לְ as a vocative particle.[21] That is not impossible (the usage occurs in Arabic and Ugaritic as well), but resort to an archaistic usage is again unnecessary. The whole verse is a direct address to Tyre in the second person (feminine singular).

הֲלֹא ... יִרְעֲשׁוּ הָאִיִּים:—The long rhetorical question introduced by הֲלֹא ("will not?") is translated by moving the last clause (יִרְעֲשׁוּ הָאִיִּים) to the front: "Will not the coastlands shudder ... ?" The Qal of רָעַשׁ was also used in 26:10 ("your walls will *shake*"). Van Dijk construes הֲלֹא as an emphatic particle like the Ugaritic *hl*,[22] so that the verse might be rendered as a declarative sentence and perhaps even as an exclamation.

מַפַּלְתֵּךְ—The noun מַפֶּלֶת, from נָפַל, "fall," will recur in 26:18 (again with second feminine singular suffix) and also in 27:27; 31:13, 16; and 32:10 in the Gentile oracles of Ezekiel. Elsewhere in the OT, it is used only in Judg 14:8 and Prov 29:16.

---

[17] Van Dijk, *Ezekiel's Prophecy on Tyre*, 24–26.

[18] Hummel, "Enclitic *Mem* in Early Northwest Semitic, Especially Hebrew," 107.

[19] Van Dijk, *Ezekiel's Prophecy on Tyre*, 24–25.

[20] Cooke, *Ezekiel*, 291.

[21] Van Dijk, *Ezekiel's Prophecy on Tyre*, 29. For לְ as an emphatic particle that can be used with a vocative, see Waltke-O'Connor, § 11.2.10i, including example 67.

[22] Van Dijk, *Ezekiel's Prophecy on Tyre*, 29–30.

בֵּאֱנֹק חָלָל—The verb אָנַק, "groan" (here Qal infinitive with בְּ), was used in the Niphal with the same meaning in 9:4 and 24:17. חָלָל, literally, "the pierced (one)," is translated as a collective: "victims." Since they are still groaning, "dying" or "mortally wounded" would be apt too.

בֵּהָרֵג הֶרֶג—The Niphal infinitive of הָרַג (a contraction of בְּהֵהָרֵג) is rendered "be slaughtered." The cognate noun הֶרֶג usually has the abstract meaning "murder," but is used concretely here: "the slain."

26:16 כִּסְאוֹתָם—Ancient Near Eastern "thrones" were usually either chairs on platforms or chairs set high enough that a footstool was necessary to reach them.

מְעִילֵיהֶם—The noun מְעִיל is a rather generic term, usually a sleeveless "robe." It may have indicated high rank. It had both secular and liturgical uses. Samuel's mother made one to take for her little boy when she and her husband made their yearly pilgrimage to Shiloh (1 Sam 2:19), and the term is also used of a priestly garment roughly comparable to our alb (e.g., Ex 28:4).

רִקְמָתָם—While אָרַג (e.g., Ex 28:32) is a verb for ordinary weaving, the verb רָקַם and this cognate noun, רִקְמָה, refer to a far more intricate weave, probably multicolored, and possibly even with the full pattern showing on both sides. Naturally, it was more expensive and hence was worn only by the wealthy. Very tellingly, Ps 139:15 uses the Pual of רָקַם ("I was knit together") for the formation of a baby in the mother's womb.

חֲרָדוֹת ׀ יִלְבָּשׁוּ—The singular of the noun חֲרָדָה is usually abstract, "fear, terror." חֲרָדוֹת may be an abstract plural with the same meaning: "(in) *trembling* they will clothe themselves." But Hebrew frequently uses abstracts for concretes, and חֲרָדוֹת could refer to special mourning garments, which might or might not be different than the common sackcloth and ashes. The plural matches the preceding בְּגָדֵי, the "robes" they remove. The noun חֲרָדָה is cognate to the verb in the following clause; see the next textual note.

וְחָרְדוּ לִרְגָעִים—The Qal of חָרַד, "tremble, be terrified," emphasizes the idea conveyed by the plural noun חֲרָדוֹת in the preceding clause. לִרְגָעִים, literally, "for moments," must mean "every moment, moment by moment," that is, constantly. One scholar has proposed a new sense along the lines of "with agitation,"[23] which has found some acceptance,[24] but careful word study does not seem to support the new proposal.[25]

26:17–18 "Lament" translates קִינָה in 26:17, technically a funeral lament and hence often translated "dirge." It also occurs in 2:10; 19:1, 14; 27:2, 32; 28:12; 32:2, 16. For its meaning and significance, see "Introduction to Ezekiel 19." Critics once held de rigueur that literature denoted by this term had to exhibit a 3:2 meter, a "limping" me-

---

[23] M. D. Goldman, "The Meaning of 'רגע,' " *Australian Biblical Review* 4 (1954/1955): 15.

[24] E.g., Zimmerli, *Ezekiel*, 2:30; Allen, *Ezekiel*, 2:72.

[25] Greenberg, *Ezekiel*, 2:536, notes that the meaning is inappropriate in the two other occurrences of the plural of רֶגַע with לְ: Is 27:3 and Job 7:18. The phrase is also used in Ezek 32:10.

ter that allegedly reflected the broken spirits of the mourners. That kind of dogmatism has vanished today. Some laments exhibit a 3:2 metrical pattern; others do not. While the last line of 26:17 and first line of 26:18 exhibit that pattern, any attempt to force all of Ezek 26:17–18 into that meter can only be accomplished by drastic surgery. The MT of these verses is difficult, and one who compares will note widespread variations in the various commentaries and translations, only a small portion of which I have included here.

26:17 אֵיךְ אָבַדְתְּ נוֹשֶׁבֶת מִיַּמִּים—The wording (אֵיךְ and a form of יָשַׁב) and meaning of this clause in the lament resemble the first clause of Lam 1:1 (אֵיכָה and a form of יָשַׁב): the once populous city is now deserted. נוֹשֶׁבֶת is the Niphal feminine participle of יָשַׁב, which in the Niphal means "be inhabited," as also in 26:19 (the perfect נוֹשָׁבוּ). The מִן on מִיַּמִּים ("from the seas") indicates the source of Tyre's traffic and wealth. In place of אָבַדְתְּ נוֹשֶׁבֶת, the LXX has κατελύθης, "you were destroyed," perhaps as if translating נִשְׁבַּתָּ, a Niphal of שָׁבַת (in 26:13 the LXX uses καταλύω to translate the Hiphil of שָׁבַת). Critical scholars offer various reconstructions of how an original unvocalized נשבת could have developed into both נִשְׁבַּתָּ and נוֹשֶׁבֶת in the two traditions.[26]

However, since the MT requires no textual reconstruction, the odds, it seems to me, tip in its favor. RSV, NRSV, and most commentators, even Block,[27] follow the LXX, usually alleging that "be inhabited" makes little sense. However, I remain unconvinced, especially in this semi-poetic context. That Tyre was probably colonized by seafaring people and still owed her very existence to her maritime activities seems eminently suited to the context. The rare use of the plural יַמִּים might indicate the vastness of the oceans on which the people were dependent. KJV has "of seafaring men," which communicates the same idea.

הַהֻלָלָה—This is the Pual third feminine singular perfect of הָלַל, meaning "be praised," with the prefixed definite article used as a relative, as happens occasionally, especially in late Hebrew (cf. GKC, § 138 i, k). The versions translate as if it were a Pual participle without the preformative *mem* (with the article still serving as relative pronoun). The difference in translation is negligible.

אֲשֶׁר הָיְתָה חֲזָקָה בַיָּם—Hebrew has no comparative or superlative forms for the adjective; the context or construction can indicate such a meaning (Joüon, § 141). The adjective חֲזָקָה here is usually considered a superlative: "that was the *strongest* in the sea."

הִיא וְיֹשְׁבֶיהָ—"She and her inhabitants" refers to Tyre.

אֲשֶׁר־נָתְנוּ חִתִּיתָם לְכָל־יוֹשְׁבֶיהָ׃—The subject of the first phrase still must be Tyre and her inhabitants: literally, "who placed their terror." חִתִּיתָם is the noun חִתִּית, "terror," which occurs elsewhere only in 32:23–27, 30, 32, and is derived from the verb

---

[26] Van Dijk, *Ezekiel's Prophecy on Tyre*, 33–38, differs considerably from others. His arguments are cogent enough to merit mention, although I have not followed them. Taking מִיַּמִּים as יַמִּים plus enclitic *mem* (see the last textual note on 26:12), he can capitalize it in translation and make it an exmythological reference to Yamm, a personification of chaos and evil. He emends נוֹשֶׁבֶת to נִשְׁבַּתָּ, resulting in "how you have perished and are you shattered."

[27] Block, *Ezekiel*, 2:43, including n. 92.

חָתַת. Its third masculine plural suffix must have an objective meaning: others were terrified at the Tyrians.

The temptation is to take לְכָל־יוֹשְׁבֶיהָ ("to all her inhabitants") as referring to the sea's inhabitants (NIV: "on all who lived there"), but יָם is never feminine. Since "Tyre" is the only possible feminine singular antecedent, Zimmerli and Greenberg[28] seem to be correct in construing the prepositional phrase with לְ as referring to "all of [Tyre's] inhabitants" as those who "placed their terror" upon others. לְ can be used for further specification, "with respect to, regarding" (see Williams, *Hebrew Syntax*, § 273; BDB, s.v. לְ, 5 e). The construction here is different from that in 32:23–26, 32, where the verb נָתַן is used with the noun חִתִּית and the preposition בְּ (not לְ) for "place terror upon" others. The sense is not that Tyre terrorized its own citizens (as NKJV, ESV, and NASB take the phrase), but that the city's distinction as terrifying was a reflection on the entire citizenry; all of them were intimately involved in garnering this reputation, just as all of them were in garnering the city's maritime prowess.

RSV ("who imposed your terror on all the mainland") apparently emends יוֹשְׁבֶיהָ to יַבָּשָׁה, "dry land," which is different than שָׂדֶה, the term rendered "mainland" in 26:6, 8. This involves a radical change in the consonantal text.

26:18 הָאִיִּן—"The coastlands" uses the Aramaic plural ending –*in*, possibly to avoid the succession of three words in a row with *mem*. Although this form occurs occasionally in much earlier texts, it could simply be the accidental writing of a more familiar form by a later Aramaic-speaking scribe. The regular Hebrew ending is used for הָאִיִּים in the second half of the verse.

יוֹם מַפַּלְתֵּךְ—One might expect בְּיוֹם ("*on* the day"), but the preposition may be omitted in an adverbial phrase such as this. For מַפַּלְתֵּךְ, see the third textual note on 26:15.

Note the almost perfect parallelism between 26:15 and 26:18, framing or forming an inclusio of a unit of thought and sharing lexically the words אִיִּים (or אִיִּן) and מַפַּלְתֵּךְ. Thus, although the LXX lacks a translation of the second half of 26:18 (and so Zimmerli deletes it as tautological),[29] the verse plays a clear structural role and undoubtedly should be included as part of the קִינָה. The use of an inclusio appears to follow a common pattern in ancient Near Eastern expressions of grief. The whole קִינָה expresses a clear contrast between what once was and what soon will be. It is a brief lament, but in a pattern common in Ezekiel, the lament genre is dropped only temporarily and resumed again in the very next chapter.

הָאִיִּים אֲשֶׁר־בַּיָּם—This phrase with the relative אֲשֶׁר occurs only here in the OT; elsewhere the construct phrase אִיֵּי־הַיָּם is used (Joüon, § 130 f).

מִצֵּאתֵךְ:—This is the Qal infinitive construct of יָצָא, to "depart" (BDB, Qal, 1 e), with second feminine singular suffix preceded by the preposition מִן in a causative sense: "by/because of your departure." Note the virtually perfect synonymous parallelism between the two halves of the verse, since this balances מַפַּלְתֵּךְ at the end of

---

[28] Zimmerli, *Ezekiel*, 2:31; Greenberg, *Ezekiel*, 2:537–38.

[29] Zimmerli, *Ezekiel*, 2:31.

the first half. Van Dijk derives this infinitive from נָצָה III, "fall in ruins" (BDB), as- suming a by-form נָצָא, whose infinitive would be צֵאת [30] Greenberg equivocates.[31]

26:19 The simile of abandoned, ruined cities is clear enough, especially in the light of what has been forecast about Tyre earlier in the oracle. נֶחֱרֶבֶת, "ruined," is the Niphal feminine singular participle of חָרֵב, whose Hophal ended 26:2.

בְּהַעֲלוֹת עָלַיִךְ אֶת־תְּהוֹם—The Hiphil (infinitive construct with בְּ) of עָלָה has a causative meaning, "bring up." It lacks a suffix, which would clarify who is per- forming this action. Some commentators think that the last two letters were trans- posed (בְּהַעֲלֹתוֹ). Others suppose that the suffix on the preceding infinitive בְּתִתִּי ("when I make," Qal of נָתַן) does double duty, which certainly is possible. But such omissions are not all that rare, and no problem exists when the context indicates who the subject must be. Yahweh was the subject of the Hiphil first common singular per- fect וְהַעֲלֵיתִי in 26:3.

More problematic is how to render תְּהוֹם, the verb's object. When treated as a proper noun, as here, it naturally never takes the article, and when used as a direct ob- ject, as here, it is preceded by אֶת־. Hence, technically we should transliterate and cap- italize it: "Tehom." But that will hardly communicate to a modern audience. The syntactical singularities just noted about the word betray its ultimate origins in the world of pagan mythology. Tiamat (linguistically cognate with Tehom) was in Mesopotamian mythology a primordial ocean goddess who annually did battle with other gods about the fate of the universe. In the Bible, the concept and the word have long since been demythologized; that is, they are used without the pagan theology, just as the Scriptures refer to Baal and Artemis as divinities who really are not gods at all. תְּהוֹם, like יָם ("sea," e.g., Job 7:12; 38:8), continues to be used in the OT poet- ically and metaphorically of the ocean, especially its deepest part.

Since there is only one God, the Creator of all, including Tehom, it can no longer be a threat, but is only another part of God's creation, to be used as he sees fit. It cov- ered the earth at creation (Gen 1:2; Ps 104:6), and in the deluge, God had allowed it to reclaim the whole earth in manifestation of his total judgment against human sin. Now God will allow it to reclaim the island Tyre, which had risen, as it were, from the depths. The poetry of the verse does not attempt to explain the mechanics of how this will happen. Whether we should think of a huge tsunami or a tidal wave or of the island simply sinking in some tectonic movement is beside the point. But talk of the underworld in 26:20 seems to favor the latter metaphor.

הַמַּיִם הָרַבִּים:—Parallel to Tehom is the "many waters," familiar to Bible read- ers as one of the forces of chaos often appearing in the Psalter (e.g., Pss 18:17 [ET 18:16]; 32:6; 144:7). Ezekiel uses the phrase eleven times (sometimes without the ar- ticle). A good parallel to its use here is in Ezek 31:15, but it has different connotations in Ezek 1:24.[32]

---

[30] Van Dijk, *Ezekiel's Prophecy on Tyre*, 39.

[31] Greenberg, *Ezekiel*, 2:538, claims that "the balance is even between an unusual meaning of a common verb (*yṣ'*) and the regular meaning of an uncommon verb (*nṣ'*)."

[32] Song 8:7 affirms that "many waters" are not able to extinguish the love that is "the flame of Yah" (8:6). One may see Mitchell, *The Song of Songs*, 1192–97.

26:20   This verse takes a more personal-sounding tone and depicts Tyre as an individual descending into the realm of the dead. OT pictures of life after death are not systematized and should not be forced into one. Various expressions are used, some of which appear here. The topic is discussed only briefly here and will appear in greatly expanded form regarding Egypt in 31:14–18; 32:17–32.

אֶת־יוֹרְדֵי בוֹר—This phrase, repeated in the verse, has the Qal masculine plural participle of יָרַד, "descend," in construct with בוֹר, basically a "pit" or cistern of almost any kind. Applied to the individual grave, it could easily be expanded to describe the entire realm of the dead as a universal grave. Elsewhere, as in 31:15–17, בוֹר is often paired with שְׁאוֹל, Sheol, a more technical term for that realm. As Greenberg rightly points out, יָרַד can have a stative meaning, "be low," as well as being an active verb, meaning "descend."[33] Then the יוֹרְדֵי בוֹר are not only "those who descend to the pit," but also "those who *have descended* to the pit," that is, those already dead. יוֹרְדֵי בוֹר recurs in 31:14, 16; 32:18, 24–25, 29–30.

The אֶת־ here is the preposition, "with." Some critics want to emend it to אֶל־, which is in the next clause, but the related passages (31:16–17; 32:18–32) unanimously support the MT, whose sense here is sharing the destiny "with" (אֶת) those already in the pit. Cooke calls this a "pregnant" sense.[34]

The parallel expressions following in 26:20 confirm this interpretation of בוֹר and its inhabitants, described as an עַם עוֹלָם ("people of old") who reside in a place כָּחֳרָבוֹת מֵעוֹלָם ("like ancient ruins"; some manuscripts have the preposition בְּ, "in"). This pictures entire cities now lying in ruins, which the dead haunt. It is a picture without other attestation, although it would easily be applicable to Tyre in this context.

Both those parallel expressions have עוֹלָם, whose traditional translation, "eternity/eternal," may be misleading here, although it does have that meaning elsewhere. The connotation of עוֹלָם here probably is more "hidden, covered," since it is derived from the verbal root עָלַם, "conceal." Thus, "ancient" or even "primeval, immemorial (unremembered)" are possible renditions. At times, עוֹלָם may be used more substantively, as in, for example, Eccl 12:5, where the dead are described as living in a בֵּית עוֹלָם, "everlasting house," that is, the underworld. Similar expressions are known from the literature of ancient Israel's neighbors. In any case, the emphasis here is on the finality and irreversibility of death. The theological implication is that the heathen Tyrians will be consigned to everlasting judgment with all the dead unbelievers.

Yahweh next describes the dead as being בְּאֶרֶץ תַּחְתִּיּוֹת, literally, "in the land of the lowest places/depths." This expression, unique to Ezekiel, appears again in 32:18, 24. In 31:14, 16, 18, the singular feminine adjective תַּחְתִּית modifies אֶרֶץ and serves as a superlative: literally, "the lowest land." תַּחְתִּי is also used with שְׁאוֹל in Deut 32:22, and the plural תַּחְתִּיּוֹת occurs in several other OT books, with either בוֹר (Ps 88:7 [ET 88:6]; Lam 3:55) or אֶרֶץ (Is 44:23; Pss 63:10 [ET 63:9]; 139:15). These idioms suggest a picture of the underworld as an isolated, self-contained realm. They have also spawned debate about levels in the underworld. The Scriptures affirm that just as there

---

[33]   Greenberg, *Ezekiel*, 2:538.

[34]   Cooke, *Ezekiel*, 295.

will be degrees of glory for redeemed believers in eternal life (e.g., Dan 12:3; 1 Cor 3:8; 2 Cor 9:6–7), so there are degrees of punishment and dishonor in hell (especially Ezek 32:19, 23). See Ap IV 356–74.

וְנָתַתִּי צְבִי בְּאֶרֶץ חַיִּים׃—This clause is of disputed meaning. The easiest option would be to take it as a contrast to the land of gloom and half-living just described: Yahweh declares, "I will establish glory/splendor in the land of the living." However, such a comment sounds banal and intrusive in the context. I am attracted to the interpretation of van Dijk and Block,[35] who take וְנָתַתִּי, the perfect Qal of נָתַן with *waw* consecutive, not as first person singular, but as an archaic second feminine singular form, like the second feminine singular perfect verbs ending in תִּי- in 16:13, 18, 22, 31, 43, 47, 51. See Joüon, § 42 f, and the textual note on אָכַלְתִּי in 16:13. If so, the verb's subject is Tyre, who clearly is the subject of the verb in the preceding clause, לֹא תֵשֵׁבִי. The negative לֹא does double duty, and the parallelism is perfect: "so that you will not be dwelt in or manifest glory in the land of the living."

Following the LXX's μηδὲ ἀνασταθῇς, many emend וְנָתַתִּי צְבִי to וְתִתַיַצְבִי, but the omission of the MT's *nun* is not easy to explain unless one postulates an original וְתִתְנַצְבִי, a form without parallels.

26:21 בַּלָּהוֹת—The noun בַּלָּהָה, "terror, horror," is almost always plural in the OT. It probably is to be derived ultimately from the verb בָּהַל, "be terrified" (as is the noun בֶּהָלָה, "terror, ruin"), changed by metathesis into בלה. The plural is for the sake of intensification or amplification. The rest of the verse intensifies still further. As Zimmerli notes, the city's nonexistence will be no mere vacuum, but horror or terror to the highest degree, and the continuing vain search for her signifies "a continuing restlessness which prevents us from misunderstanding the non-existence as peace and rest."[36] Block similarly points to the use of the construct phrase מֶלֶךְ בַּלָּהוֹת, "the king of terrors," in Job 18:14 as clearly chthonic. In exmythological language, Tyre is being handed over to that terrifying king in the underworld.[37]

Commentary

A certain similarity between 26:1–6 and the oracle against Ammon in the previous chapter (25:1–7) has often been noted. Only these two of the oracles against other nations formulate the charge as a direct quotation. Both also contain the gloating "aha!" over Jerusalem's misery (הֶאָח, 25:3; 26:2; also 36:2).

However, the connection of 26:1–6 with what follows in its present context should not be overlooked. Ezek 26:7–14 will expound on the judgment pronounced in 26:3–6 and shift the focus from Yahweh to his agent, Nebuchadnezzar. Finally, 26:15–21 will describe the reaction to that judgment by the nations that witness it. Chapters 27 and 28 are entirely independent oracles, as evidenced partly by the word-event formula introducing each.

---

[35] Van Dijk, *Ezekiel's Prophecy on Tyre*, 46; Block, *Ezekiel*, 2:47, including n. 116.

[36] Zimmerli, *Ezekiel*, 2:39.

[37] Block, *Ezekiel*, 2:50.

Judgment on Tyre (26:1–6)

26:1 Tyre stands out from the other subjects of Ezekiel's Gentile oracles in a number of ways. First of all, whereas all the states targeted in chapter 25 were populated to a large extent by relative newcomers (arriving more or less the same time as the Israelites, who, after the exodus from Egypt, entered Canaan ca. 1400 B.C.), Tyre, like other Phoenician states, represented the remnants of the autochthonous Canaanite population before the Israelite arrival.

Even more striking was Tyre's geographical situation. Its name (צוֹר or צֹר, a synonym of צוּר), literally means "rock," after the island on which it was situated, some six hundred yards off the coast and some thirty-five miles north of Mount Carmel. Its location "in the middle of the sea" (26:5; 27:32; cf. 27:4) kept its defenses from being penetrated until 332 B.C., when Alexander the Great built a mole out to the "rock" and could bring his normal war machines to bear against it. In the meantime, would-be conquerors had to content themselves with overcoming Ushu on the mainland opposite Tyre, as well as Sidon and other coastal communities. Over the centuries, alluvial deposits have so broadened Alexander's causeway that today Tyre simply sits at the end of a peninsula.

In the era of friendly relations between Hiram I and David and Solomon, Hiram is always called "the king of Tyre" (e.g., 2 Sam 5:11; 1 Ki 5:15 [ET 5:1]). In the ninth century, Ethbaal I is identified as "the king of the Sidonians" (1 Ki 16:31), and the latter seems to be the common designation throughout the ancient Near East. "Sidonian" was apparently the common equivalent of our "Phoenician." Sidon had been the dominant power earlier and would again be later, but "the king of Tyre" accurately reflects the city's political preeminence at the time of David and Solomon.

Although never actually conquered by Assyrian kings, by cutting Tyre's supply lines, they had forced the city into some sort of accommodation with Assyria, and this tie to Assyria continued after Nebuchadnezzar came to power in Babylon. Josephus reports that Nebuchadnezzar engaged in a thirteen-year siege of Tyre, which probably began shortly after the fall of Jerusalem.[38] There is evidence of Nebuchadnezzar's personal presence during at least part of the siege. The ruler of Tyre at the time, Ethbaal III, even seems to have been taken captive to Babylon and a more favorably disposed monarch was placed on his throne, with a "keeper of the seal" installed to keep him in line.[39] Thus, Ezekiel's prophecy, suggesting a breaching of Tyre's walls as was usual with cities, never came to pass literalistically in that era, but the difference was quite nominal.

---

[38] Josephus, *Antiquities*, 10.228 (10.11.1).

[39] Zimmerli, *Ezekiel*, 2:23–24, including n. 20, citing Eckhard Unger, "Nebukadnezar II. und sein Sandabakku (Oberkommissar) in Tyrus," *ZAW* 44 (1926): 314–17, and Unger, *Babylon: die heilige Stadt nach der Beschreibung der Babylonier* (Berlin: Gruyter, 1931), 36–37. See also Block, *Ezekiel*, 2:31.

The fact that Ezekiel devotes three entire chapters to Tyre (chapters 26–28)—more than any other prophet—invites an explanation. A partial answer is suggested by the gleeful "aha!" we hear in 26:2. Jerusalem's fall would enable the Tyrians to expand their commercial interests still further, especially with Transjordanian areas to the east. But this is hardly the main reason. Ezekiel understood clearly that Babylon was God's appointed agent to carry out judgment upon Israel, and any attempt to thwart that role was intrinsically at odds with the irrevocable divine decree. When Jerusalem fell in 586, the only states still resisting Babylon were Tyre and Egypt. So it is no accident that when Ezekiel is finished with Tyre, he will devote four chapters to Egypt (Ezekiel 29–32).

26:2 A series of four barely connected exclamations after the initial "aha!" express Tyre's glee at the fall of its competitor and its expectation to profit handsomely as a result. "Gateway to the peoples" summarizes Tyre's perception of Jerusalem's position as a commercial power. The expression with (literally) "doors" may indicate either an entranceway or a barrier; trade tends to move in both directions. In 27:17 Ezekiel will mention "wheat from Minnith," east of the Jordan, among Judah's exports to Tyre, indicating its role as a middleman in at least that commodity. The fact that Tyre and Sidon often sent envoys to Jerusalem in plots against Babylon indicates its importance as a trade emporium. If my interpretation of the chronological problem in 26:1 is correct, Tyre's expectations are anticipatory (see the textual note on 26:1). This prophecy is delivered in spring 586, when Tyre expects Jerusalem to fall soon (as it will in summer 586, after an eighteen-month siege). Tyre can hardly wait until an old competitor has been eliminated, and her coffers will be filled to overflowing.

While Tyre may not have realized it, "gateway to the peoples" (26:2) can apply to the central role of Jerusalem not just in commerce, but also for the spread of the Gospel to all peoples throughout the world (cf. Acts 1:8). Already in the OT era, God intended for his people Israel to carry out an evangelistic mission,[40] though it was not until the NT era that Christians, as citizens of the new Jerusalem (Gal 4:26), began to fulfill that mission on a large scale.

26:3 This verse, like the text through 26:5a, depicts the judgment as Yahweh's direct personal intervention. Even the surf is no mere act of nature, but evidence of Yahweh at work. In the realm of history, Yahweh's agents are "many nations" (again in 31:6; 38:23; 39:27).

26:4 This verse contains an obvious play on the city's name. The fortified city wall literally became what it once was and what its name proclaims, nothing but a rock jutting up from the sea. Again Yahweh is described as personally involved in the demolition.

---

[40] See the excursus "Mission in the Old Testament" in Lessing, *Jonah*, 151–69.

26:5 The contrast continues. The once-bustling trade center will be so desolate that only fishermen will use it as a place to dry their nets. A similar picture will recur in the eschatological vision of 47:10, where the general picture, however, will be one of the fructification of a previously desolate area.

The final clause of the verse (which really connects with 26:6) describes a turning of the tables. The punishment will fit the offense—a common biblical motif (e.g., Lk 12:47). The city that once exploited other nations for her own enrichment will now, as she is plundered, become a source of their enrichment.

Nebuchadnezzar Is Yahweh's Agent of Judgment (26:7–14)

26:7 Yahweh's long address directly to Tyre (26:7–14) begins with an announcement of Yahweh's fearsome agent accompanied by his formidable war machine with all its components, more of which will be added in the following verse. Throughout the section, one notices many echoes and expansions of what has already been threatened in the previous speech (26:3–6).

26:8 The style changes to that of second person (direct address: "you"), which has the effect of sounding as if Ezekiel is proclaiming the oracle to Tyre, but this usage probably accords with Yahweh's command for Ezekiel (in Babylon) to "set" his "face toward/against" the enemy (25:2; 28:21; and often elsewhere; see the second textual note on 6:2).

The attack on Tyre's "daughters," her satellite cities, is repeated almost verbatim from 26:6, where they were added at the end of the address, almost as an appendage. Here they are mentioned first, undoubtedly following the natural course of events, since these villages on the mainland would need to be conquered before the assault on the offshore city of Tyre itself. Ezek 26:3 had moved immediately into the result of the attack, while details of the attack were omitted. Ezek 26:8b–11a will fill in that omission and will not speak of results until 26:11b.

26:8b–12 After a brief preview of the siege and destruction of the city in 26:3–4, these verses expand on the scene and offer about as detailed and vivid a picture of standard siege and assault practices on a walled city in ancient times as we find in Ezekiel—and all of the OT, for that matter. There is only one tiny problem: as far as we know, Nebuchadnezzar never carried out these actions. In fact, these procedures, which could be and often were implemented in the conquests of mainland cities, could not happen to an island city like Tyre, where instruments like battering rams could not approach. It seems that nothing of the sort happened to Tyre until Alexander the Great built his massive mole out to the island, so that his war machines could be brought to bear (see the commentary on 26:1). Nebuchadnezzar, like Assyrian armies before him, subdued, blockaded, and exercised some political control over Tyre, but an investment of the type Ezekiel describes was not possible. In fact, in 29:17–20 Ezekiel himself acknowledges that Nebuchadnezzar's efforts against Tyre were less than fully successful and that Yahweh would give him Egypt in compensation (a prophecy with its own problems; see the commentary there). It appears, at least, as if Ezekiel had a sort of stock, stereotyped repertory of idioms to describe the fall of cities.

Obviously, this raises problems of unfulfilled prophecy, or possibly even false prophecy (see the commentary on Ezekiel 13). For those who regard the Bible just as another piece of human religious literature, that is no problem. But for those with the true and high view of Scripture as God's inspired and inerrant Word, it certainly does.

Perhaps the problem is not as great with a prophet like Ezekiel, who is so given to hyperbole in general. It does remind us that prophecy, even in its predictive mode, is not the simplistic "history written in advance" that it can easily be described as being. If God himself often "relents" or "changes his verdict" (usually the Niphal of נָחַם, e.g., Ex 32:14),[41] it surely is no problem if he inspires his prophet to utter oracles that cannot always be milked dry. A more relaxed attitude toward "fulfillment" can easily get out of hand, of course, and lead in thoroughly agnostic directions. But it need not, if the rest of Scripture and the hermeneutical circle it engenders and empowers remain operative. In any event, the prophecy certainly was fulfilled in that the people of Tyre did eventually all die and face God's judgment.

26:14 This verse is a repetition and summary of earlier threats (26:4–5), emphasized by Yahweh's own signature,[42] that Tyre's demise as the great city she now is will be permanent.

The Nations React to Tyre's Judgment (26:15–21)

26:15 If the fate just described could befall mighty Tyre, what will happen to far less defensible coasts and islands with which Tyre traded? The reactions of the other nations will heap shame upon proud Tyre. Similar expressions occur frequently in Gentile oracles, and evidently this was one of the standard idioms of the genre.

26:16 The gestures of the neighbors were apparently the conventional ones for such situations. Many parallels can be cited. The description is very similar to that of the king of Nineveh, who repented at Jonah's preaching (Jonah 3:6).[43] Such actions may be taken as representative of the great debasement of human pretensions whenever they challenge him who alone "will be exalted in that day" (Is 2:11).

26:17–18 This lament continues the direct address to Tyre, begun by Yahweh in 26:15 as indicated by the citation formula[44] there ("thus says the Lord

---

[41] See the excursus "When Yahweh Changes a Prior Verdict" in Lessing, *Jonah*, 324–41.

[42] For the signatory formula, "says the Lord Yahweh," see pages 8–9 in the introduction and the second textual note on 5:11.

[43] See Lessing, *Jonah*, 286–87, 307–10.

[44] For this formula, see pages 8–9 in the introduction and the fourth textual note and the commentary on 2:4.

Yahweh to Tyre"). A new citation formula in 26:19 will signal the beginning of a new unit.

26:19–21 In contrast to 26:15–18, and like 26:3–4, 13–14, in this final section Yahweh clearly and repeatedly specifies that he is the actor ("I make … I bring …"). Stereotyped and exmythological themes (see the textual notes) are freely used to describe a judgment of unparalleled horror and severity in "the land of no return" (an ancient Mesopotamian description of the realm of the dead), for which there is no adequate analogical language of human experience in "the land of the living" (26:20).

A Lament over Tyre

Translation

27 [1]The Word of Yahweh came to me: [2]"You, son of man, utter a lament over Tyre: [3]Say to Tyre, who dwells at the entrances to the sea, international merchant to many coastlands, 'Thus says the Lord Yahweh:

" 'Tyre, you say,
  "I am a perfect beauty."
[4]Your borders were in the heart of the seas;
  your builders perfected your beauty.
[5]Of junipers from Senir they built for you
  a whole double deck,
a cedar from Lebanon they took
  to make a mast upon you.
[6]Of oaks from Bashan
  they made your oars,
your planks of ivory-inlaid cypresses
  from the coasts of Cyprus.
[7]Your sail was brightly embroidered linen from Egypt,
  which also served as your flag.
Your awning was a bluish or reddish purple
  from the coasts of Elishah.
[8]Inhabitants of Sidon and Arvad were your rowers;
  your own skilled men, O Tyre, who were already in you, manned your sails.
[9]Skilled veterans from Byblos were on board you,
  serving as your repairmen.
All the ships of the sea and their sailors
  were in you[r harbor] to engage in your trade.
[10]Among your personnel were warriors
  from Persia, Lydia, and Put.
They hung shields and helmets on you,
  thus contributing to your splendor.
[11]Men of Arvad and Cilicia
  were all around on your walls,
and Gammadites
  on your towers.
They hung their quivers all around on your walls.
  They made your beauty perfect.

¹²" 'Tarshish was your trader because of your great wealth of every kind. In silver, iron, tin, and lead they sold your exports. ¹³Ionia, Tubal, and Meshech also were your dealers. For human beings and articles of bronze they sold your wares. ¹⁴From the house of Togarmah, horses, horsemen, and mules were given to you for export. ¹⁵The men of Rhodes were your dealers, many coastlands were agents of your trade, bringing back ivory tusks and ebony in payment to you. ¹⁶Edom was your trader because of the abundance of your products. Turquoise, red-purplish and finely embroidered cloth, linen, coral, and rubies they sold as exports to you. ¹⁷Judah and the land of Israel were your dealers; for wheat of Minnith, flour, honey, oil, and balm they sold your wares. ¹⁸Damascus was a trader with you in the abundance of your products, because of the abundance of wealth of all kinds. Wine of Helbon, wool from Sahar, ¹⁹and wine casks from Izalla they sold as exports. Wrought iron, cassia, and calamus were for your import. ²⁰Dedan was your dealer in saddlecloths for riding. ²¹Arabia and all the sheiks of Kedar traded as your agents in lambs, rams, and goats—your agents for those. ²²Merchants of Sheba and Raamah were your dealers in all choice perfumes and in all precious stones and gold, which they sold you for export. ²³Haran, Canneh, and Eden, dealers of Sheba, Assyria, and Kilmad were your dealer(s). ²⁴They were your dealers in gorgeous clothes, in cloaks of bluish purple and finely embroidered cloth, in carpets of multicolored trim, and in tightly wound ropes for your merchandise. ²⁵Tarshish ships traveled for you with your imports.

" 'So you were full and very heavily loaded
    in the midst of the seas.
²⁶Into deep waters
    your rowers brought you out;
an east wind broke you up
    in the heart of the seas.
²⁷Your wealth, your exports and your imports,
    your sailors and your pilots, your repairmen,
and those who bring you imports,
    all your warriors on board—
in fact, all your company who were on board
    will sink into the heart of the seas on the day of your fall.
²⁸At the sound of the outcry of your pilots,
    the mainland suburbs will quake.
²⁹All who handle the oar
    will come down from their ships;
the sailors and all the pilots of the sea
    will stand ashore.
³⁰They will shout loudly over you
    and cry out bitterly.
They will throw earth on their heads
    and dust themselves with ashes.

³¹They will make a bald spot on their heads on account of you
    and put on sackcloth.
They will weep bitterly over you,
    a bitter lament.
³²In their grief, they will raise a lament over you
    and lament over you:
"Who is like Tyre
    in the midst of the sea?
³³When your exports were unloaded from the seas,
    you satisfied many peoples;
by your abundant wealth and your imports,
    you enriched the kings of the earth.
³⁴Now you have been broken up by the seas
    in the watery depths.
Your merchandise and the entire company on board
    have fallen.
³⁵All the inhabitants of the coastlands
    are appalled over you;
their kings' hair stands on end;
    their faces show distress.
³⁶Traders among the peoples
    whistle at you.
You have become a horror
    and will be no more forever." ' "

Textual Notes

27:1–36 See the map "The Ancient Near East."

27:2 קִינָה ... שָׂא—As in 19:1; 28:12; 32:2, the Qal masculine singular imperative of נָשָׂא is used for "lift up, utter" a קִינָה, "lament, dirge." A finite form of the verb will be used in 27:32 (וְנָשְׂאוּ ... קִינָה). For קִינָה, see "Introduction to Ezekiel 19" and the textual note on 26:17–18.

27:3 Throughout chapter 27, one is struck by the unusually long description of Tyre, the addressee whom the prophet is to address. Already 27:1–3 adopts a relatively neutral tone, devoid of charges of wrongdoing, that will continue throughout the chapter. In contrast, the oracle against Tyre that constituted chapter 26 began with a specific accusation (26:2), and 28:1–19 will be almost totally accusatory.

וְאָמַרְתָּ לְצֹור—The לְ before "Tyre" might be a vocative (see the first textual note on 26:15), but I have taken it as a simple dative.

הַיֹּשֶׁבֶת֫י—The Qere, הַיֹּשֶׁבֶת, is the normal form of the Qal feminine participle of יָשַׁב with article. It, like many modifiers later in the chapter, is feminine because Tyre, like all city names, is feminine. The additional *yod* of the Kethib, הַיֹּשַׁבְתִּי, may be poetic and ornamental, or it may be influenced by the "i" of the feminine pronoun in Aramaic. At any rate, grammarians have given it the fancy title of *hireq compaginis*, coming along, as it were, to keep the word company (see GKC, § 90 m–n). The identical Kethib form here also appears in Jer 10:17; 22:23; and Lam 4:21.

מְבוֹאֹת יָם—The LXX, Vulgate, and Peshitta translate the plural of מָבוֹא by a singular: "entrance to the sea." They appear to have a case of faulty historical memory, because we now know that insular Tyre had two harbors: a natural harbor to the north, called the "Sidonian," and an artificial one on the opposite or southeastern side, called the "Egyptian" because of the direction it faced. The latter was more celebrated in antiquity because it apparently had been developed much more, consisting of both an inner and an outer harbor and various anchorages. The natural harbor still exists, but the south one was later neglected and silted up, so that later writers often make no mention of it. מָבוֹא has both a masculine and a feminine plural form; the masculine was used in 26:10, while the feminine is used here. An article could have been used before יָם here, but there are many other comparable construct phrases with anarthrous wordings.

רֹכֶלֶת הָעַמִּים אֶל־אִיִּים רַבִּים—Most revealing are these two modifying phrases—which come close to summarizing all the rest of the chapter. Participles of רָכַל (here, feminine singular: רֹכֶלֶת) occur ten times in the oracle. The root indicates a "merchant," "trader," or "dealer" who transfers products from port to port all over the world. In 27:12–25, many such dealers are named. Probably related to that root is רָכִיל, a "gossiper" or "slanderer" (22:9), an almost natural association, as is still evident in eastern bazaars. The "coastlands" (אִיִּים) that Tyre served probably included a good share of the then-known world.

אַתְּ אָמַרְתְּ אֲנִי כְּלִילַת יֹפִי:—Many critics are disturbed by the unannounced shift to the metaphor of the ship starting in 27:4, as though a poet must specify his metaphor before using it. They propose various emendations of 27:3 to prepare for the metaphor. Zimmerli deletes אָמַרְתְּ in the interests of his 3:2 metrical rewrite.[1] Van Dijk repoints the verb as a Pual, אֻמַּרְתְּ ("you are called"),[2] but the Pual occurs nowhere in the OT. Either change must be accompanied by an emendation of אֲנִי, "I," to אֳנִיָּה, "ship," or it must be revocalized to אֳנִי, "ship," attested in only one Amarna letter. However, the careful reader will note that nowhere in the entire poem is "ship" expressly applied to Tyre. The nautical meaning is communicated by other vocabulary and sound associations, as 27:4 will illustrate. That is, the transition is not as abrupt as imagined. The rest of 27:3 in conjunction with 27:4 indicates that a certain double entendre of city and ship is being introduced.

The adjective כָּלִיל, "perfect," is applied to Tyre's beauty again in 28:12. However, in other passages it is applied to Jerusalem. Greenberg cites Lam 2:15, reporting that before her ruin Jerusalem had been called כְּלִילַת יֹפִי ("perfection of beauty"), and Ps 50:2, where, using a related word, Zion is termed מִכְלַל־יֹפִי (also "perfection of beauty"). He especially appeals to Ezek 16:14, where the beauty of the woman representing Jerusalem is "perfect" (כָּלִיל) because of the "splendor" (הָדָר) God has bestowed upon her, and he compares that description to this oracle, where הָדָר is used in 27:10 of Tyre, and the verb כָּלַל, "make perfect," is used in 27:11 (also in 27:4).

---

[1] Zimmerli, *Ezekiel*, 2:42.

[2] Van Dijk, *Ezekiel's Prophecy on Tyre*, 56–57. Allen, *Ezekiel*, 2:80, calls it a Qal passive.

Greenberg plausibly argues that in Tyre's boast about her beauty in 27:3, she is appropriating an epithet that is rightfully Jerusalem's.[3] That may be, but if so, there is no explicit reproach of Tyre for the unfounded conceit. It is the type of boast one would be less surprised to find in the next chapter. Perhaps it merely manifests the excessive urban pride evident in many great cities, including those of the world today. Whether Greenberg intimates correctly or not, one should note that Ezekiel has a near monopoly on the key vocabulary. In the OT, the verb כָּלַל, "make perfect," occurs only in 27:4, 11. And of the nineteen occurrences of the noun יְפִי, "beauty" (in pause: יֹפִי) in the OT, ten (over half) occur in Ezekiel.

27:4 בְּלֵב יַמִּים גְּבוּלָיִךְ—The duality in meaning is apparent throughout the verse, which could refer either to Tyre or a ship. "In the heart of the seas," poetic for "in the water" (though here probably close to shore), could be the location of the island city or of the metaphorical ship being built or loaded. Later on, in 27:26–27, there is no doubt: the phrase means "on the high seas." Likewise, "your borders" might apply just as easily to the boundaries of the city as to the rim or circumference of a ship.

בֹּנַיִךְ כָּלְלוּ יָפְיֵךְ:—"Your builders" (Qal masculine plural participle of בָּנָה with second feminine singular suffix) can refer as easily to shipwrights as to urban construction workers on land. The verb כָּלַל, "to perfect," occurs in the OT only in 27:4, 11. יָפְיֵךְ (repeated in 27:11) is the noun יְפִי, "beauty," from 27:3, with second feminine singular suffix.

27:5 With this verse, Ezekiel, clearly speaking metaphorically, begins a description of the magnificent construction of the ship, described as a superb human achievement. Ezek 27:4–6 portrays its superior construction of the best materials, 27:7 its outstanding decoration, and 27:8–11 the top-notch personnel to man it.

Four kinds of wood are described in 27:5–6, together with their geographic origin and their use on the ship. Greenberg admits our modern ignorance about the ancient terminology: "The names of the woods/trees used in constructing the ship are all uncertain."[4] Other commentators sound more certain. Many of the names have traditional translations, and little seems gained by departing from them. One can hardly expect the biblical text to distinguish subspecies and the like, after the manner of a modern scientific text. One can be confident that by ample experience the Tyrians had learned which woods served their various needs. Nor would they have lacked any supply of timber. There were not only the heavily forested mountains east of them, but their allies would probably be only too happy to supplement the native supply.

בְּרוֹשִׁים מִשְּׂנִיר—For בְּרוֹשׁ, "juniper" seems to command as much assent as any translation. KJV had "fir," and the handbooks indicate it may be included. Solomon included בְּרוֹשׁ in the construction of the temple (1 Ki 5:22, 24 [ET 5:8, 10]; 6:34; 9:11).

Its source, "Senir," was, according to Deut 3:8–9, the Amorite name for Mount Hermon, while the Sidonians called it Sirion. The name occurs also in Song 4:8 and 1 Chr 5:23. The Assyrians referred to it as Saniru.

---

3   Greenberg, *Ezekiel*, 2:548.
4   Greenberg, *Ezekiel*, 2:549.

לְחֹתָיִם—Commentators divide on the meaning of this term in this context. The noun לוּחַ is used most often of a special writing "tablet," but also of other boards or tablets of either wood or stone, as used for the Decalogue (e.g., Ex 24:12). Here the plural לְחֹות receives a dual ending (־יִם) in pause (־יָם; see Joüon, § 91 b; cf. GKC, § 87 s). Some think of the two sets of ribs of the ship, one corresponding to the other. Rather than the hull, it probably is better to think of the dual referring to a double deck, with each deck composed of many planks (hence the plural). The word's position at the head of the lists of the ship's parts and its association with the mast, followed by the oars, are apparently intended to describe the double-decked design of the ship, in which rowers occupied the lower deck and sailors the upper one. Such Phoenician ships are shown in palace reliefs from Nineveh.

אֶרֶז מִלְּבָנוֹן—"Cedar" is still the traditional translation of אֶרֶז, the famed cedar of Lebanon that still adorns the national flag of modern Lebanon. There is no cogent reason to abandon it, although, of course, it is disputed, mostly on the grounds that now the tree does not seem to grow high enough to serve as a mast. In Ezekiel's time, a ship's sails were held up by a single mast, so that its strength and height were of the utmost importance. The role of אֶרֶז in the construction of Solomon's temple (1 Kings 5–7) is not relevant here, but should not be forgotten.

תֹּרֶן—This noun is used only two other times in the OT (Is 30:17; 33:23), but its meaning here is not in doubt: the ship's "mast."

27:6 Many details of the translation of this verse are debatable. אַלּוֹן seems to be a rather generic word, but it is obviously closely related to אֵלוֹן and אַלָּה (subspecies or spelling variations?), usually translated "oak," "terebinth," or the like. Traditionally, an "oak" of some sort has been taken as the raw material for the "oars" (מִשּׁוֹטָיִךְ is the plural of מָשׁוֹט with second feminine singular suffix; cf. the cognate מָשׁוֹט, "oar," in 27:29). Assyrian reliefs depict biremes, with one row of oarsmen visible on the lower deck and a second invisible row extending their oars from openings in the ship's hull.

קַרְשֵׁךְ—In Ex 26:15–29 and Num 3:36; 4:31, the plural and true singular of קֶרֶשׁ are used repeatedly for the "boards" or "planks" of the wooden walls of the tabernacle. Here the singular probably is collective in meaning. A Ugaritic cognate is used of some sort of pavilion or dwelling place for El. Whether קֶרֶשׁ here refers to the material for the deck or for a cabin on it is not made clear.

עָשׂוּ־שֵׁן בַּת־אֲשֻׁרִים—The noun שֵׁן basically means "tooth," but then derivatively "ivory," an elephant's tooth. The full form שֶׁנְהַבִּים (with the *hab* element from the Egyptian word for elephant) occurs only in 1 Ki 10:22 ‖ 2 Chr 9:21. Mention of "ivory" here strikes many as strange. Some commentators would delete שֵׁן as a dittograph of the last two consonants of עָשׂוּ; some would also delete the following בַּ.[5] But use of ivory inlay is mentioned already in the *Aeneid*,[6] and Phoenician involvement in the ivory trade is documented. Such a touch of luxury would not be out of place at all in a vessel as grand as the one Ezekiel is describing here.

---

[5] So Zimmerli, *Ezekiel*, 2:44; cf. Block, *Ezekiel*, 2:56, including nn. 24–25.

[6] Virgil, *Aeneid*, 10.136–37.

The phrase בַּת־אֲשֻׁרִים, literally, "the daughter of the Assyrians," is nonsensical. Of the ancient versions, only the Targum supports what is now commonly accepted, that the MT's division into two words was faulty and that this should be read as בִּתְאַשֻׁרִים, the plural noun תְּאַשֻׁרִים preceded by the preposition בְּ. The singular תְּאַשּׁוּר appears in Is 41:19 and 60:13 and refers to some kind of tree, perhaps "box-tree" (BDB), though "cypress" is generally preferred today.

מֵאִיֵּי כִּתִּים:—In any case, the trees came "from the coasts of Cyprus," the modern counterpart of ancient Kition (modern Larnaca), an important Phoenician colony on the southeast coast of Cyprus. Important remnants of it have recently been exposed by archaeological excavation. The plural gentilic "Kittim" was later extended to the entire area of the Greek islands. In Dan 11:30 the region even includes territory controlled by the Romans. Compare the textual note on אֱלִישָׁה, "Elishah," in 27:7.

27:7 שֵׁשׁ־בְּרִקְמָה מִמִּצְרַיִם הָיָה מִפְרָשֵׂךְ—The noun מִפְרָשׂ is, literally, a "spreading." It occurs elsewhere only in Job 36:29 of clouds, but the verb פָּרַשׂ, "to spread out," with various other objects, is common. In this context, the meaning is surely "sail." This is such a prominent element of tall ships (those with a mast, 27:5) that it would almost have to be mentioned. שֵׁשׁ־בְּרִקְמָה is, literally, "linen with embroidery." Egyptian שֵׁשׁ, "linen," was a highly prized item in antiquity. It was never dyed, but often embroidered with colored threads in bold and striking patterns. The בְּ with רִקְמָה is a *bet* of accompaniment. Texts speak of the great pleasure taken in the colored sails of temple barges (luxurious vessels) in Egypt's New Kingdom.

לְנֵס—Such sails would not only catch the wind, but serve as identifying marks. This is apparently the point of the addition of נֵס, a military "standard" or "flag" set on a prominent position as a rallying point (Is 13:2; Jer 51:27). Although there are no depictions of Phoenician ships with flags, נֵס might have been used in some such secondary sense. Van Dijk quite preemptively insists that נֵס must mean "sail," but the evidence he adduces is scant and unconvincing.[7]

תְּכֵלֶת וְאַרְגָּמָן—These two colors were highly prized dyes (usually used on wool) and derived mostly from a shellfish (murex) found along the Phoenician coasts, occasionally from the secretions of certain insects. As a result, "born to the purple" has even entered English idiom. It is strange that Phoenicia imported dyed cloths since it was so famous for its dyes that its name is derived from the Greek Φοῖνιξ, "purple." Conceivably, the dye derived from elsewhere, especially one of its colonies, was even more highly valued than the domestic product.

אֱלִישָׁה—"Elishah," usually called "Alashiya" in extrabiblical sources, is often mentioned in ancient texts of various provenances, especially Assyrian ones. But its exact location remains uncertain. Gen 10:4 mentions Elishah as a son of Javan, whose name (יָוָן in Ezek 27:13, 19) came to denote "Ionia," or eastern Greece (now Turkey), but that helps little in locating the place name "Elishah." A minority position thinks of Carthage, named here after Elissa/Dido, a Tyrian princess who was its legendary founder. Majority opinion thinks of Cyprus, especially since some Amarna letters

---

[7] Van Dijk, *Ezekiel's Prophecy on Tyre*, 65. The previous מִפְרָשׂ, then, he renders "canvas," which is possible, but rather general.

from Cyprus mention its export of copper. (Our word "copper" comes, via Latin, from "Cypress.") Some even wish to be more specific and point to the region around Enkomi, a major archaeological site on the east coast of Cyprus. That territory, occupied first by the Achaeans and later by the Greeks, would thus be distinguished from Kition (Larnaca), which was occupied and ruled by the Phoenicians. However, no export of purple dye or cloth from this region has yet been attested. So the exact location of this once quite important site remains totally up in the air.

מְכַסֵּךְ:—The Piel participle of כָּסָה, "to cover" (with second feminine singular suffix), must refer to an "awning" or something similar that would protect passengers, especially in the cabin of the ship, from the Mediterranean sun. Such coverings are often attested in ancient art. Because of the parallelism between this term and גַּם, many wish to emend the participle to the noun מִכְסֶה, which refers to some sort of covering of Noah's ark (Gen 8:13) and often to the coverings of the tabernacle. The case for the change seems less than convincing.

27:8 I have offered a relatively free translation of this verse in the hope of better conveying in English what the Hebrew is really saying. At the same time, many critics offer emendations that change the meaning, and not clearly for the better.

יֹשְׁבֵי צִידוֹן וְאַרְוַד הָיוּ שָׁטִים—The Qal participle of יָשַׁב (masculine plural in construct), "inhabitants," strikes many critics as too colorless and general, partly in the light of terms in the ancient translations that indicate more dignity, and partly because more skilled workmen are mentioned in succeeding verses. But no exceptional skills are involved in being "rowers" (or "oarsmen," as some translators, rather pompously to my ear, render שָׁטִים, the Qal participle of שׁוּט; cf. מְשׁוֹטֵיךְ, "your oars," in 27:6). Further, the participle of יָשַׁב was already used neutrally of the Tyrians themselves in 27:3, and the two uses of it may be linked.[8]

Sidon (צִידוֹן), Tyre's major competitor, although of secondary importance at the moment, was only about twenty-five miles to the north. Arvad (אַרְוַד), modern Ruad, was about eighty-five miles still further north. Like Tyre, Arvad was an island city, some two miles off the coast, barely visible on a clear day from the coast and easily accessible by small ferry or other craft from modern Tartus on the Syrian mainland. It appears as early as the Amarna letters as an opponent of Tyre and is frequently mentioned in reports of Assyrian campaigns.[9]

חֲכָמַיִךְ צוֹר ... חֹבְלָיִךְ:—A second common emendation in this verse (so RSV) is to alter צוֹר to צֶמֶר (Zemer), a Phoenician city referred to in Gen 10:18 between Arvad and Hamath as a place from which descendants of Canaan spread out. That emendation makes the Tyrian skilled workers (חֲכָמַיִךְ, literally, "your [Tyre's] wise men") into foreigners. However, that emendation, at best, seems to deny the attribute of wisdom to Tyre itself, and the next chapter explicitly credits the prince of Tyre (and thus by extension the Tyrians) with "wisdom" (חָכְמָה, 28:4, 5, 7, 12, 17).

---

[8] As before, van Dijk, *Ezekiel's Prophecy on Tyre*, 66–71, takes יֹשֵׁב as "king," and חֲכָמִים he interprets as "senators, counsellors or noble people."

[9] See, for example, *ANET*, 275, cited by Zimmerli, *Ezekiel*, 2:58, n. 37.

The labor assignment for the Tyrians on the ship makes sense because great skill was necessary to be a חֹבֵל, literally, a "rope man." In form, a participle of חָבַל, the verb is attested only as this participle, and it is undoubtedly related to the common noun חֶבֶל, "rope." חֹבֵל is often simply translated "sailor," but that seems too general, although at times all hands might assist in managing the ropes in order to catch the wind properly. I have rendered חֹבְלָיִךְ (literally, "your rope men") as those who "manned your sails." Tyrians would most likely entrust this position of responsibility to their own natives, whose patriotic loyalty would be above suspicion.

In Jonah 1:6, we meet רַב הַחֹבֵל, a "shipmaster" (KJV), not merely a "captain" (RSV), who would direct the men in properly handling the ropes. As helmsman, then, he also steered the ship.

27:9 זְקֵנֵי גְבַל וַחֲכָמֶיהָ הָיוּ בָךְ—The subject of this clause is, literally, "the elders of Gebal and her wise/skilled men." "Gebal" is translated as "Byblos" (whence the word "Bible") because the ancient city is almost universally known by that name today. Its ancient name was גְּבַל, to which it has reverted in the modern "Jebeil." As excavations have shown, it had perhaps the most notable history of all the Phoenician ports. Egyptian texts mention it as early as the third millennium, and it appears frequently in ancient texts afterwards. Here it appears as only one coastal city among many. It is located about sixty miles north of Tyre, twenty miles north of modern Beirut.

Critics often delete וַחֲכָמֶיהָ as a dittograph from 27:8b and/or as disruptive of the structure, but their reasons are not compelling. For the tasks of maintaining a ship— caulking seams, repairing leaks, and undoubtedly hundreds of other tasks—men of the utmost expertise and experience would be of the highest priority.

מַחֲזִיקֵי בִּדְקֵךְ—This construct phrase recurs in 27:27. Elsewhere in the OT, the noun בֶּדֶק, "fissure, rent, breach" (BDB), usually is the object of the Piel of חָזַק, "to strengthen, repair." Here and in 27:27, it is the object of the Hiphil of חָזַק (masculine plural participle in construct) with the same meaning. For this phrase, I have deliberately used the rather general "repairmen." Common translations such as "those who strengthen your leaks" or "those who caulk your seams" are probably too specific. The corresponding Piel phrase is used in 2 Ki 12:6–13 (ET 12:5–12) for unspecified repairs needed on the temple. Since the Piel is used in Kings, some wish to emend the Hiphil here, but the Hiphil appears to be identical in meaning, so no change is needed.

וּמַלָּחֵיהֶם—The noun מַלָּח seems originally to have been a Sumerian loan word. But from there it passed into many Semitic languages. It may be related to מֶלַח, "salt," and in the OT it always seems to refer to any kind of sailor, that is, one of no specific type. The form of מַלָּח is a *nomen opificum* ("name of a profession"; see GKC, § 84[b] b), for which a *qattal* formation often was used. It was probably heard in a sense similar to our colloquial "[old] salt."

הָיוּ בָךְ—My translations have not revealed it, but this clause, "they were in you," appears in both 27:8 and 27:9. Possibly already in the first half of 27:9, and certainly in the second half, the picture has plainly shifted away from the ship to the city. To capture both, I have rendered it here, "in you[r harbor]." The focus on the city will continue until 27:25b, where the ship metaphor once again dominates and then seems to alternate with that of the city until the end of the chapter.

לְעֲרֹב מַעֲרָבֵךְ:—The verb עָרַב (here Qal infinitive construct) and the cognate noun מַעֲרָב have occasioned much debate. Only here does this precise combination occur (but see the use of the words also in 27:27). At least four homonyms of עָרַב appear in standard lexica, and discoveries of new uses of those root letters have complicated things still further. Hence, choices vary widely, and I have chosen about as general and appropriate a rendition as I could think of: "to engage in your trade." Traditionally, most attempts at understanding proceeded from the assumption that עָרַב means "give/take in a pledge," hence, presumably, RSV's "barter for your wares." An ערב appears in Phoenician, Syriac, and South Arabic in the sense of "offer, bring in." Greenberg thinks he detects it in Hos 9:4 and hence would translate the phrase here "bringing you imports."[10] The general sense is clear enough, but precisely what kind of transaction is not.

27:10 Until now, everything in the chapter has sounded peaceful. But this verse and the next remind us that it was a world at war. Nebuchadnezzar's hostility is probably uppermost in Ezekiel's mind. But even in the best of times, pirates would have been lurking, so it would have been foolhardy to launch even an ordinary freighter without the ability to defend itself. The ship's difference in that respect from a man of war might have been slight. The verse may be speaking of ship and city at the same time, but the ship metaphor has not yet been dropped. Part of its crew was definitely soldiers, as will be explicitly stated in the account of the shipwreck in 27:27.

Place names begin to proliferate in 27:10, and this will continue through 27:25a. Some are well-known and easily identifiable, as was true in 27:8–9. Others are not, either subject to debate or purely a matter of speculation. The translation is faced with the dilemma of either simply transliterating the disputed or obscure names, leaving the reader to make his own guesses or to render with what seems to the translator to be the most likely intelligible modern equivalent. On the whole, I have tried to follow the latter alternative.

פָּרַס וְלוּד וּפוּט—These are, literally, "Paras, Lud, and Put." Major questions are raised about the identification of this "Paras." The form is identical with that usually used for "Persia," but it is debated whether Persia was well enough known in Ezekiel's time. Since Persia did not become a world power until the late sixth century, Zimmerli evades the issue by construing 27:9b–11 as a prose insertion from that period.[11] If we do not take that way out, there appears to be ample evidence that Persia was known long before Ezekiel's day. And since we are doubtlessly dealing with mercenaries, the political states of their homelands is largely beside the point. Persia is mentioned in Assyrian annals as early as the ninth century B.C. "Paras" is mentioned in 38:5–6 alongside Cush, Put, Gomer, and Togarmah as allies of Gog, strengthening the case for identification with Asiatic Persia. Block thinks of a "Pathros" somewhere to the south of Egypt, or of some power not yet attested in extrabiblical records,[12] but that reasoning seems tortured.

---

[10] Greenberg, *Ezekiel*, 2:551.

[11] Zimmerli, *Ezekiel*, 2:59–60.

[12] Block, *Ezekiel*, 2:64–65.

A slight question also arises with "Lud," that is, Lydia, since Genesis 10 gives two different genealogical lines, the first one Hamitic, with "Ludim" (the Hebrew plural of "Lud"), and the second one Semitic, with "Lud." Gen 10:13 states that Mizraim ("Egypt") fathered "Ludim," while Gen 10:22 names "Lud" as a descendant of Shem. The Semitic line is to be preferred as the origin of the "Lud" here, because in Gen 10:22, "Lud" is grouped with Elam and Asshur (Assyria). The LXX and the Vulgate already make this identification, and Ashurbanipal in the middle of the seventh century complains that Gyges of Lydia had stopped sending him help against the Cimmerians and had transferred his loyalty to Psammetichus, king of Egypt.[13]

Virtually no debate is engendered by "Put," which refers either to Libya or to some part of it. Already in the Egyptian Old Kingdom and still in its New Kingdom, both Nubian and Libyan mercenaries appear as important elements in Egyptian forces. The LXX, the Vulgate, and Josephus[14] make this identification, and in 30:5 Put appears together with Lydia as a helper of Egypt. In a fragmentary record of an Egyptian campaign, Nebuchadnezzar mentions a "Putu of Yaman," possibly a Greek colony in Cyrene, next to Egypt.[15]

With all three names, Ezekiel seems to be singling out peoples toward the limits of the then-known world—all to the greater glory of Tyre. These peoples are generally to Tyre's east and south. Allies to the north will be the subject of 27:11.

הָיוּ בַחֵילֵךְ אַנְשֵׁי מִלְחַמְתֵּךְ—The noun חַיִל by itself can mean "army," but it is often also used more broadly in the sense of "power" (also "wealth"). Since אַנְשֵׁי מִלְחַמְתֵּךְ duplicates it, or defines it more closely, I have freely merged the two expressions into "among your personnel were warriors."

מָגֵן וְכוֹבַע תִּלּוּ־בָךְ—The Qal of תָּלָה commonly means "hang," but 27:10–11 are the only OT verses with the Piel (תִּלּוּ, third common plural perfect), which has the same meaning. The Tyrian custom of hanging shields on both city walls and ship railings is frequently illustrated (see also 27:11b). The custom later spread to Greece. Song 4:4 also attests to the practice (cf. 1 Macc 4:57). On the other hand, no evidence has yet appeared that proves that helmets were also attached to ships or walls, although one is known from Minoan times. Here the nouns "shield" and "helmet" are used collectively. Possibly, "shield(s) and helmet(s)" (מָגֵן וְכוֹבַע), repeated in 23:24 (with the alternate spelling קוֹבַע) and 38:5, may simply be a stereotypical phrase.

נָתְנוּ הֲדָרֵךְ:—Here, as often, the pronominal suffix (second feminine singular on the noun הָדָר) has dative force: literally, "they gave your splendor," it means, "they gave splendor to/for you." The clause indicates that Ezekiel's interest in the mercenaries lies less in their military abilities than in their contribution to Tyre's glorious image.

27:11 בְּנֵי אַרְוַד וְחֵילֵךְ—The word חֵילֵךְ here is identical in form with חֵילֵךְ (with בְּ) in 27:10 ("your personnel"). Ancient and medieval translations universally understood it the same way here. While there may be a deliberate play on its prior use,

---

[13] Zimmerli, *Ezekiel*, 2:59, citing (in note 54) the Rassam Cylinder 2, 95–96; 111–15.

[14] Josephus, *Antiquities*, 1.132–33 (1.6.2).

[15] See *ANET*, 308.

it is now widely accepted, on the basis of modern studies, that the word here is a toponym, "Ḥilakku" (Cilicia).[16] Its parallelism here with Arvad also calls for it to be another place name. It is unusual for a word in construct (בְּנֵי) to govern two genitives (אַרְוַד וְחֵילֵךְ), but see Waltke-O'Connor, § 9.3b, examples 8–10.

וְגַמָּדִים—The "Gammadites" have the only name in 27:10–11 that is gentilic in form: גַּמָּדִי, a hapax. They remain of uncertain identification. The best current guess for the location of Gammad seems to be a Syrian town, Kumidi, mentioned in the Amarna letters.

שִׁלְטֵיהֶם תִּלּוּ עַל־חוֹמוֹתַיִךְ—For the hanging of shields on the wall, see the fourth textual note on 27:10. However, the precise meaning of שֶׁלֶט is still debated. Song 4:4 pairs it with מָגֵן, "shield," and both are hung on a tower. But other passages suggest a more general meaning like "arms." Only here does the LXX render it by φαρέτρα, "quiver." The Peshitta translated שִׁלְטֵיהֶם with the Syriac cognate ܩܶܠܬܳܐ, which also means "quiver." Jer 51:11 (literally, "polish the arrows; fill the quivers") seems to make that translation certain.

הֵמָּה כָּלְלוּ יָפְיֵךְ:—This final clause echoes Tyre's own boast in 27:3, which had the same noun, "beauty" (יָפִי, here with second feminine singular suffix), and the adjective "perfect" (כָּלִיל), cognate to the verb here and in 27:4, כָּלַל, "to perfect." This makes a perfect inclusio, concluding this section of the chapter.

27:12–24 All of a sudden, Ezekiel shifts to a list of Tyre's trading partners and the goods in which they trafficked. Most critics deny the originality of the list and assume Ezekiel borrowed it from some other source. There is no reason why the prophet could not have started with a commercial list, then, under divine inspiration, adapted it for its present purpose here, but obviously Yahweh could have moved him to compose it from scratch. The question of source is really irrelevant, but Ezekiel, as a priest (1:3), before his deportation would have had access to various sorts of temple and palace lists, perhaps including trade.

Basic vocabulary terms are repeated throughout the list. סֹחַרְתֵּךְ (27:12) is the Qal feminine singular participle סֹחֶרֶת (with second feminine singular suffix), "trader, agent" from סָחַר, "trade, act as a broker or wholesaler," normally in order to make a profit, as the noun סַחַר indicates. The feminine participle is used for cities or countries that were Tyre's trading partners (27:12, 16, 18), while the masculine participle is in 27:21, 36. The cognate noun סְחֹרָה, "merchandise," occurs in 27:15.

A synonym is the Qal participle of רָכַל (most often masculine plural with second feminine singular suffix: רֹכְלַיִךְ) used as a substantive, "dealer, trader, merchant," for Tyre's trading partners in 27:13, 15, 17, 20, 22, 23, 24. The feminine singular רֹכֶלֶת had been used in 27:3 for Tyre herself.

In commercial contexts, נָתַן can mean "sell, offer, deliver." נָתְנוּ is used in the commercial sense in 27:12, 13, 14, 16, 17, 19, 22. Sometimes a *bet* of price or exchange (BDB, s.v. בְּ, III 3) is attached to the object that is sold or exchanged; it denotes trading "in" a commodity. The use of this בְּ is inconsistent: compare נָתְנוּ בְּעִזְבוֹנָיִךְ in 27:12 to נָתְנוּ עִזְבוֹנָיִךְ in 27:16.

In the OT, the noun עִזָּבוֹן occurs only in the plural and only in this chapter (27:12, 14, 16, 19, 22, 27, 33), always with second feminine singular suffix (עִזְבוֹנַיִךְ). It refers to goods "left behind" (עָזַב) for someone else, that is, "exports."[17] Thus it is an antonym of מַעֲרָב (e.g., 27:9).

A certain literary structure is evident in the fact that the list begins and ends with "Tarshish" (27:12 and 27:25a). The list follows an alternating pattern, though it dissolves toward the end. The basic pattern is this:

1. The name of the trading partner.
2. The name is qualified by some form of סֹחֵר or רֹכֵל, "trader," essentially synonymous terms, perhaps interchanged for variation.
3. Sometimes the reason is given that the partner traded with Tyre "because of the abundance" (מֵרֹב) of Tyre's "wealth" (הוֹן) and/or "products" (מַעֲשַׂיִךְ, plural of מַעֲשֶׂה with second feminine singular suffix). This reason is given in 27:12, 16, 18 (cf. 27:27, 33).
4. A list of the wares traded.
5. Whether the goods were imports or exports. In either case, the wares probably were transshipped to some further destination by Tyre, which served as broker or middleman.

Variations in the pattern show some deliberate attempt to avoid monotony.

Greenberg argues that far from simply a dry commercial inventory, Ezekiel's list is a deliberate, poetic adaptation of such an inventory, with other ancient parallels. He cites two catalogs in the *Iliad*, Homer's list of Greek ships[18] and another of Trojan forces.[19] In even higher antiquity, Greenberg cites from a third-millennium Sumerian myth a list of the trade engaged in by the Sumerian paradisiacal city of Dilmun, which has a similar pattern of listing names of trading partners in opposing directions (east-west, north-south), although Greenberg claims no direct links between that list and Ezekiel's two millennia later. Greenberg proposes the following pattern of ordering the trading partners in order to demonstrate Tyre's worldwide connections:

1. Partners west and north of Tyre, the Japhethites according to Gen 10:2–4: "Tarshish … the men of Rhodes" (Ezek 27:12–15), exemplifying the outermost zone of the then-known, inhabited world
2. Partners near Tyre, to the east or northeast, including "Edom/Aram," "Judah," "Israel," and "Damascus" (27:16–19)
3. Arabian partners to the southeast, including "Dedan" and "Sheba" (27:20–22)
4. Partners to the far east, including "Haran," "Eden," and "Assyria" (27:23)[20]

Inevitably, the names of some items on the ships' manifests are unknown to us and invite speculations of various sorts. Block states, almost classically, that the rare words in this list may actually have been rather common in commercial records, but

---

[17] Cf. van Dijk, *Ezekiel's Prophecy on Tyre*, 75–76.

[18] Homer, *Iliad*, 2.494–785.

[19] Homer, *Iliad*, 2.786–877.

[20] Greenberg, *Ezekiel*, 2:566–67.

the Bible has only preserved for us a small portion (or a small number of occurrences) of the ancient vocabulary:

> Rather than interpreting the high number of hapax legomena among the articles of trade as evidence that the author's mind is elsewhere, ... these strange words simply confirm that the Hebrew OT is but a linguistic fragment, missing many expressions from the everyday world of economic production, trade, and commerce.[21]

The cargo found on a single Mediterranean shipwreck from the fourteenth century B.C., long before Ezekiel's day, shows how incredibly varied were the items an ancient merchantman could carry. This ship was discovered off the southwest Turkish town of Ulu Burum, and its inventory was first published in 1987. Many other shipwrecks have been found in the general area since then, and now that archaeological investigation of such undersea finds has been put on a firm scientific basis, our list of the possibilities is likely to grow. The multifarious cargo in Ezekiel's list is anything but fantastic.

27:12 תַּרְשִׁישׁ—Tarshish probably was in the western Mediterranean, although there is some uncertainty about its precise location. Ps 72:10 speaks of Sheba and Tarshish as two geographical extremes of the world. The Table of Nations associates it with other Mediterranean names (Gen 10:4; 1 Chr 1:7), and Jonah 1:3 indicates that it was normally reachable by ship from Joppa. For a time, Albright's suggestion of Sardinia[22] found some following, but most opinion has now returned to the older view that Spain was meant, probably Tartessus, a Phoenician colony on the Guadalquivir River. Already classical writers refer to deposits of various metals in the region.[23] Jer 10:9 mentions "beaten silver imported from Tarshish." Another possibility advocated recently is that Tarshish could be Tarsus in Asia Minor.[24] In any event, Ezek 27:12 clearly connects Tyre's "great wealth" with its trading partnership with Tarshish.

מֵרֹב כָּל־הוֹן—The noun הוֹן, "wealth," lacks a pronoun referring to Tyre, whereas it has the second feminine singular suffix in 27:27 (הוֹנֵךְ) as does its plural in 27:33 (הוֹנַיִךְ). Some want to add the suffix here. However, הוֹן again lacks a suffix when the identical phrase here reappears in 27:18. Since the context here so obviously makes Tyre the subject, even Zimmerli defends the MT as the *lectio difficilior.*[25]

27:13 יָוָן תֻּבַל וָמֶשֶׁךְ—The Ionians (יָוָן, "Javan/Ionia") were the Greeks of western Asia Minor and its islands. "Tubal" (תֻּבַל) and "Meshech" (מֶשֶׁךְ) were located farther in the interior in central and southeastern Anatolia. They appear in the same order in Gen 10:2 (‖ 1 Chr 1:5) as sons of Japheth. Is 66:19 includes "Tubal" and "Ionia" as

---

[21] Block, *Ezekiel*, 2:53, n.7.

[22] W. F. Albright, "New Light on the Early History of Phoenician Colonization," *BASOR* 83 (1941): 17–22.

[23] Cooke, *Ezekiel*, 300, citing Strabo, *Geography*, 3.2.8–9, and Diodorus Siculus, *Library*, 5.35–38, which discuss the precious metals in Iberia.

[24] See "Tarshish" in the textual notes on Jonah 1:3 in Lessing, *Jonah*, 70–73.

[25] Zimmerli, *Ezekiel*, 2:46.

distant nations to which the glory of Yahweh will be proclaimed. "Meshech" and "Tubal" (in that order) recur in Ezek 32:26; 38:2–3; 39:1

This verse suggests that all three were involved in the slave trade, and Ionian involvement also indicates the sale of Jewish captives to the Ionians by the Phoenicians (Joel 4:4–6 [ET 3:4–6]; cf. Amos 1:6, 9). Cuneiform texts and archaeological finds confirm the trade of copper vessels by Tubal and Meshech. We have no way of knowing whether the transactions described here were in the form of barter or sales.

27:14 מִבֵּית תּוֹגַרְמָה—"The house of Togarmah" is an expansion of the name of Togarmah, who is mentioned in Gen 10:3 as one of the sons of Gomer, a son of Japheth. (Compare Gen 10:2, which refers to Meshech and Tubal, names also mentioned in Ezek 27:13.) Many ancient sources mention Togarmah, including as a place that brought tribute to Assyria. Ezek 38:6 states that Beth-togarmah (literally, "the house of Togarmah") was located in "the remotest regions of the north." "The house of ..." (בֵּית) is used frequently in the Semitic world before names, often indicating the founder of a dynasty. However, the area of Togarmah was not Semitic, and the presence of the prefix here is unexplained.

סוּסִים וּפָרָשִׁים וּפְרָדִים—The trading of "horses" and "mules" is clear, but uncertain is the identity of the intermediate item, פָּרָשִׁים. For it, the LXX has ἱππεῖς, here meaning "riders" or "horsemen," and the KJV has "horsemen" as well. They are probably correct even though many modern interpreters do not agree. If the term meant "horses," the expected vocalization would be פְּרָשִׁים, like the following פְּרָדִים. The vocalization of פָּרָשִׁים is unusual because the initial syllable retains *qamets* (-ָ). Probably the reason is because the term, meaning "horsemen," is a *nomen opificum* (occupation; see GKC, § 84[b] b), whose normal form is *qattal*. However, the middle radical of פָּרָשִׁים is ר, which generally cannot accept a *daghesh*, so the preceding vowel remains lengthened in the plural as a virtual doubling of the ר. Thus the form is -פָּרָ (in place of -פַּרָ). This explanation for the vocalization supports the meaning "horsemen."

Not everybody agrees; others consider פָּרָשִׁים to be at least a partial synonym of the other equine terms. Greenberg has "horses and steeds."[26] Zimmerli gives "draughthorses and saddle-horses."[27] Allen proposes "draft horses" and "war horses"[28] (cf. RSV: "horses, war horses"), and Block has "horses and chariot teams."[29] Draft horses are not difficult to learn to drive nor very particular about who drives them, while war horses and their jockeys were often a nearly inseparable pair (cf. modern race horses).

27:15 All three clauses of this verse are difficult and obscure.

בְּנֵי דְדָן—This is, literally, "the sons of Dedan." With most scholars, I have followed the LXX (υἱοὶ Ῥοδίων) in reading "Rhodes" instead of "Dedan." An original רֹדָן could have become דְדָן because of the similarity between ד and ר (cf. the second textual note on 27:16). Dedan, a northwest Arabian oasis, will be featured in 27:20,

---

[26] Greenberg, *Ezekiel*, 2:546.

[27] Zimmerli, *Ezekiel*, 2:46.

[28] Allen, *Ezekiel*, 2:79.

[29] Block, *Ezekiel*, 2:66.

but the following "many coastlands" (אִיִּים רַבִּים) here obviously fits Rhodes, a large island off the southwest coast of Anatolia. That judgment is far from universal, however. Block prefers a "Danuna" north of Tyre, mentioned in the Amarna letters.[30] Other places with similar names have also been suggested.

סְחֹרַת יָדֵךְ—The noun סְחֹרָה (in construct), "merchandise" (BDB), is a hapax, but is cognate to the participle סֹחֵר, "trader," that is frequent in this context (see the textual note on 27:12–24). Similar, but using the participle, is the phrase סֹחֲרֵי יָדֵךְ, used for Arab tribes in 27:21. Greenberg probably surmises correctly that it is an example of the occasional Hebrew tendency to use abstracts for concrete terms.[31] Thus the literal "merchandise of your hand" means "trade agent of your hand." The abstract functions as a collective singular, so I have translated the phrase as "agents of your trade."

The following two trade items are relatively exotic. Such items might have originated in Africa, India, or Sri Lanka and could have reached the Mediterranean coast by various routes.

קַרְנוֹת שֵׁן—This is, literally, "horns of tooth," meaning "ivory tusks." The LXX renders ὀδόντας ἐλεφαντίνους, "elephantine teeth."

וְהָובְנִים—This hapax is an Egyptian loan word that also made its way into Ugaritic, Greek, and other languages. Traditionally it has been understood as "ebony" (a partial English transliteration), the prized black wood, but the meaning is not certain. The Qere is וְהָבְנִים, while the Kethib probably should be vocalized וְהֹובָנִים.

אֶשְׁכָּרֵךְ:—The noun אֶשְׁכָּר is a Sumerian loan word that occurs elsewhere in the Bible only in Ps 72:10. It has also appeared on an ostracon from about Ezekiel's time. The context demands some meaning like "payment." In Psalm 72 the parallelism suggests "tribute," but Tyre's trading partners were hardly her tributaries. On the basis of the Akkadian cognate, Greenberg defends "product to be delivered [under agency contract]."[32] I have rendered, "in payment to you."

27:16   The verse teems with words of uncertain meaning.

אֲרָם—This is "Aram," but I have followed Aquila and the Syriac, which has ܐܕܘܡ, "Edom." The mention of Damascus in 27:18 would duplicate "Aram," of which it was virtually the capital. The Hebrew ד may have been confused for ר (cf. the second textual note on 27:15). The Vulgate has *Syrus*, which supports "Aram." The LXX has ἀνθρώπους, apparently translating אדם (which it vocalized as אָדָם), the same consonants in "Edom." If "Edom" is read here, one also obtains a better south to north movement, with Edom to the south of Damascus, the chief Aramean kingdom, which will be featured in 27:18.

בְּנֹפֶךְ—"Turquoise" is the usual translation of נֹפֶךְ based on an Egyptian word for a product mined in Sinai. It appears in the list of jewels in the Israelite high priest's breastpiece (Ex 28:18; 39:11) and similarly in the pectoral of the king of Tyre (Ezek 28:13).

וּבוּץ—"Linen" here translates בּוּץ, a Late Biblical Hebrew word, occurring otherwise only in Chronicles and Esther. It simply displaces the Egyptian-derived שֵׁשׁ,

---

[30] Block, *Ezekiel*, 2:74.

[31] Greenberg, *Ezekiel*, 2:555.

[32] Greenberg, *Ezekiel*, 2:555.

"linen," named in 27:7 as coming to Tyre from Egypt. Thus בוּץ is more appropriate here for an Edomite (or Aramaic) context. Greenberg's comment is worth quoting: "The occurrence of both words for linen in the same oracle accords with Ezekiel's straddling early and late Hebrew."[33]

וְרָאמֹת—This noun occurs elsewhere in the OT only in Job 28:18 with another word of uncertain meaning. A cognate appears in an Ugaritic epic describing an ornament on a female's breast. The LXX simply transliterates, rather than translating it. "Coral" is the most common and ancient guess.

וְכַדְכֹּד—This noun occurs also in Is 54:12, obviously of some kind of gem. "Pearl" and "ruby" seem to be the favored conjectures.

27:17 יְהוּדָה וְאֶרֶץ יִשְׂרָאֵל—Yahweh places Ezekiel's own country, "Judah," and its former sister country, "the land of Israel," in the middle of his list of those with whom Tyre had trade relations. Usually in Ezekiel the phrase for Israel is אַדְמַת יִשְׂרָאֵל. Here אֶרֶץ יִשְׂרָאֵל is contrasted with Judah. The only other uses of the phrase in Ezekiel are in the context of the eschatological vision given the prophet in chapters 40–48. In 40:2 אֶרֶץ יִשְׂרָאֵל includes the city of Jerusalem, and in 47:18 it also includes all of Cisjordan. In a political sense, "Israel" had ceased to exist well over a century earlier, when it fell to Assyria in 722 B.C. However, Yahweh seems to ignore such secular realities when he refers to the region as of "the land of Israel," even though under foreign domination. The Chronicler uses the phrase in the same sense (2 Chr 30:25). The territory can still be called "Israel" even though it was no longer a political entity.

בְּחִטֵּי מִנִּית—"Wheat of Minnith" is not completely clear. It might refer simply to some special, high-quality variety, or the reference may be geographical. The only other OT reference to מִנִּית is a site mentioned in Judg 11:33, and Eusebius' *Onomasticon* identifies it as a place "four miles out of Heshbon on the road to Rabbah."[34] If the reference here is to that geographical location, this would seem to exceed the preceding reference to "the land of Israel," which nowhere, not even in eschatological texts (Ezek 40:2; 47:18), includes Transjordan. Perhaps all Yahweh means to say here is that Judah and Israel acted as brokers in transshipments from that area. That area's productiveness in grain is also attested by 2 Chr 27:5, where a large amount of wheat and barley was paid to King Jotham of Judah in tribute.

וּפַנַּג—The noun פַּנַּג is a hapax of completely uncertain meaning. An apparent Akkadian cognate suggests the usual identification with some kind of meal or flour. The context would support an agricultural product. Others, looking ahead to צֳרִי (see the next textual note), think of some kind of medicinal plant.[35] (KJV had simply transliterated the word, taking it as a place name, following Minnith.)

וָצֹרִי—This noun occurs six times in the OT, usually vocalized as צֳרִי, of which צֹרִי here could be the pausal form. It is vocalized as צְרִי in Gen 37:25. Its meaning, "balm" (mastic, the resin of a balsam tree), is well-attested. It is associated with Gilead

---

[33] Greenberg, *Ezekiel*, 2:555.

[34] Eusebius, *Onomasticon*, 132.1, cited in Greenberg, *Ezekiel*, 2:556.

[35] Block, *Ezekiel*, 2:66 and 2:76, including n. 135, argues for "resin," understood as a medicinal product.

and its medicinal value is affirmed in Jer 8:22; 46:11; 51:8. It seems to have been about as typical a product of that region as honey and olive oil were of Israel (Deut 8:8).

27:18 We confront textual difficulties in this verse, which has to be considered together with 27:19. Ezek 27:20 is also curiously short. The apparent redundancy of the "abundance" phrases (בְּרֹב מַעֲשַׂיִךְ מֵרֹב כָּל־הוֹן) may be a way of expressing the extraordinary importance of Damascus, the most important of the Aramean city-states, for Tyre's economy.

חֶלְבּוֹן—Helbon is modern Helbun, about ten miles north of Damascus. Both Babylonian and Persian sources attest to the fame wine from this region enjoyed in antiquity.

וְצֶמֶר צָחַר:—Literally, "wool of Sahar" is more problematic. The context suggests that צָחַר is another place name, possibly a Zuhru mentioned in the Amarna letters. Others think of an area called aṣ-Ṣaḥrā², northwest of Damascus, and render "white wool" on the basis of the Syriac (ܚܘܪ ܥܡܪ) and the modern Arabic term for "desert."[36]

27:19 וְדָן וְיָוָן מְאוּזָּל—Some commentators and translations (RSV, ESV) disregard the MT's punctuation at this point and read the last part of 27:18 together with the first part of 27:19, as I have done. If וְדָן means "and Dan" (rather than the place name "Vedan" in NASB), it is hard to understand the juxtaposition of Dan, in Israel's far north, with יָוָן, "Ionia," on the western Turkish coast. A relatively recent, but widely accepted, series of emendations first changes וְדָן וְיָוָן to וְדַנֵּי יַיִן, "vats/casks of wine." The noun דַּן does not occur in the OT, but is conjectured on the basis of cognates in Akkadian and Aramaic (see *HALOT*, s.v. דַּן). Then it repoints the initial *mem* of מְאוּזָּל as the preposition מִן, resulting in "from Uzal" (NIV, ESV) or "from Izalla," a town in the Anatolian foothills of the eastern Taurus mountains, between Haran and the Tigris. In Neo-Babylonian records of wine trade, Izalla is often linked with Helbon, named in 27:18.

בְּעִזְבוֹנַיִךְ נָתַנּוּ—The word order is the reverse of the same phrase, נָתְנוּ (בְּ)עִזְבוֹנָיִךְ, in 27:12, 14, 16. The meaning is unchanged. The pausal form נָתָנּוּ here has a euphonic doubling of the second *nun* with *daghesh forte affectuosum* (GKC, § 20 i).

בַּרְזֶל עָשׁוֹת—The hapax עָשׁוֹת is usually taken as an adjective, literally perhaps resulting in "smooth iron," but translated "worked/wrought iron" by the versions. It may refer to iron worked at lower temperatures and perhaps mixed with other ingredients to make it more malleable than cast iron.

קִדָּה וְקָנֶה—The noun קִדָּה is "cassia," an expensive perfume from east Asia that was used in preparing the anointing oil for the tabernacle (Ex 30:24). קָנֶה, "calamus," was another spice plant, prepared from an aromatic grass and used not only in cosmetics, but also for medicine and flavorings. The identifications seem quite certain and indicate how well-established such lengthy trade routes were already in Ezekiel's time.

---

[36] See Greenberg, *Ezekiel*, 2:557.

הָיָה:—The singular verb הָיָה is used after a plural subject also in 16:49 and 40:21.

27:20 וְדָדָן רֹכַלְתֵּךְ—Why this verse is so short is not clear. Is it more than stylistic variation? Dedan supplies something to Tyre, but the payment or what it received in exchange is unmentioned. Perhaps the verse should be read as transitional from the more northerly oriented trade just discussed to the desert and southerly items in the following verses.

Dedan (דְּדָן) was mentioned already in 25:13 in loose connection with Edom, and it will reappear in 38:13 accompanying Sheba (see 27:22). Dedan's location is fairly certain: the northwest Arabian oasis of al-ʿUla, a major station on the trade routes from south Arabia to points north.

בְּבִגְדֵי־חֹפֶשׁ לְרִכְבָּה:—The item Dedan is credited with selling or trading "in" (בְּ of price) was some kind of "garments" or "cloths" (plural construct of בֶּגֶד). Usually בֶּגֶד refers to "clothes," but the connection is about like "clothes-cloth" in English. Each of the following two words is a hapax. An Arabic cognate to חֹפֶשׁ means "blanket," or it could be an Akkadian loan word for "woollen material" (*HALOT*). More certain is the meaning of לְרִכְבָּה, "for riding," since the verb רָכַב, "to ride," is common. לְ indicates purpose. רִכְבָּה could be a verbal noun or a feminine form of the Qal infinitive construct (elsewhere in the OT the Qal infinitive of רָכַב is רְכֹב). If there is any connection between חֹפֶשׁ and the Hebrew adjective חָפְשִׁי, "free," possibly the saddlecloths connoted the type of "freedom" available only to nobility since they were expensive, as trade items might be expected to be.

27:21 עֲרַב—"Arabia" was still a quite general word in the OT without some of the more specific, especially ethnic, connotations attached to its modern derivative. It was the home of the עַרְבִי, the desert bedu (nomads) occupying the north Arabian steppe. (The related word "bedouin" already contains the Arabic plural -*in*, so "bedouins" betrays linguistic ignorance.) They were (and are) of various ethnic stocks, often culturally and physically quite distinct from other "Arabs" today. עַרְבִי in the OT (Is 13:20; Jer 3:2) is used in a general sense of "steppe-dweller" (BDB), and Is 21:13–17 speaks of "Dedanites," "those living in the land of Tema," and "the sons of Kedar" as residents of Arabia.

וְכָל־נְשִׂיאֵי קֵדָר—"All the sheiks of Kedar" is more specific. נְשִׂיאִים, "chiefs, sheiks," suggests some federation. Kedar was a son of Ishmael (Gen 25:13 ‖ 1 Chr 1:29), and the tribe consisting of his descendants was closely associated with the major oasis of Dumah (Is 21:11). Is 21:13–17 associates the tribe with Tema and Dedan, and Jer 49:28 pairs Kedar with "sons of the east." Assyrian, Aramaic, and Old South Arabic texts attest to the prominence of the Kedarites.

סֹחֲרֵי יָדֵךְ ... בָּם סֹחֲרָיִךְ:—The first phrase is, literally, "traders of your hand," but is rendered "traded as your agents." (It is similar to סֹחֲרַת יָדֵךְ; see the third textual note on 27:15.) At the end of the verse, the participle is repeated (סֹחֲרָיִךְ, "your agents") with בָּם, "for them," the *bet* of price with third masculine plural suffix referring to the three kinds of small livestock (see the next textual note). The different phraseology here for Tyre's partners may be for variety.

בְּכָרִים וְאֵילִים וְעַתּוּדִים—That the sheiks of Kedar traded "in" (בְּ) "lambs [כָּרִים], rams [אֵילִים], and goats [עַתּוּדִים]" is no surprise. A list of booty taken by Ashurbanipal in a campaign against the Kedarites is similar.[37] In a different context, this list of small livestock will be repeated (in a different word order) in 39:18.

27:22 שְׁבָא וְרַעְמָה—"Sheba" is a well-known name from the OT, but many questions surround the origins of the people of this region and their relationships to others. "Raamah" (the person and later tribe) is attested in the OT only in Gen 10:7 ‖ 1 Chr 1:9; Ezek 27:22, always in connection with "Sheba," and its location is totally unknown.

In Gen 10:7 (‖ 1 Chr 1:9), Seba (סְבָא) and Raamah are sons of the Hamitic Cush; then Raamah becomes the father of Sheba (שְׁבָא) and Dedan. In Gen 10:28, Sheba appears among various descendants of Shem who were mostly, it seems, centered in southern Arabia. In Gen 25:3 (‖ 1 Chr 1:32), Sheba appears with Dedan as a grandson of Abraham and Keturah, and Ezek 38:13 has the same pairing of Sheba with Dedan. Obviously, the history of the man Sheba and the tribe consisting of his descendants is complicated. We lack sufficient information to decipher whether Sheba originated in the north and started the later, well-known southern kingdom of Sheba as a commercial colony—or the other way around. The same question arises about the provenance of the queen who visited Solomon (1 Kings 10).

The people of Sheba may have originally been nomads, but by Solomon's time they had probably settled in what is now eastern Yemen with its capital at Marib. Because of Sheba's control of the narrow straits of the Red Sea between Arabia and Africa, and because of favorable meteorological conditions for the growth of both frankincense and myrrh trees, it undoubtedly soon became a very prosperous locale.

בְּרֹאשׁ כָּל־בֹּשֶׂם וּבְכָל־אֶבֶן יְקָרָה וְזָהָב—It is interesting that the luxury items mentioned here, "spices/perfumes" (the collective בֹּשֶׂם), "precious stones" (אֶבֶן יְקָרָה), and "gold" (זָהָב) are identical with those brought by the queen of Sheba to Solomon (1 Ki 10:10). The list here is also largely congruous with the tribute offered by defeated Arabians to Tiglath-Pileser III.[38] The phrase בְּרֹאשׁ כָּל־בֹּשֶׂם, literally, "with head/finest of all spices," is similar to the phrase בְּשָׂמִים רֹאשׁ, meaning "finest spices," in the recipe for the tabernacle's sacred anointing oil (Ex 30:23).

27:23 חָרָן וְכַנֵּה וָעֶדֶן—"Haran, Canneh, and Eden" pose no problem as the prophet looks to the far northeast of Tyre. Haran is well-known from its connections with the patriarchs (Gen 11:31–32; 12:4–5; 27:43; 28:10–31:21). The name is simply the Akkadian word *ḥarrānu*, "road," and it is situated on the Balikh River, some sixty miles north of its confluence with the Euphrates, today just a little north of the Turkish border. Canneh once was often associated with Calneh (Amos 6:2; see also Is 10:9), the capital of an Assyrian province, but the tendency today is to try to locate it in Aramean territory further west, as indicated by some private Assyrian documents, but a precise site has not yet commended itself. The "Eden" here is not the site of the original paradise, but shortened from Beth-eden (Assyrian Bit-adini), a sizeable Aramean state on the upper Balikh River west of Haran, annexed by Assyria in 857–855 B.C.[39]

---

[37] *ANET*, 299.

[38] *ANET*, 283.

[39] When used in this sense as the name of a country, the first syllable has a short vowel (*seghol*); a long vowel (*tsere*) indicates paradise.

The rest of the verse has textual problems.

רֹכְלֵי שְׁבָא—"Dealers of Sheba" seems out of place, also geographically, since Sheba was just mentioned in 27:22. In its place, the LXX has only the stock phrase "they were your merchants."

אַשּׁוּר כִּלְמַד רֹכַלְתֵּךְ:—"Asshur Kilmad" is curiously asyndetic. Asshur, of course, is a possibility as one of Tyre's brokers. It was not only the name of the country (Assyria), but of one of its various capitals. Kilmad, on the other hand, is a hapax and is totally unknown. כִּלְמַד is transliterated by the Vulgate (*Chelmad*) and, with a different spelling, by the LXX (Χαρμαν), while the Syriac has ܟܠܡܕ. The feminine singular participle רֹכַלְתֵּךְ (רֹכְלָה with second feminine singular suffix) does not fit with the plural subject, if both Asshur and Kilmad are intended (cf. 27:20a, where רֹכַלְתֵּךְ followed a feminine singular toponym).

27:24 A series of unique words besets us in this verse. Much of it appears to deal with clothes or fabrics of some sort.

בְמִכְלָלִים—The hapax מַכְלוּל, which has some cognates, may refer to an "ornate robe" (*HALOT*). Greenberg thinks of a combination of Akkadian *makla/ulu*, some kind of garment, and מִכְלֹל, "perfectly/splendidly," in the phrase לְבֻשֵׁי מִכְלוֹל in 23:12[40] (that phrase also occurs in 38:4). The LXX and Syriac lack a translation of it, and the Vulgate merely indicates a multiplicity of clothes.

בִּגְלוֹמֵי תְכֵלֶת—Similarly, the hapax noun גְּלוֹם has cognates, including Aramaic גְּלִימָא, "cloak," and the verb גָּלַם, "to wrap up" (2 Ki 2:8), that support "cloak, **wrap**" (*HALOT*).

וּבְגִנְזֵי בְּרֹמִים—The noun גֶּנֶז is used in Esth 3:9 and 4:7 of the royal treasury, but probably that is not the meaning of the word here, which perhaps is a homograph. An Aramaic Targum of Esth 1:3 leads many to translate "woollen" (*HALOT*, s.v. גֶּנֶז II), referring to blankets or coverings for couches. The hapax noun בְּרֹמִים is cognate with Akkadian and Arabic words meaning something like "multicolored trim" (see *HALOT*).

בַּחֲבָלִים חֲבֻשִׁים וַאֲרֻזִים—The syntax makes it difficult to decide whether these "ropes" (חֲבָלִים) were an additional luxury item (introduced by בְּ of price) or whether the preceding textiles were tied up "with" the ropes (בְּ of means). The more natural construal is that the ropes were merchandise. In either case, their high quality is indicated by the following two Qal passive participles, both modifying "ropes" (NIV). Probably חֲבֻשִׁים means "wound" (see *HALOT*, s.v. חבשׁ, Qal, 2) and אֲרֻזִים, "tight," yielding "tightly wound ropes." אֲרֻזִים may be related to an Arabic cognate, *'araza*, "be firm/drawn into oneself." An alternative translation in the major ancient versions and the KJV relates the word to the common noun אֶרֶז, "cedar," suggesting that the ropes were covered with cedar oil as a preservative (see *HALOT*, s.v. ארז).

בְּמַרְכֻלְתֵּךְ:—Presumably the absolute form of this noun (with בְּ and second feminine singular suffix) would be מַרְכֹּלֶת, a hapax. Since its root is the verb רָכַל, whose participle, "dealer, trader," is frequent in this chapter, it is often translated "for your trading/merchandise." It could also mean "in your place of trade." Zim-

---

[40] Greenberg, *Ezekiel*, 2:560.

merli[41] and others divide it into two words, בָּם וְכֻלָּתֵךְ, and take the phrase as essentially synonymous with the phrase בָּם סֹחֲרָיִךְ at the end of 27:21.

27:25 אֳנִיּוֹת תַּרְשִׁישׁ—The composite list of the cargo on the manifests of ships of Tyre came to a close in 27:24. Formally, this is signaled by the inclusio of "Tarshish" here, pointing clearly back to "Tarshish" in 27:12 (see the textual note on it in 27:12). But a typically Ezekelian shift in meaning has also occurred, as indicated by my translation of 27:25, which uses "Tarshish" as an adjectival modifier of "ships." The construct phrase אֳנִיּוֹת תַּרְשִׁישׁ may have originally referred to "ships of Tarshish," meaning ships plying the specific route to Tarshish, servicing the Tyre-Tarshish shipping lane. But later this phrase, meaning "Tarshish ships," became a more general term designating top-quality freighters ready for use anywhere on the high seas. Other biblical uses of the phrase (or the related phrase אֳנִי תַרְשִׁישׁ) confirm this understanding (Is 2:16; 1 Ki 10:22; 22:49 [ET 22:48]; and especially Isaiah's Gentile oracle against Tyre, Is 23:1–14). This subtle shift in the meaning of "Tarshish" is part of the transitional role of 27:25.

שָׁרוֹתַיִךְ מַעֲרָבֵךְ—This phrase casts a retrospective glance on the extensive trade just described in 27:12–24. This is, literally, "your travelers [with] your imports." A few Hebrew manuscripts prefix בְּ to מַעֲרָבֵךְ, and the versions supply such a preposition in their translations. Without it, the two words could be considered appositives. Most seem to agree that שָׁרוֹת is best understood as a Qal feminine plural participle (modifying the feminine plural noun אֳנִיּוֹת, "ships") of a verb שׁוּר with Arabic and Akkadian cognates, meaning "travel, descend" (see *HALOT*, s.v. שׁוּר II). Its second feminine singular suffix has a dative meaning: "traveled *for* you." The verb may also appear in Song 4:8: "travel" [תָּשׁוּרִי] from the top of Amana."[42]

The first half of 27:25 also harks back to 27:9b in which "all the ships of the sea" were said to be "in" Tyre's harbor. So here too the plurality of ships recedes, and Tyre herself is again the ship that is the subject of the קִינָה (27:2).

The second half of 27:25 is again fully in the world of *the* ship, Tyre. It sits low in the water, loaded down with merchandise from all over the world. The sense of בְּלֵב יַמִּים, "in the midst of the seas," is just offshore, poised to set sail. The Niphal verb וַתִּכְבְּדִי may involve a double entendre: not only "heavily loaded/weighted down" with cargo, but also "weighty" in the sense of "honored" and ready to impress the world with its grandeur and importance. Poetically the senses form a unity: both the ship's weight and its sense of self-importance will contribute to its sinking.

27:26 Much like the Santa Ana winds of coastal southern California, places like Tyre, where the mountains virtually touch the coast, are subject to incredibly strong winds that can suddenly whip down the slopes and arouse dangerously high waves just offshore. Ps 48:8 (ET 48:7) refers to the shipwreck of "Tarshish ships," conceivably a reminiscence of the dashing of Jehoshaphat's maritime hopes at Ezion-geber (1 Ki 22:49 [ET 22:48]).

---

[41] Zimmerli, *Ezekiel*, 2:51.

[42] See the discussion in Mitchell, *The Song of Songs*, 827–28.

27:27 הוֹנֵךְ וְעִזְבוֹנַ֫יִךְ מַעֲרָבֵ֫ךְ—These first words in the verse are drawn from 27:12–13. The rest of the verse, denoting the crew and others on board, comes from 27:8b–10.

וּבְכָל־קְהָלֵךְ—The *waw* is explicative, "namely, in fact." קָהָל is often translated "crew" but is possibly broader, including passengers.[43]

27:28 מִגְרָשׁוֹת:—The noun מִגְרָשׁ is of somewhat uncertain meaning here, and versions and commentaries vary widely. Usually elsewhere it refers to the common pasture land surrounding walled cities. Here it appears to mean the mainland opposite Tyre, including both villages and open countryside. Greenberg, following others, defends "*waves* will toss,"[44] but I find the reasoning unpersuasive and the result banal.

27:29 חֹבְלֵי הַיָּם אֶל־הָאָרֶץ יַעֲמֹדוּ:—The participle חֹבְלִים, "pilots," was used three times previously with a suffix (27:8, 27, 28). Here it is in construct with הַיָּם to highlight the contrast with הָאָרֶץ following: now "the pilots of the sea" are standing "on the land." This verse does not state whether their stance ashore was an action they took in fear that they, in their smaller ships, would suffer the same fate as the ship Tyre or whether it was some gesture of respect. The following verses indicate that fear was their predominant motive.

27:30 The two conventions in this verse of showing grief are mentioned elsewhere: covering the head with dust (Josh 7:6; Job 2:12) and tossing ashes on oneself (Jer 6:26). The precise picture presented in יִתְפַּלָּשׁוּ (פָּלַשׁ occurs only in the Hithpael) is uncertain, and the versions vary widely. "Wallow" is currently popular, but that seems excessive. Something like "sprinkle" (the LXX in Jer 6:26), "rub" (Targum), or "dust themselves with ashes" seems more likely.

27:31 Again parallels to these customs are numerous, not only in Israel, but in the entire Syro-Palestinian area. For the bald spot shaved on the head, see Is 22:12 and Ezek 7:18. וּבָכוּ ... בְּמַר־נֶפֶשׁ is, literally, "they will weep ... in bitterness of נֶפֶשׁ," that is, with their inmost being.

27:32 וְנָשְׂאוּ אֵלַיִךְ בְּנֵיהֶם קִינָה וְקוֹנְנוּ עָלָיִךְ—A rather awkward and prolix announcement in 27:32a signals the beginning of the קִינָה ("lament") within the lament (the entire chapter). The reader has been anticipating a קִינָה since the term was first introduced in 27:2.

The LXX and Syriac read בְּנֵיהֶם as בְּנֵיהֶם, "their sons," which is clearly out of place here. Most likely בְּנֵיהֶם is the noun נְהִי, "lament," with the preposition בְּ and third masculine plural suffix, "in their lament/dirge." The *he* has elided (as happens elsewhere), abbreviating נְהִי into נִי. The noun נְהִי is a semantic equivalent to קִינָה and to the following cognate verb וְקוֹנְנוּ (Polel of קִין), "to lament." I have tried to avoid repetition by rendering בְּנֵיהֶם as "in their grief," although I am aware that it is too psychologically reductive. In fact, "in their wailing" might not be too strong.

מִי כְצוֹר כְּדֻמָה בְּתוֹךְ הַיָּם:—The noun דֻמָה (with כְּ) is a hapax, so the precise meaning of this first sentence of the dirge is somewhat unclear. There are at least three

---

43   See van Dijk, *Ezekiel's Prophecy on Tyre*, 83–84.

44   Greenberg, *Ezekiel*, 2:561 (emphasis added).

homographic roots דמה in Biblical Hebrew. All have their champions, and possibilities offered by possible cognates in other Semitic languages add up to a staggering number of proposals.

One common דמה root is represented by the verb דָּמָה, "be like, resemble" (Ezek 31:2, 8, 18; 32:2) and the cognate noun דְּמוּת, "likeness" (sixteen times in Ezekiel; used with כְּ in Gen 1:26). If this is the root present here, the rhetorical question may literally ask, "Who is like Tyre, like (its) likeness in the midst of the sea?" This verse then would express a rhetorical question that affirms the incomparability of the true God. It can be compared to other verses that also express God's incomparability, including Ezek 31:2, 8, 18; 32:2, which use דָּמָה to say that Pharaoh likened himself to a god, but the one true God degrades Pharaoh. As it is, anyone biblically literate can hardly resist hearing an implicit analogy and confession of faith that the question can ultimately be answered with total positivity only of the true God. Compare "Michael," which means "Who is like God?" and "Micah/Micaiah," meaning "Who is like Yahweh?" The last verses of the book of Micah are virtually a meditation by the prophet on the meaning of his own name.

In antiquity, the Syriac (ܝܘ, ܐܝܟ) and Targum (לֵית דְּדָמֵי לַהּ) seem to have understood כְּדָמָה as meaning "be like."

Much of the picture of fallen Babylon in Revelation 18 is all but a paraphrase of Ezekiel 27, and Rev 18:18 asks, τίς ὁμοία τῇ πόλει τῇ μεγάλῃ, "Who is like the great city?"

Van Dijk interprets דְּמָה as the Hebrew equivalent of the Ugaritic *dmt* and the Akkadian *dimtu* and translates, "fortress," here in apposition: "... Tyre, a fortress."[45] The suggestion is attractive, but the connection with the alleged cognates is imprecise. Others relate the word to דָּמָה II, "cease, destroy," so it would mean "one who is destroyed," or to דָּמַם, "be silent" (Ezek 24:17), hence meaning "one silenced" (BDB, s.v. דָּמָה; similar are NIV, NASB). Still others emend to נִדְמָה, the Niphal masculine singular participle of one of the דָּמָה verbs, which could then mean either "like one destroyed" (ESV; similar is KJV) or "be likened to."

27:33 בְּצֵאת עִזְבוֹנַיִךְ מִיַּמִּים—Language about Tyre (27:32b) has shifted to a direct address to Tyre in the second person feminine. בְּצֵאת is the Qal infinitive construct of יָצָא with בְּ. יָצָא is not the verb one would normally expect for "unload" (usually עָלָה). The picture is almost one of the sea floating the goods (which had sprung out of the sea) to land, almost as part of the order of creation. But derivatives of יָצָא are also used of exports, e.g., in 1 Ki 10:28; 2 Chr 1:16.

בְּרֹב הוֹנַיִךְ וּמַעֲרָבַיִךְ—Tyre made much of her wealth by the profit she made in the exchange or barter of goods, plus other fees that would be imposed. This is the only place where the plural of הוֹן is used. Apparently both it and מַעֲרָבַיִךְ, "imports" (also plural only in this verse), have been assimilated to the plural form of עִזְבוֹנַיִךְ, "exports," earlier in this verse and in preceding verses. Apparently there was such a

---

45 Van Dijk, *Ezekiel's Prophecy on Tyre*, 85–86, including n. 87, citing Mitchell Dahood, "Accadian-Ugaritic *dmt* in Ezekiel 27, 32," *Biblica* 45 (1964): 83–84.

superabundance of merchandise moving in both directions that only plurals were adequate.

27:34 עֵת נִשְׁבֶּרֶת מִיַּמִּים—The lament moves from a reminiscence of Tyre's past glory to a statement of its present collapse. A few attempt to read the initial עֵת as an adverbial accusative ("at the time"), but virtual unanimity reads it as a defective spelling of עַתָּה. One would expect a finite verb instead of the Niphal participle נִשְׁבֶּרֶת, but there are other instances where a participle's subject pronoun is provided by the context (e.g., Jer 2:17). The reuse of the verb שָׁבַר obviously looks back to the beginning of the report of the tragedy in Ezek 27:26 (שְׁבָרֵךְ, Qal perfect with second feminine singular suffix). The *mem* with מִיַּמִּים should be taken as causal ("by"), as in Gen 9:11 (the waters of the flood).

מַעֲרָבֵךְ וְכָל־קְהָלֵךְ בְּתוֹכֵךְ נָפָלוּ—This is a virtually verbatim reprise of 27:27. Technically, the contents of the ship are described as "your imports" (מַעֲרָבֵךְ), but the word alternates with עִזְבוֹנַיִךְ, "your exports," in the manifest lists of 27:12–25, and so either or both can mean "trade, merchandise," often with no clear effort to distinguish them.

27:35 שָׂעֲרוּ שַׂעַר—The rare idiom that literally says "to hair (with) hair," that is, the denominative verb followed by its noun, is reproduced by "hair standing on end" or "bristling." This idiom appears only twice elsewhere (Jer 2:12, which lacks the cognate noun; Ezek 32:10), and as here, both times it is paired with the verb שָׁמֵם, "be appalled," and some other expression of horror. Greenberg equates שָׂעַר with סָעַר, "to storm," which he takes as meaning "be in turmoil" here,[46] but his argument strikes me as very weak.

רָעֲמוּ פָּנִים—The verb רָעַם normally means "to thunder." However, there may be a homonym that occurs only here and in 1 Sam 1:6 (so *HALOT*, s.v. רעם II). The Qal here would mean "be agitated, upset, confused," which is a good parallel to bristling hair. The Hiphil in 1 Sam 1:6 refers Hannah's co-wife taunting her about her inability to conceive (cf. 1 Sam 1:18, which states that she no longer had her downcast face after Eli gave her a sympathetic hearing).

27:36 שָׁרְקוּ—Whistling has different connotations at different times and places, including our own. We have no way of knowing what its range of applications may have been in Ezekiel's day. In the OT, this verb is used of derisive hissing (e.g., Jer 19:8) and of an expression of appallment when passing ruins (1 Ki 9:8), uses not unthinkable in our own culture. Here it is often taken as indicating mockery or even glee, but the context suggests that the intent was more likely to express intense grief or shock.

בַּלָּהוֹת—For this intensive plural noun, "horror," see the textual note on 26:21. It will be used in almost identical circumstances of the king of Tyre in 28:19. Contexts suggest a possible connection with the underworld.

וְאֵינֵךְ עַד־עוֹלָם—There is no signatory formula ("says the Lord Yahweh") or recognition formula ("then you/they will know that I am Yahweh") at the end of the chapter. Instead, this clause, literally, "and you are not, unto eternity," in principle re-

---

[46] Greenberg, *Ezekiel*, 2:563–64.

peats similar clauses with אֵין in 26:21 and 28:19. With nonexistence there is nothing more to be said. From the top of charts, Tyre has been dropped from the list.

Commentary

The basic outline of the chapter is simple. After the short preamble in 27:1–3a, we have a long poetic "lament" (קִינָה) in 27:3b–11, 25b–36, bisected by a basically prose catalog of the types of goods carried by Tyrian ships (27:12–25a). Outlines offered in other commentaries often vary by a verse or two from that given above, because the transitions are not always clear-cut. One may also note a lament within the lament. While the entire chapter is a lament, in 27:32b–36, a second lament appears, emanating from the lips of the doomed sailors. In fact, it is, strictly speaking, closer to the original use of a "lament" (קִינָה), uttered at the death of an individual, but the lament genre was widely adapted for the fall of also cities and nations. Especially Zimmerli[47] expends great effort in attempting to reconstruct the presumed original 3:2 rhythm of much of the oracle, but this involves such wholesale emendation and reconstruction of the MT that the approach is today largely considered abortive.[48]

The chapter opens without indication of date or setting, nor is any to be detected within the body of the chapter. There is no indication of Tyrian submission to Babylon nor of Yahweh's later amendment to this prophecy in 29:17–21. Hence, a plausible hypothesis is that it is a slightly later expansion of the "lament" (קִינָה) in 26:17–18, which is dated to the eleventh year of Jehoiachin's exile (26:1), that is, perhaps spring 586, not long before Jerusalem's fall in summer 586 (see the textual note on 26:1). There are other indications of some close connections with the previous chapter. There is a similarity between the lament at the end of this chapter and the brief one in 26:17–18. In addition, 27:2 begins with Yahweh addressing Ezekiel by וְאַתָּה, "(and) you," which elsewhere in Ezekiel always signals a subdivision within a larger oracle.[a]

The contents of the chapter itself dictate that this part of the commentary be very brief. After the word-event formula in 27:1, "the Word of Yahweh came to me,"[49] and the citation formula in 27:3b, "thus says the Lord Yahweh,"[50] the divine name is not heard again.

It may well have been that some in Judah secretly admired the way in which Tyre, in her virtually impregnable position, could all but laugh off Babylonian ambitions to dominate her.

(a) E.g., Ezek 2:6, 8; 3:19, 21, 25; 4:1; 5:1; 19:1

---

[47] Zimmerli, *Ezekiel*, discusses Ezekiel 27 on 2:41–71.

[48] Older scholars assumed that a "lament" (קִינָה) always should have a regular meter, but that assumption is not supported by the biblical text. See "Introduction to Ezekiel 19" and the textual note on 26:17–18.

[49] For this formula, see page 8 in the introduction and the textual note on 3:16.

[50] For this formula, see pages 8–9 in the introduction and the fourth textual note and the commentary on 2:4.

But, obviously, we misread if we think the chapter is but a "secular" interlude in the midst of heavily theological material. Its very position, sandwiched between chapters 26 and 28, virtually guarantees that it is not. In chapter 26, all the sea chiefs loudly lament Tyre's fall, but the dimensions of the catastrophe are not revealed. In this chapter, the background of that nearly universal mourning is detailed. And in chapter 28, the justification for Tyre's fall is spelled out at length: it is her hubris at her unrivalled skill and success. After reaching chapter 27, the basis of her hubris, by any human standard, is obvious. But all her expertise and success has not exempted her from divine judgment, which she shall receive on "the day of Yahweh" (the phrase is used explicitly for the day of Egypt's judgment in 30:3). Like the "Babylon" of the NT Apocalypse (see Revelation 17–19), which was also "seated upon many waters" (Rev 17:1), Tyre too must meet her Judge because she has challenged and denied the one true God, who is the Lord of history.[51]

---

[51] For the interpretation of Babylon the harlot, riding upon the beast, see Brighton, *Revelation*, 434–55.

Tyre's King Is Expelled from Eden

Translation

28 [1]The Word of Yahweh came to me: [2]"Son of man, say to the prince of Tyre, 'Thus says the Lord Yahweh: Because you became arrogant and said, "I am a god, and I occupy a divine throne in the heart of the seas," but you are a mere man and not a god, and you regard your wisdom as divine wisdom— [3]you are indeed wiser than Daniel; no mystery baffles you; [4]by your wisdom and your shrewdness you have gained wealth for yourself and put gold and silver in your treasuries; [5]by your great wisdom in trade you increased your wealth, but you became conceited because of your wealth— [6]therefore, thus says the Lord Yahweh: Because you regard your wisdom as divine wisdom, [7]therefore, I am about to bring against you barbarians, the most ruthless of nations. They will unsheathe their swords against the beauty of your wisdom and desecrate your radiance. [8]To the pit they will cast you down, and you will die a violent death in the heart of the seas. [9]Will you still say, "I am a god" in the face of your killer? [It will be clear that] you are merely a man and no god [when you are] in the hands of those who slay you. [10]You will die the death of the uncircumcised by the hand of barbarians, for I have spoken, says the Lord Yahweh.' "

[11]The Word of Yahweh came to me: [12]"Son of man, raise a lament over the king of Tyre, and say to him, 'Thus says the Lord Yahweh: You were a guarantor of symmetry, full of wisdom, and perfect in beauty. [13]You were in Eden, the garden of God. Every precious stone was your covering: carnelian, topaz, and emerald, chrysolite, onyx, and jasper, lapis lazuli, turquoise, and beryl; your tambourines and your settings were worked in gold. They were prepared on the day you were created. [14]You were a cherub, the anointed guardian. I appointed you. You were on the holy mountain of God, and you walked about amidst fiery stones. [15]Your conduct was blameless from the day you were created until iniquity was found in you. [16]In your widespread trade, you were thoroughly filled with illicit profit, and you sinned. Since you became defiled, I banished you from the mountain of God and expelled you, O guardian cherub, from amidst the fiery stones. [17]You became arrogant because of your beauty, and you corrupted your wisdom together with your splendor. So I hurled you into the netherworld and set you in front of kings to gloat over you. [18]By your many sins in your unscrupulous trade, you defiled your entire sanctuary. So I made fire break out from within you, and it devoured you. I reduced you to ashes on the ground in the sight of all who were watching. [19]All your friends among the peoples are appalled at you. You have become a horror and will be no more forever.' "

[20]The Word of Yahweh came to me: [21]"Son of man, set your face toward Sidon, and prophesy against it, [22]and say, 'Thus says the Lord Yahweh: I am

against you, Sidon. I will display my glory in your midst, and they will know that I am Yahweh when I inflict on it punishments and display my holiness in it. ²³I will release the plague in it, blood in its streets, and the slain will fall in its midst when the sword comes against it from all sides. Then they will know that I am Yahweh.'"

²⁴"Never again will the house of Israel have all around them those who deride them, like prickling briars or painful thorns. Then they will know that I am the Lord Yahweh."

²⁵Thus says the Lord Yahweh: "When I gather the house of Israel from the peoples where they have been scattered, I will display my holiness through them in the sight of the nations. Then they will live on their own land, which I gave to my servant Jacob. ²⁶They will live on it in security, build houses, and plant vineyards. They will live on it in security when I inflict punishments upon all those around them who deride them. Then they will know that I am Yahweh, their God."

Textual Notes

28:1–26 See the map "The Ancient Near East."

28:2 לִנְגִיד צֹר—Considerable discussion has turned on why the ruler of Tyre here is styled a נָגִיד. Although נָגִיד is common elsewhere in the OT, this is its only occurrence in Ezekiel. In 28:12, Tyre's ruler is called מֶלֶךְ (the same synonymity of both terms occurs in Ps 76:13 [ET 76:12]). Some passages use נָשִׂיא in a sense that is comparable to that here of נָגִיד, which perhaps was chosen only for the sake of literary variation. But if we are to look for further explanation, a clue may be found in the fact that while מֶלֶךְ can be used of either a divine or human "king," נָגִיד is used only of humans. In earlier OT texts, it is used especially of charismatic or dynastic rulers in Israel (e.g., 1 Sam 9:16; 10:1; 13:14; 2 Sam 7:8), and possibly its formation bears this out. Its *qatil* formation (resembling an Aramaic passive participle) may suggest someone "chosen" or "designated" by God, a thought developed more in Ezek 28:12–14, and, if so, a stance spurned by the ruler of Tyre. We have no way of knowing what the preferred term for Tyre's king was at the time in Tyre itself. We do know his name, Ithobaal II, but little more about him. In the absence of any certain alternative, I have retained the traditional "prince."

יַעַן, "because," governs the whole accusation, that is, everything through the end of 28:1–5. Then לָכֵן, "therefore," in 28:6 introduces the punishment. Therefore 28:1–5 is a protasis of a single large sentence, whose apodosis does not come until 28:6–7.

In 28:2, three parallel statements after יַעַן begin the accusation: "because you became … and said … you regard …" Between the second and third is an interrupting negated statement: "but you are a mere man and no god." Ezek 28:3–5 is God's concession that there is some basis for the prince's pride, misapplied though it is.

גָּבַה לִבְּךָ—This is the first of the three parallel statements. Like the oracle against Ammon in chapter 25, Yahweh addresses Tyre's ruler (and through him the entire principality) directly. The basic charge is, literally, "your heart is high." The common Hebrew word for "heart," לֵב, is used seven times in this chapter, and the related word

לֵבָב is used twice. לֵב has no exact English equivalent. The best translation must be determined by context, but usually the mind, will, emotions, and attitudes are all involved in one way or another. Its predicate, גָּבַהּ, "to be high," obviously has some metaphorical sense: "be haughty, arrogant, conceited," or the like. I have construed it ingressively ("*became* arrogant") because the condition tends to be an acquired trait, unless controlled or countermanded. We have already heard the theme that God exalts the humble but humiliates the proud in 17:22–24; 19:11–14; and 21:31 (ET 21:26; this theme is repeated in various ways throughout Scripture), and we might guess that it is the essence of what follows.

The two words here will be phrased only slightly differently in 28:5 (וַיִּגְבַּהּ לְבָבֶךָ), creating an obvious inclusio around the accusation (28:2–5). The identical wording here will begin 28:17, aiding in the transition to the judgment theme there.

וַתֹּאמֶר אֵל אָנִי מוֹשַׁב אֱלֹהִים יָשַׁבְתִּי בְּלֵב יַמִּים—This is the second of the three parallel statements. This single quote of what the prince says includes two related aspects of the prince's hubris.

His first claim, אֵל אָנִי, "I am a god," really says it all. In Ezekiel only here and in 28:9 is אֵל used in the sense of a rival deity besides Yahweh (the word occurs once in reference to Yahweh, in 10:5). אֵל could be a proper noun, that is, El, the head of the Canaanite pantheon. The hypothesis was once seriously entertained that that was the prince's specific claim here,[1] but that notion has now been almost universally abandoned. The following words are its best refutation. The very next clause uses the usual Hebrew generic term for "God" or "gods," אֱלֹהִים, and that is also the word used when the bald claim is repeated in 28:9. Possibly the predicate-subject word order (אֵל אָנִי) is to be heard as a deliberate contrast to the reverse order in Yahweh's repeated self-introduction throughout the book, אֲנִי יְהוָה. The shorter form אֵל is probably also intended to match the terse rebuttal that follows (see the next textual note). Both Num 23:19 and Hos 11:9 use אֵל to refer to the one true "God" when they state that he "is not a man" (לֹא אִישׁ). Similar to the following rebuttal of Tyre's prince is the statement in Is 31:3 that Egypt is "man [אָדָם] and not God [אֵל]."

His second claim in this quote is that he possesses divine authority by virtue of his throne. The verb יָשַׁב may mean "sit (down), be seated" (as well as "live, dwell"). The cognate accusative noun here, מוֹשָׁב, can mean "seat" (BDB, 1; *HALOT*, 1) or "throne" (as well as "residence"). If one were to think of Canaanite mythology, the boast could be associated with the Ugaritic tradition that each god had his abode, especially El, head of the pantheon, whose residence is described as "at the source(s) of the rivers, in the midst of the springs/sources of the two oceans."[2] But having ruled out that analogy (see above), we must translate "throne." Hebrew has a separate word for "throne," כִּסֵּא, but מוֹשָׁב is obviously chosen here for the sake of assonance with

---

[1] Pope, *El in the Ugaritic Texts*, 98–102, conjectured that underlying this passage was a Ugaritic myth of the fall of El, the head of the Canaanite pantheon.

[2] Andrée Herdner, ed., *Corpus des tablettes en cunéiformes alphabétiques découvertes à Ras Shamra-Ugarit de 1929 à 1939* (Paris: Geuthner, 1963), 4.4.21–22; 6.1.33–34; 17.6.47–48.

the verb יָשַׁבְתִּי. Here, then, בְּלֵב יַמִּים, "in the heart of the seas," must be a reference to Tyre's insular situation,[3] its remoteness strengthening the picture of godlikeness beyond human reach.

It may not be coincidental too that יָשַׁב is the preferred verb in the OT for Yahweh "sitting" on his heavenly throne, in contrast to שָׁכַן, the usual verb for his incarnational "dwelling" in the tabernacle and temple, above the ark of the covenant (although the two horizons often merge). Here too Yahweh rendered his judicial decisions (שְׁפָטִים, e.g., 28:22) determining the course of human history, with special attention to his worshipers' praise and petitions.

וְאַתָּה אָדָם וְלֹא־אֵל—Yahweh's direct contradiction of the king's claims is expressed by the parataxis of idiomatic Hebrew. English idiom demands that the conjunction on וְאַתָּה be rendered disjunctively: "*but* you are a man and not a god." Many commentators point to Is 31:3 (directed against Egypt) as the inspiration for the expression here, though it was Yahweh who inspired both prophets.

וַתִּתֵּן לִבְּךָ כְּלֵב אֱלֹהִים:—This is the third of the three parallel statements. The third aspect of Tyre's arrogance is not formulated as the king's boast (spoken in first person), but as a charge by the prophet (second person). A literal translation would be "You set/regard your heart as a god's heart." But, as the next verse shows, לֵב is here plainly used in the sense of "mind" or "will," and specifically as the seat of wisdom, hence my periphrastic translation. לֵב (or לְבָב) is used in the sense of or in connection with "wisdom" frequently in the OT, for example, Ex 31:6; 1 Ki 5:9 (ET 4:29); Prov 23:15; Job 12:3.

28:3 הִנֵּה חָכָם אַתָּה מִדָּנִאֵל—The LXX and Syriac take both this clause and the second one in the verse as questions. But of modern commentators and translators, as far as I know, only NIV does so. Van Dijk mentions it as a possibility, appealing to the Ugaritic equivalent of הֲלֹא in its sense of "behold," which, he contends, corresponds to הִנֵּה.[4] But that linguistic explanation is quite a stretch, and nothing in 28:4–5 indicates that God is questioning the fact of the king's wisdom.

We confront "Daniel" again, as in 14:14, 20; see the commentary there. Those verses stress his righteousness, while this one his wisdom (which agrees with חָכְמָה, "wisdom," in Dan 1:4, 17, 20; 2:23; 5:11, 14). Here too the Kethib, מִדָּנִאֵל, has the defective orthography, while the Qere, מִדָּנִיֵאל, has the full spelling of Daniel, as it is always written in the biblical book by that name, and in other ancient Semitic languages.

כָּל־סָתוּם לֹא עֲמָמוּךָ:—This rest of the verse uses relatively rare words. סָתוּם ("mystery") is the Qal passive participle of סָתַם, "to shut, conceal, keep secret." The verb עָמַם, "to darken, dim," is used only two other times. Ezekiel uses it in 31:8 of cedars that did not "overshadow, shade" the pharaoh pictured as a cedar "in the garden of God/Eden," that is, a setting parallel to the lament beginning in 28:12. In Lam 4:1, the Hophal is used to describe gold as "darkened, tarnished," alluding to the crown

---

[3]   See the commentary on 26:1.

[4]   Van Dijk, *Ezekiel's Prophecy on Tyre*, 99.

of Judah's king now exiled. With Greenberg and Block, I have found "baffles" to be an attractive rendition.[5]

Since עֲמָמוּךָ is third common plural (Qal perfect with second masculine singular suffix), כָּל־סָתוּם could be an adverbial accusative: "with any mystery they could not baffle you." Alternatively, כָּל־סָתוּם could be a collective: "all mysteries did not baffle you." But most commentators and translations take the impersonal plural verb as a passive and its suffix as an indirect object: "no mystery is hidden for/from you." For verbal suffixes with a datival force, see Joüon, § 125 ba.

28:4 בְּחָכְמָתְךָ וּבִתְבוּנָתְךָ—The two nouns חָכְמָה and תְּבוּנָה, "wisdom" and "understanding," are a conventional pair. See, for example, Ex 36:1, where they are endowments of the builders of the tabernacle. Sometimes דַּעַת, "knowledge," is added. Here the application is obviously to business sense and the ability to prosper at business. In the context, "skill" might better translate חָכְמָה, but "wisdom" is retained to maintain continuity with the surrounding context, for example, חָכָם, "wise," in 28:3.

עָשִׂיתָ ... וַתַּעַשׂ—Twice עָשָׂה is used idiomatically. BDB (Qal, II 7) calls attention to the comparable English idiom "make money."

חָיִל—In 28:4 and twice in 28:5 (חֵילֶךָ ... בְּחֵילֶךָ), the noun חַיִל is not merely "wealth," although the accent is plainly there, but the power and prestige that usually accompany it.

28:5 This verse slightly expands but virtually repeats the previous verse (inevitably triggering critics to doubt its genuineness). It adds רֹב, "greatness," in an idiomatic Hebrew construct chain, בְּרֹב חָכְמָתְךָ, "in the greatness of your wisdom." In such construct chains, one element is often best rendered adjectivally ("great wisdom").

בִּרְכֻלָּתְךָ—Here רְכֻלָּה does not mean "merchandise," as it meant in 26:12, but the "trade" of merchandise.

וַיִּגְבַּהּ לְבָבְךָ בְּחֵילֶךָ:—The verse ends with a clause similar to גָּבַהּ לִבְּךָ, which began the indictment in 28:2, thus making a perfect frame or inclusion for the accusation part of the oracle.

28:6 לָכֵן—"Therefore" finally begins the apodosis expected ever since the יַעַן ("because") clause in 28:2. But due to the expansion of the accusation in 28:3–5, the initial יַעַן has almost been forgotten, and so 28:6b (יַעַן תִּתְּךָ אֶת־לְבָבְךָ כְּלֵב אֱלֹהִים) reiterates the last clause of 28:2, using the Qal infinitive construct of נָתַן with second feminine singular suffix (תִּתְּךָ) instead of the second masculine singular Qal imperfect with *waw* consecutive (וַתִּתֵּן) used in 28:2 and using לְבָב in place of the first occurrence of לֵב in 28:2.

28:7 זָרִים—The participle זָר (from זוּר) is often translated "stranger, foreigner," which, while not incorrect, may be too weak. The word implies someone or something completely strange. Van Dijk's suggestion for the plural, "barbarians,"[6] seems appropriate, especially with the following construct phrase, עָרִיצֵי גּוֹיִם, which serves as a superlative, "the most ruthless of nations." The reference is to the Babylonian army. The Babylonians have already been described similarly in 7:21–22. Hab 1:6–10

---

5 Greenberg, *Ezekiel*, 2:574; Block, *Ezekiel*, 2:91.

6 Van Dijk, *Ezekiel's Prophecy on Tyre*, 109–10.

describes them in similar language (presuming they are the subject; see commentaries on Habakkuk).

בְּיִ וְחָכְמָתֶךָ—"The beauty of your wisdom" is a strange-sounding expression. Apparently we must think of "beauty" as the *result* of his wisdom: the magnificence of his commercial savvy as evidenced in the buildings, fortifications, and maritime fleet he had constructed, not to speak of his bulging treasury (cf. 28:4–5). In 27:3 the city had used the same noun (יְפִי, in construct here) to boast that it was a "perfect beauty" (see the last textual note on 27:3). In 28:12 "beauty" and "wisdom" will be used synonymously.

וְחִלְּלוּ יִפְעָתֶךָ:—The final noun in the verse, יִפְעָה (with second masculine singular suffix), makes an attractive assonantal connection with the preceding noun יְפִי, but etymologically the words are unrelated. In the OT יִפְעָה appears only here and in 28:17. It may be Ezekiel's own coinage. It is manifestly derived from the verb יָפַע, used especially of theophanic manifestations, meaning "shine forth," in, for example, Deut 33:2; Pss 50:2; 80:2 (ET 80:1). That here it is the object of the Piel verb חִלֵּל, "to profane, desecrate," indicates the religious quality inherent in it. It is probably the Hebrew equivalent of a common Akkadian epithet *melamma*, an aura or luminosity that supposedly surrounded deities and even royalty, indicating their sanctity or divinity. The halo common in Christian art may be an adaptation of it. That the Babylonians will desecrate it is a way of saying that the "prince" (28:2) who claims divinity is being demoted to what he really is: only another mortal.

28:8 לְשַׁחַת יוֹרִדוּךָ—"Pit" (שַׁחַת) is in emphatic position at the beginning of the sentence. "Pit" is a common surrogate for "Sheol" or "hell." The most common Hebrew word for "pit" in that sense is בּוֹר. In other books, שַׁחַת is often used in the same sense (e.g., Is 38:17; Jonah 2:7 [ET 2:6]; Ps 16:10; Job 33:18), but in Ezekiel שַׁחַת is used in only one other passage: in 19:4, 8 it means "trap." יוֹרִדוּךָ is the Hiphil (third masculine plural imperfect with second masculine singular suffix) of יָרַד, "to bring down," whose Qal participle was used of those who had "descended" to the pit (בּוֹר) in Ezek 26:20; 31:14, 16; 32:18, 24, 25, 29–30.

וָמַתָּה מְמוֹתֵי חָלָל—Literally, this is "and you will die the death of one slain," that is, not a natural death, but of one murdered or executed. For חָלָל, see the third textual note on 6:4. NIV's paraphrase, "and you will die a violent death," seemed attractive to me. The construction with וָמַתָּה, the Qal (second masculine singular perfect with *waw* consecutive) of מוּת, "to die," and the cognate accusative noun מְמוֹת (plural in construct), "death," occurs elsewhere only in Jer 16:4. The more common noun for "death" is מָוֶת. The use of the plural of מְמוֹת here, and the plural of מָוֶת at the beginning of 28:10, is explained by some as a species of hyperbole, suggesting a death so painful as to be equivalent to dying many times. Others explain it as an intensive plural, or perhaps implying a long, slow death. Is 53:9 has a parallel use of the plural of מָוֶת.[7]

בְּלֵב יַמִּים:—Mention of "the heart of the seas" fit chapter 27 (27:4, 25–27), but seems strange here. Apparently the idea is to contrast Tyre's island position of false

---

[7] See Mitchell, *Our Suffering Savior*, 115–16.

security with the world of the dead for which the king is headed. Jonah used an almost identical phrase (בִּלְבַב יַמִּים, 2:4 [ET 2:3]) when he was in "the belly of Sheol" (2:3 [ET 2:2]).[8] Greenberg remarks that if "in the heart of the seas" was originally figurative psalm language for life-threatening troubles, as in Jonah 2:4 (ET 2:3), its application to the location of Tyre would be noteworthy.[9]

28:9 הֹרְגֶךָ—This Qal participle (with second masculine singular suffix) is singular ("your killer"), but many other Hebrew manuscripts have the plural הֹרְגֶיךָ, which is supported by the ancient versions. I have retained the singular, but the difference is inconsequential. The parallel Piel participle מְחַלְלֶיךָ, "those who slay you," at the end of the verse is plural, but in Hebrew poetic parallelism, the inconsistency in number would not matter. Elsewhere, the Piel of חָלַל means to "desecrate" (as in 28:7), which is possible here, but more likely is "pierce, kill, slay," as most of the ancient versions translate, parallel to the preceding הָרַג. But for that meaning, one would expect a Poel form, מְחֹלְלֶיךָ. Greenberg arrives at the same meaning by construing מְחַלְלֶיךָ as a denominative from the adjective and noun חָלָל, "slain," as in 28:8.[10] The Piel form may be some idiosyncrasy of Ezekiel's own idiom, because in 32:26 we will meet a Pual instead of an expected Poal. Whatever the rationale, English translations (even KJV) have "slay" (or, in RSV and NRSV, "wound").

28:10 מוֹתֵי—Only here in the OT is the plural of מָוֶת used in construct. See the second textual note on 28:8.

28:12 שָׂא קִינָה—The identical imperative (of נָשָׂא) and the noun קִינָה, "lament, dirge," were in 19:1 and 27:2 and will be in 32:2. For קִינָה and its usual genre, see "Introduction to Ezekiel 19" and the textual note on 26:17–18. However, here it must be understood as being used very loosely. Not only does "lament" not correspond to the contents of 28:12b–19 (see the commentary), but formally it is not really descriptive either, since the passage does not exhibit any signs of a 3:2 meter. Even Zimmerli, who sometimes makes almost desperate attempts to reconstruct the putatively original meter (e.g., in chapters 19 and 27), here concedes that it can be reconstructed here only with difficulty, especially in the first part of the piece.[11] In fact, it is so irregular in form that often it is hard to know whether to classify it as prose or poetry. Interestingly, many modern English translations print it in poetic form, while *BHS* formats it as prose!

Instead of נָגִיד as in 28:2, the head of the city is addressed as מֶלֶךְ, a term usually used in Ezekiel for an earthly "king" (but of the eschatological "King," the new David, in 37:22, 24) and thus anticipating the condemnation of this king's arrogation of divine status to himself, which will ultimately dominate this part of the chapter as much as it did the first part of the chapter. Although the title מֶלֶךְ has not yet been docu-

---

[8] See the excursus "Sheol" in Lessing, *Jonah*, 249–55.

[9] Greenberg, *Ezekiel*, 2:575.

[10] Greenberg, *Ezekiel*, 2:575.

[11] Zimmerli, *Ezekiel*, 2:87–89; see 1:391–93 for Zimmerli's analysis of chapter 19 and 2:53–56 on chapter 27.

mented in Tyre, it was known in Byblos to the north centuries earlier, and, interestingly, the name of the patron deity of Tyre, Melkart, translates as "king of the city."

וְאָמַרְתָּ לּוֹ—This clause has two unusual features related to each other. First, since the verb is a second masculine singular perfect with *waw* consecutive, the accent normally would shift to the final syllable. Instead, it remains on the penultimate syllable (-מַ-) to prevent two accented syllables in a row (-לֹּ תָּ-). See GKC, § 29 e. Second, the accented *lamed* has a conjunctive *daghesh forte* that links לּוֹ to the preceding verb. This conjunctive *daghesh* is often used when the accent on the preceding verb has retracted from its expected position, as here. See GKC, § 20 f. These phonetic changes do not alter the meaning (literally, "and you will say to him"), but reflect the traditional pronunciation of the text in reading or chanting.

אַתָּה חוֹתֵם תָּכְנִית—Three summary statements are made about the initial state of the king before his unique status "went to his head." This first one is obscure and much debated. The problems are both textual and semantic.

The Masoretes pointed חוֹתֵם as a Qal participle, resulting in "you [אַתָּה] are a sealer, one who seals." The ancient versions all seem to have read their unpointed consonants as the noun חוֹתָם in construct (חוֹתַם), "you are a seal of," and virtually all modern translations (including NKJV) follow suit or use a synonym, "signet" (RSV) or "model" (so NIV freely). The chief objection to this is that the following parallel phrase, "full of wisdom" only makes sense in reference to a person ("one who seals"), not an inanimate object ("a seal"). "Full of wisdom" is missing entirely in the LXX, perhaps because the translators could not understand it in this context.[12] Block suggests that in the second phrase, the prophet's attention momentarily shifted from the signet to the person it represents.[13] However, in the third epithet ("perfect in beauty"), Ezekiel again refers to the person. Therefore if the interpreter assumes that the first phrase alone refers to an object, the result is a rambling pattern of speaking; this is not unthinkable of Ezekiel, especially in this chapter, but difficult and seemingly forced.

The ancient versions considered the third word (תָּכְנִית) to be the *nomen rectum* of the construct phrase, but seem to have read it as תַּבְנִית and so rendered the phrase as "you are a seal of likeness." Many modern translations are inconsistent in that they follow the versions for the second word but not for this third word. The noun תָּכְנִית occurs in the OT only here and in 43:10, which refers to the perfect proportions of the eschatological temple. Modern versions usually translate it "perfection" here, and with the previous emendation, חוֹתַם, the clause comes out as something like "you were the signet of perfection" (ESV), apparently meaning a perfectly wrought signet ring. But that translation is free, at best. The feminine noun תָּכְנִית is an apparent derivative of the verb תָּכַן, "weigh, measure, regulate," and so could mean "measurement, proportion" (BDB; for other possibilities see *HALOT*). If its sense is the same here as in 43:10, its translation should be something like "proportionality, symme-

---

[12] Predictably Zimmerli, *Ezekiel*, 2:82, dismisses the phrase as a secondary insertion.
[13] Block, *Ezekiel*, 2:105.

try." Aquila and Theodotion apparently derived the noun from the verb כּוּן, "prepare," resulting in "seal of preparation," that is, a seal so perfect that one prepared other seals in imitation of it. KJV rendered the clause as "thou sealest up the sum," but that needs translation in itself!

As far as I am aware, no modern scholar has pursued the possibilities in the versions' apparent reading of תַּבְנִית (from the verb בָּנָה). Ezekiel uses תַּבְנִית only in a neutral sense of a "figure, image" (8:3, 10; 10:8). The LXX, Syriac, and Vulgate translations mean "seal [impression] of likeness." Often "likeness" is expressed in Biblical Hebrew by דְּמוּת. The triune God declared that he would make man "according our likeness" (כִּדְמוּתֵנוּ, Gen 1:26); thus God made Adam "in the likeness of God" (בִּדְמוּת אֱלֹהִים, Gen 5:1), and Adam fathered his son "in his likeness" (בִּדְמוּתוֹ, Gen 5:3). Thus Adam was both made in God's likeness, and like a seal, he stamped it on following generations.

But תַּבְנִית can have theological and specifically cultic connotations of which Ezekiel would surely have been aware. In Ex 25:9, 40, it is used of the heavenly "archetype" or "model" according to which Moses is to build the tabernacle and all its appurtenances. The word is repeated of the temple in 1 Chronicles 28. The "archetype" of the tabernacle is referred to several times in the NT using τύπος, "type" (Acts 7:44; Heb 8:5), as the LXX had translated the word in Ex 25:40. In the context of Ezekiel 28, it would describe the one who "sealed" or maintained everything in "the garden of God" (28:13) exactly as God had created it, the "garden" being an antitype of heaven itself—an instance of vertical typology, according to which that on earth corresponds to the model in heaven.

Attractive as that option is, I have retained the MT's word. Neither am I inclined to revocalize the participle חוֹתֵם as a noun, mostly because the following phrase, "full of wisdom," seems to require a personal subject here—the participle. However, the designation of humans as a "seal, signet" is certainly possible (see Jer 22:24 and Hag 2:23 of Jehoiachin and Zerubbabel, respectively),[14] but retaining the MT's "sealer" requires no emendation, not even a minor vocalic one.

Hence, I have given the interpretative translation "guarantor of symmetry," which is both faithful to the MT and compatible with the rest of the verse. A veritable myriad of emendations and variant interpretations have been offered by others, but there is no point in trying to catalog them all. I shall mention only one of the more farfetched, predictably from van Dijk. Taking the final *mem* of חוֹתֵם as enclitic, he repoints the remaining consonants as חַוָּה, from חַוָּה, which in the Hebrew Bible is the personal name "Eve," but which in Phoenician and Aramaic means "snake, serpent." Of course, a snake plays a prominent role in Genesis 3, but in this context, van Dijk compares it to the two divine beings, the *karibu* (cherub) and the *lahmu* who guarded royal dwellings in the mythology and architecture of Mesopotamia. The two beings he compares to the "cherubim" and "flaming sword" that were posted to prevent reen-

---

[14] See also the Shulammite's petition that Solomon place her as a חוֹתָם, "seal, signet," upon his heart (Song 8:6).

try into the garden of Eden after the fall (Gen 3:24). Thus he translates the phrase as "Serpent of perfection."[15] But I judge that no refutation is needed.

מָלֵא חָכְמָה וּכְלִיל יֹפִי:—The second ("full of wisdom") and third ("perfect in beauty") summary statements about the king use vocabulary familiar from the oracle in chapter 27. See the commentary.

28:13 The first major hurdle in this verse is to determine the correct meaning of מְסֻכָתֶךָ, the hapax noun מְסֻכָה with second masculine singular suffix. The possible (see the commentary) connection of the following list of stones with that of the Israelite high priest's breastpiece as well as the final part of the verse that speaks of appointments of some sort on the person of the king seem to favor the traditional translation of the word as "your covering," so the LXX, Vulgate, and Targum in antiquity, and, as far as I know, all English translations as well as (NIV's "adorned you" conveys the same meaning). Probably this implies that מְסֻכָה is derived from סָכַךְ, "to cover" (so BDB), even though we would expect the double consonant כ to be evident in the noun derivative by a *daghesh forte*, that is, מְסֻכָּה. In Micah 7:4, the similar word מְסוּכָה is used in the sense of "hedge, fence," without doubling of the כ because it is a different word derived from the verb סוּךְ II, "to hedge, fence in" (so BDB). A different spelling of מְסוּכָה, "hedge, fence" is מְשֻׂכָה in Prov 15:19, derived from שׂוּךְ, "to hedge, fence in," a by-form of סוּךְ II. Another noun for "hedge, fence" is מְשׂוּכָה in Is 5:5, with שׂ and doubled *kaph* (כ), which suggests that it is derived from a verb שָׂכַךְ, although that verb (שׂכךְ III) is not attested in the OT.

The existence of those nouns for "hedge, fence" (מְשֻׂכָה, מְסוּכָה, and מְשׂוּכָה) prompts the question whether or not that is the meaning of the word used here by Yahweh. Ancient Near Eastern temples were not merely buildings, but buildings enclosed by a wall, either of stones or thick shrubs. One may compare the picture in Is 54:11–12, where the eschatological Jerusalem will have walls of precious stones. In Rev 21:19–20 precious stones, reminiscent of those in the high priest's breastpiece (Ex 28:15–21), are the foundations for the wall around the new Jerusalem (cf. Song 5:14). Certainly it is possible that מְסֻכָתֶךָ could mean "your wall," especially in the light of the difficulties at the end of Ezek 28:13, but I have opted to retain the traditional translation, "your covering."

אֹדֶם פִּטְדָה וְיָהֲלֹם תַּרְשִׁישׁ שֹׁהַם וְיָשְׁפֵה סַפִּיר נֹפֶךְ וּבָרְקַת—There is little agreement on the English equivalents of the various stones. The most unanimity is about יָשְׁפֵה and סַפִּיר, mostly because the Hebrew words have equivalent English transliterations. Thus יָשְׁפֵה is "jasper." English also reflects סַפִּיר by "sapphire," as most translations dutifully reproduce it. However, the identity of those vocables is misleading. Our "sapphire" was scarcely known in antiquity, and סַפִּיר should be rendered "lapis lazuli," a stone well known and highly prized by the ancients.

One major factor determining translation is just how Ezekiel envisioned the stones being used at Tyre. This partly depends on one's translation of the rest of the verse. Some think that Ezekiel is mixing metaphors here and not only describing the

---

[15] Van Dijk, *Ezekiel's Prophecy on Tyre*, 114–16.

king himself as an engraved seal (assuming a revocalization of the MT's חוֹתֵם to חוֹתָם in 28:12; see above) but thinking of the stones on his "covering" as worked. If so, the stones would have to have been soft enough to be engraved. For most of the stones, I have rather arbitrarily followed NIV with two exceptions: I have rendered סַפִּיר by "lapis lazuli" (not "sapphire") and for אֹדֶם I have replaced NIV's "ruby" with "carnelian," because there is no evidence that rubies were known as early as Ezekiel's time, and it is a rather hard stone.

Block has a convenient table comparing many modern English translations (but not KJV, NKJV, or RSV).[16] If further discussion is desired, the reader can find it in some major commentaries and in biblical reference works. But since neither Ezekiel nor other biblical writers seem to attach any theological significance to specific stones as such, it is a question of relatively marginal exegetical significance.

וְזָהָב מְלֶאכֶת תֻּפֶּיךָ וּנְקָבֶיךָ בָּךְ—Obscurity reigns here. Commentators and translators, ancient and modern, make widely varying guesses, and I cannot claim to be an exception. The Masoretic punctuation (*athnach*) indicates that וְזָהָב ("and gold") concludes the preceding list of precious stones, and many ancient versions reflect that syntax, but it seems highly unlikely. Although gold was used copiously in the construction of the tabernacle and temple, its inclusion in a list of gems would be unparalleled. Most commentators and modern translators are probably correct in understanding it as a kind of accusative of material (cf. Waltke-O'Connor, § 10.2.3c) referring to the following words.

Usually the noun מְלָאכָה means "business, occupation, craft," but can readily be understood as a reference to special craftsmanship with gold and jewels. תֻּפֶּיךָ is the plural of תֹּף (with second masculine singular suffix), which ordinarily means "tambourine, timbrel." In Jer 31:4 what at least appears to be the same word is used in a way that seems to refer to an ornament worn by dancers, possibly one shaped like a tambourine. וּנְקָבֶיךָ is the plural (with second masculine singular suffix) of the noun נֶקֶב, a hapax, probably a technical term for a "jeweller's work, prob[ably] some hole or cavity" (BDB) based on the verb נָקַב, "to pierce." It might refer to the settings or housings for the jewels. Cooke translates, "thy tambours and ouches."[17]

But there is another whole line of interpretation. Appealing to Ezekiel's use of יָפָה, "be/become beautiful" (16:13; 31:7) and noun יֳפִי (e.g., 28:7, 12, 17), תֹּף is taken as a noun derived from the root יפה or from a by-form, ופי. The form here (with a prefixed ת) could then be vocalized תֹּפִיךָ. For מְלֶאכֶת תֻּפֶּיךָ Block suggests "the craftsmanship of your beauty," and he notes that in Ugaritic texts *tp* is paralleled with *n'm* (in Hebrew, נֹעַם), "delight, charm, kindness."[18] Similarly, van Dijk gives, "the gold of your work of beauty."[19]

Others suggest that וּנְקָבֶיךָ is not the plural of the unique masculine noun נֶקֶב, but of the common noun נְקֵבָה, "female," whose plural is unattested elsewhere in the OT.

---

[16] Block, *Ezekiel*, 2:108.

[17] Cooke, *Ezekiel*, 317.

[18] Block, *Ezekiel*, 2:110, including n. 104.

[19] Van Dijk, *Ezekiel's Prophecy on Tyre*, 118.

The masculine-looking plural could be formed after the analogy of words such as נָשִׁים, "women," and פִּילַגְשִׁים, "concubines." Thus Keil can argue for interpreting the phrase as the performance (מְלָאכֶת) of "the odalisks who beat the timbrels" in the king's harem.[20] The word derived from נקב leads the Targum to give the phrase an anatomical interpretation, applied to the king's pride: "you didn't consider that your body is made with cavities and orifices (nqbyn) needful for you—since you cannot live without them—fixed in you from the day you were created."[21] Still others press this line of thought further; since *tp* and *nʿm* appear in an erotic context in Ugaritic, the words are taken to be euphemisms for "penis" and "vulva."[22] But having moved from the perplexing to the absurd, one has only given more than ample illustration of the obscurity of this phrase—and much of the verse. (There are other interpretations, but this must suffice.)

28:14 This verse too has textual and exegetical problems, some of which involve the basic meaning of the verse.

אַתְּ־כְּרוּב—The noun כְּרוּב (28:14, 16) is the same one used for the "cherub(im)" in chapter 10, who evidently are the same four creatures as in chapter 1. See the second textual note on 1:5 and commentary on 1:5–11.

Since the king of Tyre is masculine and in the surrounding context all the forms that refer to the king are masculine, nearly everyone agrees that אַתְּ is not the feminine pronoun, but the masculine ("you"). This form of the second masculine singular pronoun is found also in Num 11:15 and Deut 5:27. See GKC, § 32 g (which erroneously lists Deut 5:24 instead of 5:27). The LXX read it as the preposition אֵת, "with," and at least since Cooke's commentary (1936),[23] this has proved quite popular with many commentators[24] and translations (RSV, NRSV). The decision here whether the king *was*—or was *with*—a cherub must interact with 28:16, where the king is called כְּרוּב הַסֹּכֵךְ, which is similar to the phrase מִמְשַׁח הַסּוֹכֵךְ in 28:14. Thus 28:16 supports the MT of 28:14: "you (were) a cherub."

That כְּרוּב is anarthrous implies the presence of other cherubim; compare the four in chapter 10, and the singular in 9:3, probably referring to the two over the ark (see the second textual note on 9:3). No article is used with כְּרוּב in 28:16 either. Zimmerli asks, apparently rhetorically, "Does כרוב here have the quality of a proper name?"[25] but an affirmative answer would be entirely unparalleled.

מִמְשַׁח הַסּוֹכֵךְ—The noun (or adjective ?) מִמְשַׁח is a hapax. Both words are missing in the LXX, but the Vulgate's translation of מִמְשַׁח by *extentus*, implying outstretched wings, has often been influential (see *HALOT*). It must have been based on the Aramaic verb מְשַׁח, "to measure, extend," and might imply something like "colos-

[20] Keil, *Ezekiel*, 1:412.

[21] Translation in Greenberg, *Ezekiel*, 2:583.

[22] E. Lipinski, "Les conceptions et couches merveilleuses de 'Anath," *Syria* 42 (1965): 49–50, cited in Block, *Ezekiel*, 2:110, n. 104.

[23] Cooke, *Ezekiel*, 317.

[24] E.g., Zimmerli, *Ezekiel*, 2:85, and Allen, *Ezekiel*, 2:91.

[25] Zimmerli, *Ezekiel*, 2:85.

sal," as the winged sphinxes guarding many ancient Near Eastern temples were. If this is correct, one would have to note that the Bible uses the verb פָּרַשׂ to describe the outstretched wings of the cherubim in the temple and tabernacle (e.g., Ex 25:20; 1 Ki 8:7). By his use of a different term here, Yahweh might be deliberately dissociating the Tyrian cherub from the Israelite cherubim.

However, it seems most natural to me to associate מִמְשַׁח with its root, the verb מָשַׁח, with its common meaning "to anoint" a priest or king. Relevant here would be the verb's meaning, to "*anoint, as consecration … to an office*" (BDB, Qal, 2). Most English translations render מִמְשַׁח by the adjective "anointed," as have I. According to the MT's punctuation, מִמְשַׁח is connected with הַסּוֹכֵךְ, the Qal participle (with article), "the one who covers, shelters." The Qal participle of סָכַךְ is used for the cherubim "covering" the mercy seat in Ex 25:20; 37:9; 1 Ki 8:7. (Compare also the noun מְסֻכָתֶךָ, "your covering," in Ezek 28:13.) Thus KJV has "anointed cherub that covereth." However, no ark is in view in this passage. סָכַךְ may have the nuance of providing "protection" (so *HALOT*, s.v. סכך I, Qal, 1), so the participle may mean "protector" or "guardian," as I have rendered it in 28:14, 16.

The four words, then, probably have the literal meaning "you (were) a cherub, anointed who covers/protects." The entire clause translated by ESV is "you were an anointed guardian cherub."

וּנְתַתִּיךָ—The Qal of נָתַן can mean "appoint" (BDB, 2 c) or "station, establish." It is used in a similar, absolute sense in 37:26. Here "I appointed you" probably has to be understood as saying that Yahweh had appointed the king for the position or role described by the context. The disjunctive *rebia* accent (-ﬦ-) isolates this verb from the following clause, which has its own verb (הָיִיתָ).[26] However, the *athnach* on the preceding word (הַסּוֹכֵךְ) is a stronger disjunctive, indicating that this verb goes more closely with the following clause than with the preceding.

The LXX (after omitting the previous two words) ignores the conjunction on וּנְתַתִּיךָ and connects it with what precedes: μετὰ τοῦ χερουβ ἔθηκά σε ("I placed you with the cherub"). RSV and NRSV too connect the verb with the preceding, ignoring the conjunction. I am attracted to connecting the verb with what precedes. The remaining two verbs in the verse also come at the end of their clauses.

On the translational level, the rest of the verse is clear.

28:15   תָּמִים אַתָּה בִּדְרָכֶיךָ—The Hebrew reads, literally, "blameless (were) you in your ways." תָּמִים is a singular adjective even though it appears to be a plural. When "blameless" is applied to fallen sinners, it implies forensic justification through faith, so that the person (who remains a sinner as well as a saint [Romans 7]) is "blameless" before God; see, for example, Gen 6:9; 17:1; Job 1:1. For people it does not implying strict sinlessness, although in this context in reference to the primeval paradise before the fall, it probably does.

---

[26] Greenberg, *Ezekiel*, 2:584, floats the possibility of a conflation of two versions behind this, but there is no evidence of that.

הִבָּרַאֲךְ—This Niphal infinitive construct of בָּרָא is repeated from 28:13, except that here it is pausal, so its second masculine singular suffix (normally ךָ) appears to be second feminine singular (ךְ).

נִמְצָא עַוְלָתָה—When a verb precedes its subject, it is not unusual for the verb to be masculine (נִמְצָא is the Niphal third masculine singular perfect of מָצָא) even though its subject is feminine. עַוְלָתָה exhibits the old accusative case ending (ה-) on the feminine noun עַוְלָה, "iniquity." Possibly, as in Ps 92:16 (ET 92:15), עַוְלָתָה may have been chosen to avoid the juxtaposition of two stressed syllables (here, עַוְלָה בָּךְ). The synonymous masculine noun עָוֶל is a favorite word in Ezekiel. עַוְלָה is a rather generalized term for sin, essentially synonymous with the more common nouns עָוֹן, פֶּשַׁע, and חַטָּאת, the three main OT words in that category.

28:16 The sense of the verse is reasonably clear, but it is not easy to reconstruct it into idiomatic and intelligible English, hence my relatively free translation.

בְּרֹב רְכֻלָּתְךָ—This is, literally, "in the abundance of your trade." NIV's "widespread trade" struck me as a felicitous way to express that thought.

מָלוּ תוֹכְךָ חָמָס—The verb is an abbreviated form of מָלְאוּ, exhibiting the increasing tendency of later Hebrew to assimilate final-*aleph* forms to final-*he* ones (as though the root were מלה). The verb is transitive (not stative) and impersonal with an indefinite subject used instead of a passive construction (which Hebrew, like English, tends to shy away from). Literally, "they filled in your midst," the first two words are translated, "you were thoroughly filled." Some, for example, van Dijk, propose repointing מָלוּ as an infinitive absolute to be coordinate with the following וַתֶּחֱטָא: "you have filled yourself ... and you have sinned."[27] Cooke considers the (probably free) LXX and Syriac translations, which suggest the reading מִלֵּאתָ (Piel; transitive), to be even "better,"[28] but no such changes are necessary.

The noun חָמָס, an adverbial accusative, is traditionally translated "violence," but in this context it is a rather comprehensive term for "lawlessness." Greenberg renders it as "lawless gain" (cf. Amos 3:10),[29] and I have translated, "illicit profit." That Israel was "full of violence" (מָלְאָה חָמָס) is a term of reproof used previously in Ezekiel (7:23; see also the two words in 8:17 and חָמָס in 7:11; 12:19; 45:9). Isaiah's oracle against Tyre expands the picture given here by describing Tyrian profit-making as a harlot's hire (Is 23:15–17).

וַתֶּחֱטָא—The verb חָטָא, "to sin," is parallel in meaning to the noun עַוְלָה, "iniquity," in the previous verse. This verb concludes the first half verse as climactic, although the preceding clause about "illicit gain" fleshes out its rather general meaning.

וָאֶחַלֶּלְךָ מֵהַר אֱלֹהִים—After the protasis, "since you became defiled," the verb with conjunction forms a result clause, "[therefore] I banished you ... ," equivalent to the many result clauses introduced with לָכֵן ("therefore ...") that are followed by judgment speeches in longer oracles. The Piel of חָלַל usually means to "profane, de-

---

[27] Van Dijk, *Ezekiel's Prophecy on Tyre*, 93, 121.

[28] Cooke, *Ezekiel*, 324.

[29] Greenberg, *Ezekiel*, 2:585.

sacralize, declare/regard as secular" (as in 28:18). It is not ordinarily used with מִן (on מֵהַר, "from the mountain" of God). Thus it is a pregnant construction that implies an additional verbal idea, namely, that of expulsion. It cannot easily be reproduced by any one English word; its translation is "since you became defiled, I banished you." Since the king's behavior demonstrated that he was not only no god, but also an unclean, defiled person, he was no longer fit to occupy a holy mountain.

וָאַבֶּדְךָ כְּרוּב הַסֹּכֵךְ—The expulsion implicit in the verb in the preceding clause is made explicit here with the parallel verb, a contraction of וָאֲאַבֶּדְךָ, the Piel first common singular imperfect of אָבַד with second masculine singular suffix. The Qal is intransitive ("to perish") while the Piel is causative, "to destroy, exterminate, banish." כְּרוּב הַסֹּכֵךְ uses the same noun and participle as in 28:14a, and this vocative phrase ("O guardian cherub") is in apposition to the object suffix on the verb (ךָ-, "you"), referring to the king of Tyre. However, some English translations (e.g., RSV) follow the LXX and Syriac in construing the cherub as the subject who does the expelling. This is in harmony with their reading of אֵת as "with" in 28:14a (see the second textual note on 28:14), which put two creatures on the mountain, the cherub and the king of Tyre.

28:17 Earlier themes, especially in 28:2 and 28:7, are repeated and underscored in this second accusation. As in 28:2, לִבְּךָ, "your heart," in this context simply stands for the whole person.

שִׁחַתָּ חָכְמָתְךָ עַל־יִפְעָתֶךָ—"You corrupted [second masculine singular Piel perfect of שָׁחַת] your wisdom" is obscure in English; "misused" seems to communicate its sense better. עַל is probably best taken in the sense of "together with" as in 16:37 (so already the LXX and Syriac). יִפְעָתֶךָ ("your splendor")was also the last word in 28:7.

עַל־אֶרֶץ הִשְׁלַכְתִּיךָ—This is commonly translated, "I hurled to you to the earth/ground," and that is very possible here. But it is now widely recognized that אֶרֶץ can mean "netherworld, underworld," as in cognate languages, a surrogate for Sheol or "pit" (שַׁחַת, as in 28:8, or בּוֹר as in 26:20). Its use in the comparable oracle against Egypt (32:18, 24) makes this meaning even more likely.

לְרַאֲוָה בָךְ:—The verb רָאָה with the preposition בְּ implies more than simply observing or looking at, but gloating, rejoicing in someone else's misfortune (*Schadenfreude*). Here Ezekiel uses an unusual feminine form of the infinitive construct (GKC, § 75 n) gerundivally: literally, "for gloating at you."

28:18 מֵרֹב עֲוֹנֶיךָ—Since the plural of עָוֹן occurs nowhere else in Ezekiel, and the singular does appear in some manuscripts here, some would read עֲוֹנְךָ here. But the plural is not absent from the rest of the OT (e.g., Is 64:5 [ET 64:6]; Jer 14:7; Ezra 9:6) and רֹב ("'multitude, many") is used with plural as well as singular nouns, so there is no compelling reason to emend. Van Dijk sees the *yod* in עֲוֹנֶיךָ as a remnant of the old genitive case ending,[30] but there is no need to posit an archaism either. The meaning is not substantially different in any case.

---

[30] Van Dijk, *Ezekiel's Prophecy on Tyre*, 122.

A similar problem may exist in the plural מִקְדָּשֶׁיךָ. In a pagan city like Tyre, a plurality of sanctuaries would not be surprising. But if the "sanctuary" is the entire holy garden, the mountain of God, the plural may be read as one of extension or complexity. Greenberg plausibly suggests "holy precincts."[31] I have ventured "entire sanctuary."

וָאוֹצִא־אֵשׁ מִתּוֹכְךָ הִיא אֲכָלָתְךָ—This is, literally, "I will cause fire to come out from your midst, and it will consume you." וָאוֹצִא is the Hiphil first common singular imperfect of יָצָא (with *waw* consecutive), and אֲכָלָתְךָ is the third feminine singular (prophetic) perfect of אָכַל with second masculine singular suffix. The precise nature of this punishment is unclear. It may refer to the cherub-king himself burning from the inside out. Or if the reference is to the entire sacred precinct, it could be that the "fiery stones" (28:14, 16) flare up and reduce him to ashes.

28:19 יוֹדְעֶיךָ—Cooke and van Dijk are surely correct in rendering the Qal masculine plural participle of יָדַע (with second masculine singular suffix) as "thy/your friends."[32] Here, as often, "know" does not do justice to the broad connotations of יָדַע.

בַּלָּהוֹת הָיִיתָ וְאֵינְךָ עַד־עוֹלָם:—The identical wording, but with second feminine singular forms instead of the second masculine singular ones here, was in 27:36. See the second and third textual notes on that verse.

28:21–26 The last verses of the chapter could serve as a summary statement for all of Ezekiel's Gentile oracles. The first section (28:21–23) is ostensibly against Sidon, but very little specific is said about it, except that Yahweh was against it (28:22). There is no listing of Sidon's offenses, only judgment statements. The fact that the recognition formula occurs four times within five verses indicates what the major concern of these verses is.

Much of the content of 28:21–26 consists of typical Ezekelian formulae and phrases, beginning with "son of man" (בֶּן־אָדָם) and "set your face toward" (שִׂים פָּנֶיךָ אֶל־, 28:21; see the second textual note on 6:2). The question naturally arises as to why this oracle was placed here. Two major factors were probably Sidon's proximity to Tyre (some twenty-five miles north) and also the political situation. Since about the time of Solomon, down through Ezekiel's era, Sidon had lived in Tyre's shadow. Earlier, as a variety of sources attest, it had been the premier Phoenician city. Thus in the Table of Nations (Gen 10:15), Sidon is introduced as the firstborn of Canaan. Even after it was eclipsed by Tyre, "Sidonian" stood for "Phoenician," or the two labels were read interchangeably. The Tyrian father of Jezebel is called "king of the Sidonians" in 1 Ki 16:31. Later, after the Assyrian and Babylonian assaults, Sidon appears to have recovered faster than Tyre, and by the early Persian period (later sixth century), it again stood at the head of Phoenician city-states. Yet another factor may have been Sidonian participation in the anti-Babylonian alliance at the beginning of Zedekiah's reign (Jer 27:3).

---

[31] Greenberg, *Ezekiel*, 2:586.
[32] Cooke, *Ezekiel*, 320; van Dijk, *Ezekiel's Prophecy on Tyre*, 122.

In my judgment, the answer is to be found along editorial lines. Many commentators surmise that the nominal mention of Sidon here was motivated by a desire to obtain a total of seven nations in the present collection of oracles against the nations in Ezekiel 25–32. That hypothesis is strengthened by the fact that chapters 29–32 contain seven oracles against Egypt. A minor possibility along the same line is a correspondence to the list of seven Canaanite nations to be defeated by Israel in Deut 7:1.

Similar is the idea that the oracle against Sidon is placed here to produce symmetry. As Block notes, 28:24–26, where Ezekiel focuses on his own people for the first time since chapter 24, divides the entire collection of Gentile oracles into two halves of almost equal length. There are exactly ninety-seven verses on each side of 28:24–26, namely, in 25:1–28:23 and in 29:1–32:32.[33]

Naturally, when we speak of editorial activity, we assume that it was done by Ezekiel himself under inspiration. In contrast, many other commentators affirm the authenticity of few or none of these verses. In a rather acerbic survey of such commentators and their criteria for authenticity, Greenberg notes that "the product of such operations can be persuasive only to partisans of the operators."[34]

28:22 The shift to the third person in the recognition formula ("they will know …") shows that Ezekiel's primary audience is not Sidon, but his fellow Israelite exiles. This temporary change may anticipate the major focus on Israel in 28:24–26. (The LXX incorrectly tries to harmonize by reading a second person singular verb here and continues that change in the pronominal suffixes of this verse and 28:23.)

28:23 וְשִׁלַּחְתִּי—The Piel of שָׁלַח (as in 5:16–17) tends to imply more than Yahweh merely "sending" punishments. Rather, the picture is one of him releasing, letting go—as though these scourges were straining at the leash to attack, but could do nothing until God allowed them.

וְנִפְלַל חָלָל—The two words together exhibit alliteration. The verb נִפְלַל appears to be a third masculine singular perfect of נָפַל in a Piʿlal conjugation. See GKC, § 55 d (which, however, regards נִפְלַל as arising from confusion with חָלָל). Similar rare conjugations attested in the OT include the Piʿlel and Paʿlel, for which see Joüon, § 59 b; Waltke-O'Connor, § 21.2.3a.

בְּחֶרֶב עָלֶיהָ מִסָּבִיב—Greenberg aptly compares this verbless phrase, literally, "with sword against her from around," with psalmic phrases like בַּצַּר־לִי in, for example, Ps 18:7 (ET 18:6).[35]

28:24 This verse is very compact, and some additional English words are unavoidable in attempting a fluent, intelligible translation (so even KJV and NKJV).

סִלּוֹן מַמְאִיר—סִלּוֹן, "briar, thorn," is apparently the singular of סַלּוֹנִים in 2:6; the word occurs only in these two passages in the OT. Exactly what kind of thorn is meant is uncertain, but the land of Israel has no lack of various varieties. Here the word is modified by the Hiphil masculine singular participle of מָאַר, used elsewhere only in

---

[33] Block, *Ezekiel*, 2:122–23.

[34] Greenberg, *Ezekiel*, 2:597–99 (the quote is on p. 599). He calls Zimmerli relatively "conservative"; see Zimmerli, *Ezekiel*, 2:99.

[35] Greenberg, *Ezekiel*, 2:595.

Lev 13:51–52 and 14:44 of a malignant form of "leprosy." The phrase is translated as "prickling briars."

וְקוֹץ מַכְאִב—This parallel phrase uses more common words. קוֹץ is a common, general word for "thorn, thistle," appearing first in Gen 3:18. The Hiphil participle used adjectivally with it is of the more common verb כָּאַב, which in the Hiphil means "cause pain," hence "painful thorns."

הַשָּׁאטִים—This Aramaic-type Qal masculine plural participle of שׁוּט refers to Israel's neighbors "who deride" them with scorn and insults. The immediately preceding verses illustrate what types of attitudes and comments it refers to. This root שׁוּט occurs only in Ezekiel, represented by the Qal participle of the verb (16:57; 28:24, 26; the verb used in 27:8, 26 is a by-form) and by the noun שְׁאָט (25:6, 15; 36:5).

וְיָדְעוּ כִּי אֲנִי אֲדֹנָי יְהוָה:—The recognition formula with both אֲדֹנָי and יְהוָה occurs only four other times (13:9; 23:49; 24:24; 29:16). Its usual form has only יְהוָה. Perhaps אֲדֹנָי was added here because now it is Israel who will "know ... the Lord Yahweh." Most commentators and translators delete or omit אֲדֹנָי, as do a few Hebrew manuscripts.

Commentary

Of the three major oracles directed against Tyre in chapters 26–28, none is as intriguing—and puzzling—as this one. While its basic message is crystal-clear (overweening pride as cause of downfall), its details emphatically are not. The reader will immediately note parallels with the biblical narrative of the creation and fall in Genesis 1–3, as well as with aspects of the high priestly vestments in Exodus 28.

The precise literary relationships between this chapter and those earlier texts are really impossible to ascertain with any certainty. Some radical scholars have denied that part or even all of this chapter was authored by Ezekiel himself, but that is no solution.[36] Cooke is probably more typical of mainstream critical thought: "The story belonged, no doubt, [!] to the common stock of Semitic myths. ... A select few are to be found in Genesis, purged by the genius [*sic!*] of Hebrew religion; in Ez. the purifying process has not gone so far."[37] Others hypothesize that besides Genesis 1–3, another version of the Eden "tradition" was in circulation, and Ezekiel has adapted it. However, there is no literary evidence to support such theories. No Phoenician myths are extant that might illuminate that supposition, and the Phoenician god was Melkart ("king of the city"), a proper noun not comparable with the appellation "the king of Tyre" in 28:12. I shall simply assume that Yahweh inspired Ezekiel to compose this chapter, drawing in part on a wide range of earlier canonical material and tailoring it to the rhetorical needs of the situation.

For all of the chapter's uniqueness, there are many points of contact with other parts of the book of Ezekiel. For example, the reference to trade in 28:5

---

[36] See, for example, Zimmerli, *Ezekiel*, 2:76.

[37] Cooke, *Ezekiel*, 315.

harks back to chapter 27, and the references to Sheol in 28:8–10 are parallel to those in 32:18–32.

It is almost impossible not to make a general comparison of most of this chapter with Isaiah's great dirge over the fall of "the king of Babylon" in Is 14:3–21. There the king's fall in worldly history is portrayed in astral terms as the fall of a personified meteorite, which typifies the fall of Satan from heaven and his expulsion from paradise. In both Is 14:3–21 and Ezekiel 28, there are also similarities to the fall of the first human being, Adam, in Genesis 3.

We have warrant to move a step even further back than Adam's fall in the history of creation. The Scriptures give us no detailed account of the fall of Satan and of the evil angels (cf. 2 Pet 2:4; Jude 6; Rev 20:10), but there may be intimations of that fall in these two chapters, which portray the kings of Babylon (Isaiah 14) and Tyre (Ezekiel 28) as embodiments of Satan within history. Although these human beings were created a "little lower than God" (Ps 8:6 [ET 8:5]), they were not content with second rank, but thought equality with God was something to be seized (cf. ἁρπαγμός, Phil 2:6), in contrast to Jesus Christ, the "last Adam" (1 Cor 15:45), God the Son, who humbled himself in obedience to death and thus brought justification and life where Satan and the first Adam had brought only sin and death (Rom 5:12–21; Phil 2:5–11).

The bulk of chapter 28 easily divides into two counterbalanced sections, 28:1–10 and 28:11–19. The first can easily be subdivided into an indictment or accusation (28:1–5), followed by the sentence of judgment in 28:6–10. Then 28:11–19 takes the form of a lament. The usual literary devices separate these sections from one another. Internally in each, the interpreter often meets "polymorphism,"[38] that is, abrupt changes of persons and settings from stanza to stanza.

Two further units are appended to the chapter. Ezek 28:20–23 is ostensibly another Gentile oracle against Tyre's sister city, Sidon, although its contents give no specifics and almost epitomize a Gentile oracle.[39]

The concluding verses of the chapter (28:24–26) constitute a short salvation oracle. Within the classic prophetic outline, we do not expect oracles of salvation until later,[40] but Ezekiel has a number of short salvation oracles that in many respects anticipate chapters 34–48, where the salvation of reconstituted Israel is the main theme. The repetition of the recognition formula ("and/then they will know that I am Yahweh")[41] four times in five verses (28:22–26) indicates what Yahweh's real concern is in these virtual appendixes,

---

[38] Greenberg, *Ezekiel*, 2:589.

[39] For the Gentile oracles in general, see "Ezekiel 24:25–27 and the Composition of Ezekiel 25–32" in the commentary on 24:25–27, and "Introduction to Ezekiel 25–32: Oracles against Other Nations."

[40] See pages 10–12 in the introduction.

[41] For this formula, see page 9 in the introduction and the commentary on 6:7.

and reminds us to what an extent this formula is God's signature formulation of the Gospel promise.

It may be of passing interest to note that Tyre is the location of the earliest building known to have been constructed to be a church (A.D. 314), in contrast to earlier house churches.

Indictment and Judgment of the King of Tyre (28:1–10)

The Indictment (28:1–5)

28:2 The syntax is complicated, and although the conclusion of the thought does not really come until 28:6 ("because … *therefore*"), the essence of Yahweh's indictment against the king of Tyre is summarized in this opening verse. More details of the setting will follow, but the accusation of self-deification is not all that different from the sin of "be[ing] like God," which the snake dangled before Adam and Eve in Genesis 3, and in which they readily indulged. This *Ursünde* (the primal sin) is the cause of *Erbsünde*, original sin, which all children of Adam inherit, and from which only Christ can redeem us (e.g., Rom 5:12–21). The application here is not universal, just to one sinner—the king of Tyre—but the theological point is the same. As a violation of the First Commandment and thus of God's entire Law, this sin is a constant of human history, even if it often is not recognized or acknowledged. And in recent times, especially in some versions of "New Age" thought, the quest to be like God is quite explicitly and crassly urged as the essence of "spirituality."

28:3 There is no justification for taking the verse as two questions (as NIV does, with the LXX and Syriac in antiquity). Neither does the context suggest sarcasm, as some construe it. There is nothing reprehensible about wisdom, as such. In fact, the Bible often regards it as one of God's greatest gifts. The problem arises in the response, what one does with God's gift. If one momentarily factors out the condemnation for the arrogant response, this and the following verses remind one of the neutral way in which chapter 27 had discussed Tyre's commercial prowess; it too was a good gift that was sinfully misused.

28:4–5 These verses illustrate the usual usage of "wisdom" in the OT. It is not always an overtly religious or theological term; here wisdom is ascribed to a pagan. Nor does it refer to any theoretical, intellectual power of any sort. Of course, the Scriptures, especially the book of Proverbs (see also Job 28), acknowledge that God is the source of all wisdom, but ordinarily that is simply taken for granted in the biblical text. "Wisdom" has to do with the art of mastering life, and hence the hundred and one situations addressed in the sentential collection of Prov 10:1–22:16 or the proper behavior vis-à-vis the opposite sex in Proverbs 1–9. Very often, however, it concentrates on some specific skill, gift, aptitude, and so on. Its application here is to Tyre's business acumen. As far as that "wisdom" is concerned, about all that is new here is that the prosperity described in chapter 27 was no happenstance, but deliberate and official royal policy, achieved by the wisdom that God the Creator had given Tyre's king. The reader must note that it is not that "wisdom" that is condemned

as such, but the extreme pride, even the arrogation of divinity to himself that that wisdom engendered.

Of course, the basic hermeneutical principle of "Scripture interprets Scripture" must ultimately be brought to bear also on passages such as this. It is risky to try to fit the different nuances of "wisdom" into a chronological framework, but the total biblical context gives very explicit theological meaning to "wisdom." It is developed by Solomon in Prov 1:20–33 and the following parts of the book where wisdom is personified, and flowers when wisdom is hypostasized as the preincarnate Christ in Prov 8:22–23. Inevitably, then, the NT identifies "wisdom" with the Word incarnate, Christ himself, or speaks of the essence of all true wisdom as the confession and practice of the Gospel.[42]

The Sentence of Judgment (28:6–10)

28:6–7 The punishments for the king's arrogance will be threefold. Two are summarily mentioned in 28:7; the third is developed in more detail in 28:8–10. The first two replicate the way an idol would be treated by an invading army. First, the "beauty of [his] wisdom" would be eliminated, here probably referring to the destruction of all the king's tangible accomplishments (buildings, navies, fortifications, etc.). Second, his "radiance" or halo (see the textual note on יִפְעָתֶךָ in 28:7), which he, claiming divinity, had dared to place upon himself would be "desecrate[d]," indicating that as a mere mortal he had no legitimate claim to such divine glory.

28:8–10 The final verses of the judicial sentence dwell on the third, climactic aspect of the judgment, namely, the king's ignominious and everlasting death. He will be cast down into the "pit" (28:8). The Hebrew term refers to the grave, often poetically enlarged to describe the whole realm of the dead, as though it were a mass grave. "The pit" (שַׁחַת, see the first textual note on 28:8) connotes the eternal grave of all unbelievers, who in OT language are called the "uncircumcised" (28:10). That is, they are outside God's covenant of grace and "righteousness" through faith (Gen 15:6), which he established with Abraham, to whom he also gave circumcision as the sign and seal of the covenant (Genesis 17), corresponding to Christian Baptism in the new covenant (Col 2:11–13).

In "the pit," any and all illusions that the king is an immortal deity will be falsified forever. The same idea will be developed in more detail (and in a way more reminiscent of Isaiah 14) in 32:17–32 of Egypt. Ezek 28:9 initially expresses the denial of the king's divinity with a rhetorical question, and then 28:10 follows it with the obvious answer. The "violent death" of 28:8 and "the death of the uncircumcised" in 28:10 are substantially synonymous. That uncircumcision was a disgrace to the Israelites is expressed many times, especially regarding the Philistines and Canaanites.[43] Herodotus attests that the

[42] One may see "Solomon, Wisdom, and Christology" in Mitchell, *The Song of Songs*, 34–38.

[43] Greenberg, *Ezekiel*, 2:576, compares it to our "die like a dog" or "a dog's death."

Phoenicians practiced circumcision,[44] as apparently did many of Israel's neighbors. Hence, the expression is insulting to the Tyrians, just as it would be if it were said of apostate Israelites. In both cases, the point is that, regardless of the physical mark, they are excluded from the covenant that grants eternal life.

Van Dijk proposes that עֲרֵלִים should not be translated "uncircumcised," but "castrated." He reasons from the practice of mutilating the genitals of the corpses of uncircumcised enemies as a sign of contempt, even for the dead. For example, in 1 Sam 18:25–27, David produced the foreskins of two hundred slain Philistines as the bride price of his first wife. With further abandon, van Dijk claims that "foreskin" in 1 Sam 18:25–27 is a euphemism for penis, so that the slain were castrated.[45] However, the OT evidence does not support van Dijk's claims. There is some extrabiblical evidence, such as Egyptian texts and base reliefs that make plain that the Egyptians, who also practiced circumcision, often amputated the penises of slain enemies, partly as a way of tallying how many of the enemy had been killed. But this does not change the well-attested meaning of עָרֵל in the OT from "uncircumcised" to "castrated"!

Still, those other texts may help the modern reader understand different kinds of "death" in the ancient world, and why to "die the death of the uncircumcised" (Ezek 28:10) was considered particularly ignominious. Many commentators understand the expression to imply that the uncircumcised dead would be consigned to the most undesirable part of the netherworld, the lowest part of hell, together with other vile and unclean persons. Just as Scripture suggests that there will be degrees of glory for the redeemed in heaven,[46] other passages do indicate degrees of punishment and dishonor in hell (see Ezek 26:20; 32:19, 23).

The verdict is sealed by final appeal to God's Word ("for I have spoken") and the signatory formula ("says the Lord Yahweh," 28:10).[47]

A Lament over the King of Tyre (28:11–19)

28:12 Already this first verse, as well as what follows, does not sound like a קִינָה ("lament/dirge"). Expressions of grief are entirely lacking. Instead the prophet first describes the Tyrian king's self-image in order to explain why judgment was necessary. Yahweh's judgment speech begins in earnest in 28:15, and the preceding verses serve to indicate why it was necessary and inevitable.

Three phrases are used to describe the king of Tyre before his fall. The first one, however, is very unclear, and much debated (see the textual notes). I have understood "guarantor" as using the metaphor of a seal, which will stamp the symmetry of God's "very good" creation (to borrow language from Genesis 1)

---

[44] Herodotus, *Histories*, 2.104.

[45] Van Dijk, *Ezekiel's Prophecy on Tyre*, 113. There he also claims that the Hiphil verb אֲמִילַם in Ps 118:10–12 means "I castrated them."

[46] See, for example, Dan 12:3; 1 Cor 3:8; 2 Cor 9:6–7; Ap IV 356–74.

[47] For this formula, see pages 8–9 in the introduction and the second textual note on 5:11.

on everything. The other two attributes we have met before. "Full of wisdom" echoes 28:3–5, as well as recalling the "wise," that is, expert sailors in 27:8. "Perfect in beauty" repeats Tyre's boast in 27:3, with which, as in 27:11, Yahweh seems to be in agreement.

Here, as in the following material, Yahweh affirms the king's incomparable splendor and position prior to his *hubris,* which is ample justification of the coming divine judgment. The strategy is similar to that of chapter 27: Yahweh does not deny that the city had beautifully constructed ships and flourishing trade, but then he exploits their pride in their accomplishments by turning the ship into a figure of disaster.

28:13 Interpretation would be difficult enough, even if the translation were reasonably clear (see the textual notes). Fortunately, the first and last sentences (in my punctuation) are clear enough on their surface, even if the middle of the verse is rife with difficulties and/or obscurities. To what degree Ezekiel is reproducing Tyre's own garbled version of the creation narrative or selecting elements from a variety of sources according to his purposes is impossible to determine.

It appears as if Yahweh is deliberately breaking up the phrase from Genesis, "the garden of Eden" (e.g., Gen 2:15), into "in Eden" (בְּעֵדֶן) and "the garden of God" (גַּן־אֱלֹהִים). He is careful to describe it as "the garden of God [אֱלֹהִים]," not "the garden of Yahweh," in order not to associate the revealed, covenant name of God with this pagan who worshipped other gods. "Eden" and "the garden of God" will appear together again in 31:8–9 in an oracle against the pharaoh of Egypt.

The use of the Niphal of the verb בָּרָא, "created," at the end of 28:13 (and again in 28:15) is assuming that the king of Tyre is a *creature*, not the creat*or* he apparently claimed to be. The plural form of "prepared" (כּוֹנָנוּ) indicates that the precious stones listed previously are the subject; their origin was more or less simultaneous with God's creation of the king.

The similarity of the list of precious stones here with those on the breastpiece of the Israelite high priest (Ex 28:17–20) is obvious. As claimant to divinity, the association with gems would be familiar; statues of idols were often arrayed with precious stones (cf. the "man," apparently the angel Gabriel, of Dan 10:5–6). Although Ezekiel, a priest (1:3), utilizes a list familiar to him, he seems to be at pains to make plain that he is not comparing the king of Tyre with the Israelite high priest. Already the phrase "guarantor of symmetry" in the previous verse points to the first man, Adam, as God's deputy and representative, not to a high priest. The only possible connection would be if Tyre were one of those places where the king usurped the role of high priest, but of that we have no evidence.[48] Depending on translation, the jewels are described

---

[48] Some critical theories think that postexilic [!] composers of the Pentateuch derived their description of the sacerdotal vestments from those traditionally worn by Israel's kings. Of course, the critical dating schemes for the Pentateuch must be rejected. Nevertheless, there is evidence that some Israelite kings usurped priestly prerogatives (and perhaps attire as

as inlaid in gold settings, not in any חֹשֶׁן מִשְׁפָּט, "breastpiece of judgment" (Ex 28:15).

Besides the similarities in the lists of Exodus (28:17–20) and Ezekiel (28:13), there are also differences, and it is not certain whether those have any significance. Both lists group the stones in triads, presumably reflecting their arrangement in rows. Both lists begin with the same two stones, but from there on the order differs. Ezekiel's second triad is identical to the fourth triad in Exodus. If these shufflings have any significance, it would seem to be to warn the reader not to associate the two lists in any substantial way. More likely of significance is the absence of one entire triad in Ezekiel. (The LXX restores it, but whether that represents the original text, part of which has been accidentally omitted in the MT, or whether it is an artificial harmonization is impossible to say.) In Exodus, a total of twelve was important, because each stone represented one of the twelve tribes, but in Tyre the total might have been without significance. My judgment is that Ezekiel's purpose in listing the gems is simply to illustrate concretely the fabulous wealth and splendor of the king of Tyre before his fall.

28:14 Especially the beginning of the verse bristles with difficulties (see the textual notes), but, if my translation is correct, the king of Tyre is addressed as a cherub, "anointed" as a "guardian"—presumably of the garden. Apparently the king is called a "cherub" because that was his own claim. Archaeological finds amply illustrate that this idiom was common coin of the Tyrian realm, because Tyrian art is replete with cherubic figures, and some of them have faces or are found in settings that at least suggest royalty. There appears to be no connection with the cherubim in Ezekiel's visions in chapters 1–11, which are described quite differently.

A cherub is a creature, in contradiction of the king's claim to divinity, but there is no expression of disapproval by God to the Tyrian king's styling himself as a "cherub." In the biblical view (cf. God's address of human potentates as "gods," אֱלֹהִים, in Ps 82:11) and in accord with Luther's view of the kingdom on the left hand, God has established human authority (Rom 13:1–7), no matter how it wishes to be addressed.

Exactly what he had been appointed to protect or guard is not specified, but the idea appears to be in accord with God placing Adam "in the garden of Eden to till it and keep it" (Gen 2:15). A less likely parallel is the placing of cherubim (plural instead of the singular here) "to guard the way to the tree of life" after the expulsion from paradise (Gen 3:24). Equally unlikely in my judgment is some analogy with the cherubim who "covered" the ark; the same verb whose participle is here translated "guardian" is used in both Ex 25:20 and 1 Ki 8:7 for cherubim "covering" the ark. If the purpose of the "covering" was protective, the possibilities of parallel are perhaps thinkable. This interpreta-

---

well). That could account for the marginal role the king will play in Ezekiel's eschatological vision at the end of the book (44:1–3; 46:1–2).

tion could fit the cherubim erected in the holy of holies of the temple (1 Ki 6:23–28; 8:7) as well as the cherubim over the ark (Ex 25:20). No doubt Tyre had sanctuaries, and in pagan ones idols usually occupied the adytum, but it seems doubtful that a god would need cherubic protection.

That the cherub was also "on the holy mountain of God" (Ezek 28:14) nonpluses some interpreters. How can he be both in God's garden and on his mountain? If the reference is to some Tyrian tradition, we know nothing of it, and the question cannot be answered. But if the point of departure is biblical, there are possibilities. Genesis 2–3 does not clearly situate the garden of Eden on a mountain, but if gravity operated before the fall as it has since, the garden would have had to have been elevated so that the four rivers could flow out of it. But even if only metaphorically, it is clear that the association of garden and mountain was known in Israel.

The "mountain" of God is most often associated with Mount Zion (and with Mount Sinai, which is called "the mountain of God" [e.g., Ex 3:1], but that is probably not relevant here), and since part of the meaning of the temple was that of a prolepsis of paradise restored, the mountain picture might have been retrojected to paradise itself. Furthermore, paradise restored is clearly labeled a mountain, and sometimes it is debatable whether the reference is to the present or the future Zion (or both!). This language is especially common in Isaiah. Is 11:9 is clearly eschatological: "They shall not hurt or destroy in all my holy mountain." Equally clearly are several references in Isaiah 25: "On this mountain, … [Yahweh] will swallow up death forever" (Is 25:7–8, quoted or alluded to three times in the NT, but without the mountain reference: 1 Cor 15:54; Rev 20:14; 21:4), and "The hand of Yahweh will rest on this mountain, and Moab will be trampled down under him" (Is 25:10). In the famous parallel passages of two eighth-century prophets, Is 2:2–4 and Micah 4:1–3, the prophecy is clearly eschatological, but also Zion-centered: "In the latter days, the mountain of the house of Yahweh will be established as the highest of the mountains." And in Isaiah 14, a pericope already mentioned as having many parallels with Ezekiel 28, "Helel son of dawn" (Vulgate: *lucifer*, Is 14:12) is described as aspiring to "sit on the 'mount of assembly' [הַר־מוֹעֵד] in the far north" (Is 14:13). In addition to the "mount," that passage has two other clear exmythological[49] metaphors; in biblical context, the heavenly "assembly" would be occupied by angels (1 Kings 22; Job 1–2), not gods. The second metaphor is the location of the mountain in the "north." That appears again in Ps 48:2–3 (ET 1–2), where Yahweh describes Zion as "his holy mountain … in the far north," applying the imagery of Mount Zaphon ("Mount North," i.e., Mount Casius, the Canaanite equivalent to Mount Olympus) to Jerusalem.

Finally, even aside from the above biblical references, the merger of "garden" and "mountain" locations here may be no problem if Ezekiel is merely

---

[49] For "exmythological," see the textual notes and commentary on 26:19, 21.

echoing Tyrian language. It must be remembered that mytho*logy* has a "logic," which is not that of Western thought. Compare the fluidity in the roles—and even the genders—of many pagan deities.

Parenthetically, we can note yet that the idea of Eden being on top of a mountain has been very influential in religious poetry (e.g., both Dante and John Milton). Apparently, there are many similar Muslim traditions, presumably adapted from Jewish and/or Christian sources.

The "fiery stones" among which the cherub-king "walked about" (or "back and forth," as הִתְהַלָּכְתָּ, the Hithpael of הָלַךְ, could be rendered) are, arguably, the most obscure of all in this verse. They will be mentioned again in 28:16. Guesses, naturally, are abundant, some of them quite wild sounding. There are possible parallels in both Akkadian and Ugaritic texts, but both of them of uncertain meaning. There is considerable sentiment equating the "fiery stones" with the "precious stone[s]" mentioned in the previous verse. Poetically speaking, and perhaps reflecting a touch of Tyrian pagan magic, that is very possible. Depending on their location, and especially if מְסֻכָה, "covering," in 28:13 had something to do with a "hedge" or "fence, wall," they might have signaled the inaccessibility associated with divinity.

28:15 This verse begins a major shift in the oracle. The rest of it (through 28:18) sounds like a judgment oracle, describing Yahweh's judgment on the king for his abuse of an originally divine appointment. It can be subdivided into three parts (28:15–16, 17, and 18). Each contains an accusation and uses prophetic perfects (or imperfects with *waw* consecutive) to describe the judgment. One would be surprised to find any parallel to this in Tyrian mythology.

The description recalls the fall of Satan (see the beginning of the commentary on chapter 28). Moreover, almost certainly Yahweh is applying to the king of Tyre a description of the fall of Adam and Eve (precipitated by Satan, Genesis 3). This is evident by the use of "created" (בְּרָא, 28:13, 15; the same verb used in Gen 1:1, 21, 27; 2:3–4), just as it was evident by the use of "garden" previously (Ezek 28:13). Ezek 28:15 gives no specifics about his sin except the general term עַוְלָה, "iniquity," perhaps here "sin*ful*ness" more than mere "sin," which implies a basic change in his דֶּרֶךְ, "conduct, behavior," perhaps even "character." The remaining verses will give us some concrete details, which we have heard before, particularly his pride in his success in trade.

28:16 Finally, Ezekiel returns to the theme of Tyre's trade as the occasion and manifestation of its claim to divinity (cf. 28:2–5 above). If the king were really divine, he could make his own rules or at least regard himself as above the law of ordinary mortals. It is another application of the dictum that any infraction of God's moral law is ultimately disobedience to the First Commandment (Ex 20:3; Deut 5:7). Tyre apparently had a reputation in antiquity for subethical business practices. Compare the Bible's use of כְּנַעֲנִי, "Canaanite," in the often pejorative sense of a dishonest businessman, most relevantly in Is 23:8 (Isaiah's oracle against Tyre). Tyre was the main survivor of the original Canaanite population after Israel conquered the promised land under

Joshua. "Illicit profit" and other translations may obscure just how strong the language is here; usually חָמָס refers to physical violence, even murder (e.g., Ezek 7:23). The Bible nowhere condemns trade or "capitalism," as such, but the fraud and other dishonest behaviors to which it is vulnerable.

In 28:16b, the resultant judgment, Ezekiel may reveal his priestly background by using a liturgical verb, literally, "profane, desacralize," when God says, "I expelled you." Certainly in OT usage, the liturgical and the ethical were connected. Just as "holy" applies to worship, so "clean" applies to daily life. The holy and the unholy are mutually exclusive—yet God justifies the ungodly, sanctifies and restores holiness to sinners by his grace in Christ. God declared the king "defiled" (unclean and unholy), seeking to move him to repentance, but the proud king of Tyre would not have repented; if he had, only God's declarative statement of forgiveness (justification) could have altered the king's state of being "defiled." The use of such liturgical language continues into the NT, and into our own usage, as when we confess that we are "sinful and unclean."[50]

28:17 The second accusation and ensuing punishment in this verse are sequels to the first ones (28:15–16). Here the themes of 28:2 and 28:7 are highlighted: overweening pride in "beauty/splendor" and "wisdom." They were gifts of God to be received with thanksgiving and to be used to his glory, not a means of self-aggrandizement. As the king of Tyre had once flaunted them before his fellow kings, now they will gloat over his downfall into "the netherworld," that is, hell, often called Sheol (see the textual note on אֶרֶץ in this sense here in 28:17). He who was once ensconced in the garden on "the holy mountain of God" (28:14) is now consigned to the underworld.

28:18 The third accusation returns once again to the unscrupulous trading practices of Tyre, focusing on its king. Such behavior "defiled, profaned, desecrated" (the verb חָלַל again, as in 28:16) the sacred place. Again a liturgical term is used in a moral sense.

Whatever the details of the punishment (see the textual notes), the theological point is the familiar one of sin causing its own destruction; its own punishment is inherent in the iniquitous behavior itself. "Whatever a man sows, that he will also reap" (Gal 6:7). The ashes after the conflagration will give little evidence of the former glory.

28:19 The oracle ends on words almost identical to the final ones of the previous oracle (27:36). As its use in Job 18:14 intimates, בַּלָּהָה, conventionally translated "horror," probably implies the netherworld again. Perhaps the metaphors are slightly mixed, but, although empirically he is exterminated, in another sense he has become a denizen of the underworld, a horrible end, as far removed from the holy mountain as conceivable. The very thought of the finality and irreversibility of death is always, from an earthly perspective, a

---

50 E.g., *LSB*, 151.

horrifying prospect. But the Bible (and thus the OT too!) has much more to say about death, so that all who believe in the resurrected Christ do not "grieve as others do who have no hope" (1 Thess 4:13).

An Oracle against Sidon (28:20–23)

28:22 "I will display my glory" (וְנִכְבַּדְתִּי, 28:22) pinpoints Ezekiel's overriding concern in 28:20–23. The Niphal form theoretically could be translated as a passive, but is better understood in a reflexive sense: "I will show myself glorious" or the like. The Niphal of כָּבֵד appears in Ezekiel again only in 39:13, where God displays his glory by destroying Gog (cf. "I will establish my glory among the Gentiles" in 39:21).

Its most important antecedent is probably in Ex 14:4, 17–18, where Yahweh's display of his glory is given as his motivation for the rout of the Egyptians in the exodus. The recognition formula is repeated there, "Egypt will know that I am Yahweh" (Ex 14:4, 18), just as it is repeated here, "and/then they will know that I am Yahweh" (Ezek 28:22–23). I will endorse Allen calling this a "typological parallel."[51] It is a classical example of inner-OT typology, of which there are many examples.

As Christians recognize, the correspondence extends into the NT, possibly expressed most explicitly in the Johannine theme of Christ's "glorification" in his crucifixion, which was simultaneously his triumph over death and Satan (see John 17). To complete the typological picture, it applies to believers, who daily die and rise with Christ in Baptism (Rom 6:1–4; Col 2:11–13), until Christ returns again in glory, ushering in the bodily resurrection and the final victory over all opposition at the consummation. Thus not only this oracle, but all the Gentile oracles can begin to be appropriated as an intrinsic part of the Gospel, of a piece of what Christ did climactically in being incarnated "for us men and for our salvation" (Nicene Creed).

The שְׁפָטִים, "punishments" (28:22), will be detailed slightly at the beginning of 28:23. Although these will, indeed, be judgments, the forensic background of the word should not be forgotten. These are basically "verdicts" of the heavenly court, by which all history is constituted.

Parallel to "I will display my glory" (וְנִכְבַּדְתִּי, 28:22) is "I will display my holiness" (וְנִקְדַּשְׁתִּי, 28:22). Sometimes God's glory and holiness are two sides of the coin: his holiness is his glory concealed, while his glory is his holiness revealed. But here the two verbs are used almost synonymously. (In Ex 29:43 the two together form a hendiadys.) Everywhere else in Ezekiel, the Niphal of קָדַשׁ has a public character, effecting confession of Yahweh (20:41; 28:25; 36:23; 38:16 [of the defeat of Gog again, like the Hithpael in 38:23, and developed in 39:27]). That idea is probably implicit here as well, although localized in one city. But in "holiness" the accent is not, as such, on Yahweh's

---

[51] Allen, *Ezekiel*, 2:99.

"weight" and dignity, as on the zealous fire[52] native to his essence that burns up all resistance. His "holiness" can also bring blessings, as when he provided water in the desert (Num 20:13). The two concepts, but with the functional accent on "holy," are paired also in Lev 10:3 in connection with the destruction of Nadab and Abihu by divine fire after they had "offered profane fire before Yahweh" (Lev 10:1) by unauthorized use of incense.

28:23 Yahweh's agents of judgment are now unleashed (see the first textual note on 28:23) to do their deadly work in Sidon's midst. The accent is totally on Yahweh as the cause of the judgment, which is the confession Yahweh wants the people to make, however grudgingly; there is no reference to Nebuchadnezzar as Yahweh's agent in carrying out the judgment. Instead, here we have the agency of "plague," "blood," and "sword," similar to the agency of "plague," "famine," and "sword" in 5:12 and 6:12, and "famine," "wild animals," "sword," and "plague" in 14:12–20.

Yahweh Will Regather Israel and Save His People from Derision (28:24–26)

28:24 As we have seen, Yahweh has the habit of repeatedly interjecting brief oracles of hope or salvation (e.g., 11:14–21; 16:59–63; 20:33–44) in the midst of extended judgment oracles. The real purpose of his judgment oracles is to elicit repentance and prepare the people to receive his Gospel promises in faith; those promises become his major theme in chapters 33–48. The *waw* ("and") at the beginning of the verse connects it syntactically with what precedes, so technically we must regard it as transitional to what follows. Here the Gospel is stated in terms of Israel's permanent release from the obloquy of its pagan neighbors, of which Sidon is only the last named example. One might have expected this Gospel promise not to come until chapter 33, after the end of the oracles against Egypt (chapters 29–32), but in a way, its impact is greater here.

In the great reversal, God's own people, the new Israel, finally will be freed from their rebellious tendencies and will confess the lordship of their God and all that follows from that.

28:25 The citation formula, "thus says the Lord Yahweh,"[53] indicates that the essence of the promise prepared for by the transitional 28:24 has definitively begun. A major part of the great reversal will be the regathering of God's people and their resettlement on their own land. This by itself will demonstrate Yahweh's holiness in the eyes of the nations. Ezek 36:16–32 will develop this theme at length. The NT terms the Christians scattered throughout the world as the "diaspora" (διασπορά, James 1:1; 1 Pet 1:1), and the Gospel promise

---

[52] Compare Ezekiel's use of קִנְאָה in 5:13; 8:3, 5.

[53] For this formula, see pages 8–9 in the introduction and the fourth textual note and the commentary on 2:4.

is that at the return of Christ, God's new Israel, consisting of all baptized believers (Gal 3:26–29), shall be gathered together into the new Jerusalem (Revelation 21).

From the OT perspective, only one land could be their "own," namely, that promised to "my servant Jacob" (Ezek 28:25). The phrase occurs again in Ezekiel only in 37:25, but is frequent in restoration oracles of Isaiah and Jeremiah. Why is Jacob singled out? The patriarchal promise was first given to Abraham, of course. The traditional answer is that all of the sons of Jacob were heirs of the promised land, whereas Abraham and Isaac each had one son (Ishmael and Esau, respectively) who was excluded from the promise.

28:26 The "security" of the reconstituted Israel is emphasized by repetition. Concrete signs of security in permanent repatriation will be the building of houses and planting of vineyards. Secure living is often comparably described as occurring under one's own vine (arbor) and/or fig tree (2 Ki 18:31 ‖ Is 36:16; Micah 4:4; Zech 3:10). But this security is not one that is sufficient by and for itself as the ultimate possession. Rather, it involves the recognition and confession of Yahweh as "their [his people's] God" (Ezek 28:26), an allusion to the oft-repeated (in slightly different words) and basic covenant promise, "I will be your God, and you will be my people" (e.g., Lev 26:12; see also, e.g., Gen 17:8; Ex 6:7).

Like all OT promises, this one is couched in terms of the old covenant, the not-totally-known future in terms of the known past. It is not annulled in the NT, but fulfilled in Christ, where all the terms are filled with their ultimate Christological intent. "Israel" is no longer a theocratic nation; "the Israel of God" (Gal 6:16) consists of all baptized believers in Christ, Jew and Gentile alike (Gal 3:26–29). The present "promised land" is not to be defined or limited geographically; as in the formulation of the promise to Abraham (Gen 12:3), the parameters of the present kingdom of God extend to the ends of the earth. Yet they are still concrete: God's kingdom comes and is present where the Gospel of Jesus Christ is preached faithfully and his Sacraments, Baptism and his Supper, are administered rightly. Thus the "body of Christ" is where Christ's body and blood are sacramentally present and received in faith (1 Cor 10:16–17; 11:23–32). His Word and Sacraments promise the resurrection of the body and life in the eternal heavenly land. And the security from enemies is not any mortal's own achievement, but the ultimate gift of Christ himself and his victory over Satan and all his cohorts. Thus in the eschaton, God will dwell with his redeemed people in Christ; "they will be his people, and God himself will be with them as their God" (Rev 21:3).

Introduction to Ezekiel 29–32:
Oracles against Egypt

(a) See, e.g.,
Gen 1:1–2:3;
Rev 1:4, 20;
5:6; 6:1; 8:2;
16:1; 21:9

(b) Ezek
29:1–16;
29:17–21;
30:1–19;
30:20–26;
31:1–18;
32:1–16;
32:17–32

From Genesis to Revelation,[a] the number seven plays a pivotal role in Scripture in symbolizing completeness, as also in Ezekiel's oracles against Egypt (chapters 29–32). Egypt is the seventh and last of the countries to be addressed in Ezekiel's oracles against the nations (Ezekiel 25–32),[1] and seven separate oracles are addressed against it.[b] These seven can again be divided into two segments that somewhat parallel each other, 29:1–31:18 and 32:1–32. Each segment describes Egypt's destruction by the Babylonians, concluding with the picture of Pharaoh descending into Sheol. (The "seven days" in Ezek 3:15–16, as well as the seven angels in 9:2, also connote completeness.)

That the choice of seven was deliberate is shown by the fact that two Gentile oracles occur outside chapters 25–32, one against Ammon in 21:33–37 (ET 21:28–32) and another against Edom in chapter 35. These could have been included among the other Gentile oracles, but apparently were placed elsewhere to preserve the number seven. The practice of gathering oracles against seven Gentile nations is not unique to Ezekiel, although his collection is more central and structural in comprising an entire section of his prophetic book (about one-twelfth of the entire book).[2] Similar collections of seven appear also in Amos 1–2 and Jeremiah 46–49.[3] Probably the biblical pattern is founded by the assertion in Deut 7:1 that Israel must defeat seven Canaanite nations in order to possess its inheritance. The symbolism of seven can also be documented in extrabiblical literature.

Also striking is the concentration of dates for these oracles against Egypt. All are in chronological order except for the second (29:17–21). (The third oracle, 30:1–19, is undated.) Throughout the book, all but one of the dates are calculated, as 1:2 indicates, from the exile of King Jehoiachin in 597 B.C. (which coincides with the exile of Ezekiel too). The first date in the oracles against Egypt, in "the tenth year" (29:1), is about a year after Nebuchadnezzar began his siege of Jerusalem (see the textual note on 24:1 and figure 1), which would last two and a half years. The date in 29:1 is two years before a fugitive brings

---

[1] See "Introduction to Ezekiel 25–32: Oracles against Other Nations."

[2] For the role of this section within the classical prophetic outline, see pages 10–12 in the introduction.

[3] Amos includes an oracle against both Israel and Judah in addition to six neighboring countries, but Judah was not Gentile, whereas the apostate Northern Kingdom could easily be considered as bad as the Gentiles. In Jeremiah 46–49, we can count more or less than seven oracles depending on how the text is divided. Another Gentile oracle follows in Jeremiah 50–51, but it has a different introduction, a greater length, and a different character, and it ends with an action prophecy.

the news of the city's fall to Ezekiel and the exiles in Babylon (33:21). Thus, 29:1–16 is the earliest of Ezekiel's Gentile oracles, even earlier than chapter 26 (see 26:1).

By contrast, the second oracle (29:17–21) is the latest dated oracle (as well as one of the shortest) in the entire book. Apparently it was placed in Ezekiel 29, the first chapter of oracles against Egypt, in order to locate it close to the oracles against Tyre in chapters 26–28. According to this second oracle, Nebuchadnezzar was not able to capture Tyre fully, and so he will be given Egypt as a kind of consolation prize. Once this second oracle breached the chronological order of the oracles against Egypt, it was apparently easy to place next the undated one in 30:1–19. Topically, 30:1–19 fits well after chapter 29 because it contains the threats against Egypt's הָמוֹן, "horde/army" (30:4, 10, 15), mentioned previously 29:19. In addition, these two oracles are the only ones among the oracles against Egypt to mention Nebuchadnezzar by name (29:18–19; 30:10; he is also named in 26:7 in an oracle against Tyre).

Ezekiel himself never names the pharaoh who apparently triggered at least some of the oracles against Egypt, but it is easy to identify him as Hophra (Greek: Apries). Jer 37:5–8 records that when Nebuchadnezzar began to besiege Jerusalem, Hophra dared to challenge him, forcing him to lift the siege at least temporarily. But, as Jeremiah predicted (37:7), the Egyptian feint was easily disposed of (and may well have been only a token effort to begin with). From Ezekiel's standpoint, then, Hophra simply joined the list of others who attempted to thwart Yahweh's intent to use Nebuchadnezzar to punish Jerusalem.

But that relatively minor incident can scarcely have been the only occasion for the extensive attention Yahweh pays to Egypt in Ezekiel 29–32. While it is the only concrete event to which we, with our limited knowledge of ancient history, can point, in a way it was only the last in a long series of contacts between Israel and Egypt, which began with Abram's sojourn there (Gen 12:10–20) and culminated with the four hundred years (Gen 15:13) the Israelites spent there before the exodus (mid-fifteenth century B.C.).

Not long after the exodus under Moses, Egypt ceased to be a world power, but it was not for lack of desire. Hophra's foray into Israelite territory was only the most recent of Egyptian incursions, although previous ones had usually been with hostile intent against Israel. And Egypt was still smarting from the defeat Nebuchadnezzar had inflicted upon its armies at Carchemish in 605 B.C. in the contest to determine who would replace Assyria in world dominance. But whatever the details, Egypt remained the major threat to Babylonia, which was God's agent for punishing Jerusalem, and Yahweh really needed no further motivation than that for the oracles in Ezekiel 29–32.

In light of Egypt's antagonistic role throughout Israel's history, it is remarkable that Yahweh issues a salvation oracle for Egypt (29:13–14; cf. Is 19:18–25). In those verses, Yahweh describes the restoration of Egypt in iden-

tical terms used elsewhere for the eschatological restoration of Israel, for example, "gather" and שׁוּב שְׁבוּת, "bring about the restoration of."[4] Thus Egypt itself will undergo a kind of "new exodus" deliverance and receive the same salvation promised to reconstituted Israel. This is a depiction in OT language of the present church age, in which believing Jews and Gentiles are equal members in the body of Christ, "the Israel of God" (Gal 6:16). All baptized believers in Jesus Christ are heirs of God's covenant promises to Abraham (Gal 3:26–29; cf. 1 Cor 12:13; Eph 2:11–22). Therefore the Gospel is to be proclaimed to all peoples, and in the eternal state, the church triumphant shall consist of the redeemed from all nations and languages (Rev 5:9; 7:9–17; 14:6).

---

[4] For קָבַץ, "gather," in salvation oracles for Israel, see 11:17; 20:34, 41; 28:25; 34:13; 36:24; 37:21; 39:27. For שׁוּב שְׁבוּת, "bring about the restoration of," in reference to Israel, see 39:25. It was also used for Sodom and Samaria in an eschatological salvation oracle in 16:53. It is a comprehensive phrase for God's entire eschatological goal, to be completed at the return of Christ, the bodily resurrection, and the inheritance of the new heavens and earth by all believers (e.g., Mt 25:34; 1 Cor 15:50–57).

Judgment for Egypt, Recompense for Babylon, and a Horn for Israel

Translation

29 ¹In the tenth year, in the tenth [month], on the twelfth [day] of the month, the Word of Yahweh came to me: ²"Son of man, set your face against Pharaoh, the king of Egypt, and prophesy against him and against all Egypt. ³Speak and say, 'Thus says the Lord Yahweh:

" 'I am against you, Pharaoh, king of Egypt,

the great monster who lies amidst his Nile channels,

who says, "Mine is my Nile, and I made it for myself."

⁴But I will put hooks in your jaws and make the fish of your Nile channels stick to your scales.

I will haul you up from amidst your Nile channels with all the fish of your Nile channels clinging to your scales.

⁵I will hurl you out into the desert—you and all the fish of your Nile channels.

You will lie fallen in the open country, neither collected nor gathered up.

To the wild animals of the field and the birds of the air I will give you as food.

⁶Then all the inhabitants of Egypt will know that I am Yahweh.

" 'Because they were a reed used as a staff for the house of Israel— ⁷when they grasped you with the hand, you would splinter and tear open all their shoulders; when they leaned on you, you would break and make all their hips unsteady— ⁸therefore, thus says the Lord Yahweh: I am about to bring a sword against you and cut off people as well as animals from you; ⁹the land of Egypt will become a desolate ruin, and they will know that I am Yahweh.

" 'Because he said, "The Nile is mine; I myself made it," ¹⁰therefore, I am against you and against your Nile channels, and I will make the land of Egypt ruins, parched desolation—from Migdol to Aswan, that is, to the Nubian border. ¹¹The foot of man will not pass over it, nor shall the foot of beast pass over it, and it will remain uninhabited for forty years. ¹²I will make the land of Egypt a desolation among desolated lands, and its cities will be a desolation among ruined cities for forty years. I will scatter the Egyptians among the nations and disperse them among the countries.

¹³" 'Furthermore, thus says the Lord Yahweh: At the end of forty years I will gather the Egyptians from the peoples where they were scattered. ¹⁴I will bring about the restoration of Egypt and return them [the Egyptians] to Upper Egypt, the land of their origin, and there they will be a lowly kingdom. ¹⁵It will be the lowliest of kingdoms, and it will never again exalt itself above other nations. I will make it so weak that it will never again rule over the nations. ¹⁶It will never

again be an object of trust for the house of Israel, a reminder of their iniquity when they turned to them for help. Then they will know that I am the Lord Yahweh.' "

[17]In the twenty-seventh year, in the first [month], on the first day of the month, the Word of Yahweh came to me: [18]"Son of man, Nebuchadnezzar, king of Babylon, made his army labor hard against Tyre. Every head was made bald, and every shoulder rubbed raw, yet neither he nor his army received any recompense from Tyre for the labor they had expended against it.

[19]"Therefore, thus says the Lord Yahweh: I am about to give to Nebuchadnezzar, king of Babylon, the land of Egypt. He will carry off its horde, despoil it of its spoil and loot its pillage. That will be recompense for his army. [20]As his pay for which he labored I have given him the land of Egypt because they did it for me, says the Lord Yahweh.

[21]"On that day I will make a horn sprout for the house of Israel, and I will cause them to give you a hearing. Then they will know that I am Yahweh."

Textual Notes

29:1–21   See the map "The Ancient Near East."

29:1   On the significance of this date in 587 B.C., see "Introduction to Ezekiel 29–32: Oracles against Egypt" (see also figure 1). Only here, in 1:2 (which follows a different pattern), and in 40:1 does וַיְהִי fail to precede a date. Possibly the omissions signal major transitions in the book, although, if so, one might have expected the pattern to be followed more consistently. The Vulgate has "eleventh (day)," but the "tenth year" in the MT is supported by the LXX and is clearly the superior text.

29:2 בֶּן־אָדָם—For Ezekiel as "son of man," see the textual note and commentary on 2:1.

שִׂים פָּנֶיךָ עַל־פַּרְעֹה—For the idiom שִׂים פָּנֶיךָ, "set your face," which is unique to Ezekiel and used nine times in the book, see the second textual note on 6:2. Only here and in 35:2 does it use the preposition עַל ("against") instead of אֶל (the usual preposition) or דֶּרֶךְ (used like a preposition once). The substitution of עַל for אֶל may reflect Aramaic influence, but it was apparently ancient in Hebrew as well.

"Pharaoh" (פַּרְעֹה) is a Hebrew adaptation of Egyptian for "great house" (living quarters), but by extension early came to stand for the occupant and hence was used as a personal name. The appositional phrase מֶלֶךְ מִצְרַיִם, "the king of Egypt," expresses it in Hebrew terms, but one doubts if it was really necessary. Since "Pharaoh" was an embodiment of all Egypt, the following Hebrew pronouns and suffixes vacillate between masculine singular (referring to the pharaoh), feminine singular (referring to the land), and masculine plural (referring to the inhabitants of the land).

29:3 דִּבֶּר וְאָמַרְתָּ—Critics are tempted to delete the seemingly redundant דַּבֵּר before וְאָמַרְתָּ (as the LXX apparently did), but this combination occurs also in 14:14; 20:3, 27; and 33:2, as well as elsewhere in the Bible.[1]

---

[1]   A defense of the idiom is given by Boadt, *Ezekiel's Oracles against Egypt*, 21–23. Boadt's

הַתַּנִּים֙ הַגָּדֹול—The noun תַּנִּים appears to be plural, but the singular adjective shows that it is not (there is a word תַּן, "jackal," whose plural is spelled like this, but that word plainly does not fit). The proper singular of the word used here is תַּנִּין, used, for example, in Is 27:1; 51:9; and Ps 74:13. Its plural is a regular תַּנִּינִם. Both here and in 32:2 the Ezekelian text has תַּנִּים for the singular. It is unclear whether the final *mem* is a case of hypercorrection of the sometimes mistakenly written Aramaic plural in -*in* or whether the occasional confusion of *mem* and *nun*, evidenced also elsewhere, was already established by Ezekiel's time. Compare 26:18, which had both הָאִיֹּן and הָאִיִּם, and 30:13, where נֹף is written for מֹף, Memphis, the ancient capital of Lower Egypt.

יְאֹרָיו ... יְאֹרִי—The noun יְאֹר is a Hebraization of the Egyptian word for "river." Since there almost literally was no other river in Egypt besides the Nile, it virtually always has that specific meaning; thus it is a common noun used as a proper noun. Only very rarely is it used in the OT in a generic sense of any stream (e.g., Is 33:21). Since the Nile delta consisted of various branches (crisscrossed by many irrigation canals), the Egyptians themselves referred to at least any of the major ones as "a Nile," a usage accurately reflected in the plural יְאֹרָיו, "his Nile channels." Perhaps Yahweh puts the accent on it because Sais, the capital city of the Saitic (Twenty-sixth) Dynasty, contemporary with Ezekiel, lay in the west-central part of the delta.

וַאֲנִי עֲשִׂיתִנִי:—The pronoun is emphatic and redundant: "I myself." The suffix on the verb (first common singular Qal perfect of עָשָׂה) can hardly be a first common singular direct object, which would result in "I made myself." Claims to self-creation by certain Egyptian deities are known, but if such a boast had been intended, one would have expected to see it before Pharaoh's assertion of ownership of the Nile. Cooke and Zimmerli, among others, wish to emend to עשׂיתיו or עשׂיתים.[2] However, recent scholarship prefers to take it in a dative sense, "for myself." This usage was once thought to be rare (GKC, § 117 x), but partly due to Ugaritic studies, it is now recognized at various places in Ezekiel and other biblical books.[3] The suffix here then corresponds to לִי in לִי יְאֹרִי ("mine is my Nile") at the beginning of the Pharaonic boast.

29:4 וְנָתַתִּי חַחִיִּים֙ בִּלְחָיֶיךָ—This expression will be repeated in 38:4. Compare the references to "hooks" also in 19:4, 9. The Kethib, חַחִיִּים, is the plural of חָח, "hook," with dittographic double י. The Qere is the normal plural חַחִים.

יְאֹרֶיךָ—For all three occurrences of "your Nile channels," the LXX has the singular. Given Ezekiel's tendency toward prolixity, the repetition of the word is not at all surprising and is perhaps intended to underscore God's rejoinder to the pharaoh's boast about the Nile in 29:3.

---

work is an important monograph devoted solely to Ezekiel's Egyptian oracles. It is generally more restrained and balanced than the work of van Dijk on the Tyrian oracles (*Ezekiel's Prophecy on Tyre*). Boadt is also the author of the entry "Ezekiel, Book of" in *ABD* 2:711–22.

[2] Cooke, *Ezekiel*, 326; Zimmerli, *Ezekiel*, 2:106–7.

[3] See Boadt, *Ezekiel's Oracles against Egypt*, 29–30.

וְאֵת כָּל־דְּגַת יְאֹרֶיךָ בְּקַשְׂקְשֹׂתֶיךָ תִּדְבָּק׃—This final clause of the verse's second line nearly duplicates the final clause of the first line, וְהִדְבַּקְתִּי דְּגַת־יְאֹרֶיךָ בְּקַשְׂקְשֹׂתֶיךָ, which used the Hiphil of דָּבַק (literally, "I will cause to cling"). This clause uses the intransitive Qal imperfect תִּדְבָּק. Its subject is the feminine singular noun דָּגָה (in construct: דְּגַת). However, the subject phrase (וְאֵת כָּל־דְּגַת יְאֹרֶיךָ) is introduced by the direct object marker אֵת. Perhaps the use of אֵת was triggered by the Hiphil of דָּבַק in the first line, which could have taken אֵת with its direct object. It might also be the result of the nearer Hiphil of עָלָה, which would have two direct objects without the final two words of the second line: by itself, וְהַעֲלִיתִיךָ מִתּוֹךְ יְאֹרֶיךָ וְאֵת כָּל־דְּגַת יְאֹרֶיךָ would mean "I will haul up from amidst your Nile channels [both] you and all the fish of your Nile channels." But as the texts stands, אֵת may be understood as emphatic—an unexpected, but not rare use of the particle. In any case, syntactically we seem to have a sort of anacoluthon, and most English translations are, like mine, a bit free. KJV and NKJV seem simply to ignore the אֵת.

29:5 וּנְטַשְׁתִּיךָ הַמִּדְבָּרָה—The verb נָטַשׁ normally means "leave, abandon," and this is reflected in some English translations (KJV, NKJV, NIV), but the LXX and Vulgate as well as the adjacent verbs suggest a basic sense of "throw, hurl." The verb occurs in the same sense in 31:12 and 32:4.

הַשָּׂדֶה—This common noun usually means "field." It can refer to cultivated land, but the close connection with מִדְבָּר ("desert") here makes that unlikely. Crocodiles can travel a considerable distance out of water, but survival in a desert is a different matter.

תֵּאָסֵף וְלֹא תִקָּבֵץ—The verbs are the Niphals (second masculine singular imperfects) of אָסַף and קָבַץ, which are virtual synonyms meaning "gather" and which are often paired in parallel cola. Here, where one or the other seems redundant, many critics, following the Targum and several Hebrew manuscripts, emend תִקָּבֵץ to תִּקָּבֵר ("be buried"), a change possibly supported by the use of אָסַף and קָבַר together in Jer 8:2; 25:33 (so RSV and NRSV here). That sense may be correct, but emendation is not necessary to achieve it. אָסַף can be used of gathering for burial, as in the frequent biblical idiom "be gathered to one's people/fathers" (e.g., Gen 25:8; Judg 2:10). The LXX's use of περιστέλλω for קָבַץ (similar is the Syriac's translation) suggests that a corpse is "laid out" or prepared for burial, a natural sequel to the initial "gathering" of the remains. The Vulgate's support of the MT as well as the use of קָבַץ in 29:13 (the application of the prophecy) are further support.

29:6 The MT's versification is misleading. As so often, the recognition formula concludes a section, as 29:6a obviously does, while 29:6b begins a new paragraph. The metaphor shifts abruptly from that of a monster/crocodile to that of a reed.

But the MT's versification does, undoubtedly, reflect the understanding of the Masoretes that the subject of הֱיוֹתָם in 29:6b is "all the inhabitants of Egypt" in 29:6a. The versions, however, reflect a singular suffix (possibly הֱיוֹתְךָ), which many assume to be the original (e.g., Zimmerli and even Block),[4] which more easily coincides with

---

[4] Zimmerli, *Ezekiel*, 2:107; Block, *Ezekiel*, 2:136, n. 32.

the second person singulars in the following verses and the greater focus on the pharaoh himself. But such a change must assume a very fluid text until very late, contrary to all we know of the history of the text. The change is not substantively different because of the simultaneity of the pharaoh's fate and that of his subjects. Some ingenious emendations have been proposed.[5] But the simplest solution is to understand יַעַן ("because") in 29:6b as the beginning of a protasis, and the apodosis commences with לָכֵן ("therefore") in 29:8, a standard Hebrew sequence in prophecy. יַעַן requires a subsequent conclusion.

מִשְׁעֶנֶת קָנֶה—Most translations literally translate this construct phrase with these two nouns as "staff of reed." But I am not sure this readily communicates in English, so I have paraphrased slightly. There probably was no difficulty in understanding the Hebrew because of the obvious derivation of מִשְׁעֶנֶת, the *nomen regens*, from שָׁעַן, "to lean, depend on."

29:7 The Kethib בְּכַפְּךָ ("in your hand") must be mistaken. Perhaps a scribe inadvertently copied the suffix from the preceding בְּךָ. The Qere, probably correctly, reads בַּכַּף, "in the hand," without a suffix, as in 21:16 (ET 21:11). The LXX and Syriac reflect בְכַפָּם, probably to conform to the same suffix on the Qal infinitive construct (בְּתָפְשָׂם) at the beginning of the verse. More radically, Zimmerli and Allen wish to delete בַּכַּף as superfluous,[6] because it is not used in the following parallel, but that is a clear non sequitur.

תֵּרוֹץ ... תִּשָּׁבֵר—Two relatively synonymous words are used for "break," רָצַץ and שָׁבַר. Partly for variation and partly because of its object, the first is often rendered "splinter," as I have also. They are both imperfect (durative) and followed by perfects with *waw* consecutive, implying a standard pattern, hence, the translations, "would ... and ..." Thus the statement virtually becomes a proverb in its own right.

וּבָקַעְתָּ לָהֶם כָּל־כָּתֵף—The exact intent of this clause is not clear. Literally, it reads "and you tear open for them every (the whole?) shoulder." "Shoulder" is not quite as broad a term as the Hebrew כָּתֵף, which can refer to the entire shoulder area, both front (upper arm and chest) and back (shoulder blade). Perhaps the best sense is derived here if כָּתֵף is taken as the shoulder viewed from underneath, the armpit, which could be pierced by the sharp end of a splintered reed. The LXX and Syriac here speak of the כַּף instead of the כָּתֵף. Zimmerli spins out two theories as to how the presumably original כַּף was changed,[7] but the more likely reason was the influence of the Rabshakeh's words in Is 36:6 ‖ 2 Ki 18:21, where, however, a different verb (נָקַב) is used instead of בָּקַע here.

וְהַעֲמַדְתָּ לָהֶם כָּל־מָתְנָיִם:—Nearly everyone agrees that the Hiphil of עָמַד, which would have some sense like "cause to stand, set upright, make stiff and rigid," is just the opposite of what must be intended. KJV gamely renders, "madest all their loins to be at a stand." NIV, appealing questionably to the LXX's συνέκλασας and similar Vulgate and Peshitta renditions, offers a footnote rendition, "you caused their backs

---

5   E.g., Allen, *Ezekiel*, 2:102, and Boadt, *Ezekiel's Oracles against Egypt*, 36–37.

6   Zimmerli, *Ezekiel*, 2:107; Allen, *Ezekiel*, 2:102.

7   Zimmerli, *Ezekiel*, 2:107.

to stand," and in its main text has "their backs were wrenched." But this seems to me to be a counsel of desperation and appears to exhibit a reluctance to admit even the most routine text criticism. Among other modern translators and commentators, there is remarkable agreement that we must witness here a case of metathesis of the first and second root consonants. If we make that change to וְהִמְעַדְתָּ (Hiphil of מָעַד), we get the necessary meaning of "make shake, wobble, be unsteady." A comparable statement appears in Ps 69:24 (ET 69:23). Some translations have "collapse," but this is probably stronger than the Hebrew. The English idiom of knees "knocking" in fright might be comparable. The "loins," that is, hips and lower back, are commonly described in the Bible as the seat of the body's strength.

29:8 As expected, לָכֵן here introduces the apodosis after the protasis (יַעַן) in 29:6b. Both halves of the compound sentence in 29:8 employ stereotypical doom phraseology, with many parallels in Ezekiel (the first expression evidenced also in Lev 26:25, part of the so-called "Holiness Code" with which Ezekiel has so many affinities). Feminine singulars are used because "the land of Egypt" (29:9) is being addressed, as also in the next verse.

29:9 I have followed Greenberg in taking לִשְׁמָמָה וְחָרְבָּה as a hendiadys because of the absence of לְ before the second noun.[8] Ezekiel frequently uses חָרְבָּה or related forms. חָרְבוֹת will be used with שְׁמָמָה again in the next verse and in 35:4.

Once again the recognition formula ("and they will know …") concludes a section in the middle of a verse.

As in 29:6b, a new part of the oracle begins with יַעַן (the indictment, quoting Pharaoh's boast in 29:3), but it is followed immediately in the next verse by the apodosis, beginning with לָכֵן. This third part of the oracle (29:9b–16) sums up and expands both of the preceding parts of the oracle of judgment, but concludes, surprisingly, with a prophecy of clemency for Egypt.

אָמַר—I have retained "he said," although most translators, ancient and modern, read the second person ("you said"), which also moves more smoothly into the second person forms of 29:10. The MT is defensible, in my judgment because of the general tenor of the following verses. On the whole, the oracle centers on the Nile and/or the land, not the pharaoh. The Pharaoh becomes irrelevant, but passing attention must be given to him because of this quotation from him—spoken not by the Nile or the land, but by its ruler, whose last words in this oracle become virtually his self-judgment.

29:10 Syntactically, the sequence לְחָרְבוֹת חֹרֶב שְׁמָמָה either can be construed as an extended construct chain ("ruins of dryness of desolation"), or one can make one member an appositive. The meaning will be about the same, but I have opted to take the first word as the lead noun, modified by the next two ("ruins, parched desolation"). These or related words occur together also in Is 61:4 and Jer 49:13. The LXX read the middle word as חֶרֶב and seems to have transposed the first and third words, resulting in "to desolation and sword and destruction," which is possible but seems less

---

8   Greenberg, *Ezekiel*, 2:605.

felicitous. The scalpel of modern critics[9] often wishes to delete that middle word as a dittograph or gloss, but this is arbitrary.

מִמִּגְדֹּל סְוֵנֵה—"From Migdol to Aswan" (also in 30:6) probably functioned comparable to "from Dan to Beersheba" (e.g., 1 Sam 3:20) in the Bible, defining traditional boundaries, and in both cases happening to move from north to south. "Migdol" is really a Hebrew word ("tower"), and its use reflects Semitic influence in Lower Egypt. The name appears in several Egyptian place names in the northeastern delta. It appears already in the Exodus narrative (Ex 14:2). Jer 44:1 indicates the presence of Judahites there (probably either refugees or mercenaries), and in Jer 46:14 it is included in that prophet's Gentile oracle against Egypt. It was probably located a little east of the modern Suez Canal near the Mediterranean coastal road.

"Syene," the modern Aswan, is famous today as the site of the high dam on the Nile, just north of the first cataract of the Nile. Is 49:12 indicates that Israelites were there already that early (the Hebrew form is "Sinim"), and the syncretistic Jewish mercenaries stationed on the island of Elephantine, opposite Aswan, in the fifth century are well-known. The מִן before Migdol suggests that סְוֵנֵה could be revocalized סְוֵנָה with a *he* of direction to give "from … to," but the identical form (סְוֵנָה) is also used in 30:6.

וְעַד־גְּבוּל כּוּשׁ:—The *waw* should be understood as explicative ("that is"). כּוּשׁ or Nubia (essentially the modern Sudan) was the usual Egyptian designation of all the territory to the south, and Egypt had extensive contacts with the Nubians. The precise boundaries may well have fluctuated a bit from time to time, but probably never too far from Aswan. Many translations from KJV to NKJV have "Ethiopia," but the modern country by that name is farther south, and it is doubtful if the ancient Egyptians had much to do with it.

29:11 The perfect chiastic structure of the Hebrew original should be noted, though regrettably, that poetic flourish is lost in an idiomatic translation:

תַעֲבָר ... רֶגֶל ... וְרֶגֶל ... תַעֲבָר

"Forty years" is a common semi-symbolic designation for a generation. Often it is hard to know to what extent it is to be taken literally and/or figuratively. In 4:6 (which see), Ezekiel was instructed to lie on his right side for forty days, a day for each year,[10] corresponding to the duration of the Israelite exile. "Forty years" is best known to describe the generation the refractory Israelites would wander in the desert until almost all had died (Num 14:20–35; 32:13). It is also used to describe a full term for some "judges" and kings (e.g., Judg 8:28; 2 Sam 5:4). Since even King Mesha of Moab describes the Israelites' occupation of his country as lasting forty years,[11] it obviously was also a cultural idiom elsewhere in the Levant besides Israel.

---

[9] E.g., Cooke, *Ezekiel*, 327; Zimmerli, *Ezekiel*, 2:108.

[10] Compare the discussion of "seventy years" (Jer 25:11–12; 29:10) and its two biblical termini in Hummel, *Ezekiel 1–20*, 157.

[11] *ANET*, 320.

29:12 בְּתוֹךְ, used twice in this verse, is sometimes taken as having superlative force (e.g., "the most desolate of desolated lands"). The interpretation is not universally accepted, however, and it is hard to imagine a superlative topping the sweeping assertion of 29:11. Greenberg in particular disputes that construal: "Membership in a class is the point, not superlative exemplification of it."[12]

The Hophal feminine singular participle מֳחֳרָבוֹת ("ruined"), from חָרֵב, will be replaced by the synonymous Niphal feminine singular participle נַחֲרָבוֹת in 30:7.

29:13 The initial כִּי does not have its usual force of "for/because," but is contrastive or deictic, introducing a new stage in the oracle, specifically in clarifying the meaning of the "forty years," which is repeated.

29:14 וְשַׁבְתִּי אֶת־שְׁבוּת—On the idiom שׁוּב שְׁבוּת, "bring about the restoration of," which has nothing, as such, to do with either captivity or luck/fortune, see in "Introduction to Ezekiel 29–32: Oracles against Egypt." See also the discussions of the same phrase in the first textual note and the commentary on 16:53, where it referred to Sodom and Samaria, and the commentary on 39:25, where it refers to eschatological Israel.

פַּתְרוֹס—I have followed NIV in rendering the Hebrew "Pathros" (פַּתְרוֹס) as "Upper Egypt," which, hopefully, will communicate better. The name will reappear in 30:14. In the Table of Nations (Gen 10:13–14) and the parallel 1 Chr 1:11–12, the "Pathrusim" (people of Pathros) are listed among the descendants of "Mizraim" (Hebrew for "Egypt"), the grandson of Noah. Its location in the south is based on the sequence in Is 11:11, also found in Assyrian sources, that moves from Mizraim (presumably lower or northern Egypt) through Pathros to "Cush" (Nubia; see the last textual note on 29:10). The Egyptian form of the name means "the southern land," reinforcing the other evidence.

אֶרֶץ מְכוּרָתָם—"The land of their origin" uses מְכוּרָה, found in the OT only in 16:3; 21:35 (ET 21:30); and here. The Egyptians themselves had a tradition of the South, probably centered at Thebes or the vicinity, as the area from which the unification of the North (Memphis) and South originated. It is a historical fact that the unification of the country did begin by southern rulers gaining control of the North, and that scenario was repeated several times in the course of Egypt's history. The anti-delta and anti-Saite stance of this oracle, reflecting current conditions, probably encouraged this insistence, expanded in the rest of the section, that the future will be vastly different from the present.

מַמְלָכָה should not be pressed to indicate a political system with a מֶלֶךְ at its head, but is used generally of a nation under any type of government. In 17:14 מַמְלָכָה שְׁפָלָה had referred to Zedekiah's vassal status, and vassalage may be the intended application to Egypt here.

29:15 וְהִמְעַטְתִּים—The Hiphil of מָעַט (first common singular perfect with *waw* consecutive and third masculine singular suffix) is, literally, "to make small, few," but

---

[12] Greenberg, *Ezekiel*, 2:607.

the point is probably not geographic or demographic size, but political and military strength.

29:16 יְהְיֶה—This singular verb is difficult in a context of masculine plurals and feminine singulars, and hence many emend to the plural יְהְיוּ, as the ancient versions translated. Meaning is unaffected, but it is not clear that a textual change is necessary in the context of the interchangeability of king, land, and people.

לְמִבְטָח מַזְכִּיר עָוֺן בִּפְנוֹתָם אַחֲרֵיהֶם—The syntax here can be taken in several ways. The noun מִבְטָח, "object of trust," clearly refers to Egypt, which Israel had relied upon or trusted instead of Yahweh. The referent of the following מַזְכִּיר עָוֺן, "one causing [someone] to remember iniquity" (with the Hiphil participle of זָכַר), is less certain. Sometimes מַזְכִּיר refers to a spokesman of some sort; in 21:28 (ET 21:23), Ezekiel had used it of a prosecutor who accused Israel of perjury. Here, however, the meaning seems more impersonal, a "reminder." But who reminds whom? I added "their," referencing the Israelites, in my translation, but the Hebrew has no suffix. By trusting in Egypt, the Israelites reminded Yahweh of their own iniquity, but with Egypt humiliated, the Israelites would no longer trust it, nor would they thereby remind Yahweh of their iniquity. Alternatively, the subject could be Egypt, with Yahweh as the object; no longer would an arrogant Egypt remind God of Israel's misplaced trust in someone besides him. However, the third plural possessive suffixes on the words following this phrase clearly refer to Israel. The Hebrew is asyndetic; the translation has a comma after "Israel" to separate מִבְטָח and מַזְכִּיר. "Their [Israel's] turning after them [Egypt]" is a strange expression if one translates בִּפְנוֹתָם אַחֲרֵיהֶם literalistically, but we probably have an Aramaism, where פָּנָה אַחֲרֵי regularly replaces the standard Hebrew פָּנָה אֶל.

Greenberg notes the similarity to Ps 40:5 (ET 40:4): "Blessed is the man who makes Yahweh the object of his trust and does not turn to [פָּנָה אֶל] the Rahabs." Since Rahab was a name of the monster of chaos in Canaanite mythology, more or less synonymous with תַּנִּין (the usual spelling for the "monster" in Ezek 29:3; see also Is 51:9), and since in Ps 87:4 Egypt is called "Rahab," he suggests plausibly that "our Ezekiel verse may be a specific application of Ps 40:5."[13]

29:17 As noted in "Introduction to Ezekiel 29–32: Oracles against Egypt," 29:17–21 is the latest of the dated oracles in Ezekiel. It came two years after the eschatological vision in chapters 40–48, about sixteen years and four months after the previous oracle (29:1), and sixteen years after the next dated oracle in the book (30:20). (See figure 1, "The Dates in Ezekiel.") It is also the only one of the chronological notices in chapters 29–32 that is out of actual sequence, apparently because of the topic it addresses, a year or two after the end of Nebuchadnezzar's aborted siege of Tyre. With only five verses, it is one of the shortest in the book.

29:18 הֶעֱבִיד אֶת־חֵילוֹ עֲבֹדָה גְדֹלָה—The Hebrew, with the Hiphil of עָבַד and the cognate noun עֲבֹדָה as an adverbial accusative, is, literally, "he made his army labor (with) great labor." This describes the extraordinary effort Nebuchadnezzar made to

---

[13] Greenberg, *Ezekiel*, 2:607.

capture Tyre, an island city. That heads were rubbed bald and shoulders raw evidently refers to the protracted carrying of burdens on those parts of the body. Since Nebuchadnezzar was apparently never able to get close enough to the city to heap up the usual siege mounds and ramps, the reference would seem to be the earthworks erected to blockade the land approaches to the city. Conceivably, Nebuchadnezzar attempted to build a causeway out to the island, but lacked the resources to accomplish that feat, which only Alexander succeeded in doing centuries later. See the commentary on 26:1.

Normally, שָׂכָר refers to wages or payment someone receives for services rendered, but ancient Near Eastern idiom also used the word for booty taken upon a city's surrender, whatever its form. While Tyre did evidently reach some sort of accommodation with the Babylonians to cause them to lift the siege, it was a far cry from a literalistic fulfillment of Ezekiel's prophecy in 26:3–14 (which see). Since Yahweh is speaking, the implication is that Yahweh is the ultimate paymaster (see 29:20), and he will pay the Babylonians something for doing his work.

29:19 וְנָשָׂא הֲמֹנָהּ—Nebuchadnezzar's "consolation prize" is described with three nouns referring to the booty. The first is הֲמֹנָהּ, "its [Egypt's] horde," which he will be able to "carry off" (וְנָשָׂא). The noun הָמוֹן can mean "riches." However, throughout the Egyptian oracles in Ezekiel 29–32, the word is used sixteen times and means "horde, crowd," presumably of prisoners of war and perhaps even of a wider enslavement of Egyptians.

וְשָׁלַל שְׁלָלָהּ וּבָזַז בִּזָּהּ—These two cognate accusative constructions use synonyms, literally, "take its spoil as spoil and plunder its plunder."

29:20 פְּעֻלָּתוֹ אֲשֶׁר־עָבַד בָּהּ—The noun פְּעֻלָּה can mean "work," but also "reward/recompense," and here most likely it is simply a synonym of שָׂכָר, "wages," near the end of 29:19. The Hebrew continues, literally, "which he worked for it." The feminine suffix on בָּהּ, "for it," refers back to the feminine noun פְּעֻלָּה. The LXX, Syriac, and Vulgate, however, take the antecedent to be Tyre in 29:18. This makes a neat parallel with 29:18b and brings out the compensatory nature of the gift of Egypt, but the great distance between בָּהּ and Tyre as antecedent makes that interpretation less likely.

נָתַתִּי—This is probably as classical an example of the prophetic perfect as one will find. Regardless of the earthly timetable, the irrevocable decision has already been made in heaven.

אֲשֶׁר עָשׂוּ לִי—A major textual problem is that a translation of this clause is absent in the LXX and Peshitta, causing many to delete it as a gloss. If one construes אֲשֶׁר as introducing a relative clause ("which they did for me"), it remains intelligible, but it has no clear antecedent and seems to be rather awkwardly placed. However, the syntactical problem is alleviated if אֲשֶׁר is understood as causal ("because"), as virtually all English translations (already KJV) do. (It is hard not to suspect that theological motives are involved in the alacrity with which many critics declare it a gloss.) Boadt even takes the first אֲשֶׁר in the verse as causal ("as compensation *because* he worked for it"),[14] which is possible too. This causal use of אֲשֶׁר is not com-

---

[14] Boadt, *Ezekiel's Oracles against Egypt*, 51–52; emphasis added.

mon, but recognized as a possibility. Theologically, of course, it is beautiful: even though events had not turned out precisely as originally foretold, Yahweh would see to it that his agent (however unwitting) is rewarded. See the commentary on 29:17–21 for the hermeneutical issue of true prophecy.

29:21 See the commentary.

Commentary

This chapter consists of two oracles. The first (29:1–16) focuses almost exclusively on the judgment of Egypt. The second (29:17–21) continues the theme of divine judgment for Egypt, but at the hands of the king of Babylon, who, by subduing Egypt, receives a recompense for his labor (only partially successful) in attacking Tyre. The second oracle concludes with a striking Gospel promise of a "horn" for Israel.

Judgment for Egypt, the Monster and Splintering Staff (29:1–16)

This first oracle is replete with typical Ezekelian diction and formulae. Both "the Word of Yahweh came to me"[15] and Yahweh's address to the prophet as "son of man"[16] also begin later oracles about Egypt (29:17–18; 30:1–2, 20–21; 31:1–2; 32:1–2, 17–18). Various subdivisions of this oracle are possible, but the threefold occurrence of the recognition formula,[17] "then/and they will know that I am (the Lord) Yahweh" (29:6, 9, 16) seems to offer the most helpful pointer. Since this formula normally signals the end of an oracle or section thereof, we can divide this oracle into three sections: (1) 29:3–6a; (2) 29:6b–9a; and (3) 29:9b–16. The logic of this division is further demonstrated by the pattern of the protasis יַעַן ("because") followed by the apodosis לָכֵן ("therefore") in the second and third subdivisions. The first and third subdivisions score Pharaonic hubris, while the second is more concerned with Egyptian-Israelite relations.

29:2 In all of Ezekiel's oracles against Egypt, the message is almost simultaneously against the pharaoh, the land over which he rules, and the people inhabiting it. Even when one of the three is singled out, the other two are implicated. Hence, the pronouns and predicates vary freely in number and gender, although the variation is less obvious in English than in the more inflected Hebrew language.

29:3 The rather general challenge formula "I am against you" links this oracle with the preceding ones against Tyre and Sidon (26:3; 28:22). Specific Egyptian coloration begins with the direct address to the pharaoh as "the great monster" (הַתַּנִּים הַגָּדוֹל). No single English word reproduces the Hebrew fully because of its multivalence. The description of the creature's capture in 29:4

---

[15] For this word-event formula, see page 8 in the introduction and the textual note on 3:16.

[16] See the second textual note and the commentary on 2:1.

[17] For this formula, see page 9 in the introduction and the commentary on 6:7.

makes one think of a crocodile, reinforced by the similar language in an account by Herodotus of a crocodile's capture.[18] תַּנִּין is usually rendered "snake/serpent" (although that is normally expressed in the OT by נָחָשׁ). תַּנִּין is used of the "snake" into which Moses' staff turned before the first plague (Ex 7:9–10, 12), and hence often understood as the reptilian crocodile (perhaps also in Deut 32:33; Ps 91:13). But by itself "crocodile" is scarcely adequate because of the following claim that it created the Nile. Neither is it to be entirely dismissed, partly because of the known veneration of the crocodile god, Sobek, in parts of Egypt, especially in the delta region. In addition, the ancient Egyptians regarded their Pharaohs as actual deities.

But this only begins to hint at the exmythological overtones that Ezekiel will have intended. Hence, many translations have "dragon" (KJV, RSV, NRSV), but in my judgment, that word sounds like functional mythology to modern ears, although it continues to be used even in the NT. See Rev 12:3–13:11, where, for the Greek δράκων, all English versions use "dragon." "Monster" (as in NKJV and NIV) has seemed better to me here, although it is paler. Possibly "sea monster" (cf. Gen 1:21 and Ps 148:7) would be even better. The original Canaanite myth described the annual, autumnal triumph of Baal (Hadad) over Moth ("death") and Yammim ("sea"). "Exmythological" means that Israelite believers would have recognized that Ezekiel is using language adapted from the pagan myths, but, of course, he is using it to proclaim the one true God over against the pagan "gods," who at most, in biblical thought, represent the devil and the forces of evil. Similar exmythological uses of sea-monster language for the evil defeated by God are in, for example, Is 27:1; 51:9; Pss 74:14; 89:10 (ET 89:9).

Sometimes the sea monster, god of chaos, is called Rahab and Leviathan (the latter known in Ugaritic). In its demythologized form in the Bible, the tale was used to describe Yahweh's winning battle over idols or would-be gods. As already Gen 1:21 (using תַּנִּינִם) had indicated, in its various manifestations, it was finally only another creature and no possible threat to the almighty Creator, and so "Leviathan" is described in Is 27:1 and Ps 104:26 (and probably Job 41 as well). But creatures, especially in human form, can rebel and play god, that is, represent Satan, and in Revelation 12–13, such creatures will represent Satan himself. Thus here, although the language is a demythologized metaphor, the pharaoh is indicted for virtually the same arrogance as the king of Tyre, who had flatly said "I am a god" (28:2). Possibly it is coincidental, but the pharaoh's braggadocio sounds like an explicit challenge to Yahweh's assertion in 17:24; 22:14; and elsewhere: "I, Yahweh, have spoken, and I will accomplish it." Isaiah had expressed the same thought even more strongly in Is 47:8, 10, where arrogant Babylon boasts: "I am, and there is none besides me." Not only hegemony, but the existence of another bona-fide God is at issue.

---

[18] Herodotus, *Histories*, 2.70.1–2.

At the risk of overexegesis, one may even detect exmythological overtones in the description that the monster "lies" (רֹבֵץ) in the water. The word may only connote a creature at ease, sprawling or couching. But the biblical scholar will note that God had used the same verb in his warning to Cain before his fratricide (Gen 4:7), where "sin" (הַטָּאת) had been pictured as a monster "couching" (the same Hebrew participle) at the door. In Akkadian, the cognate *rabiṣum* is a term for a demon.

29:4 By virtue of the very exclusivity of his nature, Yahweh must respond to such hubris. Syncretism of any sort is incompatible with the very essence of biblical faith. Hence the overtones of monstrosity in which the pharaoh's boast had been couched is now shown to be the figment of human imagination that it is by simply disappearing from sight. Instead the figure of a sea monster is replaced by that of an ordinary fish, not only incapable of eluding capture himself, but dragging along with himself all the other fish caught in his scales. The mention of the capture of the "big fish" and all the "small fry" together with him corresponds to the way in which the entire pericope alternates in consideration of the pharaoh himself and the inhabitants of Egypt, whose fate is inextricably bound up with his.

29:5 So unimportant is this pompous Pharaoh that he not only will not be given a grand state burial, but his carcass and that of his people will be abandoned to the elements or left to be eaten by animals (a common curse or threat in ancient literature). The metaphorical language here anticipates historical prophecies, first the scattering of the Egyptian populace in 29:12 and then in 29:13 their gathering again in their homeland.

29:6 The verse should be divided into two (see the first textual note on this verse). The recognition formula in 29:6a emphasizes that Yahweh has been the real actor all along and that when he changes the pharaoh's arrogance into ignominy, even the Egyptians will acknowledge Yahweh's supremacy.

In 29:6b the specific charge of the pharaoh's interference in Israelite affairs comes to the fore. The metaphor of trying to use a hollow Nile papyrus reed as a crutch or cane arises to express Hophra's inability to be of any real help to Israel and Israel's desperate gullibility in even entertaining the notion that it might be otherwise. The weakness and brittleness of the reed was proverbial. We meet it first in Scripture in the taunt of the Assyrian Rabshakeh to besieged Jerusalem (Is 36:6 ‖ 2 Ki 18:21), describing Egypt over a century earlier as a broken "reed" that is a poor "staff" (using the same vocabulary as here). This metaphor is also known in Assyrian, Hittite, and Indic literature.

29:7 The metaphor of the unreliable reed is expanded in two directions. It will cause debilitating injury to both the upper and lower parts of the body, as the Israelites should have learned long ago. Addressing the Egyptian people as a single individual, they are faulted for leading Israel into a state of false trust. Egyptian blandishments had made them even less willing to repent and lean on Yahweh's promises. Egypt's guilt was compounded by assisting Zedekiah's resistance to Yahweh (the obverse of 17:15–18, where Zedekiah had appealed to Egypt for help), and thus standing in the way of Yahweh's inexorable plan for Israel.

29:9 As in 29:6, the second part of this section of the oracle, after initial prophecies of judgment on Egypt, ends with the recognition formula in midverse. With 29:9b the final section of the oracle (through 29:16) begins by quoting the pharaoh's bombastic boast in 29:3. But how empty the boast was is shown by the fact that this is the last we hear of the pharaoh. When he claims divinity in confrontation with the only true God, he is quickly exposed (and deposed) as a non-entity. God has given rulers a legitimate ministerial function (Rom 13:1), but to claim more inevitably brings confrontation and destruction.

There are only minor differences between the form of the pharaoh's boast in Ezek 29:3 and its quotation here. The variations seem to have some significance. In 29:3 לִי ("mine," calling attention to the pharaoh) came first, while here it follows. That "Nile" comes first here and lacks the first person possessive suffix accents the river, not Pharaoh's ego. The same effect is achieved by the absence here of the first person object suffix on the verb.

29:10 The punishment, introduced by לָכֵן, "therefore," begins by repeating the challenge formula of 29:3, although as already noted, the pharaoh is fading from view, and Yahweh's wrath is concentrated on the land and the Nile channels. The second half of the verse is almost thetical for the material through 29:12. Ezekiel begins here by piling up words for the utter desolation to come, and prophecies that it will encompass all of Egypt from its northern to its southern border.

29:11 The land will be completely devoid of life for a generation ("forty years"; see the textual note). The threefold repetition of the number in 29:11–13 emphasizes it.

29:12 As he had prophesied earlier that Judah would be scattered among the nations (e.g., 5:10, 12; 12:14–15; 20:23; 22:15), Ezekiel now predicts that the Egyptian population too will be scattered. It is hard not to compare Ezekiel's prophecies here with the earlier historical accounts of Jeremiah 43–44. Jeremiah does not seem to describe such utter devastation as Ezekiel, but his oracles are more vivid and detailed: Nebuchadnezzar attacking the pharaoh's palace in Tahpanhes, burning the temples of the Egyptian gods, breaking up the obelisks at Heliopolis, and bringing disaster on the Judahite exiles in that land. Interestingly, though, in his anti-Egyptian Gentile oracle in 46:13–26, Jeremiah's language more closely approximates Ezekiel's.

29:13–16 It is hard to know how to deal with these verses exegetically. It strikes one that the language employed to describe both Egypt's judgment and its restoration is very similar to that which is otherwise used of Israel.[19] But why is Egypt favored with a promise of restoration when the other foreign nations are condemned to annihilation? Part of the answer must lie in the differ-

---

[19] See "Introduction to Ezekiel 29–32: Oracles against Egypt."

ent attitude of Egypt. While the other nations had gloated over Jerusalem's misfortune, we read nothing of that sort about Egypt. After all, in the near past, Egypt had tried to come to Israel's aid, even though it had failed. In contrast to the king of Tyre's crass claim to divinity, Egypt's *hubris* had stopped short of that. Egypt's real fault had been in tempting Israel to a false trust, in deflecting it from reliance solely on Yahweh and his promises. That problem Yahweh could solve by something less than the country's total annihilation. Its reduction to "third world" status would suffice for that.

Later, in 30:23, when the prophecy of the dispersal of the Egyptians is repeated, there is no mention of a forty-year limitation (as in 29:11–13), nor a promise of their eventual restoration. Many critics raise suspicions that 29:13–16 is simply a mitigating afterthought, inserted at some later time. But militating against that notion is the fact that other prophets also envisioned some exceptional status for Egypt in the future. We glimpse this thought briefly in Jer 46:26b and in detail in Is 19:18–24, where the vision has moved into full-blown eschatology (including even a restored Assyria). There is something eschatological about this oracle in Ezekiel as well, although his focus is limited more to Israel's near restoration, to be described in more detail in chapters 34–48. But whether short or long range, prophecy is typically couched in terms of present, known realities. One can no more deduce a this-worldly political program (ancient or modern) from it than some millennialists who seek to interpret modern Near Eastern history on the basis of biblical history. God's program of restoration is universal, as had been promised already to Abraham (Gen 12:3). The Gospel of God's redemptive work in Jesus Christ is to be proclaimed throughout the world, to the ends of the earth (Acts 1:8). Yet the message is not universalistic; sinners are only saved through repentance and faith in Jesus, whose atonement on Calvary and whose empty tomb have procured redemption for all.

A Recompense for Babylon and a Horn for Israel (29:17–21)

Before considering the import and the special hermeneutical problems posed by this separate oracle at the end of the chapter, I shall address first the exegesis of its last verse (29:21).

A simple, surface translation of the verse is easy, but the import of those words is anything but clear. "On that day" binds this final verse with the previous four, for in a way it treats a separate topic: the aftermath and consequences of what has just been prophesied. "That day" is indefinite. The immediate referent must be Nebuchadnezzar's imminent conquest of Egypt, something that should happen soon enough that the booty obtained then should clearly be compensation for his failure to receive any "pay" for his siege of Tyre. But at least in my understanding, an eschatological element is intertwined with it—the kind of double application one frequently encounters in prophecy.

To "make a horn sprout" is obviously a mixed metaphor. "Horn," applied to the house of Israel, is itself plainly metaphorical. In fact, it is often given as a classical illustration of the difference between "formal" and "dynamic equivalence," the two main theories of translation. In the "formal" method, one will simply translate literally "horn" and leave it to the reader to decide for himself what the metaphor means. In contrast, the "dynamic" procedure will usually offer some interpretation of the metaphor. If that interpretation is correct, a much more intelligible translation will be the result; if it is incorrect, confusion or damage of various sorts may ensue. The translator's presuppositions will inevitably evidence themselves much more in the "dynamic equivalence" method. While, in general, I have much sympathy for the "dynamic" approach, in this instance I have retained the literal "horn" translation, simply because of my own (and a common) uncertainty as to what precisely is meant.

Since an animal's strength often expressed itself through its horns, the word is often a figure for strength,[20] often as a gift of God's grace in various contexts, but also in the negative sense of "arrogance." For example, in Lam 2:3 God had cut off Judah's "horn" when he caused its fall (see also Ps 75:5–6 [ET 75:4–5]). A classical example of the positive usage would be in the Song of Hannah (1 Sam 2:1): "my horn is exalted in Yahweh," transmuted by Mary into "my soul magnifies the Lord" in the Magnificat (Lk 1:46). In the Benedictus Zechariah, filled with the Holy Spirit, prophesies:

> Blessed be the Lord God of Israel,
> > for he has visited and worked redemption for his people
> and has raised up *a horn of salvation* for us
> > in the house of his servant David,
> as he spoke by the mouth of his holy prophets from of old. (Lk 1:68–70)

In Rev 5:6, Christ himself is seen as a Lamb who has been slain "with seven horns and seven eyes."

A major issue is whether the "strength" apparently indicated by "horn" here is messianic. The identical idiom is used in Ps 132:17, where Yahweh promises, "I will make a horn sprout for David; I have prepared a lamp for my anointed one." Many other passages relate a "horn" to God and his salvation.[a]

(a) 2 Sam 22:3 ‖ Ps 18:3 (ET 18:2); Pss 89:18, 25 (ET 89:17, 24); 112:9; 148:14

Until recent times, some sort of messianic or at least eschatological interpretation of Ezek 29:21 was widespread, with the Babylonian conquest of Egypt as a harbinger of Israel's restoration, ultimately in Christ. Even Keil limits its application to "the Messianic salvation" without reference to a personal Messiah,[21] but sometimes this is almost a distinction without a difference. Zimmerli argues that Messianism was "fairly unimportant" in Ezekiel and wishes to limit the expression's meaning to "a general reference to an approaching deliverance for Israel."[22] However, this is not entirely convincing because Ezekiel

---

[20] Mesopotamian gods are regularly shown with horns (see *ANEP*, §§ 525–26). Altars normally had four horns, but there is no agreement at all as to their possible significance. Compare the various horns in the visions of Dan 7:7–8, 24; 8:5.

[21] Keil, *Ezekiel*, 2:14.

[22] Zimmerli, *Ezekiel*, 2:120.

had concluded the oracles against Tyre and Sidon with an eschatological picture (28:25–26), and, as Block argues, Ezekiel will shortly make some explicitly messianic predictions (34:24; 37:24).[23] Just possibly, we may even see a reinforcement of the messianic idea in the verb "sprout" (Hiphil of צָמַח) used in 29:21, since the noun derived from that root, צֶמַח, "branch, shoot," is frequently a metaphor, sometimes almost becoming a proper noun, for the messianic king.[b]

For the promise to Ezekiel himself that "on that day" Yahweh will give him (literally) "openness of mouth" (29:21), my free translation is anything but a formal equivalent. One's initial reflex is to think of a lifting of the prophet's muteness (3:26–27; 24:25–27, and the report of that occurring in 33:21–22). But that issue is tethered to the fall of Jerusalem, not of Egypt, and, if that were the intent, one would have expected the simple "I will open your mouth" (cf. 24:27; 33:22). The more oblique idiom here suggests that it has other overtones. It may be related to a cognate Akkadian idiom referring to part of the ritual by which sacred images were consecrated, that is, empowered to function as believed. Applied to Ezekiel, that would imply a vindication of his ministry so that the people would "give [him] a hearing," that is, actually listen to his message and know that Yahweh is God (nowhere does the recognition formula flow more naturally out of its context than here in 29:21). The use of the expression once before in Ezekiel (16:63; which see) seems to confirm this interpretation; there it is used negatively of repentant Jerusalem's inability to find an audience for its boast of supposed superiority over its "sisters."

If so, it sounds as if Ezekiel's whole credibility as a prophet had been called into question because of the failure of Tyre to capitulate, at least in the way predicted in chapters 26–28. (Earlier in 12:27 already the people had tended to dismiss Ezekiel's messages because they referred to "distant times" that did not seem relevant to the people's current plight.)

This raises the question of true versus false prophecy, which is at issue in this entire appendix-like conclusion to the chapter.[24] In fact, the problem may even be exacerbated by the present prediction about Egypt. External evidence for an invasion of Egypt by Nebuchadnezzar is scanty, at best. A damaged and fragmentary cuneiform tablet does refer to some kind of military action against Egypt in Nebuchadnezzar's thirty-seventh year (568/567), that is, within three years of this prophecy. Reference seems to be made to Amasis, who, at least according to Herodotus, succeeded Hophra in connection with a civil war that erupted upon the latter's death.[25] It can be hypothesized that Nebuchadnezzar took advantage of the disorder in Egypt to launch some kind of military action. But at about the same time, the Egyptians are describing Amasis' defeat of some Asiatic invaders, very possibly Babylonians. But whatever the facts, the in-

(b) Jer 23:5; 33:15; Zech 3:8; 6:12; cf. Is 4:2; 61:11

---

[23] Block, *Ezekiel*, 2:152.

[24] For true versus false prophecy, see also the commentary on Ezekiel 13.

[25] Herodotus, *Histories*, 2.163, 169.

cursion into Egypt does not seem to be nearly as devastating as 29:19 would lead one to believe. We are hampered enough, however, by exiguous (and contradictory) evidence that one hesitates to make definite assertions. Jeremiah is implicated as much as Ezekiel, for in Jer 43:8–13 he also predicts in different, but more detailed, language major depredations in Egypt by Nebuchadnezzar.

So the whole hermeneutics of the fulfillment of prophecy come into focus here. According to Deut 18:21–22, if a prophecy failed to come to pass, it proved that a false prophet was speaking. Of course, the question immediately arises: how precisely must the fulfillment match the prediction? The prophets often spoke in highly figurative and hyperbolic poetry where literalism can easily raise unnecessary questions. As far as we know, Tyre's walls were never breached by battering rams and so on, as 26:6–14 would indicate, because Nebuchadnezzar could never bring such war machinery to bear against the island city. Yet it does seem clear that Tyre did make enough concessions that the Babylonians seem to have declared victory and bothered Tyre no more. Something comparable may have occurred in Egypt, as we just noted. One should not forget that Deuteronomy cites yet another criterion of true prophecy, namely orthodoxy or "Mosaicity" (Deut 13:2–6 [ET 13:1–5]).

Then there is the so-called "contingency" of prophecy. Whether enunciated or not, a conditional clause appears to accompany virtually all prophecy, pivoting on whether or not the hearer(s) repent and/or continue to be faithful or not. The Bible itself records many instances where God "relents/changes his verdict,"[26] sometimes for reasons not revealed to humanity. If some unknown factor required a shift in strategy, that was all in the inscrutable mystery of the Godhead. This understanding of prophecy is obviously capable of abuse, which if used carelessly, could evacuate prophecy of all solid, meaningful content. The prophets were themselves aware that they, under inspiration, spoke more than they knew, as the NT also informs us (1 Pet 1:10–12). The subject cannot be trivialized, but, as especially some millennialistic "evangelists" in our day illustrate, "preoccupation with the fulfillment of predictions has a tendency to deafen hearers to the primary message of God and his agent in any age."[27]

Finally, some commentators read this pericope as primarily God's message of reassurance to Ezekiel himself, who supposedly had begun to doubt his own vocation. This is certainly not out of the question, and Scripture does record such moments in the lives of prophets (perhaps classically Elijah in his flight from Jezebel in 1 Kings 19; see also Jeremiah's lament in Jer 20:14–18; cf. even the Servant in Is 49:4). But Ezekiel virtually never reveals his inner feelings, so that even if it were the case, we could hardly expect him to verbalize it, and I see nothing in the words of the text itself to lead us to such a conclusion.

---

[26] See the excursus "When Yahweh Changes a Prior Verdict" in Lessing, *Jonah*, 324–41.

[27] Block, *Ezekiel*, 2:154.

Egypt Will Fall and Pharaoh's Arm Will Be Broken

Translation

30 ¹The Word of Yahweh came to me: ²"Son of man, prophesy and say, 'Thus says the Lord Yahweh: Wail: alas for the day! ³For a day is near; yes, near is the Day of Yahweh. It will be a day of clouds, a time for the nations. ⁴A sword will enter Egypt, and there will be panic in Nubia, when the slain fall in Egypt, and they take away its horde, and its foundations are demolished. ⁵Nubia, Lybia, Lydia, all the mixed units, Kuv, and the men of the land of the covenant with them will fall by the sword.

⁶" 'Thus says Yahweh: The supporters of Egypt will fall, and its proud might will sink. From Migdol to Aswan those within it will fall by the sword, says the Lord Yahweh. ⁷It will be desolated among desolate lands, and its cities will be among ruined cities. ⁸They will know that I am Yahweh when I set fire to Egypt and all its helpers are crushed. ⁹On that day, messengers will go out from me in ships to terrify confident Nubia, and there will be panic among them on the day of Egypt, for it is surely coming.

¹⁰" 'Thus says the Lord Yahweh: I will put an end to the horde of Egypt by the hand of Nebuchadnezzar, the king of Babylon. ¹¹He and his army with him, the most ruthless of nations, will be brought in to destroy the land. They will unsheathe their swords against Egypt and fill the land with the slain. ¹²I will dry up the Nile channels and sell the land to fierce men. I will desolate the land and everything in it by the hand of foreigners. I, Yahweh, have spoken.

¹³" 'Thus says the Lord Yahweh: I will destroy the fecal deities and eliminate the non-gods from Memphis. A prince from the land of Egypt will never again exist, and I will put fear in the land of Egypt. ¹⁴I will desolate Upper Egypt, set fire to Zoan, and inflict punishments on Thebes. ¹⁵I will pour out my wrath on Pelusium, the stronghold of Egypt, and cut off the horde of Thebes. ¹⁶I will set fire to Egypt; Pelusium will writhe in pain; Thebes will be breached; and Memphis will face enemies by day. ¹⁷The young men of Heliopolis and Bubastis will fall by the sword, and the women will go into captivity. ¹⁸At Tahpanhes the day will grow dark when I break the yokes of Egypt there, and there its proud might will cease. A cloud will cover it, and its daughters will go into captivity. ¹⁹I will inflict punishments on Egypt, and they will know that I am Yahweh.' "

²⁰In the eleventh year, in the first [month], on the seventh [day] of the month, the Word of Yahweh came to me: ²¹"Son of man, I have broken the arm of Pharaoh, the king of Egypt. Note that it has not been dressed so that it might heal, nor wrapped in a bandage to bind it, so that it might become strong enough to grasp a sword.

[22]"Therefore, thus says the Lord Yahweh: I am against Pharaoh, the king of Egypt, and I will break his arms, both the strong one and the one that was broken, and cause the sword to fall from his hand. [23]I will scatter Egypt among the nations and disperse them among the countries. [24]I will strengthen the arms of the king of Babylon and put my sword in his hand. Then I will break the arms of Pharaoh, and he will groan before him with the groans of one mortally wounded. [25]I will strengthen the arms of the king of Babylon, but the arms of Pharaoh will fall limp. They will know that I am Yahweh when I put my sword in the hand of the king of Babylon, and he stretches it out against the land of Egypt. [26]I will scatter Egypt among the nations and disperse them among the countries. Then they will know that I am Yahweh."

Textual Notes

30:1–26   See the map "The Ancient Near East."

30:2 הֵילִילוּ הָהּ לַיּוֹם:—The Hiphil imperative of יָלַל, "wail," is plural; its singular was used in 21:17 (ET 21:12) to summon the prophet himself to lament for his people. The plural here indicates that it is addressed to all who will be affected by the "day," primarily the Egyptians, but also their allies (30:4–5). Since every divine judgment is but a miniature of the final judgment of the entire world when Christ returns, it is always appropriate to call all people to repentance.

The interjection הָהּ is a hapax, probably a form of אֲהָהּ (e.g., 11:13; 21:5 [ET 20:49]) abbreviated here for the sake of alliteration with the preceding verb. Related particles with similar meanings appear in Ezekiel: אָח (e.g., 6:11; 21:20 ET 21:15]) and הֶאָח (25:3; 26:2; 36:2).

Since the interjection does not require a preposition to connect it with the following word in other contexts, it is sometimes suggested that the *lamed* before יוֹם should be construed here as either vocative or emphatic: "O day!"[1] But I have preferred to retain the traditional prepositional rendering.

30:3 כִּי־קָרוֹב יוֹם וְקָרוֹב יוֹם—Boadt would take the initial כִּי as asseverative.[2] The word may have that force, but its usual explicative force seems more likely here. Quite a number of indicators of emphasis are built into the text as it stands.

The *waw* added when the phrase is repeated (וְקָרוֹב יוֹם) seems to me to be a valid candidate for an emphatic sense. Many critics omit the repetition as a dittograph, as the LXX evidently did. But, as Block points out, the LXX could just as easily be guilty of the haplographic omission.[3]

יוֹם לַיהוָה—The usual OT phrase is a simple construct chain, יוֹם יהוה, "the Day of Yahweh," as in the parallel passage Is 13:6. The periphrastic insertion of a *lamed* does not alter the meaning. It alliterates better with the opening הֵילִילוּ הָהּ לַיּוֹם (30:2).

יוֹם עָנָן עֵת גּוֹיִם יִהְיֶה:—The singular עָנָן is translated as a collective: "clouds." "A time [עֵת] of/for the nations" is evidently an end time of judgment (cf. 21:30, 34

---

[1]   Boadt, *Ezekiel's Oracles against Egypt*, 58–59; Block, *Ezekiel*, 2:156, including n. 7.

[2]   Boadt, *Ezekiel's Oracles against Egypt*, 59.

[3]   Block, *Ezekiel*, 2:156, n. 9.

[ET 21:25, 29], where עֵת is used near קֵץ). The LXX has a more concise translation of the whole verse that omits several Hebrew words and uses πέρας, "end," which could translate קֵץ. Probably it reflects the influence of chapter 7, where קֵץ was prominent. יוֹם and עֵת are common parallels in contexts of imminent judgment. The LXX's shorter translation of the verse, resulting in the loss of its parallelism, probably reflects the general difficulty the LXX seems to have had with pairs of words and its tendency to eliminate one member as redundant.

30:4 וּבָאָה ... וְהָיְתָה—These two Qal third feminine singular perfect verbs with *waw* consecutive are anomalously accented on the ultima instead of the normal penultimate syllable. The reason is unclear, and there are only a few parallels in the entire Masoretic Text.

The noun חַלְחָלָה is usually rendered "(great) anguish" or the like, but Greenberg is probably correct in protesting that a stronger word is needed,[4] and I have chosen "panic." The word is a reduplicative derivative of the verb חוּל, associated with labor pains and childbirth. The noun is repeated in 30:9, and the verb appears in 30:16. The assonance between this word and חָלָל ("slain") in the next clause should be noted.

וְלָקְחוּ הֲמוֹנָהּ—The subject of "they will take" is indefinite, but obviously refers to any enemy. Its object, הֲמוֹנָהּ ("its horde"), was also in 29:19; see the textual note there. הָמוֹן is also in 30:10, 15 and is a key word in the Egyptian oracles. Of eighty-four occurrences in the Bible, twenty-four occur in Ezekiel and sixteen in chapters 29–32.

30:5 This verse is sometimes read as a prosaic addition in a more poetic context, but it need not be so construed. As it stands, it serves as a transition from the general vision of 30:2–4 to the extended announcement of the fall of Egypt's allies together with her—so אִתָּם, "with them," already in this verse. The verb "fall" (נָפַל) binds 30:4, 5, and 6 together.

The first three countries (כּוּשׁ וּפוּט וְלוּד) can be identified with considerable certainty, but the last three entities are uncertain and much disputed. The first three appear in the same order in Jer 46:9 (using the gentilic לוּדִים) as part of Pharaoh Neco's army at Carchemish in 605 B.C. (see also Ezek 29:10). The second and third (פוּט וְלוּד) were also mentioned in reverse order in 27:10 (which see).

Just what group of allies is intended by כָּל־הָעֶרֶב is unclear. עֶרֶב is a common noun, appearing already in Ex 12:38 of a "mixed rabble" or the like, that is, apparently non-Israelites who seized the occasion to join the Israelites in escaping from slavery in Egypt. They are a salutary reminder that the exodus should not be viewed from any ethnic or racial perspective; from the very start God's redemption of Israel did not exclude, but was intended to include also Gentiles. The noun appears similarly in postexilic times (Neh 13:3). Here the "mixture" is probably of mercenaries drawn from many points. Jeremiah uses the term similarly of groups in both Egypt (25:20) and Babylon (50:37). RSV, NRSV, and NIV follow the Syriac in translating "all Arabia," which assumes a different vocalization (עֲרָב). This appears unlikely, however, because Arabs were not significantly represented in Egypt until around the time of the Muslim conquests in the sixth–seventh centuries A.D.

---

[4] Greenberg, *Ezekiel*, 2:621.

The word כּוּב is a hapax and completely unknown. With others, I have simply transliterated it as Kuv. Since it is another monosyllabic name, one might have expected it to follow immediately after the three at the beginning of the verse. The LXX's Λίβυες, "Lybians," suggests that it might be a scribal error for לוּב, "Lybia," although elsewhere the LXX uses Λίβυες to translate פּוּט, already mentioned in this verse. (RSV, NRSV, and NIV, which translate כּוּב as "Lybia," simply transliterated פּוּט earlier.) But לוּב does not occur in the OT; only the gentilic form לוּבִים occurs (Nah 3:9; Dan 11:43; 2 Chr 12:3; 16:8). Perhaps most relevant here, in Nah 3:9 both פּוּט and לוּבִים are mentioned as allies of Egypt. Thus if one must guess, it might be that two different parts of what we know as simply "Lybia" are in view. There are numerous other conjectures.

The final group, וּבְנֵי אֶרֶץ הַבְּרִית, literally, "the sons of the land of the covenant," is equally unclear. בְּרִית can be a "treaty, pact, contract" of almost any sort. Hence the reference could be to some unknown group bound by treaty with Egypt, although why it alone should not be mentioned by name in this context is anyone's guess. Usually in the OT, of course, בְּרִית refers to Yahweh's specific "treaty/covenant/promise" to his people. Although the expression "the land of the covenant" never occurs elsewhere in either Testament of Israel, some label for Israelites still seems to be the most likely reference here. We know that there had been sizable Judahite communities in Egypt at least since the deportation of 597 (Jer 24:8). There is evidence of Judahite mercenaries being involved in various Egyptian military campaigns. Ezek 17:13–21 may even suggest that the "covenant" was a mutual assistance pact between Zedekiah and Saite Egypt. Ezekiel may use the oblique phrase here because he does not care to include the Judahites among the עֶרֶב ("rabble, mixed units") mentioned earlier, nor does he wish to imply that they were directly involved in Egypt's disaster.

30:6 כֹּה אָמַר יְהוָה—On this shorter form of the citation formula, see the third textual note on 11:5.

The participial סֹמֵךְ often implies a personal helper (in other contexts Yahweh), but here probably refers to allied warriors. The same duality is true of עֹזֵר in 30:8, which parallels it.

"Its proud might" uses the idiomatic Hebrew construct phrase "the pride of its strength" instead of the English adjective.

"Sink/descend" (יָרַד) parallels נָפַל in this verse and 30:4–5. נִשְׁבַּת carries the same thought (30:18; 33:28).

On "from Migdol to Aswan," see the textual note on the identical phrase in 29:10.

It is debatable whether בָהּ refers to the sword or to the inhabitants. The net result is the same. I have opted for the latter connection.

30:7 The verse simply rephrases much of 29:10 (which see). Both gender and number are confused in both the MT and the LXX.

30:9 מִלְּפָנַי—The literal *"from* before me," that is, from Yahweh's heavenly court, occurs in a few early passages (e.g., Gen 23:4, 8; Lev 22:3) but is much more common in Late Biblical Hebrew and here may be an Aramaism.

בַּצִּים—Probably for the sake of local color, Ezekiel does not use the ordinary Hebrew word for "ship" (אֲנִיָּה, as in 27:9), but an Egyptian loanword, appearing in

Hebrew in the form צִי. This (בַּצִּים) is the plural with the preposition בְּ. The word is used elsewhere only in Num 24:24; Is 33:21; and Dan 11:30. The last two verses suggest no simple dhow, but a sturdy military vessel, while the Isaiah passage indicates the usual inaccessibility of certain areas to these ships; this verse asserts that that inaccessibility will be penetrated. The LXX evidently did not understand the word wherever it was used and so translated "in haste" here, a misunderstanding apparently reflected here in RSV's "swift."

בֶּטַח is an adverbial accusative, "*in* confidence, security." Usually in Ezekiel it qualifies יָשַׁב, "dwell." Here there is no verb, but the word directly follows כּוּשׁ, and there can be little doubt as to its meaning. Gen 34:25 uses the word as here (of Shechem before the attack by Dinah's avengers). The verb חָרַד (Hiphil infinitive construct: לְהַחֲרִיד) is commonly used as an antonym, as here.

בְּיוֹם מִצְרַיִם—"On the day of Egypt" is pleonastically expanded to "on the day of Egypt's doom" in RSV, NRSV, and NIV. The following verses indicate that the reference is to Nebuchadnezzar's campaign against Egypt. See the commentary on 30:2, 9.

30:10–19   Critics tend to treat this entire section as a hodgepodge of Ezekelian banalities, collected here by disciples or glossators. But nothing prevents us from understanding it as a summary statement by the prophet himself, perhaps delivered on an entirely different occasion. Gentile oracles rarely tell us anything about their *Sitz im Leben*. Ezekiel's generally tell us as much as any because so many of them are dated. At any rate, textual problems in these verses are generally rare and minor, except for in 30:16. Some are considered in the commentary.

30:12   זָרִים—Literally, "strangers/foreigners," in the ancient Near East this was tantamount to "enemies." Similarly, Latin *hostis*, "stranger," usually meant "(hostile) enemy."

30:13   גִלּוּלִים—For "fecal deities," see the fourth textual note on 6:4.

30:16   This verse has no new place names, but several other difficulties.

חוּל תָּחִיל—A *waw-yod* variation is involved in the Kethib and Qere here. After the Qal infinitive (חוּל), the Kethib is תָּחִיל, while the Qere is תָּחוּל. Hebrew has both middle-*waw* and middle-*yod* verbs (חוּל and חִיל), which occasionally overlap slightly in meaning. Either could be the verb source of the reduplicated noun form, חַלְחָלָה, "panic," in 30:4 and 30:9. Both verbs normally would have a Qal infinitive absolute form of חוּל (with וֹ as its characteristic vowel), and that is the form we would expect here. For this kind of construction, the infinitive must be the absolute, not the construct. Apparently the infinitive absolute was vocalized as חוּל by vocalic assimilation to the following finite form of the Qere (תָּחוּל).

סִין—Instead of the MT's סִין (Pelusium) again (as in 30:15), the LXX apparently read סְוֵנֵה (Syene, that is, Aswan), as in 29:10 and 30:6. Since a *waw-yod* confusion is textually very easy to understand, it is hard to choose between the two readings here. In the other two references, Aswan had been contrasted with Migdol as representing the southern and northern frontiers of Egypt. Since Migdol and Pelusium were probably not far apart, the two formulations could be read as virtually synonymous. At the same time, Pelusium and Thebes also represent the same two frontiers, so the effect is the same in either case. And, as Cooke comments: "But *Nō'* [Thebes] is repeated in this v[erse], and why not *Sîn*?"[5] Nothing is at stake.

לְהִבָּקֵעַ—That Thebes (נֹא), that is, its walls, will be "split/breached" (the intransitive Niphal infinitive construct of בָּקַע) is paralleled in 2 Ki 25:4, which describes the fall of Jerusalem.

וְנֹף צָרֵי יוֹמָם:—This final clause is difficult because it lacks a verb. After נֹף we have simply "oppressors [of?] by day." The masculine plural of צַר, "adversary, foe" (BDB, s.v. צַר III, under the root צרר II) is in construct with an adverb. This is an unusual construction, but not without parallel (e.g., Prov 3:25; 26:2). We apparently have to reckon with simple ellipsis of the verb. Those who consider the MT corrupt have suggested many emendations, but with none winning wide consent. The LXX has a totally different reading, literally, "and waters will be dispersed," which would seem to be based on an entirely different Hebrew text. Is there a connection, as some suggest, with Nah 3:8, which describes Thebes as "situated by the rivers, (with) waters around her, whose rampart was the sea, and whose wall was from the sea"? For all of its difficulty, the MT here seems to describe Thebes as under incessant attack, even in broad daylight.

30:21 The verb חָבַשׁ, "bind, bandage," is used twice in this verse. The first time it is probably used somewhat generally of "dressing" a wound. חֻבְּשָׁה is probably a Qal passive (not a Pual) since most uses of the verb are Qal, with the Piel occurring only in Ps 147:3 and Job 28:11.

לָתֵת רְפֻאוֹת is usually understood in an absolute sense, literally, "to give healing," as I have taken it, but it may be more concrete, "to administer medicines." The other two biblical uses of רְפֻאוֹת in Jer 30:13 and 46:11 do not resolve the issue.

The parallel לָשׂוּם חִתּוּל is uncertain, because חִתּוּל is a hapax. But it is cognate with "swaddled" in 16:4 and a noun in Job 38:9 meaning something like "swaddling band" (RSV). Hence it most likely refers to a bandage of some sort. NIV has "splint,"[6] which is a logical guess, but more speculative. (The LXX guessed "to put plaster on it.")

לְחָבְשָׁהּ לְחָזְקָהּ לִתְפֹּשׂ בֶּחָרֶב:—Since the verb חָבַשׁ is now repeated and is not present in the LXX, it is often deleted as a gloss.[7] But stylistically the use here of three infinitives in a row is striking. The first two are Qal with לְ and third feminine singular suffixes. The suffix on לְחָבְשָׁהּ is objective: "to bind it." The Qal of חָזַק is intransitive, so the suffix of לְחָזְקָהּ is subjective: "it might become strong." לִתְפֹּשׂ with the preposition בְּ is technically not transitive, but "to grasp with the sword." תָּפַשׂ is more often used with an accusative.

30:22 The change in tense should not be overlooked. Now we have perfects with *waw* consecutive, that is, futures instead of the previous past tenses.

Before לָכֵן one would normally expect a יַעַן protasis or other enumeration of guilt. We must mentally supply one, the implication being that Pharaoh failed to learn

---

[5] Cooke, *Ezekiel*, 334.

[6] Boadt, *Ezekiel's Oracles against Egypt*, 87, has "splints."

[7] E.g., Zimmerli, *Ezekiel*, 2:136.

his lesson from having one arm broken. Therefore, it will be necessary for God to break the other arm as well. Ezek 30:21 already spoke of the breaking of one arm, but as a way of saying that God will see to it that both arms are broken, the text now rhetorically speaks as though both are just being broken.

30:23 The verse is a verbatim repetition of 29:12c.

30:25–26 As usual in the recognition formula,[8] the subject of יָדְעוּ (in 30:25–26) is indefinite. The LXX is surely pointing in the right direction by adding πάντες, "*all/everyone* will know," in 30:26.

Commentary

Content-wise, chapter 30 contains relatively little that is essentially different from chapter 29. Ezek 30:1–4, 6–8, 13–19 supplements 29:8–12, and likewise 30:10–12 may be compared with 29:17–21. The style is generally Ezekelian in tone. The Hebrew is easier than in many of the other Gentile oracles.[9] The first oracle of the chapter is easily divided into four divisions: (1) the announcement of the Day of Yahweh on Egypt (30:1–5); (2) the reaction of Egypt's allies, who also suffer Yahweh's judgment (30:6–9); (3) the agent by which Yahweh will accomplish the judgment on Egypt (30:10–12); and (4) the comprehensive scope of the judgment (30:13–19). The second oracle, consisting of the final verses (30:20–26), functions as a sort of appendix-summary of Yahweh's impending judgment on the pharaoh.

As in 29:1–2, this chapter too begins with the word-event formula, "the Word of Yahweh came to me," and God's address to Ezekiel as "son of man."[10] Both recur in 30:20–21 at the start of the second oracle. Since the first oracle (30:1–19) is undated and general in its contents, it is impossible to make even a confident guess about its precise setting. Its strong anti-Egyptian tone suggests two likely possibilities: (1) sometime in connection with Hophra's campaign to aid Jerusalem[11] or (2) when Nebuchadnezzar abandoned his attempt to capture Tyre and turned his attention to Egypt.[12]

Egypt Will Fall by the Sword (30:1–19)

The Announcement of the Day of Yahweh on Egypt (30:1–5)

30:2 The oracle opens on a rather shrill note, reminiscent of chapter 7, which also speaks of the "day." See the third and fourth textual notes on 7:7

---

[8] For this formula, see page 9 in the introduction and the commentary on 6:7.

[9] Predictably, some critics consider most of the chapter to be an epigonic addition by someone who thought the description of Egypt's fall in chapter 29 was not strong enough. See, for example, Zimmerli, *Ezekiel*, 2:127–28, and Eichrodt, *Ezekiel*, 415. Greenberg, *Ezekiel*, 2:629, trenchantly observes: "Critics do not allow Ezekiel to produce anything less than the best quality (that he is capable of, in their estimate). ... Hence they agree in relieving him of responsibility for authoring these verses, and foist them on his 'school' or his 'editors.' "

[10] For the word-event formula, see page 8 in the introduction and the textual note on 3:16. For "son of man," see the second textual note and commentary on 2:1.

[11] See Jer 37:5–8 and "Introduction to Ezekiel 29–32: Oracles against Egypt."

[12] See the commentary on 29:17–21.

for "day" terminology and theology. There the threat had been addressed to Israel; here it has been transferred to Egypt and its neighbors.

There has been much futile speculation about the origin of the concept of "the Day of Yahweh." As such, the phrase refers to any signal intervention by Yahweh in human history. Instead of the possessive "of Yahweh," we frequently meet the objective genitive phrase "the day of [a people or country]," that is, naming the one upon whom the terrors of the "day" will fall (e.g., 30:9 on Egypt). This phraseology appears in the eighth-century prophets, including Isaiah ("the day of Midian," Is 9:3 [ET 9:4]) and Amos (5:18–20), where it clearly is already a well-established concept. The populace plainly expects the "day" to be one of deliverance and salvation, but Amos proclaims the precise opposite, and this is the general import of the phrase in the rest of Scripture.

Eschatological overtones are commonly present, but to what degree is often hard to determine. Ezekiel 38–39 will describe the eschatological battle with Gog in "day" terms. "The day of the Lord" and similar phrases with "day" continue to be used in the NT (1 Cor 5:5; 2 Cor 1:14; 1 Thess 5:2; 2 Pet 3:10). We know the concept best in the phrase "Judgment Day," where, unfortunately, the accent is usually only on the negative, on condemnation of the wicked. But for OT and NT believers, the day of God's judgment can be heard as the time when God will issue his public verdict, and for the believer that day is the day of final acquittal and vindication because of the imputed righteousness of Jesus Christ (e.g., 2 Cor 5:21). After Christ returns in glory, all the dead shall be raised, and believers shall enter the everlasting paradise of which Ezekiel is given a glimpse in chapters 40–48 (paralleled by Revelation 21–22).

30:3 The theme that the Day of Yahweh is "near" is common in prophecy (see Is 13:6, which also has "wail"; Joel 2:1; 4:14 [ET 3:14]; Zeph 1:7, 14). The nearness is according to celestial time, not necessarily according to human chronology. Just as no individual knows when his day will come to meet his Maker (or something penultimate), so application on a wider canvass cannot be computerized. Also traditional is the description of the "day" as one of clouds, often accompanied by synonymous or stronger expressions, perhaps most famously the *dies irae* passage of Zeph 1:15, but also Joel 2:2; 4:15 (ET 3:15). What transpired on Good Friday, when darkness covered the land, was the imposition of God's judgment upon his own Son, that all who trust in him may be spared judgment on the Last Day.

"Time" is a momentous, decisive period, an alternate term for "day." RSV, NRSV, and NIV all add "of doom," lest there be misunderstanding, but I doubt if it is necessary. "Nations" translates גּוֹיִם, although here "Gentiles" might be better to emphasize that the judgment theme commonly directed against Israel is here universalized. This is the theme of the Gentile oracles as a whole.[13] That the word is anarthrous in Hebrew may underscore its universality. Thus the ap-

---

[13] See "Introduction to Ezekiel 25–32: Oracles against Other Nations."

plication is much broader than merely Egypt and its neighbors mentioned in 30:5. Just as the Gospel will be proclaimed to all nations, so also no nation (its unbelievers) shall escape judgment.

30:4 Strong language is used in this verse to describe the judgment coming upon Egypt. The "sword," a metonym for war in general, is almost personalized as Yahweh's agent. The "panic" that will engulf Nubia at the same time picks up an ancient theme of "holy war," such as the panic of the Midianites upon Gideon's attack (Judges 7). This theme will be amplified in Ezek 30:9. "Slain" may be too weak for חָלָל, "pierced," which does not specify how, but suggests judicial execution. The "demolishing" of the foundations is perhaps an intentionally stronger term than the merely "laying bare, exposing" (Niphal of גָּלָה) of Israel's in 13:14. As archaeologists know well, in war buildings were commonly simply leveled with the foundations still in the ground; to dig up the entire foundation implied unusual fury. Possibly the expression is metaphorical here: not only the "horde" or "masses" (הָמוֹן, 30:4, 10, 15) are affected, but also the "foundations" (leadership, etc.).

Egypt's Allies Will Also Be Judged (30:6–9)

30:6–8 The magnitude of the judgment on not only Egypt but also its allies is expressed at length in these verses. Again pride is the root of the problem, and the end result will be recognition, however grudging, of Yahweh's agency. The themes of "fire," "crushing," not to speak of "sword" are standard, not only in Ezekiel, but in biblical Gentile oracles in general.

30:6 It is unusual to have a short verse both introduced by the citation formula (here, "thus says Yahweh") and concluded by the signatory formula ("says the Lord Yahweh").[14] Otherwise 30:6 follows naturally from 30:4 and flows easily into 30:7. The two formulas simply highlight Yahweh's determination. Perhaps this is why the Tetragrammaton stands alone in the messenger formula here (rather than "the Lord Yahweh"), something which happens only twice otherwise in Ezekiel (11:5; 21:8 [ET 21:3]).

30:9 In prose style, "that day," described in 30:8, is expatiated a bit more. The divine terror will reach not only Egypt, but even Nubia, cockily supposing itself to be safe because of its remoteness and relative inaccessibility. The same "panic" (חַלְחָלָה) already promised Nubia in 30:4 will characterize that country on "the day of Egypt" (see the commentary on 30:2). Influence from Isaiah is usually noted in this verse, not only in the analogy of "the day of Egypt" with "the day of Midian" (Is 9:3 [ET 9:4]) but in Ezekiel's reversal of Is 18:1–2. There ambassadors from Nubia had come downstream. Here envoys from Yahweh's heavenly court come upstream—and not in papyrus vessels but in sturdy men of war (see the second textual note on 30:9).

---

[14] For the citation formula, see pages 8–9 in the introduction and the fourth textual note and the commentary on 2:4. For the signatory formula, see pages 8–9 in the introduction and the second textual note on 5:11.

This portion of the chapter ends somewhat as it had begun with a warning (הִנֵּה is translated "surely") about the inexorability and propinquity of "that day."

Babylon Is Yahweh's Agent (30:10–12)

30:10 As 26:7–14 did after 26:1–6, the three verses of this short section concentrate on Yahweh's agent, Nebuchadnezzar, who is immediately mentioned by name. The clause וְהִשְׁבַּתִּי אֶת־הֲמוֹן, "I will put an end to the horde," uses a favorite verb of Yahweh in Ezekiel, and links this verse specifically with 26:13, where the verb has the same object. And הָמוֹן, "horde," as in 30:4, 15, is multivalent, including wealth, pride, and so on, together with troops, multitude, and such.

30:11 But immediately after specification of the agent, the passive (Hophal) participle of בּוֹא, "be brought," is used to emphasize that he is only that—someone executing Yahweh's purposes. This is a variation of the use of the active (Hiphil) participle with Yahweh as subject in 28:7.

עַם in this and similar contexts is obviously the army, but it represents "the most ruthless of nations," עָרִיצֵי גוֹיִם (the phrase is used also in 28:7; 31:12; 32:12; cf. "the most wicked of the nations," רָעֵי גוֹיִם, in 7:24). גּוֹיִם עָרִיצִים, "ruthless people," had appeared in Is 25:3 (cf. עָרִיצִים also in Is 25:4–5).

As in 28:7, the Hebrew idiom is literally, "empty" (the scabbards of) "their swords," meaning "unsheathe their swords." Here "empty" forms a contrast with the transitive use of מָלֵא, "fill the land [with] the slain." "Slain" (חָלָל) echoes 30:4 and many other passages.

30:12 Yahweh's activity is now unmediated. In the semi-arid Near East, and especially in Egypt, almost totally dependent upon the Nile, the drying up of water supplies would indeed make the land desolate (cf. 30:7), to put it mildly. The threat often appears in ancient literature. This is Ezekiel's only use of חָרָבָה, "dry," but it alliteratively connects with the Niphal participle of חָרֵב ("ruined") in 30:7 and the חֲרָבוֹת ("swords") of 30:11.

This verse also contains Ezekiel's only use of מָכַר, "sell," in the sense of selling a person or country to his/its enemies, a metaphor especially frequent in the book of Judges. The Hebrew continues with בְּיַד־, "into the hand," unnecessary in English idiom. The idiom is repeated shortly, but with a different meaning. In 30:12a the literal "into the hand of" differs in sense from the agential "by the hand of" in 30:10 and 30:12b. For רַע, instead of "evil," "fierce" better matches עָרִיץ, "ruthless," of 30:11; morality, as such, is not the point here (cf. also 7:24; 28:7, 10; 31:12).

The Comprehensive Scope of Egypt's Judgment (30:13–19)

30:13 As at the exodus, destruction of Egypt would be coterminous with the destruction of its gods, just as of other ancient countries in pagan thought. Two major words from the extensive Hebrew vocabulary for "idols" are paralleled here: (1) the almost scatological favorite of Ezekiel, גִּלּוּלִים, "fecal deities" (Ezekiel has thirty-nine out of forty-eight biblical occurrences) and (2) אֱלִילִים, "nonentities/non-gods," found nowhere else in Ezekiel, but common in Isaiah and also found in the Torah (Lev 19:4; 26:1). The word אֱלִיל is of uncertain derivation, but usually a diminutive of אֵל, "god," is assumed. On the basis of the Ugaritic, Boadt (following Dahood) suggests "old rags,"[15] making this another derogatory term for idols.

"A prince" (נָשִׂיא) in this context is a bit of a crux. It is known in cognate languages as a title of divinity, and so Boadt suggests that it implies the diminution of the pharaoh from king-divinity to mere "tribal chief" (apparently its basic sense).[16] Similarly, Greenberg translates, "a native chief" (literally, "a chief from the land of Egypt").[17] The apparent meaning is that, after being conquered, Egypt will never have a native ruler again.

Deprived of both deity and ruler, the twin repositories of authority, "fear," יִרְאָה, will engulf the land. Although the word was used in 1:18 in the sense of something fearsome in the inaugural vision and is used elsewhere of the "fear" of God (e.g., Is 11:3), its sense here of dread of anarchic chaos is unique in Ezekiel, and perhaps in the entire OT.

Memphis (נֹף here and in 30:16, or מֹף in Hos 9:6; both derive from the Egyptian name for the city) was situated just south of modern Cairo or some fifteen miles south of the southern apex of the Delta. Although Thebes (Ezek 30:14–16) in Upper Egypt was more often the political capital of Egypt, Memphis was an important cultural and religious center throughout Egypt's history, and often the residence of the pharaoh. The city also had a sacred name from which the Greek Αἴγυπτος ("Egypt") is derived, totally unrelated to the Hebrew מִצְרַיִם, a name which occurs six times in this part of the oracle (30:13–19).

30:14 "Punishments" translates שְׁפָטִים, although "judgments" would be appropriate here. The place names indicate that these punishments would be experienced from one end of the country to the other, a pattern that will continue in the following verses.

Pathros is not a city, but a region, Upper (southern) Egypt. See the second textual note on 29:14.

Zoan in the eastern Delta, twenty-nine miles from the Mediterranean, was an important city in that region, and often served as the official royal residence. It is mentioned seven times in the OT (according to Num 13:22, it was established seven years after Hebron). The name was Hellenized as Tanis, but since that is probably no more familiar to moderns than Zoan, I have retained the Hebrew form of the name.

No (נֹא), situated some 450 miles south of the Mediterranean, is better known by its Grecized name of Thebes. Its full name was No-amon (Nah 3:8),

---

[15] Boadt, *Ezekiel's Oracles against Egypt*, 78, including n. 49, citing Dahood, *Psalms*, 2:358.

[16] Boadt, *Ezekiel's Oracles against Egypt*, 77.

[17] Greenberg, *Ezekiel*, 2:625.

that is, "the city of (the god) Amon," the state god of Egypt during its glory days on the world stage at the time of the exodus (see Ex 12:12; Num 33:4) under the New Kingdom in the last half of the second millennium. Ezekiel refers to the city two other times (30:15–16), reflecting its importance, which is still evident in the impressive temples of the major tourist sites of Karnak and Luxor on the east shore of the Nile and the Valley of the Kings on the west.

30:15 The new name in this verse is סִין, probably derived from an Egyptian word for "fortress/stronghold," for which the following מָעוֹז, "stronghold," is a virtual translation. It is usually identified with Pelusium, a fortress city on Egypt's extreme northeast frontier, on "the way of the land of the Philistines" (Ex 13:17), east of the Delta and not far from the Mediterranean Sea. In that location, it was inevitably a key point in relations with Asia, hostile or otherwise, in all historical periods.

Because of the rhyme, some have suggested that הֲמוֹן נֹא, "horde of No/Thebes," is a play on the name of the god Amon, whose worshiped centered there. But this seems unlikely after 30:13, nor is הִכְרַתִּי ("I will cut off") the expression one would expect in that case.

30:16 See the textual notes on this verse.

30:17 Either Ezekiel or later Hebrew scribes deliberately distorted the vowels of אֹן (On) into אָוֶן, "evil/wickedness." Biblical writers and/or scribes frequently made such changes with names of foreign gods or their cults. In its other occurrences (Gen 41:45, 50; 46:20), אֹן is correctly vocalized (Joseph's wife, Asenath, was "the daughter of Potiphera priest of On"), but in Jer 43:13, the city is referred to as "Beth-shemesh," the Hebrew equivalent of "Heliopolis" (the city of the sun), by which On was known to the Greeks. The Egyptian for "On" means "city of the pillar," and Jeremiah refers to the pillars (obelisks) of the city (Jer 43:13). The Greek name derives from the fact that the city was the center of the worship of Ra and Atum, the Egyptian sun gods, of which the pharaohs were believed to be the earthly embodiment. It was located at the apex of the delta, six miles northeast of Cairo. The archaeologically minded tourist can still see magnificent remains there.

Bubastis is the Greek adaptation of the Egyptian for "house of Bastet," a major Egyptian cat/lioness goddess, for whom major temples were built and elaborate festivals celebrated. The ruins of Tell Basta are located on the outskirts of the modern Zagazig on the easternmost of the three major Nile branches, some thirty-nine miles north-northeast of Cairo.

"The women will go into captivity" (Ezek 30:17) assumes that the subject of the feminine plural verb is "women." Since "city" (עִיר) is feminine in Hebrew, the subject could be the two cities themselves. But I have followed the LXX, which supplies αἱ γυναῖκες, "the women." Not only does this counterbalance "the young men" at the beginning of the verse, but Ezekiel may well be alluding to the prominence of women in the festivals in honor of Bastet.

30:18 The judgment is described in somewhat more cosmic terms in this verse. The MT reads חָשַׂךְ ("withhold/restrain"), in which case we have another ellipsis and must supply "its light" or the like. However, other manuscripts and the versions read חָשַׁךְ ("be/grow dark"), which seems much more likely and should probably be read (so slight a change that one can hardly label it an emendation). Possibly the MT's pointing reflects assimilation to the *samek* at the end of the preceding place name (originally a slightly different sound, but probably no longer distinguished in biblical times).

The MT vocalizes the place name here as "Tehaphnehes." It is better known by its shorter form, Tahpanhes, found, for example, in Jer 43:7–9, where it is mentioned as a frontier town to which the Judahite rebels under Johanan had fled and forcibly taken Jeremiah along. It was known to the Greeks as Daphnae and is located some fifteen miles southwest of Pelusium.

"Yokes" (the two parallel beams above and below the head of the animal pulling an implement) is a common metaphor for slavery, and release from them implies liberation from slavery. There probably is a specific reference to the exodus (cf. Lev 26:13, which uses this language), but the metaphor appears more generally for deliverance from the universal human condition of sin through the Messiah (Is 9:3–5 [ET 9:4–6]), as in Ezek 34:27. Here the reference would be to the freeing of Egypt's vassals.

Without change in the consonantal text, the word can also be read מַטּוֹת ("scepters") instead of מֹטוֹת, as the LXX and other ancient versions do, and preferred by some modern commentators. The sense might be essentially the same, or since מַטֶּה often means "staff/support," the reference might be to "the supporters of Egypt" of 30:6, where "its proud might" follows, just as it does in this verse.

As at the beginning of the chapter (30:3), gloom and darkness accompany Yahweh's "day" (30:18), a common theme (Is 13:10; to appear again in Ezek 32:7–8; and passim in Joel).

"Daughters" (Ezek 30:18) may be taken either literally (cf. 30:17), or this may be the common Hebrew idiom for outlying, dependent villages (NRSV: "daughter-towns").

30:19 Obviously this is a summary statement, but the infliction of punishments (שְׁפָטִים, "judgments") on Egypt not only repeats 30:14b (the word is also used some nine other times in Ezekiel), but surely the word harks back to Ex 12:12 as Yahweh announces the final plague about to come upon Egypt. As there the punishment was preparatory for the redemption of God's people, so it is promised to be here, so it is constitutively in the Law-Gospel, Good Friday-Easter proclamation of the Christian faith.

Pharaoh's Arm Will Be Broken (30:20–26)

30:20 This dated oracle indicates the time in 587 B.C. when Pharaoh Hophra was attempting to lift the siege of Jerusalem, that is, almost four months after the oracle of 29:1–16. For these dates, see "Introduction to Ezekiel 29–32: Oracles against Egypt" and figure 1. It compares to the previous verses as 29:17–21 did to 29:1–16 and has a similar structure. Nebuchadnezzar is never mentioned by name, although referred to by title three times (in 30:24–25). Many parts of the oracle, as it stands, are often questioned because of its repetitiousness, but that can also be viewed as its strength.

30:21 "Arm(s)" is obviously a keyword in this section, used six times. To "break arms," an expression is often used elsewhere, plainly means to deprive the pharaoh of his aggressive power. Egyptian iconography frequently depicts the flexed arm of the king holding a sword or club, ready to bludgeon an enemy. The Egyptian word for "arm/power" had been common in pharaonic titles since Hyksos times, and Hophra in particular often styled himself the "possessor of a strong arm." Ezekiel's audience was probably well aware of this usage and would not have had doubts about the oracle's target.

The verb שָׁבַר, in "I have broken," is a non-converted perfect with its usual sense of something already past. The particle הִנֵּה, often left untranslated in English, I have rendered here with the imperative "note." The implication is that enough time has elapsed since the arm was broken that Egypt would have taken remedial measures if it could have. The fact that it has not implies that the injury is irreparable.

30:22 Naturally, one wonders what historical circumstances Ezekiel is referring to by the pictures of Yahweh breaking first one arm, then both. Unfortunately, we lack sufficient collateral information to enable us to answer such a query with any certainty. Most think of some sort of two-pronged campaign by Hophra, one of which has already been defeated. Others think that the land forces aimed at aiding Jerusalem have already been repulsed, but that Hophra's navy is still able to assist in the defense of Tyre. Only after it too has been subdued will Egypt itself be ripe for destruction. Still others point to fragmentary sources indicating a pitched battle between Egypt and Babylon already in 601 B.C., which had not been decisive, and to the fact that one is coming shortly in which Egyptian forces will be completely routed.

30:24 The first person forms ("I," "my") in this verse make it clear that Yahweh is the real actor. He puts his sword into Nebuchadnezzar's hand, and (repeated from 30:22) he will break Pharaoh's arms. The verb נָאַק for "groan" represents a transposition of the first two radicals of אָנַק in 26:15; the verbs are synonymous. So far, "Pharaoh" has tended to stand collectively for Egypt, but here he is individualized in his death; he groans at the feet, as it were, of Nebuchadnezzar. "Mortally wounded" is slightly free for חָלָל, "pierced/slain."

30:25–26 The last two verses simply reiterate previous themes. With NIV I have added "limp" to "fall" for the sake of vividness. For the third time (after 29:12 and 30:23), we hear of the fragmentation of Egypt and the scattering of Egyptians throughout the world so that one will no longer be able to speak of a single, united Egypt.

When will all this be fulfilled? One can find at least partial fulfillments at many points in history. But if one remembers that *sub specie aeternitatis*, "in light of eternity," all of salvation history is prophecy, we will let Yahweh give the final answer in the ἀποκατάστασις πάντων, "restoration of all things" (Acts

3:21), a NT counterpart to the Hebrew idiom שׁוּב שְׁבוּת, "bring about the restoration of" (Ezek 16:53; 29:14; 39:25).[18] The date itself is never the salient feature of biblical eschatology. The point is that it will be a "new creation," "paradise restored and transcended," signifying that the primal sin of Adam and Eve and its consequences will finally and definitively be overcome and reversed. Christians celebrate this great reversal every Easter, and in a derivative sense, every day is a little Easter as the baptized believer dies to sin and rises to new life in Christ (Rom 6:1–4). Yet we await the consummation at the second coming of Christ, when we shall be raised bodily, and sin and death shall be no more.

---

[18] Remarkably, the expression is used for the conversion and salvation of Gentiles: Sodom and Samaria in 16:53 and Egypt in 29:14. See first textual note on 16:53, and for 29:14, see "Introduction to Ezekiel 29–32: Oracles against Egypt." In 39:25 the expression is part of a salvation oracle for Israel; see the commentary there.

Like Assyria, the Cedar, Pharaoh
Will Descend to Sheol

Translation

31 ¹In the eleventh year, in the third [month], on the first [day] of the month, the Word of Yahweh came to me: ²"Son of man, say to Pharaoh, king of Egypt, and to his horde, 'To whom are you comparable in your greatness? ³Consider Assyria, a cedar in Lebanon, with beautiful branches, a thicket giving shade, of great height, and with its top among the clouds. ⁴The waters made it grow; the deep gave it height, making its main channels flow around the place where it was planted, but sending its smaller canals out to all the other trees of the field. ⁵So its height was greater than all the other trees of the field. Its branches multiplied, and its boughs grew long, because of the abundant water in its channel. ⁶All the birds of the sky nested in its boughs; all the wild animals of the field gave birth under its branches; and all the mighty nations lived in its shade. ⁷It was beautiful in its grandeur and in the length of its branches because its roots reached down to abundant water. ⁸The cedars in the garden of God did not eclipse it; the junipers were not the equal of its boughs; and the plane trees could not rival its branches. No tree in the garden of God could equal it in beauty. ⁹I made it so beautiful by the abundance of its branches that all the trees of Eden that were in the garden of God envied it.

¹⁰" 'Therefore, thus says the Lord Yahweh: Because you were of great height, and it stretched its top up between the clouds, and its heart became haughty because of its height, ¹¹I will deliver it into the hand of a chief of nations, and he will deal with it. According to his wickedness I banished him. ¹²Foreigners, the most ruthless of nations, cut it down and discarded it. Its branches fell on the mountains and in all the canyons. Its boughs lay broken in all the watercourses of the land, and all the peoples of the earth came down from its shade and abandoned it. ¹³All the birds of the sky lodged on its fallen trunk, and all the wild animals of the field were on its branches. ¹⁴All this happened so that all the well-watered trees would never again reach such heights or stretch their tops up between the clouds, and their chiefs—all drinkers of water—will not stand in their loftiness, because they have all been handed over to death, to the underworld, along with mortals, to those who have descended to the pit.

¹⁵" 'Thus says the Lord Yahweh: When it went down to Sheol, I caused mourning; I covered the deep because of it; I restrained its main channels; and the abundant waters were held back. I darkened Lebanon because of it, and all the trees of the field wilted because of it. ¹⁶I made the nations quake at the sound of its fall, when I brought it down to Sheol to be with those who have descended to the pit. In the underworld, all the trees of Eden, the choicest and best of

Lebanon, all drinkers of water, consoled themselves. [17]These too went down to Sheol with them, to those slain by the sword, and its arm who lived in its shade among the nations. [18]To whom, then, are you comparable in glory and in greatness among the trees of Eden? Yet you shall be brought down together with the trees of Eden to the underworld. You shall lie among the uncircumcised together with those slain by the sword. This is Pharaoh and all his horde, says the Lord Yahweh.' "

Textual Notes

31:1–18   See the map "The Ancient Near East."

31:1   The date in 587 B.C. is a few days shy of two months after the previous oracle (30:20) and about five and a half months after the first oracle against Egypt in 29:1–16. See "Introduction to Ezekiel 29–32: Oracles against Egypt" and figure 1. Unlike the date in 30:20, we know of no event on this date that might have precipitated the oracle.

31:2 הֲמוֹנוֹ—The noun הָמוֹן is used for Egypt's "horde" sixteen times in chapters 29–32. See the textual note on it in 29:19.

אֶל־מִי דָּמִיתָ בְגָדְלֶךָ:—The verb דָּמָה, "be like, resemble," will recur in 31:8 (twice), 18. בְגָדְלֶךָ is the noun גֹּדֶל, "greatness," with בְּ (as also in 31:7, 18) and second masculine singular suffix. Many scholars find difficulty in the use of מִי ("who?") instead of מָה ("what?"), considering that the text goes on to speak of a tree—probably Assyria under the figure of a tree (see 31:3). There are other OT instances that may exhibit the same use of מִי, perhaps most strikingly in two of Isaiah's rhetorical questions on the incomparability of Yahweh: Is 40:18 and 40:25. As there the objective answer had to be "nobody," so here the use of מִי is determined by the objective intent of the question. The answer comes from the prophet immediately in the next verses, which summarize the entire chapter: Pharaoh is like another king (of Assyria), who was greater, but who fell—and so will Pharaoh. After that point has been made, the question אֶל־מִי דָמִיתָ will be repeated in the last verse of the chapter (31:18).

31:3 הִנֵּה אַשּׁוּר אֶרֶז בַּלְּבָנוֹן—With אַשּׁוּר, "Assyria," we meet a major crux, which will influence much of how we view the rest of the chapter. The vast majority of critical commentators[1] assume that a reference to Assyria would be out of place in an oracle against Egypt and posit an original תְּאַשּׁוּר, "cypress," with the *taw* allegedly dropped by pseudo-haplography (similarity, not identity of consonants) after the final *he* of the preceding הִנֵּה. (Sometimes they also omit "a cedar in Lebanon" as an explanatory gloss.) In their view, the bulk of the oracle likens Pharaoh to a cypress and a cedar, instead of first portraying Assyria as a cedar and then declaring that Pharaoh will share the same fate as Assyria.

But there are many cogent arguments against emendation. First, the ancient versions unanimously support the MT. Second, תְּאַשּׁוּר is a rare word, occurring only in Is 41:19 and 60:13, where it refers to a literal tree and is not used figuratively. Third, it would be strange to have two trees ("cypress" and then אֶרֶז, "cedar") mentioned at the outset with the first one explained or paralleled by the second, common one.

---

[1]   E.g., Cooke, *Ezekiel*, 339; Allen, *Ezekiel*, 2:122; Zimmerli, *Ezekiel*, 2:141–42.

Fourth, nowhere else does Ezekiel compare or identify Pharaoh with a tree, but with animals (see 29:3; 32:2).

RSV succumbed to the critical reasoning by translating, "Behold, I will liken you to a cedar in Lebanon," so that the passage is about Pharaoh alone (not Assyria), but NRSV and ESV have returned to the text, which most modern translations follow. NIV fittingly renders הִנֵּה with "consider," which I have followed.

יְפֵה עָנָף וְחֹרֶשׁ מֵצַל וּגְבַהּ קוֹמָה—Ezekiel characterizes this cedar, a widespread ancient symbol of majesty (cf. Is 35:2, "the glory of Lebanon"), with three two-word phrases, which are then elaborated upon in succeeding verses. The first and third ones each use an adjective (יָפֶה and גָּבֹהַּ) in construct with a noun (עָנָף and קוֹמָה). However, the middle one is the noun חֹרֶשׁ, "a thicket," modified by מֵצַל, the Hiphil participle of צָלַל, "to cause shade," hence "a thicket giving shade." It is also functional rather than descriptive. Since it is missing in the LXX and interrupts the two construct chains, critics often delete it as a gloss on עֲבֹתִים, which they understand as a singular meaning "branch," not a plural, "clouds."[2] Boadt would repoint the noun חֹרֶשׁ as another adjective in construct, חָרָשׁ, meaning "skilled in shade-giving,"[3] but this seems a stretch since חָרָשׁ elsewhere does not serve as an adjective, but as a noun signifying a craftsman of some sort.

The change in person from second person address to Pharaoh in 31:2 to a third person description of "Assyria" should be noted. This kind of abrupt change in person is not unusual. Ezekiel provides numerous similar examples, and they can also be found in other prophetic literature (and elsewhere in the Bible). In 31:9 we have a sudden shift to the first person, with Yahweh himself speaking, which tends to dominate the rest of the chapter until the very end (31:18), when the rhetorical question of 31:2 is repeated.

31:4 מַיִם גִּדְּלוּהוּ תְּהוֹם רֹמְמָתְהוּ—The verbs are both intensive conjugations of stative verbs with third masculine singular suffix: the Piel (third common plural perfect) of גָּדַל and the Polel (third feminine singular perfect) of רוּם. The verbs (in these conjugations) are paired elsewhere only in Ps 34:4 (ET 34:3), and in Is 1:2 and 23:4, where they refer to rearing and raising children. Here the reference is clearly to the nourishment and growth of the tree.

The two subjects, מַיִם and תְּהוֹם, raise the issue of distant mythological backgrounds again. מַיִם is the ordinary Hebrew word for "water," but because of its pairing with תְּהוֹם, everyone (already KJV) renders it with the plural form, "waters." When the two are parallel, as, for example, in Jonah 2:6 (ET 2:5), מַיִם can refer to the ocean depths, conceived of as subterranean in ancient thought. More often, as here, the two seem to be contrasted, with מַיִם referring to rainwater or other surface waters, while תְּהוֹם refers to the subterranean springs. For example, in Gen 7:11 "the windows of heaven" (rain) combine with תְּהוֹם below to inundate the earth (cf. Gen 8:2). Whenever תְּהוֹם appears in the Bible, some scholars cannot resist comparing it with Tiamat, the monster of the Mesopotamian creation myth. While the words are undoubtedly

---

[2] E.g., Allen, *Ezekiel*, 2:123; Zimmerli, *Ezekiel*, 2:142.

[3] Boadt, *Ezekiel's Oracles against Egypt*, 103.

related etymologically and fossilized mythological language is occasionally retained in the Bible (cf. Gen 49:25), all vestiges of the hostility and conflict involved in Tiamat's mythological appearances have been expunged, so that the demythologized biblical תְּהוֹם is merely a common noun, as when it makes its first appearance in Gen 1:2.

אֶת־נַהֲרֹתֶיהָ ... וְאֶת־תְּעָלֹתֶיהָ—In 31:4b and 31:4c, these direct objects are placed before the verbs that govern them because Ezekiel wishes to contrast them. נָהָר ordinarily means "river," though it can refer to subterranean currents (e.g., Jonah 2:4), and here the plural probably refers to large "channels." תְּעָלָה refers to a trench, ditch, aqueduct, or the like (e.g., 1 Ki 18:32; 2 Ki 18:17; Is 7:3), which would normally not carry as much water as a river. With that understanding, the *waw* on וְאֶת must be understood as adversative, "but." The point of the verse as a whole, then, is that all the waters directed their main "channels" to irrigate the important tree, Assyria, while all the other trees were served by smaller watercourses or "canals." I have added "main" and "smaller" to my translation to make this clear.

In form הֹלֵךְ appears to be a Qal participle, but the Qal of הָלַךְ is intransitive, so it would not take a direct object, as אֶת־נַהֲרֹתֶיהָ must be. The context requires that תְּהוֹם must be the subject, and תְּהוֹם is normally a feminine noun, so a feminine form like הֹלִיכָה (Hiphil of הָלַךְ) would be expected. (Its parallel verbs are feminine singular: רֹמְמָתְהוּ, the Polel third feminine singular perfect of רוּם with third masculine singular suffix, and שִׁלְחָה, the Piel third feminine singular perfect of שָׁלַח.) The versions translate the clause with a transitive verb, and most critics emend accordingly.[4] Their understanding of the text is correct, but emendation is not necessary to achieve it. Disagreement in gender between the verb and its subject occasionally occurs when the object comes first, but a much happier solution is to understand הֹלֵךְ as a Hiphil infinitive absolute, written defectively for הוֹלֵךְ.[5] Infinitive absolutes, which are not inflected, often continue the thought after a finite verb.

The feminine suffix on the noun (מַטָּעָהּ, "the place where *it* was planted") must refer either to the land of Assyria or to אֶרֶץ (31:3) as its metaphor. Usually אֶרֶץ is masculine, but sometimes it is construed as feminine, as in Ezek 17:22. The feminine suffix might also be due to attraction to the feminine suffix on the preceding נַהֲרֹתֶיהָ.

כָּל־עֲצֵי הַשָּׂדֶה:—The point made by the next verse, contrasting the size of the trees, should eliminate the critical suspicion[6] that these words are a dittograph from the line below.

31:5 עַל־כֵּן גָּבְהָא קֹמָתוֹ מִכֹּל עֲצֵי הַשָּׂדֶה—Literally, this is, "so its height was higher than all the trees of the field." This elaborates on the phrase וּגְבַהּ קוֹמָה, "of great height," in 31:3. גָּבְהָא is an Aramaicized form with final א instead of the Hebrew ה. The expected form of this Qal third feminine singular perfect would be גָּבְהָה (not גָּבְתָה because the ה of גָּבַהּ is consonantal).

Ezek 31:5b–6 now expound on חֹרֶשׁ מֵצַל ("a thicket giving shade") in 31:3. The two subjects in 31:5b, the plurals of סַרְעַפָּה (a hapax) and פֹּארָה (also in 31:6, 8, 12–13,

---

4   Zimmerli, *Ezekiel*, 2:142; Allen, *Ezekiel*, 2:123.

5   So Greenberg, *Ezekiel*, 2:638; Block, *Ezekiel*, 2:182, n. 18.

6   So Zimmerli, *Ezekiel*, 2:142, and even Block, *Ezekiel*, 2:182, n. 20.

and elsewhere only in 17:6, of the shoots of a vine) are synonymous, apparently causing the LXX to telescope the entire line. סַרְעַפָּה is another Aramaism, since Aramaic tends to insert a *resh* between the first two radicals (e.g., כָּרְסֵא in Dan 5:20 and 7:9 for כָּסֵא, "throne"). The Hebrew form סְעַפָּה begins Ezek 31:6. The Aramaisms cause many critics[7] to dismiss the verse as secondary, but that does not follow at all.

מִמַּיִם רַבִּים בְּשַׁלְּחוֹ:—The phrase "many waters" often has exmythological connotations, but they are probably irrelevant here (although in 26:19 it is paralleled תְּהוֹם). It is used eleven times in Ezekiel. בְּשַׁלְּחוֹ is the Piel infinitive construct of שָׁלַח with בְּ and third masculine singular suffix, literally, "in its sending" (cf. NKJV: "as it sent them out"). Keil proposes "in its spreading out" (of branches, roots, etc.),[8] but at best the phrase seems tautologous. It must relate to the Piel perfect שִׁלְּחָה in 31:4 ("*sending* its smaller canals") and probably also to שִׁלֹחַ in Is 8:6. Some repoint it as בְּשִׁלְחוֹ, "in its channel/water conduit" (the noun שֶׁלַח used in Neh 3:15), which, if correct, would mean the great cedar now has a water channel all its own, and the lesser trees are ignored.

31:6 While the congregating of birds and animals around the tree is more or less what we would expect from the realm of nature, the phrase "all the mighty nations" reminds us of the ultimate political intention of the metaphor. The threefold repetition of כֹּל, "all," makes a pleasing triad, representing comprehensiveness. If רַבִּים is translated "mighty," as it can mean, the awkwardness and redundancy of "all the many nations" disappears. "Many/mighty nations" is a stock prophetic phrase used three other times in Ezekiel (26:3; 38:23; 39:27), usually of nations hostile to Israel, but here probably of those subjugated by Assyria. The sudden shift to the imperfect יֵשְׁבוּ (Qal third masculine plural of יָשַׁב) with perfect verbs fore and aft is not abnormal in poetry (so again in 31:13, and many examples in the Psalter). As the birds and animals reproduced without fear of predators, so here "lived" has overtones of tranquillity and security—in the immediate political context as long as they behaved properly with respect to their suzerain. "Shade" as a translation of צֵל fits the immediate metaphor best, but in the wider political context, "shadow" would probably be better, implying both the king's protection of his subjects and his subjects' dependency upon him. The figure of the king's "shadow" is widespread in ancient Near Eastern literature.

31:7 In 31:7–9, Ezekiel expands on יְפֵה עָנָף (literally, "beautiful of branch") in 31:3.

וַיְיִף is an odd third masculine singular Qal imperfect with *waw* consecutive of יָפָה (GKC, § 76 f), possibly a mixed Qal-Piel form. The expected Qal form would be וַיִּיף. Because אֹרֶךְ in 31:7 is replaced in 31:9 by רֹב, and the LXX so reads in 31:7, Zimmerli would read רֹב here too,[9] but the proposal is without merit. "Abundant water" again translates מַיִם רַבִּים, as in 31:5 (which see), with its possible extra-mundane possibilities.

31:8 לֹא־עֲמָמֻהוּ—This is the Qal (third common plural perfect with third masculine singular suffix) of עָמַם, "to darken, dim," which occurred in 28:3 in the sense of "baf-

---

[7] E.g., Zimmerli, *Ezekiel*, 2:150.

[8] Keil, *Ezekiel*, 2:32.

[9] Zimmerli, *Ezekiel*, 2:143.

fle." Here it probably means that the other trees "did not eclipse [it]" (BDB, s.v. עָמַם II; cf. *HALOT*, s.v. עמם), that is, were shorter and so did not shade it. בְּרוֹשׁ is often translated "juniper," as I have translated it here and in 27:5 (its only other occurrence in Ezekiel), but some prefer "cypress." עַרְמוֹן (or עֶרְמוֹן) occurs elsewhere only in Gen 30:37, but is usually translated as "plane tree."

31:9 The first clause is missing in the LXX and hence critics often delete it as a theological gloss.[10]

וַיְקַנְאֻהוּ—The Piel (third masculine plural imperfect with *waw* consecutive and third masculine singular suffix) of קָנָא with a direct object ("they envied it") is unusual in this sense, but it occurs also in Gen 26:14 and Is 11:13.

31:10 לָכֵן signals that a judgment speech begins here.

Person, tense, and referent often vacillate frustratingly in this and some of the following verses. The prophet moves between reference to Assyria and his real target, Egypt, and back and forth from tree metaphor to political-theological application. Even when the grammatical gender of the Hebrew pronouns does not change, the translator must decide whether "he," "she," or "it" is best, and sometimes a reference to both the thing and the person it represents might be appropriate at once. Often the MT's punctuation and/or versification is not above challenge.

Grammatical inconsistency is immediately apparent in 31:10, where the tree itself is first described in the second person, but in the following clauses it is spoken of in the third person. Already the Syriac and Vulgate and many moderns harmonize the initial inconcinnity away, but MT is the *lectio difficilior*, and it does accord with the direct address of 31:2b and 31:18.

31:11 This verse is inconsistent in the tense of the verbs. It begins with a simple future (imperfect) and ends with a past tense (perfect). Not everyone agrees, but the best sense seems to be obtained if we take the future as referring to Yahweh's forthcoming judgment on Egypt, while the past tense is a reminder to the pharaoh of what Yahweh has already done to Assyria. NRSV follows the LXX in treating the first verb as past also, but such harmonization does not appear to be necessary.

וְאֶתְּנֵהוּ בְּיַד אֵיל גּוֹיִם—The verb is the Qal imperfect (first common singular with third masculine singular suffix) of נָתַן with conjunctive (not consecutive) *waw*, hence translated as future tense. Yahweh says, literally, "I will give it into the hand of a ram of/over nations." Obviously אַיִל is a figure for a leader over nations. The Bible, like other ancient Near Eastern literature, uses various animal epithets for leaders, for example, "bulls" in 39:18, (literally) "young lions" in 38:13, and "goats" in 34:17. Of these, "ram(s)" is easily the most common, but its use with גּוֹיִם here is unique, evidently indicating this ram's international stature.

עָשׂוֹ יַעֲשֶׂה לּוֹ—The future tense continues with the Qal infinitive absolute and imperfect of עָשָׂה, "he certainly will do to/deal with him/it." It is left to the reader to picture how Nebuchadnezzar will "deal with" the pharaoh. According to the MT's punctuation, a period or the like must be placed after לּוֹ, and I have translated ac-

---

[10] E.g., Zimmerli, *Ezekiel*, 2:143.

cordingly. Others follow Boadt in linking גֵּרַשְׁתִּהוּ with 31:12 and leaving כְּרִשְׁעוֹ to explain יַעֲשֶׂה.[11] The argument is based on the parallelism achieved: "I will deliver it/him ... a chief of nations ..." paralleling "I banished him; foreigners ..." But this leaves בְּיַד hanging, and the theological/moral implications of רֶשַׁע have more weight when it explains Yahweh's actions in contrast to the political/military motivations of the Babylonians.

31:12 The superlative phrase "the most ruthless of nations" (עָרִיצֵי גוֹיִם) we already met in 28:7 and 30:11. וַיִּטְּשֻׁהוּ is used twice in this verse; it is the Qal (third masculine plural imperfect with *waw* consecutive and third masculine singular suffix) of נָטַשׁ, used in a similar sense in 29:5 and again in 32:4. The verb contains two ideas, both of discarding and of abandoning. The two nuances coincide somewhat, but the first dominates in its first use in the verse, the second at the end of the verse. In both uses, the suffix is attached directly to the third plural ending, characteristic of late Hebrew usage. Ezekiel frequently includes "mountains," "canyons," and "watercourses" (in varying order) in descriptions that connote "everywhere." In the other verses, Ezekiel adds גְּבָעוֹת, "hills" (and in one verse still more terms), to stress the comprehensiveness or universality even further (6:3; 35:8; 36:4, 6).

וַיֵּרְדוּ מִצִּלּוֹ—There is often puzzlement about the use of יָרַד, "they came down from its shade," in this connection. Many dismiss any idea of descent or interpret (as does NIV) that they "came out from under its shade." But it seems to me most likely that there is an assumption that the cedar was growing on a mountain, so the people "came down" the mountain and thus also out from the fallen tree's shade. The mention of "canyons" suggests rather rough terrain!

In a somewhat parallel passage in 35:8, corpses cover the landscape, so there is at least a hint that the scattered "branches" and "boughs" of the tree here represent the Assyrian dead. The next verse will speak of the actions of the denizens of the tree after its fall. In 29:5 and 32:4, the birds and beasts feed on the carcass of the monster (being left as food for the birds and the animals is a common curse on cities or nations in Near Eastern languages), but, although the next verse, 31:13, moves in that direction, a fallen cedar does not lend itself to the development of such a picture.

כָּל־עַמֵּי הָאָרֶץ—"All the peoples of the earth" replaces "all the mighty nations" in 31:6. עַמִּים a common variation for גּוֹיִם.

31:13 עַל־מַפַּלְתּוֹ יִשְׁכְּנוּ—Many suggestions are made to explain the unexpected imperfect יִשְׁכְּנוּ. Allen suggests either pseudo-dittography of the *yod* (after a preceding *waw*) or a frequentative imperfect.[12] Probably better is Boadt's suggestion that it, with the following perfect הָיוּ, exhibits the *yqtl-qtl* sequence of "tenses" that ancient Semitic poetry frequently employs for the sake of variety.[13]

The noun מַפֶּלֶת is derived from נָפַל and can refer to a "carcass" of an animal (Judg 14:8) or the "fall, overthrow" of a city or its king, sometimes (as here) in

---

[11] Boadt, *Ezekiel's Oracles against Egypt*, 113–14.

[12] Allen, *Ezekiel*, 2:123.

[13] Boadt, *Ezekiel's Oracles against Egypt*, 115.

metaphorical language (Ezek 26:15, 18; 27:27; 31:13, 16; 32:10), or the "downfall" of the wicked (Prov 29:16). Here it refers to the fallen tree. The birds and animals can hardly feed on it, but they can live in it and exploit it. The idea seems to be that many nations took advantage of fallen Assyria and made a new life of their own from its remnants. That is consistent with the next phrase, "the wild animals of the field were on its branches."

31:14 לְמַעַן אֲשֶׁר—This combination is used to introduce telic (purpose or result) clauses (see BDB, s.v. לְמַעַן, 2 a, under the root ענה I). The paraenetic contents of this verse can be understood as dependent on 31:10–11, with 31:12–13 as simply an expansion of the thought expressed in גֵּרַשְׁתִּהוּ (31:11): "I banished him" because of his haughtiness. Thus 31:14 becomes a summary of the point of the entire oracle and a transition to 31:15–18. Like many other translators, I have inserted a few initial words in order to make the syntactical connection clear.[14]

כָּל־עֲצֵי־מַיִם—Literally, "all trees of water," this is translated, "all the well-watered trees." Much of the rest of the language of 31:14a–b repeats that found in 31:10.

וְלֹא־יַעַמְדוּ אֲלֵיהֶם בְּגָבְהָם כָּל־שֹׁתֵי מַיִם—This is, literally, "so their chiefs will not stand in their loftiness—all drinkers of water." The phrase כָּל־שֹׁתֵי מַיִם (with the Qal masculine plural participle of שָׁתָה in construct) will recur at the end of 31:16. אֵלֵיהֶם is the plural (with third masculine plural suffix) of אַיִל, "ram; chief," used in 31:11. What is the relationship between "their chiefs" and the "drinkers of water"? Despite the intervening בְּגָבְהָם (the noun גֹּבַהּ with בְּ and third masculine plural suffix), most likely the latter phrase is in apposition to the former, so "their chiefs" are "all drinkers of water." To whom or what does "their" refer? Back to the "trees" or to human beings, who are the main referent of the last part of the verse? Most likely both.

Instead of אֲלֵיהֶם, the LXX (πρὸς αὐτά) and the Targum (לְהוֹן) apparently read אֲלֵיהֶם, "all drinkers of water will not stand *over them*" (LXX). Some English translations (e.g., KJV) simply ignore the word, while others render יַעַמְדוּ אֲלֵיהֶם as "reach up to them" (RSV, ESV, NKJV) or "stand erect" (NASB).

אֶל־יוֹרְדֵי בוֹר:—As in 26:20, יָרַד functions here as a stative verb (see the second textual note on 26:20). יוֹרְדֵי בוֹר recurs in 31:16; 32:18, 24–25, 29–30.

31:15 הֶאֱבַלְתִּי כִּסֵּתִי עָלָיו אֶת־תְּהוֹם—This is, literally, "I caused mourning; I covered over it the deep." The verbs are asyndetic. The MT accents separate them, and I have respected that tradition. In the only other passage with the Hiphil of אָבַל, it takes a direct object (Lam 2:8), but it is used here in an absolute sense with no object. The objects (those who are caused to mourn) will become evident as we move further into the verse. The LXX lacks "I covered," which results in "I made the deep mourn." In the other direction, on the basis of a highly debatable Akkadian cognate meaning "gate," others, including Block[15] and NRSV, eliminate "mourn" and offer something like this: "I closed the deep over it and covered it" (NRSV), yielding two virtually synonymous statements. Boadt proposes a hendiadys and suggests "I cover with

---

[14] Zimmerli, *Ezekiel*, 2:151–52, would delete the verse.

[15] Block, *Ezekiel*, 2:195.

mourning garments the Tehom" (NIV is similar).[16] All in all, the MT seems to be the least difficult text, and the ancient versions support it.

וְכָל־עֲצֵי הַשָּׂדֶה עָלָיו עֻלְפֶּה:—The last word can hardly be translated literally since it is a noun. Following the LXX, it is often revocalized as עֻלְּפוּ, a Pual verb. עָלַף is a rare verb that occurs only in the Pual (Is 51:20 and Song 5:14) and Hithpael. Its meaning is apparently to "faint (with grief)," or (of trees) to "wilt," or possibly "languish." Syntactically, the noun is the predicate of a nominal sentence, literally, "all the trees of the field were over it languishment." Greenberg compares 16:22, "you were nakedness and nudity," that is, "[you were] stark naked."[17] Here English idiom requires use of a verb, but there is no need to emend the Hebrew.

31:16   אֶת־יוֹרְדֵי בוֹר—The identical phrase was in 26:20 (twice); see the textual note on it there. Cooke probably correctly senses that the אֵת has pregnant force: "*so as to be with* those who are gone down [to the pit]."[18]

מִבְחַר וְטוֹב־לְבָנוֹן—This phrase, "the choicest and best of Lebanon," has two governing nouns in construct with the same *nomen rectum* (Waltke-O'Connor, § 9.3b, example 6). The LXX translates with only one governing word. More problematic is that both Hebrew words in construct are collective singulars in a verse otherwise filled with plurals (leading Zimmerli to consider וְטוֹב a gloss),[19] but Hebrew idiom easily equates collectives and plurals.

31:17   I have used a strictly "formal equivalent" translation of this verse because of its obscurity. That is, I have reproduced the Hebrew words as exactly as possible, praying that the reader can extract meaning from them. There is minimal agreement among commentators and translators, ancient and modern, on the verse's meaning, and I do not find grounds for claiming certainty myself.

גַּם־הֵם—The pronoun הֵם, literally, "they," appears to have "all the trees of Eden … Lebanon" of 31:16 as its antecedent, and 31:17a sounds like an explanation for their presence in Sheol. These are more or less further identified as "those slain by the sword" (חַלְלֵי־חֶרֶב), using חָלָל, a word we have frequently encountered from 6:4 on. Evidently they were killed by Assyria in its imperialistic wars, but now in death they occupy the same place as the royalty who fell in battle (a theme to be expanded in 32:17–32).

וּזְרֹעוֹ יָשְׁבוּ בְצִלּוֹ בְּתוֹךְ גּוֹיִם:—This is, literally, "and its arm—they lived in its shade among the nations." I have added the relative pronoun "who" after "arm," although the following verb is plural and "arm" is singular, presumably a collective. "Its arm" could be an appositive to the preceding "sword," wielded by Assyria, so the reference might be to Assyria's allies (so NIV and NRSV) or at least to its vassals who had been incorporated into its army. Those nations, which had previously lived in its "shade," would then seem to have preceded the tree (Assyria) to Sheol and wel-

---

[16] Boadt, *Ezekiel's Oracles against Egypt*, 118, crediting an oral proposal by Mitchell Dahood (n. 70).

[17] Greenberg, *Ezekiel*, 2:643.

[18] Cooke, *Ezekiel*, 345; emphasis added.

[19] Zimmerli, *Ezekiel*, 2:145.

come it upon its arrival. But how do we reconcile this understanding with 31:12, where those who had previously lived in its shade have already abandoned it?

For whatever reason, the LXX translates very differently and/or had a different Hebrew text in front of it, but it raises as many questions as it answers. Instead of "and his arm," וּזְרֹעוֹ, the LXX translators vocalized וְזַרְעוֹ, "and his seed." Instead of the Qal perfect יָשְׁבוּ, they read a plural participle in construct, יֹשְׁבֵי (consonantly, only a *waw-yod* variation). The LXX's total rendering of 31:17b is "and its seed, those dwelling under its shade/shelter, perished in the midst of their life." Obviously, the predicate has no connection with the MT. Those attracted to the LXX have proposed various reconstructions of the original Hebrew, but "everything here is very uncertain."[20]

31:18 אֶל־מִי דָמִיתָ כָּכָה—The first three words are repeated from the last clause of 31:2. כָּכָה generally means "so, thus, under such circumstances." It apparently is used to accent the question and half anticipate the answer: the insanity of Pharaoh's supposition that his fate will be any better than Assyria's.

Commentary

Rarely are the boundaries of an oracle indicated so clearly by formal markers that coincide almost exactly with one entire chapter. After the date notice, 31:1–2 opens with the word-event formula, "the Word of Yahweh came to me,"[21] and Yahweh's address to the prophet as "son of man."[22] Then 31:18 closes with the divine signatory formula, "says the Lord Yahweh."[23] After the introductory material, the chapter divides naturally into three parts: (1) a description of a cosmic tree (31:2–9); (2) the destruction of the tree because of its pride (31:10–14); and (3) the descent of the felled tree into Sheol (31:15–18). The second and third parts are set off by the citation formula, "thus says the Lord Yahweh,"[24] at their outset (31:10, 15). In contrast, the recognition formula, "(then) you/they will know that I am Yahweh," is absent from the chapter.

Predictably, critics, to one degree or another, deny that a good share of the chapter was authored by Ezekiel. Among those verses most commonly considered inauthentic are 31:5 and 31:9. The most radical (here and throughout his 1924 German commentary on the book) is Hölscher, who allows only parts of five verses (31:3–4 and 31:6–8) to be genuinely Ezekelian.[25] Form critics had an unusually difficult time deciding how to classify the chapter because it

---

[20] Zimmerli, *Ezekiel*, 2:145. Greenberg, *Ezekiel*, 2:644, opines about 31:17b: "Altogether this clause looks like a stray or mutilated passage whose placement here is secondary."

[21] For this word-event formula, see page 8 in the introduction and the textual note on 3:16.

[22] See the second textual note and the commentary on 2:1.

[23] For this formula, see pages 8–9 in the introduction and the second textual note on 5:11.

[24] For this formula, see pages 8–9 in the introduction and the fourth textual note and the commentary on 2:4.

[25] Gustav Hölscher, *Hesekiel, der Dichter und das Buch: Eine literarkritische Untersuchung* (BZAW 39; Giessen: Töpelmann, 1924), 152–53.

really fits none of their categories. Elements of many genres are present. Perhaps there is a slight plurality in favor of viewing at least 31:10–15 at the oracle's core as an announcement of judgment. "Therefore" (לָכֵן, 31:10) normally introduces the sentence of judgment in such an oracle, but no list of charges precedes it, and יַעַן ("because") follows it in the same verse (31:10). This is contrary to the normal structure of a judgment oracle, where first יַעַן ("because") introduces the (usually long) accusation, and then לָכֵן ("therefore") introduces the punishment.

Assyria Was a Cosmic Cedar (31:1–9)

31:2–7 The rhetorical question in 31:2 asking Pharaoh to whom he is comparable is answered immediately by Yahweh in the following verses. The comparison is to Assyria, described under an extensive metaphor of a cedar of Lebanon. Thus, Greenberg fittingly entitles the chapter "Assyria: A Lesson to Egypt."[26] Somewhat similarly, Keil uses the word "type,"[27] although he is using the word in a general, everyday sense, not in the technical sense of biblical typology.

A comparison of a person (Pharaoh) with a country (Assyria) would be incommensurate if we did not remember that in antiquity the ruler is reckoned as the personification of the people under him. With the pharaoh this had been implied already in 31:2, where Ezekiel is commanded to address "Pharaoh, king of Egypt, and … his horde [הֲמוֹנוֹ]." And then "Assyria" must be read in the same sense of a country embodying a people. Isaiah had done this very thing with "Assyria" in Is 10:5–11. Bearing this in mind will also resolve the problem that some perceive in the use of מִי, "who?" instead of מָה, "what?" in the question (see the second textual note on 31:2).

Only the framework (31:2, 18) connects the oracle specifically with Egypt. Ezekiel's anti-Egyptian oracles usually keep that country in full view, but here the accent is almost totally on Assyria, albeit metaphorically. In 28:12–17, the fall of the prince of Tyre was depicted like the fall of Satan, whose arrogance led to his downfall, and like the fall of Adam, who originally was entirely good in Eden before his sin caused his expulsion. The same is true of Assyria here. That is intended to drive home the chapter's point that "pride goeth before destruction, and an haughty spirit before a fall" (Prov 16:18 KJV).

Although now defunct at the time of Ezekiel's ministry (early sixth century B.C.), Assyria had dominated the historical stage in the ancient Near East for centuries. Although Babylon bested Egypt at Carchemish in 605 in the contest to succeed Assyria, the Babylonian Empire was relatively short-lived (not much over a half-century), and Egypt had not abandoned its ambitions. Ezekiel's view of Assyria as the archetypal imperial power will be evident in

---

[26] Greenberg, *Ezekiel*, 2:635.

[27] Keil, *Ezekiel*, 2:28.

the oracle of the next chapter, where Assyria heads the list of those who welcome the fallen pharaoh to Sheol (32:22–32). And the memory of having lived long in Assyria's shadow will still have been very much alive among the Israelites themselves.

In ancient art, the Assyrian kings are most often associated with the date palm. But Assyrian literature makes plain that they were well aware of the grandeur and desirability of the cedar of Lebanon. But already 31:3 indicates that this cedar is no ordinary tree, and this will become even more evident in succeeding verses. Many pagan mythologies have what is often referred to as the "world tree" or "cosmic tree" motif. It represents what the great historian of religion Mircea Eliade described as an *imago mundi*, that is, an image of the totality of the world. The three regions of the universe, considered vertically, are heaven, earth, and the underworld. The tree connects them, since it reaches to the heavens and has roots underground.[28] The tree is also a habitation that sustains life. This tree motif is prominent in Indian and Scandinavian mythology. It is present in Sumerian creation myths and elsewhere in Mesopotamian literature, probably most famously in the Gilgamesh Epic. It sometimes overlaps with, but should not be confused with, the "tree of life" motif so well represented in Mesopotamian glyptic art—a motif that is undoubtedly a pagan precipitate of the biblical theme. (Ancient pagan religions may contain garbled remnants of the true story of creation, the fall, the flood, and so on, as recorded accurately in the Scriptures.) In paganism, certain trees were often considered sacred to certain gods, but that theme is unparalleled in Scripture, which distinguishes Creator and creation too strictly for that. And because they were often considered at least semi-divine, trees (especially the tree of life) were often associated with kings.

If Ezekiel's use of the tree metaphor were appropriated from the realm of ancient Near Eastern mythology, one might be tempted to label it as "exmythological," a term I have used at other points.[29] However, while the Israelites likely were familiar with Mesopotamian mythology, we have no evidence that any story or mythology similar to this chapter had ever developed on Canaanite soil. Hence, "exmythological" may say more than we want to. Of course, that very term implies that what was functional mythology in paganism is instead in Scripture only a metaphor that serves to proclaim the supremacy and salvation of the one true and triune God, to the exclusion of all other "gods." But in this instance, where no actual native Canaanite mythology is known, perhaps

---

[28] Mircea Eliade, *The Sacred and the Profane: The Nature of Religion* (trans. Willard R. Trask; New York: Harcourt, Brace, 1959), 42–46, 52–54.

[29] This means that Scripture writers may use terminology or motifs found also in pagan religions, but of course the inspired biblical writers use them to convey religious truths, free from the presuppositions and associations that the terms had in paganism. For possible "exmythological" language, see, for example, the textual notes and commentary on 26:19, 21; the commentary on 28:14; 29:3; and the first textual note on 31:4.

we should be content with simply saying that Ezekiel's language is metaphorical.

Ezekiel 31 is not the only place where such a tree metaphor makes its appearance in the Bible. Yahweh himself has worked around the edges of the picture in Ezekiel 17 (which see). In Daniel 4, Nebuchadnezzar's dream, portending his punishment, plainly is based on the same metaphor. And even our Lord's parable of the mustard seed, related by all three synoptic evangelists, concludes with the image (Mt 13:31–32; Mk 4:30–32; Lk 13:18–19).

31:8 After the long discourse on the magnificence of the tree in 31:3–7, the text suddenly takes a more theological turn by stressing that not even various majestic trees in "the garden of God" were its match. The proper noun "Eden" does not appear until the next verse, but there can be no doubt that "the garden of God" is the same thing. In chapter 28, where the application was to Tyre, it was debatable whether the referent was to some Tyrian version of the biblical story, or to the biblical story plus details not mentioned in Genesis 2–3, but now revealed to Ezekiel by Yahweh. Here, there is no reason to suppose that anything but the Genesis narrative is in mind.

31:9 That all this grandeur was Yahweh's doing is now stated almost matter-of-factly. None of the other trees in paradise had the glory God had given to this cedar. Yet Assyria would not have given the one true God credit for its grandeur. Ancient heathen kings were not given to saying, *Soli Deo gloria!* When the tree became arrogant and incurred God's wrath (as described in 31:10), it was no more its Maker's fault than was the fall of Adam and Eve. Their fall brought sin and death upon the entire creation (e.g., Rom 5:12–21; cf. Rom 8:19–23). Echoes of that fall and its consequences may be heard in this chapter, which serves as an illustration of that point.[30]

The great cedar among "the trees of Eden … in the garden of God" (Ezek 31:9) recalls the depiction of Eden in Genesis 1–3, with "the tree of life" in its midst (Gen 2:9). The fall of Adam and Eve caused their expulsion from paradise and exclusion from that tree (Gen 3:22–24). Yet access to "the tree of life, which is in the paradise of God" (Rev 2:7), is gained through Jesus Christ. After his return, all the dead shall be raised, and believers shall enter the new garden paradise (Revelation 22), which shall have "the tree of life" (Rev 22:2, 14).

This may help explain the dendrite descriptions of the Messiah as the "Branch" (Is 4:2; 11:1; Jer 23:5; 33:15; Zech 3:8; 6:12), perhaps rooted in the selection of this one son of Jesse from the family tree, and of his cross as a "tree" (ξύλον, Acts 5:30; Gal 3:13; 1 Pet 2:24) that was both an instrument of his death and the source of life for all who believe. Part of a traditional prayer used as the Proper Preface for Holy Week is this:

---

[30] Zimmerli, *Ezekiel*, 2:150, attempts to contrast this context's accent on the beauty of the trees of Eden with the concern of Genesis with their fruit. But at best, this is cavil, and not even completely accurate. See Gen 2:9: "And out of the ground Yahweh God made to grow every tree that is pleasant to the sight and good for food."

On the tree of the cross you gave salvation to mankind that, whence death arose, thence life also might rise again and that he [Satan] who by a tree once overcame likewise by a tree might be overcome, through Jesus Christ our Lord.[31]

The Tree Was Destroyed because of Its Pride (31:10–14)

31:10 Yahweh through the prophet here tells Pharaoh what he had once said to the king of Assyria. Much of the vocabulary in this verse (and some of the following verses) is familiar from preceding ones, but special note should be made of the play on the roots גָּבַהּ, "be high," and רוּם, "be haughty." Earlier they had referred to the physical height of the tree (31:4–5), but here with לֵבָב, "heart," they take on the metaphorical sense of pride, arrogance, and so on, reflecting what in prophetic usage is virtually the primal sin. This is the only place in Ezekiel where רוּם is used in this derived sense of "haughty," although that sense is found elsewhere in the OT. Ezekiel usually uses גָּבַהּ, "be high," for "be arrogant, proud," as in 28:2, 5, 17.

31:11–14 Arrogance will lead to divine destruction and dismemberment, described in some detail, with the tree metaphor and the application often intertwining. But the ultimate point comes in the כִּי clause of 31:14, "because they have all been handed over to death, to the underworld." The haughtiness of those who were nourished by the mighty waters (31:4–5 and 31:14b) will come to naught. Like all mortals, they are ineluctably journeying toward the grave. As unbelievers, unless they repent and believe in Israel's true God, they will be consigned to eternal perdition in hell. One does not ordinarily think of trees as inhabiting the underworld alongside humans, but Yahweh continues the metaphor there nonetheless. The piling up of words for death, to which Yahweh has handed them over, is a reminder that the depths to which they must inevitably "go down" will be commensurate with the heights that they arrogantly claimed—heights of which Yahweh is sole master, and to which only his believers may be exalted (cf. 17:24; Mt 11:23; 23:12; Lk 1:52).

The phrase אֶרֶץ תַּחְתִּית (with a singular adjective, 31:14, 16, 18), translated "the underworld," is probably synonymous with the similar phrase אֶרֶץ תַּחְתִּיּוֹת (with a plural adjective, 26:20; 32:18, 24), also translated "the underworld." It is possible that these could be understood in a comparative or superlative sense, "the lower/lowest parts of the earth/underworld," and so point to the biblical doctrine of degrees of punishment in hell (e.g., Mk 12:40; Lk 12:47–48; James 3:1). Those unbelievers who were loftier in this life and used their greater power to commit more heinous sins will receive greater punishment in the lower regions of hell, as implied also in Ezekiel 32.

Ezek 31:14 happens to have the only occurrence in the book of the plural בְּנֵי אָדָם (31:14), literally, "the sons of Adam/men," translated "mortals," a universal expression that generalizes the singular "son of Adam/man" by which

---

[31] *LW*, p. 147.

Yahweh consistently addresses the prophet himself.[32] We have already met בּוֹר, "pit," picturing the realm of the dead as one mass grave, in 26:20 (which see; the word occurs again in 31:16). Ezek 31:15–17 will use the more common synonym שְׁאוֹל, "Sheol."

The Descent of the Felled Tree into Sheol (31:15–18)

31:15 The motif of the journey to Sheol of the tree representing Assyria, and portending the fate of Pharaoh, is now expounded. The Tyre oracles (26:19–21; 28:8) had touched on the theme, and it will shortly receive its fullest treatment in the book of Ezekiel in 32:17–32.

The two asyndetic verbs at the beginning of the apodosis of the verse, "I caused mourning; I covered," make for difficult Hebrew (see the textual note), but seem to provide the keys to the message of the entire unit. Signs of mourning pervade the entire verse. The deep is so incapacitated that it cannot perform its watering functions, and nature itself languishes because of the demise of the great cedar. That result somewhat precedes the cause, which is God's covering the deep, that is, putting a cover on it,[33] so that, without water, a drought results.

The language approximates that often used of Judgment Day. Although the text does not develop the eschatology as such, the judgments that befell Assyria and Pharaoh in OT history—and indeed, every divine judgment in history—can and must be understood as a miniature or even a "type" of the final judgment of all people at the end of the world, upon the return of Jesus Christ. Christians view judgment via the cross, where Christ suffered the entirety of divine judgment for humanity's sin. All in Christ receive the free gift of his righteousness (2 Cor 5:21) and so will be acquitted on the Last Day. The cross is the hermeneutical key for reading the judgment oracles of the OT and, *sub contrario* (God working "under the guise of opposites"), the means by which he justifies all who believe. But those (like Pharaoh) who do not believe in the Son remain under God's wrath and on the Last Day will be condemned to hell for eternity (e.g., Jn 3:18, 36; 6:40; 12:48).

We grasp much of the detail of the verse if we read it as an undoing of what was described in 31:2–5. The final judgment is often pictured as a dissolution of the present order of creation in order to enable a new creation. This is expressed classically in Jer 4:23–28, where the *tohu wa-bohu* (תֹהוּ וָבֹהוּ) of the primeval void returns (see Gen 1:2). See also, for example, 2 Pet 3:10–13.

The theme of mourning becomes even more vivid in the last two clauses. The Hiphil of קָדַר, "to darken," occurs elsewhere only in the parallel 32:7–8, but the Qal is often used in connection with mourning (e.g., Jer 4:28). Scripture often expresses that nature mourns because of man's evil. Of course, in

---

[32] See the second textual note and the commentary on 2:1.

[33] Regarding this point, see Zimmerli (*Ezekiel*, 2:152) and Block (*Ezekiel*, 2:194–95, including n. 91).

other contexts, the opposite is also true: all nature rejoices in God's redemption of man (e.g., Pss 96:11–12; 98:7–9; and many others). It is idle to try to compare this biblical language with nature's mourning in mythology, where it expresses the change of the seasons in a divinized nature. In the Bible, nature is as much a part of creation as man himself is. The creation is not an inert stage upon which God's interaction with man takes place, but an integral part of the cosmic drama (cf. Joel 4:18 [ET 3:18]; Amos 9:13; Rom 8:19–22). It is a case where the poetic details (e.g., trees clapping hands in Is 55:12) must not be taken literalistically, but seriously nonetheless. This is expressed in the Christmas hymn "Joy to the World":

No more let sins and sorrows grow Nor thorns infest ground;
He comes to make His blessings flow Far as the curse is found.[34]

Finally, in all of this, one must not lose sight of the overall emphasis that everything is totally under Yahweh's control—the cedar, Assyria, Egypt, the reaction of the nations, and—be it noted—also Sheol. It is not a place he frequents, but also not a place beyond his reach, which is true also of Hades in the NT (see Rev 1:18). In some passages, Sheol refers to the grave as the common destiny of all people since the fall into sin. In others it denotes the eternal realm of the damned (e.g., Num 16:30), but God in Christ has redeemed his people from that fate, and so Scripture can speak of God delivering believers from Sheol (1 Sam 2:6; Jonah 2:3 [ET 2:2]), even as he did Christ himself (Ps 16:10; translated with ᾅδης, "Hades," in Acts 2:27, 31).[35]

31:16 The quaking of the nations at the tree's fall apparently parallels or amplifies the wilting/fainting of "the trees of the field" in the preceding verse.

The rest of the verse takes place in Sheol. Those who have already gone there are the other choice, but fallen, trees of Eden and Lebanon—which here are combined. Three essentially parallel phrases describe the company found there. "All the trees of Eden" are other powerful and noble princes and/or the empires they ruled that had preceded Assyria/Egypt. "The choicest and best of Lebanon" has the same import. Third, the repetition of "all drinkers of water" (from 31:14) combines the figure and what it represents—trees and humans who together share a common need for water and a common mortality.

All these find a macabre consolation (נחם, "be comforted, relieved, quieted") in the fact that the cedar tree, formerly incomparable in its power and beauty, which they had once envied (31:9), has joined them in "the democracy of the dead,"[36] and like all human potentates, it has become as impotent as they. This theme will surface again briefly in 32:31, but its incomparable parallel is Is 14:10–17, applied to the king of Babylon, which may well have influenced Ezekiel here.

---

[34] *LSB* 387:3.

[35] See the excursus "Sheol" in Lessing, *Jonah*, 249–55.

[36] Cf. G. K. Chesterton, *Orthodoxy* (London: John Lane, 1909), 83 (chapter 4).

31:18 The chapter ends with the same rhetorical question with which it began (31:2), thus forming an inclusio, a format of which Ezekiel was apparently rather fond. And again we have direct speech, Yahweh addressing Pharaoh and asking him to compare himself with Assyria. If he deludes himself into thinking that he is Assyria's legitimate heir, let him ponder the oblivion now besetting Assyria. And so the initial question is expanded by a prediction of Pharaoh's forthcoming journey to the realm of the dead together with all his congeners, even those he found repulsive in this world, including the "uncircumcised" (see the commentary on 28:10). The final epigraph removes all possible doubt that the subject of the oracle is, indeed, Pharaoh (who has not been mentioned since 31:2), even though the focus of most of the chapter has been Assyria. The signatory formula, "says the Lord Yahweh," functions almost as authorization for immediate implementation.[37]

---

[37] For this formula, see pages 8–9 in the introduction and the second textual note on 5:11.

Pharaoh Will Descend to Sheol

Translation

32 ¹In the twelfth year, in the twelfth month, on the first [day] of the month, the Word of Yahweh came to me: ²"Son of man, raise a lament over Pharaoh, king of Egypt, and say to him, 'You consider yourself a young lion of the nations, but you are really like a monster in the seas. You thrash around in your Nile channels; you roil the water with your feet; and you make their channels turbid. ³Thus says the Lord Yahweh: I will cast my net over you by an assembly of mighty nations, and they will haul you up in my seine. ⁴I will hurl you down on land and throw you on the open field. I will let all the birds of the sky settle on you and let all the wild animals of the earth feed on you to their fill. ⁵I will put your flesh on the mountains and fill the ravines with your carcass. ⁶I will water your river bottom with your blood up to the river bluffs, and the tributaries will be filled with your body fluids. ⁷When you are snuffed out, I will cover the sky and darken their stars. I will cover the sun with a cloud, and the moon will not give its light. ⁸All the luminaries in the sky I will black out over you and set darkness over your land, says the Lord Yahweh. ⁹I will trouble the minds of mighty peoples when I bring word of your calamity to the nations, to countries you do not know. ¹⁰I will make mighty peoples appalled at you, and their kings' hair will stand on end because of you, when I brandish my sword before them. They will tremble at every moment, each for his own life, on the day of your fall.

¹¹" 'For thus says the Lord Yahweh: The sword of the king of Babylon will come against you. ¹²By the swords of [his] warriors I will fell your horde; the most ruthless of nations are they all. They will devastate the pride of Egypt, and its whole horde will be shattered. ¹³I will exterminate its livestock from beside great waters, and the foot of man will never trouble them again, nor will the hooves of cattle ever trouble them. ¹⁴Then I will let their waters settle and make their channels flow like oil, says the Lord Yahweh. ¹⁵When I cause the land of Egypt to be deserted, the land is devoid of all its contents, and I have struck down all its inhabitants, then they will know that I am Yahweh. ¹⁶This is a lament, which they will keen. The daughters of the nations will keen it. Over Egypt and all its horde they will keen it, says the Lord Yahweh.' "

¹⁷In the twelfth year on the fifteenth [day] of the month, the Word of Yahweh came to me: ¹⁸"Son of man, wail over the horde of Egypt, you and the daughters of majestic nations, and bid it go down to the underworld, to be with those who have descended to the pit. ¹⁹Are you more favored than others? Go on down and lay yourself with the uncircumcised. ²⁰They will fall among those slain by the sword. A sword has been appointed. They have carried it [Egypt] off and all it hordes. ²¹The leaders of warriors will speak to him and to his allies from the

midst of Sheol. The uncircumcised, those slain by the sword, have come down and lain down. ²²Assyria is there with its whole army, its graves around him, all of them slain, fallen by the sword. ²³Its graves are set in the deepest part of the pit, and its army all around its grave, all of them slain, fallen by the sword, who had spread terror in the land of the living. ²⁴Elam is there with its whole horde around its grave, all of them slain, fallen by the sword, who went down uncircumcised into the underworld, who had spread terror in the land of the living. They bear their shame with those who have descended to the pit. ²⁵A bed is made for it among the slain, with its whole horde around its graves, all of them uncircumcised, slain by the sword, for terror of them was spread in the land of the living, and they bear their shame with those who have descended to the pit. They are placed among the slain. ²⁶Meshech-Tubal is there with its whole horde around its graves, all of them uncircumcised, slain by the sword because they had spread terror in the land of the living. ²⁷Do they not lie with other fallen, uncircumcised warriors, who went down to Sheol with their weapons of war, with their swords placed under their heads, and evidence of their iniquity on their bones, because of the terror these warriors had wreaked in the land of the living? ²⁸You too[, Pharaoh,] will be broken in the midst of the uncircumcised and will lie with those slain by the sword. ²⁹Edom is there, its kings and all its chiefs, who, despite their strength, are put with those slain by the sword. They lie with the uncircumcised, with those who have descended to the pit. ³⁰The princes of the north are there, all of them, and every Sidonian, who went down with the slain despite the terror they caused. Let down by their strength, they lie uncircumcised with those slain by the sword, and they bear their shame with those who have descended to the pit. ³¹Pharaoh will see them [all] and console himself concerning his whole horde. Slain by the sword is Pharaoh and his whole army, says the Lord Yahweh. ³²For I have set my terror in the land of the living, and he shall be made to lie among the uncircumcised with those slain by the sword, that is, Pharaoh and his whole horde, says the Lord Yahweh."

Textual Notes

32:1–32 See the map "The Ancient Near East."

32:1 The versions translate the date notation in widely divergent ways. They may have tried to make the two dates in this chapter (32:1, 17) earlier than 33:21, when word of Jerusalem's fall reaches Ezekiel. (See figure 1, "The Dates in Ezekiel.") Special credence is often given to the variant "the eleventh year"[1] (instead of "the twelfth year"), but that change partly depends on the interpretation of 32:17 (which see).

32:2 בֶּן־אָדָם שָׂא קִינָה—The identical clause was in 28:12, and שָׂא קִינָה was in 19:1 and in 27:2, with the two words separated by "over Tyre" in the latter verse. I have,

---

[1] Some Hebrew manuscripts, LXX manuscript Alexandrinus, and the Syriac read "the eleventh year" in 32:1, and some Hebrew manuscripts and the Syriac read "the eleventh year" in 32:17.

as before, retained the traditional translation of קִינָה, as "lament," that is, a funeral dirge. See "Introduction to Ezekiel 19" and the textual note on 26:17–18. The following oracle illustrates that Hebrew uses the word in a relaxed, multivalent way. However rendered, the repetition and accent on the word again in 32:16 indicates an intent to use it as an inclusio or frame around the entire first oracle (32:1–16).

כְּפִיר גּוֹיִם נִדְמֵיתָ—This is the only use of the Niphal of דָּמָה, "be like, resemble," in the OT. Since Hebrew has two (or possibly three) דָּמָה homonyms, the traditional translation "be like" here is often challenged, and instead the verb is interpreted as derived from the homonym meaning "be destroyed/cut off," as in Is 6:5. In isolation, that might make sense, but the immediate context here casts a strong veto. The versions consistently translate it as a verb that compares. The Niphal here can be taken as having the passive meaning of the Qal used in 31:2, 8, 18, hence, "you could be compared to," or in the reflexive sense often found in the Niphal, as I have taken it ("you compare/consider yourself"). Is 14:14 uses the Hithpael in about the same sense ("you put yourself on a par with ..."), and for many verbs a Niphal can have the same meaning as a Hithpael.

One might have expected the preposition כִּי before כְּפִיר, as found before תַּנִּים in the next clause, but it is not indispensable.

וְאַתָּה כַּתַּנִּים בַּיַּמִּים—In this context, the conjunctive *waw* demands to be understood adversatively. Instead of a young, vigorous lion, the pharaoh is really a "monster," a תַּנִּים, as in 29:3 (which see). Here too Ezekiel does not use the expected spelling, תַּנִּין. Also here too there may be vague exmythological connotations, especially if יַמִּים ("seas") is taken as an allusion to Yamm, the Canaanite sea monster, but the creature here is clearly described in crocodilian terms.

וַתָּגַח ... וַתִּדְלַח ... וַתִּרְפֹּס—These three relatively rare verbs are all Qal second masculine singular imperfects with *waw* consecutive and are all more or less synonymous. They are used to belittle and ridicule the pharaoh's "accomplishments," of which he is so proud. (One thinks of Genesis 11, where the people of Babel thought they were building up to the heavens, but their accomplishment was so puny Yahweh "came down" [Gen 11:5] to see what they were actually up to.) First, גִּיחַ is used elsewhere with מִן in a sense of "gush, burst out" (Judg 20:33; Job 38:8; cf. the Gihon, the spring supplying ancient Jerusalem's water, which naturally pooled and then gushed out). Its use here with בְּ may indicate a comparable "thrashing around," but only within the confines of the banks of the Nile channels. דָּלַח, "roil, trample," is used only here and in 32:13. The creature's feet are unable to carry him far, and all he accomplishes by his trampling is to foul and muddy (רָפַס) the streams, thus impairing their usefulness for both animals and people.

בְּנַהֲרוֹתֶיךָ ... נַהֲרוֹתָם:—For the plural of נָהָר, referring to the "Nile channels," see the second textual note on 31:4. When the noun is repeated, Yahweh switches from a second masculine singular to a third masculine plural suffix, perhaps changing the application from the pharaoh alone to his subjects. Such variation is typical in Ezekiel.

32:3—בִּקְהַל עַמִּים רַבִּים—The preposition בְּ with קְהַל may simply be locative, as this is often translated: "you ... together with many peoples." But it seems preferable to take it as parallel to the following בְּחֶרְמִי (בְּ with חֵרֶם, "in my seine"), that is, in an instrumental sense: "by (means of) an assembly of mighty nations." As before (31:6), רַב is not so much quantitative ("many") as qualitative ("mighty.") That the nations are not mere bystanders is indicated by the plural verb following (וְהֶעֱלוּךָ, "they will haul you up," Hiphil of עָלָה), although they are not pictured as so actively involved in 32:9–10. The verb וְהֶעֱלוּךָ should not be changed into a first common singular verb (like וּפָרַשְׂתִּי) as in RSV and NRSV (part of a LXX-inspired emendation; see below). Yet "my net" (רִשְׁתִּי) and "my seine" (חֶרְמִי) remain Yahweh's. Yahweh is plainly pictured as the commander in chief of a huge, multinational army, possibly more specifically the various components of Nebuchadnezzar's army. In 29:4 Pharaoh, the marine creature, had been captured by hooks. רֶשֶׁת is a generic word for any kind of net for hunting, while חֶרֶם is a seine, a net more specifically applicable to a water habitat.

Because the LXX omits a translation of בְּקָהָל, many commentators view this entire phrase as an addition that disrupts the parallelism,[2] forcing them to propose various theories of how the MT took shape, and involving other emendations, for example, changing "they will haul up" to "I will haul up" as in the LXX, thus making Yahweh the subject.

32:4 For נָטַשׁ in the sense of "throw, hurl," see the first textual note on 29:5.

וְהִשְׁבַּעְתִּי ... וְהִשְׁכַּנְתִּי—The two Hiphil verbs, both perfect with *waw* consecutive, have a permissive sense, "I will *let* ... settle on you and let ... feed on you," as much as a strictly causative one.

חַיַּת כָּל־הָאָרֶץ—This is a unique phrase, literally, "the beasts/wild animals of all the earth," but its meaning is similar to that of the common כֹּל חַיַּת הַשָּׂדֶה, "all the wild animals of the field," as in 31:6, 13.

32:5 רְמוּתֶךָ—The noun רְמוּת is a hapax. The preceding parallel noun בְּשָׂרְךָ, "your flesh," indicates that its general force must be. It is an accusative of material, and translation requires adding a preposition, "with your carcass." Etymologically the most likely source would seem to be the root רוּם, with a resultant sense of "heap, bulk." Others cite the Syriac and take it as a plural of רִמָּה, "worms/maggots," evidently referring to putrescent flesh—a slight heightening of בָּשָׂר, and Hebrew parallelism often heightens or intensifies the second parallel member. The association of בָּשָׂר with רִמָּה is found in Job 7:5: "My flesh is clothed with worms." The LXX (ἀπὸ τοῦ αἵματός σου) and the Vulgate (*sanie tua*) both render the word in Ezek 32:5 as "with your blood/bloody matter."

32:6 This is a very difficult verse. The gory general picture seems clear, but the exact details emphatically are not. Neither ancient nor modern translators agree completely, and I have proceeded somewhat independently myself.

וְהִשְׁקֵיתִי אֶרֶץ צָפָתְךָ מִדָּמְךָ אֶל־הֶהָרִים—The first hurdle is the meaning of צָפָתְךָ, the noun צָפָה, a hapax, with suffix. Most likely it is a derivative of צוּף, a rare verb meaning to "flood/flow over" (cf. Lam 3:54). The Masoretic accents link together אֶרֶץ צָפָתְךָ, and one must decide whether to follow them or not. I have, although I am in a decided minority, and my translation of the entire verse is premised on that deci-

---

[2] Allen, *Ezekiel*, 2:129; Greenberg, *Ezekiel*, 2:651–52; Zimmerli, *Ezekiel*, 2:154–55.

sion. As a compound object of the Hiphil of שָׁקָה, the expression would literally mean something like "I will water the land of your flood, from your blood (up) to the bluffs." "Land of your flood" would refer to the bottom land, subject to flooding with Pharaoh's blood. Virtually every river has bottom land of varying widths subject to flooding, and also "bluffs" (הָרִים) of varying heights on one or both sides. But nowhere in the world is that phenomenon so prominent and virtually constitutive of its history as in Egypt with its annual inundations of the Nile. Even today one can literally stand with one foot on some of the richest soil on earth, from the annual deposit of silt, and with the other foot on totally arid ground incapable of supporting any vegetation.

The noun צָפָה is understood differently in the various versions. One meaning that could be appropriate here is that of Symmachus (an early Greek translation), ἰχώρ, the fluid that was thought to flow in the veins of gods, and possibly applicable to the unearthly "world beast" spoken of here. The LXX and other versions separate אֶרֶץ from צָפְתְךָ, yielding a meaning something like "I will water the land (with) your issue/what flows out of you." The Vulgate leaves that phrase quite vague (*pedore sanguinis tui*), but other versions were more interpretive. The LXX has "excrement," which perhaps suggests a different text with צְפִיעַ (see 4:15) or even צֹאָה, used as the Qere in 2 Ki 18:27 ‖ Is 36:12 for human feces. Similarly, the Targum has "manure." Any of these other readings make מִדָּמְךָ awkward, leading critics to suppose that it is either an interpretive gloss or a misplaced correction of the final מִמֶּךָ. The LXX lacks a translation of מִדָּמְךָ. Some translators attempt to salvage it by rendering "with your flowing blood" (RSV, NRSV, NIV), but this seems possible only if it is meant as a free version of NKJV's "with the flow of your blood." KJV's "I will also water with thy blood the land wherein thou swimmest" hardly makes sense and must be a desperate guess.

וַאֲפִקִים יִמָּלְאוּן מִמֶּךָ:—The short second part of the verse, literally, "and channels will be filled from you," complements the first part. אֲפִקִים are the deepest water channels of a valley. Since the first part of the verse has already stated that the entire valley will be flooded, I have ventured "tributaries." In wetter climates, these will usually contribute some water of their own to the main channel, but in deserts they will only contain water that backs up into them when the river itself is in spate. The Niphal יִמָּלְאוּן counterbalances the Piel מִלֵּאתִי of the previous verse (32:5). Its final *nun* is the so-called "energic *nun*," apparently a poetic flourish, although more common in Aramaic, and possibly attracted by the concentration of liquid *mem*s near it. Usually מָלֵא is followed by an adverbial accusative of the substance (liquid). The usage here, where the Niphal takes מִן for the source of the material, also appears in Eccl 1:8. Many translations have something like "filled with you." If blood is understood as the essence of physical life, as is common in biblical thought, one can understand the clause, but it still seems strange. I am attracted by Boadt's suggestion of a defectively spelled מֵימֶיךָ,[3] ordinarily "your water(s)," although the word can be used of other body fluids.

---

[3] Boadt, *Ezekiel's Oracles against Egypt*, 140.

32:7 וְכִסֵּיתִי בְכַבּֽוֹתְךָ֙ שָׁמַ֔יִם—This is, literally, "and I will cover—in the snuffing out of you—the heavens." The Piel infinitive construct of כָּבָה has no subject, and Cooke and Greenberg are probably correct in understanding the active form with an indefinite subject as having a passive meaning,[4] "when you are snuffed out."[5] The LXX translates it with an aorist passive infinitive, ἐν τῷ σβεσθῆναί σε. Some wish to repoint the form as a Qal infinitive or follow the Vulgate (*cum extinctus fueris*) in using a finite form, but in the first person, "when I snuff you out," with Yahweh as subject (so Block[6] and most English translations). However, it is self-evident in the context that Yahweh is the actor.

כֹּֽכְבֵיהֶ֔ם—The third masculine plural suffix ("*their* stars") is a bit puzzling. Grammatically, the nearest possible antecedent is שָׁמַיִם, technically a dual form, which, more easily than the English "sky/heaven," can be used with plural suffixes, adjectives, and verbs.

32:8 מְאֹ֤רֵי אוֹר֙—This is, literally, "luminaries of light." The inflection of מָאוֹר as a masculine plural (in construct) occurs only here in Biblical Hebrew, although the feminine plural appears three times in Genesis 1 (1:14–16). Both masculine and feminine plurals of natural features are not infrequent (e.g., רֹאשׁ, עָפָר, שָׁנָה, יוֹם).

The translation of both occurrences of עַל in the verse are inherently debatable. Both "over" and "on account of/against" are theoretically possible. The analogy of 31:15b would point in the latter direction (the luminaries as metaphors for other kings), but in 32:8b, "I will set darkness עַל your land" must be non-metaphoric, and that sense probably extends back to 32:8a to a certain extent.

32:9 בַּהֲבִיאִ֤י שִׁבְרְךָ֙—The verb is the Hiphil infinitive construct of בּוֹא with בְּ and first common singular suffix, literally, "when I bring your breaking." However, here the noun שֶׁבֶר, "breaking" (with second masculine singular suffix), is used in the pregnant sense of "news/sound of you being broken" (cf. Jer 4:20; 50:22; Zeph 1:10), or "word of your calamity," as I have translated it. In Ezek 26:15 and 31:16, a similar idea had been made more explicit by using קוֹל in the expression קוֹל מַפֶּלֶת, "sound of your/its fall." Here שֶׁבֶר may have concrete connotations too: "your broken army/your shattered remains." Hebrew abstract forms often have concrete meanings. That interpretation would approximate the LXX translation "your captivity" (perhaps reading שִׁבְיְךָ), followed by RSV and NRSV. However, Boadt has noted that Ezekiel does not phrase threats of sending Israel into exile with שְׁבִי and בּוֹא, but rather, in Ezekiel שְׁבִי is always used with הָלַךְ (12:11; 30:17–18).[7]

32:10 יִשְׂעֲר֤וּ עָלֶ֙יךָ֙ שַׂ֔עַר—I saw no reason not to give a relatively literal translation of "hair standing on end." The Qal verb שָׂעַר is a denominative of the noun שַׂעַר or

---

[4] Cooke, *Ezekiel*, 356; Greenberg, *Ezekiel*, 2:653.

[5] Greenberg, *Ezekiel*, 2:653, cites these verses for comparison: literally, "and on the day of the erecting of the tabernacle" means "and on the day the tabernacle was erected" (Num 9:15), and literally, "the time of giving Michal" means "at the time Michal was given" (1 Sam 18:19).

[6] Block, *Ezekiel*, 2:203.

[7] Boadt, *Ezekiel's Oracles against Egypt*, 145.

שַׂעֲרָה, "hair." The cognate accusative construction would be, literalistically, "to hair (with) hair," impossible in English. The same idiom was used in 27:35. The verb is used without the cognate noun in Jer 2:12 (and possibly Deut 32:17, although the verb there may be a homonym).

בְּעוֹפְפִי חַרְבִּי—The verb is the Polel infinitive construct of עוּף, "to fly," with בְּ and first common singular suffix. The poetic intensive conjugation is used to signify "fly back and forth." Various needless emendations have been proposed, but the only real question is whether the verb is to be understood in an intransitive or a transitive sense. Birds (Gen 1:20) and seraphim (Is 6:2) can simply "fly" (using the Polel), and similarly here, חַרְבִּי could be the subject of the intransitive verb: "when my sword flies back and forth." However, most interpreters, probably correctly, prefer the transitive alternative (which also accounts for the suffix on the infinitive), "when I brandish my sword," because Nebuchadnezzar had previously been termed the bearer of God's sword (Ezek 30:24) and because of the attribution of lightning flashes to the sword in 21:15, 20, 33 [ET 21:10, 15, 28]).

וְחָרְדוּ לִרְגָעִים—"They will tremble at every moment" repeats the idiom in 26:16 (see the fifth textual note on that verse).

מַפַּלְתֶּךָ:—The noun מַפֶּלֶת was previously used of the "fall" of Tyre (26:15, 18; 27:27) and of the tree representing Assyria (31:13, 16).

32:11 תְּבוֹאֶךָ:—The second masculine singular suffix on the Qal third feminine singular imperfect of בּוֹא is obviously datival: "come *to/against* you." The subject, חֶרֶב, is a feminine noun.

32:12 גִּבּוֹרִים—"Warriors, heroes" will be used again in 32:21, 27, and in 39:18, 20.

עָרִיצֵי גוֹיִם—This superlative construction, "the most ruthless of nations," was used in 28:7; 30:11; 31:12, all referring to the Babylonians, as here.

וְשָׁדְדוּ ... וְנִשְׁמַד—For literary reasons, the Qal (active) plural is followed by the Niphal (passive) singular, creating paronomasia of שָׁדַד and שָׁמַד. Correspondingly, "the pride of Egypt" is the object of the Qal, while the subject of the Niphal is "its [Egypt's] whole horde."

32:13 For the exmythological overtones of מַיִם רַבִּים, see the second textual note on 26:19 and also Rev 17:1. The Nile is obviously meant here, but by being so labeled, is invested with a significance beyond a surface meaning. In the light of what follows, we probably should think of Yahweh redeeming Israel in the exodus through the Red Sea, which can also be described in exmythological language (see Is 51:9–10; Ps 89:10–11 [ET 89:9–10]), although the connection is to redemption in general, and is not to be pressed.

In both content and chiastic form, 32:13b echoes 29:11a, although adapted to this context. The disagreement in number between the plural of פַּרְסָה ("hooves") and the singular verb תִּדְלָחֵם ("trouble them," Qal third feminine singular imperfect with third masculine plural suffix) is not unusual, and perhaps is here a result of viewing the noun as a collective, like the singular רֶגֶל in the preceding colon. The verb דָּלַח occurs in the Bible only here (twice) and in 32:2. It apparently is rather general in meaning ("trouble"), although its import is to "stir" and "muddy" (so NIV freely), as the next verse will make plain. It is unusual, but not irregular to use the same verb in both halves of a bicolon, although the LXX sounds as though in the second colon it had רָפַס ("make turbid") as in 32:2. It is hard to say whether it translated from a different text than the MT or was simply being free.

32:14 אָז אַשְׁקִיעַ מֵימֵיהֶם—The otherwise common אָז, "then," occurs in Ezekiel only here, and suggests an archaism. Perhaps Ezekiel has used or adapted an older poetic fragment for his salvation oracle here (see the commentary). "Then" is more precisely defined by the next verse, that is, at the same time the devastation also takes place.

The verb שָׁקַע means "to sink," and the Hiphil (first common singular imperfect) has a causative meaning, "cause/let their waters settle," referring to the silt that had formerly befouled the waters because of the crocodile's thrashing about (32:2). With the elimination of the monster, the natural limpidity of pure water can return. Possibly, Ezekiel also had in mind the Nile's annual deposit of silt after flooding. In 34:18 Ezekiel will use a noun derivative of שָׁקַע to describe limpid water.

32:15 בְּתִתִּי אֶת־אֶרֶץ מִצְרַיִם שְׁמָמָה וּנְשַׁמָּה אֶרֶץ מִמְּלֹאָהּ—This is, literally, "when I place the land of Egypt (as) desolation and destroyed—(the) land from its fullness." The noun שְׁמָמָה is derived from the verb שָׁמֵם, whose Niphal feminine singular participle follows (וּנְשַׁמָּה), literally, "devastation and destroyed." Elsewhere Ezekiel uses as a hendiadys two noun derivatives of שָׁמֵם in the phrase שְׁמָמָה וּמְשַׁמָּה (6:14; 33:28–29; 35:3).

In translation, אֶרֶץ מִמְּלֹאָהּ becomes a lame, isolated phrase without a verb. With virtually all translators and commentators, ancient and modern, I have connected it with the preceding verb וּנְשַׁמָּה, yielding "the land is devoid of all its contents," referring especially to the loss of human inhabitants. The verb is usually translated "devastate, destroy," but it also has psychological connotations and implies a sinister, silent desolation. Since the line (וּנְשַׁמָּה אֶרֶץ מִמְּלֹאָהּ) speaks of the land being stripped of its "fullness" (probably both people and economy), my translation of the line (necessarily a little free) accents that aspect. Yahweh causes this act of devastation (בְּתִתִּי, Qal infinitive of נָתַן with בְּ and first common singular suffix), as emphasized in the next clause ("I have struck …").

32:16 קִינָה הִיא וְקוֹנְנוּהָ—This verse, a little postscript or "colophon," as it is sometimes termed, is an expanded version of a similar statement in 19:14b. It anticipates obedience to Yahweh's command in 32:2 that Ezekiel was to utter a "lament," so the repetition of קִינָה here forms an inclusio around the first oracle (32:1–16). Such an oracle can functionally be treated as a "lament, dirge." In three incremental statements, the denominative verb קוֹנֵן, appearing in the OT only in the Polel, is used to assert that it will be so used. The verb is not easy to translate, because our culture has no counterpart to a profession of this nature. "To lament," "sing," or "chant" are all too general. "Keen" is probably the best counterpart, although it is not in common usage. As this verse and Jer 9:16 (ET 9:17) indicate, this professional mourning was normally done by women. One might compare the "ululation" of women in modern Arabic culture, used for occasions of both great joy and great grief.

After the recognition formula ("then they will know that I am Yahweh") in 32:15, some scholars speculate on when and by whom the "colophon" of 32:16 was added. The question is non-productive to discuss or debate, because there is no basis for any

but a speculative answer. The concluding signatory formula, "says the Lord Yahweh," bids us to take it as a divine Word, just as authoritative as the surrounding material.
32:17 The new date notice unmistakably indicates that a new oracle is beginning. Ezek 32:17–32 is the last of Ezekiel's against Egypt, and also against foreign nations as a group (chapters 25–32). The specification of which month is absent here as in 26:1 (some speculate due to scribal haplography after the preceding "twelfth"). The specification of the "twelfth month" in 32:1 suggests that the same month should be assumed here. That is, this oracle then comes only two weeks after the preceding one, thus serving as a conclusion to the preceding one. Similarly, 31:15–18 had concluded 31:1–14, and this oracle, in turn, serves as an expansion of 31:14c and 31:15–18.

The LXX, however, instead of assuming "twelfth," fills in the lacuna with "in the first month." A few critics have followed the LXX, as have, unfortunately, RSV and NRSV. But although there is no definitive way to settle the matter, the LXX is almost certainly a harmonizing addition in order to place this date in chronological order, preceding the date in 33:21 (see the textual note on 32:1 and figure 1).

In a way, this textual question in 32:17 is a harbinger of the nightmarish textual problems following. Let Block summarize the situation:

> The greatest difficulty posed by this literary unit is probably the text itself. Seldom since Ezekiel's opening vision has a unit been plagued by such a concentration of truncated sentences, grammatical inconsistencies, and redundancy, yielding a literary/rhetorical style some consider ill befitting the prophet so renowned for his creativity. The plethora of deviations from the MT in the LXX suggest that the Alexandrian translators ... were as frustrated with the text as modern interpreters are. On the one hand, this early Greek version omits 15–18 percent of the material found in MT; on the other hand, it fills in several lacunae. It also simply changes the reading where it is deemed appropriate. ... Stylistically, the oracle lacks color, being composed from a limited pool of expressions, drawn mostly from the vocabulary of death, and crafted in morbidly repetitious fashion.[8]

The unit does have a certain surface organizational logic, however. It may be divided in various ways, of course, but a sixfold division is perhaps most helpful. The first and last sections (32:18–21 and 32:31–32) describe Egypt in Sheol, thus as an inclusio keeping Ezekiel's main target unmistakable. In between, we have a list of dishonored dead from various nations.[9] Following the first section on Egypt (32:18–21), the others are presented in this order: Assyria (32:22–23); Elam (32:24–25); Meshech-Tubal (32:26–28); and Edom, all the princes of the north, and every Sidonian (32:29–30), obviously a sort of "etc." at the end of that catalog. Of the six groups listed, three are or were world powers, and three are smaller neighboring nations. Chronological considerations clearly were not used to determine the order of these nations. There may be an inclination toward the number seven as sym-

---

8   Block, *Ezekiel*, 2:212–13.

9   Block, *Ezekiel*, 2:219; labels 32:22–32 "The 'Dishonor Roll': Egypt's Company in Sheol."

bolic of all nations,[10] but if so, this is muted by the combination of Meshech and Tubal as well as the catchall reference to "the princes of the north" (32:30). Except for Sidon, which was addressed briefly in 28:20–23, none of the other nations has been targeted in the previous corpus of Gentile oracles (unless we count Assyria, which ostensibly is featured in chapter 31, but the fall of Assyria portrayed there anticipates Egypt's fall). One will note that Babylon is almost conspicuous by its absence; at Ezekiel's writing, Babylon is still playing the role of God's instrument of judgment upon Israel.

32:18   נְהֵה—This is the Qal imperative of נָהָה, used only here; Micah 2:4; and possibly 1 Sam 7:2. It might have been translated "to lament," but after using "lament" to translate קִינָה in 32:2, 16 (and elsewhere in Ezekiel), a near synonym was sought. What differences in nuance the two roots may have had is impossible to say.

וְהוֹרִדֵהוּ—This Hiphil imperative of יָרַד (with third masculine singular suffix) is translated "bid it go down," theologically meaningful because it implies the power of the divine Word to be spoken by the prophet (see the commentary). It is perhaps obscure if translated literally, "cause it to go down."

אוֹתָהּ וּבְנוֹת גּוֹיִם אַדִּרִם—The feminine singular pronoun אוֹתָהּ ("her") would have to be a direct object, duplicated after the objective third masculine singular suffix הוּ- on the preceding verb, but the masculine suffix does not agree with the feminine pronoun. One *can* explain the resulting grammatical impropriety if the masculine suffix refers to "horde" (masculine) and the feminine pronoun refers to "Egypt" (as the name of a land, feminine), or alternatively, the feminine land name may stand for its masculine king (as "Assyria" did in 31:3), but this seems more than a little forced. Furthermore, the relation between "her" and "the daughters of majestic nations" would be difficult. In 32:16 בְּנוֹת הַגּוֹיִם ("the daughters of the nations") were the keening women who lamented the demise of Egypt; they were the subject of the verb תְּקוֹנֵנָּה ("they will keen") there. Therefore an emendation of אוֹתָהּ ("her") to the masculine singular pronoun אַתָּה ("you") seems advisable here. The most likely construction is for the women, together with resumptive אַתָּה, to form a compound subject of the preceding singular imperative וְהוֹרִדֵהוּ ("bid it go down"), and perhaps also of the earlier imperative נְהֵה ("wail"). Hebrew can use a singular verb with a plural subject especially when the verb precedes its subject, particularly if one individual (here Ezekiel, "you") is the most prominent part of a compound subject. It is much more natural grammatically and makes better sense to revocalize the word and understand it as a resumptive subject for the preceding two imperative verbs (נְהֵה ... וְהוֹרִדֵהוּ).

אֶרֶץ תַּחְתִּיּוֹת—For this phrase, literally, "the land of the lowest places," with the feminine plural of the adjective תַּחְתִּי, see the second textual note on 26:20.

אֶת־יוֹרְדֵי בוֹר:—In this expression, יָרַד functions as a stative verb (see the second textual note on 26:20). Hence יוֹרְדֵי בוֹר means "those who *have descended* to the pit," and אֶת means "(to be) with/together with." יוֹרְדֵי בוֹר also occurs in 26:20; 31:14, 16; 32:24–25, 29–30.

---

[10] Thus seven nations are included in the oracles against the nations (Ezekiel 25–32), and Ezekiel has seven oracles against the seventh nation, Egypt, in chapters 29–32.

32:19 מִמִּי נָעַמְתָּ—The Hebrew question, using מִי with attached comparative מִן, is, literally, "More than whom are you pleasing/favored?" Ezekiel often uses such initial rhetorical questions (e.g., 19:2; 31:2; 32:19). The verb נָעֵם is used in a variety of contexts and is multivalent enough that its translation must be adjusted to suit them. It is often translated as "be pleasant, lovely, beautiful," and these may be appropriate in some contexts (cf. the name Naomi in Ruth 1:20), but the point of departure in understanding it must be divine favor. Boadt notes that the word can also be a title for Tammuz (Adonis), whose cult among apostate Jerusalemites is witnessed by Ezekiel himself (8:14) and has been archaeologically established as widespread in Canaan as early as the third millennium (Early Bronze Age III).[11] Tammuz was a chthonic deity, and if that is part of the implication here, it would make the question even more sarcastic, highlighting Pharaoh's pretensions to elude Sheol.

רְדָה וְהָשְׁכְּבָה—These two masculine singular imperatives are both lengthened by the paragogic *he*, which is usually considered a stylistic flourish, but here just might function to highlight the irony of the preceding question. רְדָה is the Qal imperative of יָרַד, "go down" (whose Hiphil imperative was in 32:18). The rendition "go *on* down" seems to me to fit the sardonic tone of the verse. הָשְׁכְּבָה is the Hophal masculine singular imperative of שָׁכַב, "lie down." (The Hophal perfect וְהָשְׁכַּב is used in 32:32.) It is one of only two Hophal imperatives in the entire OT (the other is in Jer 49:8). It is debatable whether it should be translated as a passive, "be laid out," or a reflexive, "lay yourself." Such language sounds as strange in English as it does in Hebrew, but the reflexive meaning seems to me to fit the ironic context better.

In the MT, God directs the prophet to speak this verse to command Pharaoh, bidding/sending him down. But in the LXX, it appears in place of most of 32:21b as the welcome spoken to Pharaoh by those already in Sheol upon his arrival.

32:20–21 Textually, these two verses must be treated together because the grammatical problems of both are of a piece. These problems include the following: (1) the absence in the LXX of any equivalent for חֶרֶב נִתָּנָה in 32:20; (2) the feminine (singular) suffixes on אוֹתָהּ and הֲמוֹנֶיהָ in 32:20, referring to Egypt, conflict with the masculine (plural) verb יִפֹּלוּ in 32:20 and the masculine (singular) suffixes referring to Egypt in 32:21a; (3) the imperfect יִפֹּלוּ in 32:20 clashes with the following perfect, מָשְׁכוּ; (4) Egypt is referred to by singular forms in 32:18–19, 21a, but apparently it is the subject of the plural verb יִפֹּלוּ in 32:20 and the plural verb יָרְדוּ in 32:21b; and (5) the verb מָשְׁכוּ in 32:20 lacks a subject. Sometimes critics reposition the first three words of 32:20 at the end of 32:19 as a sort of appositive to "the uncircumcised" (that collocation does occur at the end of 32:21), but in so uncertain a text, one runs the risk of confounding confusion if one starts rearranging elements. Various scholars propose ingenious explanations of what went allegedly wrong with the text,[12] but usually they create a considerably different text and/or consider all of it to be a later accretion. Even though the text does not follow the usual rules of grammar, our only

---

[11] Boadt, *Ezekiel's Oracles against Egypt*, 154 (see the sources cited in his n. 59).

[12] E.g., Allen, *Ezekiel*, 2:134; Zimmerli, *Ezekiel*, 2:164–65.

alternative is to try to make sense of the MT as best we can at the same time as we disclaim certainties.

32:20 חֶרֶב נִתָּנָה—The translation "a sword has been appointed" assumes that the subject of the Niphal third feminine singular perfect of נָתַן is the feminine noun חֶרֶב. Similarly, NIV has "the sword is drawn." One must assume that the sword is being handed over to Babylon as the divinely appointed bearer of the sword against Egypt. However, KJV, NKJV, NRSV, and ESV take Egypt as the subject of the feminine verb (in the next clause feminine suffixes refer to Egypt) and have something like "she is delivered to the sword" (KJV, NKJV), similar to the Targum, but this supposes an anomalous ellipsis of the preposition לְ before חֶרֶב. RSV omits the clause with the LXX.

מָשְׁכוּ אוֹתָהּ וְכָל־הֲמוֹנֶיהָ—The subject of מָשְׁכוּ is undefined. The verb means "draw away, carry off." If Sheol is in mind, as seems likely, "drag down to" might be appropriate. If a subject must be specified, the nations or, more specifically, the Babylonians, would seem to be logical. I have taken מָשְׁכוּ as a Qal third masculine plural perfect, since it is a textbook form of it. However, there is much to be said for the Jewish tradition and some more recent interpreters[13] who take the form as a Qal masculine plural imperative, with the short "o" (*qamets chatuph*) of the first syllable as a rare variant of the normal "i" (*hireq*). The normal imperative מִשְׁכוּ occurs in Ex 12:21, but the Qal imperatives חָרְבוּ in Jer 2:12 and (feminine singular) מָלְכִי in Judg 9:10 display the *qamets chatuph*, which also appears when the imperative takes a suffix, for example, the masculine singular imperative (with first common singular suffix) מָשְׁכֵנִי in Song 1:4.

Elsewhere in Ezekiel 29–32, the singular הָמוֹן frequently refers to Egypt's "horde" (see the first textual note on 29:19). In Ezekiel, only here is the plural used. The third feminine singular suffix (הֲמוֹנֶיהָ) refers to Egypt, and so the word may refer to Egypt's allies.

32:21 יְדַבְּרוּ־לוֹ ... אֶת־עֹזְרָיו—Literally, this is "they speak to him ... and (speak) with his helpers." The masculine suffixes on לוֹ and עֹזְרָיו must refer to Pharaoh. Normally after דִּבֶּר לְ ("speak to") a quotation of the spoken words would follow, but the MT has none (at least not obviously; see on 32:21b), probably explaining why the LXX has "will say to you" and places a translation of the MT's 32:19 here. It is not clear to me that a direct quotation must follow. Many give לוֹ the anomalous sense of "speak *about/of*" (see RSV, NRSV, NIV). The preposition אֶת is often translated by its normal meaning, "with," but it can be rendered "to," since it is parallel to לוֹ.

אֵלֵי גִבּוֹרִים—The speakers, "leaders of warriors," has the plural of אַיִל (literally, "ram," as in 17:13; 31:11) in construct and written defectively, without the middle *yod*. The verse reminds us of, and may be influenced by, the malicious pleasure with which the kings already in Sheol usher the slain Babylonian king into their company in Is 14:9–10.

32:22 אַשּׁוּר וְכָל־קְהָלָהּ—The noun קָהָל can refer to any "assembly, company, congregation," but in this context probably means "army." It is not clear why this word

---

[13] E.g., Keil, *Ezekiel*, 2:51.

is used only of Assyria, while "horde" (הָמוֹן) is applied to Elam in 32:24–25, to Meshech-Tubal in 32:26, and the Pharaoh in 32:31–32 (and was applied to Egypt in 32:12, 16, 18; cf. the plural for Egypt's allies in 32:20). Is it only stylistic variation, or is there an implication that Assyria's forces were more disciplined? As one would expect, the following countries are considered feminine, as shown by the third feminine singular suffix on הֲמוֹנָהּ in 32:24–26, referring to Elam and Meshech-Tubal, and there are comparable feminine references to Edom.

סְבִיבוֹתָיו קִבְרֹתֶיהָ—Now two masculine suffixes apparently refer to the king instead of the kingdom, which thus are not kept strictly separate. סְבִיבוֹתָיו will be repeated in 32:25–26 (and without the suffix in 32:23–24). The masculine noun קֶבֶר, "grave," has both masculine-form and feminine-form plurals, but this chapter uses only the plural that is feminine in form (32:22, 23, 25, 26).

הַנֹּפְלִים בֶּחָרֶב:—In this verse and 32:24, the Qal participle נֹפְלִים is used with the article, while in 32:23 and 32:27, the participle is anarthrous, but there is no discernible difference in meaning between the two usages. The participle must be translated as perfect tense, those who have *fallen* by the sword, rather than present, "falling."

32:23 קִבְרֹתֶהָ ... קִבְרֹתֶיהָ—Besides the feminine-form plural of קֶבֶר, this verse also uses the feminine noun קְבֻרָה (with third feminine singular suffix, קִבְרֹתֶהָ; the identical form reappears in 32:24). Occasionally קְבֻרָה can describe "(the act of) burial," but, generally, as throughout this context, it is indistinguishable from the masculine קֶבֶר, "grave."

32:25 נָתְנוּ מִשְׁכָּב לָהּ—The pronominal suffix on לָהּ must refer to Elam. The verb has an indefinite subject: "they gave/made," apparently referring to whomever assigned burial plots in Sheol. In idiomatic English, it is most easily rendered as a passive: "is given/made." Etymologically, the noun מִשְׁכָּב is derived from the verb שָׁכַב and so refers to a place to "lie down" or "sleep," hence normally a "bed, couch." Sometimes the word might as well be translated "bier" or "sepulcher." This, of course, reflects the nearly universal euphemism of death as sleep. Except for literary variation, there probably is no reason why מִשְׁכָּב is used only of Elam. The word reflects the widespread construction of "bench tombs" in *loculi* hollowed out of soft rock on a hillside, where the corpse was often placed on a simulation of a bed, often including a pillow.

בְּכָל־הֲמוֹנָהּ סְבִיבוֹתָיו קִבְרֹתֶהָ—This is, literally, "with her whole horde, round about him are her graves." The identical phrase (with וְ instead of בְּ) recurs in 32:26, in only a slightly different context. My translation, "with its whole horde around its graves," takes the phrase as having a meaning similar to סְבִיבוֹת קִבְרֹתֶהָ in 32:22, as does the Syriac translation of the phrase here. The phrase (and most of the rest of 32:25) is not reflected in the LXX.

נָתַן חִתִּיתָם—This is, literally, "their terror was given." The Niphal third masculine singular perfect of נָתַן has the feminine noun חִתִּית as its subject. However, the subject is rendered as the object: "who had spread terror" since the context demands that the suffix of חִתִּיתָם be understood as "terror of them, the terror they inspired in others," not terror or dread that the Elamites themselves felt.

בְּתוֹךְ חֲלָלִים נִתָּן—This short last clause of the verse is so similar to the verse's opening clause that it may be a truncated inclusio around the verse. נִתָּן probably is the pausal form of the Niphal third masculine singular perfect נִתַּן (see the preceding textual note), but it could also be the Niphal masculine singular participle, "being given, placed." Conceivably, the three words then could be construed as a pendant participial phrase, with the masculine participle as a reference to the Elamite king, but this seems awkward. The LXX omits the entire verse except for a translation of בְּתוֹךְ חֲלָלִים from either the beginning or end of the verse. Following most other versions and commentators, I have translated as though the Niphal were a plural: "they are placed among the slain." Compare the rendition of the impersonal plural active נָתְנוּ as a passive at the beginning of the verse. Closure by inclusion that harks back to the beginning could also be achieved by assuming מִשְׁכָּב, found there, as the assumed subject of the singular verb here: "it [their bed] was placed among the slain."

32:26 מֶשֶׁךְ תֻּבַל—Meshech and Tubal are regularly mentioned together in the OT, but as two separate peoples. In the Table of Nations, Gen 10:2 and the parallel 1 Chr 1:5, they are listed as two of the seven sons of Japheth. Two other siblings are Gomer and Magog, who will reappear in Ezekiel 38–39. Their unique asyndetic mention here implies that they are a single group, "Meshech-Tubal," as confirmed by the singular pronominal suffixes following ("its"). The LXX and Syriac add the copula ("Meshech *and* Tubal"), as does also Herodotus in his mention of them.[14] The inconsistency probably arises from their geographic adjacency. See further the commentary.

מְחֻלְלֵי חֶרֶב—The Pual participle (masculine plural in construct) of חָלַל, "pierce, slay," is used here instead of the more common noun (plural in construct) חַלְלֵי. The Pual of this חָלַל occurs only here in the OT. Critics usually consider the participle to be a result of simple dittography of the final *mem* of the preceding word, עֲרֵלִים. However, Ezekiel uses the Piel participle of this חָלַל in 28:9, and the Pual has the corresponding passive meaning. He also uses the Pual participle of the homographic חָלַל, "to profane," in 36:23. I incline to agree with Greenberg that the Pual here simply exemplifies Ezekiel's penchant for slight variations in his repetitions.[15] The Pual would technically be translated as "ones made to be pierced by the sword," not substantially different in meaning from חַלְלֵי.

32:27 I have followed a minority interpretation (reflected in the LXX and NIV) and treated the opening וְלֹא as introducing a rhetorical question, as in Ex 8:22 (ET 8:26). It has the same meaning as the common הֲלֹא, as in, for example, Ezek 12:9 and 26:15. In this understanding, the verse does not distinguish Meshech-Tubal from predecessors in Sheol, but places it squarely in their midst. In my judgment, this eliminates a host of problems that the verse usually poses for interpreters, beginning with the temptation to reverse the order of 32:25 and 32:26 (see the commentary on 32:25).

נֹפְלִים מֵעֲרֵלִים—The use of מִן on עֲרֵלִים must have a partitive sense, that is, "from among" the countless other uncircumcised warriors to be found in Sheol. With NIV,

---

[14] Herodotus, *Histories*, 3.94, 7.78.

[15] Greenberg, *Ezekiel*, 2:665.

I have simplified it to "other." The LXX apparently read מֵעֲרֵלִים as מֵעוֹלָם ("from of old"), which then leads many commentators to the conclusion that Ezekiel was thinking of Gen 6:1–4, where the offspring of unions between "the sons of God" and "the daughters of men" are called "Nephilim" (traditionally translated "giants"), similar in spelling to the participle נֹפְלִים here. However, נֹפְלִים (also in 32:22, 23, 24) and עֲרֵלִים have been used so often in this context that there is no cogent reason to follow the LXX at this point. We do not need to go back to the antediluvian period to find the burial practices described in the rest of the verse.

וַיִּתְּנוּ אֶת־חַרְבוֹתָם תַּחַת רָאשֵׁיהֶם—Again, the impersonal plural verb without a subject (וַיִּתְּנוּ, literally, "and they placed") is translated as a passive ("placed") with the direct object (חַרְבוֹתָם, "their swords") as its subject. From archaeology, we have countless examples of warriors being buried with some or all of their weaponry. Nothing exactly matching Ezekiel's description of a burial with a sword as a sort of pillow has been found yet, as far as I am aware, but "absence of evidence is not evidence of absence." Daggers are often found interred beside skeletons, but not often at their heads. At Baghouz, a skeleton from the Middle Bronze II period (nineteenth–eighteenth centuries B.C.) was found buried with an axe at or slightly under his head. Geographically and chronologically closer to Ezekiel's time, at Tell es-Saʿidiyeh in the Jabbok Valley a little east of the Jordan (probably biblical Zarethan), an Iron I (1200–1000) burial excavation uncovered a warrior wrapped in a linen shroud on top of which his sword had been laid.

וַתְּהִי עֲוֹנֹתָם עַל־עַצְמוֹתָם—This clause, literally, "their iniquities were on their bones," apparently is parallel to "their swords placed under their heads." It is not easy to make sense of, although it is supported by all the versions. RSV and NRSV follow a common emendation of עֲוֹנֹתָם to צִנּוֹתָם ("their shields"), which yields perfect parallelism, and is very tempting. I have followed the MT, in which עָוֹן must be another instance of an abstract noun used for something concrete, perhaps broken bones, or some visible mark on them, but just what would give evidence of their iniquity is obscure. Keil suggests that the clause is essentially synonymous with the וַיִּשְׂאוּ כְלִמָּתָם ("they bear their shame") in 32:24 and 32:30.[16]

כִּי־חִתִּית גִּבּוֹרִים בְּאֶרֶץ חַיִּים:—This final verbless clause seems condensed. I have in effect followed the example of the LXX and Syriac and supplied a verb in translation: "because of the terror these warriors *had wreaked* in the land of the living."

32:28 A smoother English translation results if we coordinate the two verbs and take "those slain by the sword" as appositional to "the uncircumcised" (so the Syriac already and RSV, NRSV, NIV), but we lose the rhythm of the Hebrew balanced cola (with the alliteration of the verbs שֻׁבַּר and שָׁכַב, which cannot be reproduced in translation in any case). The MT treats the entire verse as prose, not as a poetic bicolon, and the LXX completely lacks a translation of תִּשָּׁבֵר.

32:29 In this and the next verse, we meet שָׁמָּה instead of the שָׁם of 32:22, 24, and 26. Technically, it should mean "thither/to there" (with *he* directive), but the form is

---

[16] Keil, *Ezekiel*, 2:57.

often eroded into a synonym or stylistic variant of שָׁם. Compare 23:3, where the two are paralleled, and the locative force of the eschatological city's name at the very end of the book (48:35).

מְלָכֶיהָ ... נְשִׂיאֶיהָ—Unlike the large kingdoms considered previously, no "horde" or "army" is mentioned with these smaller states that were near Israel. Edom had "kings" (plural of מֶלֶךְ) quite early (Gen 36:31–39), and its monarchy is also mentioned in Jer 27:3, but its "chiefs" (plural of נָשִׂיא) are not otherwise mentioned. We know too little of Edom's internal political organization to comment on the term. In Ezek 7:27, the singulars of מֶלֶךְ and נָשִׂיא were used, apparently synonymously, of leaders in Israel, but the two terms do not appear to be synonymous here.

בִּגְבוּרָתָם—The noun גְּבוּרָה (with third masculine plural suffix), "strength," occurs in Ezekiel only here and in the next verse. The preposition בְּ could mean "with/because of," but "despite" seems more likely here. That meaning of בְּ is not all that uncommon; see, for example, Lev 26:27; Is 47:9; and the common בְּכָל־זֹאת, "despite all that" (e.g., Is 5:25). I have translated the preposition the same way in 32:30 on בְּחִתִּיתָם, "despite the terror they caused."

32:30 Interpretations and translations of this verse vary.

נְסִיכֵי צָפוֹן כֻּלָּם וְכָל־צִדֹנִי—First, we do not know precisely what political significance is indicated by נָסִיךְ. Even though its plural is translated "princes," just like that of נָשִׂיא in 32:29, the two words may well have referred to distinct offices. In Josh 13:21, the two words appear in the same verse, though of different countries. In Micah 5:4 (ET 5:5), the plurals of נָסִיךְ and רֹעֶה ("shepherds," that is, "kings, rulers") are parallel, and in Ps 83:12 (ET 83:11), the plural of נָסִיךְ parallels the plural of נָדִיב, "noblemen" (?). If the political situation was feudal, one might think of vassal-princes, persons enfeoffed. But nothing depends on precise definition.

Second, what territory is referred to by "princes *of the north*"? Why is כֻּלָּם added to the phrase? And why is there an individualizing gentilic, וְכָל־צִדֹנִי, "and every Sidonian," after that? Sidonians may be well be singled out both because their territory was adjacent to Israel and because they signified all the people we know collectively as "Phoenicians," often occupying a hegemonic position among them. So the two phrases seem to want to make sure that not only all Phoenician territory is in view, but also many of the Aramean city-states still farther north.

אֲשֶׁר־יָרְדוּ אֶת־חֲלָלִים בְּחִתִּיתָם—The Hebrew of this and the following clause is easy enough, but translators and interpreters often ignore the syntax indicated by the Masoretic accents and end up with diverse meanings. The best sense is obtained, it seems to me, if we do not ignore the Masoretic *athnach* (on בְּחִתִּיתָם), as many do. The suffix of חִתִּיתָם should be understood in the same way as on the identical term in 32:25 (see the third textual note there): "the terror they caused (in others)." I have taken the בְּ in the same sense ("despite") as on בִּגְבוּרָתָם in 32:29. Much of the confusion or perplexity probably arises from the fact that גְּבוּרָתָם is also the next word here, but with the preposition מִן.

מִגְּבוּרָתָם בּוֹשִׁים—These two words fall into place as a sort of appositive to the preceding clause. The verb בּוֹשׁ, "be ashamed," is commonly used with מִן to express an immediate consequence, in this case that of being let down by something a person relied upon. The phrase reaffirms an emphasis of the previous verse: the ultimate nullity of human might. Ezekiel uses בּוֹשׁ elsewhere only in the totally different contexts of 16:52, 63; 36:32, of the shame felt by a pardoned Israel.

וַיִּשְׁכְּבוּ עֲרֵלִים—The notice that "they lie (down) as uncircumcised" is paradoxical, because all the evidence we have indicates that the Phoenicians and even the "Syrians" (Arameans) to the north practiced circumcision. Hence some are attracted to Cooke's suggestion that we should read "*with* the uncircumcised" as in 32:19, 29,[17] but that would require some major textual emendation without any external textual support, and thus is hard to justify. It would be easier if we took "uncircumcised" here in the same metaphorical, spiritual sense we have met previously, regardless of actual penile condition: these are uncovenanted peoples, excluded from God's covenant of grace by their lack of faith. See the commentary on 28:10 and 32:19.

32:31 אוֹתָם יִרְאֶה פַרְעֹה—"Them" (אוֹתָם) stands in initial position for emphasis. It is possible to reproduce the same word order in English: "them will Pharaoh see." The antecedent is *all* the nations that have just been listed in 32:22–30, and I have freely added "all" so that this emphasis is not overlooked.

הֲמוֹנָה ... חֵילוֹ—The difference between the Kethib, הֲמוֹנָה (which is the sole reading in 32:32), and the Qere, הֲמוֹנוֹ, is purely orthographic. The Kethib uses ה as an archaic *mater lectionis*, while the Qere has the standard form of the third masculine singular suffix. הָמוֹן is the most common word in this pericope. It and חַיִל are virtual synonyms. הָמוֹן, at least etymologically, places more emphasis upon the bustle and din of any large group, while חַיִל is more immediately oriented toward the idea of wealth and power, but there is a broad middle area where they overlap. The use of חַיִל here, especially in the phrase "Pharaoh and his whole army," is drawn almost verbatim from the exodus narrative (Ex 14:4, 17; cf. Ex 14:28).

32:32 כִּי־נָתַתִּי—The verse begins with a verb in the first person, which is supported by all the ancient versions, except the often periphrastic Targum. The fact that most commentators and translators prefer the Targum's reading (as well as the Kethib over the Qere; see the next textual note) is a good illustration of the extent to which theological predispositions affect such textual decisions. "Lower [text] criticism" is a much more objective endeavor than "higher criticism," but, like all human endeavors, can never be entirely so.

חִתִּיתוֹ—The Qere, חִתִּיתִי, has the first person suffix on חִתִּית, "terror," while the Kethib, חִתִּיתוֹ, has the third masculine singular. The difference is exegetically significant; see the commentary.

פַרְעֹה וְכָל־הֲמוֹנֹה—"Pharaoh and his whole horde" is the compound subject of the clause beginning with the preceding Hophal verb וְהֻשְׁכַּב. It rather hangs at the end of the verse, and so I have again inserted "that is" for the sake of clarification.

Commentary

Jerusalem had fallen in summer 586, and it took the survivor about six months to bring the news to Ezekiel and the other exiles in Babylon in January 585 (33:21). About two months later, in March 585, came Ezekiel's last

---

17 Cooke, *Ezekiel*, 355.

two oracles against Egypt, which comprise this chapter. The first one (32:1–16) was delivered two weeks before the second one (32:17–32), assuming that the second one, which mentions no month, came in the same month as the first.[18]

Both are largely reprises or elaborations of earlier oracles. The first (32:1–16) concerns the fall of Pharaoh and echoes 29:1–16, while the second (32:17–32), an elegy on his descent into Sheol, elaborates on 31:14c–18.

The Fall of Pharaoh (32:1–16)

The boundaries of the first oracle are clearly indicated by the date and the word-event formula ("the Word of Yahweh came to me")[19] in 32:1 and the sort of colophonic conclusion and the signatory formula ("says the Lord Yahweh")[20] in 32:16. The intervening material, however, is fragmented in various ways that defy easy classification. The great variety is almost irresistible bait for critical speculations about how the chapter took shape.[21] About the only unanimity is the recognition of גּוֹיִם ("nations") as a keyword that may hold the disparate material together.

32:2 That a pharaoh would compare himself with a "lion" would almost have been expected in Egypt, and to a lesser extent throughout much of the ancient world. It was not necessarily a direct claim to divinity, but not far removed from it. Often it was connected with solar symbolism, specifically Ra, the Egyptian sun god. Both the destructive potential of the sun as well as war was represented by the lion-headed Sekhmet, the bloodthirsty wife of Ptah, a god of wisdom. Semitic syncretism is evident in a plaque of Qudshu (the "holy one"!), a goddess of war and fertility, standing naked astride a lion. It is worth noting that in the Scriptures, the self-revelation of the one true God (a totally non-mythological context), Yahweh executing judgment is often metaphorically compared to a ravening lion: Is 31:4; 38:13; Hos 5:14; 11:10–11; 13:7; and Amos 3:8. Moreover, Jesus, the only Savior from judgment, is portrayed as the conquering "lion from the tribe of Judah" (Rev 5:5; cf. Gen 49:10; Ezek 21:32 [ET 21:27]).

In Yahweh's eyes, the pharaoh's claims are comic. Instead of anything comparable to the "king of beasts," he is best compared to a defeated sea monster, or better, to a crocodile, confined to his narrow channels. By using the phrase "like a monster in the seas" (כַּתַּנִּים בַּיַּמִּים, 32:2), Ezekiel does apparently briefly introduce another exmythological motif, but he does not develop it. The figures and names often fuse in mythology, but Is 51:9–10 may be in-

---

[18] These and almost all the other dates in the book of Ezekiel are calculated from the exile of King Jehoiachin in 597 B.C., which coincides with the exile of Ezekiel too. See the textual note and commentary on 1:2, and figure 1.

[19] For this formula, see page 8 in the introduction and the textual note on 3:16.

[20] For this formula, see pages 8–9 in the introduction and the second textual note on 5:11.

[21] E.g., Zimmerli, *Ezekiel*, 2:157–58, takes 32:2 and 32:16 as the core of the oracle, to which four expansions were made, 32:3–8, 9–10, 11–14, and 15, although he concedes that even later layers may be from Ezekiel himself.

structive, where in a single passage Isaiah links Yamm, Tannin, Tehom, and Rahab, using Yahweh's exodus victory through the Red Sea as a type or prophecy of the defeat of Babylon (cf. 1 Cor 10:1–4). The monster under the label "Rahab" ("arrogance"?) is applied to Egypt also in Is 30:7 and Ps 87:4, but as a foe who is anything but a threat to God.

Here Yahweh portrays Pharaoh by means of a more earthly simile, the rather repugnant one of a crocodile, and a rather helpless one at that. As it thrashes about, perhaps making futile attempts to escape its confines, all it succeeds in doing is polluting what God intends as the life-giving streams of the nations. And for this, it will pay dearly, as elaborated in the rest of the oracle.

32:3 The imagery of a net to capture enemies is very common in the ancient Near East, also in treaty curses. Even Yahweh is pictured as hunting wicked men with nets in Hos 7:12; Ezek 12:13; and Lam 1:13. Here it yields a vivid picture of Yahweh mustering many nations to effect a "final judgment" on a would-be rival. Thus figurative and non-figurative language are used side by side, a common feature in Ezekiel.

32:4 The verse is largely a reworking of 29:5 (which see). To the "hauling up" of 32:3, we now have the contrast of "hurling down." Before the two complementary activities of Yahweh, the monster is helpless.

32:5 The language here is reminiscent of that describing the felling of the tree in 31:12. If the hapax רָמוּת (translated "carcass") is derived from רוּם "be high" (see the textual note), there may be overtones of the sin of haughtiness, which was also given as the reason for Pharaoh, as the world-tree, being cast into the mountains and ravines in 31:10–12. The general similarity of the two passages would emphasize that the subject here is no ordinary beast, but a "world beast" of cosmic dimensions (cf. the dragon in Revelation 12 and the beast he conjures out of the sea in Revelation 13).

32:6 The verse bristles with difficulties, but the general gist is clear: Ezekiel paints a grotesque, almost revolting picture of Yahweh drenching the entire land with the remains of the monster, his blood and other body fluids and parts. It would be an ignominious end for a ruler who fancied himself "a young lion of the nations" (32:2), and no part of his own nation would remain unaffected by his slaughter.

32:7–8 The language becomes more eschatological, even apocalyptic in these verses, and as is to be expected in such contexts, is loaded with imagery. That Pharaoh is being regarded as one of the brightest stars in the sky is supported by the fact that 32:7 coincides closely with Is 13:10, and also by Is 14:12, where the king of Babylon is compared to the morning star. Like Ezekiel 28, these passages relate the downfalls of these evil rulers to the protological fall of Satan in paradise (see the commentary on Ezekiel 28).

The verb כָּבָה, "snuff out," when used literally, refers to the extinguishing of a fire (e.g., Lev 6:5–6 [ET 6:12–13], the altar fire, and 1 Sam 3:3, the lamp at the tabernacle in Shiloh), but figuratively of a life, especially of a leader (of royalty in 2 Sam 21:17). Death is also intimated by darkness, or even by the

verb כָּסָה, "cover," used of donning the black of mourning (Ezek 31:15) or even of burial (Num 16:33; Ps 106:17). Compare Is 50:2–3, where Yahweh redeems by drying up the seas (thus defeating the sea serpent in Is 27:1) and clothing the heavens with garments of mourning.

In typological fashion, the language points both backwards and forward. Especially in 32:8b one cannot but recall the penultimate plague on Egypt, the darkness over the whole land (Ex 10:21–23). And the eschatological import, already broached in passing in Ezek 30:3, is developed more fully in the OT in Joel 2:10 and 4:15 (ET 3:15). The overthrow of the world-power presented by Pharaoh is to be understood as "an omen and prelude of the overthrow of every ungodly world-power on the day of the last judgment," when, after the return of Jesus Christ, "the present heaven and the present earth will perish in the judgment-fire."[22]

Finally, it should be noted that Ezekiel has reversed the usual sequence of the heavenly bodies (e.g., the stars first instead of last) found in Gen 1:16–18 and in parallels such as Jer 31:35 and Ps 136:7–9. This may be only a literary flourish without exegetical significance. Possibly, however, the thought runs along the lines of Jeremiah's in 4:23–28, as the ordered cosmos gradually reverts to a state of chaos ("without form and void," Jer 4:23, as in Gen 1:2).

32:10 The verse vividly describes the international effect of Pharaoh's defeat. But the eschatological overtones have not been abandoned entirely. The horrors of the end times also appear in similar NT predictions of judgment, for example, Mt 24:20–21.

32:11 The use of the citation formula, "thus says the Lord Yahweh,"[23] indicates a transition in the oracle. The figurative language of the preceding verses is dropped and the message is summarized in literal terms: the imminent Babylonian devastation of Egypt. Ezekiel's "sword" motif[24] is featured especially in 32:11–12, emphasizing how Yahweh will carry out his preceding threat to "brandish" his sword (32:10). As in 21:24 (ET 21:19), the sword almost assumes a life and power of its own. In the wider context, it is not even the king of Babylon's sword, as such, which is in mind, but Yahweh's, and he merely uses the king as his agent.

32:12 The king does not come alone, but with all his ruthless allies. "The most ruthless of nations" was used of Babylon and company already in 28:7; 30:11; and 31:12. The opposition here is termed "the pride of Egypt," probably not referring so much to that of which Egypt is proud, but to whatever in Egypt exalts itself—perhaps Egypt itself as a challenger of Yahweh. Powerful language is used to describe the result for Egypt.

---

[22] Keil, *Ezekiel*, 2:45.

[23] For this formula, see pages 8–9 in the introduction and the fourth textual note and the commentary on 2:4.

[24] See especially Ezekiel 21 (ET 20:45–21:32) and also, for example, 5:1–2; 6:11–12; 11:8, 10; 30:4–6; 31:17–18; 33:2–6.

32:13–14 As already the Targum and the Vulgate discerned, we have in these verses another of those messianic (in the broad sense) passages that Yahweh slips in at the most unexpected places, reminding us that even God's most severe judgments are subservient to his ultimate salvific intent. Pharaoh, the embodiment of "the kingdoms of this world" under judgment here, has been challenging and obscuring the clear streams of God's grace and promise, and his blessings cannot include "Egypt" until its fallen, natural will to grasp power is destroyed. Rivers that "flow like oil" are not merely rivers that flow smoothly and viscously, but rivers that contain oil instead of water (cf. Job 29:6). Throughout the Old and New Testaments, and continuing in Christian usage and symbolism, the chrism (cf. "Christ"!) or unction of oil is used to describe the life-giving power of the Spirit and the blessings of Christ's work,[a] which the Spirit brings through God's Word and Sacraments, Baptism and also the Lord's Supper. Catholic and Orthodox churches apply chrism together with Holy Baptism.

(a) Cf. Pss 23:5; 45:8 (ET 45:7); 89:21 (ET 89:20); Heb 1:9; James 5:14

If Christological exegesis of the OT means anything, it means "reading *out of*" (not "into"!) texts like these all the specific fullness that Scripture interpreting Scripture will entail. In the OT, the beatific significance of oil occurs also in Gen 27:28 (Isaac's blessing of Jacob) and in Deut 32:13. Keil quotes even Ewald, one of the nineteenth-century pioneers of the rise of the historical-critical method, as summarizing the meaning of this weighty, but easily overlooked verse: "The Messianic times will then for the first time dawn on Egypt, when the waters no more become devastating and turbid, that is to say, through the true knowledge to which the chastisement leads."[25]

32:15 This summary of a summary expresses in three more or less synonymous clauses and in a more formulaic way (the recognition formula, "they will know that I am Yahweh"[26]) what the previous verse had asserted more poetically, that Yahweh's purpose in judgment is to move people to repentance; but if they will not repent, at least they will recognize his lordship (cf. Phil 2:10–11).

Greenberg plausibly understands the threats of this chapter as an adaptation of Lev 26:34–35, where the future desolation of the land of Israel is attributed to its failure to observe the sabbatical years God commanded: "With the desolation of the land of Israel God's dominion is affirmed through enforced sabbaticals; with the desolation of Egypt it is affirmed through enforced limpidity of the Nile."[27]

32:16 Theologically, this postscript merely predicts that the judgment oracle just concluded will be keened, or chanted as a dirge, beyond all national frontiers and thus will proclaim God's victory over any and all that presumes to vaunt itself over him. On Easter (and every Sunday), the Christian church

---

[25] Keil, *Ezekiel*, 2:49.

[26] For this formula, see page 9 in the introduction and the commentary on 6:7.

[27] Greenberg, *Ezekiel*, 2:658.

proclaims that that decisive victory has already been won and a realized eschatology is celebrated proleptically even before the lingering forces of Satan mount another futile challenge.[28]

Pharaoh Descends into Sheol (32:17–32)

32:18 The last in the collection of Ezekiel's Gentile oracles is clearly a sequel to and conclusion of the preceding one. It is focused almost completely on Egypt's descent into the "pit," or Sheol, and is, in fact, alongside Isaiah 14, one of the OT's most detailed depictions of the nether region. It begins with another command to "lament/wail," but in the light of what follows, that word could almost be translated as "taunt" (see the textual note). The content, as such, is not specified, but another command immediately follows. The charge involves the verb יָרַד, "go down, descend," used prominently in this oracle as in previous oracles against Tyre (26:11, 16, 20) and Egypt (31:12–18), which is not surprising, considering the subject matter. More surprising is its inflection as a Hiphil imperative with the prophet as the subject: "bid it go down."

This is an excellent example of the power of the prophetic word, which often does not only proclaim or predict, but brings reality to pass. But, of course, it is not the power of the prophet's word, as such, in some inherent, magical way, but the efficacious Word of Yahweh, which always accomplishes what it says (Is 55:10–11). Christian life and worship depends on this power of God's Word, as when the pastor pronounces absolution and declares, "As a called and ordained servant of Christ, and by His authority, I therefore forgive you all your sins in the name of the Father and of the Son and of the Holy Spirit."[29] Christ's Words of Institution too are efficacious: Christ is present at his Supper in such a way that communicants receive his very body and blood together with the bread and wine.

Literally, the prophet is to "make" Egypt "go down" to the underworld, that is to consign it to its posthumous existence there. Nor is he to do it alone, but in concert with the בְּנוֹת גּוֹיִם אַדִּרִם, "the daughters of majestic nations," the professional mourning women mentioned in 32:16—and thus an obvious link with that preceding oracle. Sometimes the genitive here is taken as epexegetical, "the daughters who are the nations" that will be mentioned later in the oracle, but that strikes me as unlikely. God is here described as working mediately, not only through "called and ordained" prophets, but through other agents, who have no idea who they are really serving. All his creatures, and indeed all creation, carries out the purposes of the Creator and Redeemer.

---

28 The NT declares that throughout the church age Satan will intensify his attacks against the church, culminating in a final assault (e.g., Rev 20:7–10), but at the return of Christ all opponents of God's kingdom will be vanquished forever (Rev 20:10–15).

29 *LSB*, 151, citing Jn 20:19–23. For an explanation of the biblical basis and theology of absolution, see the section on the office of the keys in the Small Catechism (*Luther's Small Catechism with Explanation*, 27; *LSB*, 326).

By labeling the nations "majestic," Yahweh reminds Egypt that many powers as great or greater than it is have met the same destiny and it should not suppose that it will somehow be exempt. At the same time, he extends his taunt of Egypt into a funeral dirge on the fall of all the heathen powers of the world—the ultimate point of all the Gentile oracles.[30]

32:19 The prophet's actual speech to Pharaoh begins here, and it fairly drips with mockery and sarcasm. The language is different, but the rhetorical force of the question is similar to earlier challenges to name anyone equal to Egypt in greatness (31:2) and glory (31:18). But here is the gist: who does he think he is, favored somewhat by God as he once had been, that he thinks it will exempt him from the universal visit of God's "grim reaper"?

The ignominy is even incomparably greater if he must lie down among the "uncircumcised." The applicability of such obloquy here is puzzling, as it was in 28:10 (see the commentary there), where the prince of Tyre was prophesied to "die the death of the uncircumcised." The problem arises from the fact that the Egyptians (at least priests and kings), like the Edomites and the Sidonians in the following list, practiced circumcision. Evidently, Ezekiel is using conventional and metaphorical language. Perhaps there is simply an assumption that the Egyptians would have found such a thought as revolting as Israelites would, and this may well have been the case, but firm evidence is lacking. It is frequently assumed that Israelite custom excluded the uncircumcised from family graves and that they were consigned to the lowest level of the underworld (see the commentary on 32:23) since they had broken God's covenant and would be cut off from their kin (Gen 17:14). Orthodox Israelites would, of course, be circumcised, and perhaps a comparable assertion could be made of Egyptians (at least, the upper classes) as well.

As a priest, Ezekiel would be especially knowledgeable and precise about such matters of the covenant. He may, at God's bidding, have been homiletically applying Israelite covenantal categories to Egyptians, according to which they would be "uncircumcised" spiritually—excluded from God's covenant of grace and hence from his redeemed people—even if circumcised in the flesh (see also the commentary on 28:10). In God's frame of reference, the dishonorability of departing this world as "uncircumcised" also extends to the underworld, and to be buried with the uncircumcised would obviously add insult to injury. In the new covenant, Holy Baptism into Christ's death and resurrection supercedes circumcision as the seal and guarantee of inheritance of all God's gracious promises.[b] Thus to express the fate of Pharaoh in NT terms, he is consigned to eternal perdition among the unbaptized, who are unbelievers (cf. Rev 20:15; 21:27).

32:20 Interpretation of so difficult a text is also difficult. One almost gets an impression of a series of disjointed sentences, each of which must be con-

(b) Gal 3:26–29; Col 2:11–13; cf. Rom 2:25–29; 1 Cor 7:19; Gal 5:6; Phil 3:3

---

[30] See "Introduction to Ezekiel 25–32: Oracles against Other Nations."

sidered independently. The subject of the initial verb "they will fall" (יִפְּלוּ) must be the Egyptians. The imperfect (future?) almost sounds like a flashback to the battles preceding their descent into Sheol. Is there a connection with the "uncircumcised" just mentioned? "The uncircumcised" and "those slain by the sword" are placed side by side in 32:21b and perhaps should be here also. Greenberg sees the connection in the fact that fallen corpses were typically stripped by the victors and their naked bodies would make their lack of circumcision evident.[31] Block argues, as he does repeatedly, that "those slain by the sword" does not mean simply casualties of war, but criminals, who after execution were not given an honorable burial, but disposed of otherwise, and in the underworld would also be separated from those who had received proper burials.[32] In this context, he appeals to 32:27 as evidence. Thus while distinguished from the uncircumcised, both groups would be sequestered, and it would be equally disgraceful to have to join them in Sheol. But the evidence for this view is weak.

32:21 Egypt's "helpers" ("allies") were mentioned already in 30:8, and their association with Pharaoh here is probably essentially synonymous. They are not mentioned in the LXX and Syriac. Their function, if anything specific, seems to be to identify themselves as the "uncircumcised" of the next clause. The import of 32:21b is uncertain. Some read it as a sort of snide aside when Pharaoh arrives ("here come …"). Others construe the entire half verse as simply a parenthetical addition. Pharaoh's warriors would presumably have been circumcised, and the point could be simply a denigrating assimilation of the Egyptians to those who were physically uncircumcised. Another attractive solution is to take "the leaders of the warriors" as the subject (spoken of here in relative clauses without אֲשֶׁר), "who went down (and) lay uncircumcised, pierced by the sword."[33] Finally, the terms may be adverbial accusatives: "they have gone down as leaders, uncircumcised." In any case, the indisputable point is the inevitable doom of Egypt.

32:22 Yahweh's "dishonor roll" (list of dishonored nations) begins here and continues through 32:30. It is scarcely surprising that Assyria heads the list. It had been two decades since Assyria had fallen for the last time at the Battle of Carchemish (605 B.C.), but memories of its preceding centuries of sadistic tyranny were doubtless still very much alive. As will be repeated several times, there appears here the first mention of the common practice of grave complexes with the king's tomb at the center and those of the royal family and other nobility nearby. Any tourist who has visited the pyramids across the Nile from Cairo can readily visualize the general picture, although the precise burial practices varied from country to country.

---

[31] Greenberg, *Ezekiel*, 2:662.

[32] Block, *Ezekiel*, 2:218.

[33] Boadt, *Ezekiel's Oracles against Egypt*, 155.

32:23 This verse adds two details, the first of which is applied only to Assyria. Its graves will be situated in "the deepest part of the pit." The noun יַרְכָּה describes the remotest, most distant, and/or most inaccessible part of something. (Ezekiel will use it again of the צָפוֹן "north," in 38:6, 15; 39:2, and of the eschatological temple in 46:19.) The only other place where it is used with בּוֹר, "the pit, hell," is in Is 14:15, where it is contrasted with remotest parts of the "north" (Is 14:13), there Mount Zaphon (in Greek, Casius, the pagan Canaanite counterpart of Mount Olympus, the home of the gods). There the opposition is specific: the Babylonian king who aspired to be a god in the highest heaven will be cast down to the lowest part of Sheol. That contrast is not articulated here, but the import is very similar. Assyria, which had in the mid-seventh century ruled most of the "civilized" world of the time, including Egypt, had ceased to exist in this world and would never rise again.

The point is a proverbial one, not far removed from our Lord's diction "everyone who exalts himself will be humbled" (Lk 14:11; 18:14; see also Lk 10:15, 18). This passage, like Ezek 31:11–14, indicates that the higher an arrogant unbeliever aspires and rises on earth, and the more egregious his sins against God and his fellow humans, the deeper he is consigned in the underworld. This is consistent with other passages that allude to degrees of punishment in hell (e.g., Lk 12:47–48; James 3:1), even as Scripture also speaks of degrees of glory for the redeemed in heaven (e.g., Dan 12:3; Lk 19:16–19).

Second, there is a charge that we shall hear again in each of the next four verses and in 32:30, namely, that these nations had caused or spread חִתִּית, "terror," in this world. This is a uniquely Ezekelian expression (also used of Tyre in 26:17). It occurs seven times in this context and perhaps comes as close as anything to giving a reason why the nations targeted are included in Yahweh's "dishonor roll." Their reign of terror in the "land of the living" (32:23) is contrasted with their utter impotence in Sheol. Again, the sinful behavior of unbelievers in this life will lead to corresponding punishments in the hereafter. "As a man sows, so shall he reap" (Gal 6:7–8; cf. 2 Cor 9:6) pertains both to the judgment of unbelievers (Hos 8:7) and to the salvation of penitent believers (Hos 10:12; Ps 126:5).

32:24–25 Elam remains one of the least known of the major civilizations of the ancient Near East. Its long history, usually considered as beginning around 3200 B.C. and ending (at least politically) with its conquest by Alexander the Great in 331, is punctuated by a recurrence of both military and mercantile contacts with Mesopotamia to its west, apparently one of those constants of ancient world history (consider the modern relations of Iran and Iraq). Elamites (or people occupying the same territory, the southwestern part of the Iranian plateau, today the Iranian province of Khuzestan) developed their own system of ideographic writing about the same time as the Sumerians, but this Proto-Elamite remains undeciphered, although presumably reflecting the same agglutinate tongue (unrelated to any other known language) known from its later history. One of its major cities, and often its capital, was Susa, the set-

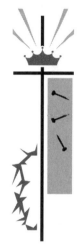

ting of the book of Esther, the writer of which was, as archaeology has demonstrated, well acquainted with the city, whether or not he actually lived there. At times, part of the area was even known as Susiana.

The region makes its first major mark in recorded history around 2200 B.C. with the destruction of the Akkadian Empire (the earliest Semitic one) by the Guti, barbarians from the Zagros Mountains. A few centuries later, Elamites play a role in the fall of Ur III (the third dynasty of Ur, at the end of the Sumerian political influence), and still later, around 1600, with the collapse of the Amorite dynasty of Babylon (Hammurabi is its best-known ruler). Elam reached its brief zenith a couple of centuries later. Much closer to Ezekiel's day, Elam was constantly dabbling in the interminable conflict between the Assyrians and Babylonians (now mostly Aramean Chaldeans), inevitably provoking Assyrian reprisals, first by Sennacherib (704–681), for aiding the Chaldean guerrilla rebel Merodach-Baladan (2 Ki 20:12 || Is 39:1), and a little later by Ashurbanipal (668–627). In 640, Ashurbanipal finally conquered the country and described (probably in somewhat hyperbolic detail, as was customary) the ferocity with which he wreaked his vengeance on an ancient foe. Some Elamites were even deported to Samaria (Ezra 4:9–10). One cannot point to any single event that caused Yahweh to include Elam in his dishonor roll, but their settlement in northern Israel after it was taken by Assyria would be a major candidate.

It is beyond our purview to sketch Elam's history further, but the name does not disappear from the historical record for a long time. While others were preoccupied with the Mesopotamian conflict, the Medes and the Persians, originally from the plateau, gradually pushed the indigenous Elamites toward the low country. At least by the time Cyrus (559–530) conquered Babylon in 539 (cf. Is 21:2), Elam had become a province of the Achaemenid Empire, which inherited many characteristics of Elamite culture. Darius (521–486) restored Susa to its ancient glory, and the city's association with Elam is reflected in the Bible (Dan 8:2; Ezra 4:9). The city continued to exist after the Hellenistic and even later the Islamic invasions, but by the fourteenth century A.D., the ancient empire finally fell into oblivion.

The Bible does not flesh out major details of Elamite history, but what is known from secular sources does explain why it is mentioned as often as it is. In the Table of Nations (Gen 10:22 || 1 Chr 1:17), Elam appears as a son of Shem, alongside Asshur (Assyria), Arpochshad (?), Lud (Lydia), and Aram. The most famous Elamite in the OT is "Chedorlaomer, king of Elam" (Gen 14:1, 9), among those four kings who captured Lot, who was rescued by Abraham, who was subsequently feted by Melchizedek. The name Chedorlaomer is unquestionably Elamite, but no satisfactory identification is known from Elamite history. Elam is mentioned several times by the prophets. Is 22:6 associates Elamites with archery, chariotry, and cavalry. Jeremiah (49:34–39) is the only prophet to devote an entire Gentile oracle against Elam. Is 11:11 speaks of an Israelite diaspora in Elam, and after Cyrus' edict (538), Israelites are mentioned as returning from Elam (Ezra 2:7, 31; 8:7). Nor are we surprised to find Elamites among the pilgrims in Jerusalem on Pentecost (Acts 2:9).

What Ezekiel says of Elam is what he has already said of Egypt, and almost in the same words. As Boadt notes: "The constant repetition of the same description for each nation ... has a calculated tolling effect that enhances the nature of a lament."[34] Ezek 32:25 virtually duplicates 32:24, except for the omission of the opening "Elam is there" and the middle clause ("who ... underworld") and a few other minor changes.[35]

32:26 Meshech and Tubal, two Anatolian nations, are usually considered semi-separately, and the MT equivocates at this point (see the textual note). In 27:13 both names had appeared, in reverse order. They apparently could act in concert, but also were often ravaged by internecine (fratricidal? see Gen 10:2 || 1 Chr 1:5) warfare. Not too much is known of the details of their history. They seem to have skirmishes repeatedly both with the barbarian Cimmerians (Gomer; see the textual note) from southern Russia and with Assyria. We have no knowledge of direct contacts with Israel, but it is usually supposed that their contacts with Assyria underlie their inclusion in Ezekiel's list here. Later they were incorporated into the Persian Empire, but appear to lose their ethnic or cultural identity after that. Ezek 27:13 mentioned them as traders with Tyre in both human slaves and in bronze. In chapters 38–39, they will reappear as included in Gog's massive (eschatological) invasion of Israel's restored land.

32:27 My decision not to treat לֹא as a negative, but as having the same meaning as הֲלֹא (introducing a rhetorical question: "do they not ... ?") yields an entirely different meaning of the verse than that found in the majority of translations and commentaries. In less stereotyped language than usual, Yahweh simply affirms that Meshech and Tubal find their place in Sheol together with generations of the "uncircumcised" before them. Except for varied language, this is thoroughly in line with what Yahweh has been asserting throughout his list of dishonored nations in hell.

If לֹא is taken as a simple negative, as many do, the verse would contrast the ignominy Meshech-Tubal would experience in the underworld with the honor some previous warriors had been accorded as indicated by their being buried with their weapons. Block compares the verse with 16:44–59, where Jerusalem is excoriated for being more wicked not only than her sister but even

---

[34] Boadt, *Ezekiel's Oracles against Egypt*, 163.

[35] Since most of 32:25 is missing in the LXX, some commentators (e.g., Cooke, *Ezekiel*, 353; Zimmerli, *Ezekiel*, 2:167; Eichrodt, *Ezekiel*, 435–36; cf. Boadt, *Ezekiel's Oracles against Egypt*, 158) consider the verse to be a secondary addition. Either haplography or dittography in one direction or the other could account for the discrepancy. Some suggest that the order of 32:25 and 32:26 should be reversed, and a section on Egypt is then comprised of 32:25, 27–28. However, this shuffling of verses lacks any external support. I personally incline to the explanation that Ezekiel was simply being his usual verbose self, and the LXX purposely abbreviated his repetitious text.

than Sodom.[36] But for Ezekiel to talk of some heathen (even very ancient ones) as having met a glorious death, their lack of circumcision notwithstanding, seems out of character to me.

32:28 The verse does not refer to Meshech-Tubal, but to Egypt ("you too"), to whom the whole ode is addressed, although we have not met direct address since the rhetorical question in 32:19a. To make this clear, I have inserted "Pharaoh" in the translation. Thus we meet a preliminary inclusio with 32:19, a sort of summary judgment on Egypt, although Ezekiel has two brief additions in 32:29–30 to his dishonor roll before he finally concludes.

32:29 One need not inquire why Edom is included in Ezekiel's roll call of the dishonorable, because it had been one of Israel's bêtes noires throughout its history, both before and after Ezekiel's day. Nothing is said of their "terror" (חִתִּית, which will be attributed again to the Sidonians in 32:30), but only their "strength," which, however, was of no avail in helping these unbelievers avoid consignment to hell. And the fact that they, though circumcised (so apparently Jer 9:24–25 [ET 9:25–26] and Josephus[37] later), had to lie with the uncircumcised in death heightens their ignominy.

A problem of tense arises with this verse. The perfect verb נִתְּנוּ ("are put") would normally imply the past, and I have construed יִשְׁכָּבוּ ("they lie") as a present, though it could imply the future. In a catalogue of those who had already been sent to Sheol, it would be strange if Edom were an exception in this context. The problem arises in the fact that chapter 35 will be totally devoted to a prophecy of Edom's *future* destruction. However, since the punishment of the unbelievers from that country being sent to hell was both something that happened (repeatedly) in the past and would recur (again, repeatedly) in the future, we probably need not posit any conflict between the two passages. At the outside, one might think of an extended prophetic perfect here or at least prophesied proleptically, but there is no hint in the present text that we need resort to such an explanation.

32:30 The verse is difficult in some details, but exegetically includes the Phoenicians and even peoples living farther north (probably Arameans) in the infernal fellowship of Sheol.

32:31 Ezekiel concludes this oracle about Egypt (and effects an inclusio for the whole oracle) by a two-verse reminder that Egypt (named explicitly in 32:18 near the start of the oracle, but not specifically mentioned after that until the mention in 32:31–32 of Pharaoh) has been the real concern all along. When Pharaoh arrives in Sheol, his reaction might have been one of anger or at least deep disappointment when he discovers that he will have to spend eternity in the ignominious company of the uncircumcised and dishonorably buried. But he will "console himself" (that reflexive meaning is better for the Niphal of נָחַם than the passive "be consoled") when he realizes that his fate is

---

[36] Block, *Ezekiel*, 2:229, n. 87.

[37] Josephus, *Antiquities*, 13.257–58 (13.9.1).

the same as any number of other unbelieving aspirants to divinity, and that he could hardly expect to fare any better than they. "Console himself" implies no honorable or penitential motive, and no true comfort. The Hithpael of the same verb is used in Gen 27:42 for Esau's intent to "console himself" by killing Jacob, and the Niphal is used in Ezek 31:16, where the well-watered trees "consoled themselves" by the fact that the greatest tree of all, the cedar of Lebanon, had also been brought down into Sheol.

The echo of exodus language (see the textual note) hints at what the next verse will make more explicit. What Yahweh had accomplished with Egypt in the prophet Ezekiel's day was not quite as constitutive a redemptive event as his defeat of "Pharaoh and his whole army" (32:31) at the exodus, but it was in the same line of salvific activity by the triune God. It was a tributary to the original exodus as its type, the definitive antitype of which would come on Easter; see ἔξοδος, "exodus," in Lk 9:31 (cf. also in 2 Pet 1:15).

The use of the signatory formula, "says the Lord Yahweh," might suggest the conclusion of the topic, but another thought is important enough that it must yet be added.

32:32 This verse is a more explicitly theological counterpart to 32:31. As in earlier verses, there is a contrast between the behavior of Pharaoh and the nations during their life, and their sentence of damnation in Sheol. But the main emphasis is on Yahweh's orchestration of—ultimately—the whole course of world history. The initial first person verb ("I have set") signals Yahweh's mastery of the whole process and virtually demands the Qere *my* terror" (instead of the Kethib, "his terror/terror of him") to bring out the full impact.[38]

"I have set my terror in the land of the living" is an assertion that God himself exercises a "terror" that trumps and finally overwhelms all human terrors. I read the verse as an excellent statement of the indispensable Law (in the Pauline sense) element in the Law-Gospel paradox. The terror of God's accusations in his Law is necessary to drive the sinner to repentance; fear of God's judgment is a prerequisite to receiving in faith the consolation of the Gospel, that Christ on our behalf has won for us full pardon, received through faith in him. God finally must overcome death by entering into death himself in the person of his Son, Jesus Christ—and triumphing over it through his resurrection from the dead. Each believer overcomes the fear of death, and all the subsidiary terrors of this fallen world, only by being baptized into Christ's death and resurrection (Rom 6:1–4; Col 2:11–13; 1 Pet 3:21).

Zimmerli correctly offers the possibility that in this verse "God in his judgment bestows saving terror on those who see it, in the hope that they awake to

---

[38] It would be grammatically possible for the initial כִּי to be causal, explaining the rest of the sentence, but at best that is an otiose thought, already, in effect, having been enunciated many times. A greater problem is that if the text were construed to mean that God had *caused* the pharaoh's terrifying behavior, that comes close to an unacceptable assertion of God as the author of evil. That implication is scarcely lessened if כִּי is translated concessively "although."

a proper fear of him and return to him."[39] Or from a slightly different perspective, Boadt concludes his exegetical discussion of the oracles against Egypt with the almost proverbial *sic transit gloria mundi*[40] ("so passes away the glory of this world"), which would serve as an appropriate epitaph for all the kingdoms against which all the prophetic Gentile oracles are addressed.[41]

In this light, the signatory formula, "says the Lord Yahweh," occurring in both 32:31 and 32:32, far from indicating that 32:31 is a later addendum, sounds like τετέλεσται, "it is finished," coming from Jesus' lips in Jn 19:30 as he completed his vicarious atonement for the sins of the world, and thereby accomplished redemption for all. Of course, this does not mean universalism; those without faith in Christ shall, if they perish in their unbelief, be damned to hell for eternity, sharing the fate of Pharaoh and the other unbelievers consigned to Sheol. But Christ's death and resurrection have opened the everlasting kingdom of God to all, including Gentiles like those addressed in Ezekiel 25–32, and entrance is gained simply by faith in him.[42]

---

[39] Zimmerli, *Ezekiel*, 2:178.

[40] Boadt, *Ezekiel's Oracles against Egypt*, 168.

[41] See "Introduction to Ezekiel 25–32: Oracles against Other Nations."

[42] One may see the excursus "Sheol" in Lessing, *Jonah*, 249–55, who emphasizes that Christ's death and resurrection have procured deliverance from hell and salvation for all.

Ezekiel 33–39

Oracles of Israel's Eschatological Restoration

The Watchman,
and the Fall of Jerusalem

Translation

33 ¹The Word of Yahweh came to me: ²"Son of man, speak to your countrymen and say to them, 'When I bring a sword upon a land, and the people of the land take one man from their midst and appoint him as their watchman, ³and he sees the sword coming upon the land and blows the horn and warns the people, ⁴and anyone who hears the sound of the horn but does not take warning, and a sword comes and takes him away, then his blood will be on his own head. ⁵He heard the sound of the horn, but did not take warning, so his own blood is on him. If he had taken warning, he would have saved his life. ⁶But if the watchman sees the sword coming and does not blow the horn so that the people cannot take warning, and the sword comes and takes one of them away, he was taken away because of his own iniquity, but I will hold the watchman responsible for his blood.'

⁷"As for you, son of man, I have appointed you a watchman for the house of Israel. Whenever you hear a word from my mouth, you are to warn them from me. ⁸When I say to a wicked man, 'Wicked man, you shall surely die,' if you do not speak to warn the wicked man against his way, he, the wicked man, will die because of his iniquity, and I will hold you responsible for his blood. ⁹But if you do warn the wicked man to turn from his way, and he does not turn from his way, he will die because of his iniquity, but you will have saved your soul.

¹⁰"As for you, son of man, say to the house of Israel, 'This is what you are saying, "Certainly our rebellions and our transgressions weigh upon us, and because of them we are rotting away. How then can we live?"' ¹¹Say to them, 'As I live, says the Lord Yahweh, I find no pleasure in the death of the wicked man, but rather that the wicked man turn from his way and live. Turn back, turn back from your evil ways, for why should you die, O house of Israel?'

¹²"As for you, son of man, say to your countrymen, 'The righteousness of a righteous man will not save him on the day of his rebellion. As for the wickedness of a wicked man, he will not fall over it on the day of his turning away from his wickedness. Likewise a righteous man will not be able to live because of it on the day of his sinning. ¹³If I say to the righteous man, "He will surely live," but he then trusts in his own righteousness and does unrighteousness, all of his righteous acts will not be remembered, and he will die because of the unrighteousness he does. ¹⁴Or when I say to the wicked man, "You will surely die," and he turns from his sin and practices justice and righteousness— ¹⁵if the wicked man returns the collateral paid him for a loan, returns what he has stolen, walks in the laws of life, and so avoids doing unrighteousness—he will surely live; he will not die. ¹⁶All of the evil acts he committed will not be remembered against him. Since

he has practiced justice and righteousness, he will surely live. [17]Yet, your countrymen are saying, "The Lord's way is not fair," although it is their way that is not fair. [18]When a righteous man turns away from his righteousness and does unrighteousness, he will die because of such acts. [19]But when a wicked man turns away from his wickedness and practices justice and righteousness, he will live on account of such acts. [20]So, even if you say, "The Lord's way is not fair," I will judge each one of you according to his ways, O house of Israel.' "

[21]In the twelfth year of our captivity, in the tenth [month], on the fifth day of the month a certain survivor from Jerusalem came to me and said, "The city has fallen." [22]Now the hand of Yahweh had been upon me the evening before the survivor came, and he had opened my mouth, so that by the time he came to me in the morning, my mouth was opened, and I was no longer mute.

[23]The Word of Yahweh came to me: [24]"Son of man, the inhabitants of these ruins in the land of Israel are saying, 'Abraham was only one man, and he took possession of the land; we are many, and surely the land has been given to us as a possession.'

[25]"Therefore, say to them, 'Thus says the Lord Yahweh: You eat over the blood; you raise your eyes to your fecal deities; you shed blood; and still you will possess the land? [26]You stand by your sword; you commit abominations; each of you defiles his neighbor's wife; and still you will possess the land?'

[27]"This is what you must say to them, 'Thus says the Lord Yahweh: As I live, those who are in the ruins will fall by the sword, and anyone in the open country I have assigned for the wild animals to eat him, and those in strongholds and caves will die by the plague. [28]I will make the land an utter desolation; its arrogant strength will cease; and the mountains of Israel will be so desolate that no one will travel through them. [29]Then they will know that I am Yahweh when I make the land an utter desolation because of all the abominable things they have done.'

[30]"As for you, son of man, your countrymen who are talking with each other about you beside the walls and in the doorways of the houses, say to one another, each to a neighbor, 'Come now and hear what the Word is that is coming from Yahweh.'

[31]"My people come to you in droves and sit in front of you. They listen to your words but refuse to act on them, because they prefer to use their mouths for obscene talk, and their heart pursues their illicit profits. [32]Look, to them you are like a singer of erotic songs with a beautiful voice and an excellent instrumentalist, for they listen to your words but are not doing them. [33]But when it comes—and come it will—they will know that a prophet has been among them."

Textual Notes

33:2 אֶ֫רֶץ כִּי־אָבִיא—The style, with a noun (here the indirect object אֶ֫רֶץ) followed by כִּי and an imperfect verb (Hiphil of בּוֹא), is similar to the pattern found in legal casuistic law of a subject followed by כִּי and an imperfect verb, forming a protasis (e.g., Lev 1:2; 2:1; 5:1; 13:2; cf. Ezek 14:3, where the verb is perfect), although the pattern is not carried out consistently here as the following conditional clauses show. Several subordinate clauses describe the "case," and the apodosis does not come until 33:4b. Then this casuistic formulation will reappear in 33:6 (וְהַצֹּפֶה כִּי־יִרְאֶה; cf. 33:9).

מִקְצֵיהֶם—Literally, "from their edge/border," that is, from within their entire circumference (see BDB, s.v. קָצֶה, 3), this is rendered "from their midst." קָצֶה is used in the OT only in the singular, and the *yod* that appears with suffixes is the third root letter (the ה originally was י). Cf. GKC, § 93 ss. The preposition מִן is prefixed, but here the qoph (-קְ-) has lost the *daghesh* because of its *shewa* (GKC, § 20 m).

33:3 The conditional clauses continue in this verse, in semi-narrative fashion.

בָּאָה—The accent on the last syllable of בָּאָה indicates that it is the feminine singular participle (not perfect) of בּוֹא, and the feminine is used because חֶרֶב is a feminine noun. The same participle recurs in 33:6.

בַּשּׁוֹפָר—The שׁוֹפָר is technically a "ram's horn," not really a musical instrument because little variation in pitch is possible. Perhaps it is best known for its use in various liturgical contexts (continuing today in the synagogue), but as this passage shows, it had other uses, as for an alarm. It is so often used in war contexts that, as here, it often signals impending attack or doom. Hence, although "horn" is a bit too broad a translation for a culture that does not use ram's horns, there is no real substitute. The LXX translation is σάλπιγξ, which the NT uses in eschatological contexts (Rev 8:2, 6, 13; 9:14), including the return of Jesus Christ (Mt 24:31; 1 Cor 15:52; 1 Thess 4:16), in passages where it usually is translated "trumpet." The horizon here is not explicitly eschatological, but, typologically and homiletically, the connection easily could and should be made. The pastor, like a watchman, is called to preach God's Law to warn his people of impending judgment, especially in light of Christ's return, so that they may repent and believe his proclamation of the Gospel and so be saved by being reckoned "righteous" (Ezek 33:12–20) through faith in Christ.

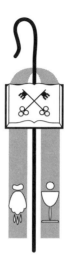

וְהִזְהִיר—In 3:17–21 too Yahweh described the prophetic role of Ezekiel the watchman as "to warn" using the Hiphil of זָהַר. Forms of the Hiphil recur in 33:7–9.

33:4 וְשָׁמַע הַשֹּׁמֵעַ—The comprehensiveness of the situation, as the prophetic warning goes out to everyone and anyone, is expressed by this, literally, "and a hearer hears." The generic article on the participle הַשֹּׁמֵעַ might even be rendered "*any* hearer."

נִזְהָר—The form could be the Niphal participle, but in this context it probably is the Niphal third masculine singular perfect of זָהַר, which could be translated as a simple passive, "was warned," but a tolerative nuance is more likely here: "he lets himself be warned, takes warning." The *qamets* under its final syllable (-הָר) is apparently pausal, although the *zaqeph qaton* is not a strong enough disjunctive accent always to accompany a pausal form. Perhaps the Masoretes intended the pausal vowel as a subtle way of accenting the thought. The identically accented pausal form here was used in 3:21 for the sinner who "takes warning" and so lives. The form recurs thrice in 33:5–6.

וַתָּבוֹא חֶרֶב וַתִּקָּחֵהוּ—After the perfects, the verse continues with imperfects with *waw* consecutive, reminding us that in Hebrew we do not deal with Western-type tenses.

דָּמוֹ בְרֹאשׁוֹ יִהְיֶה:—This is the apodosis of the conditional sentence that began in 33:2b. This idiom, "his blood will be on his head," occurs only here in Ezekiel. It is synonymous with דָּמוֹ בּוֹ יִהְיֶה, literally, "his blood will be on him," in 33:5, which is a variation of the formula in priestly texts (Lev 20:9, 11–13, 16, 27), and which Yahweh used in Ezek 18:13, which may have been determinative here. Both expressions mean that the man bears full responsibility for his own death.

33:5 וְהוּא נִזְהָר נַפְשׁוֹ מִלֵּט:—In form נִזְהָר could be a Niphal participle, but most likely this too is a pausal Niphal perfect (see the second textual note on 33:4) followed by another perfect (מִלֵּט, Piel) without a conjunction. Such perfects can be used to indicate an irreal, contrary-to-fact clause (Waltke-O'Connor, § 30.5.4a), as the context demands here: "If he had taken warning (which he did not), he would have saved his life." However, more often an irreal clause is introduced with a conditional particle such as לוּ (Judg 8:19; 13:23) or לוּלֵא (Gen 43:10).

33:6 וְהַצֹּפֶה כִּי־יִרְאֶה—The same casuistic legal construction (noun [here the subject], כִּי, imperfect verb) is used as in 33:2. Again the case is stated as hypothetical, requiring "if … ," but this may have already taken place at various times in the past and likely will in the future.

וְהוּא בַּעֲוֹנוֹ נִלְקָח—In this apodosis, the bare perfect נִלְקָח (Niphal of לָקַח) signals both certainty and suddenness. לָקַח can be used for "take away" in death (e.g., Gen 5:24), as does the Qal with חֶרֶב as subject in Ezek 33:4 (וַתִּקָּחֵהוּ) and earlier in 33:6 (וַתִּקַּח).

The preposition בְּ on בַּעֲוֹנוֹ is used in the sense that the man's death is "*because of* his (own) iniquity." See the textual notes on בַּעֲוֹנוֹ in 3:18 and on בְּחַטָּאתוֹ in 3:20. The preposition בְּ will be used in the same sense in, for example, 33:8, 9, 13.

וְדָמוֹ מִיַּד־הַצֹּפֶה אֶדְרֹשׁ:—This idiom, where God "seeks [דָּרַשׁ] blood [דָּם] from [מִן plus יָד]" someone, occurs only here in Ezekiel (cf. Gen 9:5), but it is synonymous with the idiom that instead uses בָּקַשׁ, "seek," in 3:18, 20; 33:8. See the fifth textual note on 3:18. It describes Yahweh as searching for or seeking out the person responsible for the shed blood of the guilty. Cooke suggests a slightly more literal translation of "exact an equivalent for."[1] In the background one hears echoes of the first murder (Gen 4:8–11).

33:7–9 These verses are nearly verbatim duplicates of 3:17–19; see the textual notes and commentary there. Block has a convenient table listing the two texts in parallel columns with the variations in italics.[2]

33:10 כֵּן אֲמַרְתֶּם לֵאמֹר—Yahweh's introduction to the people's popular saying is unusual. Usually a participle introduces what the people have been saying (e.g., 8:12; 11:3; 12:27; 13:6). The use of לֵאמֹר (KJV: "saying"), the infinitive construct with לְ, is a standard Hebrew idiom for introducing a quotation, of course, but Greenberg may have a point when he suggests that "the infinitive would seem to authenticate the quo-

---

[1] Cooke, *Ezekiel*, 364.

[2] Block, *Ezekiel*, 2:242.

tation; '(This is what you are saying) and I quote: …' " He compares 33:24; 35:12; as well as Gen 42:22; 2 Sam 3:18; and Jer 27:14.[3]

כִּי־כָשָׁעֵינוּ—Here כִּי may be an inert introduction to direct speech ("you say *that* …") and thus does not need to be translated.[4] RSV, NRSV, and NIV do not translate it. KJV and NKJV translate "if," which is theoretically a possible, though unusual, meaning of כִּי, but in my judgment, contrary to what the context demands. Block takes it in an emphatic sense, "certainly,"[5] and I have followed him, but little is lost if it is left untranslated.

אֲנַחְנוּ נְמַקִּים—The verb מָקַק is mostly used in the Niphal (here the masculine plural participle) for putrefying, gangrenous, or rotting flesh. The people's use of it here may derive from the realization that they are suffering from the covenant curse in Lev 26:39 that uses it: "those of you who remain will rot away because of their iniquity in the lands of your enemies."

33:11 The language of this important verse repeats that in 18:23, 32; see the textual notes there.

33:12 וְאַתָּה—This is now the second time (after 33:10) when Yahweh uses וְאַתָּה, "as for you," to introduce a command for Ezekiel to speak. Ezekiel is addressed with this expression also in 33:7, and twice in 33:9, where it is translated, "but you." It emphasizes the pivotal role he has been appointed to play as Yahweh's accredited messenger. Quite a bit of the vocabulary of the verse differs both from the immediate context and from chapter 18, with which it has no counterpart. However, the rest of this section, 33:10–20, bears many similarities to chapter 18.

בְּנֵי־עַמְּךָ—Ezekiel is commanded to address "the sons of your people" or "your countrymen," as in 33:2. Most interpreters assume that here this refers specifically to Ezekiel's fellow exiles, but these verses are phrased as general case laws applicable to all God's people.

וְרִשְׁעַת הָרָשָׁע לֹא־יִכָּשֶׁל בָּהּ—The verb יִכָּשֶׁל is the Niphal imperfect of כָּשַׁל. Both its Qal and its Niphal often mean "stumble" and take the preposition בְּ prefixed to the thing over which one stumbles (BDB, Qal, 1; Niphal, 1 b). Compare the noun מִכְשׁוֹל, "stumbling block," in, for example, 3:20 and 18:30, and in the NT, the corresponding noun σκάνδαλον in, for example, Mt 18:7; Rom 14:13; 16:17. For the verb here, Block suggests "trip up,"[6] but that implies too fleeting or temporary a circumstance for the context. I have rendered "fall." The feminine preposition on בָּהּ, "over it," refers back to the feminine noun רִשְׁעָה, "wickedness," in construct (וְרִשְׁעַת).

וְצַדִּיק לֹא יוּכַל לִחְיוֹת בָּהּ בְּיוֹם חַטֹּאתוֹ:—This clause basically repeats the first clause about the "righteous man."[7] In the preceding clause about the "wicked man," בָּהּ referred back to וְרִשְׁעַת, his "wickedness" (see the preceding textual note), so here

---

3   Greenberg, *Ezekiel*, 2:673.

4   Greenberg, *Ezekiel*, 2:673, appealing to BDB, 1 b, and citing 1 Sam 10:19 as a parallel.

5   Block, *Ezekiel*, 2:244 (ESV is similar).

6   Block, *Ezekiel*, 2:245, including n. 45.

7   Predictably, critics such as Zimmerli, *Ezekiel*, 2:181, therefore want to delete it.

בָּהּ, "by it," must refer back to צְדָקָה (in construct: צִדְקַת) near the start of the verse: the righteous man's "righteousness."

The construction with בְּיוֹם and the Qal infinitive construct with suffix, חֲטֹאתוֹ, might easily be rendered "when(ever) he sins," as it often is, but the more literal "on the day he sins" expresses a possible instantaneous and decisive change in a person's standing before God. Ezek 33:13–16 will present the change more in terms of a process.

33:13 The details of Ezekiel's first illustration by which Yahweh refutes the people's "sea of despondency" in 33:13–16 are largely a recycling of what had already been proclaimed in 18:21–22, 24, although with some significant differences; see the commentary.[8]

וְעָשָׂה עָוֶל—For the idiom "do [עָשָׂה] unrighteousness [עָוֶל]" in 33:13, 15, 18, see the third textual note on 3:20.

כָּל־צִדְקֹתָו—Here צְדָקָה is, as often elsewhere, used in a concrete sense: "righteous *acts*." The Kethib could be vocalized as the singular noun (with suffix) צִדְקָתוֹ or as a defective spelling of the plural, צִדְקֹתָו. The defective spelling may reflect an older form when the *matres lectionis* were not yet widely used. The Qere (צִדְקֹתָיו) is plural. The same Kethib-Qere variation was in 3:20 and 18:24. Here (as well as in those verses) the plural is preferable, especially since the plural verb presupposes it (see the next textual note).

לֹא תִזָּכַרְנָה—The Niphal imperfect (third feminine plural) of זָכַר, "be remembered," implies God as its agent. To "remember" (or, as here, "not remember," or elsewhere, שָׁכַח, "forget") is a common anthropomorphism for God's interaction with mankind. In the semi-legal idiom of forensic justification used here, where Yahweh is accountant, to "credit" (as in Gen 15:6) or "not credit; deduct, charge, debit" or the like would be appropriate. Nevertheless, retention of the literal "remember" reminds the reader that the idiom is not to be pressed in some impersonal, legalistic way. The idiom will be repeated in 33:16, but for the righteous man whose sins will not be remembered.

33:14 וְעָשָׂה מִשְׁפָּט וּצְדָקָה:—Here and again in 33:16, 19, Yahweh uses standard OT idiom for the sanctification or life of faith of the believer, the sinner who repents: literally, "he does justice and righteousness." See the textual note on 18:5, which has the same expression (also 18:19, 21, 27; 45:9). As touched on there, especially "justice" is fraught with possible misunderstandings as a legalistic or socio-political term, for both cultural and theological reasons, so "what is just" may be an improvement. While this language can be used for all God's people (e.g., Gen 18:19; Is 56:1; 58:2; Ps 106:3), it is especially applied to kings (e.g., 2 Sam 8:15; 1 Ki 10:9) and to God himself (Jer 9:24; Pss 99:4; 103:6) and his promised Messiah (Jer 23:5; 33:15; cf. Is 9:6 [ET 9:7]), whose righteousness is imputed to all believers (Romans 4).

33:15 חֲבֹל יָשִׁיב רָשָׁע גְּזֵלָה יְשַׁלֵּם—The sanctified, ethical behavior described here has been rendered a bit freely. The language is mostly the same as in 18:7, 12, 16; see

---

[8] See the parallel columns comparing chapters 18 and 33 in Block, *Ezekiel*, 2:249.

the textual notes on 18:7. The first example is the restoration of a "pledge" (חֲבֹל), but I doubt if "pledge" will readily communicate to a modern audience. As in chapter 18, I have used the common modern equivalent, "collateral." (NIV does not use that word, but of the modern translations consulted, it was the only one that even makes plain that a loan was involved.) The OT has fairly extensive regulations on the subject, and God's main concern always is that the necessities for life (cloak, oxen, etc.) not be taken as collateral. Otherwise it was perfectly legal for a creditor to require a "pledge," but to waive this right was considered commendable (Ezek 18:16), and refusal to return it when the loan was retired was, as this context (and 18:7, 12) shows, simply thievery. Hence, not surprisingly, the next clause simply generalizes on the example, "returns what he has stolen [גְּזֵלָה]."

In the NT (2 Cor 1:22; 5:5; Eph 1:13–14), the Holy Spirit is described as the ἀρραβών, "down payment, pledge, collateral," who assures Christians that they will receive their full inheritance after Christ returns and they are raised from the dead to life everlasting.

בְּחֻקּוֹת הַחַיִּים הָלַךְ—That he walks in "the laws of life" uses a unique phrase that requires careful theological explication. It apparently arises here because of the proximity in 18:9, 17 of "walk in my statutes" to the verdict "he will surely live" (see also 18:19, 21). Compare also 20:11, 13, 21: "my statutes ... (and) my ordinances ... by which man will live if he observes them." Obviously, such language is capable of being misunderstood as the crassest works-righteousness, and, to those who misunderstand the OT as a whole, as a summary of its theology. The subject here is sanctification, evidences in the believer's behavior of the new life God has given him by grace alone and through faith alone, but the *opinio legis* (the Law-based thinking of fallen humans) always tugs in the opposite direction.

לְבִלְתִּי עֲשׂוֹת עָוֶל—This phrase with the negated infinitive עֲשׂוֹת, literally, "so as to not do unrighteousness," supports the correct construal of "the laws of life" if it is understood as an infinitive of result or even of purpose. It too does not refer to righteousness by works (here, the avoidance of evil actions).

33:16 This verse is the obverse of 33:13.

לֹא תִזָּכַרְנָה לּוֹ—The anthropomorphic Niphal of זָכַר is used again for things (here: sins) "not remembered" by Yahweh. Here it is followed by לוֹ, which functions as a dative of disadvantage, "not remembered *against him*," that is, "will not be held against him."

33:17 Like the previous verses that had parallels in chapter 18, here 33:17–20 differs only trivially from 18:25–30.[9]

לֹא יִתָּכֵן—The precise force of this negated Niphal of תָכַן (used twice in 33:17) is hard to pinpoint, and interpretations differ. See also the textual note on 18:25, where it occurred (also in 18:29). The Qal means "examine, measure." The Niphal, then, should mean something like "be examined" and then "be in order, tested, approved," and the negative לֹא implies failure to pass the test or gain approval. The idea could

---

[9] Again, see the parallel columns in Block, *Ezekiel*, 2:251.

be simply the inscrutability of Yahweh's behavior, and the Niphal could be tolerative: God does not allow himself to be examined or evaluated by his sinful creatures, since the principles by which God acts are past our finding out. Hence some meaning like "erratic, arbitrary" might be the import. If pressed a bit more, "unprincipled," that is, amoral, might be the bitter charge. Or the cavil may be simply that Yahweh is not following his own self-revelation, the "way" he should act based on his own Word.

In the context, the more likely reference would seem to be the cases or rules by which God deals with the righteous man and the wicked man, as spelled out in this chapter (also chapter 18). Everything depends on whether, as St. Paul would put it, the people had faith in God's stated principles of judging, and there is nothing unpredictable or unfair about that. In chapter 18, the issue was whether the Israelites were suffering for ancestral sins or for their own sins. But that is not at issue here, so the people's charge here must involve some sort of challenge to the stated (and shortly to be reiterated) principle that God will judge people according to their present status before him, not any former status or way of life.

Greenberg may correctly intuit that their difficulty in understanding how they can avoid "rotting away" (33:10) in their sins "hints at reluctance to change their ways. God throws it back in their face, declaring that their way—knowing the way to life (= repentance) and not following it—is incomprehensible."[10]

33:18 וְעָשָׂה עָוֶל וּמֵת בָּהֶם—Here a plural prepositional phrase has a singular antecedent. The righteous man who apostatizes does "unrighteousness" (עָוֶל, singular) and then dies "because of *them*" (בָּהֶם). The assumption is that the "unrighteousness" will produce unrighteous actions, and so בָּהֶם is translated "because of such acts." Similarly in 33:19, the prepositional phrase עֲלֵיהֶם is rendered "on account of such acts." The idea is phenomenally similar to our insistence on the ultimate unity of justification and sanctification, in spite of the urgency of a careful theoretical distinction. That is, a justified person does righteous acts, and an unrighteous person does wicked acts. Jesus expresses this in terms of the kind of tree and its fruit (Mt 7:17–19; 12:33).

33:20 The people are addressed both individually (אִישׁ כִּדְרָכָיו) and collectively (אֶתְכֶם) in a way that English cannot match. The "house of Israel," like the NT equivalent, the church, the body of Christ, is both a corporate whole and an aggregate of many individuals.

33:21 בְּעַשְׁתֵּי—Following the pattern of most of Ezekiel's date notices, there is no word for "month" (חֹדֶשׁ) after the ordinal "tenth," but it is implied and is supplied in the versions. The postexilic book of Zechariah (8:19) mentions a fast during the tenth month, which may have commemorated this tragic occasion recorded in Ezekiel as well as the beginning of Nebuchadnezzar's siege of Jerusalem (24:1), which led to the sad result reported here. (See figure 1.)

לְגָלוּתֵנוּ—The same noun, גָּלוּת, "captivity, exile" was used in 1:2, which establishes the dating scheme Ezekiel uses throughout most of the book. The identical form here recurs in 40:1. In the translation of this verse, "of our captivity" is moved right

---

[10] Greenberg, *Ezekiel*, 2:674.

after "year" for clarity (see the next textual note), instead of following the Hebrew word order ("... on the fifth of the month of our captivity").

הַפָּלִיט— The noun פָּלִיט is traditionally translated "fugitive," usually implying clandestine, voluntary flight. But its usage elsewhere in the book of Ezekiel alone demonstrates that it refers to a "survivor" of the divine judgment, who may have escaped death, but still is subject to deportation. Compare, for example, 6:8–9, where פְּלִיטִים are among those who have been "scattered" or "carried captive" in some movement of groups. The use of the definite article with פָּלִיט here, as in 24:26, seems to be a sort of article of specification, indicating that God had appointed this one "survivor" for this specific purpose. Perhaps one may even see a back-reference here to 24:26; that is, the "survivor" who arrives now is the one God predicted in 24:26.

The major issue in the chronological notice has to do with the MT's specification of the occasion as occurring in the *twelfth* year. There is some minor versional evidence for reading "the eleventh year," and some modern commentators endorse that as the original reading.[11] An alleged problem arises from the notice in 24:1, which seems to date the beginning of Jerusalem's siege about three years earlier. If the siege of Jerusalem lasted eighteen months as some scholars maintain, the remaining eighteen months seem to be an incredibly long interval for the "survivor" to travel to Ezekiel and the other exiles in Babylon. If, however, the siege of Jerusalem lasted two and a half years, as the chronology followed in this commentary maintains, the alleged problem disappears. (See the discussion of the length of the siege and the date of the city's fall in figure 1, "The Dates in Ezekiel," in the textual notes on chapter 24.)

As noted in the textual note on 24:1, the solution appears to lie in different points of reference. In 24:1, Ezekiel uses the same date recorded also in 2 Ki 25:1 and Jer 52:4, which is figured from the regnal years of Zedekiah. Thus in 24:1, Ezekiel is departing from his own idiosyncratic system of dating events from the beginning of his deportation, as indicated by his reference to גָּלוּתֵנוּ, "our captivity" (33:21), which will appear again in 40:1 and did already without a suffix in 1:2. "The ninth year" (24:1) of Zedekiah's reign was actually the tenth year of Ezekiel's exile.

By that dating, it took the פָּלִיט slightly less than six months to reach Babylon with the news (on about January 8, 585, after the fall of the city on about July 14, 586). That figure compares favorably with the notice in Ezra 7:9 (cf. Ezra 8:31) that it took Ezra's company four months to return. That return came over a century after Ezekiel's time, when conditions were much more stable and secure. We can only speculate about the prior circumstances of the פָּלִיט, but if he was not deported until after the torching of the city, which happened about a month after it was breached (2 Ki 25:8–11 || Jer 52:12–15; cf. Jer 52:28–30), and this survivor may even have been taken elsewhere in Babylon before he could reach Ezekiel and the earlier exiles in Tel Abib (Ezek 3:15), his speed may even be reckoned remarkable.

הֻכְּתָה הָעִיר:—The meaning of the Hophal (third feminine singular perfect) of נָכָה is the passive of its Hiphil, "strike, smite," which commonly describes warfare. I have retained the traditional translation "fallen" in reference to the city. As usual in Hebrew, the verb precedes its subject (Waltke-O'Connor, § 8.3b).

---

[11] E.g., Zimmerli, *Ezekiel*, 2:191; Eichrodt, *Ezekiel*, 457–58.

33:22 עַד־בּוֹא אֵלַי בַּבֹּקֶר—The preposition עַד is used idiomatically in the sense of "before, by the time." In the preceding clause, the same infinitive construct had a subject (בּוֹא הַפָּלִיט), and so that same "survivor" must be this infinitive's subject, who came to Ezekiel "in the morning."[12]

33:24 יֹשְׁבֵי הֶחֳרָבוֹת הָאֵלֶּה—Most take the demonstrative pronoun אֵלֶּה as modifying הֶחֳרָבוֹת ("these ruins"), but there is something to be said for Greenberg's suggestion that it modifies the entire construct phrase ("these inhabitants of ruins are saying").[13] So construed, the demonstrative would express contempt for the claim made by those inhabitants and would accord well with the following response of the prophet.

"Ruins" is probably as good a translation as any for the plural of חָרְבָּה, but it may be heard too narrowly. "Wasteland," on the other hand, is too broad. Jer 40:7–12 gives us a mixed picture of the aftermath of the Babylonian invasion. Some of those left behind apparently straggled back to whatever ravaged cities or villages they could seize, while others tried to eke out a living scattered around the countryside. No new settlers were brought in to replace those deported, as the Assyrians had early done in the Northern Kingdom after the fall of Samaria, so there were no competing claimants.

וַיִּירַשׁ ... לְמוֹרָשָׁה:—The Qal of יָרַשׁ was used in the patriarchal promises that Abraham and his descendants would "inherit, possess" the land (e.g., Gen 15:7; 28:4) and again when the Israelites "took possession" of the land under Joshua (e.g., Josh 1:11, 15). It is the root of the noun מוֹרָשָׁה, a "possession," whose seven of nine occurrences are in Ezekiel and which usually refers to the land (Ex 6:8; Deut 33:4; Ezek 11:15; 33:24; 36:2, 5). The verb יָרַשׁ will be repeated in Yahweh's incredulous question repeated at the end of 33:25 and 32:26.

33:25 עַל־הַדָּם ׀ תֹּאכֵלוּ—"You eat on/over the blood" undoubtedly refers to the practice prohibited by Lev 19:26. That practice might be the offense of eating meat with blood still in it. Almost all commentators and translators assume that is the case and so take the preposition עַל in the sense of eating "accompanied by/in addition to" blood. See, for example, already KJV's "with" and Cooke.[14] But in my judgment, the offense involved more than the simple charge that they were failing to "keep kosher," that is, to drain the blood properly from the meat before eating it. See further the commentary.

וְעֵינֵכֶם תִּשְׂאוּ אֶל־גִּלּוּלֵיכֶם—The verb נָשָׂא (Qal imperfect), "lift up," with the object "eyes," can mean "look to for help," either to God (e.g., Ps 121:1) or to idols, as here and in Ezek 18:12. וְעֵינֵכֶם is simply defective spelling for the dual of עַיִן with second masculine plural suffix. For גִּלּוּלִים as "fecal deities," see the textual note on it in 6:4.

וְהָאָרֶץ תִּירָשׁוּ:—Hebrew questions need not be introduced by an interrogative, and the context is sufficient to indicate that this clause, introduced only with conjunctive *waw*, is a rhetorical question. It will be repeated at the end of 33:26.

---

[12] Zimmerli, *Ezekiel*, 2:191, argues that בּוֹא may be the result of metathesis from an original בֹּאוֹ, "his coming."

[13] Greenberg, *Ezekiel*, 2:684.

[14] Cooke, *Ezekiel*, 371.

33:26 עֲמַדְתֶּם עַל־חַרְבְּכֶם—The idiom "you stand on your sword" occurs only here. Clearly, however, the clause seems to mean something like to "live by" or "resort to the sword" (BDB, s.v. עָמַד, Qal, 7 c). Compare Mt 26:52. It describes a sort of law of the jungle where might makes right. The anarchic conditions that prevailed in Judah after the fall of Jerusalem are evidenced in the assassination of Gedaliah (Jeremiah 41) and the need for still another deportation by Nebuchadnezzar in 582/581 (Jer 52:30). Thus in essence, the charge here is the same as "you shed blood" in Ezek 33:25.

עֲשִׂיתֶן תּוֹעֵבָה—What appears to be the Qal second *feminine* plural perfect form of עָשָׂה is most likely an example of dissimilation, because a final *nun* would be easier to pronounce than a *mem* before the following *taw* (see GKC, § 44 k). Joüon, § 42 f, notes that this form is occasionally used as a masculine in Mishnaic Hebrew.

וְאִישׁ אֶת־אֵשֶׁת רֵעֵהוּ טִמֵּאתֶם—This clause clearly echoes 22:11, describing an utterly dissolute culture where wife-swapping (or "swinging," as current slang has it) was the norm.

33:27 בֶּחֳרָבוֹת בַּחֶרֶב—The assonance is too obvious to miss. It is not so self-evident, but the same literary feature probably appears again in the last of the triad of clauses: בַּמְּצָדוֹת וּבַמְּעָרוֹת.

לַחַיָּה נְתַתִּיו לְאָכְלוֹ—The Qal infinitive of אָכַל with object suffix, "to eat him," seems redundant, since the same suffix was on the preceding verb, נְתַתִּיו (Qal first common singular perfect of נָתַן with suffix). Many critics want to emend to the noun with preposition, לְאָכְלָה, "for food." However, it is probably of a piece with the singularity of the entire middle clause. God is here the explicit subject, and the victim is described by that singular suffix as direct object. In the surrounding clauses, the victims appear in the plural as subjects. In addition, נְתַתִּיו is perfect, whereas the preceding and following clauses use imperfect verbs (יִפֹּלוּ ... יָמוּתוּ). The prophetic perfect here evidently "marks a strong resolution to be carried out in the future."[15] The structure of the verse is an excellent example of Ezekiel's penchant for combining variety and repetition.

33:28 שְׁמָמָה וּמְשַׁמָּה—These two nouns display assonance again (see the first textual note on 33:27). They probably are to be considered a hendiadys ("an utter desolation"), as in 6:14 (there translated "a desolate waste"). They recur together in 33:29 and 35:3.

וְנִשְׁבַּת גְּאוֹן עֻזָּהּ—This identical clause (plus בָּהּ) is in 30:18 (also similar are 7:24; 24:21; 30:6). The verb is the Niphal of שָׁבַת, "cease." The subject is the construct phrase גְּאוֹן עֻזָּהּ, literally, "the pride of its strength," translated "its arrogant strength."

הָרֵי יִשְׂרָאֵל—As we first noticed in 6:2, and as will be prominent in chapter 36, "the mountains of Israel" is one of Ezekiel's favorite and perhaps nostalgic descriptions of his native land in contrast to the flat Mesopotamian valley to which he had been exiled.

---

[15] Cooke, *Ezekiel*, 371.

33:30 The Hebrew sentence structure is somewhat complex and has been smoothed out to a degree in translation.

בְּנֵי עַמְּךָ הַנִּדְבָּרִים בְּךָ—The article on the Niphal participle of דָּבַר functions as a relative pronoun in apposition to בְּנֵי עַמְּךָ ("your countrymen *who* are talking with each other"). The Niphal of דָּבַר, which has a reciprocal meaning, "to talk together, to one another," is rare, occurring elsewhere only in Mal 3:13, 16, and Ps 119:23, where, as here, it takes בְּ in the sense of "against." The following two phrases, literally, "one to another" and "each to a neighbor" also describe such reciprocal interaction, so it is strongly emphasized. Functionally, the initial relative clause speaks of the entire community en masse, while the following two phrases individualize. The main verb for this relative clause is the following דִּבֶּר, but its singular form (unusual, since אִישׁ … אָחִיו usually takes a plural verb, as in 4:17; 24:23) indicates that grammatically it is the predicate to the two phrases (speaking of individuals) that follow it, leaving the initial relative clause syntactically pendent and isolated.

וְדִבֶּר־חַד אֶת־אַחַד אִישׁ אֶת־אָחִיו—The adjective חַד is the Aramaic (e.g., Dan 2:31; Ezra 4:8) cognate of אֶחָד, "one," which sometimes (as here) is vocalized אַחַד. Presumably the less common pointing, אַחַד, is used for the sake of assonance with חַד.[16]

33:31 The first half of the verse has only minimal difficulties, but, in the second half, commentaries and translations are "all over the map," and many critics delete that half verse as a series of annotations.[17]

The subject of (in effect) the entire verse is עַמִּי, "my people." It does not come, as one would expect, at the beginning, but is curiously delayed until after two verbal predicates (וְיָבוֹאוּ … וְיֵשְׁבוּ …). In the context, it is hard not to hear Yahweh's use of the word for his unfaithful people as sarcastic or, at least, expressing deepest disappointment. Possibly postponing the word was intended to be more striking.

כִּמְבוֹא־עָם—"In droves" represents a commonly suggested paraphrase of the literal Hebrew "like the coming of people," that is, as people normally do under circumstances like these. Zimmerli explains correctly: "So they summon one another, come running, as people have come running through the ages whenever something sensational is to be seen."[18]

וְשָׁמְעוּ אֶת־דְּבָרֶיךָ וְאוֹתָם לֹא יַעֲשׂוּ—That "they listen to your words but them they do not do" means they do not believe or obey the prophet's message from God. This will be repeated in almost identical wording in 31:32. The language of "doing" or "not doing" God's words is employed by Jesus regarding his own divine words in Mt 7:24, 26.

כִּי־עֲגָבִים בְּפִיהֶם הֵמָּה עֹשִׂים—The conjunction כִּי, "because," introduces two participial clauses, this one and the next one. These clauses explain the preceding clause (see the previous textual note). In this clause, the key word is עֲגָבִים, which will be repeated in the next verse. The LXX and Syriac have "lies" (usually expressed by

---

[16] Cooke, *Ezekiel*, 371.

[17] See Allen, *Ezekiel*, 2:150.

[18] Zimmerli, *Ezekiel*, 2:201.

כְּזָבִים), which some commentators follow, but that is too far removed from the MT to be anything but a translation of an entirely different underlying text. Probably the word here is the plural of עֲגָבָה, which referred to sexually promiscuous behavior and was rendered "lustfulness" in 23:11 (see the second textual note there). It is found in the OT only in these three verses (23:11; 33:31–32). It is derived from the verb עָגַב, "to lust, have inordinate sexual desire," which occurred frequently in 23:5–20, a passage about the wayward sisters that well illustrates what the term means. The masculine plural ending of the noun in 33:31–32 evidently bespeaks an emotional state or activity carried on in that state. Compare רַחֲמִים, "compassion" (e.g., Ps 25:6), and דּוֹדִים, for "making love" in the context of marriage in Ezek 16:8 and Song 1:2, 4. The contexts of עֲגָבָה in Ezek 23:11 and 33:31–32 militate against attenuating the sexual component into the more neutral "love" (cf. אַהֲבָה). Some translations have simple "love" here (KJV, NKJV, RSV) or apparent derivations of the concept, "flattery" (NRSV) or "devotion" (NIV). With פֶּה here (בְּפִיהֶם, literally, "in their mouth"), it must refer to some kind of speech. ESV has "lustful talk," and if my understanding is correct, something like "obscene talk" seems to be required.[19] It has even been suggested that, in ridicule, the audience uses Ezekiel's very words for bawdy talk or song, although this carries us beyond anything clearly suggested in the text. If it is at all correct, however, it anticipates the later scandal of the profane use of the Song of Solomon, an activity which the famous rabbi Akiba, who was defending the canonicity of the biblical book, said would forfeit for the scoffer a portion in the world to come.[20]

If that was how they amused themselves in lighter moments, the final clause specifies where their "hearts" or minds were really focused: the pursuit of the "bottom line," בֶּצַע, "profit, gain," again implying that obtained by illegal or fraudulent transactions.

33:32 כְּשִׁיר עֲגָבִים—The noun עֲגָבִים is repeated from 33:31. In construct with it is שִׁיר (with כְּ), which could be the noun "song," or perhaps the Qal infinitive construct of the verb שִׁיר, "to sing." In either case, obviously it refers to Ezekiel as the "singer," so that is how it is translated. Some emend to the Qal participle שָׁר, although we probably need not resort to surgery to achieve the necessary result. The easiest solution is simply to assume that it is a case where the abstract שִׁיר, "song," stands for the concrete שָׁר, idiomatically describing the actor as the action with which he is so closely identified. There are parallels to this usage. It is also possible that the consonants could be vocalized as the nominal formation שַׁיָּר, analogous to צַיָּד, "hunter" (the plural of which is used in Jer 16:16), although such a form is unattested with the root שִׁיר.

וּמֵטִב נַגֵּן—The Hiphil participle of יָטַב, "to do well," is used with the Piel infinitive construct of נָגַן, "to play an instrument," also in 1 Sam 16:17. Similar constructions with these two verbs are in Is 23:16 and Ps 33:3. נָגַן implies a stringed instrument, but we are not sure what kind. The lyre is most likely. Compare the mu-

---

[19] Greenberg, *Ezekiel*, 2:683, 686, has "erotic talk."

[20] See Mitchell, *The Song of Songs*, 434–35.

sical term נְגִינָה, "music" (?), the plural of which is often in psalm superscriptions, for example, MT Pss 4:1; 6:1.

Commentary

By any measure, a major transition in the book commences with this chapter. So far, the bulk of the book has accented God's judgment on Israel (chapters 1–24), and on the heathen nations, which too shall incur judgment (chapters 25–32). In contrast, the rest of the book (chapters 33–48) will usually speak of God's grace to a new Israel that will consist of regenerate believers endowed with the Spirit under a new David as their Shepherd, Prince, and King (e.g., 34:23–24; 36:25–27; 37:24–25; 39:29). It is unfortunate that selected portions of these chapters are often the only ones given much attention in the church, as though a full-orbed Gospel could really be proclaimed without in-depth attention to the Law, a posture entirely at odds with any sturdy Lutheranism.

Much of the material in 33:1–20 has been stated before. Ezek 33:1–9 is remarkably parallel to 3:16–21, slightly abbreviated but often repeated verbatim. Ezek 33:10–20 differs only minimally from 18:21–25.

Why are the watchman oracles repeated here? Theologically, we answer that question most fruitfully in terms of the dialectic of judgment and salvation, Law and Gospel, which extends through the entire Scriptures. I submit that we should not attempt to read these watchmen oracles apart from the epochal report in 33:21–22 that "the city has fallen." That message gives us the historical axis upon which that entire dialectic turns in the OT—just as Christ's death is the turning point in the Gospels and the axis of the NT. It marks a major turn, not only in the book, but in Ezekiel's entire ministry and Israel's history. The responsibility to be a watchman applies to the Gospel as much as it does to the Law. God's judgment against Israel had been the main burden of Ezekiel's ministry in chapters 1–24, and now the Gospel promise of restoration is to be the central theme of his proclamation in chapters 33–48. We recall our Lord's own words: "What I say to you, I say to all: 'Watch!' " (Mk 13:37).

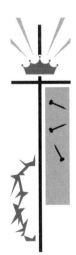

To read this chapter in its full depth, we must understand its full typological and Christological dimension. Just as Israel's new era began at its lowest ebb, so the Gospel proclaims Christ's death as the moment of his glorification, by which he accomplished salvation for all, with the promise of glorification for all in Christ (cf. Rom 8:17, 30). The Gospel of John brings this out most clearly (especially Jn 13:31–32; 17:1–26). There is no more powerful musical expression of that message than in Bach's *St. John Passion*, where the lugubrious aria "It is finished" is interrupted by the magnificent paean "The King of Judah triumphs now and ends the strife."

Naturally, all sorts of other explanations have been offered for the repetitions, and there is no point in trying to recount them all. A common approach is along redactical lines. A few critics defend the integrity of the oracles,[21] but

---

[21] E.g., Cooke, *Ezekiel*, 363–64.

most deny it.[22] Some reconstructions sought justification in Josephus' obscure statement that Ezckiel wrote two books.[23] Many appeal to the evolutionary assumption that the repetition attests to the increasing accent on individual accountability over corporate solidarity—surely a false alternative! Others think of Ezekiel's own later rearrangement and/or reapplication of the oracles he had given earlier. Even if that were demonstrable, it would bring us back to the present text.

The biblical text of 33:1–20, as it stands, clearly contains a historically separate oracle from those in 3:16–21 and 18:21–25, notwithstanding the near identity of content. A favorite understanding of many conservatives has been that 33:1–20 was intended as a sort of second call to the prophet's ministry, now that an entirely different phase of it is about to begin. (Cf. Jonah's second call in Jonah 3:1–2 and Peter's reinstatement to his apostolic office in John 21, although both Jonah and Peter needed a new call because they had forsaken their prior mission, and Ezekiel has not.) I personally have considerable sympathy for this understanding. However, the discontinuity between the two parts of the book (judgment oracles in chapters 1–32 and salvation oracles in chapters 33–48) is not absolute. God's people—and those called to minister to them—will always face some of the same old problems as long as the present, fallen world stands, as subsequent chapters of the book will show.

The allusions here are all retrospective, rather than prospective. Chapter 33 reads like an epilogue to the old ministry of doom. The material in chapter 3 was a private one intended to buoy the prophet himself at the beginning of a difficult ministry, while that in chapter 33 is public and addressed to all the exiles. The key to understanding the reuse of old material is probably best to be found in 33:10: the despairing lament of the people, "How then can we live?" Confirmation of Jerusalem's fall had not yet come, but they could easily have sensed that it was imminent and inevitable—and that Ezekiel's unwavering insistence on that fact was true after all. At the same time, the purpose of that message, to bring them to repentance, had not yet been accomplished. The only alternative seemed to be the conclusion that they had no future. So Ezekiel is commanded to reiterate in no uncertain terms what the real point of his preaching had been.

At the same time, he holds out the very real possibility of repentance and of a future under God. The people can be held responsible only for themselves and their own generation, to be sure, but the stain of the past is expungeable if that genuine repentance occurs; this is the purpose of reusing 18:4–32. The pivotal statement then comes in 33:11 (a restatement of 18:23): "I find no plea-

---

22 For example, Eichrodt (*Ezekiel*, 443–44) speculates that 3:20–21 was originally a part of chapter 33, but was accidentally omitted from this chapter when the verses were inserted at the beginning of the book. According to Zimmerli (*Ezekiel*, 2:183–84), 33:7–9 is the original wording and 3:17–21 a redactional amplification.

23 Josephus, *Antiquities*, 10.79 (10.5.1), says: "Ezekiel … left behind him in writing two books" (trans. Whiston, *The Works of Josephus*, 271).

sure in the death of the wicked man, but rather that the wicked man turn from his way and live." As Taylor writes: "This cardinal feature of Ezekiel's theology needs to be written underneath every oracle of judgment which his book contains."[24] That is to say, Ezekiel's evangelical and pastoral intent is evidenced not only in those unexpected messianic or eschatological snippets that we have been surprised to find appearing all along. Rather, it is a *cantus firmus*[25] pervading the entire book, although the times in which he lived did not invite frequent articulation of the theme until after Jerusalem's fall.

If this construal is correct, it implies that the traditional chapter division is not the most felicitous either. A much better transition-marker would have come after 33:20, with 33:21 beginning an entirely new chapter. The rest of chapter 33 plainly speaks to the *post*exilic situation, and, beginning with chapter 34, also to an eschatological Israel—the Christian church.

Regardless of where we place the major caesura, 33:1–20 is not easy to mortise into the classical prophetic outline,[26] which otherwise stands out so prominently in the book. The verses seem to be a detached portion of part 1 (chapters 1–24, judgment on Judah), or perhaps in this context, we should understand them as saying that the last measure of obduracy manifested by the exiled Judahites in these verses has, in effect, made them indistinguishable in God's eyes from Gentiles. However, God has in store a new era of redemptive history for both Israel and the Gentiles, and in Christ there will be no difference between them (Gal 3:28; Eph 2:11–22). Thus Yahweh can issue the same promise, "I will bring about the restoration," to Gentiles (Ezek 16:53; 29:14) as to Israel (39:25).

Chapter 33 is easily divisible into five sections, but they tend to coalesce into only two or three. The first two (33:1–9 and 33:10–20) go together: they proclaim the inexorability of the judgment if the Israelites do not heed the watchman's warning, but at the same time, also that the God who is their "enemy," ordaining doom, is also the redeeming God, who sends the prophets precisely so that his message of judgment will not be misread deterministically, but may be averted by repentance. After the announcement of the survivor's report in 33:21–22 are two confrontations with those who misunderstand the new situation: the remnant left in Jerusalem (33:23–29) and the exiles in Babylon, whom Ezekiel had been addressing all along (33:30–33).

The Watchman's Warning of Judgment (33:1–9)

33:2–5 One should not overlook that the entire hypothetical situation described in these verses is introduced by "when I bring" (כִּי־אָבִיא, 32:2). The

---

[24] Taylor, *Ezekiel*, 215.

[25] This Latin musical term for "constant melody" was popularized by Martin Franzmann as a term for the Gospel message that is constant throughout the Scriptures. One may see Mitchell, *The Song of Songs*, 16, especially footnote 9.

[26] See pages 10–12 in the introduction.

legal form is neutral, but the situation described is under Yahweh's control, and the conditions described, although seeming to be part of the natural, logical order of things, are really his. Disregard of the warnings of a prophetic/pastoral "watchman" will ultimately be just as fatal as in wartime. Ezek 33:5 simply recapitulates and summarizes the conclusion or apodosis of the previous verses.

33:6 A different scenario—that of a negligent, unfaithful watchman—is considered briefly here. Israel had ample experience with false and often venal prophets and prophetesses (see Ezekiel 13), but that is considered briefly because it is only marginally germane to the situation at hand.

The inclusion of the notice that the unwarned citizen nonetheless dies "because of" his own sin really belongs to application rather than to the hypothetical situation being considered. But part of Ezekiel's rhetorical strategy may be evident here, challenging the people to look beyond the obvious culpability of the watchmen to their responsibility for their own sins, even if they had not been warned "early and often" (to use a phrase from Jeremiah, e.g., 25:4; 26:5; 29:19). There is an unspoken assumption that everyone dies because of sin, and because everyone sins, every death is justified (Romans 3; 5:12–21).

33:7–9 These three verses are verbally almost identical with 3:17–19, and virtually indistinguishable in content as well. All that differs is the application (and possibly the outer circumstances, but on that we are uninformed). In chapter 3, the verses were part of Ezekiel's call or commissioning and were intended to impress upon him the (literally) life or death gravity of the vocation he was entering. There the message came in private, but here it is public and is intended to clarify to the people what he had been about all these years. As the final verses of the chapter (33:30–33) make clear, most had not understood or accepted his message.

Furthermore, in essence, these verses really add nothing to what 33:1–6 has already asserted.[27] The previous verses have stated the principles of Yahweh's administration abstractly and in legal language. Now everything is personalized: Yahweh is doing the appointing of a watchman, and Ezekiel is the one whom Yahweh has appointed. And now is the time when pleas of guilty or not guilty must be made, and the appropriate sentence imposed.

God's Pleasure Is for the Sinner to Repent and Live (33:10–20)

33:10 The absence of the word-event formula (as in 33:1) or any other introductory formula suggests that the two following exchanges between prophet and the people (33:10–16 and 33:17–20) were delivered at the same time as the preceding oracle (33:1–9). In any case, the text clearly intends for us to take 33:1–9 and 33:10–20 together.

For the first time in the entire book, the people admit that their guilt is the cause of their suffering, depicting themselves in terms of Yahweh's predictions

---

[27] Hence, many critics regard 33:1–6 as a sort of derivative or spin-off of 33:7–9, though such compositional questions can hardly be anything but speculative.

(4:17; 24:23). But "this is an empty cry for songs in the night; there is still no desire for the One who gives the songs."[28] Their question is obviously rhetorical, assuming the negative answer that survival is impossible. In Lutheran terms, it represents a classical instance when the Law has done its work (*lex semper accusat*),[29] but a Gospel-less vacuum still exists, which Yahweh will then fill in chapters 34–48.

33:11   Yahweh cannot but agree with the people's diagnosis of the reason for their plight, but must contest the despair that they are inferring from it. And first of all, they must (re)learn Yahweh's nature and his ultimate intent for them. He begins his rejoinder in the strongest possible way, by an oath based on his own life to counter their despair of life. And the Christian will not neglect to add that the God of Israel ultimately did back up that oath by sacrificing his own Son on the cross for the life of world. It is even proper to affirm that in the death of God the Son, *Gott selbst ist tot*,[30] "God himself is dead," as the hymn has it—yet of course he also rose from the dead on the third day. To emphasize that the true God is the God of life, he repeats almost verbatim again an earlier asseveration of the point (18:23; cf. 18:30b–32). In chapter 18, it had been couched as a rhetorical question, but here it is turned into an emphatic disavowal of the assumption underlying the people's despair. Yahweh parries their question with one of his own—another rhetorical one, implying the needlessness of anyone's death if he will only שׁוּב, "repent, turn, return."

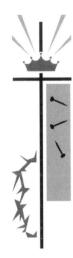

Ezekiel functions here as no mere therapist pointing the people to their own inner resources, but as a κῆρυξ ("herald")[31] of the Gospel, as he proceeds to apply Law and Gospel, expounding them in terms he has already laid down. Zimmerli does not overstate the Good News: "The complete irrationality of the divine activity is discernible in this announcement: Yahweh, the enemy of his people, who draws the sword against them to annihilate them because of their disobedience—Yahweh at the same time, however, the God who sets up a watchman for his people, who will warn them of the sword in which he himself comes, and thus tries to make that sword ineffectual."[32] Dire as the situation may look, there still is time between the present and an irreversible death sentence—if they will only "turn." God himself is the only one who can avert

---

[28]   Block, *Ezekiel*, 2:246, alluding to Job 35:9–13.

[29]   "The Law always accuses" summarizes that the purpose of God's Law is to bring the sinner to realize the full extent of his own sinfulness and that he deserves nothing but judgment and damnation. Only after this conviction by the Law is the sinner properly prepared to hear the Good News that Christ has died for his every sin to procure full pardon. Believing this, the sinner is then justified by grace alone. See AC IV; Ap IV; SA III II 4–5; III III 1–8; FC Ep and SD V.

[30]   This line is in the original German of the seventeenth-century hymn *O Traurigkeit*, "O Darkest Woe." Most English translations soften the language, for example, "God's Son is slain" (*LW* 122:2) or "God's Son is dead" (*TLH* 167:2). But *LSB* 448:2 has "Our God is dead."

[31]   St. Paul uses this term for himself in 1 Tim 2:7 and 2 Tim 1:11, and St. Peter applies it to Noah in 2 Pet 2:5.

[32]   Zimmerli, *Ezekiel*, 2:185.

death and provide everlasting life; this he has done in the death and resurrection of his Son (Psalms 16 and 22).

33:12 This verse has no precedent, as such, in chapter 18, but merely delineates the thesis and then follows the pattern established in chapter 18 in offering several illustrations. Block succinctly summarizes that thesis: "One's end is not determined by how one begins a race, but how one ends it."[33] Yet the one who ends life as a "righteous man" is so through repentance and faith that bears fruit—not through any human efforts to attain righteousness by works.

33:13–16 In the reworking of 18:21–22, 24 that largely underlies these verses, two things in particular strike us. First of all, the emphasis on divine address, absent in chapter 18, is prominent here. The two possibilities of life and death (repentance or apostasy) each begin with בְּאָמְרִי: "*If I say* to the righteous man, 'He will surely live' " (33:13) and "*When I say* to the wicked man, 'You will surely die' " (33:14).

Second, the possibility of repentance and life is highlighted more than that of apostasy and death, in answer to the people's sense of hopelessness. This is evinced by the reversal in the sequence of the cases. Ezekiel here begins with the apostatized righteous (33:13) and ends with the repentant wicked (33:14–16), the opposite of the order in 18:21–24. The same slant is evident in the detail devoted to the repentant life (33:15) in contrast to the brevity of consideration of apostasy. A didactic element thus accompanies the consolatory: the new life will involve confessing one's own sins, then turning from them and living by a faith that manifests itself in obedience to specific divine ordinances, which will bring in its wake not only a happier and more just society, but all the blessings summarized under the word "life." Doubtless, this is not yet as full a picture of the abundant life (e.g., Jn 10:10) as has now been given Christians in the NT (and there is still much not yet revealed to us [1 Jn 3:2]), but the principle and the parameters are the same.

33:17–20 The precise thrust of this second expression of the people's anomie depends on the precise meaning of the verb תָכַן, "be fair" (33:17, 20; see the textual note on it in 33:17). Our difficulty in settling on one, definitive translation may be part of the point of the entire section (33:17–20). To the people's apparent complaint that Yahweh is acting in irrational, inscrutable, or unpredictable ways, Yahweh responds that their refusal to simply accept his offer of "amazing grace" even in this very last hour is irrational and incredible. Hence there is nothing to do but repeat once again briefly the ultimately simple and clear principle by which he, the heavenly Judge, renders his verdicts.

The unbeliever is damned because of his unrighteous acts. However, a wicked man who repents and believes is justified forensically through faith, which is active in works of love (Gal 5:6), and none of his sins is remembered on Judgment Day. This same basis for God's judgment is depicted in NT pas-

---

[33] Block, *Ezekiel*, 2:248.

sages such as Mt 25:31–46, where unbelievers are condemned because of their failure to do good works for Christ, whereas believers inherit eternal life because of the merits of Christ, whose grace empowered their good works for him and his brethren (Mt 25:35–40). Similarly, in Rev 20:11–15, the unbelievers are judged according to the records of their deeds, whereas believers are saved simply because their names are written in "the Lamb's book of life" (Rev 21:27).[34]

The pericope ends abruptly without any concluding formula or hint of the people's reaction. Or in the final vocative "O house of Israel," do we, by the use of the covenant name "Israel," hear one final plaintive, poignant plea that they recall "the rock from which [they] were hewn" (Is 51:1; cf. Gal 6:16)?

The Survivor Arrives from Fallen Jerusalem (33:21–22)

33:21 One is surprised to encounter this rare autographical notice which, with the following verse, interrupts prophetic oracles. Brief though it is, its pivotality in the book, yes, in the entire OT, can hardly be overstated. It took only two Hebrew words for the survivor to confirm what the prophets had long foreseen: הֻכְּתָה הָעִיר, "the city has been smitten/has fallen." But these words represent a virtual continental divide in many respects. (I have already observed that it would have been more meaningful to the reader if a chapter division had come immediately before 33:21.) It is only slightly hyperbolic to compare this divide to the B.C.–A.D. division of the two Testaments/covenants. In 36:25–37:28 Ezekiel will use language synonymous with the "new covenant" prophecy of Jer 31:31–34. The fall of Jerusalem now vindicates the doom prophecies of Ezekiel together with Yahweh, who had shown himself to be the true Lord,[35] and yet at the same time, the "survivor" from Jerusalem and the existence of the remnant in Babylon show Yahweh also to be the Savior, whose prophecies of salvation will be fulfilled. The parousia had not yet arrived (as some of the remaining oracles will show), and we too still await the parousia, but other oracles of Ezekiel will have the ring of the opening words of our Lord's ministry (Mt 4:17): ἤγγικεν … ἡ βασιλεία τῶν οὐρανῶν, "the kingdom of heaven is at hand."[36]

33:22 Ezekiel records his authentication as a true prophet in the fulfillment of the prophecy to which his entire ministry had been devoted in terms

---

[34] See Brighton, *Revelation*, 583–84.

[35] This is an emphasis in the repeated recognition formula, "(then) you/they will know that I am Yahweh." For this formula, see page 9 in the introduction and the commentary on 6:7.

[36] Gibbs, *Matthew 1:1–11:1*, 215, comments about the verb:

> ἤγγικεν captures well this 'both present and future' of the reign of heaven. The reign of heaven has not yet fully arrived, with all of its power and salvation. At the same time, however, Jesus, the Son of God, is already here, and he is bringing a salvation that will avail *on the Last Day.*

> The same can be said already for the ministry of Ezekiel, especially from this point onward. Even though Christ's first advent lay half a millennium in the future, God was already bestowing everlasting salvation on repentant believers through the prophet's ministry.

of the "hand" of Yahweh being upon him again. We met this expression before, for example, in 1:3 (Ezekiel's inaugural vision, which see) and especially in 3:22–27 at his commissioning, when Yahweh had first rendered him mute. The theological axiom is never defined, nor is it here, although it seems to imply God's overwhelming power (hence the divine "hand" is used with the verb נָפַל, "fall," in 8:1), and it is generally connected with great visionary experiences. The experience here had started the evening before the survivor's arrival, although no emphasis is placed upon the crepuscular occasion as such, only that it was all complete by the time of the survivor's arrival. By the time the survivor arrived, Ezekiel's muteness had been lifted. The "he" referring to the one who opened Ezekiel's mouth must have Yahweh as its antecedent, because if the "hand" itself had been the agent, a feminine form would have been required. The language of the verse is a bit prolix, but the intent seems to be to emphasize two main themes: (1) that Yahweh had carefully orchestrated the scene so that the date when the prophet would regain his ability to speak (without restraint?) would coincide with the date of the arrival of the survivor to deliver his message (a day was reckoned as beginning at evening) and (2) that the prophecy of 24:25–27 had be fulfilled precisely.

Unfortunately, we are not enlightened by the report of the opening of Ezekiel's mouth as to precisely what this meant empirically and/or functionally any more than we were in 3:25–27 (which see) when his tongue began to cling to the roof of his mouth. Certainly we cannot in the words that follow detect any more verbal spontaneity or other great difference in Ezekiel's manner of conversation than in the preceding oracles throughout most of the book. All that we have been given to understand fully is that everything Ezekiel spoke that was recorded in his book was "the Word of Yahweh" (e.g., 33:1, 23).

The Apostate Remnant in Jerusalem Will Die (33:23–29)

33:23–30 The single word-event formula in 33:23, "the Word of Yahweh came to me,"[37] heads the rest of the chapter, although it obviously consists of two very distinct oracles, 33:23–29 and 33:30–33. The two are, however, internally distinguished, since each one starts with Yahweh addressing Ezekiel with the familiar "son of man"[38] (33:24, 30). That address comes each time when the prophet is commanded to respond to popular talk among the Israelites—talk that is quoted to him by Yahweh. However, the talk is by two different audiences. That in 33:24 is by the Israelites left in ruined Jerusalem, while that in 33:30 is by Ezekiel's fellow exiles.

33:24 The first of the two oracles, delivered by the prophet after Jerusalem's fall, concerns poor peasants left behind in Judah after the deportation of more wealthy and powerful elements in the society. Their claim to title to the land is conveyed to the prophet in Babylon by Yahweh himself. It is

---

[37] For this formula, see page 8 in the introduction and the textual note on 3:16.

[38] For this address, see the second textual note and the commentary on 2:1.

based on the repeated promises made to Abraham, even while still childless, that both land and countless progeny were to be his (Gen 12:2–3; 13:15–16; 15:5–7, 18; 17:7–8). The people's argument is an *a fortiori* one: if one man was enough to establish title to a land, how much more will the "many" (which they call themselves, and relatively speaking, probably they were) qualify for a title guarantee.

It is not clear against whom (if anyone in particular) the Judahites were making their claim. We have heard a similar claim before. In 11:14–15 Ezekiel had confronted the claim of those still in Judah that the first deportees, now outside the land of Israel, had been rejected by Yahweh. But here there is no hint of any claim against the exiles, and Yahweh does not assert the rights of the exiles in reply as he had in 11:16–21. Hence one may surmise that the counterclaim to the land comes from neighboring peoples. In fact, Ezekiel seems to say as much when in 35:10–12 the Edomites are quoted as asserting that the now-desolate mountains of Israel had been given them "to possess" and "for food," and in 36:2 similar sentiments are attributed to unnamed neighbors of Judah. And this seems to accord with the actual situation Ezra and Nehemiah confronted when they returned about a century and a half later, and Edomite (Idumean) incursions into southern Judah continued to affect NT events.

Those quoted in chapter 11 who wished to exclude the first wave of exiles had at least used quasi-theological argumentation by appealing to a sort of deity-people-land association (also known in contemporary paganism). But now the people's reasoning is totally secular. There is no recollection of Yahweh's oath, promise, and covenant given to Abraham. Since God's "house" (temple) had been destroyed and he no longer resided there (Ezekiel 11), he allegedly no longer had interest in or authority to determine who should live there. The people's claim that the land had now been "given" (33:24) to them does not imply any recognition of the divine gift. They seem to have forgotten that Abraham was not given permanent residency in the land, but described himself as a רֵג, "alien, sojourner" (Gen 23:4), and actual possession of the land would not come until four centuries later (Gen 15:15–21) when his progeny was indeed numerous, and Joshua led them in the conquest of the land. And the fact that the covenant with Abraham was virtually unconditional in form made it easy to appeal to him in spite of the people's depravity, which Yahweh will shortly score (Ezek 33:25–29). In place of "the faith of Abraham," it seems that those Judeans have a kind of "Darwinian materialism" if they presume that they have survived because they are "the fittest."[39]

Although Yahweh does not enunciate it here, possibly above all lay the same conviction Jeremiah had proclaimed so forcefully: the future lay with those who had experienced the exile, not with those who escaped it, neither in 597 nor in 586. As detailed earlier, this preachment is typologically of a piece

---

[39] Block, *Ezekiel*, 2:260.

with the fact that none rise with Christ who have not died with him (Baptism), that there is no Easter without Good Friday.[40]

To such a situation, Yahweh responds with consummate contempt. The salient feature of Abraham's response to the promise had not been his singleness, but his faith (Gen 15:6) and corresponding virtue, qualities conspicuousness by their absence among these squatters.

The survivors' pious-sounding appeal to Abraham has something paradigmatic about it. Protagonists of almost any cause instinctively seek to gain some higher moral ground, and, if Christian, will probably seek it (and usually somehow find it, at least to their satisfaction) in the Bible. If "a little knowledge is a dangerous thing," a "little Bible knowledge" can be even more so. The episode is a reminder that mere formal appeal to the Scriptures, even when rightly affirmed as inspired and inerrant, is not necessarily proof of anything. Apart from all the other principles of a confessional biblical hermeneutics, especially the Christological and soteriological material principle, Scripture may be bent to all sorts of invalid, even nefarious, purposes (cf. Mt 4:1–10).[41]

33:25 In his sharp rejoinder, Yahweh accuses the survivors of six specific transgressions (three in this verse, three in the following), all of which more or less define the wicked. For many of these transgressions he had already indicted the earlier inhabitants of Jerusalem. In chapter 18, homage to idols had been linked with all sorts of ethical failures. The shedding (literally, "pouring out") of blood—that is, murder—had been ascribed to Jerusalem especially in chapter 22.

The first charge in this verse is the most difficult and probably the most misunderstood. It is not an accusation of eating meat from which the blood has not been properly drained, which was, of course, an almost constitutive concern of the OT faith (and still is of orthodox Judaism). That rule was laid down as soon as permission to eat any meat was given after the flood (Gen 9:4–6) and was made a central feature of Sinaitic Torah (Lev 17:10–16). It remained so central in Jewish sensitivities that the first ecumenical council in Jerusalem decreed that even Gentile Christians were enjoined to observe the rule for a time (Acts 15:20). But the phrase עַל־הַדָּם ("upon/over the blood") appears in none of those other OT discussions. If anything, it is the preposition בְּ ("with, in") that characterizes those passages (see Gen 9:4; Lev 17:11).

The phrase "eat [אָכַל] upon/over the blood [עַל־הַדָּם]" occurs in only two other OT passages. The first, Lev 19:26, is in a context that bans various forms

---

[40] See pages 17–18 in the introduction and the commentary on 6:14; 11:14–21; 22:24; 28:22; and 32:19.

[41] The formal principle of all theology is that the Scriptures are the only source and norm for the Christian faith and life (FC Ep, Rule and Norm, 1–2; FC SD, Rule and Norm, 3; SA II II 15). The material principle is that the Gospel of justification by grace alone, through faith alone, for the sake of Christ alone, is the center of all theology and the chief article of the Christian faith (AC IV; Ap IV). See also pages 1–6 in the introduction.

of divination and occult practices. But in 1 Sam 14:32–33, the context indicates that the people were so exhausted and hungry that they ate meat with blood still in it, and so עַל־הַדָּם in 1 Sam 14:32–33 means "together with blood," as also does אֶל־הַדָּם in 1 Sam 14:34.

Here, as Maimonides already recognized, the phrase probably refers to some sort of pagan communion meal in which the participants ate meat whose blood was poured out in order to attract jinns, whom they believed would then come and give them knowledge of the future. Homer refers to such a ritual for raising shades for divination, and abundant evidence exists for similar practices all over the ancient Near East.[42] It may well have been one of those pagan practices that continued subterraneously throughout the biblical period despite the biblical prohibition. Kleinig deems it most likely that the phrase refers to the occult practice of eating beside a pit that contained the blood of the sacrificed animal.[43] Since we are never given details about the version of the rite that may have flourished in Canaan, there is little alternative but to translate the Hebrew literally as "eat over the blood."

33:26 Like Leviticus, the prophet Ezekiel, a priest (1:3), uses תּוֹעֵבָה, "abomination," comprehensively for all sorts of misbehavior, especially that which is egregiously offensive to Yahweh. Here in 33:26 it is used concretely and collectively. Often it refers to some sort of idolatry, but especially in the light of 22:11, with which this verse has affinities, sexual immorality may especially be in mind (cf. Leviticus 18), and it often seems to refer especially to homosexual behavior, prohibited in Lev 18:22; 20:13. That prohibition did not just apply to OT Israel; it continues to be normative for the church, as affirmed by passages such as Rom 1:18–27; 1 Cor 6:9; 1 Tim 1:9–10. The church must excommunicate those who engage in such "abominations" in the hope that they will repent, cease the behavior, and, forgiven through faith in Christ, be readmitted into the communion of saints. If not, just as the apostate Israelites will not "inherit/possess the land" (Ezek 33:25–26) so also, as St. Paul says, those who do such things "will not inherit the kingdom of God" (1 Cor 6:9).[44]

33:27 Yahweh's response to such turpitude comes in the form of a second command to Ezekiel to speak and the citation formula, "thus says the Lord Yahweh."[45] His three agents of wrath are sword, wild animals, and the plague.[46]

---

[42] See Greenberg, *Ezekiel*, 2:684, who cites Maimonides, *Guide of the Perplexed*, 3.46, and Homer, *Odyssey*, 11.24–50.

[43] See Kleinig, *Leviticus*, 399–400.

[44] See further Kleinig, *Leviticus*, 379–80, 387, 390, 437, and the excursus "Homosexuality" in Lockwood, *1 Corinthians*, 204–9.

[45] For this formula, see pages 8–9 in the introduction and the fourth textual note and the commentary on 2:4.

[46] Compare 14:12–21, which includes those three and adds famine as a fourth agent. Compare also 5:12; 6:11–12; 7:15; 12:16, which refer to the sword, famine, and plague as the three agents of divine wrath (cf. also 5:17).

That is, there will be no security, no escape from an unpleasant death, anywhere.

33:28   In principle, this verse adds nothing new to 33:27, but merely restates it in a superlative degree. Keil adds that the words are to be applied not only to "the Babylonian captivity, but embrace the devastation which accompanied and followed the destruction of Jerusalem by the Romans" in A.D. 70.[47] Obviously, that goes beyond the letter of the text, but to deny it would illustrate the temporal myopia that tends to stalk most modern historical exegesis. Typologically or in the cosmic sweep of *Heilsgeschichte* it must be applied to all time down to the final assize.

The Exiles in Babylon "Will Know That a Prophet Has Been among Them" (33:30–33)

33:30   In this final section of the chapter, Yahweh again quotes to Ezekiel what people are saying, and this time about him. The speakers are not the flotsam left behind in Judah, as in the previous oracle, but Ezekiel's own fellow exiles. By three essentially synonymous expressions, (1) the Niphal of דָּבַר used reciprocally, "talking with each other," (2) "say to one another," and (3) "each to a neighbor," the text accents that the prophet is on everyone's lips; he is "the talk of the town." Locating the conversations "beside the walls and in the doorways" suggests that the people seize any occasion (preferably in the shade?) to urge one another to hear what he has to say. No longer do the people listen to him only grudgingly, if at all, or delegate the chore to the elders. On the surface, Ezekiel could hardly have asked for more. The fulfillment of his basic prophecy of the fall of Jerusalem has at least convinced them that Yahweh is present and active, even on foreign soil after his "house" in Jerusalem has been reduced to ruins, and that he really does communicate through his prophet.

33:31   For all its difficulties in translation (see the textual notes), the verse portrays a very credible picture of a people whose thoughts and lives are dominated by sex and money (that is, power), two of the major drives in secular human life, "with minds set on earthly things" (Phil 3:19 RSV). No wonder they had no interest in Ezekiel's message.

33:32   Essentially repeating 33:31, Yahweh here applies it personally to Ezekiel. He is regarded as an excellent performer, both as vocalist and instrumentalist, but his words and the message they convey are about as irrelevant as those in much popular music today. The words of 33:31, to the effect that the people have not the slightest intent of repenting and believing, are repeated virtually verbatim, in order to attach the threat in the next verse.

This verse implies that Ezekiel, probably like many other prophets, did, at least on occasion, sing or chant his oracles. How frequently is impossible to ascertain. The poetic or semi-poetic form of so many prophetic oracles sug-

---

[47]   Keil, *Ezekiel*, 2:76.

gests that the practice was not unusual. Other passages reinforce the conclusion, for example, the Song of Moses after the exodus (Ex 15:1–18), the Song of Moses shortly before his death (Deuteronomy 32; see also Deut 31:30), the Song of the Vineyard (Is 5:1–7), Elisha's request for a minstrel (2 Ki 3:15).

There surely is a lesson here for worship today. It is probably natural that we wish to be entertained (and, indeed, in another, specialized sense we should "enjoy" worshiping), but even when sincere, congregation members may easily impede and blur their worship by the hymns they prefer, the liturgy they use, and so on, and the pastor may easily pander to their desires with the best of intentions. When disproportionate attention is paid to the worshipers' experience, rather than focusing on Word and Sacrament, or when the preacher's oratorical skills are admired rather than his doctrinal faithfulness, the Gospel easily gets muted or lost. "Praise songs" that are devoid of solid theological content may be repeated three times, but 3 x 0 = 0. In such churches, it will probably not be a thoroughly hypocritical audience like Ezekiel's, but scarcely a truly devout one either.

And this might be the occasion to remind ourselves that virtually all world religions, including Christianity, traditionally chant (not read) their scriptures in worship. The Masoretes supplied the Hebrew Scriptures with vowels and accents at least partly for the purpose of cantillation. Luther was concerned with the proper chants for the Scripture lessons in his liturgical revisions, even in the *Deutsche Messe* for common people. Not only is a chanted text often easier to understand than a spoken one (and it certainly was before electronic amplification was possible), it also communicates that the worshiper has left profane (in the etymological sense of the term) space and entered sacred space and time "with angels and archangels."[48] The rarity of chanting in Lutheranism today to no little extent betrays the influence of both Zwinglian iconoclasm and of a secularism that scarcely knows what "holy" means.

33:33 What is coming? The text ("when it comes—and come it will") does not specify the antecedent of the pronoun. The fulfillment of the prophecy concerning the fall of Jerusalem may have convinced the people that technically Ezekiel was a prophet, but as the previous two verses show, the real content and implications of his preaching had barely registered at all. His continued calls for repentance and warning of further judgment will continue to have behind them the full authority of the triune God, who calls prophets and apostles—and men into the pastoral office. The modified recognition formula, "they will know that a prophet has been among them,"[49] is repeated from 2:5 and is assurance to Ezekiel (as it is warning to the skeptics and mockers) that God will continue to stand by his Word, "whether they listen or do not" (2:5, 7).

The preacher needs no other security. It is no cliché to insist that the *true* prophet is called to be faithful to God's Word—not to be "successful."

---

[48] To borrow words from the Proper Preface in the Divine Service (e.g., *LW*, p. 146).

[49] For the regular recognition formula, "(then) you/they will know that I am Yahweh," see page 9 in the introduction and the commentary on 6:7.

Ezekiel 34:1–31

Yahweh Will Save His Sheep through His Messianic Shepherd

Translation

34 ¹The Word of Yahweh came to me: ²"Son of man, prophesy against the shepherds of Israel, prophesy and say to them, 'To the shepherds—thus says the Lord Yahweh: Woe, shepherds of Israel, who have been shepherding themselves. Are not sheep what shepherds are supposed to shepherd? ³You eat the curds; you wear the wool; you slaughter the fattened ones—the flock you do not shepherd. ⁴The weak you have not strengthened; the sick you have not healed; and the injured you have not bound up. The expelled you have not brought back, and the lost you have not searched for. Instead you have domineered them with force and with violence. ⁵So they scattered, because there was no shepherd, and became food for all the beasts of the field. My sheep scattered and ⁶wandered all over the mountains and on every high hill. Over the face of the whole earth my flock was scattered, with no one inquiring and no one searching. ⁷Therefore, shepherds, hear the Word of Yahweh: ⁸As I live, says the Lord Yahweh, surely, because my flock has become plunder, and because my flock has become food for all the beasts of the field for lack of a shepherd, and my shepherds did not concern themselves about my flock, but the shepherds shepherded themselves instead of shepherding my flock, ⁹therefore, shepherds, hear the Word of Yahweh: ¹⁰Thus says the Lord Yahweh: I am against the shepherds. I will hold them accountable for my flock. I will stop them from shepherding sheep, and no longer will those shepherds shepherd themselves. I will rescue my flock from their mouths, so that they will no longer be food for them.

¹¹" 'For thus says the Lord Yahweh: I myself will seek the welfare of my flock and examine them carefully. ¹²As a shepherd examines his flock when he is with his sheep that have been scattered, so will I examine my flock and rescue them from all the places where they were scattered on a day of clouds and thick darkness. ¹³I will bring them out from the peoples and gather them from the countries and bring them to their own ground. I will shepherd them on the mountains of Israel, in the valleys, and in all the settlements of the land. ¹⁴I will pasture them in good pasture, and their grazing land will be on the high mountains of Israel. There they will lie down in good grazing land, and they will pasture on rich pasture on the mountains of Israel. ¹⁵I myself will shepherd my flock, and I myself will let them lie down, says the Lord Yahweh. ¹⁶The lost I will seek; the expelled I will bring back; the injured I will bind up; the weak I will strengthen; the fat and the strong I will destroy; and I will shepherd them in justice.

¹⁷" 'As for you, my flock, thus says the Lord Yahweh: I am going to establish the rights of one animal versus another. To the rams and the goats: ¹⁸Is it not

enough for you that you feed on the good pasture, but the rest of your pastures you must trample with your feet, or that you drink the clear water and the remainder you muddy with your feet? [19]Then my flock has to feed on what your feet have trampled and drink what your feet have muddied.

[20]" 'Therefore, thus says the Lord Yahweh to them: I myself am going to establish the rights of fat versus lean animals. [21]Because you have shoved with side and shoulder and knocked down all the weak with your horns until you had scattered them abroad, [22]I will save my flock so they will not become plunder any more. Thus I will establish the rights of one animal versus another.

[23]" 'Then I will raise up over them one Shepherd, and he will tend them: my Servant David. He will tend them, and he will be their Shepherd. [24]I, Yahweh, will be their God, and my Servant David will be Prince among them. I, Yahweh, have spoken. [25]Then I will make for them a covenant of peace, and I will rid the land of wild animals, so they may live securely in the desert and sleep in the forests. [26]I will make them and the area around my hill a blessing; I will send the rain down in its season—rains of blessing they will be. [27]The trees of the field will yield their fruit, and the ground will yield its produce. They will be secure on their own land and know that I am Yahweh when I break the bars of their yoke and rescue them from the hand of those who enslaved them. [28]No more will they be booty for the nations, nor will wild animals devour them. They will live in security, with no one to make them afraid. [29]I will establish for them a land renowned for the reliability of its crops so that they will no more be carried off by famine in the land or bear the derision of the nations. [30]They will know that I, Yahweh, their God, am with them, and that they, the house of Israel, are my people, says the Lord Yahweh. [31]You are my sheep, the sheep of my pasture. You are men, and I am your God, says the Lord Yahweh.' "

Textual Notes

34:2 לָרֹעִים—After the repeated Niphal imperative הִנָּבֵא, "prophesy," and וְאָמַרְתָּ אֲלֵיהֶם (literally, "you shall say to them"), the לְ on the masculine plural participle of רָעָה with article, "the shepherds," is perplexing. NIV "solves" the problem by omitting all of לָרֹעִים. KJV through ESV take it as appositive to the preceding אֲלֵיהֶם ("to them ... to the shepherds"). That kind of construction is possible in Biblical Hebrew and common in Aramaic, the influence of which may be detected here. However, when Hebrew uses the pattern, usually the two prepositions are identical, in which case the preposition with suffix anticipates the (repeated) preposition and following noun. A second possibility, which I have followed, assumes the influence here (as throughout the oracle) of Jeremiah, who often introduces or entitles prophecies with לְ prefixed to the people or country against which the oracle is aimed (e.g., Jer 23:9; 46:2). לָרֹעִים is translated, "to the shepherds," as if it were an appositive, but connected syntactically with what follows: "to the shepherds—thus says the Lord Yahweh: Woe to the shepherds" (although לְ is not used on רֹעֵי־יִשְׂרָאֵל). A third possibility, preferred by some commentators,[1] takes the *lamed* as a vocative, but whether

---

[1] E.g., Block, *Ezekiel*, 2:277, including n. 23.

Dahood's proposal that Biblical Hebrew even had such an idiom is not universally accepted.[2] The Syriac so rendered it, but that may be only a free rendering.

הֹוֹי רֹעֵי יִשְׂרָאֵל—The interjection הוֹי is traditionally translated "woe" and followed by לְ, עַל, or other constructions. Sometimes it is followed by a vocative, as here (see *HALOT*, 2 b). In some other passages, it may simply be a vocative particle ("oh, ah") but, functionally, it seems to carry the "woe" meaning here, especially in the light of the structure of a typical woe oracle that follows: the indictment in 34:2–6, followed by the announcement of judgment in 34:7–10. By the same token, there is no need (with NRSV) to insert "you" before the translation of הוֹי, because woe oracles frequently shift abruptly from third to second person.

הָיוּ רֹעִים אוֹתָם—In English it may sound slightly artificial to use "shepherd" as both noun and verb, as I have done in this chapter, but in that way the Hebrew idiom can be reproduced almost exactly in English. Furthermore, English can reproduce precisely the periphrastic idiom here, "they were shepherding/feeding/tending themselves." For this meaning one might have expected some reflexive construction, but since the OT contains neither a Niphal nor a Hithpael of רָעָה (conjugations used for reflexive meanings of other verbs), the Qal masculine plural participle (רֹעִים) is used with the direct object marker (אוֹתָם) with the corresponding masculine plural suffix to express the idea (Joüon, § 146 k). The contrast between this clause and the following one with the feminine singular noun צֹאן, (collective) "sheep" or "flock," removes all doubt that אוֹתָם refers to the shepherds "themselves" and not צֹאן.

הֲלוֹא הַצֹּאן יִרְעוּ הָרֹעִים:—I have retained the traditional translation of הֲלוֹא as an interrogative, here requiring an affirmative answer. But like cognates in other Semitic languages, it may have affirmative or emphatic force, in which case it would probably be pointed differently. The imperfect יִרְעוּ (Qal of רָעָה) in this context has the modal nuance of an obligation, "must tend" (Joüon, § 113 m), or "should shepherd, are supposed to shepherd."

34:3 The short verse lists three things the "shepherds" have done and one—the "one thing needful" (Lk 10:42)—they have not done.

All through the verse, the objects precede the verbs. The first object is vocalized in the MT as חֵלֶב, "fat." The LXX and the Vulgate, however, apparently read the consonants as חָלָב, "milk." And since one does not normally "eat" milk, it is usually assumed that the word is used comprehensively to include solids made from milk, such as curds, cheese, or yogurt (modern Arabic *leben*), although Hebrew has another word (חֶמְאָה) more specifically for those products. Possibly, though, the idiom of "eating milk" was widely used, as even by St. Paul in 1 Cor 9:7 (ἐσθίω γάλα), in a verse that refers to shepherds partaking of milk from the flock. Some other passages speak of "drinking" liquid milk with שָׁתָה (Ezek 25:4; drinking wine and milk in Song 5:1) or the Hiphil of שָׁקָה (Judg 4:19). So linguistically, we seem to get a draw. For most modern commentators, however, the clinching argument for "curds" or some solid milk product here is logical: an animal first must be slaughtered to obtain its "fat," but that

---

[2] See Dahood, *Psalms*, 1:21; Waltke-O'Connor, § 11.2.10i, n. 96.

charge does not come until later in this verse (see the next textual note). I have agreed, but it is no crucial issue.

הַבְּרִיאָה תִּזְבָּחוּ—This and the next clause are asyndetic; we would expect both to begin with *waw*. After the *waw* at the end of the preceding word, תִּלְבָּשׁוּ, it could be a case of homoioteleuton, but for both clauses the desire to avoid repetition of the consonant (-וְ וּ-) might explain the absence of the initial *waw*. The direct object of תִּזְבָּחוּ (Qal imperfect of זָבַח), "you slaughter," is הַבְּרִיאָה, technically singular ("the fattened animal"), but probably in a collective sense, hence, usually translated as plural in English.

הַצֹּאן לֹא תִרְעוּ׃—It would be natural to add an adversative *waw*, "but," on הַצֹּאן, because this final clause is clearly adversative. But perhaps the omission of a conjunction was intended to highlight the shepherds' malfeasance, and so I have employed a simple dash: "—the flock you do not shepherd." In ordinary circumstances, the first three activities described in the verse would be normal and unobjectionable for shepherds (cf. 1 Cor 9:7), but to take care only of themselves and neglect the sheep was inexcusable.

34:4 This verse explains in detail the meaning of the last clause of 34:3. Hence it is a series of negative statements, describing all that a "good shepherd" would do, but these shepherds do not. The imperfects of 34:3 describing present behavior, some of it unobjectionable, are replaced by perfects (and imperfects with *waw* consecutive in 34:5), cataloging a long record of outrages. The negative statements here are then expressed positively about Yahweh's activities in 34:16.

אֶת־הַנַּחְלוֹת לֹא חִזַּקְתֶּם—The direct object, נַחְלוֹת (with article), is a Niphal feminine plural participle of חָלָה, "be weak." Instead of the MT's plural, the LXX, Vulgate, and Syriac all read a singular, corresponding to the singular objects in the rest of the verse. The incongruity is obscured in English translation. This plural might imply that the next two terms are examples of the "weak."

וְאֶת־הַחוֹלָה לֹא־רִפֵּאתֶם—The object here is a Qal feminine singular participle of the same verb, חָלָה. It might seem strange to find two conjugations of the same verb so close together, but it is, in fact, quite common in Ezekiel. The Niphal and Qal of חָלָה have identical semantic ranges; the specific meaning in each case is determined by the other verb used with it— here the Piel of רָפָא, "heal," implying sickness.

וְלַנִּשְׁבֶּרֶת לֹא חֲבַשְׁתֶּם—"Injured" may be too weak a rendering for the Niphal feminine singular participle of שָׁבַר, "to break," so "fractured" might better reflect the meaning. A *lamed* precedes the object of the verb (Qal of חָבַשׁ, "bind up"), as occasionally elsewhere (e.g., Num 12:13; Ps 116:16).

וְאֶת־הַנִּדַּחַת לֹא הֲשֵׁבֹתֶם—I have started a new sentence with this verse's fourth count of the indictment because the subject matter changes ever so slightly, even though the usual Hebrew parataxis does not change. This and the next clause describe those who have become separated from the main flock. The Niphal feminine singular participle of נָדַח may imply either a simple "straying" animal or one that has been "driven away, expelled" by others in the flock. I have preferred the latter alternative, both to avoid duplication with the translation of the object in the next clause (the Qal feminine singular participle הָאֹבֶדֶת must mean "the straying, lost") and to anticipate the expulsion of the weak by the strong in 34:21 (which uses different verbs).

וּבְחָזְקָה רְדִיתֶם אֹתָם וּבְפָרֶךְ:—One might have expected a separate verse for this last clause. In formulation it is positive, but in substance it is a summary of all the previous condemnations. Its general sense is clear, but it is problematic in some details. The difficulty centers on the masculine object pronoun אֹתָם, "them," incongruent with the previous feminine singular participles, whose antecedent is the feminine singular צֹאן back in 34:3. The best explanation seems to be that the application of the metaphor—the rulers' harsh oppression of their subjects—has intruded into the shepherd picture, a type of thing that happens in other extended metaphors in Ezekiel. The uncommon noun חָזְקָה, "force," always takes the preposition בְּ and has an adverbial meaning, here "forcibly, violently" (BDB, 1). The Qal of רָדָה can have a neutral meaning of "rule (over)," but the adverbial here indicates oppression. The verb can take the preposition בְּ attached to those over whom one rules, and that is how the LXX understood the text ("and the strong you rule," requiring pointing וּבְחָזְקָה). The MT's וּבְחָזְקָה must be coordinate with וּבְפָרֶךְ at the end of the sentence—an unusual separation, but not without parallel (cf., e.g., Gen 28:14b; Ex 34:27b; Deut 7:14b).[3] פֶּרֶךְ, "harshness, severity," also always takes the preposition בְּ and has an adverbial meaning. It is used in Ex 1:13–14 of the harsh treatment of the Israelites by their Egyptian taskmasters, and there may well be a reminiscence of that here. Three times the Torah forbids treating an Israelite serf בְּפָרֶךְ (Lev 25:43, 46, 53).

The LXX differs significantly from the MT, so various reconstructions are proposed, but the MT is defensible.

34:5a וַתְּפוּצֶינָה מִבְּלִי רֹעֶה—The verb, repeated identically at the end of the verse, is the Qal third feminine plural imperfect of פּוּץ with *waw* consecutive, whose Niphal will be in 34:6, 12 and whose Hiphil is in 34:21. The Qal is translated intransitively, "they scattered," and the Niphal as a passive, "was/have been scattered," while the Hiphil is transitive and causative, "to scatter." The LXX, Syriac, and Vulgate add "my flock" here, but the subject is obvious from the context. The negative adverb מִבְּלִי (מִן plus בְּלִי) often has causal force, as here: *because there was no* shepherd." Similar is the force of מֵאֵין in 34:8. The singular or plural of the participle רֹעֶה, "shepherd," is repeated frequently in following verses, once in 34:7; three times in 34:8; once in 34:9; twice in 34:10; once in 34:12; and twice in 34:23. It, together with צֹאן (see the next textual note), introduces a compassionate note that runs through 34:5–6 and connects 34:1–10 with the following sections (34:11–22 and 34:23–31). Especially in the light of the maltreatment just described, it depicts Israel as sinned against as much as sinning.

34:5c–6 וַתְּפוּצֶינָה: יִשְׁגּוּ צֹאנִי—The MT concludes the verse with the repetition of וַתְּפוּצֶינָה, which could be translated as a self-standing sentence: "They scattered." It is also possible to construe it as a temporal clause with the preceding: "and they be-

---

came food … when they scattered" (NKJV; KJV and NIV are similar). However, like ESV, I have taken it as the start of a new sentence that continues into 34:6, with צֹאנִי as the subject of both verbs: "My sheep scattered and ⁶wandered …" Yet this construal has its difficulties, since it takes the feminine imperfect with *waw* consecutive (וַתְּפוּצֶינָה) as parallel to the following asyndetic masculine imperfect without *waw* (יִשְׁגּוּ, Qal of שָׁגָה), which must refer to past time. It also makes יִשְׁגּוּ seem like an unneeded repetition of the synonymous previous verb, which is thus separated from the subject צֹאנִי. In the ancient versions, יִשְׁגּוּ is attested in the Peshitta, the Vulgate, and possibly the Targum, but not in the LXX. Even though the feminine noun צֹאן is singular, its collective meaning, "sheep," explains the use of the plural verbs, but not of the masculine יִשְׁגּוּ, unless the language moves from the metaphor to the human referents (Israelites).

In any event, the suffix "my" on צֹאנִי subtly introduces the theme of Yahweh as Israel's true and faithful Shepherd. צֹאנִי will be repeated in 34:6; four times in 34:8; twice in 34:10 (and once without the suffix); and so on throughout the chapter.

וְאֵין דּוֹרֵשׁ וְאֵין מְבַקֵּשׁ:—The two participles are near synonyms, but דָּרַשׁ (repeated in 34:8, 10, 11) implies "inquiring" about something or troubling oneself about it, while בִּקֵּשׁ (repeated from 34:4 and recurring in 34:16) signifies more the actual "searching" for the lost.

34:7 לָכֵן רֹעִים—The Hebrew has no article before the vocative רֹעִים, which most translators reflect by using "O" or "you." It has the article in the parallel 34:9 (לָכֵן הָרֹעִים). But there is considerable freedom in Hebrew usage of vocatives. An article seems to be omitted especially when the reference is to persons not present or theoretical. Possibly, its omission here is to signal the harshness of Yahweh's forthcoming reprimand.

34:8 אִם־לֹא ׀ לָבַז יַעַן הֱיוֹת־צֹאנִי—This structure is anacolouthic since it begins with the positive oath formula אִם־לֹא, meaning "surely will," but instead of the oath following immediately, a motive clause introduced by יַעַן ("because") intervenes, and the substance of the oath does not come until 34:10. Under such or similar circumstances, אִם־לֹא by itself may mean "surely" (see the textual note on 3:6). KJV and NKJV so translate it; RSV and NRSV omitted it; ESV restored it. Thus the grounds for God's reaction are hammered home before it is spelled out in 34:10.

Since wild animals do not take "plunder" (בַּז), this intrusion of the human referent (Israel plundered) is immediately restated in terms of the metaphorical sheep, repeating the words וַתִּהְיֶינָה לְאָכְלָה from 34:5b. Ezek 34:28 will express the opposite of both formulations.

רֹעַי—The suffix "my" must not be overlooked. For the first time, the miscreant "shepherds" are identified as God's agents, although all along there has been no doubt that they represent the leaders whom God stationed over his people.

וַיִּרְעוּ הָרֹעִים אוֹתָם וְאֶת־צֹאנִי לֹא רָעוּ:—The repetition of the verb רָעָה with two contrasting direct objects, positively with אוֹתָם in a reflexive sense (see the third textual note on 34:2) and negatively with צֹאנִי, highlights the shepherds' malfeasance.

34:9 The interposition of the long motive in 34:8 requires that the entirety of 34:7 be repeated before the sentence of judgment (34:10).

34:10 וְדָרַשְׁתִּי אֶת־צֹאנִי מִיָּדָם—Literally, "I will seek my flock from their hand," this is translated, "I will hold them accountable for my flock." See the second textual note on 34:11 and the commentary on 34:10.

34:11 The initial כִּי, "for," serves as a two-way transition, both connecting the citation formula, "thus says the Lord Yahweh,"[4] with the preceding denunciations and with the following description of how Yahweh will deliver his people.[5] The false shepherds now disappear completely, and in their place only Yahweh's activity is mentioned.

הִנְנִי־אָנִי וְדָרַשְׁתִּי אֶת־צֹאנִי וּבִקַּרְתִּים:—He begins with what appears to be a semi-technical self-introduction formula[6] (הִנְנִי־אָנִי, with a disjunctive accent, -אָ), which could be translated literalistically, "behold/look at me; it is I." In this context especially, it connotes firm determination. It is followed by a perfect with *waw* consecutive (וְדָרַשְׁתִּי). This sequence occurs only here and in 34:20 (הִנְנִי־אָנִי וְשָׁפַטְתִּי; see also 6:3, where a participle follows הִנְנִי אָנִי).

Ezek 34:11b is virtually thetical for the entire following section, through 34:22. First of all, Yahweh will "seek" (דָּרַשׁ) his flock—the same verb used in 34:6 (translated "inquiring"); 34:8 (translated "concern themselves about"); and 34:10, where it had a semi-legal meaning. Its use here is closest to that of 34:10, but just the obverse in application. Both have legal overtones, but in 34:10 God, as prosecuting attorney, was seeking to determine the extent of the accused shepherds' misdeeds and the appropriate penalty, while here God, as the defense attorney for the sheep, is seeking appropriate redress to correct the wrongs done to that injured party. That it has that nuance here is shown by the word with which it is paired.

In 34:6 דָּרַשׁ was paired with the near synonym בָּקַשׁ, but here it is paired with a different Piel, also a close synonym, בָּקַר, which will recur twice in 34:12. Ezekiel uses בָּקַר only in these two verses, and it is a word that betrays his priestly background. In Lev 13:36 it describes a priest's careful physical examination of a "leper" before he can be pronounced "clean." According to Lev 27:32–33 a worshiper is to give every tenth animal for sacrifice and not inspect the animals (to distinguish [בָּקַר] and withhold the good ones). Liturgical activities of an unspecified sort are probably also implied in 2 Ki 16:15 and Ps 27:4. (A similar use of the root is known from Nabatean inscriptions from the time of Christ). A semi-liturgical context is implied by the admonition of Prov 20:25 to reflection and self-examination before making a vow (normally accompanied by a votive offering).

A similar usage appears in the title מְבַקֵּר, "overseer," for the head of the Qumran community. The *Damascus Document* associated with that community describes his duties in language that appears to be derived in large degree from this verse in Ezekiel. It is unprovable, but widely surmised that similar conceptions underlie the

---

[4] For this formula, see pages 8–9 in the introduction and the fourth textual note and the commentary on 2:4.

[5] My translation of the verse largely follows that of Block (*Ezekiel*, 2:286), to whose exegesis I am indebted.

[6] See page 9 in the introduction on Yahweh's self-introduction formula.

NT term ἐπίσκοπος, "overseer, bishop, pastor." One might also compare the old LCMS idiom of circuit "visitors"[7] (before they were renamed "counselors"), and it is a reminder of the falsity of any supposed gulf between the priestly and pastoral/prophetic functions of a pastor.

34:12 כְּבַקָּרַת —This is an Aramaic-form Piel infinitive of בָּקַר in construct and with כְּ. The corresponding Hebrew form would be כְּבַקֵּר.

עֶדְרוֹ—The noun עֵדֶר, "flock," occurs only here in Ezekiel and is essentially synonymous with צֹאן.

בְּיוֹם־הֱיוֹתוֹ בְתוֹךְ־צֹאנוֹ נִפְרָשׁוֹת—This remainder of the protasis occasions some problems. The ancient versions vary widely, and a welter of emendations have been offered by modern commentators. Cooke advocates deleting בְתוֹךְ,[8] and alone among major modern translations only RSV does that, but little difference in meaning results. The indefinite Niphal participle of פָּרַשׁ appears to qualify the definite צֹאנוֹ, "his sheep," as an accusative attribute of state, "having been scattered." Since elsewhere פָּרַשׁ means "explain, declare," probably the word here is a variant spelling of פָּרַשׂ, whose Niphal in 17:21 meant "scattered." In spite of the problems, the general picture is clear enough. When Yahweh arrives among his once scattered flock, he will check the condition of the sheep.

וְהִצַּלְתִּי אֶתְהֶם מִכָּל־הַמְּקוֹמֹת אֲשֶׁר נָפֹצוּ שָׁם—Those from which Yahweh will "rescue" (Hiphil first common singular perfect of נָצַל with *waw* consecutive) "them" (the masculine אֶתְהֶם, referring now to people, not sheep) here are not the evil shepherds, but "all the places where they were scattered," the geographic locations that have grasped them away, as it were.

בְּיוֹם עָנָן וַעֲרָפֶל:—The day of that catastrophe is described, literally, as "a day of cloud and thick darkness," a common hendiadys meaning "a day of dark clouds." In Pentateuchal texts the language is typically associated with the Sinaitic theophany (עֲרָפֶל in Ex 20:21; עָנָן וַעֲרָפֶל in Deut 4:11; 5:22). In Ezekiel (13:5; 22:24; cf. chapter 7) as in other texts (cf. Ps 97:2), it is synonymous with "the Day of Yahweh," referring most immediately to the fall of Jerusalem, but that also as a prelude to the establishment of his universal lordship at the first (see "darkness" in Mt 27:45; Mk 15:33; Lk 23:44) and second (Mt 24:29; Acts 2:20) advents of Jesus Christ. Thus although the immediate application here is not eschatological, that implication is present in the wider horizon.

34:13 The only problematic word in the verse is the masculine form of the plural of מוֹשָׁב in construct (מוֹשְׁבֵי). Everywhere else in the OT a feminine plural is used. The explanation is debated. The word may be epicene (although without any other evidence of it). It could be a homonym, related to an Arabic root meaning "abound with grass," although again without supporting Hebrew evidence. Or it may be evidence,

---

[7]   These "visitors" were pastors acting under the elected presidents of the district-synods who had the responsibility to visit the other pastors and churches that comprised the circuit to ensure that their doctrine, worship, and life were sound.

[8]   Cooke, *Ezekiel*, 380.

as seen elsewhere in Ezekiel, of disintegration of the norms and structures of preexilic, classical Hebrew.

34:14 מִרְעֶה, used in Ezekiel only in 34:14, 18 (twice in each verse), is derived from רָעָה, "to shepherd," and thus the dominance of that key word throughout the chapter is continued. When מִרְעֶה is repeated in this verse, it is modified by the adjective שָׁמֵן, meaning "lush" or the like, related to שֶׁמֶן, "(olive) oil." In 34:16 שָׁמֵן refers to a "fat" animal.

וּבְהָרֵי מְרוֹם־יִשְׂרָאֵל—Literally, "the mountains of the height of Israel," the construct chain is equivalent to an adjectival phrase, "the high mountains of Israel." The LXX and Targum read a singular "mountain" (although they have the plural at the end of the verse). There is no warrant to emend the text here, but the change in number is of theological significance. In 20:40 the singular ("my holy mountain, the high mountain of Israel") had been used to contrast with the many illicit high places (20:28–29). Similarly, the parable in 17:22–23 uses the singular to specify Jerusalem, the seat of the Davidic dynasty.

נְוֵהֶם—The noun נָוֶה (with third masculine plural suffix), "pasture," is evidently intended to maintain the ovine atmosphere, although it implies human presence as well. The word has an Akkadian cognate, and in the Amorite texts of Mari, it is often used of seminomadic encampments. Naturally, good pasturage would be a major concern in choosing sites, hence it is translated "good grazing land."

תִּרְבַּצְנָה—This and the following verb (תִּרְעֶינָה) have switched from the preceding masculine forms (referring to the people) back to feminine, with "sheep" as their implied subject. רָבַץ will be repeated in the next verse. The bucolic picture of "lying down" in security is very similar to that painted in Ps 23:2, with the Hiphil of רָבַץ.

34:15 The prominent redundant and emphatic pronoun אֲנִי, "I," twice in the verse accents again Yahweh's direct agency, not some impersonal luck or historical process.

34:16 Even formally, it is clear that the verse is transitional. The first half of the verse repeats 34:4a in slightly abbreviated form and in reverse order, evidently to indicate the reversal of the traumas of the past. By replacing the negative associations of the past with positive affirmations, the replacement of the evil shepherds by the Good Shepherd is clearly proclaimed.

וְאֶת־הַחוֹלָה אֲחַזֵּק—Forms of חָלָה in 34:4 meant "sick" and "weak," but here it must mean "weak" because רָפָא ("heal") does not appear, only the (causative) Piel of חָזַק, "strengthen."

The second half of the verse foreshadows the internal conflicts among the sheep/Israelites of which 34:17–22 will speak. Here too there are surface changes: instead of a single direct object in the clauses in 34:16a, in the first clause of 34:16b, there is a double direct object (הַשְּׁמֵנָה וְאֶת־הַחֲזָקָה) of a destructive act: אַשְׁמִיד, "I will destroy." However, there is much debate about אַשְׁמִיד. It implies far more drastic action than the deposition of the wicked shepherds in 34:10 and than the flock's rescue from bullies in 34:22. The Targum agrees with the MT, but the rest of the ancient versions (also Luther![9]) apparently read אֶשְׁמֹר, "I will keep watch," plausible enough on

---

[9] WA DB 11/1.518–19: *behüten.*

the surface because of the similarity of *resh* and *dalet* in Hebrew script. "Watch" may be understood as irony, but it is still a far weaker statement. In favor of the MT is its agreement with the following מִשְׁפָּט, which need not be translated "judgment" (KJV and NKJV) to harmonize with "destroy." Even if translated "justice" or "justly," that is, giving each its due care, it implies a correction of the abuse of the weak by the strong described earlier, and it accords with the use of the verb שָׁפַט in 34:17, 20, 22. Perhaps the phrase is best taken as an oxymoron. Compare "you shall shatter them [תְּרֹעֵם] with an iron rod" in Ps 2:9, translated as "shepherd them" (using ποιμαίνω, as if the Hebrew were a form of רָעָה) by the LXX, and also in Rev 2:27; 12:5; 19:15.

אֶרְעֶנָּה בְמִשְׁפָּט:—Although English idiom requires "shepherd *them*," the energic singular suffix on אֶרְעֶנָּה continues the singular objects of the previous verbs.

34:17–22 Ezek 34:17–22 exhibits certain changes in style and content from the preceding verses, but also definite continuities. Of the latter, perhaps the most obvious is the use of the keyword שָׁפַט (34:17, 20, 22), fleshing out the noun מִשְׁפָּט at the end of 34:16. The theme of "save" (Hiphil of יָשַׁע) in 34:22 parallels the "rescue" (Hiphil of נָצַל) in 34:10.

At the same time, we hear no more of evil shepherds. Now the sheep are addressed, and directly in the second person, no longer as a third party. There is no longer any consideration of external enemies or of divine judgment upon the community itself. Here the concern is that of internal relations between members of the flock. Although 34:17 begins with another vocative and the citation formula, there is no formal conclusion at the end of 34:22, and 34:23 continues with a *waw* consecutive, forbidding segregation of this section (34:17–22) from what follows (34:23–31).

This subsection can be further divided into the accusation in 34:17–19 and a judgment oracle in 34:20–22, which begins typically, with לָכֵן and a repetition of the citation formula.[10]

34:17 וְאַתֵּנָה—This rare second feminine plural personal pronoun is used elsewhere only in 13:11, 20 as well as Gen 31:6. Here it is used as a vocative. The short form, אַתֵּן, occurs only once in the OT, in Ezek 34:31.

הִנְנִי שֹׁפֵט—The suffixed הִנֵּה followed by a participle often indicates the *futurum instans*, "about to," sometimes in an eschatological perspective. But if that is the case here, it seems to be in a rather weak sense, so I have translated, "*I am going to establish* the rights." For that meaning of שָׁפַט here, see the commentary.

שֶׂה—בֵּין־שֶׂה לָשֶׂה לָאֵילִים וְלָעַתּוּדִים:—שֶׂה appears here for the first time in this context instead of the collective צֹאן. It denotes an individual of the flock, whether sheep or goat, male or female. Usually the word is treated grammatically as masculine, although occasionally as feminine (so in 34:20 and in 45:15).

The MT, followed by the versions and virtually all modern translations, plainly connects the last two words of the verse, "to the rams and to the goats" with what precedes, that is, in apposition to "one animal versus another." But a number of things support taking the last two words as introducing 34:18, as I have translated. The two

---

[10] For this formula, see pages 8–9 in the introduction and the fourth textual note and the commentary on 2:4.

plural nouns with לְ here correspond to לְרֹעִים in 34:2, where Yahweh speaks "to the shepherds." In 34:20 we meet בֵּין־שֶׂה ... וּבֵין שֶׂה, and then in 34:22 we meet the same בֵּין שֶׂה לָשֶׂה as here, and in neither verse is there a distinction between "rams" and "goats," nor is לְ ... לְ used to make a distinction between animals. If we take the two masculine plural nouns at the end of 34:17 as beginning a new sentence, this explains why masculine forms refer to them also in 34:18 (whereas 34:17 began by referring to the animals with the feminine plural אַתֵּנָה).

אַיִל and עַתּוּד refer to male "sheep" and "goats," respectively. אַיִל is the most common metaphorical animal designation for a human "leader" in the OT. עַתּוּד was used in 27:21 of literal animals, and the word will recur in 39:18, where it metaphorically refers to leaders who have been sacrificed and judged.

34:18 The accusation is in the form of two parallel rhetorical questions (cf. the behavior of the fourth beast in Dan 7:7).

הַמְעַט מִכֶּם—The interrogative particle plus מְעַט is followed by the preposition מִן in a comparative sense: literally, "Is it too little for you ... ?" (see BDB, s.v. מְעַט, 1 e a). Often elsewhere this construction is then followed by a כִּי clause (LXX here has ὅτι), but in Is 7:13 an infinitive construct follows, and here a finite verb follows, תִּרְעוּ, which must be translated "*that* you feed." Apparently the idiom for such a question was fluid.

וּמִשְׁקַע־מַיִם—The noun מִשְׁקַע is a hapax, derived from the verb שָׁקַע, "to sink, settle," as in 32:14. The picture is that of water from which the dirt and sediment have settled to the bottom. After the strong have trampled around in it, only turbid water is left, scarcely potable.

34:20 הִנְנִי־אָנִי—See the second textual note on 34:11.

וְשָׁפַטְתִּי—For the translation of שָׁפַט, see the commentary on 34:17.

בֵּין־שֶׂה בִרְיָה וּבֵין שֶׂה רָזָה:—Both types of animals are described with feminine adjectives. The feminine form of בָּרִיא, "fat," is normally spelled בְּרִיאָה, but the form בִּרְיָה used here is common in Mishnaic Hebrew.

34:22 וְהוֹשַׁעְתִּי לְצֹאנִי—After יַעַן, "because," at the start of 34:21, one would expect לָכֵן to begin the verdict or judgment, but syntactically, the *waw* on the verb (not translated in English idiom) serves this function. Perhaps the reason is that 34:21–22 is not intended as an ordinary judgment oracle, but to announce divine intervention to stop the strong from taking unsavory advantage of the weak. The concern is not the punishment of the wicked, but the deliverance of and restoration of harmony to the flock.

34:23 וַהֲקִמֹתִי עֲלֵיהֶם רֹעֶה אֶחָד—The *waw* consecutive indicates that we are not to think of a new topic beginning here, but of the continuation of the preceding—but specifically, of course, of Yahweh's rectification of the intolerable state of affairs just described.

Ezek 34:23–24 and 34:31, built around the covenant formula, form a framework around the intervening material. In totality, the three segments enable one to label the pericope "messianic" in the narrow sense, speaking specifically of the Son of David, but also "eschatological" in a very broad sense.

The gender of the pronominal suffixes in this verse is inconsistent, anticipating the transition from the metaphor (flock, feminine) to the non-figurative language of the application (people, masculine) from 34:24 on.

The verse continues to revolve around the verb רָעָה. For the participle רֹעֶה I have continued to use "shepherd," but it seemed imperative to abandon my previous practice of consistently translating it so for the finite form וְרָעָה. Various alternatives present themselves. I have chosen "tend" as perhaps as comprehensive a term as one could find. "Feed" is probably the most common alternative.

אֶת־עַבְדִּי דָוִיד—אֵת marks "my Servant David" as the direct object of the initial verb, "I will raise up, establish." As signaling a definite object, it may also give a certain emphasis to what would otherwise be a simple appositive to the indefinite רֹעֶה. No significance attaches to the *plene* spelling of the name דָּוִיד in contrast to the defective orthography elsewhere in the book (34:24; 37:24–25). The general pattern is that the use of the vowel letters increased in the Hebrew language as time went on, but the change is uneven.

הוּא יִרְעֶה אֹתָם וְהוּא־יִהְיֶה לָהֶן לְרֹעֶה:—Typical repetitious priestly style appears here. The first clause uses the finite form of the verb רָעָה, while the second uses הָיָה followed by the participle רֹעֶה.

34:26 The verse, especially its first half, is somewhat of a *crux*. Grammatically, after אוֹתָם, we might expect אֶת also before סְבִיבוֹת גִּבְעָתִי. Materially, some critics allege that in a context of the enhanced fruitfulness of the whole country, it is out of place to mention the people and Mount Zion especially. גִּבְעָה is an unusual designation of the temple "hill," but not unparalleled; see Is 10:32; 31:4. The versions attest to something like the MT, but with variations. The LXX omits the copula before סְבִיבוֹת and a translation for בְּרָכָה, and some base reconstructions on that.[11] Some reconstruct the text into וְנָתַתִּי לָהֶם רְבִיבִים בְּעִתּוֹ, similar to Lev 26:4 and parallel to the second half of the verse. However, such reconstructions represent the rather drastic manipulation of the text based on an eclectic use of the versions. Mount Zion, as the place where God is enthroned or dwells, is often pictured in the OT as a source of blessing (e.g., Joel 4:16–21 [ET 3:16–21]; Micah 4:1–4; Ps 9:12–13 [ET 9:11–12]). The MT presents some challenges, but one can make sense of it without mutilation. See the commentary.

34:27 בְּשִׁבְרִי אֶת־מֹטוֹת עֻלָּם—The idiom "break [שָׁבַר] the bars [מֹטוֹת] of a yoke [עֹל]" occurs only here and in Lev 26:13. There too the idiom is accompanied by language for God's salvation (the exodus redemption). The figure of a yoke for enslavement is common (e.g., Is 9:3 [ET 9:4]; Jer 30:8).

הָעֹבְדִים בָּהֶם:—This is a circumlocution, literally, "those who do work by means of them," meaning "those who enslave them." This locution is relatively common in Jeremiah, but found also in, for example, Ex 1:14; Lev 25:39, 46.

34:29 מַטָּע לְשֵׁם—This literally means something like "a plantation for a name/ renown." Debate swirls around the words, both singly and in combination. It is not easy to find an adequate equivalent for מַטָּע in English. "Planting-place" sounds mod-

---

[11] Especially Zimmerli, *Ezekiel*, 2:210.

ern, and "plantation" has other overtones. The various translations offered are "plant" (KJV), "garden" (NKJV), "plantations" (RSV), and "vegetation" (NRSV). The one I have adopted is a modification of NIV's paraphrase, "a land renowned for its crops." The metaphor of God's people as his "planting," as such, is fairly common (e.g., Is 60:21; 61:3), intended as the obverse of the common figure of God uprooting his people from their land. It takes its place among the many idioms that describe God reversing the fortunes or turning of the tables for his people, especially after the Babylonian exile.

For לְשֵׁם the LXX and Syriac translate with "peace, prosperity," implying metathesis of the MT's consonants into שָׁ(וֹ)לֹם (the Targum may also support that reading). This does have a parallel in Lev 26:6, and, in view of the immunity from famine promised in the next clause, is usually taken as implying something like fertility or productivity. Some modern translations reflect this understanding: "prosperous plantations" (RSV), "splendid vegetation" (NRSV), and "a land renowned for its crops" (NIV). The point of my addition, "renowned for the *reliability* of its crops," is that in restoration prophecies, "plant(ing)" is a metaphor for permanency rather than fertility (cf. Micah 1:6). What God is doing will not be a simple hiatus in waves of invasion, exile, and return, but will be *the* fulfillment—the full dimensions of which have not even been revealed to us denizens of the interim between the first and second comings of the Good Shepherd and Son of David.

אֲסֻפֵי רָעָב—The verb אָסַף commonly means "gather, collect," but in this context, the Qal passive participle (masculine plural in construct) has the added nuance of "gather up and sweep away, carry off" (cf. Gen 30:23; Ps 26:9).

Israel's permanency of fruitful occupation will finally silence the mockery of the nations. Especially because of their devotion to the scandal of particularity—only one true God, who chose only one people, and from their lineage only one Savior—God's people often hear the gibe, "Where is their God?" Instead, the people of Israel will be renowned (שֵׁם), not for their virtues, but because it will be obvious that they are a people whom God has blessed out of his own grace.

34:30 It has been smoothed out in translation, but the combination of the symmetrical covenant formula of mutuality ("I am/will be their God, and they are/will be my people"; see, e.g., 37:27) with the assurance formula ("I am with ...") has upset the balance syntactically. If we translate the last part of the covenant formula of mutuality in the same order as the Hebrew we see this imbalance: "and they are my people, the house of Israel, says the Lord Yahweh." Meaning is not affected.

Zimmerli notes that "with them" is technically intrusive, while Allen says it "gilds the lily" and considers it a gloss bound up with another of his ingenuous reconstructions of 34:31.[12]

34:31 The clause "I am your God" does not include the usual Tetragrammaton before "your God" (as, e.g., in 20:5, 7).[13] Most of the ancient versions include it, but this

---

[12] Zimmerli, *Ezekiel*, 2:211; Allen, *Ezekiel*, 2:158.

[13] See page 9 in the introduction on Yahweh's self-introduction formula, "I am Yahweh," which

may be a harmonization because, as Zimmerli points out, the sentence also incorporates the covenant formula, which does not contain the divine name.[14]

The suffixed form מַרְעִיתִי ("my pasture") occurs only here in Ezekiel. Outside of Jer 23:1, מַרְעִית with a suffix denoting Yahweh is the language of the psalms (74:1; 79:13; 95:7; 100:3), reflected in the Venite: "we are the people *of his pasture* and the sheep of his hand."[15]

Commentary

Chapter 34 is probably one of the more familiar chapters of the book because of its shepherd theme, especially its Good Shepherd development in 34:11–31. Hence, it is naturally paralleled with Psalm 23 and with Jn 10:7–18, where our Lord Jesus identifies himself as ὁ ποιμὴν ὁ καλός, "the Good Shepherd" (Jn 10:11, 14), using language that seems to be drawn from Ezekiel 34. There plainly is a connection between this metaphor in Ezekiel and our Lord's depiction of the final judgment in Mt 25:32–46 (see the commentary on Ezek 34:17). Shepherd language also governs Lk 15:3–7. The stricture of Jude 12 against those who "shepherd themselves" clearly echoes Ezek 34:10, and in Rev 7:17, paradise is described as a place where "the Lamb ... will shepherd/feed [ποιμανεῖ] them."

In liturgical worship, Ezek 34:11–16 is the traditional Old Testament Reading for *Misericordias Domini*, the Second Sunday after Easter. In the Revised Common Lectionary and also in *Lutheran Worship* (1982) and the Three-Year Lectionary in *Lutheran Service Book* (2006), the Good Shepherd theme has been transferred to the Fourth Sunday of Easter (the Third Sunday after Easter). However, the Three-Year Lectionary substitutes pericopes from Acts in place of those from the OT during the Easter season, and so Ezekiel 34 disappears from that season. Ezek 34:11–16 is still listed for those who continue to use the One-Year Lectionary.[16]

In *Lutheran Service Book*, Ezek 34:11–16, 20–24 is the OT Reading in Series A, paired with Mt 25:31–46 as the Holy Gospel, for Proper 29, the Last Sunday of the Church Year, another traditional time for Good Shepherd Sunday. Also in *LSB*'s Three-Year Lectionary, in Series C, Ezek 34:11–24 is the OT Reading for Proper 19, whose Gospel is Lk 15:1–10, with Jesus' parable of the Lost Sheep, and whose Epistle is 1 Tim 1:5–17, with St. Paul's charge for the office of pastor.

Before we proceed with exegesis, we should recall how exceptionally widespread the metaphor of the shepherd was, not only in the Bible, but in the

---

is incorporated into the recognition formula, "(then) they/you will know that I am Yahweh" (on which, see also the commentary on 6:7).

[14] Zimmerli, *Ezekiel*, 2:211.

[15] The Venite (Psalm 95) is sung at the beginning of Matins (e.g., *LSB*, 220–21).

[16] Ezek 34:11–16 is the Old Testament Reading on the Fourth Sunday of Easter in *LW* and on the Third Sunday of Easter (the Second Sunday after Easter) in *LSB* (as in *TLH*).

entire ancient Near East. It is a classical case where the Bible adapts ("bap-
tizes") common imagery and terminology of its world in order that the whole
world can understand its message. In pagan literature, the picture is used of
both gods and men. The picture of gods as shepherds appears in some of our
earliest Mesopotamian (Sumerian) literature and is common in Egyptian literature as well. In Homer, Agamemnon, the leader of the Greeks against Troy, is
regularly styled "shepherd of the people."[17] In mythology, it is sometimes hard
to distinguish whether the shepherd is the god or his agent. In the incarnation
of God in Jesus Christ, of course, the two have fused once for all: his true human nature and true divine nature are united in his one person, as confessed in
the Athanasian Creed.

The OT usages are superficially very similar to those in the rest of the ancient world. Yahweh himself is often called or described as Israel's Shepherd,
for example, explicitly and most familiarly in Ps 23:1 (also, e.g., Is 40:11;
Micah 7:14; Ps 80:2 [ET 80:1]). Or the English noun (Hebrew participle) or
the verb "shepherd" may refer to a ruler appointed by God, for example, Moses
in Is 63:11; David in his political role in Ps 78:70–72; and even the pagan Persian king Cyrus, who had been called to deliver Israel, in Is 44:28, where the
Hebrew participle ("shepherd") is parallel to "messiah" (lowercased!) in Is
45:1.

Biblical usage seems to diverge from that of its neighbors in sometimes
pluralizing the term and applying it to the entire ruling class. Ezekiel 34 is an
example of that use of the metaphor. In the context, it appears likely that the
preexilic monarchy was primarily in Yahweh's mind, but sometimes it seems
likely the entire ruling class is included. Echoes of the motif are heard especially in the postexilic Zechariah 10–11. Ezekiel's slightly older contemporary,
Jeremiah, especially Jer 23:1–6, seems to have been influential for Ezekiel.
Both prophets are addressing their contemporary situations, but at the same
time their vision is often extended into the future eschatological and eternal
kingdom of God in Jesus Christ. Wherever we are situated on God's timeline,
unfaithful rulers and enemies must be eliminated at the same time the divine
kingdom is established, and in one way or another, the simultaneity of those
themes structures the next six chapters (Ezekiel 34–39).

Chapter 34 can readily be divided into three parts: (1) 34:1–10: the woe
oracle against derelict "shepherds"; (2) 34:11–22: Yahweh's rescue of his people from their enemies, both external and internal; and (3) 34:23–31: establishment of the messianic Shepherd and the "covenant of peace" (34:25), also
with nature, in a "new creation."

Judgment Oracle against Predatory "Shepherds" (34:1–10)

34:2–4 Without date or setting for chapter 34, it is impossible to determine just which unfaithful "shepherds" Ezekiel has in mind in these verses.

---

[17] E.g., Homer, *Iliad*, 2.243; *Odyssey*, 3.156.

But in my judgment, to try to specify a certain group at a certain time is beside the point. If one looks ahead towards the end of the chapter (especially 34:20–31), it becomes evident that Ezekiel's vision is not primarily political or this-worldly. A theocratic context might not have foreseen our (often secular) "separation of church and state." But if we use that formula, we must accent the "church" component. Yahweh's real concern is that Israel may be freed from "internal captivity"[18] and enjoy a different sort of freedom that only the Good Shepherd can establish, and that the NT repeatedly announces and proclaims. God's kingdom rarely was manifest to any great extent in the political order of ancient Israel, and likewise today, the current problems and conditions of society at most may supply the preacher with raw materials for the proclamation of what we need to be saved from.

Since the scope is biblical-eschatological, the reader will remember that a "now-not yet" soberness always attends it. Until the second coming of Christ, we shall continue to be plagued by evil shepherds of one sort or the other. If the application were political, one could easily find authorities whose chief conception of their office is self-aggrandizement. That will be our concern only to the extent that Christians in this world are involved in matters of government, "the kingdom of the left hand." But the proper application of the text is to the church in the broad, visible sense, and its relevance is always going to be apparent in the church militant on earth. The severest judgment will be for church leaders who lead their flocks astray from the truth of God's Word (Jn 17:17), particularly those who distort or ignore the person and work of Christ. It is always tempting to tone down or omit the harshness of the Law, which then empties the Gospel of its full consolation. Some infractions will likely not be with malice aforethought, but whether through incompetence or the "sin which so easily besets" (Heb 12:1) all fallen mankind, clergy certainly not excepted, Christ's flock is easily neglected, alienated, and abused by those called to be shepherds.

34:5–6 The verses describe the inevitable result of negligent and abusive shepherding. The language of sheep without a shepherd is very similar to Micaiah's description in 1 Ki 22:17 of Israel's army about to be routed. The evangelists use the same language for the lost, upon whom Christ has compassion (Mt 9:36; Mk 6:34). In Ezek 34:6 the picture of the dispersion is expanded from locales in Canaan to include "the whole earth."

The Hebrew syntax of יִשְׁגּוּ, "wandered," at the beginning of 34:6 is challenging (see the textual note). Functionally, however, it stresses that the straying was not only physical, but moral as well. The verb is used in such a sense in Ps 119:10, 21, 118, and in liturgical contexts for inadvertent or unwitting sins (e.g., Lev 4:13; Num 15:22; Ezek 45:20). It seems to be another of those cases where the literal, referential meaning (stray sheep) merges with the

---

[18] Block, *Ezekiel*, 2:277.

metaphorical and theological application to the Israelites. Their leaders' malevolence had resulted not only in the Babylonian captivity, but in syncretistic or simply pagan worship as well.

And, once again, *mutatis mutandis*, the picture is readily applicable to modern church life. Erstwhile members may be scattered for any number of reasons. Some, undoubtedly, will be found by other faithful "shepherds," but many will wander aimlessly and fall prey to sectarian blandishments or abandon the Christian faith entirely. And many a pastor knows that it is often harder to reclaim for the church the lapsed, especially if, rightly or wrongly, they feel they have been wronged, than it is to gain new converts.

34:10 This rather transitional verse describes the deposition of the unfaithful shepherds, which leads into the following description (34:11–22) of what the Good Shepherd will do for his flock. It opens with the so-called "hostile orientation formula," literally, "behold, I am against …"[19] The first assertion, which can hardly be translated literally, involves a play on the verb דָּרַשׁ. In 34:6, 8 that verb had its common force of "inquiring" or "concerning oneself about" (the unfaithful shepherds did not do that regarding the sheep). Here, followed by מִיָּדָם ("from their hand"), the verb has the semi-legal force of taking inventory of someone's stewardship, of requiring someone to give an account of what he has done with what was entrusted to him (cf. Mt 18:23; 25:19).

The direct object in the clause "and no longer will those shepherds shepherd them(selves)" (וְלֹא־יִרְעוּ עוֹד הָרֹעִים אוֹתָם), אוֹתָם is ambiguous, since it could refer to the sheep ("them"). However, in the light of the use of the same object (אוֹתָם) in 34:2 and 34:8, the reflexive translation, "themselves," seems very likely here too, and most modern translators take it in that sense. However, in the immediate context, a translation of "them" with flock as the antecedent is also possible, as the ancient versions generally construed it. Or must we choose? It makes sense if the suffix refers to both referents at the same time.

In the final two clauses, the false shepherds are described in the same way as the predatory wild beasts in 34:5, 8. This may be the background of our Lord's saying, which changes the picture only very slightly: "Watch out for false prophets, who come to you in the clothing of sheep, but inwardly are ravenous wolves" (Mt 7:15). The same strong metaphor is not completely inapplicable to the leaders of the church today in their dereliction.

Yahweh Rescues His Sheep from Their Enemies (34:11–22)

34:11–12 Again, the ministry of our Lord Jesus Christ is replete with imagery drawn from these verses (especially Mt 25:32–46; Lk 15:3–7; Jn 10:7–18). Jesus himself is the Shepherd (Heb 13:20; 1 Pet 2:25) who has come for "the lost sheep of the house of Israel" (Mt 15:24). Moreover, he sends his

---

[19] For this formula, see page 9 in the introduction and the commentary on 5:8.

apostles (and now pastors) as his undershepherds to gather "the lost sheep" (Mt 10:6).[20] That they are both to "tend" (ποιμαίνω) and "feed" (βόσκω) his "lambs" (Jn 21:15–17) has Eucharistic overtones.

The scattering of the sheep "on a day of clouds and thick darkness" (Ezek 34:12) would apply to the fall of Jerusalem in Ezekiel's day (Ezek 33:21–22) and to its destruction in A.D. 70, as well as to all the persecutions inflicted on the church (cf. the scattering resulting from the persecution in Acts 8:1; 11:19), but the apocalyptic language especially points to the return of Christ, when his elect shall be gathered from all the earth (Mt 24:29–31).

34:13 The three expressions at the beginning of the verse represent standard prophetic typology, referring to a preliminary "fulfillment" in Israel's return from the exile, but in total biblical perspective prophesying the ingathering of believers into the "promised land" of the *una sancta* ("one holy catholic and apostolic church" [Nicene Creed]), and even encompassing the final "communion of saints" of all times and places (cf. Ezek 20:34–35, 41–42; 36:24; 37:12, 21). "The mountains of Israel" (which will be featured twice again in the next verse) as the site of the ingathering of Israel represent again one of Ezekiel's favorite characterizations of the promised land. Here the phrase contrasts with its use in 34:6, where "the mountains" were the site of the people's previous leaderless dispersal.

It is interesting to note that although Ezekiel frequently speaks of "the land [אֲדָמָה] of Israel," he uses suffixed forms, "your/their land/ground," only in restoration oracles.

Although generally Ezekiel maintains the ovine and geographical metaphors, with mention of "settlements," the real referent intrudes briefly: the *people* of the true Israel, the church of both Testaments (Gal 6:16; Ephesians 2). When the return took place, the people would naturally rebuild their cities and villages. Explicit accent on the people will not become dominant until Ezek 34:25–31.

34:16 That no one was "searching for, seeking" (בָּקַשׁ, 34:4, 6) the sheep is remedied by the promise that Yahweh himself will do so (בָּקַשׁ, "seek," in 34:16), as fulfilled in the NT, when "the Son of Man came to *seek* and to save the lost" (Lk 19:10, with ζητέω, which the LXX uses in Ezek 34:4, 16; ἐκζητέω in 34:6). Likewise, Christ himself is the man who "seeks" the one lost sheep in Mt 18:12.

34:17 If there is any part of the chapter where we would love to have more historical context, it is in this verse and through 34:22. It obviously reflects conflicts within the community itself, presumably the one that had been exiled with Ezekiel in 597 B.C., possibly now augmented by some from the fresh wave of exiles that may have joined them after the city's fall in 586. Was

---

[20] For the relationship between Jesus sending his apostles in Matthew 10 and the pastoral office today, see Gibbs, *Matthew 1:1–11:1*, 507–9, 512–14.

there a reluctance by the earlier exiles to accept the impoverished newcomers? But aside from the book of Ezekiel itself, we have no other information about the community's internal affairs. The following verses indicate that the friction was partly between the ruled and the rulers, or at least those who had more power than others. One might speculate that—as the end of the previous chapter might already intimate—some within the community might have actually become repentant believers and were subjected to abuse by the majority, who remained impenitent. However, the book of Ezekiel does not give us clear evidence that any of those exiles who gathered around the prophet were yet believers. Of course, the book of Daniel reveals that some in the earliest group of exiles to Babylon were and remained believers (e.g., Daniel 1; Ezekiel in 14:14, 20 referred to Daniel as having "righteousness").

The key word is the verb שָׁפַט (34:17, 20, 22), conventionally translated "judge," together with its cognate noun מִשְׁפָּט ("I will shepherd them in *justice*," 34:16), usually rendered either "judgment" or "justice." For the verb, I have risked the rendition, "establish the rights." Talk of "rights" in our culture has become so thoroughly grounded in humanistic and various politically correct ideas that the traditional biblical and Christian use of the word has a difficult time making itself heard. But the Bible has much to say about how we treat one another, both in the church and in the realm of quotidian affairs, theologically founded in the original creation of man and woman in the "image" of the triune God (Gen 1:26–27). Lost in the fall, that image was proleptically restored in the covenant with Israel, climaxing in the "new covenant" in the blood of Christ, who is himself the image of God, and in whom the image is being restored to us.[a] In the light of the explicit Messianism at the end of the chapter (34:23–31), such a horizon cannot be dismissed. Moreover, in Ezek 34:22 Yahweh will "establish rights" (שָׁפַט) by "saving" his flock (see the commentary on 34:18–22).

If we may again extrapolate a bit farther to the interim between the first and second comings of Christ, all kinds of possible applications present themselves. The unity of the *una sancta* ("*one* holy catholic and apostolic church" [Nicene Creed]) is often anything but empirically evident. The "party spirit" exhibited by St. Paul's list of "the works of the flesh" (Gal 5:19–21) readily rears its ugly head, and on all kinds of pretexts. Techniques of "conflict resolution" may be usable, but one runs the risk of depending on secular psychology and sociology and covering it with a very thin theological veneer. What is needed is the proper application of Law, which puts to death the sinful flesh, and of the Gospel, which raises the believer to the new life of faith (e.g., Romans 6).

This pericope may well be the chief OT preparation for Jesus' famous depiction of the last judgment in Mt 25:32–46 (see also 1 Pet 5:4). This passage's similarity to the words of our Lord may be attributed to its inspiration by the Holy Spirit. However, the correspondence is not exact. Here it is a separation of "fat" sheep from "lean" sheep (Ezek 34:20, expounding on this verse), while in the Gospel the division is between sheep, who enter eternal life in the king-

(a) Rom 8:29; 1 Cor 15:49; 2 Cor 3:18; 4:4; Col 1:15; 3:10

dom prepared for them, and goats, who are consigned eternally to the flames of hell prepared for the devil and his angels. Yet the reasons for the separation are similar: both involve treatment of believers. Here within God's covenant people, the strong have marginalized and treated the weak lovelessly. In Matthew the judgment turns upon whether or not faith is evident in one's practice, specifically in respect to showing Christian love and charity to needy Christians ("my brothers," Christ calls them); such works of love are done (or not done) to Christ himself. Finally, here the conflict seems to be within the community of Israelites, which (like the visible church) included both believers and unbelieving hypocrites, while Matthew 25 is more clearly about unbelievers (especially those outside the church) versus Christians, who comprise the body of Christ.

34:18–22 The animal metaphor is perfectly clear to anyone who has worked around livestock. But, again, the precise occasion or application here eludes us. The general context suggests dysfunction in the community of Israelite exiles. Some of the vocabulary echoes the preexilic situation, for example, the "scattered" of 34:21 harks back to 34:5, and the בַּז ("plunder") of 34:22 uses language for human warfare, as in 34:8 (which see).

Possibly the most heavily laden vocable in 34:22 theologically is וְהוֹשַׁעְתִּי, "I will save," expanding on וְהִצַּלְתִּי ("I will rescue them") in 34:12, and, of course, pointing forward to the ministry of Jesus Christ, whose first advent accomplished our salvation by his cross and whose second advent will usher in our complete rescue from all the effects of sin and evil in this fallen world. Especially in this context, the negative connotation usually associated with "judge" makes that translation for וְשָׁפַטְתִּי ("I will establish the rights") completely misleading (see the commentary on 34:17).

One can hardly help but think of the misleadingly entitled book of "Judges," named after the שֹׁפְטִים (participle of שָׁפַט) therein. In the body of that book, the verb שָׁפַט, "judge, administer," is frequently used for the leaders whom God raises up to organize fractured Israel, turn them from idolatry, and lead the people to renewed faithfulness to their God and to victory over their oppressors. As the narratives illustrate, they are often and rightly referred to also as "savior[s]" who "saved" the people (Hiphil of יָשַׁע, e.g., Judg 2:16, 18; 3:9, 15, 31; 6:14–15), since Yahweh himself saved his people through them (Hiphil of יָשַׁע, Judg 6:36–37). Because the salvation God accomplished through the judges very much involved theology, we rightly consider them types (prefigurements) of *the* Savior, Jesus Christ. In Ezekiel 34, Yahweh does not speak of undershepherds who minister on his behalf, but only of his own action and that of the one Shepherd. Nevertheless, in the history of salvation, the lines of the OT judges (also of the prophets, priests, and kings) do ultimately converge with that of the Messiah in the subject matter with which the chapter continues and concludes.

One could also append the various other passages where terms for "save" (or "salvation") and "judge(ment)" are used side by side describing divine redemption.[b] And then we should recall the crucial role this breakthrough meant in Luther's understanding of Scripture, which gave rise to the Reformation: the righteousness of God and his activity of judging are revealed not only in his condemnation of the sins of unbelievers, but in his justification of believers in Christ through faith alone (e.g., Rom 1:16–17).[21]

(b) E.g., Is 33:22; 51:5; Obad 21; Pss 54:3 (ET 54:1); 72:4; cf. Hos 13:4, 10

The Messianic Shepherd, "My Servant David" (34:23–31)

34:23–24 So much is packed in these two verses that one could almost construct an OT Christology from them.

The opening verb, "I will raise up" (וַהֲקִמֹתִי, Hiphil of קוּם), is a standing expression for the establishment of some person in a position through God's interposition. Moses uses it in Deut 18:15, 18 for God's promise to establish the Prophet like Moses, that is, Christ (Acts 3:22; 7:37). Elsewhere in the OT it is employed to describe Yahweh's appointment of all sorts of figures: prophets (Amos 2:11), priests (1 Sam 2:35), and kings (1 Ki 14:14; Jer 30:9). Often it is used for God establishing his gracious covenant.[c] The point here is that this "Shepherd" will not be self-appointed nor selected by popular referendum; his sole source and authority is God.

(c) E.g., Gen 9:9, 11, 17; 17:7, 19, 21; 26:3; Ex 6:4; Lev 26:9; Deut 8:18; Ezek 16:60, 62

Some debate turns about the import of the use of אֶחָד, "*one* Shepherd" (which in other contexts can merely be the sign of an indefinite noun). The antithesis is probably twofold: both the many evil shepherds of the past and especially the two competing kings of the divided empire after the death of Solomon. Only a single ruler under Yahweh could provide the unity and consistency necessary for a united and faithful people. We probably have here an initial statement of the refrain heard in all the prophets who address the topic: the eschatological restoration of the united monarchy. As he often does in Ezekiel, Yahweh here merely suggests or adumbrates a topic he will later expand much more fully. In this case, the full treatment comes in 37:16–24, where the word אֶחָד, "one," will occur no less than eleven times.

Of course, Jesus draws on 34:23 when, in Jn 10:16, he refers to other sheep (Gentiles) that he must gather into "one flock" under himself as the "one Shepherd." The one church spanning both Testaments consists of all believers in Christ, both Jews and Gentiles (e.g., Gal 3:26–29; 6:16; Ephesians 2). All who are under the "one Shepherd" are part of God's one flock; conversely, all who refuse to submit to this one Shepherd are not.

"My Servant David" or similar phrases are standing titles of King David.[d] The noun עֶבֶד, "servant," is so structured in biblical theology that its use can hardly even be surveyed here. It is typically used of those who stood in some official position and especially of those chosen for a special task. In addition to David, phrases indicating that the person was a "servant" of Yahweh are used of Abraham (Gen 26:24; Ps 105:6, 42), Isaac (Gen 24:14), Jacob/Israel (Ezek

(d) E.g., 1 Ki 11:34, 36, 38; 2 Ki 8:19; Pss 36:1 (ET superscription); 78:70

---

[21] See, e.g., AE 25:149–53; Ap IV 67, 230; FC Ep VI 5; FC SD III 20, 54.

28:25; 37:25; 1 Chr 16:13), Moses (often, e.g., Ex 14:31; Josh 18:7), and others, particularly the Suffering Servant in Isaiah.[22] Such phrases are used of David thirty-one times in the OT. They accent not only David's obedience in contrast to the insubordination of the "shepherds" of Ezek 34:1–10, but also his election (1 Ki 11:34; cf. Is 42:1).[23]

Our concern here is with the servant David, whose forty-year reign (ca. 1000–960 B.C.) preceded Ezekiel by some four centuries. The basic source of expectations about the "house" of David is Nathan's oracle to David (2 Samuel 7 ‖ 1 Chronicles 17; cf. Is 9:5–6 [ET 9:6–7]; Psalm 89). There the promise is made of the perpetuity of David's dynasty through his Son; it will last "forever" (עוֹלָם is used repeatedly). Jeremiah summarizes it classically in 33:17, 20–21, 25–26. In the earlier pastoral context of Ezekiel 34, it is perhaps not coincidental that David had been called from the נָוֶה ("pastoral encampment," the same term in Ezek 34:14) to be a נָגִיד ("ruler") over Israel (2 Sam 7:8). Samuel avoids the label מֶלֶךְ, "king," as assiduously as Ezekiel does, and for comparable reasons.[24]

The election and survival of the people of Israel was inextricably bound up with Yahweh's covenant with David. Inevitably, the fall of Jerusalem and the carrying of the Davidic descendant King Jehoiachin into captivity with Ezekiel had called all this into question. But Yahweh's promises could not fail, and so one should not be surprised that faithful Israel's hopes in and after the exile should be formulated in terms of the kingship of David. How significant this hope was after the return is obvious, where צֶמַח, "Branch" (earlier used by Is 4:2; Jer 23:5; 33:15) has all but become a proper noun for the Messiah (Zech 3:8; 6:12). Even though among first-century Jews this hope became contaminated with dreams of political liberation, its centrality in the NT faith needs no demonstration here.[25]

For all of its importance, it is strange how infrequently the OT names "David" when speaking of the future King. (Alternate expressions of "Zion" language contribute to the thought, however.) The earliest is found in the eighth-century prophets, including Hos 3:5, where the "Israelites" (Northern Kingdom?) will return "to David their King," and Isaiah's references to the future reign of the Son on the throne of "David" (Is 9:6 [ET 9:7]); 16:5; cf. also Is 7:2, 13–14; 22:22; 55:3). Almost contemporaneously with Ezekiel, Jer 30:9

---

22 Is 42:1–9; 49:1–13; 50:4–11; and 52:13–53:12. Mt 8:17 explicitly cites Is 53:4.

23 Mt 12:18–21 quotes Is 42:1–4, the longest such explicit OT citation in Matthew's Gospel. Of course, Is 42:1 is also a key passage behind the Father's declaration about his incarnate Son on the occasion of his Baptism (Mt 3:17 and parallels). See Gibbs, *Matthew 1:1–11:1*, 182–84.

24 See further below. See also the second textual note on 7:27; the commentary on 12:10; and the second textual note on 21:30 (ET 21:25).

25 For example, Mt 2:23 quotes the word spoken by "the prophets" that Jesus would be called a Ναζωραῖος, "Nazarene," perhaps a verbal allusion to the OT prophecies of a *netser*, "Branch." See Gibbs, *Matthew 1:1–11:1*, 131–34.

prophesies that the returning exiles "will serve Yahweh their God and David their King."

Nowhere do we find metaphysical speculation about the nature of the relation between the historically past David and the coming "David." The phrase "David *redivivus*" is sometimes used, but there is no indication that this ever involved physical resurrection or something else paranormal (cf. Mt 14:2; 16:14). Other than genealogical descent, the accent is on the future Ruler who will establish God's rule, forgive sins, be completely faithful to God, and the like.

Ezek 34:23–24 seeks to explain how the future David's power will manifest the power of Yahweh himself. We can only expect to find here in the OT a foretaste of the full Trinitarian and theanthropic Christology we find in the NT. But here we have the assertion that the future Ruler will feed and govern the people in perfect unity with God, perfectly carrying out God's will, and not placing himself in opposition to God, as the evil shepherds had done. Since the advent of Christ, Jewish interpreters have tended to suppose that messianic predictions can be read as though the "Messiah" were merely an earthly administrator, rather than God incarnate (contrary to, e.g., Is 7:14; 9:5–6 [ET 9:6–7]; Ps 45:7 [ET 45:6]). The little of Judaism that still concerns itself with a personal Messiah is of such a subordinationistic and non-Trinitarian sort (and much of Judaism has devolved into the mere hope for some ill-defined "messianic age," or even into secular humanism). However, as the long historical record of OT monarchs shows, no sinful human ruler—not even David himself—could ever begin to fulfill the prophetic depiction of a wholly faithful ruler whose reign would endure forever. From a NT perspective, of course, the "difficulty" resolves itself, because Christ is both true, eternal God and also the man who is the Father's "agent" on earth to do his will perfectly.

Here the unity of purpose between God and his Ruler is formulated by quoting half of the covenant formula of mutuality, "I, Yahweh, will be their God," which is followed by the non-metaphoric "David will be Prince among them" (34:24), a restatement of the metaphoric "he will be their Shepherd" at the end of the previous verse. From here on, we have no more metaphoric language about sheep and shepherds until the closing verse (34:31), and in the final two verses, 34:30–31, both halves of the covenant formula of mutuality are also expressed: "I, Yahweh, their God, am with them, and ... they, the house of Israel, are my people" (34:30; 34:31 restates the first half of the formula, "I am your God," but emphasizes the second half using ovine imagery).

Ezekiel designates the future "David" as a נָשִׂיא, "Prince" (34:24). For the word's significance, see further the commentary on 37:25. It is conventionally translated "prince," although "ruler" or "chief" might arguably be better. In premonarchial days, it seems to have been used of the leader of a given tribe (cf. Num 2:3–29). 1 Ki 11:34 suggests that, with the rise of the monarchy, the term became more generic. Yahweh says of Solomon, "I will make him a נָשִׂיא all the days of his life for the sake of David my servant." Perhaps the term could be used synonymously with מֶלֶךְ, "king," with no pejorative connotations. In

chapters 40–48, Ezekiel continues to speak of this same Davidic ruler, Jesus Christ, as נָשִׂיא, "Prince," focusing on his role as the official sponsor and patron of the liturgical worship centered at the eschatological temple. One might see a preview of that usage here. It is also likely, both here and there, that Ezekiel prefers נָשִׂיא ("Prince") to מֶלֶךְ ("King") to underscore the difference between the coming David and the previous unfaithful rulers in David's line.

That this Prince will be among the people suggests identification with them[26] as well as authority ("over them," 34:23). (One recalls the prophecy of Deut 18:15 that the eschatological Prophet will be "from your midst.") In this case, we probably should invoke the repeated Pentateuchal affirmation, sometimes expressed as part of the covenant formula of mutuality (and "incarnated" in the tabernacle and later the temple), that Yahweh would "dwell" (שָׁכַן, an "incarnational" word) in the midst of his people (Ex 25:8; 29:45–46; Num 5:3; 35:34). That is, the future David will incarnate the gracious presence of Yahweh among his people, a presence that the Holy Spirit continues to effect among us, not only "spiritually," but sacramentally in water (Holy Baptism), bread and wine (the Lord's Supper), and the spoken Word of God.

34:25 Although connected with the preceding by a *waw* consecutive (וְכָרַתִּי), the horizon broadens considerably in the following verses. We hear no more of sheep and shepherds nor of David, although, functionally, they should be kept in mind. Rather, reusing some of the picture found in previous verses, Ezekiel paints a landscape that approaches a "new creation" (cf. Isaiah 11 and 65; Revelation 21–22).

This first verse functions as a thesis statement for the entire section. For it to be intelligible, one must remember what a deficient translation of שָׁלוֹם our usual "peace" is. Etymologically, the root (שׁלם) implies a wholeness, a harmony, or an integrity of whatever the subject is, and sometimes "salvation" is appropriate (cf. Num 6:26). And a בְּרִית, "covenant," is a pact, treaty, promise, or binding relationship. With it Yahweh uses the idiomatic כָּרַת, "to cut" (as also in, e.g., Gen 15:18; Ex 24:8; Deut 5:2–3), and probably to reinforce that this does not imply a bilateral, conditional agreement, he does not employ a preposition meaning "with," but rather לְ, "*for* them." In that way, God accents the monergistic, unconditional nature of his covenant of grace, by which he alone fully accomplishes his people's salvation.[27] That accent is especially pronounced if one compares the following verses with Lev 26:3–13, which Yahweh reworks and adapts in the following verses. In Lev 26:3–13 everything was presented as a reward by grace to his faithful people, while here all is a free gift from God to his people.

---

[26] Thus when the people are being baptized by John, Jesus presents himself among them to be baptized, and so the sinless Son takes the place of all sinners to be the bearer of their sins (Lk 3:21; 12:50).

[27] With "covenant," other passages use the verbs הֵקִים, "establish" (e.g., Gen 6:18; 9:9, 11, 17; 17:7, 19, 21; Ex 6:4) or נָתַן, "give" (e.g., Gen 15:18; 17:2; cf. Is 42:6; 49:8) to convey that same accent on God's monergism.

The concept of "a covenant of peace" is not entirely unique to Ezekiel, although he expounds it in his own unique way. A key parallel appears in Is 54:7–10 (especially 54:10), but that entire passage points back to God's postdiluvian covenant with Noah (Genesis 9) as setting the pattern for the content of "a covenant of peace." Elsewhere, the phrase itself appears only one other time outside of Ezekiel, the special context of Num 25:12, where Yahweh uses the phrase in rewarding Phinehas for his courageous behavior that had averted God's wrath. In Ezekiel, it is used again in 37:26, which is essentially an alternate version of the present text. The thought is similar to the "everlasting covenant" (בְּרִית עוֹלָם) of 16:60, where Yahweh promises to remember and restore the covenant he made with the wayward waif Jerusalem in her youth.

This verse announces the first of three types of divine activity Ezekiel uses to describe the experience of his covenant. (The second and third are in 34:26–27.) It is the elimination of predatory animals from the land, animals that had earlier been described as agents of divine punishment (5:17; 14:15, 21; 33:27). Hosea (2:20 [ET 2:18]) had already expressed this thought. In the absence of those predators, security (לָבֶטַח, "securely," Ezek 34:25, 27, 28; also 38:8, 11, 14; 39:6, 26) is repeatedly highlighted as a central gift. When God has reestablished perfect "peace" (שָׁלוֹם), as he had originally created it, there will be nothing to fear. Ezek 34:28 will restate these themes.

34:26 Second, Yahweh will give security by blessing the land with great fruitfulness, a theme reiterated in 34:29. The Hebrew idiomatic construction "to make [נָתַן] something into something else" implies a change from one state into another: "I will make them and the area around my hill a blessing." If the antecedent of "them" is the previously mentioned uninhabitable deserts and forests, here called "the area around my hill," the idea is clearly that the now destroyed temple (in contrast to the illicit cult sites on "every high hill" in 34:6) and its environs will become a "blessing." The precise nuance here is debated: "examples of blessedness," "evidences of divine blessing," or "sources of blessing" for others (as in Gen 12:2). In OT usage, "blessing" tends to imply what we would call "material blessings" as tangible evidence of God's grace, but "spiritual" blessings are by no means excluded—and, since it was assumed that God was the giver of both, probably OT believers would not even have distinguished them.

In this context, the proper amount of rain at the right time is clearly the main application. This would be of special concern for an agrarian society, but ultimately, it is anywhere. When rain is mentioned the second time and called "rains of blessing," the phrase probably parallels "in its season," that is, not גֶּשֶׁם שֹׁטֵף, "a driving rain" (as in 13:11, 13; 38:22), which can be very destructive. "In its season" probably also refers to what the Bible often particularizes as "early rain and late rain" (יוֹרֶה וּמַלְקוֹשׁ, Deut 11:14; Jer 5:24). For the farmer, it was important that the seasonal rains started early (end of October through the beginning of December), so he could get his crops into the ground early enough, and that the rains continued late enough (March–April) that the heads of grain would fill out properly, cisterns would be filled, and so on. Here the more generic גֶּשֶׁם, "rain," is used here instead of a specific term for "early rain" or "late rain."

How does the "the area around my hill," that is, the temple mount and the vicinity, enter into this picture? As mentioned earlier, Yahweh was present in a special "incarnational" way in the temple and would naturally be pictured as the controlling source of the weather. But since the picture is semi-eschatological, Greenberg may correctly remind us of a comparable picture in 47:1–12 (cf. Joel 4:18 [ET 3:18]; Zech 14:8; Rev 22:1–2) where "another melioration of nature appears," as the river of life flows from the temple (or the city) and fructifies the environs.[28] Since the garden of Eden was pictured as being on a mountain in Ezek 28:14–16 (see the commentary on 28:14), the overtones are clearly that of "paradise restored."

34:27 Third, using a modified version of the recognition formula,[29] God describes the people's liberation and restoration as a second exodus: "and (they will) know that I am Yahweh when I break the bars of their yoke and rescue them from the hand of those who enslaved them." Christians will realize that this is not yet clearly *the* exodus accomplished by Christ (ἔξοδος, "exodus," in Lk 9:31), but if one thinks in terms of phases or aspects of the totality, it clearly is one preliminary antitype, which in turn becomes a springboard for the ultimate fulfillment. As in many prophecies, how much was given to Ezekiel himself to see is impossible to say, but, again as often, probably God's whole future is being telescoped into one vision, in which the individual details or phases might be difficult to distinguish (cf. 1 Pet 1:10–12). The comparison is often made between prophetic visions and a view of a distant mountain range: the observer cannot readily discern the distances between the peaks, and closer ones might appear higher than loftier but more distant ones.

34:30 The more external aspects of "blessing" (34:26) that have been featured so far in 34:25–29 now fade into the background at the climax of the pericope, and all attention focuses on the Gospel of the "new covenant" (although that precise phrase is not used). The formulation involves another modification of the recognition formula that includes two other elements: a slightly modified *covenant formula of mutuality*, strengthened by the naming of the two parties (cf. 2 Cor 6:16; Rev 21:7), "I, Yahweh, their God, am with them, and … they, the house of Israel, are my people," which incorporates *an assurance formula*, "I … am with them" (cf. Mt 28:20; Acts 18:10). The signatory formula, "says the Lord Yahweh,"[30] serves as a divine imprimatur. Any biblically literate Christian will find it easy to flesh out these standing formulae with Christological specificity. Having been baptized into Christ's death and resur-

---

[28] Greenberg, *Ezekiel*, 2:703.

[29] For this formula, see page 9 in the introduction and the commentary on 6:7.

[30] For this formula, see pages 8–9 in the introduction and the second textual note on 5:11.

rection (Rom 6:3), we now live in Christ (Rom 6:11), and on the Last Day we will be raised to live with him forever (1 Cor 15:22).

34:31 The apparent purpose of this addendum is to relate the intervening verses (34:23–30) to the shepherd-flock imagery of the first part of the chapter (34:1–22), thus forming a sort of inclusio for the whole. We note this immediately by the same kind of inconsistency of gender we saw at the beginning. The initial feminine plural אַתֵּן, "you" (the only occurrence of this form in the OT), refers to the "flock" metaphor, and the subsequent masculine plural אַתֶּם, "you," moves from the image to the reality—the people. That the "flock" was, indeed, the people of Israel is signaled by reversing the order of the covenant formula of mutuality, first, "you are my sheep" instead of "people," and then second, "I am your God."

"You are men" (אָדָם) seems intrusive, and the LXX does omit it, leaving a much simpler, unencumbered sentence. But we have no real warrant to delete it (though RSV and NRSV do). What is the point of the word? I am attracted to Keil's quotation of Hengstenberg: the words "call attention to the depth and greatness of the divine condescension, and meet the objection of men of weak faith, that man, who is taken from the earth הָאֲדָמָה,[31] and returns to it again, is incapable of so intimate a connection with God."[32] In the incarnation of Jesus Christ, God the eternal Son condescended to become a man (but without sin) in order to redeem all people ("who for us men and for our salvation …" [Nicene Creed]). All in Christ are God's flock, which he shall preserve forevermore: "Behold, the dwelling place of God is with men. He will dwell with them, and they will be his people, and God himself will be with them as their God" (Rev 21:3).

---

[31] Hengstenberg is alluding to Gen 2:7. Note that in Hebrew, אָדָם, "man," is spelled with the first three letters of אֲדָמָה, "earth."

[32] Keil, *Ezekiel*, 2:92.

An Oracle against Mount Seir

Translation

35 ¹The Word of Yahweh came to me: ²"Son of man, set your face against Mount Seir and prophesy against it: ³Say to it, 'Thus says the Lord Yahweh: I am against you, Mount Seir; I will stretch out my hand against you and make you an utter desolation. ⁴I will make your cities ruins, and you will be desolate. Then you will know that I am Yahweh. ⁵Because you cherished an ancient grudge and turned the Israelites over to the sword at the time of their disaster, at the time of [their] final punishment, ⁶therefore, as I live, says the Lord Yahweh, I will make you blood, and blood will pursue you. As you were a blood enemy, blood will pursue you. ⁷I will make Mount Seir an utter desolation and cut off from it all who come and go. ⁸I will fill its mountains with its slain; on your hills and in your valleys and all your ravines those slain by the sword will fall. ⁹I will make you eternal desolations, and your cities will not be reinhabited. Then you will know that I am Yahweh.

¹⁰" 'Because you said, "These two nations and these two lands will be mine, and we will possess it," even though Yahweh was there, ¹¹therefore, as I live, says the Lord Yahweh, I will treat you in accordance with your anger and your fanaticism with which you, in your enmity, treated them, and I will make myself known among them when I punish you. ¹²Then you will know that I, Yahweh, have heard all the blasphemies that you uttered against the mountains of Israel: "They have been desolated and given to us for food." ¹³With your mouth you made big boasts against me and multiplied arrogant words against me. I have heard it myself.

¹⁴" 'Thus says the Lord Yahweh: When the whole world rejoices, I will make you a desolation. ¹⁵As you rejoiced over the possession of the house of Israel because it was desolate, so will I treat you. You will be desolate, Mount Seir, and the whole of Edom, all of it. Then they will know that I am Yahweh.' "

Textual Notes

35:1–15   See the map "The Ancient Near East."

35:2 בֶּן־אָדָ֫ם—For Ezekiel as a "son of man/Adam," see the second textual note and the commentary on 2:1.

שִׂ֤ים פָּנֶ֙יךָ֙ עַל—This idiom is translated "set your face *against*," as in 29:2. It may be synonymous with, or show more hostility than, the idiom שִׂ֤ים פָּנֶ֙יךָ֙ אֶל in 6:2; 13:17; 21:7 (ET 21:2); 25:2; 28:21; 38:2. See the second textual note on 6:2.

35:3 וּנְתַתִּ֤יךָ שְׁמָמָ֖ה וּמְשַׁמָּֽה—This same vocabulary was in 6:14 and 33:28–29, and as there, the two synonymous nouns are translated as a hendiadys, "a desolate waste" or "an utter desolation."

35:5 יַעַן הֱיֹות לְךָ אֵיבַת עֹולָם—This protasis of Yahweh's charge against Edom says, literally, "because there was to you enmity of eternity," that is, "you had," but something like "cherish, nurture, harbor, nurse" scarcely can be considered overexegesis. Whether individually or corporately, people really do "love to hate" someone or something. For אֵיבָה, first used in Gen 3:15!, "enmity" is commonly used, although when it smolders, lying in wait for a chance to implement itself (cf. Gen 4:7), "grudge" is also accurate. Compare the bumper sticker "Don't get mad. Get even." The same construct phrase, אֵיבַת עֹולָם, was used in 25:15 for the Philistines' animosity toward Israel, but they apparently disappear from history a little before Jerusalem's fall, while the Edomites remain on the scene at least until the time of Christ.

וַתַּגֵּר אֶת־בְּנֵי־יִשְׂרָאֵל עַל־יְדֵי־חָרֶב—The Hiphil of נָגַר (second masculine singular imperfect with *waw* consecutive) is used for "pouring out" liquids (e.g., Ps 75:9 [ET 75:8]). However, it is also used metaphorically with the same prepositional phrase as here ("to the hands of the sword") in Jer 18:21 and Ps 63:11 (ET 63:10) for giving people over to the sword. In 2 Sam 14:14 the wise woman of Tekoa uses the Niphal to compare human mortality to "water *spilled* on the ground." The metaphor here was probably occasioned by the mention of blood in the next verse. In fact, KJV paraphrases here: "hast shed *the blood of* ..." (similarly NKJV).

בְּעֵת אֵידָם—The noun אֵיד, "disaster, calamity," is not rare, but occurs only here in Ezekiel. Its suffixed form here, אֵידָם, is obviously assonant with both אֱדֹום, "Edom" (35:15), and with דָּם in 35:6. Together with עֵת, "time," here, it is almost a technical term for "day of disaster" (as יֹום אֵיד is often translated in, e.g., Deut 32:35; Jer 18:17; Obad 13). Of the four times in the OT where אֵיד refers to the fall of Jerusalem, three appear in oracles against Edom: here; Jer 49:8; and Obad 13. (In Jer 49:32 it is applied to Hazor.)

בְּעֵת עֲוֹן קֵץ—This Ezekelianism (also in 21:30, 34 [ET 21:25, 29]) is parallel to the preceding phrase for the "disaster" and is, literally, "at the time of punishment of (the) end." עָוֹן is not used in its common sense of "guilt, iniquity," but the full measure of it, which brings a "final punishment." קֵץ, "end," referring to Jerusalem's, was prominent in Ezekiel 7.

35:6 This apodosis, describing Yahweh's response to Edom's perfidy, is full of difficulties; interpretations differ. The word דָּם is used four times in various applications.

חַי־אָנִי נְאֻם אֲדֹנָי יְהוִה—Probably to emphasize how seriously Yahweh takes the matter, he opens it with an oath of self-assertion ("as I live"),[1] followed by the signatory formula ("says the Lord Yahweh").[2] Two different asseverations follow, each consisting of two clauses. The concluding part of the oath formula, starting with אִם־לֹא, does not appear until the second asseveration (see the fourth textual note on 35:6).

כִּי־לְדָם אֶעֶשְׂךָ וְדָם יִרְדְּפֶךָ—This first asseveration uses the particle כִּי, "that," which is used after חַי־אָנִי נְאֻם יהוה also in Is 49:18; Jer 22:24; and Zeph 2:9. "Into blood I will make you" clearly refers to the shedding of Edomite blood. It has a meaning similar to וּנְתַתִּיךְ דָּם, "I will make you blood," in 16:38 (which see). The country

---

[1] For this formula, see page 9 in the introduction.

[2] For this formula, see pages 8–9 in the introduction and the second textual note on 5:11.

will become "blood" (דָּם), which its Hebrew name (אֱדוֹם, 35:15) suggests. Beginning with KJV, most English translations have something like "I will prepare you for blood" (ESV), but that strikes me as too free. NIV's "I will give you over to bloodshed" is more literal and conveys the sense. So too would "I will make you bloody."

The second half of the first asseveration (וְדָם יִרְדְּפֶךָ) will be repeated as the second half of the second asseveration. In it, the metaphor changes. The language of the law of asylum is tapped, and, in fact, seems to govern the rest of the entire verse. The blood of Edom's victims (apparently murdered "in cold blood") is personified and it "will pursue" (the only place Ezekiel uses רָדַף), as its own avenger, the one who shed it, just as the victim's kinsman who was "the redeemer of blood" (גֹּאֵל הַדָּם, e.g., Num 35:19) pursued the killer, at least until the killer could reach one of the six cities of refuge and his innocence or guilt could be established (Num 35:6–34; Deut 19:1–13; Josh 20:1–9). We first hear this kind of personification of shed blood in Gen 4:10, where Abel's blood cries out to God for vengeance, and Ezekiel himself had used the image of shed blood personified in 24:7–8.

Since the entire first asseveration is missing in the LXX, many critics would delete it, alleging that it was an originally marginal dittograph of the second asseveration. But its presence in the Vulgate and Targum attests to its antiquity and originality.

אִם־לֹא דָם שָׂנֵאתָ וְדָם יִרְדֲּפֶךָ׃—This is the second asseveration. It is important to note that לֹא belongs to the oath language, and as part of an oath אִם־לֹא is a strong affirmative. Therefore the first half of the second asseveration is דָם שָׂנֵאתָ, literally, "blood you hated." Apparently it follows the same line of thought as the first asseveration, but expresses it very compactly—almost obscurely, unless it is citing some ancient maxim or formula of which we are unaware. To describe Edom as "hating blood" or as "an enemy of blood" initially sounds, at best, as the very opposite of what the context would require. It must mean that Edom in its hatred shed blood, so it is translated, "you were a blood enemy," that is, an enemy who shed the blood of its foes. Thus the MT appears to express in asylum terms a clear symmetry: the punishment (pursuit) will match the crime. Edom had acted out of sheer blood enmity, that is, sheer hostility toward life, because "the blood is life" (Deut 12:23), not inadvertently or in self-defense. Therefore justice demanded that blood pursue Edom until its own blood is shed.

Most English translations do not regard אִם־לֹא as part of the oath language and so take לֹא as negating the verb שָׂנֵאתָ, for example, "you did *not* hate bloodshed" (ESV). But that leads to an illogical assertion: "since you did *not* hate blood, blood will pursue you." Keil suggests that לֹא was separated from the verb to avoid a collision of דָם, which precedes the verb, with וְדָם, which follows the verb,[3] but this seems to me like a desperate rationalization that loses sight of the asylum metaphor. Following the LXX (εἰς αἷμα ἥμαρτες), many commentators assume that the verb here was אָשֵׁם and translate, "you have incurred guilt with respect to blood," somewhat as in 22:4 and 25:12, but that too loses the asylum metaphor.

---

[3] Keil, *Ezekiel*, 2:97.

35:7 לְשְׁמָמָה וּשְׁמָמָה—The vocalization שְׁמָמָה occurs only here in the OT. Some critics allege that it is a misvocalization, or even that this phrase is a greater scribal error for שְׁמָמָה וּמְשַׁמָּה (see the textual note on 35:3). But it seems unlikely that such a common phrase would be miscopied, and even less likely that the error would be perpetuated. שְׁמָמָה is probably a simple dissimilated form of the following common word שְׁמָמָה used for variation, but the variation is impossible to reproduce in English. Other verses attest a word repeated but with slightly different vocalization, for example, אָנֶה וָאָנָה in 1 Ki 2:36 and כָּזֹה וְכָזֶה in 2 Sam 11:25.

וְהִכְרַתִּי מִמֶּנּוּ עֹבֵר וָשָׁב:—The desolation of the land is expressed in different words by God cutting off from it עֹבֵר וָשָׁב, two Qal participles that form a merism, literally, "he who goes and he who returns," that is, all human traffic. The phrase occurs elsewhere only in Zech 7:14 and 9:8, with a similar usage in Ex 32:27.

35:8 Alternating between second and third person forms is something Ezekiel does quite insouciantly throughout the book. After the third person singular לֹו, "to him/it," in the first clause of 35:3, referring to Mount Seir, second person masculine singular forms were used in 35:3–6, until the third masculine singular forms in 35:7, which continue into 35:8a. Then 35:8b–15 uses second masculine forms. Already the ancient versions tended to try to smooth out the difference in one direction or the other.

וּמִלֵּאתִי אֶת־הָרָיו חֲלָלָיו—This first clause with "mountains" refers to Seir by third person suffixes, connecting it with 35:7. This is a double accusative construction. The Piel וּמִלֵּאתִי, "I will fill," has the first direct object אֶת־הָרָיו, "its mountains," followed by a second direct object, חֲלָלָיו (definite too, but not introduced with אֵת), "its slain (ones)," that supplies the means (material) with which the mountains are filled. For the construction, see Waltke-O'Connor, § 10.2.3e, examples 35–39. For חָלָל, "slain," see the third textual note on 6:4.

The LXX (καὶ ἐμπλήσω τῶν τραυματιῶν σου τοὺς βουνούς) omits "his mountains" (by haplography because of similarity to the following word?) and has a second masculine singular pronoun with "slain." The resultant "I will fill with your slain [your] hills" would reflect an unidiomatic use of מָלֵא, since the container should come first and the contents second. Virtually all English translations after KJV (including NKJV, NIV, ESV) have "the slain" (supported by a minor LXX manuscript) instead of the MT's "its slain" (חֲלָלָיו), but that weakens the application to Edom.

גִּבְעוֹתֶיךָ וְגֵאוֹתֶיךָ וְכָל־אֲפִיקֶיךָ—The three second masculine singular suffixes connect these words with the following verses. These topographical references particularize the preceding "mountains" into the components of such terrain. All three nouns also occur together in 6:3 and 36:4, 6. The different word order here, with גֵּיא coming last, may explain its plural form here, גֵּאוֹת (unique in the OT), instead of the usual גֵּאָיוֹת.

חַלְלֵי־חֶרֶב יִפְּלוּ בָהֶם:—The resumptive pronominal suffix on בָהֶם refers back to the preceding three nouns, which form a nominative absolute or *casus pendens*, literally, "your hills, your valleys, and all your ravines—those slain by the sword will fall on *them*." See Waltke-O'Connor, § 4.7b.

35:9 שְׁמְמוֹת עוֹלָם—This plural construct form of שְׁמָמָה occurs only here in Ezekiel, but is found elsewhere (Jer 25:12; 51:26, 62). I have translated it literally as "desolations," although "wastes" or the like might be substituted. "Eternal desolations" is Yahweh's antithesis to Edom's "eternal/ancient grudge" in 35:5.

וְעָרֶיךָ לֹא תָישַׁבְנָה—The Kethib, תֵּישַׁבְנָה, is a *plene* spelling of the usual תֵּשַׁבְנָה, the Qal third feminine plural imperfect of יָשַׁב in its intransitive sense of "be (re)-inhabited," as in 29:11. The ancient versions all reflect the Kethib, as do modern English versions (but not KJV). It is to be preferred over the Qere תָּשֹׁבְנָה, the Qal imperfect of שׁוּב, "return," which possibly can mean "be restored, return to their former state" (2 Ki 5:10; Ezek 16:55), but here that would be a dubious sense of the word. Ironically, it seems likely that the unusual *plene* spelling was used for the Kethib to prevent a derivation of the word from שׁוּב.

וִידַעְתֶּם כִּי־אֲנִי יְהוָה:—As Greenberg observes, the recognition formula shifts from second singular in 35:4, to second plural here, back to second singular in 35:12, and finally to third plural in 35:15.[4] English, of course, does not distinguish between the singular and plural for the second person ("then you will know that I am Yahweh").

35:10 אֶת־שְׁנֵי הַגּוֹיִם וְאֶת־שְׁתֵּי הָאֲרָצוֹת לִי תִהְיֶינָה—The Hebrew definite articles can be rendered as demonstrative, "these" two nations and lands (so KJV already). The license is slight because, functionally, a definite article is a weaker form of demonstrative. The object sign אֵת is used before both construct phrases even though they are subjects of the verb (תִהְיֶינָה) because of the idiom הָיָה לְ, "belong to" (see Waltke-O'Connor, § 10.3.2, example 10; cf. Joüon, § 125 j (3)). The construct phrases may also be thought of as objects of the next verb, although its object suffix is singular; see the next textual note.

וִירִשְׁנוּהָ—The Qal perfect of יָרַשׁ with *waw* consecutive is first plural, "and *we* will possess it," agreeing with the suffix on לָנוּ in 35:12b. However, the verse began by referring to Edom in the singular (the singular second masculine suffix on אָמְרְךָ, Qal infinitive of אָמַר). Edom can be thought of either as a unit or as an aggregate of its inhabitants. The object suffix הָ- is feminine singular and must refer back to the feminine noun אֶרֶץ, whose plural was in the preceding clause. Ironically, modern English versions translate the third singular as plural, "possess *them*," and in so doing, lose some of the theological import of the verse. See the commentary.

35:11 The sentence is similar to 25:14, which clarifies the syntax of this verse, whose problems fade in translation.

וְעָשִׂיתִי—Apparently an indirect object must be supplied in thought, "I will do *with you*" (translated as "I will treat you"), as if it had בְּךָ, as with בָּם in the next clause. Some versions supply one, for example, ποιήσω σοι (LXX).

אֲשֶׁר עָשִׂיתָה מִשִּׂנְאָתֶיךָ בָּם—Since the verb שָׂנֵא, "hate," and its cognate noun, שִׂנְאָה, "hatred, enmity," generally do not take the preposition בְּ, here בָּם must be the object of עָשִׂיתָה, "you [Edom] did with them [the Israelites]." The intervening word מִשִּׂנְאָתֶיךָ could be the singular noun שִׂנְאָה or a feminine form of the Qal infinitive construct of שָׂנֵא. In either case, it has מִן and the form of the second masculine singular

---

4 Greenberg, *Ezekiel*, 2:715.

suffix for a plural noun, which is unusual (Joüon, § 94 j). Allen suggests that it may have been influenced by the feminine plural noun with the same suffix, נֶאָצוֹתָיִךְ (literally, "your blasphemies"), in 35:12.[5]

35:12 נֶאָצוֹתֶיךָ—This is the plural of the noun נְאָצָה, "blasphemy" (BDB), a strong meaning that the next verse will confirm. Elsewhere in the OT, it occurs only in Neh 9:18, 26, where its plural is vocalized נֶאָצוֹת, but here the guttural א has probably caused the preceding vowel to be lengthened (GKC, § 84[b] e). In 2 Ki 19:3 ‖ Is 37:3, Hezekiah used the similar, singular נְאָצָה, "blasphemy," to describe the Rabshakeh's boast (2 Ki 18:33–35 ‖ Is 36:17–20) that Yahweh was as powerless to save Israel just as other gods had also been powerless to save their worshipers. The cognate verb נָאַץ, "disdain, despise, insult," almost always has God as its object, so "blaspheme" is appropriate for it too.

שָׁמֵמָה—The Kethib, שָׁמֵמָה is the Qal third feminine singular perfect of שָׁמֵם. Many commentators make a case for the Kethib, which must refer to the (feminine) land of Israel (rather than its people or mountains), as does the third feminine singular suffix on וְיִרַשְׁנוּהָ in 35:10. Moreover, שְׁמָמָה in 35:15 refers to the desolated land of Israel. The Qere here, שָׁמֵמוּ, is the Qal third common plural perfect, so its subject probably is the preceding הָרֵי יִשְׂרָאֵל, "the mountains of Israel," apparently used here and in 36:1, 4, 8 as an antithesis to "the mountain [range] of Seir/Mount Seir" (35:2–3, 7, 15). The Qere corresponds to the next verb נִתְּנוּ, the Niphal plural (third common perfect) of נָתַן. Virtually all English versions (KJV through ESV) follow the Qere.

35:13 וַתַּגְדִּילוּ עָלַי בְּפִיכֶם—This is the first of two expressions describing Edomite conceit. It translates, literally, "you made great against me with your mouth." "Talk big" would be an idiomatic English equivalent (see Waltke-O'Connor, § 27.2f, including footnote 17). Obviously, boastfulness is the picture. Obadiah 12 uses a similar idiom for Edom's boasting over Jerusalem, the Hiphil verb הִגְדִּיל with פֶּה as its object. Note that this and the following clause describe Edom as gloating over Yahweh himself: both have עָלַי, "over/against me."

וְהַעְתַּרְתֶּם עָלַי דִּבְרֵיכֶם—The parallelism leaves little doubt that the import of this phrase too must be Edomite boasting, even though the verb is obscure. עָתַר I means "pray, supplicate," but that does not fit in this context. Another עָתַר occurs in the Niphal in Prov 27:6, perhaps meaning "be excessive," and the Hiphil here could have the corresponding causative meaning, "ye have multiplied against me your words" (BDB, s.v. עָתַר II, Hiphil). As BDB notes, the Aramaic עֲתַר is cognate with the Hebrew עָשַׁר, "be rich, abundant." Then its Hiphil with the object "words," literally, "to enrich words," would imply logorrhea, a quantity of words in inverse proportion to substance, "a big head" manifesting arrogance. Ezekiel frequently has Aramaisms. The LXX omits the clause, presumably because it did not understand it. There is a plethora of suggestions for emending, but all of them are pure guesses.

35:14–15 These two verses conclude the oracle, or at least the anti-Edom part of it, if chapter 36 continues the same oracle (see the discussion at the beginning of the

---

5   Allen, *Ezekiel*, 2:168.

commentary on chapter 36). These verses are closely related, in fact, partly duplicating each other. Both contain textual problems, which, in part, have to be addressed in terms of their relation to the other.

35:14   כְּשִׂמֹחַ כָּל־הָאָרֶץ—I have taken כְּ with the infinitive construct of שָׂמַח in a temporal sense, as it often has on infinitives. "*When* the whole world rejoices" seems to announce a turning of the tables (which 35:15 will continue). It suggests an eschatological ambience (cf. Ps 96:1), but that idea of restoration for all creation is not developed here. Instead, the focus is that Edom will not participate in that cosmic rejoicing. Rather, as it now rejoices over desolated Israel, so it will be desolated.

שְׁמָמָה אֶעֱשֶׂה־לָּךְ:—The syntax is unusual: the verb עָשָׂה takes an indirect object with the preposition לְ (with second masculine singular suffix in pause) and the accusative noun שְׁמָמָה, literally, "desolation I will do to you." Usually the idiom is the verb שִׂים or נָתַן with a direct object plus (לְ)שְׁמָמָה, as in 35:3 and 35:7 (see also, e.g., Jer 12:11). However, the meaning is clear. Similar is כֵּן אֶעֱשֶׂה־לָּךְ, literally, "so I will do to you," in 35:15, which is then followed by שְׁמָמָה, though it starts a new clause.

Critical commentators[6] treat 35:14 as corrupt, but the LXX and Targum support it. But 35:15a is missing in the LXX, possibly by homoioteleuton, and this, together with its similarity in thought to 35:14b, leads to all sorts of speculative reconstructions.[7] But although there is repetition for the sake of emphasis, the text makes sense as it stands.

35:15   כְּשִׂמְחָתְךָ לְנַחֲלַת בֵּית־יִשְׂרָאֵל—The preposition כְּ prefixed to the noun שִׂמְחָה (with second masculine singular suffix) is used as a conjunction of comparison, "like your rejoicing," though it is translated as a verb, "as you rejoiced." The preposition לְ on the noun נַחֲלָה would, literally, be "regarding, in reference to," but is rendered as "rejoiced *over*" for the sake of English idiom.

שְׁמָמָה תִהְיֶה הַר־שֵׂעִיר וְכָל־אֱדוֹם כֻּלָּהּ—Since Yahweh in the context is addressing Edom in the second person, probably the verb תִהְיֶה is second masculine singular imperfect (not third feminine singular)[8] and הַר־שֵׂעִיר is a vocative. The addition of, literally, "and all Edom—all of it" makes the judgment as comprehensive as possible. The devastation will encompass the whole territory of the Edomites, whether mountainous or not. Partly for that reason, the ethnic appellation אֱדוֹם, "Edom," is added to the geographic term "Mount Seir," which serves as the foil to "the mountains of Israel" in 35:12 and chapter 36. But people and territory go together, so the emphatic כֻּלָּהּ ("all of it") has a feminine suffix in reference to the territory of Edom, since אֶרֶץ is feminine (cf. the second textual note on 35:10). The phrase "Edom, all of it" will recur in 36:5. The full formula כָּל־בֵּית יִשְׂרָאֵל כֻּלֹּה, "the whole house of Israel, all of it" has already been used in 11:15 and 20:40 and will reappear in 36:10.

---

[6]   Zimmerli, *Ezekiel*, 2:227; Allen, *Ezekiel*, 2:168.

[7]   Even Greenberg, *Ezekiel*, 2:716–17.

[8]   Joüon, § 150 m, takes the other view: even though the subject, הַר־שֵׂעִיר, is usually construed as masculine (e.g., עָלָיו in 35:2), its verb here, תִהְיֶה, is feminine (third singular) because of the influence of the preceding feminine direct object, שְׁמָמָה.

Commentary

The brevity of this chapter might give the careful reader his first clue that there is something different about it. If he reads further, he soon discovers that chapter 35 should be counted as only half a chapter and should really be paired with 36:1–15, where the next chapter should begin. It must rate as one of the most egregiously misleading chapter divisions in the OT.

The unity of 35:1–15 and 36:1–15 is evident formally in the fact that the word-event formula, "the Word of Yahweh came to me,"[9] which usually begins an oracle, is present in 35:1 but is not repeated in 36:1. There is a transition at 36:1, but it opens with language virtually identical with that in 35:1: "son of man, prophesy ... and say ..." When the text continues in those two places, it uses two virtually identical expressions with opposite meanings: the hostile orientation formula "I am against you"[10] in 35:3 versus "I am for you" in 36:9.[11]

The correspondence between 35:3 and 36:9 illustrates the nature of the relation between the two halves: 36:1–15 is simply the reverse of 35:1–15. Chapter 35 proclaims judgment on Mount Seir (Edom), while 36:1–15 proclaims salvation to "the mountains of Israel" (36:1, 4, 8). The resulting diptych or bifid is sometimes referred to as the result of a method of "halving," a device used elsewhere by Ezekiel. As with all the oracles against heathen nations, judgment upon the enemies is a necessary part of God bringing salvation to his own people.[12]

Inevitably, the question arises as to why we have a second anti-Edom oracle here.[13] The first had appeared where we would expect it, in the oracles against the Gentile nations (chapters 25–32), in the collection of oracles that comprise chapter 25, specifically 25:12–14. In that chapter, Ammon had appeared to be the greatest danger to God's people, and Edom's inclusion seemed rather perfunctory. Any Gentile oracle is a bit unexpected in this part of the book, since Ezekiel 33–48 is primarily concerned with Israel's restoration. But that redemptive concern probably provides the most plausible answer to the question—to the extent that current historical problems were still determining the content of Ezekiel's semi-eschatological oracles. Presuming that those problems still were somewhat operative, it follows that Edom's vengeance at the fall of Judah, cited in chapter 25, was no immediate obstacle to Israel's restoration, while its later encroachment on southern Judean territory was. (The

---

[9] For this formula, see page 8 in the introduction and the textual note on 3:16.

[10] For this formula, see page 9 in the introduction and the commentary on 5:8.

[11] Block, *Ezekiel*, 2:309–10, lists eleven similar examples for why 35:1–36:15 forms a unity.

[12] See "Introduction to Ezekiel 25–32: Oracles against Other Nations."

[13] One reason for including this oracle here, rather than somewhere in chapters 25–32, may be to preserve the orderly arrangement there of the oracles against seven nations. See "Introduction to Ezekiel 25–32: Oracles against Other Nations."

alternate text to the canonical Ezra in 1 Esdras 4:50 quotes a decree of Darius permitting Israelites to return to the land as also explicitly forbidding Edom from encroaching on Judah.) Ezek 35:10–15 will make this interpretation very likely.

It may not be immediately relevant here, but the virtually "congenital" ill will between the two countries may play at least a subliminal role. The Bible describes the conflict between Jacob (renamed "Israel" in Gen 32:29 [ET 32:28]) and Esau (the father of Edom) as beginning already in Rebekah's womb (Gen 25:21–23). Their fraternal strife was interpreted by Yahweh himself as a precursor of their descendants' future relations (Gen 25:23). Esau's rash sale of his birthright to Jacob and Jacob's deception of his aged father, Isaac, sets the stage for a series of events that continue through Genesis 36.

Relations had not improved by the time of Moses, when Edom's refusal to grant the Israelites transit rights forced a long detour (Num 20:14–21). Nevertheless, in his farewell sermon, Moses enjoins the Israelites to show special consideration to the Edomites because of their kinship (Deut 23:8 [ET 23:7]), but we are unaware of any love lost between the two nations at any subsequent time.

By the eighth century B.C., "Edom" had virtually become an archetype of all the heathen kingdoms of this world. In OT usage it is second only to Babylon as a major exemplar of all that stood in opposition to the establishment of the kingdom of God. Amos condemns Edom for its perpetually pitiless treatment of a "brother" (Amos 1:11–12), although we are given no specifics. In Obadiah, who is usually dated more or less contemporaneously with Ezekiel (early sixth century B.C.), Obad 1–14 and 15–21 quite exactly parallel Ezek 35:1–15 and 36:1–15, respectively. Comparably, in the twin chapters Isaiah 34 and 35, "Edom" is the antithesis to redeemed Zion. In Is 63:1–6 "Edom" represents the forces that Yahweh alone had to defeat in his salvation of Zion; it is aptly paraphrased and given its ultimate, Christological application in one of our infrequently used Easter hymns, "Who Is This That Comes from Edom?" (*TLH* 209). Even Malachi (1:2–5) uses "Jacob" and "Esau" to describe the mystery of divine election (*Cur alii, alii non?*),[14] which human designs cannot derail.

Although I have spoken of "Edom," it should be noted that the entire pericope uses that national designation only twice: in 35:15, in apposition to "Mount Seir," and in 36:5, where it parallels "the rest of the nations." Rather,

---

[14] The question "Why are some elected, others not?" cannot be fully answered on the basis of Scripture. What Scripture does reveal is that God has elected, even before his creation of the world, some to be brought to faith in Christ and thus to everlasting salvation, and this doctrine is to comfort believers—not make them complacent, about themselves or about evangelism. It also reveals that those who die without faith in Christ perish eternally as punishment for their own sins (not due to any fault on God's part). Nevertheless, God's desire is for all people to repent and be saved. See FC Ep and SD XI, "God's Eternal Foreknowledge and Election," and also Ezek 18:23, 32; 33:11.

most of the time Yahweh speaks of "Mount Seir," no doubt as a contrast to "the mountains of Israel," which he mentions frequently, probably harking back to 6:2–3, where he had first introduced the expression in Ezekiel. "Seir" is primarily toponymic in focus, but in most of the biblical period, it was occupied by the Edomites. Gen 14:6 states that "Seir" had originally been inhabited by "Horites" (Hurrians, centered in northern Mesopotamia). Probably in later times, pressure from Arabs to the east (cf. Geshem in Nehemiah's day [Neh 2:19; 6:1–2]) caused the Edomites, in turn, to move into southern Judah. The name "Seir" is well-attested in extrabiblical texts, at least as early as the fourteenth century B.C. Amarna texts. The territory the name refers to may have varied a bit from time to time, but in general it refers to the mountains and slopes at the southern end of the Transjordanian plateau, from the northern border with Moab at the Zered canyon and perhaps as far south as the Gulf of Aqaba. It was bordered by desert on both east and west, perhaps the Wadi Rum (of later *Lawrence of Arabia* fame) in the east, and the Wadi Arabah (the southern extension of the Dead Sea depression) on the west.

35:2–4 Beginning with the hostile orientation formulae, "set your face against" and "I am against you," the initial oracle uses typical Ezekelian doom language in the second person of direct address.[15] No reason is given at this point for Yahweh's fundamental opposition.

One literary flourish serving the message may be noted. The noun שְׁמָמָה, "desolation," is used twice in succeeding verses (35:3, 4) for Mount Seir. Moreover, the asyndetic expression in 35:3, שְׁמָמָה וּמְשַׁמָּה, "an utter desolation," will recur in 35:7, both times portending judgment for the mountains of Edom. This recalls the use of "an utter desolation" in 6:14, before the fall of Jerusalem, in a prophecy of judgment upon Israel's mountains, and also its use in 33:28–29, which, after Jerusalem's fall, proclaimed judgment for the remaining inhabitants of Judah.

35:5–6 Yahweh's first statement of his case against Edom describes the country as an ancient blood enemy of Israel, evidenced especially in its treatment of Israel at the time of the Babylonian invasions. Already after the universal flood, God had established the principle "he who sheds man's blood, by man shall his blood be shed" (Gen 9:6). Apparently using the ancient premonarchical language of asylum, Edom is described as one who shed blood vindictively and with full culpability. Hence, the blood he shed would seek its own justice, and he would find no city of refuge (see the textual notes on 35:6). The language about blood vengeance and the asylum metaphor are alien to us, but the theological point is powerful.

We must remember "Edom" as a major example of what the Gentile oracles were all about. God's judgment on the heathen enemies of his people is

---

15 For these formulae, see page 9 in the introduction, the commentary on 5:8, and the textual note on 35:2.

part of the Law-Gospel dialectic that extends throughout the Scriptures and that characterizes how God works in history to accomplish salvation.[16] These verses almost classically exemplify what still characterizes the fallen "world" in which we live. Ancient enmities, often leading to bloodshed and war, still characterize much of life, whether individual or international. Anyone who knows the modern Near East will feel that often he need only substitute biblical names for the modern ones to understand its unending conflicts. Especially since the rise of modern nationalism, Europe has nourished grudges that the "European Union" and Common Market hope finally to extinguish. But there are no permanent political or social solutions to conflicts between peoples. Lasting peace begins to come only when God's Word of Law and Gospel does its work, putting to death the sinful human nature in individuals, who then, by the power of the Spirit, can begin to lead the new life of faith in Christ (e.g., Romans 6). Ultimately, God's left-hand kingdom, with all the governments and nations of this world, must pass away at the return of Jesus Christ before his eternal kingdom will come in full. And for this we pray, "*Thy* kingdom come" (Mt 6:10).[17]

35:7–9 Yahweh now speaks about Seir (not to it, as in 35:3–6). This serves as a reminder that his audience includes not just the Edomites (most of whom will not listen), but also the Israelite exiles, many of whom may repent, believe, and be comforted by God's promises. The theme of utter desolation, heard before, is now picked up in different language in 35:7 and continued in 35:8–9. Instead of living people, Edom's rugged terrain will be filled with their corpses (35:8), and 35:9 applies the idea to the terrain itself (cf. 29:12 and 30:7). The repetition of the recognition formula,[18] "then you will know that I am Yahweh" (35:9; see also 35:4, 12, 15), especially in a context like this, is a reminder that Yahweh's ultimate desire is not the destruction of Edom or anyone else, but for "all men to be saved and to come to the knowledge of the truth" (1 Tim 2:4; see also Ezek 18:32).

35:10 A new accusation and appropriate penalty are launched with this verse: Edom's unjustifiable desire to annex and occupy the now depopulated land of Judah, even though, in God's eyes, Edom had no legitimate claim to it. Yahweh speaks of "these two nations and these two lands" at the same time that he uses the singular object "it" in his direct quotation of the Edomite ambition: "we will possess it." This is no inconsistency, but an anticipation of a thought he will shortly develop in detail (37:15–28), and which he expressed through all the prophets, namely, that the kingdom that was divided after Solomon's death really remained one kingdom. So it had been before, and so it would be again under "my servant David," the "one Shepherd" (Ezek 34:23;

---

[16] See "Introduction to Ezekiel 25–32: Oracles against Other Nations."

[17] For the eschatological orientation of this petition, see Gibbs, *Matthew 1:1–11:1*, 328–30.

[18] For this formula, see page 9 in the introduction and the commentary on 6:7.

37:24) who would gather by faith even Gentiles into his "one flock" (Jn 10:16).[19]

Since northern Israel had fallen well over a century earlier in 722 B.C., the Edomites probably thought of occupying only the one former kingdom of Judah, recently capitulated in 586 B.C., but from a prophetic perspective their intrusion into the promised land necessarily constituted an invasion against the Northern Kingdom as well. Archaeological evidence amply confirms Edomite penetration into southern Judah (even before the fall of Jerusalem, according to a letter found at Arad), but there is no evidence that they ever ventured as far north as Jerusalem, or even had hopes to do so. In any case, even calling them "two lands" heightens Edom's greed. Imperialistic ambitions being what they are in every age, it is not implausible that Edom actually did entertain such grandiose dreams, however unrealistic.

The circumstantial clause at the end of the verse, "even though Yahweh was there," magnifies the offense from mere opportunistic seizure of a neighbor's territory into an affront against Yahweh himself. In typical pagan thought, land, temple, and deity were all but inseparable. The chief god was often virtually a personification of the "spirit" of the nation. Any god who allowed his "house" to be destroyed and his people deported must have abandoned that land and people, leaving it ripe for the picking. And in the syncretistic thought of that world, the god himself would have simply been absorbed into the pantheon of the conquering nation and assigned some subsidiary role serving the chief god of the victorious people. Thus the Edomites would have interpreted even a partial conquest of Judah as proof that their gods were superior to Israel's God.

We must ask how Yahweh's assertion here accords with the earlier vision of Yahweh's כָּבוֹד ("Glory") abandoning the land (Ezekiel 9–11). In the other direction, the clause prematurely anticipates the climactic renaming of the new Jerusalem at the end of the book, "Yahweh is there" (48:35). Among other things, this type of question probably imports more of the Western sense of tense and time than is applicable. Given the position of the Hebrew verb הָיָה in the clause in 35:10, one would ordinarily translate it as "Yahweh *was* there," but this does not carry the corollary that Yahweh was no longer there in any sense. (The LXX translates, κύριος ἐκεῖ ἐστιν, "Yahweh *is* there," better bringing out the continuity.) For although Yahweh had allowed his temple, city, and land to be laid waste because of his people's abandonment of him, that did not mean that he had renounced his right to the land and had abandoned it forever. It was his grant to Jacob/Israel (28:25; 37:25), and in 36:5 he will call it "my land." Edom had received its own allotment (Deut 2:1–7) and should have been content with that. If false territorial claims from within Israel should be denounced (Ezek 11:15; 33:24), how much more so when they come from a foreigner!

---

[19] See the commentary on Ezekiel 34, a traditional OT text for Good Shepherd Sunday.

After the exile, God's people, humbled and penitent, would return to the land and rebuild the temple, and Yahweh would once again reside there. Then in the fullness of time (Gal 4:4), God would become incarnate in human flesh in the person of Jesus Christ. He will be the new sanctuary (σκηνόω, "to tabernacle," in Jn 1:14) and temple (Jn 2:14–22), and henceforth God gathers true worshipers in Spirit and truth, not to Jerusalem nor confined to any geographic land, but around the One in whom his fullness dwells.[a] Eschatologically, he will again reside in the midst of his people even more concretely than in the earthly temple (Rev 21:3, 22).

(a) Jn 1:14; 2:19–22; 4:20–24; Col 1:19; 2:9

35:11   Again God expresses the motif that his justice matches the offense. אַף, "anger," and קִנְאָה, "zeal, jealousy," are often attributed to God, who administers them in his righteousness. When God is jealous, this relates to his covenant with his people as a kind of marriage in which he tolerates no adultery.[20] When "jealousy" is attributed to people, however, it is more likely a matter of sinful, petty grudges or self-serving desires. Simple "jealousy" is common enough among people, of course, but in this case, although Edom was a competitor and an enemy of Israel, it is not clear why it should have been "jealous." I have translated, "fanaticism," in the hope that it will convey some of the irrationality the use here implies.

In Yahweh's promise "I will make myself known among them," the antecedent of "them" (בָּם), in a second-person address, is debatable. Parallel thoughts that will be expressed in 38:23 and 39:21–23 after Yahweh's destruction of Gog do not clarify the issue here. Those parallels, if relevant, would indicate that the reference is dual, both to Edom and to Israel. The next verse seems to suggest that Edom is the primary referent and will learn that Yahweh is not another god who dies or is defeated when his land and temple are desolated. The LXX specifically makes this application, translating, γνωσθήσομαί σοι ἡνίκα ἂν κρίνω σε, "I shall be known to/by you when I judge you."[21] Chapters 38–39 make possible the additional interpretation that Yahweh is faithful to his ancient promises and has not completely abandoned his people in spite of their infidelities.

35:12   The rest of the chapter is a commentary on the last clause of 35:10, "even though Yahweh was there." It is somewhat divided into two parts by the use of the citation formula, "thus says the Lord Yahweh,"[22] at the beginning of 35:14. It somewhat makes explicit what could be assumed all along. A depopulated land of Judah left a vacant territory that the Edomites believed they would be foolish not to add to their own domain, and the few poor peasants

---

[20] See the commentary on 5:13, as well as on chapters 16 and 23.

[21] Many critics think that the LXX preserves a better text and that בָּם in the MT arose by inadvertent assimilation to the בָּם in the preceding clause. However, the LXX often simplifies according to its understanding, and the MT is definitely the *lectio difficilior*.

[22] For this formula, see pages 8–9 in the introduction and the fourth textual note and the commentary on 2:4.

left after the deportation of most Israelites would be no real hindrance. The use of the passive verb in "given [נִתְּנוּ] to us for food" may even imply their assumption that heaven—Yahweh or their own god(s) or both—had given them permission to proceed. The language is similar to 29:5, where Pharaoh was given to the animals for food, or 34:5, 8, 10, where Israel as scattered sheep are vulnerable to predators.

Yahweh hears such thoughts as blasphemy because to taunt and take advantage of his people was tantamount to doing it to him personally. Jesus affirms this in his description of the final assize in Mt 25:31–46. The verb "I have heard" (שָׁמָעְתִּי) will be repeated at the end of Ezek 35:13, thus framing the two verses. In 8:18 Yahweh had asserted that he would "act in wrath" because of his people's offensive idolatry, and then he would "not hear/listen," no matter how loudly his apostate people cried for help. Here he does hear the insults of the enemy who does not know Yahweh and mocks him as a deposed ruler who has lost his claim to the land and people of Israel.

35:13 What Yahweh hears are the arrogant words of "Mr. Big Mouth," words that, however, will prove to be only "hot air" in confrontation with him who "upholds all things by the word of his power" (Heb 1:3). It is a familiar theme in Scripture that "pride goeth ... before a fall" (Prov 16:18 KJV). Even general revelation and human experience can attest to that.

35:14–15 The unexpected citation formula alerts us to the conclusion of this half (35:1–15) of the oracle (35:1–36:15). Its basic theme is the eschatological one of the great reversal, when all of God's competition will be eliminated. As we confess in the Creeds, this goal has, in principle, already been accomplished on Easter with the triumphant resurrection of Jesus Christ from the dead, having vanquished death and the devil, along with all of our sins by his atonement on the cross.

(b) E.g., Rom 8:17; Gal 3:18, 29; 4:7; Eph 1:11–18; 1 Pet 1:4

This pericope is too focused on the immediate postexilic situation to be developed in eschatological terms, although there are hints of that in "when the whole world rejoices" (35:14; cf. Rom 8:18–23) and in the singling out of Edom as representative of the whole power of Satan. No Gentile oracles will be understood correctly if they are not read eschatologically.[23]

Noteworthy here too is "the possession [נַחֲלָה, usually 'inheritance'] of the house of Israel" (35:15). The word is very prominent in the later chapters of Numbers, in Deuteronomy, and subsequently in Joshua 13–24, when the Israelites took possession of the land under Joshua. Its theological import continues in the frequent use of "inherit" (κληρονομέω and κληρόω), "inheritance" (κληρονομία), and "heir(s)" (κληρονόμος) in the NT.[b] Having been adopted into God's family through Baptism into Christ, who is himself the "heir" of all things (Heb 1:2; see also Mt 21:38), we receive an "inheritance" and are "heirs" of all God's promises, from those issued to Abraham through those uttered by

---

[23] See "Introduction to Ezekiel 25–32: Oracles against Other Nations."

Christ himself. Ultimately, our inheritance will comprise the entirety of the new heavens and the new earth (Mt 5:5; 25:34; Revelation 21–22).

God remains the ultimate owner of the land. Yahweh's vested interest in it is shown by his use of נַחֲלָה, "possession, inheritance," in 35:15 and 36:12 and thirteen times in chapters 44–48. It functions as a sort of key to the meaning of the entire pericope (35:1–36:15). The true Israel of God (Gal 6:16)—the one church that spans both Testaments—retains its inheritance, while unbelieving Edom's claims are thrown out by the heavenly Judge.

Yahweh Will Sprinkle His People with Clean Water to Give Them a New Heart and Spirit

Translation

36 ¹"Now you, son of man, prophesy to the mountains of Israel and say, 'Mountains of Israel, hear the Word of Yahweh: ²Thus says the Lord Yahweh: Because the enemy said, "Aha!" about you, that is, "The ancient heights have become our possession," ' ³therefore, prophesy and say, 'Thus says the Lord Yahweh: Because, therefore, they have devastated and crushed you from all sides, so that you could become the possession of the rest of the nations and a subject of popular gossip and slander, ⁴therefore, mountains of Israel, hear the Word of the Lord Yahweh: Thus says the Lord Yahweh to the mountains, hills, valleys, ravines, desolate ruins, and abandoned cities, which have become a source of plunder and an object of ridicule to the rest of the nations all around.

⁵" 'Therefore, thus says the Lord Yahweh: Surely, in my fiery zeal I am speaking against the rest of the nations and against Edom, all of it, which took my land as their own with whole-hearted glee and deep-seated derision, and neighboring territory as plunder.' ⁶Therefore, prophesy about the land of Israel and say to the mountains, hills, valleys, and ravines, 'Thus says the Lord Yahweh: In my zealous wrath I am speaking because you have borne the taunts of the nations. ⁷Therefore, thus says the Lord Yahweh, I swear with uplifted hand that the nations all around you will bear taunts against themselves. ⁸But you, O mountains of Israel, will grow your branches and bear your fruit for my people, Israel, because they will soon come home. ⁹For I am for you. I will look on you with favor, and you will be cultivated and planted. ¹⁰I will multiply people on you, the whole house of Israel, all of it. The cities will be resettled and the ruins rebuilt. ¹¹I will multiply both people and animals on you. They will multiply and be fruitful. I will resettle you as you were in earlier times and do more good to you than at your beginnings. Then you will know that I am Yahweh. ¹²I will cause people, my people Israel, to walk on you. They will take possession of you; you will be their inheritance; and never again will you deprive them of their children.

¹³" 'Thus says the Lord Yahweh: Because people say to you, "You devour people and keep on depriving your nation of its children," ¹⁴assuredly, you will no longer devour people or deprive your nation of its children, says the Lord Yahweh. ¹⁵No longer will I let you hear the taunts of the nations or bear the scorn of the peoples. Never again will you deprive your nation of its children, says the Lord Yahweh.' "

¹⁶The Word of Yahweh came to me: ¹⁷"Son of man, when the house of Israel was living in their own land, they defiled it by their conduct and their misdeeds; their conduct became in my sight like the uncleanness of menstruation. ¹⁸So I poured out my wrath on them on account of the blood they had poured on the ground and for the fecal deities with which they had defiled it, ¹⁹and I scattered them among the nations so that they were dispersed among the countries. In accord with their conduct and their misdeeds I punished them. ²⁰And when they came to the various nations, they profaned my holy name when it was said of them, 'These are the people of Yahweh, but they had to leave the land.' ²¹So I was concerned about my holy name, which the house of Israel had profaned among the various nations to which they had come.

²²"Therefore, say to the house of Israel, 'Thus says the Lord Yahweh: Not for your sake, O house of Israel, am I about to act, but for my holy name, which you have profaned among the nations to which you came. ²³I will sanctify my great name that has been profaned among the nations, which you profaned among them. Then the nations will know that I am Yahweh, says the Lord Yahweh, when I show myself holy through you before their eyes. ²⁴I will take you from the nations; I will gather you from all the lands; and I will bring you to your own land. ²⁵I will sprinkle clean water on you, and you will be clean. From all your impurities and from all your fecal deities I will cleanse you. ²⁶Then I will give you a new heart and put a new S/spirit within you. I will remove the heart of stone from your body and give you a heart of flesh. ²⁷I will put my Spirit within you and make it so that you will walk in my statutes and be careful to observe my covenant standards. ²⁸Then you will live in the land I gave your fathers. You will be my people, and I will be your God. ²⁹I will save you from all your impurities. I will summon the grain, make it abundant, and not bring famine upon you. ³⁰I will increase the fruit of the trees and the produce of the fields so that you will never again suffer the disgrace of famine among the nations. ³¹Then you will remember your evil actions and your misdeeds that were not good, and you will loathe yourselves on account of your iniquities and your abominations. ³²Not for your sake am I about to act, says the Lord Yahweh; let it be known to you! Be ashamed and disgraced because of your conduct, O house of Israel.

³³" 'Thus says the Lord Yahweh: On the day I cleanse you from all your iniquities, I will resettle [your] cities and the ruins will be rebuilt. ³⁴The desolate land will be cultivated instead of being a desolation in the sight of every passerby. ³⁵They will say, "This land that was desolate has become like the garden of Eden, and the cities that were ruined, desolated, and destroyed are now fortified and inhabited." ³⁶Then the nations that are left around you will know that I, Yahweh, have rebuilt the places that were destroyed and have replanted what was desolated. I, Yahweh, have spoken, and I will do it.'

³⁷" 'Thus says the Lord Yahweh: This too I will allow the house of Israel to ask me to do for them: I will multiply them so their men are like flocks. ³⁸Like flocks consecrated for sacrifice, like the flocks of Jerusalem on its feast days, so

will the ruined cities be filled with flocks of men. Then they will know that I am Yahweh.'"

Textual Notes

36:2 יַעַן אָמַר הָאוֹיֵב—In usage we associate אוֹיֵב, "enemy," more with the language of the Psalms. It occurs elsewhere in Ezekiel only in 39:27. The related abstract noun אֵיבָה, "enmity," we met in 25:15 and 35:5.

הֶאָח—The gloating "Aha!" needs no further exegesis than in the first textual note on 25:3.

וּבָמוֹת עוֹלָם—The clause beginning with explicative *waw*, "that is," spells out what "Aha!" connotes. A famous parallel with an explicative *waw* appears in Zech 9:9: "on an ass, that is, on a colt, the foal of an ass." The plural of בָּמָה here probably has its basic meaning of "back" or ridge of a mountain. Often elsewhere, including in Ezekiel, it is translated "high place" when it refers to centers of pagan worship and cultic prostitution, but it is doubtful if those features are involved in its use here. To humans, the mountains might well seem "eternal," but the sense of עוֹלָם here is more restricted, "ancient, permanent." It is used elsewhere as a designation for hills (גִּבְעוֹת עוֹלָם, Gen 49:26; Deut 33:15; Hab 3:6). Because of their permanence, mountains are often appealed to as witnesses in oaths and prophecies. They were deified in paganism, but in Israel are poetically demythologized (cf. Ps 121:1).

לְמוֹרָשָׁה הָיְתָה לָּנוּ—The singular verb הָיְתָה is not in accord with its plural subject, בָּמוֹת. The apparent disagreement in number may be explained in various ways, perhaps as due to the attraction of the preceding מוֹרָשָׁה, or as thinking of the בָּמוֹת as a collective singular.

36:3 לָכֵן—"Therefore" begins five verses in succession (36:3–7). The rest of this verse teems with difficulties and obscurities.

יַעַן בְּיַעַן—This asyndetic repetition of יַעַן is puzzling in many respects (cf. Joüon, § 170 f). The phrase with *waw*, יַעַן וּבְיַעַן, was used in 13:10 as well as Lev 26:43. In those two verses, a perfect follows, but here infinitives follow (see the next textual note). Most ancient versions and all English translations ignore the repetition of יַעַן. However, many commentaries, in their original translations, add an adverb or other expression, and in that tradition, I use "therefore," although it should not be confused with לָכֵן at the beginning of this and succeeding verses.

שַׁמּוֹת וְשָׁאֹף—There is no agreement, ancient or modern, on the meaning (or roots!) of these two verbs. They are alliterative, but that literary feature can be reflected in a variety of English translations. Probably most favored for שַׁמּוֹת is to relate it to the verb שָׁמֵם, which Ezekiel uses so often, and construe it as a rare form of the Qal infinitive in a transitive sense. But that results in an unparalleled syntax, although the form finds possible parallels in Ps 77:10 (ET 77:9; with חָנַן) and Ps 77:11 (ET 77:10 with חָלַל). A sense like "devastate, desolate" may be stronger than the context calls for as well. Compare GKC, § 67 r. The second verb, שָׁאַף, is relatively common, meaning "gasp, pant" (or of animals, "snap at"). Here its infinitive absolute evidently functions like the preceding infinitive construct, which is not problematic (Joüon, § 123 x). However, middle *aleph* and hollow verbs easily interchange, especially later under Aramaic influence, and so this could be the infinitive absolute of the verb שׁוּף, "crush." The *protevangelium* of Gen 3:15 puns on its two uses of שׁוּף, with the Seed of Eve "crushing" the serpent's head and the snake "snapping at" his heel. Some commentators propose various reconstructions that assume that the underlying verb here is נָשַׁם, used elsewhere only in Is 42:14 of a woman in labor.[1] Then here would be a hendiadys of two virtually synonymous verbs, both meaning "pant after," which may fit the context better, but one must take a rather circuitous linguistic route to achieve it. Of these two alternatives, it is even hard to say which is the more difficult, but I have opted for "devastate" and "crush." But no certainty—or even confidence—in the choice can be claimed. The legion of other guesses I shall not discuss. NIV's "ravaged and hounded" is a bit free, but attractive, although I have not reproduced it.

וַתֵּעֲלוּ—As pointed in the MT, this appears to be partly Niphal תֵּעֲלוּ, "you were brought/taken up," and partly Qal תַּעֲלוּ, "you came up." These mixed forms are always hard to explain. Is it dialectical? part of the exilic disintegration of the language? a mixed textual tradition where copyists tried to incorporate two different readings from different manuscripts?

עַל־שְׂפַת לָשׁוֹן—Whether the preceding verb is Niphal or Qal, the Israelites were, literally, "on the lip of the tongue." The "lip" (שָׂפָה) is apparently considered the organ of speech and the "tongue" (לָשׁוֹן) personified as the speaker. Compare Ps 140:12 (ET 140:11), where אִישׁ לָשׁוֹן, "a tongue-man," is a gossiper. The context here too supports the translation that Israel is "a subject of popular gossip."

וְדִבַּת־עָם:—This parallels the preceding expression. דִּבָּה, a none too common word for "slander, defamation, bad report," was used of the bad news Joseph brought to his father about his brothers (Gen 37:2) and of the unfavorable report most of the spies brought back to the Israelites in the desert (Num 13:32; 14:36–37).

36:5 אִם־לֹא—As a kind of double negative, literally, "if not" properly implies a positive oath, but used alone it can only be translated by an adverb, "surely." Most modern translations ignore it, but it helps reinforce the strong language in the rest of the verse and context.

בְּאֵשׁ קִנְאָתִי—"Fiery zeal" translates the Hebrew idiom that prefers a construct chain, "the fire of my zeal," to an adjective. This expression occurs elsewhere in Zeph 1:18 and 3:8. I judge the traditional "jealousy" for קִנְאָה to be as subject to misunderstanding here as elsewhere.

דִּבַּרְתִּי—Most commentators, including Cooke,[2] note that in such a forward-looking prophecy it is rare to have just a perfect verb. More often הִנֵּה immediately precedes a perfect, as in, for example, 3:8, 25; 4:8; 13:12. Compare הִנְנִי ... דִּבַּרְתִּי in 36:6. Here (and in 36:6) דִּבַּרְתִּי is translated in the present tense, "I am speaking"—an instantaneous perfect—because it both alludes to Yahweh's previous threats to surrounding nations and implies that he is now continuing them.

---

[1] See Greenberg, *Ezekiel*, 2:718; Cooke, *Ezekiel*, 386, 394.

[2] Cooke, *Ezekiel*, 394.

אֱדוֹם כֻּלָּא—When "Edom" refers to the land, it is construed as feminine, as in 32:29 and 35:15. The use of א for the third feminine singular suffix on כֻּלָּא probably reflects the Aramaic preference for an *aleph* in such forms. However, because of the following אֲשֶׁר, it is possible that it is simply scribal dittography.

נָתְנוּ־אֶת־אַרְצִי ׀ לָהֶם לְמוֹרָשָׁה—Similar language was used in 11:15. נָתַן, as frequently, especially in Ezekiel, no longer has its original sense of "give," although "gave to themselves" would make sense for לָהֶם ... נָתְנוּ, but has its secondary sense of "set, establish" and in this context, "take" or "claim for themselves."

בְּשִׂמְחַת כָּל־לֵבָב בִּשְׁאָט נֶפֶשׁ—Literally, their attitude is described as "in glee/delight/rejoicing of all the heart and in derision/scorn of soul/person." Fortunately, since English uses "heart" in the same metaphorical way as Hebrew, no explanation is necessary. The accompanying phrase with נֶפֶשׁ is harder to reproduce fully and accurately (cf. the use of נֶפֶשׁ in 25:6, 15). Greenberg offers "wholesouled,"[3] which, however, is hardly English. Sometimes in ecclesiastical usage, "soul" is used for the whole person. However, God originally created man with both a soul (or spirit) and a body, and although they are separated at death (cf. Rev 6:9), at the resurrection, we shall be raised whole, possessing both. No one word in English captures all the nuances of נֶפֶשׁ, but here, as often, it implies "the real you," the uniqueness of each person. I have settled for "deep-seated."

לְמַעַן מִגְרָשָׁה לָבַז׃—This final phrase is obscure and much debated. לְמַעַן usually is used with a verb in a purpose or result clause, but there is no verb here. I have hidden this difficulty in my translation by making "neighboring territory as plunder" the second object of the verb "took." Yet the force of מִגְרָשׁ in this context is anything but clear. Elsewhere in the Bible, especially in Leviticus, Numbers, and Joshua, the noun denotes the territory surrounding a city given to the Levites as "pastureland" for their sustenance. But the relevance of that meaning in this context is debatable. One ancient line of interpretation construes the form of מִגְרָשָׁה as an Aramaic-type infinitive (with prefixed מ) of גֵּרֵשׁ, "expel, empty out, drive out," with third feminine singular object suffix having "my land" is its antecedent. If the root itself is the Aramaic גרשׁ, its meaning would be "destroy," and so the LXX seems to take it. But the Syriac, Targum, and Vulgate all understand the underlying root to be Hebrew, and so evidently did KJV ("to cast it out for a prey").

Most other translations seem to take מִגְרָשׁ as a common noun, "open/adjacent land" or the like, sometimes but not always retaining the "pasture" picture. They apparently deem its usual reference to the Levites as only one specific application, not intrinsic to the word itself. I have followed this line of thought with my "neighboring territory." Apparently NKJV (departing from its exemplar) had this kind of thought in mind with its "in order to plunder its open country." RSV's "plunder it" seems to simply ignore the word, but NRSV tries to restore it with "because of its pasture," and NIV similarly. Many delete the phrase as a gloss or as hopelessly corrupt.[4]

---

[3] Greenberg, *Ezekiel*, 2:711, 718.

[4] Compare Allen, *Ezekiel*, 2:168, who develops one of those complicated and ingenious reconstructions of the history of the text in which he seems to delight.

36:6 הִנְנִי בְקִנְאָתִי וּבַחֲמָתִי דִּבַּרְתִּי—The syntax is somewhat unusual, apparently for the sake of emphasis. Commonly in Ezekiel, הִנֵּה (often with a suffix) is immediately followed by a participle (e.g., 26:7; 28:7; 34:17) or by a perfect (see the third textual note on 36:5). But here הִנְנִי is separated from the verb דִּבַּרְתִּי, which, as in 36:5, is an instantaneous or performative perfect. "In my zealous wrath" represents the literal hendiadys of בְקִנְאָתִי וּבַחֲמָתִי, "in my zeal and in my wrath," obviously equivalent to the "fiery zeal" idiom of the previous verse. As with that similar phrase in 26:5, this phrase precedes the verb for emphasis.

כְּלִמַּת גּוֹיִם נְשָׂאתֶם:—The idiom כְּלִמָּה נָשָׂא, "bear a taunt/disgrace," that is, "be taunted/disgraced," is used both in this and the next verse. It is a favorite of Ezekiel (e.g., 16:52, 54; 39:26; 44:13).

36:7 אֲנִי נָשָׂאתִי אֶת־יָדִי אִם־לֹא—"I swear with uplifted hand" is, literally, "I lift my hand," followed by the positive oath formula אִם־לֹא (used by itself in, e.g., 36:5; 38:19). The same gesture of raising the hand is standard in contemporary courts. The perfect verb נָשָׂאתִי is again instantaneous, hence translated as a present. Since the verb is inflected, the pronoun אֲנִי, "I," is technically redundant, but may have been used regularly to emphasize the necessity for the speaker to fully identify with his testimony. In this context אֲנִי probably plays the extra role of emphasizing the contrast between the shifting subjects of נָשָׂא, "bear; raise." In 36:6, "you have borne" (with no pronoun) referred to Israel; here it is Yahweh ("I") who "raises" his hand; and at the end of 36:7 it is the nations (הֵמָּה, "they") who will "bear" taunts.

36:8 כִּי קֵרְבוּ לָבוֹא—The final כִּי clause consists of the intransitive Piel perfect קֵרְבוּ followed by לְ and the Qal infinitive of בוֹא. This idiom implies imminence, literally, "they are near to come." This idiom with the Piel of קָרַב is found only here, but Gen 12:11 has a similar idiom with the Hiphil: הִקְרִיב לָבוֹא. The Hebrew says nothing about "home" as such, but since it so obviously refers to the return from the exile, I have followed most modern translations (RSV through NIV) in adopting it. Already the Targum had given it a broader eschatological interpretation: "my redemption draws near." See further the commentary.

36:9 הִנְנִי אֲלֵיכֶם—In this context, the prepositional phrase must serve as a dative of advantage, "behold, I am *for* you," connoting God's favor (BDB, s.v. אֶל, 3 (c)). The identical wording in 13:8 and the similar uses of הִנְנִי with אֶל elsewhere (e.g., 13:20; 21:8 [ET 21:3]; 29:10) constitute the hostile orientation formula, "behold, I am *against* … "[5]

36:11 וְרָבוּ וּפָרוּ—Many critics[6] would delete these two Qal perfects (of רָבָה and פָּרָה) with *waw* consecutive, "they will multiply and be fruitful," because they are missing in the LXX and interrupt the series of first person statements, but the third person reappears in 36:12. The obvious parallelism to the use of the same verbs in Gen 1:22, 28 is undeniable, and if the previous surmise of a similar reprise of the creation story is correct (see the commentary on 36:8), the case for their genuineness is very strong. At the same time, one can hardly help but note that the order of the two

---

[5] For this formula, see page 9 in the introduction and the commentary on 5:8.

[6] E.g., Allen, *Ezekiel*, 2:169.

verbs here is the reverse of their order in Gen 1:22, 28; 8:17; 9:1, 7. However, there is a fairly common tendency in Late Biblical Hebrew to reverse customary word order, and while generally there is no obvious reason for that penchant, in this case placing "multiply" first continues the focus on that verb, whose Hiphil occurred twice just before: וְהִרְבֵּיתִי at the start of 36:10 and 36:11.

כְּקַדְמוֹתֵיכֶם—"As you were in earlier times" paraphrases the literal "as in your former times." Perhaps the plural of the feminine noun קַדְמָה intends to periodize earlier history, but plural nouns in Hebrew are often abstractions to signify concrete manifestations of a singular quality or state, such as "time."

וְהֵטִבֹתִי—This Hiphil (first common singular with *waw* consecutive), "I will do good," is not used elsewhere in the OT. It appears to be a hybrid, mixing a form derived from יָטַב (הֵטַבְתִּי) with one derived from טוֹב (הֲטִיבֹתִי). See GKC, § 70 e.

36:12 The first half of the verse refers to the mountains with second masculine plural forms, but the second half refers to them in the second masculine singular. The singular can be understood as concentrating all the mountains of Israel into one (cf. Deut 3:25). It is not until the next two verses, where the idea of "land" is even more prominent, that expected feminine forms appear.

36:13 יַעַן אֹמְרִים—Usually יַעַן ("because") is followed by an infinitive construct, but a participle appears here because a quotation follows. The masculine plural participle is indefinite; I have added "*people* say" for clarity. (In the Hebrew this is not connected to אָדָם, "people, humanity," in the quotation that follows.)

לָכֶם אֹכֶלֶת—As in 36:12, the first half of the verse, ending with לָכֶם, "to you," refers to the mountains in the masculine plural, and the second half of the verse, beginning with אֹכֶלֶת (Qal feminine singular participle of אָכַל), refers to them in the singular. The singular forms in 36:13b are feminine, as one would expect in reference to land.

אַתְּ ... גּוֹיֵךְ—Both of these words involve Kethib-Qere variant readings. The first Qere is the usual אַתְּ for the second feminine singular personal pronoun, instead of the archaic form of the Kethib, אַתִּי, with a final *yod*, which occurs some half dozen other times in the OT. It apparently had ceased to be pronounced long before the main biblical period, and we cannot explain why the archaic orthography appears occasionally nonetheless.

In the second instance, the Kethib, גּוֹיֵךְ, is a suffixed singular of גּוֹי, evidently thinking of "Israel" as one unified nation, while the Qere, גּוֹיַיִךְ, has the plural of the noun, which appears to accord with the "two nations" of the divided kingdom in 35:10. The ancient versions support the Kethib, and all modern translations (but not KJV!) follow it. The same Kethib-Qere variation obtains when the word reappears in the next two verses.

36:14 לָכֵן—Usually when לָכֵן, "therefore," follows after יַעַן, "because" (36:13), it describes Yahweh's response to the previous indictment, and usually the citation formula, "thus says Lord Yahweh,"[7] follows לָכֵן. But here, where לָכֵן begins a promise, it seems to have little more than emphatic force, almost like הִנֵּה often does. I have used "assuredly."

---

[7] For this formula, see pages 8–9 in the introduction and the fourth textual note and the commentary on 2:4.

וְגוֹיֵךְ לֹא תְכַשְּׁלִי עוֹד—This clause has two Kethib-Qere variations. The clause is repeated near the end of 36:15 (but with different variants for the verb there). For the first Kethib-Qere variation, which also occurs in 36:13, 15, see the last textual note on 36:13.

In the second Kethib-Qere variation, it is hard to choose between the alternatives. Both are Piel second feminine singular imperfect. The Kethib, תְכַשְּׁלִי, is the Piel of כָּשַׁל, "cause to stumble," while the Qere, תְשַׁכְּלִי, is the Piel of שָׁכַל, "to bereave, make childless, deprive of children," which was used in 36:12–13. If the Qere is correct, then the Kethib is the result of a simple case of metathesis of the first two consonants of the root. The versions support the Qere, and most English translations follow it as well. Most commentators seem to follow the Kethib ("cause to stumble"). The Kethib might be defended and retained on the basis of *lectio difficilior*, but after some debate, I have opted in favor of the Qere on the logic that to blame the land for making the people "stumble," that is, causing them to sin, is alien to the context and a weird thought. See further the commentary. Other OT passages indicate that the land suffers because of, but is not the cause of, the people's sin. The Qere ("deprive of children") is consistent with 36:12–13; both of those verses use the Piel of שָׁכַל, and 36:13 (like this verse) describes the land as "devouring" (אֹכֶלֶת) its inhabitants.

36:15   וְגוֹיַיִךְ לֹא־תַכְשִׁלִי עוֹד—For the Qere-Kethib variants involved in וְגוֹיַיִךְ, see the last textual note on 36:13. תַכְשִׁלִי is the Hiphil imperfect (second feminine singular) of כָּשַׁל, which would mean "*you will* no longer *cause* your nation *to stumble*." There is no Qere-Kethib variation here. But several Hebrew manuscripts have תְשַׁכְּלִי, "you will deprive of children," which was the Qere in the corresponding clause in the preceding verse (see the second textual note on 36:14), and which is supported by the Targum here. In both verses, I have translated, "deprive of children."

The LXX and Syriac lack a translation for this entire clause. Some suggest that it is a dittograph from 36:14, a copyist's eye apparently having strayed back to the first עוֹד there. However, the LXX often omits repetitious phrases.

36:17   בֵּית יִשְׂרָאֵל יֹשְׁבִים עַל־אַדְמָתָם וַיְטַמְּאוּ אוֹתָהּ—"House of Israel" is the subject of the Piel imperfect וַיְטַמְּאוּ, "they defiled" it. The three intervening words, beginning with the participle יֹשְׁבִים without the article, form a circumstantial (here temporal) clause, literally, "when they were living on their land," although an idiomatic English translation blurs the construction.

(a) Ezek 14:22–23; 20:43–44; 24:14; 36:17, 19

בְּדַרְכָּם וּבַעֲלִילוֹתָם—The two nouns דֶּרֶךְ and עֲלִילָה are a fixed pair in Ezekiel[a] The terms are nearly synonymous. דֶּרֶךְ is a bit more comprehensive a term for "conduct, behavior, lifestyle," while עֲלִילָה points more to specific manifestations of the first, "misdeed."

כְּטֻמְאַת הַנִּדָּה—The noun טֻמְאָה, "uncleanness," is cognate to the Piel of טָמֵא, "defile," earlier in the verse. The noun נִדָּה is abstract, "menstruation," or semi-metaphorically, "pollution." To describe the menstruant herself, it must be used in apposition to a preceding אִשָּׁה, as in 18:6, although here many of the versions freely render it in a concrete sense ("menstruating woman"). The article on הַנִּדָּה is generic, that is, anything in that category, although in practice, menstruation is almost sui generis, a metaphor for the most extreme and revolting pollution.

36:18 שָׁפַכְתִּי ... וָאֶשְׁפֹּךְ—This verse has an obvious play on the verb שָׁפַךְ in both a metaphorical ("*I poured out* my wrath") and a literal ("blood *they had poured*") use. Many times before, Ezekiel has used the verb with the object חֵמָה, "wrath,"[b] and the object דָּם, "blood."[c]

עַל־הַדָּם אֲשֶׁר־שָׁפָכוּ ... וּבְגִלּוּלֵיהֶם טִמְּאוּהָ:—Prepositional phrases introduce two motive clauses, each giving a reason why Yahweh poured out his wrath. עַל־הַדָּם is "on account of the blood," and it is followed by a relative clause with אֲשֶׁר, literally, "that they had poured." For the last two words (וּבְגִלּוּלֵיהֶם טִמְּאוּהָ), we should infer another relative clause, "and by their fecal deities *with which* they had defiled it" (cf. Joüon, § 158 d). For גִּלּוּלִים as "fecal deities," see the textual note on it in 6:4. The LXX lacks a translation of both motive clauses, and Zimmerli and Allen consider them misplaced additions to 36:17a, wishing to include them in a more general picture of the grievous conduct described there,[8] but there is no overriding reason to delete them.

36:19 וָאָפִיץ אֹתָם בַּגּוֹיִם וַיִּזָּרוּ בָּאֲרָצוֹת—Yahweh's judgment of "scattering" Israel has been mentioned many times before (e.g., 12:15; 20:23). Although the Hebrew has its usual parataxis, the relation between the two virtually synonymous verbs ("scatter" and "disperse") is really one of cause and effect. וָאָפִיץ (Hiphil imperfect of פּוּץ), "I scattered," expresses the causative action, and its result is expressed by וַיִּזָּרוּ (Niphal imperfect of זָרָה), the passive "they were dispersed." In all other instances where these two verbs (פּוּץ and זָרָה) are parallel, both are active.[d] That may explain why the LXX and Syriac render them both as active here too. Greenberg suggests that by the change to the Niphal of זָרָה here, the prophet intended "a closure of the series."[9]

36:20 וַיָּבוֹא אֶל־הַגּוֹיִם אֲשֶׁר־בָּאוּ שָׁם—The first verb is singular, but the second verb and forms later in the verse are plural ("they"). See the textual note on וַיָּבוֹא in 14:1 and also the second textual note on 20:38, which has the singular יָבוֹא where we might expect a plural. Some consider וַיָּבוֹא to be a metathetical error for וַיָּבֹאוּ. Many ancient Hebrew witnesses as well as the versions support the plural reading. But, as the following verse shows, the antecedent of "they" is "the house of Israel," and Hebrew more easily shifts between the collective singular and the individualizing plural than English, so there is no urgency in making the change.

The Hebrew sounds redundant, literally, "they came to the nations which they came thither." I have condensed it to "when they came to the various nations," similar to the same idiom in 36:21–22, where the verb is used only once in each verse. This *idem per idem* ("the same by the same") seems to accent imprecision, when there is no desire to specify exactly where the scattered Israelites went, but at the same time it intensifies the thought of their dispersal. Zimmerli quotes Vriezen as translating, "Everywhere, wherever they came."[10] A close parallel to the idiom of coming to the nations appears in 12:15 and elsewhere.

(b) Ezek 7:8; 9:8; 14:19; 20:8, 13, 21, 33–34; 22:22; 30:15

(c) Ezek 16:38; 18:10; 22:3–4, 6, 9, 12, 27; 23:45; 33:25

(d) Ezek 12:15; 20:23; 22:15; 29:12; 30:23, 26

---

[8] Zimmerli, *Ezekiel*, 2:241; Allen, *Ezekiel*, 2:176.

[9] Greenberg, *Ezekiel*, 2:728.

[10] Zimmerli, *Ezekiel*, 2:241, quoting Theodorus Christiaan Vriezen, "*ʾEhje ʾašer ʾehje*," in *Festschrift Alfred Bertholet zum 80. Geburtstag* (ed. Walter Baumgartner et al.; Tübingen: Mohr [Siebeck], 1950), 504.

36:21 וָאֶחְמֹל עַל־שֵׁם קָדְשִׁי—The verb חָמַל usually means "have compassion, pity." See the textual note on it in 5:11. The word definitely implies some positive regard for its object, but with Yahweh as subject and "my holy name" as the beneficiary, "have pity on" seems inappropriate. We dare not jump to the conclusion that the real object is Israel (even though indirectly the Israelites were), because 36:22 specifically rejects that thought. Hence, although KJV literalistically has "had pity for," NKJV and other English translations, including NIV, have rendered, "I had concern for my holy name."

It is exegetically significant that the imperfect וָאֶחְמֹל appears here with *waw* consecutive, implying the past tense. One would expect a statement about the future. The implication could be that Yahweh is now informing Ezekiel about something that has already taken place, even if the people know nothing about it yet. More likely, however, it alludes to the fact that the salvation of the people had long since been proclaimed to them, but it was not clear how he of the "holy name" could possibly forgive a people who had not hallowed that name. Thus the verb prepares for the *sola gratia* ("salvation by grace alone") of the following verses. Apart from that, the people's prospect was bleak indeed. In this context, the imperfect with *waw* consecutive becomes functionally a prophetic perfect, speaking of the future as already done.

36:22 Although לָכֵן ("therefore") links the following material with what precedes, both the citation formula, "thus says the Lord Yahweh," and the command to speak signal a major shift. No longer does Yahweh only communicate to Ezekiel; the prophet is commanded to speak to the people, and so the oracle (36:22–32) appears in the form of the second person of direct address. The assertion "not for your sake …" is repeated in 36:32, so it frames the entire unit at the same time as it summarized its main point.

לֹא לְמַעַנְכֶם אֲנִי עֹשֶׂה—The negative לֹא might echo the negatives in the previous verses (36:12, 14–15), sounding as though another judgment oracle is about to come, but really it is only the foil to the positive notes that follow. A noun clause is more commonly negated by אֵין rather than לֹא, and the expected wording here might be אֵינֶנִּי עֹשֶׂה לְמַעַנְכֶם ("I am not acting for your sake"). The use of לֹא with a noun clause is emphatic and indicates that the force of the negation falls on the following word (GKC, § 152 d), which is מַעַן (לְמַעַנְכֶם) with לְ and second masculine plural suffix), literally, "*not* for your sake I am acting." The negative does not extend to the participle עֹשֶׂה. The inversion of the normal word order (with אֲנִי עֹשֶׂה following instead of preceding) also underscores the negation. עָשָׂה without an object occurs also in 20:9, 14, 22, 44, where Yahweh declares that he acts for the sake of his name.

כִּי אִם־לְשֵׁם־קָדְשִׁי—The positive antithesis to the preceding negative is then introduced by כִּי אִם ("but") and the simple לְ of advantage, "for my holy name." The uncommon use of לְ in parallel with לְמַעַן is found also in Is 55:5.

36:23 The appearance of the signatory formula, "says Lord Yahweh," in the middle of the recognition formula, "they will know that I am Yahweh … when …" is unusual. The signatory formula does not appear in the LXX and some Hebrew manuscripts. But as the MT stands, the formula is obviously an emphatic expression of Yahweh's determination and of the power of his divine Word.

בְּהִקָּדְשִׁי בָכֶם לְעֵינֵיהֶם:—The Niphal (infinitive construct with בְּ and first common singular suffix) of קָדַשׁ has a causative-reflexive meaning, "when I show/reveal myself as holy," in which the subject causes the action to happen to himself (cf. Waltke-O'Connor, § 23.4h). Instead of בָכֶם ("through you"), many ancient Hebrew manuscripts read בָהֶם, "through them," which might be supported by the parallel in 28:25. That could emphasize God's punishment of the nations, if that were how he displayed his holiness "through them." The wording here, literally, "through you to their eyes," implies Yahweh's merciful activity through his people in the eyes of the astonished nations. Since that is the theme of the following verses (36:24–38), it is easily the preferred reading here.

36:26 See the textual notes on the same and similar vocabulary in 11:19. For the translation of וְרוּחַ חֲדָשָׁה as "a new S/spirit," see the commentary on 11:19. This phrase here might refer to a new human spirit, a new spiritual disposition that God gives to his people, but in 36:27, רוּחַ plainly refers to Yahweh's "Spirit"—the Holy Spirit.

36:27 וְעָשִׂיתִי אֵת אֲשֶׁר־בְּחֻקַּי תֵּלֵכוּ וּמִשְׁפָּטַי תִּשְׁמְרוּ וַעֲשִׂיתֶם:—A literal translation, admittedly awkward in English, would be "and I will make which [so] in my statutes you walk, and my judgments you guard and do." Here אֲשֶׁר introduces a relative clause that is the direct object of the verb וְעָשִׂיתִי (see Joüon, §§ 157 f and 158 l). This usage increases in frequency in Late Biblical Hebrew. Instead of "do, make," here עָשָׂה has the nuance of "cause," as also in Eccl 3:14: "God has made it so they [people] revere him." See BDB, s.v. עָשָׂה, Qal, 9, and Cooke,[11] who is often cited.

36:28 וְאָנֹכִי—Virtually all commentators note that only here in Ezekiel is the long form of the first person personal pronoun found. In the later books of the OT, the preponderance of אֲנִי over אָנֹכִי is evident. Thus in Ezekiel the shorter form occurs one hundred sixty-nine times in contrast to the solo appearance of the long form here. The probable reason for the long form here is the influence of Jeremiah. Ezekiel's slightly older contemporary still uses אָנֹכִי quite frequently (thirty-seven times compared to fifty-four of אֲנִי); among the places he does so is in the covenant formula of mutuality (see Jer 11:4; 30:22; and especially 24:6–7, a promise of future restoration, as is Ezek 36:28). An additional possibility is that "the land I gave your fathers," which also occurs only here in Ezekiel (cf. 20:42; 37:25; 47:14), may indicate that the long form אָנֹכִי is a deliberate archaism on Ezekiel's part. There is no intrinsic difference in meaning in the two forms, and the feature is lost in translation.

36:30 Two expressions in this verse are rare or unique, although the meanings are clear. וּתְנוּבַת הַשָּׂדֶה, "the produce/crops of the fields," with שָׂדֶה being used in a collective sense, occurs only here. The related expression תְּנוּבֹת שָׂדָי occurs only in Deut 32:13 and Lam 4:9. The noun תְּנוּבָה, which occurs two other times in the OT, is from the rare verb נוּב, "grow." Second, the common verb לָקַח, usually "take," in context here with the object "disgrace," means "receive," a usage paralleled only in Hos 10:6. I have translated, "suffer the disgrace." There are comparable English idioms, for example, "take," that is, endure something, whether one likes it or not.

---

[11] Cooke, *Ezekiel*, 395.

36:34 תַּחַת אֲשֶׁר הָיְתָה—Literally, "instead of which it was," the combination תַּחַת אֲשֶׁר is used as a conjunction with the following verb הָיָה elsewhere only in Deut 28:62. See BDB, s.v. תַּחַת, II 3 a. Usually תַּחַת אֲשֶׁר is used without the verb, meaning "because/inasmuch as."

לְעֵינֵי כָּל־עוֹבֵר—This expression, "in the sight of every passerby," is unique to Ezekiel, and its only other occurrence was in 5:14 (see the second textual note there). The shorter phrase כָּל־עוֹבֵר occurs also in, for example, Jer 18:16; 19:8; 49:17; 50:13; Ezek 16:15, 25.

36:35 הָאָרֶץ הַלֵּזוּ—The feminine demonstrative pronoun הַלֵּזוּ, "this," is a hapax. It apparently is a feminine form of the masculine הַלָּזֶה, which appears twice (Gen 24:65; 37:19). Those masculine and feminine forms are both related to הַלָּז, which seems to be epicene (modifying both masculine and feminine forms, seven times in the OT). It is impossible to say whether these pronouns are archaic, dialectical, poetic, or slightly emphatic. The nouns they modify usually have a definite article, and there are indications that the pronouns were used especially when the subject was at a remove from the speaker, both of which conditions apply here. See BDB on those words and Waltke-O'Connor, § 17.2a.

וְהֶעָרִים הֶחֱרֵבוֹת—The feminine plural form חֱרֵבוֹת ("ruined") of the adjective חָרֵב occurs only here and in 36:38. We would expect the vocalization to be -חֲ with *chateph patach* instead of *chateph qamets* (short "o" vowel) here. The anomaly probably arises from the influence of the noun חֳרָבוֹת at the end of 36:33.

בְּצוּרוֹת יֵשֵׁבוּ:—"(They) are now fortified and inhabited" is a free translation of the feminine plural Qal passive participle (בְּצוּרוֹת, modifying the preceding הֶעָרִים), used circumstantially with the prophetic perfect (in pause), יֵשֵׁבוּ, literally, "the cities … (as) fortified they inhabit."

36:37 אַרְבֶּה אֹתָם כַּצֹּאן אָדָם:—This clause is not easy to translate. The first two words are clear enough: "I will multiply [Hiphil first common singular imperfect of רָבָה] them." In 36:38 צֹאן אָדָם is a construct phrase (see the fourth textual note on 36:38), but here כַּצֹּאן אָדָם cannot be a construct chain ("like the flock of men") because כַּצֹּאן has the article (indicated by the *patach*, -כַּ), which words in construct cannot have. כַּצֹּאן must be in apposition to אֹתָם, "I will multiply them (to be) like flocks." Then אָדָם may be in apposition to כַּצֹּאן, yielding, "… like flocks, human ones." But more likely in my judgment, the Hiphil verb אַרְבֶּה takes a double accusative, so both אֹתָם and אָדָם are direct objects. Verbs indicating abundance often take a double accusative of the affected object (Joüon, § 125 u), so the meaning is "I will multiply them (in) men." By itself "multiply them" might just indicate an increase in their possessions or territory, but the addition of "men" indicates their human population. The comparison כַּצֹּאן then yields "I will multiply them (so) their men (are) like flocks (of sheep)." Technically, צֹאן can include goats as well (German: *Kleinvieh*), but "sheep" stands for both. The next verse develops the picture more vividly.

36:38 The two added similes use semi-technical OT liturgical vocabulary, which is not easy to render into English.

כְּצֹאן קָדָשִׁים—As in 36:37, צֹאן is a collective, so translated "flock*s*." קָדָשִׁים is the plural of קֹדֶשׁ, which usually has the abstract meaning "holiness," but it can be used for holy "things consecrated at sacred places," including sacrificial animals (BDB, s.v. קֹדֶשׁ, 3 b), hence the translation "flocks consecrated for sacrifice." Since the fall (Genesis 3), nothing in this world is holy by nature until it is consecrated to or sanctified by Yahweh. Since God provided for many common, ordinary (חֹל) things to be so hallowed, קָדָשִׁים is often a generic term for almost anything connected with the temple and liturgical worship, especially sacrifices. See קֹדֶשׁ in, for example, 42:13–14, 20.

בְּמוֹעֲדֶיהָ—"Feast days" is a pale facsimile of "appointed/fixed times," the plural of מוֹעֵד (with בְּ and third feminine singular suffix referring to יְרוּשָׁלַ͏ִם). The noun commonly refers to the three great pilgrimage festivals, Passover, Pentecost (Weeks), and Booths (Sukkoth), when massive throngs of pilgrims flocked (no pun intended) to Jerusalem, each man with his own sacrificial gift.

צֹאן אָדָם—This phrase is similar to כַּצֹּאן אָדָם in 36:37. However, here צֹאן lacks the article, and this is a construct phrase, probably a genitive of genus, "human cattle" (Joüon, § 129 f (3)) or "flocks *of men*" (Waltke-O'Connor, § 9.5.3i, example 56).

Commentary

Except for the words "son of man, prophesy ..." (36:1), found also in 35:2, there is no indication, such as a word-event formula,[12] that a new chapter begins here. In fact, functionally, 36:1–15 should be designated 35:16–30. But practically, for commentary purposes, we have no choice but to follow the traditional chapter and verse divisions.

If one feels compelled to outline chapter 36, one can describe 36:1–15 as addressed to the mountains of Israel, while 36:16–38 is an address to the people of Israel. But it is more fruitful to consider chapter 35 and 36:1–15 to comprise a single oracle, consisting of two parts, each beginning with a corresponding vocative. Ezek 35:1–15 is addressed against "Mount Seir," while 36:1–15 is addressed for "the mountains of Israel." In fact, Yahweh's overriding interest to proclaim salvation to "the *mountains* of Israel" in 36:1–15 probably explains why in chapter 35 he had virtually always spoken against "*Mount* Seir" rather than using the country's name, "Edom" (only in 35:15). See further the first part of the commentary on chapter 35.

For those concerned with "logical" structure, 36:1–15 is nightmarish. Let Block, a quite conservative commentator, summarize:

> If ch. 35 seems disjointed, 36:1–15 is even more so. Numerous repetitive and disruptive prophetic formulae appear to chop it up into little fragments. Indeed, it is difficult to determine when Yahweh is addressing his messenger and when he is addressing the mountains. The result looks like a patchwork quilt, except that quilts usually reflect more deliberate design.[13]

---

[12] For this formula, "the Word of Yahweh came to me," see page 8 in the introduction and the textual note on 3:16.

[13] Block, *Ezekiel*, 2:322.

Block puts forth a reconstruction that explains the text in terms of an original core (36:1–2, 6–11) to which additions (36:3–5 and 36:12–15) were later added. However, he does not attribute the additions to later editors, but to miscellaneous logia that Ezekiel himself uttered on other occasions and subsequently inserted here.[14] And, of course, there are no lack of other reconstructions, which need not be detailed here.

I personally have no problem with Block's observations, but, as this commentary has shown elsewhere, it is not the type of problem that significantly concerns me. Regardless of how the present text took shape (humanly speaking), the level of subjectivity in putative reconstructions is almost unacceptably high. We have little choice but to take the text as it has been handed down, dealing with problems individually as we confront them. In the end, we must affirm that the Scriptures, in their extant form, were inspired by the Holy Spirit (2 Pet 1:20–21) and possess normative authority for the church.

Oracle for the Mountains of Israel (36:1–15)

36:1 The address to "the mountains of Israel" is similar to that first heard in 6:2–3, except that the tone is entirely different. There it had been used to denounce their idolatrous associations. Here the immediate contrast is with 35:12, describing Edom's blasphemous boasts against the mountains of Israel. Now the phrase describes the land and its people whose deliverance has already been announced in veiled terms by the judgment oracle against Edom in chapter 35. As we said about the oracles against the nations in chapter 25–32, judgment against enemies is part of God saving his own people. Ezek 36:1–15 promises salvation to Israel through the form of antitheses to that threat against Edom.

36:2 The boast put in Edom's mouth here is very similar to those we have already heard in chapter 35. The noun "possession" (מוֹרָשָׁה) is derived from the verb יָרַשׁ, which may mean either "possess" or "dispossess," since occupation by one people usually involves expulsion of another. The noun and verb are used in God's promises of the land and Israel's conquest of Canaan (see the second textual note on 33:24), although more prominent in Deuteronomy and Joshua is נַחֲלָה, "inheritance," used in Ezek 36:12. Similar claims to the land using "possession" (מוֹרָשָׁה) had been made in 11:15 and 33:24 by the Judeans who had escaped deportation. As such, it here expresses Edom's intent to take definitively for itself land that had long been Israel's gift from God; thus Edom wanted to do to Israel what Israel had done to the prior heathen Canaanite inhabitants.

36:3 In spite of uncertainties in translation (see the textual notes), the general sense of the verse is clear. It functions as an expansion of 36:2 in the form of a direct address to "the mountains of Israel" (36:1). They have been so battered and pummeled that they can offer no resistance to any occupier. Ezekiel usually uses שְׁאֵרִית, "rest, remnant," of those who have survived divine judg-

---

14 Block, *Ezekiel*, 2:322–23.

ment (5:10; 9:8; 11:13), but here it must refer to any and all groups, including the Edomites, who were still intact after the Babylonian invasions. And the slanderous gossip probably involved a jibe at Israel's earlier confidence in the inviolability of Jerusalem as God's elect.[15] So violated a land as Judah might have colloquially been referred to as one that devoured its own people, as the faithless Israelite spies had once described the land (Num 13:32).

The careful reader will not fail to notice that every verse from Ezek 36:3 through 36:7 begins with לָכֵן, "therefore." Even critics acknowledge the word's genuineness since it is hard to imagine editors so careless that they would allow such repetition. Keil's approving quotation from the critic Ewald seems in order:

> Ezekiel is seized with unusual fire, so that after the brief statement in ver. 2 "therefore" is repeated five times, the charges brought against these foes forcing themselves in again and again, before the prophecy settles calmly upon the mountains of Israel, to which it was really intended to apply.[16]

36:4 This verse, obviously an expansion of the previous verses, is the beginning of Yahweh's reply. The list of four topographical expressions, "the mountains, hills, valleys, ravines," comes from 6:3 and is obviously intended to say that this oracle of salvation is intended to reverse the judgment oracle in which it had earlier been used. It is strengthened by the addition of "desolate ruins" and "abandoned cities." The mention of "plunder" parallels the use of "food" (אָכְלָה) in 34:8 and 35:12. "Ridicule" (לַעַג, used in Ezekiel only here and in 23:32) parallels the two expressions at the end of the previous verse. "Plunder" translates בַּז, a derivative of the geminate verb בָּזַז, but its similarity to the third-*he* verb בָּזָה, "to despise," suggests paranomasia. Plundering and ridiculing the defeated victims often go together, so one may take "a source of plunder and an object of ridicule" as a near hendiadys here as well. The objective element of desolation and the subjective one of ridicule easily merge.

36:5 The same thoughts are reiterated in heightened form, stating some of the reasons for Yahweh's wrath, and in the form of an oath. The same fiery "zeal" that had once been stoked by Israel's affronts (e.g., 5:13) is now fanned by the arrogance of "the rest of the nations." But for the first and only time in 36:1–15, "Edom" is specified as representative of all the nations who coveted or actually seized Israelite territory and as the main country against which, just as in chapter 35, this oracle is aimed (although, factually, we already knew it was "Edom" because of 35:15). What the Edomites intend to appropriate for themselves, Yahweh calls "my land," reminding us of 35:10, when he had insisted that he was still there. And finally, the unrestrained glee and visceral malice with which they were proceeding simply rubbed salt in the wounds. Yahweh

---

[15] The unfaithful Israelites misapplied God's Zion promises to the city of Jerusalem. See Hummel, *Ezekiel 1–20*, 256–57, 274–75, 371, 471. See also the commentary on 21:28 (ET 21:23); 24:20–21.

[16] Keil, *Ezekiel*, 2:102.

could not allow such an insolent and disdainful challenge to his Word to go unanswered.

36:6–7 As 36:1–15 moves into the oracle of salvation, which it mainly is, it summarizes the coming punishment upon the adversaries in terms of the great reversal, the turning of the tables, measure for measure—a common OT theme. The concluding verses of the oracle (36:12–15) will return to this theme, forming a sort of frame or inclusio.[17]

36:8 Before he addresses his people (36:16–38), Yahweh first speaks to the land upon which they will again live. The salient feature of that land is the very hilly or mountainous character of most of it. Such terrain is not conducive to any large-scale cultivation of grains and vegetables, but trees and shrubs will flourish even on steep slopes, which in Israel were apparently terraced at an early date, as is still evident today. This accounts for the importance attached to fruit trees in this and many other passages. Compare Deut 8:8, where five of the seven things with which the land is blessed are fruit trees or shrubs or their products.[18] God had created those mountains to be "mountains of Israel," and instead of the present war-ravaged and desolate landscape, they will again perform their God-given function for his people.

Greenberg nicely observes the parallel with the creation narrative of Genesis 2. As God had planted fruit-bearing trees in Eden before placing Adam in it—"and arboriculture preceded agriculture (Gen 2:5–16; 3:17–19)"—so here the growing of edible fruit precedes the return of the people.[19] Greenberg does not mention the "new creation" motif, and it goes beyond the surface perimeters of this pericope, but in the quasi-eschatological atmosphere, it is relevant. In total biblical perspective, Israel's return is a type of returns of infinitely greater scope, part of the realization of which still awaits us at the end of history. After the return of Jesus Christ, the present fallen creation itself will give way to a new heavens and a new, abundantly fruitful earth (Isaiah 11; 65; Revelation 21–22) that can be likened to "the garden of Eden" (Ezek 36:35), as Yahweh will reveal more fully to Ezekiel in chapters 40–48.

How "soon" (Ezek 36:8) the return home would be was not revealed to Ezekiel. Earlier eschatological imminence had been predicted of judgment on Israel in 7:7–19 in terms of the "day" of Yahweh (in 30:3 also applied to Egypt) and similarly in 12:22–28. Precise dates were not given then either, and usually are not in genuinely biblical eschatology. (An exception was the revela-

---

[17] Not here, but a common prophetic summarizing formula elsewhere is שׁוּב שְׁבוּת (16:53; 29:14; 39:25), unfortunately often translated as "reversal of fortunes," as though it were the work of Lady Luck, rather than of Yahweh, who acts in judgment upon unbelievers, but in grace for believers.

[18] Greenberg, *Ezekiel*, 2:719, quotes this observation from J. Feliks, *Plant World of the Bible* [in Hebrew] (Tel Aviv: Massada, 1957), 12–14. The five fruit trees or shrubs are (grape)vines, fig trees, pomegranates, olive trees, and date trees. דְּבַשׁ, "fruit syrup" (traditionally translated "honey"), is most often made from dates. See Kleinig, *Leviticus*, 73.

[19] Greenberg, *Ezekiel*, 2:719.

tion to Jeremiah that the exile would last "seventy years" [Jer 25:11–12; 29:10].) Part of the reason why God generally does not reveal his timetable is the existential element that always accompanies the "day" language in Scripture: every day is a judgment day as God acts to condemn and punish sin, and every day is the day of salvation, at least for the believer (see Heb 3:7–8, 15; 4:7). But there have always been those who were not satisfied with such uncertainty, and, at best, have succeeded only in skewing the main biblical message as a result. Greenberg notes that Jewish chiliasts of the fourth century A.D. were cautioned by Rabbi Abba that the "sign of the end-time" in this verse was as explicit as they would get,[20] by which, Greenberg surmises, Rabbi Abba intended to discourage such speculation. Greenberg adds mordantly, "In the event, it has inspired theurgic fantasies down to the present."[21] And Christians will be only too aware that they have had to endure comparable impulses all through their history, as people wrongly predict the return of Christ on a certain date or espouse false millennial eschatologies, such as the current "left behind" scenarios (based on premillennial dispensationalism).[22] Some millennial groups are even based on anti-Christian heresy, such as the Jehovah's Witnesses and similar caricatures of Christian faith.

36:9 Both formally and materially, Ezekiel expresses the great reversal by changing the hostile orientation formula, which usually means "I am against you" (most recently in 35:3), into its opposite, "I am for you," or "I am on your side," as some paraphrase it. This is the only time in the OT that this clause appears with this meaning. "I ... will look on you with favor" is NIV's paraphrase of the literal "I will turn toward you," which again is the opposite of a common hostile idiom, where God "hides his face from" those with whom he is angry (e.g., Deut 31:17–18). The language here differs only slightly from that of the Aaronic benediction (Num 6:24–26), with which Ezekiel, a priest (1:3), would have been well-acquainted. Clearly this and the following verses are connected to the covenant blessings of Lev 26:9, although in the context there, God's blessing is contingent (see Lev 26:3), while in the context here, blessing is predicted absolutely.

36:10 This and the next verse are concerned with the repopulating of the land. How and when this should happen Ezekiel again does not say. On the empirical plane, Canaan had its ups and downs—and still does. Its ultimate application must be to the Christian missionary mandate to preach the Gospel to the ends of the earth (e.g., Acts 1:8). By adding "all of it" (כֻּלֹּה), Ezekiel probably intends to include also the "ten lost tribes" of northern Israel, which had politically, but not theologically, been sundered from "Israel." After this and

---

[20] Talmud, *Sanhedrin*, 98a.

[21] Greenberg, *Ezekiel*, 2:720.

[22] For a survey of Jewish and Christian views and a stout defense of the historic Christian view, one may see the excursus "The Millennium" in Brighton, *Revelation*, 533–41.

other intimations in the book, Ezekiel will develop this idea in detail in 37:15–28.

36:11 This is a restatement and amplification of 36:10, as is immediately apparent in the inclusion of animals in the coming plenitude of life. The assertion that the land's fertility will exceed anything previously known again hints at a paradisiacal state, like "the garden of Eden" in 36:35. Since Christology should be included in the ultimate picture, theology's *felix culpa* ("blessed fault") formulation inevitably comes to mind: in Christ, the "last Adam" (1 Cor 15:45), mankind gained more than he lost in the fall of the first Adam.

36:12 Repopulation means repossession. The use of the verb "walk" seems strange. It could imply a contrast to the curse on Edom (35:7) that God would cut off from it "all who come and go." But Greenberg may correctly discern in the word "the popular legal conception that ownership of land may be established by walking through it." He cites God's command to Abraham to do just that (Gen 13:17) as well as God telling Joshua how he caused Abraham to walk through the land (Josh 24:3).[23]

That Israel will "take possession" (יָרַשׁ) of the land sounds as though it intends to counter the hopes of other nations to occupy it as their own "possession" (מוֹרָשָׁה, 36:2–3, 5). And in near parallelism stands the more theologically loaded noun נַחֲלָה, "inheritance," frequent in Deuteronomy and Joshua. The Israelites were no mere squatters or migrants, but as people of the promise, they could claim the land by divine right, just as Christians do with their "land," a promise already fulfilled at the first advent of Christ, but also awaiting its consummation at his return.[24]

The last phrase in the verse clearly uses the verb שָׁכַל (in Piel, transitive), which means to cause a miscarriage or otherwise bereave someone of children. The idea is taken up again in the next verses, and 36:14 and 36:15 probably use the same Hebrew verb (see the textual notes). The expressions that the land deprives the people of their children (36:12–15) and devours people (36:13–14) hardly make sense literally, but must be metaphorical of the land, pictured as a mother, being invaded and depopulated, thus losing her children (cf. Is 47:8–9). This view of the land was ancient, having been heard and repeated (using the verb אָכַל, "devour") already by the faithless spies in Num 13:32. We know too little of Canaan's pre-Israelite history even to guess what underlay that reputation at that early date, but the defeat of the Canaanites by invading Israelites meant the land had vomited them out because of their abominations (Lev 18:25, 28; cf. Lev 20:22). In turn, the deportations of the

---

[23] Greenberg, *Ezekiel*, 2:721.

[24] For the way in which the OT land promises pertain to the church and Christians as heirs (Gal 3:26–29), see page 3 in the introduction and the commentary on 37:14, 22, 25, as well as Heb 11:13–16; 2 Pet 3:13.

northern Israelites by the Assyrians and of the Judeans by the Babylonians would seem applicable here.

36:13–15 These verses are a sort of summary of 13:1–15. The subjectless אֹמְרִים, literally, "they are saying," must refer to all who observe Yahweh's miraculous restoration of his land and people. The masculine plural of the dative לָכֶם, "to you," must have the "mountains of Israel" (36:1, 4, 8) as its antecedent. The idea of the land depriving the nation of its children (36:13–15) continues the thought introduced in the previous verse, and "the taunts of the nations" (36:15) refers back to 36:6. Formally, throughout these verses, the land is personified as the owner of its inhabitants, and hence the predominance of feminine Hebrew forms.

Noteworthy in 36:14 is Yahweh's characterization of the restored population as a גּוֹי, "nation." Most often גּוֹיִם (the plural, "nations") appears in reference to the "Gentiles, heathen." Yet its usage partially overlaps with עַם, "people," since ancient Israel was a political as well as an ethnic, cultural, and religious unit. But there is no doubt that עַם, "people," is the preferred term when there is a desire to accent Israel's special status as the elect, covenanted people, especially with the first person suffix, "*my* people" (e.g., Ex 3:7, 10). עַם is so applied hundreds of times in the OT, and the same theology largely continues with the use of λαός, God's "people," for Christians in the NT (e.g., Mt 1:21; Lk 1:17; Titus 2:14; 1 Pet 2:9–10). In contrast, גּוֹי, "nation," rarely is suffixed, and its usage often resembles that of ἔθνη for "Gentiles, heathen, pagans" in the NT (e.g., Mt 6:32; Lk 2:32). Yet already in the promise to Abraham, God spoke of Abraham's descendants becoming "a great nation" (Gen 12:2). But only in (the Qere of) Zeph 2:9 does Yahweh call Israel "my nation" (גּוֹיִי), and only in Ps 106:5 is Israel referred to as "your [Yahweh's] nation" (גּוֹיֶךָ). By using גּוֹי, "nation," of Israel here, Yahweh wishes to emphasize that the people of God will be a divinely governed entity on the repopulated land. The Christian heirs of OT Israel can no longer claim any "land" (in its ordinary sense of real estate) by divine right, but neither is the church a purely spiritual (subjective) entity of the heart. God comes to us now in physical ways in his Sacraments. Through Baptism we are heirs of God's promises to Abraham, and in the Lord's Supper, we receive a foretaste of the feast to come—the wedding supper of the Lamb, to be celebrated in the new heavens and new earth, our true promised land, where God shall dwell with his redeemed in Christ for eternity (Revelation 19–22).

Zimmerli suggests that the oracle addresses some "hidden despondency on the part of the exiles" and gives assurance that Yahweh will not ultimately forsake his people, even though they had been judged severely, and all this only as a result of God's own "inner faithfulness," what Zimmerli calls "the logic of His faithfulness."[25]

---

[25] Zimmerli, *Ezekiel*, 2:239–40.

Some Hebrew texts speak of the land causing the people to stumble.[26] Ezekiel uses many bold and unusual metaphors, but nowhere in either Ezekiel or the rest of Scripture is it suggested that the *land* caused the Israelites to sin. Neither did the land cause Adam and Eve to sin, although the fruit of the tree became enticing to them after Satan's misrepresentation of it. Fallen Adam (and all subsequent men, until the curse be lifted at the return of Christ) was required to earn a living "in the sweat of [his] face" because the ground was much less fruitful as a result of his sin (Gen 3:19; cf. the commentary on Ezek 44:18).

Therefore, I have followed the Hebrew readings in 36:14–15 that state that the land will no longer deprive the nation of her children. Metaphorically speaking, the land had bereaved the people when God sent judgments against them in such forms as famine, disease, and wild beasts (see 5:17; 14:21; also Rev 6:8). In modern times, many diseases have been eradicated, and at least in the Western world, famine and wild beasts rarely claim lives. Nevertheless, tragedies can deprive people of their children, which is the most grievous loss possible ("every parent's worst nightmare"). One might also think of the modern specter of abortion, whereby parents take the lives of their own children, a heinous sin akin to ancient child sacrifice (see the commentary on Ezek 16:21; 20:26, 31; 23:37). But God promises that in the coming age his redeemed and sanctified people will be free from such sins, and they need not fear for their children.

The signatory formula, "says the Lord Yahweh,"[27] is repeated at the end of both 36:14 and 36:15, doubly guaranteeing his promise.

Salvation Oracle to the People of Israel (36:16–38)

Arguably, this oracle (36:16–38), especially 36:25–27, is theologically one of the most significant in the entire book. At the very least, it must be ranked with Ezekiel's inaugural vision and commissioning (chapters 1–3) and the following section on resurrection (37:1–14). Certainly, it is one of the clearest expressions in all Scripture of *sola gratia*, that salvation comes "by grace alone"—and, by extension, also its opposite, the total depravity of human nature due to original sin, so that we can contribute nothing to our salvation, and all must be done by God. I am always reminded of the beautiful words of one of our collects, assigned to the Third Sunday after Trinity in *TLH* and to the Tenth Sunday after Pentecost in *LW:* "O God, the Protector of all who trust in you, without whom nothing is strong and nothing is holy ..." The full extent to which Yahweh would go to demonstrate his grace and make it available to his people is not yet revealed to Ezekiel, but it is the same grace given us in Christ, and as always, the Christian expounder is obligated to make explicit that fullness.

---

[26] "Cause to stumble" is the Qere in 36:14 and the sole reading of most manuscripts in 36:15. See the second textual note on 36:14 and the textual note on 36:15.

[27] For this formula, see pages 8–9 in the introduction and the second textual note on 5:11.

As we work though Ezekiel's exposition of these themes, we become aware of singularities of Ezekiel's language—language with which we are not quite so familiar, at least in these applications. It is language that Lutherans tend to associate with the Calvinist tradition, namely, God's "glory"[28] and his "holy name," which are Yahweh's repeatedly stated reasons for bringing his people home. As Zimmerli observes:

> Here too Ezekiel is devoid of all soft-hearted features and warmer tones. There is no mention of mercy, love, covenant faithfulness, the justice that brings salvation. This whole vocabulary is missing from the book of Ezekiel. חסד, רחמים, אמונה, ישועה, ישע, אהבה are sought in vain in the book of Ezekiel. צדקה ["righteousness"] and אמת ["faithfulness"] are attested only in a strictly forensic use, while אהב ["love"] occurs only in chapters 16 and 23 of human lovers. Only the verb הושיע ["to save"] occurs three times (34:22; 36:29; 37:23). In place of these in Ezekiel the dominant concept is that of the majesty of Yahweh and the revelation of his honor and glory. ... From this majesty there comes also his work of deliverance for his people.[29]

Undoubtedly, this accent and vocabulary in Ezekiel partly explains why Lutherans (beginning with Luther) seem never to have warmed to or made as much use of Ezekiel as of other prophets, especially of Isaiah. But we easily erect a false antithesis if we are not careful. In the biblical kaleidoscope of God's attributes and his relation to us, each prophet forms one part of the total picture and is incomplete without the rest. An obvious casualty of avoiding Ezekiel and similar texts will probably be the loss of solid proclamation of the Law, of God's wrath over sin, and a sentimentalizing of his love. To "hate the sin, but love the sinner" is a helpful maxim for humans to follow, since we cannot read the heart, but if God is made the subject of that maxim, it is simply unscriptural and indefensible. Where is abstract "sin" to be found except in flesh and blood sinners? When sin becomes an abstraction, our confessions of sin become perfunctory, and the subsequent absolution an almost mechanically self-evident result. Not for nothing do refrains such as *soli Deo gloria* ("to God alone be the glory") and *ad maiorem Dei gloriam* ("to the greater glory of God") reverberate throughout our theological and devotional literature.

The word-event formula, "the Word of Yahweh came to me"[30] (36:16), and the address to Ezekiel as "son of man"[31] (36:17) signal the beginning of a new oracle, continuing until the recognition formula, "then they will know that I am Yahweh,"[32] in 36:38. On this much, there is broad agreement among scholars, but little beyond that.

---

[28] While chapter 36 does not mention Yahweh's "Glory," the book as a whole emphasizes it, especially in chapters 1–3, 8–11, and 43–44. See also 39:13, 21.

[29] Zimmerli, *Ezekiel*, 2:247–48.

[30] For this formula, see page 8 in the introduction and the textual note on 3:16.

[31] See the second textual note and the commentary on 2:1.

[32] For this formula, see page 9 in the introduction and the commentary on 6:7.

As so often, the basic question asked by critics is whether we are to regard 36:16–38 as a coherent whole or as a composite of various stages and accretions. They especially call into question the unity of the material because of the "intrusion" of various prophetic formulae—all typically Ezekelian—at seemingly random points. Their proposed solutions range all the way from denial of any Ezekelian involvement at all, to the prophet himself making additions to an original core at various times later in his ministry. To the latter alternative, there would be no intrinsic theological objections, although details would undoubtedly remain hypothetical.

Ironically, regardless of how one views the history of the text, it is readily divisible (with minimal debate) into three or four sections: (1) 36:16–21, in the form of a divine address to Ezekiel, referring to Israel in the third person, describing the damage Israel's exile is doing to Yahweh's "name" or reputation (these verses are sometimes regarded as the original core, to which later attachments were made); (2) 36:22–32, in the form of a divine speech Ezekiel is to relay to his audience, describing what Yahweh will do to remedy the situation; and (3) 36:33–38, a final recapitulation (or two, since 36:37–38 sometimes is distinguished as a separate addendum), with a little extra detail about the restored land and redeemed people.

The text-critical problem is at points complicated severely by comparison with the LXX, especially in 36:23c–38, which does not appear in Papyrus 967, our oldest extant witness to the LXX, dating to the second or third century A.D., and there are other divergences from the MT in the entire surrounding LXX text. This has led to various theories of an originally shorter autograph at this point, but this evidence is now effectively cancelled out by the unpublished Masada Hebrew text, which cannot be later than the first century A.D. and which contains clear remains of 36:24–34, all identical with the MT.[33] Even without that evidence, Zimmerli had concluded that the LXX variation poses "a problem for the history only of 𝔊, but not of 𝔐."[34]

Possibly abetting doubts about the MT's textual integrity is the unusually high number of stylistic anomalies in the Hebrew text of 36:23–38. Block cites another writer's calculation of some thirteen words or expressions that are rare or unique in Ezekiel, and sometimes in the entire OT.[35] Some critics take these as evidence of some non-Ezekelian hand. Considerable Jeremianic influence is evident, although, to some extent, that is characteristic of much of the book, as one would expect of two near-contemporaries. But another explanation is the most congenial. It is rather characteristic of Ezekiel that when he expounds on a theme he has previously mentioned only briefly, he typically enriches it with new and even unusual language. So, especially in a passage such as this

---

[33] As reported to Greenberg by Sh. Talmon, who is to publish the text (*Ezekiel*, 2:740).

[34] Zimmerli, *Ezekiel*, 2:245.

[35] Block, *Ezekiel*, 2:339, n. 10, citing Johan Lust, "Ezekiel 36–40 in the Oldest Greek Manuscript," *CBQ* 43 (1981): 521–24.

one, which is near the zenith of the book's theology, it is not surprising that we encounter an exalted literary style that matches the subject.

Israel's Exile Profaned Yahweh's Holy Name (36:16–21)

36:17 Yahweh's address begins with a reminder of why it had been necessary for him to expel Israel from its own land and scatter it among the heathen. The reason is summarized as the defilement of the land, described under the simile of the defilement or uncleanness caused by menstruation. Although Ezekiel elsewhere speaks of people defiling (or not defiling) themselves (e.g., 4:14; 14:11; 20:7, 18), the temple (5:11; 9:7; 23:28), Yahweh's holy name (43:7–8), and a neighbor's wife (18:6, 11, 15; 22:11; 23:17; 33:26), this (36:17–18) is the only place he speaks of the land itself as defiled. A land could be defiled either by pagan invasion (Ps 79:1) or by the misbehavior of its occupants, the case here. In Lev 18:25–28, Yahweh described the land as defiled by the Canaanite inhabitants to the extent that the land vomited out its defilers, referring to the Israelite invasion of Canaan and the removal of the previous population. In Lev 20:22 he warned that the land would likewise vomit out the Israelites if they defiled the land in the same ways. Both ceremonial and moral infractions (not always strictly distinguished in the OT itself) could defile, but the latter were more serious and required more than some ritual act of cleansing, including also repentance and sacrifice for removal.

Those labeled an "abomination" (תּוֹעֵבָה) were the worst. Thus homosexuality (see the commentary on 33:26), incest, bestiality, child sacrifice, and occult practices are abominations that defile the land and require the inhabitants to be expelled (Leviticus 18 and 20). The land could also be defiled by other kinds of sexual unchastity, unexpiated bloodshed, overnight exposure of an executed criminal, touching a carcass, experiencing a bodily discharge, as well as idolatry of any sort. The simile here must not be pressed beyond its intent: the accent is on the people's behavior, which pollutes the land, but the land itself does not become culpable, any more than a menstruant was considered morally guilty because of her discharge. The point is more that menstrual uncleanness required separation or segregation from the community for a given period of time (Lev 15:19–24; cf. Lev 15:25–33).

36:18 The two motive clauses ("on account of … and for …") help explain the transgressions described in the preceding verse. Apparently they included both moral and liturgical offenses, all of which are sins against the First Commandment. "Fecal deities" (36:18) relates to "uncleanness" (36:17) because idolatry involved unclean rites and liturgical abuses (e.g., the "abominations" in chapter 8). "The blood they had poured on the ground" (36:18) alludes to the "menstruation" (נִדָּה) element of the simile "like the uncleanness of menstruation" (כְּטֻמְאַת הַנִּדָּה) in 36:17. Their outpouring of "blood" implies murder, a moral offense. This pouring of blood on the land has its own defiling consequence, as we have noticed previously,[36] classically in Abel's blood

---

[36] See the third textual note on 35:6 and the commentary on 35:5–6.

in Gen 4:10–12. Since the people had "poured" out blood, God correspondingly "poured out" his "wrath."

36:19 Block plausibly suggests that the analogy of a menstruous woman was evoked by the ancient covenant curse that the land would be devoid of its inhabitants until the land had received its divinely allotted sabbatical rests, a command that the preexilic population had ignored (Lev 26:33–45; cf. 2 Chr 36:21). As a menstruant was considered unclean for a fixed period of seven days (Lev 15:19–30) and was not to be approached in the meantime, so the land would be unclean until the sum of the years when it had not been left fallow, as it should have been, had been made up. Block builds part of his case on the similarity between the phrases "when you live on it" (בְּשִׁבְתְּכֶם עָלֶיהָ) in Lev 26:35 and (literally) "they were living on their land" (יֹשְׁבִים עַל־אַדְמָתָם) in Ezek 36:17.[37]

36:20–21 The sense of the statement that Israel "profaned" (וַיְחַלְּלוּ and חִלְּלוּהוּ) Yahweh's "name," repeated in these verses, is somewhat of a crux. Since the Piel verbs are transitive, the translation "profane," "defile," or the like is beyond dispute. But in what sense? God's name in 36:21–24 perhaps does not quite have the hypostatic connotations it often has in Deuteronomy, especially with the Hiphil of שָׁכַן, where God promises that he "will cause his name to dwell" at the sanctuary (Jerusalem) he will choose,[e] where he was present "incarnationally," dispensing his grace through divine worship. Nevertheless, the "name" still appears here almost as a personal manifestation of God, capable of suffering—as indeed God would suffer in Christ, who bore the curse, shame, and defilement of crucifixion. Here God's "name" is not specifically related to his dwelling place and worship, but to the land Yahweh had given his people (20:15; 28:25; 37:25). The primary problem is in the perception that Yahweh is unable to hold his people and his land together.

(e) Deut 12:5, 11; 14:23; 16:2, 6, 11; 26:2

The expression "profane (God's) name" was probably originally at home in liturgical contexts, since it occurs first in Lev 18:21; 19:12; 20:3; 21:6; 22:2, 32, referring to child sacrifice, idolatry, false swearing, and improper behavior in connection with offerings brought to the sanctuary (cf. "defile my sanctuary" in Ezek 5:11; 23:38). In ethical contexts, to profane God, his name, or his holy things implies a deliberate flouting of his will, in violation of his commandments, as in 13:19 and 22:26 (with חָלַל, "to profane," as in 36:20–21) and also in 43:7–8 (with טִמֵּא, "defile, make unclean"; cf. 23:7, 13, 17). Yahweh tends to relate desecration of his name to historical events, and three times in chapter 20 (20:9, 14, 22), he explains how he acted for the sake of his name in ways that seem very similar to the language of 36:20 here: unless he acted for the sake of his name, he would be discredited by the misfortune of his people, when the nations to which they came drew negative and false conclusions about the Israelites' "god" (as they would view him), as though he was unable

---

[37] Block, *Ezekiel*, 2:347, including n. 57.

to protect his own people or had been bested by the gods of the nations who conquered Israel. Israel's condition of exile from its land and dispersion to other ones reflects negatively on its God. Probably a majority of interpreters understand this passage in that way.

It is worth noting that already Moses in his intercessions on behalf of the people had expressed similar fears. In Num 14:15–24, after the people had rebelled upon hearing the negative majority report of the spies and Yahweh threatened to disown them and choose other people, Moses expresses the fear that the nations will conclude that Yahweh was powerless to bring the people to the land he had promised them. Even worse, after the golden calf apostasy (Ex 32:12–13), Moses expresses the fear that the Egyptians will conclude that Yahweh was really malicious and destructive, and by appealing to Yahweh's reputation, the intercession of Moses gains the people's pardon.

However, there is another line of interpretation of Ezek 36:20–21, which commends itself. We must consider the possibility that the Israelites had profaned God's name by their behavior during their exile among the heathen. Many other passages in the book describe the deportees as exemplars of depravity. In 12:15–16, in a passage similar to ours, the scattered survivors will relate all their abominable acts "among the nations where they go." Similarly, in 14:22–23, the survivors will convince the exiles that the disaster was deserved because of "their behavior and their actions." Later in this chapter (36:31), there is a retrospection where the redeemed will loathe themselves for their sins and abominations. One may add Yahweh's characterization of Israel's deportment as worse than that of the heathen (5:6–7) or, again, as shocking even by Gentile standards (16:27).

I find it difficult to choose between these two alternatives. Other commentators seem not to take into consideration the second as much as the first. Yet both are plausible in the general context, and perhaps both were intended.

Yahweh Will Sprinkle Clean Water on His People to Give Them a New Heart and Spirit (36:22–32)

This salvation oracle can be subdivided into three sections: (1) Yahweh's motive in restoring Israel (36:22–23); (2) the actions Yahweh will perform on Israel's behalf (36:24–30); and (3) Israel's fitting response to Yahweh's grace (36:31–32). In many ways it is parallel to 11:14–21, where God promised to create a regenerated remnant by giving his people "one heart" and "a new S/spirit" (see the commentary there).

Yahweh Saves His People for the Sake of His Holy Name (36:22–23)

36:22–23 By all kinds of syntactical devices (see the textual notes), Yahweh stresses that the grace he is about to show his people is not motivated in the slightest by any merit or virtue in them (cf. Ps 115:1). This passage thus contributes to the biblical doctrine that justification cannot be by works; it is *sola gratia*, "by grace alone" (see, e.g., AC and Ap IV). Participles are intrinsically tenseless, but because of the futuristic context, "I will act" or "I am about to act" seems required for God's promise here in 36:22. The people have long since forfeited any claims to Yahweh's compassion or other obligation to help them in their plight. This profound perception of total human depravity supports the dictum *non posse non peccare*, that since the fall, humans are "not able not to sin."[38] In contrast, for Jesus Christ, who is true but sinless man and also God the Son, this expression applies: *non posse peccare*, Christ was "not able to sin."[39]

One notes the surface divergence of this passage, with its accent on human sin, from a passage like Is 43:1–44:5, where the accent on Yahweh's love is much more up front. Of course, the two are not contradictory, but Ezekiel's language is at this point much more theocentric. He expresses his thoughts under more formulaic language that stresses God's name and his holiness. Yahweh's people cannot be vindicated and restored as long as Yahweh himself is in the disrepute in which the nations now hold him—or at least the cosmic and redemptive import of his actions will never be grasped. Here too we need to remember the importance of the First Commandment as *first* (see, e.g., Ex 20:3; Deut 6:5; Mt 22:37; 1 Jn 5:2).

Since God's holiness implies his aseity, his inner essence, the way he is as true God, the use of the Piel verb קָדַשׁ ("I will *sanctify* my great name," Ezek 36:23) implies more than what we usually hear under the translations of either "glorify" or "sanctify." In this context, it implies not only evidence of his triumph over all other "gods," but the winning of the awe and dread of his name, manifested through his mighty acts (see Josh 7:9). As in Ezek 20:41, the reversals in Israel's condition will manifest God's dread sanctity in all in whose sight it had been impugned. And since the Israelites in their unbelief had despaired in their apparent abandonment by God, it was necessary that Yahweh also reestablish his "great name" among them also.

Yahweh Will Gather His People, Sprinkle Them, and Endow Them with His Spirit (36:24–30)

36:24 Ezek 36:24–30 is a detailed exposition of "I am about to act (אֲנִי עֹשֶׂה) in 36:22. These verses reverse 36:19 and expand on 11:17–20. Block calls this section "the most systematic and detailed summary of Yahweh's restorative agenda in Ezekiel, if not in all the prophetical books."[40] That Yahweh is the explicit subject of most of the verbs in the section hammers home the "not for your sake" (36:22), *sola gratia* motif of the previous verses. The promises are arranged in an ABA' pattern, with the internal spiritual dimension at the center (B: 36:25–29a) and the external promise of return from the exile to the homeland on the exterior (A: 36:24, and A': 36:29b–30).

---

[38] See, for example, AC and Ap II; FC Ep and SD I.

[39] See, for example, Mt 4:1–11; FC SD I 43–44; Pieper, *Christian Dogmatics*, 2:76–77.

[40] Block, *Ezekiel*, 2:352–53.

Ezek 36:24 clearly uses "new exodus" terminology, which occurs nine other times in Ezekiel (once, in 29:13, for the Egyptians)[f] and becomes most prominent in the context of the restoration oracles in chapters 34–39. Its antitypical use here by Ezekiel, some eight centuries after the original exodus under Moses, in turn becomes a type of the still greater exodus in the life and work of Jesus Christ, whose suffering, death, and resurrection are *the* "exodus" (ἔξοδος, Lk 9:31) that has procured redemption for all people. The baptismal language that the NT uses for the original exodus (1 Cor 10:1–2) supports relating the water imagery in Ezek 36:25 to the Sacrament of Christian Baptism, through which the benefits of Christ's redemptive "exodus" are applied to the baptized (e.g., Acts 2:38–39; Rom 6:1–4; Titus 3:5–6). The language here is especially close to that of Ezek 34:13 except for the replacement of הוֹצִיא, "bring out," a classical exodus verb (e.g., Ex 3:10–12; 6:6–7), with the unusual לָקַח, "I will *take* you from the nations" (as in Deut 30:4), and the inconsequential change of עַמִּים ("peoples") to גּוֹיִם ("nations").

(f) Ezek 11:17; 20:34–35; 20:41–42; 28:25; 29:13; 34:13; 37:12, 21; 39:27

36:25 As the regathering in 36:24 was a reversal of the exile in 36:19, this verse promises a reversal of 36:17–18, an absolution of the accumulated impurities caused especially by bloodshed and idolatry. The metaphor of the uncleanness of a menstruant (36:17) will no longer be applicable. The verb זָרַק, "sprinkle," is most often used in connection with the sprinkling of blood. It is the verb used when Moses sprinkled "the blood of the covenant" on Israel to inaugurate the covenant (Ex 24:8), which forms the background to "the new covenant in my blood" in Jesus' Words of Institution (Lk 22:20; 1 Cor 11:25). זָרַק, "sprinkle," is often used in Leviticus for the sprinkling of sacrificial blood (e.g., Lev 1:5, 11; 3:2, 8, 13). זָרַק is a synonym of נָזָה, also meaning "sprinkle," used in Lev 4:6, 17; 5:9 for the sprinkling of the blood of the sin offering, and climactically for the sprinkling of blood in the rituals of the Day of Atonement ceremonies in Lev 16:14–19. Such passages are the OT background for NT expressions that speak of the blood of Jesus Christ cleansing us from all sin (1 Jn 1:7), particularly with "sprinkling," such as, "the sanctification of the Spirit into obedience and sprinkling of the blood of Jesus Christ" (1 Pet 1:1–2; see also Heb 12:24).[41]

Ezekiel, however, here seems to mix the metaphors of blood-sprinkling and other priestly cleansing ceremonies featuring the sprinkling of water. Rituals that involved sprinkling or washing with water included the consecration of priests (Ex 29:4) and Levites (Num 8:6–7), the ablutions of the high priest on the Day of Atonement (Lev 16:4, 24), the red heifer ceremony (Numbers 19), and the ceremonial washing of garments (Ex 19:10). In metaphorical texts that speak of cleansing, the use of water probably should not be divorced from that of blood. The expression in Rev 7:14 rings in one's ears: "they *washed* their robes and made them white in the *blood* of the Lamb." See also Heb 10:22:

---

[41] For a discussion of נָזָה and זָרַק, "sprinkle," in the OT in relation to the atonement of Jesus Christ, one may see Mitchell, *Our Suffering Savior*, 101–5.

"with our hearts sprinkled clean from an evil conscience and our bodies washed with pure water" (RSV).[42]

Ezekiel uses the phrase מַיִם טְהוֹרִים, "pure/clean water" (36:25). It is a unique phrase. It could be a euphemism for מֵי נִדָּה, "water of impurity" (Num 19:9, 13, 20), a lustration for those who were unclean. More likely here, however, the adjective is resultative: water that renders people clean, removes their impurity. That is supported by verses such as Lev 14:8–9; 15:13; 17:15, where a person who follows Yahweh's command to wash in "water" (מַיִם) is then rendered "clean" (the verb טָהֵר).

Using other words, there are other references to Yahweh "washing" and thus cleansing his people from sin (Is 4:3–5; Ps 51:4, 9 [ET 51:2, 7]). There are other passages that challenge hearers to "wash themselves" as a sign of repentance (Is 1:15–16; Jer 4:14). It is impossible to determine whether these are mere figures of speech or correspond to either fixed or voluntary ritual actions. In these passages, as in Ezek 18:31, the contextual emphasis is on personal human responsibility.

In any case, it was just as true for the OT faithful as it remains today according to orthodox Christianity: it is impossible for people to cleanse themselves spiritually, even by synergistic cooperation with God; he alone can cleanse sinners so that they are clean. Although psychologically it may appear that *we* repent, believe, and seek Christian Baptism, we confess that our repentance, faith, and cleansing in Baptism are ultimately all God's work, made possible through the sacrifice of his Son. Hence Saul of Tarsus was invited, "Be baptized and wash away your sins, calling on his name" (Acts 22:16; see also, e.g., Acts 2:38–41; 8:12, 35–38).

Only a Protestant prejudice will try to contrast or separate the ceremonial from the spiritual. OT rituals, performed in faith engendered by God's Word, were means through which God bestowed the forgiveness of sins and salvation, just as the Christian Sacraments are. A careful word study of the roots טהר, "to be clean," and טמא, "to be unclean," will readily reveal that at the same time they are bound up with ceremonies, their predominate concern is with people's faith-based relationship to God. The OT rites were no more *opera operata* or "magic" than Baptism and the Lord's Supper are. Neither are they mere symbols, memorials, or ordinances. Rather, they are efficacious means through which God bestows his grace, which is received through faith alone.[43]

---

[42] In Luther's baptismal theology, he often combined the biblical motifs of water and blood. See the excursus "Death and Resurrection Motifs in Luther's Baptismal Theology" in Lessing, *Jonah*, 256–64. Lessing summarizes (pp. 261–62):

> What unites the images of death and resurrection with washing and cleansing is not only the theme of drowning in the water of Baptism, but also biblical passages that ascribe cleansing power to the shed blood of Jesus Christ, who was crucified, died, and was buried, then rose from the dead. In this way Luther connects both of the Sacraments, Baptism and the Lord's Supper, with the redemptive blood of Jesus Christ.

[43] The Latin phrases *opus operatum*, "a work done," and *ex opere operato*, "(effective simply) by being done," both describe the view that the Sacraments are automatically efficacious,

Even the priest Ezekiel (1:3) says nothing of ceremonies in this and the following verses, but only of divine monergism: it is God alone who accomplishes the full redemption of his people. It is a section comparable to Deut 30:6–8, promising the Israelites that if they choose "life" (Deut 30:19–20), Yahweh will circumcise their hearts so that they may love God wholeheartedly and obey his commandments.[44]

The context here is eschatological, phrased in the future tense. On the Last Day, God will finally cleanse his people by the removal of their sinful nature so that they shall never again sin or be unclean (1 Cor 15:42–43; Rev 21:27). Yet God acts already now to cleanse his people, even though in this present life they (we), sinners and saints at the same time, continue to sin, repent, and be forgiven. The rest of the book alone refutes the idea that God's people attain sinless perfection already in this life (although there have repeatedly been sects which so misunderstand the Gospel).

Traditionally Christians have understood the verb יַזֶּה, "he will *sprinkle* many nations," in Is 52:15 as a prediction of the Suffering Servant's atoning work by the shedding of his blood and its application to all believers in Christ (1 Pet 1:2; Heb 10:22; 12:24).[45] Ultimately, we must invoke the "now/not yet" eschatological tension, *simul iustus et peccator* ("saint and sinner at the same time"), and the Law-Gospel paradox here. Through faith in Christ, and by means of God's Word and Sacraments, already now we are cleansed by the shed blood of Christ and so are rendered "saints" according to his Gospel promises. Yet as long as we still live in this fallen world, our sinful nature wars against our regenerated nature as new creations in Christ, and we remain vulnerable to and often succumb to sin and uncleanness (the autobiographical struggle St. Paul confesses in Romans 7). At the same time, we understand the divine words of absolution delivered through the mouth of an ordained pastor to be a prolepsis of eternal life itself. On the Last Day, the old shall have passed away completely, and all will be made new (Revelation 21–22).

A final question to be considered is the exact relation of our verse to Christian Baptism. On the one hand, there is nothing in either the OT text or the NT

---

even without faith in Christ. Lutherans reject that view and instead affirm the biblical teaching that the Sacraments are efficacious because God works through them to create and sustain saving faith in Christ according to his promises in his Word. See AC XIII; XXIV 30; Ap IV 61–74; XII 12; XIII 18–23; XXIV. For an exegetical study of NT passages that describe how God creates faith in Christ, and bestows the forgiveness of sins, the Holy Spirit, and salvation through Christian Baptism, one may see "Baptism in Luke-Acts" in Just, *Luke 1:1–9:50*, 135–43. For exegetical studies of what Jesus' Words of Institution teach about the Lord's Supper, one may see Just, *Luke 9:51–24:53*, 819–38, and Lockwood, *1 Corinthians*, 386–95, 400.

[44] This "choice" is a response to God's prior grace and his Word. God had already redeemed his people from slavery in Egypt and had established his covenant with them through Moses. So their "choice" was not an independent human decision, but one wrought in them by God himself. See also Harstad, *Joshua*, 783–85, on "choose" in Josh 24:15.

[45] For an exegetical discussion of Is 52:15 and a homiletical application to Maundy Thursday, one may see Mitchell, *Our Suffering Savior*, 100–12.

to warrant our understanding of the text as being exclusively a prophecy or type of that Sacrament alone, and not also a prophecy of the general cleansing from sin that takes place through faith in Christ (faith that can be created by the Holy Spirit working through the Word apart from the Sacrament; see, for example, Lk 23:40–43; Rom 10:17; Gal 3:2). On the other hand, by accommodation or analogy, the words serve admirably as a prophecy of Baptism.

From the standpoint of historical development, we are unable to trace extrabiblical and postbiblical developments in any detail, but it is clear that in the intertestamental period, or in the transition from the salvific OT faith in the one true and triune God to the different (anti-Trinitarian) faith known as Judaism, there was a considerable proliferation of water rites. The *mikvah*, "pool" for ceremonial washing (cf. מִקְוֶה, Lev 11:36; מִקְוָה, Is 22:11), is well-known also from archaeological excavations, and strict rabbinical regulations about its construction and use developed. Many of these rites continue in conservative Judaism today. Of special interest here is the practice of proselyte "baptism"

(טְבִילָה). We know that such a rite was also observed at Qumran. John the Baptizer, of course, was well-known for his baptism. Many history-of-religion scholars posit Christian Baptism as merely an adaptation of a similar ceremony in both mainstream and sectarian Judaism. If formulated in humanistic and historicistic fashion as merely another aspect of man's "search for truth" or the like, the thesis is thoroughly objectionable, of course. We have no other way to test the possible connection than to examine the NT itself, which gives no origin for John's baptism other than God's express command ("the one who sent me to baptize," Jn 1:33). Likewise, for Christian Baptism, our Lord's mandate in Mt 28:19–20 (cf. Mk 16:16; Jn 3:5; Acts 1:5) as well as the numerous instances of Christian Baptism recorded in Acts and the baptismal teaching in other books[g] are the normative foundation for Baptism as the Sacrament of initiation into the Trinitarian Christian faith and a means of grace.[46]

36:26 If one does not press the comparison or divorce the two, one might say that the cleansing from sin spoken of in 36:25 corresponds to justification, while this verse speaks of the sanctification that follows. That is to say, one might assert that 36:25 expresses in brief what is summarized fully in the Second Article of the Creed, while 36:26 corresponds to the Third Article. Ezek 36:26 is a virtual quotation of 11:19, and it simply repeats the promise made there. On the surface, it contrasts with 18:31 ("get for yourselves a new heart and a new spirit"), but in total biblical context that verse does not imply self-salvation, but simply the need for each individual to believe and live God's promise.

Regeneration is here formulated in terms of a new "heart" and a new "spirit."[47] The Hebrew pronominal suffixes throughout the verse translated

(g) E.g., Acts 2:38, 41; 8:36, 38; 16:15, 33; Rom 6:1–4; 1 Cor 12:13; Gal 3:26–29; Eph 4:5; Col 2:11–13; 1 Pet 3:18–21; Titus 3:5–6

---

46 For exegetical studies of John's baptism, the Baptism of Jesus, and Christian Baptism, one may see Gibbs, *Matthew 1:1–11:1*, 172–74, 184–86; Just, *Luke 1:1–9:50*, 135–43. For Christian Baptism alone, one may see Lockwood, *1 Corinthians*, 444–46; Deterding, *Colossians*, 103–7.

47 For "Spirit" or "spirit," see the first textual note on 11:19 and the commentary on 36:27. See also the textual note on 1:12 and the commentary on 1:12, 20, where there was a similar

"you" and "your" are plural, but in good Hebrew idiom, the singular forms of לֵב, "heart," and רוּחַ, "spirit," may be used for constituents that are common to a number of persons. The concept is essentially parallel with the "new covenant" of Jer 31:31–34.

The promise is that both will be made "new." Sometimes, when the adjective is used in theological contexts, it does not imply complete discontinuity with the "old" (but here it certainly does). The word generally carries a certain dialectical dynamic with it, as well as eschatological implications involving "now but not yet." Already now, all in Christ are "a new creation" (2 Cor 5:17), yet not until the Last Day will the old sinful nature be completely gone, and God will declare, "Behold, I am making all things new" (Rev 21:5). Not for nothing have Lutherans traditionally prayed David's earlier equivalent of Ezek 36:26 in Ps 51:12–13 (ET 51:10–11) as their Offertory every Sunday: "Create in me a clean heart, O God, and renew a right spirit within me. Cast me not away from Thy presence, and take not Thy Holy Spirit from me."[48]

"Heart" and the human "spirit" are near synonyms, but are not to be totally fused. "Heart" has to do with rational faculties, but in Hebrew psychosomatic thought it involved emotion and will as well. What is implied by a "new heart" is defined more closely in 36:26b. A heart of "stone" obviously implies obduracy, obstinacy, incorrigibility, coldness, unresponsiveness to God. Ezekiel had ample experience with that kind of "heart," for example, the obduracy of the people at the time of his call (2:4–10; 3:4–11), and had learned that such refractoriness could be overcome only by miraculous divine intervention. God in the Hebrew idiom literally speaks of removing the heart of stone from the "flesh" (בָּשָׂר) and replacing it with a heart of "flesh" (בָּשָׂר, the same word; English usage requires "body" in the first case for the sake of clarity). That is, like the flesh (meat) on a body, the new heart will be impressionable and malleable—yielding to God, his will, and his Spirit, who works through his Word. The implication is that "the heart of stone" (obdurate sinful nature) is incompatible with the creaturely frame that God had originally given Adam and Eve, and incompatible with God's redemptive purposes. The sinful nature cannot simply be trained or tamed; it must be surgically removed. This is essentially the same as the Pauline teaching that we must die to sin by baptismal burial with Christ, so that we may rise to new life with him (Rom 6:1–4; Col 2:11–13).

"Spirit" (רוּחַ) is an even more elusive, multivalent word than לֵב ("heart"), but perhaps one may summarize by saying that the human spirit refers to one's attitudinal, energizing, and animating impulse. That the two words are not interchangeable is shown by the different prepositions used after נָתַתִּי. The new heart will simply be given to (לְ) the Israelites after the excision of the old organ, while the "new spirit" will be placed (literally, "given") בְּקֶרֶב ("within/in-

---

ambiguity as to whether the reference is to the "spirit" of the angelic creatures or to Yahweh's Spirit.

[48] *LSB* 192–93.

side") them. The distinction will be further explained in the following verse (36:27), where it is God's own "Spirit" that he promises to put in his people. Thus the new human "spirit" in 36:26 is intertwined with the gift of the Holy Spirit in 36:27, just as in Ps 51:12–14 (ET 51:10–12). There it is difficult to decide whether רוּחַ in 51:14 (ET 51:12) and possibly in 51:12 (ET 51:10) should be capitalized in English ("Spirit") as in 51:13 (ET 51:11) or whether it refers to the regenerated "spirit" of the believer (and translations vary). Thus the Third Article of the Apostles' and Nicene Creeds begins, "I believe in the Holy Spirit," who effects the believer's regeneration and sanctified life of faith. See further the commentary on 11:19–20.

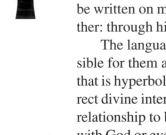

36:27 The source of the "new heart" had not been identified in 36:26, but here it is. It will be "my Spirit," Yahweh's own רוּחַ. Restated in the language of fulfillment, that is, of the NT, we do not hesitate to speak in explicitly Trinitarian terms. In Rom 8:1–17 Paul describes how God the Father has sent his Spirit—the Spirit of Christ—to dwell in us and give us resurrection life. Endowed with the Holy Spirit, the third person of the Trinity, bringing to the believer a new divine energy, it will finally be possible to do God's will and live accordingly. This had been promised already in Ezek 11:20, but without so explicit a reference to "my Spirit," which appears in the book first here and will be repeated in 37:14 and 39:29. The formulation is also very similar to Lev 26:3 (see the commentary on Ezek 36:29). The parallel is also very close to Jeremiah's "new covenant" prophecy that God's תּוֹרָה, "Torah," will be written on men's hearts (Jer 31:33), but, in a way, this verse goes even further: through his Spirit Yahweh participates directly in man's new obedience!

The language almost sounds coercive, as though God is making it impossible for them any longer to be anything but faithful and obedient. Obviously, that is hyperbolic, but it is a way of emphasizing again that nothing short of direct divine intervention will ever make it possible for God's intended covenant relationship to be implemented. Sinful man is completely unable to cooperate with God or even begin to lead a life pleasing to him.[49] The "new obedience"[50] is made possible only as the Holy Spirit works saving faith, so that the believer abhors his old way of life and lives "in the newness of the Spirit" (Rom 7:6; see also Rom 8:2–16). Compare Ezek 2:2, where the prophet was like a dead man until the "Spirit," working in conjunction with God's oral Word, raised him to his feet, and 3:12, 14, 24; 8:3; and 11:1, where again the prophet is pas-

---

[49] Thus AC II confesses:

> Since the fall of Adam all men who are born according to the course of nature are conceived and born in sin. That is, all men are full of evil lust and inclinations from their mothers' wombs and are unable by nature to have true fear of God and true faith in God. Moreover, this inborn sickness and hereditary sin is truly sin and condemns to the eternal wrath of God all those who are not born again through Baptism and the Holy Spirit. Rejected in this connection are the Pelagians and others who deny that original sin is sin, for they hold that natural man is made righteous by his own powers, thus disparaging the sufferings and merit of Christ.

[50] See, for example, Romans 6; AC VI; Ap IV 122–44; LC II 53; FC Ep and SD IV; VI.

sive and is lifted up and sometimes transported by the "Spirit." Orthographically, Biblical Hebrew has no distinct capital or lowercase letters, and it was debatable whether "spirit" should be capitalized or not in 36:26, though there is no doubt here because of the pronoun ("my Spirit"). In one sense, the springs of energy do not cease to be those of the believer, who remains a sinner at the same time that he, regenerated ("born of water and the Spirit," Jn 3:5), is a saint through forensic justification, but God's "Spirit" in the OT is so often hypostatic (already in Gen 1:2; see also Gen 41:38; Ex 31:3; Num 11:25–29) that his occupation in the "temple" of man's body is but an extension of his "incarnational" dwelling in the OT temple and its NT antitypes. As St. Paul says in Gal 2:20, "I have been crucified with Christ; it is no longer I who live, but Christ who lives in me; and the life I now live in the flesh, I live by faith in the Son of God," and in 1 Cor 6:19, "Your body is a temple of the Holy Spirit within you."

36:28 That the Israelites will live in the land implies a permanent stay there, because it had been their faithlessness to the covenant (see 36:27b) that had caused the exile in the first place. The clause "(that) I gave to your fathers" occurs only here in Ezekiel (cf. 20:42; 37:25; 47:14), but it and similar expressions are frequent in Jeremiah, upon whom Ezekiel seems dependent in this section (both deriving their message from Yahweh). And bound up with the gift of the land had been the pact of covenant mutuality, which Ezekiel repeats here: "you will be my people, and I will be your God." In it, the suffixed "*my* people" and the pronoun "I" have a contrastive function: no longer will the people have any "fecal deities" (36:25), but instead Yahweh will be their sole God to the exclusion of any possible alternatives.

36:29 At first blush, it seems strange that Yahweh should promise, "I will save you from all your impurities" (טֻמְאוֹתֵיכֶם, literally, "your uncleannesses") because in 36:25 he had already promised the removal of "all your impurities" (the same word, טֻמְאוֹתֵיכֶם). Hence predictably some critics consider 36:25b–36:29a to be secondary, thereby—by no accident one suspects—removing some of the most profoundly theological material in the book. The reference here can only be such defilements as are still possible after the renewing of the people, during the "not yet" time (this present earthly life) in which they still live. In, for example, Romans 7, St. Paul details his own (and every believer's) ongoing struggle (sometimes unsuccessful) against relapsing into the old pre-conversion sins, a struggle that shall cease only after death in Christ, and in that way, the believer shall finally attain the victory over all sin, death, and the devil (Rom 7:24–25). In light of that future victory, Yahweh can proceed to make still further promises.

That the "impurities/uncleannesses" are energized, nearly personified, is not due to primitive, dynamistic thinking, but because they fracture covenant solidarity and evidence the work of a competing spirit. Evil deeds proceed from the evil one. A possible, and perhaps preferable, translation of the final petition of the Lord's Prayer asks for deliverance not merely from abstract "evil" but

from the personal devil, "the evil one" (ὁ πονηρός, Mt 6:13; see the same phrase in, e.g., Mt 5:37; 13:19, 38).

That conception may explain why the verb "save" (Hiphil of יָשַׁע) is used here. Although this Hebrew verb is one of the most common OT words for "save," in Ezekiel it occurs elsewhere in the book only in 34:22 and 37:23. The idiom הוֹשִׁיעַ מִן, "to save [someone] from," usually denotes rescue from some person or power that holds one captive or by whose authority one is oppressed. The language here implies that the Israelites have been and can again be held captive, not so much by human enemies as by their own uncleanness.

Perhaps the influence of Leviticus 26 can still be detected in that Lev 26:3, which prescribes obedience to God's commands, is followed in Lev 26:4 by a promise of "rains in their season," and here in Ezekiel fertility and productivity of the land follow in 36:29b–30. Yet that connection between inner obedience and the external condition of the land pervades the entire OT, as is evident even in so late a book as Haggai (1:7–11).

The verb translated "summon" the grain is, literally, to "call to" it (קָרָא אֶל, Ezek 36:29). God is personally involved in what especially our secular age considers the impersonal processes of "nature." A land that had been considered by observers as one that devoured its inhabitants (36:13), undoubtedly by famine as well as other means, will be shown to be fruitful under God's blessing. Both thoughts continue in the next verses.

Ironically, some contemporary "Earth Day" observers who chatter about "earth justice" come close to deifying nature again. Indeed, some neo-pagans do believe in a "mother goddess" and/or worship "mother earth." The old myths (which pagans believed described realities) have never really been expunged from our language and culture. The religion of native Americans is a good example of their continuing existence. Even Christians may carelessly use terms like "mother nature," but if they do, it is only as a metaphor, and so a modern example of what I call "exmythological" language, used without believing the myth. But it is better for Christians to speak creedally of God as Father and Creator of the world.

36:30 This verse is little more than a restatement of 36:29. The "disgrace/reproach/scorn of famine" is apparently part of "the scorn of the peoples" in 36:15, as is clear from 34:29. Famine is specified in both 36:29 and 36:30, perhaps because of Canaan's vulnerability to droughts and the inevitable out-migrations that would follow (e.g., Ruth 1:1).

Israel's Fitting Response to Yahweh's Grace (36:31–32)

36:31 The oracle returns sharply to its starting point in 36:16–21. This verse is almost identical with 20:43, and the various parallels with the entirety of chapter 20 suggest that this restoration oracle is intended as a sort of sequel. Both chapters manifest the somber tone even of Ezekiel's messages of hope, in contrast to the celebratory atmosphere of many other prophets. Together with the next verse, 36:31 emphasizes that only after God acts *sola gratia* in restoring the people will they be capable of true contrition over their past behavior. The simple indicative verbs, "you will remember your evil actions and your misdeeds that were not good, and you will loathe yourselves," suggest that these actions are a natural, inevitable, almost involuntary part of true repentance.

The word translated "misdeeds" here is מַעֲלָלִים. This is the word's only occurrence in Ezekiel. However, it is common in Jeremiah, where it is commonly paired with דֶּרֶךְ, "way, path," as it is here and as is the related Hebrew word for "(mis)deed," עֲלִילָה, in Ezek 36:17, 19. (עֲלִילָה, in turn, is not used by Jeremiah.) In other contexts, מַעֲלָל ("deed") can be neutral, but here it is qualified by the litotes אֲשֶׁר לֹא־טוֹבִים, "that were not good (ones)," which echoes 20:25. "Loathe yourselves" is, literally, "feel nauseous in your face" (cf. 6:9 and 20:43).

36:32 The revulsion is not to be suppressed, but is commanded. Repentance is no mere generalized feeling of being less than perfect, but is a particularized self-examination, with a confession of sins of omission and commission—to the extent that one is aware of them— combined with the knowledge that one's whole being is sinful. It is for this reason that the church historically encourages *private* confession and absolution.[51] In the liturgy we confess ourselves to be "poor, miserable sinners."

The use of two Niphal imperatives, "let it be known" and "be disgraced," suggests that true knowledge of sin and grace inevitably involves such a reaction of disgrace. And as the ultimate reason for such a reaction, the words of 36:22 are repeated ("not for your sake I am about to act"), underscoring the rejection of all self-glorification or illusions about deserving God's grace, which dominates this entire oracle.

Zimmerli deserves to be heard again in comparing this penitential mood of Ezekiel with the notes of joy and celebration prominent in comparable oracles of other prophets:

> However little an isolated proclamation of a call to repentance which is unable to break through to rejoicing over that activity of God which makes repentance possible will be able to come fully alive, so on the other hand a message of mercy to the elect which does not rest upon the solid foundation of repentance and of knowledge of the "justificatory" לא למענכם ("not for your sake") can become a diabolical temptation.[52]

Cleansed Israel Will Inherit an Edenic Land (36:33–38)

36:33 A repetition of the citation formula, "thus says the Lord Yahweh,"[53] begins the addendum (or two addenda, 36:33–36 and 36:37–38), which somewhat repeats already familiar themes: the vindication of Yahweh's honor, and the restoration of life on the renewed land.

---

[51] Thus Luther counsels: "Before God we should plead guilty of all sins, even those we are not aware of, as we do in the Lord's Prayer; but before the pastor we should confess only those sins which we know and feel in our hearts" (SC V 18; *Luther's Small Catechism with Explanation*, 24; *LSB* 326).

[52] Zimmerli, *Ezekiel*, 2:250.

[53] For this formula, see pages 8–9 in the introduction and the fourth textual note and the commentary on 2:4.

Ezek 36:33a largely repeats 36:25b. Ezekiel here speaks in more general terms of purification from "iniquities" (עֲוֹנוֹת) than the somewhat more specific offenses mentioned in 36:25. It surely is no accident that the verse speaks of Israel's religious cleansing before it turns to the promise of territorial restoration in 36:33b–36. They form a link with the previous oracle, especially 36:9–10.

36:35 The subject of וְאָמְרוּ (a perfect with *waw* consecutive), translated as future tense, "will say," is an indefinite "they," probably referring to the "every passerby" of the previous verse. These people's wonderment at the nation's restoration is cast in the form of a direct quotation, just as their reaction to the Israelites' exile had been in 36:20. What impresses the observers here, as one would expect, is not the return as such or even the spiritual regeneration of the Israelites, but the physical transformation of the land. Ezekiel referred to the original paradise of "Eden" in 28:13 and 31:9, 16, 18, but this promise looks forward to the eschatological state, when God's redeemed shall inhabit a new but greater Eden-like paradise, described further in chapters 40–48 (see also Lk 23:43; Rev 2:7; and especially Relation 22). Isaiah similarly referred to Eden (Is 51:3). The change in Joel 2:3, where the land that was like "the garden of Eden" is devastated in a conflagration, is the opposite of the change here, where the desolated land becomes like the garden of Eden.

Since passers-by (36:34) and surrounding nations (36:36) witness the transformation of the land, the speakers in 36:35 may be converted Gentiles, since elsewhere Ezekiel speaks of the conversion of Israel's neighbors and even of their inclusion in God's covenant (e.g., 16:53–58).

No less than three semi-synonymous terms are used to describe the utter devastation before the rebuilding: "the cities that were ruined, desolated, and destroyed" (36:35). This trio appears together only here in Ezekiel. What especially strikes the people are the walls (fortifications) surrounding the cities, a sign of permanent and secure settlement. Here we confront a seeming conflict with the assertion of 38:11 that the future Israelite cities will be unwalled and need no defenses. However, even the eschatological new Jerusalem in Revelation 21 has a city wall, though its four gates remain perpetually open because of the absence of any danger or evil.

Zimmerli predictably gives a redaction-critical explanation: the "theological statements" of 38:11 were not yet available to the author of 36:35. Zimmerli suggests that the language here is a figure of the spiritual protection Yahweh offers Jerusalem (cf. Zech 2:9).[54] Greenberg suggests rather a non-literalistic reading of both verses depending on the different rhetorical effect intended: "not working to a systematic theology," here Ezekiel simply describes a typical city in contrast to ruins, while in 38:11 his point is that the unwalled cities will tempt the distant hordes to invade Israel.[55]

---

[54] Zimmerli, *Ezekiel*, 2:250–51.

[55] Greenberg, *Ezekiel*, 2:732.

36:36   What is probably the real aim of this entire addendum emerges here: the confession of the surrounding nations that Yahweh has not permanently abandoned his people, but has seen to their return and the reconstruction of what had been thoroughly devastated. In 36:3–5 these nations had been mentioned three times, and in 36:4 they had been pictured as gloating over Israel's fall. Now they must sing a different song. The description "the nations that *are left*" (Niphal of שָׁאַר, related to nouns for "remnant") suggests that they themselves had been decimated, but not annihilated. The historical reference in the OT era is probably to those who had survived Nebuchadnezzar's campaigns, some suffering more than others, but all having been ravaged to some degree already in Yahweh's implementation of judgment against Israel by means of Babylon (cf. 30:3 with 29:21). The fact that they have not completely perished in that judgment makes them independent, outside witnesses to Yahweh's faithfulness to his promises of salvation to Israel and his continued commitment to his people.

Twice in this verse אֲנִי, "I," and the Tetragrammaton are juxtaposed. I have taken the divine name as appositive to אֲנִי: "I, Yahweh, have …" But it is possible to punctuate the sentences so that they read like this: "I am Yahweh. I …" The first instance is then part of the standard recognition formula, "you will know that I am Yahweh."[56] One LXX manuscript does use εἰμί, "I am," indicating that understanding. The ultimate difference in meaning would be negligible, but with the accent so strongly here on Yahweh's action, not his nature, it seems preferable to retain the "holy/great name" (36:20–23) as the subject of the series of active verbs.

Although not formulated as an oath, the two verbs in "I, Yahweh, have spoken, and I will do it," are, in effect, asseverations of the power and certainty of Yahweh and his almighty Word.

36:37   Another citation formula (like that beginning 36:33) indicates another postscript, almost as an afterthought of Yahweh, but no less important for that reason. In these final two verses, the accent is not so much on the holiness of Yahweh's name (as in the previous part of the oracle) as on Yahweh's relation to his people. In the previous verses (36:33–36), Yahweh had addressed the subject of the repopulating of the land from the land's perspective, but here the human population itself is the issue.

The initial עוֹד זֹאת, "this too," sounds almost like a "P.S." at the end of a modern letter, but at the same time, it firmly integrates this piece with the preceding. The phrase had occurred twice before (20:27; 23:38), both times in descriptions of Israel's transgressions against God, but here it introduces what he will do for his people. What Yahweh wishes to add is no minor item, but speaks of a radical change in his relation to his people in the renewed covenant relationship. Covenant and population increase had been linked from the beginning of the OT (e.g., Gen 17:2; Lev 26:9). "I will *allow* the house of Israel *to*

---

[56]   For this formula, see page 9 in the introduction and the commentary on 6:7.

ask me" uses the tolerative Niphal (אִדָּרֵשׁ) of דָּרַשׁ, "seek," in its common sense of prayer or petition. Twice before, in chapters 14 and 20, Yahweh had curtly rebuffed attempts to be sought by the people because of their sins (14:3, 7, 10; 20:3, 31; see also 8:18). But now in the "new covenant" (or an OT harbinger of it), the people's many requests for prayer are allowed, and God's promises to hear those prayers are restored. What the people pray for and what Yahweh promises to grant is a great increase in population, using the simile of a huge flock of sheep (see the textual notes). The next verse expands the simile.

36:38 We must use our imagination to picture the scene Yahweh describes, but most of Ezekiel's audience would be quite familiar with it. This verse does not even give proverbially numerous numbers, but for the sake of comparison, King Hezekiah in his reformation sacrificed 3,600 animals (2 Chr 29:33), and Josiah's paschal sacrifices involved 41,400 animals (2 Chr 35:7–9). The real application of this verse is not to animals, but to the consecrated people, who thus expressed their repentance and renewed devotion to the Lord. The verse also makes plain that the entire land is involved, not only Jerusalem and its feast days. Thus the passage carries forward the message of salvation begun in chapter 34, where the people, now owned as "the sheep of my [Yahweh's] pasture" (צֹאן מַרְעִיתִי, 34:31), recognize who Yahweh really is.

Now that the Good Shepherd has come in the flesh,[57] all Christians know that they too are participants in this promise, which has already begun to be fulfilled, thanks solely to his grace for his name's sake.

---

[57] Readings from Ezekiel 34 and John 10 are traditional for Good Shepherd Sunday. See the first part of the commentary on chapter 34.

Resurrection of Dry Bones to Become a People United under the New David

Translation

37 ¹The hand of Yahweh came upon me, and he brought me out by the Spirit of Yahweh and set me down in the middle of the valley, and it was full of bones. ²He led me all around them on all sides. There were very many on the valley floor, and they were very dry. ³He said to me, "Son of man, can these dry bones come back to life?"

And I answered, "Lord Yahweh, you know."

⁴Then he said to me, "Prophesy to these bones and say to them, 'Dry bones, hear the Word of Yahweh. ⁵Thus says the Lord Yahweh to these bones: I am about to make spirit enter you so you will come back to life. ⁶I will put sinews on you, make flesh come upon you, cover over you with skin, and put spirit in you, and you will come back to life. Then you will know that I am Yahweh.'"

⁷So I prophesied as I had been commanded, and as I was prophesying there was a noise, in fact an earthquake, as the bones came together, bone to proper bone. ⁸As I watched, sinews appeared on them, then flesh arose, and he covered over them with skin from above. But there was no spirit in them.

⁹Then he said to me, "Prophesy to the wind. Prophesy, son of man, and say to the wind, 'Thus says the Lord Yahweh: From the four winds, come, O breath, and blow into these slain that they may come back to life.'"

¹⁰So I prophesied as he commanded me. Breath entered them, and they came back to life. They stood on their feet, a very, very large army.

¹¹Then he said to me, "Son of man, these bones are the whole house of Israel. They are saying, 'Our bones are dried up; our hope is lost; we have been completely cut off.' ¹²Therefore, prophesy and say to them, 'Thus says the Lord Yahweh: I am going to open your graves and raise you up from your graves, O my people, and bring you into the land of Israel. ¹³Then you will know that I am Yahweh when I open your graves and when I raise you up from your graves, O my people. ¹⁴I will put my Spirit in you, and you will come back to life. I will settle you on your own land, and you will know that I am Yahweh. What I have spoken I will do, says Yahweh.'"

¹⁵The Word of Yahweh came to me: ¹⁶"Now you, son of man, take one writing board and write on it: 'Belonging to Judah and belonging to the sons of Israel associated with it.' Then take another writing board and write on it: 'Belonging to Joseph, Ephraim's piece of wood, and the whole house of Israel associated with it.' ¹⁷Then bring one board close to the other to make for yourself a single board, so that they may be a unity in your hand. ¹⁸When your countrymen say to you, 'Won't you tell us what these things mean to you?' ¹⁹say to them,

'Thus says the Lord Yahweh: I am going to take the board of Joseph, which is in the hand of Ephraim, and the tribes of Israel associated with it, and I will place them on it, that is, [on] the board of Judah. Thus I will make them one board, so that they will be one in my hand.' ²⁰The boards on which you will write should be in your hand for them to see. ²¹Then say to them, 'Thus says the Lord Yahweh: I am going to take the sons of Israel from among the nations where they have gone, and I will gather them from all around, and I will bring them to their own land. ²²I will make them one nation in the land, on the mountains of Israel, and one King will be King for all of them. Never again will they be two nations, and never again will they be divided into two kingdoms again. ²³Never again will they defile themselves with their fecal deities, with their disgusting practices, and with all their rebellious actions. I will save them from all their apostasies by which they have sinned, and I will cleanse them. They will be my people, and I will be their God. ²⁴My Servant David will be King over them, and they will all have one Shepherd. They will follow my ordinances and be careful to keep my statutes. ²⁵They will live in the land I gave my servant Jacob, where your fathers lived. They will live there—they, their children, and their grandchildren—forever, and David my Servant will be their Prince forever. ²⁶I will make a covenant of peace with them. It will be an everlasting covenant with them. I will establish them, and I will multiply them and set my sanctuary in their midst forever. ²⁷My tabernacle will be over them; I will be their God, and they will be my people. ²⁸Then the nations will know that I, Yahweh, sanctify Israel when my sanctuary is in their midst forever.' "

Textual Notes

37:1 הָיְתָה עָלַי֙ יַד־יְהוָֹה֙—The abrupt beginning of the chapter with a simple perfect verb without *waw* is striking (הָיְתָה, Qal feminine, since יָד is a feminine noun). Idiomatic Hebrew commonly begins major divisions (chapters) and even books with an imperfect with *waw* consecutive. After the initial verb here, perfects with simple *waw* conjunctive continue in 37:2, 7, 8, and 10, as, in fact, happens throughout the book of Ezekiel. Although this phenomenon (continuing with perfects with conjunctive *waw*) occurs occasionally in early texts (e.g., Judg 5:26, after an initial simple imperfect), it becomes much more common in Late Biblical Hebrew. Since Aramaic (like postbiblical Hebrew) has no *waw* consecutive forms, it is very possible that we witness Aramaic influence on Hebrew here (so GKC, § 112 pp, and also Joüon, § 119 z, regarding וּבֵאתִי in 37:7 and וְהִנַּבֵּאתִי in 37:10).

This first clause recurs identically in 40:1, which has a date notice. Hence attempts have been made to supply one here, but we have no basis for even an intelligent guess about the date, except perhaps shortly after the fall of Jerusalem. Possibly no date is given in order to link this chapter more closely to the preceding one, which in one sense it reinforces. Links between the chapters include the promises "I will give you a new heart and put a new S/spirit within you. I will … give you a heart of flesh. I will put my Spirit within you. … Then you will live in the land" (36:26–28), which are fulfilled by the action of the Spirit, the gift of spirit, and settlement in the land in 37:1–14.

וַיּוֹצִאֵנִי בְרוּחַ יְהוָה—Since the preceding clause had the feminine subject יָד, Yahweh's "hand," we might expect a feminine verb here (וַתּוֹצִאֵנִי), but instead the masculine Hiphil imperfect of יָצָא (with *waw* consecutive and first common singular suffix) is used because Yahweh himself is considered the real actor. The same happens in 40:1, where יַד־יְהוָה is followed by וַיָּבֵא (see also 33:22; cf. 3:22).

It seems slightly redundant to say "he [Yahweh] brought me out by the Spirit of Yahweh." Evidently רוּחַ־יהוה is a fixed phrase that here could be translated "by his own Spirit" (equivalent to בְּרוּחוֹ). Elsewhere in Ezekiel רוּחַ יהוה occurs only in 11:5, but בְּרוּחַ אֱלֹהִים ("by the Spirit of God") in 11:24 parallels the use of the phrase with the Tetragrammaton here. As in Yahweh's promise to give רוּחִי, "my Spirit" (36:27; 37:14; 39:29), these phrases plainly refer to the Holy Spirit, the third person of the Trinity.

וַיְנִיחֵנִי—This form, which recurs in 40:2, is the regular Hiphil form (third masculine singular imperfect with *waw* consecutive and first common singular suffix) of נוּחַ, which has two distinct Hiphil paradigms. This paradigm with undoubled *nun* usually means "give rest to," but here and in 40:2, it means to "set down" (BDB, s.v. נוּחַ, Hiphil A, 2). That meaning is usually expressed by the other Hiphil paradigm of נוּחַ, whose forms have doubled *nun* (and are generally synonymous with שִׂים, "put, place"). Consequently, critics suggest repointing this form as וַיַּנִּיחֵנִי (cf. וְהִנַּחְתִּי in 37:14). However, it is difficult to imagine the Masoretes making a mistake of this sort. Although the meanings overlap slightly, the picture here is one of gently letting someone down. It does not appear to be of major exegetical significance.

הַבִּקְעָה—The noun בִּקְעָה can be translated as "plain," but usually the reference is to the broad alluvial plain of a river valley. Compare the Bekáa today, the Arabic cognate used of the valley between the Lebanon and Anti-Lebanon Mountains in the country of Lebanon. "Valley" is the traditional translation here, and there is no reason to abandon it.

37:2 וְהֶעֱבִירַנִי עֲלֵיהֶם סָבִיב ׀ סָבִיב—The text is clear, but it has various nuances that are all but impossible to reproduce in good English. The Hiphil (perfect with suffix) of עָבַר with עַל apparently means simply "cause one to pass over/beside/by." A few have pressed the idiom to imply a literal walking over heaps of bones. This is not impossible, but seems to paint a more gruesome picture than we have in the more likely rendition, "he led me around." סָבִיב is repeated to indicate *all* around them *on all sides*, so that this thorough inspection would impress Ezekiel with the gravity of the situation.

וְהִנֵּה רַבּוֹת מְאֹד ... וְהִנֵּה יְבֵשׁוֹת מְאֹד׃—Both the interjection הִנֵּה (traditionally "behold") and the noun מְאֹד used as an adverbial accusative, "very," are used twice, obviously for emphasis or to express astonishment on Ezekiel's part. We would not have been surprised if Ezekiel, a priest (1:3), had become alarmed at the danger of becoming unclean by such close contact with the dead, prohibited for priests in Lev 21:1–4 (and for the high priest in Lev 21:11). He probably also would have been appalled at the failure to give the bones a proper burial; see Deut 21:23 and contrast Ezek 39:12–16, where great care is taken to keep the corpses from contaminating the land. But at this moment, the overriding concern is death versus life, not unclean versus clean.

"Dry" (יְבֵשׁוֹת) implies bleached, desiccated, perhaps crumbling from long exposure to the merciless Mesopotamian sun. Water is a prerequisite for life, and some poetic passages speak of bones as the center of life,[a] so "very dry" bones are completely devoid of any sign of life. Modern archeologists often speak of the opposite as "green" bodies, that is, ones not long buried, some with tissue still attached. The adjectives רַבּוֹת and יְבֵשׁוֹת are both feminine plural to match עֲצָמוֹת at the end of 37:1. However, earlier in 37:2, the masculine suffix on עֲלֵיהֶם referred to them, and starting again in 37:4 and continuing throughout this section, other masculine verbs and suffixes will refer to the bones. This may simply be more evidence of the general preference for masculine forms in Late Biblical Hebrew, but possibly it has exegetical significance, anticipating the bones' revivification into men.

37:3 הֲתִחְיֶינָה הָעֲצָמוֹת הָאֵלֶּה—Elsewhere Ezekiel uses the verb חָיָה with the meaning "to live, be alive." However, since the subject of הֲתִחְיֶינָה (Qal imperfect with interrogative הֲ) is הָעֲצָמוֹת, and "the bones" presumably had once been alive, but now are dead, the appropriate meaning for the verb is *"come back* to life, revive, live *again."* Forms of חָיָה are translated similarly in 37:5, 6, 9, 10, 14. In the question here in 37:3, the imperfect undoubtedly also has a modal meaning, *"can* they … ?"* (cf. Joüon, § 113 l).

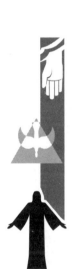

The verb חָיָה has that same meaning in the revivifications in 1 Ki 17:22; 2 Ki 8:5; 13:21. Most consider those not to be "resurrections" in the full NT sense.[1] Jesus Christ was the first to rise from the dead with a glorified, immortal body (Acts 26:23; "firstfruits" in 1 Cor 15:20; "firstborn" in Col 1:18). The three OT revivifications (1 Ki 17:17–24; 2 Ki 4:18–37; 13:21), like the raising of Lazarus and others in the NT (e.g., Lk 7:12–15; John 11), were restorations to natural earthly life, but eventually the people so "raised" likely died again. Only on the Last Day shall all the dead be raised permanently—the righteous to everlasting life and the wicked to eternal damnation.[b]

אַתָּה יָדָעְתָּ:—Compare the deferential reply "you know" (σὺ οἶδας), spoken by Peter to Jesus (Jn 21:17) and by John to the angel (Rev 7:14), submitting themselves to their questioners' greater knowledge of the divine.

37:4 הִנָּבֵא עַל־הָעֲצָמוֹת הָאֵלֶּה—Ezekiel elsewhere uses the Niphal imperative הִנָּבֵא, "prophesy" (also in 37:9, 12) with אֶל (e.g., 6:2; 13:2; 37:9) or עַל (e.g., 11:4; 13:17; 38:2), both of which can mean either "to" (as אֶל must mean in 37:9) or "against." "Prophesy over these bones" (ESV; cf. KJV) is possible here, but I have translated "to" in harmony with the following command to speak "to them" (אֲלֵיהֶם).

37:5 הִנֵּה אֲנִי מֵבִיא—Ezekiel often uses הִנֵּה with a participle (here מֵבִיא, Hiphil of בּוֹא) as a *futurum instans*: "I am about to …" (see GKC, § 116 p). Instead of the usual pronominal suffix on הִנֵּה, here he uses the pronoun אֲנִי.

רוּחַ—The many possible meanings of רוּחַ (37:1, 5–6, 8–10, 14) include the Holy "Spirit" (37:1, 14); the "spirit" of living humans, which departs at death (Ps 78:39;

(a) E.g., Pss
31:11 (ET
31:10); 38:4
(ET 38:3);
Job 20:11;
21:24; Prov
3:8

(b) See, e.g.,
Is 25:6–8;
26:19;
Dan 12:1–3;
Jn 5:28–29;
1 Cor
15:53–54;
Rev
20:11–15

---

[1] See "The Structure and Themes of Matthew 8–9," the commentary on Mt 8:17, and footnote 15 in the commentary on 10:5–15 in Gibbs, *Matthew 1:1–11:1*, 402–6, 424–28, 510.

Eccl 12:7); "breath"; or "wind" (the first three occurrences in Ezek 37:9). The translation "spirit" in 37:5–6, 8 connects 37:5–10 to Yahweh's final promise of his "Spirit" in 37:14, as well as to his promises of a new "S/spirit" in 11:19 and 36:26–27. Conversely, one might paraphrase 37:11 by saying that the discouraged exiles were "dispirited." See the further discussion in the textual note on 37:9–10.

Jesus in Jn 3:3–8 plays on the similar multivalence of the Greek noun πνεῦμα, "Spirit, spirit, wind," and verb πνέω, "blow."

וִחְיִיתֶם:—This form, repeated in 37:6, 14, is the usual pointing of the Qal second masculine plural perfect of חָיָה with *waw* consecutive. The expected form for a verb with an initial ח would be -וַחְ, but חָיָה (and הָיָה) behave unusually. See GKC, § 63 q.

37:6 וְנָתַתִּי עֲלֵיכֶם גִּדִים—The noun גִּיד, "sinew, tendon," occurs only five other times in the OT (Gen 32:33 [twice; ET 32:32]; Is 48:4; Job 10:11; 40:17).

The description of God assembling the human body in Job 10:11 uses the same four Hebrew terms as Ezek 37:5–8. Their order there is עוֹר, "skin," בָּשָׂר, "flesh," עֲצָמוֹת, "bones," and גִּידִים, "sinews."

וְקָרַמְתִּי עֲלֵיכֶם עוֹר—The verb קָרַם, "to cover," occurs in the OT only in 37:6 and 37:8, but is known in Akkadian and Syriac, and there are derivative nouns in the Mishnah. See further the textual note on 37:8.

37:7 צֻוֵּיתִי—This verse contains several uncommon forms. Ezekiel uses the Pual of צָוָה to say he did as he "was commanded" only in 12:7; 24:18; and here, all using this identical form (first common singular perfect).

וַיְהִי־קוֹל כְּהִנָּבְאִי וְהִנֵּה־רַעַשׁ—The construction of וַיְהִי followed by הִנֵּה occurred also in 17:7 and is found elsewhere (e.g., Gen 15:12, 17; 24:15; 29:25). Ezekiel uses the Niphal infinitive construct of נָבָא, "prophesy," only in 11:13 and here, both times with כְּ and first common singular suffix (כְּהִנָּבְאִי) to form a temporal clause, "as/while I was prophesying." The noun קוֹל, "sound, noise, voice" (omitted by the LXX) precedes the infinitive, and following is, literally, "and behold, an earthquake." רַעַשׁ usually refers to an "earthquake" (Amos 1:1), and Ezekiel uses it in that sense in 38:19, but in 12:18 it referred to human trembling. In 3:12–13 these two nouns were in a construct relation in the phrase קוֹל רַעַשׁ גָּדוֹל, literally, "noise of a great rumbling," in reference to the theophany. One gets the impression that here Ezekiel has separated קוֹל and רַעַשׁ in order to heighten the effect, presenting them in slow motion, as it were.

וַתִּקְרְבוּ עֲצָמוֹת—The absence of an expected definite article on the subject (עֲצָמוֹת) occurs occasionally elsewhere in semi-poetic high prose (and, of course, is common in poetry). Since עֲצָמוֹת is feminine plural, the verb form must be the third feminine plural (not second masculine plural) Qal imperfect of קָרַב, "draw near, approach." The expected form would be תִּקְרַבְנָה. However, analogous Qal second feminine plural imperfects occur in Jer 49:11 and Job 19:15 with feminine plural subjects; see Joüon, § 44 da (cf. GKC, § 60 a, footnote 1; Waltke-O'Connor, § 31.1.1a, footnote 2). A bit free for "approached"—and then arrived—is my "came together."

עֶצֶם אֶל־עַצְמוֹ:—Literally, "a bone to [אֶל] its bone," here the suffix on עַצְמוֹ refers to "its" proper, connected bone. For the masculine suffix referring to the feminine עֶצֶם, see the second textual note on 37:2.

37:8 וַיִּקְרַם עֲלֵיהֶם עוֹר מִלְמָעְלָה—The Qal verb קָרַם, "to cover" (*HALOT*), occurs in the OT only here and in 37:6, where it was transitive, וְקָרַמְתִּי עֲלֵיכֶם עוֹר, "I will cover over you with skin." Here it could be intransitive with עוֹר as its subject: "skin covered over them from above," like the preceding intransitive verb, וּבָשָׂר עָלָה, "then flesh *arose*." The LXX translates literally and intransitively: καὶ ἀνέβαινεν ἐπ᾽ αὐτὰ δέρμα ἐπάνω ("and skin arose over them above"). However, it would be unusual for Qal forms of a verb to have both a transitive and an intransitive meaning. Some critics want to emend the verb to be Niphal here (וַיִּקָּרֵם).[2] Yet another possibility is that the verb is transitive here too (as in 37:6), with Yahweh as the implicit subject and "skin" as its object (an accusative of material): "and he covered over them (with) skin from above."

Ezekiel uses the adverb מִלְמָעְלָה, "(from) above," elsewhere (e.g., 1:11, 22, 26). Here it suggests that the skin came down upon the reconstituting bodies. It is a combination of מַעַל with prefixed prepositions מִן and לְ and directional *he* ending (see BDB, s.v. מַעַל, 2 d, under the root עלה).

37:9–10 Structurally, 37:9–10 is basically parallel to 37:4–8, the only substantive difference being the addressees of Ezekiel's prophecy. In 37:4–8, he prophesied to the עֲצָמוֹת, "bones." Here he addresses הָרוּחַ, and the singular in 37:9–10 always has the definite article. But how should it be translated? All three meanings, "spirit, breath, wind," come into view, and all three could be defended as at least the primary referent (perhaps all three at once, although that is manifestly impossible to translate). KJV chose "wind" in 37:9a, and then "breath." But NKJV and other modern translations prefer "breath" throughout. In my judgment, KJV is to be preferred because of the reference to the "four winds."

The Holy "Spirit" is not appropriate as a translation in 37:9–10, but must be in the picture implicitly. As a person's body is "dust from the earth" (Gen 2:7), his breath is the same element as the wind or air that covers the earth. But no combination of the two will produce life without God's Spirit providing the life (see Job 33:4). "Breath" resonates with the verb וּפְחִי (Qal feminine singular imperative of נָפַח), "breathe, blow" (Ezek 37:9), the same verb used for God "breathing" the breath of life into man in Gen 2:7.

37:9 מֵאַרְבַּע רוּחוֹת—There is no doubt about the meaning of the plural of רוּחַ in this phrase, which clearly means "from the four winds," referring to the four geographical directions, as on a compass. The picture seems to have been Mesopotamian in origin and does not appear until later OT books, for example, again in Ezek 42:20 (see also 42:16–19), and also in Jer 49:36 and Zech 6:5. In the NT, see Mt 24:31, and Rev 7:1, where "four angels" stand at "the four corners of the earth" holding back "the four winds [τοὺς τέσσαρας ἀνέμους] of the earth." Variations of these expressions with "four" occur many other places in Scripture.

---

[2] Greenberg, *Ezekiel*, 2:744, suggests that since the Niphal of קרם did not survive in postbiblical Hebrew, the Masoretes did not recognize what he speculates was the original Niphal here.

37:10 וְהִנַּבֵּאתִי—Instead of the Niphal of נָבָא as in 37:7 (וְנִבֵּאתִי, "so I prophesied"), this is the Hithpael (first common singular perfect). The preformative ת has been assimilated to the following radical, resulting in the doubled *nun* (-נַּ-). See GKC, § 54 c; Waltke-O'Connor, §§ 21.2.3c, including footnote 30, and 26.1.1c, including example 27. The same happened with וְהִנֶּחָמְתִּי in 5:13. For the quiescent א and the *sere* vocalization (-בֵּאתִי), see GKC, § 74 c, and Joüon, § 78 a, c.

37:11 הָעֲצָמוֹת הָאֵלֶּה כָּל־בֵּית יִשְׂרָאֵל הֵמָּה—This is a tripartite nominal (verbless) clause. It has a suspended (*casus pendens*) subject (הָעֲצָמוֹת הָאֵלֶּה), a predicate, (כָּל־בֵּית יִשְׂרָאֵל), and a resumptive pronoun (הֵמָּה) that functions as the subject, literally, "these bones—the whole house of Israel (are) they." See Joüon, § 154 i. This kind of nominal clause with a final pleonastic pronoun is common in the interpretation of visions, dreams, or other symbols (e.g., Ex 3:5, Moses at the burning bush). In spite of the feminine gender of עֲצָמוֹת at the start of the clause, the masculine pronoun הֵמָּה is used because the nearer predicate contains the masculine noun בַּיִת, "house."

הִנֵּה אֹמְרִים— Yahweh has reminded the prophet of the people's words a number of times, but this is the only instance where they are introduced by הִנֵּה, traditionally, "behold." It probably functions to shift Ezekiel's attention from the preceding vision to the immediate problem and leads up to Yahweh's response (לָכֵן, "therefore") in 37:12. Often plural participles (here אֹמְרִים) without a stated subject are entirely indefinite, but here the context provides a definite subject: those who comprise "the whole house of Israel" (in the preceding clause) are the ones "saying."

The people's lament is structured in a tripartite form. Each of the three clauses consists of two Hebrew words. The three clauses rhyme because the second word of each ends with the first common plural suffix נו- ("our"). In fact in the third clause, both words end with נו-.

יָבְשׁוּ עַצְמוֹתֵינוּ—The verb יָבֵשׁ, "be dry," is a homograph of the adjective יָבֵשׁ, "dry," in 37:2, 4. "Our bones are dried up" means that they lack the moist marrow or vital sap of healthy bones, and the saying signifies despair, dispiritedness, listlessness. The pulled-apart "bones" and "dried up" strength expressed in Ps 22:15–16 (ET 22:14–15) would be true literally for a crucified victim; compare Jesus' quotation from that psalm on the cross (Mt 27:46, quoting Ps 22:2 [ET 22:1]). The converse, healthy bones, signifies joy (Is 66:14; Prov 15:30).

וְאָבְדָה תִקְוָתֵנוּ—"Our hope has perished/is lost" (the verb אָבַד and the feminine noun תִּקְוָה) is a nonmetaphorical explanation of the first clause. The same clause, but with third feminine singular suffix (אָבְדָה תִקְוָתָהּ), occurred in 19:5. Critics often excise the initial copula, not reflected in the LXX and Targum, as dittographic, since the preceding word too ended with *waw* (עַצְמוֹתֵינוּ). In any case, "and" is readily omitted in idiomatic English. But Hebrew loves its *waws* far more than English does conjunctions, and there is no reason why it would not be used as explicative (there are many parallels).

נִגְזַרְנוּ לָנוּ:—This final expression is semi-figurative again and difficult to reproduce fully in translation. The Niphal of גָּזַר (here perfect) means "*be cut off*, separated, excluded" (BDB, 1). It can be used for someone dead and buried, as in the well-known parallel where the Suffering Servant is "cut off from the land of the living" (Is 53:8) and then buried (Is 53:9). See also Ps 88:6 (ET 88:5). The preposition לְ is used here as a dative of disadvantage (Joüon, § 133 d), "against us." It is centripetal in force, focusing attention back on the subject represented by the suffix. I have ventured the translation "we have been completely cut off."

A famous suggested emendation retains the consonants but divides the two words differently, forming נִגְזַר גּוֹלֵנוּ, "our thread [of life] is cut off." This assumes a hypothetical noun גֹּל, "thread," parallel to a Syriac cognate, allegedly to provide a better parallel with the preceding clause. But the normal Hebrew word for "thread" is חוּט (e.g., Josh 2:18; Judg 16:12), and there is no analogy to this language and imagery elsewhere in the OT, so this emendation is usually rejected.

37:12 עַמִּי—"My people" relates the resurrection promise of this verse to the covenant status of the people in relation to Yahweh. Many critics take it as a later interpolation by someone who wished to stress the importance of the covenant, but such an argument cuts both ways: why should not Yahweh have wished to make such a point himself? One might have expected it to come at the beginning of the quotation (where NIV repositions it). The evidence of the ancient versions is ambiguous. A translation of it is missing in the Syriac Peshitta and most LXX recensions. However, עַמִּי appears again at the end of the next verse, where the LXX does reflect it, but not the Peshitta. Some critics speculate that it was first added to the end of 37:13 and then it crept into 37:12 by assimilation, but such speculation is unwarranted.

37:14 וְהִנַּחְתִּי—This is the second Hiphil conjugation of נוּחַ (first common singular perfect with *waw* consecutive), in which *nun* is doubled (-ִנּ-), and which regularly means "place, put" (BDB, Hiphil B, 1), here probably with the added nuance "settle, let stay, allow to dwell securely," as in Is 14:1 (cf. Judg 2:23). Compare the third textual note on 37:1, which discusses the first Hiphil conjugation of נוּחַ.

37:15–16 The word-event formula, "the Word of Yahweh came to me,"[3] and the different contents of the following verses would justify a new chapter. The Syriac Peshitta even inserts a superscription. But the discontinuity should not be overstated. וְאַתָּה at the beginning of 37:16 is usually a mark of continuation, although it can be used at the beginning of an oracle (e.g., 7:2). Both halves of the chapter have in common an interest in "the whole house of Israel" (37:11, 16). Yahweh will both "raise up" (37:12a) his people from their graves, that is, "take" them from their exile (37:21a), and "bring" them (37:12b, 21b) into their own land.

37:16 קַח—This is the normal form of the Qal imperative of לָקַח, which generally behaves like a first-*nun* verb with "a" characteristic vowels. When the imperative is repeated later in the verse, its form is לְקַח, unusual, but also in Ex 29:1 and Prov 20:16 (cf. 1 Ki 17:11). Presumably the different form is used simply for the sake of variation.

לְיוֹסֵף עֵץ אֶפְרַיִם—After "belonging to Joseph" (for this use of לְ, see BDB, 5 a), the construct phrase "Ephraim's piece of wood" is generally taken as an explanation

---

[3] For this formula, see page 8 in the introduction and the textual note on 3:16.

of the uncommon "Joseph" as a designation for the northern tribes. Again in 37:19 "Joseph" is associated with "Ephraim" (עֵץ יוֹסֵף אֲשֶׁר בְּיַד־אֶפְרַיִם). "Ephraim" was the leading tribe of the tribes in the north after their secession from Judah and Benjamin in the south; it was the usual term for what remained of the northern Israelites after their territory was annexed by Assyria in 722 B.C.. Hosea and Jeremiah both use the term as a parallel for "Israel" (cf. Is 17:3). Some critics advocate deleting עֵץ אֶפְרַיִם based on debatable arguments about "parallelism," but the ancient versions include it, and there is no overriding reason to consider it a gloss. See further the commentary.

37:17 וְקָרַב—This is the Piel imperative of קָרַב, whose Piel has a transitive meaning, "bring (something) near, together." The paradigmatic form would be קָרֵב, but the same anomaly occurs with פַּלַּג ("divide") in Ps 55:10 (ET 55:9). See GKC, §§ 52 n, 64 h.

לַאֲחָדִים—The plural of אֶחָד, "one," ordinarily means "a few," but plainly not so here. Here it seems to imply "a composite one" or "unity," that is, "one" made out of two. In 37:19 when God explains the action prophecy, he uses the expected singular in the phrase לְעֵץ אֶחָד. Greenberg proposes, I think correctly, that in the difference between the wordings in 37:17 and 37:19 is the message that "what God joins together is a seamless unity, unlike the human product."[4]

37:18 The beginning of the temporal clause "when …" with a simple וְכַאֲשֶׁר is rather abrupt. Idiomatic Hebrew would normally preface it with וַיְהִי. The LXX supplies a translation for that by inserting ἔσται, but the terse MT may be deliberative. See the commentary.

לֵאמֹר—This, introducing a direct quote, is absent in comparable queries by the people (12:9; 21:5, 12 [ET 20:49; 21:7]), so some critics consider it a later addition, but that is a weak argument for deleting so ubiquitous an idiom, and the meaning is unaffected.

מָה־אֵלֶּה לָּךְ:—Whereas לְךָ in 37:16 (קַח־לְךָ, literally, "take for yourself") and 37:17 (אֶחָד אֶל־אֶחָד לְךָ, literally, "one to another for yourself") was the reflexive or ethical dative (see BDB, s.v. לְ, 5 h), here it (לָּךְ, pausal with *daghesh forte conjunctivum*, GKC, § 20 f) is a full-fledged prepositional phrase. The literal "what are these [two boards] to you?" is equivalent to "what do you mean (by them)"? The same idiom was used in 24:19.

37:19 דַּבֵּר—This verse too (like 37:18) begins abruptly, presumably for the same reason; see the commentary. Again the LXX smooths it out by translating as though the Hebrew were the perfect with *waw* consecutive, וְדִבַּרְתָּ, instead of the Piel imperative דַּבֵּר. In Ezekiel, Yahweh more often employs the imperative אֱמֹר than דַּבֵּר in commands to speak.

וְנָתַתִּי אוֹתָם עָלָיו אֶת־עֵץ יְהוּדָה—I have translated this literally: "and I will place them on it, that is, [on] the board of Judah." We can understand the MT if the plural suffix on אוֹתָם refers to the tribes that the board represents and the singular suffix on עָלָיו refers to the board that represents primarily Judah. The phrase אֶת־עֵץ יְהוּדָה is

---

[4] Greenberg, *Ezekiel*, 2:754.

an appositional explanation of the suffix on עָלָיו. By the end of the verse, a clear explanation of the prophet's actions has not emerged, except that they reflect something which God, the real subject, will execute.

There is near unanimity among critical commentators that at least 37:19b is corrupt. The major cause of their difficulty appears to be the mixture of tribes and boards. The problem is reflected already in the readings of the LXX and Vulgate. Twice in this verse, when עֵץ is the *nomen regens* of first Joseph and later of Judah, the LXX translates עֵץ as φυλήν, "tribe," and thus aligns it with Israel's φυλάς, the LXX's accurate translation of שִׁבְטֵי. Toward the end of the verse, עֵץ אֶחָד is rendered ῥάβδον μίαν, "one *scepter.*" שֵׁבֶט, "tribe," can also mean "scepter," and apparently the LXX translates עֵץ אֶחָד as "one scepter" to anticipate what will be clearly revealed in 37:22, 24, namely, the restoration of the "one King" over united Israel, "my Servant David." (Similar was God's promise in 34:23–24 of "my Servant David" who would be "one Shepherd" and "Prince" over his people.) This LXX interpretation of 37:19 is an important part of the history of exegesis, but at this point, it is not evidence for a different Hebrew text.

A common critical "solution" is to delete אוֹתָם, but this would have the effect of implying the superiority of "Joseph," scarcely the point Ezekiel wants to make.

37:20 לְעֵינֵיהֶם:—Literally, "to their eyes," this is translated "for them to see."

37:21–28   It should be noted parenthetically that there is widespread critical debate about the authenticity of the rest of the chapter, beginning with this or the previous verse. Many find here only a verbose amalgam of restoration hopes from many quarters of the Ezekiel school. In general, the great variety of reconstructions is the best refutation of the very premise of later additions. A relatively "conservative" sample can be found in Zimmerli, who posits a first supplement by Ezekiel or a member of his school in 37:20–24a and then a later miscellany in 37:24b–28.[5]

There is undeniably a shift in thematic and chronological focus in these final verses, most obviously the use of עוֹלָם, "forever," which occurs five times (37:25 [twice], 26 [twice], 28). The text as it stands exhibits a deliberative and logical progression, as the action prophecy gradually fades from view and the accent is on Yahweh's original and ultimate plans for his people.

37:22   וּמֶלֶךְ אֶחָד יִהְיֶה לְכֻלָּם לְמֶלֶךְ—Ezekiel rarely uses מֶלֶךְ, "king," favorably. However, he does so twice here and in 37:24 for the eschatological David. In both 37:22 (translating only the first occurrence) and 37:24, the LXX renders it by ἄρχων, "ruler," rather than βασιλεύς, which the LXX frequently uses for the heathen kings of the ancient Near East (e.g., 17:12; 19:9; 29:2, 18, 19). One other time in Ezekiel the LXX uses ἄρχων for מֶלֶךְ (28:12), but usually the LXX uses ἄρχων for נָשִׂיא (e.g., 12:10; 34:24) or another word for an official (e.g., 22:27; 28:2; 31:11). Since Ezekiel generally shows a decided preference for נָשִׂיא in reference to Israel's kings, many commentators emend the text here in supposed agreement with LXX. But LXX's renderings of מֶלֶךְ are not consistent, and Zimmerli makes the convincing point that the

---

5   Zimmerli, *Ezekiel*, 2:275–76.

double parallelism of גּוֹי ... מֶלֶךְ in 37:22a with גּוֹיִם ... מַמְלָכוֹת in 37:22b strongly favors the MT.[6]

וְלֹא יֵחָיֶּה־עוֹד—The plural Qere יִהְיוּ, "they [the two nations] will be," is almost certainly to be preferred to the singular Kethib, יִהְיֶה, which apparently would have גּוֹי אֶחָד ("one nation") near the start of the verse as its subject. All the versions read the plural, and it obviously makes a much better parallel with the rest of the line.

וְלֹא יֵחָצוּ עוֹד לִשְׁתֵּי מַמְלָכוֹת עוֹד:—The final עוֹד, "again," is superfluous. In Ezekiel עוֹד is often placed immediately after the verb (as is the first one here: יֵחָצוּ עוֹד), although there are exceptions (e.g., 19:9; 39:7). Allen suggests a conflation of two texts,[7] but this is not necessary. The second עוֹד simply underscores the unrepeatability of the schism, never mind the redundancy.

37:23 יִטַמְּאוּ—This form is the reading in Leningradensis and hence *BHS*. It is the Hithpael of טָמֵא, but with the anomalous omission of *daghesh* in the ט. Most other Hebrew manuscripts have יִטַּמְּאוּ, which is the same Hithpael form that was in 14:11. In that form, the preformative ת (יִתְטַמְּאוּ) has been assimilated and is marked by the *daghesh* (-טַּ-). The Hithpael of טָמֵא has a reflexive or middle meaning, "defile oneself, render oneself unclean," and echoes the Levitical laws of purity for Israel. The following series of nouns with instrumental בְּ favor translating the verb as an action, "defile themselves with" (like most English translations from KJV on) instead of a state ("be unclean, defiled").

וְהוֹשַׁעְתִּי אֹתָם מִכֹּל מוֹשְׁבֹתֵיהֶם—In this context, after "and I will save them from all of ... ," מוֹשְׁבֹתֵיהֶם can scarcely mean "their dwellings" (plural of מוֹשָׁב with suffix). Perhaps the MT was influenced by the triple use of that noun's root (the verb יָשַׁב) in 37:25. No doubt, some of the outrages vividly described in the previous clause did occur in houses as well as elsewhere, but the people would not need to be saved from their dwelling places. As sensed already by the LXX's ἀνομιῶν, "iniquities," we probably have in the MT a variant spelling (some allege a metathetical error of the *waw* and the *mem*) of the plural of מְשׁוּבָה, "backslidings, apostasies." Although מְשׁוּבָה is used nowhere else in Ezekiel, it is frequent in Jeremiah (and used elsewhere), and we may see another example of Jeremianic influence on Ezekiel. KJV and NKJV retain "dwellings"; most other English versions have "backslidings." In any case, מוֹשְׁבֹתֵיהֶם has a double plural marker (see Joüon, § 94 f), the feminine plural ending (-וֹת-) with the third masculine plural suffix form for plural nouns (-ֵיהֶם-). The plural of מוֹשָׁב usually takes such suffix forms, but not always: מֹשְׁבֹתָם is in Gen 36:43 and Num 31:10.

37:24 וְעַבְדִּי דָוִד מֶלֶךְ עֲלֵיהֶם וְרוֹעֶה אֶחָד—This terminology, "my Servant David" and "one Shepherd," was used in 34:23–24. See the textual notes on 34:23 and the commentary on 34:23–24. However, 34:24 used נָשִׂיא, "Prince" (as in 37:25), instead of the stronger מֶלֶךְ, "King," here (also 37:22).

37:25 אֲבוֹתֵיכֶם—Instead of "*your* fathers," the LXX and Syriac, apparently influenced by the context, read "*their* fathers," which is preferred also by some modern

---

[6] Zimmerli, *Ezekiel*, 2:269, 275.

[7] Allen, *Ezekiel*, 2:190.

commentators. But "your" does not clash with the preceding clause.[8] Allen defends the MT as the *lectio difficilior*.[9] In Ezekiel "*their* fathers" always occurs in reproofs (2:3; 5:10; 20:4, 24). "*Your* fathers" sometimes occurs in reproofs (20:18, 27, 30, 36), but it also occurs in salvation promises (20:42; 36:28; 47:14) similar to the one here, which recalls God's promise to give the land to the patriarchs.

וְדָוִד עַבְדִּי נָשִׂיא לָהֶם לְעוֹלָם:—Here the eschatological David is labeled a נָשִׂיא, "Prince." Compare מֶלֶךְ, "King," in 37:22, 24. The LXX's translation here is ἄρχων, as one would expect, unlike 37:22, 24, where the LXX had translated also מֶלֶךְ as ἄρχων. See the first textual note on 37:22.

37:26 בְּרִית עוֹלָם יִהְיֶה אוֹתָם—Here אוֹתָם, usually the sign of the direct object (with third masculine plural suffix), must be a form of the preposition אֵת, "with" ("an everlasting covenant *with* them"). The books of Kings, Jeremiah, and Ezekiel frequently use such forms of the preposition that appear to be the direct object marker (see BDB, s.v. אֵת II). Already the LXX renders μετ' αὐτῶν, and from KJV on English translations do likewise ("with them"). בְּרִית, "covenant," was used with -אוֹת, "with," also in 16:60 (see also 16:8), and Block may correctly surmise a dialectical variation.[10] בְּרִית was used with the expected form -אֶת, "with," in 16:62; 17:13.

וּנְתַתִּים—Here נָתַן is used in an absolute sense, as in 28:14 (see the fourth textual note there). I have translated, "I will establish them," as do NKJV and NIV, a meaning that נָתַן often has. RSV and NRSV follow the Targum and translate, "I will bless them." Block sees here a truncated form of the land-grant formula, "[I] will give to them [the land of Israel]," as a corollary to the preceding covenant promise, and he appeals to similar promises elsewhere in the book (11:17; 36:28; 37:21–22).[11] ESV has "I will set them in their land."

Critics often propose ingenious theories of the history of the text. The LXX apparently omitted a translation of וּנְתַתִּים וְהִרְבֵּיתִי אוֹתָם, as though the translator's or an earlier copyist's eye had skipped from one אוֹתָם to the next.

Commentary

With the possible exception of the inaugural vision (chapter 1), this is easily the best known chapter of the book—not least because of the well-known African-American spiritual "Dry Bones," based on the first half of the chapter (37:1–14). The remaining verses (37:15–28) are clearly set off by the word-event formula, "the Word of Yahweh came to me" (37:15),[12] and the customary address to the prophet as "son of man" (37:16, as in 37:3, 9, 11).[13] It is probably safe to assert that the second half of the chapter is generally as unfamiliar as the first half is familiar.

---

[8] Contra Zimmerli, *Ezekiel*, 2:270; cf. even Greenberg, *Ezekiel*, 2:757.

[9] Allen, *Ezekiel*, 2:191.

[10] Block, *Ezekiel*, 2:408, n. 84.

[11] Block, *Ezekiel*, 2:419–20, including n. 124.

[12] For this formula, see page 8 in the introduction and the textual note on 3:16.

[13] See the second textual note and the commentary on 2:1.

It is a bit hard to fit the chapter into neat form-critical categories (thus illustrating the weakness of that approach). "Vision" would probably be the label one would first think of, but the chapter lacks one of the usual nouns for "vision" (מַרְאֶה or חָזוֹן), and the verb רָאָה, "to see," occurs only in the Qal (in 37:8), not the Hiphil ("to show, cause the prophet to see"), which is commonly used in connection with visions (as in 11:25; 40:4). In favor of interpreting it as a vision, however, is the frequent use of הִנֵּה,[14] traditionally "behold," characteristic of dream and vision reports. The initial statement of Ezekiel's seizure by Yahweh's "hand" (37:1; see the commentary on 1:3; used also in 3:14, 22; 33:22; 40:1) would tend to describe more of a prophetic trance or ecstasy. But such labeling is of minimal value in understanding. All in all, "vision" seems the most appropriate term. Greenberg points out that scenes littered with bones are frequent in Mesopotamian curses and/or victory boasts.[15] Yahweh may have chosen to reveal such a scene to Ezekiel because it was familiar to his fellow captives in exile, so its impact upon them would be greater.

Resurrection of the Dry Bones and of God's People from Their Graves (37:1–14)

The first ten verses of the pericope describe the dialogic vision, in which the prophet participates, as he does in other comparable scenes in the book (1:1–3:15; 8:1–11:25; and 40:1–48:35). The prophet is led around the scene by Yahweh himself, whereas in 8:1–11:25 he was led by Yahweh's Christological representative, as he will be again in chapters 40–48 (see the commentary on 40:3 and on 43:6). In this vision Ezekiel's prophesying has a direct bearing on what happens. Then 37:12–14 is entirely a speech by God, giving his prophet the words he is to prophesy. Linking the two sections (37:1–10 and 37:12–14) is a popular saying by the exiles (37:11), expressing their hopelessness in two metaphors. The first metaphor, of dried bones, relates to the preceding vision. The second, of being "cut off," relates to the following prophecy of disinterment. Some critics are disturbed by the supposed inconsistency of a scene of a valley full of disarticulated bones (37:1—10) alongside one of corpses rising from graves (37:12–14), but this is probably a typical case of attempting to impose Western notions of "logic" upon God's inspired Word, in the form of ancient Oriental literature.

One should note the repetition of certain key words in 37:1–14, which together with the detail of the narrative, contribute to its impressiveness: (1) רוּחַ, "Spirit, spirit, breath, wind," ten times, and in several senses; (2) עֶצֶם or עֲצָמוֹת, "bone(s)," ten times; (3) the verb נָבָא, "prophesy," seven times; and (4) the verb חָיָה, "to live again, come back to life," six times.

Beyond the exegesis (in its usual philological sense) of a pericope such as this one, many other issues arise. Foremost will be the question whether God

---

[14]   Although I have not translated it, it occurs in 37:2 (twice), 5, 7, 8, 11, 12, 19, 21.

[15]   Greenberg, *Ezekiel*, 2:748.

1075

intends anything further than Israel's *national* "resurrection," its return from exile in Babylon to the land of Israel, in the direction of a bodily resurrection of the people, if not also the resurrection of individual believers from the dead. Of course, one may argue that God's people ("O my people," 37:12–13) are composed of individuals, but the question remains whether the text implies any such conception as a literal bodily resurrection from the dead. Older critics and most modern critical commentators answer the question with an emphatic negative. At the other extreme, church history has known allegorists who read the OT as written in code that simply is to be equated with the NT, without taking seriously the original historical context and application to God's OT people. In my judgment, neither extreme will pass muster.

Basic Christian confession insists on the unity of Scripture, although not uniformity, and not denying a certain progression or development in revelation. God reveals himself and his salvation more fully as one moves from Genesis to the "fulfillment" of the OT at Christ's first advent, and then toward Revelation and the "consummation" of all things at Christ's return. There is no airtight, universally agreed-upon way of expressing the complex relationship between the two Testaments, but Christian commentators agree on the basics. We are not to read *into* the OT arbitrary and fanciful meanings that are utterly alien to the original text and context, but I like to speak of reading *out* of the OT all that the NT teaches is latent there, as St. Augustine said: "The New Testament is latent in the Old; the Old Testament becomes patent in the New" (*In Vetere Novum lateat, et in Novo Vetus pateat*).[16]

We cannot read Ezekiel's mind and make his words say more than they do. At the same time, we know that we have received the OT anew at Christ's hand and now read it with a veil lifted from our faces (2 Cor 3:12–18). We can begin by casting a wider net in the rest of the OT.[17] Christians have long recognized that the OT teaches a tradition of life with God after death, which sometimes surfaced explicitly.[18] We may note the miracles of revivification performed through Elijah and Elisha (see the first textual note and the commentary on 37:3). The template of Adam's creation in Genesis 2, which clearly underlies the reconstitution of the bodies (bones, sinews, flesh, skin) and endowment with "breath" in Ezek 37:4–10, could also be applied to an eschatological resurrection. Very early OT texts celebrate Yahweh as the one who kills and makes alive (Deut 32:39; 1 Sam 2:6). While some biblical passages, such as Ezekiel 31–32, depict Sheol as the gloomy place where dead unbelievers languish forevermore (similar to the view in the Semitic world), other passages speak of Yahweh's ability to save his faithful from Sheol (e.g., Jonah 2:3, 7 [ET

---

[16] Augustine, *Quaestionum in Heptateuchum*, book 2, question 73 (PL 34:623; CCSL 33:106).

[17] Some commentators seek to connect the chapter with surrounding paganism, Egypt, dying and rising Canaanite gods, later Zoroastrianism, or so forth, but the OT suggests a repudiation of all such ideas.

[18] See, for example, Gen 5:24; 2 Kings 2; and Ps 73:24, all with the verb לָקַח, "take."

2:2, 6]).[19] The Psalms often speak poetically of sickness and sundry other woes as the power of "death" invading this life, but from Yahweh comes rescue from them all, even from death and Sheol.[c] However this language may have been read in the OT era, it is only a small step between a metaphorical understanding and a historical application to life after death in a literal sense.[20] Certain other passages about resurrection stand out, especially Hos 6:1–3; Is 25:6–8; 26:19; and Dan 12:1–3, especially since Daniel dates to the same exilic period as Ezekiel (who refers to Daniel in Ezek 14:14, 20; 28:3). Finally, we should not fail to note that Jonah's three-day interment in the great fish (Jonah 2:1 [ET 1:17]) and "on the third day he will raise us up" in Hos 6:2 seem to be the OT basis for Jesus' repeated assertion that it was necessary for him to rise "on the third day" to fulfill the Scriptures (e.g., Lk 9:22; 18:33; 24:7, 46; see especially 1 Cor 15:4).[21]

(c) E.g., Pss 16:10–11; 49:15–16 (ET 49:14–15); 116:8–9

Apparently in the intertestamental period, in the transition from the OT faith (Yahwism) to the (different) religion of early Judaism, views about the resurrection diverged, as attested in the NT about the Pharisees and Sadducees (e.g., Mt 22:23–34; Acts 23:6–10). Critics once widely held that the Pharisaic defense of the resurrection was a relative novelty, while the Sadducees were on this point the traditionalists. More recently, many scholars have reversed the roles of these two parties and construe the Sadducean position as a conscious departure from earlier beliefs grounded in the OT. In general, the early Jewish evidence is mixed, although a resurrectionist view seems to have been the dominant one.

Special note should be made of the painting on one wall of a third-century A.D. synagogue unearthed at Dura-Europos on the middle Euphrates, today in eastern Syria not far from the Iraqi border. A Christian house church, a mithraeum, and various pagan temples were also found, almost all of them at least with partially painted inside walls, but the synagogue is the only one relevant for Ezekiel 37. (Today it may be viewed in the Syrian National Museum in Damascus.) The painting pictures the four winds (in the form of winged Psyches) entering dead bodies and next to them an assembling of men standing in a posture of praise. It is impossible to tell from the painting whether the artist intended to convey a reality or a metaphoric vision.

Eastern Christian art continued to show a fascination with the theme of resurrection based on Ezekiel 37, though it was less attested in the West. The interpretation seems generally to have been that the chapter depicts the eschatological resurrection of all dead believers in Christ. A major Eastern example was found at Dara in northern Syria, a center of Christian activity in the Byzantine period. One tomb painting at the site shows Ezekiel walking toward

---

[19] See the excursus "Sheol" in Lessing, *Jonah*, 249–55.

[20] For a good, but usually neglected, survey of possible passages in the Psalms that speak of believers enjoying life with God after death, see Dahood, *Psalms*, 3:xlii–lii.

[21] One may also see "The Sign of Jonah" in Lessing, *Jonah*, 228–39.

a mound of skulls, and above him is the hand of God along with the four winds, holding the key to life. In front of the prophet, two figures emerge from a sarcophagus.[22]

The NT may not directly cite Ezek 37:1–14 as fulfilled by NT events, but it contains a number of allusions that may be more than coincidental. Mt 27:50–54 usually heads such lists: when Jesus expired, "the earth quaked" (cf. "earthquake" in Ezek 37:7), "and the graves were opened. And many bodies of the saints who had fallen asleep were raised. And coming out of the graves after his resurrection they went into the holy city and appeared to many." The atoning death of Christ is thereby shown to be the basis for the resurrection of all believers to everlasting life. On the Last Day, after the return of Christ, all believers shall be raised with immortal, glorified bodies like that of the risen Christ (e.g., 1 Cor 15:48–55). Since the NT declares that Jesus himself was the first to rise from the dead, the saints who were raised at his death (and others who were raised in the OT and NT periods) probably were only temporary revivifications or restorations to mortal life, so that Christ himself on Easter is the first to be raised with a glorified, immortal body.[23]

John's Gospel and Apocalypse have strong allusions. Jesus declares, "Truly, truly, I say to you that an hour comes and is now when the dead will hear the voice of the Son of God, and those who hear will live. ... An hour is coming when all in the tombs will hear his voice and come out" (Jn 5:25–29). Jesus then calls forth Lazarus from the tomb (Jn 11:43; see also Jn 11:23–26). The visionary passage Rev 11:11 quotes from Ezek 37:5, 10: "The spirit of life [πνεῦμα ζωῆς] from God entered them [the two witnesses], and they stood on their feet."[24] And the apostle John answers, "Lord, you know," as does Ezekiel in 37:3, when asked about the great multitude that comprises the church triumphant after the resurrection (Rev 7:14).[25]

Various references to the giving of the Holy Spirit may also be expressed in the light of this chapter. The ambiguity of πνεῦμα ("Spirit, spirit, wind") in

---

[22] See Oliver Nicholson, "Shall These Bones Live? A Dakhma at Dara?" *AJA* 89 (1985): 667–71, especially p. 669, cited in Block, *Ezekiel*, 2:391, including n. 114.

[23] See the first textual note and the commentary on 37:3.

[24] The two witnesses who are resurrected in Rev 11:11 are not specific persons, but figures who represent the entire witnessing church, whose members will be persecuted (some martyred). But by God's grace the church will live anew to continue witnessing until the return of Christ, whereupon all dead believers will be raised to everlasting life on the Last Day. See Brighton, *Revelation*, 300–301.

[25] See Brighton, *Revelation*, 193, 199–201. To counter widespread misconceptions of the tribulation and millennium, here we may affirm briefly the eschatology set forth in the NT, which is consistent with that in the OT. The present church age is the "millennium" spoken of in Rev 20:1–7. During the present era, upon death all believers immediately enter the nearer presence of God (they are the souls under the altar in Rev 6:9), while unbelievers immediately enter a state of torment. Persecution of the church shall intensify as time goes on, especially as the return of Christ draws near. At his return, all the dead shall be raised bodily, and unbelievers shall be damned to hell, while believers shall inherit eternal life (Rev 20:11–15; see also Jn 5:28–29).

Jn 3:5–8, with "born again/from above" (γεννάω ἄνωθεν, 3:3, 7; cf. 3:31) as a kind of resurrection motif, recalls the multivalence of רוּחַ ("Spirit, spirit, breath, wind") here. In Jn 20:22, the risen Christ breathes on his disciples and says, "Receive the Holy Spirit"—a verse that might echo Gen 2:7 as well as Ezek 37:14. St. Paul's reference in 1 Thess 4:8 to God "who gives his Holy Spirit to you" likewise may have Ezek 37:14 as its background. Finally, discussions of the subject often include reference to the difficult Romans 11, where Paul speaks of the possible conversion of unbelieving Jews to faith in Christ, so that they would be received by God, as being "life from the dead" (Rom 11:15). All believers in Christ, both Jewish and Gentile, comprise the "all Israel" that "shall be saved" (Rom 11:26).

If one does wish to formulate an organic "prophecy" connection with the NT, perhaps the Matthew 27 reference provides the best illustration. One may debate, however, how best to formulate the connection (other than the generic "prophecy"). "Typology" does not seem to work well here since, at least as I understand and use the term, it implies actual history or another objective fact in the OT era, and the resurrections Ezekiel sees are in a vision, not bodily resurrections that occurred in his day. Perhaps this is an instance where "from OT metaphor to NT reality" might be more fitting.

Not surprisingly, liturgical use of Ezek 37:1–14 has been extensive, both in the synagogue and the church. Its interpretation as a new exodus probably contributed to its synagogal assignment as the הַפְטָרָא (*haftara*ʾ) for the Sabbath of Passover, corresponding to the סְדָרוֹת (*sedaroth*) of Ex 33:12–34:26 and Num 28:19–25.

St. Jerome declares that "all the churches of Christ" read this pericope.[26] Christian use of it has centered on Lent and Easter, especially at the Baptism of catechumens during the Easter Vigil on Easter Eve. Some ancient Eastern traditions used it at Matins on Holy Saturday, and some Syriac lectionaries assign it to Easter Day itself. There is also a tradition of using it at the commemoration and burial of the dead (so the Nestorians) and in Russia at the burial of a priest. At one time, at least, Anglicans read it at Matins on the Tuesday after Pentecost. I have not surveyed the entire Lutheran tradition, but I am aware that it is the Old Testament Reading (with Jesus breathing the Spirit in Jn 20:19–31 as the Gospel) for the Second Sunday after Easter in the One-Year Lectionary, and in the Three-Year Lectionary, for the Fifth Sunday in Lent (with the raising of Lazarus in John 11 as the Gospel) in Series A and for Pentecost (with readings from Acts 2 and John 15–16 about the Spirit) in Series B.[27]

37:1 Two agents of Yahweh are mentioned at the outset as active in placing Ezekiel on the scene of this chapter's events, at least of its first fourteen verses. Yahweh's "hand" (יָד) was active in the inaugural vision (see the com-

---

[26] Jerome, *Commentariorum in Hiezechielem* (CCSL 75:512).

[27] *LSB* xiv, xvii, xxi.

mentary on 1:3) and has appeared a number of times since (3:14, 22; 8:1; 33:22; and again in 40:1). It is not easy to define except as an anthropomorphic, and hence somewhat "incarnational," form of Yahweh exerting his supernatural power, which snatches the prophet out of the everyday realm and locates him in a position where he hears and sees divine revelation.

In 2:2 the "Spirit" accompanied the spoken divine Word, but here it is "the hand of Yahweh" that functions in conjunction with "the Spirit of Yahweh." As noted in the introduction to the chapter, רוּחַ (translated "Spirit" here and in 37:14) is a major keyword of the pericope, used in 37:1–14 with several different nuances, which are not always easy to distinguish. By itself the word can mean simply "wind," and closely associated is its sense of "breath," a produced "wind" that connotes life and so often parallels נֶפֶשׁ (traditionally "soul" or "life"), נְשָׁמָה ("breath"), and even חַיִּים, "life" (cf. רוּחַ וִחְיִיתֶם, literally, "... spirit so you will come back to life," in 37:5–6). In 11:5, the only other place in the book where "the Spirit of Yahweh" is used, it is followed by a command to prophesy, so it signifies the Spirit's enablement for the prophet to receive and transmit messages from God. Such passages with "Spirit," together with the related description "God-breathed" (θεόπνευστος, 2 Tim 3:16), constitute the theological and also the etymological basis of our dogmatic use of "in*spir*ation," although the Scriptures use other kinds of language to describe the mystery of their divine origin as well. The "Spirit" (רוּחַ) may also be an agency of conveyance, a transporting agency, as, for example, in 11:24 where the "Spirit" (רוּחַ, not "hand"!) brought me "in the vision by the Spirit of God" (בַּמַּרְאֶה בְּרוּחַ אֱלֹהִים). Similarly, in 40:2, a passage corresponding to this one, God transports the prophet "in visions of God," that is, "in divine visions" (בְּמַרְאוֹת אֱלֹהִים). All of this indicates how fluid and semi-interchangeable the terms for the divine are.

The immediate issue is whether we should think of a change of Ezekiel's physical location, or of "events" that transpired in his head, as it were, under inspiration. The balance of evidence, to judge by parallels in the book, would point to visionary experiences of some sort. Yahweh's "hand" first comes upon Ezekiel in 1:3 when he is already "by the Kebar Canal," but we are not told of its location with respect to the main exilic community in Tel Abib, so it might or might not have been the same as the "valley" here. When Ezekiel is "brought" to Jerusalem in chapter 8, "hand," "Spirit," and "vision(s)" are all mentioned. Even if all these instances are visionary, a mental image of some specific geographical location is not ruled out. Grammatically, this affects how we should render the Hebrew definite article on הַבִּקְעָה, "the valley." Many translators apparently consider it generic (any valley) and so offer us "*a* valley." In a vision, indeed, one valley might serve as well as any other. But being the weak demonstratives that definite articles intrinsically are, "*the* valley," that is, some specific valley, seems more likely. It could have been the specific valley intended by God, or more likely, the same locale as the "valley" (בִּקְעָה) in 3:22–23, the last part of his prophetic commissioning.

In prior OT books "the Spirit of Yahweh" (רוּחַ יהוה) had become a fixed semi-technical expression, that is, virtually a hypostasis or manifestation of Yahweh himself.[28] If we can cite the later canon of Trinitarian dogma *opera Trinitatis ad extra indivisa sunt*, "the external works of the Trinity are inseparable," meaning that all three persons of the Godhead are present and active when God works in the world, "the Spirit of Yahweh" comes very close to expressing that dogma. Yet there are other times when Yahweh's "Spirit" and the Tetragrammaton are not so tightly linked, and in such cases we cannot simplistically attempt to limit the reference to just one person of the Trinity. Only the full revelation of the second person of the Trinity, Jesus Christ, makes the clear formulation and confession of the doctrine of the Trinity possible. But we surely see here in Ezekiel part of the *praeparatio evangelica* ("preparation for the Gospel"), one of the building blocks or adumbrations of what in the fullness of time would indeed become the doctrine of the Trinity.

When Ezekiel arrives at the valley, he finds it "full of bones" (37:1), that is, not skeletons, but a sea of scattered, disarticulated bones. The next verse (37:2) describes the scene in greater detail.

37:3 Instead of narration, direct speech now dominates through 37:6, and except for 37:3b, it is all Yahweh's. Divine questions are standard elements in visions, probably to help wrest significance from a scene (e.g., Jer 1:11, 13; Amos 7:8; 8:2; Zech 4:1–2, 5).

Ezekiel's reply is properly deferential. Had another human being asked the question, it would have been ridiculous, laughable. But with Yahweh as the questioner, Ezekiel can only plead human ignorance and impotence versus divine omniscience and omnipotence (similarly John in Rev 7:14). Ezekiel's reply tells us very little about how much he (or believing Israel in general) knew at this time about "the resurrection of the body" and "the life everlasting" (Apostles' Creed). But it does provide us with a minimum that must be accepted before we attempt to enlarge the picture. First of all, Ezekiel plainly does not dismiss the very possibility of resurrection out of hand, as many an agnostic would today. That God, the Creator of life, was Lord over both life and death is implicit in the OT from the outset, even when nothing explicit is said about the relation of the two. As early as Num 27:16, we meet the description of Yahweh as "the God of the spirits [הָרוּחֹת] of all flesh [בָּשָׂר]." And Ezekiel would have been aware of the resuscitations of dead people by Elijah (1 Ki 17:17–24) and Elisha (2 Ki 4:18–37), even as the result of a corpse touching Elisha's own bones (2 Ki 13:21). But all those involved recent deaths, of people whose bodies had only begun to decay, and whose bones were far from being "very dry" (Ezek 37:2). So this is something entirely different, and Ezekiel can do no more than refer the question back to God.

---

[28] It occurs almost thirty times in the OT, first and often in Judges (e.g., 3:10; 6:34), then in the books of Samuel and Kings. Isaiah (11:2; 40:7, 13; 59:19; 63:14), Hosea (13:15), and Micah (2:7; 3:8) are the only other prophets besides Ezekiel to use it.

37:4–6 "The prophet is suddenly transformed from being the spokesman of human impotence into the spokesman of divine omnipotence."[29] Using the citation formula, "thus says the Lord Yahweh" (37:5),[30] he is to prophesy to the bones as though they were a living audience. He proclaims that what is about to be done will be accomplished through the medium of God's Word, by which Yahweh has the power to fulfill whatever he promises to his people.

Ezek 37:5 summarizes the restoration to life in general terms, and 37:6 describes the process in greater detail, although the last half of 37:6 simply repeats the assertion of 37:5, adding only that all of it will be done in order that they come to understand the mystery and power of Yahweh—the recognition formula, "then you will know that I am Yahweh."[31] The ultimate concern is not biological life as much as spiritual, everlasting life through faith and knowledge of God (cf. Jn 6:69; 17:3; Gal 4:9).

Both Ezek 37:5 and 37:6 emphasize רוּחַ, "spirit," as the crucial element for life, a theme that will be reiterated in 37:9–10. The LXX highlights the point even more by placing the last two words of 37:5 in a genitive relationship, πνεῦμα ζωῆς, "spirit of life" (quoted in Rev 11:11), and expanding the simple רוּחַ, "spirit," of 37:6 into πνεῦμά μου, "my Spirit," probably under the influence of "my Spirit" in 36:27 and 37:14.

37:7–8 As Ezekiel watches in amazement, the divine words of his prophecy are effective, and the scattered, bleached bones are reconstituted into human bodies. But the reader is brought up short by the final disjunctive clause: "but there was no spirit in them." All Ezekiel has accomplished so far is to make bodies or corpses; without רוּחַ ("spirit, breath") in them, they remain lifeless.

37:9–10 The urgency of the one thing needful (cf. Lk 10:42) is expressed by the repetition of Yahweh's command to prophesy to הָרוּחַ, "the wind," which should come from all four "winds" (directions) and by the power of the "Spirit" become the "breath" of life (all of the preceding words in quotes are implied by the same Hebrew noun, רוּחַ; see the textual notes). As the context shows, a whole, vast army is to be given life, so Yahweh calls on the "breath" from the four "winds," which are elsewhere pictured as his servants (Pss 104:3–4; 148:8; Heb 1:7), to do his bidding.

The scene is plainly modeled after the creation narrative of Genesis 2. The lump of clay that Yahweh had molded does not become a living being (חַיָּה נֶפֶשׁ) until God "breathed, blew" (the same verb, נָפַח, as used here) the "breath of life" (נִשְׁמַת חַיִּים, Gen 2:7). Yet this is not a first creation of natural life, but a new creation, as will be made clear by the gift of "my Spirit" in 37:14, hence akin to the rebirth by the Spirit in Jn 3:3–8; Titus 3:5–6.

---

[29] Zimmerli, *Ezekiel*, 2:260.

[30] For this formula, see pages 8–9 in the introduction and the fourth textual note and the commentary on 2:4.

[31] For this formula, see page 9 in the introduction and the commentary on 6:7.

By labeling the reassembled corpses as הַרוּגִים (Qal passive participle of הָרַג, "kill," 37:9), literally, those who had been "killed, slain," the perspective changes slightly. The bodies are those of "a very large army" (חַיִל), as they are called at the end of 37:10 after the "breath" has entered into them and they have stood up. חַיִל can have other connotations besides "army," but Ezekiel uses it in that sense in 17:17; 29:18–19; 32:31; 38:4, 15, and it accords with הַרוּגִים, "slain," as in battle.

These had not been buried, however. Ezekiel does not say why, but the curse of being left unburied to be eaten by wild animals appears frequently in treaty oaths of the ancient Near East. The OT is well aware of the practice (cf. Rizpah's eerie vigil in 2 Samuel 21), and covenant curses mention it (Deut 28:25–26; Jer 34:17–20, the latter with explicit reference to the covenant-making ceremony). The command in Deut 21:22–23 to bury a criminal executed by being impaled (the precursor to crucifixion) also was because of the curse involved (Gal 3:13).

Nothing indicates that these soldiers were worthy of being restored to life. If we were to ask why they were selected, the explanation must be the general reference to God's undeserved grace, which informs this entire pericope.

37:11 The "are" in "these bones are the whole house of Israel" is a required English insertion in the Hebrew nominal clause, so it should not be pressed. "Represent" or "stand for" would be more accurate. "The whole house of Israel" intimates what will be the subject of the second half of the chapter (37:15–28), the united kingdom, including those whom the Assyrians had exiled about 130 years previously (as has been already affirmed in 36:10 and will be reiterated in 39:25 and 45:6—a consistent prophetic theme in general). The martial picture in 37:9–10 is now abandoned, and the purely visionary form of the previous verses with it.

Representatively, then, it is the entire eschatological nation that voices the despair quoted in 37:11b. All three expressions of despair are essentially synonymous, although the first is more figurative, connecting with the vision just seen (see the textual notes). The remaining verses in the pericope are God's refutation, divisible into two parts, 37:12–13 and 37:14, each containing promises of divine action.

37:12 This verse contains a triad of promises, corresponding to the triad of popular laments in 37:11b. Like the laments, they too are introduced by the deictic particle הִנֵּה (untranslated) to arouse the people's attention. The metaphor now changes drastically to that of a cemetery, something probably not perceived as jarring a transition in Ezekiel's day as it is for a modern, Western audience. Yahweh first promises to "open" their graves (which theoretically might have been done for other reasons, but compare the NT accounts of Jesus' resurrection), then promises also to "raise/bring [them] up" from those graves. The verb "I will raise/bring up" is plainly exodus terminology (see the Hiphil of עָלָה also in, e.g., Gen 50:24; Ex 3:17; 32:1; Deut 20:1; Josh 24:17). This leads into the third promise, "I will bring" (וְהֵבֵאתִי), with restoration of

Yahweh's people to their homeland, where even the grave terminology is abandoned. This too is part of the same exodus typology that lies at the heart of most of Ezekiel's restoration oracles (20:42; 34:13; 36:24; 37:21).

37:13 The recognition formula, "then you will know that I am Yahweh" (repeated for emphasis in the next verse), shows that "as ever in the book of Ezekiel, salvation is to be a means to a divine end. The redeeming act of God would bring with it the revelation of his true self."[32]

37:14 This verse features רוּחַ again, not as "breath" or "wind" or (human) "spirit" but plainly (as in 37:1) the Holy Spirit, רוּחִי, "*my* Spirit." As we noted earlier, the agency of the Spirit was implicit in the word's earlier translations as "spirit," "breath," and "wind," but could not easily be expressed in a simple translation. The expression inevitably merges with the promises of "my Spirit" in the previous chapter (36:27) and again in 39:29.[33] The promise of "my Spirit" echoes throughout the OT Scriptures and into the NT, for example, Is 42:1, quoted in Mt 12:18; Is 44:3; 59:21; Joel 3:1–2 (ET 2:28–29), quoted on Pentecost in Acts 2:17–18; Hag 2:5; Zech 4:6; 6:8. The vista goes beyond mere revivification to the inner transformation of the individual as well, "renewal by the Holy Spirit" (ἀνακαινώσεως πνεύματος ἁγίου, Titus 3:5). The Christian will inevitably be reminded that biblical doctrine attributes all this sort of activity to the third person of the Holy Trinity, "the Lord and giver of life, who proceeds from the Father and the Son" (Nicene Creed; cf. 2 Cor 3:17–18), culminating in "the resurrection of the body" and "the life everlasting" (Apostles' Creed).

The exodus typology has been extended into a new settlement after the pattern of Joshua's conquest of Canaan. Biblical hermeneutics will extend it further into the "land" of the church, ultimately also that of the church triumphant.[34] The OT land promises are fulfilled in Christ, and so Christians enter their "promised land" by being part of the body of Christ, the church, with the promise of entering the new heavens and earth after the resurrection (Mt 25:34). Thus the "very, very large army" (Ezek 37:10) of risen people that will dwell securely in their own land is an OT depiction of the church triumphant, the multitude from every nation, glimpsed by John the Seer (Rev 7:9–17), which, raised bodily after the return of Christ, shall dwell forever in the new heavens and new earth with God in their midst (Revelation 21–22).

The pericope closes with redundant, but maximally emphatic asseverations: the recognition formula (in 37:6, 13) is repeated once more, with the reminder that God's Word of promise will certainly be fulfilled (cf. 22:14), and

---

[32] Allen, *Ezekiel*, 2:187.

[33] See the textual notes and commentary on 11:19–20 as well as on 36:26–27 and 39:29.

[34] See page 3 in the introduction. Further, one may see "The Central Theme" in the introduction and the excursus "Geography and Theology of the Holy Land" in Harstad, *Joshua*, 25–31 and 489–96, respectively.

his final signatory formula, "says Yahweh,"[35] is added as a still further personal guarantee.

Israel Reunited as One People under God and His Servant David (37:15–28)

37:16 The divine commands in this and the following verse initiate the last action prophecy in the book of Ezekiel,[36] and the only one in connection with the salvation oracles. Usually this genre consists simply of the action and its explanation. In this case, however, the pattern is more complicated. After a brief explanation in 37:18–19, another command follows in 37:20 and then a long divine speech, which gradually relates less and less to the action prophecy itself and more to the Christological new David.

The initial imperative, "take" (קַח, 37:16), is followed (as is often the case in action prophecies), literally, by "for yourself" (לְךָ, the so-called "ethical dative" or "dative of advantage"), often left untranslated in modern, idiomatic English. Its meaning, if discernible, seems to focus attention on the actor, apart from the audience. That understanding in this case would be reinforced by the audience's question about the act's meaning in 37:18.

The command is, literally, to take "one/a [אֶחָד] piece of wood," which together with the following אֶחָד means "one ... another." "One" (אֶחָד) is a keyword in the pericope, summarizing the major point of the action prophecy. Its use eight times in 37:16–19 will be echoed by a threefold use in the divine speech later for "one nation ... one King ... one Shepherd" (37:22, 24).

A major exegetical issue is the precise meaning of the common word עֵץ here. It is much more multivalent (or ambiguous) than any English equivalent. Most commonly it is translated "tree" or "wood." That "wood" can be of almost any sort: "stick," the rare, but otherwise attested traditional translation here and retained in most modern versions, or other "piece of wood" (which could have been used because it seems as noncommittal or ambiguous as the context seems to require). Analogous usages in English would include: (1) the use of "tree" as a synonym for "cross" in both Scripture (Gal 3:13; 1 Pet 2:24) and our liturgy[37]—probably technically merging crucifixion and impalation; and (2) especially in older rural settings, talk of "single trees" and "double trees" for horse-drawn vehicles or implements. Ezekiel himself has already used the word in various senses: trees in general (6:13; 17:24); fruit trees

---

[35] This verse has one of the four instances of the shorter formula (13:6–7; 16:58; 37:14). The longer form is "says *the Lord* Yahweh." See pages 8–9 in the introduction and the second textual note on 5:11.

[36] See "Ezekiel's Action Prophecies" in Hummel, *Ezekiel 1–20,* 148–50.

[37] See especially the Proper Preface for Holy Week: "On the tree of the cross you gave salvation to mankind that, whence death arose, thence life also might rise again and that he who by a tree once overcame likewise by a tree might be overcome, through Jesus Christ our Lord" (*LW*, p. 147).

(34:27); wood from which a skilled craftsman can make something (15:2–3); and fuel for a fire (15:6; 24:10; 39:10). The issue is in what sense he intends it here.

The traditional "stick" is by no means out of the question. Ezekiel commonly uses ordinary objects in his action prophecies, and in this case it was part of the ambiguity that elicited the request for interpretation in 37:18. We are not told their size, but they would not have to be too large for Ezekiel to inscribe a few words on them. We have an Egyptian parallel where staffs were inscribed over most of their length with epithets of the god Amun and a dedication to him.

Perhaps the most favored interpretation today depends on the Greek rendering as ῥάβδος, understood as "scepter" or "staff." In the LXX ῥάβδος usually translates שֵׁבֶט or מַטֶּה, and both Hebrew terms can be used for a ruler's "staff" or royal "scepter" (e.g., see the Christological use of שֵׁבֶט in Gen 49:10; Num 24:17; Ps 45:7; and of מַטֶּה in Ps 110:2). It is often thought that this verse reminded the LXX translators of Num 17:16–26 (ET 17:1–11), where Moses writes the name of the נָשִׂיא ("leader") of each of the tribes on twelve staves. Ben Sirach appears to had this idea in mind in his reflections on the perpetuity of the Davidic covenant (Sirach 47:20–22). If this was Ezekiel's intention, his audience did not grasp it, as is shown by their question in 37:18. Furthermore, if he meant royal scepters, it would imply a unification not only of the divided countries, but of their ruling houses as well. But neither Ezekiel nor any other orthodox biblical figure ever conceded legitimacy to any of the various northern dynasties. In fact, Ezekiel here seems to be quite careful to specify a unification of the kingdoms, not their kings. The only legitimate royal line was that of David, culminating in the new David (34:23–24; 37:24–25).

Another line of interpretation would understand the pieces of wood as shepherds' rods or staffs. The eschatological "David" is referred to as a "Shepherd" (רֹעֶה) in 34:23 and 37:24. Appeal is also made to the apparent dependence on this Ezekiel passage by Zechariah (11:4–17), who has two staffs labeled "Grace" and "Union." But even if that dependence is granted, it is odd that Ezekiel would describe a shepherd's staff with עֵץ instead of one of the usual terms, מַטֶּה (not used by Ezekiel in this sense), מַקֵּל (39:9), or מִשְׁעֶנֶת (29:6).

In my judgment, the Targum is closer to the mark by using לוּחַ, "tablet," to reproduce עֵץ. (The Targum uses לוּחַ, "tablet," also for גִּלָּיוֹן, "writing tablet," in Is 8:1.) A "writing board" or "diptych" would translate it more precisely. These writing boards were typically two or more leaves (called "doors") of flat, hinged pieces of wood with a writing surface filled with a compound of beeswax and orpiment on which a message could be etched, and which, after use, could be heated slightly and reused. These were widely used in antiquity and very ancient. They are attested as early as the Sumerian period in the third millennium, and an actual example was recently excavated from a fourteenth-century-B.C. ship that sank off the coast of southeastern Turkey. Besides גִּלָּיוֹן

in Is 8:1, also לוּחַ in Is 30:8 (where it parallels סֵפֶר) and לוּחַ in Hab 2:2 probably refer to such a "writing tablet." Some object that if such a writing board was Ezekiel's instrument, there would have been no necessary association with a kingdom, but it was the writing on them that conveyed the message. Also, the two leaves would not suggest oneness until the diptych was closed.

One must also decide as to the force of the preposition לְ before "Judah," "the sons of Israel," and "Joseph." In addition to a host of specialized idioms, this preposition is the usual way to express the dative "to, for." Hence, most English translations from KJV on simply translate "for." But as a meaningful translation, that seems evasive to me. The best alternative seems to be a *lamed* of possession or ownership (BDB, s.v. לְ, 5 a, b), hence, my translation, "belonging to." In some cases, English "of" might be appropriate, especially if the instance here may be compared to the superscriptions of the Psalms and similar labels in Ugaritic epics. That so-called "*lamed* of authorship" is usually translated "of." In the second command to write here, the fact that a construct chain, עֵץ אֶפְרַיִם, "Ephraim's piece of wood," stands in apposition to the previous לְיוֹסֵף, "belonging to Joseph," seems to confirm that understanding of the preposition. Extrabiblically there are the parallels of the hundreds of stamped bullae and stamp seals from the biblical period, not to mention the jar handles, often stamped *lmlk*, "for the king," found on containers of wine or other commodities. Within the Bible again, we may even adduce the two goats involved in the Day of Atonement ritual, one goat לַיהֹוָה, "belonging to, to be sacrificed to Yahweh," and the other לַעֲזָאזֵל, "belonging to Azazel" and released in the desert (Lev 16:8). See also לַיהוָה, "belonging to Yahweh," in Is 44:5 (twice). It has been objected that this use of לְ applies mostly to individuals, not groups, but if taken collectively here of entire groups or their eponyms, that concern is neutralized.

To each designation of ownership, Ezekiel appends חֲבֵרָיו (the plural suffix of the Qere is almost certainly preferable to the Kethib's singular). The word חָבֵר occurs only here and in 37:19 in Ezekiel, but is common enough otherwise, and its meaning is quite general, "companion, associate, ally." In this context the reference must be to the smaller tribes or other groups historically associated with the ones named, by which they were probably absorbed. With Judah one would think of the priests and Levites (2 Chr 11:13–14), Simeon, Benjamin, and perhaps also the Calebites, Kenizzites, Jerahmeelites, and northerners who had defected to the South at the time of the schism. With Joseph, better known after its dominant tribe, Ephraim, one would include all the other of the tribes.

In both inscriptions, "Israel" is used consistently of the undivided covenant nation as a whole, but the much larger size of the northern contingent may be indicated by the phrase "the *whole* house of Israel associated with it" in connection with the North, in contrast to the simple "the sons of Israel associated with it" for the South.

37:17 My translation may be free, depending on the precise meaning of עֵץ, "board, writing tablet," which is crucial for visualizing exactly what was happening. A literal translation might be this: "bring them together, one to the other for yourself into one board, so that they may be united in your hand." The verb קָרַב is usually translated "join," and naturally so if we understand the prophet as simply holding two sticks end to end in his hand. But the verb is not that precise; it simply means "bring near." If we think of diptychs, the method of "joining" would consist of linking two tablets edge to edge by means of hinge pins or leather cords. It may be coincidental, but the language here is redolent of the "joining" (same Hebrew verb) of bone to bone in 37:7.

37:18 One almost gets the impression that Yahweh is so eager to have the prophet complete his action prophecy so that a full explanation can be given that he interrupts his own instructions to give Ezekiel advance notice that the people will not understand and will interrogate him as to the meaning.

37:19 At first reading, this rather opaque verse (see the textual notes) does not clarify much, except that the shift from second to first person pronouns shows that the real significance lies not in the prophet's strange actions, but in what they represent, namely, what Yahweh will perform. Upon closer scrutiny, however, one discerns little changes that accumulate to make the ultimate point: the reunification of the two kingdoms.

First of all, the "board" of Joseph is now mentioned before that of Judah (the reverse of their order in 37:16). Then when that board is placed on the Judahite counterpart, the implication is of the foundational superiority of the Southern Kingdom. The boards are not the ultimate concern, but the two kingdoms that they represent. The board of Joseph is described as being in Ephraim's hand (slightly expanded from 37:16) because of that tribe's dominance in the North. The tribes "associated with it" (חֲבֵרָיו, the same Qere form as twice in 37:16) are mentioned, but not those associated with Judah, probably accurately reflecting the greater cohesion in the South throughout the preceding history.

The second textual note on 37:17 pointed out that the unusual plural אֲחָדִים, "ones," used in that verse implies only an apparent "unity," which in 37:19 is replaced by the normal אֶחָד, "one," indicating something genuinely and definitely united—as only God could do. This divine monergism is strengthened at the end of 37:19 by "in my hand," probably intended as an antithesis to "in the hand of Ephraim" earlier in 37:19, implying that God himself will reverse "the sins of Jeroboam (the son of Nebat)," the recurring condemnatory description of the idolatry instituted by Jeroboam and perpetuated by the northern kings in the book of Kings.[d] Thus as Zimmerli summarizes, 37:19 is not really a further interpretation of the action prophecy, but a divine promise that Yahweh will personally heal the ancient breach and fulfill his promise.[38]

(d) E.g., 1 Ki 14:16; 15:30; 16:31; 2 Ki 10:29, 31

---

[38] Zimmerli, *Ezekiel*, 2:275.

37:20 This verse completes the description of the prophet's prophetic action. It probably implies a certain durative significance: Ezekiel is to continue to hold the united tablets in front of the people, or let them publicly rest in his hands, sufficiently long so that this visual, concrete circumstance will be understood as a sure promise of the realization of the verbal message that will now follow.

37:21–28 Various outlines of the concluding verses are possible, but the section constitutes a unity. The covenant formula of mutuality, "they will be my people, and I will be their God," in 37:23 and (in reverse order) in 37:27, is a formula that stands at the end of oracles or major sections elsewhere in the book (11:20; 14:11; 34:30–31). The first subsection of these concluding verses (37:21–23) is concerned with the ingathering of the Israelites from the Diaspora into their own land and their purification from all their sins, while the second (37:24–28) concentrates on their undisturbed and everlasting blessedness under "my Servant David" (37:24–25) in "a covenant of peace" (37:26). The whole promissory section of 37:21–28 is really but a repetition (and reemphasis!) of the promises found in 34:11–13 and 36:22–30.

37:21 The promise of restoration continues what had begun in the visionary language of 37:12 and 37:14. The common translation "Israelites" obscures intended overtones of the original, which is, literally, "the sons of Israel." Ethnic consciousness is much more prominent in that literal phrase, and also with "the house of Israel," a phrase overwhelmingly preferred elsewhere in the book. Both hark back to the eponymous ancestor "Israel/Jacob" and ultimately all the patriarchs. "From all around" indicates that the restoration will involve not only the present Babylonian exile but also a much wider Diaspora, most immediately that of the northern tribes whom the Assyrians had dispersed all over their empire (2 Ki 17:6 and 18:11). But whatever the fortunes of those northern expatriates, the books of Ezra and Nehemiah give ample witness to the virtual impossibility of reintegration of all "the sons of Israel," especially with the multi-ethnic population of Samaria at the time. As Block observes: "The reconciliation envisioned by Ezekiel could no more be achieved by their own initiative than the Judeans could perform their own heart transplant (36:26–27), or the dead bones could of themselves come back to life (37:1–14). Every phase of the restoration required direct and miraculous divine intervention."[39]

On Pentecost, the worldwide restoration of God's Israel through the inclusion of Gentiles, grafted in through faith and Baptism into Christ, would begin in earnest (Acts 2). Thus the "all Israel" that will be saved consists of all believers in Christ, Jewish and Gentile alike (Rom 11:22–27; cf. Acts 4:12).

Second, we should not overlook the new exodus typology implicit here. The more explicit term for expressing that concept is the verb הוֹצִיא, when God

---

[39] Block, *Ezekiel*, 2:412.

promises to "bring out" his people (e.g., 34:13), but here, "take" (לָקַח) is used in harmony with the command to Ezekiel to "take" (imperative of לָקַח in 37:16) the writing boards for "Judah" and "Joseph" (see the verb also in 36:24).

37:22 Now comes the third factor in the scenario of national rehabilitation in the first act of divine grace: reunion as one people after they are gathered out of the nations and restored to the land of Israel, as God promised in the previous verse.

"I will make them one nation" under "one King" seems to interpret "I will make them one board" toward the end of 37:19. "Nation" translates גּוֹי, not עַם, accenting for the moment not the relational aspects of the covenant, but the political aspects. Not only in the cultural context of the times, but also if it was to be a genuine antitype of the united monarchy under the historical David, there would have to be a king who would undo the rebellion of Jeroboam and rule in such a way that it would no longer be possible for the people to be divided into two political entities. In that world, a "nation" (גּוֹי) was by definition a monarchy or "kingdom" (מַמְלָכָה), which had to be ruled by a "king" (מֶלֶךְ).

It is often argued that Ezekiel was antimonarchic on principle, but the evidence renders that assumption simplistic. In fact, 37:25 will indicate that he has no difficulty in describing the eschatological David, who surely is "King" (מֶלֶךְ, 37:22, 24), as "their Prince forever" (נָשִׂיא לָהֶם לְעוֹלָם). At most, Ezekiel seems to shy away from "king" (מֶלֶךְ) because of the malodorous record of most of the historical monarchy,[40] but in 37:22–25 (as in 34:23–24 and often in chapters 40–48 by way of "the Prince") he is talking about the future Son of David, Jesus Christ, who will reign over God's people in perfect fidelity and righteousness.

When we have an unqualified use of אֶרֶץ with the article, "the land," as at the beginning of the verse, it means the land of Israel, the chosen land—in the messianic 2 Sam 7:23 described as a nation unique on earth. Essentially the same idea is conveyed by the appositive "the mountains of Israel," one of Ezekiel's beloved phrases referring to the homeland. There is where the restoration would take place, ultimately through Jesus' cross and empty tomb, yet the one people of God would transcend the geographic boundaries of the land where their redemption was accomplished. Their unity consists in their baptismal[41] incorporation into the one King and Shepherd.

37:23 Especially the first part of the verse is full of Ezekelian commonplaces: Israel's sins against Yahweh, which he has often condemned in the past and from which in the new aeon he will free them. "Fecal deities" or "dung-gods" (גִּלּוּלִים) is one of Ezekiel's favorite dysphemisms.[42] "Disgusting prac-

---

[40] See the second textual note on 7:27; the second textual note on 21:30 (ET 21:25); the commentary on 12:10; and the commentary on 34:23–31.

[41] See the commentary on 36:25.

[42] See the fourth textual note on 6:4; compare also the second textual note on 4:12.

tices" (שִׁקּוּצִים, often paralleled with תּוֹעֵבוֹת, "abominations," e.g., 5:11) covers any number of loathsome abominations abhorrent to a faithful Yahwist. All are labeled "rebellious actions" (פְּשָׁעִים), since they are not simply the result of ignorance or weakness.

Two verbs are used to describe how Yahweh will make such a "lifestyle" a matter of ancient history. The Hiphil verb הוֹשִׁיעַ, "to save," is one of the OT's major terms for salvation. Often it has deliverance from external enemies in mind, but here, as in biblical theology in general, the people's inveterate sinfulness is thought of as the real enslaving power. Due to the original sin we inherit from Adam, we are "not able not to sin" (*non posse non peccare*). The Piel verb טָהַר, "to cleanse, purify," which in other texts may involve liturgical sacrifice and priestly absolution, described the creation of a new heart and a new S/spirit in 36:25–28, and that is its sense here as well. All of this is finally summarized as a covenant renewal so comprehensive that it involves establishment of a new covenant, and the use of the classical covenant formula proclaims that "God" and "God's people" will express the fullness of what God intended. Looking back in the book, the verse reminds one of 14:11 in terms of covenant renewal and expressly announces a reversal of 5:11. Looking forward, this anticipates the new covenant established by the shed blood of Jesus Christ, which cleanses us from all sin (Mt 26:28; Lk 22:20; Heb 12:24; 1 Jn 1:7).

37:24 The first half of the verse is very similar to 34:23. Spiritual renewal will be concretized in the fulfillment of Nathan's promise to David in 2 Sam 7:16 and parallels on the perpetuity of the Davidic dynasty through the eternal Son of David (Is 9:5–6 [ET 9:6–7]; Mt 22:42–45; Lk 1:32–33). As was stated explicitly in Ezekiel 34, the promise of the coming David as the "one Shepherd" (34:23; 37:24; cf. John 10) is simultaneously an indictment of the bad "shepherds" who had led the people astray, perhaps especially those of the North who had preempted the covenant term "Israel" and proclaimed themselves to be legitimate "shepherds" of the God who led Israel out of Egypt. The true David's special relationship with Yahweh is summarized by עַבְדִּי, "my Servant" (37:24–25), a title of great honor in the ancient Near East, and here emphasizing that his rule will not be characterized by self-service, all too often the way of earthly monarchs, but will embody the portrait painted by Moses in Deut 17:14–20. As miscreant leaders had been responsible for earlier apostasies, the future Good Shepherd will be credited with his people's faithfulness, both by example and by providing them with the power to comply. See further the commentary on 34:23–24, which also named the coming David "my Servant."

As always, it is difficult to find good equivalents of the nearly synonymous terms (plurals of מִשְׁפָּט and חֻקָּה) translated "ordinances" and "statutes" (37:24). Although the specifics sometimes were different in the OT, it is important to emphasize that the fundamental theological principles are no different than in the NT. As the basic "new covenant" promise of Jer 31:31–34 makes plain, the new heart God will give his people through Baptism and faith in Jesus Christ will not even be open to sinning. At the same time, as long as the interim between his first and second advents lasts, our old Adam still influences us, and we remain sinners as well as saints during this earthly life. Therefore we daily repent, receive the forgiveness of Christ, and seek to live in accord with God's Word, whose commandments inform and guide our life of faith (Rom 13:9; 2 Jn 6), so the third use of the Law (FC SD VI) will remain indispensable.

37:25 Many scholars wish to begin a new section with 37:24b (or as critics would have it, another appendix). I see no reason to quibble about the versification, but, no doubt, there is a clear shift of emphasis from the action prophecy with its focus on the unification of the nation to the permanence of the new circumstances in Christ, as evidenced in the use of the word עוֹלָם, "forever," five times in 37:25–28. In other contexts, the word does not necessarily imply "eternity" (it may refer only to some unspecified remote period), but here it does. This is clear in its usage: in four of the five occurrences, either עַד־עוֹלָם (literally, "until forever") or לְעוֹלָם (literally, "to forever"). It is doubtful if those two idioms can be distinguished, but if they can, the latter may accent futurity even more, while the former may suggest gradual progress into the future.

It is not entirely clear why the promise of perpetual occupation of the hereditary land is associated here with "Jacob" (Gen 28:13–15; 35:11–12) rather than with Abraham (e.g., Gen 13:14–17; 17:1–8). God's promises to the two patriarchs are virtually identical. But in Ezekiel there is a general reluctance to name Abraham at all; the only time we hear it is on the lips of apostate Judahites (33:24) immediately after the fall of Jerusalem. Presumably Jacob is preferred because his "baptismal" name is Israel (Gen 32:29 [ET 32:28]), and thus he became the eponymous ancestor of the people of God—a usage that continues into the NT, where the church is called "the Israel of God" (Gal 6:16).

The definite nature of the coming salvation is expressed not only in the unconditional rejection of any renewed threat of exile but also in the promise of the eternal duration of the eschatological David's rule (see Lk 1:32–33). In contrast to the earlier accent, where the stress was on the Savior's role as "King" over God's united people (Ezek 37:22), here Yahweh concentrates on the Son of David's spiritual role as Yahweh's "Servant" (עֶבֶד) and "Prince" (נָשִׂיא) over them.[43] The term "Prince," among other things, stresses his ties with the people and his function as a regent under Yahweh. This language prepares for the vision of chapters 40–48, where this same "Prince" functions primarily as a religious leader.[44] Yet the underlying thought is no less messianic than when "King" and related terms are employed. The language is clearly dependent

---

[43] See the first textual note on 37:22 and the second textual note on 37:25 for a discussion of the LXX, which translates both מֶלֶךְ, "King," in 37:22 and נָשִׂיא, "Prince," in 37:25 with ἄρχων, "Ruler."

[44] In the eschatological vision of chapters 40–48, the same term (נָשִׂיא) will be used for "the Prince" in 44:3; 45:7–9, 16–17, 22; 46:2, 4, 8, 10, 12, 16–18; 48:21–22.

upon the key OT messianic prophecy of 2 Samuel 7, where David is also called Yahweh's "servant" twice (2 Sam 7:5 and 7:8), and where he acknowledges this role ten times (7:19–29). Another key word here in Ezekiel, עוֹלָם, "forever," appears eight times in 2 Samuel 7.

Unfamiliarity with Ezekiel's language is one of the reasons for its neglect by many Christians, including many Lutherans (beginning with Luther himself). In the retrospect of NT Christology, it makes no difference whether the Messiah is described directly as "King" (Lk 19:38; Jn 1:49; 12:13; Rev 17:14; 19:16) or as a regent under God the "King" (1 Tim 1:17; 6:15), the Son who does his Father's will, precisely because of his theanthropic person.[45] Yet Ezekiel's language here for him as "Prince" (similar to various expressions used by other OT authors) is infinitely less familiar than passages like Is 9:5–6 (ET 9:6–7); 11:1–9; Micah 5:1–3 (ET 5:2–4); Zech 9:9. But the OT should not be read through such narrow Christomonistic lens that only such passages are recognized as testifying to the Messiah, lest much of its eschatological content, which is virtually always also "messianic" in its fullest sense (cf. Lk 24:27, 44; Jn 5:39), would remain, as it were, a book sealed with seven seals. All of the OT Scriptures testify to Jesus Christ, as he himself declared (Lk 24:27, 45–47; Jn 5:39). Those prophecies that concentrate on the blessings he would bring are just as "messianic" as those that concentrate explicitly on his person and work.

This may also be the place to review two other common difficulties or misunderstandings that Christians often have with the OT, specifically in passages such as these in Ezekiel. It is not hard to understand how those who read these sorts of land prophecies literalistically, apart from NT enlightenment, apply them to modern politics, whether it is fanatical Zionists in their settlements in modern Israel or many Protestants in their one-sided support of Israel and utter disregard for Palestinian claims. From an amillennial Lutheran standpoint (see AC XVII), such conceptions or debates are, at best, theologically besides the point, since Ezekiel 37 and similar OT passages are not about such political or territorial issues. He whose kingdom is not of this world (Jn 8:23; 18:36) does not address or answer the specific political or military debates of this world (Acts 1:6–7). Nor does the Second Petition of the Lord's Prayer, "thy kingdom come," concern national boundaries, since God's gracious reign comes now through faith in Jesus Christ, with the promise of the full arrival of God's kingdom after the resurrection to everlasting life in the new creation (2 Pet 3:1–13).[46]

> Canaan, as the site of the Old Testament kingdom of God, would be a symbolical or typical designation of the earthly soil of the heavenly kingdom, which has appeared in the Christian church. ... Palestine has ceased to be the

---

[45] "Theanthropic" is from the Greek for "God-man." It affirms the divine nature and the human nature in the one person of Jesus Christ. See AC and Ap III; SC II 3–4; LC II 25–33; FC Ep and SD VIII; Chemnitz, *The Two Natures in Christ* (originally published in 1578).

[46] For the proper interpretation of the OT land promises, see also page 3 in the introduction.

chosen land of the revelation of the saving grace of God, and … the Israel of the new covenant, the church of Jesus Christ, is spread abroad over the earth, and … Zion or Jerusalem is to be sought wherever Christendom worships God in spirit and in truth, wherever Christ is with His people, and dwells in the hearts of believers through the Holy Spirit.[47]

It is thoroughly understandable that the NT avoids express "land" language because of the false, political messianic hopes of the Jews of the first century A.D. False understandings of "land" and false messianic expectations stand and fall together. But when the NT speaks eschatologically of the "new Jerusalem," the everlasting habitation of God's redeemed in Christ after their resurrection, the land idiom returns (Revelation 21–22). It is only during the present interim (the true "millennium" in Rev 20:1–6, the church age[48]) that the problem persists, and the land promises can wrongly be construed as fulfilled only in a Platonic abstraction or in the solipsism of individual piety.

We must understand the "forever" (עוֹלָם) component of these prophecies in the same vein as their King and kingdom components. We believe, teach, and confess that "in Christ" (ἐν Χριστῷ, e.g., Rom 8:1), we have already received everlasting life (e.g., Jn 3:36; 5:24; 6:54; 17:3)—the life of the world to come (Heb 2:5)—and so we have entered into "forever," both a spatial and a temporal concept. In principle, with Christ's death and resurrection, our redemption is already accomplished ("it is finished," Jn 19:30), and we do not look for another. Yet Scripture also speaks of the future time when we shall enter into the fullness of everlasting life (Dan 12:2–3; Mt 25:46; Jn 12:25; Gal 6:8), when our present life with Christ will extend beyond time and space as we know them.[49] Thus εἰς αἰῶνα, *in saecula saeculorum*, "forever and ever," or "world without end" (misleading if taken as referring to the present world) has concluded Christian creeds and prayers in all ages.

37:26 Numerous promises are accumulated in this verse, most of which are familiar, both in Ezekiel and other biblical texts. "Covenant of peace" is really too literalistic a rendering of בְּרִית שָׁלוֹם, although all translations seem to retain it. The phrase was used already in 34:25, where the application included general environmental security. "Peace," however parsed specifically, is probably part of the package, but words like "well-being," "salvation," and the like must be included. The expression really comprehends all the saving good that God has and will bestow upon his sanctified people in Christ. Two factors of

---

[47] Keil, *Ezekiel*, 2:138. For a more extensive discussion, see further pages 138–57.

[48] For a discussion, one may see the excursus "The Millennium" in Brighton, *Revelation*, 533–41.

[49] This is the language of the Athanasian Creed: "At His [Christ's second] coming all people will rise again with their bodies and give an account concerning their own deeds. And those who have done good will enter into eternal life, and those who have done evil into eternal flame. This is the catholic faith; whoever does not believe it faithfully and firmly cannot be saved" (*LSB* 320).

this salvation are specified in 37:26b–28: the multiplication of the people on the earthly side and the establishing of his eternal sanctuary in their midst on the spiritual side.

Of course, the "covenant of peace" will be "an everlasting covenant" (עוֹלָם בְּרִית), an expression used first in Gen 9:16[e] and found in other prophets.[f] Ezekiel makes no attempt to specify the various OT covenants that we often differentiate—Noachian, Abrahamic, Mosaic, Davidic. They all are combined as fulfilled in this definitive "everlasting covenant" in Jesus Christ.

"I will establish them [the people]" (see the second textual note on 37:26) simply reinforces what was implicit in the "everlasting covenant." A Hebrew *waw* ("and") connects that clause to the following "I will multiply them," as though the two had become a near-hendiadys. This promise is inextricably connected with the first messianic promise to Abraham in Gen 12:1–3 and repeatedly reaffirmed. Ezekiel had already emphasized it in 36:10–11, 37.

Finally, and climactically, Yahweh's "sanctuary" (מִקְדָּשׁ) will be set "in their midst," a promise made and accomplished already long ago, in the days of Moses (see מִקְדָּשׁ in, e.g., Ex 15:17; 25:8; Lev 16:33; 19:30), but never again to be interrupted by further destructions, as at the capture of the ark from the tabernacle at Shiloh (1 Samuel 4) and recently (586 B.C.) at the destruction of Solomon's temple in Jerusalem (Ezek 33:21). Yahweh will shortly resume a discussion of this topic in the most detailed discussion in the entire book (chapters 40–48), although he has already alluded to it in previous chapters.[50] That the sanctuary will be "in their midst" will in chapter 40 be illustrated more concretely in the way the land is allocated.

This discussion of the "sanctuary" (מִקְדָּשׁ, 37:26, 28) is inseparable from the alternate term used in 37:27, "tabernacle" (מִשְׁכָּן). Yahweh often uses "sanctuary" in the book for the Solomonic temple in Jerusalem, which the Israelites defiled (e.g., 5:11; 8:6; 9:6; 23:38–39), whereas he speaks of "my tabernacle" only in 37:27.[51] "Sanctuary" and "tabernacle" complement one another. Initially here, the accent is that Yahweh will dwell among his people as the one who is קָדוֹשׁ, "holy," of which מִקְדָּשׁ, "sanctuary," is a nominal derivative, etymologically parallel to the connection of "sanctuary" with the Latin *sanctus*, "holy." At the beginning of the book, there was great accent on Yahweh's presence as his כָּבוֹד, "Glory."[52] As stressed there, God's holiness and his glory tend to be correlative, and if, as the formula goes, "God's glory is his holiness revealed,"[53] the implication would be that now in the end time, the distinction

(e) Also, e.g., Gen 17:7, 13, 19; Lev 24:8

(f) Is 24:5; 55:3; 61:8; Jer 32:40; 50:5

---

[50] In 11:16 he promised, "But I will be for them a sanctuary [מִקְדָּשׁ] for a little while in the lands to which they have come." See the commentary there and also on 20:40–42.

[51] The only other occurrence of מִשְׁכָּן in Ezekiel is in 25:4, where its plural refers to human "dwellings" set up by invaders from the East.

[52] For the divine "Glory" understood Christologically, see pages 1, 11, and 13 in the introduction, as well as the textual notes and commentary on 1:26–28.

[53] See page 13 in the introduction.

will be erased, as God will be fully and forever revealed among his people (see God's "glory" among his people in the eternal state in Rev 21:11, 23).

37:27 The alternate term מִשְׁכָּן, "tabernacle," is in the OT primarily associated with the tabernacle constructed under Moses in the desert, also often called the אֹהֶל מוֹעֵד, "tent of meeting" (e.g., Ex 27:21). By extension, the term is sometimes applied to the tabernacle's successor, Solomon's temple, although other vocabulary is often associated with that temple. (Ezekiel makes no point of it here, but some other OT and NT passages accent the original wilderness tabernacle instead of the temple, which was the site of so many gross apostasies; see, for example, Amos 9:11; "tabernacled" in Jn 1:14; and "tabernacle" in Acts 7:44; 15:16; Heb 8:2–5; 9:1–11, 21; Rev 13:6; 15:5; 21:3.) Beginning with RSV, מִשְׁכָּנִי has been translated as "my dwelling place," a rendering that cannot be called incorrect, but which loses much of the theological import of the word. The same issue pertains to Rev 21:3, where the noun σκηνή and verb σκηνόω are often similarly translated: "the dwelling place of God is with men, and he will dwell with them." However, the noun and verb "tabernacle" would better capture the fulfillment of the OT. While מִשְׁכָּן can be used of human "dwellings" (as in Ezek 25:4), most often it is used of the tabernacle, which was indeed God's "house" on earth, but in an "incarnational" sense. We have no better word in English to express that than "tabernacle." Again, this gracious "indwelling" of God on earth among his people is often labeled "immanental," which, unfortunately, has philosophical overtones that lose sight of the fact that God's residence on earth was not a matter of nature, but of election, of his condescending grace and salvific will to redeem. His presence on earth does not diminish his presence in heaven; in the vertical typology of the Bible, the ark of the covenant, which resided in Holy of Holies in the tabernacle and then in the temple, is both throne (e.g., 1 Sam 4:4; Ps 80:2 [ET 80:1]) and footstool (1 Chr 28:2).

Literalistic, millennial interpretations must again be combated here.[54] St. Jerome confronted that problem here by translating מִקְדָּשׁ in the surrounding verses (37:26, 28) with *sanctificatio* ("sanctification") instead of his usual (and theologically correct) *sanctuarium* ("sanctuary," e.g., 9:6). He is often quoted:

> This the Jews interpret with regard to the temple which was built under Zerubbabel. But how can it be said to stand "for ever" since that temple which was built by Zerubbabel and afterwards restored by many was destroyed by fire by the Romans? All these things are to be applied to the church and to the time of the Savior when his tabernacle was set up in the Church.[55]

The "sanctuary" and "tabernacle" of which Ezekiel speaks in 37:26–28 must be assimilated to the vision of the sanctuary seen by Ezekiel in chapters

---

[54] For a broader discussion, one may see the excursus "The Millennium" in Brighton, *Revelation*, 533–41.

[55] Jerome, *Commentariorum in Hiezechielem* (CCSL 75:521), translated by Zimmerli, *Ezekiel*, 2:271.

40–48, which, in turn, is a figurative representation of God dwelling in the midst of his people in the incarnation of his Son and through the gift of the Holy Spirit during the church age, to be consummated in the eschaton (Revelation 21–22), where, however, there will be no temple structure, only God and the Lamb (Rev 21:22). The realization of God dwelling with men in the incarnation of the Logos is described classically in Jn 1:14 in the words "the Word became flesh and *tabernacled* among us" (ἐσκήνωσεν ἐν ἡμῖν), as well as in Christ's declaration that his body, to be destroyed and raised, is the true temple (Jn 2:19–22). This true temple is continued in the spiritual indwelling of God in the heart of believers (1 Cor 3:16; 6:19) and will be completed at the second coming of our Lord when "the tabernacle [σκηνή] of God is with men" (Rev 21:3) in the new Jerusalem, of which God himself and the Lamb are the temple (Rev 21:22). Thus we have in Ezek 37:26 and 37:27 one of the most central of biblical truths and one of the major lines linking the two Testaments together and extending on into the parousia.

The classical covenant formula of mutuality is repeated once more in 37:27 because it represents the theological substance of the concrete, sacramental realities just described. Just preceding it, one other variation in the language should not be overlooked. In 37:26 and 37:28, Yahweh's מִקְדָּשׁ, "sanctuary," is described as being בְּתוֹכָם, "in their [his people's] midst." Here in 37:27, the "tabernacle" (מִשְׁכָּן) is described as עֲלֵיהֶם, "*over* them." The roots of this language are probably in the theophany of the divine cloud and pillar of fire accompanying Israel during the exodus and desert wanderings (e.g., Ex 13:21–22; 14:19, 24; Num 14:14), especially over the tabernacle (Ex 40:35–38; Num 9:15–22). The implication of this theophany is most fully developed in Is 4:5–6, where the Christological, eschatological tabernacle is described as a canopy or pavilion that will shelter the people of God from the elements. Other pictures may have flowed into it, for example, Ex 40:35 where Yahweh's "Glory" (כָּבוֹד) is described as filling the tabernacle, or the sight of the temple towering over the city of Jerusalem (Ps 68:30 [ET 68:29]), reminding the faithful of the protective power and grace of God, who had deigned to make it his dwelling place among them.

The Bible itself does not use the noun "Shekinah" (a derivative of the verb שָׁכַן, "dwell") for the divine sheltering presence, but later Jewish sources use it, though without acknowledging that the sole dwelling place of God's grace is in Christ. Some Christians have adopted "Shekinah" to refer to Christ and the indwelling Holy Spirit, who makes Christ present and protective among us through God's Word and Sacraments.

37:28 A final modified form of the recognition formula, "then the nations will know that I, Yahweh, sanctify Israel,"[56] emphasizes that Yahweh's "sanctuary" in our midst (37:26, 28) and his "tabernacle" over us (37:27; both ful-

---

[56] For the usual recognition formula, "(then) you/they will know that I am Yahweh," see page 9 in the introduction and the commentary on 6:7.

1097

filled in Christ) are the central event by which he must be recognized and confessed anywhere in the world. The purpose of the sanctuary is to sanctify, and it is there that the Gospel of the forgiveness of sins is dispersed through preaching of the Gospel, absolution, Holy Baptism, and our Lord's Supper. Without these means of grace properly administered according to God's Word, the sanctuary is meaningless, if not condemnatory. Also requisite is the sanctification of the members gathered at the sanctuary. That God will sanctify his people is a promise as old as Ex 31:13 and Lev 20:8, and the promise of the new covenant (Jer 31:31–34) includes the assurance that written on our hearts will be the sanctified response to what God has first given us by tabernacling among us— a life of faith and obedience by the power of the Spirit (the "new spirit" and "Spirit" promised in Ezek 11:19; 18:31; 36:26–27; 37:14; 39:29). But in this interim, we are then all the more aware that we "daily sin much"[57] and so daily die to sin and rise again to new life by his grace, all the time praying, *Marana tha*, "Come, Lord (Jesus)" (1 Cor 16:22; Rev 22:20).

---

[57] Luther explains the Fifth Petition of the Lord's Prayer, "And forgive us our trespasses as we forgive those who trespass against us," by saying in part:

We are neither worthy of the things for which we pray, nor have we deserved them, but we ask that He would give them all to us by grace, for we daily sin much and surely deserve nothing but punishment. So we too will sincerely forgive and gladly do good to those who sin against us. (SC III 16 [*Luther's Small Catechism with Explanation*, 19; *LSB* 324])

Introduction to Ezekiel 38–39:
The Final Battle and the Defeat of Gog

All commentators seem to agree that chapters 38 and 39 are really a unit and their division into two chapters is artificial. Chapter 39 partially reiterates (especially in 39:1–6) and partially continues chapter 38. The boundaries of the unit are signaled by the word-event formula, "the Word of Yahweh came to me,"[1] at its beginning in 38:1 and the signatory formula, "says the Lord Yahweh,"[2] at its conclusion in 39:29.

But there is no agreement on how best to outline the chapters. Taylor[3] and others find seven units, each introduced by the citation formula, "thus says the Lord Yahweh"[4] (38:3, 10, 14, 17; 39:1, 17, 25). Some version of Zimmerli's view is widespread: the original core, consisting of parts of 38:1–9 along with 39:1–5, 17–20, is interspersed with a series of interpretative expansions.[5] Some explain the division into two chapters as evidence of an analysis into two divisions. There is considerable feeling that 39:23–29 functions as a sort of epilogue, uniting these two chapters with the emphases of chapters 33–37: the ultimate security of God's people even in the face of the worst threats, the outpouring of the Holy Spirit, and the fundamental promise of the return of God's people to dwell in the promised land. All this variation among interpreters indicates the rather kaleidoscopic structure of the chapters, which gradually add new (and increasingly surreal) themes, rather than displaying Western-type logical coherence. That is, one does better following the chapter's ideas seriatim, as I shall largely do.

The oracle is undated and leaves no clues as to any historical occasion that might have elicited it. Closely related is the question of the positioning of the sermon at just this point in the book, especially because initially it appears to interrupt the sequence of chapters 33–37 and 40–48. Those earlier chapters promise the advent of the new David, Jesus Christ, and the regeneration of God's people (e.g., 34:23–25; 36:25–28; 37:22–28). The later chapters (40–48) give us an eschatological picture of a golden age of everlasting peace, security, and proper worship in the transformed promised land—the new heavens and new earth—parallel to the portrait of the eternal state in Revelation 21–22.

But here in Ezekiel 38–39 we have a description of a fearsome, climactic battle between the forces of evil and the people of God, who have already been

---

[1] For this formula, see page 8 in the introduction and the textual note on 3:16.

[2] For this formula, see pages 8–9 in the introduction and the second textual note on 5:11.

[3] Taylor, *Ezekiel*, 242.

[4] For this formula, see pages 8–9 in the introduction and the fourth textual note and the commentary on 2:4.

[5] Zimmerli, *Ezekiel*, 2:296–99.

redeemed and restored (e.g., "gathered" in 38:8; "peaceful … resettled … re-gathered" in 38:11–12). If we read Ezekiel 33–48 as presenting a chronological end-time sequence, this means that after the first advent of Jesus Christ (as prophesied in chapters 33–37), those who believe in him will be raised to new spiritual life already now. Thus the resurrection in Ezek 37:1–14 corresponds to dying and rising with Christ in Baptism (Rom 6:1–4) and to the "first resurrection" in Rev 20:5–6. Baptized believers in Christ have already undergone this spiritual "first resurrection," though we still await the bodily resurrection at the return of Christ.[6]

Yet during this NT era, the powers of darkness are still present on earth, and they continue to wage war against the church. Eventually they will mount a final attack against God's redeemed in Christ, but they will be overthrown (Ezekiel 38–39) before the dawning of the eternal state (Ezekiel 40–48). To amillennialists, including Lutherans, this chronological sequence fits the common biblical picture that persecution shall increase in intensity during the present church age and reach its peak before the parousia of Christ. That biblical picture is presented by Christ himself in Matthew 24 and is the gist of the entire book of Revelation. Thus both Ezekiel 38–39 and Rev 20:7–9, which alludes to these Ezekiel chapters by way of "Gog and Magog" (Rev 20:8), describe the warfare that Satan and his minions now wage against the church, with a final all-out battle coming before the end.

Therefore Ezekiel 33–48 supports the traditional understanding of biblical eschatology. In particular, chapters 38–39 offer no support for any of the complicated dispensational schemes involving a seven-year tribulation and a rapture of believers to be followed by an earthly reign of Christ on the present earth for a literal millennium.[7]

---

[6] According to amillennialists, the thousand years in Rev 20:1–6 depict the present church age, during which believers in Christ are spiritually raised to new life and begin to reign with Christ. Then Rev 20:7–9 describes the increasing persecution of the church, which will culminate in a last battle before Christ returns. At his return all the dead will be raised and judged (Rev 20:11–15). Then all believers in Christ will enter the new heavens and new earth, which will be their home for eternity (Revelation 21–22). There is no "rapture" apart from the bodily resurrection of all the dead at the return of Christ. Neither is there a literal thousand-year reign of Christ on earth apart from the present church age, when his church is his kingdom on earth. After his return, his everlasting reign will be over his people in the new heavens and new earth. See also "Introduction to Ezekiel 40–48."

For a survey of various millennial views throughout church history and for a defense of the church's traditional amillennial eschatology, one may see the excursus "The Millennium" in Brighton, *Revelation*, 533–41, as well as Brighton's commentary on the passages cited. An excellent and more detailed discussion of biblical eschatology from a Reformed amillennial perspective is Hoekema, *The Bible and the Future*.

Since "amillennialists" affirm the teaching of the "millennium" in Rev 20:1–6 and consider the number to be figurative (10 x 10 x 10 represents a triply complete time period determined by God) and the millennium to have begun already with the first advent of Christ, a term such as "inaugurated millennialism" would actually be more accurate than "amillennialism" for describing the traditional Christian view.

[7] Dispensational millennialists usually consider Ezekiel 38–39 to describe an attack by earthly armies against the nation of Israel toward the end of the "tribulation," a seven-year period of persecution that precedes a return of Christ to set up an earthly kingdom for a literal mil-

Since Ezekiel 38–39 has some similarities with the Gentile oracles (chapters 25–32), some ask why they were not placed there. However, one will note that those oracles dealt with close and easily identifiable neighbors of Jerusalem, who were her enemies during the OT era. These chapters deal with enemies who are more distant, both geographically (see the commentary on 38:2–3) and temporally ("in the latter years/days," 38:8, 16).

A related issue is the genre of the material. First proposed in the middle of the nineteenth century and more recently seconded by Cooke[8] and others, the chapters are often labeled "apocalyptic," and Ezekiel himself is labeled "the father of apocalyptic." That appellation is debatable, partly because of the imprecision with which some interpreters use the label. If used with any care, "apocalyptic" has more to do with the content and style of a text than with its form. Typically, the genre of apocalyptic features God, as an otherworldly being, revealing an eschatological salvation ("salvation *from* history, rather than *of* history") that brings his people into another, supernatural world. The theme of a climactic battle between good and evil, God's people and the demonic, is found in some pseudepigraphical works (*1 Enoch* 56:5–8; *4 Ezra* 13:5–11), as well as in Qumran's *War of the Sons of Light and the Sons of Darkness*. Highly symbolic (and even cryptic) symbolism is characteristic of the descriptions. Certain aspects of such an "apocalyptic" literature can be found in Ezekiel 38–39 (and elsewhere in the book), but Ezekiel's paternity of the genre of apocalyptic must be rejected because so many of those aspects are found in earlier OT books as well (e.g., Isaiah 24–27; Joel 2–4 [ET Joel 2–3]; Amos 9): conflict between Yahweh and Israel's enemies, the ultimate deliverance of Israel, and Yahweh's universal sovereignty. Ezekiel 38–39 certainly suggests a future, final battle, and the picture of a cosmic shaking in 38:18–23 will lead into a consummation of earthly history in the eschatological state pictured in chapters 40–48. The focus remains on the salvation of God's Israel,[9] the defeat of

---

lennium. They believe Ezekiel 40–48 predicts the rebuilding of a temple in Jerusalem and the resumption of animal sacrifices during that millennium.

8   Cooke, *Ezekiel*, 406–7.

9   As one would expect in an OT book, Ezekiel describes God's redeemed people as "Israel" (e.g., 38:8, 14, 16, 18). However, already Ezekiel himself does not use that term primarily as an ethnic designation, but as a theological term. Repeatedly he refers to apostate, ethnic Israel as "a rebellious house" (see second textual note on 2:5) instead of "the house of Israel" (see the third textual note and the commentary on 3:1 and also the commentary on 4:4–8). In contrast, the restored "Israel" to be attacked in chapters 38–39 is the people united as one (37:15–28) under the new David, the one Shepherd, Jesus Christ (see especially the beginning of the commentary on chapter 34 as well as the commentary on 34:23–25; 36:25–28; 37:22–25). The book of Ezekiel as a whole supports the traditional Christian view that the OT promises about the true (faithful) Israel are fulfilled in the Christian church, which is "the Israel of God" (Gal 6:16), the "all Israel" that will be saved through faith (Rom 11:22–27). The "one holy catholic and apostolic church" (Nicene Creed) consists of all believers in Christ, Jewish and Gentile alike.

Dispensational millennialists reject that continuity between OT Israel and the NT church. Many propose that God has two plans of salvation: Gentiles are saved through faith in Christ, but God will save ethnic Israel through another plan, and Jews need not become part of the

all evil enemies, and, as reiterated many times previously in Ezekiel, the vindication of Yahweh's holiness and the people's recognition of him. Yet the symbolism is tame compared to the more typical apocalyptic variety found in Daniel and Revelation.[10]

Taylor appropriately admonishes: "Interpretation therefore needs to correspond to contents, and attempts to read too much into the incidentals of the prophecy betray the ingenuity of the speculator rather than the sobriety of the exegete."[11] His footnote makes plain that the comment is applicable especially to the Scofield Reference Bible (so beloved by many Protestant dispensational premillennialists), which unhesitatingly identifies "Rosh" with "Russia," "Meshech" with "Moscow," and "Tubal" with "Tobolsk."[12]

That is just one modern example of the long history of subsequent interpretation of Gog and Magog. This interpretive history can be traced in Jewish and Muslim traditions too, but we must limit ourselves to Christian reuse, and even so, consider only St. John's allusions in his portrayal of the eschatological conflicts in Revelation 19–22, and so let Scripture interpret Scripture.

The first major biblical reuse occurs in Revelation 19. Preparations are being made for the celebration of the marriage feast of the Lamb: at the return of Christ, all believers, who comprise his church and bride, will dine with him (Rev 19:7–9). The counterpart to that feast is the scene of the birds gathered for their great feast on the carnage of the enemies of God and his people in Rev 19:17–21, which is clearly a reworking of Ezek 39:17–20. Gog is never mentioned by name here, but plainly the "beast" (θηρίον, Rev 19:19–20) represents him.[13] Like Gog, he leads a worldwide coalition against God's church, accompanied by a false prophet and his various charms. At the conclusion of the last great battle, in which the beast and his coalition are defeated, the beast and the false prophet are cast alive into the lake of fire (Rev 19:20).[14]

Christian church. While liberal Protestants approach the issue from a different perspective, they too protest the "supercessionist" view that the church is the fulfillment of OT Israel, and contend that Jewish people need not believe in Jesus to be saved because they supposedly still are united with God through the old covenant.

However, consistent with the OT, the NT proclaims that for all people, salvation is only through faith in Jesus Christ (e.g., Jn 14:6; Acts 4:12; Rom 1:16–17).

[10] Likewise, the host of extracanonical apocalyptic writings that proliferated after the Maccabean crises have much more extreme symbolism.

[11] Taylor, *Ezekiel*, 243.

[12] See further the commentary on 38:2–3.

[13] This "beast" is the one that Satan, who is the "dragon" in Revelation 12, had conjured out of the sea in Rev 13:1. This beast morphs into different guises throughout the church age, throughout which it, as Satan's puppet, tries to destroy the followers of Christ. For this beast, one may see Brighton, *Revelation*, 341, 343, 445–47, and for its defeat in the final battle, see pages 520–22.

[14] This last great battle is the same one that had been depicted earlier in Rev 16:12–21 as taking place at "Armageddon." As there, so also in Revelation 19, the great battle takes place shortly before the second coming of Christ, which is the event that causes the final defeat of the evil foes. The beast and false prophet are cast into the lake of fire immediately after the return of Christ (Rev 19:11–20).

"Gog and Magog" figure explicitly in the account of the defeat of the beast in Rev 20:7–10. Yahweh putting hooks in Gog's jaws and summoning him from the far north to wage war on Israel (Ezek 38:4–23) is OT language for the same event now described as God releasing ὁ σατανᾶς, "Satan," the adversary, from his prison for a short time after the millennium (toward the close of the church age) so that he can assemble his army, consisting of "Gog and Magog." One should note that while Ezekiel describes God as orchestrating the whole scenario, Revelation gives prominence at this point to Satan. This is, of course, no ultimate contradiction, and Keil nicely compares this contrast to the famous one between 2 Sam 24:1 and 1 Chr 21:1 (on who prompts David to take a census).[15] Again, the miraculous defeat of the army coincides with the return of Jesus Christ. Ultimately, the deceiver of the nations, now identified as ὁ διάβολος, "the devil," is recaptured and thrown into the fiery lake to join the beast and his false prophet (Rev 20:10; cf. Rev 19:20).

What has happened is that Ezekiel's prophecy of a penultimate event in human history ("the latter years/days," 38:8, 16) has become a prophecy of the final, ultimate, universal victory by the Messiah over the cosmic forces of evil. In NT context, this means that the victory Jesus won on Calvary over our sin, death, and the devil is in principle complete ("it is finished," Jn 19:30), but still awaits its consummation at the end of human history. Every time we partake of the Eucharist, we proleptically join the celestial victors in "a foretaste of the feast to come."[16]

---

[15] Keil, *Ezekiel*, 2:162.

[16] From "Let the Vineyards Be Fruitful" (*LSB* 955). Text © 1978 *Lutheran Book of Worship*.

In the Latter Days, Gog Will Attack and Be Defeated by God

Translation

38 ¹The Word of Yahweh came to me: ²"Son of man, set your face against Gog of the land of Magog, the prince of Rosh, Meshech, and Tubal, and prophesy against him, ³and say, 'Thus says the Lord Yahweh: I am against you, O Gog, prince of Rosh, Meshech, and Tubal. ⁴I will mislead you; I will put hooks in your jaws; and I will bring out you and your whole army, horses and horsemen, all of them magnificently arrayed, a vast horde [armed] with body shields and hand shields, all of them wielding swords. ⁵Persia, Nubia, and Libya are with them, all of them with hand shields and helmets, ⁶also Gomer and all its troops, Beth-togarmah from the remotest regions of the north and all its troops—many peoples are with you. ⁷Ready yourself; prepare yourself, you and your whole horde gathered around you; and keep watch over them. ⁸After many days you will be given your orders; in the latter years you will invade a land restored from the sword, whose population had been gathered from many peoples on the mountains of Israel, which had lain waste for a long time. Its population had been brought out of the peoples, and all of them now live securely. ⁹You will come up like a devastating storm; you will be like a cloud to cover the land, you and all your troops and many peoples with you.

¹⁰" 'Thus says the Lord Yahweh: On that day thoughts will come into your mind, and you will scheme a scheme of evil. ¹¹You will say, "I will go up against a land of unwalled villages. I will attack the peaceful people who live in security, all of them living without walls, with neither bars nor gates, ¹²in order to seize spoil and carry off booty, to assault resettled ruins and people regathered from the nations, who are acquiring livestock and other property, who live at the navel of the earth." ¹³Sheba, Dedan, the merchants of Tarshish, and all its leaders will say to you, "Have you come to seize spoil? Have you gathered your horde to carry off booty, to carry away silver and gold, to take away livestock and other property, to seize much spoil?" '

¹⁴"Therefore prophesy, son of man, and say to Gog, 'Thus says the Lord Yahweh: On that day, when my people Israel are dwelling securely, will you not take note of it? ¹⁵You will come from your place, from the remotest regions of the north, you and many peoples with you, all of them riding on horses, a great horde, a mighty army. ¹⁶You will come up against my people Israel, like a cloud covering the land. In the latter days this will happen: I will bring you against my land in order that the nations may know me when I prove myself holy through you before their eyes, O Gog.

[17]" 'Thus says the Lord Yahweh: Are you he of whom I spoke in earlier days through my servants the prophets of Israel, who prophesied in those days for years that I would bring you against them? [18]On that day when Gog comes against the land of Israel, says the Lord Yahweh, my wrath will be evident in my face. [19]In my zeal and the fire of my fury, I have spoken: on that day there will surely be a great earthquake in the land of Israel. [20]They will quake before me: the fish in the ocean, the birds in the sky, the animals in the open country, every creeping thing that creeps on the ground, and every human being on the face of the earth. The mountains will be overthrown; the hillside terraces will collapse; and every wall will fall to the ground. [21]I will summon against him a sword on all my mountains, says the Lord Yahweh. Every man's sword will be against his brother. [22]I will punish him by plague and by bloodshed; and torrential rain, hailstones, and burning sulfur I will rain down on him and on his troops and on the many peoples who are with him. [23]Thus I will prove myself great, and I will prove myself holy, and I will make myself known in the sight of many nations. Then they will know that I am Yahweh.' "

Textual Notes

38:2 בֶּן־אָדָם—For Ezekiel as a "son of man/Adam," see the second textual note and the commentary on 2:1.

שִׂים פָּנֶיךָ אֶל־—For this idiom, "set your face against," see the second textual note on 6:2.

גּוֹג אֶרֶץ הַמָּגוֹג נְשִׂיא רֹאשׁ מֶשֶׁךְ וְתֻבָל—Not only are the identifications of these names difficult (see the commentary), but also the syntax is uncertain. גּוֹג אֶרֶץ הַמָּגוֹג would most naturally identify "Gog" as a person from "the land of Magog," the name of a country where Gog lived. Then "Gog" would also be the "prince" (נְשִׂיא) of the following regions. The Vulgate and Targum follow the MT without clarifying the syntax. The definite article before מָגוֹג is a conundrum if it is a place name, which would already be definite without the article. Keil suggests that the article marks a people well-known from the time of Genesis (see Gen 10:2) and that the phrase thus refers to "the land of the Magog (-people),"[1] but if so, we have an irregular Hebrew usage. In Ezek 39:6, "I will also send fire on Magog," מָגוֹג lacks the article and could refer to a person and/or his people, but probably it is the same place name as here.

However, besides 38:2 and 39:6, "Magog" appears elsewhere in the OT only in Gen 10:2 and 1 Chr 1:5, where it is the name of a person, the second son of Japheth, alongside six brothers. Here in Ezek 38:2, the LXX (καὶ τὴν γῆν τοῦ Μαγωγ ἄρχοντα …) and the Syriac add a copula before "the land," which might allow for Magog to be understood as a name of a person[2] who then is the "prince," although later verses (38:3 and 39:1 in both the MT and LXX) identify Gog as the "prince." In much later

---

[1] Keil, *Ezekiel*, 2:159.

[2] Cooke, *Ezekiel*, 409, and Block *Ezekiel*, 2:433, say that the LXX apparently takes "Magog" as the name of a people.

literature, including Rev 20:8 and extrabiblical writings,[3] "Gog and Magog" became a standard pair of personal names for the enemy leaders in descriptions of the final eschatological battle.

Many critics take the easy way out and consider the phrase "of the land of Magog" a gloss. Others suggest a different word division. For example, Cooke and Zimmerli propose אַרְצָה מָגוֹג, that is, after the command שִׂים פָּנֶיךָ אֶל־, "set your face against," the noun אֶרֶץ has a locative *he* (paralleled in 21:2 [ET 20:46] with תֵּימָנָה), resulting in "set your face against Gog, toward the land of Magog."[4] Allen suggests that the original might have been אַרְצֹה מָגוֹג, "his land is Magog."[5]

No absolute certainty is possible, but the MT clearly understands הַמָּגוֹג as a place name.

The next two words, נְשִׂיא רֹאשׁ, are repeated identically in 38:3 and 39:1, each time immediately after גּוֹג, so 38:3 and 39:1 identify "Gog" (not "Magog") as the "prince." Since the noun נְשִׂיא is in construct (-נְ) with רֹאשׁ, the MT implies that "Rosh" is another place name, as reflected in my literal translation: "(the) prince of Rosh, Meshech, and Tubal" (38:2–3; 39:1).

If נְשִׂיא were not in construct, רֹאשׁ could be appositional, thus qualifying it: "the prince, the head/chief, of Meshech …" KJV has "the chief prince of Meshech and Tubal," as do RSV and many other modern versions, but that is abandoned by NKJV: "the prince of Rosh, Meshech, and Tubal."

The ancient versions are divided. The LXX's ἄρχοντα Ρως agrees with the MT, but Aquila (a very literalistic Greek version), the Targum, the Syriac, and Jerome[6] take רֹאשׁ as in some sense appositional. That understanding of רֹאשׁ finds possible support in phrases like הַכֹּהֵן רֹאשׁ, "the high priest," in 1 Chr 27:5. If we take that route, the implication of "chief prince" would be that Gog was not only one of many princely figures, but somehow above his peers. That appellation possibly could have been based on specific knowledge of the political system at a certain place (in "the land of Magog").

Some object to taking רֹאשׁ as a place name because of the difficulty of determining what area it denotes. But to my mind this objection is a less than convincing reason to reject the MT. Earlier scholars[7] often cited the mention in Byzantine and Arabic writers of a Scythian tribe called Rûs that occupied the northern Taurus Mountains. More recently, if a geographical location is sought, scholars tend to adduce a Râshu/Rêshu/Arashi in neo-Assyrian records and Ugaritic texts.[8] That location, how-

---

[3]   See the extrabiblical writings cited in Block, *Ezekiel*, 2:434, n. 35.

[4]   Cooke, *Ezekiel*, 415; Zimmerli, *Ezekiel*, 2:284.

[5]   Allen, *Ezekiel*, 2:199.

[6]   Block, *Ezekiel*, 2:432, n. 28, says that the Vulgate, *principem capitis Mosoch et Thubal*, literally, "leader of the head of Meshech and Tubal," takes רֹאשׁ as an intensification of נְשִׂיא.

[7]   E.g., Keil, *Ezekiel*, 2:159–60.

[8]   E.g., Block, *Ezekiel*, 2:435, including n. 42, who cites James D. Price, "Rosh: An Ancient Land Known to Ezekiel," *GTJ* 6 (1985): 69–73.

ever, was on the border between Babylon and Elam, far to the east, and hence thought by some to be too distant from "Meshech" and "Tubal," which are mentioned next. However, as we proceed, it becomes evident that Ezekiel's vista covers a broad horizon, so that hardly seems to me to be a disqualifying argument either. See the map "The Ancient Near East."

The only identification to be rejected unconditionally is the fatuous attempt of some dispensational premillennialists to identify Ezekiel's ראֹשׁ with modern Russia, mostly because of the assonantal similarity. The association is hopelessly anachronistic because all evidence indicates that "Russia" is of northern Viking derivation and was first used in the Middle Ages of the Ukraine,[9] today an independent state south of Russia.

הִנְנִי אֵלֶיךָ גּוֹג—This is the hostile orientation formula, "behold, I am against …"[10]

38:4 וְשׁוֹבַבְתִּיךָ—The identical Polel perfect (first common singular with second masculine singular suffix and *waw* consecutive) of שׁוּב recurs at the start of 39:2 (there spelled defectively). (The Polel infinitive of שׁוּב in 39:27 has a different meaning.) Most English translations follow the KJV: "and I will turn thee back." But without some place in the context as the initial goal from which Yahweh would "turn back" Gog, that translation seems meaningless. The rendering "mislead, lead astray" seems much more pertinent here and also in 39:2 and is supported by the Polel in Is 47:10. For these three verses, BDB (Polel, 3) gives "*lead away* (enticingly)." So understood, the verb summarizes the gist of much of chapters 38–39: what Gog and his company think is their own enterprise is really masterminded by Yahweh.

וְנָתַתִּי חַחִים בִּלְחָיֶיךָ—The LXX omits a translation of these words, so critics predictably argue that at some point, under the influence of 29:4, "I will place hooks in your jaws" was introduced, even though it is allegedly an alien thought.[11] But the logic of that argument eludes me. The metaphor again expresses the point that Gog is not really acting by his own free will, but is doing Yahweh's bidding.

The LXX has καὶ συνάξω σε, which is also its translation of וְשׁבַבְתִּיךָ in 39:2, and then it skips to a translation of וְאֶת־כָּל־חֵילֶךָ and the rest of the verse. Therefore the LXX apparently omits וְנָתַתִּי חַחִים בִּלְחָיֶיךָ וְהוֹצֵאתִי אוֹתְךָ, unless καὶ συνάξω σε is its translation of וְהוֹצֵאתִי אוֹתְךָ, in which case it omits וְשׁוֹבַבְתִּיךָ וְנָתַתִּי חַחִים בִּלְחָיֶיךָ. In either case, the LXX lacks a translation of וְנָתַתִּי חַחִים בִּלְחָיֶיךָ.

סוּסִים וּפָרָשִׁים—For these terms, see the second textual note on 27:14.

לְבֻשֵׁי מִכְלוֹל—The identical construct phrase was used for the Assyrian soldiers in 23:12. The plural Qal passive participle of לָבַשׁ, "to wear," is in construct with the clothing (see Joüon, § 121 o): literally, "clothed *in* completeness/perfection." In this military context, מִכְלוֹל must refer to armor and the like. The word as such is an ab-

---

[9] Block, *Ezekiel*, 2:434, n. 40, citing Edwin Yamauchi, *Foes from the Northern Frontier: Invading Hordes from the Russian Steppes* (Grand Rapids: Baker, 1982), 20–21.

[10] For this formula, see page 9 in the introduction and the commentary on 5:8.

[11] For example, Allen, *Ezekiel*, 2:200, indulges again in what appears to be one of his favorite hobbies: a convoluted speculation about how the MT reached its present form.

stract noun. A concrete cousin, מַכְלוּל, was used in 27:24, but not in a martial context. The same syntax, with a participle in construct, appears at the end of the verse: תֹּפְשֵׂי חֲרָבוֹת. Both construct phrases conclude with a semi-redundant כֻּלָּם.

צִנָּה וּמָגֵן—For these two terms, see the fourth textual note on 23:24. They form a syntactically independent phrase, apparently added to say that the soldiers carried defensive arms as well as swords.[12]

38:5 פָּרַס—"Persia" is not known to have been of much importance in Ezekiel's time. See the commentary.

כֻּלָּם מָגֵן וְכוֹבָע:—The final clause, literally, "all of them [with] hand shield and helmet," is again very clipped, perhaps to be diagrammed as a nominal clause used adverbially. Both כֻּלָּם and מָגֵן are repeated from 38:4.[13]

38:6 גֹּמֶר וְכָל־אֲגַפֶּיהָ—This verse does not begin with a *waw* and is not a separate thought, but continues the previous verse. אֲגַף, "army, troop," is a word unique to Ezekiel, occurring only in 12:14 and 17:21 besides 38:6, 9, 22; 39:4.

38:7 הִכֹּן וְהָכֵן לְךָ—Two assonantal forms of the verb כּוּן open Yahweh's command to Gog. Ezekiel is fond of such double expressions (e.g., 14:6; 18:30; 20:4). The first here is Niphal, the second Hiphil (imperative). The reflexive force inherent in the Niphal may be expressed for the Hiphil by the following reflexive לְךָ, "for yourself." הִכֹּן could be either the imperative or infinite absolute, since the two forms are identical. Some of Ezekiel's doublings repeat the identical aspect, so two imperatives in different conjugations would not be surprising here. But if it is infinite absolute used as a surrogate, it is emphatic. (The same alternatives with the same root confront the exegete in Amos 4:12.)

וְכָל־קְהָלֶךָ הַנִּקְהָלִים עָלֶיךָ—"Horde" is used to translate קָהָל as before (38:4; cf. also, e.g., 27:27, 34), but here it is followed by the cognate verb in the form of a Niphal participle, הַנִּקְהָלִים, "gathered," which is plural because of the collective sense of קָהָל. The rhetorical effect of the cognate construction cannot be reproduced in English without using a different translation of קָהָל and thus perhaps confusing the meaning.

וְהָיִיתָ לָהֶם לְמִשְׁמָר:—The meaning of this final clause is uncertain, as attested by the variety of translations. The noun מִשְׁמָר can mean "prison," "act of guarding," or "band of guards." Here it may carry some specific military nuance that eludes us. It is from the common verb שָׁמַר, "watch, guard, keep." Thus KJV translates literally, "and be thou a guard unto them," followed in essence by NKJV and RSV. NIV has "and take command of them," that is, be the one who guards or leads them, which may well be the intent. NRSV, following an old suggestion (see BDB, s.v. מִשְׁמָר, 2) is more venturesome: "and hold yourselves in reserve for them," that is, taking מִשְׁמָר in the passive sense of a "force *kept* in reserve." This is possible, but a usage unattested elsewhere.

---

[12] Zimmerli, *Ezekiel*, 2:285, and Allen, *Ezekiel*, 2:197, 200, consider the whole line (everything after רְב) a gloss.

[13] Because of the repetition, Zimmerli, *Ezekiel*, 2:285, and Allen, *Ezekiel*, 2:200, take the clause as a sort of reflex from 38:4.

38:8 בְּאַחֲרִית הַשָּׁנִים ... מִיָּמִים רַבִּים—These two temporal phrases are eschatological. The first is "after many days." For the temporal meaning "after" for the preposition מִן, see BDB, 4 b. The second is, literally, "in the latter part of the years." The feminine noun אַחֲרִית often means "latter part, close, end" and is used as "a prophetic phrase denoting the final period of the history so far as the speaker's perspective reaches; the sense thus varies with the context, but it often = the ideal or Messianic future" (BDB, b). It recurs in the phrase בְּאַחֲרִית הַיָּמִים in 38:16.

תִּפָּקֵד—The verb פָּקַד can have a variety of applications, but in military contexts tends to mean to "muster, summon, call to duty, give marching orders," so the Niphal is translated here "you will be given your orders." The older "visit" is archaic and no longer communicates clearly. פָּקַד often implies punishment, but that theme does not appear explicitly until 38:18–23.

מְשׁוֹבֶבֶת מֵחֶרֶב מְקֻבֶּצֶת—The two participles are feminine because they modify the preceding feminine noun אֶרֶץ, "land." The Polal of שׁוּב is used only here in the OT and means "restored," though "from the sword" (מֵחֶרֶב) points toward the restoration of the population. As again later in the verse, "land" is used metonymically of also the people inhabiting the land, a thought that must be supplied in translation. That is reinforced by the Pual participle מְקֻבֶּצֶת, "gathered." Everywhere in Ezekiel, the verb קָבַץ, "gather," is used only for living beings.

אֲשֶׁר־הָיוּ לְחָרְבָּה תָּמִיד—The plural verb here refers to הָרֵי יִשְׂרָאֵל, "the mountains of Israel"—the land itself. Note the assonance of חָרְבָּה, "desolation, waste," and the preceding חֶרֶב, "sword." The adverb תָּמִיד (occurring elsewhere in the book in 39:14 and 46:14–15) usually indicates continuous or regular action (e.g., the diurnal sacrifices in the temple [e.g., Num 28:6]), but here the sense is more durative ("for a long time"), complementing the two chronological phrases at the beginning of the verse. See the commentary.

וְהִיא מֵעַמִּים הוּצָאָה—The antecedent of the feminine pronoun וְהִיא and the subject of the feminine verb (Hophal of יָצָא) is the "land," but "brought out from the peoples" clearly must refer to God's people, as does the last clause, וְיָשְׁבוּ לָבֶטַח כֻּלָּם, literally, "and they will dwell securely—all of them."

38:9 וְעָלִיתָ כַּשֹּׁאָה תָבוֹא—Literally, this is, "you will come up; like destruction you will come." The verb תָבוֹא likely is second masculine singular (imperfect of בּוֹא) rather than third feminine singular with the feminine noun שֹׁאָה as its subject. שֹׁאָה is a general term for "devastation, ruin," but in light of עָנָן, "cloud," in the next clause, here it must mean "devastating storm" (BDB, s.v. שׁוֹאָה, 1, under the root שׁוא). In modern Hebrew שׁוֹאָה is the term for the Holocaust during World War II.

כֶּעָנָן לְכַסּוֹת הָאָרֶץ תִּהְיֶה—This is, literally, "like a cloud to cover the land you will be." The reference must be to the ominous cloud cover of a violent thunderstorm. The Piel infinitive כַּסּוֹת with לְ forms a purpose clause. Ultimately, it is not Gog's purpose, but Yahweh's purpose that Gog fulfills. The same is true in 38:16, where the purpose clause is repeated (כֶּעָנָן לְכַסּוֹת הָאָרֶץ).

וְעַמִּים רַבִּים אוֹתָךְ:—This is almost identical to the ending of 38:6. The textbook form of the preposition אֵת with second masculine singular suffix, "with you," is אִתְּךָ, but in pause אִתָּךְ, as at the end of 38:6. However, about half of the time, including

1109

אוֹתָךְ here, Ezekiel uses forms that appear to be from the sign of the direct object (-אֵת). See the third textual note on 2:1.

38:11 אֶעֱלֶה עַל־אֶרֶץ פְּרָזוֹת אָבוֹא הַשֹּׁקְטִים—The verbs עָלָה and בּוֹא (both Qal first common singular imperfect) are paired, probably to make a deliberate link with 38:9, where they were paired (as also in 38:16). Many critics feel that after אֶעֱלֶה the form of בּוֹא should be cohortative, and so they propose the word division אָבוֹאָה שֹׁקְטִים (the cohortative with an anarthrous object). The change is minor, but hardly imperative. בּוֹא in the sense of "attack" is usually followed by some preposition, but a direct object, as here (the participle הַשֹּׁקְטִים), is possible. The verb שָׁקַט, "be quiet, peaceful," was used in 16:42 and 16:49, but in quite different contexts.

The noun פְּרָזוֹת (only plural in the OT) means "villages," which by definition at that time meant they were unwalled. It occurs elsewhere only in Esth 9:19 and Zech 2:8 (ET 2:4), where in his third night vision that prophet is assured that Yahweh himself would be a protective wall of fire around Jerusalem (Zech 2:9 [ET 2:5]), which after its fall in 586 remained unwalled until Nehemiah rebuilt its wall in the middle of the fifth century. Some commentators attempt to date chapters 38–39 to the postexilic era by assuming that it implies that the Jerusalem of Ezekiel's vision is still unwalled (as in the Zechariah reference), but that probably overlooks the rhetorical concerns of Ezekiel, which outweigh any desire to give semi-photographic reports.

יֹשְׁבֵי לָבֶטַח—The syntax of the plural participle in construct (יֹשְׁבֵי) with a prepositional phrase (לָבֶטַח) is attested elsewhere; see Joüon, § 129 m, and Waltke-O'Connor, § 9.6b. The same construction will occur in 38:12 with the same participle (יֹשְׁבֵי עַל־טַבּוּר הָאָרֶץ).

38:12 לִשְׁלֹל שָׁלָל וְלָבֹז בַּז—The verse division is artificial since 38:11–12 comprises one sentence and 38:12 begins amid a purpose clause, "… in order to seize spoil and carry off booty …" The two cognate accusative constructions use the Qal infinitive constructs (with לְ) of essentially synonymous verbs, שָׁלַל, "despoil," and בָּזַז, "plunder." (For the form of וְלָבֹז, see Joüon, § 82 k.) Each has its cognate noun as the direct object: שָׁלָל, "spoil," and בַּז, "plunder." The same cognate accusative constructions will recur in 38:13 (see also 29:19; 39:10). However, in these instances, there is no passable way to reproduce the literary flourish in English.

לְהָשִׁיב יָדְךָ עַל־חֳרָבוֹת נוֹשָׁבֹת—At this point, the Hebrew text shifts from first person discourse (Yahweh's quote of Gog speaking) to second person address, Yahweh speaking to Gog, literally, "to return *your* hand against ruins reinhabited." My free translation smoothes over the transition by omitting the pronoun: "to assault resettled ruins." In any case, the change in person is unavoidable in the translation of 38:13, which requires "you." The literal translation of the Hiphil infinitive of שׁוּב, "to *return* your hand," means that this assault recalls earlier assaults in preexilic times, when foreign nations had raided and plundered Israel with their "hand." The free translation "assault/assail" fails to convey the historical reminiscence, but the Niphal participle (of יָשַׁב) as its object, נוֹשָׁבֹת, "reinhabited, resettled," by referring to restoration, implies that there had been earlier assaults that had killed or exiled the population. Likewise, in the next phrase, "regathered" (the Pual participle מְאֻסָּף) implies prior deportation.

עֹשֶׂה מִקְנֶה וְקִנְיָן—The participle עֹשֶׂה (literally, "making," translated "acquiring") is singular, evidently because its subject, עַם in the preceding phrase, is collective. But because the following clause has a plural participle (in construct), יֹשְׁבֵי, some would read עֹשֵׂי here, but the difference probably represents Ezekiel's apparent delight in such variations. The two objects of עֹשֶׂה are the nouns מִקְנֶה and קִנְיָן, both derived from the verb קָנָה, "acquire," used in Ezekiel only in 7:12, where the participle meant "purchaser, buyer." The nouns occur in Ezekiel only in 38:12–13. מִקְנֶה always refers to domesticated animals or livestock, either large (cattle) or small (sheep and goats). קִנְיָן (an Aramaic-type formation) is less common in the OT and refers to property purchased or gained through commerce. The LXX telescopes the two into a single word, the plural of κτῆσις. The two words are used together also in, for example, Gen 31:18. Here they may imply that Israel's wealth was acquired not only by raising "livestock" and agricultural pursuits, but also by commerce, as the next verse may suggest.

In any case, fulfillment of prophecy (34:26–27) appears to be in mind again. The promise of blessing will have been fulfilled (at least in part, incipiently) already in the present life of God's people (applicable to the present church age) before the rise and attack of "Gog" against them (prior to the return of Christ).

יֹשְׁבֵי עַל־טַבּוּר הָאָרֶץ:—For the syntax of the plural participle in construct (יֹשְׁבֵי) with a prepositional phrase (here עַל־), see Joüon, § 129 m. Much interest and debate have focused on the description that the Israelites live at the טַבּוּר, "navel," of the earth. Far behind the metaphor may lie some ancient animistic conception of "Mother Earth," but in no literal sense was such thought operative in Israel. Hebrew has another near (?) synonym, שֹׁר, which Ezekiel had used in 16:4 for the newborn girl's "umbilical cord," and שֹׁר literally means "navel" in Song 7:3 (ET 7:2) and Prov 3:8.[14] Since "navel" and "umbilical cord" are related, of course, but not exact synonyms, שֹׁר is used somewhat broadly, as perhaps טַבּוּר could be as well. The exact relation of שֹׁר to טַבּוּר is uncertain. טַבּוּר occurs elsewhere in the OT only in Judg 9:37 in the identical construct phrase used here, טַבּוּר הָאָרֶץ, "the navel of the earth," in a syncretistic context as the place from which Abimelech's armies are descending to attack Shechem. Probably there it alludes to Mount Gerizim, an old sacred mountain, and later the site of the Samaritan temple. That suggests that טַבּוּר had more of a mythological than an anatomical connotation.

We should note the idea of height connected with the word (clear in Judg 9:37, where the foes are יוֹרְדִים, "descending," from it). However, Block overstates his case when he translates טַבּוּר here in Ezek 38:12 as "top" and defines it "as an elevated plateau without external fortifications" (paralleling the previous reference to "unwalled villages").[15] Shrines and whole villages tended to be built on mountains or hilltops, and the Mesopotamians, lacking mountains, erected shrines atop artificial mountains or "ziggurats." In 38:8 Ezekiel had referred to "the mountains of Israel" again, so the idea was probably in his mind.

---

[14] One may see the discussion of שֹׁר in Mitchell, *The Song of Songs*, 1055–57.

[15] Block, *Ezekiel*, 2:445, 448.

Orthodox Israel would have demythologized the idea of "navel" into a metaphor of the "middle" of the earth, as Ezekiel himself had described Jerusalem in 5:5. But Ezekiel had no qualms about using the metaphor. Neither did later Judaism, since the LXX translated literally as ὀμφαλός, nor did Christendom, since St. Jerome rendered it with *umbilicus*. Certainly the idea that a city was the center of a land or the nurturing origin of a people was widespread in the ancient world and can be documented of any number of major cities and/or shrines: Delphi, Athens, Miletus, Babylon, and many others. Homer even uses ὀμφαλός of Calypso's island Ogygia as the center of the ocean.[16] Islam today applies the expression "navel of the world" to Mecca.

In the Byzantine era, the term "navel of the world" was connected with the church of the Holy Sepulchre in Jerusalem, indicating the term's role in Christian thought. At the foot of the rock identified with Golgotha is the small Chapel of Adam, so named because of an ancient belief that the first Adam was buried there. Whether or not Adam was, the belief intends to affirm that Christ is the second Adam (see Rom 5:12–21; 1 Cor 15:22, 45). On the crusader floor of the Katholikon directly under the dome of the church stands an urn labeled the "navel of the world" because of its central position between Golgotha and the edicule containing the traditional tomb from which Christ rose from the dead.

Ancient cartographers naturally depicted the idea. From the sixth century B.C. (about Ezekiel's time), we have a circular map from Mesopotamia depicting the center of the universe at either Babylon or Nippur. We have many Christian counterparts with Jerusalem as the center. We misconstrue the maps if we read them literalistically as merely showing antiquity's lack of the Mercator projection. As with the corresponding texts, the message is theological rather than topographical. See further the commentary.

38:13 The verse recalls Tyre's trade list in chapter 27. The locations have been discussed previously. For Sheba, see the first textual note on 27:22 (see also 27:23). For Dedan, see the second textual note on 25:13 and first textual note on 27:20 (it is also in the MT of 27:15). For Tarshish, see the first textual note on 27:12. These locations are listed in a generally east to west order, representing major players in the international commerce of the day.

כְּפִרֶ֫יהָ—A crux comes in the interpretation of the plural of כְּפִיר (with third feminine singular suffix). Literally, it means "her young lions," but it must be used in some metaphorical sense here. The LXX has αἱ κῶμαι αὐτῶν, "their *villages*," which agrees with the Syriac (ܩܘܪ̈ܝܗ) and is followed by RSV and NIV. That presupposes that the word is the plural of כְּפָר with a plural suffix. It seems less likely to me than interpreting the MT. The Vulgate has *leones eius*, "her/its *lions*," followed by KJV and NKJV, which leave the modern reader to puzzle out the meaning of the metaphor. NRSV ventures "its young warriors," which is possible. However, the way כְּפִיר is used metaphorically in 19:2–6 and 32:2 suggests that some meaning like "rulers, leaders" is more likely here, as in ESV, "its leaders." Whether or not some implication of the impulsiveness of youth carries over into the application is debatable.

---

[16] Homer, *Odyssey*, 1.50.

38:14 תֵּדָע ... הֲלוֹא—As part of the rhetorical question introduced by the negative הֲלוֹא, the final word, the imperfect of יָדַע, "know," must mean, "will you not take note?" As is common in Hebrew idiom, the object of יָדַע is not stated, but is obvious from the context. The verb is supported by the Syriac, Targum, and Vulgate, yet is challenged by most critical commentators. The LXX translation, ἐγερθήσῃ (followed by NRSV), may imply that its Hebrew text had *resh* instead of the similar-looking *daleth* and transposed the last two letters: תֵּעֹר, "rouse yourself." But a mistake might just as easily have been made in the text translated by the LXX (or made by the translators themselves) as in the MT, and there appears to be no compelling reason to emend.

38:16 בְּאַחֲרִית הַיָּמִים תִּהְיֶה—Literally, בְּאַחֲרִית הַיָּמִים is "in the latter part of the days," and is traditionally rendered "in the latter days." The import of the eschatological phrase is similar to that of בְּאַחֲרִית הַשָּׁנִים; see the first textual note on 38:8. The antonymous phrase in 38:17, בְּיָמִים קַדְמוֹנִים, "in earlier days," refers to the lifetimes of the OT prophets, so "the latter days" are far in the future from their OT perspective. תִּהְיֶה, the imperfect of הָיָה, probably is third feminine singular, "in the latter days *it will happen*" (similar are KJV, NKJV, NASB), although the form could also be second masculine singular, "... you will be." Most English translations subsume תִּהְיֶה into the temporal clause "in the latter days" and move straight to the following verb וַהֲבִאוֹתִיךָ, for example, ESV: "In the latter days I will bring ..."

38:17 יְהוָה הַאַתָּה־הוּא—The major ancient versions did not translate with an explicit interrogative to reflect the interrogative *he* on the pronoun (הַאַתָּה), so they may have read the sentence as declarative rather than a question. On that basis, some critics argue that the *he* is a dittograph from the preceding Tetragrammaton (ה- הַאַתָּה). Many modern translations and commentators take the sentence as declarative. But, as usual, the argument cuts both ways, and the ancient versions may be haplographic. The interrogative form is rhetorically stronger. See further the commentary.

עֲבָדַי נְבִיאֵי יִשְׂרָאֵל—To many critics, the allegedly non-Ezekelian language of "my servants the prophets" is a major problem. However, that phrase, or "his/your servants the prophets," is frequently found in 2 Kings (9:7; 17:13, 23; 21:10; 24:2) and Jeremiah (7:25; 25:4; 26:5; 29:19; 35:15; 44:4) and occasionally in other books (Amos 3:7; Zech 1:6; Dan 9:6, 10; Ezra 9:11). Since critical commentators think "Deuteronomic" activity began with Josiah's reformation in 622 B.C. and was even more prevalent during and after the exile (often in supposed tension or even conflict with priestly circles, like those of Ezekiel!), critics suppose they can use this language to locate the origin and perhaps even the date of this allegedly interpolated verse.[17] Since this same phrase occurs in Zech 1:6, who in 1:4 had referred to "the former prophets" (הַנְּבִיאִים הָרִאשֹׁנִים), critics intimate that this "distanced" reflection of past prophecy in Ezek 38:17 may date a good half century after the genuine Ezekelian prophecies. Obviously, such argumentation bespeaks a set of prepossessions that are

---

[17] Zimmerli, *Ezekiel*, 2:312, can even deny such language to Ezekiel, "who himself, even when he clearly goes back to older prophetic oracles (chapters 16, 23, 34), still stands directly in the prophetic experience of the word."

a cosmos removed from the hermeneutics and theology in the Scriptures themselves, which govern this commentary. Since Ezekiel probably was no more than slightly younger than his prophetic contemporary Jeremiah, it is not surprising that the phrase common in Jeremiah should also be found in this book inspired by the same God.

הַנִּבְּאִים בַּיָּמִים הָהֵם שָׁנִים—The first three words are syntactically normal, and the Niphal participle with article begins a relative clause: "who prophesied in those days." (For the form נִבְּאִים instead of נִבָּאִים, see Joüon, §§ 78 h, 96C b.) But the plural of שָׁנָה following asyndetically is awkward. The LXX and Syriac add a copula: "... in those days and years." Others have suggested a conflation of two textual traditions, but we have no way of testing such guesses. Most likely, שָׁנִים is an adverbial, temporal accusative, "for years," answering the question "For how long did they prophesy?"

38:18 תַּעֲלֶה חֲמָתִי בְּאַפִּי —This main clause is, literally, "my wrath will go up in my nose." The feminine noun חֵמָה is the subject of the feminine verb (Qal imperfect of עָלָה). This exact anthropopathic expression is unique in the OT but has a few near parallels (Ps 18:9 [ET 18:8] ‖ 2 Sam 22:9; Ps 78:21, 31). Many other passages use אַף in the sense of "anger," either by itself or in conjunction with other verbs, especially חָרָה, "be hot, angry" (e.g., Ps 106:40).

Since the LXX takes its translation of וּבְקִנְאָתִי at the beginning of the next verse (καὶ ὁ ζῆλός μου, which ignores the בְ) as a second subject of the verb (ἀναβήσεται for תַּעֲלֶה), some commentators want to change the MT verse division to match the syntax of the LXX (which requires discarding the בְ). Meaning is scarcely affected, and there appears to be no good reason to abandon the MT.

38:20 וְנָפְלוּ הַמַּדְרֵגוֹת —The precise meaning of the plural noun מַדְרֵגוֹת is uncertain. The word's only other OT occurrence is in Song 2:14, where the singular is parallel to סֶלַע, "cliff, rock," and denotes an inaccessible place.[18] The ancient versions vary (here the LXX has φάραγγες, "valleys") as do modern ones: KJV and NKJV have "steep places," while most recent versions give "cliffs." The root is cognate with the Arabic for "step, stairs." Aramaic and Rabbinic Hebrew support the meaning "terraces," which are held up by retaining walls that could "fall, collapse" (וְנָפְלוּ), so that seems the most likely meaning to me.

38:21 וְקָרָאתִי עָלָיו לְכָל־הָרַי חֶרֶב —Usually for a first common singular perfect with *waw* consecutive, the accent shifts to the final syllable (see the next textual note). Sometimes it does not when the next word begins with א, and here on וְקָרָאתִי it does not with עַ following (GKC, § 49 l). This clause is, literally, "I will summon against him to all my mountains a sword." "Sword" at the end of the sentence is unusual, but may be emphatic and/or intended to lead into the rest of the verse, which should elucidate it. "My mountains" occurs elsewhere in the OT (e.g., Is 14:25; Zech 14:5), but not in Ezekiel, although Yahweh has frequently expressed his zeal for "the mountains of Israel" (especially chapters 6 and 36; see also 34:13–14). It is debatable whether לְ is distributive, "*throughout* all my mountains," or indicates direction "to." The LXX translates (?) the words לְכָל־הָרַי חֶרֶב by πᾶν φόβον, resulting in "I will summon

---

[18] For a discussion, one may see Mitchell, *The Song of Songs*, 714–15, 730.

against him *all fear.*" On that basis Zimmerli argues for an original לְכָל־חֲרָדָה.[19] RSV follows the LXX with its "every kind of terror." But the LXX itself may have been uncertain of the meaning, and the MT, though problematic, should be allowed to stand.

38:22 וְנִשְׁפַּטְתִּי אִתּוֹ—The idiom with the Niphal of שָׁפַט and the preposition אֶת, "with," usually means "enter into judgment with, bring to trial," as in 17:20 and 20:35–36. But here, since the guilt has already been established, it probably implies the execution of the sentence, so it is translated, "I will punish."

38:23 וְהִתְגַּדִּלְתִּי וְהִתְקַדִּשְׁתִּי—In these two perfect Hithpael verbs (first common singular) with *waw* consecutive the accent moves to the final syllable, and the expected *patach* under the middle root letter (- דַּ-) is attenuated to short *hireq* (-דִּ-). See Joüon, § 53 f (cf. the alternative explanation in GKC, § 54 k). The force of each Hithpael can be called "estimative-declarative reflexive" in meaning, "and I *will show* my *greatness* and *display* my *holiness,*" similar to the force of the following Niphal וְנוֹדַעְתִּי, "and I will make myself known" (Waltke-O'Connor, § 26.2f, including example 11).

Commentary

Hordes Prepare to Attack God's Restored People (38:1–9)

38:2–3   The oracle is introduced by the last occurrence in Ezekiel of the formula whereby Yahweh commands his prophet, "set your face against …" (38:2). It portends the hostile orientation formula, where Yahweh himself declares, "I am against you" (38:3; for both formulas, see the textual notes).

Vast efforts have been devoted to the identification of the people and places mentioned, some of which are easier than others. I shall proceed on the assumption that they are historical names. But it is possible that they are artificial creations, and, in either case, their functional significance is more important than their identity. Allen aptly suggests a comparison with someone today speaking of "a new Hitler."[20]

The most agreement is found with "Gog," who is usually identified with a powerful king of Lydia in west Asia Minor in the early seventh century B.C., known to the Greeks as Gyges and to the Assyrians as Gugu. The name is also attested in an archaeological excavation in the area. Since he ruled a century before the time of Ezekiel, it may be a dynastic name that his successors also bore. Much earlier, a "Gaga" also appears at Ugarit (second millennium B.C.) and in the Amarna letters (fourteenth century B.C.).

"Magog" is clearly a place name in the Hebrew here, but also appears as a personal name in the Bible (Gen 10:2; 1 Chr 1:5; see the third textual note on Ezek 38:2). Possibly we have an eponym. Its location, otherwise unknown, must be determined from the personal names with which it is associated, and that suggests Lydia-Cappadocia in Anatolia. If the names "Gog" and "Magog" are ciphers of some sort, there may be an attempt at a certain rhyming of names

---

[19]   Zimmerli, *Ezekiel*, 2:289.

[20]   Allen, *Ezekiel*, 2:205.

as with "Eldad" and "Medad" in Num 11:26. If the two are so related, we have a sort of chicken-and-egg question of priority. Some see in "m-g-g" a sort of cryptography, comparable to "ath-bash," as found in Jeremiah's "sh-sh-k" = "b-b-l" (Babel, Babylon; Jer 25:26; 51:41), where the first letter of the alphabet is replaced with the last, the second with the second last, and so on, continuing throughout the alphabet.[21] According to this view, instead of "b-b-l" Ezekiel here has used the corresponding next letters in the Hebrew alphabet, that is, "g-g-m." (In the order of letters in the Hebrew alphabet, "b" is followed by "g," and "l" by "m.") When each of the letters in "g-g-m" is reversed using "ath-bash," they become "m-g-g" ("Magog"). Such devices are common in later apocalyptic. However, most such approaches assume that Ezekiel is depicting the Babylonians as God's enemies, whereas he consistently describes them as God's agents to punish unfaithful Israel.

Another attempt to understand "Magog" assumes a Hebrew adaptation of the Akkadian way of writing "the land of Gugi." "Land" in Akkadian is *matu*, but before proper nouns, it is usually written (though probably not spoken) as a preceding determinative (of the category of subject to follow) and normally transliterated *mat* *Gugi*. Then "Gog" and "Magog" together would mean "Gog of the land of Gog." But this is pleonastic and sounds desperate. Albright once proposed some sort of blend with "Manda," an abbreviation of "Umman Manda," a generic Mesopotamian label for "barbarian."[22] But few have followed this suggestion either.

Finally, it may be helpful to remember that Josephus identified Magog with the Scythians.[23] And if "Rosh," the name mentioned next, was Scythian, as was once commonly held, some connection may be made there. Discussion of "Rosh" is stymied until we decide whether it is another place name or a common noun meaning "head, chief." See the third textual note on 38:2 for a summary of that debate. I incline toward the view that it is a place name.

The final two nations, "Meshech" and "Tubal," form a standard pair in biblical writings, and we have encountered them previously in Ezekiel: in 27:13, where they appear (in reverse order) on Tyre's trade list, and in 32:26, where they are listed among the slain in Sheol. See the textual notes on those verses for a discussion of their importance.

Thus if our assumptions and conclusions are at all correct, we get the picture of an alliance of Anatolian powers against Israel: Gog (Lydia) is the farthest west, and moving eastward, Meshech and then Tubal (see the map "The

---

[21] "Ath-bash" is so named by the application of this substitutionary system to Hebrew. Thus the first Hebrew letter, א ("a"), is replaced by the last letter, ת ("th"), yielding "ath." Then the second Hebrew letter, ב ("b"), is replaced by the second-last letter, ש ("sh"), yielding "bash."

[22] W. F. Albright, "Contributions to Biblical Archaeology and Philology," *JBL* 43 (1924): 383, cited by Block, *Ezekiel*, 2:434, n. 38.

[23] Josephus, *Antiquities*, 1.123 (1.6.1).

Ancient Near East"). Although much debated, in my judgment, we should also include Rosh (which was possibly located in the Taurus Mountains). They are all too distant from Jerusalem to be likely ever to have had frictional contacts with Israel in the OT era. Block is probably correct in his perception:

> The peoples in the distant north were shrouded in mystery. The reports of these mysterious people groups that filtered down spoke of wild peoples, brutal and barbaric. This combination of mystery and brutality made Gog and his confederates perfect symbols of the archetypal enemy, rising against God and his people.[24]

(a) Rev 20:4, 6; cf. Rom 5:17, 21; Eph 2:6; 2 Tim 2:12; Rev 5:10

That fits with the sole mention of any of these peoples in the NT. When the imminent return of Jesus is bringing the "thousand years" of the present reign of Christians with Christ[a] toward its glorious conclusion, Satan, who had been bound at Christ's first advent (Rev 20:2; see also Mt 12:29; Mk 3:27), will be given enough freedom "to deceive the nations that are at the four corners of the earth, Gog and Magog, to gather them for battle" against God's saints (Rev 20:8–9). But God shall rain down fire and sulfur upon these enemies (Ezek 38:22; Rev 20:9), and at the return of Christ they, along with the devil who misled them, shall be cast into the lake of fire for eternity (Rev 20:10, 15). In the NT too, then, rather than specific human, national, or political figures, "Gog and Magog" primarily represent the demonic powers and principalities that wage war against God's redeemed (Eph 6:12) but that have been defeated by Christ (Eph 4:8; Col 2:15), whose victory over them will be consummated at his second coming.

38:4   Ezek 38:4–9 summarizes how Yahweh will use Gog for his own purposes. These verses divide into two parts, ending at 38:6 and 38:9, as is obvious from the repeated conclusion "many peoples (are) with you [Gog]." The phrase "hooks in your jaws" (38:4) is probably reused from 29:4, where Yahweh applied it to his conquest of Pharaoh as a crocodile in the Nile. It pictorially summarizes what the following verses elaborate: at least from God's perspective, Gog's pretentious and exhaustive preparations to attack and plunder Israel are involuntary. God uses all things, even the forces of evil, for the good of his people (see Jn 11:50; Rom 8:28).

38:5–6   These verses add five more peoples allied with Gog. All except one have appeared previously in Ezekiel. In 27:10 פָּרַס ("Persia"?), Lydia, and Put (Libya) were partners of Tyre, and in 30:5 Nubia, Libya, and Lydia were allied with Egypt. Beth-togarmah was listed in 27:14 as bartering with Tyre. See the map "The Ancient Near East."

In 38:5 the major problem arises with פָּרַס, which in later Hebrew texts certainly refers to "Persia," but here, as in 27:10 (which see), it perhaps refers to some other nation. Questions are raised by both its geographical distance from the other two countries mentioned after it in 38:5 ("Nubia" and "Libya")

---

[24] Block, *Ezekiel*, 2:436.

and chronological considerations, since we do not know of other evidence that Persia was active in international politics in Ezekiel's day (early sixth century B.C.). The alternative would be some power not yet attested in extrabiblical sources or an Egyptian spelling for "Pathros," the original homeland of the Egyptians (29:14; cf. 30:14). However, although it is true that Ezekiel shows no other interest in the region of Persia, his contemporary, Jeremiah, does concern himself with the neighboring Medes (Jer 25:25; 51:11, 28). Our knowledge of the international affairs of the time is tenuous enough that it is rash to pontificate beyond our documentable knowledge.

"Gomer" in 38:6 has not appeared previously in Ezekiel, but Gen 10:2–3 mentions a person so named as a brother of Meshech, Tubal, and Magog, and father of Togarmah. It is generally agreed that the name in Ezek 38:6 refers to the Cimmerians from somewhere north of the Black Sea who for a time gave Assyria no little trouble. With most translations I have retained "Gomer," however, because it will be no more unfamiliar than "Cimmerian."

(Beth-)Togarmah was apparently a somewhat more easterly area, probably on the upper Euphrates (in eastern Turkey today) and later incorporated into Media. Especially earlier commentators identify it with the area of modern Armenia. In any case, from Ezekiel's perspective it qualifies to be labeled as situated in "the remotest regions of the north" (38:6). In 39:2 that phrase is applied to Gog, and in connection with 38:17, is often interpreted as saying that Ezekiel is signaling his awareness that he is thinking of the fulfillment of earlier prophecies, especially in Jeremiah (1:13–15; 4:6–17; 6:1–30) of the foe from the north.[25] This is an intriguing thought, but probably should be stated with caution. The application here in 38:6 of "from the remotest regions of the north" seems to be to Beth-togarmah, rather than to Gog, but Ezekiel may be using the phrase generally enough that it need not be restricted to just that one nation out of those mentioned in 38:2–6. If the phrase also has exmythological overtones, after Mount Zaphon ("mount north," the pagan Canaanite equivalent of the Greek Mount Olympus), it adds to the eschatological urgency of the pericope.[26]

Finally, it should be noted that the number of evil allies is seven, the same as the total number of nations addressed in the Gentile oracles (chapters 25–32; cf. those who accompany Egypt in Sheol in 32:17–32). "Seven years" (39:9) and "seven months" (39:12, 14) appear symbolically later. This common numerical symbol of completeness makes the point that no localized skirmish is

---

[25] Jeremiah does not use the exact phrase "the remotest regions of the north" (יַרְכְּתֵי צָפוֹן). He does, however, speak of nations "from the remotest regions of the earth" (מִיַּרְכְּתֵי־אָרֶץ) in 6:22; 25:32; 31:8, and in 50:41 that phrase is parallel to "from the north" (מִצָּפוֹן).

[26] For the possible exmythological significance of "north," see the commentary on 1:4. For other possible exmythological usages in Ezekiel, see the textual notes and commentary on 26:19, 21; the commentary on 28:14; 29:3; the first textual note on 31:4; and the commentary on 31:2–7.

in mind, but rather a universal conspiracy against God's people. The same point is made by the wide geographical range of Ezekiel's names of nations, extending from the northern to the southern extremes of the world known to Israel.

38:7 The second part (38:7–9) of the summary of Yahweh's purposes with Gog (38:4–9) begins with two singular Hebrew imperatives, translated as "ready yourself; prepare yourself." Then singular imperfects with a kind of imperatival force follow in 38:7b–9. The singular verbs indicate a primary preoccupation with Gog, while the accompanying phrases make plain that all his allies are included as well. Ironically, of course, Gog has no idea who is giving these commands; he thinks he is acting independently. Similarly, in Is 45:1–5 Cyrus is unknowingly led by God to conquer Babylon to fulfill God's redemptive purpose.

38:8 The exiles, who must still be Ezekiel's primary audience, would surely receive from the previous verse the impression that the invasion was imminent. This verse rectifies such a misunderstanding by the use of two expressions. The first, מִיָּמִים רַבִּים, means "after many days," and is deliberately general. It occurs otherwise only in Josh 23:1, where it describes the time elapsing between Israel's entrance into Canaan and Joshua's farewell address (cf. Ezek 12:27). The second, בְּאַחֲרִית הַשָּׁנִים, literally, "in the latter part of the years," occurs only here in the OT, but is clearly only a variant of the phrase בְּאַחֲרִית הַיָּמִים, traditionally translated "in the latter days," which occurs a good dozen times throughout the OT, including 38:16. The noun אַחֲרִית, traditionally translated "latter," means "last" or "(distant) future." There is some debate about how distant a future Ezekiel has in mind, but in the parallelism of the verse, the two phrases should be essentially synonymous. In Dan 2:28 and 10:14, "in the latter days" is a full-fledged eschatological phrase that looks to the coming of God's eternal kingdom at the first advent of Jesus Christ. That may be true of the phrase in other OT passages, but not always. Ezekiel's vision seems to be moving in that direction. Yet the reappearances in this chapter of themes from chapters 34 and 36–37 (regathering of the people, rebuilding of ruins, and God's people living in perfect security) seem to presuppose that this battle will take place *after* the fulfillment of those salvation oracles, and that fulfillment comes preeminently in the first advent of the new David, Jesus Christ (34:23–24; 37:24–25). This warfare is no punishment upon God's Israel for disobedience (as the Babylonian captivity had been), but a malicious assault by the unconverted long after the return of OT Israel after the exile and then the dispersion of the new Israel throughout the world. This is consistent with the NT depiction of the church as God's regenerated Israel (e.g., Gal 3:26–29; 6:16; see also Luther's use of "new Israel" in AE 35:288, 290), presently scattered throughout the earth (e.g., διασπορά, "diaspora," in James 1:1; 1 Pet 1:1), finally to be regathered permanently at the second coming of Christ (e.g., Mt 13:30; 24:31).

But as stressed before, if we try to fit this into a more precise chronological sequence, we are making Ezekiel answer questions that he is not address-

ing. Chiliasts might try to relate this prophecy to the seven-year "tribulation" or the like in their scheme (with a "rapture" of Christians before or halfway through that "tribulation"), to be followed by a return of Christ to an earthly reign lasting a literal thousand years, before the arrival of the eschaton. But we must understand the "millennium" of Rev 20:1–6 to be the present church age, the time of the "now but not yet." The "end" came with the fulfillment of the OT at Christ's first coming (see τέλος in Lk 22:37; cf. Jn 13:1; τελέω in Jn 19:30), but still to come is the final "end" (τέλος, Mt 24:6, 13–14; cf. Rom 6:22; 1 Cor 15:24; Rev 21:6), the consummation of all things at his second coming. During this present time, Satan is now waging his last-ditch battles against the redeemed, and the Scriptures suggest that his warfare, manifest in antichrists (1 Jn 2:18, 22; 4:3; 2 Jn 7) and "the man of lawlessness" (2 Thess 2:1–12), will intensify before the final defeat of all evil at Christ's parousia. Thus we arrive at a "chronological" conclusion in harmony with other biblical notices of the end times in which we now live (e.g., Acts 2:17; Heb 1:2).

38:9 Two meteorological similes ("like") are used to describe the massive incursion led by Gog. In the first, the verb עָלָה, "come up," indicates hostile advance, and עָנָן, "cloud," in the second indicates that both similes refer to a storm (see the textual notes). The same verb and the plural of עָנָן, "clouds," are in Jeremiah's description of the enemy from the north (Jer 4:13). The key noun שֹׁאָה, translated adjectivally here in Ezek 38:9 as "devastating," seems to depend on the storm coming from afar in Is 10:3.

What can be viewed as a sort of prologue closes with this verse, before the citation formula in 38:10, "thus says the Lord Yahweh,"[27] opens a new verse and a new theme. It should be stressed that, so far, Yahweh alone has been the speaker, addressing Gog in the second person and describing him. Everything has been arranged objectively and is being guided by God, and to a large extent, this radically theocentric perspective continues through the end of chapter 39 and beyond.

Gog's Evil Intent Serves God's Purpose to Prove Himself Holy (38:10–23)

38:10 A series of typical Hebrew idioms comprise this sentence, describing Gog's subjective involvement in what is about to happen. דְּבָרִים, ordinarily translated "words," is somewhat broader in Hebrew. Often it implies actions, but here "thoughts," unspoken words. They take shape in Gog's "heart" (לֵבָב) in the sense of "mind" (in 11:5 and 20:32 a similar idiom used רוּחַ, "spirit"). What these thoughts are we hear in 38:11–12, but first they are described as "a scheme of evil" (מַחֲשֶׁבֶת רָעָה). The cognate accusative construction "to scheme a scheme" (חָשַׁב מַחֲשֶׁבֶת) is common Hebrew style, and I have retained it in my literalistic translation.

---

[27] For this formula, see pages 8–9 in the introduction and the fourth textual note and the commentary on 2:4.

38:11–12 These verses express the total depravity of unregenerate man, who by nature is held in slavery to sin and the devil (e.g., Rom 6:16–20; Titus 3:3; cf. Ap II). Zimmerli nicely summarizes it:

> There is in Gog's heart … the evil desire to commit an atrocity against the defenseless, who are to be attacked where they least expect it—a desire which is rooted deep in the mysterious depths of the human heart. …

> With this evil intention of attacking the weak there is instantly associated in Gog also the greedy desire for enrichment by the possessions of the defenseless.[28]

Again there is back reference to the prophecies of new blessing in the land in 34:25–31 and 36:6–38, prophecies which Yahweh cannot allow Gog to nullify.

The metaphor of the land situated "at the navel of the earth," odd though it sounds to us, was in antiquity a common idiom associated especially with shrines (see the fourth textual note on 38:12). Here part of the point is that Israel's prominent position at the "navel" of the earth excites the envy and cupidity of Gog and his allies all the more. Israel itself may well have associated more with the expression. Because of the long history of God working salvation at this location, Israel and especially Jerusalem are the hinge of history, and possibly also in a vertical sense, implying a bond of heaven and earth in one place. For Christians, of course, our understandings of the metaphor are only magnified by the realization that God became incarnate in Jesus Christ, whose atoning death and resurrection at Jerusalem have reconciled God and humanity. "In him all things hold together" (Col 1:17). Ezekiel does not again use the language of "navel" or "middle" (in the sense it was used in 5:5 for Jerusalem), but in chapters 40–48 the importance of the temple mount is virtually the total theme. In this context of a looming attack, "navel" emphasizes that this will not be merely another war, of which the pages of history are full, but a war that will have decisive significance in world history, and since it occurs at the theological center of the world, it will involve space as well as time. All of this is close to the "new creation" language of Christological eschatology (2 Cor 5:17; Gal 6:15; see also Jn 19:41; 2 Pet 3:13; Rev 21:1–5). The old must perish, as it will in this battle, to make room for the new.

38:13 The possibility of acquiring much booty arouses the interest of others as well, which they express by peppering Gog with verbose questions, which to a large extent simply repeat his own language from 38:12. Conceivably, a challenge to Gog is implied, but more likely the questions simply represent the desire of others to share in Gog's attack against God's people, as well as the vision of easy spoils in which they can also share. Whether on a large international scale or in smaller, even personal, contacts, the picture of sinful human nature's greed and covetousness rings all too true.

---

[28] Zimmerli, *Ezekiel*, 2:310.

38:14–16 These verses mostly only restate what has already been said earlier in the chapter. Ezek 38:14 underscores that the nations involved are deliberately taking advantage of Israel's perceived security and launching their massive invasion when its guard is completely down.

One notes the explicit covenant bond in these verses in God's repeated reference to "my people Israel" (38:14, 16) and to "my land" (38:16). Previously there had been mostly only generalities about returnees and restoration.

With the verb "I will bring you" (וַהֲבִאוֹתִיךָ, 38:16b), we reach the main point of these verses. Yahweh is not merely allowing Gog to come, but summoning him as his agent. The common "in the latter days" (בְּאַחֲרִית הַיָּמִים) is used here instead of the unique variant in 38:8 (see the commentary there), but the meanings are essentially the same.

Finally, the purpose of the whole confrontation will be a worldwide manifestation of Yahweh's holiness, as reaffirmed in 38:23. Previously in the book, the recognition formula, "(then) you/they will know that I am Yahweh,"[29] often referred to knowledge gained by Yahweh saving his people and judging his enemies. The formulation with God as the direct object, "that the nations may know me," occurs in Ezekiel only here. This leads Zimmerli, Allen, and others to see a later interpolation,[30] but that sort of "logic" eludes me. The virtual universalism of the clause, implying that all will know God by experiencing either his judgment (upon unbelievers) or his salvation (for believers), is of a piece with the semi-eschatological ambience of all of chapters 38–39.

38:17 There really can be no doubt that the question God addresses to Gog requires a positive answer, as implied at the end of the verse: "I would bring *you* against them." That answer is made more emphatic by approaching it indirectly through a question, which does not simply make the assertion, but suggests an inquiry for the sake of getting a definite answer.

Who are the prophets of (literally) "former days" (a counterpart to "latter days" in 38:16), who had made such prophecies? If one looks for specific OT proof texts about Gog (apart from Ezekiel 38–39 themselves), one will look in vain. But if one considers all the many earlier prophecies of Yahweh's Day of Judgment upon the heathen, it is possible to include a vast percentage of all earlier prophecies. None of them specifically mention Gog, of course, but this verse affirms that Gog and his many attacking allies are fulfillments of what the earlier prophets had spoken, and likewise with his imminent destruction at the hand of Yahweh. The great showdown battle is not at all at variance with the promise of the ultimate restoration of Israel, although for a time it might seem otherwise, just as the ongoing persecutions of the church cause her to yearn all the more for the final deliverance when her warfare shall have ceased. The parallels are not precise, of course, but such an understanding is instructive for the study of specifically "messianic prophecy." After the fulfillment in

---

[29] For this formula, see page 9 in the introduction and the commentary on 6:7.

[30] Zimmerli, *Ezekiel*, 1:39; 2:288, 297; Allen, *Ezekiel*, 2:201.

Christ, one can look back and see how the earlier Scriptures were indeed fulfilled perfectly, even if in prior times the details seemed unclear (cf. Lk 24:27,
44).

This verse is also very instructive about the history of the canon. There is
ample evidence that prophetic sayings were recorded and collected already during a prophet's lifetime (e.g., Jeremiah's relation with Baruch as evident in Jer
36:1–4 and 45:1–2, and, less clearly, Isaiah and his sons in Is 8:16). Already
Moses in Deuteronomy (especially chapters 13 and 18) evinces an awareness
of prophecy, both true and false. 2 Ki 17:13–23 describes the demise of the
northern kingdom as a fulfillment of prophecy, and Amos 3:7 indicates an
awareness of God's regular revelation through his prophets. We cannot trace
the details of a "prophetic tradition," but there obviously was one—probably
two, both true and false, as the running conflicts between the two make plain.[31]
And with the fall of Jerusalem, Ezekiel's own prophetic ministry was authen-
ticated (Ezek 24:25–27; 33:21–22), as were those of other faithful prophets
who had predicted the same, and the addition of their books to the definitive
canon of inspired books was, humanly speaking, a rather natural development.

38:18–20   The language of Yahweh's wrath has occurred before, of
course, and also of earthquakes (3:12–13; 37:7). Ezek 38:18 announces the
eruption of Yahweh's wrath; 38:19 in oath language announces that Yahweh
will manifest it through an earthquake; and 38:20 details how all creation, animate and inanimate, will be affected. (The list of creatures resembles Gen 1:26,
28 and 9:2.) Every symbol of stability, whether natural or manmade, will be
shattered. That it is Yahweh's activity is expressed by "before me/in my presence" (מִפָּנַי) near the beginning of 38:20, as well as by the passive verb "will
be overthrown" (Niphal, וְנֶהֶרְסוּ) for the mountains later. The theophanic language is reminiscent of the revelation at Sinai. The language of cosmic up-
heaval accompanying Yahweh's advent occurs often in Scripture (e.g., Is
24:17–23; frequently in Joel; Pss 18:7–16 [ET 18:6–15]; 144:5–6). In Hag
2:6–7 and Zech 14:4–5, earthquake is a harbinger of Yahweh's eschatological
acts of salvation, as also in the NT: Mt 24:29–31; Mk 13:24–27. The earthquake at the death of Christ signals the impending end of the old, fallen creation (Mt 27:54), and the one at his resurrection (Mt 28:2) announces that the
believers' hope of resurrection on the Last Day has already been accomplished
in Christ. After the seventh angel pours out his censer and God announces, "It
is done!" (Rev 16:17), there shall be one final, climactic earthquake greater
than all others that shall take place at the second advent of Christ (Rev 16:18).[32]

Critical consensus dates this kind of language as late and "apocalyptic,"
but we have formal parallels from seventh-century Assyria, indicating its antiquity.

---

[31] For true versus false prophecy, see also the commentary on Ezekiel 13.

[32] This earthquake is also mentioned in Rev 6:12 and 11:19 (cf. Rev 8:5; 11:13). See Brighton,
    Revelation, 151, figure 3.

38:21 The "sword" is highlighted as Yahweh's instrument of punishment, as previously, especially in chapter 21 (see also chapters 5–6). It appears to specify internecine warfare in the enemy camp as its precise mode of action. It is a standard motif in the biblical "war of Yahweh" (often preferred today to "holy war" to avoid confusion with Muslim *jihad*). Classical examples of the motif occur in Gideon's war with the Midianites (Judg 7:22) and in Jehoshaphat's battle with a Transjordanian coalition (2 Chr 20:23).

38:22 Yahweh will use other agents besides the sword. They are grouped in three pairs: (1) "plague" and "bloodshed," as in 5:17 and 28:23; (2) "torrential rain" and "hailstones," as in 13:11, 13; and (3) literally, "fire and sulfur" (traditionally "fire and brimstone"), which God rained down on Sodom and Gomorrah in Gen 19:24 (cf. Deut 29:22 [ET 29:23]), perhaps by means of volcanic activity, because of their abominations, including homosexuality.[33] "Fire" was an instrument of judgment in Ezek 10:2; 21:3, 36 (ET 20:47; 21:31); and other verses. "Sulfur/brimstone" occurs only here in Ezekiel, and the LXX renders it here (also in Gen 19:24; Deut 29:22 [ET 29:23]; and other passages) by θεῖον, which the NT employs in its depiction of hell as the "lake of fire burning with sulfur" (Rev 19:20; see also Rev 20:10; 21:8; cf. Lk 17:29; Rev 14:10).

38:23 As the previous verse had echoed 38:6 and 38:9, this final verse picks up the theme of world recognition of Yahweh in 38:16. All the verbs in the first sentence are reflexive. The first two are the only occurrences in Ezekiel of the verbs גָּדַל and קָדַשׁ in the Hithpael, "I will prove myself great, and I will prove myself holy" (see further the textual note). "I will make myself known" translates the Niphal of יָדַע, which had been used before for Yahweh's self-disclosure (20:5, 9; 35:11; 36:23). That sentence is then capsulized in the simple, but characteristic recognition formula, "then they will know that I am Yahweh,"[34] which to a large extent summarizes and consummates not only the chapter, but the whole book—and the whole Bible.

The recognition of God's holiness (the Sanctus or Trisagion) is the ceaseless acclamation of the angels surrounding him (Is 6:3; Rev 4:8), and his greatness, glory, and honor are the unending hymn of the angels together with all the redeemed in heaven (Rev 5:9–14; 7:9–12). The scenes of the end at the return of Christ, many replete with eschatological signs as in Ezek 38:19–22, remind us that God displays his holiness and righteous not only in the vindication of his faithful servants, but also in his final judgment and destruction of unbelievers, the devil, and his minions (e.g., Rev 11:16–19; 14:7–11; 19:1–6; 20:7–15).

---

[33] For homosexuality as an "abomination" (תּוֹעֵבָה), see the commentary on Ezek 33:26 and 36:17.

[34] For this formula, see page 9 in the introduction and the commentary on 6:7.

Yahweh Will Defeat Gog and Pour Out His Spirit on His People

Translation

39 [1]"Now you, son of man, prophesy against Gog, and say, 'Thus says the Lord Yahweh to you: I am against you, O Gog, prince of Rosh, Meshech, and Tubal. [2]I will mislead you; I will show you the way; I will lead you up from the remotest regions of the north; and I will bring you against the mountains of Israel. [3]But there I will knock your bow from your left hand, and I will make your arrows fall from your right hand. [4]On the mountains of Israel you will fall—you, all your troops, and the peoples who are with you. To scavenger birds of every kind and to the wild animals I will give you as food. [5]In the open country you will fall, for I have spoken, says the Lord Yahweh. [6]I will also send fire on Magog and on those who live in security on the coastlands. Then they will know that I am Yahweh.

[7]" 'I will make my holy name known among my people Israel. I will not let my holy name be profaned any more, and the nations will know that I am Yahweh, the Holy One in Israel. [8]It is coming! It will surely take place, says the Lord Yahweh. This is the day of which I have spoken. [9]Then those who live in the cities of Israel will go out and set on fire and burn the weapons, the hand shields and body shields, bows and arrows, clubs and spears. They will make fires of them for seven years. [10]They will not take wood from the open country or gather it from the forests because they will make fire from the weapons. They will despoil those who had despoiled them and plunder those who had plundered them, says the Lord Yahweh.

[11]" 'On that day I will give to Gog a burial place there in Israel, the valley of those who travel [east] toward the [Dead] Sea, and it will block the travelers. There they will bury Gog and all his horde and call it the Valley of Gog's Horde. [12]The house of Israel will spend seven months burying them in order to cleanse the land. [13]All the people of the land [of Israel] will join in burying them, and it will redound to their honor on that day when I display my glory, says the Lord Yahweh. [14]In addition, they will set apart permanently employed men who will pass through the land and who, together with others who pass through, will bury those who are left on the surface of the land in order to cleanse it. At the end of seven months, they will make their search. [15]When those who go through the land see a human bone, they shall erect a marker beside it until the buriers have buried it in the Valley of Gog's Horde. [16]Also the name of a city will be Its Horde. And so they will cleanse the land.'

[17]"And you, son of man, thus says the Lord Yahweh: Speak to birds, every winged creature, and to all the wild animals, 'Assemble and come, gather from all around to my sacrificial meal, which I am preparing for you, a great sacrifi-

cial meal on the mountains of Israel. You will eat meat and drink blood. ¹⁸You will eat the meat of warriors and drink the blood of the princes of the earth as if they were rams and lambs, goats and bulls, all of them fatlings of Bashan. ¹⁹You will eat fat until you are full and drink blood until you are drunk from my sacrificial meal, which I have prepared for you. ²⁰At my table you will be filled with horses and chargers, with warriors and all the men of war, says the Lord Yahweh.'

²¹"Thus I will establish my glory among the Gentiles, and all the nations will see my justice, which I have executed, and my hand, which I have laid upon them. ²²The house of Israel will know that I am Yahweh, their God, from that day on. ²³And the nations will know that the house of Israel went into exile because of their iniquity, because they were unfaithful to me. So I hid my face from them and delivered them into the hand of their adversaries, and they all fell by the sword. ²⁴I dealt with them according to their uncleanness and their rebellion, and I hid my face from them.

²⁵"Therefore, thus says the Lord Yahweh: Now I will bring about the restoration of Jacob; I will have mercy on the whole house of Israel; and I will be zealous for my holy name. ²⁶They will bear their shame and all the unfaithfulness they showed toward me even when they live in security in their own land with no one to make them afraid. ²⁷When I bring them back from the nations and gather them from the lands of their enemies, I will prove myself holy among them in the sight of many nations. ²⁸They will know that I am Yahweh, their God, in that I sent them into captivity among the nations, but also gathered them again to their own land and will never again leave any of them behind. ²⁹Nor will I ever hide my face from them again because I will have poured out my Spirit on the house of Israel, says the Lord Yahweh."

Textual Notes

39:1 Throughout this chapter, the verses are essentially a reprise of corresponding material in the previous chapter. Ezek 39:1 is a condensation of 38:2–3. The hostile orientation formula, הִנְנִי אֵלֶיךָ גּוֹג, literally, "behold, I am against you, O Gog," is repeated from 38:3, and it applies to the entire chapter, which emphasizes Yahweh's actions against Gog. As is typical of Ezekiel, he repeatedly reverts to previous statements and enlarges them. As a result, the text does not have the kind of linear progression and consecutiveness that modern Westerners may expect, but, as noted in chapter 38, that expectation is generally alien to ancient Near Eastern literature. In spite of what seems to us to be the chapter's fragmented form, Yahweh keeps hammering away at themes that are already very familiar to any reader of the book.

39:2 This verse has affinities with 38:4, 15, but lacks the crocodilian "I will put hooks in your jaws" in 38:4.

וְשֹׁבַבְתִּיךָ—For the identical Polel of שׁוּב (there spelled plene), see the first textual note on 38:4. The Polel infinitive occurs in 39:27 in a different sense. The meaning "mislead," found also in Is 47:10, seems preferable here to the common "turn you around" (from where?).

וְשִׁשֵּׁאתִיךָ—This verb, a first common singular perfect with second masculine singular suffix, is a hapax. There is no agreement on either its derivation or its meaning. It appears to be the Piel of שָׁשָׁא, but it would be exceptional for the first two consonants of a Hebrew verb to be identical. Therefore some propose that it is a Pilpel of a biliteral root שֵׁא, perhaps expanded to שָׁאָא or שׁוּא (see GKC, § 55 f). For its meaning, the context may be as reliable an indicator as any, so I have basically followed the LXX (καθοδηγήσω σε) with "I will show you the way." Compare the Vulgate, *seducam te*. KJV's "leave but the sixth part of thee" follows the medieval association of the word with the numeral שֵׁשׁ, "six," but I think that is universally abandoned today. Commonly, the word is related to an Ethiopic *sosawa* ("to proceed, walk along"),[1] but there are any number of other proposals and/or emendations.

39:3 The picture of the archers corresponds to reality, because, assuming that most of them would be right-handed, they would naturally hold their bows in their left hands and their arrows in the right.

39:4 The first half of the verse repeats vocabulary from 38:6, 9, 22.

לְעֵיט צִפּוֹר כָּל־כָּנָף—The noun עַיִט is relatively rare, used only five other times in the OT. The singular is usually collective. In its various contexts it seems to describe birds for whom carrion was the chief food, so it probably denotes various types of vultures and/or eagles (Hebrew does not always distinguish the two). Perhaps partly because of its infrequency, it is further defined by being in construct with צִפּוֹר, a generic term for "bird," another singular that often is collective. Thus, literally, "vultures of birds" probably means "scavenger birds." Probably to indicate how widespread their food supply will be, the construct chain continues with כָּל־כָּנָף, literally, "vultures of birds *of every wing*," that is, "scavenger birds *of every kind*."

In 29:5 Ezekiel had used the more common phrase עוֹף הַשָּׁמַיִם, "the birds of the air," to refer to all kinds that would feed on victims of God's judgment. Compare that phrase also in 31:6, 13; 32:4; 38:20.

וְחַיַּת הַשָּׂדֶה—Parallel to all kinds of scavenger birds is this generic phrase, literally, "the beasts of the field." The singular collective חַיָּה (in construct) here probably would refer primarily to hyenas and jackals, but possibly includes any other carnivore.

נְתַתִּיךָ לְאָכְלָה—"Giving" (the verb נָתַן) someone "for/as food" (the noun אָכְלָה) is a punishment previously found in 29:5 and 35:12 (cf. 15:4, 6).

39:7 וְלֹא־אַחֵל אֶת־שֵׁם־קָדְשִׁי עוֹד—Since God himself would not profane his name, the first common singular Hiphil imperfect of חָלַל (אַחֵל) must have a tolerative sense: "I will not *let* my holy name *be profaned* any more" (see BDB, s.v. חָלַל III, Hiphil, 1 a). Compare the Niphal infinitive of חָלַל in 20:9, where God acted so that his name would not be profaned. It is quite rare for a Hiphil verb to have a tolerative meaning (Waltke-O'Connor, § 27.5c, cites only Ps 89:43 [ET 89:42]). That nuance is more typically associated with Niphal verbs (Waltke-O'Connor, § 23.4f–g).

Hebrew characteristically employs a construct chain to express an adjectival relationship (Joüon, § 129 a and f (1)). Thus שֵׁם קָדְשִׁי (twice in 39:7), שֵׁם in construct

---

[1] So Cooke, *Ezekiel*, 423; Zimmerli, *Ezekiel*, 2:290; Allen, *Ezekiel*, 2:201.

with the noun קֹדֶשׁ (with first common singular suffix), literalistically, "name of my holiness," means "my holy name." This is confirmed by the later clause in 39:7 with the adjective קָדוֹשׁ, "holy," used as a substantive: אֲנִי יְהוָה קָדוֹשׁ בְּיִשְׂרָאֵל, "I am Yahweh, the Holy One in Israel."

39:8 הִנֵּה בָאָה וְנִהְיָתָה—The identical expression was in 21:12 (ET 21:7). The accent on the ultima of בָאָה shows that it is the feminine singular participle, not the third feminine singular perfect of בּוֹא. The Hebrew feminine can be used for an abstract idea, as here: "*it* is coming!" Likewise, the Niphal of הָיָה is feminine, and a prophetic perfect, and so it is translated, "it will surely take place."

39:9 וּבִעֲרוּ וְהִשִּׂיקוּ—These two verbs evidently form a hendiadys; the LXX telescopes them into one verb, καὶ καύσουσιν. Since a fire must be kindled *before* something is burned up, I have translated in the logical order: "set on fire and burn." Usually בָּעַר means "to burn up, consume," but its Piel can mean "kindle, light" a fire (see BDB, Piel, 1). In form, וְהִשִּׂיקוּ may be the Hiphil of נָשַׂק (so *HALOT*, which gives "to kindle fire"), with the assimilated נ marked by the *daghesh* in the *sin* (-שִּׂ-). The only other verbs in the OT from the same root are the Hiphil יַשִּׂיק in Is 44:15, paired with בָּעַר, as here, and the Niphal in Ps 78:21. Traditionally, however, these three verb forms are understood to be from שָׂלַק (so BDB, which gives "make a fire, burn"). If so, the middle ל assimilates; see GKC, § 66 e. It may be related to סָלַק, "go up, ascend," whose ל assimilates; that verb occurs in the OT only in Ps 139:8, but is common in Aramaic.

בְּנֶשֶׁק וּמָגֵן וְצִנָּה בְּקֶשֶׁת וּבְחִצִּים וּבְמַקֵּל יָד וּבְרֹמַח—Of the seven kinds of weapons burned, only the second and third (וּמָגֵן וְצִנָּה) are not preceded by the preposition בְּ, although prepositions are attested for them in the LXX.[2] Perhaps one of the two verbs (see the preceding textual note) preferred the use of the preposition, while the other did not; the Piel of בָּעַר usually takes an accusative object, but when the Qal transitively means "burn, consume," it often takes בְּ (see BDB, s.v. בָּעַר I, Qal, 3). Hebrew commonly uses a single preposition intended to cover two or more objects (doing "double duty"), so the preposition need not be repeated every time in such a list.

A question remains about the precise nature of מַקֵּל יָד, literally, "rod of a hand." The rendition "club" is plausible. However, after the initial generic collective נֶשֶׁק, "weapons," the weapons are grouped in natural pairs, and "club" is hardly a good mate for the following רֹמַח, a common word for "lance" or "spear." Hence, many interpret מַקֵּל יָד as "javelin," a much smaller weapon, usually thrown.

39:10 וְשָׁלְלוּ אֶת־שֹׁלְלֵיהֶם וּבָזְזוּ אֶת־בֹּזְזֵיהֶם—The cognate accusative constructions with the Qal perfects (with *waw* consecutive) taking the Qal participles as their objects is similar to the cognate accusative constructions of these same two verbs in 29:19; 38:12–13. See the first textual note on 38:12.

39:11 מְקוֹם־שָׁם קֶבֶר בְּיִשְׂרָאֵל—Literally, this is "a place there, a grave, in Israel." Ordinarily in idiomatic Hebrew one would expect the relative pronoun אֲשֶׁר, "a place *which* is a grave there in Israel" (cf. מָקוֹם אֲשֶׁר ... שָׁם in 6:13 and 46:20) or the in-

---

[2] To Allen, *Ezekiel*, 2:201, and other critics predictably this is a sign of a gloss.

finitive לִהְיוֹת, "a place there *to be* a grave in Israel" (cf. לִהְיוֹת בְּ in 44:7). Compare also בְּמָקוֹם אֲשֶׁר ... בָּאָרֶץ in 21:35 (ET 21:30). Some such connective is presupposed here even though קֶבֶר is asyndetic.

גֵּי הָעֹבְרִים—Here the feminine noun "valley" is written defectively as גֵּי (the א was quiescent or silent), but it is written plene in the last phrase of the verse. The participle with article (הָעֹבְרִים) serves as a relative clause: "valley of those who travel, pass by."

וְחֹסֶמֶת הִיא אֶת־הָעֹבְרִים—The verb חָסַם occurs elsewhere only in Deut 25:4, where the Qal means "to muzzle" an ox. The cognate noun מַחְסוֹם occurs only in Ps 39:2 (ET 39:1), where it refers metaphorically to a "muzzle" that would be placed on a person's mouth to avoid spoken sins. Here the Qal participle חֹסֶמֶת (feminine because its antecedent is גֵּי) must mean something like "obstruct, block" the travelers. Allen argues for "stop up the valley"[3] since the LXX and Syriac translated as if the object of the participle were the "valley" rather than the "travelers." The difference in meaning would be slight.

גֵּיא הֲמוֹן גּוֹג—Here "valley" is written plene: גֵּיא. This whole phrase could be transliterated as a proper place name, "Gey Hamon Gog," but it is translated according to its obvious meaning, "the Valley of Gog's Horde." Ezekiel has frequently used the noun הָמוֹן, "multitude, horde," for foreign armies (e.g., 31:18; 32:12, 16, 18, 20), as here and again in the place name in 39:15.

39:13 וְקָבְרוּ כָּל־עַם הָאָרֶץ—"All the people of the land" must be the subject of the verb "they will bury" (וְקָבְרוּ). Since 39:11–12 stated that Gog and his horde would be buried, they must be the implied object, which can be omitted when it is obvious. "Them" must be supplied in English, as it was already in the LXX (αὐτούς).

39:14 וְאַנְשֵׁי תָמִיד יַבְדִּילוּ עֹבְרִים בָּאָרֶץ מְקַבְּרִים—The phrase אַנְשֵׁי תָמִיד, literally, "men of perpetuity," must mean "men permanently employed, on constant duty, professionals," or the like. They are the object of the Hiphil verb יַבְדִּילוּ, "they will set apart." The two participles עֹבְרִים ... מְקַבְּרִים (literally, "passing through ... burying") are secondary predicates, forming circumstantial clauses that modify the "permanently employed men": "who will pass through the land and who ... will bury ..." The asyndetic relation of the participles leaves grammatically unclear whether all the appointed men are to carry out both activities or whether the appointed men are divided into two groups, each with its distinct job. The next verse, 39:15, makes clear that the appointed men are divided into two groups: one group is to "go through the land" and simply mark the bodies for the second group, consisting of "the buriers" who actually inter the remains.

אֶת־הָעֹבְרִים אֶת־הַנּוֹתָרִים עַל־פְּנֵי הָאָרֶץ—After the preceding participle מְקַבְּרִים, referring to the permanent buriers, אֶת־הָעֹבְרִים is obscure, and many expedients are suggested. If אֵת is the sign of the definite direct object, הָעֹבְרִים could be the object of מְקַבְּרִים, resulting in "burying the travelers." Then אֶת־הַנּוֹתָרִים (Niphal participle of יָתַר, "the remaining ones") is an appositional phrase modifying the "travelers," as

---

[3] Allen, *Ezekiel*, 2:201.

in ESV, "bury those travelers remaining." But "the travelers" (הָעֹבְרִים) in 39:11 were living Israelites (and 39:11 had seemed to say that the burial mound had blocked the way for those "travelers"). Or are the "travelers" here stragglers from Gog's horde who had escaped the earlier slaughter? That apparently is what NRSV means by "bury any invaders who remain." Block has a unique interpretation of הָעֹבְרִים as a sort of euphemism for the dead,[4] and one must concede that, as such, here that would make sense.

However, if we take אֵת as the preposition "with," then the permanently employed buriers might draft any fellow Israelite "travelers" (as in 39:11) who chance by to join them in their labor of burying the dead. I have adopted this alternative as possibly the least difficult of the various proposals, but out of no conviction. Then the following אֶת־הַנּוֹתָרִים עַל־פְּנֵי הָאָרֶץ refers to the dead (literally) "who remain on the face of the land" and who are buried by the permanent buriers and travelers together.

Cooke thinks that אֶת־הָעֹבְרִים is a gloss.[5] Allen suggests that it is a misplaced phrase meant to qualify "all the people of the land" in 39:13, but mistakenly linked with מְקַבְּרִים here rather than with וְקָבְרוּ there.[6] The omission of אֶת־הָעֹבְרִים in the Syriac and the original hand of the LXX lends plausibility to some text-critical explanation, although the MT clearly is the *lectio difficilior.*

39:16 וְגַם שֶׁם־עִיר הֲמוֹנָה—The Hebrew nominal (verbless) sentence could be cast in translation either in the present or future tense. The future gives the detail an eschatological cast in keeping with the entire context: "also the name of a city will be Its Horde." The form הֲמוֹנָה occurs in the OT only here. It may be a feminine proper name, "Hamonah," or a feminine noun corresponding to the masculine הָמוֹן, "horde." More likely it is הָמוֹן with a third feminine singular suffix written without *mappiq,* as attested elsewhere, hence "Its Horde," although it is not clear what the referent of the suffix would be. Perhaps it is an example of a "vague suffix" (Joüon, § 146 j (2)). In 39:11 הֲמוֹנֹה, "his horde," had an archaic form of the third masculine singular suffix, also spelled with final ה. For both unusual suffix forms, see GKC, § 91 e. The LXX translates/interprets הֲמוֹנָה as πολυάνδριον, "full of men," a term for a "common/mass grave" also used in LXX Jer 2:23 and 19:2, 6, verses where the Hebrew has "valley" or the longer "Valley of the Son of Hinnom," that is, Gehenna.[7] Similarly, the LXX had translated גֵּי in Ezek 39:11a and הָמוֹן in 39:11b, 15 as πολυάνδριον.

Predictably, critics imagine that this clause was a gloss added to the margin, which later crept into the text,[8] although some more cautiously think of scribal misunderstandings.[9] However, all the ancient versions attest to its presence.

---

4   Block, *Ezekiel,* 2:471.

5   Cooke, *Ezekiel,* 424.

6   Allen, *Ezekiel,* 2:201.

7   See the textual notes and commentary on 16:21 and 20:31, where Yahweh condemned Israel for child sacrifice by fire, which likely would have been at Gehenna.

8   E.g., Zimmerli, *Ezekiel,* 2:293; Allen, *Ezekiel,* 2:202.

9   E.g., Cooke, *Ezekiel,* 424.

39:17 The citation formula, "thus says the Lord Yahweh," comes unusually early in this verse. If the ordinary pattern in Ezekiel were followed, it would not come until after "the wild animals," immediately before the quote of Yahweh's words to them. The Syriac "corrects" the MT by placing it there, though no change in meaning is involved. However, evidently Ezekiel's penchant for variation triumphs over the abruptness of placing the formula before the command to speak to the fauna.

עַל־זִבְחִי אֲשֶׁר אֲנִי זֹבֵחַ לָכֶם—The noun זֶבַח can be a generic term for any kind of "sacrifice." It can be more specifically used for the "communion offering" (traditionally, "peace offering") in the phrase זֶבַח שְׁלָמִים,[a] the only sacrifice in which part of the offering was returned to the worshipers for a meal to be eaten in the tabernacle/temple precincts.[10] KJV and NIV translate with simple "sacrifice," but since most readers will not immediately associate a sacrifice with a meal, NKJV's "sacrificial meal" or the "sacrificial feast" of RSV and NRSV is preferable. I have adopted the first of those alternatives.

(a) E.g., Lev 3:1, 3, 6, 9; 7:15, 18; 19:5; 22:21; 23:19

Hebrew uses the cognate construction with the verb זָבַח (here participle: זֹבֵחַ) and the noun זֶבַח again in 39:19. "My sacrifice, which I am sacrificing" would be possible in English, but a slight paraphrase for the verb as "prepare" is more idiomatic.

39:20 סוּס וָרֶכֶב—Ezekiel used the collectives "horse and chariot(ry)" in 26:7 (cf. 38:15). However, "chariot(ry)" is an unlikely part of even so surreal a banquet as this one. For רֶכֶב KJV retains "chariots." But the major ancient versions render, "horseman, rider, charioteer," as do most modern English translations, which may require repointing to רֹכֵב. But since the same combination occurred in 26:7, it should not be abandoned lightly. In 2 Sam 8:4 David hamstrung most of the רֶכֶב, suggesting that there it means "chargers, chariot horses," which is also appropriate here, essentially a synonym of סוּס.

39:25 אָשִׁיב אֶת־שְׁבִית יַעֲקֹב—This is essentially the same idiom used in 16:53 and 29:14. Those verses used the Qal of שׁוּב in a transitive sense, and this verse uses the Hiphil, אָשִׁיב, which must have the same transitive meaning, "I will return/restore." The equivalence of these Qal and Hiphil forms is supported by 29:14, which uses both (וְשַׁבְתִּי ... וַהֲשִׁבֹתִי).

The Qere form of the noun is שְׁבוּת, while the Kethib is שְׁבִית. The same Kethib-Qere variation was in 16:53 (29:14 has only the reading שְׁבוּת), but in some other OT passages they are the reverse. The Kethib שְׁבִית suggests that the noun is derived from שָׁבָה, "to carry into exile." The Qere שְׁבוּת would seem to be derived from שׁוּב, "return." In this context, the Kethib's apparent primary force would seem preferable, but in any event, the verb and noun are a fixed expression, regardless of etymology. See also the first textual note on 16:53. For the theology of the phrase in 29:14, see "Introduction to Ezekiel 29–32: Oracles against Egypt."

KJV's "bring again the captivity of Jacob" could be misunderstood as an announcement of another judgment. NKJV's "bring back the captives of Jacob" hap-

---

[10] One may see Kleinig, *Leviticus*, 92–96, commenting on Lev 3:1–17. While Kleinig uses the traditional term "peace offering," he relates it to Holy Communion, in which the sacrificed body and blood of Christ is furnished as a meal for the worshiper.

pens to fit this context better, but as such, it is an application rather than a translation of a phrase that has broader meaning. NIV paraphrases slightly into "bring Jacob back from captivity." RSV, NRSV, and many others use "restore the fortunes," but that sounds too much like the pagan "Lady Luck" to me. I have resorted to my own paraphrase, "bring about the restoration of," as also in 16:53 and 29:14.

39:26 וְנָשׁוּ אֶת־כְּלִמָּתָם—The Qal perfect verb is a defective spelling for וְנָשְׂאוּ, "they will bear," and illustrates the occasional writing of third-*aleph* verbs as though they were of the third-*he* type. Ezekiel often uses this idiom with נָשָׂא and the noun כְּלִמָּה,

(b) Ezek 16:52, 54; 32:24–25, 30; 34:29; 36:6, 7; 39:26; 44:13; cf. 36:15

"shame, disgrace," as its object.[b] However, except for KJV and NKJV, most English versions translate as if the verb were וְנָשׁוּ, "they will forget," apparently because of the context of salvation here. But Zimmerli defends the MT for a host of cogent reasons: the ancient versions all follow the MT; Ezekiel does not use נָשָׁה, "forget," elsewhere, and its Qal is rare (only in Jer 23:39; Lam 3:17); the idiom here is common in Ezekiel, and in 16:54, as here, it also follows the idiom שׁוּב שְׁבוּת (16:53).[11]

וְאֶת־כָּל־מַעֲלָם אֲשֶׁר מָעֲלוּ־בִי—For the cognate accusative construction with the verb מָעַל and the noun מַעַל, see the first textual note on 14:13.

39:27 בְּשׁוֹבְבִי—This Polel of שׁוּב (infinitive construct with בְּ and first common singular suffix), followed by מִן, means "bring back" from (BDB, Polel, 1) so as to regather, restore. Ezekiel used another Polel form of שׁוּב in 38:4 and 39:2, where it had a different meaning.

לְעֵינֵי הַגּוֹיִם רַבִּים:—Clearly this means "to the eyes of/in the sight of many nations," as in 38:23. However, in 38:23 both terms in גּוֹיִם רַבִּים were anarthrous, and here the noun is definite (הַגּוֹיִם), while its adjective modifier (רַבִּים) lacks the article. There are other examples of that inconsistency of determination, but they are rare. Since רַבִּים is not represented in the LXX, critics usually dismiss it as a gloss that was not fully assimilated into the syntax.[12] Nothing major is at issue, and the MT may be defended.

39:28 וְכִנַּסְתִּים עַל־אַדְמָתָם—The Piel of כָּנַס, "to gather," was used once before in Ezekiel, in 22:21. It replaces the usual verb in Ezekiel for Yahweh gathering his people, קָבַץ (e.g., 11:17; 20:34, 41; 34:13; 36:24). כָּנַס becomes common in Rabbinic Hebrew and again reflects Ezekiel's position at a major transitional point in Israel's history and language—plus ultimately also its religion. A few centuries later, in the intertestamental period, much of ethnic Israel will leave behind the OT faith and form the various branches of Judaism, a different religion altogether.

וְלֹא־אוֹתִיר—The Hiphil of יָתַר here in the promise "I will not leave behind" probably has overtones of God's "remnant" promises. Compare the negated Hiphil with "remnant" in Jer 44:7. The Hiphil was used for leaving survivors of judgment in Ezek 6:8; 12:16, as also in Is 1:9, and the Niphal in Ezek 14:22.

39:29 אֲשֶׁר שָׁפַכְתִּי אֶת־רוּחִי—There is some debate whether אֲשֶׁר should be taken temporally, "*after/when* I have poured out my Spirit," as Zimmerli argues,[13] followed

---

[11] Zimmerli, *Ezekiel*, 2:295.

[12] E.g., Zimmerli, *Ezekiel*, 2:295; Cooke, *Ezekiel*, 424.

[13] Zimmerli, *Ezekiel*, 2:295.

by RSV and NRSV, or causally, "for/because," as the LXX and Vulgate took it, followed by other English translations and defended by Cooke.[14] I have followed the latter option. I have cast the entire clause in the future, in keeping with the context, and so have rendered the Qal perfect verb שָׁפַכְתִּי as a future perfect, "because I will have poured out my Spirit."[15]

Commentary

Yahweh Will Disarm Gog and His Troops (39:1–6)

39:1–2 With only slight and inconsequential variation, these verses repeat 38:1–3. Yahweh is the real subject of the action for reasons already stated and soon to be repeated and expanded upon.

39:3–6 These verses expand on what was asserted in 38:1–9. There the invaders were described as horsemen, and here, also as archers. Since Scythians were among the invaders,[16] this is not surprising because also extrabiblical sources (e.g., Xenophon[17]) attest to Scythian expertise with bow and arrow. But somehow Yahweh will disarm them so they are incapable of fighting (cf. Pss 37:15; 46:10 [ET 46:9]). Second, their defeat will be so swift and widespread that they will not even be accorded burial; their corpses will be left in the field to be devoured by scavengers of any sort. Finally, Yahweh declares, "I will also send fire" upon them (39:6). The idiom שִׁלַּח אֵשׁ occurs only here in Ezekiel, but is repeated in Amos' Gentile oracles, as Yahweh makes the same declaration (Amos 1:4, 7, 10, 12; 2:2), which he also makes against Judah in Amos 2:5 and against Israel in Hos 8:14. "Fire" to destroy walls, chariotry—anything of use or value to the enemy—is always a major part of the predations of war, and as mentioned in 38:22 already, has overtones of destruction inflicted directly by God. Rev 20:9 alludes to this: when "fire came down from heaven and consumed them."[c]

(c) See also Gen 19:24; Ex 9:23; 2 Ki 1:10–14; Job 1:16; Lk 9:54

Ezek 39:6 and its "fire" is targeted not only for Gog, but also to the outer reaches of his imperium. It incinerates not only "Magog," which, according to 38:2, was Gog's place of origin,[18] but also the "coastlands," that is, the Mediterranean islands, which in 38:13 had been represented by Tarshish. The proximity of Tarshish to Javan (Ionia; Greece) in the trade list of 27:12–13 (cf. Gen 10:4, where Tarshish is among the sons of Javan) indicates what a wide area the prophet has in mind. In 38:13 it might have seemed that these distant groups were only envious spectators, but here it is plain that they are fully involved in the invasion of Israel. That they lived "in security" (39:6), the same phrase used

---

[14] Cooke, *Ezekiel*, 424.

[15] Allen, *Ezekiel*, 2:199, somewhat similarly suggests "once I have …"

[16] See the third textual note on 38:2 and commentary on 38:2–3.

[17] Xenophon, *Anabasis*, 3.3.10.

[18] However, in Rev 20:8, "Magog," together with "Gog," appears to be a personal name for a leader of the invading enemies. See "Introduction to Ezekiel 38–39: The Final Battle and the Defeat of Gog."

earlier of God's provision for Israel (לְבֶטַח, 38:8, 11, 14; in fulfillment of the Christological promise in 34:25, 27, 28), is ironic. Those who attack Israel with such levity must learn who alone provides real security: "the Holy One in Israel" (39:7).

Yahweh Will Reveal His Holy Name as the Weapons Are Burned (39:7–10)

39:7   The verse functions as a sort of commentary on the recognition formula at the end of 39:6, "then they will know that I am Yahweh."[19] It emphasizes that that recognition will not simply be a coincidental result of the defeat of Gog, but that it has been Yahweh's purpose all along. "Knowing" that he is Yahweh means a recognition or confession of his very being or character: "I am Yahweh, the Holy One in Israel." His dynamic attribute of holiness is emphasized by the triple use of the root קדשׁ, "holy," in the verse. First, in 39:7a, Yahweh declares, "I will make my holy name known among my people Israel"; the covenant people will be the first to make confession of him. Second, 39:7b emphasizes its permanence: "I will not let my holy name be profaned any more." Third, in 39:7c, other nations will be brought to confess Yahweh's holiness: "the nations will know that I am Yahweh, the Holy One in Israel."

It is not repeated here, but in the background stands the earlier disastrous history of Israel, which had almost habitually profaned Yahweh's holy name (cf. 20:9, 14, 22, 39; 36:20–23). Yahweh had specifically spoken of Israel profaning "my holy name" in 20:39 and 36:20–22. Positively, he will again refer to "my holy name" in 39:25 and 43:7–8. By Yahweh's defeat of the universal conspiracy of evil, the Gog debacle will signal the final triumph of God's long struggle to keep his name holy in Israel. What is more, this will reveal his holy name also among the nations, who will know him by a new name, "the Holy One in Israel." This phrase is unique in the OT, but one cannot help but compare it to Isaiah's frequent epithet for Yahweh, "the Holy One *of* Israel,"[20] and the recognition by the demons and by Jesus' disciples that he is "the Holy One of God" (ὁ ἅγιος τοῦ θεοῦ, Mk 1:24; Lk 4:34; Jn 6:69). Ezekiel may well be prophesying the eschatological achievement of the meaning of Isaiah's earlier label, which will be fulfilled when Christ has defeated all the human and demonic powers of evil, and his redeemed people are radiant with the holiness of God (Rev 21:1–11). Ezekiel the priest (Ezek 1:3), in his characteristic liturgical way, here refers to the Holy One as located "in Israel," as God had been at the temple and will be again in the eschatological vision (43:1–12; cf. Rev 21:22–26). Similar is the locative affirmation at the end of the book about the new Jerusalem: "Yahweh is there" (Ezek 48:35; cf. Rev 21:2–3).

---

[19]   For this formula, see page 9 in the introduction and the commentary on 6:7.

[20]   Isaiah uses this phrase twenty-five times. See, for example, Is 1:4; 5:19, 24; 43:3, 14; 49:7; 60:9, 14. Compare also the famous Trisagion, Is 6:3.

The NT affirms that already at the first advent of Christ, the heathen Gentiles together with unbelieving Israelites conspired to attack God's Anointed, but were defeated by his atoning death and victorious resurrection (see, e.g., Acts 4:26–30). During the church age, the proclamation of the Gospel reveals the holy name of Jesus, to the salvation of all who believe. The church militant uses no literal weapons, but relies on God's Word and Sacraments (cf. Eph 6:10–20). Thus Jesus is the Holy One who now is in his Israel, the church, through his means of grace. Yet we await the final defeat of all evil at Christ's second coming and the consummation, when all spiritual warfare will have ceased, and the triune God shall dwell in the midst of his people in a far more intimate way (Rev 21:3).

39:8 The double assertion "It is coming! It will surely take place" occurred already in 21:12 (ET 21:7), but there it referred to the impending destruction of Jerusalem (in summer 586 B.C.). Here it asserts the inevitability of the coming salvation even more strongly because of the absence of the necessity of any intervening judgment on Israel. But there will be judgment—on Gog—and here it is finally asserted that the judgment on Gog is the day of which Yahweh has previously spoken. Commentators debate whether the reference is to Ezekiel's own prophecy of Gog's defeat or to a continuation of 38:17, where Ezekiel had spoken of the prophecies of his predecessors. But there is surely no reason to decide between the two; it is a case of "both … and." The key word הַיּוֹם, "the day," often refers to some decisive intervention by Yahweh, as classically in "the day of Midian" (Is 9:3 [ET 9:4]). In the context here, it probably also evokes the eschatological "Day of Yahweh."[21]

39:9 The Israelites suddenly emerge and burn the weapons of the defeated troops. Apparently they simply were passive spectators until God annihilated Gog and his horde (cf. 2 Kings 7 and 19), perhaps with literal fire from heaven (see the commentary on Ezek 39:6), or perhaps the attacking armies killed each other off in a kind of civil war (cf. Judg 7:22). The total of *seven* weapons (including the general term נֶשֶׁק, "weapon, weaponry," used in Ezekiel only in 39:9–10) is complemented by the "seven years" it takes to complete the task of burning them as fuel. Obviously, we have symbolism here, expressing the completeness of the divine judgment. This also hints at the eschatological theme of the elimination of armaments from the earth, as in Is 9:3 (ET 9:4) and Ps 46:10 (cf. Is 2:4 ‖ Micah 4:3).

39:10 The eschatological theme of the great reversal, the turning of the tables, is again implied (see further the commentary on 39:25), but in terms of the normal aftermath of wars: "they will despoil those who had despoiled them and plunder those who had plundered them." This could be a sort of "second exodus" theme since Israel plundered the Egyptians in the first exodus (Ex 3:22; 11:2–3; 12:36). Again, the NT applies this already to the first advent of Christ,

---

[21] See the third and fourth textual notes on 7:7 and the commentary on 30:2 for "day (of Yahweh, etc.)" terminology and theology.

the "stronger man" who has despoiled the devil (Lk 11:22; cf. Eph 4:8; 1 Jn 3:8) by freeing us from his tyranny, though again, the final vanquishing of all the powers of evil will not come until the second coming of Christ, and "death is swallowed up in victory" (1 Cor 15:54, quoting Is 25:8).

The Burial of Gog's Horde (39:11–16)

39:11 There is great debate—and no consensus—on the location for the mass burial site. Much depends on how one translates or interprets at least three words (see the textual notes), and even after agreement on those points, no clearly identifiable site emerges. One key word, repeated in the verse, is הָעֹבְרִים, the participle of עָבַר, meaning "those who pass by, the travelers," or the like. No other OT passage refers to a valley by that name, but it is similar to הָעֲבָרִים, "Abarim." The OT mentions two sites by that name, one apparently east of the Sea of Galilee (Jer 22:20) and the other in the region around Mount Nebo (e.g., Num 27:12; 33:47–48), but both of these sites are east of the Jordan and thus no longer "in Israel," as required by Ezek 39:11, and in 47:18 Ezekiel considers the Jordan to be the eastern boundary of Israel. Block would translate הָעֹבְרִים as "those who have passed on," that is, have died, and Block takes the word to be a deflation of Gog's grandiose self-conception by saying he and his horde will descend to Sheol just as surely as Egypt in chapter 32 and other great powers.[22] But that seems to me to introduce a tangential idea into the context.

The phrase קִדְמַת הַיָּם must mean that the travelers are going eastward "toward the [Dead] Sea." It does not mean that these Israelites are traveling "east of the [Dead] Sea," because that would again be outside of Ezekiel's "Israel." קִדְמָה occurs elsewhere in the OT only in Gen 2:14 and 4:16, where it means "facing east" and thus located to the west, and in 1 Sam 13:5, where it is ambiguous. Similarly, by etymology, our word "*orient*ation" means "face the East," that is, the "Orient." The Dead Sea is referred to as הַיָּם הַקַּדְמוֹנִי, "the Eastern Sea," in 47:18. So "the Sea" (הַיָּם) here must likewise mean the Dead Sea. (If the phrase meant "east of the [Mediterranean] Sea," it would be tautological since all of Israel lies east of the Mediterranean).

While no certainty on the location is possible, if Ezekiel is thinking in terms of pre-eschatological topography, the north side of the Dead Sea would seem most plausible, both because it, as the broadest part of the valley, would be (and still is!) a principal crossing point, and because it would be spacious enough for all the bodies.

Finally, a suggestion by Zimmerli merits consideration. The first two words of the construct chain גֵּיא הֲמוֹן גּוֹג, literally, "*the Valley of the Horde* of Gog," are intended by loose assonance to recall גֵּיא הִנֹּם, "the Valley of Hinnom,"[23] that is, Gehenna, the site of child sacrifice and burial site of criminals and an-

---

[22] Block, *Ezekiel*, 2:469.

[23] Zimmerli, *Ezekiel*, 2:317.

imals (e.g., Jer 7:31), to remind the reader of that locus of all sorts of abominations. The burial of Gog there thus represents the complete end of all such evils.[24]

39:12 In addition to the "seven years" spent burning the enemy's armaments (39:9), it will take "seven months" to bury all the dead. Unburied bodies would defile the land (cf. Num 19:11–12), so they must be interred "to cleanse the land" (Ezek 39:12). When Ezekiel speaks of the Holy Land in this way, it is not touristy, market-oriented language, but the same literal, priestly picture of the new heavens and new earth (Isaiah 11 and 65; Revelation 21–22) that will pervade all of Ezekiel 40–48.

39:13 Gog's fall is regarded as complete after all the people of God have joined in and completed the burial. That will be the day, says Yahweh, "when I display my glory." The Niphal of כָּבֵד could be translated as a passive, "be glorified," but as in 28:22 (its only other occurrence in Ezekiel), a reflexive meaning, synonymous with a Hithpael form, is preferable: Yahweh is not merely a recipient of glory, but effects his own glorification by the annihilating victory, which he himself accomplishes for the sake of his people. Yahweh was the subject of the same verb when he described how he would achieve glory through his exodus triumph (Ex 14:4, 17–18; see also Lev 10:3; Is 26:15; Hag 1:8). The NT fulfillment in Christ is a theme in the Gospel of John.[d]

Israel, however, does not receive "glory," but a שֵׁם, literally, only a "name," that is, "honor" (as I have translated it), fame, and a good reputation by God's grace. That is, the victory over and destruction of Gog remain entirely Yahweh's work; Israel's job is limited to clearing up the battlefield. But by God's grace, his people receive the salvation he alone has accomplished.

39:14 Certain details are unclear (see the textual notes), but the general gist is clear. After the heptad of months of mass burials is finished (39:12), "permanently employed men" will be appointed to scour the entire land again for any corpses that may have escaped earlier attention. No effort is spared to insure the total cleansing of the land; no unclean thing shall remain. This priestly concern is reflected in Rev 21:27, where "no unclean thing" (including the unbelievers listed in the verse) shall ever enter the new Jerusalem, the eternal habitation of all God's redeemed in Christ.

39:15 The verse clarifies and adds details to the preceding verse. It makes plain that the men appointed in the previous verse are further divided into two distinct groups. One consists of "those who go through the land" and search intensively for any unburied bones, then erect a "marker" beside them. צִיּוּן is used in Jer 31:21 of a "road sign," but in 2 Ki 23:17 it denotes a "grave marker,"

(d) E.g., Jn 1:14; 2:11; 8:54; 12:16, 23, 28; 13:31–32; 16:14; 17:1–5; cf. Rom 15:6, 9; Rev 15:4

---

[24] See the textual notes and commentary on 16:21 and 20:31, where Yahweh condemned Israel for child sacrifice by fire, which likely would have been at Gehenna in idolatrous worship of Molech. Modern equivalents of that OT abomination include the abortion of unborn children and infanticide, as children are sacrificed on the modern "altar" of the parents' freedom to choose to murder their own children for the sake of their own convenience and ease of life.

similar to its use here. We probably must not think of any permanent grave-stone, but of a cairn or a single upright object that would not be overlooked. The second group, "the buriers," then will inter the remains.

39:16 Yet a further detail is that "the name of a city will be Its Horde [*Hamonah*]." Block recalls earlier uses of הָמוֹן, "horde," in Ezekiel. In 5:7 and 7:12–14 it had referred to Israel in verses that summarized her riotous and re-bellious behavior, which was not all that different from its application to other nations in the Gentile oracles, especially the final oracle against Egypt in chapter 32. Then, by associating the statement here about the city's name with the somewhat similar naming of the eschatological city at the conclusion of the book, "Yahweh is there" (48:35), Block suggests that this one too intimates a "new Jerusalem":

> In the present context *Hamonah*'s primary function is to memorialize the demise of Israel's last and greatest enemy, but by association it also memori-alizes the transformation of the city, and with it the nation. … Once the city (and the entire land) has been purged of every vestige of defilement, the stage is set for Yahweh to return (43:1–7) and to replace the retrospective name with a new, forward-looking (*mîyyôm* [48:35]) one. Hamonah is gone, Yah-weh is there![25]

Top that if you can! The thought is congenial and agrees with the general gist of the last chapters of the book.

"And so they will cleanse the land" (39:16) is plainly the conclusion of the unit (39:11–16) and reiterates the purpose, "in order to cleanse it," from 39:14.

God Will Prepare a Sacrificial Meal (39:17–20)

39:17 The citation formula, "thus says the Lord Yahweh,"[26] begins a new unit. Following pictures of the burning of weapons (39:7–10) and burial of the dead (39:11–16), this verse begins an imaginative account of the third and last (39:17–20) of the three tableaux Ezekiel presents to describe the total de-struction of Gog's forces. This one describes a huge banquet literally called a "sacrifice" (see the second textual note on 39:17), where the menu is the fallen unbelievers and their horses, and the guests are the birds and wild animals. Logic might inquire how this is possible after the previous section had re-counted the meticulous care taken that no corpses remain unburied. But it is really one of the clearest indications among many that literal, chronological considerations were not among Ezekiel's priorities. Block labels these verses a "literary cartoon" and observes that, as we have gone along, "the scenes have become increasingly bizarre, climaxing here in a scene more fantastic than all."[27] This becomes even clearer if one reflects on the scene in the light of Is-

---

[25] Block, *Ezekiel*, 2:472.

[26] For this formula, see pages 8–9 in the introduction and the fourth textual note and the com-mentary on 2:4.

[27] Block, *Ezekiel*, 2:473.

raelite ceremonial law in the Torah of Moses. Here Yahweh hosts unclean creatures and even serves them blood, in contrast to the dietary laws, which specified that blood was to be drained off completely before any meat was eaten
(e.g., Lev 7:26–27; 17:10–14; 19:26). All this indicates that Ezekiel 38–39 does
not depict a literal series of events, but is a figurative description of the continuing war of unbelievers against the church, which will climax in the most
intense persecution before the second coming of Jesus Christ.[28]

The picture of Yahweh's victory celebrated as a sacrificial feast (זֶבַח) is not
at all unique to Ezekiel, but he develops it to an extreme degree, as he typically
does with many previous OT motifs. Perhaps the earliest appearance of the
theme of a sacrificial feast comes in Isaiah in the eighth century B.C. Is 34:5–8
(with זֶבַח in Is 34:6), celebrates Yahweh's victory over Edom. Jer 46:10 mentions such a זֶבַח after the defeat of Pharaoh Neco by Nebuchadnezzar at Carchemish (Jer 46:2). Another possible parallel appears in Zeph 1:7–8, but there
the "sacrifice" (זֶבַח) is in a judgment oracle against Judah.

All these prophetic applications suggest that there was an eschatological
component in all of Israel's sacrificial rituals, even though the ritual texts in
Leviticus articulate little explicit eschatology. But typologically, via Christ, the
OT sacrifices—and especially the "peace" or "communion" sacrifice, which
furnished a meal for the worshiper[29]—relate to the celebration of the Eucharist,
a feast in which our crucified and risen Lord furnishes us his body and blood,
given and shed for the forgiveness of our sins, in a way that both proclaims his
past death and anticipates his future return (1 Cor 11:23–26).[30] Even the common table prayer "Come, Lord Jesus, be our Guest, and let thy gifts to us be
blessed" alludes to the continuing prayer of the church, *Marana tha*, "Come,
Lord (Jesus)" (1 Cor 16:22; Rev 22:20).

Because alimentation of the deity played such a prominent role in the pagan rituals of Israel's neighbors, the OT usually does not highlight the picture
of Yahweh as the host of Israel's regular sacrifices, but this and other texts make
plain that the picture was not absent. In paganism, the god was depicted as being fed, but mortals were not invited to participate. In contrast, the Bible is not
at all adverse to portraying Yahweh as hosting banquets for earthly guests. One
had climaxed the sealing of the Sinaitic covenant (Ex 24:9–11), and the motif
surely underlies much of the imagery pervading Psalm 23, whose "you prepare
a table before me" has eucharistic implications. In Is 25:6–9, the feast is clearly
described in eschatological terms: it is not a slaughter of enemies, but a banquet of rich food and aged wine, furnished by Yahweh himself in celebration

---

[28] See further "Introduction to Ezekiel 38–39: The Final Battle and the Defeat of Gog."

[29] Kleinig, *Leviticus*, 92–96, commenting on Lev 3:1–17, relates this sacrifice to Holy Communion, in which the sacrificed body and blood of Christ is furnished as a meal for the worshiper.

[30] For a fuller explication, one may see Lockwood, *1 Corinthians*, 386–95.

of the day when he will "swallow up death forever" and "wipe away tears from all faces," to be fulfilled upon the return of Jesus Christ (the wedding feast of the Lamb in Revelation 19; see also Rev 21:4).

Here in Ezek 39:17, Yahweh calls the meal זִבְחִי, "*my* sacrificial meal," and in 39:20 he refers to the spread as שֻׁלְחָנִי, "*my* table." Already in 39:4, Yahweh had announced that he would give Gog as food to wild creatures, but here he sends his prophet officially to invite them to come and enjoy the feast he has personally prepared for them (39:17, 19).

But here, Ezekiel, a priest (1:3), grossly caricatures any ordinary זֶבַח, "sacrifice." Instead of a human worshiper slaughtering animals in the presence of Yahweh for expiatory and eucharistic purposes, here Yahweh slaughters people for the sake of animals, who are invited to come from all over the world to "the mountains of Israel" to join him in his gigantic victory celebration (39:17).

The final clause of 39:17, which will be described further in the next verse, gives the menu for the banquet, בָּשָׂר, "meat," and דָּם, "blood," a common biblical merism for the entire body or carcass. When humanity is contrasted with divinity, "flesh" is an appropriate translation of בָּשָׂר (e.g., in Gen 6:3; Is 40:6), but when it is simply a matter of food to be eaten, "meat" is more natural.

39:18 Ezekiel describes the famous warriors and aristocracy of Gog in metaphors derived from the fare that might normally be found at a sacrificial meal. אֵילִים, "rams," and עַתּוּדִים, "goats," were already used metaphorically for abusive leaders in Israel in 34:17. The Hebrew itself does not state that the animals listed are descriptive comparisons of the slain people, but this is implied. Following NIV, I have added, "*as if they were* rams and lambs …"

The final phrase, describing them all as "fatlings of Bashan" (מְרִיאֵי בָשָׁן) is transitional to the next verse. That exact phrase appears only here in the OT, but מְרִיא, "fatling," is common enough and is sometimes used specifically for desirable sacrificial animals (e.g., 2 Sam 6:13; Is 1:11; Amos 5:22). Bashan, fairly equivalent to the modern Golan Heights, east of the Sea of Galilee and north of the Yarmuk River, was famous for its fertility and suitability for agriculture and grazing cattle, and hence it has spawned innumerable wars between Israel and Syria for control of the territory. After the defeat of Og (Num 21:33–35), Moses assigned the territory to the half-tribe of Manasseh (Deut 3:13). It had been annexed by Assyria about a century and a half before Ezekiel's day (early sixth century B.C.).

39:19 The banquet loses all decorum as Yahweh encourages unrestrained gluttony. Until the modern era, when our high-fat diets have made cholesterol a worry, fat was a desirable part of a meal, and even Yahweh's eschatological banquet celebrating the death of death features "fat things full of marrow" (Is 25:6). In Israel's sacrifices, the internal fat and suet around the vital organs was burned on the altar (e.g., Lev 3:3–5), not eaten, but a well-fattened animal would still provide an ample quantity of other fat that could be eaten.

Drunkenness was an entirely different matter, of course, and is universally condemned in the Scriptures.

39:20 This grotesque scene closes with a reminder of the referent of the metaphor: all those involved in the battle against God's people are slain (cf. Is 66:24), not excluding their horses.

Yahweh Will Restore and Pour Out His Holy Spirit on His People (39:21–29)

39:21 The remainder of the chapter is not so much an appendix to chapters 38–39 as a summary of their total import, although Gog and his troops disappear from the picture from here on. Ezek 39:21–29 may be subdivided in many ways, although, contrary to some critics, the overall unity of these verses is not hard to defend. A weak division into 39:21–24 and 39:25–29 can be supported by noticing that לָכֵן, "therefore,"[31] begins 39:25, and that both 39:23–24 and 39:29 refer to Yahweh "hiding his face" (a phrase otherwise absent from the book). Block convincingly observes a chiastic construction of both halves: each half both begins and ends with divine action, and in between describes human responses.[32] Ezek 39:21–24 is mostly retrospective, reviewing the results of God's judgmental activity on Israel, while 39:25–29 summarizes the blessings promised as a result of his saving activity.

Both of those perspectives are present in the transitional 39:21. The immediate declaration, "Thus I will establish my glory among the Gentiles," indicates that the primary purpose of the Gog oracle (like most of Ezekiel's oracles) is revelatory. The Hebrew phrase (נָתַן כָּבוֹד בְּ) is not a common Ezekelian formulation, and the verb נָתַן is multivalent enough that it is hard to settle on any one adequate English equivalent. Taking its force as "establish, put in place," Ezekiel seems to express a semi-objective and personal aspect of Yahweh's "Glory" (כָּבוֹד), that is, the same sort of "incarnational" and "Christological"[33] vision as he had witnessed when the "Glory" first appeared to him in chapter 1; when he saw the "Glory" forsake the temple in 10:4, 18–19 and 11:22–23; and which he will observe again when the "Glory" returns to the eschatological temple in 43:1–5. That may also be evidenced in Ezekiel's verb in the next clause, "all the nations will *see* [רָאָה] my justice" (39:21), instead of the usual יָדַע, "to know" (found in the modified recognition formula in 39:23), although its immediate object is מִשְׁפָּט, "justice," not the כָּבוֹד, "Glory." And here the revelation is more to the nations than to Israel.

Ezekiel does not pursue that line of thought, however—and, of course, it would be hard to do until the "Glory" became incarnate in our Lord Jesus (Jn

---

[31] For its importance, see the first textual note on 5:7.

[32] Block, *Ezekiel*, 2:479–80.

[33] For the divine "Glory" understood Christologically, see pages 1, 11, and 13 in the introduction, as well as the textual notes and commentary on 1:26–28.

(e) Cf. also
Lk 2:32;
24:26; Jn
11:40; 12:41;
17:5, 24

1:14).[e] In the OT era generally, the "Glory" was largely tied to the temple, although Ezekiel 1 and 10–11 prepare for its greater mobility in the person of Jesus Christ, the new temple (e.g., Jn 2:19–22; cf. Jn 4:20–24). But with the ascension of Christ and the gift of the Spirit on Pentecost, the church's missionary outreach began to be extended in earnest to all nations, revealing the glory of God in the one Savior, Jesus Christ (e.g., 1 Cor 2:7–8; 2 Cor 3:7–18; 4:4–6; Col 1:27).

Through Ezekiel, what Yahweh emphasizes is that "my Glory" has been manifested to the Gentiles by "my justice," rendering מִשְׁפָּט (39:21), another notoriously elusive word for translators. "Judgment, punishment" upon the unbelieving enemies of God's people is surely involved. In 5:8 Yahweh used עָשָׂה מִשְׁפָּטִים to say that he would "perform judgments" on unfaithful Israel, and he used עָשָׂה with a plural of שֶׁפֶט for (literally) "performing judgments" against heathen nations in 25:11 and 30:14, 19. In 38:22, speaking of Gog, Yahweh used the Niphal of שָׁפַט to say he would "enter into judgment with" or "punish" him. The point here is that the attacking nations' cowardly attempt to take advantage of God's vulnerable people deserved to be punished. Yahweh has the authority to vindicate his name and cause the offenders to acknowledge his justice. The result of Yahweh showing himself as a God of justice in the forensic finding of guilt and subsequent punishment seems to be the point of the following expression, "my hand, which I have laid upon them" (39:21). The Hebrew expression (שִׂים יָד בְּ) occurs only here in Ezekiel (and elsewhere in the OT only in Ps 89:26 [ET 89:25]), but "hand" is clearly anthropomorphic for God using his power to put Gog in his proper place. To be sure, this will apply to the return of Christ, which will accomplish the final defeat of all the forces of evil arrayed against the church, but it has also applied already to God's defeat of the unbelieving Jewish and heathen Gentile forces that attempted to do away with Christ and his church—forces overcome by the resurrection of Christ and the church's ongoing witness to him during the present era (e.g., Acts 3:13–26; 4:25–30; 13:27–41).

39:22 Before he returns to consider the nations further, Yahweh adds this declaration that is similar to the common recognition formula, "(then) you/they will know that I am Yahweh" (see 39:6–7, 28). This verse is the only time in the book when Israel is expressly the subject of the verb יָדַע, "to know," and the reference is to knowledge of God. Possibly we should even contrast Israel "knowing" God (in the pregnant sense, connoting true saving faith) with the nation merely "seeing" what God has done (cf. 39:21). The chronological notice "from that day on" implies again that Ezekiel is referring to an era in earthly history (although the true "Israel" certainly will retain faith and knowledge of God after the parousia of Christ). This verse points to the beginning of the new era that Christians know as the "new testament," the present church age, when God's true "Israel" consists of all Jewish and Gentile believers in Christ, the One through whom God has revealed his glory and established his justice through forensic justification (e.g., Romans 4–5).

39:23–24 The Gentiles, who will know God through the revelation of his glory in Christ (Lk 2:32), also will know that Yahweh had applied his justice to Israel. The OT people of Israel had not been exiled because Yahweh had been unable to defend them or had abandoned his covenant with them, but because of their faithless attitude and behavior. A number of expressions are used to describe the dimensions of their guilt. The first and last are major expressions of sinfulness: "their iniquity" (עָוֹן in this context might be translated "perversion") and "their rebellion" (פֶּשַׁע). In between come the verb מָעַל, "were unfaithful," which implies infidelity or treason against Yahweh, their Lord, and the noun טֻמְאָה, "uncleanness," both abstract and concrete, that is, a state of uncleanness as well as acts (both immoral and liturgically perverse) that cause or manifest that state.

Both 39:23 and 39:24 describe the punishment as God "hiding his face" (הַסְתִּיר פָּנִים), which occurs only in this context in Ezekiel (also in 39:29), but is frequent elsewhere in the OT (twenty-six times), especially in the Psalms. Throughout the Near East this was a common idiom indicating divine disfavor. Its opposite is well-known from two clauses in the Aaronic blessing: "Yahweh cause his face to shine toward you" and "Yahweh lift up his face toward you" (Num 6:25–26).

What was evident by Yahweh hiding his "face" was shown experientially by his delivering his people into the power (literally, "hand," יָד again) of their "adversaries" (צָר, elsewhere in Ezekiel only in 30:16, but frequent in the Psalter). That is, the fall of Jerusalem had been the result not of the might of the Babylonian army nor of Marduk's superiority over Yahweh, but of Yahweh's own deliberate reaction to his faithless people. The Gentiles will recognize Yahweh's justice in how he had treated his people in the past, as well as in how he is now treating them—graciously in Christ, yet with the warning of everlasting judgment upon all unbelievers.

39:25 Easter comes after Good Friday, and for those who repent and believe, death is followed by resurrection to eternal life. Now that Israel's "Good Friday" is past, Yahweh turns to the resurrection. The idiom "bring about the restoration of" was also used for Sodom and Samaria (see the first textual note and commentary on 16:53) and in a salvation oracle for Egypt in 29:14 (see "Introduction to Ezekiel 29–32: Oracles against Egypt"). Rather than merely indicating that the Judean exiles will return, as some translations render it (see the textual note), it is much more comprehensive and indicates a complete restoration to God's original intent for humanity, a reversal of all that human sin has caused, including rupture of communion with God and physical death itself. As in chapter 37, the message is eschatological, pointing to what will be fully accomplished only at the return of Christ: "the resurrection of the body, and the life everlasting" (Apostles' Creed).

"I will *have mercy* on the whole house of Israel" uses the verb רָחַם, not used elsewhere in Ezekiel, although frequent elsewhere in the OT for God showing mercy.[f] Ezekiel had used the synonym חָמַל, "have pity, compassion," but except in 36:21 it was always negated (e.g., 5:11; 7:4, 9). The affirmative "have mercy" parallels the force of the preceding expression, "bring about the

(f) E.g., Ex 33:19; Is 49:13; 54:8; 55:7; 60:10

restoration of." We should also note the parallelism of "the whole house of Israel" here with "Jacob" in the previous clause, pointing to a restored people broader than just the Judean exiles. (Just "Israel" was parallel to "the house of Jacob" in the judgment oracle of chapter 20 [20:5]; "Israel" and "Jacob" are often parallel elsewhere in the Bible.) Surprisingly, the expression "be zealous for my holy name" is unique in Ezekiel, although both components, "be zealous" and "my holy name," have appeared separately before. What Yahweh's zeal for his name consists of is evident from 39:7 and, in more detail, from 36:21–23, namely, that by means of his just judgment he shows himself to be the holy God.

39:26 We have heard this refrain, "bear (their) shame," before in Ezekiel (first in 16:52), and we will meet it again (44:13). It addresses a perennial, endemic problem in God's Israel—the OT people and now the Christian church. If the repentance described by this verse does not correspond to reality, it means that in those people a substitute faith (what Bonhoeffer famously labeled "cheap grace"[34]) has replaced the genuine article. The temptation is to understand grace as a birthright or entitlement, rather than sheer, unmerited divine favor: "while we were yet sinners, Christ died for us" (Rom 5:8). We must constantly remember the fact that, in spite of ourselves, "we daily sin much and surely deserve nothing but punishment."[35] Or the problem can be formulated in Law-Gospel terms: the Gospel of plenary forgiveness in Christ should increase our awareness of our unworthiness according to the Law, but for some, it becomes a source of pride, exclusivism, and even a license to flout God's Law, to engage in sins condemned by Scripture, as is evident in many denominations today.

39:27 The verse is largely an expansion of 39:26b, and the language is heavily dependent on previous pronouncements. The enemies led by Gog are no longer specifically in the picture, but in 38:16 and 39:7, God had asserted that he would manifest his holiness through his judgment of them. Here, however, he manifests his holiness through his people, whom he regathers. "The lands of their enemies" appears only here in Ezekiel and appears to depend on the covenant curses in Lev 26:36–39. Thus God will have carried out his curses upon his unfaithful OT people, but then will regather a new Israel that will manifest his own holiness (1 Pet 2:5–9; 3:15).

39:28 One final recognition formula[36] is expanded with a reiteration of the fact that not only will the nations acknowledge God's holiness (39:27), but above all, the new Israel to be gathered will recognize and confess who "Yahweh" is and what his actions mean—both by their recollection of the well-de-

---

[34] Dietrich Bonhoeffer, *The Cost of Discipleship* (trans. R. H. Fuller; rev. ed; New York: Macmillan, 1963), 45–60.

[35] Luther's explanation of the Fifth Petition of the Lord's Prayer (SC III 16 [*Luther's Small Catechism with Explanation*, 19; *LSB* 324]).

[36] See the commentary on 39:7. For the formula, see also page 9 in the introduction and the commentary on 6:7.

served exile and by their repatriation to their homeland. The promise "I will never again leave any of them behind," that not a single straggler will be left behind in the restoration of God's people, is without parallel in the OT. The NT issues similar promises in terms of election by God's grace in Christ: not one believer in Jesus will be lost (Jn 10:28–29; 17:12; 18:9).

39:29 The final and climactic message of chapters 38–39 links the permanence of Yahweh's presence in his new Israel with the pouring out of his Holy Spirit. In the context of Ezekiel's usual language, this promise is all the more surprising because Ezekiel has so often used God's wrath as the object of שָׁפַךְ, "pour out" (e.g., 7:8; 14:19; 20:8).

This is the only occurrence of the "outpouring of the Spirit" in Ezekiel. The triune God had spoken of giving "my Spirit" in 36:27 and 37:14, but in the idiom (נָתַן רוּחַ בְּקֶרֶב), "put my Spirit within" his people. The idioms are related, but not entirely synonymous, at least not in their original contexts. The earlier formulations expressed in the context of the rebirth of the nation, which only God could accomplish. Here the context is rather a sealing of the eternal covenant and of Yahweh's salvific activity on behalf of his chosen people. That accent is also present in the other OT passages with the idiom שָׁפַךְ, "pour out," with רוּחַ, God's "Spirit" (Joel 3:1–2 [ET 2:28–29]; Zech 12:10; cf. the similar idiom in Is 44:3).

Of course, the best known of those parallel passages is Joel 3:1–2 (ET 2:28–29), part of the OT text upon which St. Peter based his sermon on Pentecost (Acts 2:17–21). This text provides a classical case for faithful exegesis. On one hand, we must refrain from reading *into* the OT text by assuming that the original audience perceived all the Trinitarian fullness revealed with such language after the advent of the Messiah, Jesus Christ. At the same time, we must be diligent in reading *out* of the ancient text all that God himself would reveal about its full meaning in the fullness of time (cf. Gal 4:4).

Since the Christian church is "the Israel of God" (Gal 6:16), we confess ourselves, by God's grace, to be among the beneficiaries of this and similar promises. The end-time event prophesied by Joel and Ezekiel took place already at Pentecost and recurs every time a person is baptized in the triune name of God (Mt 28:19) and so receives the promised gift of the Holy Spirit, along with the forgiveness of sins and everlasting salvation in Christ (e.g., Acts 2:38–39; 22:16; Rom 6:1–4; 1 Cor 12:13), becoming an heir of all God's OT promises (Gal 3:26–29). Therefore we are already in the "latter days" (e.g., Ezek 38:16) envisioned by the OT prophets, the interim between Christ's first and second advents. During this time, God's people are called, gathered, and preserved in the faith by the Holy Spirit,[37] until the parousia comes, when we will understand fully, even as we have been fully understood (1 Cor 13:12).

---

[37] Thus the Third Article of the Apostles' Creed begins, "I believe in the Holy Spirit," the one who creates and sustains "the holy Christian church" through God's Word and Sacraments, and the Third Article ends with "the life everlasting."

Ezekiel 40–48

Vision of the New Temple, the New Creation, and the New Israel

Introduction to Ezekiel 40–48

Theological Interpretation

From almost any perspective, these chapters are among the most formidable and challenging in the entire Bible. The reader must attempt to grasp what God, writing through the exiled priest Ezekiel, intended for Israel with these chapters, as well as attempt to determine in what respect these passages of the inspired, authoritative Scriptures pertain to the life and future of the NT believer and church.[1]

Critical scholarship has generally failed to provide any assistance for that effort. Part of the problem is accurately pinpointed by the Jewish scholar Jon Levenson in the introduction to his work: "The fact that critical inquiry into biblical tradition was conceived and nurtured mostly by men whose outlook was molded by theologies whose origins lay in the Protestant Reformation has not aided the emergence of a serious and sympathetic appreciation of the place of law and priesthood in the Hebrew Bible."[2] Levenson may have been aware that many of those "Protestants" were Lutherans, but since their Lutheranism was often quite nominal and certainly not confessional, they shared with Protestants a deficient appreciation of the liturgical and sacramental aspects of Scripture and church life, so Levenson's assertion remains essentially true.

We find in these chapters not only a plethora of ceremonial detail that will naturally be of more interest to an orthodox Jew than to a typical modern Christian but also a mentality that might be more readily intelligible to a traditional Catholic than to a Protestant (not excluding many protestantized Lutherans). A traditional Catholic or Orthodox worshiper tends to be sensitive to ceremonial and symbolic details in worship, but Protestants, for whom the sermon has often all but displaced the weekly Eucharist and its accompanying liturgy, may hardly notice.

In fact, Protestant prejudices are often not only unmindful of but also suspicious of or even hostile to liturgical ceremony. Ritual is assumed to be almost necessarily ritual*ism*, and a veritable cult of simplicity holds sway. The "externals" of worship are airily dismissed as adiaphora, or, if accented at all, are considered legalistic. The reality of what Scripture promises in its sacramental language (e.g., "this is my body," Mt 26:26; "Baptism now saves you," 1 Pet 3:21) is demoted to being true only in a merely "spiritual" way. Simultaneously, the corporate dimension is dissolved into individualistic "spiritualization." And if such attitudes reign with respect to Christian worship, one does not have to think too hard to understand what theological-ideological hurdles must be cleared to approach Ezekiel 40–48 sympathetically.

---

[1] Keil, *Ezekiel*, 2:382–434, provides a thorough and excellent discussion of how Ezekiel 40–48 should be interpreted in light of its fulfillment in Christ and in harmony with the eschatology of the entirety of the Scriptures, particularly Revelation. Keil argues for a Christological and typological interpretation ("the symbolico-typical view appears to be demanded" [p. 388]) and vigorously denounces literalistic millennial interpretations.

[2] Levenson, *Theology of the Program of Restoration of Ezekiel 40–48*, 1.

The comment of Block, a conservative Protestant, on the last verse of the book (48:35) also applies to all of chapters 40–48:

> Where God is, there is order and the fulfillment of all his promises. Further-more, where the presence of God is recognized, there is purity and holiness. Ezekiel hereby lays the foundation for the Pauline spiritualization of the temple. Under the new covenant, even Gentiles' communities may be trans-formed into the living temple of God (1 Cor. 3:16–17). Moreover, through the indwelling presence of the Spirit of God, individual Christians become temples, residences of deity (1 Cor. 6:19).[3]

All that certainly is true, but we must first emphasize the fulfillment of Ezekiel's vision in the incarnation of Jesus himself, the new temple.[4] The temple itself in Ezekiel 40–48 may be the central feature of the vision that prefigures the Messiah, but it is not the only part of the vision that does so. The supernatural guide who leads Ezekiel through the vision has certain Christlike features (see the commentary on 40:3 and also on 43:6). Earlier in Ezekiel the promised Son of David was called the coming "Prince" (34:24; 37:25), and he is frequently referred to by that same title in chapters 40–48 (see further below). Also, the divine "Glory" who takes up residence in the new temple (43:1–12) should be identified as the same divine Glory to be manifest in the Word made flesh (Jn 1:14).[5] After emphasizing the fulfillment in Christ himself, we then must add the relevance of Ezekiel 40–48 for the ongoing liturgical and sacramental worship of the corporate church, the body of Christ, during this NT era. It is through God's Word and Sacraments that Christ is present with his people already now, and through these means of grace God fashions us Christians into his holy temple. Finally, we must stress the ultimate fulfillment of Ezekiel's vision in the new heavens and new earth, the new creation to be inaugurated after the second coming of Christ and the bodily resurrection of all believers to eternal life therein (Isaiah 11 and 65; 2 Pet 3:1–13; Revelation 21–22).[6]

---

[3] Block, *Ezekiel*, 2:506.

[4] See the commentary on Ezek 37:26–28, especially 37:27. In the NT, see, for example, Jn 2:19–22.

[5] For the Christological interpretation of the divine "Glory," see pages 1, 11, and 13 in the introduction, as well as the textual notes and commentary on 1:26–28.

[6] This view is in basic agreement with that of Luther in his 1545 "Preface to the Prophet Ezekiel" (AE 35:292–93):

> Therefore this building of Ezekiel is not to be understood to mean a physical building, but like the chariot at the beginning [1:4–28] so this building at the end [chapters 40–48] is nothing else than the kingdom of Christ, the holy church or Christendom here on earth until the last day.
>
> As to how all the parts of the prophecy are to be interpreted and arranged, we will leave that until that life [in eternity] in which we shall see the whole building finished and complete. We cannot see it all now, since it is still under construction, and much of the stone and wood that belong to it are not yet born, let alone prepared for use in building. It is enough that we know it to be the house of God, his own building in which we all are.
>
> Whoever has the leisure and the inclination can look into it and investigate it extensive-ly, if he will take up the word of God and the sacraments, with their powers and the

At the very least, these chapters carry the message that we must take worship seriously, not as a legalistic command by which merit will be accumulated, but as God's gracious gift. Through the outpouring of the Holy Spirit, who works through God's Word and Sacraments, the "new heart" and "new spirit" are created in the corporate new Israel,[7] as prophesied in 11:19; 36:26–27; 37:14; 39:29. The emphasis on restored liturgical worship appeared earlier in chapter 20, and in fact, 20:40–44 sounds like a précis of chapters 40–48. The topic also appears fleetingly at the end of chapter 37, in 37:26–28, which at least one LXX manuscript places just before chapter 40.[8]

The command to the prophet to relate the details of the coming vision to the Israelites (40:4; and more extensively, 43:10–11) indicates the theological significance attached to all of it, even if it is difficult for us to visualize how the command was obeyed. It obviously implied more than simply regaling the Israelites with a naked catalogue of measurements! Hals comments:

> It simply boggles our minds to contemplate the "preaching" of such dull details. Beyond a certain degree of clarity in overall intention, such as the reality of a restoration and a legitimate, divinely authorized new sanctuary, we find this wealth of minutiae extremely uncommunicative. ... What a shock it is, then, to learn how this material, together with the to us equally dull details of the visions in chs. 1 and 10, became an integral part of later Jewish mysticism.[9]

Did God really intend his prescriptions in Ezekiel 40–48 to literally be followed? Do these chapters furnish a plan for a temple that Israel was to build after its Babylonian exile? Or could they be meant for an earthly "millennium," a literal thousand-year reign of Christ on this earth, during which time God intends a temple to be rebuilt in Jerusalem with a resumption of animal sacrifices? The biblical answer to all these questions is negative.[10]

---

effects which the Holy Spirit works in the church through them, and bring these things into agreement. The Revelation of John can also be of help in this regard.

[7] The regenerated Israel of which Ezekiel speaks includes the OT faithful remnant of believers and continues in the NT church, consisting of all Jewish and Gentile believers in Christ. There is no salvation apart from Christ (Jn 14:6; Acts 4:12), and there are no separate plans of salvation for Jews versus Gentiles. All believers from both the OT and NT eras comprise "all Israel" that "will be saved" (Rom 11:26), "the Israel of God" (Gal 6:16), the "one holy catholic and apostolic church" (Nicene Creed). Luther in his preface to Ezekiel spoke of the church as the "new Israel" (AE 35:288, 290). In Revelation, the unity and continuity of this one people of God (OT Israel and NT church) are depicted by the twenty-four elders before God's throne (Rev 4:4, 10; 5:8; 11:16; 19:4): twelve represent the tribes of Israel and all OT believers, while the other twelve represent the apostles and all NT believers.

As was true in OT Israel, so also in the present church, one must distinguish the believers from the apostate unbelievers who may gather with and outwardly belong to the same people, but who are not part of God's true Israel (cf. Rom 9:6, 27; 1 Jn 2:9–29).

[8] This sometimes leads to speculations about the provenance of chapters 38–39. But for their place in relation to chapters 40–48 and in the eschatology of Ezekiel 33–48, see "Introduction to Ezekiel 38–39: The Final Battle and the Defeat of Gog."

[9] Hals, *Ezekiel*, 301.

[10] The historic, mainstream Christian view is that the "millennium" of which Rev 20:1–7 speaks is the present church age, during which Satan is bound so that the Gospel can be

Ezekiel, like other prophets, including his predecessor Isaiah and his contemporary Jeremiah, was told that there would be a "second exodus," a return of Israel from captivity in Babylon, although Ezekiel gives us no timetable.[11] Just as ancient Israel had encamped at Sinai after the first exodus and received its basic constitution there, including plans for the tabernacle, it might be plausible that Ezekiel, as a sort of "second Moses" in the sequel, would now offer modifications for the temple, worship, and resettlement in the promised land. However, Ezekiel never develops that thought typologically by suggesting that these chapters are to be implemented literally by postexilic Israel, and he himself never purports to be a "new Moses." Instead, he foresees a new David, who will be Israel's "one" eternal Shepherd and King (34:23–24; 37:24–25).

The absence of any word such as תַּבְנִית, "pattern, plan," describing Ezekiel's temple vision is a major clue that God did not intend it as a blueprint for construction by his people in any era. In contrast, both Moses (Ex 25:9, 40) and Solomon via David (1 Chr 28:11–19) are commanded to build their earthly sanctuary (the tabernacle and temple, respectively) according to the celestial model or prototype revealed to them. But no such word as "pattern, plan," nor any command to build and replicate the vision, can be found in Ezekiel 40–48. (In 43:10–11 God commands Ezekiel to write down the temple plan so that the Israelites may contemplate it and keep his statutes, but even there we find no command to build it [see on 43:11].) In fact, in Ezekiel's vision, the temple is already there in Jerusalem, already built—by God. This divine house is not to be built by any human hands, neither those of OT Israelites, nor of Christians or Jews in a future millennium. "Chapters 40–42 present instead the proleptic revelation in a transcendent way of what God gives to his people when he reestablishes his presence in their midst."[12] In harmony with the "now but not yet" quality of biblical eschatology, the temple vision has already been fulfilled

---

spread. Christians on earth have already been raised to new life (cf. Rom 6:1–4) and have begun to reign with Christ. But persecution of the church will continue and culminate before all evil is defeated at the return of Christ. At Christ's second coming all the dead will be raised bodily and judged (Rev 20:11–15). All who do not believe in Christ will be damned, and all believers in Christ will enter the new heavens and new earth, their home for eternity (Revelation 21–22).

See also "Introduction to Ezekiel 38–39: The Final Battle and the Defeat of Gog" and the commentary on 38:8. For a discussion of different views and a defense of historic amillennialism, one may see the excursus "The Millennium" and the commentary on Revelation 20 in Brighton, *Revelation*, 533–87. For a fuller presentation of biblical eschatology from an amillennial Reformed scholar, one may see Hoekema, *The Bible and the Future*.

[11] Ezekiel uses "new exodus" terminology at least ten times in his book: 11:17; 20:34–35; 20:41–42; 28:25; 29:13; 34:13; 36:24; 37:12, 21; 39:27. (Once, in 29:13, he applies it to the Egyptians.) This theme becomes most prominent in the context of the restoration oracles in chapters 34–39. The original exodus under Moses in the fifteenth century B.C. is the OT type, and the return from Babylon in the sixth century is an OT antitype that in turn anticipates the still greater exodus redemption through Jesus Christ, whose suffering, death, and resurrection are the "exodus" (ἔξοδος, Lk 9:31) that has procured salvation for all. See especially the commentary on Ezek 11:17; 34:13; 36:24; 37:12, 21; and 39:27.

[12] Hals, *Ezekiel*, 303.

by the death and resurrection of Christ, yet we await its consummation at the return of Christ and the inauguration of the eternal state.[13]

In addition, Ezekiel himself would have been perfectly aware of other problems. Too many aspects of the temple construction, as well as later elements in the total vision of the promised land, are simply impossible to implement literally in the topography of Jerusalem and the rest of Cisjordan on the present earth. Their realization requires a new creation, a new heavens and new earth. The perfect square of the temple plan plus the "building" (בִּנְיָן, 40:5; 41:12, 15; 42:1, 5, 10) to its west simply would not fit on the narrow peninsula of land on which the former temple stood. Later in the vision, the east-west allotments of the tribes do not accord with the lay of the land or the natural routes for movement of people and goods (47:13–48:29). And, of course, the vision of the fructifying water flowing out from under the temple (47:1–12) is not of the present fallen order of nature, but hearks back to Eden (Gen 2:10) and anticipates the paradise to come (Rev 22:1–2).

All this suggests that the entire section of chapters 40–48 is a vision (as it is termed in 40:2) and must be read accordingly. Ezekiel himself realizes in 43:3 that his "vision" of the divine Glory is the same kind (genre) of "vision" as he had received in chapter 1 and chapters 8–11. Sometimes the term "apocalyptic" is applied to chapters 40–48, but they lack virtually all the distinguishing features of apocalyptic, even more so than chapters 38–39. "Eschatological" in a sense it certainly is, but not as fully as Revelation 21–22, for Ezekiel 40–48 still pictures the future in terms of OT realities (temple, animal sacrifices, altar) rendered obsolete by the first advent of Christ, and entirely absent in John's vision of the eschaton.[14]

Many have observed that the emphases in chapters 40–48 have as an overarching purpose "the repair of history,"[15] correcting all that went wrong in Is-

---

[13] The fulfillment in Christ is affirmed by the quote of Jesus' words about the Jerusalem temple and the new temple of his own body: "We heard him saying, 'I will destroy this temple that is made by hands, and in three days another, not made by hands, I will build'" (Mk 14:58; cf. Jn 2:19–22). Yet the future completion is affirmed by St. Paul's expression of the Christian hope: "For we know that if our earthly home of a tent is destroyed, we have a building from God, a house not made by hands, eternal in the heavens" (2 Cor 5:1).

[14] The sacrifice of Christ on the cross was the once-for-all atonement for humanity's sin that rendered all other sacrifices, and indeed the whole earthly temple, obsolete. This is the theme of the book of Hebrews. Thus God allowed the Jerusalem temple to be destroyed in A.D. 70. Any rebuilt temple and any resumption of sacrifices would show contempt for the completed atonement and bodily resurrection of Christ. Thus in John's vision of the eternal state, there is no temple (Rev 21:22).

Nevertheless, Revelation still uses the OT language of "temple," "tabernacle," "ark of the covenant," and even "altar" to describe present heavenly realities (Rev 6:9; 8:3, 5; 11:19; 14:15, 17; 16:1, 7, 17), and also the "temple" in promises to be fulfilled in the eternal state (Rev 3:12; 7:15).

[15] Levenson, *Theology of the Program of Restoration of Ezekiel 40–48*, 87, makes this point about chapters 17 and 34, where God promises to restore his relationship with Israel through a messianic Ruler and Shepherd who will repair the damage done by the unfaithful rulers and abusive shepherds.

rael's past. Looking back in the OT, there certainly are parallels with the Pentateuchal revelation to Moses, but of course these chapters are far briefer than the tabernacle description and priestly legislation in the Torah. Some have supposed that Ezekiel envisioned a much simpler temple and fewer ceremonies than in Solomon's temple, but to an extent that is an argument from silence. The priesthood is smaller, restricted to the Zadokites, who did not go astray as the other Levitical priests did (44:15; 48:11).

(a) Ezek 44:3; 45:7–9, 16–17, 22; 46:2, 4, 8, 10, 12, 16–18; 48:21–22

Since the kings had brought trouble to the earlier temple (43:7–9; see also the references to past oppression in 45:8; 46:18), the messianic "Prince" (נָשִׂיא) is to be completely unlike them. God had expressed this concern when he spoke of this same "Prince" earlier as "my Servant David," the one "Shepherd" and "King" who would unite God's people, care for them, and protect them (34:23–24; 37:24–25), in contrast to Israel's past, unfaithful, and abusive "shepherds" (chapter 34), the rulers who divided the people and led them into idolatry (37:22–23). The "Prince" is mentioned frequently,[a] but sometimes obliquely, and usually not in the terms familiar from the better-known messianic prophesies in other OT books. While "Prince" is a royal title, his role is often priestly. He has the unique privilege of eating before Yahweh in the temple's east gate, closed to all other humans because Yahweh had entered it (44:1–3). He also provides the sacrifices for atonement (45:17). Christians can see foreshadowed in such passages about the "Prince" Christ's office as Priest (and to a lesser extent, as King), which is expounded at length in Hebrews 3–10. Other passages about the "Prince" elaborate his liturgical role and extensive property rights (something neither OT priests nor kings had) in the sacred reserve (45:7–9; 46:16–18; 48:21–22).

The inequities in the original land distribution and the earlier deportation of the northern tribes because of their own defection from Yahweh will be corrected (48:1–29). The rules about the closed east gate (44:1–2) and the arrangement of the temple plan so as to give preeminence to the east (see figures 2 and 5) probably also have to do with the undoing of past evil, even if the precise motivations elude us. But all this "negativity" should not obscure the positive point that is being made: Yahweh will return to his restored people and never again leave them, but dwell among them forever (48:35).

There is not the slightest indication that Ezekiel's contemporaries ever understood the vision to be a literal program for rebuilding the temple. Many aspects of these chapters, including the allotment of the entire land and the supernatural river, were far beyond their ability to implement. When Zerubbabel's temple was built in 520–516 B.C., a little more than half a century after Ezekiel prophesied these chapters, the returnees apparently labored to replace Solomon's temple as best they could and made no attempt to replicate Ezekiel's vision. The ark of the covenant is among the items Ezekiel does not mention, nor do the descriptions of the rebuilt temple include it. Probably it had been destroyed along with the Solomonic temple in 586 B.C. and was considered irreplaceable. Therefore, the absence of the ark in both the rebuilt temple and the temple seen by Ezekiel is by necessity and is no indication that the rebuilders were following Ezekiel as a model. According to the prophecy of Jer 3:16, God intended the ark (and indeed, the entire old covenant) to be superceded by the coming new covenant in Christ.

At many points, Ezekiel 40–48 seems to conflict with the Pentateuch.[16] As noted earlier, Jewish mysticism was fascinated by such esoteric learning as could be found in Ezekiel 40–48, but mainstream, orthodox, rabbinic Judaism had concerns about its deviations from the prescriptions in the Torah of Moses. One rabbi, Ḥananiah ben Hezekiah, is credited with burning three hundred barrels of oil in his room until he had reconciled the divergences.[17] The sectarian Jews at Qumran, probably in the second century B.C., composed their *Temple Scroll*, which was somewhat modeled after Ezekiel 40–48, but largely has its own vision of the eschatological fulfillment.

To an extent Ezekiel 40–48 can apply to the present "interim," where the end has begun (at Christ's first advent), but is not yet consummated (at his parousia).[18] That is, we can see at least the partial fulfillment now of Ezekiel's vision in the Christian church, which the NT describes as the fulfillment of Israel and its temple and altar.[b] This is supported by Rev 11:1 (parallel to Ezek 40:3–5), where the apostle John is given a "measuring rod" and told to "measure the temple of God and the altar and those worshiping there," and what follows is a description of the church in the NT era, represented by the two witnesses (evangelists).

(b) E.g., 1 Cor 3:16–17; 6:19; 2 Cor 6:16; Gal 6:16; Eph 2:21; Heb 13:10

However, for biblically minded Christians, the ultimate fulfillment of Ezekiel's vision is to be found in Revelation 21–22. Some older commentators held that Ezekiel's vision had no meaning for his contemporaries and was di-

---

[16] For example, many of the sacrifices and rites prescribed for the major festivals in 45:21–25 and for the minor festivals in 46:1–15 differ from those in the Torah. Perhaps most striking is that 46:13–15 only prescribes the daily sacrifice to be offered in the morning, whereas the Torah prescribed the daily sacrifice to be offered in both the morning and the evening (Num 28:1–8). In Ezekiel's vision, the Prince receives two large tracts of land (45:7–8; 46:16–18; 48:21–22) even though the Torah and Joshua allotted no special land grant to the royalty. The allotments of land to the twelve tribes in Ezekiel 48 is quite different from the arrangement anticipated in the Torah and carried out in Joshua 13–21.

[17] Talmud, *Shabbath*, 13b. The Talmud hyperbolically claims that without this rabbi's effort, "the Book of Ezekiel would have been hidden [נִגְנַז, Niphal of גָּנַז, 'prohibited, suppressed'], for its words contradicted the Torah" (Soncino ed.).

[18] A good discussion of the issue can be found in Hengstenberg, *Christology of the Old Testament*, 3:58–64. He points out that Ezek 47:22–23, which places foreigners on the same footing as Israelites, is fulfilled by the inclusion of both Jews and Gentiles in the church, which is the NT antitype of the OT temple. He concludes (p. 63):

> The temple was the symbol of the kingdom of God in Israel, and a type of the church, … the restoration of the kingdom of God could not possibly be represented in a more appropriate manner, than under the image of a restored and glorified temple. …

> The reason, for describing so minutely the details of the building, was *to give a forcible proof of the prophet's firm belief in the continued existence of the kingdom of God.* So long as the church lay prostrate and the sanctuary was in ruins, this ideal temple of Ezekiel was to serve as a support to the weak faith of the nation.

rectly intended for future Christianity, but such an ahistorical hermeneutic is indefensible for the Scriptures. Rather, we should affirm that Ezekiel was given a vision of the eternal state (the church triumphant in the new heavens and new earth, after the second coming of Christ) that is still very much pictured in OT terms that would be familiar to Ezekiel, a priest (Ezek 1:3). God gave this vision to comfort and encourage Ezekiel and his contemporaries (exiles who yearned for Jerusalem and the temple; see 24:21), as well as other believers in the OT and NT eras (including us), with its Gospel message.

A misguided viewpoint currently popular in "evangelical" circles (although very much a minority view in Christianity as a whole) is usually labeled "dispensational premillennialism." It was popularized in the Scofield Reference Bible (first published in 1909), and more recently in the Left Behind series of popular books (whose first volume was published in 1995), which show a fascination with esoterica (and neglect of the clear teachings of Scripture) like that of Jewish mysticism, but from a different viewpoint. This viewpoint has various, frequently warring, factions, but generally agrees that before the end of earthly time all the prophecies concerning the glorious future of Israel will be literalistically fulfilled. There will be a seven-year "tribulation," culminating in an earthly battle against the modern state of Israel.[19] There is disagreement whether a "rapture" of Christians will occur before, halfway through, or at the end of the "tribulation." But the "tribulation" will be followed by a return of Christ to set up a kingdom on this earth, which he will rule for a literal thousand years. During this "millennium," the temple will be rebuilt according to Ezekiel 40–48 and animal sacrifices will be resumed. Politically, dispensationalism throws its weight behind a blindly Zionist, pro-Israel stance because it holds that the modern state of Israel must triumph before the rest of the supposed scenario can proceed.

To be sure, dispensationalists and other millennialists are to be commended for their high view of the inerrancy of Scripture,[20] which is shared by other conservative Christians, including confessional Lutherans. However, the key question is whether God intended passages such as Ezekiel 40–48 to be understood as requiring a literal fulfillment in earthly history, or whether God intended that such an OT vision should be interpreted in light of the fuller revelation of later Scripture passages. Scripture is to interpret Scripture; clear passages are to interpret the unclear ones; and in general, the Scriptures are characterized by progressive revelation, as over time, God reveals more and more detail—about what he has already done and will yet do. Thus the NT is the authoritative in-

---

[19] Usually Ezekiel 38–39 is taken as a description of that battle. See "Introduction to Ezekiel 38–39: The Final Battle and the Defeat of Gog."

[20] Allen, *Ezekiel*, 2:214, is unduly acerbic and betrays another agenda when he criticizes them for their high view of Scripture: "To resort to dispensationalism and postpone them [Ezekiel 40–48] to a literal fulfillment in a yet future time strikes the author as a desperate expedient that sincerely attempts to preserve belief in an inerrant prophecy."

terpretation of the OT, and God's plan of salvation finds its fulfillment in Christ, who is the goal and center of all biblical theology.

Dispensationalists tend not to observe such distinctions within Scripture and require an equally literal fulfillment of all prophecy, even when later Scripture passages indicate otherwise. Rather than harmonize passages with surface differences (e.g., Ezekiel 40–48 and Revelation 21–22) and see them as fulfilled simultaneously, they attempt to construct complex chronological sequences so that every detail can be fulfilled (often sequentially). Moreover, they do not see all prophecy as finding its fulfillment in Christ and his church. Many entertain two plans of salvation, one for Gentiles (via the church) and the other for Jews (ethnic Israel), which contradicts the ecclesiology of the NT, which portrays the church as the new Israel and the fulfillment of OT prophecies about the restoration of Israel.[21] Their two-plan scheme requires either some future mass conversion of Jewish people (allegedly based on Rom 11:26), or the possibility of salvation apart from faith in Christ, in direct contradiction of the NT.

We, therefore, will allow the NT to interpret the OT. A reading of Revelation 21–22 shows a metamorphosis of Ezekiel's vision: certain features remain unchanged, but other ones are dramatically different. We should expect such differences in details because, even though both visions ultimately foresee the same eternal state (God's redeemed in glory, worshiping him in the new heavens and new earth), the first one is couched in OT language and was given to a priestly OT prophet over six centuries before the revelation to the apostle John, who had already witnessed the completion of Jesus' earthly ministry.

Among the visionary details that remain the same in Revelation are these: (1) The prophet[22] is transported to a high mountain (Rev 21:10). (2) Jerusalem is at the center of a new world (21:1–2, 10). (3) God's dwelling is in the midst of his people (21:3–4). (4) God's "glory" is present in the city (21:11). (5) An angelic being uses a measuring rod to measure the city (21:15–17). (6) Jerusalem is a "foursquare" city with twelve gates, one for each tribe (21:12–16). The geographical order in which these gates are presented (east, north, south, and then west) is the same in both Ezek 42:15–20 and Rev 21:13. (7) There is an emphasis on the purity and holiness of its inhabitants (21:27). And (8) a river of life proceeds from God (22:1).

But there are also fundamental differences in Revelation: (1) Besides the dimensions of length and width, height dimensions are given as well, resulting in a city that is not only a square, but cubical (Rev 21:16). (2) The city is built of precious stones and metals (instead of the ordinary stones implied in Ezekiel; 21:18–21). (3) The "holy city" is unhesitatingly called the "new

---

[21] See, for example, Acts 2; Rom 1:16–17; Gal 3:26–29; Ephesians 2. The one church, consisting of Jewish and Gentile believers in Christ, is the one "Israel of God" (Gal 6:16).

[22] Revelation both begins (1:3) and ends (22:7, 10, 18–19; cf. 19:10) with the description that it is a "prophecy."

Jerusalem" (τὴν πόλιν τὴν ἁγίαν Ἰερουσαλὴμ καινήν, 21:2) instead of "Yahweh *Shammah* [Yahweh is there]" (Ezek 48:35). (4) Instead of the temple at the center of everything, the apostle John is shown that there is no temple structure, "for the Lord God Almighty and the Lamb are its temple" (Rev 21:22). (5) There are also no sacrifices, because the sacrificed and risen Lamb, the antitype of all the OT sacrifices, lives among his redeemed people. (6) There is no longer any need to distinguish the holy from the profane, or clean from unclean, because all the people and things in the city are holy already, and everything impure has been excluded (21:26–27; 22:14–15). And finally (7) in contrast to Ezekiel's limited vision of the Israelites, John sees the Christians from all nations coming into the city through its perpetually open gates (21:24–27).[23]

The NT supported a Christological interpretation of the Glory of Yahweh, who appeared in the opening chapters of Ezekiel.[24] Since the Glory comes to dwell in the visionary temple in 43:1–12, it too can be interpreted in reference to Christ and his indwelling in his church, his body. This might explain why, in the corresponding NT vision, the new Jerusalem represents the redeemed in Christ, and the only temple is God and the Lamb (Rev 21:22). If Ezekiel saw the Lamb who would be slain in the visionary form of a temple with an altar, that would then be a point of fundamental continuity between Ezekiel 40–48 and Revelation 21–22, rather than a discrepancy. It would also help explain why this temple was deemed worthy of such a detailed description that takes up such a large portion of the sacred Scriptures.

Obviously, we understand Revelation 21–22 as a vision, but also as a promise of a future reality that is certain for us in Christ, and that has already been at least partially inaugurated among those in Christ. For the eternal state, no human word-pictures will ever be adequate. Instead, we sing and pray in the words of the ancient Christmas macaronic: "Oh, that we were there!"[25]

Text, Composition, and Outline

The Hebrew of chapters 40–48 (especially chapters 40–43) poses an unusually high number of textual and exegetical difficulties. Much of the problem inheres in the special topics discussed, which required technical Hebrew architectural terms, the precise meanings of which often are uncertain or even unknown to us. If this loss of understanding happened at an early enough date, it would make ancient copyists' errors much more likely. Whether or not that

---

[23] While John speaks of "the nations" and their "kings" entering the city, he clearly means that these are Christians from all nations, and unbelievers are excluded, because Rev 21:27 states that only those whose names are written "in the Lamb's book of life" are able to enter the new Jerusalem.

[24] See pages 1, 11, and 13 in the introduction, as well as the textual notes and commentary on 1:26–28.

[25] This is the final line of the hymn "Now Sing We, Now Rejoice" (*LSB* 386), a fourteenth century A.D. Latin and German hymn, whose final line in German is *Eia, wär'n wir da!*

was the reason, the LXX often seems to have preserved a better text, but one concedes that with some hesitation, because we have no way of testing whether the easier Greek readings preserve the original Hebrew text (while the Hebrew in the MT tradition was miscopied) or whether the hard Hebrew (preserved in the MT) was simplified and paraphrased by the Greek translators, whose clear rendition is simply an educated guess. Be that as it may, when we are confronted with a choice between a reading in the MT that is unintelligible to us and an apparently lucid LXX, it is tempting to choose the latter.

Until relatively recently, critical scholarship was reticent to acknowledge any genuine Ezekelian material in chapters 40–48, and remnants of that critical stance are still to be found in modern commentaries. Yet fortunately a more conservative viewpoint has gained ground in the past half century, gradually and in varying degrees. There is space here to mention only a few important names in this process of change, some of which will be cited on individual points in the commentary.

The dissertation of Carl Howie, *The Date and Composition of Ezekiel*, in 1950, hypothesized a relatively simple compositional history with all the oracles collected by a disciple in "the thirtieth year" (1:1), but with all the material being virtually Ezekiel's. The dissertation was directed by W. F. Albright. However, because of a common animus against Albright, the work did not have the influence it should have, except among other students of Albright.

Much more influential was Hartmut Gese, *Der Verfassungsentwurf des Ezechiel (Kap. 40–48): Traditionsgeschichtlich Untersucht* in 1957. With the translation of Zimmerli's massive Ezekiel commentary into English (the second volume of which was published in 1983), Gese's influence penetrated the English-speaking world because, in the main, Zimmerli tends to follow him. Gese attributes a good share of the material to Ezekiel himself with the exception of what he calls the "prince (נָשִׂיא) stratum" (44:1–3; 45:21–25; 46:1–10, 12); a "Zadokite stratum" (44:6–31); 45:13–15; and a "land-division stratum" (48:1–29); plus sundry alleged glosses.[26]

Meanwhile, more holistic studies and commentaries have appeared, of which I can again mention only a few. Not directly addressing the question of authorship, but generally implying substantial authenticity, were Jon Levenson, *Theology of the Program of Restoration of Ezekiel 40–48* (1976), and Ronald Hals, *Ezekiel* (1989). Finally, we must note Moshe Greenberg, the Jewish scholar who completed commentary on Ezekiel 1–37, but died before writing his commentary on the later chapters. Nevertheless, he authored an essay in the journal *Interpretation* in 1984 entitled "The Design and Themes of Ezekiel's Program of Restoration" that simply assumes the unity of chapters 40–48.

Since Yahweh through his messenger commanded Ezekiel to "tell everything you see to the house of Israel" (40:4; see also 43:10–11), we should con-

---

[26] See the summary in Gese, *Der Verfassungsentwurf des Ezechiel*, 109–15.

clude that Ezekiel himself recorded the entire vision in writing, soon after its revelation, to accomplish that purpose. There is no reason to suppose that any of the material was added by other authors. The date of these final chapters is given in 40:1, and its possible significance will be discussed in the commentary there. According to that date, Ezekiel saw the vision recorded in chapters 40–48 more than a decade later than the latest dated oracle in the rest of the book except for 29:17–21 (the latest dated passage in the book). We know of no particular occasion for the revelation of this extended vision at this time.

In broad strokes, the nine chapters are readily divisible into three main divisions: (1) chapters 40–43 are the vision of the new temple, with 43:13–27 concentrating on the altar; (2) chapters 44–46 envision the new organization of worship, accenting especially rules governing access to the temple and activity in it; and (3) chapters 47–48 depict the vivifying water issuing from the temple (47:1–12) and the apportionment of the land among the people. This neat outline is breached particularly in the central section, where descriptions of parts of the temple appear, which we would have expected in the first section. We can imagine Ezekiel digressing briefly to add details he may have neglected earlier.

A more detailed outline can be given as follows:

1. Vision of the new temple (40:1–42:20)
2. Return of the Glory of Yahweh to the temple (43:1–12)
3. Measurements of the altar of burnt offering (43:13–17)
4. Consecration of the altar of burnt offering (43:18–27)
5. The closed outer east gate and the Prince (44:1–3)
6. Vision of the Glory and admonition to pay close attention (44:4–5)
7. The legitimate officiants for worship (44:6–31)
8. Property for Yahweh, the priests, the Levites, and the Prince (45:1–8)
9. Need for proper weights and measures for the required offerings (45:9–12)
10. The contribution for the Prince and his liturgical supervision (45:13–17)
11. The major festivals (45:18–25)
12. The minor festivals and the Prince (46:1–15)
13. Legislation on the Prince's property (46:16–18)
14. The two kinds of sacrificial kitchens (46:19–24)
15. The life-giving water issuing from the temple (47:1–12)
16. The new allotment of the land among the people (47:13–48:29)
17. The city, its gates, and its name (48:30–35)

Figure 2

The Temple Compound in Ezekiel

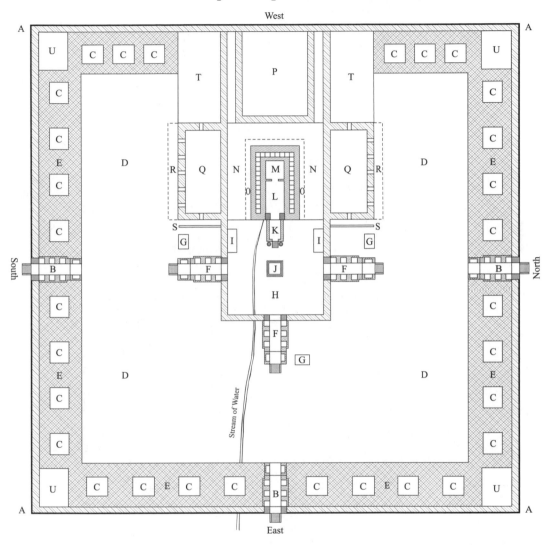

A Outer wall (40:5)
B Outer gates (40:6–16, 20–27)
C Worshipers' rooms (40:17)
D Outer court (40:17–19)
E Lower pavement (40:17–18)
F Inner gates (40:28–37)
G Rooms for washing sacrifices (40:38)
H Inner court (40:44, 47)
I Priests' guard rooms (40:44–46)
J Altar (40:47; 43:13–17)
K Vestibule of the temple (40:48–49)

L Nave of the temple (41:1–2)
M Holy of Holies (41:3–4)
N Large open area around the temple (41:9b–10)
O Small open area around the temple (41:11)
P West building (41:12)
Q Priests' sacristies (42:1–14; 44:19; 46:19;
   perhaps also 41:10)
R Walkway (42:4, 11–12)
S Wall (42:7)
T Kitchens (46:19–20)
U Kitchens (46:21–24)

Adapted from C. F. Keil, *Biblischer Commentar über den Propheten Ezechiel* (2d ed.; Leipzig: Dörffling und Franke, 1882).

Figure 3

The Outer Temple Gates in Ezekiel

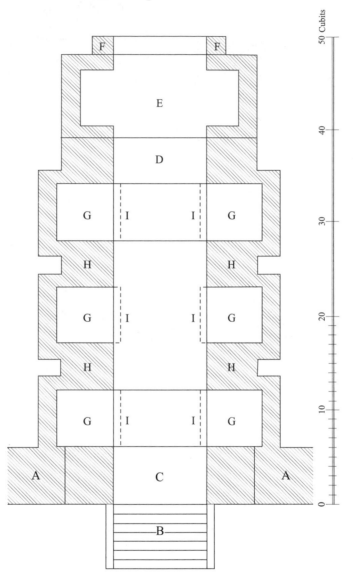

The outer gates are described in 40:6–16, 20–27.

- A Wall of the temple compound
- B Steps
- C Threshold of the gateway
- D Threshold of the vestibule
- E Vestibule
- F Gateposts of the vestibule
- G Guardrooms
- H Walls between the guardrooms
- I Barriers in front of the guardrooms

Adapted from C. F. Keil, *Biblischer Commentar über den Propheten Ezechiel* (2d ed.; Leipzig: Dörffling und Franke, 1882).

Figure 4

The Inner Temple Gates in Ezekiel

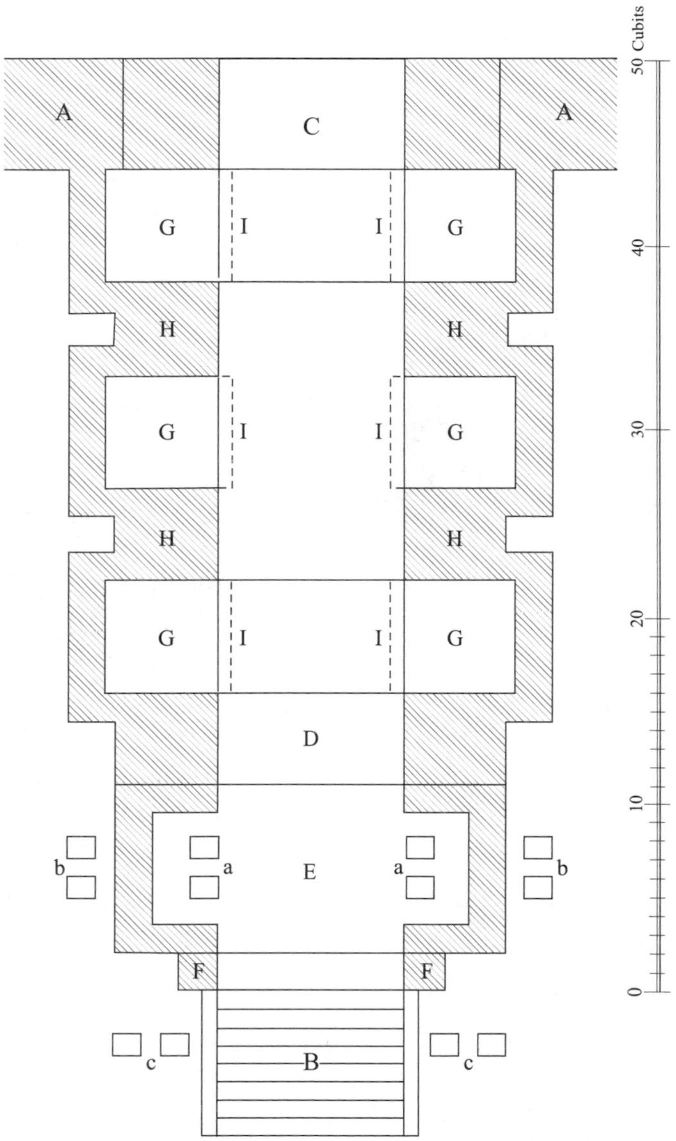

The inner temple gates are described in 40:28–37.

- A Wall of the inner court
- B Steps
- C Threshold of the gateway
- D Threshold of the vestibule
- E Vestibule
- F Gateposts of the vestibule
- G Guardrooms
- H Walls between the guardrooms
- I Barriers in front of the guardrooms

Tables for preparing the sacrifices are discussed in 40:39–43.

- a Tables in the vestibule of the inner gate (40:39; see also 40:41, 43)
- b Tables by the outside wall of the vestibule of the inner gate (40:40; see also 40:41, 43)
- c Tables of hewn stone (40:42; see also 40:43)

Adapted from C. F. Keil, *Biblischer Commentar über den Propheten Ezechiel* (2d ed.; Leipzig: Dörffling und Franke, 1882).

Figure 5

The Temple and the Altar in Ezekiel

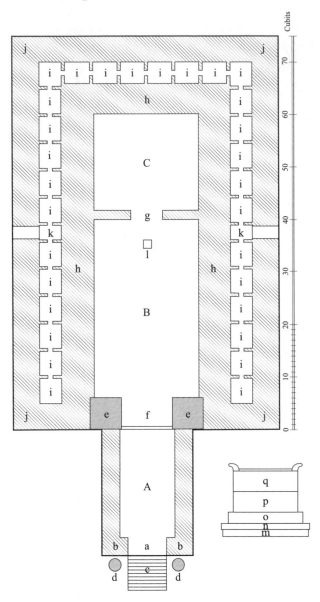

A Vestibule (40:48–49)
B Nave (41:1–2)
C Holy of Holies (41:3–4)
a Doorway of the vestibule (40:48)
b Doorposts of the vestibule (40:48–49)
c Steps (40:49)
d Pillars (40:49)
e Doorposts of the nave (41:1)
f Entrance of the nave (41:2)
g Entrance of the Holy of Holies (41:3)

h Wall of the temple (41:5)
i Side rooms (41:5–7)
j Outer wall of the side rooms (41:9)
k Entrance of the side rooms
l Table (41:22)
m Gutter (43:13–14; perhaps also 43:17)
n Ridge (43:13; perhaps also 43:17)
o Smaller, lower ledge (43:14; perhaps also 43:17)
p Larger, upper ledge (43:14; perhaps also 43:17)
q Hearth (43:15–16)

Adapted from C. F. Keil, *Biblischer Commentar über den Propheten Ezechiel* (2d ed.; Leipzig: Dörffling und Franke, 1882).

Ezekiel 40:1–49

Vision of the New Temple: Part 1

Translation

40 ¹In the twenty-fifth year of our captivity, at the beginning of the year, on the tenth of the month, in the fourteenth year after the city had fallen, on that very day, the hand of Yahweh came upon me, and he brought me there. ²In divine visions he brought me to the land of Israel and set me down on a very high mountain on which were buildings resembling a city, to the south. ³When he brought me there, a man was there whose appearance was like bronze. A linen cord was in his hand, and a measuring rod, and he was standing at the gateway. ⁴The man said to me, "Son of man, watch closely, and listen carefully. Pay attention to everything that I am about to show you, because you were brought here in order that I might show it to you. Tell everything you see to the house of Israel."

⁵Now there was a wall all around the temple compound. In the man's hand was the measuring rod, six cubits long (by the long cubit). When he measured the thickness of the structure, it was one rod, and (its) height was one rod.

⁶Then he approached the gateway that faced east and climbed its steps. He measured the threshold of the gateway; it was one rod deep. ⁷Each guardroom was one rod wide and one rod long. Between the guardrooms [the walls were] five cubits [thick], and the threshold of the gateway by the vestibule of the inside gate was one rod long. ⁸He measured the vestibule of the inside gate; it was one rod. ⁹Next he measured the vestibule of the gateway, which was eight cubits, and its gateposts, two cubits. The vestibule of the gate was at the inner end. ¹⁰As for the guardrooms beside the east gateway, there were three on either side. All three were of the same size, and the gateposts on either side were also of the same size. ¹¹Then he measured the width of the opening of the gate; it was ten cubits, and the length of the gate was thirteen cubits. ¹²There was a barrier in front of the guardrooms, one cubit wide on either side. Each guardroom was six cubits on each side. ¹³Next he measured the gateway from the ceiling of one guardroom to the ceiling opposite it. The total width was twenty-five cubits. The openings of the guardrooms were opposite each other. ¹⁴He determined [the height of] the gateposts at sixty cubits, and the court all around the gateway reached to the gateposts. ¹⁵From the front of the entrance of the gate to the front of the vestibule of the inner gate was fifty cubits. ¹⁶The guardrooms and their doorposts had openings slanting inward toward the gate all around, and likewise the vestibule had openings all around inward. The doorposts had palm-like decorations.

¹⁷Then he brought me into the outer court. There were rooms and a pavement made all around the court. Thirty rooms faced the pavement. ¹⁸The pavement ran along the side of the gates, the same length as the gates; this was the lower pavement. ¹⁹He measured the width from the front of the lower gate to the outside of the inner court: one hundred cubits (the east and the north).

²⁰As for the gateway facing north leading into the outer court, he measured its length and its width. ²¹Its guardrooms, three on either side, its gateposts, and its vestibule were of the same measurement as the first gateway, fifty cubits long and twenty-five cubits wide. ²²The openings of the vestibule and its palm decorations were also of the same measurement as those of the gate facing east. By seven steps one would ascend it, and its vestibule was ahead of them. ²³A gate of the inner court was opposite the northern gateway (as on the east), and he measured from one gate to the opposite one: one hundred cubits. ²⁴Next, he led me toward the south, and there also was a gateway facing south. He measured its gateposts and its vestibule, and the measurements were like the others. ²⁵It and its vestibule had openings all around like the openings of the others. Its length was fifty cubits and its width twenty-five cubits. ²⁶It had seven steps ascending with its vestibule ahead of them, and it had palm decorations on either side on its gateposts. ²⁷The inner court also had a gateway facing south. He measured from one gate to the other toward the south: one hundred cubits.

²⁸Then he brought me into the inner court through the south gate. He measured the south gate, whose measurements were like those [of the previous gates]. ²⁹Its guardrooms, gateposts, and vestibule had the same measurements [as the others]. Both the gate and the vestibule had openings all around. It was fifty cubits long and twenty-five cubits wide. ³⁰(These were vestibules all around. They were twenty-five cubits long and five cubits wide.) ³¹Its vestibule faced the outer court, palm decorations were on its gateposts, and its stairs had eight steps. ³²Next he brought me into the inner court facing east, and he measured the gate, and its dimensions were the same as the others. ³³Its guardrooms, gateposts, and vestibule were the same size as the others. It and its vestibule had openings all around. It was fifty cubits long and twenty-five cubits wide. ³⁴Its vestibule faced the outer court, and there were palm decorations on its gateposts on either side. Its stairs had eight steps. ³⁵Then he brought me to the north gateway and measured it. It had the same measurements [as the others]. ³⁶[This was also true of] its guardrooms, its gateposts, and its vestibule. It had openings all around. It was fifty cubits long and twenty-five cubits wide. ³⁷Its vestibule faced the outer court, and there were palm decorations on its gateposts on either side. Its stairs had eight steps.

³⁸There was a room with its opening by the gateposts [at] the gateways where they washed the burnt offering. ³⁹In the vestibule of the gateway, there were two tables on either side, to use when slaughtering the burnt offering, sin offering, and reparation offering. ⁴⁰By the outside wall, as one goes up to the entrance of the north gateway, were two tables. By the other wall of the vestibule of the gateway were two tables. ⁴¹That is, there were four tables on one side and four on the other side of the gateway—eight tables on which they were to slaughter. ⁴²The four tables for the burnt offering were made of hewn stone. They were one and a half cubits long, one and a half cubits wide, and one cubit high. On them they placed the instruments with which they slaughtered the burnt offering and the other sacrifices. ⁴³Double-pronged hooks, each a handbreadth long, were fas-

tened to the building all around, but the meat for the sacrifice was placed on the tables.

⁴⁴Outside the inner gate, in the inner court, were two rooms, one at the side of the north gate facing south and the other at the side of the south gate facing north. ⁴⁵He said to me, "This room that faces south is for the priests who guard the temple, ⁴⁶and the room that faces north is for the priests who guard the altar. They are descendants of Zadok, the only Levites who may approach Yahweh to minister to him."

⁴⁷Then he measured the court. It was one hundred cubits long and one hundred cubits wide—a square. The altar was in front of the temple.

⁴⁸Next he brought me to the vestibule of the temple. He measured each doorpost of the vestibule: five cubits on either side. The width of the doorway was three cubits on either side. ⁴⁹The length of the vestibule was twenty cubits, and its width was eleven cubits. One ascended it by [ten] steps, and there were pillars by the doorposts, one on either side.

Textual Notes

40:1 Ezek 40:1–4 serves as an introduction or preamble to the "temple tour" itself.

בֶּעָשׂוֹר לַחֹדֶשׁ—Instead of the usual ordinal form for "tenth," עֲשִׂירִי, used in the date notices in 24:1; 29:1; and 33:21, we here have an apparent cardinal form, עָשׂוֹר, "ten," used in 20:1 and 24:1 and elsewhere in the OT in date formulae. As usual in Ezekiel, the numeral stands before לַחֹדֶשׁ ("to/of the month") without יוֹם.

אַחַר אֲשֶׁר—The usual form of the preposition "after" in this combination is אַחֲרֵי אֲשֶׁר. Ezekiel here uses אַחַר, found in this combination elsewhere only in Ruth 2:2. See Waltke-O'Connor, § 38.7a, example 9.

הֻכְּתָה הָעִיר—See the fourth textual note on 33:21 for the identical clause in the initial report of Jerusalem's fall: literally, "the city was struck/smitten." The verb is the feminine Hophal perfect of נָכָה since the noun עִיר is feminine.

הָיְתָה עָלַי יַד־יְהֹוָה וַיָּבֵא אֹתִי שָׁמָּה:—These two clauses emphasize God's activity and the prophet's characteristic passivity, evident throughout the book. So too do the various forms of the guidance formula that recur throughout chapters 40–48 (see the second textual note on 40:2).

Most body parts that occur in pairs, including יָד, "hand," are grammatically feminine. In the construct phrase יַד־יְהֹוָה ("the hand of Yahweh"), יָד is the subject of the feminine verb הָיְתָה, but then, as in 3:22 and 37:1 (see also 33:22), the next verb (וַיָּבֵא) is masculine because Yahweh is the real actor in the event.

The final adverb, שָׁמָּה, is שָׁם, "there," with the locative *he*, which here has true directional force: "*to* there." (Sometimes elsewhere, as in 48:35, שָׁמָּה simply means "there.") It may refer back to הָעִיר, "the city" that had fallen, but the earthly temple in Jerusalem had been destroyed when the city fell in 586 B.C. Other features, such as the "very high mountain" (40:2) also transcend the earthly place. The location is within the "divine visions" (40:2) as will become clearer in 40:3, which begins with the same three words that ended 40:1, but with the first two words spelled plene (וַיָּבִיא אוֹתִי שָׁמָּה).

40:2 בְּמַרְאוֹת אֱלֹהִים—The identical construct phrase, literally, "in visions of God," was in 8:3, where it was translated "in a divine vision," and מַרְאוֹת אֱלֹהִים was also in 1:1. In 1:1 and 8:3, the visions were of God himself, at least in the "incarnated" form of his "Glory," but here it is God's city and temple that Ezekiel sees. The "Glory" does not appear until 43:1–12. Therefore, here "God" is used in a sort of adverbial sense in the phrase. In the OT God is heard in OT visions, but never seen directly in his heavenly majesty. However, he can be seen in various "incarnational" hypostases. Thus Moses cannot see his "face" in Ex 33:20–23, but does see his "back," and terrified Isaiah sees Yahweh "incarnated" in his temple (Isaiah 6), as does Ezekiel in chapter 8. The Christian confession is that the gulf between God and man was bridged in the incarnation: "no one has ever seen God," but we have seen Christ, "the only-begotten God," "who has made [God] known" (Jn 1:18). See also Jn 6:46 and especially Jn 14:7–11. This confession divides Christians from Jews, Muslims, and others who deem it blasphemy.

הֱבִיאַנִי—"He brought me," the Hiphil perfect of בּוֹא with suffix, is synonymous with וַיָּבֵא אֹתִי in 40:1b and וַיָּבִיא אוֹתִי in 40:3. It too emphasizes that God is the actor and the prophet is the passive recipient of divine revelation. The Hiphil imperfect of בּוֹא with suffix, וַיְבִיאֵנִי (sometimes *ḥaser*: וַיְבִאֵנִי) has the same meaning and is repeated in 40:17, 28, 32, 35, 48; 41:1; 42:1; 44:4; 46:19. The implied subject of "brought" here is (masculine) "Yahweh" (in "the hand of Yahweh") in 40:1.

These clauses in Ezekiel 40–48 with the Hiphil of בּוֹא and a first common singular suffix are often called the "guidance formula" because the prophet is guided throughout the vision. Essentially synonymous are six other forms of the guidance formula, all of which also use a Hiphil verb with first common singular suffix: (1) the Hiphil imperfect with *waw* consecutive of נוּחַ: וַיְנִיחֵנִי, "he set me down," in 40:2 (see the next textual note); (2) וַיּוֹלִכֵנִי, the Hiphil imperfect with *waw* consecutive of הָלַךְ, "he led me" (40:24; 43:1; 47:6); (3) the Hiphil perfect, or imperfect with *waw* consecutive, of יָצָא, "he led me out" (42:1, 15; 46:21; 47:2); (4) the Hiphil imperfect with *waw* consecutive of שׁוּב, "he brought me back," in 47:1, 6, and also in 44:1, where instead of a suffix the verb takes the direct object particle (וַיָּשֶׁב אֹתִי); (5) the Hiphil imperfect with *waw* consecutive of עָבַר, "he led me past/through," in 46:21; 47:3, 4 (twice); and (6) the Hiphil imperfect of סָבַב: וַיְסַבֵּנִי, "he brought me around," in 47:2.

In most instances, the guidance formula does not have a named subject. The supernatural guide will be introduced in 40:3, and in particular 43:6 reveals how Yahweh speaks to Ezekiel through the agency of this guide. It is possible that throughout Ezekiel 40–48 Yahweh guides Ezekiel (and speaks to him) by means of this guide, even in the passages (e.g., chapters 44 and 45) where the guide is not mentioned and where Yahweh is named as the one who speaks to the prophet.

The role of the guide as Yahweh's intermediary can be explained whether he is an angel (cf. Heb 1:7, 14) or whether he is a preincarnate appearance of God the Son, Jesus Christ (cf. Jn 8:38; 14:10, 24). See further the commentary on Ezek 40:3 and 43:6.

In the comparable vision in Rev 21:9–22:6, the apostle John on Patmos states, καὶ ἀπήνεγκέν με ἐν πνεύματι, "he brought me in the Spirit" (Rev 21:10). The (feminine) "Spirit" had also been the transporter in Ezek 8:3 and will be again in 43:5, where the verbs are feminine, וַתִּשָּׂאֵנִי רוּחַ וַתְּבִיאֵנִי, although that distinction is lost in the identical translation of the Hiphil of בוא with suffix: "the Spirit lifted me up and *brought me.*"

וַיְנִיחֵנִי אֶל־הַר גָּבֹהַּ מְאֹד—For the verb, see the third textual note on 37:1. This Hiphil form of נוח would ordinarily mean "cause to rest," but in 37:1 and here, it must mean "set down, place." The use of this form with this meaning may be another sign of the decay of classical Hebrew in and after the exile. Throughout the vision, אֶל ("to") is used in the sense of עַל, hence, "he set me down *on* a very high mountain."

כְּמִבְנֵה־עִיר מִנֶּגֶב:—The preposition כְּ was used frequently in chapter 1 to indicate that the vision transcended ordinary experience and can only be described via simile as being "as, like." It will be so used again in 40:3 for the man who looked (literally) "like the appearance of bronze" (כְּמַרְאֵה נְחֹשֶׁת). The noun מִבְנֶה is a hapax, although obviously derived from the common verb בָּנָה, "to build." In a Phoenician parallel, the word has a collective sense, and so I have taken it here as the plural, literally, "like *buildings* of a city," although it could be singular, "like the construction of a city." The reference is clearly not to Jerusalem, but to the temple, described as "like/resembling" a city, probably because of its walls and gates and the other structures besides the temple proper described in 40:5–42:20.

"To the south" (מִנֶּגֶב) is troublesome to many critics, who sometimes regard it as a gloss or later addition.[1] They argue that it is awkward and that aside from here, דָּרוֹם is always used for "south" elsewhere in chapters 40–42.[2] However, presuming Ezekiel came along the Fertile Crescent he would approach Jerusalem from the north and would naturally see the temple to the south. In 8:3 the prophet had also approached from the north. Here the LXX translated with ἀπέναντι, "opposite (me)," which may mean that its Hebrew text had מִנֶּגֶד or that it tried to smooth out the MT, but the meaning is not substantially changed.

40:3 וַיָּבִיא אוֹתִי שָׁמָּה—The last three words of 40:1 are repeated to resume the main line of thought. But the normal form וַיָּבֵא in 40:1 is replaced by וַיָּבִיא. This may simply be a late plene spelling, since the use of vowel letters increased in Late Biblical Hebrew (and even more in Qumran and Rabbinic Hebrew). Similarly, *haser* אֹתִי in 40:1 becomes plene אוֹתִי here. Some suggest that the consonants could be vocalized וַיְבִיא since occasionally in Biblical Hebrew a *waw* consecutive is attached to a regular imperfect form instead of the shortened (jussive) form. See the discussion in GKC, § 74 l.

וּפְתִיל־פִּשְׁתִּים—Literally, "a cord of linen" has the noun פָּתִיל, derived from the verb פָּתַל, "twist." Thus the noun means something "twisted," and usually refers to a "cord," "thread," or "rope." In Gen 38:18, 25 it refers to the cord through the cylinder seal that Judah gave in pledge to Tamar. It refers to the cord for fastening the high priest's breastpiece to his ephod (Ex 28:28; 39:21); the cord for fastening the gold

---

[1] E.g., Zimmerli, *Ezekiel*, 2:331.

[2] In Ezekiel, נֶגֶב is in 21:2–3, 9 (ET 20:46–47; 21:4); 40:2; 46:9; 47:1, 19; 48:10, 16, 17, 28, 33, while דָּרוֹם is in 21:2 (ET 20:46); 40:24, 27–28, 44–45; 41:11; 42:12–13, 18.

plate with the inscription "Holy to Yahweh" (Ex 28:36; 39:30) to the high priest's turban (Ex 28:37; 39:31); decorative gold threads in the high priest's ephod (Ex 39:3); a cord on the tassels the Israelites were to put on their garments (Num 15:38); and a rope used to tie up Samson (Judg 16:9).

וּקְנֵה הַמִּדָּה—Literally, "a reed of measurement," this means "a rod for taking measurements," "a measuring rod." The genitive could be described as one of purpose or intention (cf. Waltke-O'Connor, § 9.5.1e). Ezekiel had used קָנֶה (here in construct) in 29:6 to refer to Egypt as an unreliable crutch. The noun מִדָּה, "measurement," occurs twenty-five times in Ezekiel 40–48. It is derived from מָדַד, "to measure" (see the fourth textual note on 40:5). Even though הַמִּדָּה has the article, it should be translated as indefinite; it is an example of where the article is added to an object used for a certain purpose (see Joüon, § 137 m).

בַּשַּׁעַר—The noun שַׁעַר is sometimes translated simply "gate" (on one set of hinges), and there probably were such gates on the interior of houses. But for cities or other major structures, "gate*way*" is technically mandatory for שַׁעַר, because these were rather complicated structures, as the description following here will make plain. It is interesting to note that Ezekiel's description of the gateway of the temple compound ("resembling a city," 40:2) is fairly parallel to city gates that we know well from archaeological excavations at Megiddo, Gezer, Hazor, and elsewhere. Nevertheless, for purposes of brevity, I have often simply used "gate."

40:4 רְאֵה בְעֵינֶיךָ וּבְאָזְנֶיךָ שְׁמָע וְשִׂים לִבְּךָ—The directions to Ezekiel are, literally, "look with your eyes, and with your ears hear, and set your heart/mind …"

אֲנִי מַרְאֶה אוֹתָךְ—A pronoun plus a participle is often a *futurum instans*: "I am *about* to show you." See GKC, § 116 p. In form מַרְאֶה is identical to the noun "appearance," used numerous times in Ezekiel, including in 40:3, but here it is the Hiphil participle of רָאָה, "see." אוֹתָךְ is אוֹתְךָ in pause.

לְמַעַן הַרְאוֹתְכָה הֻבָאתָה הֵנָּה—This is a purpose clause with an infinitive: "in order to make you see/show you, you were brought here." The Hiphil infinitive הַרְאוֹתְכָה has a classic instance of a suffix used as a direct object. Its second masculine singular suffix is written with *he* as a vowel letter. Similarly, the final *qamets* in the Hophal second masculine singular perfect הֻבָאתָה (from בּוֹא; see GKC, § 74 d) takes *he* as a vowel letter. Again (see the first textual note on 40:3), such vowel letters are more common in Late Biblical Hebrew, and even more in postbiblical Hebrew. This is the only Hophal second masculine singular perfect of בּוֹא in the OT.

40:5 וְהִנֵּה חוֹמָה מִחוּץ לַבַּיִת—Elsewhere in the OT בַּיִת often refers to the temple proper, but throughout Ezekiel 40–48 it refers to the entire temple compound or sacred precinct. Modern scholarship often refers to the temple compound as the *temenos*, a transliteration of the Greek term τέμενος, used in LXX Ezek 6:4, 6, where, however, it translates חַמָּן, a term for a pagan "shrine." τέμενος is also used in LXX Hos 8:14 (for pagan shrines) and in 1 Macc 1:47; 5:43–44; 2 Macc 1:15; 10:2; 11:3; 3 Macc 1:7, 13.

סָבִיב ׀ סָבִיב—"All around" translates the repeated adverbial. As in 37:2, this duplication is not emphatic, but an indication of Late Biblical Hebrew style. The duplicated סָבִיב סָבִיב appears often in Ezekiel, especially chapters 40–42, and nowhere else in the OT except 2 Chr 4:3.

שֵׁשׁ־אַמּוֹת בָּאַמָּה וָטֹפַח—Literally, "six cubits by a cubit and a handbreadth," this is translated, "six cubits long (by the long cubit)." The detail that these "six cubits" each measured "an (ordinary) cubit plus a handbreadth" had to be added because ancient Israel knew three different cubit measures. The ordinary cubit is referred to in Deut 3:11 as an אַמַּת־אִישׁ. Estimates of modern equivalents vary, but the ordinary cubit is usually considered equivalent to about 44.6 centimeters (17.4 inches) or six handbreadths. If a טֹפַח, "handbreadth" (four fingers), was about 7.4 centimeters (almost 3 inches), that gives us a "long cubit" of some 52 centimeters or 20.3 inches. From here on, the measurements in Ezekiel are assumed to be by this long cubit (43:13, like 40:5, explains explicitly that the cubit being used is the long cubit: אַמָּה וָטֹפַח, "an [ordinary] cubit and a handbreadth"). This long cubit seems to have been a sacred and possibly also a royal cubit, and is close to a similar measure used at times in both Egypt and Babylon.

וַיָּמָד אֶת־רֹחַב הַבִּנְיָן—The Qal of מָדַד, "to measure," occurs thirty-six times in Ezekiel 40–48, often in this form (third masculine singular imperfect with *waw* consecutive): literally, "and he measured." The noun רֹחַב, "width," occurs fifty-five times in Ezekiel 40–48. The noun בִּנְיָן, another derivative of בָּנָה, "build" (like מִבְנֶה in 40:2), occurs in the OT only in Ezek 40:5; 41:12, 15; 42:1, 5, 10 (and in the Aramaic of Ezra 5:4). A synonym, בִּנְיָה, is found in Ezek 41:13. Apparently בִּנְיָן could refer to anything "built," that is, a "structure" of any sort. Here it refers to the wall, so "the width of the structure" could be translated "the thickness of the wall" (ESV).

40:6 וַיָּבוֹא אֶל־שַׁעַר—Ordinarily the imperfect of בּוֹא with *waw* consecutive could be translated as "entered, went in," but the context makes plain that would be premature here. First, "he *approached* the gateway" by climbing the steps and measured the threshold—the subject of this verse—before entering. For unknown reasons, שַׁעַר, "gateway," is anarthrous here, as it is frequently later, but the article must be supplied in translation. The expected article is used later in this verse and in other verses, for example, 40:3, 7–11, 13–16, 18–22; 42:15; 43:1 (first occurrence).

אֲשֶׁר פָּנָיו דֶּרֶךְ הַקָּדִימָה—This is, literally, "which its face [was] toward the east." The noun דֶּרֶךְ, "way," is used as a preposition, "toward."

וַיַּעַל בְּמַעֲלוֹתָו—The Qal of עָלָה, "go up, ascend," occurs together with the plural of the cognate noun מַעֲלָה, "steps," here and again in 40:26, 49, and perhaps also in 40:22. Here the verb is translated "climbed." The Qere of the noun, בְּמַעֲלוֹתָיו, "by its steps," has the form of third masculine singular suffix for a plural noun. The Kethib probably should be vocalized בְּמַעֲלוֹתָו and is the same plural noun, "steps," but with the suffix written defectively. The same defective spelling of the third masculine singular suffix (וֹ- for יו-) occurs frequently in Kethib forms in this vision and apparently represents an archaic convention or a scribal idiosyncrasy. The MT does not say how many steps there were. Instead of a translation of the verb, the LXX has "seven" steps to harmonize this verse with 40:22 and 40:26.

וַיָּמָד אֶת־סַף הַשַּׁעַר קָנֶה אֶחָד רֹחַב—The noun סַף refers to the "threshold," here "of the gateway." Since the "width/thickness" of the wall was one rod (רֹחַב, 40:5),

the same measure is repeated here, literally, "one rod (in) width," although in the translation "deep" is chosen for the threshold. The measurement is from an outer surface inward. Hebrew sometimes uses רֹחַב ("width") and אֹרֶךְ ("length," 40:7, 11, etc.) loosely.

וְאֵת֙ סַ֤ף אֶחָד֙ קָנֶ֣ה אֶחָ֔ד רֹֽחַב׃—This is a major crux. After "he measured the threshold of the gateway; it was one rod deep," this adds another object of the verb and its dimension: "measured … the one threshold, [and it was] one rod (in) width/depth." The Targum and Vulgate reflect the MT, but the LXX has a much shorter reading. The Syriac seems to have read אֶחָד, "one," as אַחֵר, "other," which presumably is the source of that rendition in KJV and NKJV. The next verse will, indeed, describe another threshold leading into the vestibule, and its dimensions are again one rod, but its mention here is premature and redundant.

These words probably are best taken as a slightly garbled dittograph of the preceding ones, and so I, with most recent translators and commentators, have omitted them in translation.

40:7 וְהַתָּ֗א—Lexicons give various translations for the noun תָּא, including "chamber" (BDB) and "niche" (*HALOT*, 2), but functionally, we know from 1 Ki 14:28 ‖ 2 Chr 12:11 that it refers to a room for guards. These spaces were normally associated with warfare in fortresses and cities. Their function here is not stated, but subsequent chapters will make their "military" role plain: they were manned by Levites to protect the sanctity of the space within and to control access to it. Probably the outrages in the temple described in Ezekiel 8 illustrate the type of behavior that guards had to thwart.

Instead of translating it, the LXX, perhaps unsure of its meaning, always transliterates it as θεε.

The definite article on תָּא is translated "each" since 40:10 indicates that there were six "guardrooms" at each gateway, three of them on each side, all identical in size, a pattern amply attested by archaeology. Their size was a rod square: קָנֶ֤ה אֶחָד֙ אֹ֔רֶךְ וְקָנֶ֥ה אֶחָד֙ רֹ֔חַב. See figure 3.

וּבֵ֤ין הַתָּאִים֙ חָמֵ֣שׁ אַמּ֔וֹת—This is simply "between the guardrooms [were] five cubits." It is somewhat of a deduction to add that this refers to the thickness of "the walls" between the guard rooms, but this area between the guardrooms must not have been open or unenclosed, since then there would have been so many entrances into the outer court that the gateway would not be closed and guards would be useless. Hence, we must assume side walls separating one chamber from another. Except for the thickness we have no further description of these walls.

וְסַ֣ף הַשַּׁ֗עַר מֵאֵ֨צֶל אוּלָ֧ם הַשַּׁ֛עַר מֵהַבַּ֖יִת קָנֶ֥ה אֶחָֽד׃—Finally, we come to the second threshold (for the first one, see the fourth textual note on 40:6). It is described as, literally, "the threshold of the gateway by the vestibule of the gateway from the house (temple), one rod." For translation, "by the vestibule of the inside gate" seems adequate and clear for the last part of the phrase. For שַׁעַר here, "gate" or even "entrance" might be suitable because the picture is probably of an opening leading from the guardroom passage into the vestibule just inside the gate and then into the outer court. אוּלָם, which retains its long ultimate vowel (-לָ-) even when in the construct, as here, is rendered "vestibule" (KJV: "porch"). More often it is spelled defectively as אֻלָם, as already in 40:8–9. Its plural is usually אֻלַמּוֹת (see the third textual note on 40:16), and its form with suffixes is אֻלַמָּיו (e.g., 40:21–22a) or sometimes plene, אֵילַמּוֹ- (e.g., 40:24, 25). Perhaps these different forms reflect changes in pronunciation just coming into use.

Again, instead of translating, the LXX always transliterates it, the singular and sometimes the plural as αιλαμ and other occurrences of the plural as αιλαμμω.

40:8–9 The versions have widely different texts for 40:8. Numerous Hebrew manuscripts, as well as the Syriac and Vulgate, omit 40:8b–40:9a (the last three Hebrew words of 40:8 and the first four Hebrew words of 40:9). Apparently problems were caused because of the repetitiousness of the MT and because the MT gives two different measures for the vestibule: 40:8 states that it was "one rod," that is, six cubits, while 40:9 gives "eight cubits." Most modern commentators simply assume dittography and omit 40:8b–40:9a.

One must admit that little would really be lost if 40:8 were absent, but it does give us a clear idea of the inside length, or depth, of the vestibule (for the east gate, the length from east to west). Then 40:9 apparently gives (for the east gate) the length from east to west of the north or south wall of the vestibule on the outside, thus enabling us to append to this the dimensions of the "gateposts" (for אַיִל, see the next textual note) and calculate the entire length of the gateway. See the second textual note on 40:15 and figure 3.

40:9 וְאֵילָו שְׁתַּיִם אַמּוֹת—The precise meaning of אַיִל as a technical architectural term is not known. English versions vary. KJV's simple "posts" for the plural here is unclear. RSV and NIV have "jambs," while NRSV offers "pilasters." NKJV's "gateposts" seemed the most satisfactory to me. (In some other places in chapters 40–41 [e.g., 40:16, 48–49], "doorpost" seems most appropriate for אַיִל.) The Kethib וְאֵילָו has a defectively written third masculine singular suffix, while the Qere, וְאֵילָיו, has the normal suffix form for a plural noun. The same Qere-Kethib variants of the word recur nine more times in the chapter,[a] which may attest to scribal scrupulosity in reproducing even an unusual form. (For the same Qere-Kethib variants of the third masculine singular suffix on a different word, see the third textual note on 40:6.) The suffix ("*its* gateposts") refers to אֻלָם הַשַּׁעַר, not merely to שַׁעַר. Ezek 40:14 reports that these "gateposts" were sixty cubits high, so the depth stated here, "two cubits," would be needed to give the strength required to support gateposts of that height. The text does not describe how these gateposts attached to the north and south gateway walls. Whatever the details, they functioned as the west wall of the structure.

40:10 When he arrives at the exit from the gate structures, the guide returns to the entrance in order to fill in certain details about it. He points out that there were three guardrooms on either side, all of equal size, and then adds that the gateposts (already measured in 40:9) were also both of the same size. The phrase מִפֹּה ... מִפֹּה, literally, "from here ... from here," is translated "on either side." It is an idiom unique to Ezekiel 40–41. הַשַּׁעַר דֶּרֶךְ הַקָּדִים, literally, "the gateway toward the east," is translated more concretely as "the east gateway." The terse Hebrew here is an abbreviation for the full

(a) Ezek 40:21, 24, 26, 29, 31, 33, 34, 36, 37

phrase שַׁעַר אֲשֶׁר פָּנָיו דֶּרֶךְ הַקָּדִימָה (literally, "the gate which its face is toward the east") in 40:6.

40:11 This verse gives the width of "the opening of the gate" as "ten cubits." But it is unclear what is meant by "the length of the gate was thirteen cubits." One proposal is that the ten cubits of "the opening of the gate" (פֶּתַח־הַשַּׁעַר) may measure the width of the space occupied by the leaves of the door, while "the length [אֹרֶךְ] of the gate [הַשַּׁעַר]," which is thirteen cubits, may refer to "the full width of the gateway, inclusive of the jambs and the sockets."[3] This explanation builds on the distinction between פֶּתַח־הַשַּׁעַר and הַשַּׁעַר in the text and is followed by many scholars. But why this distance is referred to as the "length," אֹרֶךְ, is unclear.[4] Many other interpretations have been offered, but it is not rewarding to recount all the others. Keil, whose figures were adapted for this commentary, views the total width of the gate opening as ten cubits[5] (see figure 3).

40:12 The general meaning of גְּבוּל is "boundary." The exact nature of this boundary, presumably a small wall of some kind, is not entirely clear. We are given only its width, and, as with many other structures, not its height. The evident purpose of these barriers (in front of the guardrooms) was to enable the sentries to come in and out of the guardrooms without disturbing or being disturbed by those going through the gateway (see figure 3). Since the barriers apparently projected a cubit apiece into the passageway, it means that eight or eleven cubits' width remained for those who were going through the passageway, depending on the total width of the gateway (see the textual note on 40:11). Ezek 40:12b is essentially a repetition of 40:7a.

40:13 מִגַּג הַתָּא לְגַגּוֹ—This is, literally, "from the ceiling of the guardroom to its ceiling." The noun גַּג ordinarily means "roof," but if these measurements are being taken from the inside (see below), "ceiling" is more appropriate here. RSV and NRSV, who translate it both times as "back," follow the LXX, which translates it both times as τοῖχος, "wall," perhaps as if it read גַּו, "back (wall)." NIV equivocates with "the top of the rear wall … the top of the opposite one." But all the other ancient versions support the MT, so the case for its retention is stronger. The idiomatic לְגַגּוֹ, "to its ceiling," could have been written more fully as לְגַג הַתָּא, "to the ceiling of the (other) guardroom," and so it is translated, "to the ceiling opposite it." The final phrase of the verse has a similar idiomatic meaning, פֶּתַח נֶגֶד פָּתַח, literally, "opening opposite opening."

How the twenty-five cubits given in this verse are to be accounted for depends on how one reads 40:11 (see the textual note there). If the total width of the gateway was thirteen cubits, these measurements would have been taken from the inside, and to that thirteen cubits would have been added six cubits for each of the two guardrooms (40:7), for a total of twenty-five cubits. According to this view, the measure-

---

[3] Block, *Ezekiel*, 2:518, n. 20.

[4] The total length of the entire gateway structure (from east to west), fifty cubits, is given in 40:15 (see the second textual note on that verse).

[5] Keil, *Ezekiel*, 2:193–94; see his discussion on those pages for his view of the last half of the verse.

ments were apparently taken at the point where the ceiling and the walls met (hence the variation in the LXX, RSV, and NRSV). Keil, who reads 40:11 as saying that the total width of the gateway was ten cubits rather than thirteen, adds to the six cubits for each of the two guardrooms also a cubit and a half for each of the two exterior walls,[6] which aren't elsewhere measured in Ezekiel's vision. According to this view, the measurement would have been from the outside. See figure 3.

40:14 The import of this verse is somewhat obscure, and the various translations reflect uncertainty or speculation. Predictably, critics emend or delete.[7] I have depended largely on Keil[8] and NKJV in wresting the sense.

וַיַּעַשׂ אֶת־אֵילִים שִׁשִּׁים אַמָּה—The initial verb is not another וַיָּמָד, "and he measured" (as in, e.g., 40:13), but from עָשָׂה, "and he did, determined, fixed," perhaps reflecting that the measuring stick could not be used to obtain the result. That fits if the dimension is the height, which could not be measured from the ground, but had to be calculated by other means. That also comports with the object, אֵילִים, "gateposts," and their large measure of "sixty cubits," which does not conform to the horizontal dimensions of other structures in the context. Hence, the best alternative seems to be that this is one of the exceptions where we are given a height dimension. The Vulgate and the Targum seem to support such an interpretation.

The LXX has an entirely different reading. RSV and NRSV emend אֵילִים, "gateposts," to אוּלָם, "vestibule," but that is not appropriate for "sixty cubits." Apparently to allow for that large distance, NIV speculates that the reference is to a horizontal circumference: "He measured along the faces of the projecting walls all around the inside of the gateway—sixty cubits."

וְאֶל־אַיִל הֶחָצֵר הַשַּׁעַר סָבִיב ׀ סָבִיב:—Literally, this says, "toward the gatepost of the court the gate was all around." If we take אַיִל in a collective sense, translated as plural, then חָצֵר would seem to be the outer court of the temple, and, if not pressed, it was naturally "all around the gateway," because the gateway led into it and at least its gateposts may have extended a bit into it.

40:15 The general sense of the verse seems clear, even if some details are difficult. The opening phrase וְעַל פְּנֵי seems to say "on/against the face (of the gate)," where we might expect the preposition מִן, "from."[9] Perhaps, however, that sense was taken for granted because the phrase is obviously intended to balance the later phrase עַל־לִפְנֵי (not found elsewhere), which points in the other direction, "to the front of" the vestibule, as the terminal point. Sometimes עַל overlaps in meaning with עַד when used of the direction in which one is going (e.g., Ps 19:7; Is 10:25). The two balancing phrases here may be abbreviated in Ezek 40:19 by מִלְּפְנֵי ... לִפְנֵי, with the same meaning as here.

---

6   Keil, *Ezekiel*, 2:195–95.

7   Zimmerli, *Ezekiel*, 2:335, follows Gese (*Der Verfassungsentwurf des Ezechiel*, 140–48) in taking the easy way out by deleting the entire verse as a corrupt combination of parts of 40:15–16. Allen, *Ezekiel*, 2:220, relying in part on Gese, offers another of his torturous, labyrinthine speculations on how the verse may have taken shape.

8   Keil, *Ezekiel*, 2:187, 195–96.

9   Zimmerli, *Ezekiel*, 2:335, suggests reading מִלְּפְנֵי.

הַשַּׁעַר הָרִאשׁוֹן עַל־לִפְנֵי אֻלָם הַשַּׁעַר הַפְּנִימִי—The first "gate" is modified by a word whose Qere is הָרִאשׁוֹן. The Kethib apparently is the same word but with metathesis of its first two consonants. Whatever its original spelling, it is a hapax of uncertain meaning, although obviously an architectural term of some sort. The best guess seems to be something like "entrance," assuming a derivation from the verb אָתָה, "to come." It stands in apposition to הַשַּׁעַר, literally, "the gate, the entrance" (syntax one would expect if it were an adjective), but it must be translated as if in construct: "the entrance of the gate." The LXX's τὸ αἴθριον τῆς πύλης ἔξωθεν, "the front *of the gate from the outside*," seems to reflect a similar idea. The phrase seems to refer to the entrance to the gate structure at the top of the flight of steps. At the opposite end of the gate structure was "the inner gate" (not to be confused with the gates to the inner court described in 40:28–37). The measurement was made to "the front of the vestibule" of that gate, that is, to the west end, or exit, of the gate structure. Thus the length of the entire gate structure (from east to west for the eastern gate) is fifty cubits, and, satisfyingly, if one adds up all the measurements already given in 40:6–10, we get a total of fifty cubits: six cubits for the threshold of the gateway (40:6); three guardrooms per side (40:10), each six cubits (40:7a); two walls between the guardrooms, each five cubits (40:7b); six cubits for the threshold of the vestibule (40:7c); eight cubits for the vestibule itself (40:9a); two cubits for the gateposts (40:9b), that is, 6 + 18 + 10 + 6 + 8 + 2 = 50! See figure 3.

40:16 The verse bristles with difficulties or matters we do not understand, and so it is hard to get a clear picture. I doubt if any two translations, ancient or modern, agree, and the commentaries debate. The verse opens by speaking of וְחַלֹּנוֹת אֲטֻמוֹת. The noun חַלּוֹן is often translated "window," but really refers to an aperture of any kind. The versions seem to derive אֲטֻמוֹת from אָטַם, "close, shut." This might imply completely blocked or shuttered openings, but usually it is taken to imply only a partial closing of some sort. The translation I have chosen, "openings slanting inward," approximates the Vulgate's *fenestra obliquas* or the Syriac's paraphrase, "windows open on the inside, narrow on the outside." These places may have militaristic overtones (openings through which archers could shoot arrows), but in this context, if the translation is at all correct, they would have been for observational purposes only. The LXX guessed strangely, "secret windows." KJV had "narrow windows," which NKJV finessed to "beveled window *frames*" (emphasis added). RSV offers "*windows … narrowing* inwards into their jambs" (emphasis added), while NRSV has "windows, with shutters." NIV thinks of "narrow parapet openings." Finally, Block's venturesome translation "closed niches" (blocked windows or cupboards, perhaps for storage) is based on a cognate phrase in Qumran's *Temple Scroll*.[10] Obviously, we have no certain understanding of what the phrase means. Let the reader decide!

אֲלֵיהֵמָה—This form of third masculine plural suffix (on the plural of אַיִל, "their doorposts"), occurs only here in the OT, but is common in the Hebrew of the Dead

---

[10] Block, *Ezekiel*, 2:519, 522–23.

Sea Scrolls (Joüon, § 94 i, footnote 1; cf. GKC, § 91 l). The corresponding feminine form of the third plural suffix was used on גְּוִיֹתֵיהֶנָה in 1:11.

וְכֵן לְאֵלַמּוֹת Since this seems to introduce the second half of the verse, most commentators suggest moving the *athnach* from לְאֵלַמּוֹת back to the preceding סָבִיב. In preceding verses, "vestibule" was spelled אוּלָם or אֵלָם (see the third textual note on 40:7). But here through 40:36, the spelling is consistently אֵלַמּ-, the plural or suffixed form of אֵילָם or אֵלָם. The plural לְאֵלַמּוֹת is hard to understand here because there was only one vestibule in the gate structure. (Questionable plural suffixed forms of the word occur in 40:21–36.) Perhaps the plural here can be explained text critically: the plural ending on the following וְחַלּוֹנֹת was retrojected by a scribe, and this then required the unneeded copula on וְחַלּוֹנֹת. Others speculate that אֵלַמּוֹת and similar plurals in 40:21–36 represent a homonym with some entirely different meaning, but evidence for that is lacking.

וְאֶל־אַיִל תִּמֹרִים:—The singular אַיִל could be translated "each doorpost," but I have followed most others in translating it as plural: "the doorposts." Instead of the plural of תָּמָר, an actual "palm tree," the plural of תִּמֹרָה is used here for artificial "palm-like decorations," which also decorated Solomon's temple (1 Ki 6:29, 32, 35; 7:36). Archaeology has provided many examples of the use of the motif on the proto-Aeolic capitals of the Iron Age.

40:17 Finished with the east gate, the guide now leads the prophet over the court to the other two gates, first the north one (40:19b–23) and then the south gate (40:24–27). On the way, however, the outer court is measured and described (40:17–19a). See figure 2. Again we encounter difficult Hebrew with technical architectural terms whose meanings are disputed.

לְשָׁכוֹת—This is the plural of לִשְׁכָּה, a fairly general noun meaning "room, chamber, hall." Nothing is said about the function of these rooms here. In Jer 36:12 the word is used of a room in the king's palace. However, usually we find it in a worship context. In 1 Sam 9:22 it refers to a room on the high place where Samuel and others fete Saul before he is anointed king. That points to what seems to have been their most common role in cultic contexts: rooms where the worshipers could eat a sacrificial meal, such as that of the communion offering, or peace offering.[11] But they are mentioned also in other roles, as residences for the officiating priests and Levites (e.g., 1 Chr 9:33) and for storage of temple dues, which came in various forms (e.g., Neh 10:38–40 [ET 10:37–39]).

Nor are we informed as to their arrangement. But since the verse later states that there was a total of thirty, a likely positioning would be four on either side of each gateway of the north, south, and east outer walls (thus eight on each of those walls for a total of twenty-four) and six on the west side, three on either side of the temple itself, next to the priests' sacristies.

וְרִצְפָה עָשׂוּי—A bit more information is given about the רִצְפָה, "pavement." Note that the פ is regularly spirantized to distinguish this word from רִצְפָּה, "ember, glowing coal." What kind of a "pavement" it was is not specified. The use of the word in

---

[11] See the second textual note and the commentary on 39:17 and the textual notes on 40:39.

Esth 1:6 suggests either flagstone of some sort or possibly mosaic. The former practice is demonstrably very ancient, while mosaics were certainly very common in Roman and Byzantine construction, but it is not certain how far back that technology goes. The type of construction may explain the use of the Qal passive participle of עָשָׂה, "made." A puzzle is the lack of gender agreement between the masculine passive participle עָשׂוּי and its feminine subject, רִצְפָה. The temptation is strong to omit עָשׂוּי (as the LXX did), but עָשׂוּי appears again in 41:18–20, 25 (see the textual note on it in 41:18). Zimmerli constructively suggests that עָשׂוּי was a technical term used as a noun.[12] If so, it may say something about the nature of the room-pavement interface.

שְׁלֹשִׁים לְשָׁכוֹת אֶל־הָרִצְפָה:—There were "thirty rooms." Their relationship to the pavement is described somewhat enigmatically by the prepositional phrase אֶל־הָרִצְפָה, "to the pavement." Since אֶל frequently interchanges with עַל, the phrase may say that the rooms were built "on the pavement." More likely, however, we should understand אֶל in its basic sense of "toward, facing." That could imply that the rooms were left unpaved, with the pavement simply coming up to the lower edge of the rooms' walls, but the statement is too brief and imprecise to conclude that with any certainty. The front of the rooms would seem to be open to the courtyard, but that is not stated explicitly either.

40:18   וְהָרִצְפָה אֶל־כֶּתֶף הַשְּׁעָרִים לְעֻמַּת אֹרֶךְ הַשְּׁעָרִים—This is, literally, "the pavement [was] to the shoulder of the gates, corresponding to the length of the gates." That is, apparently the pavement flanked the gates, the "shoulder" being the area on either side of the gate building along the wall. The noun עֻמָּה, "juxtaposition," is always in construct, and except in one verse, it always has the preposition לְ. The combination לְעֻמַּת is always used as a preposition. Often it means "alongside, adjacent," as in 45:6–7, but here it probably means "agreeing with, corresponding to" (BDB, b). That the pavement was, literally, "corresponding to the length of the gates" indicates that it ran the perimeter of (at least three of) the outer walls, projecting into the outer court an area equal to the length of the gates. See figure 2. "Gates" is plural. Ezekiel is probably already thinking of all three gates, even though two will not be described until later. The pavement may or may not have run along the west wall, which had no gate.

הָרִצְפָה הַתַּחְתּוֹנָה:—Specification of this as "the lower pavement" accords with the notice in 40:31, 34, 37 that eight steps led up to the gates into the inner court. Nothing is said of any pavement in the inner court, but it would be very strange if it were less elaborate than in the outer one, and later literature seems to assume that it was not.

40:19   I have given a simplified (and hopefully more intelligible) rendering of what is, literally, "he measured the width from in front of the lower gate to in front of the inner court from without: one hundred cubits." The starting point of the measurement is expressed with מִלִּפְנֵי, "from in front of … ," and the ending point is לִפְנֵי הֶחָצֵר, "to in front of the inner court," giving not only the direction of movement, but also

---

12   Zimmerli, *Ezekiel*, 2:337.

the terminal point. Using good Hebrew idiom, מִחוּץ, "from without," defines that point more precisely. Keil explains that "the gateways of the inner court were built into the outer court" (see figure 2) and that "מִחוּץ simply affirms that the measuring only extended to the point where the inner court commenced within the outer," that is, to the front of the inner gate, not to the wall of the inner court. That seems to be confirmed by 40:23, where a measurement of one hundred cubits is given for the distance between the north outer gate and the north inner gate, and by 40:27, which gives the same information about the distance between the south gates.[13] The information in this verse seems to apply to the east side of the court (see the next textual note).

The MT has simply רֹחַב, "width," but the LXX adds "of the court," which is obviously fitting, but unnecessary in the context.

The reference to the "lower gate" (הַשַּׁעַר הַתַּחְתּוֹנָה) points again to the difference in elevation between the two courts. This will become clearer in 40:31, 34, 37, which mention the eight steps leading up to the gates of the inner court. Grammatically, there is a problem because the feminine adjective הַתַּחְתּוֹנָה does not agree with the masculine noun הַשַּׁעַר, which it modifies. Unless it is a scribal error or a sign of late Hebrew decay, the only possible way it can be understood is if the prophet really has in mind already חָצֵר, "court," a noun that is usually feminine.

הַקָּדִים וְהַצָּפוֹן: אַמָּה—The MT has the disjunctive *athnach* on אַמָּה, "cubit," and also leaves a long space afterward. Both the accent and the unusual space indicate that the last two words are separated somewhat from the earlier part of the verse, and so I have placed the two words in parentheses in my translation: "(the east and the north)." Most English translations ignore the space and simply include the last two words as part of the verse: "a hundred cubits on the east side and on the north side" (ESV; similar are KJV, NKJV, NIV). The *BHS* editors suppose that הַקָּדִים וְהַצָּפוֹן is a later gloss, but the two words are reflected in the LXX's translation, although other words are in between them: πήχεις ἑκατόν τῆς βλεπούσης κατ᾿ ἀνατολάς καὶ εἰσήγαγέν με ἐπὶ βορρᾶν ("one hundred cubits of the [gate] facing east, and he brought me to the north"). The additional words in the LXX suggest that the long space in the MT could have been left by scribes who realized that some Hebrew words had been mistakenly omitted there. The LXX makes it explicit that "the gate" mentioned earlier in the verse (τῆς πύλης) is the gate that faces east. The LXX then includes "north" in a guidance formula that is similar to its translation of 40:24, the next major transition, where the LXX accurately translates the MT. RSV follows the LXX in principle. Block is influenced by it, and his is probably the best effort to translate the MT intelligibly: "So far the eastern [gate]; now to the northern [gate]."[14] That proposal brings out the transitional character which, all agree, the last two words have.

40:20–23 Since the east gate has already been described so thoroughly, a summary statement in 40:20–23 suffices for the north gate, as will also be true of the south gate

---

[13] Keil, *Ezekiel*, 2:204.

[14] Block, *Ezekiel*, 2:524.

(40:24–27). The differences between the descriptions of the three gates are minor, mostly in manner of presentation. Plainly, all three gates were virtually identical. See figures 2 and 3. No mention is made here of the pavement flanking the northern gate, but 40:18 made it clear that this pavement flanked all of the gates in the outer wall. However, the detail is added in 40:22 that seven steps led up to the northern gate from outside the outer wall (undoubtedly true of the eastern gate as well). Ezek 40:23 also notes for the first time that the gates to the inner court were directly opposite those of the outer court.

40:20 The MT leads directly into a sketch of the northern gate of the outer wall, without a guidance formula used in similar instances ahead ("he led/brought me," 40:24, 28, etc.). But a transition is indicated by placing, in effect, the object of the verb first (וְהַשַּׁעַר אֲשֶׁר פָּנָיו דֶּרֶךְ הַצָּפוֹן) and by using the perfect verb מָדַד instead of the usual imperfect with *waw* consecutive, וַיָּמָד (e.g., 40:23). Likewise, the perfect מָדַד is also used in the transitional verses 40:24 and 40:35, and later in 41:13, 15 and 42:15–20.

This verse begins with a *casus pendens* ("as for the gateway …") and uses retrospective pronominal suffixes ("he measured *its* length and *its* width") (cf. GKC, § 143 b).

40:21 The verse has three Qere readings of a plene third masculine singular suffix (יו-ָ, the usual form on a plural noun), where the Kethib (ו-) is either a *ḥaser* spelling of the same suffix (ו-ָ) or the form for a singular noun (ו-ִ). See the third textual note on 40:6. The same phenomenon will occur in many of the following verses until 40:38, so regularly that no further comment will be made about it, unless other issues are involved. In this verse, the Kethib וְאֵלַמּוֹ ("its vestibule") is to be preferred over the Qere וְאֵלַמָּיו ("its vestibules") because there was only one vestibule per gate. This is confirmed by the following verb הָיָה, the singular form being determined by the number of the nearest subject (although it could hark back to שַׁעַר in 40:20 as well). The same will hold true in 40:24–26, 29, 31, 33–34, and 36, which again have singular Kethib and plural Qere forms of "vestibule."

הַשַּׁעַר הָרִאשׁוֹן—"The first gateway" is the east one, just measured.

אַמָּה ... בָּאַמָּה:—The second time אַמָּה, "cubit," has the preposition בְּ, often used in measurements, perhaps, literally, "by the cubit." Here it seems simply to represent a desire for variation.

40:22 וְחַלּוֹנָו וְאֵלַמּוֹ—The Hebrew is "its openings and its vestibule," but this is suspect for two reasons. The vestibule has already been mentioned in 40:21, and parallel passages refer to the vestibule *having* openings (40:16, 25, 29, 33). Nowhere else in Ezekiel is חַלּוֹן used with a pronominal suffix. Hence, with most commentators, I have acceded to an emendation to וְחַלּוֹנֵי אֵלַמּוֹ.

וּבְמַעֲלוֹת שֶׁבַע יַעֲלוּ־בוֹ—The verb יַעֲלוּ (Qal imperfect of עָלָה) is an impersonal plural, literally, "by seven steps *they* ascend by it," but translating it as a singular seems a preferable accommodation to English idiom.

לִפְנֵיהֶם:—There is some debate whether the antecedent of "before *them*" is the "steps" or the people climbing up them. If the "steps" (מַעֲלוֹת), we would expect a feminine plural suffix, not the masculine plural on לִפְנֵיהֶם. The LXX has ἔσωθεν, "inside," followed by RSV and NRSV, but this requires emendation to לִפְנִימָה, and is unnecessary, although the resultant picture would be essentially the same.

40:24 כַּמִּדּוֹת הָאֵלֶּה—Literally, "like these measurements," this means "like the measurements of the others." This phrase will be repeated in 40:28–29, 32–33, 35.

40:25 וְחַלּוֹנִים ... כְּהַחַלֹּנוֹת—The plural of חַלּוֹן appears in masculine and feminine forms in close proximity here. A "window, opening" could be construed in either gender. The pointing in *Leningradensis* (but not in most other manuscripts) of the feminine plural כְּהַחַלֹּנוֹת (with כְּ and the article) exhibits the peculiarity of a shortened (*chateph*) vowel in a closed syllable (-חֲל-, -*ḥal-lo*-). הַחַלֹּנוֹת appears also in Song 2:9.

40:26 וּמַעֲלוֹת שִׁבְעָה עֹלוֹתָו—The gist of the first three words (literally, "and steps, seven, its ascenders") is clear enough and essentially parallel to 40:22b, but details of the Hebrew seem inscrutable. What immediately strikes us is the violation of the Hebrew rule of chiastic concord: numerals from three to ten normally are of the opposite gender from the enumerated noun, but here both מַעֲלוֹת and שִׁבְעָה are feminine. The last word's Qere, עֹלוֹתָיו, is the plural with the regular suffix form, while the Kethib probably is to be vocalized עֹלוֹתָו with a *ḥaser* suffix form and the same meaning. BDB (s.v. עֹלָה II) takes it as a hapax noun meaning "stairway." Its plural with the third masculine singular suffix could mean "its stairs." Alternatively, the word could be the Qal feminine plural participle of עָלָה with suffix, meaning "its ascenders/ascents," and again referring to stairs, although the verb is never used with that meaning elsewhere. Whatever the form is here, it is clearly related to the use of the verb meaning "to ascend" with "steps" (plural of מַעֲלָה) in 40:6, 22, 49 (see BDB, s.v. עָלָה, Qal, 1 f).

Zimmerli suggests that the ungrammatical ה at the end of שִׁבְעָה was mistakenly written by some early copyist for an original מ, which had been the first consonant of the following word, which then would be מַעֲלוֹתָיו,[15] which might be a form of מַעֲלֶה (with *seghol*), meaning "its stairs, ways of ascent." Thus it would be different than מַעֲלוֹת at the beginning of the sentence, which is the plural of מַעֲלָה (with final *qamets*), meaning "steps." Then we would have an original very similar to what we will meet in 40:31, 34, and 37 (which see).

40:27 Keil calculates that the outer court covered an area of two hundred cubits on each of the north, south, and east sides (see figure 2): fifty cubits for the length that the outer gateway projected into the court (40:15, 21, 25); one hundred cubits from one gate vestibule to the opposite one (40:19, 23, 27); and fifty cubits for the length that the inner gateway projected into the outer court (40:29, 33, 36). Then, drawing on other dimensions given in chapters 40 and 41, he notes that the temple complex (enclosed by the outer walls) formed a square (see figure 2). The distance from east to west was five hundred cubits (about eight hundred fifty feet or two hundred sixty meters[16]): starting from the east gate, two hundred cubits for the depth of the outer court; one hundred cubits for the inner court (40:47); one hundred cubits for the tem-

---

[15] Zimmerli, *Ezekiel*, 2:340.

[16] See the third textual note on 40:5.

ple with the open space around it (41:13–14); and one hundred cubits for the building to the west of the temple and the restricted area (41:13). The distance from the north entrance to the south entrance was also five hundred cubits: two hundred cubits each for the north and the south sides of the outer court plus one hundred cubits for the inner court (40:47).[17] These calculations accord with the linear dimensions of the outer walls given in 42:15–20: five hundred cubits (about eight hundred fifty feet or two hundred sixty meters) on each side (if the unit of measure there is the cubit; see on 42:16).

40:28–46 The reader should be aware of a major subdivision of the chapter beginning in 40:28. The section 40:28–46 might have even merited being a new chapter. We move now to the *interior* features of the temple compound, considering (1) the gates of the inner wall (40:28–37); (2) the room for washing sacrifices and tables for preparing them at the northern gate (40:38–43); and (3) the priestly rooms (40:44–46). See figures 2 and 4. With two exceptions, noted in 40:31, 34, 37, it will be clear that the inner gates are almost exact duplicates of the outer ones in construction, dimensions, and features.

40:28 In this verse, the heavenly guide leads the prophet into the inner court through the south gate, which is opposite the south gate of the outer wall, which the guide had last measured. חָצֵר, "court," is anarthrous, as it is again in 40:31. Quite a few other words through the tour are anarthrous where we would expect them to have the article. The ancient versions translated חָצֵר as if it were definite, and some Hebrew manuscripts have the article. Perhaps the word was considered definite enough in itself that the article could be dispensed with.

40:30 This entire verse is suspect for various reasons. I have followed NIV in parenthesizing it. The verse is missing in the LXX and lacks counterparts in the descriptions of the other gates. The plural וְאֵלַמּוֹת, "vestibule*s*," is hard to make any sense of. The measurements disagree with previous information. One can only guess how the problem arose. The verse may be partially dittographical. Some speculate that a copyist collated two manuscripts, one of which had a blurred text. There are many other proposals.

40:31 This verse notes two differences from the gates in the outer wall (40:34 and 40:37 will note these same differences in connection with the other two inner gates). First, while those in the outer wall projected inward, with the vestibule to the outer court, the vestibules of the inner gates are at the end facing the outer court. Thus the inner gates form a mirror image of the outer gates. See figure 2.

Second, and of greater symbolic significance, eight steps led up to the inner gates, one more step than the seven that led up to the outer gates (40:22, 26). That means that the inner court stood on a higher platform than the outer one. As we shall see in 40:49, the temple itself stood on a higher platform still. We see reflected here the same gradation of holiness that was reflected in various aspects of tabernacle and Solomonic temple construction, and even reflected somewhat in the sacerdotal vestments. It was

---

[17] Keil, *Ezekiel*, 2:208–9.

this increasing sanctity the nearer one approached the Holy of Holies in the heart of the temple complex that, in Ezekiel's vision, requires two sets of gateways and guard-rooms

וְאֵלַמּוֹ—The Kethib singular, וְאֵלַמּוֹ, "its vestibule," is to be preferred to the Qere plural, וְאֵלַמָּיו. The same is true in 40:34 (see also the textual note on 40:37).

40:32 The Hebrew is clear, but the information given is strange. The prophet, who was already in the inner court, is now again reported as being led into it. This could imply that the guide had gone out at the south gate, and then led the prophet back into the inner court by the east gate, but it does not need to imply that. The verse could represent an awkward (humanly speaking!) repetition of information already given.

"The gate" is referred to baldly as הַשַּׁעַר without being specified as the "east" one because the direction has already been included in the guidance formula, "he brought me into the inner court facing east." Instead of "he brought me into the inner court facing east, and he measured the gate," the LXX has "he brought me into the gate facing east, and he measured it." Many propose to emend the MT accordingly, but Zimmerli judiciously notes that since the LXX already mentioned τὴν πύλην, it must translate הַשַּׁעַר when it appears in the MT by the pronoun αὐτήν, so that the LXX emended the MT twice. Hence he prefers to retain the MT as the *lectio difficilior*.[18]

40:34 לֶחָצֵר—The preposition לְ is used here, and also in the parallel passage of 40:37, instead of אֶל־חָצֵר as in 40:31. Then in the following clause in both 40:34 and 40:37 (as in 40:31), אֶל (more commonly used to indicate direction toward) is used with אַיִל for "on its gateposts" where we might expect עַל. This is one of many indications of the ease with which these prepositions were interchanged in Biblical Hebrew.

40:36 תָּאָו אֵלָו וְאֵלַמּוֹ—These first three words of the verse appear to continue the thought of the last part of 40:35, as indicated in the translation. One would expect this verse to begin with *waw*, וְתָאָו, which begins 40:21, 29, and 33. The omission of the *waw* is probably of a piece with the generally more concise wording of this verse. This probably also explains why "and its vestibule" is not mentioned as having openings. The LXX adds that, apparently to harmonize with 40:29 and 40:33.

40:37 וְאֵילָו—This first word is "and its gateposts," but the sense and the parallels in 40:31 and 40:34 require that we consider it as a scribal error for וְאֵלַמּוֹ, "its vestibule," as most of the ancient versions translated.

At the conclusion of this discussion of the gates (outer gates in 40:6–16, 20–27 and inner gates in 40:28–37), we note that there were no western gates. Instead, in 41:12, Ezekiel will see a building to the west of the temple. See figure 2.

40:38–43 The alert reader will note at once a change of subject in 40:38 but no guidance formula (which we do not meet again until 40:48). Instead 40:38 opens abruptly on the subject of a room by the north inner gate. The discussion then moves to tables used for preparing the sacrifices (40:39–43). In fact, this interruption in the flow of the tour (40:38–43) is the first of two. The other concerns rooms reserved for

---

[18] Zimmerli, *Ezekiel*, 2:341.

certain priests (40:44–46). In these sections, there is no mention of the guide, and while measurements are given in 40:42 for the stone tables, no measurements are made by the guide until 40:47. However, the verses do contain considerable detail. As Block nicely summarizes: "As anyone who has been led around a new site by a tour guide knows, the leader often pauses along the way to describe a particular feature with greater detail, thereby adding both understanding and interest to what could otherwise become routine."[19]

Unfortunately, the accounts are so brief and our own knowledge of possibly useful background so limited that many things remain unclear. At many points it is difficult to find any two commentators who are in full agreement.

40:38 וְלִשְׁכָּה וּפִתְחָהּ בְּאֵילִים הַשְּׁעָרִים—The disagreement begins on the question of where this "room" (לִשְׁכָּה) is located. Literally, this first part of the verse reads, "and a room and its opening in/into/by the gateposts, the gates." One hypothetical possibility is that this verse is describing a room located in (one or both of) the gateposts (presuming they were not solid). However, 40:9 indicates that the gateposts were two cubits (almost forty-one inches) deep, a space into which little more than a closet could be fitted (see also 40:35–36).

The main difficulty centers on the relationship between last two words and the fact that they are plural. The Syriac (ܟܦ̈ܝܣܐ ܘܐܝܠ̈ܝ) supports both words (בְּאֵילִים הַשְּׁעָרִים) while the LXX (καὶ τὰ αιλαμμω αὐτῆς) and the Vulgate (*in frontibus portarum*) partially support the MT. Some commentators suggest that the last two words should be בְּאֻלָם הַשַּׁעַר, "in the vestibule of the gateway," a phrase used in 40:39 (see the first textual note there). However, my interpretation follows that of Keil, who argues that the "room" (לִשְׁכָּה) was located outside of the gateway near one of the gateposts. He explains the connection between אֵילִים and שְׁעָרִים as "loose coordination" and argues that the words are plural to indicate that there was such a room near the other two inner gates as well.[20] Ezek 46:1–2 might indicate that that was indeed the case, since those verses imply that the Prince's offering was taken in by the east gate. See figure 2.

שָׁם יָדִיחוּ אֶת־הָעֹלָה:—The second half of the verse summarizes the function of the room by stating what was done "there" (שָׁם). The rare verb דּוּחַ, "wash," always Hiphil, occurs only three other times in the OT (Is 4:4; Jer 51:34; 2 Chr 4:6). The procedure for washing sacrificial animals is discussed in the Torah (Lev 1:9, 13), and 2 Chr 4:6 reports that Solomon's temple had ten bronze basins for that purpose (see also 1 Ki 7:38). The parts that are specified to be washed are the entrails (קֶרֶב) and the lower legs (כְּרָע, Lev 1:9, 13). Since the latter would commonly be soiled naturally and the former (always burned on the altar) easily dirtied during disembowelment, the practice probably concerned physical cleanness as much as anything ceremonial. There is never any explicit mention of such washing for any other sacrifices besides the "burnt offering" (עֹלָה), but it likely was done also for other types.

---

[19] Block, *Ezekiel*, 2:531. Critics suggest that we have an interpolation or two at this point. However, they could well be elaborations by Ezekiel himself.

[20] Keil, *Ezekiel*, 2:214–16.

Here עֹלָה here seems to be a synecdochical designation for all kinds of animal sacrifices, since it was one of the most important types (see Leviticus 1). The next verse mentions most of the other types of sacrifices. A closely parallel passage in 2 Chr 4:6 also uses עֹלָה in such a comprehensive sense.

40:39 The main question in this and the following verses is how to envision the sparse information given in relationship to the total picture of the temple complex.

If my understanding is correct, the actual slaughter did not take place in the vestibule, which was not an abattoir, but simply a space where those who entered the gate could assemble. Hence here I have translated לִשְׁחוֹט אֲלֵיהֶם, literally, "to slaughter upon them," as simply "to use when slaughtering." Ezek 40:42–43 will speak of facilities just outside the gate for the actual slaughter. The purpose of the tables mentioned in this verse was to receive the meat for sacrifice, possibly after it had been washed in the room mentioned in 40:38, and further prepare it, if need be, for the altar. The priests would then take the meat when it was ready and lay it on the altar. See figure 4.

שְׁנַיִם שֻׁלְחָנוֹת—In spite of the feminine form of the plural שֻׁלְחָנוֹת, "tables," שֻׁלְחָן is generally a masculine noun, and hence the masculine numeral שְׁנַיִם, "two," is used in this and the following verse. Similarly, in 40:41–42, שֻׁלְחָן also seems to be masculine in spite of its feminine plural since the same feminine plural form is modified by אַרְבָּעָה, a feminine form of "four," thus displaying the usual chiastic concord (a masculine noun modified by a feminine number or vice versa) used with numerals from three to ten. A masculine noun having a feminine plural form is a type of inconsistency we have often met in Ezekiel.

הָעוֹלָה וְהַחַטָּאת וְהָאָשָׁם:—I have used the most familiar translations of these three sacrifices. "Burnt offering" for עֹלָה is misleading in that all sacrifices involved some burning, but in this one the entire victim was consumed on the altar, hence sometimes it is called the "whole burnt offering."

Some scholars prefer "purification offering" for חַטָּאת, arguing that it was used to decontaminate places and objects (see Ezek 43:19–27),[21] but "sin offering" is appropriate both because the noun itself often means "sin" and because this sacrifice was for atonement from sin (e.g., Ex 29:36; 30:10; Lev 4:20; 5:6).

Finally, the אָשָׁם, traditionally rendered "guilt offering," is better described by "reparation offering," because its underlying idea was one of restitution or reparation for misuse of a sacred object or damages to a person (a monetary equivalent could be required in addition to the sacrifice; see Lev 5:14–26 [ET 5:14–6:7]).[22]

Conspicuous by its absence in this list is the "peace offering," better called "communion offering." Why it is absent is unknown, but it was the one sacrifice where some of the meat was returned to the worshiper to eat on sanctuary premises (see the second textual note and the commentary on 39:17). Perhaps one of the priorities here is to maintain a strict distinction between the priests and the laity.

---

[21] See the discussion of this view in Kleinig, *Leviticus*, 100–101.

[22] For an overview of the purpose and procedure for these offerings in Leviticus 1–7, see Kleinig, *Leviticus*, 33–39.

40:40 וְאֶל־הַכָּתֵף מִחוּצָה—Literally, "to the shoulder from the outside," this is rendered, "by the outside wall." In its metaphorical use, "shoulder" often means "side," so the verse refers to the right and left sides of the outside wall (although we would appreciate more detail; see figure 4). The orientation is indicated by לְ with the Qal participle, לָעוֹלֶה, "to someone going up (entering by)" the seven steps. Zimmerli argues that the use of לָאֵלָם in the second half of the verse requires reading the same toward the beginning and taking לָעוֹלֶה as a scribal error[23] (RSV and NRSV are similar). But I fail to see the logic of that, especially considering how often the verb עָלָה and nouns derived from it have been used in previous verses.

The reference to "the north gateway" in 40:40 indicates that the activities described in 40:38–43 take place there, although Ezekiel seems clearly to envision the activities as also going on at the east and south gates as well. Lev 1:10–11 says that the particular sacrifice under discussion there (a burnt offering from the flock) was to be slaughtered on the north side of the altar, which some scholars think is indicative of tabernacle and Solomonic temple practice for all sacrifices. If so, it is unclear how that is to be reconciled with Ezekiel's vision. Is it a result of Ezekiel's addition of another court? Or an attempt to distance the unseemliness of animal slaughter from the temple itself? I have no answer.

40:41 This verse appears merely to summarize 40:39–40.

אֲלֵיהֶם יִשְׁחָטוּ:—As in 40:39, here too the verb שָׁחַט, "to slaughter," apparently is used with אֲלֵיהֶם ("upon them [the tables]") in a broad sense, meaning that the animals, which had been slaughtered just outside the gate (not here), were prepared on these tables.

40:42 אַבְנֵי גָזִית—These last four tables mentioned were built from "stones of hewing," that is, hewn stone or ashlar. This implies that the other tables were of wood. This is the first mention in Ezekiel 40–48 of a material for an element of the temple furnishings. The location of these tables is unknown, but they are shown on figure 4 on either side of the stairs leading up to the inner gates.

אֲלֵיהֶם וְיַנִּיחוּ אֶת־הַכֵּלִים—Apparently אֲלֵיהֶם is placed first for emphasis: "*on them* they placed the instruments." The imperfect וְיַנִּיחוּ (Hiphil of נוּחַ) implies customary or frequentative action. The unexpected *waw* on it would seem to imply that it begins a new clause or sentence. The versions ignore the *waw*, and so do KJV and all modern translations.

וְהַזָּבַח:—Critics often delete this noun (זֶבַח in pause), but it is often generic for any type of "sacrifice." If the preceding עוֹלָה is here taken in its strict sense of "burnt offering," the following "(other kinds of) sacrifice" is appropriate.

40:43 וְהַשְׁפַתַּיִם—Translations and interpretations of this word vary widely. Elsewhere in the OT, it occurs only in Ps 68:14 (ET 68:13), in the same dual form as here, and its meaning there too is debated, but is usually understood as "panniers, saddlebags," although sometimes as "sheepfolds." Neither of those meanings seem to be applicable here. The LXX, Vulgate, and Peshitta translate with something like "lip(s),

---

[23] Zimmerli, *Ezekiel*, 2:363.

edge(s)," probably assuming a derivation from שָׂפָה, "lip." Those versions would have translated an unpointed text with שׁ (not distinguished as שׁ or שׂ). Allen derives the word from the verb שָׁפַת, "to put [a pot, etc.] on," and posits a meaning of "places on which to set down things."[24] If anything of this sort is the meaning, the last clause of 40:42 would make better sense after 40:43a, and many critics would rearrange the text accordingly. The tables of 40:42 are only a cubit and a half wide, but these "ledges" (if that is what they are) are even narrower.

BDB follows the Targum's עוּנְקְלִין with "hook-shaped pegs, hooks," and most modern translations from KJV on translate it "hooks" (cf. the discussion in *HALOT*). The dual form of הַשְׁפַתַּיִם is reflected by my "double-pronged hooks," as NIV also translated. This translation also goes better with מוּכָנִים, "fastened" (see the next textual note), than "ledges" would. On these hooks the carcasses would be hung for skinning and other aspects of butchering. Many modern butcher shops and slaughterhouses have similar hooks.

מוּכָנִים בַּבַּיִת—The Hophal participle of כּוּן, "set, establish," with בְּ means "fastened to." Somewhat ambiguous is the meaning of בַּיִת here. It can, of course, refer to the temple as God's "house," but that is not the scene here. Most translations from KJV on have interpreted it adverbially as "within, inside." NIV has "wall." Keil suggests that it means "the buildings," which he interprets as the outer walls of the vestibule structures.[25] Following that suggestion, I have translated it as "the building." In any case, we are left with a generality and no clear picture.

וְאֶל־הַשֻּׁלְחָנוֹת בְּשַׂר הַקָּרְבָּן:—I have taken this final clause as beginning with the *waw* in an adversative sense ("but the meat …"), closing the paragraph with the meat on the tables ready to be sacrificed (and part to be eaten if a communion offering). Thus we are brought back to a topic that has been quite central to all of 40:38–43.

It may be no accident that the paragraph closes with the noun קָרְבָּן, the most comprehensive term in the language for sacrifice. It might technically be translated "offering" or "oblation" instead of "sacrifice," but that is almost a distinction without a difference. Functionally, the noun is explained by the frequent use of the Hiphil of the verb from which it is derived, קָרַב, literally, "to bring near (to God), offer (something for sacrifice)," as in, for example, 43:22–24; 44:7, 15. Ezekiel uses the noun only once elsewhere, in 20:28, where it is applied to invalid or syncretistic worship on the high places. But the noun and verb are frequent in Leviticus and occur together already in the programmatic Lev 1:2–3.

40:44–46 A new section, 40:44–46, focuses our attention on a second set of rooms, reserved for priests. See figure 2.

40:44 The LXX has a new visionary guidance formula here. RSV followed suit, but NRSV and ESV remain with the MT. For reasons past finding out, this verse teems with egregious textual problems, so flagrant that most commentators (even Keil[26]) and

---

[24] Allen, *Ezekiel*, 2:222.

[25] Keil, *Ezekiel*, 2:219.

[26] Keil, *Ezekiel*, 2:220–22.

translations (except KJV and NKJV) agree in most cases that emendations are necessary.

וּמֵחוּצָה֙ לַשַּׁ֣עַר הַפְּנִימִ֔י—"From the outside to the inner gate" is ambiguous: either before one enters the gate or after having gone through it. Hence it is clarified by the following phrase, בֶּחָצֵ֣ר הַפְּנִימִ֗י, "in the inner court." That means Ezekiel is here observing rooms or (semi-?) separate structures apparently just after entering the inner court. They stand opposite one another, one by the north gate facing south and one by the south gate facing north. See figure 2. Some of the language describing their position will be repeated in the following two verses when the function of the rooms is described.

לִֽשְׁכ֣וֹת שָׁרִ֔ים—The plural of לִשְׁכָּה in construct with the plural Qal participle of שִׁיר, "sing," clearly means "rooms of/for singers." However, I have translated it "two rooms," following the LXX (δύο ἐξέδραι), with the assumption that a scribe misread a *taw* (שְׁתַּ֫יִם) as a *resh* (שָׁרִ֔ים). The Vulgate reproduces the MT, and the Syriac (ܪ̈ܘܡܐ܂) supports its consonantal text (but vocalizes שָׁרִים as שָׂרִ֔ים). The Targum paraphrases the MT (see below). "Singers" did play a prominent role in Israel's liturgy, at least in the temple, as amply witnessed in Chronicles and Ezra-Nehemiah, but there they are never referred to by the Qal participle שָׁרִים, but rather by the Polel participle מְשֹׁרְרִ֔ים. The Qal participle שָׁרִים, "singers," does appear in texts about the reigns of David and Solomon,[b] but never denoting official temple functionaries. But above all, the temple singers are classified as Levites, never as priests. Ezekiel not only maintains the distinction between priests and (other) Levites, but strengthens it by limiting altar service to descendants of the priest Zadok (40:46), who replaced Abiathar as high priest (see further on 44:15). The Targum's paraphrase, לִשְׁכַּת לֵיוָאֵי, "a room of (for) Levites," shows an awareness of the problem, but doesn't solve it.

(b) 2 Sam 19:36 (ET 19:35); 1 Ki 10:12 ‖ 2 Chr 9:11; Ps 68:26 (ET 68:25); Eccl 2:8

Other textual emendations in the verse include reading אֲשֶׁ֤ר as אַחַת, with the LXX, making אַחַת אֶל־כָּתֵף parallel to אֶחָ֣ד אֶל־כָּתֵף֮ in the second part of the verse, and reading שַׁ֣עַר הַקָּדִ֗ים, "east gate," as שַׁעַר הַדָּרוֹם, "south gate," with the LXX, since it faces "north" and as required by the contrast with the previous "north gate" and by the contrasts between "north" and "south" in 40:45–46. Inconsistencies in gender in reference to the feminine לִשְׁכ֕וֹת, "rooms," include the masculine אֶחָ֣ד, "one" (instead of the feminine אַחַת) and the masculine plural suffix on וּפְנֵיהֶ֖ם (cf. also פְּנֵ֣י) where we might expect וּפָנֶ֖יהָ, "its face," that is, "facing."

40:45 The heavenly guide, last mentioned in 40:35, interrupts the primarily visual tour with a verbal explanation in 40:45–46 of the function of these two rooms.

זֹ֣ה הַלִּשְׁכָּ֗ה—The feminine demonstrative adjective זֹה, "this," occurs eleven times in the OT (six in Ecclesiastes). It appears to be a dialectical variation of the common classical form, זֹאת, which it gradually displaced, until in the Mishnah זֹו is the regular form. Its position, preceding the object to which it refers, indicates that here it is technically in apposition to הַלִּשְׁכָּה, "this, the room," a syntactical usage with parallels (see GKC, § 136 d, footnote 2).

לַכֹּ֣הֲנִ֔ים שֹׁמְרֵ֖י מִשְׁמֶ֥רֶת הַבָּֽיִת׃—This idiomatic cognate accusative construction, "for the priests watching/guarding the watch/guardianship of the temple," has the first instance in Ezekiel of the noun מִשְׁמֶ֫רֶת, which will recur in 40:46; 44:8, 14–16; 48:11.

This entire phrase is repeated in 40:46 but with הַמִּזְבֵּחַ, "the altar," in place of הַבַּיִת, "the temple" (see the next textual note).

Most translations take the idiom שָׁמַר מִשְׁמֶרֶת in a rather general sense of supervision: "have charge of" (NKJV, NIV, ESV). However, in Gen 26:5 it refers to Abraham faithfully carrying out God's covenant stipulations, and it is also used in reference to the priests and Levites scrupulously carrying out God's commands as they serve at the tabernacle (e.g., Lev 8:35; Num 1:53; 3:7–8, 28, 32, 38). In other passages the idiom has a primary sense of "stand guard faithfully, have guard duty," for example, in 2 Ki 11:4–7 of Joash's Carite guards of the palace and temple. Hence we may conclude that the priests in Ezekiel's vision, in addition to having specifically liturgical functions, are to be guardians of the holy space. (One might compare the colorful Swiss guards at the Vatican, although that role has become largely ceremonial.) Thus the concern here is of a piece with Ezekiel's overriding concern that the holy space not be violated, as evidenced, for example, by the construction of the wall around the temple compound (40:5). Perhaps the sacrileges described in chapter 8 summarize the kinds of behavior that those on guard here were to prevent.

Perhaps the "two rooms" described in 40:44–46 served as sleeping or rest quarters for those on active duty. Naturally, they are located adjacent to the (north and south) gateways to the inner court. See figure 2.

40:46 וְהַלִּשְׁכָּה—The demonstrative in the corresponding phrase in 40:45 (זֹה הַלִּשְׁכָּה, "*this* room …") does double duty, so וְהַלִּשְׁכָּה could be rendered, "and *that* room …" הַמִּזְבֵּחַ, "the altar," is simply a more specific definition of הַבַּיִת, "the temple," in the otherwise identical construct chain in 40:45. Compare Num 18:4–5, which has מִשְׁמֶרֶת in three construct phrases. First, in construct with אֹהֶל מוֹעֵד in Num 18:4, it refers to the non-Aaronic Levites, who shall "keep guard over the tent of meeting," but are not to carry out priestly duties. In Num 18:5, מִשְׁמֶרֶת is used twice, in construct with הַקֹּדֶשׁ and then with הַמִּזְבֵּחַ, to say that the sons of Aaron are to be the priests who will "keep guard over the sanctuary" and "keep guard over the altar."

בְּנֵי־צָדוֹק הַקְּרֵבִים מִבְּנֵי־לֵוִי אֶל־יְהוָה לְשָׁרְתוֹ:—In Num 18:1–7 God designates all the sons/descendants of Aaron to be the priests, whereas the other Levites are to carry out ministerial service at the sanctuary, but not approach the holy place or the altar. However, in Ezekiel's vision, out of all the sons/descendants of Aaron, only those who are "sons/descendants of Zadok" are permitted to serve as priests. Much more detail about this will be given in 44:9–16; see on 44:15 (also 43:19; 48:11). In form הַקְּרֵבִים is a Qal participle (with the article), but the lexica have a separate entry for it as a verbal adjective (BDB and *HALOT*, s.v. קָרֵב) describing these descendants of Zadok as (literally) "the ones who approach, come near" to Yahweh (אֶל־יְהוָה), who is "incarnated" in the temple. קָרֵב recurs in the same sense in 45:4. The adjective קָרוֹב is used with the same meaning in 42:13 and 43:19, as is the Qal finite verb קָרֵב in 44:15–16. The preposition מִן on מִבְּנֵי־לֵוִי is not comparative ("nearer than …") but partitive, literally, "from the sons of Levi," since the Zadokites, like all the Aaronides, were from the tribe of Levi. The Piel infinitive construct with לְ and suffix, לְשָׁרְתוֹ, forms a purpose clause: "to serve/minister to him." The object suffix obviously refers to Yahweh and semi-anthropomorphically speaks of him as of any other potentate who commands servants or aides. שָׁרֵת need not, but usually does, refer to specifically liturgical service, somewhat synonymously to the verb עָבַד and the noun עֲבֹדָה in liturgical contexts.

40:47 This one-verse description of the inner court is even briefer that the three verses devoted to the outer court (40:17–19). Little information is given beyond its dimensions. מְרֻבַּעַת is the Pual feminine participle, "square," whose plural was in the description of Solomon's temple in 1 Ki 7:31. The masculine singular will be used in Ezek 45:2. More common is the synonymous Qal passive participle רָבוּעַ, used in the descriptions of the tabernacle (e.g., Ex 27:1; 28:16; 30:2) and temple (1 Ki 7:5). Later, in Mishnaic Hebrew, the Pual participle displaced the Qal passive participle completely.

It is no surprise that the court is a perfect square, as are the guardrooms (40:7, 12) and various other structures. See figure 2.

The altar is merely described as "in front of the temple." More on the subject need not be said here because the altar will be described in some detail in 43:13–17. Neither passage specifies its precise location within the courtyard. Commentators generally assume that, in accordance with the overall concern for symmetry, the altar was located at the exact center of the square, at the intersection of hypothetical lines running diagonally from the four corners, but there is some debate about this. For example, Zimmerli argues that, as indicated by the goal of the prophet's tour, everything is oriented toward the Holy of Holies, so that even the altar would be oriented toward it and would stand somewhat closer than the center of the court: the altar "stands submissively in front of the sanctuary whose core is in the holy of holies."[27] In the total structure of the temple complex, there is no gainsaying Zimmerli's contention that the ultimate focus is on the Holy of Holies. But that really determines little about exactly where the great bronze altar was situated. Apparently it was not a matter of much concern to Ezekiel (or to his guide).

In our modern paragraph divisions, we could debate whether to include 40:47 with what precedes or with what follows. One can find both positions in modern translations. The MT clearly includes it with what precedes. In a sense, since it is the only verse devoted to the court and altar, it is a paragraph unto itself.

40:48–49 A bigger puzzle is why 40:48–49 is appended to chapter 40. The verses could begin a new chapter because now the guide leads us into the temple structure itself—the subject that, together with consideration of ancillary buildings, will occupy us until the end of chapter 41. As usual, no certain answers can be given to the vagaries of chapter division, but a possible answer here is that those responsible for this one reasoned that the vestibule was still a transitional zone to the two inner areas of the temple. Alternatively, since the desert tabernacle contained no vestibule, it is not impossible that we witness here a manifestation of the attitude that the tabernacle exhibited a primordial purity or exemplarity that had been lost in Solomon's temple with its various modifications of the tabernacle template (such as the vestibule), not to speak of the many apostate "abominations" the temple had witnessed (see espe-

---

[27] Zimmerli, *Ezekiel*, 2:355.

cially Ezekiel 8). Such a tabernacle preference is certainly very evident at points in the NT; see "tabernacled" in Jn 1:14 and the emphasis on "tabernacle" (and not "temple") in Acts 7:44; 15:16; Heb 8:2–5; 9:1, 11, 21; Rev 13:6; 15:5; 21:3.

An evidence of the diminished holiness of the vestibule is that in Ezekiel we are never told how it functioned. Its nebulous role carries over even into uncertainty as to how אֵלָם should be translated in this context. Since KJV's "porch" carries other connotations today, most, myself included, have settled for "vestibule," although it certainly is no duplicate of the vestibules in the gateways. Because we are dealing with a worship structure, I would be tempted to use "narthex," a sort of counterpart in ecclesiastical architecture, if that were not utterly anachronistic in an OT book.

Unfortunately, all kinds of difficulties swirl around the full comprehension of these final two verses of the chapter. Much as in 40:44, the major problem is textual, and again the LXX seems to have preserved a text superior to the MT. Not many commentators disagree in principle.[28]

40:48 וַיָּמָד אֵל אֵלָם—This must mean "he measured each doorpost of the vestibule," with אֵל being a defective spelling of אֵיל (the construct of אַיִל), as implied by the LXX's transliteration αιλ. The LXX also has the definite article with "the vestibule" (τοῦ αιλαμ), whereas אֵלָם is strangely anarthrous.

וְרֹחַב הַשַּׁעַר שָׁלֹשׁ אַמּוֹת מִפּוֹ וְשָׁלֹשׁ אַמּוֹת מִפּוֹ:—Literally, this is "and the breadth of the gate was three cubits on this side, and three cubits on that side" (KJV; similar are NKJV and NASB). Here שַׁעַר is better rendered as the "doorway" into the vestibule. Many modern translations and commentators assume that the longer LXX text is superior: καὶ τὸ εὖρος τοῦ θυρώματος πηχῶν δέκα τεσσάρων καὶ ἐπωμίδες τῆς θύρας τοῦ αιλαμ πηχῶν τριῶν ἔνθεν καὶ πηχῶν τριῶν ἔνθεν, "the width of the doorway was *fourteen cubits, and the shoulders* [side walls] *of the doorway of the vestibule were* three cubits on either side." The words πηχῶν … θύρας could represent an omission by homoioteleuton of five Hebrew words, אַרְבַּע עֶשְׂרֵי אַמָּה וְכִתְפוֹת הַשַּׁעַר, after וְרֹחַב הַשַּׁעַר. However, the measurement of the doorway as given in the MT, three cubits on either side, could be two halves of a six-cubit doorway.[29]

40:49 אֹרֶךְ הָאֻלָם עֶשְׂרִים אַמָּה וְרֹחַב עַשְׁתֵּי עֶשְׂרֵה אַמָּה—This verse states that "the length of the vestibule was twenty cubits, and its width was eleven cubits" (about thirty-four feet by nineteen feet), as pictured in figures 2 and 5. Literally, אֹרֶךְ is "length" and רֹחַב is "breadth, width." Since the two inner sections of the temple, the nave and the Holy of Holies, were twenty cubits wide (41:2, 4), some commentators argue that the twenty-cubit figure given here must refer to the width rather than the length. Block, for instance, argues that the terms אֹרֶךְ and רֹחַב are being used loosely: "the former refers to the width from the standpoint of the observer (the longer side); the latter to the distance to the wall in front of him."[30]

---

[28] A labored defense of the MT can be found in Keil, *Ezekiel*, 2:223–26.

[29] See Keil, *Ezekiel*, 2:225, and figure 5 in this commentary.

[30] Block, *Ezekiel*, 2:539, n. 4, following Gese, *Der Verfassungsentwurf des Ezechiel*, 124–26. Block's figure 4 (*Ezekiel*, 2:541) pictures the vestibule that way. But neither BDB nor *HALOT* gives support for the view that אֹרֶךְ and רֹחַב are used to mean, in effect, the opposite, in this or any other verse.

Block includes the vestibule in his calculation of the hundred-cubit length given for the temple in 41:13.[31] But since the total length of the temple would not add up to a hundred cubits if the vestibule were eleven cubits long, as the MT of 40:49 would indicate following Block's interpretation, Block appeals to the LXX for the number, δώδεκα, "twelve."[32] Apparently the LXX read שְׁתֵּי for עַשְׁתֵּי, perhaps in connection with the correction of אֲשֶׁר to עֶשֶׂר for the steps (see the next textual note).

וּבְמַעֲלוֹת אֲשֶׁר יַעֲלוּ אֵלָיו—The MT is, literally, "and by the steps which they would go up to it." To make sense of it, KJV adds "he brought me up": "and *he brought me up* by the steps …" (emphasis added). NKJV connects it to the following phrase, "and by the steps which led up to it *there were* pillars … ," but that contradicts the placement of the pillars by the doorposts according to the MT. Hence we have little choice but to follow the LXX, which apparently read the numeral עֶשֶׂר, "ten," in place of אֲשֶׁר, "which." Regardless of the number, the "steps" clearly indicate that this is now the climactic increase in elevation as one approaches the temple itself.

Seven steps led up to the outer wall (40:22, 26); eight led into the inner gateways (40:31, 34, 37); and now ten lead into the temple building itself. The symbolism of this climb up a total of twenty-five steps would have been impressive to the worshiper as he ascended the mountain of Yahweh (Ps 24:3; cf. Rom 10:6). The higher elevations represent greater degrees of holiness. Compare Psalms 120–134, the Psalms of Ascent, probably sung during the annual pilgrimages up to Jerusalem to worship at the temple, and "go up to the temple" in Lk 18:10; Jn 7:14; Acts 3:1. The "twenty-fifth" year in 40:1 also appears to have symbolic significance; see the commentary on 40:1.

וְעַמֻּדִים אֶל־הָאֵילִים—Ezekiel gives us no information on the nature or function of the "pillars" (עַמֻּדִים) by the "doorposts" (אֵילִים). (See figure 5.) But it is hard to imagine that he has in mind anything other than counterparts to the apparently free-standing (supporting nothing) pillars described in 1 Ki 7:15–22 and briefly in 2 Chr 3:15–17. Those texts give their names as "Jachin" and "Boaz" and describe in some detail their elaborate workmanship, but their precise significance and/or function eludes us. Since parallels in other ancient Near Eastern temples are known, many opine that, whatever God's original intent may have been for their construction by Solomon, they later became a magnet for syncretistic practices in the temple. This is speculative, however. Ezekiel gives no hint of such a syncretistic association; if it existed, it is doubtful whether the pillars would have been included in his vision of the eschatological temple.

Commentary

The Setting of the Temple Vision (40:1–4)

40:1 An unusually complex date notice opens Ezekiel's temple vision. The entire vision (chapters 40–48) was revealed on this date. The notice con-

---

[31] See on 41:13–15a for the calculation followed in this commentary.

[32] Block, *Ezekiel*, 2:539, n. 5, and 2:541 (figure 4).

tains three points of reference. The first and third relate to the deportation to Babylon in 597 (see figure 1, "The Dates in Ezekiel").

By "our captivity," Ezekiel expresses his solidarity with his audience. We cannot be certain, but there is considerable agreement among commentators that "the twenty-fifth year" is more than a simple chronological notice. Since Jeremiah had predicted that the exile would last seventy years (Jer 25:11–12; 29:10), and historically we calculate that it lasted from 605–538 B.C., "the twenty-fifth year" here (573 B.C.) should not be pressed to imply the exact midpoint of the exile, although it is close. Nevertheless, it may suggest a turning point when the exiles could look forward with greater expectation to the return to their homeland.

Every fiftieth year was to be a Jubilee, when land lost through foreclosure was to be returned and all Israelite slaves released. This year in which Ezekiel is writing may have been a Jubilee Year, or perhaps the midpoint between Jubilee Years. But even if it was neither, the "twenty-fifth year" likely would have symbolic significance as half the Jubilee number. Lev 25:10 states that on the Jubilee, the Israelites are to proclaim דְּרוֹר, "liberty," which Ezekiel uses in 46:17 in his reference to the Jubilee as "the year of liberation." In Is 61:1 the Suffering Servant uses דְּרוֹר more generally: "Yahweh has anointed me ... to proclaim liberty to the captives." Jesus quotes that passage in his inaugural sermon in Nazareth (Lk 4:18) to summarize the Gospel proclamation that will characterize his ministry, and it also characterizes the continuing proclamation of the church throughout the NT era, until he returns in glory.

The liberty associated with the Jubilee, and the connotation of "twenty-five" as half of the way to it, might also explain why twenty-five and multiples of it appear so often in the rest of the book. Thus when the dimensions of the temple and its compound so frequently involve twenty-five (40:13, 21, 25, 29, 30, 33, 36) and its multiples (e.g., 40:15, 19; 42:16–20), and the sacred reserve of land is twenty-five thousand units (cubits?) long (45:1–6; see also 48:8–21), one should sense an evangelical significance.

The second point of reference given in 40:1 is "at the beginning of the year, on the tenth of the month." Considerable debate has swirled around these phrases. רֹאשׁ הַשָּׁנָה (ro'sh hashanah), "the head of the year," in later Hebrew (as in modern Hebrew) means "New Year's Day." A generation ago there was much speculation that ancient Israel celebrated such a festival, but that critical fad has now been almost totally abandoned since the rest of the OT betrays not even a hint of its presence. This is the only appearance of the phrase in the OT, and here, where the *tenth* day is specified, it must mean "the *beginning* of the year." Modern Israel does observe a Rosh Hashanah on the first day of Tishri (the *seventh* month of the liturgical calendar), but the *tenth* day of that month is the climax of the liturgical calendar: Yom Kippur, the Day of Atonement. Even if a calendar whose year began in the autumn had already been accepted in everyday life in the OT era, there is no indication that the liturgy had ever abandoned its ancient method of beginning the year in the spring (Nisan), and of all people, we would scarcely expect Ezekiel, a priest (1:3), to do so. That he did not is confirmed by the liturgical rituals he prescribes in 45:18–25, which also presuppose a spring New Year.

Why, then, does Ezekiel specify the *tenth* day of the month? The tenth of Nisan was the day the Passover lambs were selected (Ex 12:3), and that festival's connection with the general theme of salvation (cf. above on the Jubilee) would seem appropriate here. But Ezekiel mentions the Passover only once (45:21), and he mentions the Day of Atonement in the fall not at all. Block suggests that Ezekiel's intent here is polemical: to counter the *akītu* festival, the great Babylonian New Year festival celebrating Marduk's supremacy.[33] That would have great plausibility if Ezekiel were thinking of an autumnal New Year celebration, but the unlikelihood of that has already been noted. So perhaps we do best to seek no particular significance in "tenth"; the vision simply happened to come on that day. The tenth day of the first month of the twenty-fifth year of Ezekiel's exile was around April 28, 573.

The third point of reference in Ezekiel's date notice, "in the fourteenth year after the city had fallen" (40:1), agrees with the first point of reference and so adds no additional information.[34] "Fallen" translates a (Hophal perfect) form of נָכָה, "smite, destroy," the same form used in 33:21, and the verb's Hiphil imperative (הַכּוּ), "smite, strike, slaughter" had been used in 9:5 when Yahweh commanded the execution of all whose foreheads had not been marked with the *taw* (see 9:4). The motif of the reversal of the temple's destruction will be especially evident in 43:1–12, where God's Glory returns to the city it abandoned in 11:22–23.

The addition of "on that very day" (40:1) suggests, humanly speaking, Ezekiel's recollection of the anniversary of his own deportation "at the turn of the year" (2 Chr 36:10) and all the subsequent tragedies.

The anthropomorphic reference to "the hand of Yahweh" catapults us back to the inaugural vision (1:3; cf. 37:1). In 8:1–3 the "hand" had been rather violent in transporting the prophet in a vision to pre-fall Jerusalem.

40:2 The "hand" (40:1) brings Ezekiel to "the land [אֶרֶץ] of Israel" (40:2), which appears elsewhere in the book only in the trade list of 27:17 and later in 47:18. Ezekiel's usual phrase is, literally, "the ground [אֲדָמָה] of Israel" (e.g., 7:2; 11:17; 37:12; 38:18–19), though English versions usually translate both the same way. The reason for the different Hebrew terms is uncertain, but אֶרֶץ, "land," does have more territorial overtones. Because of the people's sin, they forfeited "the land of Israel" during the exile, but chapters 40–48 focus on an eschatological restoration, so it is fitting that the phrase appears in 40:2 and 47:18.

---

[33] Block, *Ezekiel*, 2:513.

[34] The "fourteenth year" after the fall of the city in 586, counting inclusively, is 573. See figure 1, "The Dates in Ezekiel," on the fall of the city in 586.

A bit more specificity follows in the description of the locale as "a very high mountain" (40:2). The reference recalls descriptions of Sinai (e g , Ex 19·11) or Zion (e.g., Is 4.5) as a mountain, but the picture is applied metaphorically and eschatologically to a place suitable for receiving a transcendent vision. Thus the mount of transfiguration, where Christ revealed his divinity, was "a high mountain" (ὄρος ὑψηλόν, Mt 17:1 ‖ Mk 9:2; cf. Lk 9:28), and it was upon "a great and high mountain" that the apostle John was shown the eschatological new Jerusalem (ὄρος μέγα καὶ ὑψηλόν, Rev 21:10). Ezekiel had already used the metaphor in 17:22–24. Its classical OT expression appears in Is 2:2–4 ‖ Micah 4:1–3.[35]

That Yahweh does not name either the mountain or the city undoubtedly reflects the abuse of Jerusalem and its temple mount before the destruction in 586 B.C. and the exile. In Ezekiel God seems averse to the very name "Jerusalem" (which isn't used at all in chapters 40–48) and ends the book by giving the city a different name (48:35). The temple itself had "buildings resembling a city" (40:2), and the city does not enter the vision until briefly in 45:6–7 and then in chapter 48 when the entire new land distribution is discussed.

40:3 The appearance "like bronze" of "the man" recalls the creatures that supported the throne in 1:7 and identifies him as a supernatural being. A longstanding Christian view held by some Lutherans[36] is that this is an appearance of the preincarnate Christ, the architect (cf. Heb 3:3) of his church, the new temple (1 Cor 3:16–17; 2 Cor 6:16). Keil explains: "This figure suggests a heavenly being, an angel, and as he is called Jehovah in ch. xliv. 2, 5 [44:2, 5], the angel of Jehovah."[37] Compare Rev 21:9, 15–16, where an angel with a measuring rod measures the new Jerusalem, and Jesus calls him "my angel" (Rev 22:16). In a number of OT passages there is a certain ambiguity as to whether an angel is simply an angel, that is, a created spirit being, or whether it is *the* Angel of the Lord, a preincarnate appearance of God the Son, the Word not yet become flesh, Jesus Christ. A corresponding ambiguity is present in some NT passages too.[38]

The "man" will address Ezekiel as "son of man" (40:4; 47:6), which is the same address for the prophet that Yahweh himself regularly uses throughout the book.[39] This same "man" (אִישׁ, 43:6) is present beside Ezekiel when he hears Yahweh speaking to him, and so it seems that the Word of Yahweh comes

---

[35] See Levenson, *Theology of the Program of Restoration of Ezekiel 40–48*, 7–53, for a thorough discussion of the mountain in 40:2 in light of Mount Zion, the garden of Eden, Mount Sinai, and Mount Abarim.

[36] A Lutheran study Bible first published in 1640 and reprinted often through the nineteenth century explained that the man is "the Son of God, who in the fullness of time became man, who is the architect of his church" (Kesler, "Hesekiel," 1003).

[37] Keil, *Ezekiel*, 2:185. See also Keil, *Ezekiel*, 2:278, quoted in the note on 43:6.

[38] For a discussion of OT and NT passages that involve this topic, see Charles A. Gieschen, *Angelomorphic Christology: Antecedents and Early Evidence* (Leiden: Brill, 1998).

[39] See the second textual note and the commentary on 2:1.

to Ezekiel through this "man" (see further on 43:6). In fact, throughout most of chapters 40–48 Yahweh apparently speaks to and guides Ezekiel through the agency of this man, probably even in those passages (e.g., chapters 44–45) that do not explicitly refer to this guide.

This man's two functions are introduced in 40:3. First, he will measure the temple area, and second, he will guide Ezekiel around and through it. The two devices he carries are a cord made of twisted flax fibers used to measure long distances and, literally, "a reed of measurement," that is, a rod (a longer version of our yardstick or meter stick) for shorter distances. Its exact length is given in 40:5. His standing "at the gateway" (40:3) indicates the place where in 40:6 the measurements will begin. It is not specified, but since Ezekiel had come from the north (40:2), it is probably the north gate of the outer wall that is meant. From there, in 40:6 the man leads Ezekiel to the east gate.

40:4 This admonition indicates that Ezekiel is to preach all the details of the vision to Israel. A similar but fuller admonition to "describe," "teach them," and "write" the vision will follow in 43:10–11 after the Glory takes up residence in the new temple (43:1–9). Ezekiel is to be no mere tourist or spectator. Rather his reporting (and presumably explaining) to the Israelites everything he sees is presented as integral to his prophetic vocation. If only we had a transcript of his commentary!

The apostle John repeatedly received similar admonitions to "write" the contents of the vision he saw,[c] which strengthens the view that Ezekiel 40–48 is to be interpreted in light of Revelation.[40]

(c) E.g., Rev 1:11, 19; 2:1; 14:13; 19:9; 21:5; contrast 2 Cor 12:4; Rev 10:4

The Temple Compound (40:5–47)

40:5 Ezekiel is first shown the exterior features of the temple compound. Although the "man" is standing at one of the gateways (40:3), he first calls the prophet's attention to the outer wall. If the prophet is approaching the temple compound from the outside, the massive walls would naturally be the first feature to catch his attention. From a literary standpoint, mention of the wall both here and at the conclusion of the temple vision in 42:20 forms an inclusio.

Unusual is the report of the wall's height. Usually Ezekiel gives us only horizontal ground plans and pays no attention to vertical dimensions. But the purpose may be to accent the wall's purpose, that is, to separate the sacred and the profane (42:20) and keep the interior "most holy" (43:12). If our calculations of the length of the "long cubit" are correct (see the third textual note on 40:5), the wall, whose height and thickness were both six cubits, was over ten feet high and ten feet thick.

The length of the wall was five hundred cubits on each side (see the textual note on 40:27). We are not informed of what materials it was constructed, nor are we told the material of most of the other components of the compound.

---

[40] See further "Introduction to Ezekiel 40–48."

While some details are obscure or debatable (see the textual notes), it may be most helpful to comment further by way of the figures on the following pages. After the wall around the compound (40:5), Ezekiel sees the following (in order):

1. The east outer gate (40:6–16; see figures 2 and 3)
2. The rooms for worshipers around the outer court (40:17; see figure 2)
3. The lower pavement of the outer court (40:17–18; see figure 2)
4. The north outer gate (40:20–23; see figures 2 and 3)
5. The south outer gate (40:24–27; see figures 2 and 3)
6. The south inner gate (40:28–31; see figures 2 and 4)
7. The east inner gate (40:32–34; see figures 2 and 4)
8. The north inner gate (40:35–37; see figures 2 and 4)
9. The rooms for washing sacrifices (40:38; see figure 2)
10. The tables for preparing sacrifices (40:39–43; see figure 4)
11. Guard rooms for priests in the inner court (40:44–46; see figure 2)
12. The altar (40:47; see figure 2)

The Vestibule of the Temple Proper (40:48–49)

These verses begin the description of the temple itself (see figure 5), which continues in chapter 41. Since the external *realia* of the temple *are* the message throughout the following chapters, beyond this point we shall combine the textual notes and commentary into a single section. In Ezekiel 40–48 it is rarely realistic (or even faithful to authorial intent) to try to separate the details of the text from their theological implication.

Vision of the New Temple: Part 2

Translation

41 ¹Then he brought me to the nave and measured the doorposts, six cubits wide on either side—the width of the tabernacle. ²The width of the entrance was ten cubits, and the side walls of the entrance were five cubits on either side. Then he measured its [the nave's] length, forty cubits, and [its] width, twenty cubits. ³Then he entered the inner room and measured the doorposts of [its] entrance, two cubits, and [the width of] the entrance [was] six cubits [and the side walls of the entrance were seven cubits on either side]. ⁴He measured its length, twenty cubits, and its width was twenty cubits at the front of the nave. Then he said to me, "This is the Holy of Holies."

⁵Next he measured the wall of the temple; it was six cubits [thick], and the width of each side room was four cubits. [The side rooms were] all around the temple. ⁶The side rooms were one over another, in three stories, thirty in each story. They rested on ledges in the wall of the temple for the side rooms all around, so that they would be supported, but not by the supports being inserted into the temple wall itself. ⁷The side rooms became wider all around as one went up from story to story, for the temple was surrounded upward all around the building [with side rooms]. Accordingly, the width of the building increased as one went up from the lowest story to the highest through the middle one. ⁸I saw an elevation all around the temple, a foundation of the side rooms. A full measuring rod, six cubits, was its top terrace. ⁹The thickness of the outer wall of the side rooms was five cubits. The open area between the side rooms of the temple ¹⁰and the other rooms was twenty cubits wide all around the temple. ¹¹As for the opening of the side room to the open area, one opening was toward the north, and another opening was toward the south. The width of the place of the open area was five cubits all around. ¹²The building in front of the restricted area on the western side [of the temple] was seventy cubits wide. The wall of the building was five cubits thick all around, and its length was ninety cubits.

¹³Then he measured the temple. Its length was one hundred cubits. The restricted area and the building with its walls also had a length of one hundred cubits. ¹⁴The width of the front of the temple, including the restricted area on the east side, was one hundred cubits as well. ¹⁵He also measured the length of the building facing the restricted area at the rear of the temple, along with its balconies on either side: one hundred cubits.

The inside of the nave and the vestibules of the court, ¹⁶the thresholds and the openings slanting inward, and the balconies all around on their three sides, opposite the threshold, were paneled with wood all around, from the floor to the openings, and the openings were covered, ¹⁷to the space above the entrance, both inside the temple and outside. On all the walls all around, both inside and out, were measured-off [18]and carved cherubim and palm-like decorations. A palm decoration was between each cherub. Each cherub had two faces: [19]the face of a man turned toward the palm on one side and the face of a lion turned toward the palm on the other side. They were carved on the whole temple all around. [20]From the floor up to the space above the entrance, cherubim and palms were carved, even on the walls of the nave.

[21]As for the nave, its doorposts were square, and the front of the Holy of Holies had the same form. [22]The altar was of wood, three cubits high; its length was two cubits [and its width was two cubits]. Its corners, its base, and its sides were also of wood. He said to me, "This is the table that is before Yahweh." [23]Both the nave and the Holy of Holies had double doors. [24]The doors had two leaves apiece, two swinging leaves—two for the one door and two leaves for the other. [25]Carved on them—on the doors of the nave—were cherubim and palm decorations, as were carved on the walls. There was a wooden canopy in front of the vestibule outside. [26]There were also openings slanting inward and palm decorations on either side on the side walls of the vestibule. The side rooms of the temple also had canopies.

Textual Notes and Commentary

Although Ezekiel does not expatiate on it, this part of the vision shown to him obviously follows the theology that informed the tabernacle and Solomonic temple. That theology must be gleaned from a variety of biblical texts. Most relevant, but mostly with only implicit theology, are the tabernacle texts (Ex 26:1–31:11; 36:8–39:43) and those describing the Solomonic temple (1 Ki 6:1–38; 7:13–51). Ezekiel's variations, and especially his omissions, seem, on the whole, not to repudiate the divine intent of those predecessors, but to intensify it. Another purpose here is to correct abuses that had crept in under apostate and syncretistic kings and priests.

The decorative features (cherubim, palms, etc.) of the temple (e.g., 1 Ki 6:29–35; Ezek 41:18, 20, 25) suggest a "paradise restored" ambience. Because it was God's earthly "house" and "dwelling place," it was the focal point of his redemptive activity until that goal would be realized, first in Christ, and then in the eschaton (Revelation 21–22). It is the heart of the Gospel that in Christ that goal was reached when "the Word became flesh and tabernacled among us" (Jn 1:14), and by his life, death, and resurrection, he opened the gates of paradise, whither baptized believers will follow at "the end of the age" (Mt 28:20).

Because God in the OT era dwelt in the Holy of Holies, that is the focal point of the temple in Ezekiel, just as in its two predecessors. It was the Most Holy Place because of the presence of him who alone is holiness itself. All sacrifices were ultimately offered to him who sat on the throne (above the lid of the ark of the covenant), and his promise was to forgive the sins of the worshipers through those OT "sacraments" (types and partakers of the final, all-availing sacrifice on Calvary).

That holiness "radiated" outward from the Holy of Holies through the nave or Holy Place into the courtyard and thence to Jerusalem and, potentially, to the ends of the earth has a missionary implication, but one that was not fully implemented until Pentecost.

The NT gives no prescriptions for church architecture, but the altar, whence the Eucharist is distributed, remains central, whether in the basilica-type "long house" model dominant in the west or in the slightly different structures of the eastern churches. All other aspects of biblical worship are to express that sense of sacred space and sacred time as the basis from which the new creation in Christ will ultimately be formed. Especially the final two chapters, Ezekiel 47–48, envision the coming new creation.

In keeping with the style I have adopted for chapters 40–48, the following notes on the specifics of the Hebrew text also include theological reflection.

The Measurements of the Nave and the Holy of Holies (41:1–4)

41:1 For the so-called "guidance formula," "he brought me" (here וַיְבִיאֵנִי), see the second textual note on 40:2.

Finally, we arrive at the main part of the temple itself. Following the pattern of its historical predecessors, the Mosaic tabernacle and the Solomonic temple (Ex 26:31–33; 1 Ki 6:16), this sanctuary is divided into two sections: the larger section measured in Ezek 41:1–2 and the inner sanctum measured in 41:3–4.

The first and largest room is labeled הַהֵיכָל, "the nave." Like the Holy Place in the tabernacle and the temple, this nave follows the "long room"[1] architectural design, and thus the whole temple is also of that design (see figure 5).

Ezekiel used the word הֵיכָל twice before, in 8:16, but there it referred more broadly to the entire temple building in Jerusalem (for which he usually uses בַּיִת, God's "house," e.g., 8:14, 16). That broader sense is closer to its earlier etymological history, for the term and its cognates go all the way back to the Sumerian *e-gal,* literally meaning "big house," which in Akkadian appeared as *êkallu,* which can signify the "palace" of a lord or potentate. הֵיכָל is used of a royal "palace" occasionally in the OT (e.g., 2 Ki 20:18 ‖ Is 39:7; Nahum 2:7 [ET 2:6]). Since Yahweh is Lord and King, הֵיכָל can be used of his "palace" in heaven (Pss 11:4; 18:7 [ET 18:6]; 29:9; cf. Is 6:1) as well as his tabernacle at Shiloh (1 Sam 1:9; 3:3) and temple in Jerusalem (e.g., Jer 7:4), specifically its "nave" or Holy Place (e.g., 1 Ki 6:17) just outside the Holy of Holies. Here the word is used in that specialized sense. One may quibble about its best English equivalent, but "nave," used by many translations, is probably the best, suggesting as it properly does a counterpart—and even a sort of type—of the

---

[1] This means that the entrance is on a short side of the rectangle, so that the structure appears long to a person standing at the entrance. A "broad room" structure has the entrance on a long side of the rectangle.

corresponding space in traditional Christian church architecture. In some of the ancient churches of the Near East that still use Aramaic, an Aramaic cognate of הֵיכָל is regularly used for the nave of churches.

The doorposts of the entrance into the nave are "six cubits wide," one cubit wider than those leading into the vestibule (40:48). See figure 5.

For "and he measured" (וַיָּמָד), see the fourth textual note on 40:5. For the idiom מִפּוֹ ... מִפּוֹ, translated "on either side," see the textual note on 40:10.

Literally, רֹחַב הָאֹהֶל is "the width of the tent." This apparently refers to the tabernacle of Moses, which is called אֹהֶל מוֹעֵד, the "tent of meeting" (e.g., Lev 1:1, 3), or just הָאֹהֶל, "the tent" (e.g., Num 11:24, 26; Deut 31:15). The dimensions of the erected tabernacle are not given in the Bible. Scholars have attempted to deduce its size from the dimensions given for the frames and the curtains.[2] One view holds that the tabernacle was six cubits wide.[3] In that case, this verse could be saying that the width of these doorposts was the same as the width of the tabernacle. A more common view is that the width of the tabernacle was ten cubits.[4] If that is correct, it is possible that these last two words of Ezek 41:1 anticipate the entranceway at the start of 41:2, which says that "the width of the entrance was ten cubits." In that case, the words might better be translated as a separate sentence: "the width [was the same as that] of the tabernacle." However, then we might expect these words to be in 41:2 rather than at the end of 41:1.

Most critics dismiss רֹחַב הָאֹהֶל as an early comparative gloss. However, the Syriac, Vulgate, and Targum all attest to the MT.

41:2 The ten-cubit width of the entrance (doorway) is larger than the entrance to the Holy of Holies, since that entrance is six or seven cubits wide (see on 41:3), evidently accenting the greater sanctity of the Holy of Holies (see figure 5).

41:3 "Then he entered the inner room" translates וּבָא לִפְנִימָה. Instead of a Qal imperfect of בּוֹא with *waw* consecutive (וַיָּבוֹא, as in 40:6), the verb is a perfect with conjunctive *waw*. Some critics suspect a corruption. However, we have met the analogous Qal perfect וּמָדַד, "he measured" (e.g., in 40:20, 24,

---

[2] See the discussion in R. E. Friedman, "Tabernacle," *ABD* 6:295–98.

[3] This view holds that the six frames of the west side, or back, of the tabernacle (Ex 26:22), each a cubit and a half wide (Ex 26:16), were overlapped in such a way that the total width of the tabernacle was six cubits. According to this view, the corner frames were placed in such a way that they did not contribute any additional width. The twenty frames on each of the north and south sides (Ex 26:18, 20), similarly overlapped, would make a total length of twenty cubits.

[4] This view holds that the six frames (see the previous footnote) were placed side by side, for a total of nine cubits. The additional cubit needed to make a total width of ten cubits could be accounted for by the two corner frames somewhat overlapping two of the other frames or by the thickness of the two side frames. This view calculates the length of the tabernacle as thirty cubits. It then would have been on a scale of 1:2 with the temple, which was twenty cubits wide by sixty cubits long (1 Ki 6:2).

35), where we would have expected the imperfect with *waw* consecutive (וַיָּמָד, as, e.g., in 41:1–5), so such variation seems to be acceptable in Ezekiel.

If any significance can be attached to the verb form here, it may be that the guide enters the Holy of Holies by himself and does not invite Ezekiel to accompany him. As a priest (1:3), Ezekiel has easy access to the nave, but only a high priest could enter the Holy of Holies and only on the Day of Atonement (Leviticus 16). Apparently the usual temporal and spatial restrictions do not apply to the supernatural guide (see the commentary on Ezekiel 40:3).

The MT is very restrained in describing where the guide has gone. לִפְנִימָה is, literally and simply, "to the inside." Later (41:4) the guide will clearly identify it as "the Holy of Holies," but at this point anyone without background knowledge of the basic temple pattern would find the expression here opaque.

The phrase וְהַפֶּתַח שֵׁשׁ אַמּוֹת is "and the entrance was six cubits." It is translated literally by the LXX. If we follow the MT in the rest of this verse, we must assume that this refers to the height. Some translations add that assumption: NASB and NKJV give "six cubits high." Most of the other dimensions given in Ezekiel 40–48 are horizontal, but a few are vertical (e.g., in 40:5, 14). The alternative, which I have followed, is to assume that this "six cubits" refers to the width of the entrance. If we make that assumption, then we must follow the LXX in the rest of the verse.

The Hebrew continues, וְרֹחַב הַפֶּתַח שֶׁבַע אַמּוֹת, "and the width of the entrance, seven cubits." This would contradict the previous "six cubits" if we assume that it refers to the width. The LXX has a much longer text here: καὶ τὰς ἐπωμίδας τοῦ θυρώματος πηχῶν ἑπτὰ ἔνθεν καὶ πηχῶν ἑπτὰ ἔνθεν, "and the shoulders [side walls] of the entrance were seven cubits on this side and seven cubits on that side." Many interpreters advocate following the LXX, in harmony with the analogy 41:2, which gives a measurement of the width of an entrance and a measurement of the shoulders (side walls) on either side of it (the LXX reading of 40:48 is similar). These interpreters reconstruct a Hebrew text that had five more words: וְרֹחַב כִּתְפוֹת הַפֶּתַח שֶׁבַע אַמּוֹת מִפֹּה וְשֶׁבַע אַמּוֹת מִפֹּה. In my translation of 41:3, the clause in brackets at the end of the verse is a translation of the LXX reading.

41:4 The innermost room is perfectly square. See figure 5. We are not told its height. In the Solomonic temple, the Holy of Holies was a cube: twenty cubits in each of the three dimensions (1 Ki 6:20). In Ezekiel's vision, its width and length are the same as in Solomon's temple, so it is likely that its height too would have been twenty cubits, forming a perfect cube, no doubt indicative of holiness and perfection.

For only the third time, the guide speaks. The first time was his instruction in 40:4 for Ezekiel to pay attention to the details so he could relate them to the Israelites, and in 40:45–46, the guide explains the function of the two rooms described in 40:44–46. Here in 41:4 he simply gives the name of the room: קֹדֶשׁ הַקֳּדָשִׁים, "the Holy of Holies." A construct chain with a noun (קֹדֶשׁ) in construct with its plural (here with the article: הַקֳּדָשִׁים) functions as a superlative, so it could be rendered "the Most Holy Place" (see Waltke-O'Connor, § 9.5.3j, including example 61).[5] Ezekiel himself, a priest (1:3), would not have needed such an explanation, but it may be given for the benefit of the Israelites to whom Ezekiel is to preach the details of his vision (see the commentary on 40:4).

"The Holy of Holies" is used for the corresponding space in the tabernacle of Moses (Ex 26:33–34) and the temple (e.g., 1 Ki 6:16; 7:50; 8:6; 2 Chr 3:8, 10). In the temple of Solomon, it is also labeled a דְּבִיר, "adytum" (e.g., 1 Ki 6:19–23; 8:6, 8; 2 Chr 3:16; 4:20), but that word never occurs in Ezekiel. The phrase used here explains why no further description is given. The overriding concern at this point is to demarcate the boundaries and zones of holiness and to defend them.

The Temple Wall, the Side Rooms, and the West Building (41:5–12)

41:5–12   Having reached a sort of a climax in the "tour" at the Holy of Holies, it is not mentioned again, and for the final time, until 45:3.[6] No guidance formula ("he brought me," as in, e.g., 41:1) introduces the new topic that continues in 41:5–11: the side rooms of the temple. See figure 5. The boundaries of this section are delineated by forms of מָדַד, "to measure," at the beginning of 41:5 and of 41:13, a verse that begins a new section. Ezek 41:12 describes a separate structure, not a side room, but is considered to be in the same section as 41:5–11.

The entire section of 41:5–12 is difficult, not only because of a host of technical architectural expressions, often of uncertain meaning, but also because of its consistent nominal sentence style, which in the MT is interrupted only by subordinate verbal clauses in 41:6b and 41:7 and a parenthetical verbal clause in 41:8. Thus we have little more than a catalogue of architectural features. There are echoes of the description of corresponding features in Solomon's temple in 1 Ki 6:5–8 (see also 1 Ki 6:10). Although 1 Ki 6:5–8 is less than a model of lucidity itself, it is sometimes helpful here.

41:5   Ezek 41:5 gives us the thickness of the side walls of the temple building, which had not been included in the description of the entrances. The figure of six cubits means they were just as thick as the walls around the entire compound (40:5). Six cubits is also the width of the doorposts of the nave (41:1). That the doorposts of the vestibule, however, measured only five cubits (40:48) is another indication that the vestibule was not really considered part of the temple structure.

---

[5]   The phrase without the article, קֹדֶשׁ קָדָשִׁים, "holy of holies," is used for things that are "most holy" (e.g., Ex 29:37; 30:10; 40:10; Lev 2:3, 10; Ezek 43:12), and sometimes the phrase with the article, קֹדֶשׁ הַקֳּדָשִׁים, has the same meaning (e.g., Lev 21:2; Num 4:4, 19; 18:9–10; Ezek 42:13; 44:13).

[6]   There the phrase occurs without the article, the only place in the OT where the phrase without the article refers to the Holy of Holies.

The text's real interest in this section is in the צְלָעוֹת. The noun צֵלָע can mean "rib" (Gen 2:21–22), but here it means "side room." The same term was used for the side rooms in Solomon's temple (1 Ki 6:5, 8; apparently יָצוּעַ, the Kethib in 1 Ki 6:5, 6, 10, is a synonym). They appear to have surrounded Ezekiel's temple on all sides except the front. The singular צֵלָע is used in this verse, as also in 41:6, 9, 11, but otherwise this section uses the plural. Depending on context, the singular may either have collective force or speak of only a single room. When measured, each צֵלָע was found to be four cubits wide. On one side is the temple wall itself, and in 41:9 (after a digression on ways of access to these rooms), there is an outer wall, one that is five cubits thick. That is, each of the walls is thicker than the rooms themselves!

41:6 The MT, literally, says, "and [as for] the side rooms, [there was] room upon room, three, and [that] thirty times." Less tersely, that seems to say that there were three side rooms situated one above the other. (In צֵלָע אֶל־צֵלָע, the preposition אֶל means "above, on," a meaning more common for עַל.) This stack of three occurred thirty times. In other words, there were three stories of side rooms, and each story had thirty rooms. The rooms in the second and third stories were directly above those in the first story. Nothing is said about the distribution of the rooms, but presumably it was uniform, with more (twelve?) along each of the long (north and south) walls and less (six?) along the short (western) wall. See figure 5.

The rest of 41:6 describes the relationship between the side rooms and the temple building. Considerable paraphrase is necessary to achieve an intelligible translation. Literally, the MT reads, "there were things coming [ledges] on the wall which the temple had for the side rooms all around, so that there would be supports, but the supports would not be in the wall of the temple." בָּאוֹת is the feminine plural Qal participle of בּוֹא, "go, come." Here it must be a technical building term, something "coming" on the wall and wide enough for the supports of the side rooms to rest on, hence "ledges, terraces." It corresponds to what in 1 Ki 6:6 are called מִגְרָעוֹת, a hapax noun derived from the verb גָּרַע, "reduce, diminish," describing the terraced form of the side rooms around Solomon's temple.

Another plural participle (Qal passive, masculine) used as a technical architectural term is אֲחוּזִים, used twice in this verse. Since אָחַז can mean "grasp, hold," this participle apparently means "supported," though I have translated its second occurrence as the noun "(the) supports." This derivation is confirmed by the language of 1 Ki 6:6 regarding supports for the corresponding side rooms in Solomon's temple: לְבִלְתִּי אֲחֹז בְּקִירוֹת־הַבָּיִת, "in order that they would not be fastened in the walls of the temple."

The side rooms were built against the temple wall in such a way that one end of the horizontal supports that formed, in effect, the ceilings and/or floors of the side rooms did not need to be fastened into the wall itself. This could be accomplished only by building the temple wall so that it had ledges on its outer side on which the supports of each story could rest. That is to say, the outer side of the wall narrowed with each story, and thus (as the next verse tells us) the rooms themselves became successively wider, going from bottom to top. The obvious purpose of this type of construction was to avoid doing violence to the sanctity of the temple building by directly attaching these rooms to its walls, potentially damaging the walls. The side rooms, constructed as an external building, also would not disturb the visual integrity of the sanctuary.

41:7 This verse follows from the preceding one. The method of construction described in the preceding verse occasioned the widening of the side rooms from story to story as one ascended. This much is clear in the verse, but little more, and understandings and translations vary widely. 1 Ki 6:6 gives specific figures: the rooms in the lowest story were five cubits wide, and they widened by a cubit each story until the top (third) story was seven cubits wide. If this was also true for Ezekiel's temple, the temple wall, which was six cubits thick at the bottom (Ezek 41:5), must have narrowed to only three cubits thick at the top.

As I understand the first clause of the verse, the initial feminine singular verbs וְרָחֲבָ֨ה וְנָסְבָה֩ are impersonal: "it spread out and it was surrounded." I have assumed that they refer to the rooms, and have translated freely: "the side rooms became wider all around." These verbs are further explained by their cognate nouns מוּסָב (translated "surrounded") and רֹחַב ("width") later in the verse. וְרָחֲבָה is the Qal perfect of רָחַב, "be wide," but many versions treat it as a noun, "a widening." וְנָסְבָה is the Niphal perfect of סָבַב, "turn, encircle, surround." The absence of a *daghesh forte* in the ב can be explained as due to Aramaicizing influence. The LXX ignores the word, but the Targum reads a noun equivalent to the Hebrew מְסִבָּה, which here could mean "a ramp, circular passage, winding staircase." Many critics consider that an attractive emendation and assume that the initial *mem* was misread as a *nun* and that the final ה of וְרָחֲבָה originally was a definite article on מְסִבָּה. With that change, the resultant translation would be something like "a widening ramp spiraled up to the side rooms," partially anticipating the last part of the verse.

The double לְמַעְלָה לְמַעְלָה seems to imply continuing ascent and so is translated, "as one went up from story to story." That is, the higher one went, the wider the rooms became. Since those words are connected to לַצְּלָעוֹת ("to/regarding the side rooms"), the widening did not take place gradually, but at each story.

The following כִּי clause is nominal. The noun מוּסָב is a hapax, but clearly derived from סָבַב, "surround," and so the construct phrase מוּסַב־הַבַּיִת must mean that the side rooms, though not mentioned here, were "what surrounds the temple." I have added in brackets "the side rooms" as the adverbial accusative that the sense seems to imply. Some suggest repointing מוּסָב to the Hophal participle מוּסָב, "was surrounded."

The import of the verse's final sentence is the most difficult. רֹחַב־לַבַּיִת here can hardly mean "the width of the *temple*" because that would imply that the temple walls became wider the higher one climbed. But this is architecturally improbable and appears to contradict 41:6, which spoke of ledges that would narrow the walls with each story. The sentence is intelligible, however, if בַּיִת is taken here to refer to the totality of side rooms, viewed as one "house" or building, hence, "the width of the building increased ..."

The Qal imperfect יַעֲלֶה, "as one went up," would seem to imply some means of ascending, but its location and nature are unclear. Some picture a large exterior ramp or stairway around most of the building, but this would seem to make lighting the rooms very difficult. For Solomon's temple, 1 Ki 6:8 describes access to the upper stories by saying וּבְלוּלִּים יַעֲלוּ, "they would go up by staircases" (לוּלִים could also be "trapdoors"). Such a means here is more likely and accords with extrabiblical analogues.

41:8 This verse has no parallel in Kings. It describes a platform six cubits (about ten feet) high on which the temple and side rooms stood, elevating an already high structure considerably more. The point can only be to emphasize its centrality and sacredness. גֹּבַהּ is the ordinary word for "height," used in, for example, 40:42. However, some cite גַּב, "back," used in, for example, 1:18 and 43:13, and conjecture that here we should read גַּבָּה, an otherwise unattested feminine form (cf. Γαββαθα in Jn 19:13), but such tinkering with the text will clarify nothing.

The Qere, מוּסָדוֹת, is the sole reading in some manuscripts. It is the plural of the feminine noun מוּסָדָה, which occurs elsewhere only in Is 30:32 meaning "appointment," but here it must mean "foundation," as does the masculine noun מוֹסָד. The Kethib, מיסדות, could be intended to be vocalized as מְיֻסָּדוֹת, the Pual feminine plural participle of יָסַד, meaning "furnished with foundations."

מְלוֹ is simply a defective phonetic spelling (the quiescent *aleph* is not written) for מְלֹוא, "fullness." Elsewhere it is sometimes used in connection with measurements (e.g., Ex 16:33). The construct phrase מְלֹו הַקָּנֶה means "a full measuring rod."

Finally, אַצִּילָה apparently is a technical architectural term, the meaning of which is not at all clear. Its plural occurs in Jer 38:12 and Ezek 13:18, where it is used anatomically of "joints" on the human body. It is conceivable that here "joint" is used architecturally of the place where one part of a building joins another, but its specific application here escapes us. The guesses are many, and I have followed Zimmerli in rendering "top terrace."[7]

41:9–10 The verse division is infelicitous. Ezek 41:9a is a separate thought from 41:9b, and 41:9a is a sort of continuation of 41:5. Ezek 41:9b begins a sentence that continues into 41:10. In Ezek 41:9b–11, a new topic, the "open area," enters the description.

41:9a With this information that "the thickness of the outer wall of the side rooms was five cubits," we can calculate the width of the exterior of the

---

[7] Zimmerli, *Ezekiel*, 2:372.

temple (including the side rooms) as fifteen cubits: six cubits for the thickness of the wall of the temple (41:5); four cubits for the width of the side rooms (41:5); and five cubits for the width (thickness) of this outer wall of the side rooms. (See figure 5.) When we add fifteen cubits for the width on both sides to the width of the nave and the Holy of Holies of the temple, twenty cubits (41:2, 4), we arrive at a total for the width of the building as fifty cubits. Ezek 41:13 tells us that the length of the temple was one hundred cubits. This gives the symmetry of a perfect rectangle, fifty by one hundred cubits. These numbers, like many others in the temple description, are multiples of twenty-five. See the commentary on 40:1.

41:9b–10 Attention is now turned to וַאֲשֶׁר מֻנָּח, literally, "and that which is left alone." מֻנָּח is the Hophal participle of נוּחַ, "left behind, abandoned." The same participle will be used as a noun (לַמֻּנָּח, with article and לְ) in 41:11. It is usually translated something like "the open area."

The final phrase of 41:9, בֵּית צְלָעוֹת אֲשֶׁר לַבָּיִת, means "between the side rooms that belonged to the temple," and it begins a sentence that continues in 41:10. בֵּית can be used as a preposition, meaning "between," as also in Prov 8:2 and Job 8:17 (see BDB, s.v. בַּיִת, under בֵּין [p. 108]; cf. BDB, s.v. בַּיִת, 7 and 8). So used, בֵּית is a synonym of בֵּין, which begins 41:10.

It is unclear what the לְשָׁכוֹת ("rooms") in 41:10 were. Since it is the same term used in 40:44–46 to describe the priests' quarters, that may be its meaning here (so NIV), but possibly it refers to some other rooms. Keil thinks these are the same as the ones described in 42:1–14.[8] Whatever they were, the open area is measured as twenty cubits wide. There is also a five-cubit open area mentioned in 41:11, but it seems to be distinct from this twenty-cubit open area. See figure 2 and the calculation in 41:13–15a.

41:11 The singular phrase וּפֶתַח הַצֵּלָע, "the opening of the side room," is puzzling. Perhaps all three initial words, וּפֶתַח הַצֵּלָע לַמֻּנָּח, are best understood syntactically as thetical: "as for the opening of the side room to the open area." On that topic, the verse goes on to say that there was one such opening toward the north and another toward the south. See figure 5.

In the phrase וְרֹחַב מְקוֹם הַמֻּנָּח, "the width of the place of the open area," the noun מָקוֹם ("place") seems redundant. The LXX has an entirely different text with no clear relation to the MT, Zimmerli's speculation (following Gese) notwithstanding.[9]

41:12 Before the entire temple compound is measured in 41:13–15a, this verse is devoted to still another previously unmentioned building, a large structure behind the temple (on its western side). It covers almost the entire space from east to west on that side. Instead of using מֻנָּח, "open area" (41:9, 11), for the space in which this building is located, 41:12–15 uses גִּזְרָה, "restricted

---

8   Keil, *Ezekiel*, 2:239.
9   Zimmerli, *Ezekiel*, 2:373, referring to Gese, *Der Verfassungsentwurf des Ezechiel*, 172.

area." Probably גִּזְרָה has different connotations, although we are not certain what they were. In the OT גִּזְרָה occurs only in Ezek 41:12–15; 42:1, 10, 13; and Lam 4:7, where its meaning is too uncertain to be helpful. It appears to be derived from the verb גָּזַר, "cut off," which in the Niphal can mean "be separated, excluded." Probably it is cognate with the Arabic *jezira*, "island, cut off place," which appears in the modern names of various localities with biblical relevance. In this context, then, it would imply not merely vacant space, but restricted space, off-limits to most people, possibly even to the priests. Its application to the area in front of the temple in 41:14 would support this understanding of the word.

Nothing is said of this building's function. Ezek 43:7–8 may indicate that various civic monarchical buildings behind Solomon's temple had tended to encroach upon sacred space. Perhaps the building behind the temple in Ezekiel's vision functioned as a barrier to that happening again. Another possibility is that this building was meant to prevent idolatrous and syncretistic outrages such as those reported in Ezekiel's vision in chapter 8 and that may have occurred in the comparable location to the west of Solomon's temple. 1 Chr 26:18 mentions a structure "to the west" of the Solomonic temple called a פַּרְבָּר. Some commentators think that the plural of that word occurs in 2 Ki 23:11: פַּרְוָרִים (see BDB, s.v. פַּרְוָר). In 2 Ki 23:11 פַּרְוָרִים are associated with the idolatrous worship of the sun. Compare Ezek 8:16, where idolaters or syncretists had faced east (toward the rising of the sun) in worship, with "their backsides to the temple of Yahweh."

With internal measurements of ninety cubit by seventy cubits and external dimensions (including the five-cubit wall all around) of one hundred cubits by eighty cubits (41:12), this was a larger building than the temple itself. Hence, in Ezekiel's mind, it must have been a structure of considerable importance, although we cannot be sure of what that significance was.[10] In 41:13 the length of this building with its wall is expressly given as one hundred cubits (a measurement given also in 41:15a). Presumably the width of the area in which the building sat was also one hundred cubits, the same as the width of the inner court (40:47) and the width of the temple and the open area around it (41:14). (See the following discussion of 41:13–15a.) Since the width of the building was eighty cubits, perhaps it stood in the center, with ten cubits of open space on either side of it. See figure 2.

The Measurements of the Temple Compound (41:13–15a)

41:13–15a The temple compound is measured in these verses. They pull together a number of measurements and details, most of which have either been mentioned previously or which one could easily obtain by a little elementary mathematics. The picture that emerges in these verses is a picture of three

---

[10] Zimmerli, *Ezekiel*, 2:380, hypercritically suggests that it was a purely theological construct for blocking off the western side of the temple.

squares, each measuring one hundred cubits by one hundred cubits: the inner court (40:47), the temple and the open area around it (see below), and the re stricted area behind the temple (see the previous discussion of 41:12). See figure 2.

Keil spells out how the one hundred cubits length and width of the temple area can be obtained. His view excludes the vestibule, which he pictures as in the inner court, and includes the open areas around the temple (see figure 2). The length (east to west) of one hundred cubits includes the following: forty cubits for the nave (41:2); twenty cubits for the Holy of Holies (41:4); six cubits for the western wall behind the temple (41:5); four cubits for the side rooms on the west (41:5); five cubits for the outside wall of these side rooms (41:9); five cubits for the small open area onto which the side rooms opened (41:11); twenty cubits for the large open area behind that (41:10). The width was also one hundred cubits: twenty cubits for the temple (nave and Holy of Holies; 41:2, 4); six cubits each for the wall of the temple on the north and the south sides (twelve cubits total; 41:5); four cubits each for the side rooms on the north and the south (eight cubits total; 41:5); five cubits each for the outside wall of those rooms (ten cubits total; 41:9); five cubits each for the small open areas on the north and the south (ten cubits total; 41:11); and twenty cubits each for the large open areas on the north and the south (forty cubits total; 41:10).[11]

Twice, at the beginning of 41:13 and also of 41:15, we meet the *waw* conjunctive with the perfect (וּמָדַד, "and he measured") instead of the usual classical use of the imperfect with *waw* consecutive (וַיָּמָד in 41:1–5) with the same meaning. While 41:12, 15 used the masculine noun בִּנְיָן to refer to the "building" in the restricted area behind the temple, for it 41:13 uses the feminine synonym בִּנְיָה, which occurs only here in the OT.

In 41:15, for אֲשֶׁר עַל־אַחֲרֶיהָ, literally, "which is at its rear," I have translated "at the rear of the temple," following the NIV.

Problematic in 41:15 is the meaning of the plural noun with suffix whose Qere is וְאַתִּיקֶיהָא, while its Kethib probably is to be vocalized וְאַתּוּקֶיהָא. The Qere clearly is the plural of the noun אַתִּיק, whose singular occurs in 42:3 and whose plural recurs in 41:16 and 42:5. The Kethib, undoubtedly a synonym, is the plural of אַתּוּק (or אָתּוּק), which occurs only here. The *plene* writing of its third feminine singular suffix (ָ־יהָא) is unique in Hebrew (GKC, § 91 l; Joüon, § 94 i), but א was commonly used as a vowel letter in Aramaic.

As for the meaning of אַתִּיק or אַתּוּק, I have chosen "balcony." For them BDB gives "gallery, porch." KJV rendered the plural "galleries," as do most English translations. Two main alternatives have been suggested on the basis of cognate languages or Hebrew etymology, but none have found widespread acceptance: (1) "passageway, corridor" from an Akkadian word; (2) "ledge," that is, describing the way a window frame may recede in steps, based on an

---

[11] Keil, *Ezekiel*, 2:239–40.

alleged derivation from נָתַק, "tear, cut off," with prosthetic א. Similarly, *HALOT* includes "overhang." Whatever the word referred to, this verse mentions some that were visible outside the west building, while 41:16 indicates that there were some inside the nave, and 42:3 and 42:5 indicate that some could be seen from the inner and outer courts, in the latter two instances also with reference to three levels. Apparently the ancients were in as much of a quandary as we are. In 41:15, the LXX translates it with the plural of ἀπόλοιπος, its usual translation for גִּזְרָה, "restricted area," including earlier in the verse, while in 41:16, the LXX suggests some sort of windows. In 41:15–16, the Vulgate simply transliterates the word, as does the Targum in 41:16, probably because they did not understand it. Their translations of the other occurrences vary.

The Interior Decorations and Appointments of the Temple (41:15b–26)

41:15b–26 In 41:15 the MT has a large space between the two words אַמָּה וְהַהֵיכָל ("one hundred cubits" and "the temple"), which probably antedates the verse numberings. This space indicates that 41:15b really goes with the beginning of 41:16. Keil launches a lengthy, but unconvincing, defense of the later versification.[12] The verse divisions between 41:16–17, 17–18, and 18–19 likewise come in the middle of sentences, but the MT does not indicate that with spaces there.

Ezek 41:15b–26 reveals additional aspects of especially the interior decorations of the temple. Interpreters agree that these verses are rife with obscurities and difficulties, perhaps more so than any other part of the book. Any comparison of translations and commentaries will remove any doubt on that score. Part of the difficulty in comprehending the material lies in the changing vocabulary. We would have expected the descriptions found here to have been revealed when the guide[13] and the prophet were still inside the temple (41:1–4). Nor does the material in 41:15b–26 connect readily with the sequel in chapter 42. Naturally, critics have a field day in hypothesizing multifarious later glosses and redactions, but their speculations really solve nothing.

41:16 KJV translates the plural first occurrence of סַף as "door posts" and later in 43:8 as "post(s)" (NKJV is similar), but I know of no reason to depart from the word's normal meaning of "threshold." Perhaps the reference is to a prominent sill that ran all around the room beneath the "openings slanting inward" (וְהַחַלּוֹנִים הָאֲטֻמוֹת, repeated without articles in 41:26; see the first textual note on 40:16, which has the same phrase as here, but with the feminine form of the noun: וְחַלֹּנוֹת).

KJV takes לִשְׁלָשְׁתָּם (the noun שְׁלֹשָׁה with לְ and third masculine plural suffix) as "on their three stories" (NASB is similar), like שָׁלוֹשׁ in 41:6. This agrees

---

with 42:3, which describes other balconies "in three stories" (בַּשְּׁלִשִׁים). However, most English versions render it "the/all three of them " I have translated,
"on their three sides." As for the antecedent of its pronoun, according to the
rule of chiastic concord of the numerals three through ten, the most likely grammatical referent of the feminine form of the numeral (שְׁלֹשָׁה) would be the masculine noun אַתִּיקִים, "balconies" (or "galleries"?), but the context suggests that
it refers also to the preceding "thresholds" and "openings," and possibly also
to the "nave" and "vestibules" in 41:15b.

The phrase נֶגֶד הַסַּף, "opposite the threshold," might use סַף in a collective sense for every threshold. The LXX and Syriac omit the phrase.

The construct phrase שְׂחִיף עֵץ refers to something, literally, "of wood."
שְׂחִיף is a hapax. An Akkadian cognate makes most think of some kind of wood
paneling or veneer.

The phrase וְהָאָרֶץ עַד־הַחַלֹּנוֹת ("and the ground until the openings") must
mean "from the floor to the openings," as the LXX translates (ἐκ τοῦ ἐδάφους
ἕως τῶν θυρίδων).

Other verses in chapters 40–41 refer to "openings" (חַלֹּנוֹת or חַלֹּנִים), but
only at the end of 41:16 are they described as "covered." In וְהַחַלֹּנוֹת מְכֻסּוֹת,
the Pual participle (מְכֻסּוֹת, from כָּסָה) is anarthrous, so it is not a nominative
modifier ("the covered openings") but a predicate: "and the openings were covered." Is that participial adjective a synonym of אֲטֻמוֹת, "slanting inward" (?),
which is used as a nominative modifier for the "openings" earlier in 41:16 and
also for "openings" in 40:16 and 41:26? Does מְכֻסּוֹת mean they were completely "closed" or perhaps merely "latticed"? All the versions attest to the
phrase here, but interpret it variously. The Hebrew does not enable us to form
a very clear picture of what is being described.

41:17 If my understanding of 41:17a is correct, עַל־מֵעַל הַפֶּתַח here has
the same meaning as עַד־מֵעַל הַפֶּתַח in 41:20a. The meanings of the prepositions עַל and עַד can overlap.

With 41:17b and through 41:20 attention is turned to the decorative features of the building. At the end of 41:17, מִדּוֹת, "measures," is unclear. The
LXX omits it, but other versions witness to its originality. Many emendations
are proposed, but Zimmerli suggests that it refers to measured-off areas.[14] I
have taken it as referring to the carefully designed nature of the reliefs mentioned in 41:18.

41:18 The term for "cherub," כְּרוּב (41:18, 20, 25), is the same as that used
in chapters 9–11, but here the reference is to artwork, not the living creatures.
They are first called "cherub(im)" in 9:3, but in 10:20 Ezekiel identifies them
as the same creatures he saw in chapter 1. See the second textual note on 1:5
and the commentary on 1:5–11.

Both nouns, כְּרוּבִים וְתִמֹרִים, "cherubim and palm decorations," are plural,
so it is odd if they are the subject of the singular passive participle (of עָשָׂה),

---

[14] Zimmerli, *Ezekiel*, 2:384.

וְעָשׂוּי, "made." We also encountered the difficult singular עָשׂוּי in 40:17, and it will be repeated in 41:19. However, 41:20 has the expected plural, עֲשׂוּיִם. Apparently the singular was a fixed technical term. "Made" is probably too general; with others, I have rendered, "carved."

The clause וְתִמֹרָה֙ בֵּֽין־כְּר֣וּב לִכְר֔וּב, literally, "a palm decoration was between a cherub and to [another] cherub," employs the late idiom of בֵּין ... לְ instead of the classical Hebrew בֵּין ... וּבֵין.

41:19 The cherubim Ezekiel saw in his earlier visions (chapters 1 and 9–11) had four faces (e.g., 1:6). These have only two, probably because a mostly flat, two-dimensional carving of them (in wood upon a wall) could only show only two faces. Both cherubim and palm-like decorations, described by the same Hebrew terms as here, had adorned Solomon's temple (1 Ki 6:29–35), but other features described there, including gold overlay and open flowers, do not appear here. The general pattern of animals or hybrid creatures on either side of a tree is well attested in various art forms throughout the ancient Near East. The OT does not delve into the theological meaning of these symbols, probably to minimize their significance in relation to Yahweh, lest they receive idolatrous attention. Yet we can easily assume that they conveyed the ideas of life and security, provided by Yahweh.

41:20 The final phrase, וְקִ֖יר הַהֵיכָֽל׃, clearly means "the wall of the nave," and the *waw* probably has the nuance *"even on."* The dots above every letter of הַהֵיכָֽל are called *puncta extraordinaria*. They appear on fifteen words in the OT, though scholars are unsure of their origin and meaning.[15] Since they are present in both Babylonian and Tiberian texts, they predate the Tiberian system of vowels and accents in the MT. Probably they indicate that ancient scribes had misgivings whether the consonants should be in the text.

It is possible that הַהֵיכָל could be a dittograph of the identical first word of 41:21, or vice versa, but I see no cogent reason why its repetition should cause any major problem. One might have expected וּבְקִיר־הַהֵיכָל, but apparently the construction is to be attributed to the enumeratory style of this entire section of the book.

For the three Hebrew words וְקִ֖יר הַהֵיכָֽל׃ הַהֵיכָל֙ spanning the end of 41:20 and the beginning of 41:21 the LXX (καὶ τὸ ἅγιον καὶ ὁ ναός) translates as if there were two, וְהַקֹּדֶשׁ וְהַהֵיכָל, "the Holy Place and the nave," apparently reading or interpreting וְקִיר as וְהַקֹּדֶשׁ in anticipation of that word's use later in 41:21. The Vulgate too reflects only one הַהֵיכָל, but translates *in pariete templi*, "on the wall of the temple."

41:21 The syntax of הַהֵיכָל מְזוּזַת רְבָעָה is a *casus pendens* (see Joüon, § 156 a), "as for the nave ... ," followed by a construct phrase, "doorpost of square." The last item of the construct phrase functions as an adjectival geni-

---

15 See Israel, *Introduction to the Tiberian Masorah*, §§ 79–80; Tov, *Textual Criticism of the Hebrew Bible*, 55–57.

1212

tive (see Waltke-O'Connor, § 9.5.3b): "it had square doorposts." רְבֻעָה is the feminine Qal passive participle (of רָבַע), which does not have a passive meaning ("squared"), but instead is used to describe "square" objects, such as an altar (e.g., Ex 27:1; 30:2) or doorways (1 Ki 7:5). Thus the meaning is that the doorposts themselves were four-cornered or square, or perhaps had quadruple gradations.

In 41:20–21, the Syriac Peshitta begins a new sentence with וְקִיר, reads only one הַהֵיכָל, and omits מְזוּזַת, so it renders, "the wall of the temple was square." The LXX includes a word for מְזוּזַת, but apparently did not understand it, since it translated it as ἀναπτυσσόμενος, "opening, unfolding." מְזוּזַת is the construct of מְזוּזָה, "doorpost." It refers to the projecting framework of entrances. In modern Hebrew usage, "mezuzah" denotes a small container with excerpts from the Torah affixed to the doorpost of an orthodox Jewish dwelling, an attempt to fulfill literally the command in Deut 6:9; 11:20.

The phrase הַמַּרְאֶה כַּמַּרְאֶה, literally, "the appearance/form (was) like the form," ends the verse in the MT, and I have rendered it, "and the front of the Holy of Holies *had the same form*." In the LXX the last half of 41:21 seems to begin a new sentence that extends into 41:22: κατὰ πρόσωπον τῶν ἁγίων ὅρασις ὡς ὄψις θυσιαστηρίου ξυλίνου, "along the face of the Holy Place was an appearance as the face of a wooden altar." The Syriac is similar, as are RSV, NRSV, and ESV: "in front of the holy place was something resembling an altar of wood." In the visions of chapters 1, 8, and 10, Ezekiel often used מַרְאֶה to describe the "appearance" of supernatural beings or things by comparing them to the "appearance" of familiar, worldly things (e.g., 1:5, 13–14, 16, 26). If הַמַּרְאֶה כַּמַּרְאֶה here refers to the structure in 41:22, that might help explain why it is first described as (having the "appearance" of) an "altar," but then the guide clarifies that it really is a "table." See further on 41:22.

41:22 The abrupt change of subject to "the altar" (הַמִּזְבֵּחַ) is thoroughly in keeping with Ezekiel's periodic style in this section. In 41:23 he will return to the (doors of) the nave and Holy of Holies, and then shortly again to decorative features of the building.

In some respects this verse seems to have been as puzzling to Ezekiel as it is to us. Hence the guide interjects an explanation that in form resembles his announcement of the Holy of Holies in 41:4. First of all, the composition of the altar is of wood. The material is expressed as the predicate of a nominal clause: הַמִּזְבֵּחַ עֵץ, literally, "the altar (was) wood." Normally wood would be incongruous for an altar, because the sacrificial fires would consume the altar itself. Perhaps that incongruity explains why the guide identifies it as "the table" (הַשֻּׁלְחָן). That word indicates that the object was not really an altar (as usually understood), but the table perpetually set with the "bread of the Presence" (KJV: "shewbread") in the tabernacle and temple (Ex 25:23, 30; 1 Ki 7:48).

How could it then be referred to as an "altar" at the start of 41:22? Evidently the answer lies in the sacrificial and "sacramental" role of the table in Israel's liturgy. The altar of incense was an inner (in the nave) counterpart to

the great altar of burnt offering in the outer courtyard, where usually the meat of animals was offered. So too, the table of "shewbread" in the nave corresponded to the unbloody grain offerings, which were also sacrificed on the great altar in the outer court, and thus the table was a sort of non-burnt offering to Yahweh. Even so, this juxtaposition of "altar" and "table" is otherwise unattested in the OT. Undoubtedly the reason why the rest of the OT never connects the "altar" and "table" is to defend Israel against the belief that sacrifice was for alimentation of the Deity—a motif that was central to the sacrificial ritual of Israel's pagan neighbors, but something which the Bible not only rejects, but ridicules (Ps 50:7–13).

From our NT vantage point, we cannot help but think of the Sacrament of the Altar, wherein our Lord prepares his Table for us (cf. Ps 23:5), and we partake of his body and blood, given and shed for us on the cross for the forgiveness of sins (Mt 26:26–28; 1 Cor 11:23–34).

This "table" seen by Ezekiel must have been constructed in a way that in some respects resembled an altar. The mention of מִקְצֹעוֹתָיו ("its corners") signals something of that sort. That word is used twice in connection with the tabernacle (Ex 26:24; 36:29) but not ever specifically for an altar. Nevertheless, it is plausible that it implies a design somewhat similar to the "horns" that were virtually always found on altars (e.g., Ex 29:12; 37:25; Lev 4:7, 18; 1 Ki 2:28).

The measurement that "its length [וְאָרְכּוֹ] was two cubits" is expressed using the construct phrase שְׁתַּיִם־אַמּוֹת, a later idiom, instead of using the dual form אַמָּתַיִם preferred in earlier Hebrew, including the tabernacle description (e.g., Ex 25:10, 17, 23). The additional measurement that "its width was two cubits," placed in brackets in the translation, is supplied from the LXX. It seems to have fallen out of the MT by homoioteleuton.

In the clause וְאָרְכּוֹ וְקִירֹתָיו עֵץ ("its length and its sides were wood") וְאָרְכּוֹ is almost universally[16] taken to be a copyist's error for וְאַדְנוֹ, "and its base," as reflected in the LXX. KJV and NKJV retain "length," but the verse has already stated, "its length [וְאָרְכּוֹ] was two cubits," and one can hardly speak of "length" as being "wood"!

Idioms aside, the dimensions of Ezekiel's table differ radically from the one in the tabernacle (Ex 25:23–30). Ezekiel's table is higher than both its width and length. The tabernacle version had been rectangular, and its length (two cubits) was greater than its width (one cubit) and its height (one and a half cubits), and all of it was overlaid with gold. Presumably, the one in the temple (1 Ki 7:48) was the same. No wonder Ezekiel may have been perplexed about what it was!

41:23–24 As in Solomon's temple (1 Ki 6:31–34), the nave and the Holy of Holies both had double doors with swinging leaves. דֶּלֶת can be used for the

---

16 Even by Keil, *Ezekiel*, 2:251.

whole "door" or for just its swinging "leaf." Each door must have been set in its own pivot hole next to the jamb. "Swinging" translates מוּחַדּוֹת, a Hophal participle denoting capability, "that can be turned." Thus being reversible, whether going in or out, the leaves would easily swing in the right way to allow access.

41:25 Here the feminine (equivalent to a neuter?) singular passive participle וַעֲשׂוּיָה, "carved," is used with masculine plural subjects, כְּרוּבִים וְתִמֹרִים. See the discussion of the masculine singular וְעָשׂוּי in 41:18. Without knowing the precise meaning of the participle, it is hard to react to the inconsistency.

A more insoluble issue arises with וְעָב עֵץ. The plural of עָב is also the last word of 41:26 (וְהָעָבִים). The noun עָב is common meaning "cloud," but the term here, and also in Solomon's temple (1 Ki 7:6), must be a homograph that is an architectural term. We have no clue what it meant, and, apparently, neither did the ancients. I have chosen "canopy" with NKJV, RSV, and NRSV.

41:26 The syntax of the last three words (וְצַלְעוֹת הַבַּיִת וְהָעָבִים) is uncertain. וְהָעָבִים may be coordinate with וְצַלְעוֹת הַבַּיִת and conclude the series: "palm decorations" were "on the side walls of the vestibule [and on] the side rooms of the temple [and on] the canopies." Or these three words may make their own independent statement, as I have translated: "the side rooms of the temple also had canopies."

Vision of the New Temple: Part 3

Translation

42 ¹Then he led me out to the outer courtyard, toward the north, and he brought me to a set of rooms opposite the restricted area and opposite the building toward the north. ²Its length was one hundred cubits on the north side and its width fifty cubits. ³Opposite the twenty [cubits] that belonged to the inner court and opposite the pavement belonging to the outer court, balcony faced balcony in three stories. ⁴In front of the rooms was a walkway ten cubits wide on the inside and one hundred cubits long. Their entrances were on the north. ⁵The upper rooms were narrower because the balconies took away space from them, more than from the building's bottom and middle ones. ⁶For they [the priests' sacristies] were in three stories and had no pillars like the pillars in the courts, and hence the upper story had to be shortened more than the lower and middle ones (from the ground). ⁷There was also a wall outside parallel to the rooms toward the outer court in front of the rooms. It was fifty cubits long. ⁸The length of the rooms relating to the outer court was fifty cubits, whereas those facing the temple were one hundred cubits long. ⁹At the foot of these rooms was an entrance from the east, when one entered them from the outer court. ¹⁰In the thickness of the wall of the court, on the south side, opposite the restricted area and opposite the building, were rooms. ¹¹They also had a passageway in front of them. Just like the appearance of the rooms on the north, like their length and so also their width, all their exits, their designs, and their entrances, ¹²identical were the entrances to the rooms on the south, at the head of the passageway, the passageway opposite the corresponding wall, as one enters them from the east. ¹³Then he said to me, "The northern and southern rooms in front of the restricted area are holy rooms where the priests who approach Yahweh will eat the most holy offerings. There they will deposit the most holy offerings, the grain offering, the sin offering, and the reparation offering, for the place is holy. ¹⁴When the priests enter them, they must not go out from the holy place to the outer courtyard until they have deposited there their vestments in which they have ministered, because they [the vestments] are holy. They must put on other clothes before they approach the area that is for the people."

¹⁵Thus he had finished the measurements of the interior of the temple area. Then he led me out through the gate facing east and measured it [the temple area] all around. ¹⁶He measured the east side using the measuring rod; it was five hundred [cubits] using canes, the measuring rod. ¹⁷Then he turned and measured the north side: it was five hundred [cubits] using canes, the measuring rod. ¹⁸Then he turned and measured the south side: it was five hundred [cubits] using canes, the measuring rod. ¹⁹He turned to the west side and measured: it was five hun-

dred [cubits] using canes, the measuring rod. **²⁰Thus on all four sides he measured it [the temple area]. It had a wall all around it, five hundred [cubits] long
and five hundred [cubits] wide, in order to separate the holy from the common.**

Textual Notes and Commentary

42:1 The chapter division is almost arbitrary, since this chapter concludes the description of the temple and its environs begun in chapter 40. The
same supernatural guide (see the commentary on 40:3) continues to lead the
"tour," but this fact is explicitly mentioned only in 42:1 and 42:15, which form
the beginnings of the two main sections of the chapter: (1) the priests' sacristies
(42:1–14) and (2) the external dimensions of the temple complex (42:15–20).
Only the second section refers to his act of measuring (the verb מָדַד), although
the first section gives results of that action (measurements).

For the guidance formulas וַיּוֹצִאֵנִי, "he led me out," and וַיְבִאֵנִי, "he brought
me," see the second textual note on 40:2. A variation of the first one occurs in
42:15.

The Hebrew הַדֶּרֶךְ דֶּרֶךְ הַצָּפוֹן is, literally, "the way was the way of the
north," that is, toward the north. Apparently Ezekiel is led out of the north inner gate into the north part of the outer court and then westward to the north
side of the area behind the temple building. See figure 2.

In 42:1 he uses הַלִּשְׁכָּה, which must be a singular collective, "*set* of rooms."
From 42:4 on he will always use the plural לְשָׁכוֹת, "rooms." The same word is
used for the rooms mentioned in 41:10, which may or may not be the same as
those described here. Based on the explanation of these rooms in 42:13–15,
they are usually referred to as something like the "priests' sacristies." See figure 2.

For הַגִּזְרָה, "the restricted area," and הַבִּנְיָן, "the building," in it, see on
41:12.

42:2 The difficult phrase אֶל־פְּנֵי־אֹרֶךְ אַמּוֹת הַמֵּאָה is, literally, "to the face
of length, cubits the one hundred." The meaning clearly is that the length was
one hundred cubits, as I have translated. Various translations and interpretations are offered. אֶל־פְּנֵי recurs in, for example, 42:3, 7, 10, 13. The following
three words appear to exhibit both transposition of words and a wrong word
division; we would expect אָרְכָּה מֵאָה אַמּוֹת.

It is hard to know what to make of פֶּתַח הַצָּפוֹן, literally, "the entrance of
the north" or "north door." To delete it as a gloss, as many critics do, explains
nothing. A less radical alternative is to emend פֶּתַח to פְּאַת, resulting in "the
north side," since פְּאַת is used in 41:12. This is supported by the LXX and followed by Zimmerli[1] and others. I too have so translated for want of a more convincing rendition.

The "width" of this set of rooms is "fifty cubits."

---

[1] Zimmerli, *Ezekiel*, 2:392.

42:3 After the numeral twenty (הָעֶשְׂרִים), the MT has no אַמּוֹת ("cubits"). This is not all that unusual, and there is little doubt that it is implied by the context. This twenty-cubit area that "belonged to the inner court" could refer to the northern twenty-cubit open area mentioned in 41:9b–10, especially if the priests' sacristies described in 42:1–14 are the same as the rooms mentioned in 41:10 (see figure 2). This would mean that there were balconies on the south side of the set of rooms mentioned in 42:1. For the רִצְפָּה, "pavement," see the textual notes on 40:17–18 and figure 2. It is debatable, but apparently here וְנֶגֶד רִצְפָּה, "opposite the pavement," was on the other (north) side of the set of rooms, meaning that balconies were on the north side as well.

The noun אַתִּיק occurred in 41:15–16; see on 41:15. Since its precise meaning is unknown, it is impossible to be sure what the final part of this verse is communicating. Whatever they were, they were אֶל־פְּנֵי, "to the face of," that is, "facing" one another. בַּשְּׁלִשִׁים, literally, "in the thirds," implies an area divided into thirds. I have translated that as "in three stories." Similar is לִשְׁלִשְׁתָּם in 41:16, which describes the balconies discussed there. In 42:6 the Pual participle מְשֻׁלָּשׁוֹת is used, apparently with the same meaning: "in three stories." Some critics wish to substitute the participle here, but בַּשְּׁלִשִׁים is probably a stylistic variation expressing the same thing.[2]

42:4 The phrase אֶל־הַפְּנִימִית, "to/on the inside," does not specify what the walkway is inside of, but probably it is inside the outer court (see figure 2). The MT goes on to say דֶּרֶךְ אַמָּה אֶחָת, "a way, one cubit." The reference is presumably to length, but a walkway only a cubit long is manifestly absurd. Hence virtually all commentators[3] and modern translations (from RSV on) assume, with support from the LXX and Syriac, an original אֹרֶךְ מֵאָה אַמּוֹת ("length of one hundred cubits"). The verse already gave the ten-cubit "width" (רֹחַב) of the walkway, and the combination of רֹחַב followed by אֹרֶךְ is common enough (e.g., 40:11; 41:2, 12; 45:6). The result, describing a passage along the whole length of the building, fits the context. More radical conjectures have been made, of course.

The final statement that the rooms' doors faced north implies that one could enter the rooms directly from the walkway in front of them.

42:5 That the upper rooms are "narrower" is described by קְצֻרוֹת, a Qal passive participle, literally, "narrow*ed*." (Contrast the three stories of side rooms in 41:6, which became successively wider, going from bottom to top.) The sense of the כִּי clause must be "because the balconies took away space from them," as surmised from the context. יוֹכְלוּ may be an irregular Qal imperfect from אָכַל, "eat," a picturesque term, since some manuscripts have its

---

[2] Keil, *Ezekiel*, 2:253, 259–61, translates this as "in the third storey" and views this verse as describing balconies only on the upper story, which would explain why that story only, and not the middle one also, is narrowed (42:5–6).

[3] Even Keil, *Ezekiel*, 2:259–60.

regular imperfect form (יֹאכְלוּ) as a Qere (cf. GKC, § 68 h). Elision of the quiescent א is common. Other manuscripts have יוּכְלוּ, the Qal imperfect of יָכֹל, "be able," which can mean "prevail against," although it seems a bit forced to derive from it the sense of "take away space." Some advocate revocalization to יָכְלוּ, the Qal perfect of יָכֹל. In any case, the verb here may be used as a technical architectural term.

The מִן prefixed to both words in מֵהַתַּחְתֹּנוֹת וּמֵהַתִּכֹנוֹת is comparative: literally, "more than the lower ones and more than the middle ones." The verse seems to say that the rooms of the upper story were narrower than those of the other two stories by the width of their balconies.

42:6 "In three stories" is a free rendition of the Pual participle מְשֻׁלָּשׁוֹת, "thirded," that is, "divided into three parts."

The absence of pillars (to support the balconies?) now gives the reason for the slanting backward of the upper story. Zimmerli prefers the LXX's ἐξωτέρων (as if the Hebrew were חִיצֹנוֹת) to the MT's חֲצֵרוֹת and translates, "<outer> (chambers)." His assumption is that this verse is later commentary on the "basic text" of 40:17, where only rooms were mentioned.[4] But that is conjectural, at best.

Since much of Ezekiel's temple is patterned after that of Solomon, this verse probably implies that the courts of the Solomonic temple were colonnaded, although that is never mentioned in Kings and Chronicles. We know from Jn 10:23 and from Josephus[5] that there were colonnades in the courts of the Herodian temple.

The meaning of נֶאֱצַל as "had to be shortened" is an intelligent guess from the context. It is the Niphal participle of a rare verb, אָצַל, used elsewhere in the related sense of "withdraw, take away." It may be another of those technical architectural terms that we are no longer able to understand fully. Some attempt to relate it to the noun אַצִּיל in 13:18 or אֲצִילָה in 41:8. Its subject is unspecified, but in context it must be the upper story that "had to be shortened." NIV interprets: "so they [the rooms on the third floor] were smaller in floor space."

"From the ground" (מֵהָאָרֶץ) apparently intends to clarify the reference point for "lower," "middle," and "upper," but in English seems redundant, so I have placed it in parentheses.

42:7 The גָּדֵר, "wall," may be protective. It is fifty cubits long, most likely running along the east side of the building (see 42:9), not along the north side, where its length would more likely be one hundred cubits, corresponding to the length of the מַהֲלָךְ ("walkway") of 42:4. See figure 2.

42:8 The length of the rooms mentioned in the previous verse and also in the next is given in this verse as fifty cubits; these rooms seem to be the ones

---

4 Zimmerli, *Ezekiel*, 2:394.

5 Josephus, *Antiquities*, 15.413–16 (15.11.5).

on the short side of the building facing east. But 42:8b is much disputed. The use of וְהִנֵּה, "and behold," is unexpected because it appears nowhere else in 42:1–14 and because in chapters 40–48 it usually is used only when a new aspect of the vision is introduced (although 47:2 is one exception). Some suggest changing its vowels to form the adverb הֵנָּה, "here, on this side." The second half of the verse refers to another set of rooms, although לְשָׁכוֹת is absent. The part of the temple referred to would be the long side facing north. Ezekiel generally uses הֵיכָל for the "nave" and prefers בַּיִת ("house") for the entire temple structure, but here he must use הַהֵיכָל for the temple structure. Although the MT uses unusual idioms, it is attested by Vulgate, Syriac, and Targum.

Some, on the basis of the LXX, emend עַל־פְּנֵי הַהֵיכָל to עַל־פָּנֶיהָ הַכֹּל. Together with the change to הֵנָּה, that results in something like this: "as they were facing it, the whole [measured] one hundred cubits." The two readings differ substantially and are typical of the exegetical morass presented by these chapters, amply evident in the ancient versions, and not clarified by modern "scientific" study.

42:9 The Qere וּמִתַּחַת הַלְּשָׁכוֹת הָאֵלֶּה is "from under these rooms." The Kethib apparently would be vocalized וּמִתַּחְתָּה לְשָׁכוֹת הָאֵלֶּה, "and from under it [them], these rooms." The feminine singular suffix on וּמִתַּחְתָּה would have to refer to the feminine plural לְשָׁכוֹת. The suffix is of the form normally found on singular nouns, but the preposition תַּחַת regularly takes the suffix form for plural nouns (which here would be וּמִתַּחְתֵּיהָ). The Kethib also lacks a definite article on לְשָׁכוֹת, while the following demonstrative pronoun הָאֵלֶּה has the article. However, other examples of such lack of concord can be found. "Under" (תַּחַת) here must imply "at the foot, base," so NKJV correctly gives "at the lower chambers."

The Kethib, הַמָּבוֹא, clearly means an "entrance." The Qere, הַמֵּבִיא, is the Hiphil participle of בּוֹא (with article), "bringing," which normally would require a direct object. Practically all translations, starting with KJV, follow the Kethib.

Apparently the picture is that it was impossible to enter the building directly from the court. Entrance was only via the walkway on the north (42:4) or this entrance on the east, which was shielded by the wall (42:7). This prevented unauthorized entry and protected the sacrality of the building. Only the priests could enter (42:13–14).

42:10 This verse begins a brief description of the southern sacristies. This topic continues through 42:12. These rooms turn out to be mirror images of the northern sacristies (42:1–9), and it is precisely this theme that 42:10–12 seems most concerned to emphasize, that is, the perfect symmetry of the entire temple complex. But the very brevity of the descriptions, magnified by continued textual difficulties, combine to make the translator's and exegete's task a rather daunting one.

This verse begins with בְּרֹחַב ׀ גֶּדֶר הֶחָצֵר, "in the width of the wall of the court," implying that the rooms to be described were within the wall and their size corresponded to the width of the wall. Most translations follow the MT fairly literally (e.g., KJV, ESV, NASB), as do some commentators,[6] However, RSV ("where the outside wall begins") and some commentators[7] take these words as the end of the sentence begun in 42:9 and emend רֹחַב to רֹאשׁ, "head, top, beginning." רֹאשׁ also appears (in a different context) in 42:12. The LXX supports "at the beginning" but has a different text: κατὰ τὸ φῶς τοῦ ἐν ἀρχῇ περιπάτου, "according to the light of the walkway at the beginning."

The MT states that the rooms are דֶּרֶךְ הַקָּדִים, "on the east side." The Vulgate and some English translations reflect that (e.g., KJV, NKJV, NASB). Others, following the LXX (τὰ πρὸς νότον), give "south side" (e.g., RSV, NIV, ESV). The context, especially "south" in 42:12 and "the northern and southern rooms" in 42:13, clearly requires "south" here. Perhaps מֵהַקָּדִים in 42:9 caused a scribe to write הַקָּדִים here also in place of הַדָּרוֹם, "the south." The description of their location obviously parallels that of the northern rooms in 42:1. Here אֶל־פְּנֵי ("opposite") is used twice as an equivalent for נֶגֶד twice in 42:1.

42:11–12 I have translated the first two Hebrew words, וְדֶרֶךְ לִפְנֵיהֶם, as a separate sentence, but they could easily be linked with the end of 42:10, although the sense is the same in either case.

I have taken the rest of 42:11 as part of the same sentence that continues in 42:12. The syntax of the rest of 42:11 and first part of 42:12 is debatable and English translations and commentaries disagree, although the main point is clear: the southern rooms were identical to the northern ones. Probably the next sentence continues through the end of 42:12. Its first part, beginning with כְּמַרְאֵה and extending through the end of 42:11, describes the northern rooms and their features. Many of the terms are prefixed by the preposition כְּ, "as, like." Once, before רָחְבָּן, "their width," we find כֵּן, "so also," which here probably is used as an equivalent for כְּ, and so the LXX rightly translates it in the same way (κατά) as it does כְּ. Then the southern rooms are described in 42:12, beginning with the preposition כְּ on וּכְפִתְחֵי (literally, "and like the entrances of …"). Hebrew can repeat כְּ "to signify the completeness of the correspondency between two objects" (BDB, s.v. כְּ, 2). To indicate this, the translation renders the כְּ at the beginning of the sentence in 42:11 as "just like" and the כְּ on וּכְפִתְחֵי at the beginning of the description of the southern rooms in 42:12 as "identical were."

In 42:11, one might have expected another כְּ instead of וְכֹל before מוֹצָאֵיהֶן, and many critics[8] emend accordingly. However, the versions clearly support the MT, although some omit כְּ before the following words.

וּכְמִשְׁפְּטֵיהֶן is the plural of the noun מִשְׁפָּט (with כְּ and suffix) in the sense of "their designs, layouts, arrangements." This an excellent illustration of the

---

[6] For an attempt to retain and understand the MT, see Keil, *Ezekiel*, 2:264–65.

[7] E.g., Zimmerli, *Ezekiel*, 2:395; Block, *Ezekiel*, 2:562, including n. 134.

[8] E.g., Zimmerli, *Ezekiel*, 2:395.

polyvalence of the word, which in other contexts can mean "custom, ordinance, justice, judgment, law suit, legal claim."

42:12 Since the first Hebrew word (וּכְפְתָחֵי) of 42:12 is not translated in the LXX, many treat it as basically dittographical and emend it in various ways, but it is retained in my translation.

The "passageway" (דֶּרֶךְ) in 42:11–12 is presumably the counterpart to the "walkway" (מַהֲלָךְ) in 42:4. In דֶּרֶךְ דֶּרֶךְ (42:12), the second occurrence of the word begins a new phrase, set off by commas in the translation, that defines this "passageway" more precisely. However, the phrase הַגְּדֶרֶת הַגִּינָה is obscure. גְּדֶרֶת is a feminine counterpart of the more common גָּדֵר, and both mean "wall." Even though it has the article, הַגְּדֶרֶת appears to be in construct (a rare phenomenon; see Joüon, § 131 d, footnote 1; cf. GKC, § 127 f–g). The meaning of הַגִּינָה is uncertain. It is a hapax and apparently another architectural term. The versions make various guesses. The rabbinical tradition understood it in a sense like "appropriate, corresponding," which I have followed (so also NRSV, ESV, and NIV). Other common guesses are "protective" or "intervening." One suspects a parallelism with the wall described in 42:7, but there is no way to claim any certainty.

The words דֶּרֶךְ הַקָּדִים בְּבוֹאָן are an abbreviated repetition of 42:9, meaning "the way of (from) the east as one comes" to these rooms. The third feminine plural suffix on בְּבוֹאָן (Qal infinitive of בּוֹא; Gen 30:38 has the identical form), literally, "when they come," perhaps is influenced by the feminine plural "rooms" (הַלְּשָׁכוֹת, 42:11–12) or by the many third feminine plural suffixes on nouns in 42:11–12.

42:13 The reader should note the uniqueness of 42:13–14 within the context of chapters 40–42. For the first time the usually silent guide (see the commentary on 40:3) identifies and also explains in some detail the significance of the rooms Ezekiel observes. The exegete will also be aware that the many textual difficulties that often frustrate us in other parts of these chapters are virtually absent here. The copyists were obviously familiar with the vocabulary and procedure described. A trivial textual problem is the absence of a *waw* on לְשָׁכוֹת to connect "the northern rooms *and* the southern rooms." The LXX, Syriac, and Vulgate inserted a copula, as do modern translations.

The rooms are unhesitatingly called "holy rooms." The construct phrase לִשְׁכוֹת הַקֹּדֶשׁ, "rooms of holiness," is an attributive or qualitative genitive. In biblical thought, the quality of holiness is an attribute of God himself, who alone is holy (Rev 15:4). When he imparts holiness, it is not only ethical, but also temporal and spatial. Paganism, however, tended to omit the ethical dimension and identify the holy with nature. But in biblical theology, since all creation has been corrupted by man's fall into sin, holy things in this world are not so by nature in the order of creation. Rather, they are holy by God's gracious election and command in the order of redemption, according to his Word. The theology is parallel to that of the NT Sacraments, whereby ordinary elements (water, bread, wine) become sacred means of grace according to God's

Word and Christ's institution. Although there is no exact NT parallel to the OT application here, "sacristies," and, in light of 42:14, also "vestries" (perhaps the pastor's study) are the nearest ecclesiastical counterpart.

Twice in this verse (and once in 42:14) the adverb שָׁם, "there," is used emphatically for these "holy rooms." The first is difficult to render into English: אֲשֶׁר יֹאכְלוּ־שָׁם is, literally, "*which they shall eat there* the most holy offerings." The second can be translated literally: שָׁם יַנִּיחוּ ׀ קָדְשֵׁי הַקֳּדָשִׁים, "*there* they will deposit the most holy offerings."

Twice the construct phrase קָדְשֵׁי הַקֳּדָשִׁים, "the holies of holies," functions as a superlative, "the most holy (offerings)." It is a semi-technical term for that portion of the sacrifices that was not burned on the altar, but was to be eaten by the priests themselves as representatives of Yahweh. It was also used in Lev 21:22 (cf. the singular קֹדֶשׁ הַקֳּדָשִׁים in, e.g., Num 4:4; 18:9). The laity and even the priests' own families were excluded from eating the most holy offerings. The phrase is almost the same as that for the most sacred space, "the Holy of Holies, the Most Holy (Place)," the innermost room of the temple (as in 41:4), except that the word in construct here is plural (קָדְשֵׁי) instead of singular (קֹדֶשׁ).

The adjective קָרוֹב in 42:13 and 43:19 describes the priests (the sons of Zadok) as those "who draw near, approach God for liturgical service" (see BDB, s.v. קָרוֹב, 2 e), the same meaning that the participle קָרֵב has in 40:46 and 45:4, and that the Qal finite verb has in 44:15–16. The adjective here parallels the use of the Hiphil of the verb, הִקְרִיב, literally, "bring near, offer," regularly used for offering sacrifices (43:22–24; 44:7, 15, 27; 46:4; also, e.g., Lev 1:2–3, 5). Cf. the approximate Greek transliteration κορβᾶν in Mk 7:11, where Jesus condemns a warped theology of offerings.

The priests are first to "deposit" (יַנִּיחוּ, imperfect of the second Hiphil conjugation of נוּחַ) the most holy things in these "holy rooms" before eating them. Basically, this stipulation is made because these offerings could not be eaten anywhere the priests desired, but only in a holy place (as commanded in Lev 6:9, 19 [ET 6:16, 26]; 7:6; 10:13) and because they had to be prepared properly first, boiling in the case of meat (Lev 6:21 [ET 6:28];) or baked without yeast in the case of grain (Lev 6:10 [ET 6:17]).

The triad of types of sacrifice mentioned here (וְהַמִּנְחָה וְהַחַטָּאת וְהָאָשָׁם) is the same as in 40:39 except that מִנְחָה here replaces עוֹלָה. In Ezekiel there is no significance in the variation.[9] מִנְחָה is, of itself, a very generic word, meaning a "gift" of almost any sort, but in sacrificial contexts it applies to the eucharistic aspect of all sacrifices that are joyful gifts from the worshiper to God. Etymologically, עוֹלָה is simply a feminine participle of עָלָה (modifying the implied but unstated feminine noun מִנְחָה). In the revelation to Moses, however, both came to refer to discrete types of sacrifices. מִנְחָה often refers specifically to the unbloody "grain offering," which under certain circumstances

---

[9] For an overview of all these offerings in Leviticus 1–7, see Kleinig, *Leviticus*, 33–39.

(especially penury) could be substituted for the עוֹלָה, "burnt offering." Although expiation was not their main emphasis, it plainly is present in both. In fact, one could almost assert that all the biblical motifs of sacrifice were present in all the types of sacrifice, although each type tends to accent one particular motif.

On the "sin offering" (חַטָּאת) and "reparation offering" (אָשָׁם), see the fourth textual note on 40:39. For אָשָׁם, "reparation offering" is more accurate than the traditional "guilt offering." For חַטָּאת, instead of the traditional "sin offering," there is a tendency in modern scholarship to prefer "purification offering," but that paints too restricted a picture of its significance, although the terms are not mutually exclusive. Almost conspicuous by its absence in this list are the שְׁלָמִים, "communion offerings" (traditionally "peace offerings"). Although a portion of that meat too went to the priests, it was not "most holy," and the accent is more on the larger portions of meat, which were returned to the laymen bringing the sacrifice.[10]

42:14 The initial clause בְּבֹאָם הַכֹּהֲנִים is, literally, "when they enter, the priests," meaning "when the priests enter." The Qal infinitive construct of בּוֹא (with בְּ) has a proleptic pronominal suffix (ם-ָ, "they") that anticipates the subject, "the priests." The following clause, וְלֹא־יֵצְאוּ מֵהַקֹּדֶשׁ, literally, "they shall not go out from the holy place," makes clear that the place they had entered is הַקֹּדֶשׁ.

The next clause, וְשָׁם יַנִּיחוּ בִגְדֵיהֶם, literally, "and there they shall deposit their vestments," refers to the holy place by the same adverb שָׁם, "there," that referred to the holy place emphatically twice in 42:13 (see the note there). The same verb, יַנִּיחוּ (imperfect of the second Hiphil conjugation of נוּחַ), "deposit," here for storing the sacred vestments, was used in 42:13 in the command that the priests "deposit" the most holy offerings in the holy place before eating them. The reason for the command about the vestments is כִּי־קֹדֶשׁ הֵנָּה, "because they are holy." The third feminine plural pronoun הֵנָּה must be chosen to clarify that this refers to "their vestments" (בִגְדֵיהֶם) rather than to the (masculine) priests. Likewise, יְשָׁרְתוּ בָהֶן means that the priests "serve" (Piel imperfect of שָׁרַת) "in them," and the third feminine plural suffix on בָהֶן again refers to the vestments. Elsewhere in the OT בְּגָדִים is usually construed as masculine, but in Ezekiel the exegete is accustomed to inconsistencies in gender (and number) by this time.

In the injunction for the priests to "put on other clothes," the Qere (וְלָבְשׁוּ) is the perfect with *waw* while the Kethib (יִלְבְּשׁוּ) is the imperfect without *waw*. The imperfect is customary in a command and so accents the change more.

---

[10] For that portion of the "communion offerings" that belonged to the priests, see Lev 7:28–36 and Kleinig, *Leviticus*, 180–82. For this sacrifice in general and for the portions that were to be eaten by the worshiper, see Lev 3:1–17 and 7:11–21 and Kleinig, *Leviticus*, 89–96, 168–74.

Because holiness is contagious, it dare not come into contact with the חֹל, "common, profane" (the term used in 42:20, which see). In many respects—theological, sacramental, ethical—it is part of the essence of the church as God's people separate from the world to maintain the distinction between the holy and the common. The pastor should constantly bear in mind God's holiness as he carries out his holy office. He is to be a faithful steward of the mysteries of God as he celebrates, proclaims, and communicates God's holiness. He is to administer the Sacraments (antitypes of the OT sacrifices) according to Christ's institution and mandate, not indiscriminately.[11] Likewise, the pastor's vestments traditionally are worn only in appropriate worship settings and are treated with due reverence. The stipulations about "the most holy offerings" (42:13) might also find application in such things as the wise stewardship of church offerings, which are not to be squandered on worldly programs that may be unobjectionable, but rather they are for the ministry of the Gospel of Jesus Christ.

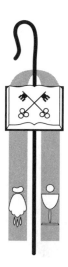

Yet with Christ as our ἀρχιερεύς, "High Priest" (the theme of Hebrews; cf. John 17), the OT distinction between priesthood and laity no longer obtains in the same way. During Christ's earthly ministry, he crossed the spatial and temporal boundaries between the sacred and the common, perhaps most obviously by ministering on the Sabbath and also by casting out demons and touching to heal, even grasping the unclean to raise the dead (Mt 9:25; Lk 7:14). On the cross, "the Holy One of God" (Jn 6:69; also Mk 1:24; Lk 4:34) allowed himself to be blasphemed and profaned to garner our salvation. And he comes even now, through his Word and Sacraments, precisely to forgive sinners and heal the sick and dying with everlasting life. At the very end of his commentary on 42:1–14 (and apparently with specific reference to 42:14), Zimmerli makes this point, which the reader is likely to miss:

> The thought that the sacred, precisely in the assertion of its character as "wholly other," finds its greatest realization at the point where it is holy, not in detachment from, but in turning to, the sick world round about (on this see 47:1–12) could easily come off badly. ... In the middle of the Bible there can be heard the proclamation of the holy God who, precisely as the "wholly other," was there in his wholeness on the side of the world of the sinners and the lost.[12]

42:15 This verse states that the first part of the great measuring process, which began at 40:5, is now complete: "thus he had finished the measurements of the interior of the temple area." These words almost have the character of a superscription.[13] The guidance formula then reappears: "he led me out" (see

---

[11] Thus the apostle Paul declares that the unworthy communicant who does not discern the body and blood of Christ in the Sacrament profanes the body and blood of Christ (1 Cor 11:27–29). This then has implications for how the pastor is to administer the Supper. See Lockwood, *1 Corinthians*, 399–410.

[12] Zimmerli, *Ezekiel*, 2:401.

[13] Most critics believe this concludes a section of the original "basic text," which was 40:1–37, 47–49; 41:1–15a; 42:1–15a; and possibly 43:1–12. They suppose that the other verses in

the second textual note on 40:2). The expected Classical Hebrew form (וַיּוֹצִאֵנִי, Hiphil imperfect with *waw* consecutive) was in 42:1. Here, with the same meaning, is וְהוֹצִיאַנִי, the Hiphil perfect with conjunctive *waw* (and first common singular suffix). The following clause too (וּמְדָדוֹ) uses a perfect verb with conjunctive *waw*, which becomes common in Late Biblical Hebrew (and the norm in postbiblical Hebrew) as the imperfect with *waw* consecutive declines (and is absent from Rabbinic and Modern Hebrew). Similarly, the four almost identically formulated statements in 42:16–19 use the asyndetic perfect מָדַד, "he measured" (see also 42:20).

The suffix of וּמְדָדוֹ, "and he measured it" (42:15), is not specified, but in context it soon becomes clear that "it" must be a contrast to the preceding הַבַּיִת הַפְּנִימִי, literally, "the inner temple," that is, "the interior of the temple area." The following measurements must be of the temple perimeter, after the interior tour has been completed. (Otherwise, we become embroiled in major contradictions.)

42:16–19 In measuring the four sides, the guide begins at the east gate (42:16). Then in 42:17–19 he moves to the north, south, and west sides. This is the same order in which the gates on the four sides of the new Jerusalem are described in Rev 21:13, strengthening the view that Ezekiel 40–48 is an OT equivalent to, and is fulfilled by, Revelation 21–22. See further "Introduction to Ezekiel 40–48." Throughout 42:16–20 the geographical "side" is expressed by a rare use of the word רוּחַ, "spirit, wind, breath." The idiom likely arose with reference to the direction from which the wind would blow directly on a side. Similar was מֵאַרְבַּע רוּחוֹת, "from the four winds," referring to the four geographical directions, in 37:9 (see the textual note there).

The measurement according to the Qere (חֲמֵשׁ־מֵאוֹת) is "five hundred." This is obviously superior to the Kethib (חֲמֵשׁ־אַמוֹת), "five cubits," probably an error of metathesis (אמות for מאות). In this and the similar phrases in 42:17–20, the translation adds "cubits," since that has been the unit of measurement throughout most of chapters 40–42. This unit is frequently not stated but assumed (e.g., in 43:16–17; 45:1; 46:22).

However, in 40:5–8 and 41:8, the unit of measurement had been the קָנֶה, "cane, rod" (always singular in those verses; 40:7 uses "cubit" as well), which was six cubits long (40:5; 41:8). Therefore one possibility for קָנִים in 42:16–19 is that it refers to six-cubit "canes" as the unit (instead of "cubits"). The identical phrase קָנִים בְּקָנֶה הַמִּדָּה סָבִיב is repeated at the end of 42:16 and 42:17. קָנִים בְּקָנֶה הַמִּדָּה is repeated in 42:18–19. The Vulgate and Targum support the MT with fairly literal translations of these phrases in 42:16–19. The Syriac supports קָנִים in all four verses. In contrast, the LXX has nothing for קָנִים in any of the verses. The LXX includes πήχεις, "cubits," in 42:17, but no unit of mea-

---

chapters 40–48 were added later as supplements. However, that contradicts the fact that these chapters begin with a single date notice (40:1), indicating that the entirety of chapters 40–48 was revealed at one time.

sure (neither "cubits" nor "rods, canes") in any of the other verses until 42:20, where it once specifies "cubits" (πηχῶν).

Most scholars advocate deleting קָנִים in 42:16–19. Allen assumes that it was an erroneous gloss on בְּקְנֵה הַמִּדָּה.[14] Block observes that it is strange that the same mistake would be made four times and plausibly suggests that, if retained, it could be construed as an instrument rather than a unit of measurement.[15] Certainly בְּקְנֵה הַמִּדָּה in 42:16–19 is instrumental: literally, "with/by the measuring cane." (For the construct phrase קְנֵה הַמִּדָּה, see the third textual note on 40:3.) For it in all four verses, the LXX (ἐν τῷ καλάμῳ τοῦ μέτρου) and the Vulgate (in calamo mensurae) have an instrumental dative, reflecting the MT statement (בְּקְנֵה הַמִּדָּה) that the measuring was done "with the measuring rod." Hence in 42:16–19, קָנִים בְּקְנֵה הַמִּדָּה can be translated "using canes, the measuring rod."

The measurements given in 40:15–41:14 indicate that the temple compound was five hundred cubits from east to west and five hundred cubits from north to south (see the textual note on 40:27 and figure 2). The measurements given in 42:16–20, then, if given in cubits, reiterate the same thing: that the outer wall of the temple compound (40:5) was five hundred cubits (eight hundred fifty feet or two hundred sixty meters) on each side, resulting in a total area of almost seventeen acres or seven hectares.

Keil argues that קָנִים is to be taken literally as the unit "canes,"[16] and among English translations, KJV, NJKV, and NASB all give "five hundred reeds/rods." This agrees with the Vulgate (quingentos calamos in calamo mensurae per circuitum, 42:16; it translates similarly in 42:17–19). Since each cane is six cubits, and the cubit is the "long" cubit of about 20.3 inches or 52 centimeters (see the third textual note on 40:5), if each side was three thousand cubits long, this would be about 5,075 feet, almost a mile or 1.6 kilometers. Obviously, this results in a vastly greater area, about a square mile or 2.6 square kilometers.

Ezek 42:20 reiterates that each side of the area was five hundred units long but does not specify whether the units are cubits or canes.

In the MT, both 42:16 and 42:17 end with the adverb סָבִיב ("all around"). This is a bit strange with reference to a straight wall. In both verses, the Targum supports it by its double סְחוֹר־סְחוֹר. The Vulgate supports it with per circuitum at the end of 42:16 (also 42:18) and per gyrum at the end of 42:17 (both used elsewhere in the Vulgate of Ezekiel for סָבִיב [e.g., 40:14, 16–17]). The Syriac (ܚܕܪ ܚܕܪ) supports סָבִיב at the end of 42:17.

However, the LXX has καὶ ἐπέστρεψεν at the beginning of 42:17, 18, 19. The LXX apparently read סָבִיב at the end of 42:16 and 42:17 as סָבַב and took it as the first word of the following verse (42:17–18). I have followed the LXX. If the adverb סָבִיב should be the verb סָבַב, it is most naturally considered part

---

[14] Allen, *Ezekiel*, 2:227.

[15] Block, *Ezekiel*, 2:568, n. 161.

[16] Keil, *Ezekiel*, 2:269–72.

of the next verse, as in the LXX and my translation. In the MT סָבֵב does begin 42:19, and so the LXX corresponds to the MT there.

42:20 The concluding summary verse does double duty in the literary structure of Ezekiel 40–48. First, the surrounding "wall" creates an inclusio with 40:5, which began the description of the temple compound by noting (but not measuring) this same "wall." Second, the wall's purpose, "to separate the holy from the common," prepares for the climactic advent of the holy "Glory," the divine resident of the temple, in 43:1–12. All the preceding detail has been preparation for this arrival.

The final measurements, like most of those in chapters 40–42, are merely two dimensional. Whether each side of the square is five hundred cubits or rods (see on 42:16), it is dwarfed by its fulfillment in Rev 21:16, where the new Jerusalem is twelve thousand stadia, or about 2,220 kilometers or 1,380 miles, on each side—and also is of equal height, forming a perfect three-dimensional cube.[17]

The purpose of the wall לְהַבְדִּיל בֵּין הַקֹּדֶשׁ לְחֹל, "to separate the holy from the common," is almost a verbatim quote from Yahweh's definitive pronouncement about the purpose of the office of the priests in Lev 10:10, in conjunction with their ministry of teaching the people in Lev 10:11. The same language had been used in Ezek 22:26, where Yahweh declared that Israel's unfaithful priests had failed in their liturgical and teaching ministry: they were "profaning what is holy to me, by not distinguishing between the holy and the common or teaching the difference between the unclean and the clean." Almost identical language will be used again, but positively, in 44:23, where Yahweh will declare that in the future the priests will carry out these aspects of their office.

This divine purpose virtually summarizes the theme of all of chapters 40–48. Jewish tradition coined the noun הַבְדָּלָה, "separation, division," from the Hiphil verb הִבְדִּיל used here (and already in Gen 1:4, 6–7, 14, 18). The goal of ritual purity and holiness, attempted through deeds of the Law and avoidance of what is "unclean" (Ezek 22:26; 44:23), is central to traditional Judaism, which, however, fails to attain it (cf. Rom 9:31–33). Instead, the divine purpose in the OT is fulfilled in Christ; justification and sanctification freely come to all believers simply through faith in him (cf. Rom 9:30). The "scandal of particularity" is that it is only through faith in Jesus Christ that we sinners can be and are reconciled to the holy God and that we gain entrance into the eternal city through its gates (cf. Jn 10:1–9; Rev 7:13–17; 21:7–8; 22:14–15). To retain her holiness in Christ, the church must vigilantly remain countercultural in many aspects of faith, ethics, and worship practice and thus keep herself "unstained from the world" (James 1:27).

---

[17] For an interpretation of the new Jerusalem that takes into consideration the background of Ezekiel 40–48, see Brighton, *Revelation*, 608–21.

Ezekiel 43:1–27

The Return of Yahweh's Glory, and the Altar

Translation

43 ¹Then he led me to the gate, the gate that faces east. ²Look, the Glory of the God of Israel was coming from the east. His voice was like the sound of many waters, and the earth shone with his Glory. ³The appearance of the vision I saw was like the vision I saw when I came to destroy the city—visions like the vision I saw by the Kebar Canal, and I fell on my face. ⁴The Glory of Yahweh entered the temple through the gate facing east. ⁵Then the Spirit lifted me up and brought me to the inner court, and the Glory of Yahweh filled the temple. ⁶I heard someone speaking to me from the temple while the man was standing beside me. ⁷He said to me, "Son of man, this is the place of my throne, and this is the place for the soles of my feet, where I will dwell in the midst of the sons of Israel forever. Never again will the house of Israel defile my holy name, neither they nor their kings, neither by their whoring nor by the monuments of their dead kings at their high places. ⁸Whenever they placed their threshold next to my threshold and their doorpost beside my doorpost with only a wall between me and them, they would defile my holy name by their abominations that they did, so I exterminated them in my anger. ⁹Now let them remove their whoring and the monuments of their dead kings from me, and I will dwell among them forever.

¹⁰"As for you, son of man, describe to the house of Israel the temple, so that they may be ashamed of their sins, and then let them measure its perfect pattern. ¹¹If they are ashamed of everything they have done, teach them the design of the temple and its layout, its exits and its entrances, all its forms and all its ordinances, all its forms and all its regulations. Write [them down] in their sight so that they may keep its whole form and all its ordinances and do them. ¹²This is the Torah of the temple. On the top of the mountain its whole territory surrounding it all around will be most holy. This is indeed the Torah of the temple."

¹³These are the measurements of the altar in cubits, a [long] cubit being an [ordinary] cubit and a handbreadth: its gutter is one cubit deep and one cubit wide with its ridge of one span around its edge. This is the height of the altar: ¹⁴From the gutter on the ground to the lower ledge is two cubits and the width is one cubit, and from the smaller ledge up to the larger ledge is four cubits, with a width of one cubit. ¹⁵The hearth is four cubits [high], and extending upward from the hearth are four horns. ¹⁶The hearth is twelve cubits long by twelve cubits wide, a square with four equal sides. ¹⁷The ledge is fourteen cubits long by fourteen cubits wide, with four equal sides. The ridge around it is half a cubit, and it has a gutter of one cubit all around. Its steps face east.

¹⁸Then he said to me, "Son of man, thus says the Lord Yahweh: These are the ceremonies for the altar on the day it is erected for offering on it burnt offering and for sprinkling blood on it. ¹⁹You are to give the Levitical priests who are from the descendants of Zadok, who draw near to me—says the Lord Yahweh—to serve me, a young bull for a sin offering. ²⁰You are to take some of its blood and put it on its [the altar's] four horns, on the four corners of the ledge, and on the ridge all around, and so you are to absolve it and make atonement for it. ²¹Then you are to take the bull that is the sin offering, and he is to burn it in the appointed place of the temple area outside the sanctuary. ²²On the second day you are to offer a male goat without blemish as a sin offering, and the altar is to be absolved as it was absolved with the bull. ²³When you have finished the absolution ritual, you are to offer a young bull without blemish and a ram without blemish. ²⁴You are to present them before Yahweh, and the priests are to throw salt on them and offer them up as a burnt offering to Yahweh. ²⁵For seven days you are to offer a goat for a sin offering each day, as well as a young bull and a ram from the flock; they are to offer [all of them] without blemish. ²⁶For seven days they are to make atonement for the altar, cleanse it, and so consecrate it. ²⁷When they have fulfilled those days, on the eighth day and onward, the priests are to offer on the altar your burnt offerings and your communion offerings, and I will accept you, says the Lord Yahweh."

Textual Notes and Commentary

Chapter 43 consists of two easily divisible sections: (1) the return of Yahweh's "Glory" (כָּבוֹד), a hypostasis of Yahweh himself, to the temple (43:1–12); and (2) the description and measurements of the great altar, along with the rites to be used in its consecration (43:13–27). Earlier the measuring tour paid virtually no attention to any of the temple appurtenances, with the exception of a different "altar" that turned out to be a "table" (41:22, which see). Here in 43:13–17, the sacrificial altar is introduced and considered in detail (as will be the priestly kitchens, where the sacrifices are prepared, in 46:19–24).

In the eschatological temple in Ezekiel 40–48, there are no references to some of the other appointments, notably the ark (see on 43:7), and also the lampstand and the incense altar, which were central features of the tabernacle and Solomonic temple. Hence this vision is transitional from the OT to the eschatological vision in Revelation 21, where there is no temple besides God and the Lamb (Rev 21:22).

The Return of Yahweh's Glory (43:1–12)

No other part of chapters 40–48 has such close links to other parts of the book as this first unit of chapter 43. This is evident on the level of the vocabulary used. Connections can readily be seen between the return of the Glory and the vision of the Glory at Ezekiel's call in chapter 1. The prophet's reference to "the vision I saw when I came to destroy the city" (43:3) clearly is to the scene in 9:1–11 where Yahweh commissioned the destroying angel. But the closest connection is with 10:4, 18–19 and 11:22–23, when the Glory had for-

saken the temple through the same east gate where this chapter begins (43:1). The return of the Glory here is a promise of a reversal of that departure. The return of the Glory is what makes the bare structures measured in chapters 40–48 become what they are intended to be: God's "house,"[1] his incarnational dwelling among his redeemed people "forever" (43:9).[2] As Block notes:

> This vision proclaims the glorious mercy of God, who invites sinners into a relationship with himself and provides the means whereby that relationship can be expressed, though without contaminating his own holiness. ... He comes to dwell among them, though without sacrificing any of his glory. ... Christians recognize the ultimate expression of the divine desire in Jesus, who is not only the restored temple (John 2:19–22) but the physical manifestation of divine glory—full of grace and truth (John 1:14).[3]

The pattern in Ezekiel 40–43, with the description of the sanctuary first (40:1–42:20) followed by the advent of the Glory (43:1–12), is the same pattern that God had followed for both the tabernacle (Exodus 25–40) and Solomon's temple (1 Kings 6–8).[4] A similar pattern can be said to pertain to God's church as the body of Christ and the new temple,[5] since we are nothing but abject sinners utterly lacking divine glory (Rom 3:23) until, through Holy Baptism and faith in Christ, God comes to dwell within us, so that we have the hope of everlasting glory.[a] That Christ, the Lord of Glory, already dwells within us now may explain why this same pattern is not strictly followed in the final NT fulfillment, which depicts the dwelling of God with his redeemed people in the eternal state. When the apostle John sees the new Jerusalem descending from heaven, she is already endowed with "the Glory of God" (Rev 21:11), and a further description with measurements then follows (Rev 21:14–22). The Christological significance of the "Glory" is affirmed by the parallel statements that "the *Glory* of God illuminates her, and her lamp is the *Lamb*" (Rev 21:23), which echoes Ezek 43:2, "the earth shone with his Glory" (see further on 43:2).

(a) See Rom 5:1–2; 6:4; 2 Cor 3:18; 4:4, 6; Eph 3:16; Col 1:27; Titus 2:13

Since this unit follows the grand temple tour of 40:1–42:20, it is appropriate to meditate a bit on what its "Torah" (43:12) means in the Christian era. The NT contains no comparable body of material about divine Glory inhabiting church buildings (nor does the NT describe church furnishings in a way comparable to 40:1–42:20 or 43:13–27). We Christians are perfectly free to worship in any kind of structure we wish—or, at the extreme, even in none at all (cf. Jn 4:23–24). However, from the earliest house churches to the grandest

---

[1] The term הַבַּיִת in, for example, 43:4–6, 10–12, is literally "the house," although it is almost always translated as "the temple."

[2] The book of Ezekiel as a whole, like the book of Revelation, has an "internal outline" centering on the divine Glory. See page 11 in the introduction.

[3] Block, *Ezekiel*, 2:590.

[4] There are formal parallels in Assyrian and Babylonian literature as well, although of course their temples were not dwelling places of the divine Glory.

[5] For a Christological exposition of the theology of the tabernacle and temple, see the commentary on 37:26–28 as well as "Introduction to Ezekiel 40–48."

Gothic cathedrals, Christians have virtually always erected "houses" of worship. It is a reminder that, as creatures of space and time, our worship is enhanced by the observance of sacred spaces and times, and, as a familiar saying goes, "he who does not worship/pray at specific times and places probably does not worship/pray at all."

Ezek 43:1–12 is a salutary reminder that it is the presence of the divine Glory—that is, Jesus Christ—that constitutes the Christian church and divine worship. He comes as God's Word is rightly proclaimed and the Sacraments are rightly administered. Without that, there is no valid worship, no matter how ornate or simple the structure may be. To speak of God's "presence" applies most easily to the bodily presence of Christ in the Lord's Supper, where he gives his body and blood for the forgiveness of sins and pledge of the resurrection to eternal life. But in a related sense, it applies no less to Trinitarian Baptism and the proclamation of the Word. We can never accent too often that the one holy Christian church

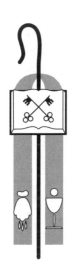

> is the assembly of all believers among whom the Gospel is preached in its purity and the holy sacraments are administered according to the Gospel. For it is sufficient for the true unity of the Christian church that the Gospel be preached in conformity with a pure understanding of it and that the sacraments be administered in accordance with the divine Word. (AC VII 1–2)

The Word and Sacraments are the means of grace, the sine qua non of the church, because through them God creates and sustains saving faith in Christ, and through such faith God grants life everlasting (see AC IV, V, IX, X, XIII).

Therefore we should view with due, evangelical caution any glib assertion that such things as the worship space, its furnishings, its art and music, its hymns and liturgies can be dismissed as of no concern because they are adiaphora. We may safely conclude from Ezekiel that God—the same triune God we worship—has great concern for the settings and forms in which he is worshiped. To be sure, we who live in the NT era know that the separation of sacred and secular no longer means exactly what it did before the incarnation of our Lord. Nevertheless, the external aspects of worship can either enhance or obscure (or even reverse) the message that God graciously comes to us in Christ, and that, secondarily, we then come to him.

43:1   For the guidance formula "he brought me" (וַיּוֹלִכֵנִי), see the second textual note on 40:2. The implied subject is Yahweh, although he is guiding his prophet by the agency of the supernatural guide (see the commentary on 40:3). Ezekiel is brought to the same east (outer) gate where the tour began (40:6; see figure 2) and where the guide had already led him at the end of the temple tour (42:15). That it is the east gate that is featured, as before (40:6; 42:15) and again later (44:1; 47:2; cf. the east inner gate in 46:1, 12), probably indicates its special liturgical significance. It was in a direct line with the main entrance to the temple, so that those who entered by it would not have to turn their backs on the "face" (presence) of Yahweh, as pagans regularly did in their deification of the sun, and as Israelite apostates were seen doing in the vision of 8:16.

The repetition of שַׁעַר in the phrase אֶל־הַשַּׁעַר שַׁעַר אֲשֶׁר פֹּנֶה דֶּרֶךְ הַקָּדִים, literally, "to the gate, a gate that faces the way of the east," may be a stylized way of beginning a new unit (43:1–12). The versions omit the second שַׁעַר, but the fact that it is anarthrous (as in 43:4; also in, e.g., 9:2 and 40:6 [which see]) makes it unlikely that it was a dittograph. It may be a way of emphasizing this gate, which the following relative clause reveals was the one "that faces east." The phrase אֲשֶׁר פֹּנֶה (with the Qal participle of פָּנָה), "that faces," occurs only here in the OT. It is only a stylistic variation. Emendation, which Zimmerli and Allen advise, is unnecessary.[6] Usually Ezekiel has only the participle פֹּנֶה or uses אֲשֶׁר פָּנָיו, literally, "which its face," as in 43:4.

43:2 The verse begins with וְהִנֵּה, literally, "and behold," to indicate a new or surprising sight, especially in a vision. It also began 40:5 and occurred near the start of, for example, 1:4, 15; 2:9. The long designation "the Glory of the God of Israel" highlights the significance of the event. In וְקוֹלוֹ כְּקוֹל מַיִם רַבִּים, "his voice was like the sound of many waters," the repeated קוֹל, which can mean either "voice" or "sound," must be translated in the first and then in the second way, according to the context. The comparison of his "voice" to "the sound of many waters" recalls 1:24 in the inaugural vision, where the rustling of the wings of the living creatures (identified as cherubim in 10:5, 20) is compared to the sound of "many waters" and then to "the voice of the Almighty." The cherubim are not explicitly mentioned here. The optical theme of light and fire had been present in Ezekiel 1:4, 13 too, but here it is presented as cosmic and eschatological. Compare the song of the seraphim at Isaiah's call: "the whole earth is full of his Glory" (Is 6:3).

"Glory" is capitalized in my translation, because we know it is Yahweh himself in visible manifestation, with what Ezekiel had described as "the likeness of the appearance of a man" (1:26), one of the three hypostases (persons) of the triune God, as confessed in the Athanasian Creed: *unum Deum in Trinitate et Trinitatem in unitate*, "one God in Trinity and Trinity in Unity."[7] This is the preincarnate Christ, the *logos asarkos*, "the Word not yet made flesh," who, in the fullness of time (Gal 4:4), would become flesh (Jn 1:14).[8] The end of the verse declares, וְהָאָרֶץ הֵאִירָה מִכְּבֹדוֹ, "and the earth shone from/with his Glory," corresponding to Rev 21:23, which declares that the illuminating Glory is none other than "the Lamb." The Hiphil of אוֹר can have the intransitive meaning "to shine, give light" (cf. BDB, Hiphil, 1 and 2). The third feminine singular perfect הֵאִירָה must have the feminine noun אֶרֶץ ("earth") as its subject. The preposition מִן on מִכְּבֹדוֹ has a causal sense, as it often does with an impersonal thing (BDB, s.v. מִן, 2 e (b)), but it can also have such a sense with a personal

---

6 Zimmerli, *Ezekiel*, 2:407; Allen, *Ezekiel*, 2:242.

7 *LSB* 319.

8 For a Christological understanding of the divine "Glory" in Ezekiel, see pages 1, 11, and 13 in the introduction, as well as the textual notes and commentary on 1:26–28.

agent (BDB, 2 e (a); cf. 2 d), such as the divine Glory, so this might be paraphrased, "his Glory made the earth shine." This is reminiscent of the Epiphany theme expressed in Is 60:1.

43:3 Throughout the book Ezekiel rarely writes in the first person, but does so here (also in, e.g., 41:8; 44:4). This verse interrupts the account of the Glory's entrance to describe Ezekiel's reaction and his recollection of two previous encounters with the same theophany (chapter 1 and chapters 8–11). The noun מַרְאֶה, "appearance, vision, sight" is used four times in this verse to emphasize the correspondence of this theophany with the previous ones. Chapter 1 used מַרְאֶה often, especially in 1:26–28, to indicate the transcendent nature of the theophany, which could only be described as appearing somewhat like familiar sights. The Hebrew וּכְמַרְאֵה הַמַּרְאֶה אֲשֶׁר רָאִיתִי כַּמַּרְאֶה אֲשֶׁר־רָאִ֫יתִי, literally, "and like a sight of the sight which I saw, like the sight that I saw," appears overloaded and prolix, but the construction וּכְמַרְאֵה ... כַּמַּרְאֶה, with repeated כְּ, emphasizes complete correspondence (BDB, s.v. כְּ, 2). Ezek 41:21 had הַמַּרְאֶה כַּמַּרְאֶה, two words also here. The LXX has a shorter text, but that may simply be the result of translational freedom.

The MT has the first person suffix on the first of the two infinitive constructs (Qal of בּוֹא and Piel of שָׁחַת), בְּבֹאִ֫י לְשַׁחֵת, "when *I* came to destroy," which the LXX and Syriac reproduce. In chapter 9 Ezekiel witnessed Yahweh's destruction of the city by means of his avenging angels. Cognate to the Piel infinitive of שָׁחַת here was the noun מַשְׁחֵת in 9:1, referring to each angel's "weapon of *destruction.*" The infinitive of purpose here, לְשַׁחֵת, provides a verbal link with the prophet's own outcry in 9:8 of what he was witnessing: "Ah, Lord Yahweh! Are *you destroying* [Hiphil participle, מַשְׁחִית] the entire remnant of Israel?" To explain 43:3, Keil quotes his contemporary Hitzig approvingly: "The prophet destroyed the city ideally by his prophecy, of which the fulfillment simply forms the objective reverse side."[9] This is supported by the Targum's rendition of 43:3, בְּאִתְנַבָּיוּתִי לְחַבָּלָא, "when I prophesied to destroy." It is also supported by the event Ezekiel reports in 11:13, "While I was prophesying, Pelatiah son of Benaiah died," which elicited another outcry from Ezekiel, "Ah, Lord Yahweh, you are making a complete destruction with the remnant of Israel!" Obviously these passages affirm the power and efficacy of the preached Word of God, in harmony with what Jesus declares in the NT about absolution (e.g., Mt 6:12; 18:21, 35) and the office of the keys, which he gave to his apostles (Mt 16:19; Jn 20:23).

The Vulgate translates in the third person, *quando venit,* "when *he* [Yahweh] came," and a few Hebrew manuscripts have בְּבֹא, which surely is the easier reading. Some scholars have suggested that the original reading was בְּבֹאוֹ but it (in many manuscripts) was altered to בְּבֹאִ֫י to avoid speaking of Yahweh himself destroying Jerusalem (by attributing the destruction to

---

[9] Keil, *Ezekiel*, 2:277, quoting Ferdinand Hitzig, *Der Prophet Ezechiel* (Leipzig: Weidmann'sche Buchhandlung, 1847), 341–42.

Ezekiel). However, Ezekiel's own prophecies include Yahweh's warnings that he would destroy the city (e.g., שָׁחַת in 5:16; 22:30), and such an alteration would violate the Hebrew scribes' desire for fidelity in the transmission of the text. Cooke suggests that בְּבֹאִי is a miswritten or misunderstood abbreviation of בְּבֹא יהוה.[10]

Whatever the textual history, Ezekiel's recollection of the earlier vision does not accent the Glory's abandonment of the temple in chapter 11, but the visionary destruction in chapter 9.

Ezekiel also has a "flashback" to his first encounter with the Glory, in chapter 1. In the MT he recalls that first encounter with וּמַרְאוֹת כַּמַּרְאֶה, "and the visions were like the vision …" The plural מַרְאוֹת, "visions," was also used in 1:1 and 8:3. The two complex visions of the Glory that began in those places could indeed be factored into various components. But here the LXX and Targum have the singular "vision," and the Syriac omits the term.

Ezekiel's reaction of prostration before the Glory (וָאֶפֹּל אֶל־פָּנָי, "and I fell on my face") is repeated almost verbatim from 1:28 and 3:23. He shows the same awe and submission, even though almost twenty years have intervened since that first sight.

43:5   Once again we meet the "Spirit" (רוּחַ), the third person of the Trinity, the divine manifestation who was able to transport the prophet to a different locality in 3:12, 14; 8:3; 11:1, 24. (In 40:1 Yahweh's "hand" had transported him.) In 2:2 the Spirit had set Ezekiel on his feet and enabled him to hear the divine commission. Of the two functions, the second seems to be the main interest here also, as the following verses show.

The report that "the Glory of Yahweh entered the house/temple" is restrained, at least compared to the historical precedents in Ex 40:34–35 and 1 Ki 8:10–11, probably because the implications of Yahweh's "Glory" have already been described in detail in earlier chapters of Ezekiel. (Some cavil that the event is not described in terms of a "cloud," but that is surely hypercritical; the cloud had been mentioned in 10:3.) In מָלֵא כְבוֹד־יהוה הַבָּיִת, the Qal of the verb מָלֵא, in form a stative (intransitive), apparently is used with a transitive meaning, "to fill (something)." The Piel is always transitive, but the two seem not to have been rigidly distinguished, and already in Gen 1:22 the Qal is used transitively. Alternatively, since there is no direct object marker (אֵת) before הַבָּיִת, the verb could be intransitive with הַבָּיִת as its subject and with כְבוֹד־יהוה as an accusative of specification: "the temple was full of the Glory of Yahweh." The meaning would not be significantly affected.

In 43:1 Ezekiel began at the east gate of the outer court. Here the Spirit brings him into the inner court, probably through its east gate, so he can observe that the Glory has filled the temple (see figure 2). At this location he can also study the altar, which is the subject of 43:13–27. Then in 44:1 he will be brought back to the east gate of the outer court.

---

[10]   Cooke, *Ezekiel*, 474.

43:6 Ezekiel says he hears "someone speaking to me." The Hebrew wording is almost identical to that in 2:2 (see the second textual note there). מְדַבֵּר is the Hithpael participle of דָּבַר with the expected ת prefix (מִתְדַּבֵּר) assimilated and marked by *daghesh forte* (-דּ-). In 2:2, Ezekiel heard Yahweh addressing him directly, with no intermediary present, but here he says that, literally, "a man was standing beside me" (וְאִישׁ הָיָה עֹמֵד אֶצְלִי). The syntax of the participle מְדַבֵּר followed by הָיָה may have a circumstantial or temporal force: "I heard someone speaking to me from the temple *while* a man was standing beside me." See Joüon, § 121 g, and Waltke-O'Connor, § 37.7.1b, including example 5. This indicates that the speech from God in the temple was mediated to Ezekiel through the "man."

The medieval Jewish scholar Rashi is often quoted as saying that while the Piel is used of conversation between people, the Hithpael denotes the speech of the Shekinah (a postbiblical circumlocution for God, who would indwell his temple) overheard by a messenger.[11] Such a statement could be appropriated in biblical, Trinitarian terms as pointing to Christ, the (spoken) Word of God. Thus the "man" in 43:6 who was God's mouthpiece would be the preincarnate Christ. The same possibility presented itself when the supernatural "man" was introduced in 40:3 (see the commentary there).

Although וְאִישׁ is anarthrous, we have noted a certain penchant for omitting the article in this section (e.g., שַׁעַר is unexpectedly anarthrous in 43:1, 4). The versions supplied the article, as do virtually all modern translations ("the man"), although NKJV (following KJV) has "I heard *Him* speaking." Even without the article, the most natural assumption is that this is the same "man" who has guided the prophet throughout the temple vision since 40:3. Since there can be no doubt that the spoken words that follow are Yahweh's, Keil believes that the "man" here must be "the angel of Jehovah, God's own speaker, ὁ λόγος τοῦ θεοῦ ['the Word of God,' as in Jn 1:1; also Rev 19:13]. But according to his outward *habitus*, this angel of the Lord … is identical with the angel [sic!] who showed the prophet the temple [40:3]."[12]

The "man" fades from view in the rest of the chapter, unless we are to understand that Yahweh communicates to the prophet through the man.

We are faced with the same question at the beginning of 43:7, since וַיֹּאמֶר אֵלַי ("he said to me") does not reveal (or distinguish) whether Yahweh speaks to Ezekiel directly or through the mediation of the "man."

43:7 God speaks from his reoccupied house. "He said to me, 'Son of man'" are precisely the same words used in 2:1 to describe how Yahweh addresses Ezekiel there (also, e.g., 2:3; 3:1). The first two clauses in the speech here (אֶת־מְקוֹם ... וְאֶת־מְקוֹם) each begin with אֶת, which has been variously interpreted. Ezekiel has unusual uses of אֶת also in 17:21; 20:16; 35:10; 44:3;

---

[11] Greenberg, *Ezekiel*, 1:62, quotes Rashi: "The Shekinah speaks in its majesty to itself; its messengers only overhear it."

[12] Keil, *Ezekiel*, 2:278–79.

47:17–19 (GKC, § 117 m). Virtually all English translations render the particle here as "this is," possibly following the Targum. According to Joüon, § 125 j (5), this is one of a few OT passages in which וֹ אֵת has "a strong meaning equivalent to a pronoun" and so should be translated "here is the place." Cooke takes it as a sign of emphasis, as in postbiblical Hebrew.[13] Usually in Biblical Hebrew אֵת introduces a definite direct object, but the first half of 43:7 lacks a transitive verb that could take these two clauses as objects. The LXX supplies a verb, "you have seen … ," with these clauses as objects; similar are GKC, § 117 m, Keil, and Zimmerli.[14] Allen construes these clauses as anacoluthon, indirectly as the objects of the later negated Piel verb יְטַמְּאוּ ("they will not defile/desecrate"), possibly placed first for the sake of emphasis, and then he supposes that by the time Ezekiel used that verb, his thought had taken a different turn and so he used a new object ("my holy name"); Block is similar.[15]

Ezek 43:7a and 43:12 probably form the kernel of Yahweh's message. The language used is at once a classical biblical expression of both divine kingship as well as of the OT "incarnation" of God in the tabernacle and temple. The "incarnation" is emphasized by the expressions "the place of my throne" and "the place for the soles of my feet" (the latter often described as God's הֲדֹם, "footstool," as in Is 66:1; Ps 110:1) and especially by the promise "I will dwell there" (שָׁכַנְתִּי־שָׁם, 43:7) using the verb שָׁכַן, the root of מִשְׁכָּן, "tabernacle." Both it and the temple are fulfilled in the Word made flesh who "tabernacled" among us (ἐσκήνωσεν, Jn 1:14). Yahweh's "incarnation" in the temple received eloquent expression in Solomon's prayer at its consecration (1 Ki 8:12–13, 27). Yahweh's "incarnation" in the tabernacle and temple is a major biblical expression of what I know as vertical typology, a real, dynamic, but not mechanical, correspondence (not identity) between things celestial and things terrestrial. Typology is usually horizontal, from OT prophecy to fulfillment at Christ's first advent and/or second advent, from Adam to the last Adam, from David to Christ as the Son of David, and so on. Yet both may be involved; as the book of Hebrews explains, OT worship on earth typified heavenly realities (Heb 8:5; 9:23), and it typified what Christ would accomplish both on earth and in heaven (e.g., Heb 9:11–12, 24). Yahweh's wars through Israel are another major biblical example of typology.

Of course, the omnipresent God is always present everywhere, both vertically and eternally in heaven and horizontally on earth in history. However, he chooses to manifest himself in wrath and grace especially in certain times and places. The correspondence between the tabernacle constructed under Moses and Yahweh's heavenly home is first enunciated in Ex 25:9, where Moses is to build according to a heavenly תַּבְנִית, "pattern, model, miniature," and the thought is repeated for the temple (1 Chr 28:19; cf. Acts 7:44; Heb 8:5; 9:23).

---

[13] Cooke, *Ezekiel*, 474.

[14] Keil, *Ezekiel*, 2:279; Zimmerli, *Ezekiel*, 2:409.

[15] Allen, *Ezekiel*, 2:242; Block, *Ezekiel*, 2:575, note 12.

Thus within the Holy of Holies, the ark (or the cherubim above it) is both Yahweh's earthly throne room (e.g., 1 Sam 4:4; 2 Sam 6:2; Ps 80:2 [ET 80:1]) and his footstool (Is 60:13; Pss 99:5; 132:7; Lam 2:1; 1 Chr 28:2). Often the two perspectives are merged, as classically in Isaiah 6. Just as Yahweh's heavenly throne can be said to encompass all the heavens, so on earth his seat on the ark is often extended to include all of Zion (e.g., Jer 14:21).

Ezekiel makes no mention of the ark, neither in the destroyed Jerusalem temple (not even in chapters 8–11 in the vision of the departing Glory enthroned in the temple prior to its destruction) nor in the eschatological temple in chapters 40–48. Most commentators, almost instinctively, seem to understand the omission as intentional. For example, Keil explains: "The ark of the covenant is not mentioned, because, as is stated in Jer. iii. 16 [3:16], in the Messianic times the ark of the covenant will not be remembered, neither will it be missed."[16] Jer 3:17 goes on to promise that Jerusalem will be Yahweh's earthly throne, and to it all nations shall be gathered (as on Pentecost [Acts 2] and eschatologically [see Rev 21:24, 26]).

Iconoclastic, non-sacramental Protestant commentators have long assumed that the OT prophets had the same disregard for the concrete elements of worship as they have, and that is the motive for Jer 3:16–17 and the absence of the ark in Ezekiel, but we must seek a better explanation.

In his inaugural vision, Ezekiel, in Babylon, had seen the cherubim carrying the throne of Yahweh (1:26), and this was the heavenly reality depicted and typified by the ark and cherubim in the temple (which at that time still stood in Jerusalem). We know that when the city fell to the Babylonians, the temple was destroyed and presumably the ark was too. In his book, Ezekiel does not reveal whether he was aware of the disappearance of the ark in the Jerusalem temple or whether that (assumed) historical event is connected to the absence of an ark in Ezekiel 40–48 (whose vision was revealed in the fourteenth year after Jerusalem fell; see the commentary on 40:1 and figure 1). Presumably, as a faithful priest (1:3), Ezekiel would have mourned its loss (but compare the command in 24:16–24 that he and the people not mourn).

After the destruction of the temple in 586 B.C., the ark was never replaced.[17] Nevertheless, as Yahweh's Glory had forsaken the Jerusalem temple in chapter 11, so now he returns to a new Jerusalem and—explicitly—to a new and eternal temple. In neither case is the ark specified, because it was merely a vehicle of his presence in the prior OT era (from Moses to the destruction in 586 B.C.), and the point here is the presence and dwelling of God with his people. In that light, despite the emphasis on the temple building in Ezekiel 40–48, these chapters are in harmony with Revelation 21, where again the central point

---

[16] Keil, *Ezekiel*, 2:279–80.

[17] See C. L. Seow, "Ark of the Covenant," *ABD* 1:390–91, on theories of when and how it disappeared.

is the presence and eternal dwelling of God among his people (Rev 21:3), and the temple has given way to God and the Lamb (Rev 21:22).

Yahweh, speaking to Ezekiel from the new temple, promises, "I will dwell [שָׁכֵן] there [שָׁם] in the midst of the sons of Israel forever" (Ezek 43:7). This language recalls the first temple (and ark!) that had been the focal point of his "incarnational" presence, but anticipates something superior and permanent. This same promise was expressed in different terminology in 37:26–28, where Yahweh promised to set his sanctuary in the midst of his people for all time—a promise now fulfilled in Christ, but to be consummated in the eschaton (Revelation 21–22). When God reveals himself to Ezekiel, an OT priest (1:3), and expresses himself in familiar terms of the OT temple and its appointments, Christological exegesis naturally must connect that language with the NT counterpart, where Christ declares himself the fulfillment of the temple (e.g., Jn 2:18–23), and who, through his Spirit, makes us baptized believers in Christ the living stones in that temple of his body.[b] And the "forever" of Ezekiel's prophecy awaits the return of Christ and the new heavens and new earth, when there will be no temple in the new Jerusalem, "for its temple is the Lord God the Almighty and the Lamb" (Rev 21:22). Yet even in the NT, the eternal state can be depicted in the same sort of temple imagery found in Ezekiel 40–48 (see, e.g., Rev 3:12; 7:15).

The people of God called and gathered to be his temple are thus called to a life of holiness that does not confess anyone or anything else besides their holy God. Ezekiel makes the point negatively, and in so doing summarizes much of the concern of all of chapters 40–48. He summarizes the transgressions that must be corrected in terms of "defile, desecrate, make unclean" (יְטַמְּאוּ, Piel of טָמֵא) "my holy name." The use of "name" here may be related to God's repeated promise in Deuteronomy that he would establish one legitimate sanctuary as "the place" where he would "place his name" or "cause his name to dwell" (Deut 12:5, 11; 14:23; 16:2, 6, 11; 26:2). Thus it too is "incarnational," pointing to Jesus as the one bearer of God's saving name, the only Savior and the only one through whom access is gained to God the Father (e.g., Mt 1:21; Jn 14:6; Acts 4:12). It also points to the placing of God's triune name on his people in Holy Baptism and their consequent invocation of his triune name to begin prayer and worship.

Four examples of how Israel had defiled God's holy name in the past are specified in 43:7b–9. Each of the four begins with the preposition בְּ, thrice in the sense of means, "by," and once, at the start of 43:8, temporally ("whenever").

The first example, בִּזְנוּתָם, is the noun זְנוּת, "whoring" (with suffix), derived from the verb זָנָה, "to play the whore, be a prostitute" (43:7). This noun, which will recur in 43:9, was used previously in 23:27 in a context filled with the verb and other nouns derived from it. These nouns and this verb may be used of literal fornication, but here, as so often in the Bible, the word primarily refers to spiritual infidelity, to illicit affairs with other political powers and their gods,

(b) 1 Cor 3:16–17; 6:19; 2 Cor 6:16; Eph 2:21; 1 Pet 2:5

which often is accompanied by sexual immorality. This dual sense of promiscuity (spiritual as manifest by sexual) was developed at great length in chapters 16 and 23.

The second example is unclear because the meanings of all three words in the last phrase of 43:7, וּבְפִגְרֵי מַלְכֵיהֶם בָּמוֹתָם, are disputed. In 6:5 the plural of פֶּגֶר had been used in the sense of the "corpses" of idolaters scattered around their idols. It is used elsewhere (e.g., Lev 26:30) of lifeless idols themselves. Hence some have thought that the reference here is to royal graves in the temple precincts. But the Bible mentions royal burials in "the city of David" (e.g., 1 Ki 2:10; 11:43), that is, Ophel, or the peninsula of land between the Tyropoeon and Kidron Valleys well south of the temple area, and possible archaeological evidence confirms that location. Only Manasseh and Amon, the worst of the worst, are reported to have been buried in "the garden of Uzzah," probably on the palace grounds, closer to the temple area, but still separate from it (2 Ki 21:18, 26). For the plural of פֶּגֶר here in Ezekiel, modern scholarship has alternated between the meaning "royal stelae" (after Ugaritic usage) or "offerings for the dead" (after Akkadian *pagru* offerings), both assuming some cult of the dead is involved. I have adopted "the *monuments* of their dead kings at their high places," for which there is more evidence than I have cited.

מַלְכֵיהֶם means "their kings." However, the use of מֶלֶךְ in 43:7, 9 is its only appearance in all of chapters 40–48. Except in the messianic context of 37:22, 24, where Ezekiel uses מֶלֶךְ, "King," for the Son of David, elsewhere for him he uses נָשִׂיא, "Prince," as will be evident shortly in 44:3 and at length in chapter 46. As the messianic references show, Ezekiel is not anti-royalist on principle, but Israel's actual, historical kings from Solomon on had failed (with the possible exceptions of Hezekiah and Josiah) to respect and safeguard the true worship of Yahweh and the sanctity of the temple.[18] The unusual reference here to מְלָכִים may be illuminated by the use of *mlkm* in Ugaritic texts, where it is sometimes parallel to or synonymous with *rp'ym* (cognate to the Hebrew רְפָאִים), a term for deceased and divinized kings. (Therefore the translation of פֶּגֶר as "offerings for the dead" could also be appropriate in this context, but "monuments," in my judgment, can marshal the stronger evidence.)

I have retained the most natural translation of בָּמוֹתָם (plural of בָּמָה with suffix) as "their high places." This reading is confirmed by Vulgate, Syriac, and Targum in antiquity. The LXX misread בְּתוֹכָם ("in their midst"), and a few lesser witnesses repoint to בְּמוֹתָם ("at their death"), followed in English by NRSV. RSV seems to merge it with פֶּגֶר, "dead bodies." "High places" seem to be associated with all sorts of cultic activities; see Ezekiel's references to them in 6:3, 6; 16:16; 20:29. They certainly were not exclusively mortuary shrines, but there is no reason to exclude that element. The five monoliths ex-

---

[18] On the reason for Ezekiel's preference for other terms other than "king" for Israel's past kings, see the second textual note on 7:27; the commentary on 12:10; the second textual note on 21:30 (ET 21:25); and the commentary on 34:23–31.

cavated at Gezer are often referred to as a "high place" and would beautifully illustrate this verse, except that the once common interpretation of those mono-liths as a "high place" is no longer widely accepted.

43:8 Some translators coordinate the final phrase of 43:7 with 43:8. However, the use of the Qal infinitive construct בְּתִתָּם (from נָתַן, with בְּ and suffix), "whenever they placed," suggests that a new sentence is beginning with this subordinate clause. The main clause begins with וְטִמְּאוּ, "they would de-file."

The entire subordinate clause ("whenever … them,") is the third example. It is not as debatable as the second, but not entirely clear either. It obviously decries some encroachment of secular structures on sacred territory, but it is hard to be more precise. The expression may be slightly hyperbolic, but its general gist is clear. 1 Kings 6–7 indicates that the temple was built as one element of the total Solomonic palace complex (so much so that some critical scholars have erroneously claimed that the Solomonic temple was originally built as the king's private chapel with "democratization" not coming until the second temple, when the monarchy was no longer functioning). The contiguity of temple and palace is clearly illustrated, for example, in 2 Kings 11. The outer court certainly was not walled off to separate the temple from unconsecrated ground outside, a deficiency the temple in Ezekiel's vision rectifies (42:20). It is doubt-ful that royal tombs were adjacent to the temple (see on 43:7b), but in 2 Ki 21:5 Manasseh is reported to have erected altars for "all the hosts of heaven" in both the inner and outer courts of the temple, and there may have been much simi-lar activity by other unfaithful or syncretistic kings. Whatever the details, this verse presents those offenses not as only occasional infringements, but as cus-tomary behavior. The perfect with conjunctive *waw*, וְטִמְּאוּ, "they would de-file" (43:8; the perfect of the Piel whose imperfect was in 43:7) has frequentative, habitual force.

After the main clause, the fourth charge is בְּתוֹעֲבוֹתָם אֲשֶׁר עָשׂוּ, "by their abominations that they did," summarized by the plural of Ezekiel's favorite and comprehensive term תּוֹעֵבָה, "abomination, detestable/abhorrent practice." See the commentary on 5:9, 11 and on 33:26.

And so, when God's patience was exhausted, inevitably he acted accord-ing to his warnings and "finished off, exterminated, destroyed" them (וָאֲכַל, Piel first common singular imperfect of כָּלָה) in his righteous wrath.

43:9 This verse is a sequel to 43:7. As we have noted before,[19] even when Ezekiel is prophesying eschatologically about what will be fulfilled in the eter-nal state (after Christ's return, "forever"), some of the prophecy seems to re-treat back to the present NT era, the "now, but not yet" interim between Christ's first and second advents. So here, Yahweh in 43:7 had declared, "Never again will the house of Israel defile my holy name," looking to the time when the sin-

---

[19] See "Introduction to Ezekiel 40–48."

ful nature of believers will have been removed forever (after their death and resurrection; Revelation 21–22). But then Ezek 43:9 uses a jussive to exhort the audience not to repeat the prior sins of Israel—an exhortation appropriate for believers in this present life (*simul iustus et peccator*, "saint and sinner simultaneously"), similar to Paul's exhortation in 1 Cor 10:1–13.

Moreover, the exhortation should not be misunderstood as implying that the people can remove their sinful nature through their own efforts ("let them remove," Ezek 43:9), since it is only the gracious action of God that can accomplish their regeneration. Compare "get for yourselves a new heart and a new S/spirit" in 18:31 with "I will give you a new heart and put a new S/spirit within you. I will remove the heart of stone …" in 36:26.

"Now" (עַתָּה), here as often, introduces the main point of the speech. God's Glory comes of itself, by sheer grace. As Luther explained the Second Petition of the Lord's Prayer: "The kingdom of God certainly comes by itself without our prayer, but we pray in this petition that it may come to us also."[20] But the people can forfeit it or cause its departure from themselves once more. The Piel jussive יְרַחֲקוּ, "let them make distant, put far away, remove," is an antonym to the Hiphil הִקְרִיב, "bring near, offer" (e.g., 43:22–24; frequent in Leviticus), used of the OT sacrifices through which Yahweh's indwelling was confirmed and strengthened. With the perfect sacrifice of Christ, and after the removal of the people's sinful nature and sins, God can dwell among them "forever" (43:9, as in 43:7; cf. Rev 22:5).

43:10   The account of the return of the Glory and its implications eventuates in a second charge to the prophet to explain the meaning of the temple structure as it had been shown to him by the heavenly guide. The Hiphil imperative הַגֵּד (from נָגַד, here with a double accusative) is used, as in the first charge, in 40:4 at the beginning of the vision. There its object was "everything you see," but here it is "the temple." That necessitates a periphrastic translation of the imperative as "describe," but the basic meaning of the verb is "tell, narrate."

How does one "narrate" or even "preach" a building?[21] Part of the answer lies in connecting the sanctuary's structure with the history of salvation of which it is a part. The connection is evident already in the structure of the Pentateuch: all its laws, including cultic ones, are subordinated to the narrative of creation and redemption. The technical architectural features are meaningful only as they contribute to the proclamation and sacramental distribution of the Gospel, which is essentially the same, whether in its OT or NT form: justification, the forgiveness of sins, and life everlasting, all furnished as God's free gifts because of the atonement of Jesus Christ. Hence, one is tempted to translate הַגֵּד here as "proclaim" (as בִּשֵּׂר and κηρύσσω usually mean).

---

[20]   SC III 7 (*Luther's Small Catechism with Explanation*, 17).

[21]   See also the discussion of this question in "Introduction to Ezekiel 40–48."

The purpose clause, "so that they may be ashamed of their sins," is rather surprising initially, but it will be reinforced in 43:11. When the people understand the proclamation of salvation encoded in the temple structure, their eyes will be opened to the extent to which their idolatrous "spirituality" had really been sacrilege. In fact, this accent is characteristic of Ezekiel, who had similar purpose clauses with the Niphal of כָּלַם, "be ashamed," in salvation oracles in 16:54, 61 and 36:32. In 16:54 the shame results from the salvation Israel receives together with the converted Gentile peoples of Sodom and Samaria. In 16:61 it is from the establishment of the everlasting covenant with Israel. In 36:32 it is from the realization of the free act of grace by Yahweh for his own sake.

A Lutheran will be sure to detect a Law-Gospel theme in these verses. We often describe evangelization in terms of first preaching the Law and later the Gospel. That sequence is so that the sinner is first convicted of his own guilt, then is ready to receive the Good News that God in Christ has won pardon for all sin. But functionally, Law and Gospel are more often intertwined and alternate with each other—in the course of the pastor's ministry and even in the liturgy and readings of the worship service. There is no valid Gospel except Law-Gospel! As we Christians grow in faith and appreciation of the Gospel of God's plenary forgiveness in Christ, we also grow in appreciation of the enormity of our sin, from which Christ saves us.

The Qal perfect with *waw* consecutive, וּמָדְדוּ, has jussive force: "let them measure." This is the same verb used throughout chapters 40–48 for the guide's measuring (see the fourth textual note on 40:5). We might have expected it to precede the clause about shame, since the perfection of God's temple would, by way of contrast, deepen the people's awareness of their own prior sinfulness. As it stands, it seems to be an invitation to the audience to contemplate and ponder the prophet's proclamation for themselves. The noun תָּכְנִית was used once before, in 28:12 (see the fourth textual note), for the "perfection, symmetry" of the king of Tyre (typifying Satan and/or Adam) before his fall. Here I have paraphrased slightly to "perfect pattern." Homiletically, one may detect in the word both Law (the contrast with the people's previous lives) and Gospel: God has done everything necessary for their salvation, so that, by his grace, his people may finally attain perfection.[c]

The versions exhibit some variations from the MT. Following the LXX, Targum, and Syriac, Zimmerli would emend תָּכְנִית to תְּכוּנָתוֹ, "its arrangement, layout,"[22] but וּתְכוּנָתוֹ is used in the next verse (43:11). These two nouns are from the verbal roots תָּכַן and כּוּן, respectively, and the change does not materially affect the meaning. In place of a verb for "measure," the LXX has καὶ τὴν ὅρασιν αὐτοῦ, "and its appearance," which RSV follows, perhaps as if וּמָדְדוּ were וּמִדָּתוֹ ("and its measure").

(c) 1 Cor 13:10; Phil 3:12; Heb 12:23; James 1:4; 1 Pet 5:10; 2 Pet 1:4

---

[22] Zimmerli, *Ezekiel*, 2:410.

43:11 This verse both emphasizes and expands on 43:10, with repetitious vocabulary. The LXX evidently had before it an entirely different text, which modern critics tend to follow in various ways.[23] Even Block follows the LXX and Vulgate in changing the initial conditional clause, "if they are ashamed … ," into a declarative sentence.[24] Indeed, the conditionality here is unexpected after the unconditionality of 43:10. The MT is certainly the *lectio difficilior* and may be understood as another sign that Ezekiel again has retreated from envisioning the eternal state after Christ's parousia and is now describing this present life, in which sin remains, requiring repentance. There may still be some who are so self-satisfied and hard-hearted that no proclamation, not even Ezekiel 40–48 or Revelation 21–22, will arouse repentance and faith (cf. Rev 22:11, 18–19).

In the Hebrew of the following apodosis, the lengthy compound object ("the design … and all its regulations") is placed first for emphasis. It is the first of two direct objects of the Hiphil imperative הוֹדַע (from יָדַע), "make known, teach," and the second object follows the verb: אוֹתָם, "them," that is, the people. צוּרָה, used four times in the verse, seems to refer to the total external "design" or "form" of the temple. תְּכוּנָה may speak of its internal "arrangement, layout."

The imperative to "teach" in this context reminds us that what we might characterize as catechetical instruction was part of the priests' regular duties, although the OT gives far fewer details about it than about their liturgical obligations. Even if their instruction centered on ceremonial matters, if done properly, it would not have been simply teaching the rites, but also the attendant theology about worship that encompasses all of life.

The concern with "its exits and its entrances" (וּמוֹצָאָיו וּמוֹבָאָיו) has to do with control of access to the sacred precincts, assuring that only authorized personnel may enter. The same kind of concern is reflected in Rev 22:14: "Blessed are those who wash their robes, that their right of access may be to the tree of life, and through the gates they may enter the city" (cf. Rev 21:7–8, 27). "Its entrances" (וּמוֹבָאָיו) is the plural of מָבוֹא with suffix, but written with *holem* in the first syllable (וּמוֹ- instead of וּמְבוֹאָיו) by phonetic assimilation to the preceding וּמוֹצָאָיו.

Twice a Kethib has a defective spelling of the third masculine singular suffix while the Qere (צוּרֹתָיו … תּוֹרֹתָיו) has the normal form for a plural noun. Unusual are the pairings of "all its forms and all its ordinances [חֻקֹּתָיו]" and "all its forms and all its regulations [תּוֹרֹתָיו]." In this context, the "ordinances" may refer to the ceremonies for worship, as the word often means in Leviticus. Ezekiel has said little about them, but, as a priest (1:3), they surely were of great importance to him. Even those OT rubrics that were ceremonial in nature

---

[23] E.g., Zimmerli, *Ezekiel*, 2:410–11; Allen, *Ezekiel*, 2:243; Cooke, *Ezekiel*, 474–75.

[24] Block, *Ezekiel*, 2:586–87, including n. 67.

could not easily be sequestered from doctrinal and moral concerns. תּוֹרָה, *torah*, is more multivalent in meaning, but in this context its plural probably connotes liturgical "regulations" again, although possibly with more theological and moral content than the "ordinances." (The second וְכָל־צוּרֹתָיו is omitted in the LXX and so naturally is a catalyst for various critical rewritings of the verse.)

"Write in their sight" shows that not only is the proclamation to be oral but it is also to be accompanied by the written text, which we now have in Ezekiel's book. We might like a drawing or sketch, as commentators have seen fit to provide. As the rest of the verse shows, everything about the temple is a "sermon illustration" that unites for God's people what he has done (and continues to do) for them—their justification—with what they will do in grateful response and become by his grace—their sanctification.

As noted in "Introduction to Ezekiel 40–48" nowhere in these chapters does God command the Israelites to build or replicate the temple after they return from exile; neither is there any such mandate for the building of a temple for animal sacrifices during an future "millennium." In 43:10–11 God commands Ezekiel to record the vision so that the Israelites may "keep its whole form and all its ordinances and do them." This means that they are to contemplate the implications of this temple and live as such by the power of God at work in them, as the NT makes explicit (e.g., 1 Cor 6:19–20; 1 Pet 2:5).

In the immediate context, doing the temple's ordinances means ceasing (43:9) and repenting of (43:11) the idolatrous practices by which the Israelites had defiled the temple of Solomon, which had been destroyed in 586 B.C., some thirteen years before this prophecy was given in 573, the fourteenth year after the fall of the city (see figure 1 and the commentary on 40:1).

43:12 "The Torah of the temple" is not a new covenant to be implemented by Israel, but a renewal of the Torah revealed first to Moses and developed in this revelation to Ezekiel—the Torah to be fulfilled in Christ (Rom 10:4; cf. Rom 8:2; 1 Cor 9:21; Gal 5:4; 6:2). Because of the difficulty in translating תּוֹרָה, I have simply transliterated it here. Its all-too-common rendition as "Law" is, at best very misleading. I have argued that "Gospel" in its broad sense, doctrinally comprising both Law and Gospel, would be closer to the word's basic sense of "teaching," both because of its historical context and salvific intent, as expressed in the preceding verses.

This verse specifies one aspect of that Torah, which had been a major concern from chapter 40 on, namely, the separation of sacred and secular. גְּבוּל normally means "border, boundary," but here is used in a slightly broader sense of the "territory" within the wall around the temple complex, which formed the boundary (40:5; cf. Rev 21:12–19). What is within the wall is to be regarded as "most holy." The expression קֹדֶשׁ קָדָשִׁים is similar to that for the "Holy of Holies," the focal point of the entire sacrosanct area (see on 41:4).

There is some debate whether 43:12 should be considered a conclusion to the preceding material in the book or a heading for the following material, which is especially concerned with the worship regulations governing access to and activities within that sacred space. "This is the Torah of" (‎זֹאת תּוֹרַת־) occurs frequently in Leviticus, both before (e.g., Lev 6:2, 7, 18 [ET 6:9, 14, 25]) and after (e.g., Lev 7:37; 11:46) prescriptive legislation, so it is hard to make a case on formal precedents. My instinct is that it is more conclusion than introduction, but it does serve perfectly as a transition.

The Measurements of the Altar and the Rites for Its Consecration (43:13–27)

We noted earlier that on the measuring tour of the temple, virtually no attention had been paid to any of the temple appurtenances, with exception of passing mention of tables used for preparing the sacrifices (40:39–43); the sacrificial altar in front of the temple (40:47); and what at first appeared to be an "altar" but what the guide identified as "the table that is before Yahweh," corresponding to the table of shewbread in the tabernacle and Solomonic temple, and anticipating the Lord's Table—the Sacrament of Holy Communion (see on 41:22). Now in 43:13–27 the sacrificial altar is considered at length, as the priestly kitchens will be in 46:19–24. Other furniture that we might have expected based on the tabernacle and Solomonic temple, such as the lampstand and incense altar, are not mentioned in chapters 40–48. Yet most conspicuous by its absence is the ark (see on 43:7).

The rest of chapter 43 describes the new altar of burnt offering (43:13–17) and the rites attending its consecration (43:18–27). Legislation for other subjects is given in chapters 44–46. This pattern in 43:13–46:24, beginning a legal code with the altar, follows the pattern in the Torah of Moses, where legal codes are introduced by the following passages: Ex 20:24–26; Lev 17:1–9; Deut 12:1–27.

This shows that God's primary concern is to provide his people with sacrificial atonement for the forgiveness of sins (the altar). His will for them in all other aspects of life (the subsequent legislation) depends on this forgiveness. Therefore this pattern can be compared to that in the Pauline epistles, and indeed, the pattern of the typical Lutheran sermon. First comes Law (condemnation of human sin), then Gospel (the sacrificial atonement of Christ for the forgiveness of sins), and only on the basis of that Gospel does God (or the pastor) address the shape of the believer's life of faith (as in the OT legislation). See, for example, Law in Rom 1:18–3:23 and Galatians 1–2; Gospel in Romans 4–11 and Galatians 3–4; and the sanctified life in Romans 12–16 and Galatians 5–6.

In Ezek 43:13–27, as in the Mosaic legislation concerning the tabernacle altar, Law and Gospel are intertwined because the sacrifices (e.g., "sin offering") presuppose the human sin for which they are offered to procure forgiveness. God did indeed bestow the forgiveness of sins upon his OT people through the sacrifices he prescribed for atonement, as affirmed by, for example, his declaration in 43:27: "I will accept/favor you." But ultimately this forgiveness was *propter Christum*, "for Christ's sake," since the animals "without blemish" (תָּמִים, 43:22–23, 25; 45:18, 23; 46:4, 6, 13) were but types of Christ, the sinless Son of God, whose perfect, once-for-all sacrifice on the altar of the cross merited forgiveness for the sins of the whole world (e.g., Jn 1:29; 2 Cor 5:21; the theme of Hebrews 3–10).

Even though Ezek 43:12 is both a conclusion to the preceding verses and a possible introduction to the following, the transition still is abrupt to the series of ordinances for divine worship in the temple (43:13–46:24). Signs of connection with what preceded are scarce. Many measurements continue, as in chapters 40–42, but in 43:13–27 there is no mention of the guide (40:3–5; 43:6), of Ezekiel himself, or of the climactic return of the Glory (43:1–12). Inevitably, critics speculate about the "editorial process" that might have arranged the sections of text in their present order. There must have been some such process, but as this commentary has affirmed elsewhere, Ezekiel himself is the prime candidate for being the "editor" who, under divine inspiration by the power of the "Spirit" (e.g., 2:2; 3:12, 14, 24; 43:5), composed and arranged the book that bears his name. It is counterproductive to try to uncover anything more.

The Measurements of the Altar (43:13–17)

43:13–17 For a reconstruction of what the altar possibly looked like, see figure 5.[25] A number of small additions, inferences, and possible emendations of the Hebrew text seem necessary to make a smooth translation into English. The description in 43:13b–15 moves from bottom to top, while 43:16–17 moves in the opposite direction and ends with mention of the altar steps.

43:13 The explanation of the large cubit repeats that given in 40:5; see the third textual note there.

The translation of חֵיק (43:13, 14, 17) as "gutter" is by no means universally followed, though Block uses it.[26] The traditional rendering was "base," but that seems misleading. For a long time that tradition seemed to be reinforced by Albright's influential equation of the expression חֵיק הָאָרֶץ (the phrase at the start of 43:14, which see) with the Akkadian *irat erṣeti*, describing the "ground floor" of palaces and temples. Albright thought that in Ezekiel, חֵיק referred to a base slab placed on the surface at ground level.[27] Today, it may be conceded that, although there may be an etymological connection between Hebrew and Akkadian at this point, functionally there is no association. The common meaning of חֵיק in the OT is "lap, bosom." In this context, it is probably best understood in the light of 1 Ki 22:35, where חֵיק הָרֶכֶב refers to a "depression/cavity of the chariot," where King Ahab's blood flowed. The purpose of this "gutter" here in Ezekiel was to catch the blood of sacrificed animals and

---

[25] Cf. Block, *Ezekiel*, 2:598, figure 9.

[26] Block, *Ezekiel*, 2:597–99.

[27] Albright, "The Babylonian Temple-Tower and the Altar of Burnt-Offering," and *Archaeology and the Religion of Israel*, 150, 152.

keep it from contaminating the sacred ground around the altar, as well as making it easier for the priests to perform their functions. The phrase at the start of 43:14 may distinguish the gutter mentioned in 43:13–14 from the one mentioned in 43:17, which some view as closer to the top of the altar (see on 43:17).

Literally, וְחֵיק הָאַמָּה is "and (its) gutter (was) the cubit." The words could be divided differently as וְחֵיקָה אַמָּה, "and its gutter (was) a cubit," as the Vulgate and Syriac translate. The third feminine singular suffixes later on וּגְבוּלָהּ ... שְׂפָתָהּ (and on לָהּ in 43:17) make it clear that חֵיק was considered feminine in gender. This "cubit" is the measure of the gutter's depth, as the LXX's βάθος correctly infers, and so my translation adds "deep."

Its גְּבוּל (usually "boundary") must here refer to its "ridge" (as I have translated) or "curb," a ledge or rim that must have been intended as an additional safeguard against spillage of the blood. Being "one span" (זֶרֶת הָאֶחָד), that is, half a cubit or about ten inches high, it would easily suffice for that purpose. The article with אֶחָד is unneeded, and since זֶרֶת is always feminine elsewhere, some propose reading אַחַת, but this is probably another case of lack of gender agreement in Ezekiel. This ridge was all around שְׂפָתָהּ, the gutter's שָׂפָה, literally "lip," but often used in the derived sense of "edge, brim."

גַּב, literally "back," is often taken to refer to the torus, a rounded or convex molding of the altar base, a substructure perhaps half underground. That is possible, but it is probably preferable to follow the LXX's ὕψος and emend to גֹּבַהּ, "height," as is done by virtually all English translations (even KJV had "higher place"). If so, the verse division in the MT may be misleading, and the phrase beginning with וְזֶה ("and this is the height …") introduces the measurements in 43:14, as I have translated. Alternatively, the phrase could conclude the measurements of the features of the altar's base, as in NASB.

43:14 It is clear that the altar is built up in steps, but precise details are debated. Much of the difficulty here arises from עֲזָרָה (43:14, 17, 20; 45:19), another architectural term of unknown meaning. Besides its use in Ezekiel, it occurs elsewhere only in 2 Chr 4:9 and 6:13, where it appears to refer to the "court" of the temple (more or less synonymous with חָצֵר). Is the term in 2 Chr 4:9 and 6:13 the same word used here, or is it a homograph? Block concludes that the words are the same and translates it here as "wall" (because the temple courtyard was walled). He thinks of a row of uncut stones supporting the altar's superstructure to keep it from collapsing outward from the weight of the fill inside.[28] To the observer, this might appear as a "ledge." But we are not informed of how the altar was constructed, and if we think of more solid blocks we might envision a plinth. In either case, the translation "ledge" seems applicable, and so it is usually translated.

The description of "the height of the altar" (43:13c) commences with the distance from "the gutter on the ground" (וּמֵחֵיק הָאָרֶץ, 43:14), probably from the ridge around its edge (see 43:13), to (the top of) "the lower ledge"

---

[28] Block, *Ezekiel*, 2:599.

(עַד־הָעֲזָרָה הַתַּחְתּוֹנָה, 43:14): two cubits, thus making the lower, smaller (in height) ledge two cubits high. Then the distance is given from (the top of) that ledge, now called "the smaller ledge" (וּמֵהָעֲזָרָה הַקְּטַנָּה), to "the larger ledge" (עַד־הָעֲזָרָה הַגְּדוֹלָה): four cubits, thus making the larger ledge four cubits high. The "one cubit" dimensions of "width" may refer to the amount the gutter projected beyond the lower ledge on every side[29] and to the amount the lower ledge projected beyond the upper ledge on every side, respectively. See figure 5.[30] The total width of one of the ledges, fourteen cubits, is given in 43:17 (see the note there).

43:15 Most of the verse is straightforward, but there has been much discussion about the term(s) that I have translated as "hearth." Part of the debate centers on whether there is a distinction between הַרְאֵל (43:15a) and the term used in 43:15b–16 (see below). Keil argues that there is such a distinction, with the first term indicating the foundation of the hearth and the second term indicating the hearth itself.[31] I, however, am inclined to view the terms as variant spellings of the same word (see below), both indicating the hearth, that is, the top of the altar on which the fire would be kindled and the sacrifices burnt. This verse gives the height of the hearth as four cubits.

We do not know whether Ezekiel is using a traditional term or one of his own coinage. The spelling of the word in 43:15a is הַרְאֵל, which suggests a compound meaning: "mountain [הַר] of God [אֵל]." In 43:15b–16 the Kethib is אֲרָאֵיל while the Qere is אֲרִיאֵל. Both may mean "lion [אֲרִי] of God [אֵל]." Or if there existed a verbal root אָרָה, "to burn," both may mean "fire/hearth of God."[32] Regardless of the meaning, the Kethib spells the first element defectively and the second element plene, while the Qere spells the first plene and the second normally and defectively. The LXX (αριηλ) and Vulgate (*arihel*) merely transliterate the term in all three places. The Qere here is the sole reading in Is 29:1–2, an ancient crux, where the word is a cryptic designation of Jerusalem.

Since Hebrew has few compound words (except proper names, which frequently are compounds), many interpreters assume that the term (probably one term with these three variant spellings) is not a compound. For a long time, many followed the view of Albright, who posited an etymological connection with the Akkadian *arallû*, which was supposed to mean both "underworld" and "mountain of the gods, cosmic mountain," perhaps relating to the ziggurat, the stepped pyramid with a temple at its top.[33] But that connection has been disproven; the Akkadian (originally Sumerian) word has nothing to do with a

---

[29] Thus Keil, *Ezekiel*, 2:285.

[30] Compare the description of the altar of Herod's temple in Mishnah, *Middoth* 3:1, as a stepped altar that became progressively smaller as one moved from bottom to top.

[31] Keil, *Ezekiel*, 2:287.

[32] So Keil, *Ezekiel*, 2:287. See also BDB, s.vv. ארה II and אֲרָאֵיל.

[33] Albright, "The Babylonian Temple-Tower and the Altar of Burnt-Offering," and *Archaeology and the Religion of Israel*, 151–52.

divine mountain.[34] The Hebrew word here must have been at home in Israel's environs, because in lines 12–13 of the Mesha Inscription, the Moabite king boasts of having dragged the "ʾrʾl of David" before his god Chemosh after a victory over Israel.[35] In the inscription, it is unclear what object the term referred to; it might have been an altar, but certainly not a mountain.

Today the most commonly accepted etymology of the term in Ezekiel seems to trace it to a presumed root ארה, "burn," cognate with Arabic *ʾiryat*, "fire pit" (so *HALOT*, s.v. אֲרִיאֵל I). The final *lamed* can be explained as the same inert afformative we seem to meet in כַּרְמֶל, "Carmel," formed from כֶּרֶם, "vineyard," plus final ל. We might wish that we could divine some theological meaning from the word, but it seems to be as purely functional as the word for "altar," מִזְבֵּח (e.g., 43:13, 18), a noun formed by prefixing מ to the verbal root זבח, "to sacrifice," meaning "place of sacrifice" (GKC, § 85 k).

The same is true of the four "horns" of the altar. These projections at the four corners were apparently an intrinsic part of an altar (see, e.g., Ex 27:1–2; 30:1–3; Rev 9:13), as can be amply demonstrated from altars found by archaeologists. But neither Scripture nor archaeology has explained their significance. Several places in the Pentateuch, Yahweh commands the (high) priest to smear the blood of a sacrifice on the horns of both the incense altar (e.g., Lev 4:7, 18) and the altar of burnt offering (e.g., Ex 29:12; Lev 4:25; 16:18), but that does not suffice as a basis for any comprehensive statement of the significance of the horns. The NT does connect "horn(s)" with Jesus Christ and salvation, perhaps as a symbol of strength and victory. Zechariah, in his Benedictus, praises God for raising up in the coming Messiah "a horn of salvation" (Lk 1:69, alluding to 2 Sam 22:3 ‖ Ps 18:3 [ET 18:2]), and the apostle John sees the exalted Christ as a lamb with seven horns (Rev 5:6).

43:16 With this verse, the description reverses direction and moves from top to bottom, beginning with the hearth that was discussed in 43:15. Instead joining the measurement of its length to that of its width with a *waw* or asyndetically, the preposition בְּ is used (here on בִּשְׁתֵּים) in the sense of "(length) by (width)," as again in 43:17. The last phrase, רָבוּעַ אֶל אַרְבַּעַת רְבָעָיו, is, literally, "a square to four of its four sides." רָבוּעַ is the masculine Qal passive participle of רָבַע, also used of both the "square" altar of burnt offering (Ex 27:1) and altar of incense (Ex 30:2) connected with the tabernacle. A feminine form of the word was in 41:21 (see the note there). In Ezekiel the cognate noun רֶבַע is always plural, referring to "four sides," and always is preceded by אַרְבַּעַת (1:8, 17; 10:11; 43:16–17). If one looked down on the top of the altar from above (see figure 2), one would see a square twelve cubits by twelve cubits.

43:17 "The ledge" (וְהָעֲזָרָה) does not specify whether this is the upper or the lower ledge. Since the description is moving downward and the next item down from the hearth (43:16) is the upper or "larger" ledge (see on 43:14), it

---

[34] See the sources cited in Block, *Ezekiel*, 2:600, n. 64.

[35] C. R. North, "Ariel," *IDB* 1:218; cf. *ANET*, 320.

is often assumed that this verse refers to that ledge. Hence some interpreters would insert הַגְּדוֹלָה (as in 43:14) and/or assume that a matching description of the lower ledge has fallen out by homoioteleuton. According to this view, this verse gives the dimensions of fourteen cubits long by fourteen cubits wide for the upper ledge and describes a ridge and a gutter not previously mentioned. Keil thinks that the reference is to the lower ledge and maintains that the ridge and the gutter are the same ones mentioned in 43:13–14. He argues that the upper ledge is not mentioned because it was the same length and width as the element above it, twelve cubits by twelve cubits.[36] This view would also fit the top-to-bottom description being given in 43:16–17, with the lower ledge being mentioned first, followed by the ridge and then the gutter, in the reverse order that those elements were mentioned in 43:13–14. See figure 5.

The clause וְהַגְּבוּל סָבִיב אוֹתָה, literally, "and the ridge surrounds it [the ledge]," uses the adverb סָבִיב as if it were a verb that takes a direct object (אוֹתָה). Some advocate changing סָבִיב אוֹתָה to either סְבִיבוֹתָיו or to סוֹבֵב אוֹתָה, but סָבִיב is used in the same way in 1 Ki 6:5 (cf. GKC, § 103 o).

The article with חֲצִי הָאַמָּה ("half of the cubit") is similar to usage elsewhere; see וְרֹחַב הָאַמָּה at the end of 43:14, and also Ex 26:16; 36:21; 1 Ki 7:31–32.

We would expect an אֲשֶׁר in וְהַחֵיק־לָה ("the gutter which belonged to it"), but again numerous parallels could be cited[37] that show that this was idiomatic.

The final clause, וּמַעֲלֹתֵהוּ פְּנוֹת קָדִים, "and its steps face east," raises various questions, not least because it appears to fly in the face of the prohibition in Ex 20:26 against building steps to altars (in order to prevent what we know as indecent exposure). The tabernacle altar was three cubits high (Ex 27:1), and the heaping up of a little soil around its base might have sufficed to enable the priests to easily access its top. But in Solomon's temple (2 Chr 4:1), the altar was ten cubits high, so some means of reaching its hearth would have been necessary. Josephus and the Mishnah indicate that the altar of Herod's temple was approached by a slope or a ramp,[38] and that could be what Ezekiel is describing here.

The form of the third masculine singular suffix on וּמַעֲלֹתֵהוּ is unique for a feminine plural noun, but the analogous suffix form ־ֵיהוּ (or, written defectively, ־ֵהוּ) occurs on masculine plural nouns (or participles) or dual nouns in 1 Sam 14:48; 30:26; Nah 2:4 (ET 2:3); Hab 3:10; Job 24:23 (see Joüon, § 94 i). The expected form here would be מַעֲלֹתָיו. Compare 40:6, where the Kethib probably should be vocalized מַעֲלֹותָו since the Qere there is מַעֲלוֹתָיו. Some would emend accordingly here, but that solves nothing substantive. The plural form of מַעֲלָה here could suggest "steps" (see BDB, 1), although the plural of מַעֲלָה is used more generally for "ascents" up to Jerusalem in the su-

---

[36] Keil, *Ezekiel*, 2:288.

[37] See Cooke, *Ezekiel*, 476.

[38] Josephus, *War*, 5.225 (5.5.6); Mishnah, *Middoth* 3:3–4.

perscriptions of the Psalms of Ascent (Psalms 120–134; BDB, 5). The Targum has וּמֵאֲתַר דְּסַלְקִין לַהּ, "and from the place where they ascend to it," omitting any reference to "steps," possibly in an attempt to harmonize this vision with Ex 20:26, although the LXX, Vulgate, and Syriac translate with words that can mean "steps." The use of a ramp would obey at least the letter of the Law.

פְּנוֹת is the Qal infinitive construct of פָּנָה, "to face," apparently used as a gerundive, "its steps are to face east," a meaning more common when an infinitive has לְ (see GKC, § 114 l; Williams, § 196). Some unnecessarily advocate revocalizing to the plural participle פֹּנוֹת.

The concern that the ascent faced east was obviously intended to make sure that when the priest offered sacrifice, he faced west, toward Yahweh "incarnate" in the temple. If the ascent were on the west, then the priest would have faced east, in the direction of pagan worship of the sun god, with his back toward Yahweh—the posture of the apostate worshipers in 8:16.

The measurements of the altar indicate that it was relatively large, as also does the necessity for an ascent or stairs to reach its hearth. The total height of Ezekiel's altar from the bottom of the gutter to the top of its hearth was eleven and a half cubits: a cubit and a half for the gutter and its ridge (43:13); two cubits for the lower ledge (43:14); four cubits for the upper ledge (43:14); and four cubits for the hearth (43:15), that is, about nineteen and a half feet or almost six meters. The tabernacle altar was three cubits high (Ex 27:1), and the height of the Solomonic altar was ten cubits (2 Chr 4:1); however, those measurements were probably by the ordinary cubit rather than the long cubit being used in Ezekiel (see the third textual note on 40:5). If Josephus is correct (and he generally is, wherever he can be checked) the Herodian altar was higher still at fifteen cubits.[39]

The altar described by Ezekiel is higher than any that has been excavated in Palestine. A comparison has been attempted with a huge installation excavated at Megiddo, but it is circular (twenty-six feet in diameter and four and a half feet high) and might better be classified as a "high place" than an altar. A rectangular structure five feet high recently unearthed atop Mount Ebal is sometimes considered to be an altar, but that interpretation is hotly debated.

Rites for the Consecration of the Altar (43:18–27)

43:18–27 The beginning of a new subsection is indicated here by the direct address to the prophet as "son of man"; the citation formula, "thus says the Lord Yahweh";[40] and the introductory formula "these are the ceremonies …" The conclusion of this subsection is indicated by the signatory formula, "says the Lord Yahweh,"[41] in 43:27.

---

[39] Josephus, *War*, 5.225 (5.5.6).

[40] For this formula, see pages 8–9 in the introduction and the fourth textual note and the commentary on 2:4.

[41] For this formula, see pages 8–9 in the introduction and the second textual note on 5:11.

The altar would have to be consecrated before it could be used, as was done also with its predecessors in the tabernacle of Moses (Exodus 29, especially 29:36–46; Ex 40:10; Leviticus 8, especially 8:11, 15) and Solomon's temple (1 Ki 8:62–66 ‖ 2 Chr 7:4–10). This section generally follows the pattern of those precursors, especially the seven-day duration (Ex 29:37; Lev 8:33–35; 1 Ki 8:65; 2 Chr 7:8–9). Much of the language is standard, stylized speech familiar from God's instructions in Exodus and Leviticus. The prophetic formulae at the beginning and end of this section give the whole section a certain prophetic cast; it is not merely a series of priestly rubrics, as is common in Leviticus. "You are to give the Levitical priests ..." (Ezek 43:19) might seem to elevate Ezekiel into the status of a second Moses, but unlike the Torah given through Moses, the commands given now through Ezekiel are not to be implemented by historical Israel. Although Ezekiel may be pictured as instructing the priests, they are the ones envisioned as performing the ceremonies Yahweh commands, for example, "you are to take some of its blood ..." (43:20).

The text does not lose sight of the future orientation of all of chapters 40–48. This altar, like the temple itself, was not a present reality for Ezekiel, nor something he or his audience was to construct. Rather, the altar was something he saw from afar in a vision, whose concluding description of the transformed land (chapters 47–48) presupposes the creation of the new heavens and the new earth after the return of Christ (Revelation 21–22).[42]

43:18 The verb וַיֹּאמֶר ("he said") lacks a subject. In Ezekiel 2–39 it was Yahweh who addressed Ezekiel as "son of man,"[43] so he may be the one who speaks directly to Ezekiel here. If so, this is the first time that Yahweh himself speaks in chapters 40–48. *How* he speaks is typically not specified. The lack of subject may imply that the supernatural guide (40:4; 43:6) continues to be the agent through whom Yahweh communicates (the supernatural guide addressed Ezekiel as "son of man" in 40:4; 43:7, 10).

חֻקּוֹת, often translated "statutes," is more frequent in Ezekiel than in any other prophet, and often is linked with מִשְׁפָּטִים, "judgments," as constituent terms for God's covenant with his people (e.g., 5:6–7; 11:20). Since the topic here is specifically the consecration of the altar, "ceremonies" seems to be an appropriate translation.

Only two main activities that would be performed at the altar after its consecration are mentioned as representative of all of them: (1) the offering on it of עוֹלָה, "burnt offering" (as in, e.g., Leviticus 1), and "sprinkling blood on it," which was done, using זָרַק (the same verb used here), in connection with the burnt offerings (e.g., Lev 1:3–5), and (2) the communion offerings (e.g., Lev 3:1–2), and using the synonym נָזָה, in connection with the sin offering (Lev

---

[42] See further "Introduction to Ezekiel 40–48."

[43] See the second textual note and the commentary on 2:1.

5:9). Ezekiel could assume that his audience was familiar enough with the rituals from the Torah for the kinds of sacrifice and the sprinkling of blood (Leviticus 1–7) that there was no need to detail them here.

"Sprinkling blood" as an expression for sacrificial atonement finds its fulfillment in the NT, which speaks of the "sprinkling" of Christ's atoning blood on believers (1 Pet 1:2). See further the commentary on Ezek 36:25, which has the same verb, זָרַק, "sprinkle."

43:19 Directions for the first day's ceremonies commence at once. We are not told what day of the week that was, but most likely it was the first day of the Hebrew week, the day after the Sabbath, that is, our Sunday.[d]

(d) Cf. Mt 28:1; Mk 16:2; Lk 24:1; Jn 20:1; Acts 20:7

Many of the commands begin with a perfect verb, most second masculine singular with *waw* consecutive (e.g., וְנָתַתָּה, 43:19–20; וְלָקַחְתָּ, 43:20–21; וְהִקְרַבְתָּם, 43:24). Others use a simple imperfect (e.g., תַּקְרִיב, 43:22–23; תַּעֲשֶׂה, 43:25; יְכַפְּרוּ, 43:26). These verbs function as imperatives and so are translated something like this: "you are to …" Most of the language is standard, stylized speech found also in prescriptions in Leviticus.

"The Levitical priests" translates הַכֹּהֲנִים הַלְוִיִּם, literally, "the priests, the Levites." All of the legitimate priests were sons of Aaron, within the tribe of Levi. However, as in 40:46, here again Yahweh further limits the rolls of eligibility by specifying that the priests must be Zadokites, descendants of Aaron's son Eleazar, and not descendants of the other son, Ithamar. This concern will be elaborated upon in 44:9–16. See further on 44:15.

The adjective קָרוֹב in 42:13 and 43:19 describes the sons of Zadok as those "who draw near, approach God for liturgical service" (see BDB, s.v. קָרוֹב, 2 e), the same meaning that the participle קָרֵב has in 40:46 and 45:4, and that the Qal finite verb has in 44:15–16. Here the adjective is defined more specifically by the later purpose clause לְשָׁרְתֵנִי, the Piel infinitive construct of שָׁרַת with suffix, "to serve me." (In 20:40 and often elsewhere in the OT, the more general verb עָבַד, "serve," can be used for divine service.) Inserted between the adjective and the infinitive is the signatory formula, נְאֻם אֲדֹנָי יְהוִה, "says Lord Yahweh," apparently to underscore the gravity of drawing "near" to Yahweh in this ceremony, and to remind the officiants of the importance of performing it properly.

פַּר by itself means "young bull." The appositional construct phrase בֶּן־בָּקָר, literally, "a son of a herd," is added here (also in 43:23, 25; 45:18; 46:6) and commonly in the Pentateuch. The phrase is redundant and hence commonly not translated, but it adds specificity, making it harder to misunderstand exactly what animals are to be used for sacrifice. בָּקָר distinguishes a "herd" of (large) cattle from צֹאן, a "flock" of (smaller) sheep or goats, which were used in other sacrifices. The relative sizes are reflected in the corresponding German terms *Großvieh* and *Kleinvieh*, respectively.

This initial offering should be a חַטָּאת, a "sin offering." As mentioned in the textual note on it in 40:39, some today advocate translating this as "purification offering," but that is deficient in seeming to minimize the scope of the problem and the potency needed to remove it. The noun is derived from the Piel form of the common verb for "to sin," חָטָא, A privative Piel (וְחִטֵּאתָ in 43:20) means to "de-sin, take away sin, free from the effects of sin." Precisely how an inanimate object like an altar could "sin" and thus have need for priests to "absolve it and make atonement for it" (43:20; see the following note) probably defies rational explanation.

In fact, at no point does the OT give us any detailed theological explanation of how any animal sacrifice "worked" except in the general sense of substitutionary atonement—an animal "without blemish" (43:22–23, 25) dying in the place of the blemished sinner—and also transfer of sin to the animal, as by the laying on of hands. The NT expounds the sacrificial death of Jesus as the substitutionary atonement by the sinless Son, to whom our sins were transferred, and whose righteousness is imputed to us through faith (e.g., Jn 1:29; Rom 3:25–5:21; 2 Cor 5:21). It is in light of the NT fulfillment in Christ that we can understand how forgiveness, righteousness, and everlasting life were mediated to OT believers through the OT sacrifices instituted by God as types of Christ's perfect, all-availing sacrifice. By God's Word and provision in the OT era, animal sacrifice simply was the divinely appointed "sacrament" for the forgiveness of sins. In that respect it can be compared with the Christian Sacraments, where God employs inanimate means—water, bread, and wine—to bestow forgiveness and salvation according to his Word and institution.

The Bible presents a comprehensive picture of the results of the fall into sin, by which death and decay spread throughout "the whole creation" (Rom 8:22), affecting even the inanimate parts of creation. Likewise, the psalmic language of trees and mountains rejoicing at the Lord (Pss 96:12; 148:9) is not to be dismissed as simply pretty poetry. The well-known Christmas hymn "Joy to the World" well develops the theme with its refrain, "heav'n and *nature* sing." With regard to the altar and other appointments of the Mosaic tabernacle and Solomonic temple that needed consecration, perhaps the most we can say is that they became impure or unclean by human contact. While the temple and altar in Ezekiel 40–48 are not made by any human hands,[44] the language and indeed the necessity of consecration seems nevertheless to be drawn from those predecessors that were constructed by people.

The Bible, of course, specifies certain human acts that defile or are sinful, but the basic problem is the sin manifested in such discrete sins. Since the fall of Adam and Eve, man is a sinner; by his fallen nature, he "cannot not sin" (*non posse non peccare*). Redemption comes only through the sinless Son of God, true man and true God, who, by virtue of his divine nature, "was not able to sin" (*non posse peccare*). He lived a life of perfect obedience, culminating in his death on the cross to atone for the sins of all humanity and in his glorious resurrection, thus leading the way for our salvation (Col 1:18).

---

[44] See further "Introduction to Ezekiel 40–48."

There is no exact parallel to be found in the NT commanding the consecration of articles used in worship. The ecclesiastical practice of consecrating and blessing liturgical objects and church structures is as close as we can come to something comparable. It rests on OT precedent, but not on NT mandate. Lutheranism has varied considerably in different eras in the extent to which it follows such practice, although it is common in the Catholic and Orthodox traditions. But whatever might happen in such rites, there certainly is no biblical basis for assuming some ontological change in the object blessed. If the intent is to set them apart for sacred use, to pray that they will be used in the service of the Gospel of Jesus Christ to the glory of God, and to indicate God's concern for "the whole creation" (Rom 8:22), they are commendable. One might quibble about use of the word "bless," but it does at least communicate that God's action, and not just mere human best wishes, must be involved for that intent to be achieved. Although "dedicate" is sacral and has ecclesiastical pedigree, it has become so secularized in our culture (where even new bridges, sewers, etc., are "dedicated") that a word like "consecrate" might be preferable in signaling what the ceremony really intends.

43:20 The importance of blood in virtually all the Israelite sacrifices (except the grain offering) is in full display in this verse. Again, the OT gives no theoretical explanation of how the actions accomplished the desired result. The closest we ever come is in the pivotal Lev 17:11, which associates blood with life. In any event, the revelation of the fulfillment in Christ again is the basis for understanding the OT preparation. The NT expounds the supreme value of the shed blood of Jesus Christ in earning for us the forgiveness of sins and everlasting salvation (e.g., Mt 26:28; Jn 6:53–56; 1 Pet 1:18–19; 1 Jn 1:7). See also the commentary on Ezek 36:25 in connection with the sprinkling of blood.

Ordinary objects in the fallen world can be deemed unclean by contact with unclean people (e.g., Lev 14:33–15:26). "Uncleanness" is a near synonym to "sin," and unclean objects need restoration to the unpolluted, undefiled state in which God had originally created the world.

Two Piel verbs (both second masculine singular perfect with *waw* consecutive) commonly used in contexts of forgiveness are used here, translated "absolve" and "make atonement for." They differ only in nuance.

The first, וְחִטֵּאתָ, is the privative Piel חִטֵּא, literally, "to remove sin." For the same reasons we rejected "purification offering" as an adequate rendering of חַטָּאת in 43:19 in favor of the traditional "sin offering," "purify" is not the appropriate translation for the removal of sin. Some verb like "absolve" seems necessary. חִטֵּא was used for the consecration of the tabernacle altar already in Ex 29:36 and Lev 8:15. (In Lev 14:49, 52 it was used in conjunction with the removal of "leprosy" from a house.) In 45:18 Ezekiel will use it for consecration of the sanctuary.

The second is וְכִפַּרְתֵּהוּ (for the form of its third masculine singular suffix, see Joüon, § 62 e). כִּפֶּר was used in 16:63 in God's promise that he would "make atonement" for all the sins of the woman representing Jerusalem (see the textual note and commentary there). In the OT it appears overwhelmingly in liturgical contexts. There has been much debate about its etymological sense (never a definitive argument), but it now seems fairly certain that it is related to the Akkadian *kapāru*, "to wipe/rub off," that is, "to purify liturgically." Its association with טָהֵר, "cleanse," in 43:26 indicates that a purgative sense is present here too. כִּפֶּר can refer to paying a ransom to atone for a crime or avert death, and that implication of a ransom payment remains prominent in theological contexts. The "ransom" here is obviously the blood or life of the bull. This verb too was used for the consecration of the tabernacle altar (Ex 29:36–37; Lev 8:15). How important the root is in the total theological expression of the meaning of temple and sacrifice is seen in the noun כַּפֹּרֶת, "mercy seat," referring to the lid of the ark (Ex 25:17), the throne of the "incarnate" Yahweh (e.g., 1 Sam 4:4), who finally effected the plenary atonement for all in the person of his incarnate Son. The root's importance can also be seen in "the Day of *Atonement* [כִּפֻּרִים]" (Lev 23:27–28; 25:9; see also Leviticus 16), the climax and summation of all OT atonement rituals.

The importance of כִּפֶּר and its cognates in the OT is continued and Christologized in the NT. It is Jesus Christ who offers his life as "the ransom [the noun λύτρον] for many" (Mt 20:28; Mk 10:45). See also the verb λυτρόω, "to ransom," in its contexts in Lk 24:21; Titus 2:14; 1 Pet 1:18. The LXX of Ezek 43:20 renders וְכִפַּרְתָּהוּ by the compound verb (and object pronoun) ἐξιλάσονται αὐτό. The cognate noun ἱλαστήριον (used elsewhere in the LXX for כַּפֹּרֶת, the "mercy seat" or lid of the ark) is used in this verse (as in 43:14, 17) for עֲזָרָה, a "ledge" on the altar. The NT uses ἱλαστήριον for both the "mercy seat" (Heb 9:5) and for Christ himself, who is our source of "*propitiation/expiation* through faith in his blood" (Rom 3:25). The shedding of Christ's blood is expressly that which pays for the sins of the world. See also the NT's use of the cognate noun ἱλασμός, which involves "propitiation" (appeasing God's wrath) and "expiation" (making satisfaction for guilt and offenses), both of which are included in "atonement": Christ himself is "the ἱλασμός for our sins" (1 Jn 2:2; 4:10). Throughout the NT and the church's kerugma, the vicarious atonement of Christ remains the core of the Gospel.

43:21 The phrase הַפָּר הַחַטָּאת could be appositional, "the bull, [the one that is] the sin offering." Or it could be one of the exceptional instances where a word in construct (הַפָּר) has the article (see Joüon, § 131 d, footnote 1; cf. GKC, § 127 f–g; see also on 46:19), "the bull of the sin offering," and the genitive would be epexegetical, "the bull that is the sin offering." In either case, this phrase distinguishes this bull from the one to be used a burnt offering in 43:23–24.

The singular verb וּשְׂרָפוֹ ("and he is to burn it") has no express subject. In Lev 4:10–12, 20–21, the task of burning the animal is assigned to the priest who offers the sacrifice, but in the corresponding rite on the Day of Atonement, Lev 16:27–28 assigns that role to an unidentified person, rather than to a priest. In the complete ritual for a sin offering, a detailed blood ceremony would be performed (beyond what is mentioned in Ezek 43:20), and the inner fat or suet of the animal would first be burned on the altar (see, e.g., Ex 29:10–14; Lev 4:3–12), but it is not Ezekiel's purpose to give a detailed account. Whether the sin offering was for the priest himself or for the entire congregation, the carcass of the animal would be burned "outside the camp" (Lev 4:12, 21; see also Ex 29:14; Lev 8:17; 9:11; 16:27). The Christological application is made in Heb 13:12 to the atoning death of Christ just outside Jerusalem: "Therefore also Jesus, so that he might sanctify the people by his own blood, suffered outside the gate."

In Ezekiel's vision, the burning is to take place בְּמִפְקַד הַבַּיִת מִחוּץ לַמִּקְדָּשׁ, "in the appointed place of the temple area, outside the sanctuary." Usually מִפְקָד is translated as "appointed/designated place" based on its verbal root, פָּקַד, "appoint, designate."[45] The word is attested in Phoenician and used four other times in the OT, but none of them help us here. We have no way of determining exactly where it would be. בַּיִת must be used in its extended sense of the entire "temple area," not just the temple itself (as בַּיִת often means in chapters 40–48), since the following phrase is "outside the sanctuary," that is, outside the temple itself.

43:22 This ritual of using a male goat as another sin offering on the second day is unparalleled, unless one adduces the ritual for the Day of Atonement (Leviticus 16), when Aaron (or the later high priest) first sacrifices a bull for himself (Lev 16:11) and then (on the same day) a goat for the people (Lev 16:15). Ezek 43:22 specifies that this goat must be תָּמִים, "unblemished, without defect," as also are the animals in 43:23, 25. This is a general requirement for all sacrificial animals (e.g., Ex 29:1; Lev 1:3, 10; 3:1, 6, 9), although it was not mentioned for the bull in Ezek 43:19.

Somewhat similar to פַּר בֶּן־בָּקָר in 43:19 (literally, "a bull, a son of a herd") is שְׂעִיר־עִזִּים, literally, "a he-goat of the goats," translated "a male goat." שָׂעִיר alone means "male goat," and עֵז alone can mean "goat," but very often one meets the idiomatic construct phrase שְׂעִיר־עִזִּים found here, with the redundant עִזִּים, the plural of עֵז. The noun שָׂעִיר specifies maleness more clearly than עֵז because there is a feminine counterpart, שְׂעִירָה, "female goat" (Lev 4:28; 5:6). In absence of directions to the contrary, we may assume that the same ceremony was used with the goat as with the bull in Ezek 43:19–21.

The repeated privative Piel perfect verb וְחִטְּאוּ ... חִטְּאוּ in 43:22b is the third person plural, literally, "they shall absolve the altar just as they absolved with the bull," whereas its second person singular (וְחִטֵּאתָ) was used in 43:20 (see the note there). Since 43:22 does not state the subject of these verbs, I have followed others in paraphrasing the impersonal plurals as passives, the altar is "absolved." Person and number fluctuate throughout this section. Probably the inconsistency is the result of a plurality of agents involving both the prophet

---

[45] Block, *Ezekiel*, 2:594, ventures "temple guard" for the phrase בְּמִפְקַד הַבַּיִת.

and priests, but we cannot achieve further clarity, except in 43:24b and 43:27b, which specify priests.

43:23–26 After the two sin offerings required in 43:19–22 are "finished" (43:23), another young bull and also a different animal, a ram, are to be offered as a different type of sacrifice—a burnt offering. Ezek 43:25–26 is as explicit as can be in describing a full week (seven days, with daily sacrifices) as basically a unitary consecration ceremony. All the sacrifices (the bull and goat for sin offerings in 43:19–22 and the bull and ram for a burnt offering in 43:23–24) are to be offered on each of the seven days. While 43:19–22 had specified that a bull was to be sacrificed on the first day and then a ram on the second day, that apparently was merely a sequential description of the order of those two sin offerings, which are to be offered on each of the seven days.

43:23 The first two finite verbs in these verses are second masculine singular, followed by two third common plural perfect verbs. The Piel infinitive constructs of כָּלָה "finish," and חִטֵּא, "absolve" (see on 43:20, 22), בְּכַלּוֹתְךָ מֵחַטֵּא, are, literally, "when you finish from absolving." The same kind of redundancy used for the bull in 43:19, 23 and the male goat in 43:22 is used in 43:23 in describing the ram. וְאַיִל מִן־הַצֹּאן is, literally, "a ram from the flock," but is translated simply as "a ram." אַיִל, "ram, male sheep," needs no further description, but is often followed, as here, by צֹאן, "flock," the counterpart to בָּקָר ("herd") after פַּר in 43:19, 23, 25.

Some critics create a problem by pressing the Piel of כָּלָה to imply an absolute end to the consecrating ceremonies and then "solve" their problem by considering the rest of the chapter a later addition.[46] See Keil's rejoinder to critics of his day who reached the same conclusion on different grounds.[47]

43:24 The new element in this verse is the mention of "salt" (מֶלַח), which the priests are to "throw" (וְהִשְׁלִיכוּ) on the burnt offering. Here "the priests" (הַכֹּהֲנִים) are specified as the subjects. The plural verbs earlier in 43:22b imply that the priests would have done some of the previous actions, even though most of 43:18–27 is spoken to Ezekiel ("you") as if he were to perform the actions himself. Leviticus says nothing about the addition of salt to burnt offerings, although Lev 2:13 does command the addition of salt to the grain offerings and to every קָרְבָּן (a very general word for "sacrifice"), which makes it likely that salt was added to many, if not all, types of sacrifice. Lev 2:13 describes it as "the salt of the covenant of your God," anticipating the phrase "covenant of salt" in Num 18:19 and 2 Chr 13:5, which emphasize the perpetuity of the covenant relationship. The purifying and preservative qualities of salt made it an appropriate symbol of the covenant and hence an addition to covenant sacrifices. The Hiphil verb וְהִשְׁלִיכוּ, "they are to throw," in Ezek 43:24 (versus, e.g., זָרַק, "sprinkle," in 43:18) suggests copious amounts of salt, apparently to intensify that symbolism.

---

[46] E.g., Zimmerli, *Ezekiel*, 2:434–35.

[47] Keil, *Ezekiel*, 2:293–96.

The phrase וְהֶעֱלוּ אוֹתָם עֹלָה has a common cognate accusative construction. וְהֶעֱלוּ, the Hiphil of עָלָה, is, literally, "to cause to go up," that is, to send up a sacrifice by burning it. It takes two accusative objects: אוֹתָם ("them") and then the verb's cognate noun, עֹלָה, a "burnt offering," literally, "the one [the offering] that goes up." There is no way to reproduce in English that wordplay which comes naturally in Hebrew.

43:25 As noted about 43:22–24, the verbs in this section frequently change in person and number, although these changes are usually ignored by commentators and in translations. The first verb, תַּעֲשֶׂה, is the second masculine singular imperfect of עָשָׂה, "do, make," which is often used of making sacrifice and so is translated, "you are to offer." The same verb's third person plural, יַעֲשׂוּ, is used at the end of the verse. Probably this does not mean that the prophet is to sacrifice the goat, while the priests are to sacrifice the bull and ram. Instead, the priests would offer all the sacrifices.

43:26 This verse is parallel to 43:25. It too stresses that all the ceremonies mentioned are for the single purpose of the consecration of the altar.

The Piel of כָּפַר, "make atonement," was also in 43:20 (see the note there). Instead of the imperfect יְכַפְּרוּ here, many Hebrew manuscripts have the perfect with *waw* consecutive, וְכִפְּרוּ, which is supported by the LXX and Syriac translations with a copula. That reading would support taking יַעֲשׂוּ at the end of 43:25 as the first word of a clause continuing in 43:26. The result would be this: "[Thus] they are to do for seven days, and so they are to make atonement ..."

The Piel verb וְטִהֲרוּ, "and they are to cleanse," is the same verb God used to speak of his cleansing of his people in 36:25, 33; 37:23. See the commentary on 36:25, which has both the Qal ("be clean") and the Piel. In 39:12, 14, 16, the Piel referred to the Israelites cleansing the land defiled by dead invaders.

The third Piel idiom, וּמִלְאוּ יָדֵו, literally, "and they shall fill his/its hand(s)," is new (only here in Ezekiel) and surprising. This is the common idiom meaning "to ordain" priests.[e] Whether we follow the Kethib יָדוֹ or the Qere יָדָיו, the singular suffix, "*his/its* hand(s)," must refer to the altar, as does the singular suffix on the preceding אֹתוֹ ("cleanse *it*"). Nevertheless, both the LXX (χεῖρας αὐτῶν, "their hand") and the Syriac (ܐܝܕܝܗܘܢ, "their hands") translate as if the priests are being ordained. KJV rendered, "they shall consecrate themselves," but no other English translation that I have consulted construes the phrase as referring to the priests rather than the altar. Elsewhere in the OT, the idiom for ordination with מָלֵא always takes the singular יָד, never the dual יָדַיִם, so the Kethib is the more likely reading here. (The dual יָדַיִם is used with מָלֵא in the different idiom "fulfill with the hands" in Jer 44:25 and 2 Chr 6:4.)

Only here in the OT is the idiom for ordination applied to an inanimate object, the altar. For priests, the phrase seems to have arisen from the literal sense of "filling their hand" with the portions of the sacrifices that were regularly allotted to them as food, thus providing them with a "salary." Occasionally, by extension, the phrase is used for installing other people besides priests into an

(e) E.g., Ex 28:41; 29:9, 29, 33, 35; Lev 8:33; 16:32; 21:10

office, for example, for the Levites in Ex 32:29 (with the Qal instead of the Piel) and for the whole assembly of Israel in 1 Chr 29:5 and 2 Chr 29:31. Possibly a token initial "payment" was given to priests when they assumed their office, as evidenced by the use of the phrase אֵיל־הַמִּלֻּאִים, "the ram of/for ordination," in Ex 29:26–27, 31; Lev 8:22, 29 (and without the article in Ex 29:22). Applied to the altar, we apparently must think of a rather bold figure of speech, virtually personifying the altar and saying, in effect, that it would be sufficiently provided with sacrificial gifts that it could accomplish its divinely intended purpose. The idiom "fill the hand" (metaphorical here, since an altar has no hand) cannot be reproduced literally in English, and so, with others, I have simply used "consecrate." This verse signals that the initiatory ceremonies are now complete.

43:27 The beginning of the regular sacrificial ritual "on the eighth day and onward" (בַיּוֹם הַשְּׁמִינִי וָהָלְאָה) is one day earlier than in the case of the tabernacle altar, where the eighth day was devoted to a detailed ceremony related to the priests' ordination (Leviticus 9). The reason for the difference could be that Ezekiel envisions the priests as already consecrated.

"The eighth day" would be the first day of a new week. In biblical usage, this day can indicate a new creation, the start of a new era in God's work of redemption. Thus circumcision took place on "the eighth day" (counted inclusively; Lev 12:3; see also Gen 17:12), that is, the same day as the birth, but in the next week, and circumcision marked the entrance of the infant into God's gracious covenant and kingdom (Gen 17:9–14). The corresponding NT Sacrament is Baptism, through which one is buried and raised with Christ, so that anyone in Christ is a new creation (Rom 6:1–4; 2 Cor 5:17; Col 2:11–13). Of course, Christ's resurrection took place on the first day of the new week (e.g., Mt 28:1), thus indicating the new era of salvation through faith in his accomplished work, and this "eighth" day, our Sunday, became the traditional "Sabbath" for Christian worship (Jn 20:19; Acts 20:7; cf. "the Lord's day," Rev 1:10).

שְׁלָמִים is traditionally rendered "peace offerings," but I prefer "communion offerings" (see the second textual note and the commentary on 39:17 and the fourth textual note on 40:39).[48] That seems especially appropriate here. The "burnt offering" (עוֹלָה) accented the vertical dimension, since the entire animal was burned and sent up, as it were, to God as a visible prayer (e.g., Leviticus 1). The שְׁלָמִים were the only sacrifice where a part of the meat was returned to the worshippers for them to eat as a "communion meal," presumably on the temple precincts (e.g., Lev 7:15–16), and so it stresses the horizontal perspective of God's people communing together with each other as well as with their Lord (cf. 1 Cor 10:16–17; 11:27, 33–34).

---

[48] Zimmerli, *Ezekiel*, 2:435, proposes "final offerings." The exact meaning of the word continues to be debated.

These two sacrifices, probably the most common, are mentioned as representative of all types. More will be said of the individual types in Ezek 45:10–17.

"And I will accept you" is my translation of וְרָצִאתִי אֶתְכֶם. The verb with א is an Aramaicized spelling for וְרָצִיתִי, from רָצָה, and an example of how third-*he* verbs often behave like third-*aleph* verbs (see GKC, § 75 rr). רָצָה is frequently used for God "accepting, looking favorably" upon sacrifice and the worshipers who offer it, as in 20:40–41 (see the commentary there).

If read with tunnel vision (ignoring the total biblical context), this clause could imply God's pleasure with a mere *ex opere operato* ritualism and that worshipers who offer specified sacrifices thereby merit God's favor and reward. As today, so also in ancient Israel there undoubtedly were people who thought in that legalistic way, but that is *not* biblical, orthodox *theology*. Quite the contrary. If that were the normative OT view, the OT would represent a religion antithetical to that of the NT, when in fact the NT is the continuation and fulfillment of the OT.

It is an elementary matter of the distinction between Law and Gospel that רָצָה must be heard as a verb of grace, not of works. God definitively showed his favor and acceptance (Mt 3:17; 12:18; 17:5; Lk 2:40, 52) toward his only Son, Jesus Christ, who offered himself as the one perfect sacrifice that made atonement for all of humanity's sins—a theme applied in this entire section to the altar by means of the verbs חִטֵּא, "absolve" (43:20, 22–23) and כִּפֶּר, "make atonement" (43:20, 26). On the basis of that sacrifice, and because of the merits of Christ himself, God accepts (Rom 15:7) and looks with favor (Lk 4:19; 2 Cor 6:2; cf. Gal 1:10; 1 Pet 2:19–20) upon all believers in Christ, who are justified through faith alone, and who, like Abraham (Gen 15:6), do not simply follow laws or customs, but offer to him the "obedience of *faith*" (Rom 1:5; 16:26; see also Romans 4).

The Prince; the Glory; and Priests and Levites at the Temple

Translation

44 ¹Then he brought me back to the outer gate of the sanctuary that faces east, but it was closed. ²Yahweh said to me, "This gate must remain closed and not be opened. No man may enter through it, because Yahweh, the God of Israel, has entered through it. Therefore, it must remain closed. ³The Prince, as Prince, may sit in it to eat food before Yahweh. Through the vestibule of the gateway he must enter, and he must go out the same way."

⁴Next, he brought me through the north gate to the front of the temple. I looked, and the Glory of Yahweh had filled the temple of Yahweh, and I fell on my face. ⁵Yahweh said to me, "Son of man, pay attention; see with your eyes, and with your ears hear everything that I am telling you regarding all the regulations of the temple of Yahweh and all the instructions about it. Pay attention to the entrance of the temple and to all the exits of the sanctuary. ⁶Say to the rebellion, to the house of Israel, 'Thus says the Lord Yahweh: There has been more than enough of all your abominations, O house of Israel, ⁷when you brought in foreigners, uncircumcised in heart and uncircumcised in flesh, to be in my sanctuary and to desecrate it, my own house, when you offered my food, the fat and the blood. Thus they broke my covenant in addition to all your abominations. ⁸You have not faithfully guarded my holy things, but appointed [others] to be guards at my sanctuary for yourselves. ⁹Thus says the Lord Yahweh: No foreigner, uncircumcised in heart and uncircumcised in flesh, may enter my sanctuary—no foreigner at all who is among the sons of Israel. ¹⁰However, the Levites, who went far from me when Israel strayed away, who wandered away from me after their fecal deities, and they must bear their punishment— ¹¹they [the Levites] may be in my sanctuary serving as guards over the gates of the temple and ministering in the temple. They shall slaughter the burnt offerings and the other sacrifices for the people. They shall stand before them [the people] to serve them. ¹²But because they used to serve them in front of their fecal deities and became an iniquitous stumbling block to the house of Israel, therefore I have raised my hand [in oath] against them, says the Lord Yahweh, and they must bear their punishment. ¹³They may not come near to me to be a priest for me or come near any of my holy things or the most holy offerings. They must bear their shame and [the consequences of] the abominations that they committed. ¹⁴Yet I will make them temple guards, in charge of all its [the temple's] duties and of everything that has to be done in it.

¹⁵" 'But the Levitical priests who are the sons of Zadok, who faithfully performed the guard duty of my sanctuary when the sons of Israel strayed away

from me, they may approach me to serve me, and they may stand before me to offer to me the fat and the blood, says the Lord Yahweh. [16]They alone may enter my sanctuary; they alone may approach my table to minister to me; and they shall perform guard duty for me. [17]When they enter the gates of the inner court, they must wear linen clothes. No wool should be on them while ministering in the gates of the inner court or inside the temple. [18]They should have linen turbans on their heads and linen shorts on their hips. They should wear nothing that causes sweat. [19]When they go out into the outer court to the people, they must take off their vestments in which they have been ministering and leave them in the holy rooms. Then they should put on other clothes so that they do not transmit holiness to the people by their vestments. [20]They must not shave their heads nor let their loose hair grow freely. They certainly must keep the hair of their heads trimmed. [21]No priest is to drink wine when he enters the inner court. [22]A widow or a divorced woman they must not take for themselves as a wife, but only virgins from the seed of the house of Israel, but a widow who is a widow of a priest they may take. [23]They are to teach my people the difference between the holy and the common, and make them knowledgeable in distinguishing the unclean from the clean. [24]In case of a dispute, they are to officiate as judges, and according to my judgments they must render judgment about it. They must observe my instructions and my regulations regarding all my appointed festivals, and they must keep my Sabbaths holy. [25]He must not go near a dead person and so make themselves unclean. Only in the case of father or mother, son or daughter, brother or unmarried sister may they make themselves unclean. [26]After his purification, they should count seven days for him. [27]On the day he enters into the sanctuary, into the inner court to minister in the sanctuary, he must offer a sin offering for himself, says the Lord Yahweh. [28]This will be their inheritance: I am their inheritance. You must not give them property in Israel; I am their property. [29]They may eat the grain offerings, the sin offerings, and the reparation offerings, and every devoted thing in Israel will belong to them. [30]The first of all firstfruits of all kinds, and every contribution of any kind from all your contributions will belong to the priests. The first of your ground meal you must give to the priest in order that a blessing may rest on your house. [31]No carcass that died naturally or was torn by wild animals, whether of a bird or a beast, may the priests eat.' "

Textual Notes and Commentary

Chapter 44 consists of three parts. The first verses (44:1–3) continue the temple tour from the preceding chapters (Ezekiel 40–43). Then in 44:4–5 comes a brief reference to the Glory "incarnated" in the eschatological temple, whose return Ezekiel had witnessed in 43:1–12, along with a solemn admonition, predicated on the presence of the Glory, to pay close attention to the following instructions. Finally, Yahweh, speaking in the first person, issues detailed commands in 44:6–31 regarding the legitimate ministerial roles of the Levites and the Zadokite priests for worship at the temple. More commands will come in 45:1–46:18, and the temple tour will not resume until 46:19.

The Closed Outer East Gate and the Prince (44:1–3)

44:1 The Qal passive participle סָגוּר, "closed," occurs three times in 44:1–2, indicating the main theme. The "closed" eastern gate may be intended as an introduction to the following ordinances (44:6–31) dealing with access to the sacred precincts and proper decorum inside them. The emphasis on restricted access and holiness may explain why 44:1 uses "the sanctuary" (הַמִּקְדָּשׁ, from the verb קָדַשׁ, "to be holy") for the complex of structures on the mountain (40:2) that constituted the temple compound. "Sanctuary" (מִקְדָּשׁ) will be the usual term in this chapter (44:1, 5, 7–9, 11, 15–16) and will be common later (45:3–4, 18; 47:12; 48:8, 10, 21). Previously in chapters 40–48, the common term had been בַּיִת, "house, temple, temple area," and "sanctuary" (מִקְדָּשׁ) had not been used except in 43:21, where it referred to the temple itself. Of course, the advent and presence of the Glory (43:1–12; 44:4) had changed the temple's quality.[1]

"He brought me back" (וַיָּשֶׁב אֹתִי) is the first instance of a new Hebrew form of the guidance formula (see the second textual note on 40:2). The clause here is equivalent to the same verb with suffix, וַיְשִׁבֵנִי, in 47:1, 6. Usually the guidance formula employs a verb with an object suffix, but אֵת with a suffix was also used in 40:1, 3.[2]

44:2 This verse emphasizes the vast distance between the Creator and his creatures by the only instance in the book of the full title "Yahweh, the God of Israel." Also conveying that emphasis is the unusual word order of the initial clause, וַיֹּאמֶר אֵלַי יְהוָה (repeated at the start of 44:5, where Ezekiel is addressed as "son of man"), which could be translated, "and he—Yahweh—said to me." Normally the subject would immediately follow the verb, as in 23:36: וַיֹּאמֶר יְהוָה אֵלַי. Even though this emphasizes that Yahweh is the ultimate speaker, since the supernatural guide (40:4; 43:6; but unmentioned in chapter 44) has been God's accredited spokesman all along, his agency is not necessarily excluded here.

The construction סָגוּר יִהְיֶה (Qal passive participle of סָגַר plus imperfect of הָיָה), literally, "will be (remain) closed," emphasizes "the durative aspect in the future" (Joüon, § 121 e). Various modal nuances can be expressed by the Hebrew imperfect, and here it is appropriately rendered "*must* remain closed" (cf. Joüon, § 113 m). The finality of the gate's closing underscores the promises given in 43:7–9 and is assurance that the Glory will never again abandon the

---

[1] Earlier in the book "sanctuary" (מִקְדָּשׁ) was used for the Jerusalem temple compound, which the Israelites had defiled (5:11; 8:6; 9:6; 23:38–39) and which Yahweh himself therefore defiled by consigning it to destruction at the hands of the Babylonians (24:21; cf. 25:3). Yet Yahweh had also promised to furnish a new "sanctuary" (see the commentary on 11:16; 37:26, 28).

[2] Zimmerli, *Ezekiel*, 2:437, suggests that the use here of the fuller form, אֵת with a suffix, as at the beginning of the vision in 40:1, 3, may signal another beginning. However, it is doubtful if we have more than a mere stylistic variation of the more common verb with object suffix.

temple, as it had in 10:4, 18–19 and 11:22–23 prior to the destruction of the earthly city.

Possibly this involves an element of polemic against Babylonian myth. We know that in ancient Babylon a ceremony of "the opening of the gates" was a feature of its New Year's festival. A gate that was normally closed would be opened for Marduk to exit and later return in procession through it. It is impossible to say whether the (poetic?) summons to the preexilic temple's gates to open to "the King of glory" (מֶלֶךְ הַכָּבוֹד, Ps 24:7–10) reflects some remotely comparable ceremony in the Israelite liturgy. Many superficial parallels to gates opened only for special occasions can be adduced throughout the world, but they probably have no relevance here.

Since the Glory had entered the temple in 43:1–12, the verb בָּא must be a perfect meaning that the God of Israel "has entered" through the gate (although the form itself could also be a participle). The LXX renders it as a future, εἰσελεύσεται, "will enter," possibly considering it a distant parallel to Zech 14:4–15.

This gate in Ezekiel's vision might be reminiscent of a similar gate near the Solomonic temple. Even though Solomon's temple had no *temenos* wall, there probably were gates in the surrounding structures, allowing access to the temple compound from nearby buildings, although we can only speculate about such gates. Excavations and architectural details confirm that the Herodian temple had a gate on the site of the present Golden Gate, which was rebuilt in the early Christian era, possibly because of the assumption, probably mistaken, that it was the same as the Beautiful Gate mentioned in Acts 3:2. Already in Byzantine times, the Golden Gate may have been closed periodically, and after the Crusader interval, its external entrances were walled shut and remain so today. Many traditions focus on the spot. There is a Muslim tradition that a Christian conqueror would ride through the gate. There are also Jewish and Muslim traditions that it is the gate through which the just will enter on Judgment Day. That is the reason for the large Muslim cemetery all around it and a corresponding Jewish one opposite it on the slopes of the Mount of Olives.

Some Christians think it was the gate through which Jesus entered Jerusalem on Palm Sunday. That might connect the gate through which "Yahweh/the Lord, the God of Israel" entered (Ezek 44:2) with the entrance of the Lord Jesus Christ, acclaimed as "he who comes in the name of the Lord, the King of Israel" (Jn 12:13). Jesus subsequently cleansed the temple precincts (Mt 21:12–13), and the temple was destroyed in A.D. 70, preventing any further admittance into it (cf. "must remain closed and not be opened," Ezek 44:2). Compare also the Christological significance of "the Prince" who alone is allowed to enter the gate in 44:3.

The Scriptures affirm the virginity of Mary at the time when she, by the power of the Holy Spirit, miraculously conceived Jesus Christ. They also affirm that Joseph had no relations with her until after the birth of the Savior (Mt

1:18–25).[3] Despite references in the Gospels to "brothers" and "sisters" of Jesus (e.g., Mt 12:46; Mk 6:3), a church tradition arose (perhaps partly to safeguard the doctrine of the virgin birth) that Mary remained a perpetual virgin, and some have also held that Jesus was born miraculously in such a way that Mary's uterus remained closed. Already early on, the church found in the permanently closed east gate in Ezek 44:2 a type (better, an allegory) of the *semper virgo* ("ever virgin") and *utero clauso* ("closed womb") components of its Mariological tradition.[4]

The Lutheran Symbols affirm the virginity of Mary in their confession of the person of Christ, God the Son, who was "conceived by the Holy Spirit, without the cooperation of man, and was born of the pure, holy, and virgin Mary" (SA I). The Latin translation of that last phrase uses *semper virgo*, but Luther's original German leaves unanswered the question of whether Mary remained a virgin even after the birth of Christ. The Formula confesses this about Christ: "He demonstrated his divine majesty even in his mother's womb in that he was born of a virgin without violating her virginity. Therefore she is truly the mother of God and yet remained a virgin" (FC SD VIII 24). Luther himself maintained the belief in Mary's perpetual virginity and closed womb, as have some traditional Lutherans (especially her perpetual virginity) down to the present day.[5]

44:3 The wording אֶת־הַנָּשִׂיא נָשִׂיא הוּא, literally, "the Prince, Prince—he … ," emphasizes his person. אֵת normally is the sign of a direct object, but sometimes Ezekiel uses it with a nominative and with emphatic force (see GKC, § 117 m, and the note on 43:7). The LXX and Syriac do not evidence the second נָשִׂיא, so some advocate dropping it as a dittograph, but the LXX often omits repetitive words, and the Vulgate and Targum attest the repeated נָשִׂיא (although they offer varying translations). With the pronoun, a literal trans-

---

[3] For an interpretation of these verses that affirms that the virgin conception and birth of Christ fulfilled the cited prophecy of Is 7:14, one may see Gibbs, *Matthew 1:1–11:1*, 99–103, 105–14.

[4] See the church fathers cited in AE 45:211, n. 23, and Gerhard, *On the Nature of Theology and Scripture*, § 387. Compare Song 4:12, which speaks of the beloved bride as "a garden locked" and "a fountain sealed," which has been interpreted in reference to the Virgin Mary, but which Lutherans traditionally have interpreted in reference to the church as the virgin bride of Christ and mother of baptized believers (Mitchell, *The Song of Songs*, 197–200, 226–27, 470, 868–73).

[5] See, for example, Luther, "The Day of the Holy Innocents" [Sermon on Matthew 2:13–23; 1541], in *Sermons of Martin Luther: The House Postils* (trans. Eugene F. A. Klug; Grand Rapids: Baker, 1996), 3:256; *Sermons on the Gospel of John* (AE 22:23; cf. 22:214–15); *That Jesus Christ Was Born a Jew* (45:205–6, 211–12); Gerhard, *On the Nature of Theology and Scripture*, § 387. Luther, *Confession concerning Christ's Supper*, says that Christ passing through the closed uterus of Mary can be attributed to his spiritual (or illocal) mode of presence: "He employed this mode of presence when he left the closed grave and came through closed doors [Jn 20:19, 26], in the bread and wine in the Supper, and, as people believe, when he was born in his mother" (AE 37:222–23, quoted in FC SD VII 100; see also Pieper, *Christian Dogmatics*, 2:307–8).

lation of נָשִׂיא הוּא would probably be "he as Prince," which I have followed, indicating that his special access to the gateway is a princely prerogative; "because he is Prince" would also be an appropriate translation (similar is NKJV). Block, following Boadt, understands the emphatically repeated נָשִׂיא after אֵת as have a limiting sense and translates, "and only the prince."[6]

This verse introduces us to "the Prince" for the first time in chapters 40–48. Further references to him will be in 45:7–9, 16–17, 22; 46:2, 4, 8, 10, 12, 16–18; 48:21–22. הַנָּשִׂיא ("the Prince") has the article, which probably is anaphoric (Joüon, § 137 f (3)), referring to the same "Prince" (נָשִׂיא), the Davidic Messiah, described earlier in 34:23–24 and 37:24–25 (see the commentary on those verses).[7]

The Prince's unique privilege to enter the gate through which Yahweh himself has passed (44:3) may mean that the Prince is no ordinary human, but God the Son, Jesus Christ. At the same time, the Prince cannot simply be equated with Yahweh, for the Prince cannot enter the gate from the east (from outside the temple compound, proceeding into the outer court), as Yahweh had done. Rather, the Prince must enter the closed east gate by means of a circuitous route: he must first enter the outer court through either the north or the south gate and then enter the east gate (whose outer entrance is occluded) through the vestibule, and he must leave the same way.[8] See figures 2 and 3. Hence the description of the Prince here (and also elsewhere in chapters 44–48) does not seem to emphasize his divine nature as much as did the more typical messianic descriptions of him in 34:23–24 and 37:24–25. On the other hand, in chapters 44–45 he is given a priestly office (see below and also on 45:7, 16–17) not mentioned in the earlier chapters.

The best explanation for the varying descriptions of the Prince would seem to be similar to what we have noted before.[9] The eschatological revelation given to Ezekiel often concentrates more on the "not yet" than on what is "now" fulfilled in Christ. The beauty and finality of the messianic age inaugurated by Jesus comes through clearly enough in Ezekiel, but it is still expressed in OT language. God's OT depiction of the coming Messiah is still concerned with alleviating the arrogant abuses perpetrated by Israel's kings and priests, and so

---

6   Block, *Ezekiel*, 2:613, including n. 4, citing Boadt, *Ezekiel's Oracles against Egypt*, 31.

7   Keil, *Ezekiel*, 2:300, identifies "the Prince" here with the Davidic "Prince" in 34:23–24; 37:24. The use of נָשִׂיא, "Prince," rather than מֶלֶךְ, "King," may be due to the infidelity of Israel's past kings, who are condemned as abusive "princes" in 45:8–9. On Ezekiel's preference for "prince" over "king," the second textual note on 7:27; the commentary on 12:10; and the second textual note on 21:30 (ET 21:25). His reluctance to speak of a "king" makes it all the more remarkable that Ezekiel does speak of the Davidic Messiah, Jesus Christ, as "King" (מֶלֶךְ) in 37:22, 24.

8   וּמִדַּרְכּוֹ יֵצֵא is, literally, "and from his way [the same way the Prince used to enter] he shall go out." Ezek 44:3b is repeated with only slight variation in 46:8, in regard to the Prince's entry into and exit out of the inner east gate. Predictably, critics construe the repetition as a reason to question the authenticity of 44:3 (see Zimmerli, *Ezekiel*, 2:439).

9   See, for example, the commentary on chapter 34 and "Introduction to Ezekiel 40–48."

the Messiah, while clearly a royal and priestly figure, is portrayed in humble, understated terms. Thus in chapters 40–48, he is the "Prince" instead of the "King" (only in 37:22, 24), and Zadokite priests[10] are also present in addition to the priestly "Prince." We in the church today can resonate with that same concern: in some respects the Messiah is a King and Priest who is unlike (even the opposite of) some of the leaders and clergy now present in the church militant. All members of the church on earth are "saint and sinner simultaneously" (*simul iustus et peccator*). Moreover, adherents of many denominations and factions of what we confess to be "the one holy catholic and apostolic church" (Nicene Creed) often comport themselves in ways that are scarcely "holy" and "apostolic," and many will disinherit themselves entirely from God's kingdom unless they repent and are renewed in faith and life (cf. 1 Cor 6:9–11; Gal 5:19–21).

The Prince may enter the gateway "to eat food" (Ezek 44:3; לֶחֶם could also be "bread"). But he enters not to do his ordinary dining there, since there he will eat it "before Yahweh" (לִפְנֵי יְהוָה). That implies that this meal has some function in the public liturgy, because Yahweh's entrance through that space had transformed it into an area of special sacrality. Traditionally, this unique privilege has been understood as conferring special priestly status on the Prince, a status that exceeds that of the Zadokite priests and Levites, for whom no provision is made to eat in this gate through which Yahweh has passed.[11] In Ezekiel 40–48 God says nothing about a high priest, and in some ways "the Prince" seems to assume that office; cf. the high priestly Christology of Hebrews 3–10. Additional references to the Prince, his priestly leadership and administrative role in worship, and his land will be in 45:7–9, 16–22; 46:2–18; 48:21–22.

Vision of the Glory and Admonition to Pay Close Attention (44:4–5)

44:4 A fresh encounter with Yahweh's Glory, now resident in the temple, ushers in a new section, in its full scope comprising the rest of the chapter. The overriding concern is still control of access to the sanctuary, but after a rebuke for Israel's past failures, the chapter moves into fairly detailed regulations, in the form of divine speech, regarding temple service by the Levites and priests. Ezek 44:4–5 serves as a sort of preamble. Formally, 44:4 is very similar to 43:3, 5 and 44:5 to 40:4.

Ezekiel does not specify whether he was taken to the outer or inner north gate, but since the gates of the inner court were eight steps (about four cubits) higher than the outer gates (40:31, 34, 37), the temple would only be visible

---

10 See on 40:46; 43:19; 44:15; 48:11.

11 Others construe it as a demotion to a status below both the priests and the Levites, intended as a polemic against royal encroachments upon exclusively priestly privileges before the exile. However, in 45:17 the Prince clearly has an administrative role over the entire sacrificial cultus, and in 46:2 the Prince is to stand in a position to oversee the priests as they offer sacrifice.

from the inner court. Neither does Ezekiel give any detailed description of the "Glory" here, but he had already done so in chapters 1 and 10–11, and to a lesser extent in 43:1–12, so here it sufficed merely to identify the "Glory of Yahweh" as the subject. Ezekiel's reaction, "I fell on my face" (44:4), is the same as it had been on previous occasions when he had seen Yahweh's Glory (1:28; 3:23; 43:3). For the divine Glory understood Christologically, see pages 1, 11, and 13 in the introduction, as well as the textual notes and commentary on 1:26–28.

44:5 The verse is virtually a summary of major concerns of not only this section, but of all the lessons to be learned from the temple measurements in chapters 40–43 (cf. 40:4; 43:10). Yahweh is described as speaking directly to Ezekiel, although it is possible that he does so through the supernatural guide (40:4; 43:6). For his address of Ezekiel as "son of man," see the second textual note and the commentary on 2:1.

שִׂים לִבְּךָ, literally, "set your heart," is idiomatic Hebrew for "pay attention." Linked here with stress on the use of both his visual and his aural faculties, it emphasizes the need to reflect deeply upon the inward, theological import of the regulations. The Hebrew has a chiastic structure: "see with your eyes, and with your ears hear." The rare use of the Piel participle מְדַבֵּר (elsewhere only in 1:28 and 2:8; cf. the Hithpael participle in 2:2 and 43:6), "I am speaking/telling," accents the verbal element. The similarity to 2:8 of the clause here with מְדַבֵּר and the language of the next verse lends credence to Block's suggestion that a sort of recommissioning of the prophet is intimated.[12]

Four phrases, in two pairs, summarize what requires attention. The first pair concerns regulations for activity within the sacred area, and the second pair governs access ("entrance" and "exits"). The order of these two pairs here is the reverse of the order of similar topics in 43:11, forming a kind of chiasm. Each of the first pair of phrases, describing the topic of the speech (לְכָל־חֻקּוֹת בֵּית־יְהוָה וּלְכָל־תּוֹרֹתָיו), "regarding all the regulations of the temple of Yahweh and all the instructions about it"), begins with the preposition לְ. So too does the third phrase, לִמְבוֹא הַבַּיִת, "to the entrance of the temple," and its לְ can be assumed to apply also to the fourth phrase. לְ is often used with verbs of looking and attending "to" (BDB, s.v. לְ, 1 a), and it can introduce the topic of a verb of saying (Waltke-O'Connor, § 11.2.10g, including example 53). The Qere תּוֹרֹתָיו, "its instructions," is clearly plural, whereas the Kethib, תורתו, probably is to be vocalized תּוֹרֹתוֹ, a defective spelling of the same. Instead of the singular (construct of מָבוֹא), "entrance," the Vulgate, Syriac, and Targum translate with a plural "entrances," corresponding to the following plural "exits" (in construct, מוֹצָאֵי). RSV and NRSV personalize the nouns "entrance" and "exits" into people, "those who may be admitted" and "those who are to be excluded," arbitrarily emending them into Hophal participles. (We might have expected a conjunctive *waw* before בְּכָל).

---

[12] Block, *Ezekiel*, 2:620.

The Legitimate Officiants for Worship (44:6–31)

44:6 The first clause, וְאָמַרְתָּ אֶל־מֶרִי, literally, "and you shall say to the rebellion," uses the abstract noun מְרִי (in pause, מֶרִי) in a concrete sense. Normally elsewhere in Ezekiel, Yahweh speaks of Israel as בֵּית מְרִי (sometimes with the article), "(the) house of rebellion" or "(the) rebellious house," a condemning substitute for "the house of Israel,"[13] which is in the next clause of 44:6, the appositional "to the house of Israel." Likewise, in 2:7–8 Yahweh twice used מְרִי concretely (literally, "they are rebellion," and, speaking to Ezekiel, "do not be rebellion"). Supplying "house" in the first clause here in 44:6, as did the LXX, gives a smoother translation, but the difference is slight.

רַב־לָכֶם מִכָּל־תּוֹעֲבוֹתֵיכֶם, literally, "much to you from all your abominations," uses two idioms, the adjective רַב and the preposition מִן, each of which can be used by itself in an elliptical comparison to mean "too much" (see Joüon, § 141 i). The idiom רַב־לָכֶם is also in 45:9, as well as, for example, Num 16:3, 7. The following מִן adds the emphasis of *more* than enough (cf. the obverse idiom with נָקֵל in 8:17; cf. also Is 49:6). This might be paraphrased as "I have had more than enough of all your abominations." For "abominations," a favorite term in Ezekiel, see, for example, the textual note on 16:2 and the commentary on 5:9, 11; 8:6–17; 33:26.

44:7 The syntax of this continuation of 44:6 is sometimes problematic, but the sense is clear. It uses בְּנֵי־נֵכָר, literally, "sons of a foreign land" instead of the more common זָרִים, "strangers, foreigners" (e.g., 7:21; 11:9; 16:32). Elsewhere in Ezekiel (except 16:32), זָרִים refers to "foreigners" who either are Yahweh's agents in punishing Israel or are nations under divine judgment themselves. The preference here for the phrase בְּנֵי־נֵכָר (and the singular בֶּן־נֵכָר, "a son of a foreign land," twice in 44:9) may arise from the use of נֵכָר for "foreign gods/idols" (e.g., Deut 31:16; 32:12; Josh 24:20, 23; Jer 8:19), underscoring the offense of these unauthorized persons performing a liturgical act—the precise past problem this verse is prohibiting. According to God's command in Gen 17:12 (which Abraham fulfilled in Gen 17:27), any person bought by Israelites from a בֶּן־נֵכָר, "son of a foreign land," was to be circumcised. But the ones condemned here were uncircumcised, both physically and spiritually, so their very presence in the temple, which God calls "my (own) house" (בֵּיתִי, an appositive to the object suffix on לְחַלְּלוֹ), is offensive, and this is compounded when they are allowed to join Israelites in sacrificing. "Uncircumcised in heart" (cf. Deut 10:16; 30:6; Jer 9:25) means they lacked the faith and piety requisite for acceptable sacrifice. The sacrifices are God's "food" (לֶחֶם, "bread"). For all the different types of animal sacrifice, the (inner) fat was burned on the altar, and the blood was sprinkled on the altar or poured at its base (see Leviticus 1–7).

While those foreigners who had previously been brought into the temple (Ezek 44:7) and are now banned from it (44:9) are both "uncircumcised in

---

[13] See the second textual note and the commentary on 2:5 and the third textual note on 3:1.

heart" and "uncircumcised in flesh," the mere distinction between the two is unusual in the OT, which usually assumes that those who are physically uncircumcised are also spiritually uncircumcised—unbelievers who are outside God's covenant of grace.[14] Likewise, the common OT assumption is that physical and spiritual circumcision go together.

However, this is not the only place where the OT stresses that not just the flesh, but also the heart must be circumcised (see also on 44:9).[a] In the new covenant in Christ, there is no religious necessity for circumcision of the flesh, as St. Paul argues against the Judaizers, especially in Galatians. Instead, the NT emphasis is on spiritual circumcision through Holy Baptism, faith in Christ, and the life of faith (Gal 3:26–29; Col 2:11–14). "For in Christ Jesus neither circumcision nor uncircumcision counts for anything, but only faith working through love" (Gal 5:6 ESV).

The verb וַיָּפֵרוּ (Hiphil of פָּרַר, Ezek 44:7) means "*they broke* my covenant" and must have the "foreigners" as its subject. The presence and activity in the temple by people who did not themselves stand in a covenant relationship to Yahweh was a violation of the covenant. That clause is followed by אֶל כָּל־תּוֹעֲבוֹתֵיכֶם, "in addition to all your [the Israelites'] abominations" (with אֶל used in the sense of עַל).[15] For the verb, the LXX, Syriac, and Vulgate have a second person plural, referring to the Israelites, which agrees with the other second plurals in the context and the fact that the charge is primarily against the Israelites, whose infidelity is so grievous that it can only be described by another occurrence of "abominations" (see on 44:6).

(a) See also, e.g., Lev 26:41; Deut 10:16; 30:6; Jer 4:4; 6:10; 9:25 (ET 9:26)

44:8 The idiom שָׁמַר מִשְׁמֶרֶת (used previously in 40:45–46) is liturgical vocabulary for faithfully performing worship service according to God's Word. In Ezekiel the emphasis seems to be on the priests as guardians and protectors of God's holy things, perhaps also involving guard duty at the gates, so it is translated "guard" (see the third textual note on 40:45). It will recur in 44:14–16 and 48:11. Zimmerli finds a wordplay in the two occurrences in the verse of מִשְׁמֶרֶת: the Israelites have not only failed in the "observances" of their own religious obligations, but allowed foreigners to participate in the divine "service" (in the liturgical sense).[16] "My holy things" (קֳדָשָׁי) can include everything related to the realm of the sacred. It is too broad a term to make a more precise application here.

The form וַתְּשִׂימוּן, translated, "but (you) appointed [others]," probably has a paragogic *nun* (so Joüon, § 44 e, and Waltke-O'Connor, § 31.7.1a, including example 1e). RSV and NRSV supply "foreigners," which is undoubtedly the referent. GKC, § 58 g, takes the *nun* as a feminine suffix and a simple scribal error for the masculine suffix. Cooke and Zimmerli note the possibility that it

---
[14] See the commentary on 28:10 and 32:19 and the last textual note on 32:30.

[15] Cooke, *Ezekiel*, 491.

[16] Zimmerli, *Ezekiel*, 2:454.

1272

is a masculine suffix by dissimilation (avoidance of another *mem* after מוֹ-) for the sake of euphony.[17] Block proposes that the confusion arose in use of the ancient (Phoenician) script where final *mem* and *nun* were not as sharply distinguished as in the square (Aramaic) orthography.[18]

44:9 This verse is transitional. On the one hand, it concludes 44:6–8 by stating a permanent prohibition of the laxity of previous generations of priests, who did not guard access to the holy sanctuary and its rites. But the citation formula, "thus says the Lord Yahweh,"[19] at the beginning of the verse indicates that it also introduces a new subsection of this oracle. Yahweh permits two groups to approach and carry out their respective roles in the temple: (1) the Levites (44:10–14) and (2) the Zadokites (44:15–16).

The construction כָּל־ ... לֹא יָבוֹא is, literally, "every" foreigner "shall not enter," but I have translated it as "no" foreigner "may enter." For עֲרֶל as a construct form of עָרֵל, see GKC, § 93 hh. The initial *lamed* on לְכָל־ may be emphatic (so GKC, § 143 e; Joüon, § 125 l, which compares it to the use of אֶת to introduce a nominative (as in 43:7); see Joüon, § 125 j (5)). In other Semitic languages too, *lamed* often functions emphatically. I have translated, "no foreigner *at all*." In its emphasis, it is also comprehensive, as in NIV, "not even," or NKJV, "including."[20]

Anyone who was not both physically and spiritually circumcised (see on 44:7) must be kept at a distance from the sanctuary. Only God could spiritually circumcise a person's heart (Deut 30:6), and the same emphasis on God's gracious action is expressed in Ezekiel using the only slightly different language of a "new S/spirit" and "new heart" in 11:19; 36:25–26 (see the commentary on those verses). Here too, the NT fulfillment is accomplished through the Sacrament of Christian Baptism, the antitype of circumcision (Col 2:11–13). Through baptismal incorporation into Christ, the division between Israelite and (Gentile) foreigner is overcome, so that both, as baptized believers, may approach God in holiness as his justified children (e.g., Acts 2:38–39; Gal 3:26–29; Eph 2:11–22; 4:5). The prohibition here of access to the temple by the uncircumcised may be compared to the eschatological banishment of unbelievers from the new Jerusalem in the eternal state in Rev 22:15.

44:10 All Levites (priests and non-priests) not descended from Zadok are in view in 44:10–14, but at times the focus seems to be on non-Zadok priests, with whom the Zadokites are then contrasted in 44:15–16. Except for the Zadokites, all the other Levitical priests are, in Ezekiel's vision, demoted to occupy the same inferior status as the non-priestly Levites. God states the reason

---

[17] Cooke, *Ezekiel*, 491; Zimmerli, *Ezekiel*, 2:448.

[18] Block, *Ezekiel*, 2:621, n. 43.

[19] For this formula, see pages 8–9 in the introduction and the fourth textual note and the commentary on 2:4.

[20] Cf. Waltke-O'Connor, § 11.2.10h, including example 62, which takes the *lamed* as appositional.

for the demotion of the (non-Zadokite) Levitical priests in 44:10, 12 and his reason for retaining the Zadokites in their priestly office in 44:15.

The strong adversative in כִּי אִם־הַלְוִיִּם, "however, the Levites … ," contrasts this verse with the previous verse, which prohibited entrance, implying that the Levites are granted entrance, as 44:11 will state. "May enter" could be supplied from יָבוֹא in the previous verse, since a continuation of a verbal idea can be seen following כִּי אִם also in 33:11; 36:22; 44:22. By itself עָוֹן usually means "iniquity," but with the verb נָשָׂא, "bear, suffer," it implies the consequent "punishment."

At the golden calf incident, the Levites had remained loyal to Yahweh (Ex 32:25–29). God elected the entire tribe, as a collective "firstborn" from all the tribes (Num 3:41, 45; 8:15–19), to be his ministerial servants (Ex 32:29; Num 1:49–53; Deut 10:8–9). He had established their office as a kind of covenant (Jer 33:21; Mal 2:4–5; Neh 13:29). In particular, the Levites were charged with protecting the holiness of the sanctuary by preventing lay access (Num 18:21–23). But now the Levites are charged with having gone astray from Yahweh by participating in idolatry with "fecal deities" (Ezek 44:10, 12).[21] This participation was both by active involvement in priestly service before idols, and, passively, by failing to oppose and curtail idolatry. Examples of such apostasy can be found throughout the history of the existence of the tabernacle (Moses to Solomon) and temple (Solomon to Ezekiel's day). Already in Moses' lifetime Korah, from the tribe of Levi, led a large number of Israelites into perdition (Numbers 16). Throughout the long periods of mass syncretism and apostasy recorded in Kings, the Levites were undoubtedly just as culpable as the unfaithful priests.

The old higher-critical theory read this verse and the rest of the chapter as evidence of a political struggle between the Zadokites and the other Levitical priests for hegemony within the priesthood after the exile. According to that theory, the rest of the chapter is polemical or judgmental. That view is inseparable from critical assumptions that Ezekiel's viewpoint was adopted by "P," the alleged priestly stratum of the Pentateuch, and eventually canonized. But such a mindset is utterly incompatible with the entire biblical witness, as it stands, and for that reason cannot be entertained by any serious exegete or orthodox, confessional theologian. Furthermore, the idioms of typical judgment oracles are absent from this verse, so we must construe it as constructive in intent, not destructive. The past lapse is not overlooked, and so to "bear their punishment" (44:10, 12), the (non-Zadokite) Levitical priests are limited to serving "before them [the people]" (44:11), as did the non-priestly Levites. Of the priests, only the Zadokites will be given the privilege of performing the most sacred ceremonies (44:15–16) under the supervision of the Prince, who will supply the sacrifices (45:17).

---

[21] See the fourth textual note on 6:4.

44:11 The Piel of the verb שָׁרַת, "to serve," occurs three times in this verse, giving three duties to all the non-Zadokite Levites. At least the first two times, the verb is a technical term for liturgical service in general. Thus the (non-Zadokite) Aaronites who formerly were priests are demoted to the same level as non-priestly Levites. They will not be laymen, but, like the other Levites, a class of ministers. They will not stand before Yahweh as priests, but will "stand before them [the people] to serve them" (see below).

In apposition to מְשָׁרְתִים, "serving," is the first duty: פְּקֻדּוֹת אֶל־שַׁעֲרֵי הַבַּיִת, "(as) guards over the gates of the temple." This duty is summarized by the following וּמְשָׁרְתִים אֶת־הַבָּיִת, "and ministering in the temple." The feminine abstract noun פְּקֻדָּה, "charge, office," can be used concretely for a (male) "overseer" (BDB, 2 b), here specifically a "guard." In 9:1 the angelic פְּקֻדּוֹת were "supervisors" over Jerusalem, who were commissioned to execute Yahweh's judgment on the unfaithful. In 2 Ki 11:18 the term is used for the guards whom the priest Jehoiada posted around the temple when Joash was proclaimed king and the usurper Athaliah was deposed.

The second duty is that the slaughter of the sacrificial animals is assigned to the non-Zadokite Levites. According to Leviticus 1 and 3, laymen traditionally had killed their own sacrificial animals, but in Ezekiel's vision laymen are not even allowed in the inner court. All evidence indicates that in the second temple period laymen continued to do the slaughtering, except probably at major festivals, when enormous numbers of animals were sacrificed. That the strictures in Ezekiel 40–48 were not implemented by Israel after the exile is an indication of the vision's eschatological orientation; God does not intend for his people to attempt to implement the vision literally (see "Introduction to Ezekiel 40–48"). The same two terms for sacrifice, הָעֹלָה, "the burnt offering," and הַזֶּבַח, literally, "the sacrifice," referring to all the other kinds of sacrifices, were in 40:42 (see the third textual note there).

The third duty is general: "they will stand before them [the people] to serve them" (וְיַעַמְדוּ לִפְנֵיהֶם לְשָׁרְתָם). Both suffixes ("them") refer to the people. This is a technical expression for some official service and recalls Num 16:9, where it is stated that the Levites were commissioned "to stand before the congregation to serve them." Other contexts speak of all Israel (Lev 9:5; Deut 4:10; 2 Chr 20:13) or the Levites (Deut 10:8) "standing before Yahweh" (עָמַד לִפְנֵי יהוה).

44:12 The status and role of the Levites is rehearsed a second time in 44:12–14, but this time with greater accent on their past failures, and in contrast to the role of the Zadokites, which will be spelled out in 44:15–16. Ezek 44:12 has the standard form of a judgment oracle: "because [יַעַן אֲשֶׁר] ... therefore [עַל־כֵּן]." The Piel of שָׁרַת, "to serve," appears again, but with the charge that the Levites' service had once been in the employ of an idolatrous cult instead of Yahweh, and to the detriment rather than benefit of God's people, and so the Levites became a stumbling block (cause of sin). יְשָׁרְתוּ אוֹתָם (literally, "they served them [the people]") has a frequentative imperfect. Instead of וְהָיוּ

1275

("they became"), we might have expected an imperfect with *waw* consecutive (וַיְהִיוּ), but such forms declined in Late Biblical Hebrew. The verb forms here may have durative force: "they continually ministered and so always became …" (GKC, § 112 e, footnote 1).

The scurrilous term for the dung-idols (גִּלּוּלִים; see the fourth textual note on 6:4) is about as much a part of Ezekiel's trademark vocabulary as the result to Israel: מִכְשׁוֹל־עָוֹן, literally, "a stumbling block of (which causes) iniquity."[22] Already KJV paraphrased, "and caused the house of Israel to fall into iniquity," and many English translations have essentially followed suit. Consequently, Yahweh "raised [his] hand" to signal an oath—not to bring blessing, as the idiom is often used, but punishment. (Usually, as in 20:5–6, 15, 23, 28, the idiom uses לְ; only here is עַל used.) The use of the signatory formula, "says the Lord Yahweh,"[23] lends decisiveness to the oath.

44:13 In this verse the status of the (non-Zadokite) Levites as one rung below the (Zadokite) priests is reaffirmed. The idiom with נָגַשׁ, "to approach, come near," Yahweh, is often used for the liturgical service of priests (e.g., Ex 19:22; Lev 21:21), and so it, qualified by לְכַהֵן לִי, "to be a priest for me," is prohibited for the Levites. Two expressions, "my holy things" (קָדָשַׁי) and "the most holy things/offerings" (קָדְשֵׁי הַקֳּדָשִׁים) are used to describe objects or activities that are reserved for the priests. "Offerings" is used in the translation of the superlative because the superlative was used in Num 18:9 of the same sacrifices listed in Ezek 44:29. In Num 18:3 (as elsewhere in Numbers), the simple "holy things" had been applied to various objects associated with the tabernacle, so the superlative here would likely include temple furnishings too.

In the light of Ezekiel's usage of כְּלִמָּה, "disgrace, shame," it would be a mistake to take the statement that the Levites would "bear their shame" as synonymous with their bearing of their "punishment" (עָוֹן) in 44:10, 12. In 16:52, 54, 63, Ezekiel used כְּלִמָּה, "shame," in the context of salvation, not judgment. There and here it describes the sense of unworthiness and hence of renewed gratitude and responsibility of a penitent who has been forgiven and restored. The reference to their previous "abominations" (as in 44:6–7) must describe what they are now ashamed of.

44:14 As a sort of sequel to 44:11, this verse gives a positive statement of the role envisioned for the Levites. Being "temple guards" involved more than watching the gates and internal entrances and exits. The Levites are to assist in the maintenance of all that is involved in the sanctuary's worship activities. Like the English "divine service," עֲבֹדָה may refer to *Gottesdienst*, to liturgical service on behalf of God, as well as any other kind of service. Here the ac-

---

[22] See the textual note and the commentary on מִכְשׁוֹל in 3:20. For the phrase, see the second textual note and the commentary on 7:19 as well as the commentary on 14:3. The phrase is also in 14:4, 7; 18:30.

[23] For this formula, see pages 8–9 in the introduction and the second textual note on 5:11.

cent is more on the latter, albeit within the temple precincts. In Numbers 4, עֲבֹדָה, "service," was used of the heavy manual labor of setting up and dismantling the tabernacle as it was moved from camp to camp, but since the temple was not portable, in this context the term must refer to the work of servicing everything. The overall point is that, with their past lapses forgotten and forgiven, the Levites are now fully rehabilitated and recommissioned.

44:15 This is the first of two verses devoted to the role of the Zadokites, who alone will be priests, in contrast to all the other Levites in 44:10–14. Structurally, these two verses are formulated just as 44:10–13 were, first recollecting past behavior, and then prescribing how it will be in the future.

"The Levitical priests" (וְהַכֹּהֲנִים הַלְוִיִּם) is the phrase from Deuteronomy (17:9, 18; 18:1; 24:8; 27:9) used to distinguish the legitimate priests from illegitimate competitors, such as those later instituted in the Northern Kingdom (1 Ki 12:31). All the legitimate priests were sons of Aaron, within the tribe of Levi. Thus all priests were Levites, but not all Levites were priests. The other Levites not descended from Aaron served at the tabernacle (later, the temple) but carried out only secondary ministerial service. Aaron had four sons, but Nadab and Abihu perished (without heirs [Num 3:4]) because of their liturgical infidelity (Lev 10:1–2). Therefore all of the Levitical priests were descended from one of Aaron's remaining two sons, Eleazar and Ithamar.

In Ezekiel's vision, God adds the further stipulation that only those descended from Zadok are to be priests. Zadok the priest was the son of Ahitub, from the line of Phinehas, son of Eleazar, a son of Aaron (1 Chr 5:27–34 [ET 6:1–8]). During Absalom's rebellion against his father, King David, the priests Zadok and Abiathar (who apparently was high priest) remained faithful to David (2 Samuel 15–18). However, subsequently Abiathar participated in the ordination of Adonijah as king to succeed David, without David's approval. King David had Zadok anoint Solomon as his rightful successor (1 Kings 1). Solomon then expelled Abiathar from the priesthood, banished him, and promoted Zadok to be high priest in his place (1 Kings 2). Abiathar was a descendant of Aaron through his son Ithamar (1 Chr 24:3) and was apparently the last priest from the line of Eli (1 Sam 22:6–23; 1 Ki 2:26–27). Solomon's expulsion of Abiathar from the priesthood was in fulfillment of the prophecy given young Samuel at Shiloh that about the decline of Eli's descendants (1 Sam 2:30–36; 1 Ki 2:27).

Keil's explanation hints that just as Zadok supported David, "the prince," the Zadokites are given the role of serving as priests under the supervision of "the Prince" (see Ezek 45:16–17), who was previously described as "David" (34:23–24; 37:24–25):

> From this attitude of Zadok toward David, the prince given by the Lord to His people, it may be seen at once that he not only kept aloof from the wandering of the people, but offered a decided opposition thereto, and attended to his office in a manner that was well-pleasing to God. As he received the high-priesthood from Solomon in the place of Abiathar for this fidelity of his, so

shall his descendants only be invested with the priestly office in the new temple."[24]

The faithfulness of the Zadokites must be interpreted in relative, not absolute, terms, and in harmony with the biblical doctrines of justification and sanctification. Like all fallen humans, they too were sinners, and like all believers, those who were believers were justified by grace alone. In terms of their sanctified life of faith, the Zadokites had, by the power of God's grace, remained faithful to their divine calling and had avoided the major lapses into which other priests had fallen (beginning with Nadab and Abihu in Leviticus 10; cf. Rom 8:13).

Of course, in the Christian church the ordination of men to be pastors is not in any way based on ancestry or ethnic origin, but instead is based on the biblical requirements for the pastoral office in passages such as 1 Timothy 2–3 and Titus 1, as well as on education and training. The church readily recognizes that pastors too are sinners as well as saints justified by grace alone. All have their faults and have made their mistakes, large and small. Nevertheless, it is proper for the church to differentiate between those shortcomings that can and should be tolerated and those sins that are proper cause for removal from the pastoral office (false doctrine, scandalous behavior, or gross malfeasance). The demotion of the non-Zadokite priests serves as a reminder for every man in the holy ministry to continue to strive to serve with complete fidelity to God's Word, lest he forfeit his office in the church.

In Ezekiel's vision, the Zadokites alone can "approach" Yahweh in proper liturgical service to offer him the fat and the blood of the sacrifices (Ezek 44:15), while the other Levites could only assist the laymen in preparing the offerings (44:10–14). The verb here for "approach" (יִקְרְבוּ, the Qal of קָרַב) is cognate to the adjective קָרוֹב in 42:13 and 43:19, which also described the priests (the sons of Zadok) as those who "approach" God (the same meaning that the participle קָרֵב has in 40:46 and 45:4). These terms parallel the use of the Hiphil of the verb, הִקְרִיב, literally, "bring near, offer," regularly used for offering sacrifices (as later in this verse, as well as 43:22–24; 44:7, 27; 46:4; see also, e.g., Lev 1:2–3, 5).

While not an exact equivalent, the thought here is parallel to customary practice in the Christian church that only a called and ordained pastor is to consecrate the Lord's Supper. However, commissioned ministers, elders, or deacons may help distribute Communion under his supervision, and they, as well as lay members, may participate in worship in a variety of other ways.

44:16 Furthermore, while the Levites were restricted to the gates and courtyards, the Zadokite priests had ready access to the temple itself. Only they could function liturgically at Yahweh's "table." The same noun (שֻׁלְחָן) was in

---

[24] Keil, *Ezekiel*, 2:311.

41:22 (which see), where what appeared to be an altar turned out to be a "table." As noted there, the only piece of furniture in the tabernacle or temple that was a "table" in any literal sense was that holding the bread of the Presence or shew-bread. Functionally, that table within the nave or Holy Place was a counterpart to the grain offerings burned on the great altar outside in the courtyard. Yet that altar itself and its chief inner counterpart, the incense altar at the entrance to the Holy of Holies, were far more central objects in the Israelite ritual than was the table.

Since the preceding clause was "they alone may enter my sanctuary," the "table" would seem more likely to refer to either of the two inner objects than to the bronze altar outside (described in 43:13–17). In any case, like the reference to Yahweh's "food" in 44:7, the word must be taken as a figure of speech, and not literalistically. As mentioned earlier, the ritual of setting a table to aliment a deity was central in the surrounding heathen cultures, but is explicitly repudiated in the Bible. Like the sexual activity of the pagan gods and goddesses, that anthropomorphism too is inapplicable to the one true and triune God.

Finally, in drawing the contrast, Yahweh asserts that while the Levites guarded the "house" (temple [44:14]), the Zadokites did guard duty for God himself (44:16).

We should note that in this whole summary of priestly worship there is no mention of any high priest, the Day of Atonement, or the Holy of Holies (entered by the high priest on that day alone [Leviticus 16]). This is yet another indication that Ezekiel's vision is not a restoration of the old Mosaic legislation,[25] but eschatological, anticipating the NT era, and beyond that, the eternal state (Revelation 21–22). See further "Introduction to Ezekiel 40–48."

44:17–31 The rest of chapter 44 contains a collection of various regulations about the conduct of the priests. We hear nothing more about the Levites. Neither are "the sons of Zadok" named again after 44:15, although these priests are the implied subjects of the verbs (which in Hebrew lack explicit subjects) until 44:21. This makes for a smooth transition from the earlier part of the chapter to the present one. Most of the rules are identical with those of the Mosaic Torah, although some tightening is in evidence.

44:17–19 First, Yahweh attends to the priestly clothing. The idea underlying these verses (and also 44:20) is that their external appearance should mirror their internal, official disposition as ministers of God. The topic is not simply liturgical vestments, but that is included. Nor is the thought identical with our colloquial "clothes make the man," but neither are the two totally un-

---

[25] Critics who believe that the Torah was not given through Moses (fifteenth century B.C.) but was finalized (especially by the addition of the priestly material in "P") only in the postexilic era can entertain the possibility that these things developed later than the exilic time of Ezekiel and so the prophet does not mention them because he was unaware of them. However, such speculation obviously flies in the face of the biblical data.

related. The same thought surely applies to Christian clergymen too, whether in liturgical vestments or not.

44:17 פִּשְׁתִּים is virtually always found in the plural (of a presumed singular פֵּשֶׁת) and can refer to flax, but usually to linen cloth made from flax. (In 40:3 it was used of a cord or rope.) In his earlier vision of the Jerusalem temple, Ezekiel had seen a scribe wearing priestly garb, "dressed in linen," using בַּדִּים, the plural of בַּד, the term for ordinary linen (9:2–3, 11; 10:2, 6–7). He had also used שֵׁשׁ (e.g., 16:10; 27:7) and בּוּץ (27:16) for fine luxury linen. The first two synonyms were also used in Pentateuchal parallels for priestly garments: בַּד in, for example, Ex 28:42; Lev 6:3; 16:4, and שֵׁשׁ in, for example, Ex 28:6, 8, 39. Probably there is no significance in the choice of פִּשְׁתִּים here versus another synonym. Yahweh does, however, underscore the importance of "linen" by stating the antithesis: "no wool [צֶמֶר] should be on them."

44:18 Two items of clothing are chosen as examples. פְּאֵר is a rather general term for a "turban" or "headdress." It is used for the priestly turban in Ex 39:28; for a headdress for women in Is 3:20; and for the head covering of Ezekiel (24:17) and the Israelites (24:23). There is little doubt that the priestly "turban" is what is meant here, even though that is usually labeled a מִצְנֶפֶת (e.g., Ex 28:4, 37; 39:28) and once a צָנִיף (Zech 3:5).

The second article of clothing is the plural noun whose absolute form probably is מִכְנָסַיִם. In the OT it is always in construct with a word for "linen" and occurs elsewhere only in Ex 28:42; 39:28; Lev 6:3 (ET 6:10); 16:4, always for priestly clothing. Various euphemisms are used in translation: "breeches" (KJV, RSV), "drawers," or "undergarments" (NIV, NRSV, which is a little too broad). I have not hesitated to use the everyday "shorts," because, as its presumed dual form (מִכְנָסַיִם) indicates, it was a garment with two openings for the legs. Perhaps "boxer shorts" would be more precise, possibly reaching down to the knees (see Ex 28:42), although we do not know their exact appearance. The law in Ex 28:42; 39:28; Lev 6:3 (ET 6:10); 16:4 that a priest on duty must wear "shorts" is to avoid indecent exposure (Ex 28:42), which probably was common in the pagan fertility religions, but those passages say nothing about sweat.

The reason Ezekiel gives for the preference for linen is לֹא יַחְגְּרוּ בַּיָּזַע, literally, "and they will not gird themselves in sweat," that is, in heavy material like wool, which induces sweat. The noun יֶזַע (in pause, יָזַע) is a hapax, but is obviously related to another hapax, זֵעָה, "sweat," in Gen 3:19, and there is no doubt about its meaning. An Akkadian cognate is also known. Ezekiel does not specify the reason for avoiding "sweat," but as most commentators suggest, like other human excretions (see Leviticus 15; Deut 23:13–15 [ET 23:12–14]), sweat may have been considered to produce uncleanness, which would suggest spiritual uncleanness as well. The resulting disagreeable body odor would readily reinforce that impression. Also, since part of the curse due to man's fall into sin is that he must toil with "sweat" (Gen 3:19), the absence of "sweat" here points toward the removal of the curse, the restoration of man to his original state of righteousness before God, which is the divine purpose of OT and

NT worship, in which the priest or pastor serves as mediator between God and the congregation. Compare also the eschatological promises in Ps 121·6 and Rev 21:23.

44:19 Most Hebrew manuscripts repeat אֶל־הֶחָצֵר הַחִיצוֹנָה, "to the outer court," but the repeated phrase is absent in some Hebrew manuscripts and in the LXX, Syriac, and Vulgate, so it may be dittographical. It could possibly be defended as wishing to associate the outer court with the people, but that thought is present even without it.

Even though בֶּגֶד is a general term for "clothing," בִּגְדֵיהֶם is translated as "their vestments" to distinguish these from the priests' everyday attire. The "holy rooms" (לִשְׁכֹת הַקֹּדֶשׁ) in (בְּ) which the priests are to "leave, store" (וְהִנִּיחוּ, second Hiphil conjugation of נוּחַ) their vestments are those described earlier in the temple tour (42:1–14). The reason given for the necessity of the change of clothing must be paraphrased and explained. וְלֹא־יְקַדְּשׁוּ אֶת־הָעָם בְּבִגְדֵיהֶם says, literally, "they shall not sanctify the people by their clothes." The same concern about transmitting holiness, but by the holy sacrifices, is expressed by a negative purpose clause at the end of 46:20.

In OT liturgical theology, holiness is "contagious" in that it is transmitted by God through his means of grace and can be acquired through contact with "most holy" things.[26] Our tendency to limit holiness to ethics makes such theology difficult to understand, but the biblical concept of holiness has a dynamic to it. It could be compared to an electric current that is lethal if it comes in contact with people who are not already "charged" with it. The classical examples are of those who improperly touched or even looked at the ark of the covenant: the seventy men of Beth-shemesh in 1 Sam 6:19 and Uzzah in 2 Sam 6:6–9. Apparently, Yahweh here is tightening the Mosaic Law. While the Torah prohibited lay contact with the sanctuary and its contents in general (Num 4:15), it did not explicitly prohibit lay contact with the sacerdotal vestments.

44:20 Both extremes of hair "styles" are to be avoided. The Piel of גָּלַח means "to shave." The opposite is denoted by the idiom of the Piel verb שִׁלַּח, "let loose," with the object פֶּרַע, "loose, uncut hair." The clause כָּסוֹם יִכְסְמוּ is the Qal infinitive absolute and imperfect of the verb כָּסַם, which occurs only here in the OT, but in the context must mean "trim, clip" hair. Its direct object, אֶת־רָאשֵׁיהֶם, is only "their heads," but "the hair of" is implied and must be supplied in English.

These commands are not new. In fact, the Torah parallels are more extensive. Yahweh may take for granted that the priests should observe the additional Torah commands regarding hair, or, perchance, the improper conduct he does not mention here had fallen into desuetude and no longer needed to be prohibited. The prohibition against shaving the head (or part of it) is legislated

---

[26] See Kleinig, *Leviticus*, 5–13. For the most holy food and its transmission of holiness, see Lev 6:10–22 (ET 6:17–29).

in Lev 21:5, which adds proscriptions of shaving the edges of the beard or "cutting of the flesh." Prohibitions of uncut hair appear in connection with mourning: Lev 10:6 (death of Nadab and Abihu); 21:10. Making oneself bald is mentioned in Ezek 7:18 and 27:31 as a sign of mourning (also in Jer 16:6; Micah 1:16). When Ezekiel's wife died, he was commanded to keep his turban on, that is, not let his hair hang loose (24:17; see also 24:23).

The frequent connection of these behaviors with mourning makes it likely that these were not only private customs, but were connected with pagan cults of the dead. Furthermore, some contexts indicate that they were signs of disfigurement (see Lev 19:27–28; 21:5), and Block properly asks, "If the sacrificial animals were to be without defect or blemish, how much more those functionaries who stand before the holy God in service?"[27]

44:21 This injunction is a reformulation of Lev 10:9. The reason is not hard to find—not teetotalism, which is nowhere a biblical rule (except in special, isolated instances), but simply loss of the full, rational use of one's faculties, for some people after imbibing only small amounts of liquor. I have translated לֹא־יִשְׁתּוּ כָּל־כֹּהֵן בְּבוֹאָם, literally, "they shall not drink, every priest, when they enter," as "no priest is to drink … when he enters."

44:22 Ezekiel's formulation is again slightly briefer than its Torah antecedents. Both in Leviticus and in Ezekiel, God's concern about priests' spouses is based on concern with the spheres of holiness in which the priests work and exist.[28] God's design is for marriage to be lifelong and to display the mutual love between Yahweh and Israel (Song of Songs), and between Christ and his church (Eph 5:21–33).

Lev 21:7 prohibits priests from marrying a prostitute, a defiled woman,[29] or a divorced woman, and the reason is because "he [the priest] is holy to his God." Ezekiel says nothing about prostitutes, perhaps because such a marriage would so obviously be wrong (but cf. Hosea 1–2), or perhaps because in his eschatological vision there would be no prostitutes among God's repentant and restored people (cf. Rev 21:27; 22:15). Divorce is the result of sin on the part of one or both of the spouses and involves a violation of the holy estate of marriage (Mt 5:31–32; 19:3–12; 1 Cor 7:10–16).[30]

Lev 21:14–15 has slightly stricter prohibitions for the high priest. In addition to the prohibitions for all priests from marrying a divorced woman, defiled woman, or prostitute, it prohibits the high priest from marrying a widow and mandates that he must marry an Israelite virgin. God's reason is that "I am Yahweh, who sanctifies him." Ezekiel 40–48 says nothing about a high priest, but

---

27 Block, *Ezekiel*, 2:641.

28 For outlines of the realms and degrees of holiness, see Kleinig, *Leviticus*, 6, 9.

29 This might refer to a cultic prostitute, as was common in the pagan fertility religions, or perhaps to a woman who had been raped. For the possibilities, see Kleinig, *Leviticus*, 446.

30 On Mt 5:31–32, one may see Gibbs, *Matthew 1:1–11:1*, 290–96, and for a discussion 1 Cor 7:10–16 and its practical implications, one may see Lockwood, *1 Corinthians*, 237–44.

to some extent "the Prince" fulfills his role (see on 44:3). In Ezekiel the Levit-ical prohibition against the high priest marrying a widow is applied to all priests, probably because death is an unclean intrusion into the realm of the holy (cf. Lev 21:1–4; 11; but see also 1 Cor 7:8–9, 39–40). However, in Ezekiel, Yahweh makes an exception in the case of the widow of a priest. She had al-ready been connected with the priestly sphere through her deceased husband. Compare Lev 22:13, which speaks about the widowed daughter of a priest.

44:23–24 These verses shift from prohibitions to positive commands on public duties of the priests. Formally, they differ from the context because Yah-weh speaks in the first person in them and refers to the audience as "my peo-ple."

44:23 This verse is loosely based on Lev 10:10–11.[b] OT priests had the responsibility to teach God's Word to the people, and this is no less true for the office of pastor established in the NT.[c]

The first verb, יוֹרוּ (Hiphil imperfect of יָרָה), "teach," is related to the noun תּוֹרָה, *torah*. The second verb, יוֹדִעֵם (Hiphil imperfect of יָדַע with datival suf-fix), literally, "they will make known to them," is related to the noun דַּעַת, "knowledge," which, however, never occurs in Ezekiel.

"The holy and the common" (sacred versus profane) is a merism that is shorthand for a theological system of classification, while "the unclean" ver-sus "the clean" is a more anthropological system.[31] "Holy" implies nearness to the presence of God and his sanctifying power. "The common" stands at some distance from God, but is still good. "Clean" refers to the proper, healthy con-dition of life as intended by God for his creation, whereas "unclean" implies some loss of life or health, some disruption in God's creation caused by the in-trusion of evil. The entire worship system instituted in the OT was designed not simply to distinguish between these categories, but to provide sanctifica-tion and cleansing for the people, to save them from sin and all its evil effects, and to bring them into communion with their saving God. That divine purpose has now been fulfilled through the incarnation, holy life, atoning death, and resurrection of Jesus Christ, who sanctifies and cleanses his church through his Word and Sacraments (see, e.g., Eph 5:26).

44:24 Instead of "dispute," רִיב might be rendered "lawsuit," but of course the OT had quite a different system of jurisprudence than the modern West. Formal legal action appears to be the subject here. The "dispute" (רִיב) is the referent of the suffix on the verb יִשְׁפְּטוּהוּ (Kethib: וּשְׁפָּטֻהוּ), "render judgment about it."

The idiom יַעַמְדוּ לְמִשְׁפָּט is, literally, "they shall stand for judgment" (cf. מִשְׁפָּט and רִיב in 2 Chr 19:8). The Kethib לִשְׁפֹּט, "stand *to judge*," is supported by the LXX, Syriac, and Targum. "Stand" may reflect the later OT practice (due to Babylonian influence?) of the judge standing. The earlier practice was

(b) See also Deut 4:9–10; 6:6–7; 33:8–10; Ezek 22:26; Hos 4:6; Mal 2:7

(c) 1 Cor 4:17; 1 Tim 2:12; 3:2; 4:11; 2 Tim 2:2, 24; Titus 2:1

---

[31] For these two systems of classification, see further Kleinig, *Leviticus*, 6–10.

for the litigants to stand while the judge sat (Ex 18:13; see also Num 35:12). However, "stand" may simply be an idiom for "officiate" and imply nothing about the judge's posture. This may be supported by the use of the Hiphil of עָמַד in 2 Chr 19:8 for "appointing" priests and Levites to be judges (cf. also 2 Chr 19:5).

בְּמִשְׁפָּטַי יִשְׁפְּטֻוהוּ, "according to my judgments they shall render judgment about it," is one of those rare instances where the common Hebrew use of a verb and cognate noun as object can be idiomatically reproduced in English. The בְּ indicates the standard or principle "according to" which justice is determined.

The role of the priests in jurisprudence is very evident in early Israel (see Deut 17:8–13; 21:1–9). It may have waned or been suppressed under the monarchy (cf. Jehoshaphat in 2 Chr 19:4–11), but when kings ruled no more, the priests would naturally come to the fore again. Ezekiel probably experienced this personally in the exilic community, and after the return, the short-lived diarchy of high priest and king (Joshua and Zerubbabel) soon dissolved into an active priesthood alone.

Finally, they must set a good example in behavior. Ezekiel mentions only liturgical contexts, but in the OT, theology and ethics were bound up with them. I have avoided "laws" as a translation of תּוֹרֹת in favor of its etymological "instructions." In a theocracy, an aspect of "Law" would inevitably be entailed, but the "Gospel" aspect underlying these practices should be emphasized.

"Like people, like priest" (Hos 4:9). The experience of the church too has been that laxity, indifference, and even rank heresy starts at the top. Or whenever it starts, if it is not dealt with at that level, it will slowly but surely metastasize and spread throughout the whole body (1 Cor 5:6–7; Gal 5:9).

44:25–27 Ezek 44:25–27 concerns itself with priestly deportment around the dead. Since the triune God is the "Lord and giver of *life*" (confessed about the Spirit in the Third Article of the Nicene Creed), as exemplified in 37:1–14, death is intrinsically something antithetical to him, something unclean.

Nevertheless, Jesus had contact with the dead in order to raise them (e.g., Lk 7:11–15), and he himself died and was buried before rising on Easter. In that way he has hallowed the graves of all who die in faith. This is expressed in a traditional graveside prayer:

> Almighty God, by the death of Your Son Jesus Christ You destroyed death, by His rest in the tomb You sanctified the graves of Your saints, and by His bodily resurrection You brought life and immortality to light so that all who die in Him abide in peace and hope.[32]

In light of the ministry and resurrection of Christ, Christians have tended to attenuate the OT rules about death into mere reminders that universal mortality is "the wages of sin" (Rom 6:23). Pastors, of course, are called not to

---

[32] *Lutheran Service Book: Agenda* (St. Louis: Concordia, 2006), 130.

avoid the dead, but to minister to the dying and to grieving families, perform funerals, and commemorate the departed saints. The church properly observes many customs about the burial of the dead out of respect for the sanctity of the body—which had been created by God and received Holy Baptism and the Sacrament of Christ's body and blood—and to express the belief in the biblical doctrine of the bodily resurrection on the Last Day. In contrast, those with no hope in Christ for the resurrection of the body often treat it with disdain and may forego burial for cremation. The scriptural precedent in both Testaments favors burial, and while Scripture does not forbid cremation, that practice historically has been associated with religions that deny the resurrection of the body. The neo-paganistic assertion that "death is a part of life" is hard to distinguish from the ancient, circular "myth of the eternal return" as still found in the Hindu religion.

44:25 The first verb of the verse is singular, יָבוֹא, apparently referring to an individual priest, but is translated as plural by the LXX, Syriac, and Vulgate. Some deem it a metathetical error for יָבֹאוּ since the verse concludes with the plural verb יִטַּמָּאוּ (Hithpael imperfect of טָמֵא; see GKC, § 19 d). However, 44:26 begins with a singular reference (the suffix on טָהֳרָתוֹ) to a priest. לְטָמְאָה ("to become unclean," 44:25) is a so-called feminine form of the Qal infinitive construct of טָמֵא (see Joüon, § 49 d). The exceptions (dead people the priests may approach) are connected by *waw* except for לְאָח, though many manuscripts and versions supply it.

One may well ask why the priest's wife is not mentioned. The traditional answer is that she is implied because she is nearer to him than any of the other relatives. She would have been included in the "nearest of kin," which heads the list in Lev 21:2–3, and the rest of the list there is essentially the same as the one given here.

According to Lev 21:11, the high priest was not allowed to bury even his father or mother. However, as mentioned earlier (see on Ezek 44:3), no high priest is envisioned in Ezekiel 40–48.

44:26 The "purification" (the noun טָהֳרָה) should last seven days according to Num 19:11–13. Here, "after his purification" (וְאַחֲרֵי טָהֳרָתוֹ) seems to require an additional seven days, for a total of fourteen. That, plus the sacrifice required in 44:27, evinces again Yahweh's intense concern for purity and holiness throughout Ezekiel 40–48.

Instead of the impersonal plural יִסְפְּרוּ־לוֹ, "they shall count for him" (supported by the Vulgate and Targum), the LXX and Syriac have a singular verb, followed by some English translations, for example, RSV and NIV.

44:27 What Hebrews (5:3; 7:27) says about the high priest is also true of all the Zadokite priests according to this verse: because they are sinful, they are obligated to sacrifice a sin offering (here specified after contact with a dead person). But in contrast, Jesus Christ is the sinless great High Priest who has no such obligation, but offered himself as the unblemished sacrifice for the sins of the whole world (Heb 7:27).

The LXX has no translation for אֶל־הַקֹּדֶשׁ, "into the sanctuary," and some critics omit it.[33] It undoubtedly seems superfluous, since the following reference to the priest entering "the inner court" presupposes that he has entered the sanctuary. However, Allen points out that it can easily be read as emphatic, underscoring the gulf between the holy place and the priest's prior uncleanness.[34] This is one of those instances where one is tempted to render חַטָּאת as "purification offering" instead of "sin offering,"[35] but with the OT's somatic sense of sin, it is a distinction without a difference.

(d) See also Num 18:24; 26:62; Deut 10:9; 14:27; 18:1–2; Josh 13:14, 33; 14:3

To emphasize God's concern for the uncontaminated sanctity of priesthood and sanctuary, which has undergirded all his regulations for the priests, he closes this verse with the signatory formula, "says the Lord Yahweh."[36]

44:28–30 The subject of these verses is the priests' titled property, a topic Ezekiel will develop more fully in the next chapter (45:1–4). The final verse, 44:31, is another priestly regulation.[37] The aim of 44:28–30 is to emphasize the special status of the priests: they have Yahweh as their sole "inheritance" and "possession, property." (Ezekiel's vision of the land grants to other Israelites will be given in chapters 47–48.) The Hebrew wording echoes Yahweh's promise to Aaron in Num 18:20.[d]

To an extent, what God says here applies to NT pastors in that they receive him as their special "inheritance" by being called to serve him full time, ministering on his behalf to his people, perhaps forsaking other more lucrative professions or pursuits (cf. Mt 19:27–29). Yet from another standpoint, in the new covenant we Christians are like the OT priests in that no particular earthly territory is assigned to us. Rather, Christ is already our "promised land," but there is more to come. Our true inheritance is not of this world, but is kept for us in heaven, to be revealed on the Last Day. Finally, it consists of a share in God's kingdom and a place in the new heavens and new earth.[e]

(e) E.g., Mt 25:34; Eph 1:11–14, 18; Col 1:12; 3:24; Heb 9:15; 1 Pet 1:4

44:28 To smooth the transition from 44:27, I (with NRSV and ESV) have supplied "this." The Hebrew simply begins with the feminine verb וְהָיְתָה without a subject. We might assume that one of the feminine nouns later in the verse, either נַחֲלָה, "inheritance," or אֲחֻזָּה, "possession, property," is already implied as subject. Alternatively, since in Hebrew feminine forms can serve as abstracts, the entire topic being introduced could be the subject: "It will be for their inheritance [that] I am …" (cf. NKJV). In any event, the meaning of the verse is clear.

---

33 E.g., Zimmerli, *Ezekiel*, 2:451.

34 Allen, *Ezekiel*, 2:246, 264.

35 See the discussion of this view in Kleinig, *Leviticus*, 100–101.

36 For this formula, see pages 8–9 in the introduction and the second textual note on 5:11.

37 Some critics suppose 44:31 would go better after 44:27. Allen, *Ezekiel*, 2:246, and others propose drastic dislocations or complicated textual histories, based on problems the text may present to an Occidental mind, but they only distract us from the expository task at hand.

44:29 The OT describes the sacrifices as the priests' sustenance and due (e.g., Deut 18:1; Josh 13:14), what we might call their "salary." In this context where Yahweh is speaking, the words carry more profound connotations because, after all, the sacrifices were gifts or offerings to Yahweh himself. In effect, then, Yahweh is inviting the priests to share in his own "food" (44:7).

The three types of offerings named here appeared together previously in 42:13 (which see), following Num 18:9. After listing the three, Hebrew uses a repetitious resumptive pronominal suffix on the verb יֹאכְלוּם, "they will eat them." Two main types of sacrifice prescribed in Leviticus are not mentioned here: (1) the עוֹלָה, "burnt offering," where everything was consumed by the altar fire, and nothing was left for human consumption; and (2) the שְׁלָמִים, "peace offerings/communion sacrifices" (see on 43:27; 45:15).

A fourth item available to priests is חֵרֶם, "every devoted thing." This is the only instance of the word in Ezekiel. We have nothing comparable in our culture. The word appears especially in military contexts. In "Yahweh's war" waged by Israel in the OT, most things captured, whether animate or inanimate, were "devoted" to Yahweh, that is, either killed or contributed to the sanctuary. The classical example of violation of that sanction and its punishment is the account in Joshua 7 about Achan after the capture of Jericho.

Thus חֵרֶם has a sort of double significance, both "accursed" (by association with the conquered pagans) and "consecrated" to God. The first meaning, implying destruction, is mandated in Lev 27:28–29. The second meaning, which alone would apply here, is spelled out in Num 18:14. Ezekiel does not go into detail about the source of חֵרֶם, but in addition to war (cf. Ezekiel 38–39), a second possible source would be vows, whether things were devoted together with an initial petition to God or given in the thanksgiving for God's answer to prayer. References in the Psalms indicate that vows were often accompanied by sacrifice (e.g., Pss 66:13; 76:12 [ET 76:11]). (Archaeological excavations of pagan sanctuaries often turn up votive offerings of various sorts, often little images of the deity petitioned or sometimes representations of bodily limbs presumed healed by such intercessions.) Various regulations about vows are found throughout Leviticus and Numbers, and things "devoted" to the sanctuary presumably became part of the priestly emolument. However, if vows were made carelessly, they could become a "curse," classically illustrated in the tragic case of Jephthah's daughter (Judg 11:29–40).[38]

The LXX generally translated חֵרֶם as ἀνάθεμα ("anathema"), whence it passed into NT usage, where it usually is translated "accursed."[f] Only once in the NT is the word used positively: the older classical Greek spelling, ἀνάθημα, in Lk 21:5 refers to "devoted (objects)" adorning the temple. In the early church through the Reformation era (as Lutherans recall from the Council of Trent), "anathema" was used for excommunication.

(f) Rom 9:3; 1 Cor 12:3; 16:22; Gal 1:8–9; cf. Acts 23:14

---

[38] In many English Bibles the last word in the OT is "curse," translating חֵרֶם (Mal 3:24 [ET 4:6]).

44:30 This verse specifies three categories of offerings that belong to the priests. The first is all kinds of firstfruits. Theologically, the OT laws about first-fruits express the idea that all earthly gifts came from God and in a sense still belonged to him, and so he should receive the first portion or "helping" of the produce. Similar to the usage here, רֵאשִׁית, "first," is used in a construct chain with בִּכּוּרִים, "firstfruits," in the Torah (Ex 23:19; 34:26). Some argue that in-stead of the redundant "first of the firstfruits," in these contexts, רֵאשִׁית means "best" of the firstfruits. Others suggest that רֵאשִׁית means "first-processed" and בִּכּוּרִים means "first-ripened" because of its frequent application to fruit. רֵאשִׁית can be used with other, more specific words for produce in laws about the first-fruits (e.g., Num 15:20–21; 18:12; Deut 26:2, 10), which were to be given to the priests (Deut 18:4). The third category of offering in this verse is a specific kind of firstfruits (see below).

A second, more general category of offering that belongs to the priests is denoted by תְּרוּמָה. Only a very general word such as "contribution" seems to cover all its uses.[39] Etymologically, it might describe something that the priest would "lift up" (רוּם), and so its traditional translation is "heave offering," al-though some argue that the etymology should be related to the Hiphil of רוּם in the sense that the worshiper "reserves, dedicates" (as the Hiphil of רוּם means in 45:1, 13; 48:8–9, 20, where it is used with תְּרוּמָה as its cognate accusative) the offering to God. Different parts of an animal and a variety of other items (money, bread, produce, spoils of war) are called a תְּרוּמָה in various contexts.[40]

While רֵאשִׁית and תְּרוּמָה are feminine nouns and בִּכּוּרֵי is masculine plural (in construct), the following verb יִהְיֶה is masculine singular, apparently under the influence of the repeated key word כֹּל, "all, every."

The third kind of offering, וְרֵאשִׁית עֲרִסֹתֵיכֶם, translated "the first of your ground meal," clearly is a specific kind of firstfruits. However, the meaning of עֲרִסָה is obscure. It occurs elsewhere only in Num 15:20–21 and Neh 10:38 (ET 10:37), where too רֵאשִׁית is in construct with it and it designates a gift for the Lord and the priests. (Here the singular לַכֹּהֵן, "to the priest," probably is used only for variety.) In Num 15:20–21, the LXX rendered it "dough," fol-lowed by KJV, but NKJV prefers "ground meal," which I have adopted here. Those alternatives appear to be about equally divided among the lexicons, com-mentaries, and translations.

The final result clause, לְהָנִיחַ בְּרָכָה אֶל־בֵּיתֶךָ, is, literally, "to cause to rest a blessing on your house." לְהָנִיחַ (the infinitive construct of the first Hiphil con-jugation of נוּחַ) apparently has no subject, and its direct object is בְּרָכָה. Eng-lish requires translating "blessing" as the subject of the intransitive "rest": "to cause a blessing to rest on your house." God's blessing would follow from obe-

---

[39] For the meaning of תְּרוּמָה and the ritual used with it, see the first textual note on Lev 7:14 in Kleinig, *Leviticus*, 161.

[40] For the various contributions in the OT that are called a תְּרוּמָה, see figure 12 in Kleinig, *Leviticus*, 162.

dience to God's will, specifically here in providing adequately for his priests. Alternatively, as the KJV suggests, the preceding כֹּהֵן, "priest," may be the subject of the infinitive: "so that the priest causes a blessing to rest on your house." This understanding of the promise may be supported by the fact that only priests had the privilege of pronouncing the Aaronic Benediction (Num 6:22–27) upon the congregation.[41] If so, the promise is a reminder of the efficacy of the holy ministry: through the spoken Word of God, God does indeed confer the blessings of which he speaks.

In either case, the theology and sacrificial language are reflected in the NT: "Do not forget doing good and sharing, for God is pleased with such sacrifices" (Heb 13:16). In particular, the NT exhorts God's people to provide for their faithful clergy based on the OT precedent: "Do you not know that those who work in the temple precincts eat from the temple, and those who serve at the altar share in the altar [that is, in the sacrificial offerings]?" (1 Cor 9:13; see also Rom 15:27; Gal 6:6; 2 Tim 2:6).

44:31 For נְבֵלָה וּטְרֵפָה, see the third textual note on 4:14. Basically the same prohibition applied to the priests here was a rule for all Israelites as part of God's desire that they be "holy people" (Ex 22:30 [ET 22:31], with טְרֵפָה, "torn by wild animals"). In Lev 22:8 the same proscription as here (with both words: נְבֵלָה וּטְרֵפָה) appears among the specific rules for priests, which is a precedent for its application here. Contextually, it provides a stark, concluding contrast between food only fit for scavenging animals and the choice rations Yahweh wills for his priests.

---

[41] This point is made by Zimmerli, *Ezekiel*, 2:463.

Figure 6

The New Holy Land in Ezekiel

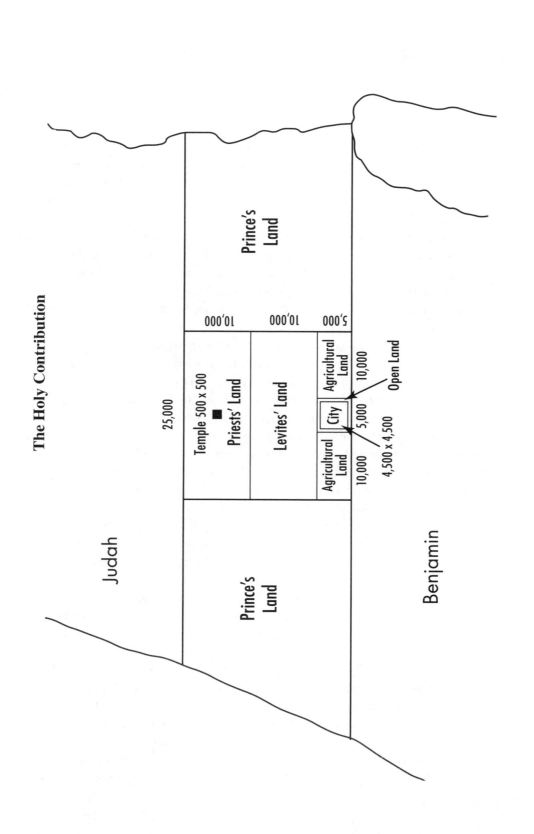

The Holy Contribution

Property for Yahweh, the Priests, and the Prince; the Major Festivals

Translation

45 ¹" 'When you allot the land as an inheritance, you are to devote a contribution to Yahweh, a holy area of the land. Its length should be twenty-five thousand [cubits] in length and its width ten thousand [cubits]. It will be holy in its entire area. ²Of this, for the sanctuary will be a square area five hundred by five hundred [cubits]. There is to be an open area of fifty cubits all around it. ³From this measured-off area, a length of twenty-five thousand [cubits] and a width of ten thousand [cubits], you should measure off [an area], and in it will be the sanctuary, the most holy place. ⁴It is to be a holy area of the land; it will be for the priests, the ministers of the sanctuary, who draw near to serve Yahweh. It will be a place for their houses, as well as a holy place for the sanctuary. ⁵And an area twenty-five thousand [cubits] long and ten thousand [cubits] wide will be for the Levites, the servants of the temple, as their possession for cities to live in. ⁶As the city's property you are to assign an area five thousand [cubits] wide and twenty-five thousand [cubits] long adjacent to the holy contribution. It will belong to the whole house of Israel. ⁷And [you are to assign] to the Prince [an area] on both sides of the holy contribution and of the city's property, alongside the holy contribution and alongside the city's property. On the west side it will extend westward and on the east side eastward, in length corresponding to one of the tribal portions, from the western border to the eastern border. ⁸This land is to be his property in Israel, so that my princes will no longer oppress my people, but will give the land to the house of Israel according to their tribes.

⁹" 'Thus says the Lord Yahweh: You have done enough of that, O princes of Israel! Remove violence and mayhem, and practice justice and righteousness. Lift the burden of your expulsions from my people, says the Lord Yahweh. ¹⁰May you have righteous scales, a righteous ephah, and a righteous bath. ¹¹The ephah and the bath should have one standard. The bath should hold one-tenth of the homer, and the ephah [should hold] one-tenth of the homer. Its standard is to be according to the homer. ¹²The shekel should be twenty gerahs. Twenty shekels, twenty-five shekels, and fifteen shekels will be your mina.

¹³" 'This is the special contribution you should dedicate: one-sixth of an ephah from each homer of wheat, and you shall take one-sixth of an ephah from each homer of barley. ¹⁴The prescribed portion of oil—the bath [is the measure for] the oil—is one-tenth of a bath from each kor. Ten baths make a kor, for ten baths are a homer. ¹⁵Further, one sheep [shall be given] from every flock, from the two hundred [sheep that comprise a flock], from the well-watered [land] of Israel, for the grain offering, the burnt offering, and the communion offerings,

to make atonement for them, says the Lord Yahweh. [16]All the people of the land will be [obligated to give] to this contribution for the Prince in Israel. [17]Upon the Prince [will be the obligation] for the burnt offerings, the grain offering, and the libation—on the festivals, on the New Moons, and on the Sabbaths, that is, at all the appointed feasts of the house of Israel. He himself will provide the sin offering, the grain offering, the burnt offering, and the communion offerings, to make atonement on behalf of the house of Israel.

[18]" 'Thus says the Lord Yahweh: In the first [month], on the first day of the month, you are to take a young bull without blemish and purify the sanctuary. [19]The priest is to take some of the blood of the sin offering and put it on the doorpost of the temple, on the four corners of the ledge belonging to the altar, and on the post of the gate of the inner court. [20]So shall you do on the seventh [day] in the month on account of anyone who sins inadvertently or in ignorance, and so you shall make atonement for the temple.

[21]" 'In the first [month], on the fourteenth day of the month, you shall have the Passover; during the feast, a week of days, unleavened bread must be eaten. [22]The Prince is to provide on that day—on behalf of himself and all the people of the land— a bull for a sin offering. [23]On the seven days of the feast he is to provide a burnt offering for Yahweh: seven bulls and seven rams without blemish for each day of the seven days, as well as a male goat for a sin offering for each day. [24]As a grain offering he is to provide an ephah for each bull and an ephah for each ram, and a hin of oil for each ephah. [25]In the seventh [month, starting] on the fifteenth day of the month, at the feast he is to provide according to these [instructions] for seven days, according to the sin offering, the burnt offering, the grain offering, and the oil.' "

Textual Notes and Commentary

The discussion of the priests and Levites as the legitimate worship officiants (44:6–31) now leads to the land allotments for the participants in that worship: Yahweh himself, the priests and Levites, and the Prince (45:1–8). After an exhortation to use proper weights and measures (45:9–12), a special contribution is proscribed for the sake of the Prince, and his supervisory role over worship is stated (45:13–17). Finally, the major worship festivals are given (45:18–25). The next chapter deals with the minor worship festivals (46:1–15) and further legislation about the Prince's property (46:16–18) as well as the kitchens used in worship (46:19–24).

Property for Yahweh, the Priests, the Levites, and the Prince (45:1–8)

45:1   This first verse of a new section includes a catchword connection with the "contribution" (תְּרוּמָה) theme, referring to offerings in 44:30, by using that same noun plus its cognate Hiphil verb (תָּרִימוּ תְּרוּמָה), "you are to devote a contribution," but here referring to land. In the covenant of Moses, the priests and other Levites received no major portion of the land besides the forty-eight scattered Levitical cities, thirteen for the priests and the rest for the non-priestly Levites (Lev 25:34; Num 35:1–8; Josh 21:1–42), because Yahweh was their inheritance (see on Ezek 44:28). In Ezekiel's vision there are no Levitical cities, but the priests and Levites still need a place to live.

This verse is about the priests' land, a rectangle twenty-five thousand cubits east to west and ten thousand cubits north to south. It is shown to Ezekiel as being a "holy area" (קֹדֶשׁ). In 45:5 the Levites will receive an equally sized rectangle, adjoining the priests' land to the south. In 45:6–7, תְּרוּמַת הַקֹּדֶשׁ "the holy contribution," will refer to the combination of these two tracts (the portions belonging to the priests and the Levites). The area reserved for the city is a narrower rectangle (half as wide north to south) adjoining the Levites' land to the south. See figure 6.

This chapter treats only the principal instructions about the holy contribution. Following a common Ezekelian pattern, what is introduced briefly here will be repeated and expanded later, in 48:8–22 (which see). The allotments of the other tribes will also be considered in 47:13–48:29.

The clause תָּרִימוּ תְרוּמָה is not easy to render into English, and inevitably, as in my "devote a contribution," the cognate construction is lost. Keil's "lift a heave" reflects the view that in Leviticus תְּרוּמָה means "heave offering" (see on 44:30), and he suggests that the sacred tract of land is to be "a portion lifted or taken by a person from his property as an offering for God."[1] In the OT, only Ezekiel uses תְּרוּמָה for real estate, both here in chapter 45 and in chapter 48 (see further on 48:8–22). The land was a gift from Yahweh, and the Israelites were to acknowledge that fact by reserving a tract for him as a sort of thank-offering. Although they are simply giving Yahweh his own, the second person plural verb (תָּרִימוּ, "you are to reserve") indicates that the Israelites are not merely passive, but are actively engaged in the process. God's justified, redeemed people have an active role in living a life of faith and sanctification (FC SD II 65–66).

The opening Hiphil infinitive (of נָפַל), וּבְהַפִּילְכֶם, literally, "when you cause to fall, cast," is an ellipsis that implies גּוֹרָל, "lot" (supplied in KJV and NKJV), as its object. Hence it means "apportion (land) by casting lots." The same idiom was used in Josh 13:6 and 23:4 for the original apportionment of the land of Israel, and the idiom will be repeated in Ezek 47:22 and 48:29 (cf. 47:14). The English verb "allot" etymologically reflects the use of "lots," but is today usually used in a more general sense.

The command here reflects God's directive to the Israelites in Num 26:53–56 and its fulfillment in Josh 18:6–10 (expressed with גּוֹרָל, "lot," and נַחֲלָה, "inheritance"), after Canaan was first conquered. In biblical theology, the use of lots or dice was not, as in our secular culture, thought of as mere random luck or chance, much less deified as in Greco-Roman Τύχη, the goddess Fortuna. Rather, it was a means by which God expressed his will, unsullied by human ambition or manipulation.

---

[1] Keil, *Ezekiel*, 2:318–19.

The object phrase here, הָאָרֶץ בְּנַחֲלָה, uses the preposition בְּ to introduce a predicate referring to the preceding noun: to allot "the land *as* an inheritance." בְּנַחֲלָה recurs in the same sense in 47:22 (cf. 46:16; 47:14). For the syntax, see Joüon, § 133 c 3.

However, it should not be overlooked that the apportioning of the land is in a subordinate clause ("when you allot …"), which, in effect, excludes the sacred tract from that process. Since Yahweh has reserved it in advance, the apportionment to the tribes must reflect his will.

There is no unified English vocabulary for the term here applied to this strip of land, קֹדֶשׁ מִן־הָאָרֶץ ("a holy area of the land"). The noun קֹדֶשׁ can have the abstract meaning "holiness," but usually it refers concretely to a "holy thing." For it here and in 45:4 the translation uses "holy area," and the construct phrase תְּרוּמַת הַקֹּדֶשׁ (45:6–7; 48:10, 18, 20–21) is rendered "holy contribution."

Its "length" (אֹרֶךְ), measured from east to west (see 48:10), is given as "twenty-five thousand." The only unit of measure given in chapter 45 is the "fifty *cubits*" in 45:2b. Keil assumes that except for 45:2b, all the other measurements in chapter 45 are in rods, but that view creates problems.[2] Most commentators assume that all of the measurements in this chapter are in cubits. I have shared that assumption, and so the translation adds "cubits" after the numbers in 45:1–6. If so, this distance is about eight miles or thirteen kilometers. The noun אֹרֶךְ is repeated both before and after the numeral. At best, the repetition is simply pleonastic; either position alone would be possible. In 45:3 אֹרֶךְ appears only before the numeral, and in 45:5 only after it, but Ezekiel tends to prefer placing the number after the dimension.

Its "width" (רֹחַב), measured from north to south, according to the MT, is "ten thousand" cubits, a little over three miles or five kilometers. This dimension is given as the same number in 48:9. עֲשָׂרָה אָלֶף is an exception to the general rule that after a number from three to ten (here עֲשָׂרָה, "ten"), the noun is plural, since here אָלֶף is singular (Joüon, § 142 d, footnote 3). "Ten thousand" is attested in the Vulgate, Targum, and Syriac. This number must refer only to the priests' tract, described further in 45:3–4 (also 48:9–12). The priests' land, which houses the sanctuary, is called a "holy place" in 45:4. While 45:5 says nothing about the Levites' land being holy, later verses indicate that it too was holy. Ezek 45:6–7 states that the city's land and the Prince's tracts are adjacent

---

[2] Keil, *Ezekiel*, 2:320. Since the measuring guide's rod was six cubits long (40:5), if the distance were twenty-five thousand rods, it would be about forty-eight miles or seventy-eight kilometers. In terms of modern geography, that would be close to (perhaps even exceed) the distance from the Jordan to the Mediterranean. That would leave no room for the Prince's two tracts of land to the east and west of the holy contribution (unless they were to extend to the east of the Jordan and west out into the Mediterranean Sea). Consequently, Keil concedes that "no regard, therefore, is paid to the natural length and breadth of the land." Keil in his figure 4 (found in the back of the German edition of his commentary) shows the two tracts of the Prince's land as very narrow (east to west) and bordering the Jordan and the Mediterranean.

to the holy contribution, and thus the Levites' land is part of the holy contribution. See also 48:13–14, which considers the Levites' land to be "holy to Yahweh."

The LXX reading here in 45:1 is εἴκοσι χιλιάδας, "twenty thousand" (about six and a half miles or ten and a half kilometers). That is the correct total of the widths of the priests' portion (45:3) and the Levites' portion (45:5), both of which were ten thousand cubits wide. Most English translations and commentators, including Keil and Block,[3] believe the number here is intended as the total, and so they follow the LXX. Some who prefer the LXX argue that עֲשָׂרָה ("ten" thousand) is the result of simple scribal confusion of ה in place of the final ם of an original reading of עֶשְׂרִים, "twenty." Confusion of ה for final ם can be attested elsewhere.

For a diagram, see figure 6. The diagram is not affected whether one follows the LXX number (twenty thousand as the total of the widths of the priests' and Levites' portions) or the MT (ten thousand as the width of only the priests' portion).

The final clause (קֹדֶשׁ־הוּא בְּכָל־גְּבוּלָהּ סָבִיב) repeats that the priests' area is "holy," obviously for emphasis. The masculine pronoun הוּא ("it") is used because of the proximity of the masculine noun קֹדֶשׁ ("holy") even though the antecedent of the pronoun is the feminine noun תְּרוּמָה, "contribution," earlier in the verse. תְּרוּמָה is also the antecedent of the feminine suffix on גְּבוּלָהּ, "its area." The adverb סָבִיב is reflected by "its *entire* area."

45:2 "Of this" (מִזֶּה) uses the preposition מִן in a partitive sense: the sanctuary occupies part of the holy area defined in 45:1. This verse is a short digression (interrupting the description of the priests' portion, introduced in 45:1 and resumed in 45:3–4) about the temple that prevents any blurring of the distinction between the divine and human habitations.[4] It is thoroughly characteristic of God's self-revelation through Ezekiel that he stresses his holy separation even from his holy priesthood. He occupies a separate "square" (מְרֻבָּע, the masculine Pual participle, whose feminine was in 40:47; cf. GKC, § 65 d, on its vocalization) five hundred cubits by five hundred cubits. הַקֹּדֶשׁ, literally, "the holy place," is rendered "the sanctuary," which normally in the OT is denoted by מִקְדָּשׁ. It will be further insulated from the surrounding area by a מִגְרָשׁ of fifty cubits (about eighty-five feet or twenty-six meters) all around. מִגְרָשׁ usually describes a belt of common pasture land surrounding walled cities (e.g., Num 35:2–5). But since it is unclear how a "pasture" would function in this context, "open area" or the like is usually used. Its function is to insure the absolute holiness of the temple itself. Even the priestly dwellings cannot come

---

[3] Keil, *Ezekiel*, 2:320; Block, *Ezekiel*, 648, including n. 3.

[4] Predictably, critics propose rearranging the text. Cooke, *Ezekiel*, 495, thinks 45:2 originally followed 45:4 and was accidentally misplaced. Allen, *Ezekiel*, 2:265, calls it "an afterthought," and Zimmerli, *Ezekiel*, 2:468, considers it a secondary addition under the influence of 42:20.

too close to the holy temple square. In 42:20 Ezekiel speaks of a wall separating "the holy from the common." How that wall and the מִגְרָשׁ relate is not entirely clear, but there need be no contradiction.[5] The dimensions given there for the temple compound agree with the numbers here: five hundred cubits by five hundred cubits.

מִגְרָשׁ will be used again for the "open area" around the city, the new Jerusalem, in 48:15, 17.

45:3 "From this measured-off area" (וּמִן־הַמִּדָּה הַזֹּאת) refers to the priests' portion, which was measured off in 45:1; those dimensions will be given again in this verse. But before those measurements intrudes the verb תָּמֹוד, which refers again (as in 45:2) to the portion measured off for the sanctuary, which is not named until the last clause of the verse. According to 45:3–4, this northern strip is to contain the sanctuary and also the priest's houses, which, as 45:2 was at pains to stress, were to be kept an appropriate distance away from the temple. See figure 6.

The singular verb תָּמֹוד, "you should measure," is unexpected in the context. Because of that and because of its unusual *plene* spelling, most commentators treat it as a metathetical error for תָּמֹדּו, "you [plural] should measure." But the versions consistently support the MT, although it is not clear who its subject is. The Qere חֲמִשָּׁה is the expected feminine form for the numeral "five" (before "twenty"), corresponding to the feminine עֲשֶׂרֶת, "ten," for the width. The Kethib חֲמֵשׁ agrees with the construct חֲמֵשׁ used with מֵאוֹת, literally, "hundreds," in 45:2.

45:4 This verse distinguishes between the area set aside for the sanctuary and the priests from that for the Levites (45:5). Earlier God had specified that only the descendants of Zadok are to be priests; the other Levitical priests are demoted to the same secondary ministerial role as all the other Levites (see on 44:15). Here and in 45:5 Yahweh uses the same verb, מְשָׁרְתֵי, the Piel participle of שָׁרַת in construct, to describe both the priests and the Levites as "ministers, servants." However, in each case the participle is in construct with a different noun. The priests are מְשָׁרְתֵי הַמִּקְדָּשׁ, "the ministers of the sanctuary," since they alone are authorized to offer sacrifice. The next clause reinforces their unique role. The priests are הַקְּרֵבִים לְשָׁרֵת אֶת־יְהוָה, the only personnel who may "draw near to serve Yahweh" for that purpose. The same adjective (הַקְּרֵבִים) and the Piel infinitive of שָׁרַת were used in 40:46 (see the second textual note there).

The final phrase consists of a repeated word, וּמִקְדָּשׁ לַמִּקְדָּשׁ. This seems to play on the etymological meaning of מִקְדָּשׁ ("holy place") and its specific reference here to the temple "sanctuary," so it is rendered "a holy place for the sanctuary." (Both at the beginning of the verse and here, many critics prefer the LXX, which differs considerably, but without convincing reason.)

---

[5] Contra Cooke, *Ezekiel*, 495.

45:5 A second strip of land, equal in size to that of the Zadokite priests, is to be set aside for the Levites. Their secondary status is indicated in several ways. First, they do not live in the strip that contains the temple. Second, they are מְשָׁרְתֵי הַבַּיִת, "the servants of the *temple*," which in this context must mean the entire temple complex. Their service too is considered liturgical (Piel participle of שָׁרַת), but in a broader sense, since they do not offer sacrifice. Third, their land is called their אֲחֻזָּה, "possession." This might seem to be a greater privilege than the priests have, since 44:28 states that the priests are to receive no land, and the strip in which the priests reside is never called their "possession" or "inheritance." However, possessing land is inferior to the privilege of the priests, who have Yahweh himself as their נַחֲלָה, "inheritance" (see on 44:28).

The Kethib, יִהְיֶה, is preferable in this context, and is the sole reading in 45:4a and 45:6b. The Qere, וְהָיָה, repeats the form at the start of 45:4b.

A major textual crux is occasioned by the last phrase of the verse, which in the MT is עֶשְׂרִים לְשָׁכֹת, "twenty rooms" (the plural of לִשְׁכָּה, which was also in, e.g., 40:17, 38). That reading is clearly attested in Vulgate, Syriac, and Targum (and followed in KJV and NKJV). However, a mere "twenty rooms" seems impossible as adequate housing for all the Levites. Hence most commentators and modern translations follow the LXX's πόλεις τοῦ κατοικεῖν, "cities to dwell (in)," presumably a translation of an original עָרִים לָשֶׁבֶת, "cities to live (in)."[6] That consonantal reading would result from עֶשְׂרִים לְשָׁכֹת by omitting שׁ and substituting בּ for כּ. Regardless of the reading, Yahweh evidently intends the arrangement, with the Levites all living close to their place of "employment," as preferable to that of Num 35:1–8, where he had prescribed forty-eight Levitical cities scattered throughout the country of Israel.

45:6 The land that is, literally, "the possession of the city" (וַאֲחֻזַּת הָעִיר) seems to have a utilitarian function: to provide produce for the city, to offer space for those making their annual pilgrimages to the temple, and the like. More details about this strip of land will be given in 48:15–20. Apparently merely for variation, this verse states the width before the length, which happens elsewhere only in 48:8 and Zech 2:6 (ET 2:2).

45:7 This verse lacks a Hebrew verb, but תִּתְּנוּ, "you are to give/assign," in 45:6 also applies to 45:7. This verse is a bit prolix, but the sense is clear.

This allocation is to the "Prince" (נָשִׂיא, 45:7–9, 16–17, 22), who receives a large special grant appropriate to his special status.[7] Israel's past kings never had their own tract of land. The Prince actually is given two large tracts, on the eastern and the western sides of the sacred presence and extending to the lim-

---

[6] Keil, *Ezekiel*, 2:319, 322–23, views the MT as corrupt but favors a different reconstruction resulting in "gates to dwell in."

[7] Besides these verses in chapter 45, in Ezekiel 40–48 the Prince appears also in 44:3; 46:2, 4, 8, 10, 12, 16–18; 48:21–22.

its of the land, bounded on the east by the Jordan River and the Dead Sea and on the west by the Mediterranean. See figure 6.

This "Prince" was previously mentioned in 44:3 as having a unique priestly role. That agrees with the placement here of his two tracts of land adjacent to those of the priests (which included the temple), the Levites, and the city (Jerusalem). Only he is given *two* allocations of land, perhaps reminiscent of the double portion given a firstborn son (cf. Deut 21:17; Rom 8:29; Col 1:15, 18; Rev 1:5). Most likely the Prince is to be identified as the same person whom God called, literally, "my Servant, David, Prince" (עַבְדִּי דָוִיד נָשִׂיא) in 34:24; 37:25 has the same name and titles but in a different order (see the commentary on those verses). In the corresponding NT fulfillment, his priestly, sacrificial role is emphasized when he is called "the Lamb" (e.g., Rev 5:6, 12; 21:22, 23), and his royal status (corresponding to "Prince" in Ezekiel) and divinity are affirmed by the references to "the *throne* of God and of the Lamb" (Rev 22:1, 3). This points to two of the three offices of Jesus Christ: Priest and King.[8]

The verse (45:7) does not specify the precise dimensions of the Prince's properties, nor does 48:21. However, 45:7 suggests—and 48:8 confirms—that the north-south width of each of the Prince's two tracts is twenty-five thousand (presumably cubits, not rods; see on 45:1), about eight miles or thirteen kilometers, which is the sum of the strip allocated to the priests (ten thousand [cubits], 45:3–4), the strip of the Levites (ten thousand [cubits], 45:5), and the tract set aside for the city (five thousand [cubits], 48:15).

From east to west, the Prince's two tracts begin at the eastern and western boundaries of the square formed by three strips of land (for the priests, the Levites, and the city). In 45:7 this beginning is described as being "alongside" (אֶל־פְּנֵי) the holy contribution (see on 48:8–22) and the city's property. The Prince's tracts then extend to the eastern and western limits of the rejuvenated land of Israel (see also 48:21). At least in its southern part, the whole land is bounded on the east by the Jordan River and the Dead Sea and on the west by the Mediterranean. See figure 6. Therefore the length of the entire holy contribution is described as "in length corresponding to one of the tribal portions" (וְאֹרֶךְ לְעֻמּוֹת אַחַד הַחֲלָקִים). For the tribal portions, see 48:1–7, 23–28.

"In length" (וְאֹרֶךְ) is accusative of direction. The plural form (לְעֻמּוֹת) of the preposition עֻמָּה occurs only here in the OT, but like the singular (e.g., 45:6) often does, it means "agreeing with, corresponding to" (BDB, s.v. עֻמָּה I, b, under עמם). In the phrase וּמִפְּאַת־קֵדְמָה קָדִימָה, the directive ה is unexpected on קֵדְמָה since the corresponding noun (יָם) in the preceding phrase מִפְּאַת־יָם יָמָּה lacks it. However, as with the last word in the book (שָׁמָּה, 48:35), the directive ה does not always have directive meaning, and so וּמִפְּאַת־קֵדְמָה simply means "and on the east side."

---

8 For Christ's threefold office as Prophet, Priest, and King, see Pieper, *Christian Dogmatics,* 2:333–94.

45:8 Many commentators and translations (e.g., ESV) take the first phrase of 45:8, לָאָ֫רֶץ ("to the land"), as concluding 45:7. In my judgment, it works better as an introduction to what I understand as the result clause in 45:8b, and the even stronger statements in 45:9. "This land" follows NIV (similar are NASB, NKJV).

In contrast to the singular "Prince" in 45:7 (also 44:3), Yahweh now turns his attention to past "princes" who abused Israel. We met the same kind of phenomenon in chapter 34, where Yahweh condemned (plural) "shepherds" (34:2, 7–10) who had oppressed Israel in the past and promised the (singular) "Shepherd" (34:23–24) who would rescue God's people and do for them what the others had not (cf. John 10).[9] By calling them "my princes" (נְשִׂיאַי) and "my people" (עַמִּי), Yahweh acknowledges that the past kings of Israel had been his appointed representatives, and the people had been in a saving covenant relationship with him. But the kings had abused their responsibilities as undershepherds of the covenant by oppressing the people. Ezekiel used the Hiphil of יָנָה ("to oppress") before, in 18:12 (contrast 18:7, 16) and 22:7, 29, for social injustices among his covenant people. Here the reference is specifically to royal confiscation of private property, as Samuel had warned already in 1 Sam 8:14, and as classically illustrated by the narrative of Ahab seizing Naboth's vineyard (1 Kings 21). "According to their tribes" (לְשִׁבְטֵיהֶם, Ezek 45:8) harks back all the way to God's original design for the tribes in the land, as outlined already in Numbers 34–35 and implemented under Joshua (Joshua 13–21). However, soon after the settlement under Joshua, various factors (including remaining pockets of Canaanites and tribal migrations) began to cause shifts in the tribal boundaries. Under Solomon (tenth century B.C.), Israel finally had control over the full extent of the promised land, but under subsequent kings, land increasingly was lost to encroaching hostile neighbors. No wonder Ezekiel abjures the title מֶ֫לֶךְ, "king," in favor of נָשִׂיא, "prince," except in messianic references to the new "David"![10]

Proper Weights and Measures for the Offerings, a Contribution for the Prince, and the Prince's Liturgical Supervision (45:9–17)

45:9 In highly idiomatic Hebrew, Yahweh addresses the malfeasant princes directly, in second person imperatives. As a frame around them he begins with the citation formula, "thus says the Lord Yahweh," and ends with the

---

[9] The plural "my princes" does not mean that Ezekiel envisions other future rulers besides the Prince, since that would contradict the promises in 34:23–24 and 37:24–25 of "one" future Shepherd, Prince, and King. Rather, as both Keil, *Ezekiel*, 2:325 (quoting Kliefoth, *Das Buch Ezechiels*, 2:248), and Block, *Ezekiel*, 2:655, explain, it refers to the many abusive kings in Israel's past.

[10] Ezekiel consistently refuses to dignify Israel's apostate rulers as מֶ֫לֶךְ, "king," especially Zedekiah, who was not in the valid line of succession. See the second textual note on 7:27; the commentary on 12:10; the second textual note on 21:30 (ET 21:25); and the commentary on 34:23–31. The new "David" is promised in 34:23–24 and 37:24–25 (see the commentary on those verses).

signatory formula, "says the Lord Yahweh."[11] For the exasperated "enough for you" (רַב־לָכֶם), see on 44:6.

As with the need for ongoing sacrifices for sin (e.g., 45:15–25), the references to continuing violence here make plain that at least some parts of Ezekiel 40–48 are not yet that of a completely realized eschatology and are not yet the eternal state depicted in Revelation 21–22, although other parts are, and the whole vision is oriented in an eschatological direction. See further "Introduction to Ezekiel 40–48."

The outrages that precipitated the exile may recur among the Israelites after their return. "Violence" is a standard translation for חָמָס (see the first textual note on 7:11 and fourth textual note on 7:23). שֹׁד, "violence, havoc," or resulting "destruction," occurs only here in Ezekiel, but was apparently part of a standard idiom with חָמָס, possibly a hendiadys ("violent lawlessness"). I have followed Allen in using the picturesque "mayhem."[12] The Hiphil imperative הָסִירוּ means "remove."

The positive antonyms to the terms for violence are מִשְׁפָּט וּצְדָקָה, "justice and righteousness," a semi-synonymous pair throughout the Scripture that summarize the theological and moral aspects of the biblical faith. See the first textual note and the commentary on 18:5, a passage that is all about the doctrine of individual justification (see also 18:19, 21, 27).

הָרִימוּ גְרֻשֹׁתֵיכֶם מֵעַל עַמִּי is, literally, "lift up your expulsions from upon my people." The Hiphil imperative הָרִימוּ probably is used as a correlative to the earlier הָסִירוּ, "remove." I have freely added "the burden of" in an attempt to reproduce the Hebrew verbal picture in English. The noun גְּרוּשָׁה occurs in the OT only here, but its form is the same as the Qal passive participle of גָּרַשׁ, "expel," which can refer to a divorced woman (Lev 21:7, 14; 22:13; Num 30:10 [ET 30:9]; Ezek 44:22). Hence "expulsions" may well refer to "divorces" as well as evictions and forcibly expelling people from the covenant community of the faith.

45:10–17 The reproofs in 45:9 are followed by a series of positive instructions, some specifically involving "the Prince" (see on 44:3; 45:7), others addressed to the people in general. Presumably the Prince will preside over the people, administer the divine mandates (as 45:16–17 emphasizes), and enforce God's will. Ezek 45:11–12 is moral and economic in orientation, while 45:13–17 (as well as 45:18–25) is more specifically liturgical.

45:10 In this verse (and extending through 45:12) the concern is for accurate and reliable weights and measures. With so much of commerce and daily life depending on their use (no modern prepackaging!), we can understand the great temptation to cheat and defraud God's people in one way or another by

---

[11] For the citation formula, see pages 8–9 in the introduction and the fourth textual note and the commentary on 2:4. For the signatory formula, see pages 8–9 in the introduction and the second textual note on 5:11.

[12] Allen, *Ezekiel*, 2:240.

their misuse. The scope of the problem in ancient Israel is evident in the frequency with which this concern is mentioned in all three parts of the OT canon: the Torah, the Prophets (e.g., Micah 6:11), and the Writings (e.g., Prov 11:1; 16:11; 20:10, 23). The commands here have special similarity to Lev 19:36 and Deut 25:13–16 in the Torah.

The Hebrew jussive at the end of 45:10, יְהִי לָכֶם, literally, "may there be for you," is translated at the start for the sake of English. The verb is singular even though its compound subject consists of three construct phrases, each of which has a word in construct (מֹאזְנֵי־, "scales"; וְאֵיפַת, "ephah"; וּבַת, "bath") with צֶדֶק, "righteousness." NIV translates צֶדֶק as "accurate," but that loses the theological motivation that must underlie the use of the measures. It could also be conveyed by "just" (ESV, NASB) or "honest" (NKJV). The point is not simply Law-based morality, but justification by God's grace: righteousness through faith, which manifests itself in righteous living.

The absolute form of "scales" would be מֹאזְנַיִם, which is dual because two objects (a weight and the commodity being sold) were balanced over a fulcrum.

45:11 There is no agreement on the exact size of these standard measures. The variation in their size at different times and in different places is undoubtedly part of the reason God spends time on the issue. We cannot determine whether this verse seeks to reestablish existing standards or define new standards. Both of the cognate nouns תֹּכֶן and מַתְכֹּנֶת (with suffix, מַתְכֻּנְתּוֹ) might mean "measurement" (so BDB), but are best rendered as the "standard" according to which various measures are determined. The Niphal of their verbal root, תָּכַן, was used in 18:25, 29; 33:17, 20 in the people's complaint that Yahweh's ways were not "fair, right, equitable" (see the commentary on those verses). Here God decrees that the homer should be the standard for both the ephah and the bath: each is "to hold, contain" (לָשֵׂאת, Qal infinitive of נָשָׂא) a "tenth" (מַעֲשֵׂר and עֲשִׂירִית) of a homer. One commonly accepted figure defines a homer as the equivalent of 220 liters (about 233 quarts or 58 gallons) so the ephah and the bath would be about 22 liters (almost 6 gallons). Evidently, the ephah was a dry measure and the bath a liquid measure.

Both הָאֵיפָה וְהַבַּת in 45:11 and וְהַשֶּׁקֶל in 45:12 use the article with a measure ("the ephah and the bath"; "the shekel") in a general way, called an "imperfect determination" by Joüon, § 137 m, who cites these examples in § 137 o. The same would also be true of further uses of הָאֵיפָה in 45:11, 13 and הַבַּת in 45:11, 14 as well as of הַחֹמֶר ("the homer") in 45:11 and הַכֹּר ("the kor") in 45:14.

45:12 The previous verse spoke of the weight or volume of the item to be sold, while this one speaks to the amount to be paid for it. It must be understood that all the terms refer to weights; coinage was not introduced until considerably later. The text fixes the weight of the shekel at twenty gerahs, Israel's smallest unit of weight. The gerah is usually calculated as weighing about 0.57 grams, and then Ezekiel's standardized shekel would weigh about 11.4 grams

(0.4 ounces). The largest unit God mentions here is the mina (מָנֶה), whose to-tal weight he computes as being 20 + 25 + 15 shekels, apparently meaning three pieces with those weights, giving us a total of 60 shekels, that is, 24 ounces (1.5 pounds) or 0.68 kilograms. The typical Israelite mina used elsewhere in the OT is usually estimated to have weighed only 50 shekels, that is, 20 ounces (1.25 pounds) or 0.57 kilograms. Perhaps the greater weight here in the MT would ensure that the offerings were generous. Block opines that "if MT is cor-rect, Ezekiel's 60-shekel minah constitutes a metrological innovation, proba-bly inspired by the sexagesimal Babylonian system."[13] The Targum adds that it is a "sacred mina" (מְנֵי קוּדְשָׁא), which hints at God's real concern: not eco-nomic stability as such, but that the full amounts be used for the holy sacrifi-cial liturgy.

The phrase עֲשָׂרָה וַחֲמִשָּׁה שֶׁקֶל, literally, "ten and five shekel," is unusual for several reasons (see GKC, § 97 e, and Joüon, § 100 h). First, it is the only time in the OT that the numeral fifteen is expressed with "ten" preceding "five" instead of vice versa. Second, since שֶׁקֶל is a masculine noun, the second nu-meral (here וַחֲמִשָּׁה) should be masculine, but both numerals are feminine. Third, we might have expected the plural שְׁקָלִים, used twice previously in the verse (with 20 and 25) instead of the singular שֶׁקֶל, although grammatically ei-ther is acceptable.

The LXX has a different text which gives the expected total of fifty shekels for a mina. The RSV and many commentators[14] (some of whom object to the odd grammar of "fifteen shekels") follow the LXX, but not NRSV or most other English translations.

45:13 Ezek 45:13, 14, and 15 give instructions about the offering of grain, olive oil, and sheep, respectively. While תְּרוּמָה ("contribution") referred to land in 45:1, 6, 7, now in 45:13, 16 it refers to a "contribution" for the regular sac-rifices, similar to its use for the choice firstfruits of the harvest (see further on 44:30). "Contribution" may be a bit misleading, because this one is not entirely voluntary. It may be compared to the expected OT tithe (Lev 27:30–32; Num 18:21–24; Deut 14:22–29).

The fraction שִׁשִּׁית הָאֵיפָה, "one-sixth of an ephah" (שִׁשִּׁית is from the num-ber שֵׁשׁ, "six"), is used for "each homer of wheat." But for the barley, the He-brew uses the denominative Piel verb וְשִׁשִּׁיתֶם, "you shall take one-sixth" (see Waltke-O'Connor, § 24.4h, which refers to analogous denominative Piel verbs from שָׁלוֹשׁ, "three," and חָמֵשׁ, "five"). (Some critics prefer to consider וְשִׁשִּׁיתֶם to be the fraction שִׁשִּׁית with a final *mem* resulting from some kind of scribal error.)

---

[13] Block, *Ezekiel*, 2:657.

[14] As usual, Zimmerli, *Ezekiel*, 2:474, and Allen, *Ezekiel*, 2:247, assume the LXX is correct and offer speculations as to how and why the MT's "corrupted" (Zimmerli) text came into being.

45:14 "Statute, ordinance" is a common translation of חֹק, but here something like the "fixed/prescribed portion" seems called for. הַבַּת הַשֶּׁמֶן, literally, "the bath, the oil," must be appositional to the preceding הַשֶּׁמֶן, specifying the measure by which the correct amount of oil will be determined. Many wish to delete the appositional phrase, but the versions support it.

With "the kor" (הַכֹּר) Ezekiel introduces a new measure. "Kor" is used only seven other times in the OT and is a synonym for "homer." Apparently for that reason, a parenthetical statement explaining it is added here. The last two clauses are virtually identical in the Hebrew, עֲשֶׂרֶת הַבַּתִּים חֹמֶר כִּי־עֲשֶׂרֶת הַבַּתִּים חֹמֶר, "ten baths are a homer, for ten baths are a homer." The LXX has a translation for only the second clause, introduced by ὅτι. Interpreters often delete the first clause as dittographical. The Vulgate has two almost identical clauses (*et decem bati chorum faciunt quia decem bati implent chorum*), but with "kor" in each, in place of "homer." I have used the Vulgate's first clause ("and ten baths make a kor") in place of the first Hebrew clause. It fits because "homer" is rarely used as a liquid measure, but "kor" is used for both dry and liquid quantities. Then the parenthesis, in effect, seems to be saying that "kor" and "homer" are equal measures. RSV and NRSV succinctly give "the cor, like the homer, contains ten baths." (Ezek 45:11 had already stated that both a bath and an ephah are to be one-tenth of a homer.)

Assuming those relative sizes for the measures, these contributions turn out to be rates of 1 percent of the olive oil (45:14) and 1.6 percent of the grain (45:13). The next verse will specify 0.5 percent for flocks of sheep.

45:15 Finally, sheep, another major fungible in Israel's economy, is considered. One sheep is to be taken from each flock, which is defined as consisting of two hundred sheep. The sheep are described as מִמַּשְׁקֵה, coming "from" (מִן) the מַשְׁקֵה, in form the Hiphil participle of שָׁקָה, "to water, give to drink." In Ps 104:13 the participle refers to God as the "waterer" of the mountains. But here and in Gen 13:10, מַשְׁקֵה is used as a noun for land that is "well-watered" or "irrigated" (cf. BDB, s.v. מַשְׁקֵה II, 1), hence amply watered pasturage. There fat, healthy animals, as required by sacrifice, will proliferate. "The well-watered [land] of Israel" reminds us of Ezekiel's frequent fond references to "(the) mountains of Israel" in earlier parts of the book (e.g., 36:1, 4; 37:22).

All of the five major kinds of sacrifice prescribed in the Torah (see Leviticus 1–7), including those three mentioned here ("the grain offering, the burnt offering, and the communion offerings"), were part of God's overarching purpose (fulfilled in Christ) "to make atonement." The two major kinds not mentioned in 45:15, the "sin" and "reparation" offerings, proportionately accented atonement and expiation even more than the others, so perhaps that is why they did not need to be mentioned here as accomplishing that purpose.[15]

---

[15] For a summary of the administration of the offerings in Leviticus 1–7 and their purpose of providing atonement, see Kleinig, *Leviticus*, figures 3–5 (pp. 37–39).

In 45:15, 17a, and 17b we have three slightly different lists of sacrifices. Their slight variations merely indicate that all of them are representative and none alone is exhaustive. The נֶסֶךְ, "libation," often translated "drink offering," is included in 45:17. Like the New Moon sacrifices (וּבֶחֳדָשִׁים, literally, "and in the months," 45:17), the offering of libations was a regular ritual observance, but the OT gives few details about either. The major sacrifice omitted in all three lists is the אָשָׁם, the "guilt/reparation offering," but it occurs often enough elsewhere in Ezekiel's eschatological vision (40:39; 42:13; 44:29; 46:20) that we should not assume that it was to be excluded here.

Of course, all of the various OT sacrifices, and all of their specific purposes and promises, are fulfilled by the perfect, all-availing sacrifice of Jesus Christ.

45:16–17 The Torah of Moses had stipulations for regular offerings for the firstborn, (e.g., Num 18:15–19), the firstfruits (e.g., Ex 23:19; Lev 23:9–22), and the tithes (e.g., Lev 27:30–32). But besides those, the people were not asked to make special contributions except for rare and important occasions, such as the building of the tabernacle in the desert (Ex 25:1–9) or the consecration of the Solomonic temple (1 Ki 8:62–66). The prescription in Ezek 45:16–17 of the special contribution to the Prince is unique and can only be compared to such other rare and important contributions. Therefore God here is not reinstituting the old covenant of Moses, but is looking forward to the new and greater covenant in Jesus Christ. Strengthening that view is the fact that God issues no commands like those in the Torah regarding provisions for the sacrifices needed for the major festivals, which will occupy the rest of the chapter (45:17–25), nor for the minor festivals in 46:1–15.

That the offering is for the Prince, who administers the sacrifices for the whole people, to make atonement for them (45:17), gives us further insight into this person (see also on 44:3; 45:7). Even though he is called by the royal term "the Prince" (see also his royal titles "David," "Prince," and "King" in 34:23–24; 37:24–25), he clearly has a priestly office too (as in Ezek 44:3), which adumbrates the office of Christ as Priest, and King. Since the vision given Ezekiel is still pictured in OT terms, we cannot expect it to reveal the person and work of Jesus Christ in the kind of detail provided by the NT, yet these verses certainly point in that direction. Whereas the covenant of Moses emphasized that atonement was made by the priests (e.g., Lev 4:20, 26; 5:6), here the Prince is charged with the responsibility "to make atonement on behalf of the house of Israel" (45:17), and thus credited with that accomplishment, even if still pictured as through the OT means of grace (grain and oil and sheep [45:13–15]). The NT will reveal that Jesus himself is "the Lamb of God, who takes away the sin of the world" (Jn 1:29), and throughout eternity his redeemed people will still recognize him as "the Lamb" who, through his death and resurrection, provided vicarious satisfaction for all their sins (e.g., Rev 5:6, 12–13; 19:7, 9; 21:9, 14; 22:1, 3).

In the vision shown Ezekiel, the people have a regular duty, although motivated by spontaneous love, to supply the offerings. Thus it might be com-

pared to the collection taken up by St. Paul for the poor saints (Jewish Christians) in Jerusalem, which was to be collected each week as the church met for worship on "the first day of the week," that is, Sunday, the day of the resurrection (1 Cor 16:1–3). Certainly it can be compared to the regular practice in all churches of receiving a collection during the worship service, accompanied by the Offertory. The NT, of course, prescribes no fixed minimum portion or tithe (a requirement of Law), nor does it place any upper limit on the percentage Christians can give. Instead, NT giving is based on the Gospel and our free and joyful response to it (2 Cor 9:7). But until the parousia of Christ arrives, there will always be those members who shirk their evangelical privilege to give according to the measure in which they have been blessed (cf. Lk 6:38), and always a concern with how the church will be able to meet its "budget," which should be not just for the congregation's own ministry, but also to support the wider ministry of the church body and its missionaries.

45:16 The construct chain כָּל הָעָם הָאָרֶץ ("all the people of the land") is one of a few examples where a noun following כֹּל has the article even though that noun (הָעָם) is in construct. Probably these examples are to be explained by the frequent occurrence of כָּל־ (כֹּל in construct) followed immediately by a noun with the article (GKC, § 127 g). Here the LXX simply dropped the second word, which some think crept in secondarily under the influence of עַם הָאָרֶץ in 45:22; 46:3, 9. Meaning is unaffected.

The idiom הָיָה אֶל ordinarily means "belong to" someone, but here it is used in the idiomatic sense that the people are under obligation to provide the contribution. The next verse uses הָיָה עַל in a similar sense, for the Prince's duty to provide the sacrifices for atonement. עַל can refer to something devolving upon a person as an obligation or duty (BDB, s.v. עַל, II 1 c). Ezekiel often uses אֶל and עַל interchangeably (see BDB, s.v. אֶל, *Note* 2).

We too can speak of giving as a duty, but we must be careful that its evangelical motivation is clear.

45:17 For the burnt offering, the grain offering, and the communion offerings, see on 45:15. For וְעַל־הַנָּשִׂיא יִהְיֶה, see on 45:16. Details about the Sabbath and New Moon sacrifices, administered by the Prince, will be given in 46:4–7. The emphatic pronoun with verb, הוּא־יַעֲשֶׂה, could mean "he himself will do/perform" (cf. KJV's "he shall prepare"), but given the earlier references to the priests in the new temple (e.g., 40:45–46; 42:13–14, 19, 24, 27), it probably means that the Prince will simply "provide" (ESV, NASB) the offerings, which the priests then would sacrifice. עָשָׂה will have the same meaning again in 45:22–25. Nevertheless, the emphasis is clearly on the Prince himself as the one who procures atonement for the sake of the entire people, in harmony with the NT depiction of "the King of Israel" (Mt 27:42; Mk 15:32) and "the King of the Jews"—the title on his cross (Mt 27:37; Jn 19:19).

In the picture of mutual obligation, after the people have supplied the Prince with the "raw materials," it is his obligation, in turn, to supply the sacrifices at Israel's liturgical activities, to perform expiation. The Piel verb כִּפֶּר,

"to atone," used in 45:15, 17, 20, occurred earlier in an eschatological context of redemption (not just for Israel, but for other peoples as well) in 16:63, and also in 43:20, 26. Only here is it used with בְּעַד, "on behalf of" (ESV), which personalizes the vicarious role of the Prince. (בַּעַד will be repeated in 45:22.) In this eschatological context, Ezekiel's use of "atone," so closely associated in the OT with the tabernacle, temple, liturgy, and sacrifices, points toward the vicarious atonement accomplished by Jesus Christ on Calvary. For the theology of atonement, fulfilled in Christ, see above on 45:16–17, as well as the second textual note and commentary on 16:63; see also "The Measurements of the Altar and the Rites for Its Consecration (43:13–27)."

The Major Festivals (45:18–25)

45:18–25 The reference to festivals in 45:17 leads into a more detailed consideration of the subject, which continues through 46:15. Both this first section (45:18–25) and the second (46:1–15) begin with the citation formula, "thus says Lord Yahweh" (45:18; 46:1).[16] This first section concentrates on the festivals themselves, while in 46:1–15 the Prince (הַנָּשִׂיא) becomes much more prominent.

The calendar used must be Israel's ancient, traditional one. There is no hint here of the Babylonian one, apparently adopted by the Israelites themselves during the exile, at least for secular purposes. Because of the date "in the first [month], on the first day of the month" (45:18), many scholars have thought of a New Year observance, analogous to that great occasion on the pagan, Babylonian calendar, although that theory is no longer nearly as popular as it once was.

The Mosaic specifications for New Moon festivals probably provide a much better entrée to understanding what God shows Ezekiel here. For most New Moons, the Torah prescribed the sin offering of a male goat in addition to burnt and grain offerings (Num 28:11–15). Additional ceremonies were prescribed for the New Moon of the seventh month (Num 29:1–6), which much later morphed into a full-fledged New Year observance, as is still true of *Rosh Hashanah* in modern Judaism.

In Ezekiel, God says nothing of about additional ceremonies on the seventh month. However, he does prescribe a "sin offering" (as it is labeled in 45:19) on the first and seventh days of the first month (45:18, 20). His specification of a bull also differs from the Torah, which usually required a male goat as a sin offering in conjunction with festivals (e.g., Num 28:15, 22; 29:5, 11, 16; see also the sin offerings provided for the dedication of the tabernacle in Num 7:16, 22, 28, etc.). The "young bull without blemish" recalls those in 43:23, 25 (for פַּר בֶּן־בָּקָר, see on 43:19). A bull was required when the sin offering was for the high priest himself (Lev 4:3; 16:3) or when the whole con-

---

[16] For this formula, see pages 8–9 in the introduction and the fourth textual note and the commentary on 2:4.

gregation had sinned (Lev 4:13–14). In Ezekiel, bulls will be required for Passover celebrations (45:21–25). The next verse will also speak of instructions concerning the use of the blood that differ from the uses of sacrificial blood described in the Torah. No reason is given for any of these differences from the covenant of Moses, but they indicate that God envisions a new covenant that is more than a reconstitution of the old, broken covenant.

It is unclear and disputed whether God in 45:18–20 speaks of an annual observance or a one-time event. When he continues in 45:21–25 to speak of the annual Passover, one might assume the former. However, the many similarities between this legislation and the one-time, initiatory purification of the altar described in 43:18–27, evident in the many correspondences in vocabulary, might indicate that what's described in 45:18–20 is also a one-time event. If we assume that it is a one-time inaugural event, a possible antecedent may be found in the consecration of the tabernacle on the first day of the year (Ex 40:2).

While the Torah of Moses was actually written in the fifteenth century B.C., advocates of the obsolete JEDP theory reversed the historical order and supposed that the Torah's "Priestly" stratum was postexilic, and thus came after Ezekiel, writing in exile in the sixth century B.C.. That wrong supposition enabled them to allege that this rite in 45:18–20 was a predecessor of the Day of Atonement in Leviticus 16, the purpose of which was also to decontaminate the sanctuary. Obviously that supposition is impossible apart from the old methodology of source criticism and its total reconstruction of the history of Israel's religion.

45:19 The blood ritual prescribed here corresponds in its totality to nothing in Mosaic ritual. No specific instructions are given in the Torah for a blood ritual on New Moons and feasts (except for the annual Day of Atonement in Leviticus 16). Perhaps the blood ritual for those other occasions was the same as for sin offerings for the high priest and for the whole congregation (Leviticus 4). For those, the priest was to enter the Holy Place to sprinkle the blood before the curtain and on the incense altar, then pour out the rest of the blood at the base of the sacrificial altar outside in the courtyard (Lev 4:5–7, 16–18).

However, there is no incense altar in Ezekiel 40–48, just the great sacrificial altar in the court (43:13–27).[17] Here God prescribes that the priest is to put blood on the doorpost(s) of the temple, on the four corners of the ledge of the altar, and on the post(s) of the gate to the inner court. Twice in 45:19, the MT has the singular מְזוּזַת, "(door)post of" (singular in construct), which could be understood as a collective. Similarly, the singular שַׁעַר, "gate," conceivably could refer to only one (probably then the east gate of the inner court). But if only one of the three gates were intended, one would expect some specification of which one, so that word too may be a collective.

---

[17] There also was what appeared to be an altar in the nave, but which turned out to be a table (see on 41:22).

45:20 We are not told what happened in the middle of the week, but if the parallel in 43:25–27 is relevant, the decontamination rituals were repeated daily during the whole week. In any case, Ezekiel mandates it for the seventh day.

Unintentional sin still is sin, and it pollutes. Thus the entire Bible (and systematic theology) accents fallen man's sin*fulness.* "Original sin," inherited from Adam, is the root cause of all the specific sins people commit, as well as the ultimate reason for death, illness, and all the human evils in the world. "On account of anyone who sins inadvertently or in ignorance" translates מֵאִישׁ שֹׁגֶה וּמִפֶּתִי, which twice uses the preposition מִן in a causal sense, attached to the person whose transgression requires the sacrifice (cf. BDB, s.v. מִן, 2 f). שֹׁגֶה is the participle of שָׁגָה, used primarily of straying livestock, but already in Lev 4:13 and Num 15:22 for unintentional human sin. פֶּתִי is common in Proverbs as an adjective (often used as a noun) describing a "simple-minded, inexperienced, naïve," or "gullible" individual. Here too it is used as a noun, a person who sins inadvertently. Both expressions here can be contrasted with sin committed בְּיָד רָמָה, "with a high hand" (Num 15:30), that is, consciously, deliberately, and impenitently.

The concluding clause וְכִפַּרְתֶּם אֶת־הַבָּיִת, "and so you shall make atonement for the temple" (with a perfect verb with *waw* consecutive), indicates both the conclusion of the occasion described in 45:18–20 and the expiatory purpose of the whole ritual.

45:21 Textually, the last half of the verse presents formidable difficulties, although there is little debate about what it must mean. The appositional phrase חָג שְׁבֻעוֹת יָמִים, literally, "a feast, weeks of days," is reflected in all the ancient versions. One interpretation is that the traditional day of Passover and the following week of Unleavened Bread is here expanded to seven weeks, corresponding to the season of Easter in the church year, extending from Easter Day to Pentecost.[18] However, since 45:23 refers to "the seven days of the feast" (וְשִׁבְעַת יְמֵי־הֶחָג), most assume that the phrase here must mean "a feast lasting a week of days," even though for that we would expect the construct chain חַג־שִׁבְעַת־יָמִים ("a feast of seven days").

The first two words here (חָג שְׁבֻעוֹת) are similar to the construct phrase חַג שָׁבֻעוֹת, "the Feast of Weeks," in Ex 34:22 and Deut 16:10, so-called because it was observed seven weeks, that is, on the fiftieth day, after the first sheaf of the barley harvest was offered during the Feast of Unleavened Bread (Lev 23:15–16). In intertestamental literature and in the NT, the Greek for "the fiftieth (day)," ἡ πεντηκοστή, that is, "Pentecost," is used for the Feast of Weeks.[a] The Feast of Weeks was when the people were to offer the firstfruits of the wheat harvest (Ex 34:22; Num 28:26). However, despite the verbal similarity

(a) Tobit 2:1; 2 Macc 12:31–32; Acts 2:1; 20:16; 1 Cor 16:8

---

[18] Kliefoth, *Das Buch Ezechiels*, 2:257–60, cited by Keil, *Ezekiel*, 2:336. However, after Keil affirms that this view is "sagacious" and "answers to the Christian view of the Easter-tide" (2:336), he concludes, on the basis of 45:23, that the phrase must refer to a feast lasting seven days (2:337).

of the Hebrew name of this festival to the expression here in Ezek 45:21, Ezekiel never refers explicitly to the Feast of Weeks (see further on 45:25).

The day of Passover (פֶּסַח) and the following week of Unleavened Bread (מַצּוֹת) were so integrally connected that each Hebrew term could be used to refer to both together, as פֶּסַח is in Deut 16:1–8, and חַג הַמַּצּוֹת is in Deut 16:16. That kind of metonymy may partially explain the expression here, although the plural שָׁבֻעוֹת, "weeks," remains difficult. Some speculate that חָג was a later addition in order to tie the preceding "Passover" (which would include Unleavened Bread) with the following "weeks," but there is no evidence for omitting חָג. Etymologically, חַג seems indisputably cognate with the Arabic *hajj* ("procession, pilgrimage"), which in Islam refers to a pilgrimage to Mecca—a site, of course, with no connection whatsoever to the one true and triune God and his salvation. But the OT applies חַג to the three annual festivals, Passover/Unleavened Bread, Weeks/Pentecost, and Succoth/Booths/Ingathering, during which adult male Israelites were expected to make a pilgrimage to Jerusalem (Ex 23:14–17; 34:22–23; Deut 16:16).

45:22–24 These Passover ordinances in Ezekiel are recognizably similar to the ones given through Moses, but again there are a number of variations. Here we immediately notice the prominent role of the Prince. In Exodus 12, the first Passover was described as a family observance by all Israelites in their homes. Later in the Torah, God gave the pilgrimage requirement for all adult men (Ex 23:14–17; 34:22–23; Deut 16:16). Especially after the conquest of the land and the centralization of worship in Jerusalem under David, the focus shifted to a national celebration. During the divided monarchy, 2 Ki 23:22 indicates that in periods of spiritual decay, the Passover was neglected, but the reforming kings (Hezekiah in 2 Chr 30:1–27 and Josiah in 2 Chr 35:1–19) revived it and provided the animals, as the Prince is to do here. Chapter 46 will address the Prince's role in the liturgy in greater detail (see also on 44:3; 45:7).

In significant respects Ezekiel's vision stops short of the NT revelation. The Prince has need to sacrifice a sin offering on his own behalf, as well as for the sin of the people (Ezek 45:22), in contrast to Jesus, the great High Priest (Heb 7:26–28). The Prince offers animal sacrifice, whereas Jesus offers his own blood (Heb 9:12). Nevertheless, the role of the Prince (rather than the people, as in the covenant of Moses) as the one who provides the sacrifices points toward the NT, where Jesus provides himself as the perfect, unblemished Lamb to be slain and raised (Jn 1:29–30; Heb 9:26; Rev 5:6, 12; 13:8). As the sinless Son of God, only his death has sufficient merit to atone for the sins of all. St. Paul boldly declares, "Christ, our Passover, has been sacrificed" (1 Cor 5:7). He also applies the theology of the Feast of Unleavened Bread to the Christian congregation's need to expel those who are sexually immoral and impenitent as "old leaven," so that the church can "celebrate the festival … with the unleavened bread of sincerity and truth" (1 Cor 5:8 ESV; see 1 Cor 5:1–13).

The type and number of the Passover victims is somewhat different in Ezekiel than in the Torah. No mention is made in Ezekiel of the Passover lamb, which was killed on the Passover itself (the fourteenth day of the first month) and eaten by the people (Ex 12:1–11). In Ezekiel, a bull is to be offered as a sin offering on that day (Ezek 45:22). On each of the seven days of the festival, seven bulls and seven rams are to be offered as a burnt offering along with a male goat as a sin offering (45:23). In comparison, the Mosaic legislation required two bulls, a ram, and seven male lambs as a burnt offering on each day of Unleavened Bread as well as a male goat for a sin offering (Num 28:16–25). Hezekiah and Josiah provided vast numbers of animals for sacrifice (2 Chr 30:24; 35:7), which makes Ezekiel's prescriptions appear modest by comparison.

As in Num 28:20–21, the animals of the burnt offering are to be accompanied by a grain offering mixed with oil (Ezek 45:24). However, in Ezekiel the amount of grain is larger and the amount of oil is specified (a "hin" is about a gallon or four liters), whereas it was not in the Torah. In sum, the burnt and grain offerings are richer and more copious in Ezekiel.

Moreover, the focus of the Passover celebration seems to have shifted. Originally the blood of the sacrificed lamb caused the angel of death to pass over and not strike down the firstborn of the Israelites, and that tenth and final plague upon the Egyptians initiated the exodus (Exodus 12). Later generations were to celebrate the Passover as God's way of incorporating them into the original exodus redemption (e.g., Num 9:1–14; Deut 16:1–12; Josh 5:10–11). That purpose probably is presupposed in Ezekiel, but the description of the burnt and sin offerings in Ezekiel emphasizes the Passover's sanctifying function to maintain the holiness of the people, lest their sin contaminate God's temple. In all these respects, we can see anticipations of the Lord's Supper, which recalls the original redemption accomplished by Christ on the cross (1 Cor 11:26); furnishes the communicant with the body and blood of Christ, given and shed for the forgiveness of sins (Mt 26:26–28); and thus sanctifies God's people, even as they are called, both individually and corporately, to live in holiness because "Christ, our Passover, has been sacrificed" (1 Cor 5:7, in the context of 1 Cor 5:1–13).

45:25 The last verse gives brief attention to a festival that is not named, but its precedent seems to be the autumnal feast of Succoth ("Booths"; also called Tabernacles or Ingathering). The salient feature here is the festival's virtual identity in observance with the Passover. Five times this verse uses כְּ in commands to perform actions "according to" the preceding instructions for Passover (see BDB, s.v. כְּ, 1 c (1)). This was not at all the case in the Mosaic ritual for Succoth (Num 29:12–34). In the aggregate, Ezekiel requires less of burnt and grain offerings for it than did the Torah.

Of the three great feasts in Israel's "church year" (Ex 23:14–17; 34:22–23; Deut 16:16), God in Ezekiel has specified only the first feast, which fell in the first month (Ezek 45:21–24), and the third feast, in the seventh month (45:25). Was it his intention to divide the calendar into two halves, each half beginning with one of these pilgrimage festivals? At any rate, left unmentioned are (1) the second great feast, Weeks/Pentecost, although שָׁבֻעוֹת, literally, "weeks," in the prescription for Passover (45:21) seems to allude to it; (2) the Day of Trumpets on the first day of the seventh month (Lev 23:23–25; Num 29:1–6); (3) the eighth day as a closing festival for Succoth and its special sacrifices (Lev 23:36b; Num 29:35–38); and (4) the Day of Atonement (Leviticus 16), which is an especially surprising omission considering Ezekiel's near obsession with atonement and cleanliness.

No one rationale explains the omission of all of these. One could assume that God saw nothing in need of change or correction in these areas. Or might we see in these omissions of foundational Torah stipulations at least the start of the transition to the NT, when the Law of Moses will be fulfilled in Christ (Mt 5:17–18; Rom 10:4) and its ceremonial aspects no longer are obligatory for Christians (see Acts 15; Col 2:16), and further still, part of the transition to the eschaton, to the new Jerusalem, where there is no temple, only God and the Lamb (Rev 21:22)? Already Jeremiah (Ezekiel's contemporary) had prophesied that not even the ark of the covenant would be remembered or missed in the new covenant era, when all nations would be welcomed into the kingdom of God (Jer 3:16–17).

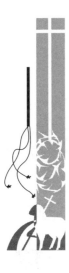

But for now in Ezekiel much of the old covenant remains, especially with the focus on the sin offerings, which reminded the OT believers of their fallen condition before God, yet which also anticipated the plenary atonement to be provided by the Lamb. We who now have the revelation of the new covenant in Christ can see clearly the fulfillment that Ezekiel was shown only from afar. Yet already to Ezekiel God promised the provision of "atonement" (45:15, 17, 20), furnishing forgiveness through the "sacramental" aspect of the OT offerings, to accomplish his standing desire that all should repent and live (18:32; 33:11).

The Minor Festivals and the Prince; Inheritance of the Prince's Property; the Sacrificial Kitchens

Translation

46 ¹" 'Thus says the Lord Yahweh: The gate of the inner court facing east must remain closed on the six days of work, but on the Sabbath day it is to be opened, and on the day of the New Moon it is to be opened. ²The Prince is to enter through the vestibule of the gateway from the outside and stand by the gatepost and the priests are to offer his burnt offering and communion offerings. He is to prostrate himself on the threshold of the gateway, and then go out, but the gate will not be closed until evening. ³The people of the land are to prostrate themselves before Yahweh at the entrance of that gate on Sabbaths and New Moons. ⁴The burnt offering that the Prince is to offer to Yahweh on the day of the Sabbath is to consist of six lambs without defect and a ram without defect. ⁵The grain offering is to be an ephah for the ram, and for the lambs the grain offering is to be as much as he can afford, with a hin of oil per ephah. ⁶On the day of the New Moon, [he is to offer] a young bull, six lambs, and a ram; they are to be without defect. ⁷An ephah for the bull and an ephah for the ram he is to provide as a grain offering, and for the lambs as much as he can afford, with a hin of oil per ephah. ⁸When the Prince enters, he is to come in through the vestibule of the gateway, and by the same way he is to go out. ⁹When the people of the land come before Yahweh at the appointed feasts, anyone who enters through the north gate to prostrate himself must go out through the south gate, and anyone who enters through the south gate must go out through the north gate. No one may return through the same gate through which he entered; he definitely must leave straight ahead. ¹⁰The Prince is to be in their midst. When they enter, he shall enter, and when they leave, [he and] they will leave. ¹¹At the pilgrim festivals and the appointed feasts, the grain offering is to be an ephah for a bull and an ephah for a ram and for the lambs as much as he can afford, with a hin of oil per ephah.

¹²" 'When the Prince makes a freewill offering, either a burnt offering or communion offerings, as a freewill offering to Yahweh, the gate facing east is to be opened for him. He is to offer his burnt offering or his communion offerings just as he does on the day of the Sabbath. When he goes out, the gate is to be closed after he leaves. ¹³You are to provide a yearling lamb without defect as a burnt offering every day to Yahweh. On every morning you are to provide it. ¹⁴You are to provide a grain offering for it every morning: one-sixth of an ephah and one-third of a hin of oil to moisten the fine flour. It is a grain offering for Yahweh. [These are] lasting statutes [to be performed] daily. ¹⁵Thus they will of-

fer the lamb, the grain offering, and the oil every morning as a daily burnt offering.

¹⁶" 'Thus says the Lord Yahweh: If the Prince gives a gift to any of his sons, it is his inheritance and will belong to his sons. It is to be their property by inheritance. ¹⁷But if he gives a gift from his inheritance to one of his servants, it will belong to him until the year of liberation, when it must revert to the Prince. It is his inheritance alone and must remain with his sons. ¹⁸The Prince may not take any of the inheritance of the people by evicting them from their property. From his own property he is to give an inheritance to his sons, so that my people will not be scattered—not a man from his property.' "

¹⁹Then he brought me through the entrance at the side of the gate to the holy rooms that belong to the priests and that face north; look, there was a place at the back toward the west. ²⁰He said to me, "This is the place where the priests will boil the reparation offering and the sin offering, and where they will bake the grain offering in order not to bring them out to the outer court and transmit holiness to the people." ²¹Then he brought me out to the outer court and led me past the four corners of the court. Look, there was a court in each corner of the court—a court in each corner of the court. ²²In the four corners of the court were enclosed courts, forty [cubits] long and thirty [cubits] wide—one measurement for the four of them, cornered. ²³A [masonry] row was all around the inside of them for the four of them, and boiling hearths were constructed beneath the rows all around. ²⁴Then he said to me, "These are the kitchens where those who minister in the temple will boil the sacrifices of the people."

Textual Notes and Commentary
The Minor Festivals and Prince (46:1–15)
The Sabbath and New Moon Offerings (46:1–11)

46:1   The division between chapter 45 and this one rests only on the citation formula, "thus says the Lord Yahweh,"[1] which signals a slight change in subject matter. Major festivals, including the Passover, were covered in 45:18–25. Now the daily and monthly minor festivals are discussed in 46:1–15. The role of the "Prince" (נָשִׂיא) as the supervisor of worship and provider of sacrifices, as described in 45:16–17, is assumed, and sometimes asserted, throughout this chapter. For the Prince's identity and role, see especially on 44:3; 45:7–9, 16–17. He is prominent enough that critics have developed considerable literature attempting to isolate a separate "prince stratum" in chapters 44–48. While they might claim to detect evidence for the compositional history, there are no grounds for positing any editor or arranger besides the author, Ezekiel himself.[2]

---

[1]   For this formula, see pages 8–9 in the introduction and the fourth textual note and the commentary on 2:4.

[2]   The date notice in 40:1–2 indicates that the entire vision of chapters 40–48 was received on that one occasion. God's commands for Ezekiel to preach and write down the vision (40:4; 43:10–11) would have caused him to record it promptly.

In 44:3 God granted to the Prince the divine and priestly privilege that he alone could go into the same eastern gateway of the outer court through which Yahweh himself had entered to dwell in the temple (43:1–12). The Prince was to enter it through a circuitous route, first entering the outer court through either the north or south outer gate, then through the eastern gate's vestibule, which opened into the outer court. Once in the gate, he would eat "before Yahweh." But the east gate of the outer court was to remain permanently closed to access from outside the temple compound.

Here we are informed about activity within the east gate of the inner court. See figures 2 and 4. Unlike the occluded outer eastern gate, the inner eastern gate "is to be opened" (יִפָּתֵחַ, 46:1)[3] until evening (46:2) on Sabbath and New Moon occasions, but not on other days. "Days of work" (יְמֵי הַמַּעֲשֶׂה) is a unique phrase in the OT that alludes to, for example, Ex 20:9; 23:12; 31:15. On these six days, the gate must "remain closed" (יִהְיֶה סָגוּר), the same periphrastic construction (הָיָה with the Qal passive participle סָגוּר) used twice in 44:2 (cf. 44:1) regarding the east gate of the outer court. The construction has a durative force. הָיָה was used with other participles in 34:2 and 43:6. While the English periphrastic construction sounds natural, the Hebrew one became common only in Late Biblical Hebrew. The "Sabbath" (שַׁבָּת) and "New Moon" (חֹדֶשׁ, literally, "month") sacrifices had been mentioned only briefly in 45:17, but details for them will be given in 46:4–7.

Like Is 66:23, Ezekiel here still describes worship in the new era in terms of the OT rites of "Sabbath" and "New Moon" that were familiar to him and his audience. However, Col 2:16 classifies both of these liturgical occasions as adiaphora. Like regulations about food and drink, the Christian is free to observe them, or not. They were but a shadow of the coming things, and what is vital is "the body of Christ" (Col 2:17). In Baptism, "the circumcision of Christ," Christians have been buried and raised to new life by faith (Col 2:11–14).

46:2 Before details on the Sabbath and New Moon observances in 46:4–7, two verses regulate the appropriate conduct of the Prince (46:2) and of the other worshipers (46:3), who are carefully distinguished from each other.

Chapters 40–48 say nothing about a high priest, but the unique privilege granted to the Prince in 44:3, although different from anything in the Torah, grants to him a leading priestly role. The same can be said about the Prince in Ezekiel 46. In this chapter too, the provisions about the Prince are different from any Torah stipulations. Nevertheless, like a high priest, the Prince has a supervisory role over the sacrifices and represents the people before Yahweh. His role may be compared to the unique High Priestly office of Jesus Christ as expounded in Hebrews 2–10 (cf. also John 17).

---

[3] Waltke-O'Connor, § 23.3b, including example 3, argues that the Niphal imperfect יִפָּתֵחַ has an adjectival meaning, "will be open," rather than a passive meaning, "is to be open*ed*." However, that explanation seems to overlook the emphasis in 46:12 on the activity of opening and closing the gate.

The Prince is obligated to be present in the gateway when the priests "offer" (as עָשָׂה, "do," is translated here and in 46:15) the offerings that the Prince is to provide (as stipulated in 45:17) using what the people have supplied to him (45:13–16). The Prince is to enter from the outer court through the vestibule (אוּלָם). See figures 2 and 4. He is then to position himself by a "gatepost" of the gateway. In chapter 40, אַיִל was used for "gatepost, doorpost," but the word here, מְזוּזָה, was used of doorposts in the temple in 41:21; 43:8; and 45:19, and of gateposts of the inner court in 45:19. The gateposts (designated by אַיִל) mentioned in the description of the inner gates in 40:28–37 were the gateposts of the vestibule (at the entrance of each inner gateway). Apparently each inner gateway also had a pair of gateposts by the exit of the gateway into the inner court, one of which is denoted here in 46:2 by מְזוּזָה. (The LXX has the plural τὰ πρόθυρα, "the gateposts.") At the gatepost near the exit of the gateway into the inner court, the sacrificial leader could supervise and observe all that happened in the inner court during the sacrifice. That the Prince remains here also apparently means that he would not venture into the sacred space, which it seems only the priests would enter.[4]

The Prince is not to be merely an idle spectator, but to lead the worship—and not only "spiritually," but through the physical act of prostration. This posture has survived in Christianity only on certain special occasions in Orthodoxy and Catholicism, for example, when a Catholic priest is ordained.[5] Older grammarians explained הִשְׁתַּחֲוָה, "prostrate himself" (whose plural, וְהִשְׁתַּחֲווּ, is in 46:3 and whose infinitive, לְהִשְׁתַּחֲוֹת, is in 46:9) as the Hithpael of שָׁחָה with metathesis of the *taw* and *shin*. Modern philologists believe the root is חָוָה and the conjugation is Hishtaphel (probably an original prefixed הׁתשׁ- underwent metathesis to הׁשׁת-). This is the only verb in the OT in this conjugation, but comparable conjugations regularly occur in some other Semitic languages.

The Prince is to prostrate himself on the "threshold," denoted by מִפְתָּן (used again in 47:1), a synonym of the term for "threshold" used earlier, סַף (40:6–7, 41:16; 43:8). The verse does not specify how long the Prince should remain prostrated, but when he is done worshiping, he is to leave; 46:8 specifies that he is to go out via the same route by which he had entered.

46:3 The "people of the land" does not mean merely "inhabitants" (let alone "landowners, aristocracy" as sometimes elsewhere in the Bible), but in Ezekiel it implies the rest of the worshiping community besides the Prince and priests. "That gate" can only be the previously mentioned east gate of the inner court, but the people are allowed to proceed only as far as its entrance, so they remain in the outer court. It is not clear whether any of the sacred cere-

---

[4] These "priests" would be only the Levitical priests descended from Zadok. See on 44:15.

[5] Prostration is standard practice for all male worshipers in Islam, but the posture does not make that worship acceptable or pleasing to God. See 8:16, where the same Hebrew verb in 46:2–3, 9 was used to describe apostate Israelites prostrating themselves toward the east in idolatrous worship of the sun. True worship is that offered in faith to the one true and triune God (cf. Jn 4:21–26; 14:6; 1 Jn 5:12).

monies are visible to them from that point. It seems unlikely that they could view the priests sacrificing in the inner court, but they may be able to observe the Prince prostrating himself.

Their worship will be "before Yahweh" (לִפְנֵי יְהוָה, at the end of the Hebrew verse, but moved earlier in the translation). The phrase implies that any activity within the temple complex was considered worship in God's presence. That phrase will be used of the people again in 46:9 and was applied to the Prince's meal "before Yahweh" in 44:3. Thus the more distant people are specifically linked with the Prince's worship and the offering of the sacrifice he provides.

The correspondence here (strengthened in 46:10) between the worship of the people and the simultaneous worship of the Prince shows that he has a vicarious role. He approaches God more intimately than any of the people can and represents them "before Yahweh" (44:3), so that, by virtue of his mediation, the people too can worship "before Yahweh" (46:3, 9). Even though the correspondence is horizontal (all taking place in the same temple complex), it might be compared to the vertical correspondence in NT worship. In Revelation 4–5, the saints in heaven (represented by the twenty-four elders, twelve for the OT and twelve for the NT) worship God and the Lamb who had been slain. The worship of the (persecuted, suffering) saints still on earth is simultaneous with and at least partially corresponds to the heavenly worship. This is expressed in the traditional words of the Preface to Holy Communion, when the pastor leading the congregation's worship on earth prays, "Therefore with angels and archangels *and with all the company of heaven* we laud and magnify your glorious name, evermore praising you …"[6]

46:4–7 These verses detour momentarily from the activities in the outer court (outside the inner east gate) to specify what sacrifices are required on the Sabbath and the day of the New Moon. The purpose is to explain what offerings the Prince, as patron of the liturgy, is to make available (cf. 45:17).

46:4 Compared to sacrifices offered during the pilgrimage festivals (45:21–25), Ezekiel's requirements for the Sabbath sacrifices are relatively modest, but compared to the Torah provision for the Sabbath (Num 28:9), they are considerably greater.

46:5 The phrase מַתַּת יָדוֹ, literally, "a gift of his hand," describes the amount of the grain offering required with the lambs. In the OT, this exact phrase appears only here and in 46:11. There are two basic interpretations. It could require the maximum amount, "as much as he can afford" (see KJV, RSV). Or it could leave the amount undetermined, to be decided by the offerer: "as much as he wishes/pleases" (see NKJV, NRSV, NIV). It appears to be synonymous with the phrase כַּאֲשֶׁר תַּשִּׂיג יָדוֹ in 46:7 (which see). The Torah has the similar phrase כְּמַתְּנַת יָדוֹ, literally, "according to the gift [the synonymous noun מַתָּנָה] of his hand," in Deut 16:17. There it describes offerings that all

---

male Israelites are to bring during the three annual pilgrimage feasts (Deut 16:16), and the phrase is parallel to "according to the blessing of Yahweh [כְּבִרְכַּת יְהוָה], your God, which he has given to you."

I have opted for the first alternative because voluntariness does not seem to be prominent in Ezekiel's prescriptions. "As much as he can afford" would mean that the Prince would base this offering on the amounts of the contributions he had received from the people (45:13–16), and perhaps also on the productivity of his own two tracts of land (45:7–8). But the point can be argued either way, and there are no grounds for any definitive decision. In any case, while this amount is left indeterminate, the amount of oil required repeats verbatim the specification of 45:24.

46:6 On the whole, Ezekiel's prescriptions for the New Moon observance are significantly reduced from those commanded in the Torah (Num 28:11–15). Throughout the Bible, Sabbaths and New Moons are frequently paired. Through the prophets, God denounced Israel's performance of them only when they became perfunctory, without faith (e.g., Is 1:13; Amos 8:5), as any worship ritual can become. Hence one can hardly draw any conclusions from Ezekiel's reduced requirements.

For the phrase פַּר בֶּן־בָּקָר, see on 43:19. It is followed by תְּמִימָם, the plural of תָּמִים, not in concord with the singular פַּר, which it modifies. Either the final *mem* is dittographical or the word is assimilated to the plural used appropriately at the end of the verse.

46:7 כַּאֲשֶׁר תַּשִּׂיג יָדוֹ, literally, "as much as his hand can overtake" (Hiphil imperfect of נָשַׂג), probably means "as much as he can afford" and is synonymous with the phrase מַתַּת יָדוֹ in 46:5, 11. Clauses with יָדוֹ as the subject of the Hiphil of נָשַׂג are used several times in the Pentateuch (e.g., Lev 14:22, 30; 25:26). In Lev 25:47, the idiom תַּשִּׂיג יָד means "become wealthy."

46:8 Attention now returns to the Prince. This verse reiterates the notice already given in 46:2 that he must enter the inner gateway via the vestibule, and it clarifies that he is required to leave via the same way he entered. The infinitive with בְּ as a temporal clause (וּבְבוֹא, "when he enters") adds precision to "the Prince is to enter [וּבָא]" in 46:2 to preclude the possible misunderstanding that when he leaves the gateway he has permission to enter the inner court and exit through another gate. Instead, he must leave the gatepost, turn around, and return to the outer court through the vestibule, the same way as he had entered. The same regulation was given in 44:3 for the Prince entering and leaving the east gate of the outer court. (The vestibules of the corresponding inner and outer gates faced each other, both opening into the outer court. See figure 2.)

46:9 Other regulations are needed when faithful laymen come "before Yahweh" to "prostrate" themselves (the same verb used for the Prince in 46:2 and the people in 46:3) in worship. The occasions spoken of are called מוֹעֲדִים, "appointed feasts." This broad term would cover all times and days holy to Yahweh, including Sabbaths and New Moons. It can be distinguished from the

more specific חַג, "feast, festival" used for the major pilgrimage festivals in
45:21, 23, 25. The two words appear together in 46:11 to encompass all occasions when huge crowds would "ascend the hill of Yahweh" (Ps 24:3).

The main concern of the verse is that worshipers exit through the opposite
gate from the one they entered. Pragmatically, this would aid crowd control by
ensuring that everyone kept moving forward. It may also indicate that turning
around within the holy space was inappropriate or even offensive to Yahweh.
In an earlier vision prior to the fall of Jerusalem, Ezekiel had seen apostate worshipers in the inner court of the temple who had turned their "backsides" to
Yahweh (8:16). The regulation here would prevent that orientation.

As in 40:2, here and in chapters 47–48, נֶגֶב is used for "south" instead of
the synonym דָּרוֹם, used throughout the rest of chapters 40–42.

I have taken כִּי as emphatic: "definitely." נִכְחוֹ is a suffixed form of נֹכַח, a
substantive always used as a preposition or, as here, an adverbial accusative.
It could mean "its opposite" and refer back to (literally) "the gate which he entered through it" (הַשַּׁעַר אֲשֶׁר־בָּא בוֹ), meaning that he is to leave by the opposite gate. Or it could refer to the worshiper and mean "opposite himself": the
worshiper is to proceed straight ahead (see BDB, s.v. נֹכַח, 1). The meaning is
essentially the same in either case. The expected form of נֹכַח with third masculine singular suffix would be נָכְחוֹ, and the vowel in -נָ would be the short
qamets chatuph, reduced from the long holem (-נֹ). The substitution of hireq in
נִכְחוֹ (the identical form is in Ex 14:2) may be due to dissimilation, that is, the
desire to avoid two "o" vowels in adjacent syllables (short qamets chatuph in
the first syllable and long holem in the second). See GKC, § 93 q.

At the end of the verse, the Qere, יֵצֵא, "he must leave," is singular, in agreement with the singular verbs in the rest of 46:9: בָּא ... יָשׁוּב ... יֵצֵא ... יֵצֵא. The
subject of the first two of those verbs is the participle הַבָּא, "anyone who enters." The subject of the last two verbs as well as of the Qere is indefinite, referring to any one of the worshipers as a representative of all of them. The
unspecified subject of the plural Kethib, יֵצְאוּ, "they must leave," must have as
its ultimate antecedent the collective עַם, "people," at the start of the verse,
which can take either a singular or a plural verb (see further on 46:10). Ezekiel
is egregiously inconsistent in his use of collectives. Keil even argues that the
Kethib plural is more correct, because two groups of people are implied: "those
who entered by the north gate and those who entered by the south."[7]

46:10 This regulation further confirms the Prince's solidarity with the people, even though he is elevated above them in other respects, and he alone carries out his unique priestly roles (44:3; 45:17; 46:2). Here he is more closely
associated with the people than are the priests, since the priests would not need
to synchronize their movements with the people. (The priests would enter the
inner court to sacrifice the offerings provided by the Prince.)

---

[7] Keil, *Ezekiel*, 2:344.

What is said about the Prince and the people here can be applied to Jesus Christ and the Christian church. It also has application to the pastor as he leads the congregation in worship. Especially on festival days, traditional Christian worship can begin with a processional into the nave with a cross, representing the presence of Christ, which is then placed in the chancel. Usually an Introit or entrance hymn is sung near the start of the service. During the service, Christ comes to his people through his Word and Sacraments and bestows his gifts of forgiveness, life, and everlasting salvation. At the conclusion of the service, the cross is carried out during a recessional. Christ goes with his people as they leave and carry out their vocations during the week. He continues to abide with his people, who have been edified by God's Word and fed in the Holy Supper. In that way, Christ can be said to enter and leave the church with his people.

The plural suffixes ("them") on בְּתוֹכָם בְּבוֹאָם ... וּבְצֵאתָם refer back to "the people of the land" (46:9). The same plural verb, יֵצֵאוּ, that was the Kethib at the end of 46:9 is the sole reading at the end of 46:10. To make sense in this context, not just the people, but also the Prince must be the subject of "they will leave." The implied compound subject is supplied in the translation.

46:11 What is said about the grain offering for the Sabbaths and the New Moons in 46:5, 7 is applied in this verse to all sacred occasions. The worship of Yahweh is to be orderly, not chaotic and ad hoc. For חַגִּים and מוֹעֲדִים, see on 46:9. For the translation of מַתַּת יָדוֹ as "as much as he can afford," see on 46:5 (cf. also on 46:7).

The Prince's Freewill Offering (46:12)

46:12 As the name indicates, a "freewill/voluntary offering" (נְדָבָה) was entirely spontaneous. In the Torah, it is often mentioned together with נֶדֶר, a votive offering in fulfillment of a vow, which could also have been entirely spontaneous, although certain self-imposed obligations would be entailed in the nature of the case. See the regulations for such offerings in Lev 22:18–25 and Num 15:1–12. God here apparently limits "freewill" offerings to burnt offerings or communion offerings, the latter of which involved communal meals.[8] In the Torah also, a freewill offering could be a burnt offering (Lev 22:18; Num 15:3) or a communion offering (Lev 22:21).

"Just as he does on the day of the Sabbath" seems to imply that the rules given in 46:1–2 for Sabbath offerings would also apply to these voluntary offerings, which could be made on any day of the week. This means that on these occasions the east gate, normally "closed on the six days of work" (46:1), would be opened for the Prince so that he could observe the priests (as in 46:2), who would actually perform the sacrifice on the altar. The only difference is that for a freewill offering, the gate is to be closed after the ceremony is over and the

---

8 For שְׁלָמִים, "communion offerings," see the second textual note and the commentary on 39:17 and the fourth textual note on 40:39.

Prince leaves, not left open until evening, as on the Sabbath and the New Moon (46:2).

Literally, וּפָתַח לֹו could mean that the Prince would "open for himself" the gate. However, virtually all commentators and translations take that clause and the later verb וְסָגַר, "and close," as impersonal. This would mean that "someone should open for him" and then "close" the gate. Impersonal verbs can be rendered as passives in idiomatic English, as do many translations, for example, the gate "shall be opened for him" and "shall be shut" (ESV).

The Daily Offerings (46:13–15)

46:13–15 The shift to second singular verbs in 46:13–14 is startling, before 46:15 reverts to the third person plural, referring to the priests. (A similar shift to the second person singular was in 45:18, 20.) Hence the instructions about the sacrifices in 46:13–14 sound as though Yahweh is speaking either to the Prince, who provides the sacrifices from what the people supply to him (45:13–17), or to Ezekiel, who perhaps is merely to convey the instructions to the people. The LXX and Vulgate harmonize with the preceding verses by continuing to use third person singular verbs, as do RSV and NRSV. Many critics naturally take the change in person as a sign of an editorial addition. However, the topics in 46:1–15 follow the precedent of Num 28:1–15, which discusses the daily (morning and evening) sacrifices in connection with Sabbath and New Moon sacrifices.

The Torah required a daily burnt offering and an accompanying grain offering and libation that were to be offered twice daily, in the morning and at twilight (Ex 29:38–40; Num 28:1–8). However, in each of the three verses here (Ezek 46:13–15), God specifies that the daily burnt offering and grain offering are to be offered בַּבֹּקֶר בַּבֹּקֶר, literally, "in the morning, in the morning," simply translated as "every morning." Does this mean that he wishes to drop the evening sacrifice?

Two OT passages indicate that at times the burnt offering alone (עֹולָה) was offered in the morning and the grain offering alone (מִנְחָה) in the evening rite. But one of these passages has to do with the apostate Northern Kingdom (1 Ki 18:29, 36) and the other (2 Ki 16:15) with Ahaz, a king notoriously unfaithful to Yahweh and his Torah, so it is not surprising that both passages depart from the Mosaic regulations. In any case, God here omits the requirement of a libation of a quarter of a hin of wine, which was required for the identical morning and evening sacrifices according to Ex 29:40 (see also Num 28:7–8).

It is possible that God assumed that Ezekiel, a priest (1:3), and his Israelite audience would be so familiar with the Torah requirement for the morning and evening sacrifices that what he says of the morning rite would have its counterpart every evening. On the other hand, by their exile they had been cut off from the temple and its rites, and this was the fourteenth year (40:1) since the temple itself had been destroyed, so the old order was gone. Throughout Ezekiel 40–48, various Torah rites and commands are abbreviated, altered, or abandoned, as we have noted at many points. So it is possible that here God does limit the daily offering to the morning. There is widespread opinion in the commentaries that this is the meaning of the text. If so, it would be a step toward the "once for all" sacrifice of the Lamb of God, Jesus Christ. His singular sacrifice fulfilled all the OT types and at the same time rendered them obsolete.

46:14 In contrast to the unspecified amounts for the grain offering that was to accompany the sacrificial lambs at periodic feasts (46:5, 7, 11), the amount of the grain offering that was to accompany the lamb for the daily offering is fixed. לָרֹס ("to moisten") is the Qal infinitive of רָסַס, a hapax, although there is no doubt as to its meaning. The plural of the cognate noun רְסִיס occurs in Song 5:2 meaning "drops of dew." Oil is used to moisten the סֹלֶת, "fine flour," that is, the flour ground from the heart of the wheat kernel, essentially what we know as Cream of Wheat. The Hebrew word is frequently used elsewhere.

The final phrase, חֻקּוֹת עוֹלָם תָּמִיד, is difficult. The plural חֻקּוֹת, "statutes," is commonly emended with the versions to the singular, חֻקַּת, definitely an easier reading, but the plural may refer to the burnt offering (the lamb) and the grain offering separately. The phrase חֻקּוֹת עוֹלָם occurs only here in the OT, but the corresponding singular חֻקַּת עוֹלָם, "a lasting statute," is common in the Pentateuch for a variety of rites and commands (e.g., Ex 12:14, 17; Lev 3:17; 7:36; 10:9; 16:29, 31, 34). In these contexts, עוֹלָם does not mean "forever," but "lasting" only as long as the old covenant persists, until the fulfillment in Christ has arrived. With the death and resurrection of Christ, "the ends of the ages" (τὰ τέλη τῶν αἰώνων, 1 Cor 10:11) has already begun.

תָּמִיד, properly a noun, is used here as an adverbial accusative for "regular repetition" (BDB, 1 b), that is, "daily" (see further on 46:15).

46:15 The third person plural verb, "they will offer" (as עָשָׂה was also translated in 46:2), implies that the priests were the ones to carry out the daily sacrifices. The Kethib, וְעָשׂוּ, is a classical perfect with *waw* consecutive, which becomes rare in Late Biblical Hebrew, while the Qere, יַעֲשׂוּ, is a simple imperfect.

The construct phrase עוֹלַת תָּמִיד (sometimes with the article on the second word), "daily burnt offering," can be used in the Torah to refer to the entire daily (morning and evening) burnt offering, both the lamb and its prescribed grain offering (Ex 29:42; Num 28:6, 10, 15, 24; cf. Num 28:3, 23). Other passages with that construct phrase add "its grain offering" (e.g., Num 28:31; 29:6, 11) to clarify that both are included. Ezekiel's contemporary in exile, Daniel, uses הַתָּמִיד, "the *tamid*," by itself for the daily burnt and grain offerings, which were offered at the temple every morning and evening (Dan 8:11–13; 11:31; 12:11; see BDB, s.v. תָּמִיד, 2 c [under the root מוד I]). It should be stressed that תָּמִיד does not mean "perpetual," but "regular, quotidian, daily." In biblical scholarship, the daily offering required in the Torah is often referred to by this term in transliteration: *tamid.*

This verse concludes Ezekiel's vision of the new order of worship. Two marginally related supplements conclude chapter 46 before totally different subjects are considered in the book's final two chapters: 46:16–18 concerns the Prince's rights for his landed property (cf. 45:7–9); and 46:19–24 offers a brief description of the sacrificial kitchens.

Inheritance of the Prince's Property (46:16–18)

46:16–18 The overriding concern of 46:16–18 is the maintenance of the divine division of the land to the Prince and among the tribes. Provision is made for the Prince to bequeath his property to his sons, but if his generosity causes him to grant land to non-familial servants, in the Jubilee, the land will revert to the Prince's sons. Similarly, each man from all the tribes is to retain his property and bequeath it to his heirs. This will prevent the tendency toward social stratification that plagues all societies, as "the rich become richer, and the poor become poorer."

Modern, secular societies view property as something to be earned by labor or acquired by shrewd business tactics. In contrast, the underlying assumption throughout the OT is that Yahweh is the real landowner: "mine is the land" (Lev 25:23). By his grace alone, he has granted to his people the privilege of living upon the promised land as his "sojourners and tenants" (Lev 25:23; cf. Mt 21:33–45) and passing it on to their heirs.[9] He granted the land to the tribes in an equitable way (Joshua 13–21), which must not be distorted by human legalism or power plays. Of course, the people's infidelity would cause them to forfeit their share in the land, as happened with all Israel at the exile, and again in A.D. 70 after the Jewish people as a whole rejected the Landowner's Son and Heir (Mt 21:33–45).

In God's eschatological scheme shown to Ezekiel, the Prince's portion had been described in 45:7–8 (which see) and will be again in 48:21–22. The stipulations in 46:16–18 about the Prince gifting his inheritance presuppose that he would give portions of that land described in those two other passages.[10] The allotments of the rest of the tribes will occupy 47:13–23 and most of chapter 48.

46:16 In casuistic form, this verse describes the first of two ways in which the Prince may dispose of some or all of his allotment, if he wishes, and the consequences. The first possibility is that the Prince gives some of his land to one of his sons. In that case, the son passes it on to his sons.

---

[9] The entire chapter of Leviticus 25 is concerned with Yahweh's possession and gift of the land and his provisions for its proper retention by his people as the heirs. Those provisions include the Sabbatical Year and the Jubilee. For a theological analysis one may see Kleinig, *Leviticus*, 547–55.

[10] That these three references to the Prince's property are spread across Ezekiel 45–48 may be due to the editorial process of the book's final shaping by Ezekiel himself under inspiration. Some commentators suppose that other editors were at work and attempt to reconstruct a detailed history of the process, but that is counterproductive.

The protasis of the conditional sentence begins with כִּי־יִתֵּן הַנָּשִׂיא מַתָּנָה, using כִּי in the sense of "if," as is common in OT casuistic laws, and the Qal imperfect of נָתַן (יִתֵּן), "to give, to gift," with the accusative noun derived from that verb, מַתָּנָה, "gift." (This same generic word for "gift," used in 46:16–17, was employed negatively for Israel's idolatrous and abominable sacrificial gifts in 20:26, 31, 39.)

The apodosis follows a Late Biblical Hebrew pattern: an asyndetic clause (נַחֲלָתוֹ הִיא, "his [the son's] inheritance it is") followed by a clause with an imperfect (לְבָנָיו תִּהְיֶה, "to his sons it will belong"). Many commentators[11] and English translations (NKJV, RSV, NRSV, NIV; but not ESV) follow the LXX and instead of just נַחֲלָתוֹ read מִנַּחֲלָתוֹ (as in 46:17): "If he gives a gift *of some* of his inheritance" (NKJV; emphasis added). But the LXX translation may reflect a dittographical repetition of the initial *mem* of the preceding word (מִבָּנָיו). That translation is also contrary to the Masoretic punctuation; the *zaqeph qaton* (-ִ֑-) on מִבָּנָיו is roughly the equivalent of an English comma, as I have translated ("… his sons, it is …"). Thus the nominal clause נַחֲלָתוֹ הִיא is not the last part of the protasis, but the first of two clauses in the apodosis. The suffix ("it is *his* inheritance") does not refer to the Prince (as it does in the next verse), but to (literally) "a man from his sons" (אִישׁ מִבָּנָיו), the son receiving the gift.

The second clause of the apodosis, לְבָנָיו תִּהְיֶה, "it will belong to his sons," could be a synonymous verbal restatement of the preceding nominal clause, but the plural "his sons" likely refers to subsequent generations of heirs: "sons" of the son receiving the gift (the Prince's grandchildren, etc.). That is reinforced by the last three words of the verse, אֲחֻזָּתָם הִיא בְּנַחֲלָה, "it is to be their property by inheritance." The property stays in the Prince's family as it is inherited by subsequent generations of his descendants.

46:17 This verse describes the second of two ways in which the Prince might bequeath his property. The protasis begins with four words that were also in 46:16, וְכִי־יִתֵּן מַתָּנָה מִנַּחֲלָתוֹ, "if he gives a gift from his inheritance." Unlike in 46:16, here the preposition *mem*, in a partitive sense ("some of"), is on מִנַּחֲלָתוֹ. If the Prince deeds some of his inheritance "to one of his servants" (לְאַחַד מֵעֲבָדָיו, with the preposition מִן in a partitive sense), that is, to someone outside of his family, that transfer of title can be only temporary.

As noted on 45:7–9, the Torah of Moses (and its fulfillment in the allotment of land under Joshua) had no provision for a king of Israel to receive any special land grant other than what he possessed as a member of his tribe. Therefore in Ezekiel, the provision of two large tracts of land for the Prince (45:7–8) is a radically different circumstance. But perhaps to relate this provision to the Mosaic Law, Ezekiel here uses the Early Biblical Hebrew pattern for the rest of the conditional sentence. In contrast to the apodosis in 46:16, which was

---

[11] E.g., Zimmerli, *Ezekiel*, 2:495.

asyndetic with an imperfect, this apodosis (וְהָיְתָה לֹּו עַד־שְׁנַת הַדְּרֹור) is syndetic (joined with the *waw* on וְהָיְתָה) and has that perfect verb with *waw con*secutive, The land will belong to the servant (לֹּו, "his," a *lamed* of possession) only "until" (עַד) "the year of liberation" (שְׁנַת הַדְּרֹור).

An exactly equivalent English noun for דְּרֹור is hard to find, but approximating it are "liberation," "liberty," "freedom," "emancipation," and "release," but in a theological sense, not simply a political or economic one. The word cannot be fully understood until one refers to Lev 25:10 and its context. (From that verse, "proclaim liberty throughout the land" is quoted on the American Liberty Bell, but one may question whether the verse should be applied to the United States, as if this country were the new Israel.) The verse refers to "the Year of Jubilee," as the Targum (שַׁתָּא דְיֹובֵילָא), freely but correctly renders the phrase here. According to Leviticus 25, every fiftieth year all Israelites indentured because of debts had to be manumitted, and all ancestral property had to be returned to the family of its original owner. Neither provision would have been very popular with the current owners, and hence it seems probable that both were ignored during much of Israel's history, especially in times of unfaithfulness. Jer 34:8–11 records a temporary manumission of Israelite slaves, but the OT never reports any return of ancestral property at the Jubilee. However, Israel's lack of obedience is no reason to doubt that the law was part of the Torah given to Moses.

LXX Lev 25:10 translates דְּרֹור as ἄφεσις, which in the NT refers to the "forgiveness" of sins and the consequent "liberation" from bondage to sin, death, and the devil, with the promise of the resurrection (cf. Ezek 37:1–14) to life in the eternal state, which is at least partially envisioned in Ezekiel 40–48, and envisioned more fully in Revelation 21–22. Jesus cites Is 61:1, which includes דְּרֹור and alludes to Lev 25:10, in his inaugural sermon in Nazareth, where he announces that the Father "has sent me to proclaim liberation [ἄφεσις] to the captives" (Lk 4:18).[12] God bestows the "forgiveness" (ἄφεσις) of sins through the Lord's Supper with Christ's shed blood (Mt 26:28), through Christian preaching (Lk 24:47), and through Christian Baptism (Acts 2:38). Compare also the bestowal of "forgiveness" through the baptismal ministry of Jesus' forerunner, John (Mk 1:4; Lk 1:77). Everyone who believes in Jesus receives "forgiveness" (ἄφεσις) simply through faith.[a]

"Revert" translates וְשָׁבַת, an archaic Qal third feminine singular perfect (Joüon, § 42 f; GKC, §§ 44 f; 72 o) of שׁוּב, "return," the verb used for the return of Israelites to their land inheritance in the description of the Jubilee in Lev 25:10, 13, 27, 28, 41.

(a) Acts 10:43; 13:38–39; see also Acts 26:18; Eph 1:7; Col 1:14; Heb 9:22; 10:18

---

[12] For the meaning of ἄφεσις (and the related verb, ἀφίημι, "forgive") and a discussion of Jesus' OT citations from Is 58:6 and 61:1 in Lk 4:18 in the context of Jesus' prophetic ministry, see the textual note on ἄφεσιν in Just, *Luke 1:1–9:50*, 190, and commentary on pages 192–94.

The second-to-last clause is introduced by the adverb אַךְ with the restrictive meaning: "it is his inheritance *alone*" (אַךְ נַחֲלָתוֹ). The *zaqeph qaton* accent on נַחֲלָתוֹ shows that it concludes the first of the final two clauses. With their ingrained tendency to prefer the LXX, if possible, many critics emend נַחֲלָתוֹ to the construct form נַחֲלַת, yielding, "the inheritance of his sons will become theirs." However, the MT is supported by the Vulgate and Targum, and it represents the more difficult reading, so for that very reason it is to be preferred. בָּנָיו לָהֶם תִּהְיֶה is, literally, "his sons—to them it will be." בָּנָיו represents a *casus pendens* (see Joüon, § 156 a), and it is followed by a verbal clause (תִּהְיֶה is feminine because its subject is the suffixed feminine noun נַחֲלָתוֹ) and a preposition with a retrospective suffix, לָהֶם, "to them," referring back to בָּנָיו, "his sons." For the construction, see GKC, § 143 b (b) (α).

46:18 This verse gives a reason for the inheritance law at this point. It suggests that "the relationship between family and property" is "a microcosm of the link between the nation and the land of Israel as a whole."[13] It is an echo of 45:8, since it too prohibits oppression using the Hiphil of יָנָה (here the infinitive with suffix, לְהוֹנֹתָם, literally, "to oppress them"). The oppression would be by evicting people from land that they alone were entitled to inherit. This form of oppression is forbidden so that the people would not "be scattered" (יָפֻצוּ, Qal imperfect of פּוּץ, which in the Qal can mean either "scatter" or, like the Niphal, "be scattered"), a vivid way of describing the inevitable dispersal of dispossessed, homeless people. The verb פּוּץ recalls the earlier prophecies that Israel would be scattered among the nations (11:16–17; 20:34, 41; 28:25). It also reminds us of the condemnation of Israel's evil shepherds, whose abuse had caused God's sheep to "scatter" or "be scattered" (forms of פּוּץ in 34:5–6, 12, 21). Moreover, the suffixed עַמִּי here, "*my* people," recalls the same phrase in 34:30 (and numerous references to "my sheep/flock" in chapter 34) in God's promise in 34:11–31 to regather his scattered flock by means of the one Good Shepherd, the Son of David, Jesus Christ (34:23–24). See further the start of the commentary on chapter 34.

The Sacrificial Kitchens (46:19–24)

46:19–24 Finally, Ezekiel turns his attention to the two sets of temple kitchens, where the sacrificial meals are prepared. Ezek 46:19–20 is about the kitchens for the preparation of sacrificial meals for the priests, while 46:21–24 is about those for the laity. Block comments:

> These kitchens affirm Yahweh's determination to commune with them. …
> Yahweh invited his people to eat at his table. Thus Ezekiel's kitchens symbolize paradoxically both the transcendence and the immanence of Yahweh.
> The concern for the sanctity of the divine residence and all that transpires therein accords perfectly with the radiance of the divine glory. However, by eating at Yahweh's table, the Israelites celebrated their covenantal peace with

---

¹³ Block, *Ezekiel*, 2:680.

God and delighted in fellowship with him. Herein lies the relevance of this text for the modern believer. True worshipers … with joyful hearts … accept his gracious invitation to eat the communion meal, the Eucharist, in his presence.[14]

We might wonder why 46:19–20 did not appear after 42:1–14, where Ezekiel was shown the holy rooms or sacristies at the back of which are the kitchens described here (see figure 2). But the guidance formula in 46:19, "he brought me" (וַיְבִיאֵנִי), indicates that the kitchens are described here simply because of the sequence in which God showed and explained the various parts of the eschatological vision to Ezekiel.[15] Logically, these verses that describe the kitchens for the sacrifices are naturally delayed until after the regulations governing the sacrifices (the consecration of the altar of burnt offering in 43:18–27; the legitimate officiants for worship in 44:6–31; the major festivals in 45:18–25; and the minor festivals in 46:1–15).

The guidance formulas in 46:19, 21 indicate that the guide who escorts Ezekiel continues to be the supernatural man, through whom Yahweh speaks to Ezekiel. For this guide, see the commentary on 40:3, and for his role as divine spokesman, see on 43:6.

46:19 In Ezek 44:4 the guide had led the prophet to the front of the temple building. Now, apparently, he is conducted back through the north (inner) gate into the outer court. Then, turning west, he comes to the north-facing priestly sacristies, the "holy rooms," considered part of the inner court. There were also holy rooms facing south. These holy rooms were described in 42:1–14 and mentioned in 44:19. Although there are entrances to the north-facing holy rooms also on the north (42:4), the latter part of 46:19 (see below) indicates that Ezekiel enters them via their east "entrance, passageway," מָבוֹא, described in 42:9. See figure 2.

For the "holy rooms, sacristies," the earlier passages used the construct chain לִשְׁכוֹת הַקֹּדֶשׁ (42:13; 44:19). Hebrew characteristically prefers a construct chain rather than a modifying adjective. Here the phrase is הַלִּשְׁכוֹת הַקֹּדֶשׁ, literally, "the rooms of the holiness," since the noun in construct (הַלִּשְׁכוֹת) has the article. This is one of "a fair number of exceptions" in the OT to the rule that the word in construct does not normally have the article (Joüon, § 131 d, footnote 1; cf. GKC, § 127 f–g). The same exception was encountered in 43:21 (which see). Either this testifies to the exilic decay of the Hebrew language, or, more likely, the article was inadvertently added by attraction to the following הַכֹּהֲנִים.

If the phrase אֶל־הַכֹּהֲנִים, "to the priests," were parallel to the preceding אֶל־הַלִּשְׁכוֹת הַקֹּדֶשׁ ("to the holy rooms"), it would mean Ezekiel is brought to the priests, something intrinsically unlikely. The following phrase, literally,

---

[14] Block, *Ezekiel*, 2:686.

[15] Before 46:19, the last instance of the guidance formula had been in 44:4. Two other forms of the guidance formula occur in 46:21: "he led me out … and led me past." For these and other forms of the formula, see the second textual note on 40:2.

"facing north," refers to the "holy rooms," so this phrase too should modify the rooms. Most likely אֶל is used for possession ("belonging to the priests"), which normally is indicated by לְ. Cooke suggests that אֶל is an abbreviation for אֲשֶׁר לְ,[16] "which belong to."

The "place" shown to Ezekiel was located "at the (very) back toward the west." יָמָּה is יָם, "sea," with a locative *he*. The difference between the Qere, בַּיַּרְכָתַיִם, and the Kethib is not substantial. The Qere is the dual form, and most commentators prefer it because that form, also followed by יָמָּה, is found in Ex 26:27 and 36:32. The dual apparently refers to the two sets of sacristies, one on the north and one on the south. The Kethib probably is to be vocalized בַּיַּרְכֹתָם, "in their backs," with the pronominal suffix evidently referring to the "holy rooms." English translations vary in their preferences. KJV alone reflects the dual Qere in its translation, "on the two sides." NIV also seems to follow the Qere, while NKJV, RSV, NRSV reflect the Kethib.

46:20 The guide relates nothing about the design or appearance of the kitchens, but only their function. The cuts of meat or portions of grain that need cooking are the portions of the sacrifices that the priests must eat on the premises in their official capacity. The portions burnt on the altar require no such preparation.

The relative clause אֲשֶׁר יְבַשְּׁלוּ־שָׁם, referring to the place (literally) "where they will boil there," is idiomatic Hebrew. The identical clause recurs in 46:24. The Qal of בָּשַׁל was used in 24:5 for "boil, cook" in a pot. The synonymous Piel is much more common in the OT and is used in 46:20, 24.

For אָשָׁם as "reparation offering," see the textual note on it in 40:39.

The second relative clause describing the place, אֲשֶׁר יֹאפוּ אֶת־הַמִּנְחָה, "where they will bake the grain offering," is asyndetic (no preposition or *waw* on אֲשֶׁר) and lacks שָׁם, "there" (although Zimmerli, following the LXX, suggests reading וְשָׁם instead of אֲשֶׁר here, thus considering אֲשֶׁר at the beginning of the previous clause to be doing double duty).[17] This is the only occurrence of אָפָה (Qal imperfect), "to bake," in Ezekiel.

The negative purpose clause at the end of the verse, "in order not to … transmit holiness to the people" (לְבִלְתִּי … לְקַדֵּשׁ אֶת־הָעָם), expresses the same danger as did 44:19 (which see) about the priests' vestments. That verse ended with a similar negative purpose clause, but with the negated Piel imperfect, וְלֹא־יְקַדְּשׁוּ. Here the negative particle לְבִלְתִּי is used since the verb is the Piel infinitive (לְקַדֵּשׁ). In the OT sacrificial and sacramental system, holiness is contagious and dangerous (even lethal) if it comes into contact with people unauthorized to use or touch objects infused with that quality.

46:21 The guide now leads Ezekiel to retrace his steps back into the outer court, where he is led from corner to corner all the way around the complex.

---

[16] Cooke, *Ezekiel*, 516.

[17] Zimmerli, *Ezekiel*, 2:498.

For both Hiphil verbs (וָאֵצִיאֵנִי ... וַיַּעֲבִירֵנִי) as forms of the guidance formula, see the second textual note on 40:2. Each of the four corners contained another miniature courtyard. The distributive idiom חָצֵר בְּמִקְצֹעַ הֶחָצֵר, "a court in each corner of the court," is repeated. Earlier this verse had the masculine plural construct form (מִקְצוֹעֵי) of מִקְצֹעַ, "corner," while the next verse will use its feminine plural construct form, מִקְצֹעוֹת, but we have grown used to such variations in Ezekiel.

46:22 There is no agreement on the meaning of קְטֻרוֹת, an adjective or Qal passive participle that describes the small courts. For the plural חֲצֵרוֹת קְטֻרוֹת, the LXX has the singular phrase, αὐλὴ μικρά, "a little court." The Vulgate has *atriola disposita*, "arranged antechambers." The Syriac cognate ܩܛܪ can mean "to tie, bind, join, frame," so קְטֻרוֹת might mean that these courts were "joined" to the walls. (KJV has "joined," but does not say to what.) The Targum has דְּרָתָא מְקַטְּרָן, which may mean "courts enclosed/fenced in," which I, with NKJV and NIV, have followed. Some propose that these courts were "framed" with timbers. Others propose "unroofed," but courtyards by definition are un-roofed. Following the LXX, some propose emending to קְטַנּוֹת, "small," adopted by RSV and NRSV. But Cooke sagely observes that that "emendation substitutes a rather weak word for one which is worth keeping."[18]

All of the consonants in the last word in the verse, מְהֻקְצָעוֹת, are marked in the MT with supralinear *puncta extraordinaria*, probably indicating that the scribes thought these letters should be omitted. However, the scribes were de-termined to transmit the text faithfully even when they had reservations about it, and so rather than omit a letter or word, they added these marks (see further on 41:20).[19] The word is the Hophal feminine plural participle of קצע, which has Aramaic and Arabic cognates meaning "cut off," and which was the root of the noun מִקְצֹעַ, "corner," used in 46:21–22. Hence it probably means some-thing like "cornered off" or "set in the corners." It is a rare example where the preformative *he* of the Hophal is retained even after the addition of the pre-formative *mem* of the participle, hence מְהֻ- (GKC, § 53 q, s). The LXX, Vul-gate, and Syriac do not contain a translation of the word, and so most commentators and translators delete or omit it. Zimmerli suggests that it arose as an approximate dittograph, perhaps added as a gloss, of מִקְצֹעוֹת earlier in the verse.[20] Allen speculates that it originated as a grammatical note on the mas-culine form of that word, מִקְצוֹעֵי, in 46:21.[21]

46:23 The masculine noun טוּר refers to a "row" of stones or masonry in a building wall, as also for Solomon's temple and palace (1 Ki 6:36; 7:12). The

---

[18] Cooke, *Ezekiel*, 514.

[19] See Israel, *Introduction to the Tiberian Masorah*, §§ 79–80; Tov, *Textual Criticism of the Hebrew Bible*, 55–57.

[20] Zimmerli, *Ezekiel*, 2:499.

[21] Allen, *Ezekiel*, 2:249.

feminine plural of טִירָה, used later in this verse, must be a synonym, though elsewhere in the OT, it usually refers to a circular encampment. Zimmerli thinks of stone walls fencing in the courts,[22] but since the "boiling hearths" (the Piel participle מְבַשְּׁלוֹת literally means "boilers") are built beneath or at the bottom of them, we should probably think of a "ledge" (NIV) or of a cooking facility made of tiered stones. In the phrase וּמְבַשְּׁלוֹת עָשׂוּי, the word עָשׂוּי is uninflected (not plural), as in 40:17 (see the textual note there) and 41:18–19. GKC, § 121 d (c), proposes that the implied subject of עָשׂוּי is a (singular) place and that the preceding וּמְבַשְּׁלוֹת is an accusative of result. If so, the phrase would mean that "(there was a place) constructed (to make) boiling hearths."

46:24 The construct phrase בֵּית הַמְבַשְּׁלִים, literally, "the house of the boilers," is a rare example of a plural of a construct phrase (meaning "the house*s* of the boilers") formed with only the genitive word in the plural (הַמְבַשְּׁלִים). All of the OT examples of this kind of construction have the singular בֵּית in construct with a plural noun. בֵּית must be translated as a plural, as confirmed by the preceding אֵלֶּה ("these are"). See Joüon, § 136 n; GKC, § 124 r. I have translated in idiomatic English: "the kitchens."

"The ministers of the temple" (מְשָׁרְתֵי הַבָּיִת) are all the Levites who are not sons of Zadok. In Ezekiel, God retains only the Zadokites as priests. The other Levitical priests are demoted to serve merely as Levites, and no longer as priests, because of their infidelity. See on 44:9–16. The participle in construct, מְשָׁרְתֵי, is the Piel of שָׁרַת, "to minister, serve," which described the (non-Zadokite) Levites in 44:11 (cf. 44:12), who merely serve before the people. The Piel was also used to describe the ministry of the priests in 44:15–17, 19, 27, who serve before Yahweh.

זֶבַח is obviously collective ("sacrifice*s*"). Here it probably refers specifically to the "communion offerings" (שְׁלָמִים, traditionally translated "peace offerings"), in which some of the meat reverted to the worshiper(s), who could eat it in the temple precincts. See on 43:27 (also the second textual note and the commentary on 39:17, and the fourth textual note on 40:39). The accounts of the specifications and construction of the tabernacle and Solomon's temple do not mention the kitchens, but other OT passages do (Deut 16:7; 1 Sam 2:12–17; 2 Chr 35:11–13). Archaeologically, we know that they were standard in pagan temples, where "feeding" the gods figured so prominently. However, in the worship of the one true and triune God, who needs no food (Ps 50:8–13), it is he who furnishes a meal for his people. In the Divine Service (so named because God serves his church as he comes to his people through his Word and Sacraments), the Sacrament of the Altar furnishes the body and blood of Christ, given and shed for the forgiveness of their sins.

---

[22] Zimmerli, *Ezekiel*, 2:501.

Life-Giving Water in the New Creation to Be Apportioned to Israel

Translation

47 ¹Then he brought me back to the entrance of the temple. Look, water was flowing out from under the threshold of the temple toward the east (for the temple faced east)! The water was flowing down from under the south side of the temple, south of the altar. ²He led me out through the north gate and brought me around on the outside to the outer gateway facing east, and look, water was trickling out from the south side. ³As the man went out to the east a measuring line was in his hand. He measured off a thousand cubits, and then led me through the water. The water was ankle-deep. ⁴Then he measured off another thousand [cubits] and led me through the water. The water was knee-deep. He measured a thousand more and led me through water that was now waist-deep. ⁵He measured a thousand more, but now it was a river that I was not able to cross because the water had risen so much that they were waters for swimming, a river that could not be crossed. ⁶Then he asked me, "Have you noticed, son of man?" and he led me and brought me back to the bank of the river. ⁷When I returned there, look, on the bank of the river was a vast number of trees, on both sides. ⁸Then he said to me, "These waters are flowing out to the eastern region. They go down to the Arabah and go into the (Dead) Sea, into the sea [whose waters are] polluted, and the waters [of the sea] are healed. ⁹Every living creature that swarms in every place where the rivers go will live. There will be vast numbers of fish because these waters have gone there, and [the Dead Sea's waters] are healed, [and so every living creature] will live—everywhere the river goes. ¹⁰It will be that fishermen will stand beside it from En-gedi to En-eglaim, and there will be places for them to spread their nets to dry. As for species, their fish will be like the fish of the Great [Mediterranean] Sea—so very many. ¹¹But its swamps and marshes will not be healed; they will be left for salt. ¹²Beside the river, there will grow on both its banks every kind of tree providing food. Its leaves will never wither, and its fruit will never fail. Every month it will bear fruit because its waters flow out from the sanctuary. Its fruit will provide food, and its leaves will be for healing."

¹³"Thus says the Lord Yahweh: These are the boundaries according to which you are to divide the land as an inheritance for the twelve tribes of Israel. Joseph is to have two portions. ¹⁴You will inherit in equal portions the land that I swore with uplifted hand to give to your fathers. Thus this land will fall to you as an inheritance.

¹⁵"This is to be the boundary of the land: on the north side, from the Great [Mediterranean] Sea by way of Hethlon to Lebo-hamath to Zedad, ¹⁶Beruthah,

and Sibraim, which is on the border between Damascus and Hamath, as far as Hazer-hatticon, which is on the border of Hauran. [17]Thus the border will be from the [Mediterranean] Sea to Hazar-enon, on the border of Damascus to the north, which also is the border of Hamath. This is the north side. [18]On the east side, [the border will run from Hazar-enon] between Hauran and Damascus. Between Gilead and the land of Israel is the Jordan; it is the border as far as the Eastern [Dead] Sea; [the border then will run] to Tamar. This is the east side. [19]On the south side southward, [the border will run] from Tamar to the waters of Meribah-kadesh, then along the Wadi [of Egypt] to the Great [Mediterranean] Sea. This is the south side to the south. [20]On the west side, the Great [Mediterranean] Sea is the border until [a point] opposite Lebo-hamath. This is the west side.

[21]"So you are to apportion this land for yourselves, for the tribes of Israel. [22]You are to allot it as an inheritance for yourselves and for the aliens who have settled among you, who have fathered children among you. They are to be to you as a native-born person among the sons of Israel. With you they are to receive allotments as an inheritance among the tribes of Israel. [23]In whatever tribe the alien has settled, there you are to give him his inheritance, says the Lord Yahweh."

Textual Notes and Commentary

47:1–48:35 All the rest of the book is a vision of the new land. Sometimes the final verses (48:30–35) on the new Jerusalem are considered a sort of an appendix, but they cannot be disassociated from the preceding material.

If there were ever any doubt about the otherworldly and eschatological orientation of chapters 40–48, they will dissipate after these final two chapters, especially the opening section, 47:1–12. The vision shown Ezekiel is nothing that could be implemented by Ezekiel's fellow Israelites after the exile, nor could it be achieved by Christians during a millennial reign of Christ on this earth. Rather, only God himself can bring about the rejuvenation of the land to an Edenic state as pictured here, and this God has promised to do after the return of Jesus Christ (Revelation 21–22). In short, Ezekiel 47–48 depicts the new heavens and new earth in which all God's redeemed believers will dwell for eternity.[1] The same implication is in Rom 8:10–23 (cf. Acts 3:21), which promises that after the return of Christ, all believers will be raised bodily to eternal life, and even "the creation itself will be freed from its slavery to decay into the freedom of the glory of the children of God" (Rom 8:21).

---

[1] See further "Introduction to Ezekiel 40–48." Some Christians wrongly suppose that the temple envisioned in chapters 40–42 is to be built during a future millennial reign of Christ on this earth and that the sacrifices prescribed in chapters 43–46 are to be offered there. However, that scenario contradicts the NT and becomes impossible as the vision continues in chapters 47–48.

Ezekiel 47:1–12 in Light of the NT and Christian Interpretation

In what is virtually a "new creation" scene, Ezekiel first describes a thorough revivification of the land as a result of the river of the water of life flowing out from the temple. Possible sources and/or parallels to this part of the vision, as well as the overview of the history of its exegesis, will be considered because of the importance of this passage.

One must be circumspect in inquiring about the sources of this vision. Critical scholars suppose that Ezekiel drew on other written and/or oral sources and combined them with his own ideas as he (and later, his followers) composed the text. However, Ezekiel himself states that the vision was revealed and explained to him by Yahweh and his supernatural guide (40:1–4). The prophet's role was largely passive: to see the vision, write it down, and preach it to the Israelites (40:4b; 43:10–11). The supernatural process of inspiration (and whatever else might have been revealed to Ezekiel in addition to what is in his book) we cannot investigate. Extrabiblical writings with surface similarities are too distant in theological content to draw any conclusions from.

The only sources available to us are the text of Ezekiel and other biblical ones. For them "parallels" would often be better than "sources," partly because we are sometimes unsure whether they precede or date after Ezekiel (sixth century B.C.), and partly because they may be independent revelations, without any literary dependency. Certain traditions (whether oral or written) may have been known among God's people before their incorporation into the inspired biblical revelation. Critical axioms that often equated simplicity and brevity with early date must be abjured.

The starting point must be the creation narrative of Genesis 1–2 itself.[2] The notes below on individual verses in Ezek 47:1–12 explain various points where "new creation" pictures possibly drawn from Genesis are evident. At several points earlier in Ezekiel, the location of Eden appears as a paradise on a "mountain" (28:14, 16; 31:12) as well as being a "garden" (28:13; 31:8–9).[3] Paradisiacal mountain references appear elsewhere, for example, Is 11:9 and 25:6 and the parallel passages Is 2:2–4 and Micah 4:1–3. Ezek 47:1–12 plainly merges two pictures, that of Eden (original or restored) and that of Mount Zion/Jerusalem. Apparently, the same "vertical typology" that made the ark simultaneously God's throne (e.g., 1 Sam 4:4) and his footstool (1 Chr 28:2) was easily extended in ever-widening concentric circles to Jerusalem, to the whole land of Israel, and ultimately, in visions of the eschaton, to the entire new heavens and new earth (Isaiah 11; 65:17–25; Revelation 21–22). Although Ezekiel's

---

[2] These chapters, of course, are part of the Torah composed by Moses in the fifteenth century B.C., some nine centuries before Ezekiel.

[3] In 28:1–19, the fall of the king of Tyre is likened to the fall of Satan and/or the fall of Adam into sin and his subsequent expulsion from Eden. Similarly, in chapter 31, Assyria is likened to a cedar in Eden that was felled, the same fate that will befall Pharaoh in Egypt.

major focus is on the environs of Jerusalem, the universal implications of the Gospel of life are implicit. Adam and Eve were expelled from Eden because of their sin, but God's salvation enables all believers to regain access to the everlasting paradise. In the OT era, this salvation was bestowed through the divine service at the Jerusalem temple, replaced by the person of Christ himself (Jn 2:18–23), who promises "paradise" to all who trust in him (Lk 23:43; Rev 2:7).

Eschatological descriptions of almost boundless fertility are rife in the OT. They are the Gospel remedy for the curse of sterility and death brought by sin. One need mention only the conclusion of Amos (9:13–15), the "great reversal" structure of Hosea 1–2, and countless examples in the Psalms and Isaiah.[a]

(a) E.g., Isaiah 11; 35; 44:1–5; 49; 54–55; 60–61; 65

Fertility requires water, and so Ps 46:5 (ET 46:4) speaks of a river with multiple streams in connection with Zion, possibly associated symbolically with the Gihon Spring in the Kidron Valley directly below the City of David (Ophel). Ps 36:9–10 (ET 36:8–9) speaks of "the river of your [Yahweh's] delights" and "a fountain of life" in connection with Yahweh's house. The closest OT parallel to Ezekiel's vision is near the end of the book of Joel (4:17–18 [ET 3:17–18]), where among other pictures of eschatological plenty we find a prediction that "all the streambeds of Judah will flow with water, and a spring will issue from the house of Yahweh and will water the wadi of Shittim."[4]

Perhaps Zech 14:5b–11 (late sixth century) is at least partially dependent on Ezekiel's earlier prophecy. It describes an even more drastic geographical change than did Ezekiel. The temple no longer plays any explicit role, but "living waters" flowing from Jerusalem are pictured, and they will flow year-round, "half of them to the Eastern [Dead] Sea and half of them to the Western [Mediterranean] Sea" (Zech 14:8).

In the NT, if not a quotation, then at least an allusion to Ezek 47:1–12 and Zech 14:8 can be seen in Jn 7:37–39, where Jesus cites "the Scripture" that speaks of "living water" flowing from within the believer. The evangelist John explains that this refers to the gift of the Holy Spirit, which believers would receive (on Pentecost, and subsequently through Christian Baptism [Acts 2:38–39]) after Jesus was glorified (on Easter and then Ascension). Another close verbal and thematic parallel to Jn 7:37–39 is Song 4:15, where Solomon's beloved bride (a type of the bride of Christ) is portrayed in Edenic terms as a verdant garden with "living waters and flowing streams from Lebanon."[5] Jn 7:37–39 caps a series of passages, beginning with the baptism and testimony of John the Baptist (Jn 1:24–36), the necessity to be "born again of water and the Spirit" (Jn 3:5), and Jesus' offer of "living water" to the Samaritan woman

---

[4] The date of Joel is uncertain. It may date to the ninth or eighth century, or it may be more or less contemporaneous with Ezekiel in the sixth century.

[5] For a Christian exposition of the water imagery in Song 4:12–15 in light of the Gospel and Revelation of John (among other passages), one may see Mitchell, *The Song of Songs*, 29–30, 868–73.

by the well (Jn 4:10–14), that associate flowing water with the gift of the Spirit, regeneration, and life everlasting. As in Ezek 47:1–12, where the flowing water enables what was dead to have life, so these other passages with "living water(s)" refer not simply to flowing water, but water that gives life through the power of the Spirit, who is "the Lord and giver of life" (Nicene Creed, alluding to Jn 6:63). This vivifying water is poured out in Holy Baptism (Acts 22:16; Eph 5:26–27; Titus 3:5; 1 Pet 3:21).[6] The LXX translation of Ezek 47:3 with ὕδωρ ἀφέσεως, which can mean "water of forgiveness," helped early church interpreters connect the river portrayed in 47:1–12 with Baptism.[7] See also the commentary on 36:25–26, where God speaks of sprinkling clean water and bestowing his Holy Spirit (similar is Is 44:3, which speaks of God pouring out water and his Spirit).

There is no doubt that the vision given the apostle John in Rev 22:1–2 is intended to recall and fulfill that given Ezekiel. The temple in its old sense no longer figures, because God and the Lamb will be the temple of the new Jerusalem (Rev 21:22), and from their throne will flow the "water of life," clear as crystal, through the middle of the street (Rev 22:1–2). "On either side of the river was the tree of life, producing twelve kinds of fruit, bearing its fruit every month, and the leaves of the tree are for the healing of the nations" (Rev 22:2)—words that repeat Ezek 47:7, 12 almost verbatim. "The tree of life" is the language of paradise restored (Gen 2:9; 3:22, 24; cf. Prov 3:18; 11:30). Christ promises, "To the one who is victorious, I will grant to eat from the tree of life, which is in the paradise of God" (Rev 2:7), and God gives that victory to every believer through enduring faith (1 Cor 15:57; 1 Jn 5:4).

Brighton summarizes:

> The fact that in Ezek 47:1–12 this water comes from the temple indicates that it is through God's covenantal presence in his Word and in the forgiveness of sins provided by divinely ordained sacrifice, which was fulfilled in Christ, that this saving power flows from God. That it also comes from Jerusalem (Zech 14:8) suggests that because of the salvation brought about in Zion, this spiritual power would go forth from the holy city. "The river of the water of life" here in Rev 22:1 refers to the spiritual power of God and of the Lamb that will sustain forever the communal life of God's people with him in the new heaven and earth. It also indicates that all physical life will also be richly supplied by pure natural water as in the first Eden.[8]

Implicit in Ezek 47:1–12 is the theme of the curse supplanted by blessing. The transgression of Adam brought the divine curse and death upon the origi-

---

[6] The *Didache*, a second-century Christian catechetical manual, recommends that Christian Baptism be performed with "living water" (ὕδωρ ζῶν), but allows that if such water is unavailable, "any other water" (ἄλλο ὕδωρ) will do (*Didache* 7:1–2).

[7] See on 47:3 below. The note on 47:4 also mentions an LXX manuscript with "water of blessing."

[8] Brighton, *Revelation*, 625.

nal creation and prevented his access to the tree of life (Gen 3:17–24). Christ absorbed the divine curse in his death on the cursed "tree" of the cross (Gal 3:13; 1 Pet 2:24). Thus his cross is, in a sense, the new tree of life, since by it the devil, who overcame Adam and Eve by means of a tree, has been overcome.[9] Moreover, God enables the believer to become a blessed, continually watered, ever fruitful tree whose leaves never wither (Ps 1:1–3; Jer 17:7–8; cf. Jn 15:1–8), just like those trees depicted in Ezek 47:12 and Rev 22:2, when "there will no longer be any cursed thing" (Rev 22:3).

While the NT does not provide a detailed verse-by-verse exegesis of Ezekiel's vision, its appropriation by the seer of Patmos certainly points to a Christological and Spiritual focus, and we must await the beatific vision we ourselves will behold in God's good time, by his grace. Excluded, of course, is the literalism of millennialists who expect a rebuilding of the temple on the present Mount Zion with water issuing out of it.

Not surprisingly, the early church expounded Ezekiel's vision freely, including the Antiochan interpreters Theodoret, Theodore of Mopsuestia, Ephraem of Edessa, and others, generally known for a more literal-typological approach than Alexandrian exegetes.[10] St. Jerome, who was of essentially the Antiochan persuasion, found in the river an image of the teaching of the church and the grace of Baptism. He said that the river flows along between two rows of trees, the books of the Old and the New Testaments, fructifying everything and even renewing the Dead Sea of the souls that died in sin.[11] Those commentaries on Ezekiel that are overtly Christian generally interpret the passage in light of the NT.[12]

Unfortunately, the traditional lectionaries now used in Lutheran and other churches do not include Ezek 47:1–12. However, if the traditional date reserved for St. Ezekiel, July 21, falls on a Sunday, this vision would be an enticing candidate for a sermon text. If the very appellation *St.* Ezekiel rings strange in our ears, it is a reminder of the extent to which we have de facto forgotten to include OT believers in "the communion of saints" (Apostles' Creed), and in "all the company of heaven"[13] who worship with us. Some liturgical churches use

---

9   See the Proper Preface for Holy Week: "On the tree of the cross you gave salvation to mankind that, whence death arose, thence life also might rise again and that he who by a tree once overcame likewise by a tree might be overcome, through Jesus Christ our Lord" (*LW*, p. 147).

10   Block summarizes the views of Theodoret and, briefly, some of the other Antiochenes (*Ezekiel*, 2:699–700, including nn. 72–73, citing Neuss, *Das Buch Ezechiel in Theologie und Kunst*, 59–60, 62–63, 75).

11   Jerome, *Commentariorum in Hiezechielem* (CCSL 75:714–15), cited in Neuss, *Das Buch Ezechiel in Theologie und Kunst*, 75, and Zimmerli, *Ezekiel*, 2:515.

12   See, for example, Keil, *Ezekiel*, 2:358–61; Hengstenberg, *Christology of the Old Testament*, 3:65–76; and Block, *Ezekiel*, 2:696–703.

13   From the Proper Preface that introduces the Sanctus in the Service of the Sacrament (e.g., *LW*, p. 146).

the canticle *Vidi Aquam*[14] in the Easter Vigil and throughout Eastertide as the worshipers reaffirm God's promises bestowed upon them in Christian Baptism. Many other hymns refer to living water or a river flowing from the temple or throne of God, or allude to this passage by way of the tree of life and its fruit and healing leaves.[15]

Regarding the Hebrew text, Block points out that in modern times, "because of its uncharacteristic lexical forms, doublets, repetitions, grammatical anomalies, substantive infelicities, and awkward interruptions, critical scholarship has not taken kindly to the text of 47:1–12."[16] But many of these peculiarities are common throughout Ezekiel. Those that seem significant, we shall consider as we meet them.

A positive observation by Block about the form of the text is that if we look beyond the verse divisions, the section divides into two parts, virtually identical in length: 47:1–7 contains a hundred Hebrew words, and 47:8–12 has a hundred and two. The two subsections are distinct in that 47:1–7 is basically narrative in form, while 47:8–12 is nearly all divine speech.[17] "Form criticism" usually helps little if any (and may hinder) in understanding biblical texts, and Block's suggestion of a "literary cartoon" (as he had also styled the Gog oracle in chapters 38–39)[18] hardly seems like the appropriate label. I doubt if we can say much more in that respect than that this is a section of "divine visions" (40:2; cf. 1:1), with all the vast variety that that may encompass.

47:1 Ezekiel was last situated near the sacrificial kitchens in the corners of the temple compound (46:21–24) and is now brought back to the פֶּתַח, "entrance" of the temple, probably at the entrance to the nave.[19] See figures 2 and 5. The one who conducts the prophet is the supernatural guide (see the commentary on 40:3 and also on 43:6). He addresses Ezekiel as "son of man" (47:6) just as Yahweh does throughout the book.[20] Several different Hiphil verbs (all third masculine singular imperfect with *waw* consecutive and first common sin-

---

[14] *Vidi aquam egredientem de templo a latere dextro. Alleluia. Et omnes ad quos pervenit aqua ista salvi facti sunt et dicent: Alleluia. Alleluia* (*Missale Basileense Saec. XI: Codex Gressly* [ed. Anton Hänggi and Pascal Ladner; Freiburg, Switzerland: Universitätsverlag Freiburg, 1994], vol. 1, § 215.2). ("I saw water coming out from the temple on the right side. Alleluia. And all to whom this water has come have been saved and will say, 'Alleluia. Alleluia' " [author's translation].)

[15] For example, stanza 4 in "The Tree of Life" (*LSB* 561) refers to the cross as "the tree of life" from which "flows life eternal" and which provides "salvation's living fruit."

[16] Block, *Ezekiel*, 2:689.

[17] Block, *Ezekiel*, 2:690.

[18] Block, *Ezekiel*, 2:690. Block maintains that "virtually every detail of the vision is unrealistic and caricatured" (2:700), and "these features suggest an impressionistic literary cartoon with an intentional ideological aim" (2:701). He had called Ezekiel 38–39 "a satirical literary cartoon strip" (2:431).

[19] Although Zimmerli, *Ezekiel*, 2:511, thinks of the front of the temple building.

[20] See the second textual note and the commentary on 2:1.

gular suffix) serve as forms of the guidance formula: וַיְשִׁבֵנִי, "he brought me back," in 47:1, 6; וַיּוֹצִאֵנִי, he led me out," in 47:2; וַיְסִבֵּנִי, "he brought me around," in 47:2; וַיַּעֲבִרֵנִי, "he led me through," in 47:3, 4 (twice); and וַיּוֹלְכֵנִי, "he led me," in 47:6. See the second textual note on 40:2.

For the water's course, see figure 2. Naturally, it flows down because of the gradually descending levels of the temple of the temple and the courts as described in chapters 40–42. However, since Ezekiel began his tour outside the temple complex, he had referred to seven steps leading up to the outer court (40:22, 26; see also 40:6), then eight steps up to the inner court (40:31, 34, 37), and finally ten steps leading up into vestibule of the temple itself (40:49).

At its source, the water flowed out מִתַּחַת מִפְתַּן הַבַּיִת, "from under the threshold of the temple" (47:1). The מִפְתָּן was the stone slab at the base of a door, part of which would be visible to an observer on the outside. The second half of the verse defines the place of the water's emergence more precisely: מִתַּחַת מִכֶּתֶף הַבַּיִת הַיְמָנִית, "from under the south side of the temple." Here מִתַּחַת is somewhat awkwardly repeated (but omitted in the versions); it is possibly more intelligible if separated syntactically from the following מִכֶּתֶף (literally, "from under, from …"). כָּתֵף, "shoulder," as an architectural term refers to a "side" or "sidewall" of the temple façade. Here we should attempt to visualize the part of the eastern wall of the nave between the door and the pillars. Since the orientation is eastward (כִּי־פְּנֵי הַבַּיִת קָדִים, literally, "the face of the temple was east"), the phrases in 47:1–2 with כָּתֵף and הַיְמָנִית, literally, "the right side," are translated as "the south side." From the corner of the southern wall of the vestibule and the eastern wall of the nave, the water flowed across the inner court past the south side of the altar of burnt offering and then across the outer court. See figure 2.

Hengstenberg opines that the indwelling of the Glory of Yahweh in the temple, which Ezekiel had witnessed in 43:1–12, was necessary for the life-giving water to flow from the temple, and that that indwelling points to the incarnation of Christ, "in whom all the fullness of the Deity dwells bodily" (Col 2:9).[21] The flow of the water past the altar suggests that sacrificial atonement (by Christ) was necessary in order for the new life brought by the river to come to the dead and barren creation (and creatures, including humanity).

47:2 Because the eastern outer gateway was closed to human traffic after the Glory of Yahweh entered the temple (44:1–3), the guide must lead Ezekiel through the northern gateway and around the outside. (The word דֶּרֶךְ is somewhat intrusive in the phrase דֶּרֶךְ הַפּוֹנֶה קָדִים since the phrase is describing the "gateway [שַׁעַר] … facing east.") Here again Ezekiel can see the flow of water. Since it is the same water already mentioned, one would expect the article with מַיִם, as in the LXX. The plural participle used to describe the water's sound, מְפַכִּים, is a hapax, the Piel of a presumed verb פָּכָה. Since it

---

21 Hengstenberg, *Christology of the Old Testament*, 3:66–67.

probably is onomatopoetic, "gurgle" or "bubble" might be more accurate translations than "trickle." The same onomatopoesis appears in בַּקְבֻּק, "flask," which gurgles when poured out. The verb here is the root of the noun פַּךְ, "juglet." The verb seems to emphasize the small amount of water at its source, comparable in size to that from the mouth of a small vessel.

47:3 The temporal clause בְּצֵאת־הָאִישׁ , "as the man went out," uses the Qal infinitive construct of יָצָא with בְּ. By itself, קַו (used only here in Ezekiel, although common elsewhere) means a "cord, line" of any sort, but can also imply a "measuring line" (explicitly expressed by קָו־הַמִּדָּה in Jer 31:39). In 40:3, Ezekiel described the man's measuring instruments as a פְּתִיל־פִּשְׁתִּים, "linen cord," and a קְנֵה הַמִּדָּה, "measuring rod." The resultant measurement here is expressed in idiomatic Hebrew, אֶלֶף בָּאַמָּה, literally, "a thousand with the cubit." A thousand cubits is about seventeen hundred feet, about a third of a mile or half a kilometer. (בָּאַמָּה is also used for "two thousand with the cubit" in Num 35:5.)

The expressions in Ezek 47:3–4 for the depth of the water, and especially "I was not able to cross" in 47:5 suggest that at each stop Ezekiel waded into the water to test its depth. The noun אׇפְסָיִם in 47:3 is technically a hapax. It is the dual form of a presumed singular אֹפֶס. Since the common cognate noun אֶפֶס means "extremity, end," the dual אׇפְסָיִם naturally can refer to the ends of the legs, or the "ankles." In the construct phrase מֵי אׇפְסָיִם, literally, "water of ankles," the genitive (אׇפְסָיִם, "of ankles") refers to the extent or measure, meaning water that "reached up to the ankles" (GKC, § 128 n). Similar construct phrases with "water" will be used in 47:4, מֵי מׇתְנָיִם, literally, "water of (reaching the) loins," and 47:5, מֵי שָׂחוּ, "waters of (deep enough for) swimming."

Early church interpreters, taking their cue from the LXX, readily expounded the river in Ezek 47:1–12 as a prefiguration of Christian Baptism. The LXX rendered מֵי אׇפְסָיִם as ὕδωρ ἀφέσεως, which may simply mean "water of a brook," since the LXX uses ἄφεσις for a "channel" (LEH) or "brook, stream" of water in Joel 1:20; 4:18 (ET 3:18); and Lam 3:48. Perhaps the LXX misunderstood אׇפְסָיִם or used ἄφεσις as a close transliteration. In any case, the LXX could also mean "water of forgiveness"[22] because the LXX also uses ἄφεσις to refer to "release" from bondage or "remission, forgiveness" of a debt.[b] In the NT ἄφεσις usually refers to the "forgiveness" of sins.[c] It was used by Christ in his Words of Institution for the Lord's Supper: "this is my blood of the covenant that is being shed for many for the forgiveness of sins" (Mt 26:28). It also refers to God's "forgiveness" bestowed through John's baptism (Mk 1:4; Lk 3:3) and through Christian Baptism in Peter's Pentecost exhortation "repent and be baptized, every one of you, in the name of Jesus Christ for the *forgiveness* of your sins, and you will receive the gift of the Holy Spirit" (Acts 2:38).

(b) E.g., Lev 25:10–13; Deut 15:1–3; Is 61:1; Esth 2:18

(c) E.g., Lk 24:47; Acts 5:31: 10:43; 13:38; Eph 1:7; Col 1:14

---

[22] That possible meaning may explain why the Complutensian Polyglot rendered the phrase as ὕδωρ ἀφαιρέσεως, "water of remission/forgiveness." See Cooke, *Ezekiel*, 523.

47:4 The translation is slightly free because of idiomatic differences between Hebrew and English, but the meaning is clear. The guide methodically measures off two more thousand-cubit intervals, and the water increases in depth to the knees and then to the waist. Instead of another construct phrase with "water" (as in 47:3, 4b, 5), the phrase מַיִם בִּרְכַּיִם, "water, knees," is appositional, with "knees" as an accusative of measure or extent, "water" "which reached to the knees" (GKC, § 131 e; see also Joüon, § 127 b).[23] בִּרְכַּיִם is the dual of בֶּרֶךְ, but its similarity to בְּרָכָה, "blessing," gave rise to one minor LXX manuscript that spiritualized the phrase as ὕδωρ εὐλογίας, "water of blessing," which of course lends itself to a baptismal interpretation of the river.[24]

47:5 After the guide measures another thousand cubits, Ezekiel declares that the trickle has become a torrent that he cannot ford. Many translations render נַחַל as a "river," which normally is נָהָר in Hebrew. נַחַל usually refers to an arroyo or wadi, which may flow slightly year-round, but more likely will simply be a dry river bed except briefly after winter storms. In desert climates, such as that east of the watershed of southern Canaan, flash floods are not unknown when the water can rise precipitously in a narrow channel. However, this river is continual, deep enough to swim in, and apparently the current is too swift to allow Ezekiel to swim across it, so "river" is appropriate.[25]

The syntax of כִּי־גָאוּ הַמַּיִם מֵי שָׂחוּ is compressed, but literally, "because the waters increased, waters of (for) swimming." The same verb, גָּאָה, "rise up, be exalted," is used in the Song of the Sea (Ex 15:1; see also Ex 15:21) with Yahweh as subject after the Israelites crossed the Red Sea but the waters drowned his foes. St. Paul offers a baptismal interpretation of that redemptive event in 1 Cor 10:1–2. The construct phrase מֵי שָׂחוּ, "waters of swimming," is in apposition to הַמַּיִם, but functions, in effect, as a result clause: "the waters increased (so much that they were) waters for swimming." The hapax noun שָׂחוּ is from the original root שׂחו, which became the verb שָׂחָה attested thrice in the OT: the Qal, "to swim," twice in Is 25:11, and the Hiphil, "cause to swim; drench, flood," in Ps 6:7 (ET 6:6). The final *waw* of the root שׂחו was consonantal but in the noun became the long *shureq* vowel (Joüon, §§ 26 d; 88C e).

Presumably the river continues to rise until it reaches the Dead Sea. There is no mention of tributaries or another natural reason for the water's increase,

---

[23] Keil, *Ezekiel*, 2:354, suggests that the absolute state מַיִם may have been used here because the construct phrase מֵי־בִּרְכַּיִם, "water of knees," might have had the same meaning as the euphemistic Qere construct phrase מֵימֵי רַגְלַיִם, "water of legs," used with a suffix in Is 36:12 ‖ 2 Ki 18:27, where the Kethib שֵׁינֵיהֶם gives the literal meaning, "their urine." Supporting that view may be an expression in Ezek 7:17 and 21:12 (ET 21:7), וְכָל־בִּרְכַּיִם תֵּלַכְנָה מַּיִם, "and all knees will flow with water." See the textual note on 7:17.

[24] LXX manuscript 967 is cited by Zimmerli, *Ezekiel*, 2:505.

[25] While נַחַל, "stream, wadi," is from a different root than נַחֲלָה, "inheritance," and נָחַל, "to inherit," perhaps the prominent use of those words in 47:13–48:29 influenced the choice of נַחַל here. If so, it would reinforce that the waters, together with the land and all its blessings, are entirely a gift of grace bequeathed by God to his redeemed people. See further on 47:13.

so obviously we are to think of supernatural causation. Hengstenberg comments:

> We have here a representation of the Messianic salvation which, though at first comparatively insignificant, will continue to expand with ever increasing fulness and glory. Compare [Ezek 17:]22, 23, where the Messiah appears as a tender twig, which afterwards grows to a large cedar; and the parables of the mustard seed in Matt. [13:]31, 32, and the leaven in [Mt 13:]33.[26]

Similarly, Keil cites Is 12:3 and 44:3 to support his view that the river represents the salvation brought by Christ: "The salvation which the Lord causes to flow down to His people from His throne will pour down from small beginnings in marvellously increasing fulness."[27]

47:6 "Have you noticed, son of man?" draws attention to the miraculous increase in the river. Joüon, § 161 b, argues that the interrogative on הֲרָאִיתָ could be exclamatory here and with other instances of this identical verb form, including Ezek 8:12, 15, 17. Note that the guide addresses Ezekiel as "son of man," just as Yahweh does throughout the book,[28] indicating that the guide is a supernatural personage (see the commentary on 40:3 and on 43:6).

The two guidance formulas וַיּוֹלִכֵנִי וַיְשִׁבֵנִי, "he led me and he brought me back" (see the second textual note on 40:2), leave unclear whether Ezekiel was led back *to* the bank of the river or *along* the bank to an earlier location beside it. There is no preposition before שְׂפַת הַנָּחַל. Since the prophet had been in the water to test its depth in 47:3–5, it seems most natural to me to understand the guide as leading Ezekiel out of the channel up *to* its bank, understanding שְׂפַת הַנָּחַל as an accusative of direction.

47:7 The initial בְּשׁוּבֵנִי is irregular since the form of its suffix (נִי-) is that for a direct object of a transitive verb, and שׁוּב is intransitive. The expected form would be בְּשׁוּבִי, as Keil notes.[29] Compare GKC, § 91 e. Since the noun and adjective are singular, עֵץ רַב מְאֹד could theoretically be translated as "a very large tree," but a collective meaning, "a vast number of trees," is required by the following phrase, מִזֶּה וּמִזֶּה, literally, "from this [side] and from this [side]," meaning "on both sides" of the river. The LXX translates it ἔνθεν καὶ ἔνθεν, and Rev 22:2 conveys the same point about the trees with ἐντεῦθεν καὶ ἐκεῖθεν.

47:8 In the remainder of this pericope (through 47:12), the guide interprets the river of life and describes the salubrious results it brings. The terms used to describe its course are basically geographical, and, if not pressed, match the well-known topography of the region, although an element of eschatological transformation may underlie them. The noun גְּלִילָה (in הַגְּלִילָה הַקַּדְמוֹנָה),

---

[26] Hengstenberg, *Christology of the Old Testament*, 3:69.

[27] Keil, *Ezekiel*, 2:360.

[28] See the second textual note and the commentary on 2:1.

[29] Keil, *Ezekiel*, 2:354.

"the eastern region") is obviously a derivative of גָּלַל, "roll, be round," and Josh 22:10–11 speaks of גְּלִילוֹת הַיַּרְדֵּן, "the regions around the Jordan." The reference is probably to the deepest part of the Jordan Valley known today as the Ghor ("depression"), probably especially the southern end where the valley broadens out for several miles before reaching the Dead Sea, ground which in a larger river might form a large estuary.

Today "Arabah" is used of the continuation of the Rift Valley south of the Dead Sea down to the Gulf of Aqaba. But in the Bible that word, עֲרָבָה, which basically means "dry/desert (region)," is used more generally of the entire valley from the Sea of Galilee down. If we include that entire distance, the river's route hardly matters, but in actual geography, the Kidron Valley, into which water from the temple would flow, follows a very southeasterly direction for some time before turning and flowing due east into the Dead Sea considerably south of the mouth of the Jordan.

If Ezekiel is envisioning that the river from the temple would flow more directly eastward, into the Jordan Valley north (upstream) of the Dead Sea, the possibility arises that in the vision, the Mount of Olives (east of Jerusalem) has been split, as in Zech 14:4, to form an eastward channel for the river. After the Mount of Olives, the river would have to cross a number of mountainous hills and valleys before reaching the Rift Valley, which obviously would require divine intervention. This would be a fulfillment of God's prophetic promise to provide rivers in the dry desert (Is 43:19–20), an antitype of the exodus redemption, when the Israelites passed through the sea on dry land.[30] Compare Lk 3:4–6.

Hengstenberg comments:

> In the Bible the desert represents a lost condition, and therefore is an appropriate emblem of a world estranged from God and shut out of his kingdom. … The Dead Sea was all the better fitted to be used as a symbol of the corrupt world, since it was in a judgment on the corrupt world that it originated, and with the eye of the mind the image of Sodom and Gomorrha [Genesis 19] could still be seen beneath the waves.[31]

After the water comes הַיָּמָּה, "to the [Dead] Sea," the Masoretic Text has אֶל־הַיָּמָּה הַמּוּצָאִים, which could literally mean "to the sea, [the waters?] which had been brought out." הַמּוּצָאִים may be the plural Hophal participle (with the article) of יָצָא, as was the identical form in 14:22. Its implied subject must be מַיִם, "waters," which would refer to the river if הַמּוּצָאִים means "brought out (from the temple)." The Qal participle יֹצְאִים in 47:12 refers to the waters "going/flowing out" from the sanctuary (and watering the trees). Keil defends "brought out" as a summary statement of the preceding description of the river's course, and Hengstenberg adds that the words "point to the higher

---

[30] Block, *Ezekiel*, 2:694.

[31] Hengstenberg, *Christology of the Old Testament*, 3:70, 72.

power, that carries out the whole counsel of salvation according to His prede-termined plan."[32] KJV, NKJV, and NIV apparently paraphrase the words with that understanding. This is possible, but an otiose construal of the Hebrew. The LXX has "the water of the breakthrough," and on that basis many emend the second הַיָּמָּה to הַמַּיִם, which at least agrees in number with the plural הַמּוּצָאִים.

Especially since Ezekiel has analogous Hophal participles of other middle *waw* verbs (מוּבָאִים from בּוֹא in 23:42; 30:11; מוּכָנִים from כּוּן in 40:43), הַמּוּצָאִים could also be the Hophal participle of a verb צוּא or צוֹא, "be filthy, polluted."[33] That verb does not occur elsewhere in the OT, but cognates exist in Aramaic, Syriac, and Arabic (see BDB, s.v. צוּא). The OT does contain cog-nates: the adjective צֹאִי and two nouns, צֹאָה and צֵאָה, both meaning "filth, ex-crement." Those words may be related to יָצָא in the sense of "go out" from a person (cf. ἐκβάλλεται in Mt 15:17). In this case, the implied subject is not the river, but the waters of the sea. This reading may underlie the Syriac's ܡܣܝܐ, "stagnant," followed by RSV and NRSV (although this seems to me to be too weak a description of the Dead Sea).

A popular but unwarranted emendation of הַמּוּצָאִים is to הַחֲמוּצִים, "the soured (waters)," the Qal passive participle of חָמֵץ, "be sour"[34] (cf. חֹמֶץ, "vine-gar").

"Healed" is a literal translation of the Niphal of רָפָא, which recurs in 47:9 and, negated, in 47:11. The noun תְּרוּפָה, "healing," in 47:12 is from the same root. The Kethib, וְנִרְפָּאוּ, is the expected form, while the Qere, וְנִרְפּוּ, lacks *aleph*, as if the third root letter were *he* (see Joüon, § 78 e, f, g). רָפָא was also used in 2 Ki 2:21–22, where Elisha "healed" water that was poisonous and had caused death and miscarriage. Compare Ex 15:25, where God through Moses made bitter, unpotable water "be sweet."

"Healed" implies that the sterility of the Dead Sea is a kind of disease. Ear-lier in Ezekiel God had spoken of sending "pestilence, disease" (דֶּבֶר) as an agent of his wrath (e.g., 5:12, 17; 6:11–12; 14:19, 21), so this healing is the Gospel counterpart as God dispenses his grace. In addition to its literal use for the healing of diseases (e.g., Lev 13:18, 37; negated in Deut 28:27, 35 in the covenant curses), the Niphal of רָפָא can also be used for spiritual healing through the forgiveness of sins brought by the vicarious atonement of the Suf-fering Savior: "by his wounds we are healed" (Is 53:5).

47:9 Especially the first part of the verse is reminiscent of Genesis 1, in-dicating that Ezekiel sees a veritable new creation! נֶפֶשׁ חַיָּה, "living creature,"

---

[32] Keil, *Ezekiel*, 2:354–55; Hengstenberg, *Christology of the Old Testament*, 3:72. Hengsten-berg (3:72, n. 1) quotes Neumann, *Die Wasser des Lebens*, 34: "It is not by following its nat-ural course, that the brook flows to the sea, it is conducted thither from the temple by a supe-rior hand, and under this guidance the waters of the sea are healed."

[33] This was first suggested by G. R. Driver, "Linguistic and Textual Problems: Ezekiel," *Bibli-ca* 19 (1938): 186–87, cited in Block, *Ezekiel*, 2:688, n. 26.

[34] This emendation is advocated by *HALOT*, s.v. צוּא, Hophal, 2 (cf. Cooke, *Ezekiel*, 520, 523).

was in Gen 1:20, 21 (with the article), 24, 30, and the verb שָׁרַץ, "to teem, swarm," was in Gen 1:20–21 (with the cognate noun שֶׁרֶץ, "swarms," Gen 1:20). יִחְיֶה, "will live," recalls the entirety of God's actions in Genesis 1, where he created everything out of nothing and brought forth life where there was none before.

The dual נַחֲלַיִם, literally, "two streams/rivers" or "double river," is a conundrum, since none of the surrounding verses refers to the river in a comparable way, although the plural suffix on דְּגָתָם ("their fish") in 47:10 could refer to the dual "rivers" (or to an implied plural מַיִם, "waters"). Zech 14:8, a later parallel passage, speaks of "living waters" flowing from Jerusalem, with half flowing to the Eastern (Dead) Sea and half flowing to the Western (Mediterranean) Sea.[35] Some think of influence from Canaanite mythology, where the Ugaritic texts locate the home of El at the source of the two rivers,[36] but even conceding the possibility of the use of exmythological language, this seems most unlikely to me. Keil cites Hengstenberg and endorses his interpretation of the dual as meaning a river with a strong current (citing the dual מְרָתַיִם in the difficult Jer 50:21 in support).[37] KJV and NKJV translate with the plural "rivers," but other versions, ancient and modern, use the singular.

The feminine דְּגָה used here is almost always collective, while the masculine דָּג usually refers to an individual fish (although English does not distinguish).

The second half of the verse repeats the vivifying and healing powers of the water. The subject of the plural Niphal imperfect (of רָפָא), וְיֵרָפְאוּ, must be supplied from the context: the formerly sterile and polluted "waters" of the Dead Sea. (At the end of 47:8, הַמַּיִם was the explicit subject of the Niphal of רָפָא.) Its conjunctive *azla* accent (וֹ-) connects it to the following וָחָי, which is the regular form of the third masculine singular perfect of חָיָה with *waw* consecutive, and whose *zaqeph qaton* (-חָ-) indicates that it concludes a clause. Its implied singular subject is a repetition of כָּל־נֶפֶשׁ חַיָּה, "every living creature," which was the explicit subject of the imperfect of חָיָה earlier in the verse, יִחְיֶה. That syntax leaves the final clause of the verse (כֹּל אֲשֶׁר־יָבוֹא שָׁמָּה הַנָּחַל) without a main verb, so it is set off by a dash in the translation. Critics commonly excise the final clause as a dittographic variant of the similar clause כָּל־אֲשֶׁר יָבוֹא שָׁם נַחֲלַיִם in 47:9a. But even though it is repetitive, the final clause (with כֹּל for the third time in the verse) underscores the thoroughness of the healing.[38]

---

[35] Cooke, *Ezekiel*, 520, cites the rabbis, who suggest a connection of this verse to Zech 14:8.

[36] See the Ugaritic epics Baal and Anat, *CTA* 3 E 14 (3 v 8), and Baal's Palace, *CTA* 4 iv 21 (Gibson, *Canaanite Myths and Legends*, 53, 59).

[37] Keil, *Ezekiel*, 2:356, citing Hengstenberg, *Christology of the Old Testament*, 3:73.

[38] Hengstenberg, *Christology of the Old Testament*, 3:73–74, opines:

This verse and the following form the basis of Peter's miraculous draught of fishes before the resurrection (Luke [5:1–10]), which the Lord explained in the words, "from henceforth thou shalt catch *men*" ([Lk 5:]10). The same may be said of Peter's miracu-

47:10 The sense is clear despite a few uncertain details. The introductory וְהָיָה, "and it will be," need not be translated, and is not in the LXX, while the Vulgate (*vivent*) apparently read it as וְחָיוּ, "and they will live." The Kethib of the next verb is the Qal imperfect יַעַמְדוּ, "they will stand," which is preferable in this futuristic context. The LXX and Vulgate translate it as future (while the Syriac has a participle). The Qere עָמְדוּ is the perfect without *waw*. The Vulgate and Syriac supply a conjunction. For both verbs, the LXX has simply καὶ στήσονται. The subject, דַּוָּגִים, "fishermen" (elsewhere only in Jer 16:16), is a noun of the *qattal* form used for a profession (*nomen opificum*, GKC, § 84[b] b) and is related to the noun דָּגָה, "fish," in 47:9–10.

The antecedent of the suffix on עָלָיו ("beside it") could be "the river" (הַנַּחַל at the end of 47:9) but because of the location of the two places named next, it probably is the Dead Sea (הַיָּמָּה twice in 47:8). En-gedi ("goat's spring") is the location that bears the same name today. It is an oasis fed by a spring at the top of a six hundred–foot escarpment, located at about the middle of the west side of the Dead Sea, today a popular Israeli national park. The location of En-eglaim ("spring of two calves"), possibly chosen for its assonance, is not so certain. For a long time, the favored identification was with modern ʿAin Feshka, just south of Qumran, today an Israeli resort. However, later discoveries in the caves south of Qumran from the time of the second Jewish (Bar Kochba) revolt (ca. 135 A.D.) indicate that on the southeastern side of the Dead Sea there existed a site called עֶגְלְתָן. Hence today the favored identification is with the Eglath-shelishiyah mentioned in the Moab Gentile oracles of Is 15:5 and Jer 48:34 in association with Zoar, although its precise location (and that of Zoar) in modern Jordan is unknown. This provides a much more powerful picture here because then, instead of two places by the northwestern quadrant of the Dead Sea, we have a topographical merismus, northwest and southeast, indicating that the healing extended all around the Dead Sea.

The fecundity of the waters is amplified by מִשְׁטוֹחַ לַחֲרָמִים יִהְיוּ, "a place of spreading for nets they will be." Nets would be spread out to dry on the shore after the day's catch had been brought in. The subjects of the plural verb יִהְיוּ are the two preceding place names, but the merismus implies that fishermen would engage in this practice all around the formerly dead sea. מִשְׁטוֹחַ is a hapax, but the synonym מִשְׁטָה, as well as the same noun for "nets," חֲרָמִים, was in 26:5, 14. There, in the oracle against Tyre, the city-site would be so denuded of buildings that there would be ample space for such activity. But here the activity is the result of God's blessing conferred through the living waters.

---

lous draught after the resurrection (John [21]), and of the parable of the net cast into the sea, in which fish of every kind were caught [Mt 13:47]. …

If the fishes represent men, who are made alive by means of the Messianic salvation, the fishermen must be the heralds of this salvation, who gather those that are made alive into the kingdom of God, and introduce them to the fellowship of the church. The Saviour alludes to this passage … in Matt. [4:]18, 19, … and in John [21:]1–14 the apostles appear as fishermen.

Finally, the variety of fishes will equal that to be found in the Mediterranean (הַיָּם הַגָּדוֹל, "the Great Sea"). לְמִינָהּ, "as to its [the fishes'] kinds," clearly alludes to Genesis 1, where the noun מִין, "kind, species," with לְ and various suffixes (Gen 1:11–12, 21, 24–25) refers to the great diversity of creatures, including fish, that God created, each designed to reproduce only its own kind (thus precluding the theory of evolution). The third feminine singular suffix on the word here (הָ-) refers to the later repeated feminine noun דָּגָה, "fish" (דְגָתָם כְּדְגַת). The suffix lacks *mappiq*, probably because of the following initial *begad-kephat* letter ת in תִּהְיֶה (so Joüon, § 94 h). The plural suffix on דְגָתָם ("their fish") could refer to the two places named earlier or to the healed "waters" of the sea or of the river (הַמַּיִם in 47:8–9), or perhaps to the dual "two rivers" (נַחֲלָיִם in 47:8), although it seems the fish are in the sea rather than the river itself.

47:11 בִּצָּה (elsewhere only in Job 8:11; 40:21) is a "swamp," which could be permanent in wetter climates, but in arid areas would soon dry up and leave a residue behind. Near the Dead Sea that residue would be salt and other chemicals. Both the Qere בְּצֹאתָיו and the Kethib (בְּצֹאתָו) reflect an Aramaicized plural form with *aleph* instead of *holem* (-וֹ-). The Qere has the normal *plene* spelling of the suffix, while the Kethib has the same defective suffix (וֹ-) found in 40:6; 43:11; 44:5. גֶּבֶא, "marsh," is used elsewhere only in Is 30:14. לְמֶלַח נִתָּנוּ is, literally, "for salt they are given" (Niphal perfect of נָתַן). "Salt" is probably somewhat generic for the raw material, which must be refined to obtain pure salt, and which (from the Dead Sea) contains many other useful minerals.

There is disagreement about whether the "salt" is a beneficial product harvested from the "swamps and marshes" or whether its presence there indicates that they are excluded from the blessed new creation. Block takes the salt as "a valuable seasoning and preserving agent; the word functions generically for a wide range of chemicals extracted from the sea."[39] Salt was also required in the sacrificial ritual prescribed in 43:24. Its provision here may be a touch of practical realism in the midst of an otherwise surreal vision. The location could be anywhere along the Dead Sea, but one thinks most naturally of the southern end, south of the Lisan (or peninsula of land nearly bisecting the Sea), which today has virtually dried up completely due to extensive industrial exploitation by both Israel and Jordan.

The opposite interpretation of the salt is offered by Keil: "Life extends no further than the water of salvation flows. Wherever it cannot reach, the world continues to lie in death."[40] Hengstenberg is even stronger: "The wicked are excluded from participating in the glorious promises … ; compare [Is 66:]24, and the threat in Jer. [30:]23, 24. In Rev. [20:]10, the 'lake of fire' corresponds

---

[39] Block, *Ezekiel*, 2:695.

[40] Keil, *Ezekiel*, 2:361.

to the sloughs and pools mentioned here. The *salt* is … a foe to all fertility, life, and prosperity."[41]

47:12 The guide concludes by returning to the theme of the trees growing along the river's banks, partially repeating but expanding on 47:7. They are now described as כָּל־עֵץ־מַאֲכָל, "every tree of food." Miraculously, their produce will not be seasonal or periodic, but perennial. לֹא־יִבּוֹל עָלֵהוּ, "its leaves will not wither," is the identical clause (but different word order) applied to the blessed believer in Ps 1:3 and contrasts with the metaphorical descriptions of apostates as withered leaves in Is 1:30 and Jer 8:13. "Its fruit will not fail" is the opposite of the covenant curse in Lev 26:20. לֶחֳדָשָׁיו יְבַכֵּר uses לְ in a distributive sense: literally, "each of its months it will bear early fruit." The verb יְבַכֵּר, "bear early fruit," is a denominative "productive" Piel (Waltke-O'Connor, § 24.4e, including example 1) derived from the noun בִּכּוּרִים, "firstfruits," generally considered the choicest and possibly the freshest, as RSV and NRSV interpret. The unusual placement of the prepositional phrase emphasizes the reason for the miraculous blessings: כִּי מֵימָיו מִן־הַמִּקְדָּשׁ הֵמָּה יוֹצְאִים, literally, "because its waters—*from the sanctuary* they are going out."

The plural Kethib וְהָיוּ ("they will be") perhaps could be explained if פְּרִיו … וְעָלֵהוּ formed a compound subject ("its fruit … and its leaves are …"), or if פְּרִיו had a collective meaning, referring to fruits from the different kinds of fruit trees. But since the other references in 47:12 to the fruit trees use singular forms, the singular Qere is preferred: וְהָיָה פִרְיוֹ לְמַאֲכָל, "its fruit will be for food." Then וְהָיָה is also implied in the last clause, וְעָלֵהוּ לִתְרוּפָה "and its leaves (will be) for healing." The noun תְּרוּפָה is a hapax but is derived ultimately from רָפָא, the verb "to heal" used in 47:8–9, 11. (BDB lists the noun under the root רוּף, a presumed by-form of רָפָא.) Several synonyms from רָפָא are attested in the OT (רִפְאוּת, רְפָאָה, מַרְפֵּא). KJV and NKJV render the word "medicine," which is not incorrect, but probably more restricted in meaning than the more literal "healing." Yet it reminds one of the role of medical missionaries in the history of the church, who combine healing of the body with the proclamation of the Gospel.

The perpetuity of the trees' fruitfulness recalls that in Eden (Gen 2:15–17) and anticipates that in the eternal garden paradise (Rev 22:2–3). What the healing waters from the temple do for the land, the healing leaves do for people. In Eden the forbidden fruit became an instrument of sin and death (Gen 2:17; 3:3, 11), but in the eschaton, the fruit and leaves of the trees will only be salutary. Therefore it is only a small step from the depiction of the fruitful healing trees in Ezek 47:7, 12 to their identification as "the tree of life" in Rev 22:2, 14, 19 (cf. Gen 2:9; 3:22, 24; Rev 2:7).[42]

---

[41] Hengstenberg, *Christology of the Old Testament*, 3:75.

[42] For a discussion of biblical passages with "the tree of life," one may see Brighton, *Revelation*, 625–27.

Introduction to the New Promised Land (47:13–48:35)

The citation formula, "thus says the Lord Yahweh,"[43] introduces the final section of the book. Logically, its topic is connected to the preceding. After the prophet and his guide leave the sanctuary and follow the course of the river into the land of Israel, the arrangements for everyday life in that land are considered. Formally, the citation formula applies to all of 47:13–48:35, which may be considered one divine speech. The signatory formula, "says the Lord Yahweh,"[44] at the end of chapter 47 (in 47:23) and again at the end of 48:29, subdivides the material and each time reinforces that the preceding is indeed divine speech.

The main topic of 47:13–23 is the overall boundaries of the land to be inherited by the reconstituted Israel. The individual allotments to the tribes, as well as the holy contribution, will be described in 48:1–29. The final subsection, 48:30–35, is the conclusion to the entire book, giving the gates and dimensions of the city in which Yahweh will reside forever.

Although we can observe both similarities and differences in comparison to the original allotment boundaries in Num 34:1–15,[45] the overall boundaries of the inherited land differ only slightly. The major difference comes in how the land is allotted among the tribes in chapter 48. In Ezekiel a certain idealization is obvious in that the overall shape of the land is roughly a parallelogram, with the tribal territories running in straight horizontal strips within it. See figure 6. A separate strip in the middle consists of the sacred district, enclosing the temple and the city, with portions belonging to the Prince, the priests, and the Levites. This idealized layout would be humanly impossible to implement in the terrestrial geography of the Holy Land, with its rugged hills and valleys, and so it is a further indication of the eschatological nature of the vision, which only God himself can implement, and only in the new heavens and new earth.

For reasons that can only be guessed, in Ezekiel, some of the tribes that were originally in the north are allotted land in the south, and vice versa.[46] Also in Ezekiel, the two and a half tribes (Reuben, Gad, and half of Manasseh) that were excluded from the original allotment because they had already received territory east of the Jordan River (Num 34:13–15) are now included, and none of the allotments in Ezekiel extends east of the Jordan from just south of the Sea of Galilee southward.

In Numbers 34, the description of the national boundaries begins with the southern one, while Ezekiel in 47:15 begins with the northern one. This may

---

[43] For this formula, see pages 8–9 in the introduction and the fourth textual note and the commentary on 2:4.

[44] For this formula, see pages 8–9 in the introduction and the second textual note on 5:11.

[45] Critics who believe in the documentary (JEDP) hypothesis for the formation of the Pentateuch often date Num 34:1–15 as roughly contemporaneous with Ezekiel. Cooke, *Ezekiel*, 525, is typical: "Whereas P idealizes the past, in Ez. the future is idealized and the ideal element predominates." However, this commentary affirms Mosaic authorship of the Pentateuch, which dates to the fifteenth century B.C., compared to the early sixth century for Ezekiel.

[46] Compare this commentary's figure 6 with map 4 in Harstad, *Joshua*, 844.

correspond to the fact that in Moses' time the Israelites viewed the promised land from the south, since they had come up from Egypt. Ezekiel and his audience in exile in Babylon viewed it from the north, since they had left northward on their way up the western leg of the Fertile Crescent, and if they were to return to their land, they would descend back down from the north. Usually Ezekiel's descriptions are much briefer than those in Numbers. The initial northern boundary is described in greater detail (47:15–17), but the east (47:18), south (47:19), and west (47:20) boundaries are given in only one verse each.

The noun נַחֲלָה, "inheritance" (47:14, 22–23; 48:29), together with the cognate verb נָחַל, "to inherit" (47:13–14), keeps at the fore the theological idea that the territory discussed is all a land grant from the Lord to loyal subjects, a gift of pure grace. Ultimately, the "inheritance" theme relates to the death and resurrection of Christ, the covenant mediator and testator, who wills the inheritance that rightly is his own to all believers as his heirs.[d] For NT believers, the inheritance is not simply a piece of real estate in the Middle East, but a place in the new heavens and new earth, the kingdom to be inherited after the resurrection (e.g., Mt 25:34; 1 Cor 15:50–58).

(d) Heb 1:2; 9:15–17; cf. Rom 8:17; Gal 3:26–29; Eph 3:6

In broader OT perspective, we must think typologically in terms of a new exodus, as God had forcibly promised for Israel already in Ezek 20:33. God's people are to be taken back to the beginnings, and this time God will ensure that his will is implemented through them, unlike their partial obedience during the first settlement.[47] This will take place after they have been led through "the wilderness of the peoples" (20:35) and have reached "the high mountain of Israel" (20:40). The new exodus theme accounts for the phrase "the twelve tribes of Israel" in 47:13. "The tribes of Israel" (שִׁבְטֵי יִשְׂרָאֵל) is used six times in this final section (47:13, 21–22; 48:19, 29, 31; see also "tribe(s)" in 47:23; 48:1, 23), but only once before, in the prophecy of the reunification of (northern) Israel and Judah in 37:19. (Throughout the earlier parts of the book Ezekiel's favorite way of referring to Israel collectively was "the house of Israel" [e.g., 3:1, 4–5, 7]). Historically, the northern tribes had effectively ceased to exist after 722 B.C. because of their widespread deportation and the settlement of foreigners in their territories. Then a series of deportations (notably upon the destruction of Jerusalem in 586 B.C.) removed the upper strata of the southern tribes. Ezekiel is shown a vision of a reconstituted Israel that could not possibly become a historical reality if the people simply consisted of ethnic descendants of the original tribes. The subsequent history of postexilic Israel (as in Ezra-Nehemiah) scarcely begins to fulfill the vision, so we must look farther ahead in salvation history.

---

[47] For land in the original allotment that Israel did not yet possess, see, for example, Josh 13:2–6; Judg 1:1–3:6. God was completely faithful in the fulfillment of his Word (Josh 21:43–45; 23:14–16), but the Israelites were not.

The NT refers to Christians as the heirs of the OT promises to Israel (e.g., Gal 3:26–29; 6:16) and as "the twelve tribes scattered in the diaspora" (James 1:1; cf. "diaspora" also in 1 Pet 1:1, and the twelve tribes in Rev 7:4–8). By no accident did our Lord choose *twelve* disciples. The defection of Judas led to his replacement by Matthias (Acts 1:21–26) to restore the number. The church militant on earth, consisting of all baptized believers, is figuratively numbered as 144,000 (Rev 7:4–8), which is the product of 12 x 12 x 1,000. Ultimately it is all believers in Christ, Jewish and Gentile alike, who will be gathered on the Last Day (Mt 24:31; Jn 11:52) to comprise the reconstituted, eschatological Israel seen by Ezekiel. This gathering of the new Israel began already with the ministry of John the Baptist, the prophetic voice in the wilderness (Mt 3:3, quoting Is 40:3). The Baptist pointed to Jesus Christ, who called twelve apostles (Lk 6:12–16 and parallels) to be his new patriarchs, the foundation of the new Israel (1 Cor 3:10–12; Eph 2:20; Rev 21:14). Jesus defined the new people of God as constituted by faith in him, rather than by ethnic descent (e.g., Lk 8:19–21; Jn 1:11–13). As Jews and Gentiles alike are called to faith in the promised Messiah, the gathering of God's people continues in the ongoing ministry of the church, until Christ returns, and "thus all Israel shall be saved" (Rom 11:26).[48]

In the final section of the book, there are a few textual problems. A greater challenge is that the exact locations of a large number of the place names are unknown. Usually, there are several guesses about each name, and there is no point in listing them all. This commentary will engage the issue only to the extent that the context makes locations fairly obvious, or when there is a general consensus about it. Complicating the issue is that a host of OT place names were applied to two or more different locations, often quite far apart. Thus Micah 5:1 (ET 5:2) specifies that the town from which the Ruler shall come is "Bethlehem Ephrathah" to distinguish it from "Bethlehem" in Zebulun (Josh 19:15).

Inheritance of the New Promised Land (47:13–23)

This speech (47:13–23) is the first subsection of Yahweh's testamental promise of a new land inheritance for his redeemed people. The heart of this speech is the outline of the land in 47:15–20. An introduction and conclusion provide a literary framework around the formal geographical descriptions in between. The introduction (47:13–14) specifies that Joseph is to receive a double portion, and the other tribes equal portions. The remarkable conclusion (47:21–23) grants aliens in the new covenant the same status as native Israelites, so that they receive an equal share in the inheritance.

Joseph's Double Portion and Equal Allotments for the Other Tribes (47:13–14)

47:13 The quote of Yahweh begins with the construct phrase גֵּה גְבוּל. The initial word is pointed as though it were a construct of גַּיְא, "valley," and is so

---

48 For the topic of the new Israel consisting of all believers in Christ, see "Introduction to Ezekiel 40–48."

translated only by the Syriac ("valley of the boundary"). All other translations, ancient and modern,[49] understand גֶּה as miscopied for זֶה (as in 47:15), some scribe having mistakenly written a *gimel* in anticipation of that letter at the beginning of the next word. Furthermore, one would expect the definite article to be used with גְבוּל ("this is *the* boundary"). The article may have been dropped by haplography (because of the preceding הֵ-).

With many others, I have translated גְבוּל in the plural, because the singular (used nine times in 47:15–20) is obviously meant collectively for the "boundaries" of the entire area involved. The following relative clause is אֲשֶׁר תִּתְנַחֲלוּ אֶת־הָאָרֶץ, "(according to) which you are to divide the land as an inheritance." The Hithpael imperfect of נָחַל must be imperatival: "you are to ..." (cf. Joüon, § 113 m). Its Hithpael occurs only here in Ezekiel and six times elsewhere in the OT, usually with a reflexive or middle meaning that could be rendered, "receive *for oneself* ..." But here the following prepositional phrase לְשְׁנֵי עָשָׂר שִׁבְטֵי יִשְׂרָאֵל, "for the twelve tribes of Israel," uses *lamed* to introduce the beneficiaries of the action, as in Lev 25:46 and Num 33:54. This suggests that the implied subjects ("you") of the plural verb may be designated leaders of the tribes.

The final appositional phrase, יוֹסֵף חֲבָלִים, "Joseph, portions," is challenging but attested in all the versions. We would expect לְיוֹסֵף חֲבָלִים, "to Joseph (belong) two portions," with a dual חֲבָלַיִם, supported by the Vulgate and Targum, and so translated in most English versions (already KJV), as required by the context. חֶבֶל occurs elsewhere in Ezekiel only in 27:24 meaning "rope," but in a fair number of other OT passages, it means "measured portion, lot, part, region" (BDB, s.v. חֶבֶל I, 3), although חֵלֶק is the more common noun for a "portion" of land (frequently in Joshua, and in Ezek 45:7; 48:8, 21). Most critics regard the two words as a gloss added by a scribe who noticed that Levi is not included among the allotments to the tribes in 48:1–7, 23–28, so another portion (the second one of Joseph) was required to add up to twelve.[50] However, the stipulation that Joseph should receive a double portion goes back to Jacob's declaration in Gen 48:5 (cf. also Gen 48:13–20) that Joseph's sons Ephraim and Manasseh would be considered sons of Jacob and each receive an inheritance equal to that of Jacob's other sons, so that Joseph effectively receives the double portion normally inherited by the firstborn son. Therefore Ezek 47:13 is reflected in Ezek 48:4–5 by the presence of allotments for both Ephraim and Manasseh equal in size to those of the other tribes (see figure 6). While Levi does not receive an allotment of land resembling that of the other tribes, the priests and Levites each receive a portion of land within the holy contribution described in 48:8–22 (as previously in 45:1–8). Levi is included in 48:31–34 when each of the twelve gates of the city (the new Jerusalem) is ascribed to one of the twelve tribes.

---

[49] Also Keil, *Ezekiel*, 2:362, among commentators.

[50] E.g., Cooke, *Ezekiel*, 526; Allen, *Ezekiel*, 2:274.

47:14 אִישׁ כְּאָחִיו is, literally, "each like his brother," but since it refers to the amount allocated to each tribe, it is translated "in equal portions." "Lifted up my hand" is the idiomatic gesture for God swearing or issuing an oath, as in, for example, 20:5–6, 15. The gesture connects Ezekiel's vision to God's ancient oath, accompanied by this same gesture, to give the land to the patriarchs (Ex 6:8; Num 14:30). In spite of the intervening centuries of frequent apostasy, meriting the conquests and exiles of first the northern and then the southern tribes, Yahweh remains faithful to his oath by its eschatological fulfillment in the new creation after the return of Christ.

The idiom of the land "falling" (Qal of נָפַל with הָאָרֶץ as subject) derives from the casting of lots. This method had been used in the original apportionment of the land (Num 33:54; 34:13). However, Ezekiel 48 describes Yahweh as dictating the allotments, so the phrase here must be understood figuratively. Nevertheless, it does help to retain the connection with the first distribution. (נָפַל recurs twice in 47:22.)

Here בְּנַחֲלָה has the preposition בְּ used to introduce a second predicate (Joüon, § 133 c 2 B): "thus this land will fall to you *as an inheritance*." See also בְּנַחֲלָה twice in 47:22.

North, East, South, and West Boundaries of the Inherited Land (47:15–20)

47:15–17 The northern border begins at the Mediterranean, whose location is not in dispute (!), but other reference points are the subject of great debate.[51] On Hethlon, Zedad, Beruthah, Sibraim, Hazer-hatticon, and Hazar-enon (sometimes Hazar-enan), we have no real knowledge. One suspects that the last three may not have been well-known even in Ezekiel's day because of the descriptive phrases that follow each of them. According to some identifications, the places do not fall along a straight east-to-west line,[52] but since all the other east-to-west tribal boundaries (and those of the holy contribution) are to form a straight line, we may assume that this ones does too.

47:15a–b In לִפְאַת צָפוֹנָה, after לְ with פֵּאָה ("to the side of"), there is no need for צָפוֹן ("north") to have the *he* directive (another "to"), but in Ezekiel the *he* directive often has lost its force. This can be seen, for example, by its absence at the end of 47:17 (פְּאַת צָפוֹן; cf. the end of 47:18–19) and by the absence of both the לְ and the *he* directive in the phrases comparable to the one here at the beginning of 47:15 that introduce the discussion of the three other directions: וּפְאַת קָדִים, "the side of the east" (47:18), וּפְאַת נֶגֶב, "the side of the south" (47:19), and וּפְאַת־יָם, "the side of the sea/west" (47:20). Likewise, the directive *he* on several words in 47:19 (see below) and on the last word in the book (שָׁמָּה, "to there," 48:35) has little force.

---

[51] For a summary of major investigations and views, see Zimmerli, *Ezekiel*, 2:528–30, and Block, *Ezekiel*, 2:711–16.

[52] See the northern boundary on map 2 in Block, *Ezekiel*, 2:711.

The phrase הַדֶּרֶךְ חֶתְלֹן has the definite article on a word in construct (הַדֶּרֶךְ), but similar examples are attested (GKC, § 127 f, including footnote 1). The article is absent when the construct phrase recurs in 48:1 (דֶּרֶךְ־חֶתְלֹן).

47:15c–16a   At the transition between the verses, לְבוֹא צְדָדָה׃ חֲמָת, "Lebo to Zedad, Hamath" probably means "Lebo-hamath to Zedad." Somehow צְדָדָה and חֲמָת may have been transposed. Lebo-hamath is a well-known place name attested elsewhere in the Bible, including the original boundary descriptions (Num 34:8; Josh 13:5) and shortly later in Ezek 47:20; 48:1. KJV and NKJV follow the Hebrew word order and take לְבוֹא as the Qal infinitive of בּוֹא, "*as one goes* to Zedad, Hamath" (NKJV), which is supported by the Vulgate's *venientibus Sadada, Emath* ("coming to Zedad, Hamath"). The LXX often renders Lebo- (לְבוֹא) as εἴσοδος, "entrance," and does so here, but its word order supports "Lebo-hamath to Zedad," which most English translations give, as have I.

The crucial name in getting our bearings for the northern border is undoubtedly Lebo-hamath. It is mentioned frequently in the OT, and at times of maximum expansion, Lebo-hamath formed Israel's northern border (1 Ki 8:65 in the reign of Solomon, and 2 Ki 14:25 in the time of Jeroboam II). Yet it is of uncertain location. The uncertainty begins with its grammatical meaning. Is it "Lebo (of) Hamath," with "Lebo" referring to a discrete place under the control of Hamath, or is it "the entrance of/to Hamath," perhaps a road or pass leading to Hamath? The city of Hamath itself is over two hundred kilometers (one hundred twenty-five miles) north of Damascus, about midway between Damascus and Aleppo on the main north-south road of modern (and probably ancient) Syria. It is much too far north to be the place in Israelite territory referenced in the OT. "The border of Hamath" (גְּבוּל חֲמָת) later in Ezek 47:16 and again in 47:17 and "beside Hamath" (אֶל־יַד חֲמָת) in 48:1 refer to the large territory to the north of Israel controlled by Hamath.

If Lebo-hamath refers to a specific place in that territory, whose southern boundary would also be the northern boundary of Canaan, there are intelligible possibilities. For instance, if Lebo-hamath was a town in that territory, an identification with modern Lebweh might be attractive. Lebweh is in the Bekáa (the "valley" between the Lebanon and Anti-Lebanon Mountains) at the watershed between the Leontes (Litani) River flowing south and the Orontes River flowing north, still nearly fifty miles north of Damascus' latitude. Or, very plausibly, if לְבוֹא means "entrance," "pass," or "approach road," Lebo-hamath would be at the southern end of the Syrian Empire, roughly near the modern Merj ꜥUyun in the very southern Bekáa, near the saddle that separates that valley in Lebanon from its continuation in the Jordan Valley to the south. Then we can sketch a boundary beginning at the mouth of the Litani River a little north of Tyre and extending more or less due east. This line is probably close to Israel's actual northern border during most of its history, as it is today of modern Israel.

47:16 After running through several places, the border continues to חֲצַר הַתִּיכוֹן אֲשֶׁר אֶל־גְּבוּל חַוְרָן, "Hazer-hatticon, which is on the border of Hau-ran." The first place is unknown, but Hauran is a well-established place even though it appears in the Bible only here and in 47:18. The territory is the mod-ern Jebel Druze, high volcanic mountains east of Galilee and separating Bashan from the desert. In Assyrian times (and probably continued by the Babyloni-ans), it was an administrative district, the northwest border of which came to its northerly limit parallel with a point just north of Tyre. Hauran is east of Galilee, but from Ezekiel's viewpoint as an exile from Judah, all these town or regions were to the north.

47:17 Minor grammatical challenges intrude here. In the summarizing וְהָיָה גְבוּל, we would expect גְּבוּל to have an article, which some allege was lost by haplography, but גְּבוּל is used anarthrously in other border descriptions (e.g., Num 34:6; Josh 13:23; 15:5, 12, 47). In the phrase מִן־הַיָּם חֲצַר עֵינוֹן, we would expect a preposition before חֲצַר or a *he* directive ending on עֵינוֹן: "*to* Hazar-enon."

The words גְּבוּל דַּמֶּשֶׂק וְצָפוֹן ׀ צָפוֹנָה וּגְבוּל חֲמָת are, literally, "the border of Damascus and north, northward and the border of Hamath." Following the LXX, critics are tempted to excise וְצָפוֹן as a partial dittograph of the follow-ing צָפוֹנָה, although the Syriac, Targum, and Vulgate all attest it. In any event, the implication is that north of Hazar-enon lay both the border of Damascene territory and the border of the territory controlled by Hamath. In other words, the northern border running from the ocean just north of Tyre to Hazar-enon coincided with the ancient boundaries separating the kingdoms of Damascus and Hamath from Israelite territory.

At the conclusions of the boundary descriptions in three verses (47:17–19), אֵת is used to introduce a construct chain (… וְאֵת פְּאַת) that is nominative (not the object of a verb). There are other OT examples of this phenomenon (see GKC, § 117 m). Some propose emending וְאֵת in these verses to זֹאת, which is finally used at the end of 47:20. The emendation is supported by ταῦτα in LXX 47:18 (as in LXX 47:20 for זֹאת) and τοῦτο in LXX 47:19. The *waw* and *zayin* are close enough in appearance that their confusion would be understandable. Many questions and debates remain about the precise location of this bound-ary, but I doubt if greater certainty can be achieved with our present state of knowledge.

47:18 The translation supplies several words in brackets for a smooth tran-sition. Continuity with the previous verse indicates that Hazar-enon is the start-ing point, so it is supplied in RSV (but dropped in NRSV and ESV). If the eastern border did not begin there, it must have been at some comparable point on the border between Hauran and territory controlled by Damascus. The par-allel in Num 34:10–12 has more specific place names, but here Yahweh uses mostly regional names.

Thus we cannot trace the exact route of the eastern boundary between Hazar-enon (or somewhere in that area) and the point just south of the Sea of

Galilee where the Jordan River clearly begins to form the eastern boundary (see below). Perhaps the Upper Jordan River, north of the Sea of Galilee, forms the northern part of the eastern border (as shown in figure 6), or if the starting point was east of there, the eastern boundary must have run southward probably to the Yarmuk River (today the border between Jordan and Syria) and from there west along the Yarmuk to the Jordan.

From where the Jordan River flows out of the Sea of Galilee or just south of there where the Yarmuk River flows into the Jordan, the Jordan clearly forms the eastern boundary, extending south to the Dead Sea, called "the Eastern Sea" (הַיָּם הַקַּדְמוֹנִי, used elsewhere only in Joel 2:20 and Zech 14:8), instead of "the Sea of Salt" (Num 34:12). עַל־הַיָּם uses עַל in the sense of אֶל, meaning "to," as often elsewhere, including in the same phrase (עַל־הַיָּם) in 48:28. Clearly excluded from the Holy Land is Gilead, the Transjordan north of Moab, where the tribes of Reuben, Gad, and half of Manasseh originally settled.

The *zaqeph qaton* accent on הַיַּרְדֵּן indicates that it ends a clause, as indicated by the semicolon after "Jordan" in the translation. A new clause begins with מִגְּבוּל (repeated in 47:20), which is, literally, "*from* the border" (so KJV), but in both verses I have translated it as "*is* the border" since מִן apparently implies traversing from one point to another along the border (in 47:18, following the course of the Jordan down to the Dead Sea). The LXX translates it in 47:18 with the compound verb διορίζω, a verb that can mean "is the boundary" (LEH), and in 47:20 with the simple ὁρίζω. Since in 47:18 the Vulgate (*disterminans*) and the Syriac (ﻣﺤﻤﻨ) also translate with a verb, some suggest emending to מַגְבִּיל, the Hiphil participle of גְּבַל, "forming the border." Other Hiphil forms of גְּבַל occur in Ex 19:12, 23.

The clause beginning with מִגְּבוּל ends with תָּמֹדּוּ, literally, "you will measure." The Qal of מָדַד has been frequent since chapter 40 (see the fourth textual note on 40:5). Keil defends the verb and explains the clauses with וְאֵת at the end of 47:17–19 as its direct objects.[53] However, 47:19 continues with מִתָּמָר, "from Tamar," which makes it likely that here the text originally had the place name "Tamar" (תָּמָר), perhaps with locative *he* (תָּמָרָה), as supported by the LXX and Syriac. מִתָּמָר ("from Tamar") recurs in 48:28 in the description of the border of Gad, the southern-most tribal allotment, and there Tamar might border on Edom. Since Num 34:12 simply gave "the Salt [Dead] Sea" as the southern terminus, some have found it confusing that the border here apparently extends south of the Dead Sea. The exact location of this presumed "Tamar" is disputed, but a favorite candidate is ʿAin Hoseb, a short distance southwest of the southern end of the Dead Sea and commanding major trade routes. According to 1 Ki 9:18, which has תָּמָר, "Tamar" as a Kethib, it was in the Judean wilderness and a building site for Solomon, as recent excavations seem to confirm.

---

[53] Keil, *Ezekiel*, 2:365.

47:19 The redundancy of two different Hebrew words, נֶגֶב תֵּימָנָה, "south, southward," at the beginning of the verse (also in 48:28) and, in reverse order, תֵּימָנָה נֶגְבָּה, "southward, southward," at the end of the verse, must be some idiomatic usage. As the note on 47:15 observed, often in Ezekiel the *he* directive has little or no force and need not be reflected in translation. The redundancy is reflected in the LXX, which both times uses synonyms joined by the copula νότος καὶ λίψ. Most English translations (except in KJV and NKJV) render with only one "south."

Most Hebrew manuscripts have the plural מְרִיבוֹת, "Meriboth," in construct with קָדֵשׁ, but some have the construct singular of מְרִיבָה, "Meribah," in construct with קָדֵשׁ. The Syriac, Targum, and Vulgate attest the singular here, which occurs in construct with קָדֵשׁ shortly in 48:28, as well as in Num 27:14 and Deut 32:51. מְרִיבָה is derived from the verb רִיב and means "strife, contention." Because the strife had to do with scarcity of water and ultimately prevented Moses from entering the promised land (Num 20:1–13),[54] the construct phrase מֵי מְרִיבוֹת, "the waters of Meriboth" here (and מֵי with the singular in 48:28, as in, e.g., Num 20:13, 24), recalls God's abundant provision of water despite Israel's grumbling and Moses' disobedience. Num 20:1 notes that when the incident occurred, the Israelites were camped at Kadesh (that is, Kadesh-barnea), the focal point of the Israelites' forty years in the wilderness. Here (as in Num 27:14; Deut 32:51) the addition of "Kadesh" indicates the proximity of Meriboth to Kadesh-barnea. Kadesh-barnea is usually identified with ʿAin Qudeirat, one of the strongest springs in northern Sinai, today just inside Egypt's border with Israel, and which has been excavated. (An ʿAin Kadeis not far away preserves the name of the biblical Kadesh but is a smaller spring.)

The following word, נַחֲלָה, is pointed the same as the common noun for "inheritance," frequently used in the context; see "Introduction to the New Promised Land (47:13–48:35)." However, that seems inappropriate here. Probably this is נַחַל, "stream, wadi" (the term used for the "river" in 47:1–12), with *he* directive, which normally would be pointed נַחְלָה, but the same vocalization here will recur in 48:28. This wadi is not named here because anyone familiar with the area would know that the reference is to the נַחַל מִצְרַיִם, "the Wadi of Egypt," the modern Wadi el-Arish, the traditional boundary between Israel and Egypt (e.g., Josh 15:4, 47; 1 Ki 8:65), flowing into the Mediterranean about fifty miles south of Gaza as the shoreline begins to head west.

47:20 It would be possible to render מִגְּבוּל by supplying words, "[the border will be] from the southern boundary," but, as in 47:18, more likely it means "*is* the border" (see on 47:18). The border follows the Mediterranean coast north to a point opposite Lebo-hamath (see on 47:15c–16a), obviously coming full circle.

---

[54] In Ex 17:1–7, the name "Meribah" is associated with an earlier contention of the Israelites with Yahweh over a water shortage, which occurred shortly after they left Egypt and were camped at a location further south in the Sinai peninsula.

Aliens and Israelites Shall Inherit Equally (47:21–23)

One might expect the specific apportionments to the tribes to be described immediately after 47:20, but another issue intervenes, and the distributions for the tribes and the holy contribution do not come until 48:1–29.

47:21 This first verse of the epilogue to the overall boundary description is an abbreviated repetition of 47:13, but uses the Piel of חָלַק with לְ, "apportion ... give a portion to" (BDB, s.v. חָלַק, Piel, 1), instead of the Hithpael of נָחַל used in 47:13. That the following verses deal with aliens or proselytes rather than hereditary Israelites may have influenced the change, but theologically the two expressions are virtually synonymous. With Yahweh as the ultimate owner,[55] he may give a חֵלֶק, "portion" (whose plural is in 48:8, 21), to whomever he chooses. נָחַל simply accents the fulfillment of the ancient covenant promises more. Ezek 47:21–22, however, erases those potential differences by summarizing all who are to receive land as members of "the tribes of Israel," even if they should become "Israel" through faith and adoption into the covenant of grace.

47:22–23 What follows in these verses is unique—even radical, in a good sense—among the legal regulations of the OT. Lev 19:33–34 approaches it, but stops short of Yahweh's specific application here. Ezekiel is sometimes pictured as narrowly interested only in Israelite problems, and indeed, as an exile awaiting a return to the homeland, it would be strange if it were otherwise. That charge can be countered in other ways also, but the clincher is surely to be found here. This section in Ezekiel substitutes for the attention given in the roughly parallel Num 34:13–15 to the allotments of land to two and a half tribes east of the Jordan—substituting a "fringe *people*" for a "fringe *territory*."[56]

Yahweh reveals to Ezekiel nothing less than an erasure of the distinction between the אֶזְרָח, "native-born" Israelite, and the גֵּר, "alien." This is the only time אֶזְרָח, "native-born," occurs in Ezekiel, but is common elsewhere in the OT. Various words could be used to translate it: "native-born, aboriginal, autochthonous, indigenous," or the like. Ethnicity undoubtedly enters the picture, but to accent it raises the specter of racism, a relatively modern concept. Except for three passages (Lev 23:42; Num 15:13; Ps 37:35), elsewhere in the OT, אֶזְרָח, "native-born," always occurs opposite the other key term in Ezek 47:22–23, גֵּר, traditionally translated "alien," although that too can anachronistically introduce modern notions into biblical interpretation. Hebrew can use the cognate verb גּוּר, traditionally rendered "sojourn," together with the noun גֵּר, "alien," but "sojourn" probably conveys more transience than was necessarily involved. In earlier OT laws, we hear unremitting admonitions not to oppress the גֵּר, "alien," along with widows, orphans, and Levites, whose status was about the same, and who were to be allowed to participate in the sacrifi-

---

[55] See "Inheritance of the Prince's Property (46:16–18)."

[56] Block, *Ezekiel*, 2:717.

cial meals in the sanctuary (e.g., Deut 14:29; 16:11; 24:17–21). Earlier in Ezekiel, God had excoriated the apostate Israelites for oppressing the גֵּר, "alien," as well as the orphan, widow, and poor (Ezek 22:7, 29).

Yahweh had also warned in 14:7 that a person who apostatizes away from him and engages in idolatry, whether that person is from "the house of Israel" or is a גֵּר, translated "proselyte" there, will get no divine answer through a prophet. That passage supports the inference that during the exile, at least some non-Israelites had been brought to saving faith in Yahweh, perhaps through contact with the exiles (who included the prophets Ezekiel and Daniel), and they too needed to be warned not to fall back into idolatry. Such non-Israelite believers in the one true God would be roughly comparable to the σεβομένοι of NT times ("worshipers, proselytes, Gentile converts," e.g., Acts 13:43, 50; 17:4).

In the preexilic period of Israel a גֵּר, "alien," could not own land, so he was inevitably a second-class citizen. After Ezekiel's ministry turned its focus to the future salvation (chapters 33–48), the question would have arisen as to the status of the "alien" in the coming restoration of God's people. Ezekiel foresees full rights, not to any and all foreigners, but to those who will reside in the land of Israel permanently, marry, and raise children. In the context, then, "proselyte" (the LXX uses προσήλυτος in 47:22–23) or even "convert" might be a better rendition of גֵּר here.

The promise here certainly finds its fulfillment in the new covenant in Christ. Jewish and Gentile believers in Christ share equally in the divine inheritance by grace (e.g., Rom 1:16; 4:11–18), finally to be received in the new heavens and new earth (Revelation 21–22). St. Paul echoes Ezek 47:22–23 when he declares to Gentile converts to faith in Christ:

> You were at that time without Christ, separated from citizenship in Israel, and *foreigners* [ξένοι] from the covenants of the promise ... now you are no longer *foreigners and aliens* [ξένοι καὶ πάροικοι], but you are fellow citizens with the saints and members of God's household. (Eph 2:12, 19)[57]

47:22 The language shows how comprehensive the integration of the two groups shall be. תַּפִּלוּ is the Hiphil of נָפַל, literally, "cause to fall," with גּוֹרָל ("lot") as an implied object, "cast lots, allot," but since God defines the boundaries in the text (rather than determining them by the outcome of lots), it means "apportion the land" (see BDB, s.v. נָפַל, Hiphil, 3). The stated direct object is אוֹתָהּ ("it"), whose feminine suffix refers back to הָאָרֶץ, "the land," in 47:21. (The Hiphil of נָפַל, "allot," has הָאָרֶץ, "the land," as its object also in 45:1 and 48:29.) Then בְּנַחֲלָה is an accusative (with a preposition) used as a predicate referring to the object: "allot it [the land] *as an inheritance*" (see Joüon, § 133 c 3).

---

57 The LXX often translates גֵּר as πάροικος (e.g., Gen 15:13), the term used in Eph 2:19. More often it uses προσήλυτος, as in Ezek 47:22–23, and sometimes another term, for example, γειώρας in Ex 12:19.

The allotment is to proceed equally for all of God's people: לָכֶם וּלְהַגֵּרִים, "for you and for the aliens." The retention of the definite article (הַ) after the preposition לְ in לְהַגֵּרִים is anomalous, but there are other OT examples, especially in later books (Joüon, § 35 e, observation).

In 47:22b, the phrase יַפִּלוּ בְנַחֲלָה uses נָפַל in the Qal, which, if correct, must have the same meaning as the Hiphil, "to allot, apportion." It takes the same prepositional phrase (בְּנַחֲלָה) as used in 45:1 and 47:14, which uses בְּ to introduce a predicate, "*as* an inheritance" (see Joüon, § 133 c 2 B, 3). The preceding Hiphil was second person plural, but the Qal here is in the third person, "they will allot," and the implied subjects are the preceding הַגֵּרִים, "the aliens." The aliens will join the Israelites as equal participants in allotting the land. Some propose emending יַפְּלוּ (Qal) to יַפִּלוּ, another Hiphil.[58] The LXX has φάγονται ("they will eat"), apparently reading יֹאכְלוּ instead of יַפְּלוּ. The Vulgate has *divident* ("they will divide"), a form of the same verb it used for the Hiphil in 45:1 (but it used *mittetis* for the Hiphil verbs in 47:22a; 48:29). The Syriac (نفلح) and Targum (יְפַלְּגוּן) both have "they will divide."

This inclusivity of the new Israel is based on unity of faith (Romans 4) instead of pluralistic indifference to doctrine or confession. It is a glorious way to conclude the chapter. The more expansive parallel of Is 56:3–8 is often cited in this connection. St. Paul enunciates a similar gift to Gentile converts of his day (Eph 2:11–22), and the seer of Patmos describes the church triumphant as "from every nation and all tribes and peoples and tongues" (Rev 7:9), an inclusiveness that the empirical church on earth still struggles to manifest.[59]

---

[58] So BDB, s.v. נָפַל, Hiphil, 3; Cooke, *Ezekiel*, 531; Allen, *Ezekiel*, 2:275.

[59] For the topic of the new Israel consisting of all believers in Christ, see further in "Introduction to Ezekiel 40–48."

The New Holy Land Whose Capital Is Named "Yahweh Is There"

Translation

48 ¹"These are the names of the tribes: From the northern border, along the road of Hethlon, Lebo-hamath, and Hazar-enon, the border of Damascus, toward the north beside Hamath, they will be his—from east to west—Dan's one [portion].

²"Along the boundary of Dan, from the east side to the west side, is Asher's one [portion].

³"Along the boundary of Asher, from the east side to the west side, is Naphtali's one [portion].

⁴"Along the boundary of Naphtali, from the east side to the west side, is Manasseh's one [portion].

⁵"Along the boundary of Manasseh, from the east side to the west side, is Ephraim's one [portion].

⁶"Along the boundary of Ephraim, from the east side to the west side, is Reuben's one [portion].

⁷"Along the boundary of Reuben, from the east side to the west side, is Judah's one [portion].

⁸"Along the boundary of Judah, from the east side to the west side, will be the contribution you are to devote. [Its] width is twenty-five thousand [cubits], and [its] length is equal to one of the [tribal] portions from the east side to the west side. The sanctuary will be in its midst. ⁹The contribution you are to devote to Yahweh is to be [in] length twenty-five thousand [cubits] and [in] width ten thousand [cubits]. ¹⁰The holy contribution will be for these: for the priests, [a rectangular area measuring] on the north twenty-five thousand [cubits] and on the west a width of ten thousand [cubits] and on the east a width of ten thousand [cubits] and on the south a length of twenty-five thousand [cubits]. The sanctuary of Yahweh will be in its center. ¹¹It will be for the priests, whoever has been consecrated from the sons of Zadok, who performed guard duty for me, and who did not go astray when the [other] sons of Israel went astray, as also the Levites went astray.

¹²"It will be a special offering for them from the [holy] contribution of the land, a most holy [district], along the territory of the Levites. ¹³The Levites [are to have a rectangular allotment] parallel to the territory of the priests: twenty-five thousand [cubits is its] length and its width ten thousand [cubits]. [Its] whole length is twenty-five thousand [cubits] and [its] width ten thousand [cubits]. ¹⁴They must not sell any part of it nor exchange [any of it]. No one can transfer this firstfruits of the land because it is holy, belonging to Yahweh.

¹⁵"The five thousand [cubits] in width that remain along the edge of the twenty-five thousand are common land for the city, for residence and for open land. The city is to be in its center. ¹⁶These are its dimensions: [a square measuring] on the north side four thousand five hundred [cubits] and on the south side four thousand five hundred [cubits] and on the east side four thousand five hundred [cubits] and on the west side four thousand five hundred [cubits]. ¹⁷The open land belonging to the city will be on the north two hundred fifty [cubits] and on the south two hundred fifty [cubits] and on the east two hundred fifty [cubits] and on the west two hundred fifty [cubits]. ¹⁸The remaining [area that runs] lengthwise beside the holy contribution will be ten thousand [cubits east-to-west] on the east and ten thousand [cubits east-to-west] on the west. It shall be beside the holy contribution and its produce shall be food for the workers of the city. ¹⁹The workers of the city who cultivate it will be from all the tribes of Israel. ²⁰The entire [holy] contribution will be twenty-five thousand [cubits] by twenty-five thousand [cubits]. [An area of] one-fourth of the holy contribution you are to devote for the property of the city.

²¹"What remains [of the holy contribution] will belong to the Prince: on both sides of the holy contribution and of the property of the city, extending along the twenty-five thousand [cubits north-to-south width of the] contribution until the eastern border, and westward, extending along the twenty-five thousand [cubits north-to-south width] until the western border, parallel to the [tribal] portions [will be the two portions] belonging to the Prince. The holy contribution and the temple sanctuary will be in the middle of it. ²²[The area] consisting of the property of the Levites and the property of the city is in the middle of the [two tracts] that will belong to the Prince. [The area] between the territory of Judah and the territory of Benjamin will belong to the Prince.

²³"As for the rest of the tribes, from the east side to the west side is Benjamin's one [portion].

²⁴"Along the boundary of Benjamin, from the east side to the west side, is Simeon's one [portion].

²⁵"Along the boundary of Simeon, from the east side to the west side, is Issachar's one [portion].

²⁶"Along the boundary of Issachar, from the east side to the west side, is Zebulun's one [portion].

²⁷"Along the boundary of Zebulun, from the east side to the west side, is Gad's one [portion].

²⁸"Along the boundary of Gad on the southern side, the border will run from Tamar to the waters of Meribah-kadesh, to the Wadi [of Egypt] and the Great [Mediterranean] Sea.

²⁹"This is the land that you are to allot as an inheritance to the tribes of Israel, and these are their portions, says the Lord Yahweh.

³⁰"These are the outside bounds of the city. On the north side, four thousand five hundred [cubits] is the measurement. ³¹The gates of the city are [named] according to the names of the tribes of Israel. Three gates are on the north: one

gate of Reuben, one gate of Judah, and one gate of Levi. ³²On the east side, four thousand five hundred [cubits in measurement], are three gates: one gate of Joseph, one gate of Benjamin, and one gate of Dan. ³³On the south side, four thousand five hundred [cubits in] measurement, are three gates: one gate of Simeon, one gate of Issachar, and one gate of Zebulun. ³⁴On the west side, four thousand five hundred [cubits in measurement], their gates are three: one gate of Gad, one gate of Asher, and one gate of Naphtali. ³⁵The circumference [of the city] is eighteen thousand [cubits], and the name of the city from that day on is 'Yahweh *Shammah* [Yahweh is there].' "

Textual Notes and Commentary

The Tribal Allotments and the Holy Contribution in the New Promised Land (48:1–29)

48:1–29 These verses comprise the second of three subsections, demarcated by formulas, within the final divine speech. See "Introduction to the New Promised Land (47:13–48:35)" after the comments on 47:12. The overall boundaries of the new inheritance were given in the first subsection, 47:13–23. In this subsection, the individual allotments to be inherited by the tribes of Israel—and ingrafted aliens alike! (see on 47:21–23)—are given in 48:1–7, 23–28, with a summary statement for both subsections in 48:29. Sandwiched between the two sets of tribal allotments is the description of the holy contribution in 48:8–22. The reason for this structure of the text is because God describes each strip of land, running from east to west, beginning with the northernmost strip, and moving down in a most orderly fashion to each adjacent strip immediately to the south. See figure 6.

Thus 48:1–29 contains three obvious units: (1) seven tribal allotments (48:1–7); (2) the holy contribution (48:8–22); and (3) the final five tribal allotments (48:23–28, with a summary in 48:29). However, due to the highly repetitive nature of the two units describing the tribal allotments, the comments below will first consider 48:1, then cover the tribal allotments in 48:2–7, 23–29 together, and finally take up the holy contribution (48:8–22).

The Allotments to Be Inherited by the Tribes (48:1–7, 23–29)

48:1 As anticipated since 47:21, the allotments of the individual tribes ensue, beginning again at the north with Dan. These continue through 48:7 for the seven tribes Ezekiel assigns north of the holy contribution. The list is interrupted by a long excursus on that area (48:8–22), which is really the heart of the chapter. The allotments of the five tribes south of the contribution are then listed in 48:23–29.

The northern boundary of Dan coincides with the northern boundary of the entire new promised land. Its description in this verse is an abbreviated version of 47:15–17 (which see). None of the problems discussed there are clarified here. The crucial issue is still "Lebo-hamath." I have continued to translate it as though it were one hyphenated place name. My interpretation treats לְבוֹא

as meaning "entrance" or "access road leading to" Hamath, so that this place likely is considerably farther south than Hamath itself. The boundary is placed about where Dan's border usually ran in preexilic times, rather than much farther north, where it would have to be if "Lebo-hamath" were another name for Hamath itself.

In וְהָיוּ־לֹו, the subject of the plural verb ("they will be") must be the areas outlined by the border description earlier in the verse. The proleptic לֹו, "(belonging) to him, his," looks ahead to "Dan" (דָּן) near the end of the verse, but it is separated from the name by the intervening פְּאַת־קָדִים הַיָּם, literally, "side of the east, the sea/west," meaning that his territory runs "from east to west." That is an abbreviated form of the longer expression that recurs (with only minor variations) in each of the other tribal descriptions in 48:2–7, 23–27, מִפְּאַת קָדִימָה עַד־פְּאַת־יָמָה, literally, "from the side of the east until the side of the sea/west" (e.g., 48:4).[1] Sometimes a conjunction is added (וְעַד), and sometimes no locative *he* is on קָדִים.

Thus the north and south boundaries of each tribal portion are a straight line running from east to west, regardless the terrain (hills, valleys, etc.). As pointed out in "Introduction to Ezekiel 40–48" and in "Introduction to the New Promised Land (47:13–48:35)" (after the comments on 47:12), such boundaries would be humanly impossible to implement in the geography of the present earth, and so they point toward a fulfillment after the return of Christ, in the new heavens and new earth, which only God can and will create (cf. Revelation 21–22).

All the tribal allotments in 48:1–7, 23–27 end with the name of the tribe followed by the numeral one: דָּן אֶחָד, "Dan, one" (48:1); אָשֵׁר אֶחָד, "Asher, one" (48:2); and so on. Block claims that this was simply an ancient way of checking off individual items in a series (cf. Josh 12:9–24).[2] Block's translation places the numeral at the start of the sentence, "First, ..." and changes the later numerals to follow the sequence.[3] However, placing the last Hebrew word of each verse first and changing "one" to "second," "third," and so forth, sacrifices literalness. Better is Keil, who takes each אֶחָד as referring to "one (tribelot)," with חֶבֶל (whose plural referred to Joseph's two "portions" in 47:13) implied. Keil explains that the numeral "one" emphasizes that each tribe receives one territory of the same size.[4] One could also understand חֵלֶק, "portion," to be implied, as in my translation, since its plural is in 45:7; 48:8, 21. For the sake of English idiom, the translation (still following the Hebrew word order) makes each tribal name possessive, "Dan's one [portion]." It could also be rendered, "one [portion] for Dan," and likewise for the other tribes.

---

[1] Cooke, *Ezekiel*, 539, believes the shorter phrase here is a corruption of the longer one used for the other tribal territories.

[2] Block, *Ezekiel*, 2:719, n. 80.

[3] Block, *Ezekiel*, 2:719–20.

[4] Keil, *Ezekiel*, 2:371–72.

A similar idiom, with similar implications, of parity for each of the tribes, repeats אֶחָד, "one," each time for the twelve city gates in 48:31–34. See on 48:31.

As a NT parallel to the equal portions of land granted to the twelve tribes, one can note in Rev 7:4–8 the equal numbers of sealed believers from each tribe that total the one hundred forty-four thousand who comprise the new Israel:

> From the tribe of Judah twelve thousand who had been sealed,
> from the tribe of Reuben twelve thousand ...[5]

"*Along* the road of Hethlon" is, literally, אֶל־יַד דֶּרֶךְ־חֶתְלֹן, "by the hand/side of the way of Hethlon." Here אֶל used in the sense more common for עַל. The idiom אֶל־יַד is repeated before חֲמָת, where I have translated it "beside."

48:2–7, 23–29   The allotments of the tribal territories are bifurcated by the long digression on the holy contribution (48:8–22), which takes up fifteen verses, one more than the number devoted to the twelve tribes (48:1–7, 23–28, with 48:29 as a conclusion). The two tribal sections plainly follow the same pattern, which conveys a certain formality in the listing. Minor variations occur only with the first, Dan (48:1, partially repeating elements from 47:15–17); with the last, Gad (48:28, repeating most of 27:19); and briefly with Benjamin (48:23), when the list resumes after the discussion of the holy contribution.

These verses have both similarities and differences when compared to the tribal inheritances promised in the Torah and possessed by the Israelite tribes in Joshua.[6] Naturally, the twelve-tribe system is retained. In the old Mosaic system, Levi had no unified territory, only scattered cities (Joshua 21). In Ezekiel, Levi receives no tribal allotment, but the priests (who in Ezekiel are only those Levites descended from Zadok) and the rest of the Levites each receive a portion of land within the holy contribution (48:8–22). That leaves eleven other tribes, but the double portion granted to Joseph (47:13, in harmony with Gen 48:5) by granting portions to Joseph's two sons, Ephraim and Manasseh (Ezek 48:4–5), brings the total number of tribal allotments back up to twelve. Ephraim and Manasseh receive adjacent tracts, as might be expected by their fraternal relationship.

---

[5] For the topic of the new Israel consisting of all believers in Christ, see "Introduction to Ezekiel 40–48." Brighton, *Revelation*, 190, comments that one hundred forty-four thousand is "twelve times twelve thousand. ... It suggests that God's Israel, the church of Jesus Christ, as it advances to battle in the mission given it, is a perfect and complete army, fully equipped and ready to do God's work." Regarding the listing of the tribes, he explains (p. 192):

> A redefined list of the twelve tribes of Israel is used in Rev 7:5–8: a list that has been cleansed of any association of apostasy and idolatry; a list that emphasizes faithfulness to God ... and in particular a list that focuses on the Messiah because of the placement of Judah [first].

[6] For the allotments in Joshua, see map 4 in Harstad, *Joshua*, 844.

As in Joshua 13–21, the tribes of Dan (see below), Asher, Naphtali, Manasseh, and Ephraim are located in the northern part of the Holy Land. As in Joshua, so also in Ezekiel 48 there are more tribes to the north of Jerusalem than to the south, with a more even balance here in Ezekiel: seven to the north and five to the south, whereas originally only Judah and Simeon were to the south of Jerusalem,[7] and seven and a half tribes were to the north—and two and a half (Reuben, Gad, and half of Manasseh) were east of the Jordan.

In the course of Israel's history, various events forced some major changes. The Transjordan territories given to Reuben, Gad, and half of Manasseh did not stay under Israelite control very long, but were subjugated by Moab and Ammon. Those tribes had originally requested to receive Transjordan because of its suitability for raising livestock (Numbers 32), even though it was outside the land promised through Moses (Num 34:1–15). At times they risked schism from the other tribes (e.g., Josh 22:10–34). Therefore in Ezekiel's vision, the allotment of territory entirely in the Cisjordan (with a small area perhaps east of the Upper Jordan River and the Sea of Galilee) may be a restoration of God's original intent for those tribes, where they would dwell in unity with the other tribes.

Perhaps Reuben is placed north of Judah because of his status as firstborn.

In fulfillment of Jacob's prophecy that Simeon (as well as Levi) would be scattered in Israel (Gen 49:5–7), Simeon received an allotment entirely within that of Judah and subsequently seemed to lose much, but not all, of its identity.[8] In Ezekiel, Simeon is allotted territory in roughly the same location in the south as its original allotment.

Dan was originally allotted territory along the Mediterranean Sea just north of Judah, but then, apparently under pressure from the original Amorite inhabitants, the Danites relocated to the Upper Jordan Valley, north of the Sea of Galilee (Josh 19:40–48; Judg 1:34; 18:1–31). In Ezekiel, Dan is the northernmost tribe, as it had been in preexilic times after it relocated.

In Ezekiel, the relation of Judah and Benjamin to Jerusalem (assuming the "city" in the holy contribution corresponds to it; see below on 48:30–35) is reversed, with Judah to the north of the holy contribution and Benjamin to the south of it. Possibly the etymological meaning of "Benjamin" (בִּנְיָמִין, "son of right hand," with "right" also meaning "south") determined its position there. Jerusalem had originally been allotted to Benjamin (Josh 18:28), but it remained unconquered, with Jebusites inhabiting it, until it was conquered by Judahites (Judg 1:8) and definitely by David (2 Sam 5:6–9), so that it literally became an extraterritorial "city of David" (e.g., 2 Sam 5:7, 9) and could scarcely be disassociated from him or his tribe, the messianic tribe of Judah (Gen 49:10; cf. Ezek 21:32; Rev 5:5). Perhaps Judah was placed to the north,

---

[7] Jerusalem was originally allotted to Benjamin (see below), but it was on the southern border of Benjamin, with almost all of Benjamin being north of it.

[8] See Harstad, *Joshua*, 597–98 and map 4 (p. 844).

together with tribes that had been among the apostate tribes of the Northern Kingdom, in order to dampen any royalist ambitions that the Judahites might still entertain. The only royalty in Ezekiel's vision is the Prince.[9] In any case, the holy contribution with the holy city ends up by being surrounded by the two tribes comprising the original Southern Kingdom.

One other major factor in determining the tribes' positions in Ezekiel is whether the tribes were descended from Jacob's wives, Leah and Rachel, or from their handmaidens, Zilpah and Bilhah, respectively (Gen 29:31–30:24; 35:16–18). A similar concern seems to be a factor in the placement of the city gates named after the twelve tribes (see on Ezek 48:31). The allotments of the tribes descended from the wives are closest to the sanctuary, while those from the handmaidens are placed at the extremities, farthest from the holy contribution. Some degree of preference also seems to be given to Leah as Jacob's first wife (the one chosen for him, not the one he chose) over Rachel, his second wife. This preference can be seen in the close proximity of the Leah tribes to the holy contribution: Judah adjoins the contribution to the north, then Reuben is the next one to the north of Judah. While Benjamin (from Rachel) is immediately to the south of the contribution, next come the Leah tribes of Simeon, Issachar, and Zebulun. The eight tribes descended from Leah and Rachel are evenly divided, with four on each side of the holy contribution: to the north are Manasseh (from Rachel), Ephraim (from Rachel), Reuben (from Leah), and Judah (from Leah); to the south are Benjamin (from Rachel), Simeon (from Leah), Issachar (from Leah), and Zebulun (from Leah). On the extremities, Dan, Asher, and Naphtali are the farthest north, while Gad is the farthest south. This is the north-to-south order of the tribes and the matriarch of each:

- Dan   Bilhah, handmaid of Rachel
- Asher   Zilpah, handmaid of Leah
- Naphtali   Bilhah, handmaid of Rachel
- Manasseh   Rachel
- Ephraim   Rachel
- Reuben   Leah
- Judah   Leah
- The holy contribution
- Benjamin   Rachel
- Simeon   Leah
- Issachar   Leah
- Zebulun   Leah
- Gad   Zilpah, handmaid of Leah

By making the allotments into twelve equal (see on 48:8a) and parallel strips, God likely intends to erase the inequities in size and position consequent

---

[9] See especially on 44:3; 45:7, 17; 48:21–22.

upon the old system. Politically, the exploitative nature of the monarchy is negated, in favor of what Block calls a "theocratic feudalism,"[10] which was the original ideal, with Yahweh as Israel's only king, and the Prince as his core-gent. God distributes the land as he sees fit, and each tribe is to receive in thanks-giving its "inheritance" (נַחֲלָה, 48:29) from him.

The plan for the tribal allotments entails several practical problems. That God does not address these problems is another sign that the fulfillment of the vision could never be on the present earth, but will only be accomplished by God himself in the new heavens and new earth.[11] Geographically, each tract is to be of the same width north-to-south. However, the uneven coastline would result in gross differences in the length of the tribal tracts from east to west, perhaps from as little as forty miles or sixty-five kilometers for the tracts in the far north to as much as one hundred miles or one hundred sixty-one kilome-ters in the tracts to the far south. The description in Ezekiel makes no al-lowances for the variations in the coast of the Mediterranean Sea, which forms the western boundary, nor for smaller variations in the eastern boundary, largely formed by the Jordan River and the Dead Sea. God's intent certainly seems to be to grant each tribe an allotment of the same size, but it seems impossible for that intent to be realized if the description in Ezekiel is superimposed on the geography of the land as it currently exists.

Just as significantly, the rigid east-west boundaries make no allowances for the varying terrain (mountains, hills, valleys, etc.) in Canaan's natural topog-raphy. Neither are there any references to roads or routes for travel and com-munication. The more distant tribes could find journeys to the geographically central holy contribution to be difficult, and this could produce the opposite of monarchical centralization: isolationism and centrifugal tendencies caused by the difficulty of intertribal collaboration, although presumably the new con-federacy would be drawn and held together by the tribes' common dedication to Yahweh's "house."

48:28 For the redundant נֶגֶב תֵּימָנָה, "south, southward," the place name מֵי מְרִיבַת קָדֵשׁ, "the waters of Meribah-kadesh," and נַחֲלָה (the noun נַחַל, "wadi," with locative *he*) referring to the Wadi of Egypt, see on 47:19.

48:29 This verse serves as a summary statement for the two preceding subsections of the final divine speech (47:13–48:35). "This is the land …" sum-marizes the overall boundary descriptions of the entire new promised land in the first subsection, 47:13–23. "And these are their portions …" summarizes the allotments to the twelve tribes (plus the holy contribution) in 48:1–28. See "Introduction to the New Promised Land (47:13–48:35)" after the comments on 47:12.

תַּפִּילוּ, the Hiphil of נָפַל, means "allot, apportion," and has הָאָרֶץ, "the land," as its direct object, as in 45:1 (similar is 47:22). מִנַּחֲלָה, literally, "from

---

[10] Block, *Ezekiel*, 2:724.

[11] See further "Introduction to Ezekiel 40–48."

inheritance," must have the same meaning as נַחֲלָה did when it had בְּ, "*as an* inheritance" (see on 47:14, 22). Compare the unusual use of מִן on וּמֵאֲחֻזַּת twice in 48:22.

The Holy Contribution (48:8–22)

48:8–22 These verses about the holy, central portion of land are, to a large extent, an expansion of what was already described in 45:1–8 (see the notes and commentary there). Here, after an introduction giving the dimensions and placement of the holy contribution in its broadest sense (48:8a), the remaining verses deal with the four components that comprise that holy contribution: (1) the land grant to the priests (48:9–12a, 14, 20a), in the center of which is "the sanctuary" (48:8b, 10b); (2) the land grant to the Levites (48:12b–14, 20a); (3) the common city property (48:15–20); and (4) the two tracts belonging to the Prince (48:21–22). See figure 6. For the issue of which tract(s) of land are under discussion in 48:13b–14, see on those verses below.

Throughout these verses the number twenty-five thousand recurs, which probably has symbolical significance comparable to that of "the twenty-fifth year" in 40:1, suggesting a turning point in the redemption of God's people (see the commentary on 40:1). The measurement of each side of the city is four thousand five hundred (48:16; also 48:30–34), and its circumference is eighteen thousand (48:35). Both of those numbers too are multiples of twenty-five (as are many other numbers throughout chapters 40–48), and they likely share some of the same redemptive significance.

The key word in this section is תְּרוּמָה, "contribution, offering, portion (given to Yahweh)." In 48:8–9, 20, it is used together with the verb from which it is derived, the Hiphil of רוּם, in a cognate accusative construction: for example, הַתְּרוּמָה אֲשֶׁר־תָּרִימוּ, "the contribution you are to devote" (48:8). The same verb and noun were in 45:1, which added לַיהוָה, "devote *to Yahweh*," as also in 48:9. The noun alone (without the verb) was translated as "contribution" in 45:6–7, 13, 16 (in the first two verses referring to tracts of land and in the last two to sacrifices). Hence the noun alone is rendered as "contribution" also in 48:10, 12, 18, 20, 21. In most of these verses, the noun is in the construct phrase תְּרוּמַת הַקֹּדֶשׁ, literally, "the contribution of holiness," an adjectival genitive rendered as "the holy contribution" (48:10, 18, 20–21). See on 45:1.

Throughout this section (as in chapter 45), the exact referent of תְּרוּמָה must be determined by the context. Its broadest meaning is in 48:8a (which see) and also 48:12. But in 48:20a and 48:21a (second occurrence), it refers to the smaller, square area occupied by the priests, the Levites, and the city. In 48:18, 20b, 21a (first occurrence), it refers to the still smaller area of the priests' land and the Levites' land together (as it did in 45:6–7). And in 48:9 (according to the MT) as well as in 48:10 and 48:21b, it refers still more narrowly only to the priests' land (as it did in 45:1).

No unit of measure is supplied in this chapter, but most commentators and translations assume that it is "cubits," so that word has been supplied in brackets in many verses of the translation. The long cubit specified in 40:5 was about 20.3 inches long. The east-to-west length of twenty-five thousand cubits would then be about eight miles or thirteen kilometers. The north-to-south width of ten thousand cubits would be over three miles or five kilometers. Keil, however, assumes that the unit is the guide's measuring rod,[12] which was six long cubits in length (40:5), and this would result in a rectangle about forty-eight miles or seventy-eight kilometers east-to-west and about nineteen miles or thirty-one kilometers north-to-south. Since the east-to-west dimension would be approximately the entire distance from the Jordan to the Mediterranean, that would leave little or no room for the two tracts (one to the east, the other to the west) allotted to the Prince.[13]

Introduction to the Holy Contribution (48:8a)

48:8a This verse defines the entire "contribution" as a swath of land extending the whole breadth of Israel, corresponding to the series of swaths for the twelve tribes. This verse semantically links the "contribution" to the tribal tracts by referring to them using the plural of חֵלֶק, "portions," instead of the plural of נַחֲלָה, which would have been "inheritances," since the "contribution" belongs to Yahweh and is not to be inherited by any of the tribes, although allowance is made for the Prince to pass on his land within the "contribution" to his sons by inheritance (see on 46:16–17).

In the next verse (48:9), as we shall see, תְּרוּמָה, "contribution," has a much more restricted application. But the word's theological meaning in this context is even more significant. In other OT contexts, תְּרוּמָה is a technical sacrificial expression, traditionally rendered "heave offering" (see the commentary on 20:40 and on 44:30; 45:1), referring to certain gifts or offerings dedicated to Yahweh. And as in 45:1, Hebrew can readily use with the noun the cognate verb, the Hiphil of רוּם, "to lift up," meaning "devote, dedicate, consecrate." But here the noun is used in a context where Yahweh is the Giver of his land, and the people give back or reserve as a sacrifice of thanksgiving a portion of his gift in recognition that none of it is theirs by birthright; it is in its entirety a divine gift of grace.

Thus, we have an excellent example of the sacrificial-sacramental duality that pervaded all of Israel's worship and continues into that of Christianity. Everything begins with and depends on God's prior gift, centering in Christ and the cross. Then, in voluntary response, believers offer their sacrifices, which are not propitiary, but eucharistic, and which God uses to convey further gifts and/or to continue and strengthen the original gift. Thus those OT sacrifices were in a broader sense "sacramental" and were types of the NT Sacraments, Holy Baptism and the Lord's Supper. Many nugatory debates about whether the OT sacrifices were also "sacraments" and whether our Sacra-

---

[12] Keil, *Ezekiel*, 2:369.

[13] See also on 45:1.

ments are also (eucharistic!) sacrifices (sometimes centering on "eucharistic prayers") could be avoided if this duality were comprehended.

The construct phrase כְּאַחַד הַחֲלָקִים has the preposition כְּ introducing a nominal predicate and not meaning simply "like," but *equal to* one of the [tribal] portions" in its east-to-west length. See BDB, s.v. כְּ, 1 d, and GKC, § 118 x.

The Holy Contribution Containing the Sanctuary at the Center of the Priests' Land and Containing the Levites' Land (48:8b–14)

48:8b While וְהָיָה הַמִּקְדָּשׁ בְּתוֹכוֹ (48:8b) is, literally, "the sanctuary will be in its midst," the temple is to be in the very center of the priests' land within the holy contribution, as 48:10b will indicate, using almost the same Hebrew expression. The antecedent of the masculine suffix on בְּתוֹכוֹ ("in its midst") is the grammatically feminine תְּרוּמָה, "contribution," but the suffix is masculine by attraction to the masculine plural of חֵלֶק, "portion." The same grammatical feature will be seen in 48:10 and the Qere in 48:15, 21.

Some interpreters take "in the midst" in 48:8b, 10b, to mean that the temple is in the geometric center of the entire "contribution," but that seems to contravene God's concern in Ezekiel to safeguard the sanctity of the temple, even by keeping it far from the city (see further on 48:20).[14]

48:9 The same textual problem that was in 45:1 reappears in 48:9. The MT gives the north-to-south width of עֲשֶׂרֶת אֲלָפִים, "ten thousand," supported by most of the ancient versions, which must refer only to the priests' land, which is the indisputable topic of 48:10–12a (with the possible exception of the first clause of 48:10; on which see). Thus if 48:9 is read together with 48:10b–12a there is no problem with the MT's number. The LXX gives "twenty thousand," which would include both the priests' land and the land of the Levites. RSV (as well as NRSV and ESV) follows the LXX and put the MT's number in a footnote. However, the Levites' land is not introduced until 48:12b–14, and it (and probably also the priests' land) is labeled "holy, belonging to Yahweh" (48:14b). Only the priests' allotment is labeled "a most holy [district]" (48:12) because it contains the sanctuary. See on 48:8–22 for the varying referents of "contribution."

48:10 English idiom requires a different word order for the first part of the verse to convey the sense. The MT begins, וּלְאֵלֶּה תִּהְיֶה תְרוּמַת־הַקֹּדֶשׁ, literally, "to these will belong the holy contribution." The plural לְאֵלֶּה, "to these," could refer only to the following לַכֹּהֲנִים, "to the priests," but more likely it also includes the Levites, although their land is not described until 48:12b–14. Possibly it could also include the city (48:15–20) and the Prince (48:21–22) since their tracts also are within the holy contribution (see on 48:8–22). But the rest

---

[14] To visualize the two different conceptions, compare figure 6 in this commentary and the sketch in Block, *Ezekiel*, 733 with those of Cooke, *Ezekiel*, 532; Allen, *Ezekiel*, 2:283; and Zimmerli, *Ezekiel*, 2:535.

of the verse clearly refers to the priests' land. Because it contains the temple, its importance is emphasized by giving its dimensions on all four sides. The final clause, וְהָיָה מִקְדַּשׁ־יְהוָה בְּתוֹכוֹ, literally, "and the sanctuary of Yahweh will be in its midst," is identical to the clause concluding 48:8 but with the addition of "Yahweh." Here בְּתוֹכוֹ can be translated as "in its center" because the temple is situated at the geometric center of the priests' land. See figure 6.

48:11 For the restriction of the priesthood to Zadokites in the book of Ezekiel, see on 43:19; 44:15.

לַכֹּהֲנִים הַמְקֻדָּשׁ מִבְּנֵי צָדוֹק is, literally, "for the priests, the one consecrated from the sons of Zadok." The construction is difficult because the plural "priests" is followed by the singular Pual participle, which apparently modifies the plural "priests." There is no doubt that the Pual participle of קָדַשׁ means "consecrated, sanctified, hallowed," since it has that meaning when it refers to the Aaronic priests in 2 Chr 26:18. (It is also used in reference to other consecrated people/things in Is 13:3; Ezra 3:5; 2 Chr 31:6.) The LXX translates the participle as plural, perhaps taking the following preposition *min* as the final *mem* of the participle (הַמְקֻדָּשִׁם בְּנֵי). With that different word division we could easily translate, "for the consecrated priests, the sons of Zadok." But the MT is defensible if the singular is taken in a distributive sense, "whoever has been consecrated," as I have translated. In either case, the meaning is essentially the same. However, the MT could imply that the priests (like pastors in the NT era) had no indelible character, but could lose their consecration by unfaithfulness, so that only the priests who remain faithful remain "consecrated."

48:12 The Masoretic ס (an abbreviation of סְתוּמָה, a "closed" or shorter space between verses) preceding the verse indicates that it begins a new paragraph, even though it continues the thought of 48:10–11. The subject of the feminine verb וְהָיְתָה ("it will be") is the feminine noun תְּרוּמָה in the construct phrase תְּרוּמַת־הַקֹּדֶשׁ, "the holy contribution," back in 48:10. The prepositional phrase לָהֶם, "for them," resumes לַכֹּהֲנִים, "for the priests," beginning 48:11.

The noun תְּרוּמִיָּה is a hapax and of uncertain significance, although clearly it is related to the common noun תְּרוּמָה, "contribution" (see on 48:8–22 and on 48:8–9). Cooke dismisses תְּרוּמִיָּה as an "accidental variation."[15] Zimmerli tries to relate it to the tithes that the Levites were commanded to pay in Num 18:26, which uses תְּרוּמָה, "contribution."[16] In formation, תְּרוּמִיָּה may be an abstract noun meaning "the *act* of lifting/contributing," but used in a concrete sense ("contribution"), as is common in Hebrew. But at the same time, תְּרוּמִיָּה may signal that this "contribution" is somehow distinct from the rest of the areas designated by תְּרוּמָה (see the introduction to 48:8–22). The versions generally do not distinguish it from תְּרוּמָה, but many English translations do, as my "special offering" does. The only detail we are given as to how it was special is the following superlative construct phrase, קֹדֶשׁ קָדָשִׁים, "a *most* holy

---

15 Cooke, *Ezekiel*, 539.

16 Zimmerli, *Ezekiel*, 2:534.

[district].” For that phrase, see on 43:12. “The contribution of the land” from which this “special offering” is taken refers to the holy contribution in its entirety as in 48:8a (which see).

The end of the verse states that the priests' area adjoins “the territory of the Levites,” thus introducing the next tract of land, to be described in detail in 48:13. Here in 48:12 and also in 48:13, גְּבוּל, which usually means “boundary, border,” refers to the “territory” of the Levites enclosed by its prescribed boundaries. Also twice in 48:22, גְּבוּל refers to a tribal “territory.”

48:13 Instead of וְהַלְוִיִּם, “and the Levites,” the LXX and Vulgate apparently read וְלַלְוִיִּם, “and *to* the Levites,” after the analogy of the prepositional phrases with לְ beginning 48:10 and 48:11. There is a certain logic to the consistency in those versions, but on the other hand, Ezekiel may have simply preferred variety of expression, and the MT can easily be translated as it stands. In either case, a few English words must be added for the sense; my translation adds “are to have a rectangular allotment.”

The second half of the verse is a repetition of the dimensions given in the first half, but introduced with כָּל־, translated, “[its] whole …” The north-to-south “width” of the Levites' property clearly must be “ten thousand,” as stated in 48:13a (וְרֹחַב עֲשֶׂרֶת אֲלָפִים), so that the total north-to-south width of the properties of the priests (ten thousand in 48:9–10), the Levites (ten thousand in 48:13a), and the city (five thousand in 48:15) adds up to twenty-five thousand, thus forming a square, as stated in 48:20. See figure 6. But when that same Hebrew phrase recurs at the end of the verse (וְרֹחַב עֲשֶׂרֶת אֲלָפִים), instead of the MT's width of “ten thousand,” the LXX (in an original hand) read “twenty thousand,” the same variant reading attested by the (unchanged) LXX in 45:1 and 48:9. RSV, NRSV, and ESV again follow the LXX. The LXX would be correct if the second half of the verse were describing the sacred area consisting of the combined territories of the priests and of the Levites, in which case כָּל־ would indicate their sum (“[their] whole …”). But the fact that (at least one manuscript of) the LXX was subsequently changed may make the case for following the LXX here even weaker than in 45:1 and 48:9. KJV, NKJV, NIV, and NASB all follow the MT here as all of them also did in 48:9 and as all but NIV did in 45:1.

48:14 The regulations in 48:14 could pertain only to the Levites' land (the immediately preceding topic in the MT of 48:13b), but this commentary takes the verse as pertaining to both the land of the Levites and that of the priests. This would almost certainly have to be the case if one followed the LXX in 48:13b, so that the immediately preceding topic was the combined tracts of the priests and Levites. The verbs (see further below) are third person plural (יִמְכְּרוּ) and singular (יָמֵר … יַעֲבִיר) with no stated subjects, who could be the Levites alone (48:12b–13a) or also the priests (48:10–11). The territory that is “the first-fruits of the land” and that “is holy, belonging to Yahweh” (48:14) could describe the Levites' land alone, but most likely it also describes the priests' land, in the center of which the temple was situated (48:10b).

This verse takes up a topic not considered in 45:1–8, but loosely based on regulations in Lev 25:32–34, namely, the possible sale or transfer of property to other hands. In Leviticus, the Levites, including the priests, were given the forty-eight scattered Levitical cities (Lev 25:34; Num 35:1–8; Josh 21:1–42), not property in a concentrated area as envisioned here. Through Moses, God had permitted some limited transfer of Levitical property, but it had to be returned in the Jubilee Year. But in Ezekiel, God is stricter on the point than in Leviticus. Here God absolutely prohibits any sale or transfer of land to other ownership. In Ezek 46:16–17 there were similar controls over the Prince's two properties, but there the concern was his retention of the correct apportionment of the land, while here the accent is on Yahweh's inalienable right of possession of the land that he has given, a "contribution" of which they return to him in thanksgiving (see on 45:1).

The twofold reason for the prohibitions is simply stated. First, the land (probably the combined tracts of the priests and Levites) is called the רֵאשִׁית הָאָרֶץ, literally, "the first/firstfruits of the land." רֵאשִׁית is often used for the offering of "firstfruits" (e.g., Lev 2:12), and also for the first or best of other things (e.g., Gen 49:3). Here the immediate reference is to land dedicated to God for the use of the (priests and) Levites, a part of the תְּרוּמָה, "contribution" (48:8a). The second reason is that כִּי־קֹדֶשׁ לַיהוָה, literally, "because it is a holy thing belonging to Yahweh." In other contexts, קֹדֶשׁ לַיהוה might simply mean that something is "holy (in relation) to Yahweh" (cf. BDB, s.v. לְ, 5 a (d), and Lev 27:14, 21–23), but the larger context here emphasizes that this portion of land "belongs to" Yahweh (cf. BDB, s.v. לְ, 5 b).

Grammatically, the verse is puzzling because of the inconsistency in the verbs, one plural and two singular. First is the negated Qal plural (of מָכַר): וְלֹא־יִמְכְּרוּ, "they shall not sell."

Then comes the negated singular וְלֹא יָמֵר (Hiphil jussive of מוּר), to "exchange" (BDB, Hiphil, 2), which one is tempted to emend into a plural to agree with the Syriac and Vulgate. The LXX reads a singular verb, but as if a form of מָדַד, "to measure," which does not fit the context.) The Targum translates with a singular verb. Possibly the intent of the singular verb is to individualize possible real estate transactions. As to why the form is jussive (normally negated by אַל rather than as here with לֹא) instead of a regular imperfect (normally negated by לֹא), Joüon, § 114 l, calls this one of several jussives that are "difficult or impossible to explain," and GKC, § 72 dd, considers it simply to be an imperfect (not jussive) spelled with the shortened form for the sake of rhythm. But the best explanation is by Waltke-O'Connor, § 34.2.1c–d, which says that such unexpected jussives should be interpreted by their sense (in context) rather than by their form.

Finally, the Kethib וְלֹא יַעֲבוּר is the intransitive Qal imperfect of עָבַר, which would have "the firstfruits of the land" (רֵאשִׁית הָאָרֶץ) as its subject: it shall not "pass into other hands" (BDB, s.v. עָבַר, Qal, 6 f; see also 4 e, referring to the exchange of money in Gen 23:16). The Qere, וְלֹא יַעֲבִיר, is the transitive Hiphil imperfect, which would have a Levite (or priest) as its subject, and "the firstfruits of the land" (רֵאשִׁית הָאָרֶץ) as its object: "he shall not cause it to pass over (to another owner)." The Qere is to be preferred because the first two verbs are transitive and also because both nouns in the phrase רֵאשִׁית הָאָרֶץ ("the firstfruits of the land") are feminine, and so the construct phrase would be an unlikely subject of the masculine verb (although Ezekiel has plenty of examples of grammatical inconsistencies in gender).

The Common City Property (48:15–20)

48:15 In this section, God returns to אֲחֻזַּת הָעִיר, "the property of the city" (48:20), which he had mentioned in 45:6–7. Here in 48:15 it is referred to as the five thousand cubits (north-to-south) that is הַנּוֹתָר בָּרֹחַב, literally, "the remainder in the width." The Niphal participle (of יָתַר) means "what remains," and here רֹחַב, "width," has the preposition בְּ and the article. (הַנּוֹתָר will recur in 48:18, referring to two smaller areas within this area, and in 48:21, referring to the Prince's two tracts outside but adjacent to this area.) This rectangle is the remaining area (after the allotments to the priests and Levites) needed to fill out the square with equal sides, each twenty-five thousand cubits long (48:20; see figure 6). This square is in the center of the entire תְּרוּמָה, "contribution" (48:8a).

The city's tract is pronounced חֹל־הוּא, literally, "it is common" (48:15). The antecedent of the pronoun הוּא ("it") is הַנּוֹתָר ("the remainder"). The form of this nominal sentence is known as a "declaratory judgment." The same form is used frequently in the Torah for verdicts about the kind or acceptability of sacrifices or other matters—mostly, but not exclusively, liturgical. For instance, God declares about sacrifices and the altar, "it is (most) holy" (e.g., Ex 29:34; 30:10; Lev 7:1, 6). The same form of sentence is used for the sacrifices themselves: for example, "it is a burnt offering" (e.g., Lev 1:13, 17); "it is a sin offering" (e.g., Lev 4:24). The form can also be used negatively, for example, "it/he is unclean" (e.g., Lev 11:38; 13:36) or "it is a perversion" (Lev 18:23). Often חֹל has negative connotations, in which cases the translation "profane" may be appropriate, implying defilement, but here its use is quite neutral: simply what is unconsecrated, common, ordinary.

The whole forensic aspect of the doctrine of justification follows the same pattern: God's declaration renders believers righteous through faith (e.g., Gen 15:6; Romans 4).

Two uses for this common space are mentioned. The first is לְמוֹשָׁב, "for habitation/residence," meaning unwalled "suburbs" that often surrounded walled cities in antiquity or temporary housing for pilgrims at the great festivals. The second use is וּלְמִגְרָשׁ, "and for open land." מִגְרָשׁ (repeated in 48:17) was the word used to designate the "pastureland" around the forty-eight Levitical cities that was used for the Levites' livestock (e.g., Lev 25:34; Num 35:2–5, 7). Its exact use here is less certain, perhaps including agricultural plots (somewhat like typical Russian dachas) for the sustenance of inhabitants, whether permanent or transient. Subsequent verses will provide context for these brief statements. מִגְרָשׁ was used in 45:2 for a border of "open area" around the temple compound.

The city (to be described in the next verse) will be in the center of the oblong tract. Hence the Qere, בְּתוֹכוֹ (or the Kethib, if vocalized בְּתוֹכֹה), could be rendered, "in its center," as also in 48:10b. The referent of the masculine suffix on בְּתוֹכוֹ is the masculine participle הַנּוֹתָר (not a feminine noun, תְּרוּמָה [48:12] or אֶרֶץ [48:12, 14], which might be the referent if the Kethib were vocalized בְּתוֹכָה).

48:16 The feminine suffix on מְדוֹתֶיהָ, "its dimensions," refers back to הָעִיר, "the city" in 48:15. The MT lists the dimension of four thousand five hundred separately for each of the four sides, emphasizing the city's symmetry. Assuming that the units are cubits, the dimension is almost one and a half miles or about two and a third kilometers. (If the units were rods, it would be about eight and three-fourths miles or fourteen kilometers.)

In the dimensions for the south side of the square, instead of the usual חֲמֵשׁ מֵאוֹת וְאַרְבַּעַת אֲלָפִים (literally, "five hundred and four thousand"), the text, חֲמֵשׁ חמש מֵאוֹת וְאַרְבַּעַת אֲלָפִים is, literally, "five, five hundred and four thousand." Obviously the second חֲמֵשׁ is a dittograph, as the Masoretes indicate by not supplying any vowel points for it. The marginal Masorah notes about it, חַד מִן ח כְּתִיב וְלֹא קְרֵי, an abbreviation for חַד מִן ח כת ולא קר, meaning that the unpointed חמש is "one of eight [words in the OT that are] written but not to be spoken/read."

48:17 This verse lists separately the four equal measurements of the מִגְרָשׁ ("open land") that surrounded the city on each side, again emphasizing symmetry. Adding the figures of 48:16 and 48:17 together gives us a total of five thousand cubits on each side for the square comprising the city and the open country together.

48:18 After the city and its surrounding open land, two areas are "remaining" (the Niphal participle וְהַנּוֹתָר, as in 48:15, but here referring to subdivisions of the area described there). Within the tract occupied by the city, one lies to the east and one to the west of the city and its open land. Each is a rectangle of five thousand cubits north-to-south and ten thousand cubits east-to-west. See figure 6, where these two areas are labeled "agricultural land" because of the description of their use in 48:18–19.

Some commentators propose that the second instance of the phrase לְעֻמַּת תְּרוּמַת הַקֹּדֶשׁ ("beside the holy contribution") is an example of vertical dittography, but it is preceded by וְהָיָה, which does not repeat any prior word in the verse, and all the ancient versions support the repetition of the phrase. (Critics counter that the *lapsus calami* occurred at some early stage of the texts' transmission.) Nothing is lost if it is omitted, but I have retained it. Here "the holy contribution" designates the combined portions allotted to the priests and the Levites (see on 48:8–22).

We are not told who exactly comprise עֹבְדֵי הָעִיר, "the workers of the city," but the next verse states that they come from all the tribes. Are we to think of a system such as reported in Neh 11:1–2, where lots were cast to bring one out of ten of the country's sparse population to live in Jerusalem (which, it is noted, they did voluntarily)? A much less likely alternative would be the מַס, or corvée, that is, compulsory service for the country, instituted by Solomon, but so hated that it ultimately led to the division of the kingdom when Rehoboam refused to relax the burden (1 Ki 5:13–14; 12:1–20). Whether they were to live in Jerusalem permanently or only temporarily on some rotation basis, Ezekiel does not say.

48:19 God specifies that the workload will be distributed evenly among the twelve tribes, but gives us no more details. The syntax of וְהָעֹבֵד הָעִיר must be appositional, "the worker, the city," but we would have expected a plural in a construct phrase, וְעֹבְדֵי־הָעִיר, "and the workers of the city" (as in 48:18), to provide a plural subject for the following plural verb, יַעַבְדֹוּהוּ, "they will work/farm/cultivate it." Perhaps the plural verb indicates that וְהָעֹבֵד should be taken as a collective: "the workforce." The masculine suffix on the verb refers back to וְהַנֹּותָר, the "remaining" area in 48:18.

48:20 The first half of this verse serves as a summary of the preceding verses about the priests' land, the Levites' land, and the tract for the city. These three tracts are said here to comprise כָּל־הַתְּרוּמָה, "the entire contribution," which clearly uses "contribution" in a narrower sense than in 48:8, 12, where the "contribution" also included the Prince's tracts (to be described in 48:21–22; see on 48:8–22). The territories of the priests, the Levites, and the city together comprise a perfect square, whose dimensions are given as twenty-five thousand cubits by twenty-five thousand cubits. See figure 6.

The words אֶלֶף רְבִיעִית תָּרִימוּ present a challenge. The MT's punctuation, with an *athnach* on אֶלֶף ("thousand"), indicates that that word ends the first half of the verse and that the rest of the verse is a new sentence (as reflected in the translation). רְבִיעִית is a feminine ordinal numeral that normally expresses a fraction, "one-fourth." (It is related to the cardinal אַרְבַּע, "four," and the masculine ordinal רְבִיעִי, "one-fourth," in 1:1 and 10:14.) Consequently, רְבִיעִית תָּרִימוּ אֶת־תְּרוּמַת הַקֹּדֶשׁ אֶל־אֲחֻזַּת הָעִיר is, literally, "one-fourth you are to devote the holy contribution for the property of the city." The meaning apparently is that the city's property consists of a strip of land that is one-fourth as large as the area allocated for the priests and Levites, whose combined territory is here called "the holy contribution" (as it is also called in 45:6–7; 48:18; and the first occurrence in 48:21). Their combined area was twenty thousand cubits north-to-south and twenty-five thousand cubits east-to-west. Therefore the size of the city's property (including its two adjacent tracts of agricultural land), five thousand cubits north-to-south and twenty-five thousand cubits east-to-west, is one-fourth of the size of the area given to the priests and Levites. For the sake of English clarity, the translation gives this: "[an area of] one-fourth of the holy contribution you are to devote for the property of the city."

Most commentators and translations emend רְבִיעִית ("one-fourth") to a Qal or Pual participle and move the *athnach* to the emended word meaning "square." Typical is ESV: "The whole portion that you shall set apart shall be 25,000 cubits square, that is, the holy portion together with the property of the city." Previously, "(a) square" has been expressed by either a Pual participle (מְרֻבָּע in 40:47; 45:2) or a Qal passive participle (רְבָעָה in 41:21 and רָבוּעַ in 43:16). All the ancient versions translate here with "square." The emendation does not produce a wrong meaning, but it is unnecessary. The statement in 48:20a that the dimensions were twenty-five thousand by twenty-five thousand already indicated that it was a square.

An advantage of following the literal meaning of the MT (as does my translation) is that it is consistent with the overall north-to-south order of the whole chapter, since 48:20b is then only about the city's tract, which is the southernmost of the three tracts that comprise the square. The priests' portion, which includes the temple, was mentioned first (48:9–12a), so presumably it lies north of the Levitical portion, mentioned second (48:12b–14). Then the city's property to the south of the Levites is mentioned third. This literary arrangement and the geography it describes both place the city as far south as possible from the temple (while still remaining in the entire holy tract), with the Levites located between the temple and the city. This safeguards the sanctity of the temple, which in OT and NT times (see Mt 21:12–13; Jn 2:14–17) had been defiled by the Jerusalemites' infidelity.

The Two Tracts Belonging to the Prince (48:21–22)

These are the last verses in the book about the "Prince."[17] In 34:23–24 and 37:24–25, Yahweh had promised a future "Prince" in explicitly messianic terms: the King and new David, the Good Shepherd who would tend and feed God's flock, through whom God would dwell with his people forever, granting them salvation and security. Presumably the "Prince" in chapters 40–48 is the same person, but his royal implications are muted, probably to distance him from the past abusive kings of Israel.[18] Yet the "Prince" has special privileges that in some ways are reminiscent of the high priest (and Ezekiel 40–48 never refers to any other high priest). Only the "Prince" may sit and eat before Yahweh in the vestibule of the outer east gate, through which Yahweh himself had entered his temple (see on 44:3). He also is the one who provides the sacrifices (see on 45:16–17 and 46:2). Thus the major accent in Ezekiel 40–48 seems to be an expression of the premonarchical conviction that Yahweh was Israel's only real King. The dilemma of the "Prince" will only be resolved by Jesus Christ, who is both true God and true man, and who combines and fulfills the offices of "King of Israel" (Jn 1:49; 12:13) and great High Priest (Hebrews 2–10).

---

[17] In the eschatological restoration of Ezekiel 40–48, the "Prince" (נָשִׂיא) is mentioned in 44:3; 45:7–9, 16–17, 22; 46:2, 4, 8, 10, 12, 16–18; 48:21–22.

[18] See especially on 45:7–9. See also the second textual note on 7:27; the commentary on 12:10; the second textual note on 21:30 (ET 21:25); and the commentary on 34:23–31.

48:21 All that "remains" (the Niphal participle וְהַנּוֹתָר, as in 48:15, 18, but now referring to other areas) in the entire holy contribution are the two tracts of land given to the Prince. For their location, see figure 6. The description here initially depends heavily on 45:6–7, and much of 48:21a is a verbatim repetition of 48:7.

The verse addresses the simple geographical fact that the square (composed of the tracts belonging to the priests and the Levites and the city) was only twenty-five thousand cubits east-to-west, and so would reach neither the Jordan on the east nor the Mediterranean on the west. That left a considerable area to be accounted for. In 48:21–22 (the verse division is artificial), the text makes essentially the same point three times: the Prince's properties extend on either side of the central square. Each tract is "extending along" (אֶל־פְּנֵי or עַל־פְּנֵי) the eastern or western twenty-five-thousand-cubit-long (north-to-south) boundary of the square (48:21a). Ezek 48:21b repeats the dimensions given in 48:21a and stresses again the centrality of the temple.

After the first mention of the twenty-five thousand cubits, תְּרוּמָה is missing in the LXX and Syriac. Since it disturbs the symmetry of the statements about the eastern and western halves of the Prince's property, Zimmerli and Allen regard it as a scribal error and replace it with קָדִימָה to obtain a parallel with the next part of the verse.[19] Except for such formal considerations, nothing is at stake, and I see no cogent reason to emend. But whereas "the holy contribution" earlier in the verse refers to the priests' and Levites' lands (since the city's property is mentioned separately), here the dimension of twenty-five thousand indicates that תְּרוּמָה, "contribution," refers to the priests' land, the Levites' land, and the city property (see on 48:20 and on 48:8–22).

Block thinks that the article has been dropped from חֲלָקִים by haplography, but Zimmerli has the better case by arguing that the article (as in the LXX) is necessary because the northern plurality of the tribes has already been described.[20]

The last sentence of the verse can be understood in at least two different ways, partly depending on whether one follows the Qere or the Kethib (if vocalized differently from the Qere). Probably the masculine suffix of the Qere, בְּתוֹכוֹ (and of the Kethib if vocalized בְּתוֹכֹה) refers back to the masculine participle וְהַנּוֹתָר, the "remaining" areas belonging to the Prince, at the start of 48:21. (The same Qere/Kethib variation was at the end of 48:15.) Then וְהָיְתָה תְּרוּמַת הַקֹּדֶשׁ וּמִקְדַּשׁ הַבַּיִת בְּתוֹכוֹ means "the holy contribution and the temple sanctuary will be in the middle of it." Thus "the holy contribution" (here referring only to the priests' land; see on 48:22 and also on 48:8–22) and "the sanctuary of the temple" (וּמִקְדַּשׁ הַבַּיִת) within the priests' land are between "it," the two "remaining" tracts belonging to the Prince, which are to the east

---

19 Zimmerli, *Ezekiel*, 2:525; Allen, *Ezekiel*, 2:275.

20 Block, *Ezekiel*, 2:733, n. 146; Zimmerli, *Ezekiel*, 2:525.

and the west. Alternatively, if the Kethib is vocalized בְּתוֹכָה, then its feminine suffix would refer to the entire "contribution" (תְּרוּמָה) consisting of the tracts for the priests, the Levites, the city, and the Prince, and the sentence would say that "the holy contribution [the priests' land] and the temple sanctuary will be in the middle of it."[21]

48:22 In essence, this verse simply continues to describe the location of the Prince's lands. It notes that the Levites' land and the city property bisect the Prince's two tracts. This implies that "the holy contribution" in 48:21b refers only to the third component of the square, the priests' land. Furthermore, the verse notes that the Prince's tracts, in turn, bisect the allotments of Judah (to the north) and of Benjamin (to the south). The latter observation serves as a transition to the resumption of the sequence of the tribal strips in 48:23–28. That the territory of the Levites, like that of the city, is described as mere אֲחֻזָּה, "property," gives it secondary status in the holy contribution compared to the "most holy [district]" of the priests (48:12), containing the temple (48:10).

The verse is written in a rather oblique way. Critics often delete the preposition מִן both times it is prefixed to אֲחֻזַּת as a scribal error,[22] but it can be read in a local sense and need not be reflected in English translation. Compare BDB, s.v. מִן, 3 b (e), which describes a rare use of the preposition "specifying the objects, or elements, of which a genus consists … *consisting of.*" Compare also מִן in 48:30, where מִפְּאַת צָפוֹן means "*on* the side of the north" (not "from …"), and also the unusual use of מִן on מִנַּחֲלָה in 48:29.

The first sentence of the verse is about the east-to-west boundaries of the Prince's tracts. וּמֵאֲחֻזַּת הַלְוִיִּם וּמֵאֲחֻזַּת הָעִיר, the area "consisting of the property of the Levites and the property of the city," is described as בְּתוֹךְ אֲשֶׁר לַנָּשִׂיא יִהְיֶה, "in the middle of the [two tracts] that will belong to the Prince."

The second sentence concerns the northern and southern boundaries of the Prince's areas. The syntax is much clearer: בֵּין ׀ גְּבוּל יְהוּדָה וּבֵין גְּבוּל בִּנְיָמִן, the area "between the territory of Judah and the territory of Benjamin," לַנָּשִׂיא יִהְיֶה, "will belong to the Prince."

The City Named "Yahweh Is There" (48:30–35)

48:30–35 These verses constitute the final subsection of the last divine speech in the book. See "Introduction to the New Promised Land (47:13–48:35)" after the comments on 47:12. In them Yahweh turns his attention to "the city," which is not named, but clearly it is an antitype of the earthly Jerusalem.

"Jerusalem" was named often in chapters 1–24, which were mainly condemnations of apostate Israel's infidelity. The last four references to it by name

---

[21] This seems to be the view reflected in the translation by Block, *Ezekiel*, 2:734. However, Block's explanation (2:734, n. 149) seems instead to support the translation of the KJV, which is a third alternative: "it shall be the holy oblation; and the sanctuary of the house shall be in the midst thereof."

[22] E.g., Zimmerli, *Ezekiel*, 2:525.

in the book were in connection with its siege (24:2), the gloating of Tyre over its destruction (26:2), the arrival of the survivor who reported that it had fallen (33:21), and in a salvation oracle that included its restoration (36:38). Thus it is striking that in the chapters that center on the coming era of redemption (chapters 33–48), the city is only named once (36:38) as a recipient of that salvation, and it is never named in the long eschatological vision that concludes the book (chapters 40–48).

Why would God not call the new city by the name Jerusalem? Part of the answer may be that in the coming era, God's salvation would not be confined to Jerusalem itself, nor would that city even necessarily be a focal point of centripetal force as in the OT, when pilgrimage to Jerusalem was required thrice a year for adult males (Ex 23:14–17; 34:22–23; Deut 16:16). Instead, in the NT era, worship is no longer centered at Jerusalem (Jn 4:20–24) because salvation spreads out centrifugally from Jerusalem to ends of the earth (Acts 1:8). A hint of that was in Ezek 48:8–22, where the city was separated from the temple by the intervening tract of land given the Levites (see figure 6 and also on 48:20), in stark contrast to the three temples (of Solomon, the second temple, and Herod's temple) that were within Jerusalem. In the church age, God meets his people in grace wherever the Gospel of Jesus Christ is proclaimed and the Sacraments are rightly administered. Ultimately, the location where he will dwell intimately with his people is not any place on this earth, but in a new city, the new Jerusalem (Revelation 21). That leads to another possible part of the answer. The sordid allegories of unfaithful Israel in Ezekiel 16 and 23 were expressed using the whore named "Jerusalem" who personified the city. The holy city described here is to be the antitype in the sense of the very opposite, representing the virgin bride of Christ (2 Cor 11:2; Eph 5:25–27; Revelation 21–22).

Yet earlier in Ezekiel, the theme of Jerusalem as the elect city had not been totally neglected. It was, after all, and remains here, הָעִיר, "*the* city" (e.g., 9:4; 10:2; 48:30–31, 35). Even points such as chapter 9 and 11:23, where the Glory forsakes the city, her former election to be the dwelling place of God's gracious name had been in the background, and that election came to the fore in the counterpart in chapter 43, when the Glory returns to the temple. But, on the whole, and especially in most of chapters 40–48, Ezekiel's interest had centered on the temple, and 48:8–22 deliberately separated the temple from the city (see on 48:20). Throughout Ezekiel, the "theology of Zion" has not been a major theme, except when the presumptuous misunderstanding of it was attacked—a virtual antipode to especially Isaiah, in which the proper proclamation of the theme is prominent.[23]

---

[23] For the idea of the inviolability of Zion, which can be either rightly or wrongly understood, see Hummel, *Ezekiel 1–20*, 256–57, 274–75, 371, 471. See also the commentary on 21:28; 24:20–21. For affirmations in Isaiah of the doctrine of the inviolability of Zion, the city as holy because of God's election and promise, see Is 1:27; 2:3; 4:3–5; 10:24; 12:6; 14:32; 18:7; 28:16; 52:1–2.

As a result, it is not surprising that critics widely regard these final verses as an addendum to the book added by another, later hand, which wished to highlight the "theology of Zion" that was neglected in the rest of the book. In one sense, 48:30–35 is undeniably a postscript. But these verses must not be separated from the rest of the chapter, or from the entire concluding vision (chapters 40–48).

It would be virtually unthinkable, even in the visionary world through which Ezekiel is guided, to think of God's temple in isolation from his holy city and the rest of the land he has promised to his redeemed people. The prominent "theological architecture"[24] at the beginning of chapters 40–48 initially described the setting of the temple (shown to Ezekiel in chapters 40–42) as "a very high mountain on which were buildings resembling a *city*" (כְּמִבְנֵה־עִיר, 40:2). That same architecture returns here, after much "theological geography"[25] has intervened. Thus while in 43:1–12 the Glory of Yahweh came to dwell in the new temple, the concluding verse of the book suggests that his dwelling place is the city, since it is named "Yahweh is there" (48:35). The temple and the city seem to have merged, as indeed they were united on earth in the OT era[26] and will be forever in the eschaton, after Christ returns, when in the new Jerusalem "the Lord God Almighty is her temple—and the Lamb" (Rev 21:22).

Formally, the use of אֶחָד, "one," after the name of each of the twelve city gates links 48:30–35 with that numeral repeated for each of the tribes in the lists of the tribal boundaries in 48:1–7, 23–27. Another link in this chapter between the whole people of God and the city is the statement in 48:19 that "the workers of the city … will be from all the tribes of Israel."

No Hebrew verbs are present in 48:30–35, so all the sentences are nominal. English idiom requires supplying "are" and "is" as well as other connectives to convey the meaning smoothly.

48:30 As a kind of topical superscription, this section begins with וְאֵלֶּה תּוֹצְאֹת הָעִיר, "these are the outside bounds of the city." Superscriptions introducing new topics also began with וְאֵלֶּה, "and these are …" in 43:13 and 48:1, 16. The noun תּוֹצָאָה (occurring only in the plural, as here: תּוֹצְאֹת, "outside bounds") is obviously derived from יָצָא, "go out." Most English versions translate it as "exits" here, but commentaries seek a somewhat broader translation. It is frequent in Numbers 34 and Joshua 15–19, chapters that describe the original Mosaic tribal boundaries. There it means "*extremity* of border of territory" (BDB, 1), either indicating the line of a tribal boundary or the point

---

[24] Allen, *Ezekiel*, 2:285.

[25] Allen, *Ezekiel*, 2:285.

[26] Of course, the temple was located in Jerusalem from the time of Solomon until its destruction along with the city in 586 B.C. (see figure 1) and then after it was rebuilt in 516 B.C. The second temple (extensively renovated and expanded by Herod) lasted until its destruction by the Romans in A.D. 70.

where a boundary ends. That latter sense, it is usually agreed, is pertinent here, and which perhaps determined its choice. For "exits" Ezekiel used a different noun, the plural of מוֹצָא, in 42:11; 43:11; and 44:5. But instead of that term, or another such as חוֹמוֹת, "walls" (which must have been present if there were gates), here God uses תּוֹצְאֹת, probably to accent that this city is the antitype (in the sense of goal and fulfillment) of the original promised land.

If תּוֹצָאֹת means "outside bounds" (rather than "exits"), it is not surprising that the next part of the description gives the measurement of the north side of the city (rather than moving on to the gates first). The initial attention devoted to the north side follows the same overall pattern as the north-to-south order of the tribal portions and holy contribution listed in 48:1–28, and even the north-to-south order of the tracts (for the priests, then the Levites, and finally the city) within the holy contribution (48:8–22). Further, the entire vision of chapters 40–48 began with Ezekiel approaching the city and the temple from the north, since he sees them "to the south" (see the last textual note on 40:2). After beginning at the north (48:30), Ezekiel is then shown the east (48:32), south (48:33), and finally the west (48:34) side. We would call it "clockwise." This is the same geographic order (north, east, south, west) as the overall boundary descriptions of the entire new promised land in 47:15–20.[27] That could imply that the city is depicted as a microcosm of the entire promised land, as also seems to be the case with the new Jerusalem (Revelation 21) in the larger context of the new earth that is a garden paradise (Revelation 22).

The city's measurements are already familiar from Ezek 48:16. The number four thousand five hundred presumably refers to cubits,[28] and so is almost one and a half miles or about two and a third kilometers. This number is repeated for each of the four sides (48:30, 32, 33, 34). The references to the sides are expressed in slightly different ways, as reflected in my varying translations. The measurements of the four sides are totaled in 48:35a for the circumference of eighteen thousand. Since each side and the circumference are both multiples of twenty-five, they probably have evangelical symbolism (see on 48:8–22 and the commentary on 40:1).

In 48:30 on the north and in 48:33 on the south, the noun מִדָּה, "measurement," is given after the number, but the dimensions of the east and west sides are expressed only with the bare number. Evidently, this variation is only stylistic. Only in 48:30 is מִן (usually "from") attached to פֵּאָה, "side," and מִן clearly has a locative sense in the construct phrase מִפְּאַת צָפוֹן, "*on* the side of the north" (not "from …"). See BDB, s.v. מִן, 1 c. Compare the locative sense of מִן on

---

[27] However, in 48:16 the order in which the sides of the city were presented was north, south, east, and west. Hence that verse also started from the north, but then moved to its opposite, and likewise (next) from the east to the west.

[28] The alternative is that the unit could be the guide's measuring rod, which was six cubits long, in which case the distance would be about eight and three-fourths miles or fourteen kilometers. For the issue of the unit, see "The Holy Contribution (48:8–22)" and also on 45:1.

וּמֵאָחֻזַּת, which occurs twice in 48:22, and also the unusual sense of מִן on מִנַּחֲלָה in 48:29.

The preposition אֶל will be used in 48:32 (וְאֶל־פְּאַת קָדִ֫ימָה, "*on* the side of the east") in the same way that מִן is used in 48:30. For the last two sides, the verses dispense with any preposition and simply use construct phrases with פֵּאָה, "side," adverbially: וּפְאַת־נֶ֫גְבָּה, "[on] the side of the south" (48:33), and פְּאַת־יָ֫מָּה, "[on] the side of the sea/west" (48:34).

48:31 This verse introduces the city gates and then details those gates on the north side, thus completing the description of the north side begun in 48:30. The verse begins with וְשַׁעֲרֵי הָעִיר עַל־שְׁמוֹת֙ שִׁבְטֵי יִשְׂרָאֵל, literally, "and the gates of the city according to the names of the tribes of Israel," and continues, שְׁעָרִים שְׁלוֹשָׁה צָפ֫וֹנָה, "three gates to the north." As Block argues contra Zimmerli, the MT needs no reconstruction.[29] צָפ֫וֹנָה, "to the north," is necessary in 48:31 (even though צָפוֹן, "north," was in 48:30) to indicate that the three gates named here are on the north side.

Multiple city gates were not unknown in antiquity, but hardly common either. They were nearly always the weakest points in a city's defenses, and the fact that this city has twelve is an indication that any dangers to God's people will have ceased. Various OT passages mention nine gates for preexilic Jerusalem,[30] although some of these may have been different names for the same gates; nevertheless, most scholars count at least six. The nine gates of Babylon were named after Babylonian deities, and an even closer parallel is provided by a temple tower of Marduk (the chief Babylonian god), which had a square sacred precinct with twelve gates. It is not inconceivable that Ezekiel, in exile in Babylon, was aware of those prominent features in his pagan environment and that God may have used images familiar to him in the vision God revealed of the new Jerusalem. However, especially for a priest (1:3) of Ezekiel's orthodoxy, it seems very unlikely that such pagan parallels would be relevant, except perhaps as antitheses.[31]

The twelve gates, neatly arranged with three per side, are in harmony with the overall concern throughout chapters 40–48 for symmetry and perfection as expressions of God's holiness. The naming of the gates after the twelve tribes—in the city named after God himself (48:35)—does not compromise strict monotheism. Rather, it shows that God's redemptive grace endows his people with his own holiness and righteousness—forensically in this life, but also with at least the beginning of the "new obedience,"[32] and in the life to come, all sin

---

[29] Block, *Ezekiel*, 2:734–35, n. 4; Zimmerli, *Ezekiel*, 2:544.

[30] Benjamin Gate (Jer 37:13; 38:7); Corner Gate (e.g., 2 Ki 14:13; Jer 31:38); Ephraim Gate (2 Ki 14:13); Fish Gate (2 Chr 33:14); Horse Gate (Jer 31:40); Middle Gate (Jer 39:3); People's Gate (Jer 17:19); Potsherd Gate (Jer 19:2); Valley Gate (2 Chr 26:9).

[31] Compare the use made of Sodom in Ezek 16:43–58 to shame unfaithful Israel.

[32] See AC VI; Ap IV 122–82; FC Ep and SD IV and VI.

(a) Gen 1:27;
Rom 8:29;
1 Cor 15:49;
Col 3:10;
2 Pet 1:4

will be gone, and we will be fully conformed to the image of our Creator and Redeemer.[a]

Gates in Jerusalem had been named after tribes before: the Ephraim Gate (e.g., 2 Ki 14:13 ǁ 2 Chr 25:23) and the Benjamin Gate (Jer 37:13; 38:7; Zech 14:10). In those cases, the apparent reason was because of the tribal territory toward which they led. That geographical connection happens to hold true for several of Ezekiel's gates (those of Judah and Reuben to the north and those of Simeon, Issachar, and Zebulun to the south), but that hardly seems to have been the basic rationale for their positioning.

Commentators agree that the reason for the arrangement of the twelve named gates is not as easy to divine as was the arrangement of the tribal divisions (see above on 48:2–7, 23–29). At the same time, there is considerable consensus that genealogical derivation was probably the dominant factor. The groupings of the names are more important than their sequence.[33]

On the north side (48:31) are the names of the three most important tribes descended from Jacob's wife Leah. Is it a coincidence that these three also stand first in the blessing of Moses (Deut 33:6–8)? Here is Jacob's firstborn in age (Reuben); then Judah, the bearer of the messianic promise (Gen 49:10; Rev 5:5) whose land was located closest to the temple (see figure 6); and third, Levi, whom Yahweh chose for his own service in place of the firstborn.

In Ezek 48:32, on the significant east side (the direction from which Yahweh entered his temple [43:1–2; 44:1–2]) are the two sons of Rachel, Joseph and Benjamin, plus Dan, one of the sons of Bilhah, Rachel's maid. In contrast to the honored position of Dan's gate here, Dan's tribal territory was the northern-most (48:1) and therefore the farthest on the north side from the temple. We may note that Dan is missing in the list of tribes in Rev 7:5–8.[34]

Opposite the gates of the three Leah tribes on the north (48:31) are the gates of the other three Leah tribes on the south (48:33): Simeon, Issachar, and Zebulun (all of whom, in the allotment of the land, had been displaced from their original tribal allocations, Simeon only slightly, but the other two from the far north). Finally, on the least-regarded western side (48:34) are three tribes from Jacob's concubines: Gad and Asher, sons of Zilpah, and Naphtali, Bilhah's second son.

Thus the description asserts that the city belongs to all the people of God. It is no political capital, as Jerusalem, the Judahite capital had been. Neither is it the city of any earthly king, as "the city of David" (e.g., 2 Sam 5:7, 9) had been.

---

[33] Block, *Ezekiel*, 2:737, includes two diagrams of possible arrangements of the tribal gates. One figure assumes that the names in 48:31–34 are in clockwise order, while the other figure assumes that the names on the north and south sides of the city are in east-to-west order, while those on the east and west sides of the city are in north-to-south order.

[34] Irenaeus, *Against Heresies*, 5.30.2, says Dan is missing in Rev 7:5–8 because the Antichrist will come from Dan according to LXX Jer 8:16, in which the verbs ἥξει καὶ καταφάγεται are singular: "[he] will come and devour ..."

It is impossible not to compare the vision shown Ezekiel with the one revealed to St. John in Rev 21:9–27.[35] In keeping with the doctrine of cumulative revelation, according to which the Scriptures reveal divine truth more fully as one moves from Genesis to Revelation, the last two chapters of the Apocalypse picture the same eschatological state of God's redeemed people as does Ezekiel 40–48, but more clearly in light of the redemption already accomplished at Christ's first advent. The Apocalypse is partly dependent on the picture of splendor described in Is 54:12 (gates of crystal and walls decorated with precious stones), but the basic design is that of Ezekiel 48. The holy city descends from heaven and is also laid out as a square. It is surrounded by a massive wall (the gates in Ezek 48:30–35 presuppose a wall), the foundation stones of which have the names of the twelve apostles, and the twelve gates, made of twelve pearls, are again named after the tribes of Israel. Of course, St. John also envisions even greater transformation by the absence of any need for a temple, because the Lord God Almighty and the Lamb are its temple (Rev 21:22; cf. Jn 2:18–23; Eph 2:19–22).

The same idiom is repeated in Ezek 48:31–34 for each of the twelve gates: שַׁעַר רְאוּבֵן אֶחָד, "the gate of Reuben, one," and so forth. Like the idiom with אֶחָד, "one," for each of the twelve tribal portions (see on 48:1), the repetition of the numeral emphasizes that each tribe is treated equally, with one gate apiece, no more and no less. Likewise, the parity of the tribes was indicated by the statement that the city workers come "from all the tribes of Israel" (48:19). In Rev 21:12–13, a similar parity is expressed regarding the tribes, representing the OT church, in the description of the new Jerusalem:

> She has a great and high wall and twelve gates, and at the gates twelve angels, and names inscribed, which are of the twelve tribes of the sons of Israel: on the east three gates, on the north three gates, on the south three gates, and on the west three gates.

The city gates in both Ezek 48:30–35 and Rev 21:13–14 are not intended to restrict access (as the wall of the temple complex had been [Ezek 40:5; 42:20]), but the very opposite: they are to allow access. The multiplicity of them (twelve) and the provision of three on each of the four sides would guarantee ready accessibility. The description of the new Jerusalem later emphasizes that the gates are perpetually open. They are never shut because there are no evil foes from which protection is needed. They freely allow God's redeemed permanent access to his presence in the city (Rev 21:25). See also Rev 22:14, which promises that "those who wash their robes" ("in the blood of the Lamb," Rev 7:14) are given the privilege of access to "the tree of life" and "through the gates they may enter the city."

---

[35] For an insightful interpretation of Rev 21:9–27, one may see Brighton, *Revelation*, 606–21. Taylor, *Ezekiel*, 285, speaking somewhat anthropocentrically, says that St. John "was not afraid to Christianize" Ezekiel's vision "because he saw that the symbolism still possessed meaning for the Christian church of his day."

One should also note that in the new Jerusalem in Revelation 21, in addition to the OT church represented by the names of the twelve tribes of Israel, the NT church is represented by the names of the twelve apostles (Rev 21:14):

> And the wall of the city has twelve foundations, and on them are the twelve names of the twelve apostles of the Lamb.

Thus the *una sancta* ("one holy catholic and apostolic church" [Nicene Creed]) consisting of all believers (OT and NT alike) is represented by the total of the twenty-four names (just as by the twenty-four enthroned elders in Rev 4:4, 10; 5:8; etc.).

48:32–34 A few minor textual issues may be noted. The versions and the parallel statements in the surrounding verses lack a conjunction equivalent to the one on וְשַׁעַר יוֹסֵף ("and the gate of Joseph") in 48:32. Conversely, the versions (except the Targum) and parallels have a conjunction where one is lacking on פְּאַת־יָמָּה ("the side of the sea/west") at the beginning of 48:34. Finally in 48:34, the suffixed שְׁעָרֵיהֶם is, literally "*their* gates," supported by the Vulgate and the Targum (but not the LXX or Syriac), while the preceding parallels have the simple plural, שְׁעָרִים, in each reference to three "gates" (48:31–33). There is no clear antecedent for the suffix.

48:35 Climactically, the city itself will be renamed. In antiquity in general, the meaning of names tended to be more closely associated with the reality or essence of the person or thing they designated than is true in our very "nominal" age. The biblical importance of naming finds expression in ecclesiastical practice in the rite for Holy Baptism, in which the person being baptized is named[36] and thus given his or her new "Christian" name. The church does well to remember the baptismal anniversaries of its members in order to remind all the baptized of the glorious promises that are theirs because of their Baptism into Christ. Compare Christ's promise in Rev 2:17 that he will give a "new name" to the one who conquers (whoever remains in faith until death). Moreover, in Rev 3:12, Christ issues this promise to the one who conquers:

> I will write on him the name of my God and *the name of the city of my God*, the new Jerusalem, which is coming down from heaven from my God, and [I will write on him] my new name.

"The name of the city from that day on is Yahweh *Shammah* [Yahweh is there]" (48:35). "Day" (יוֹם) is frequently used in the sense of "time," not necessarily of any particular calendar day. In the broadest biblical sense, מִיּוֹם, "from that day," connects with "the Day of Yahweh" theme prominent throughout the prophets.[37] It refers to the day/time when God will act decisively in earthly history in both a Law and Gospel manner, judging sin and destroying evil, yet also establishing his kingdom and revealing his salvation. Ultimately,

---

[36] Traditionally the pastor asks for the Christian name immediately prior to performing the Baptism. See, for example, *LSB* 268.

[37] See the third and fourth textual notes on 7:7 and the commentary on 30:2 for the terminology and theology of "the Day (of Yahweh)."

the prophetic OT "Day" is fulfilled in the Triduum, the "three days" from the evening of Holy Thursday to the evening of Easter Sunday, when Christ absorbed the entirety of divine judgment upon humanity's sin, then rose bodily in glory to usher in the new creation, which shall be consummated after his return. On that day all the dead shall be raised, and all believers shall inherit the new Jerusalem in the new heavens and new earth (Revelation 20–21). At that time, the name "Yahweh is there" will describe the accomplished reality (Rev 21:3):

> Behold, the tabernacle/dwelling of God is with his people, and he will tabernacle/dwell with them, and they will be his people, and God himself will be with them as their God.

Commentators debate the significance of the last Hebrew word of the book, שָׁמָּה with locative *he*, which could mean "(will come) thither, *to* there," versus a simple שָׁם, "(is) there, in that place." However, there is no rigid distinction between the two. In 23:3 and 32:29–30, Ezekiel himself had used שָׁמָּה as synonymous with שָׁם. In Late Biblical Hebrew, the locative *he* tended to lose its force, as can be seen in Ezekiel 48, where the geographical terms with it, for example, יָמָּה, "seaward, westward," צָפוֹנָה, "northward," often simply mean "west," "north," so the final *he* might be labeled "paragogic," that is, simply added for effect. Besides, Ezekiel has already seen the Glory of Yahweh come to inhabit the new temple (43:1–12), so if the locative *he* has any force, it might be akin to the second (not the first) advent of Christ. Compare the title ὁ ὢν καὶ ὁ ἦν καὶ ὁ ἐρχόμενος, "he who is and who was and who is coming" (Rev 1:4, 8; cf. Rev 4:8).[38] In Ezekiel 43, Yahweh came in the "incarnational" form of his Glory, and "incarnation" implies an enduring reality.[39]

The new name may imply an animadversion to the etymological meaning of "Jerusalem" (יְרוּשָׁלַ͏ִם), which apparently in pre-Israelite times meant something like "foundation of [the Canaanite god] Shalem," attested as early as the Egyptian Execration Texts from the early second millennium B.C. However, it seems likely to me that the name intends to evoke a certain assonance between יהוה שָׁמָּה (*Yhwh shammah*) and יְרוּשָׁלַ͏ִם (*Yerushalayim*), even though "Jerusalem" is absent from the entire vision (chapters 40–48).[40] The new name, יְהוָה | שָׁמָּה, "Yahweh is there," sounds like a play on the historical name, יְרוּשָׁלַ͏ִם, "Jerusalem," with the difference between the two suggesting discontinuity (the sinful associations will be gone), while the similarity implies continuity and eschatological fulfillment.

---

[38] On this title, one may see Brighton, *Revelation*, 39–41.

[39] For the divine "Glory" understood Christologically, see pages 1, 11, and 13 in the introduction, as well as the textual notes and commentary on 1:26–28. The risen and exalted Christ, now seated at the right hand of God the Father in heaven, continues to possess his true human nature (without sin), which he assumed at his incarnation (Mt 1:18–25), and with his full human and divine natures he will return visibly at his parousia.

[40] See the beginning of this section, "The City Named 'Yahweh Is There' (48:30–35)."

We should not overlook other poetic and theological appellations for the city of God, all of which end up being essentially synonymous with the one that concludes Ezekiel. Most similar is that of Is 60:14: "the city of Yahweh, the Zion of the Holy One of Israel." Theologically most significant in unpacking the significance of Yahweh's presence "there" (Ezek 48:35) is the promise through Jeremiah (33:15–16) of a "righteous Branch" from the line of David who will cause Judah to be saved and Jerusalem to dwell securely, and "this is [the name] that shall be called to her: 'Yahweh is our righteousness' [יְהוָה ׀ צִדְקֵנוּ]."[41] Lutherans in particular have always understood that promise as fulfilled in Christ, whose own "righteousness" is imputed to us through faith (and thus becomes our alien righteousness) by virtue of his vicarious atonement. The Hebrew יְהוָה צִדְקֵנוּ (but to the consternation of some, no translation) is inscribed on the mantel of the fireplace in the board room of Concordia Seminary, St. Louis.

So St. Ezekiel ends with a name that fulfills a basic part of the covenant formula, "[I will] be your God" (Gen 17:7 and many times later with slight variations), as well as the promise "I will dwell in your midst" (Zech 2:14–15 [ET 2:10–11] and other times with slight variations). And at the same time, the name is predictive of one name given the Incarnate One himself: "Immanuel [God with us]," born of a virgin (Is 7:14; 8:8; Mt 1:23). Although God through Ezekiel seldom speaks overtly of the personal Messiah,[42] there can be no messianic age in the biblical sense without a personal Messiah. Even though Ezekiel is afforded glimpses of life after the parousia (e.g., the resurrection in 37:1–14), he knows that he himself is not yet there, and his visions remain laden with OT imagery that will be absent from corresponding ones in the NT (e.g., the temple and sacrifices in chapters 40–48). Ezekiel never explains how he deals with this paradox. In that, he is one with all of us who are still in the church militant, where, in a sense, the paradox between the "now" (here) and the "not yet" (there) is even greater.

This is a thought that, among others, the church today would do well to ponder more. Ezekiel's often horrendous judgment oracles have been fulfilled in the horrific passion of Christ and his death, into which we have been baptized (Rom 6:1–4; Col 2:11–14), while we yet await the final judgment. So it is also with Ezekiel's oracles of salvation, including the extensive vision of the new temple that occupies much of chapters 40–48: they were fulfilled when Jesus raised up the "temple" of his own body on the third day (Jn 2:18–23), yet we wait in hope for our own resurrection on the Last Day.

---

[41] Since the noun צֶמַח, the messianic "Branch," is masculine, the referent of the feminine pronoun on לָהּ, "to her," must be וִירוּשָׁלַםִ, "Jerusalem," the nearest preceding feminine noun, to whom the name applies.

[42] However, some passages obviously speak of the personal Messiah and the salvation he brings, for example, Ezek 11:19–20; 34:23–24; 36:22–27; 37:12–14, 23–28.

"God himself is present: … God is in His temple,"[43] we sing. But in what sense are we privileged to be "there" with him? Not by birthright (cf. Jn 1:12–13), as universalists wrongly contend, but by our second birth through "clean water" and "a new Spirit" (Ezek 36:25–27; Jn 3:5). As we abide in his Word, the triune God himself comes to abide with us (Jn 14:23). Only by constant renewal of our faith in Christ through his gifts—in the places where he has promised to let himself be found, in his Word and at his Altar, which is really his Table (cf. Ezek 41:22)—will we finally arrive in the city where "Yahweh is there."

All this means that we enter his temple preeminently in worship, where he is spiritually and sacramentally present. And as the "Jerusalem above" (Ps 137:6; Gal 4:26) descends upon the pilgrim city below, momentarily erasing the boundaries of space and time, we proleptically participate in, but also empirically look forward to, the Day when the last enemy will have been destroyed (1 Cor 15:26, 54), and we, with all the saints in glory already, will forever be "there," where Yahweh is. "Amen. Come, Lord Jesus!" (Rev 22:20).

---

[43] From the eighteenth-century hymn "God Himself Is Present" (*LSB* 907:1).

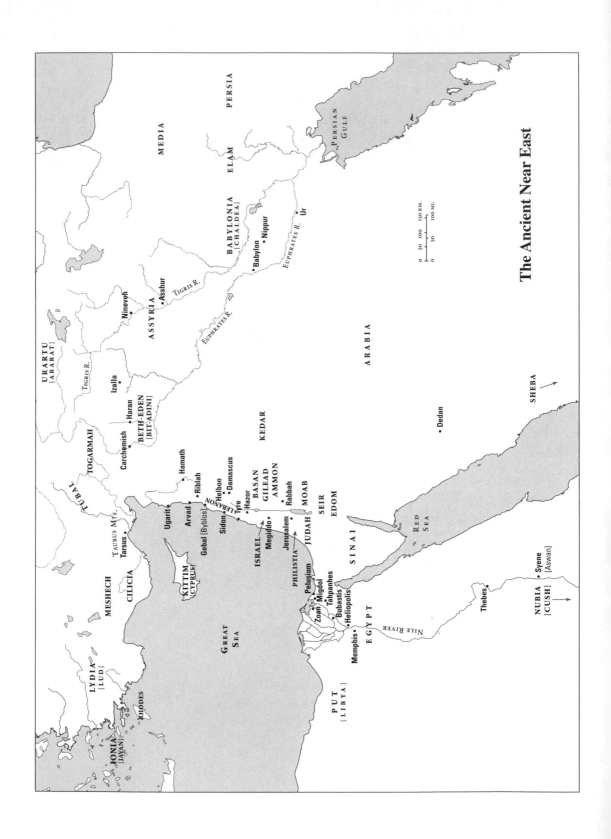

The Ancient Near East

Index of Subjects

and Scripture, 57*n22*
shepherd theme in, 997
of Tiamat, 910–11*v4*
and vision of river of life, 1344

Nabateans, 792

Nabonidus, 663

Naboth, 690

Nabu, 265*v2*

Nadab, 1277

Nahum, 680

Nakedness, 429*v7*, 468. *See also* Lewdness; Sex
exposure of, 445*v36*, 702*v10*, 729
of whoredom, 711*v29*

Name
of eschatological city, 1379–81,
1386–89
significance of, 681, 723

Name of God, 9, 14, 78, 145*v14*, 584–85,
760, 1034*v21*, 1047–49, 1061. *See
also* Baptism; Signature of God
and authority, 591
defilement of, 1239–42
and eschatological temple, 1239
as holy, 609
and pity of God, 595
profaning of, 1127–28*v7*
revelation of, 588–89, 1134–36
and salvation, 1049–50
zeal for, 1144

Naphtali, 1365

Nathan, 651

Nations
as agents of divine wrath, 481, 483
annihilation of, 649
arrogance of, 1039
assembly of, 927–28*v3*
exposure of, 481–82
gathering of, 912*v6*
imitation of, 603
and Israel, 115–16, 306*v12*, 1033*v20*
as majestic, 947
quaking of, 923
reaction to Tyre, 813–14
as remnant, 1038–39, 1061
and restoration, 1043, 1060
ruthlessness of, 931*v12*
sight of, 1132*v27*
time of, 894–95*v3*
as unclean, 162–63
wilderness of, 606–7

Natural law, 685. *See also* Law; Moral
Law

Natural man, 541–42. *See also* Original
Sin; Sin

Nave (of eschatological temple),
1200–1201. *See also* Holy Place;
Temple (eschatological)

Navel (of earth)
as Israelite home, 1111–12*v12*
metaphor of, 1121

Nebo. *See* Nabu

Nebuchadnezzar, 19
and Ammonites, 660, 788–89
army of, 883–84*v18*
and attack on Judah, 642*vv33–37*
and captivity, 506*v12*
death of, 507*v16*
divinations of, 654–55, 661
dream of, 920
as eagle, 499–500*v3*, 502*v7*, 514
and Edom, 791
and Egypt, 884–85*vv19–20*, 888–89,
891–92, 897*v9*, 899, 905–6
final campaign of, 637*v27*, 654–56
as God's agent, 809, 812–13, 870
hostility of, 824*v10*
as judge, 659
and Moab, 790
name of, 799–800*v7*
and Pharaoh, 913–14*v11*
preparation of, 634–35*v26*
rebellion against, 491
reign of, 661–62
and siege of Jerusalem, 137*v2*,
508–9*vv17–19*
and Tyre, 810, 873
and Zedekiah, 503*v7*

Neco (Pharaoh)
and Jehoahaz, 550*v4*
and Josiah, 727

Needy, 526*v12*

Negev, 621–22*v2*

Nehemiah, 978

Nephilim, 939*v27*

Net
of fisherman, 1345
of God, 515, 927–28*v3*
image of, 943

New Age (movement), 376–77

New birth, 1079. *See also* Baptism; Regeneration

New covenant, 491, 493, 1056, 1062,
1091–92
blessings of, 1008–9
Gentiles in, 1358

and judgment, 395
and judgment of Jerusalem, 314–15
and justice of God, 409
and Philistines, 786v17
and presence of God, 1097–98
and punishment of Israel, 649
and repentance, 766, 945
repetition of, 858vv21–26, 859v24,
860–61
and restoration of Israel, 1008
and salvation, 1020, 1084
and signatory formula, 1034v23
and statutes of God, 306v12
and trees of countryside, 499v1
variant of, 647
and versification, 878–79v6, 880v9
and wrath of God, 197v13

Red Sea, 1340

Redaction criticism, 770

Redeemer, 1012v6

Redemption. See also Salvation
as drawing near, 1030v8
and firstborn, 475
language of, 604
and punishment, 729–30, 905
right to, 307–8v15

Reed
as measuring instrument, 1170v3,
1196
metaphor of, 878–80vv6–7, 887

Reformation, 406

Reformed tradition, 686

Refugees
escape of, 215v16, 230
salvation of, 194v8, 202–3

Regeneration, 316–25, 546–47, 1054–56.
See also Baptism; New birth
and Baptism, 469–70, 534
and Holy Spirit, 1056
of Israel, 613–14
and Jerusalem's shame, 487

Register, 356v9
exclusion from, 369–70

Regulations
of drinking, 1282
of eschatological temple, 1244–45
on priesthood, 1279–89

Reign of God. See God, reign of

Remembering
of covenant, 492–93
of Egypt, 730
by God, 529–30v22, 685–86, 731–32,
962v13, 963v16

Remnant, 171–72v10, 202–3
destruction of, 270–71v9

and destruction of Jerusalem, 178–79
dispersion of, 183
as invisible church, 282
and Israel, 316
and Jesus Christ, 200
judgment of, 977–81
marking of, 275–79
nations as, 1038–39, 1061
preservation of, 194v8, 307v13, 315,
333v16
promise of, 129, 1132v28
return of, 490
salvation of, 244–45, 279, 281,
316–25, 488
seal of, 243
and survivors, 388v22, 408–9

Reparation offering. See Guilt offering

Repentance, 126–27
and action prophecy, 339–40
call to, 127–28, 392, 531–32vv30–31,
971–72, 1244
case of, 544–45
ceremony of, 239v16
and contrition, 1058–59
and covenant structure, 463
of Egypt, 945
of exiles, 1001
and forgiveness, 1092
God's pleasure in, 971–76
of Israel, 85, 86, 613
and judgment, 381–82v5
lack of, 209v4
and life, 530v24, 544–45
possibility of, 130
and recognition formula, 766, 945
of remnant, 202–3
and shame, 459v61, 496
and washing with water, 1052
of wicked, 103v19, 364v22,
962–63vv14–15, 975–76

Repetition, 99v16, 140v6, 209–10v5,
287v9, 302v4, 1039
and continuity, 263v1
and dittography, 307v15
of eating scroll, 112
as expression of urgency, 392
in Hebrew, 46v23
of lover's description, 729
and recognition formula, 858vv21–26,
859v24, 860–61
of rhetorical questions, 680
in vision of dry bones, 1075
and vocabulary, 200
of watchman oracles, 970–71

Representation, 152–53

Reproval, 110–11v26

Reputation, 434v14, 471

Vestments, 640*v31*
    of pastor, 1225

Vexation, 576*v28*

Victory of God, 946, 1134–35, 1137
    and sacrificial meal, 1139–41

Vidi Aquam, 1336–37

Vigilance, 122, 350. *See also* Watchman

Villages, 193*v6*

Vindication, 1050, 1059, 1102

Vine
    allegory of, 562–66
    as Davidic dynasty, 554*v10*
    destruction of, 505–6*v10*
    gender of, 555–56*v11*
    image of, 513
    metaphor of, 410*v2*, 413–15, 563
    and seeds, 500–501*v5*
    transplanting of, 503–4*vv7–8*, 514
    water for, 503–4*v7*

Vineyard, 554*v10*
    metaphor of, 563

Violence, 258–59, 802*v10*
    of Babylonians, 212*v11*
    doing of, 675–76*v26*
    of Edom, 1019
    of Israel, 271*v9*, 282, 346
    of Israelites, 240*v17*, 261
    of Jerusalem, 757–58
    judgment on, 220–21*v23*
    of princes, 1301
    of son, 525–26*vv10–11*, 542–43
    of twenty-five men, 313–14

Vision of dry bones, 1066*v2*, 1075
    as army, 1083–84
    and creation narrative, 1082
    liturgical use of, 1079
    in New Testament, 1078–79
    valley of, 1080–81

Vision of eschatological temple, 1153
    and Ezekiel's inaugural vision,
        1230–31
    fulfillment of, 1155–56

Vision of God, 33–34*v1*, 48–49*vv26–28*,
        64, 1168*v2*. *See also* Glory of God;
        Theophany

Visions, 53, 291
    of eschatological temple, 1195–96
    of false prophets, 364*v22*, 367
    of land (new), 1332
    of new Jerusalem, 1332
    and oracles, 214*v13*, 303*v4*
    and revelation, 55, 222*v26*
    of river of life, 1333–47
    of temple scenes, 245–46
    and words, 35*v3*

Vocabulary
    of architecture, 1158–59
    of death, 933*v17*
    of economics, 524*v7*
    of Ezekiel, 8, 14–15
    repetition of, 200
    sources for, 359*v18*
    of temple decorations, 1210
    of Torah, 470, 473–74
    as vulgar, 144*v12*

Voice of God, 64, 286*v5*
    and Ezekiel's call, 83
    in Ezekiel's inaugural vision,
        47–48*v25*, 49*v28*
    sound of, 1233

Vows, 1287

Wall
    breach in, 693
    construction of, 356*v10*
    demolition of, 354*v5*, 357*v11*, 358*v12*,
        367–68, 371–72
    digging through, 329–30*vv5–7*,
        331–32*v12*, 342–45
    of eschatological temple, 1203–5
    of Jerusalem, 1110*v11*
    repairing of, 678*v30*
    of temple, 851*v13*
    of temple compound, 1171*v5*
    of Tyre, 811

War
    fire of, 647
    motif of, 368
    preparation for, 634–35*v26*
    of Tyre, 799*v4*
    of Yahweh, 653, 1124

Warning
    and Ezekiel's preaching, 100*v17*
    Israel as, 393–94
    Jerusalem as, 175*v15*, 186
    of judgment, 972–73

Warriors, 931*v12*
    leaders of, 936*v21*

Washing
    Baptism as, 425*v4*
    of infant, 424–25*v4*, 427*v6*
    of sacrifices, 1184*v38*

Watchfulness, 122, 350

Watchman
    duty of, 126
    Ezekiel as, 18, 100–106*vv17–21*,
        121–22, 972–73
    and hand of God, 106*v22*
    oracles of, 970–71
    pastor as, 959*v3*

Index of Passages

**Apocrypha,
Old Testament
Pseudepigrapha, and
Other Jewish Literature**

1 Esdras